Dictionary of Pseudonyms

THIRD EDITION

Dictionary of Pseudonyms

THIRD EDITION

Adrian Room

McFarland & Company, Inc., Publishers
Jefferson, North Carolina, and London

British Library Cataloguing-in-Publication data are available

Library of Congress Cataloguing-in-Publication Data

Room, Adrian.
    Dictionary of pseudonyms / Adrian Room — 3rd ed.
      p.   cm.
    Rev. ed. of: Dictionary of pseudonyms and their origins, with stories
of name changes. 1989.
    Includes bibliographical references (p.   ).
    ISBN 0-7864-0423-X (library binding : 50# alkaline paper) ∞
    1. Anonyms and pseudonyms.   I. Room, Adrian. Dictionary of
pseudonyms and their origins, with stories of name changes. II. Title.
Z1041.R66   1998
929.4'03 — dc21   97-31640
                                                 CIP

Manufactured in the United States of America

McFarland & Company, Inc., Publishers
  Box 611, Jefferson, North Carolina 28640

Table of Contents

Aston: What's your real name, then?
Davies: Davies. Mac Davies. That was before I changed my name.

[Harold Pinter, *The Caretaker*, 1960]

Preface

This is a radically revised, expanded, and updated version of the book that first appeared in 1981 under the title of *Naming Names*, subtitled *Stories of Pseudonyms and Name Changes, with a Who's Who.*

It extends the scope of the 1989 edition even further. That was itself an expanded and updated version of the original. Now, in this third edition, the number of entries has more than doubled. Not only have hundreds of new entries been added, but all existing entries have been checked and updated through 1996 and even into 1997. I have especially striven to add the stories behind many names that were previously unexplained, or at least to enlarge on origins that may have been sketchy or even conjectural. However, it does not pay to guess the origin of a newly adopted name, and I have chosen to leave some names unexplained rather than hazard a guess as to their provenance.

In increasing the number of entries, I have consciously broadened their field, both in nature and in nationality. There are thus more magicians and mystics than before, as well as a wider representation of Welsh bards, East European writers, cartoonists, and Italian singers, these last including the specialized but noteworthy category of castrati who adopted the names of their patrons.

Readers familiar with the book's second edition will also find changes in Part I, the introductory chapters. These have been expanded in some sections and reordered in others. New material, including illustrative examples, has likewise been incorporated.

As for Part II, the dictionary proper, an enhanced representation has been given to those who changed their first name only, such as Dale Hawkins and Benny Hill, since a change of first name is as valid a name change as that of a surname. There is also now a larger proportion of temporary or as the British say "one-off" names, the latter being those adopted for a single purpose or on a single occasion. Examples are Max Bonda, who took this name for a single musical work, and Pauline Réage, who used this name for a single book.

There are some famous names that have excited greater interest (or speculation) than others, and for a few of these I have created specially detailed entries, citing material from several sources. A good example is Greta Garbo, whose name has attracted many theories over the years, both before her death (in 1990) and since. Her entry thus includes accounts from five different biographies. (Like certain other lengthy entries, it is also divided into paragraphs for ease of reading.)

There are now additions to the various appendices in Part III. Here I have retained the spectacular runs of pseudonyms used by Voltaire and Defoe, but have replaced the list of real names (cited as contrasting with pseudonyms) by further lists of different kinds, including writers who have adopted more than one pen name, French citizens who have changed their family names, and baseball players who have adopted their nicknames as their regular forenames. Although there is no longer a listing of real names, the former accounts of individuals who have deliberately *not* changed their names remain, and have likewise increased in number.

It goes without saying that the Bibliography has been updated and expanded, although some of the titles mentioned in previous editions have now been omitted on grounds of datedness or unreliability.

In short, the reader will now find not only an increase in the quantity of entries and related material, but an increase in quality as well. Pseudonyms and name changes never fail to intrigue and entertain, and this new edition of one of the few general books on the subject aims to do that subject justice and bring it before an even wider public.

Part I
Introduction

1. The Nature of a Name

With a name like yours, you might be any shape, almost (Lewis Carroll, *Through the Looking-Glass*, Chapter VI).

"What's in a name?" agonized lovelorn Juliet, for she was a Capulet, and he, her roaming romantic Romeo, was a Montague, and the two families were deadly enemies.

Shakespeare himself well knew what was in a name. One need only mention his Aguecheek and Ariel, his Benvolio and Malvolio, his Pistol and Doll Tearsheet and of course his Romeo — was there ever a more evocative name? — to see and sense the charm of well chosen names.

We shall be examining in due course and in some detail "what's in a name," but first we should touch on a more basic question: what *is* a name?

We all of us have a name. Conventionally, at any rate in the Western world, we have, as an accepted and acceptable minimum, a forename, or Christian name, and a surname, or family name. We are John Smith, or Mary Brown, or Clark Gable, or Betty Grable, or even, like the famous social leader from Houston, Texas, Ima Hogg. The names are different, and serve different purposes — a forename is essentially private property, and a surname public — but in their respective and differing ways both names carry equal weight, both actually and legally, as a means of identification.

By custom and tradition, our first name is given us soon after we are born, at a christening or baptismal or naming ceremony, while our last name is already there, and we simply become one more member of the family to share it. In most cases, we get our names from our parents, since our forename is chosen for us by our parents and we inherit our parents' surname.

Our first name is our special individual property — although there may be hundreds of other people who also bear it — and it lasts as long as our life lasts. Our surname may well have existed for centuries and generations before us, in one form or another, and will probably continue to be borne by our own children long after our own life has ended.

Assuming that our ancestors did not deliberately change the surname that we now bear, how far back can we trace this name? Theoretically, at least, must there not have been a time, going back as far as we can, when we come to the first of our forebears to be so named? How did *he* get his name? In other words, more generally, where did the very first names of all come from?

It is worth taking a look at this original process of name creation, since this is the process that is the chief concern of this book.

Many English and some Americans can trace their surnames back in written form to the Domesday Book of the late 11th century. If your name is Gridley, for example, there is a chance, admittedly an extremely slim one, that Albert Greslet was one of your ancestors. His name was recorded by the Domesday Book in Cheshire in 1086. Or if you are a Tallboy, perhaps Ralph Tailgebosc of Hertfordshire, who likewise lived nearly a millennium ago, was one of the greatest of your great-grandfathers. Both Albert and Ralph have names that to our modern eyes are recognizably personal names, in the familiar forename-surname form. A number of names cited and recorded in the Domesday Book, however, are single names, or are for example names that belong to a person who is said to be the "filius" or son of someone else. The name that today is Jarrold or Gerald, for instance, occurs in the Domesday Book as Robertus filius Geraldi — "Robert Geraldson," as it were — while people today named Bishop will find, at any rate in Northamptonshire in 1086, that their Domesday ancestor was simply called Biscop.

The Domesday Book thus also records the early stages of our present binomial (forename-plus-surname) system. Originally, therefore, people had only one name. One person with one name; quite enough. But we want to go back even further. Where did these names come from in turn? Did they have a meaning? For example, was the original Tallboy (actually Tailgebosc, as we have seen) a tall boy, and was the early Bishop a bishop? What does Gridley (or Greslet) mean, and where did Gerald come from?

The answer is both simple and complex. Simple, in that all these original names did indeed have a meaning. Complex, in that many of these early names do not mean what they seem to mean. Ralph Tailgebosc was not a tall boy but was himself the descendant of someone who was a woodcutter, from Old French *tailler*, "to cut," and *bosc*, "wood." Over the centuries his surname became smoothed and assimilated to something that had an *English* meaning and pronunciation. The original Bishop, too, although his name has not changed anything like as radically as Ralph's, was almost certainly not a bishop but a man who looked like one or, more likely, had the manners or deportment of one — an episcopal pose, if you like. His name was thus more what we today would call a nickname. Albert Greslet's surname was really a nickname, too: it means "pockmarked," literally "marked by hail," also from Old French, while Gerald, these days more common as a forename, meant "spear-ruler."

Woodcutter, Bishop-like person, Pockmarked person, and One Who Ruled with His Spear. A fearsome foursome! But we can go further back than that. We are limited by written or pictographic records, of course, but we have evidence that some time before 3050 BC there was a man named Sekhen, a predynastic king of Upper Egypt. And further back still, some two thousand years before him, in about 5000 BC, there lived a Sumerian queen named Ninziddamkiag, which is believed to mean "the queen [who] loves the faithful husband."

Our names thus have their origin where language itself has its cradle — with this Egyptian king and that Sumerian queen. More specifically, they originated where the English language did: with the Greeks, the Romans, the Celts, the Germanic peoples such as the Anglo-Saxons and the Vikings, and the Normans. All these races in fact had a naming system that was in many ways similar, since although it developed into the binomial system as we know it today, or, earlier, the famous trinomial system of the Romans (praenomen, nomen and cognomen), it originally involved the conferring of a single name that had a meaning.

As mentioned, this single meaningful name was in many cases what we might today think of as a nickname, or at any rate as a descriptive title. As such, it related directly or indirectly to the person named. If directly, it usually described his appearance, manner, gait or general image — either what he was or what he might become. The name might consist of a single element, such as the Celtic word *ruadh*, "red," for someone who was of ruddy complexion (today the name is Roy), or a double element, as the Gerald mentioned, whose name derives from Germanic *ger*, "spear," and *vald*, "rule." If a name related indirectly to a person, it would usually derive from his or her family, home area, or occupation, and if the first of these, from the name of the father or grandfather. The Greeks, for example, named the eldest son after his paternal grandfather and later children after other relatives. Sometimes, however, a Greek boy bore the same name as his father. This was the case with Demosthenes, the orator, whose name, like the

Germanic Gerald, is bielemental and meant "people-strength." (Like Gerald, too, it is a desirable image name.) Women's names were formed similarly but with a feminine ending. An unmarried Greek woman would derive her name from her father, a married woman from her husband, a widow from her son. Examples of names deriving respectively from a person's place of residence and his occupation are Anglo-Saxon Grene (modern Green), for someone who lived near the village green, and Cupere (Cooper), for a man who made or repaired wooden casks.

The categories — descriptive, familial, residential and occupational — form the basis for most modern European and transatlantic surnames.

A useful study would be to trace the fortunes and popularity of the original names as they evolved down the centuries, and to consider why many such names became fixed as surnames only (in the modern sense), while others remain in common use as Christian names or forenames. Of the few names already mentioned, for example, Bishop, Green and Cooper are more familiar today as surnames, while Gerald and Roy, although also occurring as surnames, are probably more frequent as forenames. Generally speaking, it can be said that *any* surname is capable of being put into use as a forename — Dudley and Sidney were English surnames that made this transition in the 16th century, just as later in America Chauncey and Washington were adopted as forenames — but that many surnames, in particular familial, residential and occupational, just never made it.

As to why surnames exist at all, the answer is much more straightforward. Surnames were found necessary to distinguish one particular person from others, perhaps many others, who had the same single name. A surname is thus a name that is "super," or added to, one's own. The word *surname* itself is not related to *sir*. As the English historian and antiquary William Camden concisely but carefully put it, in his *Remains Concerning Britain* (1605), "The French and we termed them Surnames, not because they are the names

of the *Sire*, or the father, but because they are *super-* added to Christian names." In recent times the dropping of a surname as a way of creating a pseudonym or as a feminist statement has sometimes been prompted by this continuing misconception. Thus Dale Spencer, in *Man Made Language* (1980), cites the case of a woman who dropped her surname because she associated the word with "sire" and regarded it as being "so closely linked socially with the ownership of women that there was no 'surname' that she found acceptable." Instead, she called herself simply Margaret Sandra.

Historically, many surnames came to incorporate an element that actually means "son." One we have already seen, for Latin *filius* in the Domesday Book's Robertus filius Geraldi survives, in assimilated French form, as the Fitz- that begins many surnames, while a number of familiar first names have become surnames by the simple process of having "son" tacked on to them. Thus both a Fitzwilliam and a Williamson had, originally, a father named William. Parallels to this paternity label exist in many other languages besides English. The Jewish equivalent, and a far more ancient one, is the *bar* or *ben*, meaning "son," in such names as the biblical Simon-bar-Jonas and the Talmudic Joshua ben Hananiah (*bar* is the Aramaic form, and *ben* the Hebrew), while although not a surname in the modern sense, the Russian patronymic, the middle name that all Russians have, as Lev *Nikolayevich* Tolstoy or Maya *Mikhaylovna* Plisetskaya, is still obligatory.

Subsequently, once a surname had been acquired, it became a family name proper and passed on, ordinarily, from father to son and daughter in a now traditional manner.

We have referred to one of the four categories of surname as *nicknames*. This is possibly not quite the right word here, for etymologically a nickname is an additional name or an extra name, and one can hardly refer to a single name as "extra" when it is the only one there is. (*A nickname* should really be *an ickname*, since the word derives from *eke* meaning "also.") On the other hand to call such names *descriptive* names is to be almost too wide-ranging, since in a sense the other three categories are also descriptive.

But we have so far mentioned only once the type of name that this book is really about, the *pseudonym*. And since we shall be using the word constantly we must define it here and now.

Literally, of course, a pseudonym is a "false name," as the two Greek elements that make up the word indicate. The term is a relatively new one. The *Oxford English Dictionary* records its earliest appearance only as late as 1846, although the adjective "pseudonymous" dates back to 1706. For the purposes of the present book, the term "pseudonym" is used for a name that a person adopts in addition to, or instead of, his or her original name. In some cases it replaces the original name, so that a full name change has occurred. In others it operates alongside the existing name, often in connection with its bearer's particular public activity, such as writer or actor.

At this point it should be observed that many dictionaries of pseudonyms are also dictionaries of nicknames, and as shown in the Bibliography (page 399), are actually titled as such. However, it does not do to mix the two, for the two types of name are quite distinctive. A pseudonym, although it may begin as a nickname, is a name consciously assumed by its bearer. A nickname is a name given by someone else, which may or may not be adopted. (If derogatory, it will usually not be!) The rock singer who was born Gordon Sumner was thus nicknamed "Sting" as a teenager for the wasp-striped T-shirt he regularly wore, and he adopted this name for his public persona. His nickname became his pseudonym. But Napoleon Bonaparte did not adopt the derisory name "Boney" by which the English dubbed him when in the early years of the 19th century there was a real danger that he might invade Britain. His nickname, which as a shortened form of his surname aimed to belittle him, did *not* become his pseudonym. His nonadoption of the name did not prevent its use by the public, however, whether in spoken form or in print.

2. Why Another Name?

A self-made man may prefer a self-made name (Judge Learned Hand, referring to Samuel Goldfish's change of name to Samuel Goldwyn, quoted in Bosley Crowther, *The Lion's Share*, 1957).

Who are the people who choose to adopt a pseudonym or to change their name, and why do they do it?

Broadly speaking people assume a new or additional name because they have to, because they are expected to, or simply because they want to. The name that they assume is then made known to the public at large, to a particular group of people, or just to one other person. An actor, for example, wants his whole public to know his new name, while a spy or secret agent operates under a cover name that is known only to a select few. An individual, on the other hand, can communicate a message to a friend or loved one in a press announcement, for example, by using a disguised name that is known to his or her correspondent alone.

Let us see who exactly the main groups of people are.

One of the most common and striking situations in which people will change their original names for new ones is the act, to a greater or lesser degree traumatic, of emigration and subsequent naturalization. A person leaves his or her native country for some reason — often driven out by war, persecution, or destitution — and, arriving in another, where very likely a new language is spoken, officially or tacitly starts a new life, assumes a new identity, and takes on a new name to go with it. One of the greatest migrations in history was the mass emigration to America by around 35 million people from all parts of Europe between 1820 and 1930. In their flight from poverty, famine and harassment, inhabitants of Great Britain and Ireland, Germany and Scandinavia, Italy and the Balkans, Russia and the Austro-Hungarian Empire, many of them Jews, poured into America in the hope of setting up a new life in a country that seemed to offer refuge and opportunities. And when they eventually reached the immigrant depot at Ellis Island — "Heartbreak Island" many of them called it, for fear of being denied entry — they were faced with a number of questions, of which the first was always, "What is your name?"

Immigrant names were a constant source of difficulty. Many of the newly arrived were barely literate and could not even spell their names, with the result that officials frequently simplified or anglicized them haphazardly. This meant that a number of immigrants left Ellis Island with a new name, perhaps not even realizing this, although many, especially the more literate, acquired a new name only in due course.

Many stories exist about "on-the-spot" name changes of this kind. Here are just two of them.

The first concerns a German Jew named Isaac. Confused by all the questioning, he replied, when asked his name, "Ich vergessen" (Yiddish for "I forget"). The immigrant officer recorded his name as Fergusson.

The second incident is an occurrence in Elia Kazan's 1963 movie *America, America*. A Greek shoeshine boy, Stavros Topouzoglou, frightened that he may not be allowed into the country, answers to the name of a dead friend, Hohannes Gardashian. The officer tells him that if he wants to be an American, he must change his name for something shorter. "Hohannes — that's *all* you need here!" And he writes the name "Joe Arness," adding, "Well, boy, you're reborn, you're baptized again. And without benefit of clergy. Next..."

Apocryphal though such tales may be, they illustrate some important realities about the process of changing one's name. First a name change can be quite an arbitrary thing. Indeed, although many of the changes recorded in this book were undertaken consciously and deliberately, thousands of American immigrants came to have their names changed by random and gradual processes — a letter dropped here, a respelling adopted there — and changed most of all, perhaps, by what Howard F. Barker, one of America's greatest authorities on surnames, called "the abrasion of common speech." Second, the immigrant officer's comment, "You're reborn," states a basic philosophy that underlies virtually all name changes. For a human being, after all, a name is far more than a mere identification tag. It is not like a placename, for example, where *London* denotes "the capital of Great Britain" and *Fort Knox* signifies "military reservation and air base in Kentucky, where most of the U.S. gold reserves are stored." Our names not only identify us, they *are* us: they announce us, advertise us and embody us. Stavros the shoeshine boy, like many other immigrants, had his name changed for him, but many people choose a new name simply because they feel that the name itself can bestow a new image and a new persona. "In assuming a new name," the French literary critic Jean Starobinski wrote of Stendhal, who assumed over a hundred pseudonyms, "he not only grants himself a new face, but a new destiny, a new social rank, new nationalities." On a rather different plane, but approached by the same path, the rock singer Elton John commented, on adopting his new stage name, "I'm still the same guy, but a new name gave me a new outlook on life, and a new drive to do things."

Short of an actual physical reincarnation, a change of name is one of the most popular and efficacious ways, many believe, of becoming a new or a different person.

For the many Jews in this great immigration, the adoption of a new name was nothing new in itself. A hundred years previously, for example, Jews in many European countries had been ordered to assume fixed family names as the result of a radical change in the political and cultural climate. It was at this time, in fact, that many Germanic Jewish names arose, such as Weiss, Schwartz, Gross and Klein. These particular four names (White, Black, Large, Little) were in turn often random names, given or acquired with no relevance to the person who came to be so named. In many communities in Hungary, for instance, Jews were divided into four arbitrary groups and each of these names was assigned to every person in one of the groups.

Now, a century later, many immigrant Jews were obliged to change their name again, to an English-style surname. So widespread was the change, and so diffuse, that today it is virtually impossible to identify a given surname as Jewish: there are thousands of Smiths, Browns and Joneses who were originally, perhaps, Kovacs, Brand or (with total dissimilarity) Edelstein. On the other hand, it is clear that today such name changes, foreign or Jewish to English, for example, are not taking place on anything like the scale that they did in the nineteenth century. In 1977 the director of the U.S. Immigration and Naturalization Service stated that each year about 142,000 people assume American nationality and of these only 7,000, or 15 percent, change their name, mainly by shortening it so that it is easier to pronounce in English. As the Russian U.S. émigré newspaper *Novoye Russkoye Slovo* commented: "In recent years the number of immigrants changing their name has fallen considerably. Many newcomers to the States prefer to maintain their ties with their homeland by keeping their real name and continuing to speak their native language" (September 1, 1977).

The practical advantages of changing a foreign name to an English-sounding one are obvious, and have already been mentioned. It is self-evident that if a person wishes to assimilate fully and successfully into a community, a name that blends with the others' will be of considerable assistance. Of course, equally, there is an obverse side to this: a person who does not change his or her name will be conspicuous as a foreigner, and this may be at least a hindrance, at most a positive and highly undesirable branding, especially in time of war. This was noticeably so in World War I, when many Anglophones with Germanic names keenly regretted their "alien" name or were prompted to change it. The English poet John Betjeman, who was ultimately of Dutch descent, relates in his verse autobiography *Summoned by Bells* (1960) how he was taunted at school about his name ("Betjeman's a German spy/ Shoot him down and let him die"), and in the British royal family King George V changed the family name from Wettin to Windsor by proclamation on July 17, 1917, while Queen Mary's family changed their name from Teck to "of Cambridge" and the Battenbergs became the Mountbattens (See page 10, Chapter 3, for more on royal name changes.)

Would people ever change their English names to foreign ones, or to ones not native to them? The immigrants, of course, changed their native names to non-native ones, but occasions when an English name has been changed to a foreign one, except for frivolous or satirical reasons, are not common, although cases have been recorded of Jews changing *back* to their original name from the English one that they adopted on immigration.

Apart from special instances such as that of disguise, when the national of one country aimed to pass himself off as the citizen of another, there have been occasions when some writers have assumed a foreign name with the aim of describing their impressions of their own country apparently through the eyes of an alien observer. Oliver Goldsmith did this for his *Chinese Letters*, republished in 1762 as *The Citizen of the World*. In their original form, these were purportedly written by a Chinese philosopher named Lien Chi Altangi. On similar lines, Robert Southey's *Letters of Espriella* (1807) claimed to be a collection of letters written from England by a young Spaniard, giving a picture of the times. There have been other examples of "foreigners' letters," most of which were inspired by Montesquieu's *Lettres Persanes* ("Persian Letters") (1721). These comprised the supposed correspondence of two Persians, Rica and Usbek, making observations about life and *mœurs* in Paris at the end of the reign of Louis XIV.

All name changes, of course, are in the last resort voluntary affairs, although political or social pressure may be very great to make the change. Possibly the only category of person who is virtually compelled to make a name change is someone who has undergone a sex change. To undergo such a radical physical and emotional transformation and retain one's old opposite sex name would seem most undesirable. In recent times one such change (of sex and name) that became widely publicized, simply because the person concerned was, and is, a distinguished writer in his — now her — own right, was that of the English writer and editor Jan Morris, formerly James Morris. Jan Morris describes the whole experience and its consequences in her book *Conundrum* (1974). (See also her entry on page 264.)

There is a noted category of name changers in criminals of all kinds, one important objective being the avoidance of detection or identification, with the name change often accompanied by an actual physical disguise. The name itself may be unimportant: what *is* important is that the criminal should have a name of some kind, since truly and permanently anonymous human beings do not exist. Ideally, to have no name at all would be an excellent idea, since then the murderer would stand a good chance of escaping undetected, and no one would know whodunit. But if you start life with a name, as we all do, you cannot simply abandon it without replacing it somehow. Even the Man in the Iron Mask had a name, although what it was has still not been established with any degree of certainty.

A special type of name assumed by a criminal, or even a suspect is an *alias*. The word is Latin in origin, meaning "otherwise," a sense that is indicated more obviously in the alternate term for an alias — "aka," or "also known as."

Like misfortunes, aliases rarely come singly, especially when a criminal or suspect is on the run, and they are changed as often as the bearer's route and disguise. The ideal alias is one that is contained in a stolen or forged passport, which is essential if the criminal is escaping to another country. Cases of criminals with forged or illegal passports are legion. One that hit the headlines in 1977, largely because of its lurid details and bizarre nature, combining sex and religion, was that of the "Mormon kidnap." A young Mormon missionary, one Kirk Anderson, claimed to have been "kidnapped and held handcuffed and manacled for three days on the orders of a wealthy lovesick woman" (*Sunday Times*, September 18, 1977). The rich and randy lady in question was Joyce, or Joy, McKinney. Among aliases used by McKinney in forged passports on her subsequent flight from the police were Mrs. Bosler, Kathie Vaughn Bare, Cathy Van Deusen, Heidi Krasler, and Mrs. Palmquist. Traveling with her as her supposed husband was Keith Joseph May, aka Bob Bosler, alias Paul Van Deusen. It was not the first time Ms. McKinney had assumed a different name. She had previously appeared as a model in a girlie magazine as Lexi Martin, and had advertised her services in the *Los Angeles Free Press* as Joey.

Somewhat similar in nature was the case of Martha Wade Kaufman, mistress of the American oil tycoon Armand Hammer, who changed her name to Hilary Gibson to get on his payroll while simultaneously altering her appearance to deceive his wife. Across the Atlantic, an English criminal and Wild West fanatic, real name Colin Tough, escaped from jail in 1992 and evaded recapture for four years by assuming the name and identity of Alan Rogers, Alan for Alan Ladd, Rogers for Roy Rogers, two of his heroes. (He had originally wanted to call himself Roy Rogers, but understandably felt that such a name might invite suspicion.)

In cases where, for whatever reason, a person assumes the guise of the opposite sex, a change of name will frequently be desirable as well as a change of dress. There have been many instances where women have assumed male names on joining the armed services disguised as a youth or man, or who claimed to have done so. Among the latter was the Englishwoman Valerie Arkell-Smith, who masqueraded as a British serving officer under the name and rank of Colonel Victor Barker in the 1920s. (In 1930 she altered her rank and expanded her name to be Captain Leslie Ivor Victor Gauntlett Bligh Barker.)

Women who did actually enlist under assumed names include Loreta Janeta Velasquez, who in 1860 joined the Independent Scouts of the Confederate Southern Army as Harry T. Buford; Emma Sarah Edmonds, who fought in the American Civil War as Franklin Thompson; Mary Anne Talbot, a British soldier and sailor under the alias of John Taylor in the 18th century; Jennie Hodgers, an American who assumed the identity of Albert Cashier to enlist in the American Civil War in 1862; Isabelle Gunn, a Scotswoman who spent two years with the Hudson's Bay Company as John Fubister; Hannah Snell, one of Britain's best known 18th-century sailors, serving as James Gray (her predictably feminine appearance earned her the nickname of "Miss Molly Gray"); Dorothy Lawrence, who joined a British Expeditionary Force in 1915 as Private Denis Smith; and Deborah Sampson, who fought for two years in the Revolutionary War as Robert Shurtleff. In some cases such adventurers changed their first name only. Ellen Watts, an Englishwoman, joined the navy in 1838 as Charles Watts, while Mary Walker worked as a sailor and barman in the 1860s as Thomas Walker.

Mention should finally be made in this particular gender- and name-change category of the 17th-century Spanish nun Catalina de Eranso, who served with the Spanish army in Chile and Peru as Alonso Díaz Ramírez de Guzmán, and of Barbara Ann Malpass, who spent four months in Jefferson County jail in 1959 claiming to be Charles Richard Williams. The latter assumed her guise and name because she reckoned she could more easily pass as a male runaway than a female.

The range of uses to which a name change can be put illegally or criminally is wide. At one end there is the murderer and his or her alias. At the other is the child at school who answers "Here!" at rollcall to cover up for a friend who is playing hookey. This last is a trivial but genuine case of impersonation. Many cases are known of one person temporarily or even permanently succeeding in passing himself off as another.

It is certainly a fact that many pseudonyms are adopted for nefarious purposes, or at least for disguise. The code names and cover names taken by spies and undercover agents are well known, from the famous, although fictional, 007 (James Bond), to the infamous Cicero, who supplied top secret documents to the Germans in World War II and who turned out to be one Elyesa Bazna. Espionage is a world of forged papers, fake identities, and secret passwords, a dark world of aliases, incognitos and assumed names. Experts in the art of espionage distinguish between a cover name and an operational name. A cover name is the name adopted by an agent when he or she embarks on the actual operation. In doing this, the agent assumes the identity of either a real person or a fictional one. If the former, he will also be impersonating that person. Thus the cover name of the Russian spy K.T. Molody was Gordon Lonsdale. An operational name, by contrast, is the name by which an agent is known to his chiefs, so that he can be identified without reference being made to his real name or his cover name. Thus the British-Russian agent whose real name was Allan Nunn May had the operational name Alek.

The general public was made aware of the use and effectiveness of cover names in World War II, especially by agents working against the Germans in occupied France. One of the best known, if only because of her fearful ordeal, was Odette (see her entry on page 276). She was fortunate enough to survive the war, but many others were not, such as the following, mentioned in a factually based account of Odette's experiences:

Miss Andrée Borrel ("Denise"— courier and co-organizer), Miss Vera Leigh ("Simone"—courier), Miss Diana Rowden ("Juliette"—courier) were to die together in Natsweiler on the 6th of July. Mrs. Yolande Beekman ("Yvonne"—radio operator), Miss Madeleine Damerment ("Martine"—courier) and Miss Elaine Plewman ("Gaby"—courier), were to live a little longer and to die side by side in the hell of Dachau [Jerrard Tickell, *Odette: The Story of a British Agent*, 1949].

Wartime agents often used several cover names. Thus the German *Abwehr* (counter-intelligence) agent Hugo Ernst Bleicher operated in France under aliases that included Monsieur Jean, Lieutenant-Colonel Henri, Jean Castel, Jean Verbeck, and Henri Botherau.

In considering the various categories of people who assume another name, we have briefly mentioned certain individual ballet dancers and writers. These are members of a creative profession whose names—stage names and pen names—are probably the most familiar to the world since they are in a most popular sector of society. But before considering these special people, in Chapter 4, let us take a look at the more common majority who change their names for traditional or legal reasons.

3. Changing Names

Why, this is flat knavery, to take upon you another man's name (Petruchio in *The Taming of the Shrew*).

Both historically and actually, in past and present, name changes have long been a feature of the human scene.

History tends to concentrate on personalities, and the consequences of their actions. But behind some of the most familiar names there are some surprises, and we find that some of the best known names are not really what they seem.

Oliver Cromwell, for example, was not really a Cromwell at all, but a Williams.

How did this come about? A certain Welsh gentleman, named Morgan Williams, married the sister, Katherine, of Thomas Cromwell, who had himself been created Earl of Essex by Henry VIII. Morgan Williams's son was Richard Williams, who received the patronage of Thomas Cromwell and who adopted his name in consequence, as sometimes happened. He was thus an ancestor of Oliver Cromwell (himself the great-great-grandson of Morgan Williams), and the Lord Protector of England was aware of his family line and former family name, even

signing himself on occasions as "Oliver Williams, alias Cromwell."

Again, look up the Duke of Wellington, the "Iron Duke" who routed Napoleon at the Battle of Waterloo (1815), in any standard encyclopedia, and you will find that his name is given as Arthur Wellesley. Yet he was the grandson of a man named Richard Colley, or Cowley, who adopted the name of an Irish cousin, Garrett Wesley, on succeeding to his estates in 1728, and who later changed this name to Wellesley.

Even the great Mowbray family, whose name became that of the Earls of Northumberland and subsequently (by marriage) of the Earls of Nottingham, was really de Albini. The baronial house was founded at the Norman Conquest by Geoffrey de Montbrai, Bishop of Coutances. His nephew and heir, Robert de Mowbray, Earl of Northumberland (died 1125), rebelled against William Rufus and was consequently imprisoned at Windsor. He had married Mathilde de l'Aigle, but when he was imprisoned his wife was granted permission by the pope to dissolve the marriage and to marry instead Nigel de Albini (d'Aubigny), another nephew of the Bishop of Coutances. Nigel thus founded the second house of Mowbray, changing his name to this from de Albini together with his son, Roger, by order of Henry I, on the king's granting him the vast estates of his imprisoned uncle. This line of Mowbrays lasted until 1476, when John Mowbray, 16th Baron Mowbray and 4th Duke of Norfolk, died without leaving any male issue. On the death of his daughter Anne (in 1481), the dukedom of Norfolk passed to the Howard family.

In similar fashion, the Dukes and Earls of Northumberland (distinct from the Mowbrays just mentioned) are traditionally associated with the family name Percy, after the Norman baron, William de Percy, who accompanied William the Conqueror to England. Yet Sir Hugh Percy (1715–1786), 1st Duke of Northumberland of the third creation, was originally Sir Hugh Smithson. He gained the honors of the house of Percy through his grandmother-in-law, Lady Elizabeth Seymour, née Percy, heiress of the 11th Earl of Northumberland, assuming her name and arms in 1750 on succeeding to the earldom through his wife, Lady Elizabeth's granddaughter, whom he had married ten years earlier. (The lady's grandfather, Charles Seymour, 6th Duke of Somerset, was not happy about the marriage, but it went ahead anyway.)

A glance through the many pages of the *Dictionary of National Biography* reveals not only these name changes, but many others of a similar nature, brought about through various terms and conditions pertaining to family inheritances and marriages. To put it fairly crudely, Mr. A inherits the estate of his uncle, Mr. B, so changes his name from A to B. Or else Mr. C marries Miss D, herself an heiress, and on her succession to the inheritance changes his name (C) to hers (D), instead of the other way around, as usually happens. (Of which more below in due course.)

The examples quoted happen to be well-known families, but the same sort of name change can be found for other, less widely known families. Here are a few more examples:

Francis Egerton, 1st Earl of Ellesmere (1800–1857), was born the younger son of George Granvile Leveson-Gower, 2nd Marquis of Stafford. On the death of his father in 1833, he changed his name from Leveson-Gower to Egerton, this being the name of his bachelor uncle, Francis Henry Egerton, 8th Earl of Bridgewater (died 1829), who left him property estimated at the then colossal evaluation of around £90,000 per annum.

Then there was Sir Thomas Hugh Clifford Constable (1762–1823), topographer and botanist, born the son of Thomas Clifford and his wife Barbara, née Aston. In 1821 he succeeded to the estates of Francis Constable, of Burton Constable, and two years later was granted royal permission to adopt the name of Constable as his surname.

Sir Thomas Constable did not acquire his new name until a few months before his death, at the age of 61, unlike Francis Egerton, who was almost half this age when he made his name change. But the changes were equally valid and equally dependent on succession to an estate, and were typical of their time.

More recently, pioneer genealogist George Edward Cokayne (1825–1911), author of *G.E.C.'s Complete Peerage* (1887–98), the now standard register of the British aristocracy, was born Adams. He changed his name to Cokayne in 1873, however, in accordance with his mother's will.

Finally, and famously, the original family name of English nurse Florence Nightingale (1820–1910) was Shore. Her father, William Edward Shore (1794–1874), adopted his new name on coming of age in 1815, when he inherited the Derbyshire estates of his mother's uncle, Peter Nightingale.

There is a nice example in literature of a name change resulting from an acquisition of property. In Thomas Hardy's *Tess of the D'Urbervilles* (1891), where the author deploys much genealogical skill, one John Stoke buys property in a part of England different from the one in which he had actually made his fortune. The acquisition prompts him to change his name, and he visits the British Museum, London, to study the county histories. He comes across the name "D'Urberville" and, in Hardy's words, "considered that D'Urberville looked and sounded as well as any of them: and D'Urberville accordingly was annexed to his own name for himself and his heirs eternally." His family thus became "Stoke-D'Urberville," but subsequently dropped the "Stoke." (The novel centers on Tess Durbeyfield, whose father John, a poor villager, has his head turned when he learns that he is descended from the ancient family of D'Urberville. Meanwhile Tess is seduced by Alec D'Urberville, son of the former John Stoke, whose claim to the name, as mentioned, is at best doubtful.)

Readers of both classical and modern literature encounter name changes and aliases as in the real world. In another of Hardy's works, *Desperate Remedies* (1871), Captain Bradleigh becomes Captain Aldclyffe, while in Agatha Christie's *Murder on the Links* (1923), millionaire Paul T. Renauld, as Georges Conneau, is involved in a crime passionnel with Madame Daubreuil, otherwise, as his mistress, Jeanne Beroldy. In W.M. Thackeray's *Lovel the Widower* (1860), actress Elizabeth Prior has the stage name Bessie Bellenden, while in Sherwood Anderson's *Dark Laughter* (1925), Chicago reporter Bruce Dudley is really named John Stockton. The true name of bootlegger Al Grecco in John O'Hara's *Appointment in Samarra* (1935) is Tony Murascho, while in R.L. Stevenson's classic *Kidnapped* (1886), Alan Breck assumes the alias of Thomson in order to help his friend David Balfour, the novel's central character. Finally (in this modest selection), the eponymous hero and narrator of Thackeray's *Barry Lyndon* (1844) gains this name only on marrying Lady Lyndon. As the novel opens he is Redmond Barry.

Name changes of a somewhat different kind have taken place over the past century in the British royal family.

British kings and queens have never had individual surnames in the accepted sense, but instead have had "house" names, that is, names of dynasties. The further back one goes in time, the more general do the dynastic names seem, with William the Conqueror, for example, regarded as belonging to the House of Normandy, and his great-grandson, Henry II, being the first of the House of Plantagenet. The latter name is essentially a nickname, given to Henry's father, Geoffrey, for his habit of wearing a sprig of broom, Latin *planta genista*, in his hat. Paradoxically, a case could be made for arguing that this name is much closer to a modern surname in its origin than many recent royal dynastic names. The only other royal house names resembling a genuine modern surname are those of Tudor, this being the family name of a line of Welsh gentry, and Stuart, originating as an occupational name, that of "steward," i.e., an officer of the Scottish royal household.

George I was the first of the House of Hanover, which concluded with Queen Victoria, who died in 1901. She was succeeded by Edward VII, of the House of Saxe-Coburg. He took this dynastic name because Victoria's husband, Albert, had been Prince of Saxe-Coburg and Gotha. The German connection, which had been all too evident in the British royal family since the accession of George I (in 1714) as the son of the Elector of Hanover, would soon become an embarrassment. Edward VII died in 1910, and his successor, George V, was a cousin of the German Kaiser, Wilhelm II. This relationship proved an embarrassment when World War I broke out in 1914, and a dilemma for the British royal family, who found themselves with a regal foot (so to speak) in the enemy's camp. At this time, too, several members of the royal family had German names and titles. What was the answer?

The solution adopted by the king was for the royal family to take a (British) surname, which would at the same time serve as a dynastic name. Similarly, British surnames were adopted in place of German family titles by other members of the royal family.

The first set of royal name changes was decreed in an order that appeared in the press on June 20, 1917 (somewhat late in the day). It ran as follows: "The King has deemed it desirable, in the conditions brought about by the present war, that those princes of his family who are his subjects and bear German names and titles should relinquish these titles, and henceforth adopt British surnames." This resulted in the creation of four new peerages: the Duke of Teck and his brother, Prince Alexander, became respectively Marquess of Cambridge and Earl of Athlone, while the Princes Louis and Alexander of Battenberg became Marquesses of Milford Haven and Carisbrooke, respectively. Other members of the Teck family took the surname Cambridge, while members of the Battenberg family assumed the surname Mountbatten. (The latter is merely a part translation of the original German name.)

The next step was for King George, at a meeting of the Privy Council on July 17, to announce his intention, set forth in a royal proclamation of the same date, that "the Name of Windsor is to be borne by His Royal House and Family and Relinquishing the use of All German Titles and Dignities" to determine that his house and family "shall be styled and known as the House and Family of Windsor."

Why Windsor? The answer, of course, is in the Royal Castle of Windsor, in the Berkshire town of this name on the banks of the Thames. Virtually every king and queen since William the Conqueror has had a hand in the building. Henry II (already mentioned) erected the first stone buildings, including the famous Round Tower, and the defenses are largely to this day those built under Henry III. Edward III was born there, and almost all succeeding monarchs down to George IV, including the two queens, expanded or altered the building. Windsor itself is also an ancient placename, recorded even before the Norman Conquest of 1066, so on that ground is equally suitable. The name itself was proposed for the royal family by George V's private secretary, Arthur John Bigge, Baron Stamfordham. But he seems not to have been aware that as long ago as the 14th century, King Edward III had been styled as "Sir Edward de Windsor, King of England"!

The subsequent history of the royal family and its new surname is also not without interest. An intriguing situation developed when Queen Elizabeth II came to the throne in 1952. Before her accession, she had been married to the Duke of Edinburgh, so that her surname would have been the same as that of her husband, in other words, Mountbatten. It was possible to argue that on her succession, the royal house was in effect not the House of Windsor, but the House of Mountbatten. The new queen clarified the situation in a declaration of April 9, 1952, just two months after her succession, when she decreed that she and her descendants, other than females who marry, and their descendants, should bear the name of Windsor.

The Duke of Edinburgh was not a British subject in origin, and was naturalized six months before his marriage to the future queen in 1947, taking the surname of his uncle, Mountbatten. Before his naturalization, as a prince of the royal house of Greece and Denmark, his surname had been the impressively Germanic Schleswig-Holstein-Sonderburg-Glucksberg.

The tale of the Windsor surname was even now not quite complete, for in 1960, when the Queen had been on the throne for eight years, she made a further declaration in Council with regard to it. This declaration brings us right up to date, and even into the future, so is worth quoting in full:

Whereas on the 9th day of April, 1952, I did declare in Council My Will and Pleasure that I and My children shall be styled and known as of the House and Family of Windsor, and that my descendants, other than female descendants who marry and their descendants, shall bear the name of Windsor. And whereas I have given further consideration to the position of those of My descendants who will enjoy neither the style, title or attribute of Royal Highness, nor the titular dignity of Prince, and for whom therefore a surname will be necessary. And whereas I have concluded that the Declaration made by Me on the 9th day of April, 1952, should be varied in its application to such persons: Now therefore I declare my Will and Pleasure that, while I and My children shall continue to be styled and known as the House and Family of Windsor, My descendants other than descendants enjoying the style, title or attribute of Royal Highness and titular dignity of Prince or Princess and female descendants who marry and their descendants shall bear the name of Mountbatten-Windsor.

This declaration could only apply to the grandchildren of the present Prince of Wales, Prince Charles, apart from the eldest grandson, and of the Queen's subsequent other sons (Prince Andrew and Prince Edward). (Under a ruling of George V, the title and style of Prince and Princess were restricted to his grandchildren.) So now, for the first time in British history, members of the royal family have a hyphenated surname. It was first used in 1973 at the marriage of the Princess Royal (Princess Anne) to Captain Mark Phillips.

As mentioned, the surname Windsor exists in its own right, as do surnames derived from many similarly ancient British place-names.

But just supposing that for some reason—not necessarily antiroyalist ones—you are named Windsor and do not like your name. How can you legally change it?

In the United States, a legal name change (except change of a woman's surname due to marriage) is a special proceeding of the local civic court. With this proceeding completed, you can then apply to the Social Security Administration for a new card (retaining your original number). The application must include Form SS5, available at local Social Security offices, and the original court document showing the name change (photocopies are not acceptable).

A woman who changes her name on marriage must also complete Form SS5 if she wishes official recognition of the change in the form of a Social Security card. Her application must include her original (not photocopied) marriage license.

In Britain, a name change is much easier. You simply change it, then advertise the fact, traditionally in the local or national press.

This is what is known in legal terms as acquisition of a new name "by use and reputation." Cases of such lawful name changes can still be spotted, if irregularly, in the press, and are usually couched in fairly formal wording, on the lines of the following: "I, William Windsor, of 246 Main Street, Windsor, Berkshire, pastrycook, heretofore called and known by the name of William Wilberforce Windsor, hereby give notice that I have renounced and abandoned the name of William Wilberforce Windsor, and that I have assumed and intend henceforth on all occasions whatsoever and at all times to sign and use and to be called and known by the name of Frederick Makepeace Cook, in lieu and in substitution for my former name of William Wilberforce Windsor. Dated this 10th day of April, 1997." (Most such announcements, however, are much less wordy. Even so, they still have full legal force.)

Some changes of this type have remained memorable, if only because an obviously undesirable name was changed to a more acceptable one. The classic example, still quoted, is that of one Joshua Bug, who placed a personal advertisement in the June 26, 1862, issue of *The Times* announcing his adoption of the new name of Norfolk Howard. Like the royal declaration above, it is worth quoting in its entirety, if only for its curiosity value:

I, NORFOLK HOWARD, heretofore called and known by the name of Joshua Bug, late of Epsom, in the county of Surrey, now of Wakefield, in the county of York, and landlord of the Swan Tavern in the same county, do hereby give notice, that on the 20th day of this present month of June, for and on behalf of myself and heirs, lawfully begotten, I did wholly ABANDON the use of the SUR-NAME of BUG, and ASSUMED, took, and used, and am determined at all times hereafter, in all writings, actions, dealings, matters, and things, and upon all other occasions whatsoever, to be distinguished, to subscribe, to be called and known by the name of NORFOLK HOWARD only. I further refer all whom it may concern to the deed poll under my hand and seal, declaring that I choose to renounce the use of the surname of Bug, and that I assume in lieu thereof the above surnames of Norfolk Howard, and also declaring my determination, upon all occasions whatsoever, to be called and distinguished exclusively by the said surnames of Norfolk Howard, duly enrolled by me in the High Court of Chancery.—Dated this 23d day of June, 1862. NORFOLK HOWARD, late Joshua Bug.

In choosing this particular name, the advertiser cheekily implied some kind of association with the Dukes of Norfolk, whose family name is Howard. As a result, "Norfolk Howard" became a slang term for a bedbug for some years subsequently. (The announcement may have actually been a spoof, but is even so a good example of the phraseology then required to effect a name change.)

The "deed poll" instanced in the above statement is a fairly common and convenient way in England to evidence a name change, and consists of a declaration similar to (but today less prolix than) the one above, but made before a witness, ideally a professional one such as Commissioner for Oaths. (The somewhat strange term originally designated a deed that was "polled," that is, the document was cut evenly along its sides, unlike an indenture, where the jagged edges of the two documents, one made by each party, were cut so as to fit into each other when the two deeds were placed together. In the case of a deed poll, the declaration is made by one person only, so there is no need for a second matching document.)

There are various situations where a name change may be desirable or even conventional. Among the latter type, one of the most common is that of marriage, the changer being the woman, who relinquishes her maiden name and takes the surname of her husband.

The custom is an old one, regarded as having symbolic significance and religious overtones. The accepted attitude was summarized by William Camden, who in his *Remains Concerning Britain* (1605), already mentioned, wrote: "Here might I note that women with us at their marriage do change their surnames, and pass into their husbands' names, and justly, for that then Non sunt duo, sed caro

una [They are not two, but one flesh]." Camden does go on to note, however, that not all countries observed this practice, and cites France and the Netherlands, where "The better sort of women will still retain their name with their husband's." (He comments: "But I fear husbands will not like this note, for that some of their dames may be ambitiously over pert and too-too forward to imitate it.")

The intention, thus, was for a unification of surname. But if two people have different names, as they of course almost always will, then naturally *one* will have to make a change. And in more recent times feminists of even the least militant kind have not been slow to point out that the change is traditionally made by the woman, not the man. The name change is thus seen as a subservient act, involving not merely a change of identity, but a loss of individuality. The abandoning of one's own family name, after all, is a highly personal and deeply felt affair. Hence the various devices used to avoid such an adoption and loss. One of the most widely favored is the practice commonly found in the United States, where a woman, on marrying, simply adds her husband's name to her own, which she retains. This results in a situation where, say, Jane Shore marries a John Strand, and becomes, however incongruously, Jane Shore Strand. In a traditional British family, the same lady would be Jane Strand, née Shore, with the latter name used only for documentation purposes, as when filling out an official form of some kind.

Another solution, of course, is for the woman either not to undertake a legally binding marriage, so that no name change is involved, or to continue to use her maiden name. Many professional women retain their maiden name after marriage, if only in order to avoid complications from the point of view of the public, who will have become accustomed to the original name. On the other hand, a compromise can be effected by which a married woman uses her husband's surname in private life, but retains her original name for her business or public life.

Whatever the solution to the situation, a

woman who does change her name on marriage has to deal with a whole host of incidental matters resulting from the change, not least involving the notification of a sizable number of official organizations or bodies to which she belongs, such as banks, building or savings societies, doctors' registers, passport authorities and the like. A man will encounter a similarly tiresome procedure only when he changes his address, when of course it is the address only that changes.

Further complications can ensue for a married woman if she obtains a divorce and then remarries. In the latter case, she may well feel that it is simply not worth all the bother of informing the relevant authorities of a further name change, even if she does actually adopt the surname of her second husband. In fact, there is evidence showing that many women do not advertise or publicly notify their new surname on remarriage, which can result in a number of potential or actual administrative problems or at least misunderstandings. One woman gave her personal account of the situation following her second marriage:

> I changed my name on paper, but not it seems in spirit. ... As time went on I felt a strange reluctance to change. I don't know why. When I remarried I had no strong feelings about losing the old name. True, I'd had it for 22 years, so you could say I was well used to it. But it was hardly a name that showed I came from ancient stock, one I felt my children and grandchildren would be proud to bear. I mean... Brown.
>
> I just went along with the convention that women change their names when they marry; and after five years of trouble, odd looks and embarrassment later, I'm still juggling with two names. Seems I'm just reluctant to let the old one go.

Ms. Brown explained that although her new married name was on her two credit cards, the old name remained on her bank account, check book, banker's card and cash card. (The new name was on the credit cards because her husband paid the bills.) This duality resulted in a host of practical problems. On one occasion, she was questioned at an airport desk when buying plane tickets in her new name while flying with a passport in her old name. As a result, a ground hostess recommended she take her marriage certificate with her when she next flew, and so avoid delay! This particular twice-married lady concluded:

> I wish I could claim I was making some kind of statement about holding on to my old name, but I'm not. I can hardly say it's a feminist thing since both names belong originally to men. I've known women who, for professional reasons, hold on to their name from a previous marriage and hyphenate it with the second. I refuse to do that since anything hyphenated with Brown sounds silly to me [Christine Brown, "The name I never dropped...," *The Times,* November 13, 1985].

But what if the divorcee does not remarry? She may well wish to retain her married name, with all its associations. But she may equally well decide to revert to her maiden name. That road may certainly be paved with good intentions, but it can involve similar obstacles and result in unexpected personal unease, even trauma.

A second writer, also in *The Times* (January 9, 1987), gives her account of what happened (Doreen Stanfield, "Rebirth of a maiden by any other name").

The lady postponed making any decision on the matter for some four years after her divorce, and only tackled the situation because she needed to renew her passport. "Having taken the plunge, gone to a lawyer and made a statutory declaration I began to feel surprisingly enthusiastic about the whole thing. I could hardly wait to shed my old identity and assume my new one in all areas of my life." She accordingly notified all the usual bodies and authorities, sent change-of-name cards to her friends, and went about her life in her new persona. But when her mail continued to arrive in the old name, she realized there was more to the business than met the eye. "The whole process seemed to have assumed a symbolic significance for me; it was rather like some sort of rebirth. I was a chrysalis which is almost a butterfly, but not quite." The writer described how she began to feel almost schizophrenic, so that when, for instance, she had to sign a check in her old name, while waiting for her new book to arrive, it "seemed to symbolize a regression into at best the cocoon of non-identity." She discovered that she attached much greater significance to her name than she had previously realized, and that she resented being reminded by correspondents who used her old name that she was still "old Mrs. X," and that she was "not quite out of the cocoon yet."

Eventually, after several months, the writer's metamorphosis was complete, and she was fully established (or re-established) in her maiden name. Now, "I am able to take the odd regressive missive addressed to Mrs. X in my stride. She now seems a different person from me, someone I once knew."

The two accounts summarized here illustrate the administrative and emotional hazards that accompany a name change. And although they respectively concern a remarriage and a divorce, there is no reason why, for some women, the mere adoption of another surname on marriage in the first place may not be equally complex and traumatic.

Some women prefer not to change their name at all. The British politician Emma Nicholson, wife of business executive Sir Michael Caine, no doubt spoke for many women when she said: "I do not believe it is necessary for women to take their husbands' names. I rather like my name and I am sticking to it. My father was in Parliament, he has no son and I want to carry it on for him. I enjoy the feeling of carrying the banner forward. People will address us as Sir Michael Caine and Emma Nicholson" (*The Times*, January 6, 1988).

Despite this, in the 1990s the pressure on women to change their names on marriage was still strong in the United States, as shown by the results of a national survey on marital naming carried out by David Johnson, professor of sociology at the University of Nebraska. "Women

who keep their birth names and never use their spouse's name ... are a tiny, tiny, majority," he said. "Most women, even college students, expect to change their name on marriage and most people do seem to feel that sharing your husband's name implies a greater commitment to the family" (*The Times*, September 1, 1996). Some women may not change their names immediately on marriage, but do so subsequently. Hillary Clinton, wife of President Bill Clinton, remained resolutely Hillary Rodham in the early years of her marriage, but as her husband's political career took off added his name to hers. A strategic message is implicit here, since most rising politicians will wish to portray themselves as family men. However, the "family factor" may not be so important where the husband need not exploit it to public advantage. Amy Carter, daughter of former President Jimmy Carter, announced her intention to keep her maiden name on her marriage in 1996 to James Wentzel, a computer consultant.

Johnson's survey showed that of the two generations of women looked at (those in their 40s and 50s, and those of their daughters' age), 95–98 percent used their husband's name in some way, with most completely changing their names. Of these, around 20 percent used both their maiden name and their married name, typically for professional (public) and domestic (private) purposes respectively. However, many found this arrangement caused complications of the type recounted above, a recurrent problem being which name to use on which occasion. Which for this mail order, for example, and which to sign that check?

A name change of another sort involves adopting a new first name (Christian name). Some people may develop an intense dislike of their first name, and wish to change it for another.

There is no legal problem in this. One simply starts using the new chosen name. The only difficulty arises when a person seeks to abandon a first name conferred at baptism. But in order to avoid ecclesiastical or other negotiations, most legal advisers recommend simply retaining the original Christian name, but not actually using it. In such instances, a person does not actually change a first name, therefore, but merely adopts an additional name.

The aversion that some people feel for a first name that has undesirable associations, real or imaginary, is typified by the following letter from a reader to the "agony aunt" of the *TV Times* (January 23–29, 1988), the latter being the Italian-born British television personality and columnist Katie Boyle (see her entry on page 103). The reader writes:

How I wish that each of us could legally choose our own Christian names when we reach the age of majority. My parents christened me Elsie Maud, after my father's favorite sisters. How I dislike my first name, and I never even admit to my second. Have you noticed that Elsie is always the least intelligent creature in a film or TV play, and in comic-book stories it is always the name chosen for dimwits? I always laugh but, deep down, I feel hurt and mad! I really think my name has given me an inferiority complex. Do you understand, Katie?

As ever, Katie did, and came up with sound practical advice and even a new name for the long-suffering name bearer.

Indeed I do. Baptized Caterina and brought up in Italy, I loathed my own name. Now I am known by lots of other versions, such as Catherine, Kate, Katie and, by many Italian friends, Caterinella. This has helped, so why don't you just switch the letters round and become known as Elise. Say straight out you have always hated the name Elsie, never felt like an Elsie, and laugh at the switch, so others laugh with you, not at you. It's the giggle which will get you over any embarrassment and keep people sympathetically on your side. I shall be the first to send you warmest wishes, dear Elise.

In short, if the Queen of England can make a declaration adopting a new name, so can any of her subjects, as famously did Joshua Bug. But the decision whether to adopt a new name at all in the first place is one for the individual, and may be the hardest aspect of the whole area of name changes.

4. Names for a Living

Goodbye Norma Jean/ Though I never knew you at all,/ You had the grace to hold yourself/ While those around you crawled./ They crawled out of the woodwork/ And they whispered into your brain,/ Set you on the treadmill/ And made you change your name (Bernie Taupin, "Candle in the Wind").

A change of name has become a tradition or even a necessity for many clearly defined professions or callings, from the very public to the much more personal. Actors and writers are perhaps the first who spring to mind, but they themselves are just part of a wider scene where name changes are the established convention. This "wider scene" embraces any person who acquires a new identity for some reason, whether as a performer, who assumes a particular role, or as someone embarking on a new direction in life. Actors are the former type, and religious the latter.

Let us consider the various categories in turn, taking the stage players first. (The fact that an actor "plays" a role, rather than actually assuming one, points up the distinction between the adopted name and the true name of its bearer.)

Many stage names are very familiar to the public, who may not even realize that they *are* stage names. Actors, after all, become stars and achieve fame and win awards, and their names take on a particularly exalted or important significance.

Why do actors adopt a different name?

Many would perhaps reply, "Because it's the tradition." Some might add, "It's automatic." But if we look at the motives more closely, we can see more specific reasons.

First, in their line of work, actors assume other identities in any case. They change their true selves and become someone else, if only for one evening. This is particularly true of professional stage and movie actors and actresses. In playing a part, whether it is major or a minor role, an actor will also assume not only the identity and character of another person, but also the name of that person. A name change is thus part of the job. Therefore a new name is assumed as if to emphasize that such "dual personality" is anyway part and parcel of the actor's real life. An actor is thus versatile and gifted, and in changing his own name adapts his own persona to the bread-winning business of becoming someone else, night after night. A stage name is, then, very important: not for nothing is an actor's name usually referred to as his or her "professional" name.

Apart from the psychological motive, there is also a historical one. For some years in the past, acting, especially in "higher" circles of society, was regarded as an inferior, degrading, or even decadent way of life. Actors would thus change their names to avoid this undesirable stigma, and to dissociate their real name, and the good name of their family, from their vocation.

Again, actors are, even today, superstitious people, believing in good fortune and fame only when it happens, and a change of name may help to avoid a possible failure on the stage. After all, if you fail to make the grade, it is not the real you that has failed but your alter ego. A different name may perhaps actually help to bring good luck in your performance, as well as ward against failure. We recall the reasoning behind the name change made by Elton John in Chapter 2. For him at any rate, the transformation seemed to work.

There are also sound practical reasons for making an actor's name change desirable. Some of these have already been mentioned and they should now be enumerated more specifically.

(1) An actor's real name may be very ordinary or common. He or she therefore wishes to change it to something rather more glamorous and memorable. Thus Peggy Middleton became Yvonne de Carlo, Merle Johnson turned into Troy Donahue, and Norma Jean Baker was metamorphosed as Marilyn Monroe. Even a change of one name is enough, so that Thomas Connery became Sean Connery, and a simple tiny addition or alteration of one letter can make all the difference: Coral Brown lost her common touch when she became Coral Browne, and Frankie Howard made people look again when he restyled his name as Frankie Howerd.

(2) A real name may be awkward or ugly or even have undesirable connotations. Change it to something euphonious and mellifluous. Thus did Virginia McSweeney become Virginia Valli, Nadine Judd turn into Nadia Nerina, and Jean Shufflebottom move upmarket to Jeannie Carson. Actresses, in particular, are anxious to avoid a name smacking of impropriety, which prompted Dora Broadbent to change to Dora Bryan, Diana Fluck to be reborn as Diana Dors, and Joanne LaCock to make her name as Joanne Dru.

(3) From the purely practical point of view, a stage name may simply be too long for billing. A shorter rather than a longer name is always more memorable, too. So it was not surprising that Michael Dumbell Smith turned into Michael Crawford, Deborah Kerr-Trimmer became trimmer as Deborah Kerr, and Roger Ollerearnshaw, TV announcer, became Roger Shaw. A shortened name can often be an improvement on the original. The popular singer Gracie Fields had a name much more melodious and pleasantly evocative than her real name of Grace Stansfield.

(4) As applies to all names, a foreign name is often best changed by an actor to an English one. So Bernard Schwartz, Dino Crocetti, and Daniel Kaminsky must have thought, to change their respectively German,

Italian and Polish-sounding names to Tony Curtis, Dean Martin, and Danny Kaye. Many stage name changes are of this type.

(5) It may happen that an actor's name is similar, or even identical, to the name of another actor. In this case he is well advised to change it, simply to avoid confusion. In fact the actors' trade union, Equity, makes it a condition that no actor may perform with the same name as another. So British movie actor James Stewart changed his name to Stewart Granger so as not to be confused with American actor James Stewart, and movie comedy writer and producer Melvin Kaminsky changed to Mel Brooks so as not to be muddled with trumpet player Max Kaminsky.

When it comes to writers, the use of a pseudonym is much more flexible, and less stereotyped, than with an actor. A written, recorded name, after all, can be much more subtly manipulated than the stage name that an actor bears in the manner of a true name. Unlike an actor's name, it can be used for a single piece of writing or genre of writing. It can be permanent or temporary, meaningful or arbitrary, resemble a real name or be quite unlike a conventional name. A writer, too, can have more than one pseudonym, even as many as a hundred, and can jettison at will one pseudonym to adopt another, for whatever reason, as easily as setting pen to paper. Indeed, by the very term "pseudonym" most people understand a writer's assumed name rather than an actor's (many dictionaries will define the word in terms of a writing name), and although a stage name will undoubtedly, because of the charisma of its bearer, often acquire a "star" quality, it is the name adopted by a writer that will almost always be the more telling.

It is worth mentioning that "ghost" writers write anonymously rather than pseudonymously. They do not assume the name of the actual supposed author, who in many cases is a celebrity. They retain their true identity, but do not disclose it to the public through the work that they write. Nor, of course, does the putative author assume the identity of the actual writer, but simply takes the credit! Thus supermodel Naomi Campbell's novel *Swan* (1995) was actually written by Carly McIntyre, and doubts were expressed in the media at the time of publication as to whether Campbell had even actually read the book.

This is the point to take a closer look at the motives for adopting a pen name, some of which, in fact, are virtually the same as the motives that lead to a stage name.

Unlike an actor, a writer may well keep two professional lives on the go at once: his "bread-and-butter" one, which exercises his conventional abilities and qualifications, and which provides him with a regular paycheck and a good degree of security—his "job," in fact—and his dedicated work as a writer, which, at any rate to begin with, may not give him the same degree of security or reward him with the same regular income, but which does give him a considerable creative satisfaction. In such cases, when a man or woman is both these, professional person and vocational writer, he or she may find it convenient or desirable to adopt a pen name for the writing activities, if only to differentiate the two sides to a single person's life. When this happens, it is the pen name that will be the better known, of course, since this is the writer's more public face. We thus know James Bridie, the playwright, much better than we know the Scottish doctor Osborne Henry Mavor; we are more likely to be familiar with the detective stories of Michael Innes than the English critical studies by J.I.M. Stewart. On the other hand, both sides of a person's creative activity may be equally well known, so that Cecil Day Lewis, the poet, has a status almost equaled by Nicholas Blake, the detective fiction writer. To distinguish, thus, the work of A.B. the breadwinner from Y.Z. the literary creator, is one of the prime functions of a pen name. Often, of course, a person's writing may be so successful that he is able to abandon his traditional career. In such a case his literary name usually "takes over" and becomes the whole individual. This happened, for example, to Richard Gordon, who gave up his professional work as a doctor in 1952 and devoted himself entirely to writing, and to John Le Carré, who as a result of the success of his third novel of espionage, *The Spy Who Came in from the Cold* (1963), was able to leave the foreign service and concentrate on full-time writing.

A writer may also assume a different name not in order to distinguish between the writing self and the professional self, but to differentiate between one aspect of his or her writing and another. A travel writer, for example, may turn his hand to mystery fiction, and will take on a second pseudonym (or a first, if he writes under his real name) to be reserved for this type of book. Or a literary critic may publish some verse under a different name. The New Zealand writer whose real name was Ruth France, for example, assumed the name Paul Henderson for her poetry. (She also adopted a male name. Such "cross-sexing" will be considered shortly.) Again, it may be convenient to use a different name for books or work written over a particular period, or even for a single publication. Christopher Caudwell, the British Marxist writer of studies of poetry and prose literature, reversed the usual process in this way, using his *real* name (Christopher St. John Sprigg) for seven detective novels written between 1933 and 1939. Welsh-born novelist Cecil Blanche Woodham-Smith adopted the name Janet Gordon for just three novels, *April Sky* (1938), *Tennis Star* (1940), and *Just Off Bond Street* (1940), while British thriller writer Leslie Seldon Truss used the name George Selmark for a single novel, *Murder in Silence* (1939). In some cases the distinction between the writer's different names for different types of writing may be minimal. Scottish writer Iain Banks, for example, names himself thus for his "mainstream" novels such as *The Wasp Factory* (1984) and *Complicity* (1993), but reserves the fuller name Iain M. Banks for his science fiction, in such novels as *Consider Phlebas* (1987) and *Excession* (1996).

For a different type of distinction, a writer may choose to take on another name for contributions to a particular magazine, or when submitting work to a different publisher.

The Scottish poet William Aytoun used the name Augustus Dun-shunner for his contributions to *Blackwood's Magazine*, and George Darley, the Irish writer, contributed to the *London Magazine* as John Lacy.

The reasons that motivate a writer to choose another name on practical grounds do not end there. Jean-Raymond De Kremer, the bilingual Belgian writer, called himself Jean Ray when writing in French, and John Flanders for his books in Flemish, while Russian writer Andrey Sinyavsky used the name Abram Tertz for his allegedly subversive writings published in the West.

A special case is that of the Portuguese poet Fernando Pessoa (1888–1935), who created four distinctive poetic personas: the fictional Alberto Caeiro, Ricardo Reis, and Alvaro de Campos, and the real Fernando Pessoa, whose own name happens to be the Portuguese word for "person," itself significantly deriving from Latin *persona*, "mask." He called these his heteronyms ("other names"), and altogether created a total 72 such names, although the three mentioned here were different. He is said to have originally invented them in connection with the literary magazine *Orpheu* that he and others founded in 1914. Poems by Campos appeared in this almost immediately, and the others followed. The four of them not only had distinctive styles—Caeiro was naive, Reis classical, Campos modern, and Pessoa innovative—but each had his own biography. Thus Reis was born in 1887 and was a doctor, Caeiro was born in 1889 but died young in 1915 of tuberculosis, and Campos was born at 1:30 P.M. on October 15, 1890 in Tavira (Algarve). The three also differed physically: Campos had a slight stoop and wore a monocle, Caeiro was a blue-eyed blond, Reis was rather swarthy. But although each persona was distinctive, they were intended to form a group, with Pessoa one of their number [Zbigniew Kotowicz, *Fernando Pessoa: Voices of a Nomadic Soul*, 1996].

A different genre, a different period, a different style, a different publisher, a different language, a different persona: a writer can identify the difference by adopting a new name.

A writer may well assume several pen names for more practical reasons than Pessoa. From the purely commercial angle, for example, a single writer can submit articles to different journals under different names, and writers who are particularly prolific may indeed prefer to "parcel out" their writings in this way. Science fiction and fantasy writers frequently employ a whole range of names, as do crime novelists, and many publishers have lists of ready-made names, so called "house names," that they allocate to their authors. These are stock names used by different writers as they come and go. Thus SF writer Chester S. Geier was assigned the house names Alexander Blade, P.F. Costello, Warren Kastel, S.M. Tenneshaw, Gerald Vance, and Peter Worth. These have all been used by other writers. By 1987, for example, Alexander Blade had been used by at least 18 writers, in some cases by two authors writing jointly.

For writers working at a less demanding creative level, such as light romantic fiction and "pulp" magazines (although some such work is more stylish than might be supposed), the adoption of several pen names has for some time been standard practice.

As to the number of names that a writer can adopt, there are few limits. The English crime novelist John Creasey wrote his 560 books under some two dozen pseudonyms. (See them in Appendix 3, page 338.) Stendhal, the French novelist, had over a hundred pen names, with "Stendhal" itself the best known, and Voltaire, itself a pseudonym, totaled at least 173, which would seem to be something of a record (see Appendix 1, page 384). For the majority of writers, however, a single pseudonym, or at most a handful, suffices for most practical purposes.

It goes without saying that many of the reasons that encourage an actor to change his name (an unsuitable real name, for dissociation, for ease of distinction from a similar name, for memorability) also apply to writers, although not perhaps to quite the same extent. An actor's name is very much part of his or her image and stage personality, and it is billed and promoted in a much more blatant and "public" way than the name of a writer. An actor's name, therefore, has a significance in itself. With a writer, on the other hand, although the name is also important, it is *what* is written that counts. It obviously helps to have a memorable and easily pronounceable and attractive name, but for a writer a name is much more a means of pure identification than it is for an actor. Anthony Trollope's novels achieved their classic status without their author's feeling it necessary to adopt another name, nor was Oscar Wilde ever tempted in this respect. But how far would mellifluously named Marilyn Monroe have got as Norma Jean Baker? It is interesting to speculate.

There are, however, particular motivations for a writer's name change that will hardly ever apply to an actor.

The chief of these is the so-called "literary mask," the need or desirability for writers to conceal their true identity (which actors will hardly wish to do). The motivation here is not so much to find a name as to escape from one. In other words, the name is regarded as a "cover-up" name, much as we saw it was for a spy or criminal in Chapter 2.

Why should a writer wish to hide his or her identity?

One reason may be a wish to avoid censorship. When a writer has something important to say, whether as fact or fiction, and when it may be difficult to say it under his real name, either because of his own standing or because it is controversial or even unlawful or hostile to authority, the adoption of a pseudonym may be the only solution. In the past many anticlerical or generally antiestablishment writers have sought refuge in an assumed name. Voltaire, imprisoned in the Bastille for writing a scurrilous lampoon on the French regent (the notorious libertine Philippe II, Duke of Orleans), assumed his pseudonym on his release (1718) with the aim of pursuing his powerful philosophical and skeptical writings. A century before him a fellow Frenchman, Agrippa d'Aubigné, an ardent Protestant, attacked the evils of the establishment, in particular French monarchs such as Catherine de Médicis and her sons Charles IX and Henri III, in his classic poem *Les Tragiques* (1616). For this he assumed the initials L.B.D.D. Only some 300 years later were these letters deciphered as standing for "Le Bouc du Désert" ("The Scapegoat"). This was known to have been a nickname used for d'Aubigné, who at one time actually lived in a small village in Brittany called Le Désert. D'Aubigné's poem was both antiroyalist and anticlerical. Specifically anticlerical was the work of yet another outstanding French writer, Blaise Pascal. For a bitter yet objective attack on the Jesuits he entitled his famous eighteen letters *Lettres de Louis de Montalte à un Provincial de Ses amis et aux RR. PP. Jésuites sur la Morale et la Politique de Ces Pères* (1656) ("Letters from Louis de Montalte to a Provincial Friend and to Their Reverend Fathers the Jesuits Concerning the Morality and the Policy of Those Fathers"). The work dealt the Jesuits a blow from which they never recovered. (It was subsequently placed on the Index and ordered to be burned by the Royal Council in 1660.)

These three literary masks incidentally give good examples of a permanent "takeover" pseudonym (Voltaire) and of names used for specific single works (L.B.D.D. and Louis de Montalte).

Thus critics and satirists of all ages have adopted a disguised name, from d'Aubigné in the 17th century to the wry American humorist Mr. Dooley (real name Finley Peter Dunne) in the 20th. It is understandable, too, that not just critics and humanists but political activists and revolutionaries will wish to adopt a "cover" name, since the publishing of their ideology in printed form will be one of the most effective ways of disseminating their message. Escaping the watchful eye of the censor here is all important. It was largely in order to publicize his views and theories on society and the economy that led Vladimir Ilich Ulyanov to adopt a whole number of pseudonyms, of which one, Lenin, would make him internationally known as a professional revolutionary. (His views and activities had in fact

caused the censor and the police to keep an eye on him even at the early age of 17. For him to have published anything under his real name would have been out of the question.) Lenin first used this particular name some time before the Revolution, in 1901. Many other Russians, both before and after the Revolution, were obliged to adopt a pseudonym for fear of censorship or reprisals.

There is another category of writers who undergo a name change. These are the plagiarists, who "steal" the writing of someone else and put their own name to it. (English "plagiarist" derives from Latin *plagiarius*, "kidnapper.") In this case, more rarely, there is not the normal change to another name but *from* another name to one's own. The filching or pirating of other people's works was common among Elizabethan playwrights, when hacks would openly steal the plays of others and present them as their own. Today the stringent laws of copyright make such thieving very difficult, if not impossible.

Even so, it still happens, as the American poet Neal Bowers discovered when in 1992 a friend faxed him a copy of a poem from the *Mankato Poetry Review* written in very much his own style. It was called "Someone Forgotten," and was signed "David Sumner." Bowers recognized it as his own "Tenth-Year Elegy," which had appeared in the Chicago magazine *Poetry* two years previously. He and his wife set out to track down Sumner. Their searches revealed that he had further poetic identities. He (or she) was Diane Compton, raised in Oregon. He (she) was also David Jones, born in Northern Ireland and raised in England but living in Oregon. And these various personae further blended as Paul Schmidt, more a writer of short stories (naturally, other people's) than a poet. Bowers and his wife finally established that the third of these, David Jones, was the true identity. When confronted with his poetic pillage, Jones acknowledged the theft and duly apologized. But the damage was done, leaving Bowers reluctant to pick up his pen in case he provided yet more material for Sumner/Jones.

The converse of such misappropriation is

to publish one's own works under the real name of a contemporary or recently deceased writer. This was the device resorted to by the English journalist and writer of children's educational books Sir Richard Phillips (1767–1840), who published works as James Adair, Rev. S. Barrow, Rev. David Blair, Rev. C.C. Clarke, Rev. J. Goldsmith, William Mavor, Mrs. (or Miss) Margaret Pelham, and Abbé Bossut. This last was for *The First French Grammar* (1806), published in France under the name of the noted French mathematician Abbé Charles Bossut (1730–1814). "Rev. J. Goldsmith," the name used by Phillips for his *Grammar of British Geography* and other works, was intended to suggest a blood relationship to the famous Oliver Goldsmith (1728–1778). As the English writer and bibliographer Ebenezer Cobham Brewer comments on Phillips in *Authors and Their Works* (1884), "It is scandalous for a publisher to palm off his books under such false names, expressly intended to deceive the public, and to trade on the reputation of another's name."

According to the pseudonymous bibliophile Olphar Hamst, in his *Handbook of Fictitious Names* (1868) (see Bibliography, p. 399), Phillips' name was itself fictitious, and he started life as Philip Richards. Phillips' *Dictionary of National Biography* entry makes no mention of this, however.

In some instances the "plagiary" may be by mutual agreement between the "thief" and his victim. At the beginning of his career, for example, George Bernard Shaw found it difficult to get his writing published. He was aided by his friend, the musical conductor George Lee. Shaw would write the musical reviews and Lee would have them printed over his own name. A similar situation in which a helping hand was given arose when Jack London aided his friend George Sterling. Sterling simply could not get his story "The First Poet" accepted. London included it in his collection of short stories entitled *Turtles of Tasman* (1916). Only some time later did Sterling reveal that he, not London, was the author of that particular story.

Many writers, of course, are influenced by the writings of others and may unwittingly borrow from them. This is not deliberate, conscious, wholesale stealing, but simply unconscious (or possibly subconscious) borrowing or adaptation, and as such is not really plagiary. Milton, for example, was greatly influenced by Spenser who in turn owed a good deal to Chaucer, and Keats was influenced by all three. This does not mean that any of the four can be accused of plagiary, even if Chaucer, in turn, had himself borrowed from French and Italian writers.

Another type of writing involving the adoption of a different name is parody. One famous case of parody was the work entitled *Les Déliquescences d'Adoré Floupette*, a collection of *poèmes décadents* that appeared in Paris in 1885. These were initially taken seriously by the critics. But who was the delightfully named Adoré Floupette? It turned out that there was no such person, but the poems themselves were clever, if rather malicious, parodies of poems by the early French Symbolist poets, Verlaine, Mallarmé, Rimbaud, Moréas and others. The *Déliquescences* ("Decayings") were actually the work of two young poets, Gabriel Vicaire and Henri Beauclair.

Many examples of parody, however, do not involve a name change at all. When Stella Gibbons wrote *Cold Comfort Farm* (1932) as a caricature of a novel by Mary Webb, she did not claim to *be* Mary Webb or anyone other than herself.

Cases of plagiary and parody may often be quite intriguing, even if one might hesitate to read the actual works. Even more interesting, and a further motive for adopting another name, are literary hoaxes. These occur when a writer claims to be someone other than who he really is. He is thus converse of a plagiarist, and closer to a parodist. Literary hoaxes involve the donning of a real literary mask.

There are some classic examples of such hoaxes.

Washington Irving, the "Father of American Literature," began his career with a double hoax. Having already used the pseudonym Jonathan Oldstyle, Gent., for a series of satirical letters published in the *Morning Chronicle* (1802–03), he collaborated with his brother William and the writer James K. Paulding to publish a series of satirical essays and poems entitled *Salmagundi; or, the Whim-Whams and Opinions of Launcelot Langstaff, Esq., and Others.* These were first published as pamphlets and subsequently (1808) in book form. But Irving was not content to stop here. The following year a number of American newspapers carried announcements signed by one Handiside, manager of the New York Columbia Hotel, to the effect that a hotel resident named Diedrich Knickerbocker had checked out of the hotel leaving a manuscript behind. The announcements described Knickerbocker's appearance and character and requested anyone who knew his whereabouts to contact Mr. Handiside who at the same time declared that if Mr. Knickerbocker did not return to the hotel he, Handiside, would publish the manuscript to recover his losses, since the aforesaid Mr. Knickerbocker had not settled his account. All this was in fact the work of Irving, intended as a build-up for his famous burlesque whose full title was *A History of New York, from the Beginning of the World to the End of the Dutch Dynasty, by Diedrich Knickerbocker* (1809). Neither Knickerbocker nor Handiside existed, of course. Thanks to this unusual publicity the work enjoyed immense success, and a few months after publication Irving revealed himself as the true author and thus "blew" his hoax. After this he published under his real name.

Irving set something of a fashion for literary hoaxes with humorous names of this kind, especially among American writers. In the March 21, 1861, issue of the Findlay (Ohio) *Jeffersonian*, for example, there appeared a letter from one "Petroleum Vesuvius Nasby, late pastor uv the Church uv the New Dispensation, Chaplain to his excellency the President, and p.m. at Confederate x roads, kentucky." This illiterate and seemingly dissolute country preacher from the South appeared to be extolling slavery and supporting those who approved of it. Astute readers

could see, however, that in fact his arguments were absurd and that his apparent support for the South was given ironically. The author of this letter, the first of a series, was in fact the *Jeffersonian*'s editor, David Ross Locke.

Locke in turn was followed by C.F. Browne, who as Artemus Ward feigned an illiterate style not simply to entertain but in order to satirize insincerities and sentimentality.

Two more literary hoaxes deserve mention here. The French writer Prosper Mérimée published in 1825, at the start of his career, a selection of plays about Spanish life in the manner of Lope de Vega. Wary of possible criticism by supporters of the classical school, he ascribed the plays to a nonexistent Spanish actress, one Clara Gazul. He did more than this. A foreword to the plays, written by someone named Joseph Létrange (significantly, "Joseph the Strange") gave an account of Clara's life to date—how she was raised, how she escaped from a nunnery to join a roving band of actors, and the like—and backed up this verbal background to the supposed authoress by an actual portrait of Clara, as a frontispiece to the plays. This portrait was executed by the painter Delescluze, and was actually of 22-year-old Mérimée wearing a mantilla and a necklace! Thus as Clara Gazul and Joseph Létrange, Mérimée not only donned a literary mask (a double one, in fact) but extended his hoax to a visual impersonation.

Pierre Louÿs (originally Louis), also a Frenchman, concocted another type of mystification. He claimed, in 1894, to have discovered and translated the songs of a hitherto unknown Greek poetess named Bilitis who lived in the 6th century BC. According to Louÿs, an archaeologist, one Dr. Heim, had discovered her tomb, and as if to prove her existence, subsequent editions of the *Chansons de Bilitis* even contained "her" portrait, as Mérimée's plays had done. But it was all fabricated by Louÿs: there had been no Bilitis, there was no Dr. Heim, and the portrait was simply a copy of a statue in the Louvre. The poems themselves were written by Louÿs in the style of Sappho.

A hoax involving a false name need not

necessarily be literary, of course. The front cover of the November 1996 number of *Esquire* magazine presented its readers with a seductive photograph of a new movie star and an equally seductive caption: "Here's Hollywood's next dream girl: the Allegra Coleman nobody knows." The latter statement was true enough. Nobody indeed knew her, for the alleged Allegra Coleman was a fiction invented by the magazine to accompany an article satirizing celebrity profiles, and the photograph was actually of a model named Ali Larder. The spoof actually made *her* a celebrity.

Such pranks must have been highly satisfying to their perpetrators.

The ultimate in literary masks, however, is to take no name at all, that is, to write anonymously. Many writers began their career in this way, believing that if what they wrote was worth reading, the public would buy it for its own sake, irrespective of whoever the author might be. Censor-dodgers, too, will obviously favor the anonymous approach. But there is a snag. If your work has no name to it, how can the public obtain more if they want it? All that can be done is to resort to a cumbersome phrase such as "The Author of 'Confessions of a Convict'" or whatever it was called. Unless the author chooses to reveal his true identity immediately, he too will have to employ a similar awkward designation in order to be recognized as the writer of the original work.

A classic case of this kind is well illustrated by Sir Walter Scott. After a writing career that had already been under way for some twenty years—so he was not the typical anonymous beginner in this respect—Scott decided to change from verse romances, in which he was anyway largely overshadowed by Byron, to novels. There duly appeared, anonymously, in 1814, his now famous historical novel *Waverley*. Would it be a success? Scott was apprehensive: he was known as a poet, not a novelist. The book was indeed well received, but Scott was still cautious, with the result that all his following novels, up to 1827, were published as "by the Author of 'Waverley'." After this, confident that his reputa-

tion as a writer of historical fiction was assured, Scott wrote under his real name.

Among other works that were first published anonymously are Tennyson's *Poems by Two Brothers* (1827), Browning's first poem "Pauline" (1833), Fenimore Cooper's first novel *Precaution* (1820), Hardy's two novels *Desperate Remedies* (1871) and (surprisingly) *Far from the Madding Crowd* (1874), and Conan Doyle's first short stories in the *Cornhill Magazine* (1879).

Thus caution, apprehension, and evasion are among the motives that prompt a writer to mask his true identity.

But why should a writer wish to disguise his or her sex?

To be more precise: why should a female writer—since in this respect the women easily outnumber the men—choose to adopt a male name?

There have been numerous occasions, some quite recent, when a female writer has been obliged to assume a male name in order that her book should be widely read, or even that it should be published at all. In the Victorian era, for example, when a woman's role was basically regarded as that of wife and mother, for a feminine pen to turn out anything more powerful or unconventional than a little light romantic verse or a cozy daily diary would have been virtually unthinkable. And that a woman should produce a stark, passionate *roman d'amour* or a radical, serious work exposing the evils of racialism would have been as unlikely as for a woman to become a corporation president or prime minister of Britain. Yet we now know, barely a hundred years later, such things are perfectly possible.

It was simply that "serious" and innovative writing of any kind, especially where it went against commonly held moral, religious, and social beliefs, was expected to come, if it came at all, from a male author, not a female. The woman's place was not only in the home, it was as a dilettante, and if a lady took to the pen it was more often for the execution of elegant artwork than for the creation of a great literary masterpiece.

The year before Charlotte Brontë wrote her masterpiece *Jane Eyre* (1847), she and her two sisters Emily and Anne had felt it prudent or even essential to adopt, if not actually male names, at any rate ones that were not so obviously feminine as their own. (For Charlotte's own account of the motive behind the sisters' name change, see her entry under Currer Bell.)

These "ambiguous" names were in fact short-lived. The following year (1848) Charlotte admitted to being the author of *Jane Eyre*, while Emily revealed herself as the writer of *Wuthering Heights* and Anne as that of *The Tenant of Wildfell Hall*. But for a while the three sisters had been so successful in masking their sex that many reviewers believed the authors to be three brothers.

It was not only the early Victorian authoresses who assumed a name of the opposite sex. Nearly forty years after Currer Bell, another woman writer would take a name that was more than masculine. This was Olive Schreiner, who in 1883 published *The Story of an African Farm* under the name of Ralph Iron. The book was a novel, but no light romance: it was an expressly feminist and anti-Christian work, which because of its fine descriptive style and originality achieved instant success. It was controversial, however, and when the sex of the author was revealed the controversy became a storm, proving that the South African writer was fully justified in her decision to adopt a cross-sex pseudonym.

Some two centuries before any of these andronymous authors, a number of French women writers had taken to adopting male pen names. Madeleine de Scudéry, known to her friends as "Sapho," wrote more than one novel under the name of her brother George. Her prolix pseudo-historical romances *Clélie* (1654–60) and *Artamène, ou le Grand Cyrus* (1649–53), each ten volumes in length, depicted distinguished persons of her day under disguised names. But Mlle de Scudéry made no secret of the fact that she was the author of these works: her pseudonym was more an incognito, which she had not assumed with any great degree of seriousness. Other well known French female novelists who wrote under a male pen name were Amandine Dudevant (as George Sand), Marie de Flavigny, comtesse d'Agoult (as Daniel Stern), and Delphine de Girardin (as Charles de Launay).

The practical advantages of adopting a male name, especially when it came to having one's work accepted for publication, were commented on by the French revolutionary writer Louise Michel: "I more than once had occasion to notice that when I submitted articles to a newspaper under the name Louise Michel I could wager a hundred to one that they would not be printed; but if I signed myself Louis Michel the chances of being published were much greater!" (*Mémoires*, 1886).

Some women writers have adopted another course, electing to publish under their initials and surname as a way of disguising their sex while retaining their true identity. This was almost certainly the case for D.K. Broster and E. Nesbit (see their entries). Children's writers who have chosen initials instead of female forenames, not necessarily in each case for pseudonymous purposes, are (forenames in parentheses) M.E. Atkinson (Mary Evelyn), L.M. Boston (Lucy Maria), H.F. Brinsmead (Hesba Fay), V.H. Drummond (Violet Hilda), E.M. Ellin (Elizabeth Muriel), S.E. Hinton (Susan Eloise), E.L. Konigsburg (Elaine Lobl), M. Pardoe (Margot Mary), and P.L. Travers (Pamela Lyndon).

A much simpler way out of the difficulty that attended a woman writer was for her to sign herself simply "A Lady." Only a few writers so called appear in this present book, but there were very many who took this title. Indeed, in 1880 the above-mentioned Olphar Hamst published a volume entitled *Aggravating Ladies: being a list of works published under the pseudonym of "A Lady."* This identifies many female writers who put their pens to paper thus. ("Perhaps," pleads Hamst in his earlier *Handbook of Fictitious Names*, "the ladies will take compassion on a poor bibliophile, when we state that he has upwards of fifty works in his list, whose authors are unknown, all 'By a Lady.'") The pseudonym is actually more satisfactory than it appears: it enables a woman writer to retain her anonymity while remaining loyal to her sex, and at the same time it has an air of respectability and refinement.

Except trivially or humorously, it has been a much rarer thing for a man to assume a female pseudonym. Whereas a female writer, to enter a male literary world, may frequently have found that the most effective passport is the adoption of a man's name, a male author is already in his man's world, and the same motives will not operate. In fact the only reason for a man to take on a female name as a writer is simply the reason that prompts him to adopt another name anyway—for any of the practical or aesthetic motives we already mentioned.

Male writers who have permanently adopted a female name are thus few and far between and mostly little known or of small consequence.

One exception, however, was the Scottish author Fiona Macleod, born William Sharp. This was primarily a "distinction" name, used consistently for his mystical and quasi–Celtic romances and plays from 1893 until his death in 1905—he had earlier written some poetry and biography under his real name—but perhaps there was also a genuine femininity in the writing or the personality of the man himself that motivated this particular choice of name. His pen name was so successful that the true identity of the author of the books by Fiona Macleod was not known until after Sharp's death. (For more about him, see his entry, page 244.)

In referring to women authors who chose to write as "A Lady" we were really dealing with a type of aristocratic name. Many writers of both sexes have chosen to devise a pseudonym that in one way or another suggests an aristocratic origin, even a royal one. This is of course a rather obvious way to enhance one's literary status, but it has been a steadily popular one over the centuries. The mechanics consist largely in assuming a name that includes an aristocratic particle or "honorific" such as the French *de* or German *von*. (For other ways of upgrading one's name, see the next chapter.) The reasoning here is fairly straightforward, the argument being: aristocrats are more important than other people and receive greater attention; if I adopt an aristocratic name or title the public will pay more attention to my writing and will rate it highly (since the author is apparently an aristocrat) even before they have read it. But such "self-promotion," in the literal sense, became overpopular as a pseudonymous device, and consequently lost its initial impact. Ralph Thomas's "aggravating ladies" were not tiresome because it was difficult attempting to track them down. It was simply that there were too many of them. And half the "mystique" of being an aristocrat, even if a spurious one, is of course the fact that you belong to the select few, not the repetitive many.

Rather more interesting is the adoption by a genuine aristocrat of an ordinary or "lowly" name. This can occur either when the writer's lofty status makes it difficult for him or her to have a work published under his or her name—as applies in particular to royalty—or when the nature of the work, and its subject matter, make it desirable for the high-ranking author to adopt a more modest stance.

Such a "flight from fame" has been resorted to on more than one occasion by a king or queen, who even for private correspondence may well choose to become Mr. or Mrs. Thus Sarah Churchill, Duchess of Marlborough (1660–1744) corresponded with Queen Anne of England as Mrs. Freeman—a doubly symbolic name—while Queen Anne in turn wrote to the Duchess as Mrs. Morley.

One of the most prolific royal writers of the 19th century was Queen Elizabeth of Romania, who published several books of verse and prose as Carmen Sylva—a name perhaps more lyrical than lowly—while Elizabeth itself was the pen name chosen by Countess von Arnim, later Countess Russell, for her novels, beginning with *Elizabeth and Her German Garden* (1898). (Elizabeth was her mother's first name.)

As mentioned at the beginning of this chapter, there are creative occupations other than acting or writing in which a name change may be traditional or desirable.

Still on the stage, or the platform, many changed or altered names have become familiar from musical performers.

Ballet dancers in the 19th and early part of the 20th centuries traditionally assumed a Russian-style name, thanks to the worldwide influence of Russian ballet, an influence and a predominance that arose in the 18th century and that remained to Soviet times and after. Thus the dancer Hilda Boot assumed the surname Butsova, Vera Clarke became Vera Savina, and Patrick Healey-Kay turned into the ballet star Anton Dolin. In some instances it comes as a surprise to find that a ballerina did not originally have the Russian name by which she became famous. Tamara Karsavina was born Tamara Karsavina, but Lydia Sokolova began her dancing career as plain Hilda Munnings. Describing the transformation of Alice Marks into Alicia Markova, the British writer on ballet Arnold Haskell commented: "She would dance just as well under the name Lizzie Smith, if we wish to be coldly logical, and yet I do not fully believe it. The adoption of the Russian name is in a way symbolical, signifying the entrance into the fine tradition, that is the living force in ballet. ... It is also a gracious compliment to those [Russian teachers] who made her and gave her the opportunity to shine" (*Balletomania*, 1934). Haskell also records the "christenings" of three members of the Ballets Russes de Monte Carlo in 1933 when celebrating the coming of age of one of their number in mid-Atlantic during the crossing to America: "Our Ballet Club girls became Russian; Prudence Hyman as Polina Strogova; Betty Cuff, Olga Nelidova; Elizabeth Ruxton, Leza Serova. The names soon passed into common usage and only their owners were still a little dazed from time to time."

Ballet is traditionally regarded as combining the craft of the actor and the skill of the singer, and musical performers generally have frequently become known under their assumed or altered names. Here the influence has been more Italian than Russian, as is evi-

dent in such names as Madame Albani, Signor Foli, Mario Lanza, Nellie Melba (although Australian in origin), Emma Nevada (although American), and Giovanni Punto (Czech). Such names have been reinforced by names that are actually of Italians but that have taken different forms with typical Italian suffixes. A distinctive group here are the castrati (male soprano or alto singers), who from the 17th century have made their names known. They include Caffarelli, Cusanino, Farinelli, Gizziello, Nicolino (or Nicolini), Porporino, Pistocchino, and Senesino. (All these have their own entries in the present dictionary.)

Prima donnas of another kind, but often also needing a distinctive name, are fashion and photographic models, who like their male counterparts may sometimes assume a single given name. The name itself here denotes not so much nationality as a glamorous allure. Certain names favored by models, such as Sue, Vicki, Debbie, and Karen, have become traditionally associated with the profession. Where a model is given or adopts a conventional name, that is, a first name and surname, it may well be chosen for its exotic or even erotic overtones. It will at least be striking. Gretchen Edgren's *The Playmate Book* (1996), with names and photographs of 516 *Playboy* centerfolds, singles out the following names of featured models as "cool," implying that most of them were specifically devised for a particular poser or pouter: Gianna Amore, Betty Blue, Lourdes Estores, Ava Fabian, Miki Garcia, Azizi Johari, Lari Laine, China Lee, Candy Loving, Jonnie Nicely, Zahra Norbo, Melba Ogle, Jackie Rainbow, Willy Rey, Mercy Rooney, Star Stowe, Victoria Valentino, Reagan Wilson, Gwen Wong. Not all the names are as obviously "modelic" as this, however. Stella Stevens is the fairly unremarkable name adopted by Estelle Eggleston, while the blandly named Michelle Hamilton began life as an arguably more memorable Roxanna Platt. English model Carol Needham became Lee Ann Michelle when taken under Hugh Hefner's American wing, while Elizabeth Jordan was Joey Thorpe as a "Bunny" girl. A former Miss Denmark, Elsa Sorensen, also modeled as Dane Arden and Alisa Davis.

Edgren gives an insight into the name creation process. Thus, Ashlyn Martin's name was suggested by Lady Brett Ashley in Hemingway's *The Sun Also Rises*, while Hefner himself rechristened Charlaine Karalus as Janet Pilgrim because he liked the name's "puritanical connotations." Gail Stanton had wanted to call herself "Gail Storm," but was advised that this "would sound like the actress who played in *My Little Margie*," in other words Gale Storm, herself originally Josephine Cottle.

Prostitutes similarly take or are given a new name when they enter a brothel or embark on their profession, although the renaming procedure for them is more obviously a rite, signaling both an acceptance of their new role and an abandoning of their former identity. Considering the renaming of prostitutes in early 20th-century America, Ruth Rosen, in *The Lost Sisterhood* (1982), comments: "Perhaps the rite of name initiation helped transform whatever individual or collective worthlessness women experienced as a stigmatized group into a more positive sense of self-esteem."

There is a clear distinction between the subculture of prostitution and the "superculture" of the religious life. Yet the renaming procedure is remarkably similar, with an initiation rite symbolizing simultaneously both a commitment to a new persona and an abnegation of a previous identity. Many religious orders today, whether female or male, retain the practice of assuming the name of a saint or venerated member of the church on their admission to the community, which in the Christian church is usually at the ceremony of clothing. Until recently some orders, such as the Catholic Friars Minor, Carmelites, and Capuchins, abandoned their surname altogether on taking their new religious name, although Capuchins added to their religious name the name of their place of origin, for example Father Pius of Chester. The adoption of a saint's name, too, is not necessarily dependent on the sex of a novice, and nuns sometimes receive the name of a male saint.

Since the Second Vatican Council of 1962–65, many Roman Catholic orders have in fact dropped the giving of a name in religion. But the custom certainly still exists, as is illustrated by the process of name selection described by Suzanne Campbell-Jones in her account of the clothing of novice Franciscan sisters: "The girl put up her own choice of names, and usually two or three devolved on a favorite saint or even a favorite sister, teacher or friend. One nun took the name Ita, not because it meant in chains, but because she knew a very nice nun by that name. Sisters still used their baptismal names for legal documents or transactions outside the convent life" (*In Habit…: An Anthropological Study of Working Nuns*, 1979). A similar procedure was described almost a hundred years earlier by Joseph McCabe in *Twelve Years in a Monastery* (1897): "The name of the novice is changed when he enters the monastery, as a sign that he is henceforth dead to the world. The surname is entirely dropped, and the Christian name is changed into that of some saint of the order, who is adopted as patron; thus my own name was changed into Antony." (See his entry, as Father Antony, on page 76.)

Not surprisingly, the names of members of the Holy Family are regarded with special favor among Christian postulants. Nuns choose Mary (the mother of Christ) and Elizabeth (Mary's cousin, and mother of John the Baptist); male novices choose Joseph (Mary's husband) and John (Elizabeth's son, the Baptist). Other popular choices are names of the apostles and disciples and outstanding New Testament figures, among them Andrew, Barnabas, Bartholomew, James, John (the Baptist or the Apostle), Luke, Mark, Martha, Mary (Magdalene, if not the Virgin), Matthew, Paul, Peter, Philip, Simon (also the name of Christ's brother), Stephen, and Timothy. For nuns, too, a desirable name to acquire is Teresa, that of the 16th-century founder of the reformed (discalced) Carmelite order. Albanian-born missionary Mother Teresa of Calcutta, however, took her name from St. Theresa of Lisieux.

Many of the later saints have come to be

known by their own Christian names, so that the mystical theologian and poet St. John of the Cross was actually baptized as John (more precisely, Juan), and St. Bernadette was christened Marie-Bernarde, with her name simply a standard French feminine diminutive (so spelled, minus the second "r") of Bernard.

It is also the usual practice in the Roman Catholic church, especially in continental Europe, for a person to take an additional name at Confirmation. The acquisition of a religious name of any kind is regarded as so significant that the bearer of the name, which is often that of a saint, will celebrate his or her "nameday" annually as a type of birthday (or "rebirthday") on the feastday of the particular saint. (In the Eastern Orthodox Church it is the baptismal name that is marked in this way, since the bearer will very likely have been named after the saint on whose feast day he or she was born.)

The motivation that lies behind the assuming of a religious name, as both a spiritual rebirth and a rejection of one's worldly identity, seems to have influenced a category of name change that has been regularly observed since the 11th century. This is the change of name undertaken by a pope upon his election. It is not actually obligatory for a pope to assume a new name, but an old custom. Although two popes, in fact, did not change their name (Adrian VI, pope in 1522–1523 and Marcellus II, in 1555), in practice every pope has changed his name since Peter, bishop of Pavia, assumed the name John in 983. It is believed that he made this change out of reverence for St. Peter, the first pope, since in his *Epitaph* he says that he took on a new name "quia Petrus antea existerat" ("because Peter existed before"). Many popes have assumed the name of a predecessor (John Paul I and John Paul II took the names of *two* predecessors), but there is one name that no pope will adopt. This is Peter, and a tradition exists that if a pope named "Peter II" is elected he will be the last of all popes.

The very early popes changed their names simply because their original names were pagan: John II (pope in 533–535) was formerly Mercurius, and John XII (955–964) was Octavianus. On similar lines, and encouraged by the example of John XIV, the former Peter, the first transalpine pontiffs, Bruno of Carinthia and Gerbert of Aurillac, changed their barbarous names to genuine Roman ones, respectively Gregory V (966) and Sylvester II (999). In more recent times the motives for a papal name change have become a good deal more complex, and have included such factors as veneration for a particular predecessor of the same name, a desire to continue the policies or works of a predecessor, or simply a coincidence of election date or of place or region of origin.

Elsewhere in the Christian church, one finds a similar renaming tradition in the Russian Orthodox Church, where the head of the Church, bearing the title of Patriarch of Moscow and All Russia, usually adopts a new name on his election. In the original patriarchate, which Peter the Great replaced with a Synod in 1700, the first patriarch Iov (Job) (elected 1589) was thus originally Ioann (John), while the last was Adrian (elected 1690), originally Andrey (Andrew). On the restoration of the patriarchate in 1917, all patriarchs except the present (Alexis II, elected 1990) took a different name. (For their original names, see their respective entries: Alexis II, Pimen, Sergius, Tikhon.)

It will be noticed that Iov and Adrian assumed names that although different, were close to the original. This has generally been the case with Russian bishops and archbishops. For example Aleksandr Fyodorovich Lavrov-Platonov (1829–1890) became Bishop Aleksy (Alexis), Aleksey Iosifovich Klyucharev (1821–1901) became Archbishop Amvrosy (Ambrosius), and Aleksey Pavlovich Khrapovitsky (1864–1936) became Archbishop Antony.

Individual names adopted by particular popes are considered separately, in Chapter 7 (page 48). In the meantime, it would be useful at this stage to examine in general how one finds or creates a new name, and this will be the subject of Chapter 5.

5. How Do You Make a Name for Yourself?

"'Oh, by-the-by, did I tell you I've cut my first name, "William," and taken the second name "Lupin"? In fact I'm only known at Oldham as "Lupin Pooter." If you were to "Willie" me there, they wouldn't know what you meant'" (George and Weedon Grossmith, *The Diary of a Nobody*, 1892).

Whatever the motivation for changing your name, temporarily or permanently, the big practical question is this: where do I get my new name from?

Taking all pseudonyms and changed names on the broadest possible basis, it may be said that the new name is either ready-made to a greater or lesser degree, that is, it is based on an already existing name, or else it is an invented name, derived from random or meaningful letters, syllables, or words. In this chapter we shall be considering the larger of these two categories. It is the one that is the more interesting, since the names mainly look like real personal names, and are what one might call "instant" or "ready-made" names. In Chapter 6 we shall then have a look at invented names.

In seeking a new name, the obvious place to start is with your own name. Your own real name, that is. Many people, especially those who are changing their name more for convenience than for special effect, will prefer to choose a name that in some way echoes or suggests their original name.

If your original name is foreign-sounding to English-speaking people, the easiest thing to do is to "anglicize" it. This can usually be arranged by modifying a section of the name to resemble an English name. In some instances, especially with Germanic names, such a modification can simultaneously be a translation, as English *-son* for German *-sohn*. In other cases it will suffice simply to switch to an English name that only vaguely resembles the original. Examples are Hardy Albrecht to Hardie Albright, Vladimir Dukelsky to Vernon Duke, Gertrude Konstam to Gertrude Kingston, and George Wenzlaff to George Winslow.

In many cases such an "anglicization" may be accompanied by a shortening, so that the surnames Reizenstein, Liebermann, Kirkegaard, and Breitenberger become Rice, Mann, Kirk, and Byrnes. Two classic examples of this type are Spiro Anagnostopoulos, whose father had anglicized the family name to Agnew, and Nathan Birnbaum, better known as the comedian George Burns. It is noticeable that transformations like this often pay little regard to the actual literal meaning of the original name, that is, there is frequently no attempt to translate the name into English, even when this would preserve the similarity. Elsy Steinberg changed her name to Elaine Stewart, not Elaine Stone, and Nathan Weinstein, the American novelist, became Nathanael West, not Nathanael Vine or Nathanael Stone.

English-style modifications form a sizable group, but bearers of foreign names who change to an English name quite unlike their own easily outnumber them. Thus Max Showalter became Casey Adams, Eugene Klass became Gene Barry, and Louise Dantzler was reborn as Mary Brian. Although such names are not based on the bearer's true name, at least they are an actual genuine or genuine-sounding English name, so in that respect are "ready-made." In practice, too, many people who favor this type of change already have an English-sounding forename which they retain: Leon Ames was Leon Waycoff, Geraldine Brooks was Geraldine Stroock, Kitty Carlisle was Catherine Holzman, and Cecil Parker was at least Cecil Schwabe.

But returning to "own-name-based" names, we find that many pseudonyms are not anglicized versions of a foreign name but merely simplified or abbreviated variants. This is the smallest concession that can be made to an English-speaking environment: at least they will be easier to read, remember, and pronounce, even if they do not actually look like an English name. Once again, it could be that a change of this type is intentionally made, so that the bearer of the name retains something of his or her native provenance, with the resulting name a convenient compromise, neither conspicuously foreign nor wholly English but somewhere between the two. In fact, such a name will still be sufficiently unusual to make it more memorable than an ordinary English name such as Jones or Adams. Examples of such names are Lionel Bart, who was Lionel Begleiter, Howard Da Silva, formerly Harold Silverblatt, Milton Berle, previously Mendel Berlinger, and Peter Tork, once Peter Torkelson. Even in non–English environments the same method can be used, with Jacques Tatischeff becoming Jacques Tati in France, and Franz von Strehlenau assuming the simplified but not specifically German name Nikolaus Lenau in Austria.

A change of this kind may often not be deliberate but result, as we have noted, from Howard F. Barker's "abrasion of common speech." A foreign-sounding name may become smoothed down and even abbreviated by the attempts of an English-speaking tongue to pronounce it. Several actual name changes have thus come about, so that such famous American names as those of Custer, Pershing, Longstreet, and Hoover were originally, several generations back, Küster, Pfoersching, Langestraet and Hüber.

If such name changes as these, incidentally, had been made in their bearers' lifetime, they would have featured individually in the main entries of this dictionary. The same goes for many other now well known names. The father of U.S. author Louisa M. Alcott (1832–1888) changed the family name to Alcott from Alcox, and David de la Garrique, grandfather of English actor-manager David Garrick (1717–1779), changed the family name to Garrick. There may have been a complete change. Scottish road builder John Macadam (1756–1836), of "macadamize" and "tarmac," was the grandson of Scottish chief Adam McGregor. The family name was changed because the latter name was proscribed by Scottish Act of Parliament in 1603, as the clan was notorious for its lawlessness.

Three further ancestral name changes, all literary, will suffice to complete the illustrations here. The English playwright Harold Pinter (b. 1930) is the son of a Portuguese Jewish father named Pinta, and the U.S. publishing house now known as Scribners was founded by a family originally named Scrivener. Finally, American novelist Leon Uris (b. 1924) was born the son of a Polish Jewish shopkeeper originally named Yerushalmi ("Jerusalemite"). He changed his name on immigrating to the USA after World War I.

How else may one vary one's real name? The answer is: in any number of ways, often combining two or more devices. Among the more popular are the following:

(1) Omit your surname. Often a person's second or middle name may actually look like a surname anyway—it is often a family name, such as one's mother's maiden name—and the advantage of such a modification is that it is both simplicity itself and that it enables a person to retain his or her original name unchanged. In such a fashion, changing your name means no change at all, since your new name is your old, and your "pseudonym" is not even "pseudo"! Not surprisingly, this is a very common procedure. Thus, Edward Ashley Cooper became Edward Ashley, William Bolitho Ryall became William Bolitho, Ernest Bramah Smith, author of the *Kai Lung* novels, dropped his prosaic Smith to assume (i.e., retain) his orientally exotic middle name as a surname, and Elizabeth Allen Gillease preferred to be known as just Elizabeth Allen. (To have a middle name that is at once a forename and a surname is indeed a stroke of good fortune.)

Variants of the surname-dropping procedure are possible. While casting off your surname, you can simultaneously change your second name in some way, as can be done to a surname proper. George Augustus Andrews dropped his surname and altered his middle name to become George Arliss, for example. Or you can alter your *first* name while dropping your surname, often assuming instead a pet form of it or a nickname. Thus James Barry Jackson became Michael Barry, and William Berkeley Enos became Busby Berkeley. If you are blessed with two middle names, you can drop both your first name and your surname and use these two as first name and surname. This is what the humorist George Anthony Armstrong Willis did, to become Anthony Armstrong. Sherwood Bonner did likewise: originally she was Katherine Sherwood Bonner Macdowell. Again, you can omit your surname and reverse the order of your two first names, even omitting a forename in the process. This was what George Barrington Rutland Fleet did, to become Rutland Barrington. Similarly, by process of omission and reversal, Edward Thomas Andrulewicz became Thomas Andrew.

The dropping of one half of a double-barreled surname is also an expedient device, whatever else you may do with the rest of your name. Angela Baddeley was born Madeleine Angela Clinton-Baddeley, and Sir Felix Aylmer was originally Felix Edward Aylmer-Jones.

The permutations and combinations that apply in this category can also, of course, be employed in other methods.

(2) More straightforwardly, you can simply use a forename on its own. This is a method favored by cartoonists, who like a short name for signing purposes, by artists of all kinds—both painters and performers—who like a single, stylish name, and is standard practice for several types of religious names, from saints to members of religious orders. Such a name is usually a person's first name, or an abbreviated or pet form of this, but can be any forename. Examples are Fabian Forte Bonaparte, who became simply Fabian, Sabu Dastagir, known better as just Sabu ("the Elephant Boy"), and the pianist Solomon Cuttner, known professionally as Solomon. Beryl Botterill Yeoman, who adopted the first name Antonia, signing her cartoons Anton, and the

political cartoonist Vicky was born Victor Weisz. Cherilyn Sarkisian LaPiere teamed with Sonny to become popular as simply Cher, and movie actress Ann-Margret has a hyphenated first name that she finds quite sufficient to enable her to drop her surname Olsson. One of the best things the Belgian wife of emperor Maximilian of Mexico did was to assume the single name Carlota. This was a variant of the second name in her original lengthy train: Marie-Charlotte-Amélie-Augustine-Victoire-Clémentine-Léopoldine. (Royalty are renowned for their lavish endowment of Christian names.) A variation of this is to use your forename as a full-length pseudonym (forename plus surname) by splitting it into two. Maybritt Wilkens did this to become May Britt, and Isaiah Edwin Leopold to be Ed Wynn. The use of a forename alone preceded by "Madame" or "Mademoiselle" or "Miss" is also popular with a number of female performers, from fortune-tellers to stage actresses. Mlle Augusta, the French ballerina, was born Caroline Augusta Josephine Thérèse Fuchs, and Mlle Clairon, the famous tragic actress of the Comédie Française, began life as Claire-Josèphe Hippolyte Léris de la Tude.

(3) As a kind of converse of this, you can simply use your surname alone. This is perhaps least of all a pseudonym, since the use of surname alone is established, in certain situations and for certain conventions, in a number of countries. For this reason, only a few examples are included in this book. However, Liberace is here, if only to prove that it was indeed the real surname of Wladziu Liberace, and the cartoonists Giles and Low are here for similar reasons: these are the actual surnames of Carl Giles and David Low. Even less of a pseudonym is a real surname preceded by "Mr." or "Mrs." Yet if we take it that a full, true name consists of a forename and a surname, this must be at least partly a pseudonym since there is an element of disguise. How many people, for example, know the first name of Mrs. Beeton, even less her maiden name? The famous cookbook writer was born Isabella Mary Mayson. Topol, incidentally, is the true surname of the actor Chaim Topol.

(4) A common disguise for one's real name, and one popular with writers of all kinds, is to use one's initials. Such a device is so frequently resorted to, both by established writers and private individuals alike—can you honestly say that you have never signed your name by your initials?—that, again, it hardly figures in our present collection of pseudonyms. But of course Q appears in our collection (see page 299), and a few other initialisms will similarly be found. (Initials that stand for something other than the bearer's real name are another matter, and they are much more obviously genuine pseudonyms.)

(5) Much more enterprisingly and ingeniously, a favorite method of forming a pseudonym is to "juggle" with one's real name in some way. This can be done by reversing the order of names, for example, by making an anagram out of it or by reading it back to front (as a reversal), or simply by "recasting" the original name in a mixture of ways, adding or subtracting letters where convenient. The thriller writer John Dickson Carr, for instance, selected as two of his pseudonyms the names Carr Dickson and Carter Dickson. Edith Caroline Rivett, writer of detective novels, took the initials of all three of her names plus the chief element of her middle name reversed to become E.C.R. Lorac (at one time she wrote also as Carol Carnac), and Patrick Reardon Connor dropped one name and altered one vowel in each of the other two to become Rearden Conner. For examples of full-blooded anagrammatic and reversal pseudonyms we need to quote the French poet and short-story writer Théophile Dondey who used an Irish-style transformation to become Philothée O'Neddy, and the English comedian Tommy Trinder who back-pedaled his surname to form the early stage name Red Nirt. A glance in the Bibliography at the end of this book will show that even one of the source authors, himself an expert on pseudonyms and already mentioned above, appears under his pseudonymous name. This is Olphar Hamst, who was in reality the English bibliophile Ralph Thomas. The classic example of an anagrammatic name is, of course, that of Voltaire, formed from his real surname of Arouet (with *u* equating with *v*) plus the initials "L.J." (*j* becoming *i*), said to stand for "Le Jeune."

(6) An extension of a pseudonym consisting solely of initials, as already mentioned, is a name that is a marked contraction of the real name. These, like the "forename only" pseudonyms, are especially popular with cartoonists for a short, snappy name that can be quickly and compactly signed. Among such names are Batt (Oswald Barrett), Jak (Raymond Jackson), Jon (W.P. John Jones), and Gus (George W. Smith). This last name is formed from initials, and thus offers another possibility for a brief name. Erté, the French costume designer, devised his name from the two initials, as they sound in French, of his full name Romain de Tirtoff, and the French cartoonist François Lejeune did similarly to produce his pen name Jean Effel. The clown Coco had a name that came from the two *ko* elements of his full name Nikolai Poliakoff, and the author of *The Book of Artemas: Concerning men, and the things that men did do at the time when there was a war* (1917), and subsequent "Artemas" books, took his name from the first syllables of his complete name Arthur Telford Mason. Here, once again, all kinds of variations are possible. Julia L.M. Woodruff, author of now unread 19th-century novels (*Holden with Cords* and *Shiloh* were two of them), took her initials, reversed them, turned the fourth into a surname, and wrote as W.M.L. Jay. The crosswordist Afrit had a name that was not only directly derived from his real name (Alistair Ferguson Ritchie) but one that additionally denotes a powerful devil in Islamic mythology, one that "inspires great dread," as every dedicated crossword compiler hopes he does in his solvers. (For a look at this fearsome class of pseudonymous devisors, see Chapter 7.)

Any name actually devised from an initial comes in this group, whether forming part of a conventional pseudonym, as Danny Kaye, who began life as Daniel Kaminsky, or used on its own, as above. Obviously, some letters of the alphabet are more suitable than others for forming a traditional English-type name, if that is what is wanted. Among them are B (Bee), D (Dee), G (Gee), J (Jay), and the popular K (Kay or Kaye).

How else can a pseudonym be evolved from your real name?

You can translate it.

Of course, you can only do this if your real name in any way resembles an ordinary translatable word or words. But to translate your name is a method of creating a pseudonym that has a well established and highly respectable antecedence. Such a method was established in the Renaissance period mainly by German scholars of the 16th and 17th centuries. These men were the "new aristocracy," and felt it appropriate to translate or in some way render their often very ordinary or even laughably earthy names into an elevated Latin or Greek form. As Paul Tabori remarked, "Schurtzfleisch (Apronflesh) or Lämmerschwanz (Sheeptail) were scarcely the right names under which to climb Mount Olympus" (*The Natural Science of Stupidity*, 1959). For examples of such classical pseudonyms and their vernacular originals, see in the main listing, among others, Agricola, Bucer, Copernicus, Fabricius, Melanchthon, Mercator, Praetorius, and Sagittarius.

Today, thinking little of it, we have come to accept the classical version of the name as the "real" one, so that we learn in school of Mercator's geographical projection and at college, possibly, of the Arminian doctrine rejecting predestination. We might even add a far more famous "classical" name to this list: that of Christopher Columbus, whose original Italian name was Cristoforo Colombo.

Some such names seemed particularly popular. Four Agricolas (or Agricolae) are cited here, but there were others. The translation was not always a faithful one. Kremer the mathematician took the opportunity of not only translating himself but promoting himself from a "tradesman" to a "wholesale merchant," *Mercator*. And where a name could not be easily translated, and even sometimes when it could, a favorite device was simply to "latinize" the name by adding "-us," as

with Copernicus and Arminius. (The French theologian born Chauvin called himself Calvinus. Today, English speakers know him as Calvin.)

In more recent times, as we have already seen (in Chapter 1), foreign immigrants to Anglophone countries have taken to translating their names, especially, like the scholars two or three centuries before them, those with German names. Schneider then becomes Taylor, Schönkind becomes Fairchild, and Weiss becomes White. Most such transformations are of Jewish names.

It is of course possible to translate or "render" from any one language to any other, as circumstances require, with the new name being a permanent acquisition or simply a temporary, even frivolous, pen name. The Laotian nationalist and author of resistance pamphlets thus adopted the name William Rabbit for one of his works, this being a translation (in part) of his real name Katay Don Sasorith, while the composer born in Italy as Giovanni Battista Lulli gallicized his name when he came to settle in France as Jean-Baptiste Lully. Some translations are almost unrecognizable, at least to an English speaker. The film star Judy Holliday started life as Judith Tuvim, her surname being Hebrew for "holiday." And how about Xanrof? This was the name adopted by Léon Fourneau, the French songwriter who wrote for the diseuse Yvette Guilbert at the turn of the century. He took his surname, translated it into Latin (*fornax*, "furnace"), then reversed it.

In North America, many historically important Native American chiefs and leaders have come to be known by the English equivalent of their original name. Among the most famous are Black Hawk (Ma-ka-tai-me-she-kia-kiak), Crazy Horse (Ta-sunko-witko), Crazy Snake (Chitto-harjo), Red Cloud (Mahpiua-luta), Sitting Bull (Tatanka-iyotake), and Spotted Tail (Sinte-galeska). Red Cloud and his wife were baptized as Christians and somewhat incongruously but quite properly took the names John and Mary. The tribal leader Susette La Flesche, daughter of an Omaha chief, came to be known by a

Native American name translating into English as Bright Eyes. (See her entry under the latter name.)

While considering translations and renderings, we should not overlook a type of converse procedure when a standard English name is turned into a foreign version. We have mentioned the need felt by a number of ballet dancers, for example, to russify their name. Hilda Boot and Patrick Healey-Kay were instanced, but there were also Ethel Liggins, who turned into Ethel Leginska, and Lilian Marks, famous as Alicia Markova. Richard Adama, the American ballet dancer who became director of the Bremen State Opera Ballet in Germany, was born Richard Adams, and—in the world of opera this time rather than ballet—the American singer Lillian Norton preferred to modify her name to the more distinguished Lillian Nordica. A variation on the theme was performed by the Scottish music hall dancer Elizabeth McLauchlan. Teaming with her husband Raoul (né Hugh Duff McLauchlan) she gallicized and prettified her first name to become just Babette.

Babette is a diminutive of Elizabeth, of course, and different enough almost to be regarded as a pet name or nickname. In this it offers another possibility for evolving a pseudonym: adopt your own pet name or nickname. There can be few people who have not had an affectionate or teasing name given them at some stage in their lives, even if only in their school days, and this could make an ideal "ready-made" pseudonym.

Many well known names, from classical times to the present, originated as nicknames. The Roman emperor Caligula had a name that arose from his upbringing among soldiers: as a boy running around camp he wore small size *caligae*, the Latin word used for the stout iron-nailed shoes worn by soldiers. His name thus literally means "Little Boots." (And how much nicer that is than Gaius Julius Caesar, his real name.) In complete contrast, the film actor Zero Mostel, originally Samuel Mostel, got "zero" for his subjects at school. In spite of the uncomplimentary nickname, he chose to adopt it as his screen name. School nicknames are notorious, in fact, and have been turned to advantage by a number of personalities for use as an adopted name. Jack Oakie (Lewis Offield) was called "Oakie" at school as he came from Oklahoma, and Dana, the singer, has a school nickname that is Irish for "mischievous" or "naughty." (It is also a first name, and even a surname, in its own right, which makes it an even better name.) Other nicknames also originate in childhood, whether at school or not, and these too can be adopted. Bing Crosby's first name was a childhood nickname, and Cyd Charisse derived her first name from her baby brother's attempt to say "sister." Bebe Daniels made her first film when she was only seven—a "baby"—and the disc jockey Kid Jensen (really David Allen Jensen) was Radio Luxembourg's youngest DJ when he was still a mere kid of 18.

In a somewhat unexpected quarter, and of much more venerable vintage, it is interesting to see that many of the names of famous artists originated as nicknames. Botticelli was thus originally Alessandro Filipepi, all those five hundred years ago. His name means "little barrel," and was the nickname used by his elder brother Giovanni. Similarly Canaletto means "little Canale" (Canale was his father's real name), Masaccio means "slovenly Tom" (it has the Italian augmentative ending), and Tintoretto means "little dyer. " The painter's father was a dyer. One of Masaccio's pupils was Masolino, whose name means "little Tom," not only in reference to his master but as a diminutive of his own name Tommaso. It may seem strange that the Italian painter Giovanni Antonio Bazzi should have chosen to adopt his hardly flattering nickname of Il Sodoma, "the sodomite," but, whether flaunting it or vaunting it, Sodoma he became.

Many nicknames actually look like real names, even Red Buttons—Aaron Schwatt was a red-haired bellboy in his teens—but some are obviously an everyday word used as a name, such as Twiggy (Lesley Hornby), and we shall be considering these "word-into-name" pseudonyms in due course.

Very many possibilities are thus open for a pseudonym to be derived from your own name—whether your real name, or part of it, or your pet name or nickname. But supposing you want to find your ready-made name some other way?

The obvious answer is, of course, that you can get your name from someone else. The only question is—who? Who is to be the person whose name you are to adopt? What is special about him or her, or his or her name? Where do you start?

Many pseudonyms begin at home. That is, within the family. And one of the commonest methods of all is to adopt your mother's maiden name.

This is an eminently satisfactory method, since it is not only a genuine surname that you are acquiring but one that is in every sense of the word a real family name. From the practical point of view, too, it enables you to extend the life of a name that might otherwise have disappeared from the family. Indeed, many people already bear their mother's maiden name as one of their own middle names, in which case to adopt such a name as a pseudonym is all too easy. You simply drop your surname.

Examples of "mother's maiden name" adoptions are easy to find. Here are a dozen people who all made this particular adoption: Constance Cummings, Ann Dvorak, Dulcie Gray, Helen Hayes, Viola Keats, Jeremy Kemp, Elsa Lanchester, Mario Lanza, Yvonne Mitchell, Anna Neagle, Romy Schneider, Simone Signoret (thus making a satisfying alliterative match). The list can be easily be extended.

And if not your mother's name, you can always take a name from some other member of the family, whether a near and dear one or a more remote relative.

Julie Andrews adopted her stepfather's name, as did Truman Capote. Diana Dors took that of her maternal grandmother. Vivien Leigh took her husband's middle name, rather unusually, and George Scrope, 19th-century English geologist and Member of Parliament, rather more unconventionally,

took his wife's maiden name. (He did this on marrying, thus reversing the usual role, by way of a compliment to his 24-year-old bride, the daughter of William Scrope, the last of the old earls of Wiltshire.) For further instances of this kind, with a man adopting his wife's name on marriage (and on inheriting), see Chapter 3, page 10.

Some people choose to take a really historic family name. Josephine Tey, the novelist, adopted that of her great-great-grandmother, and Owen Meredith, the British statesman and poet, went way back in time to take his first name from Owen Gwynnedd ap Griffith, king of North Wales, and Meredith ap Tudor, the great-grandfather of Henry VII. Edward Robert Bulwer Lytton, as Meredith is better known (his pseudonym was for his writing), was a lineal descendant of both of these royal forebears.

It is almost axiomatic that an adoptee should acquire the name of his stepparents, usually his stepfather. But he may well have had a real name of his own to begin with, which he will relinquish. This happened to Leslie Lynch King, better known as Gerald R. Ford, and to the famous author Jack London, whose biological father's name was Chaney.

The usual variations can be arranged. Paul Hamlyn, the publisher, adopted and also adapted his mother's maiden name of Hamburger, and Maria Karnilova, the American ballet dancer, changed her mother's maiden name from Karnilovich to supersede her real surname of Dovgolenko. Jacques Offenbach, the composer, took his father's nickname, "Der Offenbacher" (he was born in Offenbach-am-Main) and Kay Hammond assumed her mother's stage name. (Kay's maiden name was Standing, and her married name Clements.) Working down-family instead of up, Mike Todd, whose original first name was Avrom, took the first name of his son, Michael, and Mme Champseix, the 19th-century French writer, composed her pen name, André Léo, from the first names of both her sons.

If not from a relation, then you can always borrow someone else's name. The scope here is almost infinite, since the person whose name you choose may be known to you or not. He or she may be a public or private hero, an admired figure, a friend, a colleague—even an enemy! The act of adopting the particular person's name may be intended as a mark of homage or respect, or virtually a near-random affair. You may simply be attracted by the name itself: when pop singer Gerry Dorsey turned himself into Engelbert Humperdinck it was not because of his admiration for the German classical composer's works. The adopted name may in turn already be a pseudonym. This was the case with the American comic film actress Eve Arden, born Eunice Quedens. She based her name on that of Elizabeth Arden (Florence Graham), the Canadian cosmetician, who herself had taken her first name from that of Elizabeth, author of *Elizabeth and Her German Garden* (1898)—who was actually Mary Annette von Arnim.

Something of the wealth of possibilities can be seen by running through the names in the main listing (page 66), but among the borrowings will be found the names of a leading lady (Busby Berkeley), a schoolteacher friend (Richard Burton), an admired pop singer (Elvis Costello), a bishop (Lorenzo da Ponte), some benefactors (Carlo Farinelli), a prison guard (O. Henry), a noted golfer (Ted Ray), and an American Revolution general (John Wayne). For Lorenzo da Ponte to adopt the name of the bishop who christened him was not so much a personal tribute but a standing convention, since this was customary by many converts to Catholicism. In London similarly, in the 13th and 14th centuries, it was quite normal for an apprentice to assume the name of his master, and even earlier, for Roman slaves to take the names, as previously mentioned, of *their* masters.

The adoption of another person's name, whether permanently or temporarily, is an essential requirement for a person using a false passport or identity card, whether for criminal or legitimate purposes, for example for undercover work. In possessing and using the passport or card of another, one thus effectively passes oneself off as its actual holder. This will work, of course, if the holder himself has died or changed his name, or con-

nives in the deception, or is simply unaware of it. But what if he is ignorant of it and unexpectedly turns up? A potentially awkward situation could then be created, as described in his memoirs by the Russian revolutionary and Communist leader Valerian Vladimirovich Kuybyshev (1888–1935):

In 1908, having returned from exile in Kainsk, I was living in Petersburg with an identity card in the name of Andrey Stepanovich Sokolov. One day I was strolling along the Strelka when I bumped into a colleague I had been working with in a Siberian party group. We gave each other a big hug. Then he asked, "What name are you using these days?" Both he and I had been working under false names in the group and didn't know each other's real names. I said I was calling myself Andrey. "And what's your patronymic?" "Stepanovich." "That's strange, I'm Andrey Stepanovich, too. What's your surname?" "Sokolov." "I'm Sokolov, too!" "Where did you get my identity card?" It turned out it was his card. He had left it in Chelyabinsk, and after serving his sentence in the Orenburg region had gone to Petersburg, where they'd given him a new card. It was a tricky situation. It was lucky that Sokolov had arrived in Petersburg only a couple of days before, and that the cards, issued in different regions, had not yet met up in the Central Registration Bureau [Extract from *Episodes in My Life*, reprinted in *Molodyozhnyy kalendar'* ("Young People's Calendar"), 1978].

We shall shortly be having a special look at the name assumed by crossword compilers, but suffice it to say here that many of them gleefully (and gloatingly) adopted the names of Spanish Grand Inquisitors, a custom initiated by one of the doyen crosswordists, Torquemada.

Another special category of creative person is the Welsh bardic poet, for whom it is traditional to adopt the name of an ancient versifier: Robert Ellis, a 19th-century minister and poet, thus took as his bardic name that of the most important Welsh poet of the 12th century, Cynddelw, which itself is also some-times chosen as a suitable forename for a Welsh baby boy.

If in your search for a pseudonym all else fails in your hunt for a human being with a ready-made name that you can adopt, there is another recourse. This is to adopt a fictional name, meaning not so much a fictitious name (as already stated, all pseudonyms are ficti-tious) but a name from fiction.

There are probably characters in fiction whom we admire as much as we would if they were real flesh and blood—possibly more, since many fictional characters are idealized—and an effective way of expressing our private liking for one of them is to adopt his or her name as our own.

Here, too, the range is very wide, although naturally not as unlimited as when choosing a real person's name. And as for who, exactly, is to be the chosen character—the selection is very much a matter of personal taste and inclination. An actor or actress may choose the name of a character in a play, whether they have actually taken the part or not; a novelist or short story writer may pre-fer the name of some greater or lesser hero or heroine in a similar work—or even in his or her *own* work. The actress Elizabeth Ashley, when still Elizabeth Cole, took her new sur-name from the first name of Ashley Wilkes, as acted by Leslie Howard (originally Leslie Steiner) in the 1939 movie *Gone with the Wind*, and Tom Jones, who began life as Thomas Woodward, reputedly derived his name from the hero of the film (of Fielding's novel) *Tom Jones* (1963). (Jones himself was played by Albert Finney.) On the other hand the two famous fictional detectives Ellery Queen and Paul Temple gave their names respectively to two two-man teams of crime novelists: the Americans Frederic Dannay and Manfred B. Lee, and the British writers Fran-cis Durbridge and James McConnell (who used Paul Temple as their joint pen name for mystery novels *not* about the eponymous detective).

In a few famous instances, an author has published a purported autobiography under the name of its narrator. The title page of the original edition of Daniel Defoe's *Robinson Crusoe* (1719) thus stated that the work was "Written by Himself," while Jonathan Swift's *Gulliver's Travels* (1726), originally titled *Travels into Several Remote Nations of the World*, was "by Lemuel Gulliver." The true authorship of the latter was soon suspected, however, as Swift's friend John Gay wrote to him shortly after publication: "About ten days ago a Book was publish'd here of the Travels of one Gulliver. ...'Tis generally said that you are the Author, but I am told, the Bookseller declares he know not from what hand it came" (*Correspondence of Jonathan Swift*, 1965). A few years later, Laurence Sterne's *Tristram Shandy* (1759–67) was published as if Shandy himself had penned it.

The true authorship of these works was soon revealed. But other writers have adopted and retained the name of a fictional character as a deliberate disguise. To take the name of a character that you have yourself created is not merely a way of going on a literary ego trip, but also a kind of reward for the sweat, toil, and tears that you have experienced in creating that character. You have put some-thing, or much, of yourself into him, now let him be identified with you, his creator.

Names may be adopted from the works of others as well as from one's own creations. Pseudonyms entered in this book thus include a girl in a song (Nelly Bly), the heroine of one of the writer's own novels (Margaret Howth), the hero of an opera (Mario Lanza), a biblical hunter (Nimrod), a Shakespearean comic character (Peter Quince), and a character in Proust (Françoise Sagan). Dame Rebecca West took her name from an Ibsen play, and Dinah Shore from the song "Dinah." And what could be finer than Edward Bradwardine Waverley, the name chosen by John Croker from *two* characters in Sir Walter Scott's novel *Waverley* (1814) to reply to one Malachi Mala-growther—who was Scott himself in the guise of one of his own characters in *The Fortunes of Nigel* (1822).

Fiction, of course, covers several genres and generations, from classical times to the present, and we have already mentioned the Renaissance fashion for classical names. Classical names—those of ancient mythological characters or even actual Roman and Greek authors—have always found steady favor as a rather chic pseudonym, often, one suspects, almost as much for the impressive appearance of the name as for any actual association with the original bearer.

Janus, for example, is a good example of a symbolic classical name, being that of the "two-faced" Roman god of beginnings and endings (hence January). His name has been adopted by a number of writers, including the two German theologians Johann von Döllinger and Dr. Johannes Friedrich, and the French journalist and novelist Robert le Bonnières. We have seen how the name of Cassandra was used by William Connor. It was also adopted, perhaps less symbolically, by the Russian-born French graphic artist and stage designer (in the form Cassandre) Adolphe Mouron. The name of Alcibiades, the Athenian general and politician, was assumed by two noblemen: Albert, Margrave of Brandenberg, and George Villiers, Duke of Buckingham. It was also used by Alfred, Lord Tennyson, for an article in *Punch* published in March, 1846. The 18th- and 19th-century reformer and politician John Thelwell took the name Sylvanus Theophrastus. "Sylvanus" was a name used for one of the wood gods that followed Pan; Theophrastus was a Greek philosopher and scientist, a disciple of Aristotle. (It was also one of the real names of Paracelsus: literally it means "God-guided.") The 19th-century American novelist Emma Embury adopted the name Ianthe for her contributions to periodicals. In Greek mythology Ianthe was a Cretan girl who fell in love with another girl called Iphis, who herself subsequently (or consequently) changed into a boy and married Ianthe.

With such classical borrowings, it is often difficult to tell whether the name derives from the original character or from a later character of the same name, for example, in a play by Shakespeare or Racine. The English poet Alfred Austin, for instance, in using the name Lamia for *The Poet's Diary* (1904), may have taken this name directly from classical sources—Lamia lured strangers so that she could devour them—or from Keats's *Lamia* (1820). Again, there were often more than one classical personage of the same name, and without more precise indication it is impossible to tell whether Lady Mary Montagu, the 18th-century English writer of letters and poems, had in mind the Queen of Halicarnassus or the sister of Mausolus when she took the name Artemisia. And if she actually based the name on that of Artemis—who was also, as goddess of the moon, called Diana, Cynthia, Delia, Hecate, Luna, Phoebe and Selene—we are even more in the dark, since this name has also been alluded to scores of times by Shakespeare and several poets.

Today, the vogue for classical pseudonyms is less in evidence, although columnists and journalists frequently favor a name of this type. (One of the most popular is Atticus, who still has a regular feature in the *Sunday Times*. Atticus was an elegant Roman scholar and master of Greek, and a publisher and patron of the arts. His real name was Titus Pomponius. The pseudonym itself literally means "coming from Attica," i.e., from Athens, and was an epithet given by Romans to distinguished scholars and writers.)

If classical names do not appeal, the pseudonym searcher can always derive a name in a random fashion, by taking any name in existence and adopting it. That is to say, you can take any standard "ready-made" name and use it, without reference to a particular person of this name. Such names can be styled as arbitrary, since although real enough as names they have no specific origin.

On one of its lower levels of application "Mr. and Mrs. Smith" is an arbitrary name when used by an (unmarried) couple to check in at a hotel. They have not taken the name from a particular Mr. and Mrs. Smith, but have simply chosen the commonest surname in the English language as a transparent disguise.

Even so, there are degrees of arbitrariness, since the actual name adopted may be specifically that of a particular person, even though the adopter knows absolutely nothing about the person. In other words, the name is taken on simply as a name, nothing more. When David Cornwell became John Le Carré he is said to have taken the name from a shopfront in London which he had seen while sitting on the upper deck of a bus. Adam Faith, on the other hand, found his name in a "Naming the Baby" book. No doubt somewhere in the English-speaking world there is a real Adam Faith, perhaps several Adam Faiths, but Terence Nelhams had none of them specifically in mind when he chose his name.

Lists of arbitrary names are, or were, frequently held by agents and managers when engaging a new performer, much as many firms today hold lists of arbitrary trade names, evolved by computer, for possible use for a new product. Cary Grant came by his name from such a list. And of course an excellent source of ready-made names suitable for adoption in this way is a telephone directory. Walden Cassotto is said to have found his name Bobby Darin in a phone book, as did Martha Raye, the American radio and TV comedienne who was born Margaret Reed.

An arbitrary name can, naturally, be an invented one, such as Cantinflas or Pele, in which case it does not belong in this chapter but the next.

Some pseudonyms result from a mistake such as a misprint. They do belong here since they are certainly "ready-made," even if inadvertently.

Examples of names of this type include those of F. Anstey, the novelist, and Irving Berlin, the songwriter. They were the results of printer's errors of their real names, respectively, T. Anstey Guthrie and Israel Baline. A "mistake" name may also be a misprint of an already chosen pseudonym, not a true name. The American essayist Donald Grant Mitchell had adopted the name J.K. Marvel for his contributions to the *Morning Courier and New York Enquirer* in 1846. A typo gave him his permanent pen name of Ik Marvel. Such misprints more readily occur when the native of

one country is billed in another, in a foreign tongue. This happened to the English music hall entertainer Percy Henry Thompson, who took his stage name, Percy Honri, from the way the French printer had announced his appearance at the Folies Bergère.

When considering the evolution of personal names in Chapter 1, we saw that one source of surnames was placenames. In their more evolved form, placenames can also serve as a suitable pseudonym, especially when they indicate a place with which the name adopter has a special connection, for example as his or her birthplace. (Strictly speaking, the classical name Atticus, mentioned above, is a pseudonym of placename origin, although in translated and adjectival form.)

In this category we must interpret "placename" in its widest form, to include not just standard geographical names but names of houses, estates, streets, and fields, for example, that is, anywhere that is a place with a name. Since many placenames frequently resemble a personal name, and some of them actually are one (as Alberta or Washington, for example), it is often relatively easy to convert them or adapt them as a pseudonym.

To illustrate the scope offered by placenames in the wide sense of the word, we need only consider Conway Twitty (Conway, Arkansas, and Twitty, Texas), George Orwell (Orwell River), Clemence Dane (St. Clement Danes' church, London), Arthur Lucan (Lucan Dairy, Dublin), Cyril Hare, the British crime novelist (Cyril Mansions, Battersea, London), Gordon Craig (the Scottish island Ailsa Craig), and Cardinal Mindszenty (native Hungarian village of Mindszent). Sometimes the pseudonym refers to the place name less obviously, more allusively, as with Nellie Melba (Melbourne, Australia), the British novelist George Woden (Wednesbury, West Midlands, itself named after Woden, the Scandinavian god of war and wisdom), and Stainless Stephen, the English music hall comedian (born in Sheffield, of stainless steel fame).

Some centuries back it was in fact almost standard practice for certain sectors of society to assume the name of their native town or village. This was noticeably the case with Italian painters of the Renaissance school: Caravaggio, Perugino, and Veronese, for example, whose real names were respectively Merisi, Vanucci and Cogliari, took the names of their birthplaces Caravaggio, Perugia, and Verona. But in many cases of this kind, the native placename would have often been a conventional addition to the real name to start with, so that Caravaggio was properly Michelangelo Merisi da [from] Caravaggio. Another Renaissance painter, although German, not Italian, was Lucas Cranach, born Lucas Müller. He also adopted the name of his birthtown, then spelled Cranach (now Kronach). (This was Lucas Cranach the Elder; his son, Lucas Cranach the Younger, kept the name.) A later painter, the Frenchman Claude Gellée, became known as Claude Lorrain, from his birthplace in the historic province of Lorraine. (His name is sometimes wrongly given as Claude Lorraine. The surname has no "e," however, as it is the French adjective meaning "of Lorraine," "Lotharingian," not the name of the province itself.)

An enjoyable game is hunting for places that are named after pseudonymous persons: there are rather more than one might imagine, from all the places in the former Soviet Union named for Lenin (many of them previously for Stalin), to London Peak, Oregon, named for Jack London.

Placenames, when used as personal names, can be regarded just as properly "ready-made" as any name of a human being. The name, after all, is already there, in existence. It does not have to be invented. Moreover, as we have seen, it frequently *looks* like a personal name. To convert an ordinary word or phrase into a pseudonym, however, is to invent a name, since by definition a word (in this sense) is not already a name.

People and places, then, are the chief sources of ready-made pseudonyms. Who actually provides the name or produces it is another matter: people can adopt a name themselves or they can be suggested or noted for them. We have mentioned more than one instance of an actor or performer's being given a name by an agent or manager. Then again, as mentioned, it was noted that many foreign immigrants to the United States were presented with a new name on an *ad hoc* basis by the immigration officer almost as soon as they had set foot on land.

We now pass to the much more obviously "pseudo" class of invented names.

6. Invented Names

Francis Matthews is a lousy name for the theatre. Perhaps I should have called myself Clint Thrust (English actor Francis Matthews, interviewed in *TV Times*, May 25, 1978).

Most of the names that we have so far considered have actually looked like real names, usually comprising a "forename" and a "surname" element. Such names resemble the conventional names that we know in our daily lives.

Names that do *not* resemble conventional names we can perhaps call "invented names," and they are the subject of this chapter.

In general, invented names can be divided into three distinct types: those that are standard words, singly or grouped; those that are an artificial combination of letters or syllables (a rare category, as will be seen); and those that are represented by signs or symbols other than conventional letters. Of course, some names are a blend of one or more of these types, just as some names are a mixture of a "true" name and an invented name or element.

In the first category come many names that are essentially descriptive titles. These are very common. Oliver Goldsmith, for instance, used the name "The Citizen of the World," the novelist Chiang Yee wrote as "The Silent Traveller," Hector McNeile published his Bulldog Drummond stories as "Sapper," and one of Daniel Defoe's many pseudonyms was "An English Gentleman." Many women writers identified themselves simply as "A Lady," as already mentioned.

Some descriptive names of the type "A ...," with a following noun or noun phrase, were at one time simply standard conventions. Carty (see Bibliography, page 399) lists 10 different writers named as "A Churchman," 13 as "An Officer," 16 as "A Traveler," 18 as "A Person of Honor," 20 as "A Physician," 22 as "A Person of Quality," 23 as "A Gentleman," 24 as "A Clergyman," and no less than 63 as "A Layman." These last sought chiefly to express their views on some religious, legal, medical, or other professional matter. Carty's tally for "A Lady," incidentally, is 45.

Descriptive names of this type, especially the brief or single-word ones, are sometimes adopted by journalists and columnists, when they may belong to an individual regular contributor or to a series of writers. Examples of such names are "Spectator," "Onlooker," "Linesman" (a nice punning name for a sports journalist), or "Diplomat." Even a multiple name such as "Our City Staff," in the financial pages of a British newspaper, is really a pseudonym of this type. After all, the writers do not reveal their proper individual names. But most newspapers and magazines, even so, will now have reports and features written with a personal byline, and there has been a marked trend in the latter half of the 20th century away from pseudonymous (and anonymous) articles. Even as recently as October 17, 1996, however, *The Times* of London carried three news stories "By A Staff Reporter," and its obituaries are still anonymous. (This same newspaper's issue for June 26, 1862, by contrast, carried foreign news reports that were either anonymous or "From Our Own Correspondent.")

In the 18th and 19th centuries, the author of a first novel that sold well frequently resorted to a standard pseudonym for any subsequent book, which was published as being by "The Author of...." In his *Handbook of Fictitious Names*, Olphar Hamst identifies more than 160 such writers, from "The Author of *Abbeychurch*" (Charlotte M. Yonge, who often favored this type of pseudonym) to "The Author of *Zohrab*" (James Morier, "a great Oriental traveler, and writer of tales"). The respective works that appeared under these pseudonyms were *Scenes and Characters; or, Eighteen Months at Beechcroft* (1847) and *Ayesha, the Maid of Kars* (1834), both now largely or even entirely unread.

Not all adopters of this style of pseudonym were as obscure, however, and most readers will readily recognize the true identity of "The Author" of *Handley Cross* (Surtees), *Peter Simple* (Marryat), *Tom Brown's Schooldays* (Hughes), and *Uncle Tom's Cabin* (Harriet Beecher Stowe).

As the name or pseudonym of an author frequently follows the title of the actual work, and is (or was) preceded by the word "By...," this gives scope for the pseudonym to refer to the title itself as a factual statement. An example of such a name (quoted by Hamst) is "*The Art of Making Catalogues of Libraries; or, A Method to Obtain in Short Times a Most Perfect, Complete, and Satisfactory Printed Catalogue of the British Museum Library* By a Reader Therein." The author of this lengthily titled work was actually an Italian, the bibliographer Andrea Crestadoro, who wrote in English.

Descriptive pseudonyms are frequently allusive, even punningly so, such as "Sealion" for the English naval writer Geoffrey Bennet, and "Beachcomber" for the *Daily Express* columnist D.B. Wyndham Lewis, as well as his successor, J.B. Morton. Names of this type that consist of two words frequently come close to resembling genuine "forename–surname" names, and only the incongruity of the words themselves indicates that they are not so. An example is the name of the British wrestler "Giant Haystacks," real name Martin Ruane.

In cases where names like this have been deliberately selected to incorporate a standard word that happens to resemble or be identical to a personal name, the actual artificiality of the name may remain undetected. A classic example is the name "Mark Twain," adopted by Samuel L. Clemens. "Mark Twain" was actually the call of pilots on the Mississippi River (see the full story on page 358), but "Mark" suggests that the name is a genuine one. In such cases the adopter of the name has donned a double disguise, choosing a name that is not his own anyway, and one that is not even a personal name at all. (Twain was a great lover of frauds and hoaxes generally.) There are other forenames besides Mark that potentially lend themselves to such treatment, among them April, Bill, Bob, Cherry, Daisy, Dawn, Frank, Guy, Holly, King, Lance, May, Pat, Peg, Pip, Ray, Rob, Rose, Tony, and Will. (Fruit and flower names and pet names generally are the best candidates.) And this is to say nothing of the punning distortions familiar from our childhood as the names of bogus authors (Eileen Dover, Ivor Redhead, and so on). Of the creating of such silly names there is (fortunately) no end, and the Australians have added to the namefund with Emma Chizit, Gloria Soame, and classically, Afferbeck Lauder. These are all so-called "Strine" creations (see the last name's entry on page 227). Among real people with names of this type, we find Stepin Fetchit, Lemmie B. Good, Will B. Good, Orpheus Seeker, Marti Caine, and Luke Sharp, invented names all.

Names in other languages are not immune from exploitation in this way. The following resemble genuine names (and we make allowances for their foreignness), but they are devised from standard words in the relevant language: Caran d'Ache (Russian), Felix Carmen (Latin), Mata Hari (Malay).

Names that consist of a genuine forename with a standard word as surname also come into the "invented" category, at least partially, and obviously the scope is much wider here than when selecting a forename of this type, where the choice is restricted to existing names. Among the many examples, thus, are Jimmy Driftwood, Dion Fortune, Gary Glitter, Peter Porcupine, and Vera Vague. Again the language may not be English, as for Maxim Gorky (Russian) or Danny La Rue (French). And where the surname *does* coincide with a standard word, we have the converse of a "Mark Twain"–style name. An example is that of Veronica Lake (whose invented surname was chosen to describe her lake-blue eyes). In some cases, both forename and surname may seem genuine, but actually be standard words recruited into name service. A good example is that of Patience Strong, whose name (albeit selected from a book title) embodies the human qualities that the writer wished to personify.

In considering "invented" names, mentioned should be made of the stock name A.N. Other (of obvious origin) used in British sporting fixtures to denote a member of a team who has not yet been selected. The United States has a sort of equivalent anonym in Allen Smithee, a pseudonym conventionally used by the Directors Guild of America as a screen credit for a movie director who does not wish his name to be associated with a particular film. (This usually happens as a result of what the director judges to be interference on the part of the film's producers.) The name has a specific origin. It arose in 1967 when Don Siegel took over from Robert Totten as the director of *Death of a Gunfighter* some three weeks into shooting. Both men were dissatisfied with the final film, and neither wished their name to be associated with it. (Ironically, in 1969 a *New York Times* critic wrote approvingly that the movie has been "sharply directed by Allen Smithee.")

As another variation on the "standard word" theme, a forename may be preceded by an adjective or a noun. Popular choices here are for common words such as "Big," "Little," "Aunt," "Uncle," the latter two formerly favored by children's writers and broadcasters. Examples of such names are Big Maybelle, Little Richard, Aunt Effie, and Uncle Mac. Other adjectives can equally be commandeered, to give names such as Woody Allen (although in some names this stands for

Woodrow), Muddy Waters (the apparent surname is an invention), and Shakin' Stevens. Nouns are equally adopted, as for Giant Haystacks (already mentioned), Guitar Slim, and Washboard Sam. Placenames may function as forenames, too, as for the various people named (originally nicknamed) "Tex," while country singer Conway Twitty derived his name entirely from placenames. But of course such names are *already* names, so differ from the standard words that we are considering here.

Standard words are in particular used for a special category of pseudonym that is as much private as the ones already mentioned are public. These are the "love names" as characteristically resorted to by placers of personal ads in the press on Valentine's Day. Most lovers anyway use a standard word or words (or a pet distortion of it) for their loved one, and this is therefore the latter's name. Perhaps we should refer to such names as "intimate names," as distinct from the pet names that are fairly conventional abbreviations or alterations of a standard forename. Thus a girl named Susan will almost certainly become "Sue" or "Susie" or something similar to her close friends and family, and even at first to her boyfriend or lover. But for an intimate relationship she can progress to almost any kind of descriptive name, depending both on her personal characteristics or nature and the intimate naming habits or inclinations of her lover. (There are patterns of naming, though, as we shall see.)

A few examples of such "love names" will be enough to show the sort of descriptive techniques traditionally used by one lover to address another. The following appeared in *The Times* for Valentine's Day (February 14) 1988 (the names are extracted from the actual messages or *déclarations d'amour* and are those of the recipient): Baby Doll, Cuddly Sniggle, Chipmunk, Badger, Barrel Body, Big Nose, Bright Eyes, Bunny, Chocolate Buttons, Curly, Darling Porker, Dearest Dimples, Diddlie Wumps, Frog Eyes, Honey Bunny, Kissyface, Lady Luck, Lollipop, Monster, Pooch, Princess, Purring Lady, Scrummybum, Snug-glebum, Sweet Boy, The Lizard, Village Girl, Woolly Bear. (True, many of the ads open with the addressee's real name, but purely in order to draw his or her attention to the message.)

Such names may be nonce names or permanent designations, but they are pseudonyms right enough (the named one will acknowledge the name and doubtless use it) and are formed from standard words or "babytalk" adaptations of such words. The reduplication of sound or letter that is generally popular with pseudonym-adopters is very marked here, and is found in such names as "Grottie Smottie," "Fottlebot," "Finjin Minjin," and some of those already cited above.

Such concoctions are also found for standard "public" pseudonyms, such as Boz (for Charles Dickens, although admittedly derived from a childish pronunciation), Mistinguett (by "Miss Hellyet" out of "Vertinguette") and Woon (from the surname Wotherspoon). "Tactical" name changes of this type are a characteristic of British political elections. The new name may be deliberately outlandish. Such was Tarquin Fintimlinbinwhinbimlin Bus Stop-F'Tang-F'Tang-Ole-Biscuit Barrel, the name assumed by John Dougrez-Lewis, Cambridge candidate for the Raving Monster Loony Party at the time of the 1983 British general election. Despite it, or even because of it, he gained 286 votes. More conventionally, one Richard Huggett changed his name to Gerald Maclone in order to confuse voters supporting the Conservative candidate, Gerald Malone, in the 1996 Winchester by-election. He rationalized: "Malone is an imitator of those that have gone before. I am an innovator. I am the clone version of Gerald Malone. If I cause confusion, and damage his prospects, too bad. Politics is not an easy game" (*The Times*, November 26, 1996). (At an earlier election, Huggett had stood as a Literal Democrat, knocking the Liberal Democrat candidate into second place. This subtle ploy did not involve a name change, however.)

Further creations are the names of Grock, the circus clown, invented to match that of Brick (yet differ from that of Brock), and, at least partially, of Squibob, although this does at least suggest "squib." Completely meaningless names are thus rare, and even the name "X" conventionally indicates that its bearer prefers or has deliberately chosen anonymity.

Initials or letters are, however, a very common method of devising a pseudonym. Such letters may derive from existing names or from standard words, and it will be impossible to tell without an explanation. One famous actress was known by initials that could be interpreted both ways: "BB" denoted both Brigitte Bardot and *bébé* ("baby"). Coincidentally, Lewis Carroll adopted "B.B." as an early pen name, although it is still not certain what the letters or initials stood for.

A few pseudonymists have carried the use of letters to a deliberate excess, as did the French writer Xavier de Maistre (1763–1852), who for his 1794 novel *Voyage Autour de Ma Chambre* ("Journey Around My Room") adopted the name "M. le ch. X. o. a. s. s. d. s. M. S." This lengthy abbreviation stood for "Monsieur le chevalier Xavier, officier ancien sur service de sa Majesté Sardinienne" ("Sir Knight Xavier, former officer in the service of His Majesty of Sardinia"). A different device was resorted to by the German writer Hans Jakob Christoffel von Grimmelshausen (1621–1676), better known as "Simplicissimus," who for *Das wunderbarliche Vogel–Nest* ("The Wondrous Bird's Nest") (1672) signed himself on the title page as "A.c.eee.ff.g.hh.ii.ll.mm.nn.oo.rr.sss.t.uu," these letters being simply those of his own name arranged in alphabetical order.

But back in the world of standard invented names, we must not overlook the traditional *non*-standard method of forming a pseudonym, which is to utilize signs and symbols that are not ordinary letters. The standard symbol for anonymity or at least pseudonymity is the asterisk (*) or the dash (—), with such devices either assuming the role of individual letters or standing for an entire name. Frequently, asterisks are used in a number that corresponds to the number of letters in the real name. Thus Hamst, in his work mentioned above, succeeded in identifying one **** ******, who wrote the *Letter to *, &c., on the Rev. W.L. Bowles's strictures on the Life and writings of Pope* (1821), purportedly by "The Right Hon. Lord Byron," to be actually John Murray (1778–1843), son of John Murray, founder of the London publishing house that bears his name. The deciphering of asterisms (as they may be called) is a hard task, however, and the number of asterisks may not in fact be significant at all, but purely random. It seems to have been so in the case of **********, the author of *Letters of Advice from a Lady of Distinction to her Niece, the Duchess of *, &c., shortly after her Marriage* (1819). Hamst could not handle this one, and it is quite likely that the author was not after all a true "Lady of Distinction," nor the addressee a "Duchess." Nor did Hamst tell his readers who Ø was, as the author of *The Book of God* (1866).

Names like these, created from signs and symbols, will not occur elsewhere in this book. This is not to belittle them, however, for * is just as valid a pseudonym as George Orwell or Mark Twain, although far less original. (It also creates a practical difficulty when it comes to reading it aloud: how does one pronounce an asterism?)

7. Names with a Difference

"Ya hear the one 'bout the guy who couldn't afford personalized plates, so he went and changed his name to J2L 4685?" (Marge Gunderson in Joel and Ethan Coen's movie *Fargo*, 1996).

This chapter is dedicated to names that are special: carefully chosen names, significant names, ambiguous names, popular names, outrageous names, baffling names, vocational names, traditional names. We shall be considering names so evocative and meaningful that they almost eclipse their bearer, and names so trivial that they are mostly long forgotten. We shall also take a necessarily speculative view of certain "open-ended" names—those whose story is still incomplete or unexplained. And finally, in the light of our examination of the many aspects of pseudonyms and name changes, we shall pose once again, but this time perhaps more subjectively and philosophically, the question, "What *is* a name?"

Let us at once proceed to the specific. What did the bearers of these names have in common? Linus, Anacletus, Evaristus, Telesphorus, Hyginus, Anicetus, Soter, Eleutherius, Zephyrinus, Urban, Pontian, Auterus, Fabian, Cornelius....

Roman emperors? Greek gods? Classical authors? Esoteric underground "cover" names?

Here are some more, whose owners still have the same common identity: Paul, John, Pius, Benedict, Leo, Gregory, Clement, Innocent....

This gives the game away: all of the names are those of popes, with the "classical" names above being the (real) names of very early popes, and the more familiar names that follow being those that were assumed by some popes.

We considered papal names earlier as a special category of assumed name, when regarding them as "names for a living." Here we should take a closer look at some of the individual names that popes have taken, and

try to see why they have enjoyed such favor. Why, for example, have several popes been named John, yet none Matthew, Mark or Luke? (True, there was one pope named Mark, but this was his real name. He pontificated for nine months in 336, many years before the first assumed name.)

It is the name John, in fact, that is easily "top of the popes." No less than 23 popes have assumed it in its "neat" form, the last of these being Angelo Roncalli, who became John XXIII in 1958, with the name used in combined form by two recent popes, John Paul I (Albino Luciani, elected 1978 and in office only 33 days), and John Paul II, his successor (Karol Wojtyla, elected that same year, the first non-Italian pope since 1522).

John has long been a popular Christian name at all levels, in many countries, largely thanks to the two important New Testament characters, John the Baptist and St. John the Evangelist, "the two men who were closest to Christ the Lord"—as Angelo Roncalli designated them when explaining his own reasons for choosing the name. Roncalli's account of his motives for assuming the name John, in fact, gives us as clear a picture as any regarding the popularity of the name, as well as an insight into one individual pope's choice. Apart from the biblical pedigree, the name was dear to him, he said, since it was his father's name, it was the dedication of the village church in Lombardy where he was baptized as well as that of many cathedrals throughout the world, including the Lateran basilica of San Giovanni in Rome, and of course it was the name of 22 of his predecessors. For the future John XXIII, therefore, the name was selected on a careful combination of historical, religious, and personal grounds. Significantly, the name was in turn adopted, with specific reference to John XXIII's reforming spirit, by his two successors John Paul I and John Paul II, with the latter combining homage to both John XXIII and John Paul I, whose policies he intended to pursue.

John was thus not only the first papal name to be assumed, but flourishes as a still popular papal choice a thousand years after. What name could have a better pedigree than that?

The next most common papal name is Gregory, which has been adopted 16 times, most recently by Bartolomeo Alberto Cappellari, pope for 15 years from 1831. Just as John owes its popularity to two saints, so it is certain that Gregory owes much of its charisma to the first pope of the name, St. Gregory the Great, of *non Angli sed angeli* fame (with reference to the English slave boys he saw in Roman marketplaces). It is likely that St. Gregory himself was so named after the two fathers of the Eastern church, Gregory of Nazianzus ("The Theologian") and Gregory of Nyssa ("The Wonderworker"). The name is quintessentially "papal,", which may explain why its general use in Western Europe and the New World has not been particularly favored. In English-speaking countries, in fact, it is more likely to be associated with a surname than a Christian name.

Following Gregory in frequency comes another typically papal name, Benedict. In English-speaking countries this is even more unpopular, except among Roman Catholics, than Gregory, although it still flourishes in Latin countries. (Its meaning, "blessed," derives directly from Latin, whereas Gregory, "watchman," comes from Greek, and John, "the Lord is gracious," originated in Hebrew.) Who was the original Benedict who prompted 15 popes to assume the name, from Niccolò Boccasini in the 14th century to Giacomo della Chiesa in the 20th? As with John and Gregory and most common papal names, there were other saints of this name, the best known probably being the founder of the Benedictine order. It seems likely, however, that apart from personal references (an identification with this saint or previous pope

Benedict), many popes chose the name because of its highly favorable meaning. If a pope is not "blessed," and empowered to bless, who is?

Following Benedict in frequency comes an equally meaningful name, Clement. Fourteen popes took the name, from the 11th-century Suidger to Giovanni Ganganelli in the 18th century. Can we ascribe their name to a St. Clement? If we can, it must be to the first pope of this name, who died at the end of the 1st century AD and who has by some been identified with one of the fellow laborers of St. Paul mentioned in Paul's epistle to the Philippians (4:3). This St. Clement was famous for the letter he sent from the church of Rome to the church of Corinth, which represented the first known example of a bishop of Rome intervening in the affairs of another church. Mild (the literal meaning of Clement) the first pope of the name may have been, but certainly not meek, and subsequent popes Clement may have had him in mind when choosing the name for their pontifical position. Again, possibly the literal interpretation of the name may have been regarded as auspicious.

Clement has not been a particularly popular name for English speakers, and even less popular has been the next most common papal name, Innocent. This name of patent meaning was first borne by St. Innocent in the 5th century (it was his real name), and most recently by Michelangiolo Conti, elected as Innocent XIII in 1721. St. Innocent was hardly a distinguished man, however, either as saint or pope, and the adoption of the name by later popes would appear to be either a personal tribute to an earlier allonymous pontiff or, again, the acquisition of a favorably descriptive name. Another possibility would be a link that one of the popes of the name had with the feast day of St. Innocent (June 22) or of the Holy Innocents (December 28), or perhaps with a church dedicated to the saint or the Holy Innocents.

Seen through late 20th-century eyes, the name Innocent seems curiously bland for a pope, both meek *and* mild. But of course it also implies probity and purity, even impec-cability, hence irreproachability and ulti-mately infallibility, doctrinally the eminent papal attribute.

A much more "macho" name is Leo, "lion," adopted by 13 popes, the same num-ber as those who chose Innocent. The choice of this particular name by a pope is much more likely to be an act of homage to a pre-vious Leo than an intention to suggest a lion-like character. Indeed, we know that Leo IX, himself a saint, chose the name as a tribute to Leo the Great (Leo I), since he aimed to put the papacy, in the 11th century, on the same sound foundations as those laid by his name-sake over half a century before. Again, Leo XIII, adopting the name on his election in 1878, was paying tribute to Leo XII, whom he had always admired for his interest in educa-tion, understanding attitude towards tempo-ral governments, and desire to make active links with lapsed Catholics. The reasonable popularity of the Christian name Leo among present-day Catholics derives largely in turn from Leo XIII himself, since this pope, the last of the name, was the first world authority to codify the duties and rights of workers and their employers (1890). We thus find, coinci-dentally, that the papal bearers of this name that hints at strength and power have indeed been strong-natured and of powerful spiritual stature.

The only other name that has attracted over ten popes is Pius, which once more has a transparent meaning and an apt one, if rather obviously so. Twelve popes assumed this name, over half of them comparatively recently (seven since 1775). As with Innocent, we must assume either a personal compliment or simply a desirable, and traditional, epithet behind the adoption of the name. The first pope so called (it was his actual name) was the 2nd-century ex-slave saint who combated Gnosticism. Not until over a thousand years later, in 1458, did another pope come to adopt the name, with the most recent bearer being Pius XII (died 1958).

Pius IX (known euphoniously as "Pio Nono") had the longest of all pontificates (1846–1878), and we know that he took his name in deference to the memory of Pius VII, who had been his friend and who also, like himself, had been bishop of Imola. Earlier and later Piuses appear to have adopted the name on mostly conventional grounds. As a Chris-tian name, Pius is effectively a nonstarter, however.

Of other names favored by popes, many are unremarkable Christian names, as Stephen (selected nine or ten times, depending on the reckoning), Alexander (eight), Paul and Adrian (six each), Nicholas (five), and Victor (three). Among the typically "papal" names have been Boniface (nine popes so called), Urban (eight), and Sixtus (five). The latter three have meanings that are all of Latin ori-gin, respectively "doing good," "townsman" and, oddly, "sixth." (It is thought that the first pope Sixtus was so named as he was the sixth pope in line after St. Peter. It was Sixtus IV who gave his name to the Sistine Chapel, the pope's private chapel next to St. Peter's in Rome, famous for Michelangelo's ceiling fresco.)

In the 20th century there has been a trend away from "adjectival" names of the Benedict, Innocent, and Pius type, with a reversion to genuine Christian names. The four popes since the last Pius have thus been (apparently unoriginally but with particular personal reference) John, Paul, John Paul and John Paul. Interestingly, and almost prophet-ically, the first John Paul was instantly allot-ted the ordinal number "the First" by the media in many countries, thus prompting one letter writer to *The Times* to ask, "How long are we to wait for Pope John Paul II?" (J.C. Davis, September 1, 1978). On the last day of the month in which this letter was printed, the same newspaper would publish John Paul I's obituary.

Among the names, true and assumed, of the 265 popes elected to date, some curiosi-ties may be noted:

•Of the six popes named Adrian, the fourth was the only English (Nicholas Break-spear) and the sixth the only Dutch (Adrian Boeyens). The latter was the last non–Italian pope before the election of the Polish cardinal Karol Wojtyla as John Paul II in 1978.

•Paul VI was baptized as John the Baptist (Giovanni Battista).

•All the popes named Stephen with an ordinal number higher than II could also be one number higher, i.e., Stephen III could be Stephen IV, Stephen IV could be Stephen V, and so on. This is because there are two popes Stephen II, the first of whom was not consecrated (he died four days after his election in 752) and so was not listed in the official book of popes (*Liber Pontificalis*). This means that his successor was a "real" Stephen II or actually a Stephen III.

•Martin V, born Oddo Colonna, was elected pope in 1417. He was only the third pope so named, however, not the fifth, since the two popes, "Martin II" and "Martin III" never existed. A 13th-century scribe misread the names of the two popes Marinus as Martinus. Hence the error.

•Sixtus IV is not the only pope whose name has passed, specifically or generally, into the English language (see above). Gregory XIII gave his name to the Gregorian calendar, introduced by him in 1582 (and still in force), while Gregorian chant, or plainsong, is named after the first pope so named, St. Gregory the Great. The once popular card game called Pope Joan was *not* derived from a pope named John or even from the mythical female pope of this name (who was supposed to have been elected pope as John VIII in about 855 and who was allegedly born in England), but apparently comes from the French term for the game, *nain jaune* ("yellow dwarf").

Passing to lesser mortals, we must now turn our attention to another special category of names, one that in fact often nicely combines a distortion of a religious name and a play on words. This category comprises the ingenious names chosen by crossword compilers.

Where papal names are historically and spiritually significant, crossword compilers' names, as is to be expected, are linguistically so. Some of them, indeed, are as satisfying to "crack" as a neat clue is to solve.

As far as the English language crossword is concerned, the way was led by compilers whose classic names (in more senses than one) have gone down in cruciverbal history, in particular names derived from Spanish Inquisitors, as Torquemada (Edward Mathers), pioneer of the cryptic clue, his successor Ximenes (D.S. Macnutt), and *his* successor Azed (Jonathan Crowther). (See their entries for accounts of their names.) Some names of crosswordists pay homage, directly or indirectly, to this tortuous (and torturous) trio, such as Apex (Eric Chalkley), who aimed to "ape X," or imitate Ximenes, and Machiavelli (Mrs. Joyce Cransfield). Most names, however, are neat and apt versions of the compilers' true names, or have a similarly punning and/or erudite origin.

Some of the best British crossword compilers became known to solvers through the medium of the radio and television journal *The Listener*, which published their work regularly. For private circulation, two "Who's Whos" of *Listener* crossword setters were compiled in 1965 and 1978, giving many of the origins of setters' pseudonyms. Let us see, therefore, how some British crosswordists devised their names. (None of these names has its own entry in the present work.)

Most crosswordists favor a variation on their real name, whether using the whole name, the surname alone (or the first name alone), or simply the initials. Thus "Ad" is Alfred Adams, "Dogop" is Donald George Puttnam, "Eli" is Ivor Neame Ellis, "ffancy" (with its fancy aristocratic doubled "f") is Robert Caffyn, and "Klick" is Robert William Killick. "Mog" is J.E. Morgan, "Ram" is Reginald A. Mostyn, "Smada" is Arthur Adams, "Twudge" is Tom W. Johnson, and a pronunciation of his initials, and "Leon" is Noel Anthony Longmore. ("Noel" reversed *and* letters from his surname.)

Sometimes the wordplay, as might be expected, is more erudite. "Philipontes" is Philip Bridges, with his surname rendered into Latin to join his already Greek first name. "Ploutos" is Michael Rich, whose surname is similarly translated, although this time into

Greek. (The bearer of this name had been given a classical education, and was actually taught the subject at school by the great Ximenes already mentioned above.) "Rhombus" is not only Robert Holmes, of which name it is a partial anagram, but is also a reference to the profession of the bearer, who is a mathematician.

Some of the allusions can never be guessed, and an explanation is necessary for them to be appreciated. Thus, "Algol" is F. Fereday, who was formerly a mathematician, and "Buff," or Colin Clarke, derives from the name of a Durham pub, the Buffalo's Head, where the bearer of the name spent much time as a student. "Loki" and "Thor" not only took their respective names from Germanic mythology, but are husband and wife, the former being Eve McLaughlin and the latter Terence McLaughlin. At the same time, of course, Loki's name actually suggests her surname, and Thor's name hints at his *first* name. (In actual mythology, Loki is male, although becoming a mare in one of his manifestations, and is unrelated to Thor.)

"Sam" is in the same vein, for this was the name given Albert John Hughes when he was at school.. Similarly, it is impossible to deduce by the name alone that "Topher," otherwise John R. Cheadle, took his name from his son, Christopher. Andrew Bremner took the name "Sabre," apparently adding an initial convenient "S" to letters from his real name. "Merlin" is not only a "wizard with words," but took a name that hints at his home address, Marlin Ridge, Pucklechurch. "Smokey" is David A. Crossland, and his name derives from that of a favorite but recently deceased dog. And "Egma," who in everyday life is David Michael, adopted a Shakespearian word for his name, that of Costard's attempt at "enigma" in *Love's Labour's Lost*. The title of this play itself epitomizes the fate of many tyro crossword solvers.

Crossword setters' pseudonyms are thus frequently found in the "lit. & fig." style that they frequently favor when devising their cryptic clues.

Pseudonyms among crossword solvers seem to be rarely used, presumably since they seek publicity, not obscurity. However an instance is known of two setters-turned-solvers who assumed false names to enter Ximenes competitions. These were the co-compilers Dorothy Taylor and Alec Robins (Zander), who assumed the respective names of Mrs. B. Lewis (a neighbor of Miss Taylor, with no interest in crosswords) and L.F. Leason (Mr. Robins is Jewish: "L.F." indicates the Hebrew letter aleph—or "A"—for his first name, and his mother's name was Leah, with Robins himself thus being "Leah's son" or Leason). The couple were subsequently banned from Azed crosswords in *The Observer* for such deviousness!

Crossword setters may well have a mental tussle before hitting on a satisfactory word to fill an awkward "light," or a good clue for a word once they have entered it in their grid.

Tusslers of another sort, physical not mental, are wrestlers, and many of those who do battle in the ring will select a suitable pseudonym for themselves.

Some ring names are fairly conventional, and could apply to almost any person who has adopted a pseudonymous name. You cannot tell that Bobby Becker, Don Eagle, Paul Jones, and Dusty Rhodes, for example, are wrestlers simply by their ring names. But many wrestlers specialize in some kind of act, costume, or gimmick, or fall into a particular physical or ethnic group, and as such choose a name that reflects their special quality. Let us look at some of these categories.

•"The toffs": Some wrestlers like to pose as members of the nobility, and so have names like Lord Duncum, Lord Charles Montague, Sir Norman Charles, Lord Patrick Lansdowne, and Lord Bertie Topham. One "blue blood" wrestler in Los Angeles, James Blears, changed his name legally to Lord Blears.

•"The hillbillies": Where the "lords" enter the ring wearing cloaks and monocles, the "hillbillies" appear in blue denim and rope belts. They have names like Hillbilly Spunky, Logger Larsen, Klondike Bill, Farmer Jack, Elviry Snodgrass, and Country Boy Humphrey.

•"The Indians": If you have cowboys in the ring, then you must also have Indians. Many wrestlers in this category are called "Chief," as Chief White Owl, Chief Kit Fox, Chief Little Wolf, Chief Big Heart, Chief Thunderbird, Chief Sunni War Cloud (real name Sonny Chorre), and Chief Indio Cherokee. Women wrestlers of this kind are usually "Princess," as Princess Tona Tomah, Princess Rose White Cloud, and Princess War Star. Many of these really are Indians (Native Americans), although not chiefs or princesses. Others have names such as Billy Two Rivers, Johnny War Eagle, Danny Little Bear, and Tiny Roebuck.

•"The terrible Turks": A good guise for a wrestler, with bald head and fearsome mustache. Among them have been Ali Bey the Turkish Terror, Youssouf the Terrible Turk, and Humid Kala Pasha (so called because of his "excessive humidity" when wrestling). There has also, of course, been an Ali Baba.

•"The fatties": Their names speak for themselves: Haystack Calhoun, Giant Haystacks, Man Mountain Dean, and The Blimp. A woman wrestler in this generous group is Heather Feather. She weighs in and wades in at just under 390 pounds and trains on sausage pizzas.

•"The angels": Handsome wrestlers? Far from it! These are the big men with uneven eyes, hideous hooters, misshapen mouths, and fiddle-case feet. Their names are often variations on their category: The Golden Angel, The Swedish Angel, The Super Swedish Angel (billed as "the world's ugliest wrestler"), The Czech Angel, and the Polish Angel. There was even a bald woman wrestler named The Lady Angel.

Masked wrestlers traditionally adopt a name that relates to their visual anonymity and that hints at their fearsomeness. Typical names are The Black Demon, The Black Panther, The Executioner, The Hooded Terror, The Masked Avenger, The Mystery Man, The Red Devil, The Shadow, and of course, Zorro. Masked men in wrestling date back to around 1915, when The Masked Marvel (a name later taken up by others) was beaten by Ed (Strangler) Lewis at the Manhattan Opera House. The Masked Marvel was Mort Henderson in real life, while Ed Lewis was Robert H. Friedrich. He borrowed the name from an earlier wrestler, Evan (Strangler) Lewis.

In more recent times TV viewers have become familiar with the "power" names of contestants in the physically challenging game show *Gladiators*, a program devised in the United States but imported to Britain by LWT (London Weekend Television), where it became cult viewing. The contestants directly identify with their names, and in assuming them achieve a kind of deification. Examples, with real names in parentheses, include: Amazon (Sharron Davies, a former Olympic swimmer), Cobra (Mike Wilson), Falcon (Bernadette Hunt), Hunter (James Crossley), Jet (Diana Youdale), Panther (Helen Madderson), Phoenix (Sandy Young, formerly Bodybuilding Miss UK), Rio (Jane Omorogbe), Scorpio (Nikki Diamond), Shadow (Jefferson King), Trojan (Mark Griffin), Warrior (Mike Ahearn), Wolf (Michael Van Wijk).

Other typical names are Ace and Rebel. The names are subject to the personal approval of the contestants. Thus LWT offered Griffin a choice of three names: Trojan, Terminator, and Commando. He chose Trojan "because it didn't have any film connotations" (*Sunday Times*, May 19, 1996).

After such a show of power, both mental and physical, we should perhaps come down to more homely and familiar names.

Peter Anthony, for example, and Judith M. Berrisford. These are such ordinary names that one might not even suspect they are pseudonyms. Yet they are, and to justify their mention in this chapter are somewhat out of the ordinary run of pen names. They are in fact the names of not two individuals, but two couples, respectively Peter Shaffer and his brother Anthony, and Clifford Lewis and his wife Mary. Where two people work together like this, whether as family relatives or not, it is only natural that if they assume a pseudonym, they should take a single name.

For a couple to adopt a single pen name is fairly common, and in forming their pseudonym the usual devices are resorted to, with perhaps a wider scope for "own name" creation, since there are twice as many real names to work on. The Shaffer brothers, for example, simply used their first names as a forename and surname, while the Lewises based their joint name on the maiden name of Mary Lewis's mother (Berrisford). (Unusually, the husband-and-wife team decided in favor of a female name. Normally such double pen names are masculine.)

As with all pseudonyms, variations in formation and application are possible here. A Citizen of New York for example, was not a single citizen, nor even two, but three distinguished writers: Alexander Hamilton, "King of the Feds," James Madison, fourth U.S. president, and John Jay, jurist and statesman. The pseudonym Patrick Quentin conceals the identity of no less than four writers (Richard Webb, Hugh Wheeler, Martha Kelly, and Mary Aswell), and the clearly concocted name Smectymnuus was the joint name of five English Presbyterian ministers.

Very occasionally an inversion of this type of name occurs, when a pseudonym consisting of two names turns out to be a single individual. This is the case with "William and Robert Whistlecraft," who were not a father-and-son or fraternal team but just one man: John Hookham Frere (1769–1846), English diplomat and author. He used the name for his humorous poem *The Monks and the Giants* (1817–18), a mock-romantic Arthurian work (or the first four cantos of it) which would serve as a model for the much better known poem *Don Juan* by Byron, begun a year later (1819).

In all pseudonym creations there is often present a latent whimsicality. If you are "making a name for yourself," why not devise something witty and clever, and enjoy yourself in the process? An amusing or punning name will often be remembered much more vividly and effectively than a prosaic and commonplace one. One suspects, for example, that if English movie actress Patsy Sloots had retained her real name instead of changing it to the rather ordinary Susan Shaw, she would have made a greater impact on her fans. (Her real name actually *looks* like a stage name.)

It is not surprising that some pseudonym bearers have turned to the creation of a comical name, or several comical names, with considerable relish. The novelist William Makepeace Thackeray must have enjoyed inventing George Savage Fitzboodle, Jeames de la Pluche, Major Gahagan, Ikey Solomons, Michael Angelo Titmarsh, Charles James Yellowplush, and their kind, much as Charles Dickens and P.G. Wodehouse, in their respective fictional fields, had a genius for devising names for their characters that are often witty, occasionally outrageous, and usually entirely fitting. (The study of names of fictional characters is an important and enlightening subject, as yet mostly left untreated except by a few dedicated literary or linguistic experts. We mentioned the aptness of many Shakespearean names at the beginning of Chapter 1, for example: there is a virgin field that would richly pay the pioneer cultivator.)

Lest it be thought that humorous pseudonyms belong exclusively to writers, especially the classic American humorists (Josh Billings and Diedrich Knickerbocker among them), let us cite some of the wackier names in another creative area. These are the names used by W.C. Fields, whose love of whimsy gave us, among others: Mahatma Kane Jeeves, Otis Criblecolis, Egert Souse, Cuthbert J. Twillie, Professor Eustace McGarde, Elmer Prettywillie, Samuel Bisbee, Elmer Finch, Gabby Gilfoil, Professor Quail, Augustus Winterbottom, T. Frothingwell Bellows, Larson E. Whipsnade, and Woolchester Cowperthwaite. Silly names, of course, yet many of them not entirely implausible as actual names.

Multiple pseudonyms like this are found in several spheres of creative activity. Among names used for his recordings by George Harrison, of the Beatles, for example, were L'Angelo Misterioso, George O'Hara, Hari Georgeson, P. Roducer, Jai Raj Harisein, George H., George O'Hara Smith, Son of Harry, George Harrysong, and The George

O'Hara Smith Singers. This last name referred to the fact that the recording was of his own voice overdubbed many times.

Even John Lennon resorted to the occasional musical pseudonym, such as Noel Nohnn and John O'Cean, while Paul McCartney recorded under the names of Apollo C. Vermouth (almost a Fields creation) and Paul Ramon. Some of these are nonce usages, of course, but are genuine creations even so.

In the more familiar world of literature, there have been several multiple pseudonyms (maybe we could call them "multinyms"). U.S. crime writer Erle Stanley Gardner (1889–1970) used the names of Kyle Corning, A.A. Fair, Charles M. Green, Carleton Kendrake, Charles J. Kenny, Robert Parr, and Les Tillray, while English crime novelist John Creasey (1908–1973) used almost 30 different pseudonyms, including Gordon Ashe, Michael Halliday, Brian Hope, Kyle Hunt, Abel Mann, J.J. Marric, Richard Martin, Rodney Mattheson, Anthony Morton, Tex Riley, and Jeremy York. These are not as enterprising as Fields' names, but they are diverse enough.

Thirty pen names is chicken feed, however, alongside the "centenarians," those writers who adopted 100 or more pseudonyms. Nor are they all English speakers.

In his four-volume *Dictionary of Pseudonyms*, we find Masanov, thus, listing the 106 names used by V.M. Doroshevich (1864–1922), the Russian journalist and satirical writer (including, in translation, Ivanov, Son of Influenza, and Wandering Minstrel, Professor of Striped and Spotted Dark Green Magic), and the 107 names used by the writer, actor, and journalist A.M. Gerson (1851–1888), from the obvious "A.G." to the unexplained "S.S." The palm, however, must go to the Russian humorist Konstantin Arsenyevich Mikhaylov (1868– ?), who boasted no less than 325 pen names, from "Ab." to "Z." Most of them are abbreviations and variants of a particular pseudonym such as G., G-ver, Gl., Glv., Gllivr, and the like, which all seem to point to "Gulliver," while others are rather

pedestrian descriptive names such as (in translation) Passenger, Pedagogue and Reformer. For a humorist, indeed, the majority are not even specially amusing. Still, the record stands, and must therefore be duly noted.

Far more interesting than these are the full 173 pseudonyms adopted by Voltaire. Since, as far as I am aware, these have never appeared before in their entirety in an English-language publication, whether in original French or in translation, I am allocating Appendix 1 to them (pages 384–87) in the hopes that they will satisfy the reader's curiosity and also be a useful passage of reference for all who need them. Appendix 2, which may serve as a comparison, lists the 198 names used by Daniel Foe, otherwise Daniel Defoe, author of *Robinson Crusoe*.

With the two enjoyable names of Doroshevich, quoted above, we are reminded of the playful nature that many pseudonyms assume. Indeed, the humor and wit of many pen names is one of their most popular attributes. Everyone likes a funny name, simply because everyone enjoys a joke or relishes a pun. At the same time, the actual *use* of a humorous pseudonym may be a serious one. A frivolous name may mask a biting satire or cruel travesty. Thus Thomas Nash, the 16th-century English satirical pamphleteer and dramatist, chose the apparently lighthearted name Adam Fouleweather for his *Wonderful, strange, and miraculous Astrologicall Prognostication* (1591) that was an acrid reply to the savage denunciation of him by the astrologer Richard Harvey, and two hundred years later William Cobbett, the British author and politician, chose the seemingly frivolous name Peter Porcupine for his radical pro-British pamphlets published in America in the 1790s.

It is the lengthy, descriptive names, however, that make the most entertaining reading, whatever their purpose, and for their own sakes we may introduce a few more.

The 19th-century English statesman Lord John Russell entitled himself "A Gentleman who has Left His Lodgings" for his *Essays and Sketches of Life and Character* (1820). This originally had a preface signed

"Joseph Skillet," allegedly the lodginghouse keeper who published the essays to pay the rent that the "Gentleman" had neglected to pay. In the same style, but a few years earlier, Charles Snart, an attorney of Newark, Nottinghamshire, had published a book on fishing called *Practical Observations on Angling in the River Trent* (1812). For this purpose the author described himself as "A Gentleman Resident in the Neighbourhood, who has made the Amusement his Study for upwards of Twenty Years." In both cases, as with similar diverting titles, the name of the book would precede the pen name of the author, so that Earl Russell's essays were "By a Gentleman who…" and Snart's discourse was written "By a Gentleman…." Such names as "One who…" are also of this type, as *A Peep at the Wiltshire Assizes, a Serio-Ludicrous Poem* (1820) by "One who is but an Attorney" (George Butt, a Salisbury, Wiltshire, lawyer), and *English History for Children, from four to ten years of Age* (1832–33), by "One who loves the Souls of the Lambs of Christ's Flock" (Rev. Richard Marks, a Buckinghamshire vicar). (Hamst, quoting this last name, writes, "We dare not allow ourselves to comment upon a person who uses such a pseudonym as this.")

Infinitely more entertaining than these long-winded names, though, are those that combine description with fantasy, as the two Doroshevich names. Russian 19th-century writers, in fact, seem to have made such names something of a specialty. Dmitriyev quotes two fine specimens.

The first was devised by V.A. Zhukovsky, a minor poet, for a frivolous "Greek ballad rendered in the Russian style" entitled *Yelena Ivanovna Protasova, or Friendship, Impatience, and Cabbage* (1811). For this, Zhukovsky assumed the name "Maremyan Danilovich Zhukovyatnikov, President of the Commission on the Construction of the Muratov House, Author of the Crowded Stables, Fire-Breathing Ex-President of the Old Kitchen Garden, Knight of the Three Livers, and Commander of the Gallimaufry." Zhukovsky wrote this curiosity while staying with his friends, the Protasov family,

at their estate at Muratovo, just outside Moscow.

A friend of Zhukovsky, one Alexander Pleshcheyev, wrote some "critical comments" on this same ballad under what must be one of the longest and most eccentric pseudonyms ever devised by any writer: "Aleksandr Pleshchepupovich Chernobrysov, Active Mameluke and Bogdohan, Choirmaster of the Cowpox, Privileged Galvanist of the Canine Comedy, Publisher of a Topographical Description of Wigs, and Delicate Arranger of Divers Musical Gormandizings, Including the Enclosed Orchestrated Howlings." The preposterous personal name that heads the pseudonym, although based on Pleshcheyev's real name, has a meaning that works out something like "Alexander Splashnavelovich Darkbrownov." (The Mameluke and Bogdohan in the name are mellifluous titles of, respectively, classes of Egyptian rulers and Chinese emperors.)

Almost as bizarre in modern times are some of the names of members of pop and rock groups. Familiar examples are the "grunge" names of British punk rockers, such as Johnny Rotten, Sid Vicious, and Rat Scabies. The fad for adopting esoteric names lives on, however, and in some instances one finds that all members of a group have selected an unconventional name, not just one or two.

Some of the most original names begin as nicknames or "street names," especially among members of (usually black) rap or "hip-hop" groups. Examples are the trios Cypress Hill, formed in 1986, with Sen Dog (Sennen Reyes), B-Real (Louis Freese), and Muggs (Lawrence Muggerud), and De La Soul, formed in 1989, with Posdnuos (Kelvin Mercer), Trugoy the Dove (David Jude Jolicoeur), and P.A. Pasemaster Mase (Vincent Lamont Mason). (Mercer's name is a reversal of his nickname, "Soundsop," while Jolicoeur's is a backwards "yogurt.") Another hip-hop trio, the Digable Planets, formed in 1989, has (or had) members Butterfly (Ishmael Butler), Ladybug (Mary Ann Vieira), and Doodlebug (Craig Irving), while the vocal quartet Jodeci was created in 1990 by two pairs of brothers: JoJo (Joel Hailey), K-Ci (Cedric Hailey), Mr. Dalvin (Dalvin DeGrate, Jr.), and DeVante Swing (Donald DeGrate, Jr.).

Another 1990 trio, Massive Attack, has members 3-D (Robert Delnaja), Mushroom (A. Vowles), and Daddy G. (G. Marshall), while Public Enemy, first assembling in 1982, comprise Chuck D. (Carlton Ridenhour), Flavor Trav (William Drayton), Terminator X (Norman Lee Rogers), and Professor Griff, Minister of Information (Richard Griffin). All these are American groups, as is the female rap trio Salt-n-Pepa, set up in 1985 by Salt (Cheryl James) and Pepa (Sandra Denton). They were joined two years later by disc-spinning Dee Dee Spinderella La Toya (Deidre Roper).

The surreal element in many of these names dates from much earlier than the 1990s, however. On British soil the Rutles, created in 1959 as a parody of the Beatles, had fictional members Ron Nasty, Dirk McQuickly, Stig O'Hara, and Barry Wom (full name Barrington Womble), while stateside Spinal Tap, formed in 1961 as a sendup of a British heavy metal band, comprised David St. Hubbins (Michael McKean), Nigel Tufnell (Christopher Guest), and Derek Smalls (Harry Shearer). Mötley Crüe, a genuine heavy metal band, was formed in 1982 by singer Vince Neil (Vincent Neil Wharton), guitarist Mick Mars (Bob Deal), bassist Nikki Sixx (Frank Carlton Serafino Ferrano), and drummer Tommy Lee (Thomas Lee Bass). Two years later another U.S. band, Poison, had lead singer Bret Michaels (Bret Michael Sychak), guitarist C.C. DeVille (Bruce Anthony Johannesson), bassist Bobby Dall (Robert Kuy Kendall), and drummer Rikki Rockett (Richard Ream).

All quite a change from the conventional John Lennon, Paul McCartney, George Harrison, and Ringo Starr of the Beatles. But even Ringo began life as Richard Starkey, and the urge to fly free in name and fame, latent in all of us, cannot be resisted by some of the voguish vendors of modern popular music. Their strange names become almost as iconic as their individualistic personas.

A glance through the alphabetical listing that forms the main section of this book will show that some pseudonymous surnames seem specially favored, and have been adopted by several individuals. Among the most popular are (with variant spellings) Carol, Douglas, Field, Ford, Hay, John, Jones, Page and Williamson, and not far behind come names such as Adams, Alexander, Allan, Anthony, Barry, Bell, Blair, Brook, Brown and others. A consideration of such popular names will reveal that many of them are alternate first names and surnames (Allan, Carol, Douglas, John, and the like). It also appears that names denoting a color are often adopted (Brown, Gray, White), as are "country" names (Brook, Field, Ford, Hay, Lane). Gray (or Grey) is particularly popular, as also is Lee, a name that is in the versatile "first-name-or-surname" category.

Overall the most popular and frequently recurring names, too, are the briefest, and for a standard, run-of-the-mill surname, a monosyllabic name is often preferred. In some cases this may be because the brevity and simplicity of the name is refreshingly welcome after a difficult foreign name or an unduly long one. In other cases the ease of spelling and pronunciation, and the ready recognition of the name, are attractive factors.

Both Lynn and Carol are unusual in being girls' names popular as male assumed surnames. (They exist as real surnames, but not as widely as other names listed here.) It is tempting to ascribe the popularity of Carol to that most popular of pseudonymous writers, Lewis Carroll, but there is no evidence for this. Nor is there any evidence against it, since of the various Carrolls (or variant spellings) listed, most were born later than the author of *Alice in Wonderland* and could indeed have been inspired to adopt this name, consciously or subconsciously. Of the other names, a few may simply have occurred here as the result of random selection.

The great popularity of Page or Paige would not seem to be randomly indicated, though. Why should this name be desirable? Again, apart from being a short and simple name, it may be that one or more of the bearers suggested the name to the others, such as Patti Page or Janis Paige.

It is certainly noticeable that men who care about their specifically masculine image, for example movie actors playing tough roles, for example, tend to choose "macho" names, as Rock Hudson, Tab Hunter, and Paul Temple. Some women, too, who wish to project a distinctively feminine image likewise choose or adopt a name that has associations of romance or glamour (Renée Adorée, Eve Arden, Veronica Lake, Penny Singleton).

It should also not go unnoticed that the actual letters incorporated in a name are often important, with men frequently choosing "forceful" letters, such as "k" and "x," and women opting for soft, seductive letters, as "l" and "s." Gutturals can be gutsy, and sibilants sexy.

A large number of pseudonyms also turn out to have a common syllabic pattern. That most frequently favored is bisyllabic forename plus bisyllabic surname, as Casey Adams, Stella Martin, Henry Oscar, with the first syllable of each name accented. But this is also a fairly common phenomenon among ordinary names, and even a brief look at the *real* names of pseudonymous writers will show that there are several of this type, as David Bingley, Douglas Christie, Mary Douglas, Walter Gibson, Eric Hiscock. Perhaps an unusually high proportion of pseudonyms, however, are alliterative, with the forenames and surnames both beginning with the same letter. One has only to think of the names of some well known movie stars to see this: Anouk Aimée, Brigitte Bardot (if hers is indeed a pseudonym), Claudette Colbert, Diana Dors, Greta Garbo, Marilyn Monroe, and Simone Signoret are good examples.

But among all these facts and figures, all these personal particulars and calculated analyses, are there not any pseudonyms, it will be asked, whose real identity we cannot crack? Are there not still some disguised figures whose masks have not yet been removed? The answer, unsurprisingly, is yes. Here we are thinking not so much of the criminal or secret agent whose false name or cover name has not yet been revealed, but of the individual whose pseudonym has successfully concealed his true identity in spite of serious and scholarly attempts to unveil it.

In some cases, of course, a person's true identity may not be disclosed until after his death. This happened, for example, with the writer Fiona Macleod and the broadcaster A.J. Alan. But there are still some names whose real bearers remain unknown or at any rate uncertain.

Probably the most famous of all "uncracked" pseudonyms is that of Junius, the 18th-century author whose letters, 70 in number, in the London *Public Advertiser* between January 21, 1769, and January 21, 1772, revealed many intimate scandals of the day and were generally "agin the government" and antiroyalist (one of the letters was an impudent one addressed to King George III in person). Even today, over two hundred years later, and after much ingenious detective work and extremely thorough searching of contemporary documents, the identity of the infamous writer remains in doubt. Almost always using the name Junius, but occasionally switching to Lucius, Brutus, and possibly Nemesis, the author clearly had the objective of ruining the ministry of the Duke of Grafton, Britain's incapable and ineffective prime minister for the three years 1767 to 1770 and lord privy seal from 1771 to 1775.

Who was he? After a consideration of his style, with its original and fine command of language, of his classical name, with its apparent allusion to some particular Junius, and of all the other historical and political facets of the time, some fifty names were proposed as the real author. The most likely of these is generally held to be Sir Philip Francis (1740–1818), an Irish-born politician, who was known to have written a number of letters to the papers under pseudonyms. But this is only a conjecture. Other names suggested as the true author have been Edward Gibbon, Edmund Burke, John Wilkes, Lord Chesterfield, Thomas Paine, Lord Chatham (whom Junius loyally and actively supported),

Lord Shelburne, Horace Walpole, Isaac Barré, George Grenville, Lord Temple, Henry Grattan, Alexander Wedderburn, Lord George Sackville, and Horne Tooke.

"The mystery of Junius increases his importance," wrote the author himself, and this proved to be so, if only in the form of several imitators, with pseudonyms such as Junius Redivivus, Junius Secundus, Philo-Junius, and Junius itself. "I am the sole depository of my own secret, and it shall perish with me," also wrote the satirist, whom even sophisticated 20th-century technology has failed to unmask.

The *Letters of Junius* in fact made a significant contribution to journalistic history in that they established the fashion for the anonymity of leading articles in the press today.

Somewhat earlier than this, another literary name had attracted wide attention. This was one George Psalmanazar. As with Junius, his real name is unknown to this day, but unlike Junius he was an outrageous, if cunning, impostor. Psalmanazar claimed to be a native from Formosa, which at the time of his arrival in London in 1703 was virtually an unknown island. The following year he published an account of Formosa with a grammar of the language spoken there. This "language" was, however, a fabrication from start to finish, and he had simply concocted it. At the time literary London was taken in, but his imposture was soon exposed by Roman Catholic missionaries who had been to Formosa and who proved that the language set forth in Psalmanazar's grammar was nothing like the actual native tongue. Realizing that he had been revealed for the fraud he was, the bogus scholar publicly confessed his hoax and applied himself to more orthodox works, in particular the study of Hebrew. He died in 1763 having become a man of some repute and even the friend of Dr. Johnson.

Psalmanazar may possibly have actually been a Frenchman, or perhaps a Swiss. His year of birth is uncertain, although the year 1679 has been conjectured. He apparently took his name from Shalmaneser, an Assyrian prince mentioned in the Bible (2 Kings 17:3), although it is uncertain what particular significance this name had for him, if any. The name itself actually means "(the god) Shalman is superior." However, the Assyrian king "took" Samaria and "carried away" Israel just as the impostor "took" London and "carried away" much of the cultural world of the capital.

A man with a false name disseminating false scholarship in a country that was not even his own and claiming to be from a country where he had never set foot takes some beating for sheer audacity.

Most of the pseudonyms assumed by false claimants to the throne and bogus pretenders have in due time come to be exposed: you cannot go about calling yourself Prince Louis or Lady Maria for long without some kind of reaction and disclosure.

Two other such royal impostors may be mentioned here, both Englishwomen. The first, Sarah Wilson, lady-in-waiting to Queen Charlotte in the late 18th century, claimed to be the Queen's sister, styling herself Princess Susanna Carolina Matilda. The second, real name Mary Baker, a servant girl in the early 19th century, more exotically and esoterically claimed to be Princess Caraboo of Javasu. She spoke a "foreign" tongue that baffled English linguists, and enjoyed royal treatment for a year before she was unmasked, whereupon she fled to America and completely vanished from the public scene.

There is one royal pretender, however, who still remains unidentified. She was an almost exact contemporary of Junius, and although less well known than he, has an intriguing story.

Calling herself Princess Elizaveta Tarakanova, she was a young Russian woman born probably in 1745 who claimed to be the daughter of the Empress Elizabeth and Count Razumovsky and who in 1772, when in Paris, declared herself to be the pretender to the Russian throne under the name of Princess Vladimirskaya. Her actual origin and true name are still are mystery. All that is certainly known is her fate, typically "Russian" in that it was both romantic and tragic. In February 1775 she was arrested in Italy by Count Orlov, who thirteen years before had been instrumental in putting Catherine the Great on the throne by forcing Peter III to abdicate. Orlov brought her back to Russia and the self-styled princess was imprisoned in the notorious Petropavlovsk Fortress, in St. Petersburg, where she died of tuberculosis on December 4, 1775. (A famous picture by the Russian historical painter Konstantin Flavitsky shows Tarakanova trapped in her cell by a rapidly rising flood: the waters of the Neva rush through the prison bars while the hapless princess vainly seeks refuge by standing on her bed. This is melodramatic fiction, however, since the great St. Petersburg inundation occurred not that year but two years later, in 1777. No doubt Flavitsky, painting his picture nearly a century later, in 1864, felt that enough mystery already shrouded the subject of his portrait to enable him to depict a more dramatic fate than death from TB.)

One or two other pseudonyms used by the supposed princess are known, such as Miss Frank and Madame Tremouille, but her true identity remains a complete blank.

In the event it was Paul I who succeeded his mother Catherine to the throne in 1796.

Some impostures were freely admitted by their devisors to be hoaxes pure and simple. One such masquerader was a Mexican spinster, Concepción Jurado (1864–1931), who pretended to be a womanizing millionaire called Don Carlos Palmori. She attended hundreds of social gatherings in this guise, blithely propositioning women and brazenly regaling men with tales of bravado. At the end of each performance, however, she always tore off her mustache, let down her hair, and readily revealed her true identity.

Psalmanazar and Princess Tarakanova are not the only impostors whose true identity remains undiscovered. Another was the Scotsman calling himself Lord Gordon-Gordon who in 1872 came to New York claiming to have royal connections and great wealth. His aim, he said, was to back railroad tycoon Jay Gould during attempts to oust him as a director of the Erie Railroad. He managed to bilk Gould of $1 million in negotiable securities, and when arrested gave the names and addresses of well-placed friends and relatives at home and abroad. Before these could be checked out, however, he fled to Canada, where he committed suicide.

More recently there has been considerable speculation about the true identity of the horror and fantasy fiction writer M.Y. Halidom. The name clearly originates in the historic oath "by my halidom," with "halidom" itself a term for a holy place or thing. The name was long thought to have hidden the identity of more than one writer, and superseded the earlier name Dryasdust, which was that given for the author of the trilogy *Tales of the Wonder Club* (1899, 1900). This was reissued under the "Halidom" name in three separate parts a year or two later: Volume I in 1903, II in 1904, and III in 1905. The "Dryasdust" name had first appeared in 1890 for "The Wizard's Mantle," a story about a cloak of invisibility during the Spanish Inquisition. The story was reprinted under the Halidom name in 1903. The last story to appear under the name was "The Poison Ring" (1912).

It is now generally believed that the name was that of the English writer Edward Heron-Allen (1861–1943), professionally a marine biologist and zoologist.

Finally mention should be made of one more name that hides a still uncertain true identity. This is the poet and satirist Pietro Aretino, who lived and wrote some years before any of our other mystificators, and more than two hundred years even before Junius.

It is known that Aretino was the son of a shoemaker in Arezzo, north central Italy, where he was born on April 20, 1492. Later, he pretended to be the bastard son of a nobleman, deriving his "adopted" name from that of his native town. (Aretino means "of Arezzo.") He died in Venice on October 21, 1556, and throughout his life became widely known as a writer of vicious satires and lewd sonnets and as a leader of dissolute society in the grand style. It was his writings, especially his five comedies, that really established his reputation as a literary figure of considerable standing, above all his lively and amusing *La Cortigiana* ("Life at Court") (1534), which is an enjoyable account of lowerclass life in contemporary Rome.

We thus have a good deal of information about Aretino the man and his work. We even know what he looked like, for Titian painted his portrait (currently in the Frick Collection, New York). But the one thing that interests us here in this book—his name—remains unknown. And not knowing his name, we tend to rank him all the higher, for in a way we do not *want* to know it, lest the image be broken and the idol fall.

The world will be a duller place when the true identity of the Man in the Iron Mask is revealed.

Part II
The Dictionary

Pseudonyms and Name Changes and Their Origins

The following alphabetical listing presents some 8000 pseudonymous names to the reader, and gives not only the original names of the bearers but in many cases an account of the name change, sometimes in the bearer's own words. Where a firsthand account of a name change is not quoted, there will frequently be a "gloss" or comment on the name. In a few cases this is conjectural. In others the reader's attention is drawn to some aspect of the name change which is of interest, and which may possibly otherwise be unappreciated.

The listing does not and cannot be comprehensive. There are other books of pseudonyms that come closer to that unattainable goal, among them the compilations by Jennifer Mossman and Harold Sharp (see Bibliography, pages 402, 403). But those works do not give the stories behind the names that his present book aims to give. So that where they score in quantity, they lack in background, and where we lose by selectivity, we gain by detail and authentic documentation.

In my determined search to provide as many "name histories" as possible, I spent many hours tracking down individual biographies and autobiographies in public libraries and other holdings. (The accounts such biographies contain are sometimes dramatically colored, but one must take the facts on trust.) The more famous (or infamous) the person, the more likely it is that there will be an account of his or her life. Hence, conversely, the lack of background stories for some of the lesser lights. Even so, in casting my pseudonymous net as wide as possible, I managed to capture many specimens of interest and originality that are now displayed for the reader to admire in the pages that follow. In the final analysis, my aim was to give equal weighting to all entrants, with or without a "story." For our purposes, Ron Moody is just as important as Marilyn Monroe, and is thus supplied with the same key data.

What are the data that the reader can expect to find?

All entries aim to be consistent and to give: (a) the person's *pseudonym* or *changed name*, followed by (b) his or her *original name*, (c) *years of birth and death*, as appropriate, followed by (d) *nationality*, and (e) *occupation* or *status*.

Despite general consistency, there are departures from the norm in some instances. A person's year of birth (or death) may be unknown, for example, in which case there will be a question mark (?). The year may be uncertain, in which case it will be preceded by a question mark (to denote an approximation) or the letter "*c.*" (for Latin *circa*, "about"), this denoting a closer approximation than a question mark. A person may well have been born in one country, but lived and worked mainly in another (often as not the United States), and such "dualities" are mostly noted. The person's profession or occupation may be much fuller and more complex than it appears, and only a general indication is usually given of the relevant main activity, chiefly for purposes of identification, but also because the actual occupation may have a bearing on the professional name chosen for it.

The original or "real" name of the person is often given in full. In many cases, however, simply the forename and surname are enough for the purpose. But a married woman's maiden name may well be important, and have influenced the choice of adopted name, so that in many instances it will be quoted. Original Russian surnames of Jewish origin have the conventional form added in brackets as an aid to identification. Thus the poet Mikhail Golodny was surnamed Epshteyn (Epstein), and the actor Aleksandr Sanin was born Shenberg (Schönberg). The more familiar German forms of such names are sometimes obscured in their transliterated versions.

There are a few multiple names, chiefly of the "one for all" type, where a single name has been adopted by more than one person as a joint name. In such cases, the names of the original persons are linked by a plus sign (+). For an example, see Wade Miller (Robert Wade plus Bill Miller), or the fivefold Smectymnuus.

In a few instances, the person concerned will have acquired a familiar nickname, and I have added this where appropriate, if only for interest or for the sake of completeness. Gilbert M. Anderson (who was originally Max Aaronson) became known as "Bronco Billy," for example, and Ann Sheridan (who began life as Clara Lou Sheridan) was dubbed "the Oomph Girl."

Where a story or quotation accompanies a name, its source will frequently be given, usually (for a book) with the name of the author, the title of the quoted work, and its year of publication. Sometimes the background material or anecdote may have been taken from a work listed in the Bibliography. In such cases the author's name alone is given, together with the page(s) of the work where the quotation occurs. Several quotes come from the pages of newspapers and magazines, and in such instances the title of the periodical is given together with the date of the issue copied. The same procedure is followed for information gained directly from radio or television, with the name of the program and the date of its broadcast.

Cross references are indicated either by a direct *see* or by (*q.v.*) after the name in question. Where the readers need see no further than the previous or following entry, however, the reference will usually be simply (see above) or (see below).

The following abbreviations are used for the nationality or origin of the subjects following their dates:

Austr.	Austrian
Austral.	Australian
Belg.	Belgian
Br.	British
Bulg.	Bulgarian
Can.	Canadian
Chin.	Chinese
Cz.	Czech
Dan.	Danish
Du.	Dutch
Eng.	English
Finn.	Finnish
Fr.	French
Ger.	German
Gk.	Greek
Hung.	Hungarian
Ind.	Indian
Ir.	Irish
It.	Italian
Jap.	Japanese
Norw.	Norwegian
N.Z.	New Zealand
Pol.	Polish
Port.	Portuguese
Rom.	Romanian
Russ.	Russian
S.A.	South African
Sc.	Scottish
Sp.	Spanish
Swe.	Swedish
Turk.	Turkish
U.S.	United States

All other nationalities are spelled out. A few common abbreviations such as DJ (disc jockey), SF (science fiction), TV (television), will be familiar enough to readers.

The Alphabetical Listings

A.A.: Anthony Armstrong (*q.v.*).

Willie **Aames:** William Upton (1960–), U.S. TV actor. A new surname that will bring the actor straight to the top of any alphabetical billing.

Aleksandr **Abasheli:** Aleksandr Vissarionovich Chochiya (1884–1954), Georgian poet.

Anthony **Abbot:** Charles Fulton Oursler (1893–1952), U.S. journalist, playwright, novelist.

John **Abbot:** Vernon John (1896–1943), U.S. music hall singer.

Russ **Abbot:** Russell Allan Roberts (1947–), Eng. TV comedian. A name presumably based on the comedian's real name, though at one time he also had a pop band called The Black Abbots.

Bud **Abbott:** William A. Abbott (1895–1974), U.S. movie comedian, teaming with Lou Costello (*q.v.*).

Abd-ru-shin: Oskar Ernest Bernhardt (1875–1941), Ger. cult leader. The founder of the Grail Movement assumed his Arabic name, meaning "son of light," after World War I as a result of visits made before the war to the east. He claimed the name came from a former incarnation when, in the time of Moses, he had lived as the prince of an Arabian tribe.

Kareem **Abdul-Jabbar:** Ferdinand Lewis Alcindor, Jr. (1947–), U.S. black basketball player. Lew Alcindor (as he was usually known) adopted his new name in 1971 following his conversion to Islam in 1968, when at the University of California at Los Angeles.

Ahmed **Abdullah:** Leroy Bland (1946–), U.S. black jazz musician.

Ahmed **Abdul-Malik:** Sam Gill (1927–), U.S. black jazz musician. The musician adopted his Muslim name in the 1950s.

Rudolf **Abel:** William August Fisher (1903–1971), Eng.-born Russ. spy, of Russ. parentage, working in U.S. The Soviet intelligence officer used various aliases in the course of his work. He lived for some time in New York as an artist and photographer named Emil R. Goldfus, an approximate anagram of Rudolf Abel.

Johann Philip **Abelin:** Johann Ludwig Gottfried (*c.*1600–1634), Ger. historian.

Raymond **Abellio:** Georges Soulès (1907–1986), Fr. occultist.

Ab Ithel: John Williams (1811–1862), Welsh writer. The writer adopted the Welsh form of the surname of his grandfather, William Bethell, itself literally meaning "son of Ithael."

Ab-o'-th'-Yate: Benjamin Brierley (1825–1896), Eng. dialect writer. Benjamin Brierley was an English weaver who came to write stories and verse in the Lancashire dialect. His early stories were narrated by a character called "Owd Ab" (Old Abe), and this gave his basic pen name, with "Yate" being a Lancashire form of "gate," meaning not "gate" but "street" as in many street names in northern English towns (such as Briggate ["Bridge Street"], Leeds). Ben Brierley was thus "Abe from the street," or a typical old world townee character.

Abraham a Sancta Clara: Johann Ulrich Megerle (1644–1709), Ger. friar, preacher. The author of popular devotional works, many of them satirical, took a name meaning literally "Abraham of St. Clare."

Abu: Abu Abraham (1924–), Ind.-born Br. political cartoonist.

Acanthus: Harold Frank Hoar (1909–1976), Eng. architect, cartoonist. The acanthus is a prickly plant; maybe the cartoonist regarded himself as a "barbed" commentator and caricaturist?

Mme **Acarie:** Barbe Jeanne Acarie, née Avrillot (1566–1618), Fr. religious. The founder of the Reformed Carmelites in France was professed in 1615 under the name Marie de l'Incarnation ("Mary of the Incarnation"). This title was also adopted by the religious Marie Guyard (1599–1672), who was professed in the Ursuline order in 1631 and who introduced that order to Canada.

Stanley **Accrington:** Michael Bray (1951–), Br. folk musician. The musician took his name from town of Accrington, Lancashire, the county where he began his career as a railroad stationmaster.

Johnny **Ace:** John Marshall Alexander, Jr. (1929–1954), U.S. black rock musician.

Achad Haam: Asher Ginzberg (1856–1927), Ukrainian-born Jewish writer.

Maurice **Achard:** Marcel-Augustin Ferréol (1899–1974), Fr. writer of comedies.

Chinua **Achebe:** Albert Chinualumogu (1930–), Nigerian novelist, poet, critic. The writer abbreviated his surname to serve as a first name and abandoned his original European Christian name for a new African surname.

Cecil Adair: Evelyn Everett-Green (1856–1932), Eng. popular novelist, children's writer.

Janice Adair: Beatrice Duffy (*fl.*1930s), Br. movie actress, of Ir. parentage.

Jean Adair: Violet McNaughton (1873–1953), Can.-born U.S. stage, movie actress.

[St.] Adalbert: Vojtech (956–997), Cz. saint, martyr. The bishop of Prague received his name at his confirmation from St. Adalbert (died 981), archbishop of Magdeburg.

Brother Adam: Karl Adam Kehrle (1898–1996), Ger.-born Br. Benedictine monk, beekeeper.

Richard Adama: Richard Adams (1928–), U.S. ballet dancer. A typical Italianate adaptation for ballet purposes of a standard English (American) name.

Casey Adams: Max Showalter (1917–), U.S. movie actor.

Derroll Adams: Derroll Lewis Thompson (1925–), U.S. popular singer, songwriter. The musician took his new surname from his mother's third husband, George Adams.

Don Adams: Donald James Yarmy (1926–), U.S. TV comedian. "Adams" could be regarded as extracted from "Donald James."

Edie Adams: Elizabeth Edith Enke (1927–), U.S. movie actress, singer.

Fay Adams: Faye Scruggs (?–?), U.S. blues singer.

Joey Adams: Joseph Abramowitz (1911–), U.S. TV, movie comedian

Marie Adams: Ollie Marie Givens (1925–?), U.S. popular singer.

Maud Adams: Maud Wikstrom (1945–), Swe.-born movie actress.

Maude Adams: Maude Kiskadden (1872–1953), U.S. stage actress. The actress adopted her mother's maiden name.

Moses Adams: George William Bagby (1828–1883), U.S. humorist, lecturer.

Nick Adams: Nicholas Adamschock (1931–1968), U.S. movie actor.

Stephen Adams: Michael Maybrick (1844–1913), Eng. composer, singer.

Nora Adamyan: Eleonora Georgiyevna Adamova (1910–), Russ. writer.

Martin Adán: Rafael de la Fuente Benavides (1907–1974), Peruvian writer.

[Count] Adelaer: Cort Sivertsen (1622–1675), Norw.-born naval commander. Sivertsen entered the Dutch navy in 1639 as a cadet (*adelborst*). In 1642 he moved into Venetian service and became known as Curzio Suffrido Adelborst. He returned to Holland in 1661 but the following year accepted the command of the Danish navy with the title of Count Adelaer, from the Norwegian word for "eagle." This was originally a nickname, given him for his perspicacity and prowess at sea and punning on his original title.

Max Adeler: Charles Heber Clark (1847–1915), Ger.-born U.S. humorous writer.

Renée Adorée: Jeanne de la Fonte (1898–1933), Fr.-born U.S. movie actress. "Renée" suggests "reborn"; "Adorée" suggests both "adored" and "gilded."

Theodor Adorno: Theodor Wiesengrund (1903–1969), Ger. philosopher, sociologist, musicologist. The scholar adopted his mother's maiden name as his professional name.

Adrian IV: Nicholas Breakspear (*c.*1100–1159), Eng. pope. All popes of this name are also known as Hadrian.

Adrian V: Ottobono Fieschi (*c.*1205–1276), It. pope. The pope took his name from the church of St. Adrian (S. Adriano), Rome, of which he was appointed cardinal deacon in 1251.

Adrian VI: Adrian Florensz Dedal (1459–1523), Du. pope. This was the last pope to retain his baptismal name as a papal name.

Gilbert Adrian: Adrian Adolph Greenberg (1903–1959), U.S. movie costume designer. "Gilbert" doubtless comes from "Greenberg."

Iris Adrian: Iris Adrian Hostetter (1913–1994), U.S. movie actress.

John Adrian: John Adrian Marie Edward Warne (1938–), Br. singer, dancer.

Max Adrian: Max Bor (1903–1973), Ir.-born Eng. stage actor.

Rhys Adrian: Rhys Adrian Griffiths (1928–1990), Br. radio, TV dramatist, of Welsh parentage. Early in his career the writer used pseudonyms such as L.A. Reece and L.R. Adrian, explaining that he did not wish to be thought of as "just another Welsh playwright."

Jean Adrienne: Jean Armstrong (1905–), Eng. stage actress.

Adzhzi: Khodzhi Said-Akhmed-khodzha Siddiki (1865–1926), Tajik poet. The poet adopted a symbolic name meaning "helpless."

Æ (or AE, A.E.): George William Russell (1867–1935), Ir. poet, artist. The name derives from the initial letter of "Æon," a pseudonym used by Russell for an article, and itself meaning "eternity," from the Greek. The printer had queried the spelling of the name, so that Russell opted for the digraph alone. A current witticism was that he had chosen these particular vowels for his name "because he did not wish to be called 'I.O.U.'"

Affable Hawk: [Sir] Desmond MacCarthy (1878–1952), Br. dramatic, literary critic. The Native American-style name was chosen by MacCarthy for his articles in the *New Statesman* to match that of his predecessor, Solomon Eagle (*q.v.*).

Afrique: Alexander Witkins (1907–), S.A. music hall singer. The singer's name is French for "Africa."

Afrit: Alistair Ferguson Ritchie (1887–1954), Br. crossword compiler. The name partly derives from the initial elements of his own name (*Ali*stair *Fer*guson *Rit*chie), partly represents Afrit, a powerful devil in Muslim mythology. A crossword compiler aims to inspire dread in his hapless solvers.

Yaacov Agam: Jacob Gipstein (1928–), Israeli painter, sculptor, of Russ. parentage.

Agathon: Henri Massis (1886–1970), Fr. political writer. The name, Greek for "good," "virtuous," was used by the writer for early coauthored tracts.

Luigi Agnesi: Louis Ferdinand Léopold Agniez (1833–1975), Belg. opera singer.

Spiro Agnew: Spiro Theodore Anagnostopoulos (1918–1996), U.S. politician, of Gk. parentage. A sensible shortening of a typically lengthy Greek surname for the U.S. vice president (1969–73), who later in life preferred to be known as Ted.

Shmuel Yosef Agnon: Samuel Josef Czaczkes (1888–1970), Israeli novelist, short story writer. The writer adopted a Hebrew name taken from the story that was his literary debut, *Agunot* ("Forsaken Wives") (1908). He made the pseudonym his official name in 1924.

María de Agreda: María Fernandez Coronel (1602–1665), Sp. abbess, mystic. The abbess (also known as María de Jesus) was the head of the Franciscan monastery in the Spanish town of Agreda, where she was also born and where she died.

Georgius Agricola: Georg Bauer (1494–1555), Ger. scholar, humanist. Latin *agricola* means "plowman," "farmer," to which German *Bauer* ("farmer," "smallholder") corresponds. Compare the next three names below.

Johann Agricola: Johann Schneider (or Schnitter) (1494–1566), Ger. Lutheran reformer. Schneider first latinized his name as *Sartor* (German *Schneider*, "tailor"), but then adopted the name Agricola (see entry above).

Martin Agricola: Martin Sore (or Sohr) (1486–1556), Ger. composer, teacher, writer of music. Sore was self-taught, and was thus called to music "from the plow." Hence his adoption of the name Agricola (Latin, "plowman").

Rodolphus Agricola: Roelof Huysman (1443–1485), Du. humanist. The Dutch surname means "man of the house," here interpreted through Latin *agricola* (see above).

Ahad Ha'am: Asher Hirsch Ginzberg (1856–1927), Russ.-born Jewish writer, philosopher. The Zionist leader adopted a Hebrew name meaning "one of the people."

Ernst Ahlgren: Victoria Maria Benedictsson, née Bruzelius (1850–1888), Swe. writer.

Juhani Aho: Johannes Brofeldt (1861–1921), Finn. novelist, short story writer. The writer's name is a Finnish equivalent of his Swedish name, with Juhani corresponding to Johannes (John) and Finnish *aho*, "clearing," "glade," replacing Brofeldt, literally "broad field."

AI: Florence Anthony (1947–), U.S. poet, of mixed ancestry.

Berkley Aikin: Fanny Aikin Kortright (1821–1900), U.S.-born Br. novelist, journalist.

Gustave Aimard: Olivier Gloux (1818–1883), Fr.-born U.S. romantic novelist.

Anouk Aimée: Françoise Sorya Dreyfus (1932–), Fr. movie actress. The actress named herself after a servant girl that she played in her first movie, *La Maison Sous La Mer* (1947). She originally used the name Anouk alone.

Patricia Ainsworth: Patricia Nina Bigg (1932–), Austral. writer.

Ruth Ainsworth: Ruth Gilbert (1908–), Br. writer of children's fiction.

Catherine Aird: Kinn Hamilton McIntosh (1930–), Eng. mystery writer.

Catherine Airlie: Jean Sutherland MacLeod (1908–), Sc. writer.

Harriot Airy: Mary Darwall, née Whately (1738–1825), Eng. poet.

Jonas Aistis: Jonas Aleksandravičius (1904–1973), Lithuanian poet.

Aka Gündüz: Enis Avni (1885–1958), Turk. writer. Turkish *gündüz* means "daytime," presumably here in a symbolic sense.

Akebono: Chadwick Haheo Rowan (1969–), U.S. (Hawaiian)-born Jap. sumo wrestler.

Floyd Akers: Lyman Frank Baum (1856–1919), U.S. novelist, children's writer. Other names used by the author of the perennially popular *The Wonderful Wizard of Oz* (1900) were Laura Bancroft, John Estes Cooke, Hugh Fitzgerald, Suzanne Metcalf, Schuyler Staunton (for adult novels), and Edith Van Dyne (stories for girls). At one time Baum was on the stage as George Brooks.

Akhenaten: Amenhotep IV (*fl.* 14th century BC), Egyptian pharaoh. The famous "heretic" king was the son of Amenhotep III and originally bore the same name as his father, meaning "[the god] Amun is content." In his fifth regnal year he changed his name to Akhenaten, "glory of the [sun disk] Aten," and began to build a new capital city called Akhetaten ("horizon of the Aten"). Worship of the Aten was subsequently disavowed by his son-in-law, Tutankhamun (*q.v.*), who reintroduced the worship of Amun.

Anna **Akhmatova:** Anna Andreyevna Gorenko (1889–1966), Russ. poet. When Anna Gorenko was 17, and an aspiring poet, her father objected to her writings, calling her a "decadent poetess," and saying she would shame the family name. Anna retorted, "I don't need that name," and instead chose a Tatar name, that of her great-grandmother. The southern Tatars had always seemed mysterious and fascinating to the girl who came to be one of Russia's greatest modern poets [Amanda Haight, *Anna Akhmatova: A Poetic Pilgrimage*, 1976].

Alafon: Owen Griffith Owen (1847–1916), Welsh poet.

Alain: Emile-Auguste Chartier (1868–1951), Fr. philosopher, essayist. The philosopher took his pseudonym from his namesake, the poet Alain Chartier (*c.*1385–*c.*1430), whom Margaret of Scotland famously stooped to kiss.

Alain-Fournier: Henri Alban Fournier (1886–1914), Fr. novelist. The novelist took his new name so as to be distinguished either from his fellow writer Edouard Fournier (1819–1880) or, according to other sources, from two contemporary Frenchmen named Henri Fournier, one an admiral, the other a cycling champion. He first used the name in 1907.

Jamil Abdullah **al-Amin:** H. Rap Brown (1943–), U.S. black activist. The political activist and writer converted to the Islamic faith following his imprisonment in 1974 and adopted a Moslem name accordingly. Of the three Arabic names, Jamil means "handsome," Abdullah means "servant of Allah," and al-Amin, the name of a 9th-century Abbasid caliph, means "the faithful."

A.J. **Alan:** Leslie Harrison Lambert (1883–1940), Br. broadcaster, storyteller.

Jane **Alan:** Lillian Mary Chisholm (1906–), Eng. short story writer.

Vagram **Alazan:** Vagram Martirosovich Gabuzyan (1903–1966), Armenian writer.

Maria **Alba:** Maria Casajuana (1905–), Sp. stage, movie actress, dancer.

Antony **Alban:** Antony Allert Thomson (1939–), Br. writer.

[Dame] Emma **Albani:** Marie Louise Cécile Emma Lajeunesse (1847–1930), Can. opera singer. The singer took her professional name from Albany, New York, where her family had made their home. (This prosaic origin has its more romantic rivals, such as that quoted in the *Dictionary of National Biography*: "On the advice of her Italian elocution master, Delorenzi, she adopted the name of 'Albani', the patronymic of an old Italian noble family, practically extinct.")

Joe **Albany:** Joseph Albani (1924–1988), U.S. bop pianist.

Albert: Albert Rusling (1944–), Eng. cartoonist.

Don **Albert:** Albert Dominique (1908–1980), U.S. jazz trumpeter.

Eddie **Albert:** Edward Albert Heimberger (1908–), U.S. stage, movie, TV actor. The actor is said to have adopted the name because he grew tired of announcers referring to him as "Eddie Hamburger."

Albert L'Ouvrier: Alexandre Martin (1815–1895), Fr. worker. The socialist leader adopted this name, meaning "Albert the worker," when he was elected to the provisional French government in 1848.

Maria **Alboni:** Maria Anna Marzia (1823–1894), It. opera singer.

Martha **Albrand:** Heidi Huberta Freybe Loewengard (1914–), Ger.-U.S. spy novelist. The writer's new surname is that of her great-grandfather.

Hardie **Albright:** Hardy Albrecht (1903–1975), U.S. movie actor.

Dennis **Alcapone:** Dennis Smith (1947–), Jamaican DJ, popular musician. The singer took a name that commemorates the U.S. gangster Al Capone, since he was born in the year of the latter's death.

Alceste:(1) Alfred Assolant (1827–1886), Fr. writer; (2) Hippolyte de Castile (?–?), Fr. writer; (3) Louis Belmontet (1799–1879), Fr. writer; (4) Edouard Laboulaye (1811–1883), Fr. writer.

Doubtless one or more of these derive from Gluck or Lully's opera *Alceste* or from the character of this name in Molière's *Le Misanthrope*, where he is the misanthropic hero. But the operatic Alceste is based on Euripides' play *Alcestis*, where the name is that of the heroine.

Alcibiades: (1) Albert, Margrave of Brandenburg (1522–1557), Ger. prince; (2) Alfred, Lord Tennyson (1809–1892), Eng. poet; (3) George Villiers, Duke of Buckingham (1627–1688), Eng. courtier. The original Alcibiades was an Athenian general of the 5th century BC, appearing in later literature.

Alcipe: Leonor de Almeida Portugal de Lorena e Lencastre, Marquesa de Alorna (1750–*c*.1839), Port. poet. The poet's classical-style name was suggested to her by the Portuguese neoclassical poet Filinto Elísio (*q.v.*).

Alan **Alda:** Alphonso D'Abruzzo (1936–), U.S. stage actor. The actor created his new surname from the first syllables of his two original names, as did his father, Robert Alda (see below).

Frances **Alda:** Frances Jeanne Adler, née Davies (1883–1952), N.Z.-born U.S. opera singer.

Robert **Alda:** Alphonso Giuseppe Giovanni Roberto D'Abruzzo (1914–1986), It.-born U.S. movie actor, father of Alan Alda (see above).

Mark **Aldanov:** Mark Aleksandrovich Landau (1889–1957), Russ. writer. A name that is a near anagram of the writer's surname (Landau) while also containing letters in his patronymic (Aleksandrovich).

G.R. **Aldo:** Aldo Graziati (1902–1953), It. cinematographer.

Adair **Aldon:** Cornelia Lynde Meigs (1884–1973), U.S. novelist, children's writer. The author used the name for her earlier stories. Asked if it was some sort of pun, she replied: "I have no very subtle explanation to give. I used it for my first story of adventure for boys as I wished to keep that kind of tale separate from the historical stories I was writing at that time. The name Adair was current — not precisely in my own family, but in one with which I have close connection. As it would apply either to a man or a woman I thought it useful for my purposes and took the name Aldon to go with it, as I liked alliterative names. On the strength of the masculinity a boy's camp wrote to me and asked me to spend the summer with them as they liked one of Adair Aldon's books so much. I never felt sufficient courage to disillusion them in the matter" [Marble, p. 181].

Louis **Aldrich:** Louis Lyon (1843–1901), U.S. actor.

O **Aleijadinho:** António Francisco Lisbôa da Costa (*c*.1738–1814), Brazilian sculptor, architect. The artist was born deformed, and his name is Portuguese for "the little cripple."

Aleksandr **Aleksandrov:** Aleksandr Nikolayevich Fedotov (1903–1971), Russ. circus performer.

Grigory **Aleksandrov:** Grigory Vasilyevich Mormonenko (1903–1983), Russ. movie director.

Vladimir **Aleksandrov:** Vladimir Borisovich Keller (1898–1954), Russ. literary critic.

Aleksandra **Aleksandrova-Kochetova:** Aleksandra Dormidontovna Kochetova, née Sokolova (1833–1902), Russ. opera singer, musicologist. When actually performing, the singer used the name Aleksandra Aleksandrova, basing the surname on her own first name.

Jean le Rond d'**Alembert:** Jean-le-Rond Destouches (1717–1783), Fr. mathematician. Destouches was the illegitimate son of the hostess Mme de Tencin and one of her lovers, the chevalier Destouches. As a baby, he was abandoned on the steps of the Paris church of Saint-Jean-le-Rond, and this gave his first name. However, he was enrolled in school as Jean-Baptiste Daremberg, and the latter name was altered for reasons of euphony to give "d'Alembert."

Alexander II: Anselm (? –1075), It. pope.

Alexander III: Orlando Bandinelli (*c*.1100–1181), It. pope.

Alexander IV: Rinaldo dei Segni (*c*.1199–1261), It. pope.

Alexander V: Pietro di Candia (originally Petros Philargos) (*c*.1339–1410), It. antipope.

Alexander VI: Rodrigo de Borja y Doms (or Rodrigo Borgia) (1431–1503), Sp.-born It. pope.

Alexander VII: Fabio Chigi (1599–1667), It. pope.

Alexander VIII: Pietro Vito Ottoboni (1610–1691), It. pope.

Mrs. **Alexander:** Annie Hector, née French (1825–1902), Ir.-born Br. popular novelist. The writer took her name from that of her husband, Alexander Hector, a wealthy merchant who disapproved of her writing. She adopted the name only after his death in 1875.

Ben **Alexander:** Nicholas Benton Alexander (1911–1969), U.S. movie actor.

Dair **Alexander:** Christine Campbell Thomson (1897– ?), Br. author. Other names used by the writer were Molly Campbell, Christine Hartley, and Flavia Richardson.

[Sir] George **Alexander:** George Alexander Gibb Samson (1858–1918), Br. stage actor, theatre manager.

Jane **Alexander:** Jane Quigley (1939–), U.S. movie, TV actress.

Jason **Alexander:** Jay Scott Greenspan (1959–), U.S. movie actor.

Joan **Alexander:** Joan Pepper (1920–), Br. author.

John **Alexander:** Jeremy Taylor (1613–1667), Eng. bishop, author.

Maev **Alexander:** Maev Alexandra Reid McConnell (1948–), Sc. TV actress.

Alexis: Sergey Vladimirovich Simansky (1877–1970), Russ. churchman, patriarch of Moscow and All Russia. The head of the Russian Orthodox Church assumed his name (Russian Aleksey or Aleksiy) on taking monastic vows in 1902. See also Alexis II below.

Willibald **Alexis:** Georg Wilhelm Heinrich Häring (1798–1871), Ger. writer, critic.

Alexis II: Aleksey Mikhaylovich Ridiger (1929–), Estonian-born Russ. churchman, patriarch of Moscow and All Russia. The head of the Russian Orthodox Church, elected in 1990, retained his original name, unlike all his 20th-century predecessors. Compare Alexis (above).

Alfonsina: Alfonsina Storni (1892–1938), Argentinian poet, playwright.

Kenneth J. **Alford:** [Major] Frederick Joseph Ricketts (1881–1945), Br. popular composer, bandmaster. The composer of "Colonel Bogey," familiar from the score of the movie *The Bridge on the River Kwai* (1957), used the pseudonym W.V. Richards for the march "Namur."

Harcourt **Algeranoff:** Harcourt Algernon Essex (1903–1967), Br. ballet dancer, working in Australia, husband of Claudie Algeranova (*q.v.*). The dancer assumed his Russian-style name, based on his middle name, on joining Anna Pavlova's company in 1921.

Claudie **Algeranova:** Claudie Leonard (1924–), Fr.-born Br. ballet dancer. The dancer took her name from that of her husband, Harcourt Algeranoff (*q.v.*).

Nelson **Algren:** Nelson Ahlgren Abraham (1909–1981), U.S. writer.

Muhammad **Ali:** Cassius Marcellus Clay (1942–), U.S. black boxer. The famous boxer adopted his new name in 1964 on joining the Black Muslim movement after becoming the new world heavyweight champion as a result of his contest against Sonny Liston. The name was given him by Elijah Muhammad (*q.v.*), leader of the Black Muslims in the U.S. Ali made the following announcement to reporters in Miami Beach two days after gaining the title: "From now on my name is Muhammad Ali. Don't call me by my slave name. Cassius Clay was a slave name. It was given to my family by my white masters. I'm a Black Muslim now. That's my religion, the religion of Elijah Muhammad. And my name is Muhammad Ali. I want you to call me that from now on." The name itself means "praiseworthy noble one" [1. Muhammad Ali with Richard Durham, *The Greatest: My Own Story*, 1977; 2. Larry Bortstein, *Ali*, 1976].

Rashied **Ali:** Robert Patterson (1935–), U.S. black jazz musician. When the jazz drummer's father changed his name to Rashied Ali, Robert Patterson, Jr. followed suit.

Alien: Louisa Alice Baker, née Dawson (1858–1926), N.Z. novelist, working in U.K. The writer used this name for serials written in Britain but published in New Zealand.

Abdulla **Alish:** Abdulla Bariyevich Alishev (1908–1944), Russ. (Tatar) writer.

Valentin **Alkan:** Charles-Henri-Valentin Morhange (1813–1888), Fr. pianist, composer, of Jewish parentage. The composer's five brothers and sister, who also became musicians, adopted this same surname.

Santeri **Alkio:** Santeri Filander (1862–1930), Finn. writer, politician.

George **Allan:** Mite (or Marie) Kremnitz, née Marie von Bardeleben (1852–1916), Ger. writer.

Johnnie **Allan:** John Allan Guillot (1938–), U.S. pop musician.

Paula **Allardyce:** Ursula Torday (*fl.*1960s), Eng. crime, mystery writer. Other names used by the author were Charity Blackstock, Lee Blackstock, and Charlotte Keppel.

Henri **Alleg:** Henri Jean Salem (1921–), Algerian writer, working in France.

Chesney **Allen:** William Ernest Chesney Allen (1896–1982), Br. music hall comedian, teaming with Bud Flanagan (*q.v.*).

Corey **Allen:** Alan Cohen (1934–), U.S. movie actor, director.

Dave **Allen:** David Tynan O'Mahoney (1936–), Ir. TV entertainer. When the entertainer began his career and was eager for engagements, he changed his name to Allen, which began with "A" and would thus come near the top of any agent's list.

(Major) E.J. **Allen:** Allan Pinkerton (1819–1884), Sc.-born U.S. detective.

Elizabeth **Allen:** Elizabeth Allen Gillease (1934–), U.S. stage, movie actress.

Eric **Allen:** Eric Allen Ballard (1908–1968), Eng. children's writer. Other names used by the writer were Paul Dallas and Edwin Harrison.

F.M. **Allen:** Edmund Downey (1856–1937), Ir. humorous writer. The writer adopted his wife's maiden name as his pen name.

Fred **Allen:** John Florence Sullivan (1894–1956), U.S. radio comedian, movie actor. Sullivan was at first a juggler, taking the name Fred St. James. He then dropped the "St." to become simply Fred James. Later (1921) he grew tired of telling people that he wasn't a member of the Jesse James Gang, and so changed his name to Fred Allen "as a tribute to Ethan Allen who had stopped using the name after the revolution." (Ethan Allen was the soldier and frontiersman who captured Ft. Ticonderoga, New York, in the War of Independence.)

Mel **Allen:** Melvin Allen Israel (1913–1996), U.S. sports broadcaster.

Peter **Allen:** Peter Woolnough (1942–1992), Austral. pop musician.

Roland **Allen:** Alan Ayckbourn (1939–), Br. playwright. The name is partly from the writer's own first name, partly from his wife's maiden name. He used the name for his first three plays, but has since written under his real name.

Rosalie **Allen:** Julie Marlene Bedra (1924–), U.S. country singer, of Pol. descent.

Terry **Allen:** Edward Albert Govier (1924–1987), Br. boxer. Govier gave two accounts of his change of name. "Mate of mine called Terry Allen got killed, so I took his name for boxing. Sort of keeps it goin', like," was his original version. Later, however, he recalled how, when on the run from the Navy, he stole the identity card of an Islington, London, newspaper boy called Terry Allen. His birthday, which many of the record books have accepted as Govier's own, was August 11, 1925 [*The Times*, April 9, 1987].

Woody **Allen:** Allan Stewart Konigsberg (1935–), U.S. stage, movie actor, playwright. The following account has been given for the actor's change of name, made in 1952 when he decided to become a comedy writer and was starting to send jokes to New York newspapers. "He liked Allan and thought the more commonly spelled Allen made a good last name. But what of a first one? He thought of Max, after the writer Max Shulman. ... He thought of Mel, but Mel Allen was the broadcaster for the New York Yankees. Eventually he thought of Woody and settled on it because it had, he says, 'a slightly comic appropriateness and is not completely off the tracks.' Contrary to the popular belief that his choice was an *hommage* to one musician or another, it was, he insists, purely arbitrary and wholly unrelated to Woody Herman, Woody Guthrie, Woody Woodpecker, or even Woodrow Wilson" [Eric Lax, *Woody Allen*, 1991].

Frank **Allenby:** Francis Gatehouse (1898– ?), Austral.-born Br. stage actor. The actor adopted his mother's maiden name as his stage name.

Alfred **Allendale:** Theodore Edward Hook (1788–1841), Eng. novelist.

Mary **Allerton:** Mary Christine Govan (1897–), U.S. novelist. The writer also used the name J.N. Darby.

Ellen **Alleyne:** Christina Georgina Rossetti (1830–1894), Eng. poet.

Claud **Allister:** Claud Palmer (1891–1970), Eng. movie actor.

Alli-Vad: Aleksandr Alekseyevich Vadimov-Markelov (1895–1967), Russ. circus artist, conjuror.

Alltud Eifion: Robert Isaac Jones (1815–1905), Welsh poet, editor. The writer's name means "Alltud of Eifionydd," this being a historic district of northwestern Wales.

David **Allyn:** Albert DiLello (1923–), U.S. popular singer.

June **Allyson:** Eleanor ("Ella") Geisman (1917–), U.S. dancer, singer, movie actress. The actress's new surname derives from the pet form of her first name.

Alma: Charlotte Mary Yonge (1823–1901), Eng. novelist, writer. In her own *History of Christian Names* (1863), Charlotte M. Yonge interprets the name Alma as meaning either "fair" or "all good," and perhaps she intended this sense for herself. But she also rightly relates the name to the Battle of Alma (1854), the first of the Crimean War, and possibly she adopted the pen name at about this time for her early writing. It may be no more than a coincidence that her own Christian names contain the letters (in sequence) of "Alma."

E.M. **Almedingen:** Martha Edith von Almedingen (1898–1971), Russ.-born Eng. novelist, poet, biographer. The initials are those of the writer's two first names, reversed.

A.L.O.E.: Charlotte Maria Tucker (1821–1893), Br. writer, children's author. The initials were intended to stand for "A Lady of England," and the suggestion of "aloe" (the plant, with its bitter drug) appears to be merely coincidental. "This Aloe is not at all in keeping with her cognomen, for she has produced upwards of fifty pieces ... under the above initials, and we commend them to the reader as of exceeding beauty" [Hamst, p. 11].

Alicia **Alonso:** Alicia Ernestina de la Caridad dei Cobre Martinez Hoyo (1921–), Cuban ballet dancer.

V. **Alov:** Nikolay Vasilyevich Gogol (1809–1852), Russ. novelist, playwright. Gogol used the name, apparently formed from letters in his full name, for his early poem of German idyllic life, *Hanz Küchelgarten* (1828), published at his own expense. When it was derided by the critics, he bought up all the copies and destroyed them. At least he had preserved his true identity.

Alpha: James Fitton (1899–1982), Eng. painter, illustrator, cartoonist.

Alpha of the Plough: Alfred George Gardiner (1865–1946), Br. essayist. The pseudonym was intended to be astronomical, referring to the brightest star (Alpha Ursae Majoris) in the Plough (Big Dipper), the famous formation in the constellation of Ursa Major (Great Bear). But there are certain other links, which may or may not have been intentional. "Alpha" suggests "Alfred," and the name George, meaning literally "tiller of the soil," "farmer," appears to be echoed in the "Plough." Even Gardiner has a similar rustic association with the latter. But this could be reading too much into the name.

Mother **Alphonsa:** Rose Lathrop, née Hawthorne (1851–1926), U.S. writer, nun, medical worker. The daughter of novelist Nathaniel Hawthorne took this name after joining the Dominican Order, following the breakup of her marriage in 1895. Her religious name bears a curious (but possibly coincidental) anagrammatic resemblance to her married name.

Al. **Altayev:** Margarita Vladimirovna Yamshchikova (1872–1959), Russ. children's writer, biographer. The writer adopted her new surname from that of a character in *A Widow's Story* by the Russian poet Yakov Polonsky, who had encouraged her when she was an up and coming young author.

Peter **Altenberg:** Richard Engländer (1859–1919), Austr. writer. One can appreciate the desire to change a nationally misleading name in this instance.

Althea: Althea Braithwaite (1940–), Br. children's writer, illustrator.

Robert **Alton:** Robert Alton Hart (1906–1957), U.S. movie director.

Alun: John Blackwell (1797–1840), Welsh poet, prose writer. The name is a bardic one. John Blackwell was born in Flintshire, and the Welsh forename Alun is associated with the name of the Alyn River, which flows through that county.

Alun Cilie: Alun Jeremiah Jones (1897–1975), Welsh poet. The poet took his second name from the farm, Y Cilie, on which he was born. He was the twelfth child of a family of poets who lived here.

Luigi **Alva:** Luis Ernesto Alva Talledo (1927–), Peruvian opera singer.

Alvar: Eduarda Mansilla de García (1838–1892), Argeninian writer. The author used this name for chronicles published in *El Plata Illustrado* over the period 1871–72.

Don **Alvarado:** José Paige (1904–1967), U.S. movie actor, playing "Latin lover" roles.

Albert **Alvarez:** Raymond Gourron (1861–1933), Fr. opera singer.

Max **Alvary:** Maximilian Achenbach (1856–1898), Ger. opera singer.

Betti **Alver:** Elizabet Lepik (1906–1989), Estonian writer, translator.

Kenneth **Alwyn:** Kenneth Alwyn Wetherell (1925–), Br. orchestral conductor.

Samuil **Alyoshin:** Samuil Iosifovich Kotlyar (1913–), Russ. playwright.

Lucine **Amara:** Lucine Armaganian (1927–), U.S. opera singer, of Armenian descent.

Giuseppe **Amato:** Giuseppe Vasaturo (1899–1964), It. movie producer.

Richard **Amberley:** Paul Bourquin (1916–), Br. writer.

Don **Ameche:** Dominic Felix Amici (1908–1993), U.S. movie actor. The respelled surname was designed to prompt an accurate pronunciation of the Italian original "Amici." But does it succeed? It could even mislead, since "Ameche" could be pronounced "Ameech."

Carl **Amery:** Christian Anton Mayer (1922–), Ger. writer, translator. An altered first name and an anagrammatized surname.

Jean **Améry:** Hans Mayer (1912–1978), Austr. Jewish writer.

Adrienne **Ames:** Adrienne Ruth McClure (1909–1947), U.S. movie actress.

Jennifer **Ames:** Maysie Sopoushek, née Greig-Smith (1901–1971), Austral.-born romantic novelist.

Leon **Ames:** Leon Wycoff (1903–1993), U.S. stage, movie, TV actor.

Ramsay **Ames:** Ramsay Philips (1919–), U.S. movie actor.

Amnon: Rees Jones (1797–1844), Welsh poet.

Tori **Amos:** Myra Ellen Amos (1963–), U.S. rock singer. The singer adopted her new first name in 1985.

Alfred **Amtman-Briedit:** Alfred Fritsevich Amtmanis (1885–1966), Latvian theatrical director, actor.

Arthur **Amyand:** [Major] Andrew Charles Parker Haggard (1854–c.1923), Br. novelist, historian.

Ana-Alicia: Ana Alicia Ortiz (1957–), Mexican-born U.S. TV actress.

Anastasius IV: Corrado (di Suburra) (c.1073–1154), It. pope.

Dulce **Anaya:** Dulce Esperanza Wöhner de Vega (1933–), Cuban ballet dancer.

An Craoibhín Aoibhinn: Douglas Hyde (1860–1949), Ir. statesman, historian. Ireland's first president was the founder of the Gaelic League and a campaigner for the native Irish language. His name means "the fair maiden," and comes from the title of a traditional Irish song, "An craoibhín aoibhinn álainn óg," "The fair excellent young maid." The name is pronounced approximately "Un creen een."

Merry **Anders:** Merry Anderson (1932–), U.S. movie actress.

Martin **Andersen-Nexö:** Martin Andersen (1869–1954), Dan. writer. The writer originally used the pseudonym Nexö, taking this from the town on the island of Bornholm where his father was born. He later joined it to his surname, if only for distinction from the many other Andersens in Denmark.

Anna **Anderson:** Franzisca Schanzkowka (1896–1984), Pol.-born U.S. impostor.

Daphne **Anderson:** Daphne Carter, née Scrutton (1922–1977), Eng. stage, movie actress.

G.M. (or Gilbert M.) **Anderson:** Max Aronson (1882–1971), U.S. movie actor ("Broncho Billy").

[Dame] Judith **Anderson:** Frances Margaret Anderson-Anderson (1898–1992), Austral. movie actress. The actress appears to have selected a new first name to match those of her parents, respectively James and Jessie.

R. **Andom:** Alfred Walter Barratt (1869–1920), Eng. humorist. A rather transparent pun for a humorous writer. He also expanded the name to Robert Andom.

Fern **Andra:** [Baroness] Fern Andra von Weichs (–), U.S. movie actress.

Annette **André:** Annette Andreallo (1939–), Austral. ballet dancer, movie, TV actress, working in U.K.

Andrea del Sarto: Andrea d'Agnolo di Francesco (1486–1530), It. painter. The painter's family had been craftsmen and tradesmen, and his father was a tailor. Hence "del Sarto," from Italian *sarto*, "tailor."

Lycosthenes Psellionores **Andreopediacus:** Wolfhart Spangenberg (c.1570–1636), Ger. poet, theologian. The scholar's pseudonym is a literal Greek rendering of the original, with the third word representing his birthtown, Mansfeld, as follows (in the order Greek, German, English): *lykos, Wolf,* "wolf," *sthenos, Härte,* "strength"; *psellion, Spange,* "bracelet," *oros, Berg,* "mountain"; *andro-, Mann,* "man," *pedion, Feld,* "field."

Stephen **Andrew:** Frank G. Layton (1872–1941), Eng. novelist.

Thomas **Andrew:** Edward Thomas Andrulewicz (1932–1984), U.S. ballet dancer, choreographer.

Julie **Andrews:** Julia Elizabeth Wells (1935–), Eng. movie actress. The actress assumed the name of her stepfather, Ted Andrews, a Canadian singer. In 1969 she married the U.S. writer-producer-director Blake Edwards (*q.v.*) and used a combination of her name and his, Julie Andrews Edwards, for her book *Mandy* (1972).

Ruby **Andrews:** Ruby Stackhouse (1947–), U.S. rhythm 'n' blues singer.

Tige **Andrews:** Tiger Androwaous (1920–), Lebanese-born U.S. movie actor.

Pierre **Andrezel:** Karen Christentze Blixen, née Dinesen (1885–1962), Dan. writer, working in Kenya. The author, also writing as Isak Dinesen (*q.v.*), used the male French name for her book *Gengoedelsens Beje* (translated as "The Angelic Avengers") (1944), criticizing the German occupation of Denmark. Andrezel is the name of a village east of Paris.

Olga **Androvskaya:** Olga Nikolayevna Shults (Schultz) (1898–1975), Russ. movie actress.

Zigmas **Angaretis:** Zigmas Ionovich Aleksa (1882–1940), Lithuanian revolutionary.

Victoria de los **Angeles:** Victoria López Cima (1923–), Sp. opera singer.

Pier **Angeli:** Anna Maria Pierangeli (1932–1971), It. movie actress. The actress's surname conveniently divides to form a forename and new surname, although suggesting a man (as if "Peter Angel"), not a woman.

Fra **Angelico:** [Fra] Giovanni da Fiesole (*c.*1400–1455), It. painter. The Renaissance painter's real (lay) name was Guido di Pietro, and his religious name, as a Dominican monk, is thus the one given here, with "Fra" meaning "brother." But the name by which he is now best known originated as a nickname, "Beato Angelico," (literally "blessed angelic one"), because of the angelic beauty of his character. This name became established only after his death.

Angelina: Harriet Martineau (1802–1876), Eng. author.

[Sir] Norman **Angell:** Ralph Norman Angell Lane (1873–1967), Eng. publicist. The author of the influential *The Great Illusion* (1910) published *Patriotism under Three Flags* (1903) under his original name, but thereafter dropped "Lane."

Jean **Angelo:** Jean Barthélémy (1875–1933), Fr. stage, movie actor.

Battista **Angeloni:** John Shebbeare (1709–1788), Eng. political writer. Shebbeare used the Italian-style name for his political satire, purporting to be a translation, attacking the Duke of Newcastle. Its full title was *Letters on the English Nation, by Battista Angeloni, a Jesuit resident in London* (1756).

Maya **Angelou:** Marguerite Annie Johnson (1928–), U.S. black poet, playwright. The writer's surname is that of a Greek husband, Tosh Angelos, while her forename was originally a pet name given her by her brother Bailey.

Muriel **Angelus:** Muriel Angelus Findlay (1909–), Sc. movie actress.

Angelus à Sancto Francisco: Richard Mason (1601–1678), Eng. Franciscan priest. The name can be understood as "angel of St. Francis."

Angelus Silesius: Johannes Scheffler (1624–1677), Pol. religious poet. The poet was a native of Silesia. Hence the Latin name that he took on converting from Lutherism to Catholicism, meaning "Messenger from Silesia."

Margit **Angerer:** Margit von Rupp (1905–1978), Hung.-born Austr. opera singer.

Anise: Anna Louise Strong (1885–1970), U.S. poet, journalist. A name formed from the writer's first two names.

Mother **Ann:** Ann Lee (1736–1784), U.S. mystic, founder of Shaker movement.

Annabella: Suzanne Georgette Charpentier (1909–1996), Fr. movie actress. The actress was given her new name by the French movie director Abel Gance, who took it from Edgar Allan Poe's lyrical ballad *Annabel Lee* (1849).

Anna Livia: Anna Livia Julian Brawn (1955–), Ir.-born Br. fiction writer.

Annette: Annette Funicello (1942–), U.S. movie actress, singer.

Ann-Margret: Ann-Margret Olsson (1941–), Swe.-born U.S. movie actress.

Anodos: Mary Elizabeth Coleridge (1861–1907), Eng. poet, granddaughter of the elder brother of the poet and critic Samuel Taylor Coleridge. She adopted her name from the Greek word for "healthy."

Another Lady: Marie Dobbs, née Catton (*c.*1920–), Austral. author. The name was used by Marie Dobbs for her completion (published 1975) of Jane Austen's unfinished novel *Sandition* (written 1817), so that the combined authorship was credited to "Jane Austen and Another Lady," in the style of Jane Austen's day. Marie Dobbs also wrote as Anne Telscombe.

[Père] **Anselme:** Pierre de Guibours (1625–1694), Fr. genealogist, friar.

S. **Ansky:** Solomon Zanvil Rappoport (or Shloyme Zaynvl Rapoport) (1863–1920), Russ. Jewish writer, folklorist. The original form of the pseudonym, which had several variants, was "S. An—sky," implying missing letters. Masanov (see Bibliography, p. 402) has the writer's original name in the non-Jewish form Semyon Akimovich Rappoport, and his pseudonym is given in some sources as An-ski. The first names Solomon ("peace") and Semyon (Simon) ("hearkening") are etymologically unrelated.

F. **Anstey:** Thomas Anstey Guthrie (1856–1934), Eng. author, children's writer. The writer intended his pseudonym to be "T. Anstey," from his first two names. A printer misprinted this as "F. Anstey," which he allowed to remain.

Gilbert **Anstruther:** Russel S. Clark (1909–), Austral. writer of popular fiction.

Adam **Ant:** Stuart Leslie Goddard (1954–), Br. rock singer. Stuart Goddard was at the Hornsey College of Art, London, when he asked a friend to design a tattoo for his upper left arm. This was a heart pierced with a dagger, the word ADAM on top, PURE and SEX on either side, the whole thing set just above his vaccination mark. From then on, he called himself "Adam." "When I had the tattoo done," he said, "I really went in for it. Adam is a very strong name; it's the *first* name—you know—the Garden of Eden. I associate it with strength." The strength was further incorporated by adding "ant" to make "adamant," and "Ant" thus became his surname. ("Mr. Ant for you," said the girl on the telephone.) He soon adopted the surname for the group of four he sang with, so that he was "Adam and the Ants" [*Observer Magazine*, January 10, 1982].

Anthony: Anthony Hutchings (1946–), Eng. cartoonist, illustrator.

[Archbishop] **Anthony:** Andrew Borisovich Bloom (1914–), Swiss-born Russ. churchman.

C.L. **Anthony:** Dorothy ("Dodie") Gladys Smith (1896–1990), Eng. playwright, novelist. The writer also used the name Charles Henry Percy.

Evelyn **Anthony:** Evelyn Ward Thomas (1928–), Br. mystery novelist.

John **Anthony:** Ronald Brymer Beckett (1891–1970), Eng. writer, civil servant.

Joseph **Anthony:** Joseph Anthony Deuster (1912–1993), U.S. stage, movie actor, director, screenwriter.

Julie **Anthony:** Julie Nutt, née Lush (1952–), Austral. cabaret singer, dancer.

Lysette **Anthony:** Lysette Chodzka (1963–), Eng.-born Pol. TV actress. The actress gave the following account of the evolution of her name: "My father appeared with Ivor Novello [(*q.v.*)] in *King's Rhapsody* and decided that Chodzki was no good as a stage name: so he became Michael Anthony. When I first went to school at a convent I was asked my name and got terribly confused. I said my father's name was Michael Anthony, my mother was Bernadette Milnes and my name was Lysette Chodzka—the female version of the [Polish] family name. That was complicated enough, but then when I was ten I played a precocious kitten in *Pinocchio* in the West End and decided to call myself Lysette Elrington, after my grandmother. But at 16 I started fashion modeling and adopted my father's stage name and became Lysette Anthony—anyway, if your name starts with letter A you are always first in the casting directories" [*Telegraph Sunday Magazine*, April 17, 1983].

Piers **Anthony:** Piers Anthony Dillingham Jacob (1934–), Eng.-born U.S. SF writer.

Ray **Anthony:** Raymond Antonini (1922–), U.S. pop musician.

Richard **Anthony:** Richard Anthony Bush (1938–), U.S. pop musician.

[St.] **Anthony of Padua:** Fernando (1195–1231), Port. Franciscan friar, churchman.

Anthropos: Robert David Rowland (*c.*1853–1944), Welsh journalist, poet. Unusually, the writer chose a Greek name, meaning "human being," rather than a Welsh one.

Dr. Pessimist **Anticant:** Thomas Carlyle (1795–1881), Sc. philosopher, writer.

Antico: Pier Jacopo Alari Bonacolsi (*c.*1460–1528), It. sculptor. The artist has come to be known by his nickname, meaning "ancient," with reference to his classically inspired statuettes. He also restored ancient sculpture.

Antoine: Antek Cierplikowski (1884– ?), Pol.-born Fr. hairdresser.

Anton: Beryl Botterill Yeoman, née Thompson (1907–1970), Austral.-born Br. cartoonist. The artist originally shared this name with her brother, Harold Thompson (1911–), for the cartoons they published jointly from 1937. He explains: "Beryl, a name she hated, had recently converted to Roman Catholicism and had adopted the name Antonia. I thought 'J. Anton' had a sophisticated continental ring that the editorial staff would appreciate. We worked out the style and submitted some drawings which were accepted, but with the 'J.' dropped from the name" [*Punch*, October 12–18, 1996].

[Brother] **Antoninus:** William Everson (1912–), U.S. poet, Dominican lay brother.

Antonio: (1) Antonas Ignosovich Markunas (1915–1977), Latvian circus artist; (2) Antonio Lopez (1943–1987), Puerto Rican-born U.S. fashion illustrator. Lopez "dropped his surname only when his fame was sufficient to allow him to do so" [*Sunday Times*, February 23, 1997].

António: António Ruíz Soler (1921–1996), Sp. ballet dancer, choreographer.

Father **Antony:** Joseph McCabe (1867–1955), Eng. writer. As a boy, the writer was led to believe he had a religious vocation. At the age of 15 he thus entered a monastery to become a Franciscan monk and in due course a priest, when he was known as the Very Rev. Father Antony, O.S.F. He later realized he was mistaken in his calling and left the Church in 1896 to pursue a career under his original name as an author, journalist, and lecturer. (See also Chapter 4, p. 30.)

Hilda **Antony:** Hilda Antonietti (1886– ?), Br. stage actress, of Eng.-It. parentage.

Peter **Antony:** Peter Levin Shaffer (1926–), Eng. playwright + Anthony Joshua Shaffer (1926–), Eng. playwright, twin brothers.

Christopher **Anvil:** Harry C. Crosby, Jr. (*fl.*1970s), U.S. SF writer.

Ape: Carlo Pellegrini (1839–1889), It. caricaturist, working in England. The artist chose his pen name to reflect the essentially mischievous nature of his work, since a caricature "apes" its subject. Ape's first effort, drawn over the name "Singe" (French for "monkey"), was a caricature of Disraeli published in the fashionable magazine *Vanity Fair* in 1869. Another contributor to this journal was Spy (*q.v.*).

Apex: Eric Chalkley (1917–), Eng. crossword compiler. In typical "cryptic crossword" fashion, the name has a double sense, indicating not only a "top" compiler but one who aimed to "ape X," that is, to imitate Ximenes (*q.v.*).

Guillaume **Apollinaire:** Wilhelm Apollinaris de Kostrowitski (1880–1918), Fr. poet, of It.-Pol. parentage.

App: Barry Ernest Appleby (1909–), Eng. cartoonist.

Johnny **Appleseed:** John Chapman (1774–1847), U.S. orchardist. The name, strictly speaking a nickname, was given to the man who planted fruit trees for the frontier settlers in Pennsylvania, Ohio, Indiana, and Illinois. He adopted it, however, so can legitimately be included here.

Apsīšu Jēkabs: Jānis Jaunzemis (1858–1929), Latvian writer. The writer took his new first name from Latvian *apse,* "aspen," referring to the tree in front of his study window. The second word of the name is the equivalent of Jacob.

Mr. **Aptommas:** John Thomas (1826–1913), Welsh harpist. The musician used this name for his definitive work, *A History of the Harp,* published in New York in 1864. As Olphar Hamst comments in his *Handbook of Fictitious Names* (1868) (see Bibliography, p. 401), "This gentleman *Welshified* his name, probably for the sake of euphony." "Aptommas" would mean "son of Thomas."

Ap Vychan: Robert Thomas (1809–1880), Welsh theologian, writer. The writer's name means "little son."

Aquanetta: Burnu Davenport (1920–), U.S. movie actress.

Louis **Aragon:** Louis Andrieux (1897–1982), Fr. Surrealist poet, Communist writer, Resistance fighter. The poet and patriot was the illegitimate son of Marguerite Toucas and Louis Andrieux, a former *préfet de police* and ambassador to Spain, who named him Aragon for the historic Spanish kingdom. The quest for legitimacy and identity was one of the major themes of Aragon's work. The poet himself occasionally used pseudonyms. His poem *Panopticum* (1943), for example, an exposé of Hitler's henchmen, was signed François la Colère, as if to mean "angry France."

Shio **Aragvispireli:** Shio Zakharyevich Dedabrishvili (1867–1926), Georgian writer. The writer took his name from the Aragvi River by which he was raised.

Arazi: Movses Melikovich Arutyunyan (1878–1964), Armenian writer. The writer's pseudonym represents the Armenian name of the Araks River. This flows along the border between Iran and Azerbaijan, south of Georgia, where he was born.

Thoinot **Arbeau:** Jehan Tabourot (1519–1595), Fr. writer on dancing. The name is a precise anagram, taking "j" as "i." Thoinot is a genuine forename, as a diminutive version of "Antoine."

Madame d'**Arblay:** Frances ("Fanny") Burney (1752–1840), Eng. novelist, diarist. The writer's adopted name was that of her husband, General Alexandre d'Arblay, a French refugee in England, whom she married in 1793.

Anne **Archer:** Anne Bowman (1945–), U.S. movie actress. The actress is the daughter of John Archer (see below).

Harry **Archer:** Harry Auracher (1888–1960), U.S. popular composer, musical director.

John **Archer:** Ralph Bowman (1915–), U.S. movie actor. A synonymous name change.

Archimedes: [Sir] James Eward Edmonds (1861–1956), Eng. military historian.

Ardelia: Anne Finch, née Kingsmill (1661–1720), Eng. poet.

Don **Arden:** Harry Levy (1926–), Eng. pop musician.

Elizabeth **Arden:** Florence Nightingale Lewis, née Graham (1878–1966), Can. cosmetician. A cosmetician needs a carefully selected and suitable name. Florence Nightingale Graham was felt to be not sufficiently glamorous. Miss Graham rather liked the name Elizabeth Hubbard, which was that of the original owner of the New York salon where she set up her business. (The name was still on the window, although the lady herself had moved two doors further down Fifth

Avenue.) However Elizabeth Graham did not sound quite right, so she instead chose Elizabeth Arden. The usual explanation behind the name is that "Elizabeth" came from the author of *Elizabeth and her German Garden* (see **Elizabeth**), and that "Arden" came from Tennyson's poem *Enoch Arden*. But would Miss Graham have really been so closely familiar with these Victorian works? It is said that she made the final choice of name after posting letters to Elizabeth Arden "in care of Graham" to see what impact the name made on the envelope. Miss Arden's rival in the cosmetic field was Helena Rubinstein. Elizabeth Arden was thus the "Miss" of the cosmetics world, Helena Rubinstein the "Madame," and Coco Chanel the "Mademoiselle" [Margaret Allen, *Selling Dreams*, 1981].

Eve **Arden:** Eunice West, née Quedens (1912–1990), U.S. comic movie, TV actress. The actress is said to have adopted her name after looking over the cosmetics "Evening in Paris" (giving "Eve") and "Elizabeth Arden" (giving "Arden"). For the origin of the latter name, see the entry above.

Pietro **Aretino:** (? 1492–1556), It. satirist, dramatist (the "scourge of princes"). The writer's real name is unknown (see p. 60). "Aretino" means "of Arezzo," his native town.

La **Argentina:** Antonia Mercé y Luque (1890–1936), Argentine-born Sp. ballet dancer.

La **Argentinita:** Encarnación Lopez Julves (1895–1945), Argentine-born Sp. ballet dancer. La Argentinita was younger than La Argentina (see above), so rightly took a diminutive form of the name, "the little Argentinian."

Tudor **Arghezi:** Ion N. Theodorescu (1880–1967), Rom. lyric poet.

Argo: Abram Markovich Goldenberg (1897–1968), Russ. poet, playwright. A name formed from letters in the writer's full name, while also suggesting "argot," as one who enjoyed manipulating words. Goldenberg wrote both for the music hall and the circus.

Pearl **Argyle:** Pearl Wellman (1910–1947), S.A.-born Br. ballet dancer, stage actress.

Carina **Ari:** Carina Janssen (1897–1970), Swe. ballet dancer. An unusual extraction of a surname from an existing forename.

Arion: (1) George Laval Chesterton (1856– ?), Eng. sporting correspondent; (2) William Falconer (1732–1769), Eng. "sailor-poet." According to legend, the ancient Greek poet Arion was cast into the sea by mariners but subsequently brought back to land by a dolphin. His name is thus suitable for both sporting and maritime associations. (Atkinson and Clarke [see Bibliography] both misidentify the first Arion as the novelist G.K. Chesterton.)

Ariosto: [Rev.] Edward Irving (1792–1834), Sc. clergyman, founder of Holy Catholic Apostolic Church. The name of the epic Italian poet Lodovico Ariosto (1474–1533) was widely adopted by "great" men, or used as a nickname for important writers of the 18th and 19th centuries. Goethe, for example, was "The Ariosto of Germany," and Walter Scott "The Ariosto of the North." Possibly Irving had the latter specifically in mind.

Alan Wolf **Arkin:** Roger Short (1934–), U.S. movie actor, director.

Harold **Arlen:** Hyman Arluck (1905–1986), U.S. composer of musicals.

Michael **Arlen:** Dikran Kuyumjian (1895–1956), Bulg.-born Br. novelist, of Armenian descent. The writer's assumed name appears to be based on an anagram of "Armenian."

Richard **Arlen:** Cornelius Richard Van Mattimore (1899–1976), U.S. movie actor. It may be no coincidence that all three Arlens here were born within the same decade. This one adopted his new name in 1924, after originally being billed as Van Mattimore.

Arletty: Léonie Bathiat (1898–1992), Fr. stage, movie actress. The actress took her stage name in memory of Arlette, a character in Maupassant's novel *Mont-Oriol* (1887), as this is set in the Auvergne, near Lake Tazenat, where Bathiat's grandmother had lived. For some reason she then decided that an English final "y" was more chic than a French "e."

Joyce **Arling:** Joyce Bell, née Burge (1911–), U.S. stage actress.

George **Arliss:** George Augustus Andrews (1868–1946), Eng. stage, movie actor, father of Leslie Arliss (see entry below). The actor took his stage name from his father, William Joseph Arliss Andrews.

Leslie **Arliss:** Leslie Andrews (1901–1988), Br. movie director, son of George Arliss (see entry above).

Arlodhes Ywerdhon: Margaret Pollard, née Steuart Gladstone (1903–1996), Eng. scholar. Pollard settled in Cornwall following her marriage in 1928 and was made a bard of the Cornish Gorsedd in 1938. Her bardic name means "the Irish lady," reflecting her dedication to things Celtic.

Arman: Armand Fernandez (1928–), Fr.-born U.S. artist. In 1957 the artist decided he wanted to be known by his first name alone. The final "d" is missing through a printer's error on the front of a catalog.

Armand: Friedrich Armand Strubberg (1806–1889), Ger.-born author, working in U.S.

Mkrtich **Armen:** Mkrtich Grigoryevich Arutyunyan (1906–1972), Armenian writer. The writer's pen name emphasizes his nationality.

Armida: Armida Vendrell (1913–), Mexican movie actress.

Jacobus **Arminius:** Jakob Harmensen (1560–1609), Du. theologian, Protestant churchman. A conventional latinization of the minister's original surname.

Anthony **Armstrong:** George Anthony Armstrong Willis (1897–1976), Can.-born Br. humorist, novelist.

Henry **Armstrong:** Henry Jackson (1912–1988), U.S. boxer. What more apposite name for a "lord of the ring?" Early in his career he boxed under the name Melody Jackson.

Robert **Armstrong:** Donald Robert Smith (1890–1973), U.S. movie actor.

Dudley (or Ernest) **Armytage:** William Edward Armytage Axon (1846–1913), Eng. journalist, writer.

Georges **Arnaud:** Henri Girard (1918–), Fr. novelist, dramatist.

Desi **Arnaz:** Desiderio Alberto Arnaz y de Acha (1917–1986), Cuban-born U.S. movie, TV actor.

Peter **Arne:** Peter Arne Albrecht (1920–1983), Br.-U.S. movie actor.

James **Arness:** James Aurness (1923–), U.S. movie, TV actor.

Peter **Arno:** Curtis Arnoux Peters, Jr. (1904–1968), U.S. cartoonist, illustrator.

Sig **Arno:** Siegfried Aron (1895–1975), Ger. movie comedian, working in U.S.

Danny **Arnold:** Arnold Rothman (1925–), U.S. movie producer.

Edward **Arnold:** Guenther Edward Arnold Schneider (1890–1956), U.S. movie actor.

Françoise **Arnoul:** Françoise Annette Marie Mathilde Gautsch (1931–), Algerian-born Fr. movie actress.

Sonia **Arova:** Sonia Errio (1927–), Bulg.-born Br. ballet dancer.

Bill **Arp:** Charles Henry Smith (1826–1903), U.S. humorist. The name is almost certainly intended to suggest a comic rendering of "Wyatt Earp," the name of the famous lawman of the Wild West. Bill Arp began his career as a writer by contributing letters to a newspaper of his native Georgia addressed to "Mr. Abe Linkhorn," this being a similar eccentric spelling of a famous real name.

Arrago: Roman Semyonovich Levitin (1883–1949), Russ. circus artist, "memory man."

Pavel **Arsky:** Pavel Aleksandrovich Afanasyev (1886–1967), Russ. writer.

Artemas: Arthur Telford Mason (*fl.* 1924), Br. author. The name was formed from the first syllables of the writer's full name, but at the same time suggests a classical name such as Artemon, Artemidorus, or even Artemisia (as for the next entry below).

Artemisia: [Lady] Mary Wortley Montagu (1689–1762), Eng. writer of letters, poems. Artemisia was the name of queens of Asia Minor, one being the sister (and wife) of King Mausolus, to whom she erected the famous tomb known as the Mausoleum.

Arthénice: Catherine de Vivonne, Marquise (Madame) de Rambouillet (1588–1665), Fr. social leader. The classical-looking name is an exact anagram of "Catherine."

Bea(trice) **Arthur:** Bernice Frankel (1924–), U.S. movie actress.

George K. **Arthur:** George K. Arthur Brest (1899–1985), Sc. movie actor.

Jean **Arthur:** Gladys Georgianna Greene (1905–1991), U.S. movie actress.

Johnny **Arthur:** John Williams (1883–1951), U.S. movie actor.

Julia **Arthur:** Ida Lewis (1869–1919), Can. stage actress.

Peter **Arthur:** Arthur Porges (1915–), U.S. writer of detective stories, SF, horror fiction.

Robert **Arthur:** (1) Robert Arthur Feder (1909–1986), U.S. movie producer; (2) Robert Arthaud (1925–), U.S. movie actor, previously radio announcer.

Nikolay **Arzhak:** Yuly Daniel (1925–1988), Russ. dissident writer.

Oscar **Asche:** Thomas Stange Heiss (1871–1936), Austral.-born Br. stage actor, of Scandinavian descent.

Asdreni: Aleks Stavri Drenova (1872–1947), Albanian poet. The name is formed from letters in the poet's full name.

Clifford **Ashdown:** Richard Austin Freeman (1862–1943), Eng. mystery writer + John James Pitcairn (1860–1936), Eng. mystery writer.

Gordon **Ashe:** John Creasey (1908–1973), Br. crime novelist.

Renée **Asherson:** Renée Ascherson (1920–), Eng. stage, movie actress.

April **Ashley:** George Jamieson (1935–), Eng. transexual socialite. Jamieson was born in April. He changed his name following his sex change operation in 1960.

Caroline **Ashley:** Caroline Smith (1958–), Sc. TV actress. The actress changed her name to avoid confusion with an identically named actress. She adopted her new name from the Laura Ashley fashion shops.

Edward **Ashley:** Edward Ashley Cooper (1904–), Br. movie actor.

Elizabeth **Ashley:** Elizabeth Ann Cole (1939–), U.S. movie actress. The actress took her new surname from the forename of Ashley Wilkes, acted by Leslie Howard (*q.v.*) in the motion picture of Margaret Mitchell's novel, *Gone with the Wind.*

John **Ashton:** John Groves (1950–), Eng. stage, movie, TV actor.

Teddy **Ashton:** Charles Allen Clarke (1863–1935), Eng. journalist, writer. The Lancashire writer used this name for his popular weekly *Teddy Ashton's Magazine.*

Lena **Ashwell:** Lena Margaret Pocock (1872–1957), Br. stage actress, theatrical manager. The actress adopted her stage name from the second name of her father, Charles Ashwell Botelar Pocock.

Joseph **Askins:** Thomas Haskey (1771– ?), Eng. ventriloquist.

Grégoire **Aslan:** Kridor Aslanian (1908–1982), Fr.-Turkish movie actor. A French version of the Turkish name, with "Aslan" (meaning "lion") retained from the original name.

Aspazija: Elza Rozenberga (1868–1943), Latvian poet. The poet, wife of Jānis Rainis (*q.v.*), adopted the name of Aspasia, the 5th-century BC Greek courtesan and mistress of Pericles, renowned for her beauty and intelligence.

Asper: Samuel Johnson (1709–1784), Eng. lexicographer, critic. Latin for "rough," "severe," as a critic can be.

Assiac: Heinrich Fraenkel (1897–1986), Ger.-born Eng. journalist, writer on chess. The pseudonym is a reversal of "Caissa," the name of the muse of chess, first appearing in a poem of 1763 by Sir William Jones.

Fred **Astaire:** Frederick Austerlitz (1899–1987), U.S. dancer, stage, movie actor. The name change was not made by the dancer himself, but by his parents, Frederick and Ann Geilus Austerlitz, when the future movie star was only two years old. The suggestion of "star" in the name is appropriate. His sister, dancer and actress Adele Astaire (1898–1981), also took the name.

Mikhail **Astangov:** Mikhail Fedorovich Ruzhnikov (1900–1965), Russ. stage, movie actor.

Juliet **Astley:** Norah Lofts, née Robinson (1904–1983), Eng. historical, crime novelist. The writer also used the male name Peter Curtis (*q.v.*).

Anne **Aston:** Anne Lloyd (1948–), Sc. TV hostess. "Lloyd" is a typical Welsh name, not a Scottish one.

James **Aston:** Terence Hanbury White (1906–1964), Br. novelist.

Mary **Astor:** Lucille Vasconcellos Langhanke (1906–1987), U.S. movie, TV actress, of Ger. parentage.

Kemal **Atatürk:** Mustafa Kemal [Pasha] (1881–1938), Turk. soldier, statesman. The statesman adopted his surname, meaning "father of the Turks," in 1934 when as president of the Turkish Republic he introduced the compulsory registration of surnames.

William **Atheling:** Ezra Pound (1885–1972), U.S. poet.

Athenagoras I: Aristokles Spyrou (1886–1972), Gk. churchman. The archbishop of Constantinople adopted the name of the 2d-century AD Christian philosopher Athenagoras. His own name means "Athens marketplace," implying one who is important or influential in Greek society.

William **Atherton:** William Atherton Knight (1947–), U.S. TV actor.

Dr. **Atl:** Gerardo Murillo (1875–1964), Mexican painter, writer, revolutionary. The painter's Aztec name is the Nahuatl word for "water." He adopted it in order to repudiate his Spanish heritage on the one hand and demonstrate his loyalty to his Mexican Indian ancestors on the other.

Charles **Atlas:** Angelo Siciliano (1893–1972), U.S. bodybuilder. In Greek mythology, Atlas was the Titan god who supported the heavens on his shoulders.

Philip **Atlee:** James Atlee Philips (1915–1991), U.S. mystery novelist.

Joseph **Atterley:** George Tucker (1775–1861), U.S. essayist, satirist.

Atticus: (1) Joseph Addison (1672–1719), Eng. poet, dramatist; (2) Junius (*q.v.*); (3) Richard Hebes (1773–1833), Eng. bibliomaniac. The name of Atticus, a Roman literary patron of the 2d century BC, has been adopted by many writers and diarists.

Attila the Hun: Raymond Quevedo (1892–1962), Trinidad calypso singer.

Moshe **Atzmon:** Moshe Groszberger (1931–), Israeli orchestral conductor.

James **Aubrey:** James Aubrey Tregidgo (1947–), Br. movie, TV actor.

Cécile **Aubry:** Anne-Marie-José Bénard (1929–), Fr. movie actress.

Michel **Auclair:** Vladimir Vujovic (1922–1988), Ger. movie actor, of Serbian-Fr. parentage, working in France.

Maxine **Audley:** Maxine Hecht (1923–1992), Eng. stage actress.

Stéphane **Audran:** Colette Suzanne Jeannine Dacheville (1932–), Fr. movie actress.

Mischa **Auer:** Mischa Ounskowsky (1905–1967), Russ.-born U.S. movie actor. The actor took the name of his maternal grandfather, Leopold Auer, a violinist, who adopted him and brought him to the U.S. in 1920.

Berthold **Auerbach:** Moses Baruch Auerbacher (1812–1882), Ger. novelist, short story writer. The writer used the pseudonym Theobald Chaubert as an anagram of his adopted name.

Markos **Augeres:** Georgos Papadopulos (1884– ?), Gr. writer, critic.

Edwin **August:** Edwin August Philip von der Butz (1883–1964), U.S. movie actor, director.

Jan **August:** Jan Augustoff (? 1912–1976), U.S. popular pianist.

Joe **August:** Joseph Augustus (1931–), U.S. rhythm 'n' blues singer.

John **August:** Bernard Augustine de Voto (1897–1955), U.S. editor, essayist, writer.

Mlle **Augusta:** Caroline Augusta Joséphine Thérèse Fuchs, Comtesse de Saint-James (1806–1901), Fr. ballet dancer. Mlle Augusta was probably right to select her second name as the most "international" for professional use.

Caesar **Augustus:** Gaius Octavius (63 BC–AD 14), Roman emperor. The first of the Roman emperors was born Gaius Octavius, the son of the niece of Julius Casear. When Caesar adopted him in 44 BC he became Caius Julius Caesar Octavianus, otherwise Octavian. In this name, according to the Roman naming system,

Caius was his *praenomen*, or forename, Julius Caesar was the name of his adoptive father, and Octavianus was his *cognomen*, or extra personal name, here the adjectival form of his original *nomen*, his *gens* (clan) name.

In 27 BC he became Gaius Julius Caesar Octavianus Augustus, this last being a title (meaning "revered") that was conferred on him by the Senate and that indicated his supremacy. From then on he was known simply as Augustus, a name which, together with the designation *Imperator* ("general," the origin of English "emperor"), became part of the formal title of all later Roman emperors.

The origin of "Augustus" is explained by the 2d-century historian Suetonius as follows: "He assumed the surname of ... Augustus ... by virtue of Munatius Plancus' his sentence; for when some gave their opinion that he ought to be styled Romulus, as if he also had been a founder of the city [of Rome], Plancus prevailed that he should be called rather Augustus; not only for that it was a new surname, but also greater and more honourable, because religious and holy places, wherein also anything is consecrated by bird-flight and feeding of them, be called augusta" [Suetonius, *History of Twelve Caesars*, translated by Philemon Holland, 1606 (1930)].

Georgie **Auld:** John Altwerger (1919–1990), Can. jazz musician.

Marie **Ault:** Mary Cragg (1870–1951), Br. stage, movie actress. The actress adopted her mother's maiden name as her stage name.

Jean-Pierre **Aumont:** Jean-Pierre Philippe Salomons (1909–), Fr. movie actor, working in U.S. The actor's new surname is an approximate phonetic rendition of his original name, minus its initial "Sal-" syllable.

Aunt...: For names beginning thus, see the next word, e.g. for Aunt Charlotte see **Charlotte**, for Aunt Effie see **Effie**, etc.

Aurangzeb: Muhi-ud-Din Muhammad (1618–1707), Ind. emperor. The last of the great Mogul emperors surrounded his royal presence with pomp and luxury. Hence his assumed name (or title), meaning "beauty of the throne." On succeeding to the throne itself in 1658 he took the equally grandiose kingly title of Alamgir, "conqueror of the universe."

Auseklis: Mikelis Krogzemis (1850–1879), Latvian poet. The writer's poetic name means "break of day," "morning light."

Charles **Austin:** Charles Reynolds (1879–1942), Eng. music hall comedian.

Gene **Austin:** Eugene Lucas (1900–1972), U.S. popular singer.

Lovie **Austin:** Cora Calhoun (1887–1972), U.S. black jazz pianist.

Florence **Austral:** Florence Wilson (1894–1968), Austral. opera singer. The singer adopted her patriotic name at the start of her stage career, which opened in London, England, in 1922.

Frankie **Avalon:** Francis Thomas Avallone (1939–), U.S. pop singer, movie actor.

Claude **Aveline:** Eugène Avtsine (1901–1992), Fr. novelist.

Aventinus: Johann Thurmayr (or Turmair) (1477–1534), Ger. historian, humanist. The historian was a native of Abensberg, and adopted its Latin name as his professional name.

Richard **Avery:** Edmund Cooper (1926–), Eng. SF writer, reviewer.

Tex **Avery:** Fred Bean Avery (1907–1980), U.S. movie animator. Like other people so named or nicknamed, Tex Avery was born in Texas.

Avi: Avi Wortis (1937–), U.S. children's writer.

Kofi **Awoonor:** George Awoonor Williams (1935–), Ghanaian poet, novelist.

Axiologus: William Wordsworth (1770–1850), Eng. poet. This name, Greek for "worthy of mention," was adopted by the then youthful poet for his "Sonnet, on seeing Miss Helen Maria Williams weep at a tale of Distress," published in *The European Magazine* in 1787.

Aybek: Musa Tashmukhamedov (1904–1968), Uzbek writer, translator. The writer adopted a poetic name meaning "knight of the moon." It arose from his childhood memories, one of the most vivid being that of a moonlit night. In his own words: "A full white moon sailed in the sky and it seemed so beautiful that I held out my little arms to it and kept saying, 'Momma, give me the moon!' I still sense the ecstasy that I experienced in those times" [Dmitriyev, p. 141].

Catherine **Aydy:** Emma Christina Tennant (1937–), Br. novelist, journalist. The writer claims she got her name from an Ouija board. She used it for her first novel, *The Colour of Rain* (1964). The book had a mixed reception, however, and she dropped the name.

Aydyn: Manzura Sabirova (1906–1953), Uzbek poet. The writer chose a pen name meaning "bright."

Dan **Aykroyd:** Daniel Agraluscasacra (1951–), Can. movie actor.

[Sir] Felix **Aylmer:** Felix Edward Aylmer-Jones (1889–1979), Br. stage, movie actor.

Allan **Aynesworth:** Edward Abbot-Anderson (1864–1959), Eng. stage actor, brother of Louis Goodrich (*q.v.*).

Ayni: Sadriddin Said-Murodzoda (1878–1954), Tajik writer. The writer recounts in nice detail how he finally arrived at his pseudonym: "In my early years [at a Muslim college] in Bukhara some people, especially the mullahs, used to demean me. So I at first chose the name Sifli, i.e. belittled one. But as time went on I no longer liked the name. They might demean me, but why should I regard myself as demeaned? ... So I dropped the pseudonym Sifli and chose a new name—Mukhtodzhi, i.e. impoverished one. But I began to tire of that name in turn. 'I am hard up, it's true—I said to myself—but why should I broadcast my poverty to all and sundry?' So I dropped that name as well.

Some people, noticing my rather odd behavior, would say, 'He's a bit crazy!' As a result of those remarks I chose the name Dzhununi, i.e. madman. But I soon grew sick of that pseudonym. After all, I wasn't crazy!

Discovering that I wrote poetry, people began asking about my pseudonym and its meaning. I decided to find a name that would be as meaningful as possible. Leafing through the dictionary to that end, I came across the word 'ayni'; it had 48 meanings, of which the best known—eye, source, sun—were very suitable as a pseudonym. So I chose the name Ayni. If anyone now asked me what my name meant, I replied: 'It has forty-eight meanings, so look it up in the dictionary and find out for yourself.' That soon silenced the questioners" [Dmitriyev, pp. 111–12].

Agnes **Ayres:** Agnes Hinkle (1896–1940), U.S. movie actress.

Lew **Ayres:** Lewis Ayer (1908–1996), U.S. movie actor.

Mitchell **Ayres:** Mitchell Agress (1910–1969), U.S. jazz musician.

J. Calder **Ayrton:** Mary F. Chapman (1838–1884), Ir.-born Br. novelist. The writer's first novel, *Mary Bertrand* (1860), was published under the name Francis Meredith. Her last novel, *The Gift of the Gods* (1879), was the only one published under her real name.

Michael **Ayrton:** Michael Gould (1921–1975), Eng. artist, writer. The artist adopted his mother's maiden name as his professional name.

John **Ayscough:** [Rt. Rev. Mgr. Count] Francis Browning Drew Bickerstaffe-Drew (1858–1938), Eng. writer of religious novels. The Roman Catholic prelate had the original name of Bickerstaffe, but assumed his mother's maiden name of Drew (which he already bore) as an additional surname on coming of age in 1879.

Azed: Jonathan Crowther (1942–), Eng. crossword compiler. The compiler's crossword clues cover "A to Z," while at the same time being tortuous, or even torturous, like the Spanish grand inquisitor whose name is reversed here, Don Diego de Deza. This association is all the more meaningful when it is known that Crowther succeeded Ximenes (*q.v.*) as chief compiler for the *Observer*. Earlier, he had compiled for other publications as "Gong," an early childhood pronunciation of "Jonathan."

Maria **Azevedo:** Francisca Júlia (1871–1920), Brazilian poet.

Charles **Aznavour:** Shahnour Varenagh Aznavurjan (1924–), Fr. movie actor, singer, of Armenian parentage.

Azorín: José Martínez Ruiz (1873–1967), Sp. writer, literary critic. The writer took his pen name from that of the eponymous hero of his autobiographical novel *Antonio Azorín* (1902), with the name itself from the Spanish for "hawk-like."

Agnès **b.:** Agnès Bourgeois, née Troublé (1941–), Fr. fashion designer. On opening her first fashion shop in Paris, the designer saw that her real name was hardly suitable. She therefore needed a new name. She considered her married name (Bourgeois), but her former husband "had a certain notoriety in the publishing world," which did not seem compatible with her work. She therefore just kept the initial, "lower case, because it suits me better" [*The Times*, January 8, 1996].

Ba'al Shem Tov: Israel ben Eliezer (1698–1760), Pol. Jewish mystic, folk healer. The founder of the Hasidic movement adopted a Hebrew name meaning "master of the good name." This related to his reputation as a healer, who worked using herbs, talismans, and so on inscribed with the divine name. The acronymic form of his name was Besht.

Bab: [Sir] William Schwenk Gilbert (1836–1911), Eng. playwright, comic poet, illustrator. The writer, librettist of the famous Gilbert and Sullivan operettas, used this name for his *Bab Ballads* (1866–71). The name originated as nickname given Gilbert as a child by his parents.

The **Bab:** [Mirza] Ali Mohammad (1819–1850), Persian religious leader. Ali Mohammad claimed to be a gateway to the Hidden Imam, a new messenger of Allah who was to come. Hence his adopted name, the Arabic word for "gate." Some years after the Bab's execution in 1850, his work was taken up by the "Hidden Imam" in question, Baha-'Alla-h (*q.v.*). Mirza is a Persian title of respect, meaning literally "son of a lord."

Babette: Elizabeth McLauchlan (1925–), Sc. music hall dancer. Babette is one of the many pet forms of "Elizabeth," albeit a French one.

Gracchus **Babeuf:** François Noël Babeuf (1760–1797), Fr. revolutionary. The protocommunist adopted as his new first name that of the 2nd-century BC agrarian reformer Gaius (Caius) Sempronius Gracchus. He later effectively adopted the name as a whole, calling himself "Caius-Gracchus, Tribun du peuple."

Jean **Babilée:** Jean Gutman (1923–), Fr. ballet dancer, choreographer, actor.

Alice **Babs:** Alice Nilson (1924–), Swe. popular singer, movie actress.

Master **Babua:** Prosanta Kumar Roy (1947–), Ind. child movie actor.

Babyface: Kenneth Edmonds (1959–), U.S. rhythm 'n' blues musician. The musician adopted his nickname, given him for his youthful looks.

Baby Huey: James Ramey (1944–1970), U.S. rhythm and blues singer.

Baby LeRoy: Ronald LeRoy Winebrenner (1932–), U.S. child movie actor

Baby Peggy: Peggy Montgomery (1917–), U.S. child movie actress.

Baby Sandy: Sandra Lee Henville (1938–), U.S. child movie actress.

Lauren **Bacall:** Betty Joan Perske (1924–), U.S. stage, movie actress. The actress's mother left Romania for America when she (the mother) was only a year or two old, together with her own parents. On arriving at the immigration office on Ellis Island, the family gave their name, Weinstein-Bacal, meaning "wineglass" in German and Russian (the latter properly *bokal*, itself from French *bocal*). The immigration officer must have written just the first half of the name, so that the husband and wife were Max and Sophie Weinstein (Lauren Bacall's grandparents), with their daughters Renee and Nathalie (her mother) and their son Albert. Nathalie married William Perske, but soon divorced him, and then took instead the second half of the original "double" name for herself and her daughter. Then when the future Lauren was eight years old, her mother became Nathalie Bacal, and the little girl was Betty Bacal. By the time she was eight, Betty had added another "l" to her name, as "there was too much irregularity of pronunciation": some people rhymed the name with "cackle," others pronounced it "Bacahl." She felt the second "l" would ensure that the second syllable of the name would be pronounced correctly, as in "call."

When she began her movie career, director Howard Hawks wanted to find a good name to go with her surname, and asked if there was a suitable one somewhere in her family. Betty's grandmother's name, Sophie, did not seem to be quite right, and Hawks said he would think of something. Later, over lunch one day with Betty, he said he had found a name for her. It was "Lauren," and he was going to tell everyone that it was an old family name of Betty's, even that it had been her great-grandmother's. "What invention!" commented the actress, who is in fact said to dislike the name [Lauren Bacall, *By Myself*, 1979].

Barbara **Bach:** Barbara Goldbach (1947–), U.S. movie actress.

Sebastian **Bach:** Sebastian Bierk (1968–), U.S. rock singer. A readily made tribue or at least acknowledgment to the German composer.

Il **Baciccia:** Giovanni Battista Gaulli (1639–1709), It. painter. The name probably arose as a childish pronunciation of the artist's second name. (Giovanni Battista literally means "John the Baptist.")

Backsight-Forethought: [Sir] Ernest Dunlop Swinton (1868–1951), Br. army officer, writer. Major-General Swinton used this name for his treatise on minor tactics entitled *The Defence of Duffer's Drift* (1904), subsequently recommended reading for young officers. His better-known pen name was Ole Luke-Oie (*q.v.*).

George **Bacovia:** George Vasiliu (1881–1957), Rom. Symbolist poet. The poet took his name from his birthplace, the Moldavian town of Bacau.

Angela **Baddeley:** Madeleine Angela Byam Shaw, née Clinton-Baddeley (1904–1976), Eng. stage, movie actress, sister of Hermione Baddeley (*q.v.*).

Hermione **Baddeley:** Hermione Willis, née Clinton-Baddeley (1906–1986), Eng. stage, movie actress.

George **Bagby:** Aaron Marc Stein (1906–), U.S. mystery writer.

Eduard **Bagritsky:** Eduard Georgiyevich Dzyubin (1895–1934), Russ. revolutionary poet. The poet based his name on that of the princely Bagratid dynasty of Armenia and Georgia, and so on that of one of their descendants, the Russian general and hero of the Napoleonic Wars Prince Bagration (1765–1812). He himself commented on his new name: "It smacks of war, and has something of the flavor of my writing."

Bagritsky published an early volume of poems, *Auto in Trousers* (1915), under the name Nina Voskresenskaya. His readers were certain it was written by a woman, for one poem began with the line, "I am in love with him," while another, naming an Odessa street, concluded, "So Deribasovskaya has its poetess!"

Yelisaveta **Bagryana:** Yelisaveta Belcheva (1893–1991), Bulg. lyric poet. The poet's adopted name means "crimson."

Baha-'Alla-h: [Mirza] Hoseyn Ali Nuri (1817–1892), Persian religious leader. The founder of the Baha'i faith was a follower of the Bab (*q.v.*) who at some point in the 1860s proclaimed himself "Him Whom God Shall Make Manifest," a divine spirit foretold by the Bab. Hence his Arabic name, meaning "Glory of God." The keystone of Baha'i belief is that the Bab and Baha-'Alla-h are thus manifestations of God, and that when the latter proclaimed himself, the Bab's mission was fulfilled. Mirza is a Persian title of respect, meaning literally "son of a lord."

Guy **Bailey:** [Professor] Cedric Keith Simpson (1907–1985), Eng. pathologist, forensic expert. "Guy" is a reference to Guy's Hospital, London, where Simpson was head of the department of forensic medicine; "Bailey" refers to the Old Bailey, London, the Central Criminal Court of England.

James A. **Bailey:** James Anthony McGinnes (1847–1906), U.S. impresario. This was the man who gave the second name of the famous Barnum & Bailey Circus.

Mildred **Bailey:** Mildred Rinker (1907–1951), U.S. (white) jazz singer, movie actress.

Ba Jin: Li Fei-Kan (1904–), Chin. anarchist writer. The writer formed his pseudonym from the Chinese equivalents of the first and last syllables of the names of Bakunin and Kropotkin, two Russian anarchists that he admired.

Art Baker: Arthur Shank (1898–1966), U.S. movie actor.

Belle Baker: Bella Becker (1895–1957), U.S. vaudeville singer, actress, of Jewish parentage.

Bonnie Baker: Evelyn Nelson (1918–), U.S. popular singer

Cheryl Baker: Rita Maria Crudgington (1955–), Eng. pop singer, TV presenter.

Eddie Baker: Edward King (1897–1968), U.S. movie actor.

LaVern Baker: Dolores Williams (1928–1997), U.S. black blues singer.

Bakhori: Abdumalik Rakhmanov (1927–), Tajik poet. The writer's adopted name means "of the spring," "vernal."

Leon Bakst: Lev Samoylovich Rosenberg (1866–1924), Russ. theatrical designer, scenic artist. The artist's adopted name was that of his grandfather.

George Balanchine: Georgy Melitonovich Balanchivadze (1904–1983), Russ.-born U.S. ballet dancer.

Rev. Edward Baldwin: William Godwin (1756–1836), Eng. philosopher, novelist, dramatist. The writer, husband of the moral writer Mary Wollstonecraft, mother-in-law of the poet Shelley, used this as his main pen name. Originally a Nonconformist minister, he adopted it on becoming an atheist in 1783, rejecting "God-" in favor of "Bald-." He also wrote as Theophilus Marcliffe (*q.v.*).

Neil Balfort: Robert Lionel Fanthorpe (1935–), Eng. SF writer. A name based on the author's original name, as were many of his other pseudonyms, such as Erle Barton, Thornton Bell, Phil Nobel, and Olaf Trent.

Clara Balfour: Felicia Dorothea Hemans, née Browne (1793–1835), Eng. poet.

James Balfour: William Bruce Hepburn (1925–1992), Eng. doctor, novelist.

Ina Balin: Ina Rosenberg (1937–1990), U.S. movie actress.

Marty Balin: Martyn Jerel Buchwald (1942–), U.S. rock singer.

Bobby Ball: Robert Harper (1944–), Eng. TV comedian, teaming with Tommy Cannon (*q.v.*).

Harry Ball: William Henry Powles (?–1888), Eng. music hall singer, father of Vesta Tilley (*q.v.*).

Kaye Ballard: Catherine Gloria Balotta (1926–), U.S. movie comedienne.

Balthus: [Count] Balthazar Michel Klossowski de Rola (1908–), Fr. painter, of Pol. parentage.

Juozas Baltùsis: Albertas Juozenas (1909–), Lithuanian writer. The writer adopted his name from Lithuanian *baltas*, "white."

Micah Balwidder: John Galt (1779–1839), Sc. novelist.

Honoré de Balzac: Honoré Balzac (1799–1850), Fr. novelist. Balzac's father was Bernard-François Balssa. Wishing to "improve" on the name's peasant connotations, the writer changed this to Balzac in 1821 and added the honorific particle "de," possibly in imitation of the writer Jean-Louis Guez de Balzac (1595–1654).

Afrika Bambaataa: Kevin Donovan (1960–), U.S. black soul musician, rapper. The musician's alternate original African name is Khayan Aasim.

Peter Bamm: Curt Emmrich (1897–?), Ger. writer.

D.R. Banat: Raymond Douglas Bradbury (1920–), U.S. SF writer.

Anne Bancroft: Anna Maria Luisa (or Anne-Marie Louise) Italiano (1931–), U.S. stage, movie actress. The actress was born in New York as the daughter of Italian immigrants, and even her original name came as the result of a misunderstanding. Her father, on arriving at Ellis Island, thought he was being asked his nationality and said "Italiano, Italiano." This was recorded as his name (which was what he was really being asked). The actress began her professional career on TV in 1950 as Anne Marno. She first appeared as Anne Bancroft in her film debut in *Don't Bother to Knock* (1952), taking the name from a list submitted to her by producer Darryl Zanuck.

[Sir] Squire Bancroft: Sydney Bancroft Butterfield (1841–1926), Eng. stage actor, theatrical manager. The actor assumed his new name in 1867.

Albert Band: Alfredo Antonini (1924–), It.-born movie director, producer, working in U.S.

Billy Bang: William Walker (1947–), U.S. black jazz musician.

Darrell Banks: Darrell Eubanks (1938–1970), U.S. pop musician.

Monty Banks: Mario Bianchi (1897–1950), It. movie actor, director. Mario Bianchi not only anglicized his name but did it in such a way as to suggest "mountebank," the term for a charlatan.

Vilma **Banky:** Vilma Lonchit (or Konsics) (1898–1991), Austr.-Hung. movie actress.

Angela **Banner:** Angela Mary Maddison (1923–), Br. children's writer. The writer's name appears to match the popular insect characters Ant and Bee that first featured in her stories for young children in 1963.

Margaret **Bannerman:** Margaret Le Grand (1896– ?), Can. stage actress.

R.C. **Bannon:** Daniel Shipley (1945–), U.S. country musician. The musician adopted his new name in 1968 as a DJ in Seattle, basing it on the commercial product RC Cola.

Anna **Banti:** Lucia Longhi Lopresti (1895–1985), It. novelist, short story writer.

Banx: Jeremy Banks (1959–), Eng. cartoonist.

Bao Dai: Nguyen Vinh Thuy (1913–), Vietnamese emperor. The last reigning emperor of Vietnam succeeded to the throne in 1926 and assumed a name (or title) meaning "keeper of greatness."

R. Hernekin **Baptist:** Ethelreda Lewis (1875–1946), Eng.-born S.A. novelist. The writer used this name for four novels published in the 1930s.

Baptiste: (1) Nicolas Anselme (1761–1835), Fr. sentimental comedy actor; (2) Jean-Gaspard Deburau (1796–1846), Fr. pierrot.

Theda **Bara:** Theodosia Goodman (1890–1955), U.S. stage, movie actress. For publicity purposes, as the first "vamp," Goodman claimed to be the love child of a French artist and his Egyptian mistress, with a name alleged to be an approximate reversal of "Arab death." (It could equally have been an anagram of "Hated Arab.") But Theda clearly relates to her original first name, Theodosia. In a 1908 stage appearance she was billed as Theodosia de Coppet.

Amiri **Baraka:** Everett LeRoy (later LeRoi) Jones (1934–), U.S. black playwright, poet, novelist. The writer changed his name in 1968 on converting to Islam, usually prefixing it with the title Imamu ("spiritual leader"). Amiri means "prince," "ruler," and Baraka "shining," "lustrous."

Barbara: Monique Serf (1930–), Fr. singer, songwriter.

Johannes **Barbarus:** Johannes Varesh (1890–1946), Estonian poet. The writer's name arose in his school days, when he distributed a hectographed magazine in Russian, Estonian, and Latvian. It included his first poems and articles. He could not put his name to them, however, for that would have risked expulsion. He recalled: "I

needed a pen name. One of the teachers called me a barbarian because I was once late for a lesson. I translated the word into Latin, and that gave my pseudonym, which I have used all my life" [Dmitriyev, p. 96].

W.N.P. **Barbellion:** Bruce Frederick Cummings (1889–1919), Eng. essayist, diarist, naturalist. The writer adopted this name, taken from the front of a confectioner's shop in Bond Street, London, when he published entries from his diary in book form under the title *The Journal of a Disappointed Man* (1919). He claimed that the initials stood for "Wilhelm Nero Pilate," all men of bravado.

Antonia **Barber:** Barbara Anthony, née Wilson (*c.*1935–), Br. children's writer.

Glynis **Barber:** Glynis van der Riet (1955–), S.A.-born TV, movie actress, wife of Michael Brandon (*q.v.*).

Barbette: Van der Clyde Broodway (1899–1972), U.S. music hall female impersonator. The artist made his debut in the circus dressed as one of the Alfaretta Sisters, but subsequently developed his own individual act as an aerialist (trapeze artist) named Barbette.

Ion **Barbu:** Dan Barbilian (1895–1964), Rom. lyric poet, mathematician.

David **Barclay:** David Poole Fronabarger (1912–1969), U.S. stage actor.

Gabriel **Barclay:** Manly Wade Wellman (1903–), U.S. SF, fantasy, mystery writer.

Roy **Barcroft:** Howard H. Ravenscroft (1901–1969), U.S. movie actor.

Countess Hélène **Barcynska:** Marguerite Florence Helene Barclay, later Evans, née Jervis (1894–1964), Br. popular fiction writer. The author assumed a fictional identity to match her books, claiming her first husband, Armiger Barclay, was the son of a Polish count called Barcynsky.

The **Bard:** Edward Jerringham (1727–1812), Eng. poet, dramatist of the Della Cruscan school.

Samuel A. **Bard:** Ephraim George Squier (1821–1888), U.S. archaeologist, traveler, author.

Wilkie **Bard:** William Augustus Smith (1870–1944), Eng. music hall comedian. The actor had a high, domed forehead, like that of Shakespeare. Hence his nickname and subsequent stage name, which was originally Will Gibbard when he made his debut in 1895.

Y **Bardd Cloff:** Thomas Jones (1768–1828), Welsh poet. The poet's name means "the lame poet," referring to an accident he had as a child.

Y **Bardd Coch o Fôn:** Hugh Hughes (1693–1776), Welsh poet. The poet's name means "the red poet of the bottom."

Y **Bardd Cocos:** John Evans (1827–1888), Welsh poetaster. The rhymester earned a living by selling cockles. Hence the name by which he became known, meaning "the cockles poet."

Y **Bardd Crwst:** Abel Jones (1829–1901), Welsh balladist. The singer's name means literally "the crust poet," implying one who earns his daily bread by his street performances.

Bardd Gwagedd: Richard Williams (*c.*1805–*c.*1865), Welsh balladist. The singer's name means literally "vanity poet," alluding to his reputation as "the king of all the ballad-singers" in southern Wales.

Bardd Nantglyn: Robert Davies (1769–1835), Welsh poet. The poet took his name from his birthplace, Nantglyn near Denbigh (now in Clwyd).

Bardd y Brenin: Edward Jones (1752–1824), Welsh musician, writer. The writer was appointed bard (court poet) to the Prince of Wales. Hence his bardic Welsh name or title, meaning "King's Poet." The appointment was an honorary one.

Bardd yr Haf: Robert Williams Parry (1884–1956), Welsh poet. The poet won the chair at the 1910 National Eisteddfod with his poem *Yr Haf*, "The Summer," and so came to be known as "the poet of summer."

John **Bardon:** John M. Jones (1939–), Eng. movie, TV actor.

Brigitte **Bardot:** Camille Javal (1934–), Fr. movie actress. The actress's real name (if that is what it is) is consistently quoted in all his editions by Halliwell (see Bibliography), although biographies of the actress do not mention it. A genuine pseudonym used by Brigitte Bardot, however, was "BB" (*q.v.*).

Lynn **Bari:** Marjorie Schuyler Fisher (1913–1989), U.S. movie actress. The actress once explained that she created her new name by combining the names of the actress Lynn Fontanne and the dramatist James Barrie.

Norah **Baring:** Norah Baker (1907–), Br. movie actress.

Viktor **Barna:** Gyözö Viktor Braun (1911–1972), Hung.-born Eng. table tennis player. The sportsman changed his name to avoid anti-semitism in the years before World War II. After the war he became a British citizen.

A.M. **Barnard:** Louisa May Alcott (1832–1888), U.S. novelist, short story writer.

Barney **Barnato:** Barnett Isaacs (1852–1897), Eng. financier, diamond magnate. The speculator adopted the name of the Barnato Brothers, which he and his brother had used in London as vaudeville entertainers.

Louis **Barnaval:** Charles De Kay (1848–1935), U.S. editor, writer.

Binnie **Barnes:** Gitelle Gertrude Maude Barnes (1905–1983), Eng. movie actress.

L. David **Barnett:** Barnett D. Laschever (1924–), U.S. journalist, writer.

Baron: (1) Michel Boyron (1652–1729), Fr. actor, playwright; (2) Baron de V. Nahum (1906–1956), Eng. photographer.

Jacques **Baroncelli:** Jacques Baroncelli-Javon (1881–1951), Fr. movie director.

Ida **Barr:** Maud Barlow (1882–1967), Eng. music hall comedienne.

Richard **Barr:** Richard Baer (1917–1989), U.S. theatre director, producer.

Ray **Barra:** Raymond Martin Barallobre (1930–), U.S. ballet dancer.

Edith **Barrett:** Edith Williams (1906–1977), U.S. stage, movie actress. The actress adopted her mother's maiden name as her stage name.

Judith **Barrett:** Lucille Kelly (1914–), U.S. movie actress.

Rona **Barrett:** Rona Burnstein (1934–), U.S. gossip columnist.

Odoardo **Barri:** Edward Slater (1884–1920), Br. popular composer.

Amanda **Barrie:** Shirley Ann Broadbent (1939–), Eng. stage, movie, TV actress.

Barbara **Barrie:** Barbara Ann Berman (1931–), U.S. movie actress.

J.J. **Barrie:** Barry Authors (1933–), Can. pop musician.

Mona **Barrie:** Mona Smith (1909–1964), Austral. movie actress, working in U.S.

Scott **Barrie:** Nelson Clyde Barr (1941–1993), U.S. black fashion designer.

Wendy **Barrie:** Marguerite Wendy Jenkins (1912–1978), Br. movie actress. Marguerite Jenkins was the goddaughter of the writer J.M. Barrie, author of *Peter Pan* and she took her surname from him. She was already named Wendy, after the heroine of the play, Wendy Darling.

E. **Barrington:** Eliza Louisa Moresby Beck (?–1931), Br. romantic, historical novelist. The name repeats the initials of the writer's first and last names. She also wrote as Lily Adams Beck and Louis Moresby (*qq.v.*).

George **Barrington**: George Waldron (1755–1804), Ir. writer, adventurer. Waldron ran away from school at the age of 16 and joined a group of strolling players, changing his name to Barrington. He subsequently turned to crime, and as a persistent pickpocket was deported in 1790 to Botany Bay, Australia, where he reformed and wrote interesting accounts of his experiences. A popular verse was current following his conviction:

Two namesakes of late, in a different way,
With spirit and zeal did bestir 'em;
The one was transported to Botany Bay,
The other translated to Durham.

The namesake was Dr. Shute Barrington, bishop of Durham, son of John Shute Barrington (see below).

John Shute **Barrington**: John Shute (1678–1734), Eng. politician. In 1710 the future Viscount Barrington inherited the estate of Francis Barrington, husband of his first cousin, and according to the terms of the will adopted the name and arms of the bequeather.

Rutland **Barrington**: George Barrington Rutland Fleet (1853–1922), Eng. actor, singer.

Desmond **Barrit**: Desmond Brown (1944–), Br. stage, movie actor.

Blue **Barron**: Harry Friedland (1911–), U.S. trombonist, bandleader.

Chris **Barron**: Christopher Barron Gross (1968–), U.S. rock musician.

Charles **Barry**: Charles Bryson (1887–1963), Eng. detective novelist.

Christine **Barry**: Grace Underwood (1911–1964), Br. stage actress.

David **Barry**: Meurig Wyn Jones (1943–), Welsh-born Br. TV actor.

Don "Red" **Barry**: Donald Barry de Acosta (1912–1980), U.S. movie actor.

Gene **Barry**: Eugene Klass (1921–), U.S. movie, TV actor.

Jack **Barry**: Jack Barasch (1918–1984), U.S. TV personality, producer.

Joan **Barry**: Joan Tiarks, née Bell (1901–1989), Eng. stage, movie actress, society hostess.

John **Barry**: John Barry Prendergast (1933–), Eng. rock musician.

Len **Barry**: Leonard Borisoff (1942–), U.S. pop singer, film music composer.

Michael **Barry**: James Barry Jackson (1910–), Eng. musician, writer.

Diana **Barrymore**: Diana Blanche Barrymore Blythe (1921–1960), U.S. movie actress, daughter of John Barrymore (see below).

Ethel **Barrymore**: Ethel Mae Blythe (1879–1959), U.S. stage, movie actress. Both Ethel Blythe and her brothers John and Lionel Blythe (see below) adopted the name of their father, Maurice Barrymore (*q.v.*).

John **Barrymore**: John Sidney Blythe (1882–1942), U.S. stage, movie actor.

Lionel **Barrymore**: Lionel Blythe (1878–1954), U.S. stage, movie actor.

Maurice **Barrymore**: Herbert Blythe (1846–1905), Eng. actor, father of Ethel, John, and Lionel Barrymore (see above). Maurice Barrymore adopted his stage name from an old playbill hanging in the Haymarket Theatre, London. It was in turn adopted by his three children, who made their name on the American stage, where Maurice himself had gone in 1875.

Michael **Barrymore**: Michael Keiron Parker (1952–), Eng. TV entertainer. The entertainer was obliged to find another name since there was already a Michael Parker in show business. His agent renamed him after the U.S. actor Lionel Barrymore (see above).

Louis **Barsac**: Ernest James Oldmeadow (1867–1949), Br. journalist, writer.

Jean **Bart**: Eugen Botez (1874–1933), Rom. writer. Many of the writer's works have the sea as their setting. Hence his pen name, that of the French naval commander Jean Bart (1650–1702).

Lionel **Bart**: Lionel Begleiter (1930–), Br. lyricist, composer. The musician is said to have adopted his professional name from Bart's, the popular name of St. Bartholomew's Hospital, London, although it echoes his original name. Oddly enough, his real surname is German for "musical accompanist."

Freddie **Bartholomew**: Frederick Llewellyn (1924–1992), Br. child movie actor, working in U.S. The young actor was raised by an aunt, Millicent Bartholomew, and adopted her name.

Bartimeus: Lewis Anselmo da Costa Ricci (1886–1967), Br. author of naval stories. The best-known Bartimeus is the blind beggar healed by Jesus in the Bible story. Maybe the author intended this reference?

Sy **Bartlett**: Sacha Baraniev (1909–1978), Russ.-born U.S. screenwriter, movie producer. The writer's full adopted name was Sydney S. Bartlett.

Eva **Bartok:** Eva Martha Szöke (1926–), Hung. movie actress.

Fra **Bartolommeo:** Bartolommeo di Pagolo del Fattorino (or Baccio della Porta) (1472–1517), It. painter.

Buzz **Barton:** William Lamarr (1914–1980), U.S. juvenile movie actor.

Ganna (Hanna) **Barvinok:** Aleksandra Mikhaylovna Belozerskaya-Kulish (1828–1911), Ukrainian writer. Russian *barvinok* is the periwinkle (the flowering plant *Vinca minor* or *Vinca herbacea*).

Basho: Matsuo Munefusa (1644–1694), Jap. haiku poet. The poet's pen name is the Japanese word for the banana tree, alluding to the simple hut by such a tree where he liked to retreat from society.

Basia: Basia Trzetrzelewska (1959–), Pol.-born U.S. rock singer.

Count **Basie:** William Basie (1904–1984), U.S. black jazz musician. During a broadcast from the Reno Club, Kansas City, the announcer of an experimental radio program introduced Basie as the "Count," and he adopted the nickname. Duke Ellington (*q.v.*) had a similar "titular" name.

Colonel W. de **Basil:** Vasily Grigoryevich Voskresensky (1881–1951), Russ. impresario. "Vasily" is the Russian equivalent of "Basil."

Ivan **Baskoff:** Henri Meilhac (1832–1897), Fr. dramatist, author.

Lina **Basquette:** Lena Baskette (1907–1994), U.S. movie actress. The actress adopted the modified form of her name in 1927.

Jacopo **Bassano:** Jacopo da Ponte (*c.*1510–1592), It. painter. The painter took his name from his birth town of Bassano, northern Italy. His family adopted the name in turn.

Hogan Kid **Bassey:** Okon Bassey Asuquo (1932–), Nigerian boxer.

Florence **Bates:** Florence Rabe (1888–1954), U.S. movie actress. The actress took her stage name from the character of Miss Bates that she played in a stage adaptation (1935) of Jane Austen's novel *Emma*.

Batt: Oswald Barrett (?–?), Br. cartoonist.

Battling Siki: Louis Phal (1897–1925), Senegalese boxer, working in U.S.

Nikolay **Baturin:** Nikolay Nikolayevich Zamyatin (1877–1927), Russ. Communist activist, historian.

Steven **Bauer:** Steven Echevarria (1956–), Cuban-born U.S. movie actor.

Beryl **Baxter:** Beryl Gross, née Ivory (1926–), Br. stage, movie actress.

Jane **Baxter:** Feodora Kathleen Alice Forde (1909–1996), Br. stage, movie actress. The playwright James Barrie advised the actress early in her career that Feodora Forde was not a good stage name. She therefore chose a new name, taking it from a character in Booth Tarkington's novel *Seventeen* (1916).

Keith **Baxter:** Keith Stanley Baxter-Wright (1933–), Welsh stage actor.

Nora **Bayes:** Dora Goldberg (1880–1928), U.S. vaudeville, musical comedy actress.

William **Baylebridge:** Charles William Blocksidge (1883–1942), Austral. poet, short story writer. The writer adopted his pen name from about 1925. It is uncertain to what extent the new surname is a meaningful alteration of the original.

Beverly **Bayne:** Pearl von Name (1894–1982), U.S. movie actress.

Vladimir **Bazarov:** Vladimir Aleksandrovich Rudnev (1874–1939), Russ. philosopher, economist. The socialist philosopher appears to have adopted the name of Bazarov, the nihilist hero of Turgenev's novel *Fathers and Sons* (1862).

Hervé **Bazin:** Jean-Pierre-Marie Hervé-Bazin (1911–1996), Fr. poet, novelist, short story writer.

B.B. (1) Lewis Carroll (*q.v.*); (2) Denys James Watkins-Pitchford (1905–1990), Eng. writer of books about the countryside; (3) Brigitte Bardot (*q.v.*). (2) and (3) here normally used the name in the form "BB." Denys Watkins-Pitchford chose the initialism for *The Sportsman's Bedside Book* (1937), and derived it from the designation of the particular size of lead shot he used for shooting wild geese, BB being 0.18 inches in diameter. Brigitte Bardot's own initials are of course B.B., and "BB" was first used in print for her appearance as a cover girl on the French magazine *Elle* in 1948. The initials have added point when it is remembered that in French they are pronounced the same as *bébé*, "baby." Bardot was still a teenager at the time.

Beachcomber: (1) Dominic Bevan Wyndham Lewis (1891–1969), Br. humorous columnist; (2) John Cameron Andrieu Bingham Michael Morton (1893–1979), Br. humorous columnist. The name was passed down by (1) to (2) in 1924, when Morton succeeded Lewis as columnist on the *Daily Express*. The reference is to the essential "gleaning" activity of a beachcomber. The columnists looked for interesting news items, just as a beachcomber searches the shore for valuables. (Lewis's original first name was actually Llewelyn, but he dropped this in favor of Dominic on entering the Roman Catholic Church in 1921.)

John **Beal:** James Alexander Bliedung (1909–), U.S. stage, movie actor.

Orson **Bean:** Dallas Frederick Burroughs (1928–), U.S. stage actor, comedian. Burroughs began his stage career as a magician, and chose this randomly bizarre name for his work.

Allyce **Beasley:** Allyce Schiavelli, formerly Sansocie, née Tannenberg (1954–), U.S. movie, TV actress.

Beatrice: Anne Manning (1807–1879), Eng. novelist, miscellaneous writer.

Warren **Beatty:** Henry Warren Beaty (1937–), U.S. movie actor. Beaty made a minor adjustment to his real name by doubling a letter for his screen name. His sister, Shirley Maclaine (*q.v.*), made a similar modification.

Philip **Beauchamp:** George Grote (1794–1871), Eng. historian.

Beauchâteau: François Chastelet (*fl.*1625–1665), Fr. actor.

Douglas **Beaufort:** Douglas Broad (1864–1939), Eng. magician.

Balthasar de **Beaujoyeux:** Baldassare di Belgiojoso (? –1587), It. violinist, composer. A name that is part rendered, part translated, from Italian to French.

Pierre-Augustin Caron de **Beaumarchais:** Pierre-Augustin Caron (1732–1799), Fr. dramatist. Beaumarchais took his writing name from that of a small property owned by his first wife. There are several villages of the name (meaning "beautiful marsh") to be found in the north of France.

Mlle **Beauménard** *see* Madame **Bellecour.**

André **Beaumont:** Jean Conneau (1880–1937), Fr. aviator.

Charles **Beaumont:** Charles Nutt (1929–1967), U.S. SF writer.

Susan **Beaumont:** Susan Black (1936–), Br. movie actress.

Beauval: Jean Pitel (*c.*1635–1709), Fr. actor.

Roger de **Beauvoir:** Edouard Roger de Bully (1809–1866), Fr. novelist.

Gilbert **Bécaud:** François Silly (1927–), Fr. popular singer, songwriter.

Christopher **Beck:** Thomas Charles Bridges (1868–1944), Eng. writer of stories for boys.

Lily Adams **Beck:** Eliza Louisa Moresby Beck (? –1931), Eng. novelist, working in Canada.

The writer used this name for several books about oriental culture. She also used the names E. Barrington and Louis Moresby (*qq.v.*).

Gustavo Adolfo **Bécquer:** Gustavo Adolfo Domínguez Bastida (1836–1870), Sp. poet. The poet adopted his father's middle name as his new surname.

Cuthbert **Bede:** [Rev.] Edward Bradley (1827–1889), Br. humorist. The author of *The Adventures of Mr. Verdant Green* (1853) attended the University of Durham, and took his name from the two patron saints of that city, St. Cuthbert and the Venerable Bede.

Bonnie **Bedelia:** Bonnie Culkin (1948–), U.S. movie actress, singer, dancer.

Donald **Bedford:** Henry James O'Brien Bedford-Jones (1887–1949), Can.-born U.S. writer of historical adventures.

Demyan **Bedny:** Yefim Alekseyevich Pridvorov (1883–1945), Russ. Socialist poet. Pridvorov's pen name derives from Russian *bedny*, "poor," reflecting the conditions of the peasants and working classes before the 1917 Revolution. Compare the name of Maxim Gorky (*q.v.*). It was originally a nickname. He had brought a poem entitled "Demyan Bedny, the Harmful Peasant" to his editors, and when he next visited the office they exclaimed "It's Demyan Bedny!" Demyan (English Damian) was actually the first name of his uncle, who was a peasant. The poet would also have certainly wished to avoid the aristocratic associations of his real surname, Pridvorov, which suggests *pridvorny*, "of the court."

Widow **Bedott:** Frances Miriam Whitcher (1814–1852), U.S. humorous writer.

Jon (or George) **Bee:** John Badcock (*fl.*1816–1830), Br. sporting writer. The writer also used the name John Hinds.

Janet **Beecher:** Janet Beecher Meysenburg (1884–1955), U.S. movie actress, of Ger.-U.S. parentage.

Francis **Beeding:** John Leslie Palmer (1885–1944), Br. thriller writer + Hilary Aidan St. George Saunders (1898–1951), Br. thriller writer. A single name for a two-man writing partnership. Palmer had always liked the name Francis; Saunders had once owned a house in the Sussex village of Beeding.

Captain **Beefheart:** Don Van Vliet (1941–), U.S. pop singer. When he was 13, Van Vliet moved with his family from Los Angeles to Lancaster, California, where Frank Zappa, then his classmate at Antelope Valley High School, nicknamed him "Captain Beefheart" because he appeared to have a "beef in his heart" against the world.

Beggarstaff Brothers: [Sir] William Newzam Prior Nicholson (1872–1949), Eng. poster artist + James Pryde (1866–1941), Eng. poster artist, his brother-in-law.

Maurice **Béjart:** Maurice-Jean de Berger (1928–), Fr. ballet dancer, opera director.

Belcampo: Herman P. Schönfeld Wichers (1902–), Du. writer. The writer, a doctor by profession, took for his pen name an Italian-style translation of his third name (Schönfeld), literally "beautiful field."

Belita: Gladys Lyne Jepson-Turner (1924–), Br. ice skater, dancer, movie actress.

Ivan Petrovich **Belkin:** Aleksandr Sergeyevich Pushkin (1799–1837), Russ. poet, dramatist. Pushkin used the name for the supposed narrator of his own *Tales of the Late Ivan Petrovich Belkin* (1831). He did not use the name for any other work.

Acton **Bell:** Ann Brontë (1820–1849), Eng. novelist, poet, sister of Charlotte Brontë (Currer Bell) (see below).

Carey **Bell:** Carey Bell Harrington (1936–), U.S. blues harmonica player.

Currer **Bell:** Charlotte Brontë (1816–1855), Eng. novelist, sister of Acton Bell (above) and Ellis Bell (below). When the three sisters first published some poems in 1846, they named themselves as "Currer, Ellis, and Acton Bell," leading many people to think that the authors were three brothers, and therefore writing to them as men. Charlotte Brontë later gave the following account of the assumption of these names: "Averse to personal publicity, we veiled our own names under those of Currer, Ellis, and Acton Bell; the ambiguous choice being dictated by a sort of conscientious scruple at assuming Christian names positively masculine, while we did not declare ourselves women, because—without at that time suspecting that our mode of writing and thinking was not what is called 'feminine'—we had a vague impression that authoresses are liable to be looked on with prejudice" [Charlotte Brontë, "Biographical Notice of Ellis & Acton Bell," 1850]. Charlotte Brontë's *Jane Eyre* (1847) was originally published by Currer Bell, and that same year Emily Brontë's *Wuthering Heights* also appeared, with the author given as Ellis Bell. Their guise was soon penetrated, however, and when Charlotte Brontë received a letter from her contemporary, Harriet Martineau, it began "Dear Madam," although "Currer Bell, Esq." appeared on the envelope.

The choice of the respective first names and surname has been a matter of much speculation. Charlotte Brontë is said to have chosen the name Bell because it was the middle name of Arthur Bell Nicholls, her future husband. Currer is a Yorkshire surname and was familiar to the Brontës as that of a local benefactor, Frances Richardson Currer. Ellis is also a Yorkshire name, and was that of a local family of mill owners. Acton was a name Anne Brontë would have known from her time as governess to a family at Thorp Green, near York. All three names preserved their bearers' original initials [Juliet Barker, *The Brontës*, 1994].

Ellis **Bell:** Emily Brontë (1818–1848), Eng. novelist, sister of Charlotte Brontë (Currer Bell) (see above).

Josephine **Bell:** Doris Bell Ball, née Collier (1897–1987), Eng. detective novelist, doctor.

Marie **Bell:** Marie-Jeanne Bellon-Downey (1900–1985), Fr. stage, movie actress, theatre manager.

Neil **Bell:** Stephen H. Critten (1887–1964), Eng. novelist, short story writer.

Paul **Bell:** Henry Fothergill Chorley (1808–1872), Eng. journalist, novelist, music critic.

Rex **Bell:** George Francis Beldam (1905–1962), U.S. movie actor.

William **Bell:** William Yarborough (1937–), U.S. soul singer.

George **Bellairs:** Harold Blundell (1902–), Eng. mystery novelist.

Madge **Bellamy:** Margaret Philpott (1903–1990), U.S. movie actress.

Bellecour: Jean-Claude-Gilles Colson (1725–1778), Fr. playwright, comic actor, husband of Madame Bellecour (see next entry below).

Madame **Bellecour:** Rose-Perrine le Roy de la Corbinaye (1730–1799), Fr. actress. The actress left home when she was 13 and took up with an itinerant comic actor called Beaumènard. She adopted his name and calling and thus became known as Mlle Beaumènard. Later she married the actor Bellecour (see entry above), and became known by his name as Madame Bellecour.

Belleroche: Raymond Poisson (*c.*1630–1690), Fr. actor.

Bellerose: Pierre Le Messier (*c.*1592–1670), Fr. actor.

Belleville: Henri Legrand (*c.*1587–1637), Fr. actor. This was the name Legrand assumed for his tragic roles. For his comic parts he used the name Turlupin (*q.v.*).

Dormont de **Belloy:** Pierre-Laurent Buirette (1727–1775), Fr. dramatist.

Louie **Bellson:** Louis Paul Balassoni (1924–), U.S. jazz drummer, bandleader.

Bessie **Bellwood:** Elizabeth Ann Katherine Mahony (1847–1896), Ir. music hall artiste.

Albert **Bels:** Janis Cirulis (1938–), Latvian writer.

Vizma **Belševica:** Vizma Elsberga (1931–), Latvian poet.

N. **Beltov:** Georgy Valentinovich Plekhanov (1856–1918), Russ. Marxist revolutionary. Plekhanov adopted the name of the central character of Herzen's novel *Who Is to Blame?* (1841–46). He also wrote as Volgin (see **Lenin**).

Andrey **Bely:** Boris Nikolayevich Bugayev (1880–1934), Russ. symbolist poet, writer, critic. When Bugayev wished to publish some poetry as a student, in 1901, his father objected. The pseudonym Andry Bely was thus proposed for him by his editor, M.S. Solovyov, who devised it simply for its euphony, even though Russian *bely* means "white." Bugayev had initially preferred the name "Boris Burevoy" ("Boris Boisterous"). But Solovyov said that people would only pun on the name, seeing it as *Bori voy*, "Borya's howl." So Andrey Bely it was.

Benauly: Benjamin Vaughan Abbott (1830–1890), U.S. author + Austin Abbott (1831–1896), U.S. author, + [Rev.] Lyman Abbott (1835–1922), U.S. author, his brother. The composite name consists of the first syllables of each of the three brothers' forenames, in strict order of seniority.

Bendigo: William Thompson (1811–1880), Br. boxer, prizefighter. The name is a corruption of "Abednego," one of the three "certain Jews" (Shadrach, Meshach and Abednego) who were ordered, according to the Bible story, to be cast into King Nebuchadnezzar's burning fiery furnace for not serving his gods or worshipping his golden image. But why Abednego? "According to one account, he was one of triplets, whom a jocular friend of the family nicknamed Shadrach, Meschach, and Abed-Nego, the last of which was the future celebrity. ... The rival theory is that, when he was playing in the streets and his father appeared in the offing, his companions used to warn him by crying 'Bendy go!' This theory disregards the assertion ... that the great man was never called Bendy" [Ernest Weekley, *The Romance of Words*, 1922].

The boxer's own ring name was given in turn to the Australian mining town of Bendigo, which was developed in the gold rush of 1851 by an admirer of his who had adopted his name to boost his own reputation as a boxer.

Benedict VIII: Theophylactus (or Teofilatto) (*c.*980–1024), It. pope.

Benedict IX: Theophylactus (or Teofilatto) (?–*c.*1055), It. pope. The pontiff adopted the name of his uncle, Benedict VIII (see above), whose original name he also shared.

Benedict XI: Niccolò Boccasini (1240–1304), It. pope. The pontiff assumed the original name, Benedict (Benedetto), of his predecessor, Boniface VIII (*q.v.*).

Benedict XII: Jacques Fournier (*c.*1280–1342), Fr. pope.

Benedict XIII: Pietro Francesco Vincenzo Maria Orsini (1649–1730), It. pope.

Benedict XIV: Prospero Lorenzo Lambertini (1675–1758), It. pope.

Benedict XV: Giacomo della Chiesa (1854–1922), It. pope.

Dirk **Benedict:** Dirk Niewoehner (1944–), U.S. TV actor.

Richard **Benedict:** Riccardo Benedetto (1916–1984), U.S. movie actor.

David **Ben-Gurion:** David Gruen (1886–1973), Pol.-born Israeli prime minister. David Gruen adopted the ancient Hebrew name of Ben-Gurion when working as a farmer in northern Palestine, where he came in 1906. The name means "son of a lion" (or "son of strength"), and assimilates well to his former surname, which means "green." The specific reference is to Joseph Ben-Gurion, head of the Jewish state in ancient Palestine at the time of the revolt of the Jews against the Romans. Itzhak Ben-Zvi (*q.v.*) emigrated to Palestine in 1907, soon after Ben-Gurion. Compare the name of Micah Bin Gorion (below).

Georgi **Benkowsky:** Gavril Khlytev (*c.*1841–1876), Bulg. revolutionary.

Bruce **Bennett:** Herman Brix (1909–), U.S. movie actor.

Compton **Bennett:** Robert Compton-Bennett (1900–1974), Eng. movie director.

Harve **Bennett:** Harvey Fischman (1930–), U.S. TV series producer.

Lennie **Bennett:** Michael Berry (1938–), Eng. stage, TV entertainer.

Michael **Bennett:** Michael Bennett DiFiglia (1943–1987), U.S. ballet dancer, choreographer.

Tony **Bennett:** Anthony Dominick Benedetto (1926–), U.S. popular singer, of It. parentage. When the singer began his career at age 19 in New York night clubs, he called himself Joe Bari, after his father's hometown in Italy. One night in 1949, Bob Hope (*q.v.*) came into the club and engaged Bennett to join his touring show. "There was one condition. 'Joe Bari' should change his name to something a little classier. 'Let's call you Tony Bennett,' Hope proposed. Newly reincarnated, Bennett soon got ... a recording contract with Columbia Records" [*The Times Magazine*, December 14, 1996].

Jack **Benny:** Benjamin Kubelsky (1894–1974), U.S. stage, radio, TV comedian. When Benjamin Kubelsky began his career (1918) he called himself Ben Benny. But this was too close to the name of Ben Bernie, bandleader and comedian. He therefore changed again to Jack Benny. When he first saw the name in lights he said, "I got the strangest feelings...as if this wasn't me and I was an impostor and someday the audience would find me out" [Irving A. Fein, *Jack Benny: An Intimate Biography*, 1976].

Beno: Nikolay Konstantinovich Sheskin (?–1942), Russ. circus artist, acrobat.

Alain de **Benoist:** Fabrice Laroche (1943–), Fr. journalist, essayist.

Henry **Benrath:** Albert Henry Rausch (1882–1949), Ger. lyric poet, novelist.

Carl **Benson:** Charles Astor Bristed (1820–1874), U.S. author.

Robby **Benson:** Robert Segal (1956–), U.S. juvenile movie actor.

Brook **Benton:** Benjamin Franklin Peay (1931–1988), U.S. black popular singer.

Itzhak **Ben-Zvi:** Isaac Shimshelevich (1884–1963), Ukr.-born Israeli president. Israel's second president emigrated to Palestine in 1907, soon after David Ben-Gurion (*q.v.*), with whom he became closely associated. His adopted name means "son of a deer."

André **Beranger:** George André de Berganger (1895–1973), Austral. stage, movie actor.

Jane **Berbié:** Jeanne Marie-Louise Bergougne (1934–), Fr. opera singer.

Bernard **Berenson:** Bernhard Valvrojenski (1865–1959), Lithuanian-born U.S. art historian, working in Italy. The name Berenson simply means "son of Bernard."

Jack **Beresford:** Jack Beresford Wiszniewski (1899–1977), Br. rower, of Pol. origin.

Gertrude **Berg:** Gertrude Edelstein (1899–1966), U.S. TV, radio, movie actress.

Teresa **Berganza:** Teresa Vargas (1935–), Sp. opera singer. Spanish *varga* means "hill," and doubtless the singer chose a name that interpreted this in a more recognizable form (through German *Berg* and related words).

Polly **Bergen:** Nellie Paulina Burgin (1930–), U.S. stage, radio, TV singer, movie actress.

Veritas Leo **Bergen:** Irma von Troll-Vorostyani (1847–1912), Austr. writer, feminist.

Helmut **Berger:** Helmut Steinberger (1944–), Austr. movie actor.

Ludwig **Berger:** Ludwig Bamberger (1892–1969), Ger. movie director.

Elisabeth **Bergner:** Elisabeth Ettel (1897–1986). Pol.-born Br. movie actress, working in U.S.

Ballard **Berkeley:** Ballard Blascheck (1904–1988), Eng. stage, movie, TV actor.

Busby **Berkeley:** William Berkeley Enos (1895–1976), U.S. director of movie musicals. Berkeley adopted his new first name from the actress Amy Busby.

Milton **Berle:** Mendel Berlinger (1908–), U.S. TV, stage, movie comedian.

Irving **Berlin:** Israel Baline (1888–1989), Russ.-born U.S. composer, popular song writer. Israel Baline, the son of a penniless itinerant synagogue cantor, published his first sheet music in 1907, and the printer misprinted his surname as "Berlin." The composer kept it that way, and altered Israel to Irving.

Paul **Bern:** Paul Levy (1889–1932), U.S. movie director.

Pierre **Bernac:** Pierre Bertin (1899–1979), Fr. concert singer.

[St.] **Bernadette:** Marie-Bernarde Soubirous (1844–1879), Fr. peasant girl, visionary. The saint's name derives from one half of her own Christian name, with *-ette* a diminutive suffix. The other half would have given "St. Mary," which would have been unacceptable.

Jeffrey **Bernard:** Jerry Joseph Bernard (1932–1997), Eng. journalist. The columnist, famous for his bohemian lifestyle, begged his mother to change his first name at the age of eight. He recounts: "I got teased a lot at school in the war ... because Jerries were Germans—and chamberpots were jerries. ...My mother said, 'Well, we'll call you something else beginning with J,' and she chose Jeffrey" [Graham Lord, *Just the One: The Wives and Times of Jeffrey Bernard*, 1992]. Bernard's mother was the opera singer Fedora Roselli (*q.v.*), and his family name was originally West. It was changed to Bernard, after a French aunt, by Jeffrey's paternal grandfather, Charles West, a music hall impresario.

Sam **Bernard:** Samuel Barnett (1863–1927), Eng.-born U.S. vaudeville comedian.

Bernard-Lazare: Lazare Bernard (1865–1902), Fr. polemicist, antisemitist.

Bernardo: Boris Mikhaylovich Mukhnitsky (? –1918), Russ. circus artist, clown.

Carl **Bernhard:** Andrea Nicolai de Saint-Aubin (1798–1865), Dan. novelist, chronicler.

Göran **Bernhard:** Göran Streijflert (1932–), Dan. child movie actor.

Sarah **Bernhardt:** Henriette-Rosine Bernard (1844–1923), Fr. tragic actress. The actress was born as the illegitimate daughter of Judith Van Hard, a Dutch courtesan who had settled in Paris, and Edouard Bernard, a law student. Her Germanic-looking surname was devised to reflect the names of both.

Ben **Bernie:** Benjamin Woodruff Anzelevitz (1891–1943), U.S. bandleader.

L'Abbé **Bernier:** Paul-Henri Thiry, baron d'Holbach (1723–1789), Fr. materialist, atheist writer. The philosopher and encyclopedist used the name cynically for his *Théologie portative, ou Dictionnaire abrégé de la religion chrétienne* (1786). Holbach also wrote as Nicolas Boulanger and Jean Mirabaud (*qq.v.*).

Bert **Berns:** Bert Russell (1929–1967), U.S. pop writer, producer.

Claude **Berri:** Claude Langmann (1934–), Fr. movie director.

Judith M. **Berrisford:** Mary Lewis (1921–), Eng. writer of books on animals for children + Clifford Lewis (1912–), Eng. writer of books on animals for children, her husband. The two writers based their joint name on the maiden name, Berrisford, of Mary Lewis's mother.

Dave **Berry:** David Holgate Grundy (1941–), Eng. pop musician. Berry adopted his new surname from that of the U.S. rock 'n' roll musician Chuck Berry (1926–).

Jules **Berry:** Jules Paufichet (1883–1951), Fr. movie actor. The actor appears to have taken his name from the historic region of Berry, central France, although he was actually born in Touraine, to the west.

Berryman: Royden Ullyett (1914–), Eng. cartoonist. The artist used this name for his contributions to the *Sunday Pictorial*.

Ivan **Bersenev:** Ivan Nikolayevich Pavlishchev (1889–1951), Russ. stage, movie actor, theatrical director.

Louky **Bersianik:** Lucile Durand (1930–), Can. poet, novelist, playwright. The writer assumed the Slavic name to break free from her patriarchal lineage. Her assumed name appears to have evolved from a combination of her own first name and the surname of her father, Laurence Bissonet. Her mother was Donat Durand.

Jean **Bertheloy:** Berthe Roy de Clotte le Barillier (1868–1927), Fr. poet, novelist.

Francesca **Bertini:** Elena Seracini Vitiello (1888 or 1892–1985), It. movie actress.

Vic **Berton:** Vic Cohen (1896–1951), U.S. jazz musician.

Charles **Bertram:** James Bassett (1853–1907), Eng. magician.

Mary **Berwick:** Adelaide Anne Procter (1825–1864), Eng. poet. Procter, the daughter of Barry Cornwall (*q.v.*), contributed to Charles Dickens's periodical *Household Words* under this name. The surname seems to have been chosen as one geographically opposed to that of her father. Cornwall is in the extreme southwest of England, while Berwick is in the far northeast.

Besiki: Besarion Gabashvili (1750–1791), Georgian poet. The poet's adopted name is a diminutive of his first name.

Pavel **Besposhchadny:** Pavel Grigoryevich Ivanov (1895–1968), Russ. poet. The poet began his career as a miner in the Ukraine. The name he adopted means "merciless," "pitiless," describing the conditions he experienced and that were later experienced by the miners about whom he wrote.

Mongo **Beti:** Alexandre Biyiti (1932–), Cameroonian writer, working in France. The anticolonialist writer used the name Eza Boto for some early novels.

Don **Betteridge:** Bernard Newman (1897–1968), Br. novelist, travel writer.

Bettina: Bettina Ehrlich, née Bauer (1903–1985), Austr.-born Br. children's book illustrator, writer.

Billy **Bevan:** William Bevan Harris (1887–1957), Austral.-born U.S. movie actor.

Isla **Bevan:** Isla Buckley (1910–), Br. movie actress.

Clem **Bevans:** Clement Blevins (1879–1963), U.S. movie actor.

Turhan **Bey:** Turhan Gilbert Selahettin Saultavey (1920–), Austr.-born U.S. movie actor, of Turk.-Cz. parentage. The actor's new name represents the Turkish word for "prince" as well as the final syllable of his original surname.

Petr **Bezruč:** Vladimír Vašek (1867–1958), Cz. poet. The name adopted by the poet means literally "without responsibility." He also wrote as Ratibor Suk.

Bhaskar: Bhaskar Roy Chowdhury (1930–), Indian ballet dancer, teacher, working in U.S.

Ernesto **Bianco:** Oscar Ernesto Pelicori (1923–1977), Argentine stage actor.

Jacob **Bibliophile:** Paul Lacroix (1806–1884), Fr. historical writer.

John **Bickerdyke:** (1) Jonathan Swift (1667–1745), Ir.-born Br. satirist, cleric; (2) [Sir] Richard Steele (1672–1729), Ir. essayist, dramatist; (3) Benjamin West (1730–1813), U.S. mathematician. Swift used the name for a pamphlet of 1708 attacking the almanac-maker John Partridge. Steele used it for launching *The Tatler* the following year. West adopted it for a series of almanacs published in 1768 in Boston. Swift was thus the first to use the name, and he is said to have taken it from a smith's sign, adding the common first name Isaac. There was a real Isaac Bickerstaffe (with a final "e"), as an Irish playwright. But he lived after both Steele and Swift (from about 1735 to about 1812), so the name could have not derived from him.

Biddeshagor: Ishshorchondro Shorma (1820–1891), Ind. writer, translator. The scholar's honorary name translates as "ocean of knowledge."

Big Bopper: Jiles Perry Richardson (1930–1959), U.S. rock singer, songwriter. The musician so nicknamed himself for his ample size.

Big Daddy: Shirley Crabtree (1935–), Eng. heavyweight wrestler. The wrestler began his career as "Shirley Crabtree, The Blond Adonis," as well as simply "Mr. Universe." By the time he was in his early 30s, he was wrestling as "The Battling Guardsman." It was then that he met and married his wife Eunice, and she suggested a new name to improve his "bad guy" image, as she knew he had a gentle side to him. In 1975 "The Battling Guardsman" thus became the softer, cuddlier "Big Daddy" [*TV Times Magazine*, October 16–22, 1982].

Hosea **Biglow:** James Russell Lowell (1819–1891), U.S. humorist, satirist, poet. Lowell used the name for the purported author, a young New England farmer, of *The Biglow Papers*, two series of satirical verses in Yankee dialect published in the mid–1840s.

Big Maceo: Major Meriweather (1905–1953), U.S. blues singer.

Big Maybelle: Mabel Louise Smith (c.1920–1972), U.S. blues singer.

Big Youth: Manley Augustus Buchanan (c.1952–), Jamaican pop singer, DJ.

Bilitis: Pierre Louÿs (1870–1925), Belg.-born Fr. novelist. The famous "hoax" name is that of the supposed Greek poetess Bilitis (see full story, p. 25).

Acker **Bilk:** Bernard Stanley Bilk (1929–), Eng. jazz clarinetist. The musician was born in Somerset, where he was nicknamed "Acker," a local friendly form of address that he adopted as his first name.

Vladimir **Bill-Belotserkovsky:** Vladimir Naumovich Belotserkovsky (1884–1970), Russ. dramatist. English speakers have long had problems with Russian names, and when Belotserkovsky was in the USA, Americans gave up on his full name and called him by its first syllable, as "Bill." The writer liked this, and added it to his existing name, thus unwittingly exaggerating the problem.

Josh **Billings:** Henry Wheeler Shaw (1818–1885), U.S. humorist. Shaw used the name for his first book, *Josh Billings, His Sayings*, publication of which was arranged in 1865 by C.F. Browne (see Artemus **Ward**). The name is not as crackpot as most of Shaw's writings, which incorporate an amazing display of ridiculous spellings, deformed grammar, incongruous statements, and the like.

Billy the Kid: William H. Bonney (1859–1881), U.S. desperado. There is evidence that the gunfighter's original name was actually Henry McCarty.

Bim: Ivan Semyonovich Radunsky (1872–1955), Russ. circus clown, teaming with Bom (*q.v.*). Bim was always accompanied by Bom, and Bom always went with Bim. The team of *Bim-Bom*, in fact, was a single interdependent entity: a pair of Russian clowns who first performed under the name in 1891. (The name is a meaningless one, but suggests something like "bing-bang" or "boom-boom"). There was always a single *Bim* in the person of Ivan Radunsky, a Pole by origin, but there were no less than four *Boms*: a russianized Italian named Cortesi, a fellow Pole called Stanevsky, a Czech by the name of Viltzak, and finally a Russian named Kamsky. The duo began as an eccentric but versatile couple, both amusing and acrobatic, lively and highly literate (they spoke "good" Russian, as distinct from the broken Russian affected by a number of clowns). After the tragic death by drowning of Cortesi in 1897, the second Bom presented a different image, dressing not as a conventional clown but as a chic "man about town," wearing evening dress, complete with top hat and a chrysanthemum in his buttonhole. The pair now played down the acrobatics in favor of verbal satire. In the early 20th century the two toured Europe. After the Revolution, Stanevsky emigrated to his native Poland, and Bim followed suit. He returned in 1925, however, and in partnering Viltzak now concentrated on the musical aspect of his turns. (The third Bom was an accomplished if unorthodox musician. One of his specialties was playing on two concertinas at once.) Bim finally teamed up with Kamsky in World War II. The early 1920s produced a number of Bim-Bom imitators, notably Bib-Bob (G.L. Rashkovsky and I.A. Vorontsov), but also Viys-Vays (V.A. Sidelnikov and M.I. Solomenko), Din-Don, Rim-Rom, Fis-Dis and the like [Shneyer, p. 67].

Satane Binet: Francisque Sarcey (1828–1899), Fr. dramatic critic, novelist.

Micah Joseph Bin Gorion: Micah Joseph Berdichevsky (1865–1921), Russ. Jewish writer. The writer's name is of the same origin as that of David Ben-Gurion (*q.v.*).

Bing Xin: Hsieh Wan-Ying (1900–), Chin. (female) writer of sentimental stories, poems. The writer's adopted name means "pure in heart."

Richard Bird: William Barradell-Smith (1885– ?), Sc. writer of school stories. The name was presumably meant to evoke "dicky bird," as a teller of tales ("A dicky bird told me"). The name itself was perhaps suggested by the author's original surname.

W. Bird: Jack Butler Yeats (1871–1957), Ir. painter. The younger brother of the poet W. B. Yeats used this name for his cartoons published in the weekly humorous magazine *Punch* from 1910 to 1941.

Tala Birell: Natalie Bierle (1908–1959), Pol.-Austr. movie actress, working in U.S.

George A. Birmingham: [Rev.] James Owen Hannay (1865–1950), Ir.-born Br. author of light novels. James Hannay chose the pen name "Birmingham" not because he had some connection with that city, but simply because it was (and still is) a fairly common name in Co. Mayo, where he was rector in the town of Westport. The more usual spelling of the Irish surname, however, is Bermingham.

Miervaldis Birze: Miervaldis Berzins (1921–), Latvian writer. The writer's new name, while suggesting his original name, translates as "grove."

Joey Bishop: Joseph Abraham Gottlieb (1918–), U.S. TV, movie comedian. Gottlieb adopted the name of his roadie, Glenn Bishop.

Julie Bishop: Jacqueline Wells Brown (1914–), U.S. movie actress. The actress began her career as a child star named Jacqueline Wells. She adopted her adult name in 1941.

Stacey Bishop: George Antheil (1900–1957), U.S. novelist, opera composer. Stacey can be either a man's or a woman's name, and the novelist does not seem to have been seeking any special ambiguity in choosing it.

Zoubida Bittari: Louise Ali-Rachedi (1937–), Algerian novelist, working in France.

George Bizet: George Tulloch Bisset-Smith (1863–1922), Sc. sociologist, writer.

Brynjolf Bjarme: Henrik Ibsen (1828–1906), Norw. poet, dramatist.

Björk: Björk Gudmundsdóttir (1965–), Icelandic pop singer.

Dinna Bjørn: Dinna Bjørn Larsen (1947–), Dan. ballet dancer.

Black: Colin Vearncombe (1951–), Br. rock singer.

Cilla Black: Priscilla Maria Veronica White (1943–), Eng. popular singer, TV presenter. The singer explains how she came by her name: "My mum's name is Priscilla as well and she was always known as Big Priscilla whereas I was Little Priscilla. I lived in a very tough area [in Liverpool] and to have a posh name like that was very embarrassing. Luckily the kids called me Cilla at school. The Black bit came when a local paper, called The Mersey Beat, had a misprint. They knew my surname was a colour and guessed wrong. My manager Brian Epstein quite liked it, though, and put it into my contract. My dad went spare [was mad] because he didn't think any of his mates down at the docks would believe I was his daughter" [John Sachs and Piers Morgan, *Secret Lives*, 1991].

Don **Black:** Donald Blackstone (1938–), Br. lyricist.

Gavin **Black:** Oswald Wynd (1913–), Sc. thriller writer.

Ivory **Black:** Thomas Allibone Janvier (1849–1913), U.S. novelist.

Karen **Black:** Karen Blanche Ziegler (1942–), U.S. movie actress. "Black" from "Blanche."

Lionel **Black:** Dudley Barker (1910–1980), Eng. novelist, nonfiction writer.

[Sir] Misha **Black:** Moisey Cherny (1910–1977), Br. architect, industrial designer, of Russ. parentage. The architect's father translated his Russian name to Black when the boy was barely a year old, and the latter's first name was subsequently altered from Jewish Moisey (Moses) to Russian Misha (Michael).

Black Ace: Babe Kyro Lemon Turner (1907–1962), U.S. black blues musician.

E. Owens **Blackburne:** Elizabeth Owens Blackburne Casey (1847–1894), Ir. novelist, journalist.

Black Francis: Charles Michael Kitteridge Thompson IV (1965–), U.S. rock musician.

Bernard **Blackmantle:** Charles Molloy Westmacott (1787–1868), Eng. journalist, writer. The author also wrote as Abel Funnefello.

Harry **Blackstone:** Henri Bouton (originally, Harry Boughton) (1885–1965), U.S. magician. The illusionist shortened his original surname of Boughton to Bouton in 1910 when performing a double comedy act with his brother Pete. He then appeared under a succession of names: Martin, The Great Stanley, Francisco, Harry Careejo, Mr. Quick, C. Porter Newton, LeRoy Boughton, Beaumont the Great, and Fredrik the Great, and finally Harry Blackstone in 1918. ("Fredrik" had to be abandoned because of anti-German sentiment.) The magician explained the source of his final name variously: either it was his grandmother's maiden name, or it came from the Blackstone Hotel, Chicago, or he took it from a billboard advertising Blackstone cigars. Blackstone's first wife, Inez Nourse, claimed the third of these was correct, the billboard being in Wapakoneta, Ohio [John Fisher, *Paul Daniels and the Story of Magic*, 1987].

Scrapper **Blackwell:** Frankie Black (1903–1962), U.S. black jazz guitarist.

Hal **Blaine:** Harold Simon Belsky (1929–), U.S. drummer.

Vivian **Blaine:** Vivienne Stapleton (1921–1995), U.S. movie actress.

Betsy **Blair:** Elizabeth Boger (1923–), U.S. movie actress.

David **Blair:** David Butterfield (1932–1976), Eng. ballet dancer. The dancer appears to have created his new surname from letters in his original name.

Isla **Blair:** Isla Jean Baxter (1944–), Br. stage, TV actress. The actress's original surname was Blair Hill, "Hill" having been added to the Scottish family name of Blair in about 1880. She dropped the "Hill" when she left RADA (Royal Academy of Dramatic Art), since "Blair Hill seemed a mouthful" [private fax from Isla Blair, March 22, 1996].

Janet **Blair:** Martha Janet Lafferty (1921–), U.S. movie actress.

Joyce **Blair:** Joyce Sheridan Taylor, née Ogus (1932–), Eng. stage actress.

Lionel **Blair:** Lionel Ogus (1934–), Eng. stage actor, dancer, choreographer, TV performer.

Anne **Blaisdell:** Elizabeth Linington (1921–1988), U.S. writer of historical, mystery novels. The author also wrote as Lesley Egan, Egan O'Neill, and Dell Shannon (*qq.v.*).

Amanda **Blake:** Beverly Louise Neill (1929–1989), U.S. stage, movie actress.

Bobby **Blake:** Michael James Vijencio Gubitosi (1933–), U.S. child movie actor. The member of the "Our Gang" series performed as Mickey Gubitosi until 1942.

George **Blake:** George Behar (1922–), Br. traitor, double agent, of Du. parentage. Blake adopted his new name in World War II when he escaped to England as a member of the Dutch resistance and volunteered for the Royal Navy.

Marie **Blake:** Blossom MacDonald (1896–1978), U.S. movie actress.

Nicholas **Blake:** Cecil Day-Lewis (1904–1972), Ir.-born Br. poet. The poet's name derives from that of his son, Nicholas, and one of his mother's family names. (She was originally Kathleen Blake Squires.)

Robert **Blake:** Michael Gubitosi (1933–), U.S. movie actor.

Blakitny-Ellan: Vasily Mikhaylovich Yelannsky (1894–1925), Ukrainian poet, politician. The first part of the writer's name, prefixed to a form of his original surname, means "blue," contrasting symbolically with the "red" socialist stance taken by many of his contempories at the time of the Russian Revolution (1917).

Blam: Edmund Blampied (1886–1966), Br. cartoonist, illustrator.

Anna **Blaman:** Johanna Petronella Vrugt (1905–1960), Du. novelist.

Neltje **Blanchan:** Nellie Blanchan Doubleday, née de Graff (1865–1918), U.S. writer on nature subjects.

Alexander **Bland:** Nigel Gosling (1909–1982), Eng. ballet critic + Maude Gosling, née Lloyd (1908–), S.A.-born Eng. ballet dancer, critic, his wife.

Fabian **Bland:** Hubert Bland (1856–1914), Br. writer + E. Nesbit (*q.v.*), Br. writer, his wife. The joint pseudonym was used for the novel *The Prophet's Mantle* (1885), with "Fabian" a reference to the Fabian Society, of which Bland was a prominent member.

Ralph **Blane:** Ralph Uriah Hunsecker (1914–1995), U.S. movie music composer, lyricist.

Sally **Blane:** Elizabeth Jane Young (1910–), U.S. movie actress, sister of Loretta Young (*q.v.*).

Docteur **Blasius:** Paschal Grousset (1845–1919), Fr. journalist.

Blas Roca: Francisco Vilfredo Calderio (1908–), Cuban Communist official.

Charles Stuart **Blayds:** Charles Stuart Calverley (1831–1884), Br. poet, parodist. Calverley's father was the Rev. Henry Blayds, and a descendant of the old Yorkshire family of Calverley. The poet assumed the ancient name in 1852, when he became 21 and of full age.

Christopher **Blayre:** Edward Heron-Allen (1861–1943), Eng. writer of fantasy fiction.

Henri **Blaze:** Ange Henri Blaze de Bury (1813–1888), Fr. author.

Oliver **Bleeck:** Ross E. Thomas (1926–), U.S. mystery writer.

Emile **Blémont:** Léon-Emile Petitdidier (1839–1927), Fr. critic, dramatist, writer.

Brenda **Blethyn:** Brenda Anne Bottle (1946–), Eng. movie, TV actress.

Carla **Bley:** Carla Borg (1938–), U.S. jazz, rock composer. The musician's performing name is that of her husband, Paul Bley, although she used her maiden name initially.

Rose **Blight:** Germaine Greer (1939–), Austral.-born Br. literary critic, reviewer, journalist. The writer used this punning name for *The Revolting Garden (1979)*.

Mathilde **Blind:** Mathilde Cohen (1841–1896), Ger.-born Eng. poet, translator. The writer came to be known by the name of her stepfather, Karl Blind. She also wrote as Claude Lake.

Belinda **Blinders:** Desmond F.T. Coke (1879–1931), Br. army officer, schoolmaster, novelist. The writer also used the name Charbon (French for "coal," punning on his original name) for articles in *Hearth and Home* magazine.

Helen **Bliss:** Helena Louise Lipp (1917–), U.S. stage actress, singer.

Reginald **Bliss:** Herbert George Wells (1866–1946), Eng. novelist, sociological writer. Wells used the name for his novel *Boon* (1915), in which Reginald Bliss was the friend and literary executor of the main character, the popular playwright and novelist, George Boon.

Levi **Blodgett:** Theodore Parker (1810–1860), U.S. religious writer.

Pyotr Grigoryevich **Blokhin:** Grigory Iosifovich Sverdlin (1887–1942), Russ. revolutionary.

Max **Blonda:** Gertrud Schoenberg, née Kolisch (*c.*1894–1967), Austr. musician. The musician was the second wife of the Austrian-born American composer Arnold Schoenberg, whom she married in 1924. She used this name as librettist of his comic opera *Von Heute auf Morgen*, composed in 1928–9. The name itself appears to pun vaguely on that of her husband, with Schoenberg literally meaning "beautiful hill." Reading from right to left, the final *-a* can be seen as representing his first name, *blond* as meaning "fair," "beautiful," and *max* as denoting something high or lofty, like a hill.

Charles **Blondin:** Jean-François-Emile Gravelet (1824–1897), Fr. tightrope walker. The performer took his name from his tutor in the art, Jean Ravel Blondin.

Johnny **Blood:** John Victor McNally (1904–1985), U.S. American football player. When at college, McNally and his friend Ralph Hanson decided to set up a semi-pro football team. In order to play for the semi-pros, yet protect their eligibility for collegiate teams, they knew they would have to use assumed names. The story goes that on their way to the try-outs they passed a cinema showing *Blood and Sand*. "There are our names," said McNally, "I'll be Blood and you be Sand." It is not known what became of Sand.

Buster **Bloodvessel:** Douglas Trendle (1958–), Br. rock singer.

Claire **Bloom:** Patricia Claire Blume (1931–), Eng. stage, movie actress, of Pol.-Latvian descent.

Luka **Bloom:** Barry Moore (*c.*1955–), Ir. folk singer, working in U.S. The musician adopted his new name to be distinguished from his elder brother, the revered Irish folk singer Christy Moore (1945–), taking Luka from Suzanne Vega's 1987 hit so titled and Bloom from Leopold Bloom, the central character of James Joyce's novel *Ulysses* (1922).

Fannie **Bloomfield:** Fannie Zeisler, née Blumenfeld (1863–1927), Austr.-born U.S. concert pianist. The pianist performed under this name until her marriage (1885), after which she appeared under her married name.

Kurtis **Blow:** Kurt Walker (1959–), U.S. black rock singer, rapper.

Ben **Blue:** (1) Benjamin Bernstein (1901–1975), Can. vaudeville comedian, dancer; (2) S. David Cohen (1941–1982), U.S. pop music writer. Cohen was renamed by his friend Bob Dylan (*q.v.*).

David **Blue:** S. David Cohen (1941–1982), U.S. folk rock musician.

"Little" Joe **Blue:** Joseph Valery (1934–1990), U.S. black blues musician

Miss **Bluebell:** Margaret Leibovici, née Murphy (originally Kelly) (1912–), Ir. dancer, teacher, founder of "Bluebell Girls" dancing troupe. The dancer was born in Dublin to a Mrs. Kelly. Only a fortnight after the birth, however, her mother gave away her baby to a spinster, Mary Murphy, who would raise the child. Later, a doctor visiting the little girl, who was thin and delicate, was mesmerized by her clear blue eyes and nicknamed her "Bluebell." Margaret Murphy adopted the name for herself and passed it on to her dancers [*Sunday Times Magazine*, August 23, 1981].

Blue Boy: Austin Lyons (1955–), Trinidad calypso singer.

Jake **Blues:** John Belushi (1949–1982), U.S. soul singer.

Peter **Blume:** Piotr Sorek-Sabel (1906–1992), Russ.-born U.S. painter.

Nellie **Bly:** Elizabeth Cochrane Seaman (1867–1922), U.S. journalist. Elizabeth Seaman's name was suggested by the managing editor of *The Pittsburgh Dispatch*, for which she began writing at the age of 18. The name comes from the character in an 1850 song by Stephen Foster.

Larry **Blyden:** Ivan Lawrence Blieden (1925–1975), U.S. stage actor, director.

Betty **Blythe:** Elizabeth Blythe Slaughter (1893–1972), U.S. movie actress.

Jimmy **Blythe:** Sammy Price (1908–), U.S. black jazz pianist.

Capel **Boake:** Doris Boake Kerr (1895–1944), Austral. novelist.

Tim **Bobbin:** John Collier (1708–1786), Eng. writer, caricaturist. The writer used this name for satirical poems in the Lancashire dialect published from 1739 to 1771.

Bobèche: Jean-Antoine-Aimé Mardelard (or Mandelard) (1791–*c.*1840), Fr. comic actor, teaming with Galimafré (*q.v.*). French *bobèche* is a slang word for "head," so can be understood as something like "nut," "noddle."

Willie **Bobo:** William Correa (1934–), U.S. jazz musician, of Puerto Rican parentage. The musician was nicknamed "Bobo" by jazz pianist Mary Lou Williams during a recording session in the early 1950s.

Bob Tai'r Felin: Robert Roberts (1870–1951), Welsh folksinger. The singer's name means "Bob of the millhouse," referring to his home near Bala.

Bocage: Pierre-Martinien (or François) Touzé (1797–1863), Fr. actor.

Dirk **Bogarde:** Derek Gentron Gaspart Ulric van den Bogaerde (1921–), Br. stage, movie actor, of Du. descent.

Aleksandr **Bogdanov:** Aleksandr Aleksandrovich Malinovsky (1873–1928), Russ. socialist writer, Proletkult leader.

V. **Bogucharsky:** Vasily Yakovlevich Yakovlev (1861–1915), Russ. revolutionary historian. The writer also used the name B. Bazilevsky.

Boisgilbert: Ignatius Donnelly (1831–1901), U.S. writer, politician.

Maurice **Boissard:** Paul Léautaud (1872–1956), Fr. novelist, essayist. The writer used this name as a drama critic.

Marc **Bolan:** Mark Feld (1947–1977), Br. pop musician, of Pol.-Russ. descent. Feld cut his first disc in 1965 as Mark Bowland, a name said to have been given him by his recording company, Decca. That same year he made this more distinctive as Marc Bolan. However, according to another account, he took his new name from the first and last syllables of the name of Bob Dylan (*q.v.*). He had earlier called himself Mark Riggs, after Riggs O'Hara, an actor friend, and had been nicknamed Toby Tyler, for the young waif who is the central character in James Otis's 1881 novel for boys so titled.

Rolf **Boldrewood:** Thomas Alexander Browne (1826–1915), Eng.-born Austral. romantic novelist. The writer took his pseudonym from a placename mentioned in Sir Walter Scott's poem *Marmion* (1808): "Through Boldrewood the chase he led" (Introduction to Canto I).

Richard **Boleslawski:** Boleslaw Ryszart Srzednicki (1889–1937), Pol.-born U.S. stage director.

William **Bolitho:** William Bolitho Ryall (1831–1930), S.A.-born Br. journalist, author.

Florinda **Bolkan:** José Suarez Bulcão (1941–), It. movie actress, of Brazilian parentage.

Isabel **Bolton:** Mary Britton Miller (1883–1975), U.S. poet, novelist. Possibly the writer's middle name suggested her adopted surname.

Michael **Bolton:** Michael Bolotin (1953–), U.S. rock balladist. The musician slightly adjusted his name because his original surname "sounded too Russian."

Bom:(1) F. Cortesi (? –1897), It.-born Russ. circus clown, teaming with Bim (*q.v.*); (2) Mechislav Antonovich Stanevsky (1879–1927), Russ. clown, of Pol. parentage, teaming with Bim; (3) Nikolay Iosifovich Viltzak (1880–1960), Russ. clown, of Cz. parentage, teaming with Bim; (4) N.A. Kamsky (1894–1966), Russ. clown, teaming with Bim.

Bombardinio: William Maginn (1793–1842), Ir. author.

Fortunio **Bonanova:** Luis Moll (1895–1969), Sp. movie actor, singer.

Father **Bonaventura:** Charles Edward Stuart (1720–1788), Sc. prince ("Bonnie Prince Charlie"). The Young Pretender adopted this name on visiting England from France incognito in 1753.

[St.] **Bonaventure** (or Bonaventura): Giovanni di Fidanza (*c.*1217–1274), It. theologian, scholar, mystic. The saint is said to have been given his new name, meaning "good fortune," by St. Francis, whose order he joined in about 1243.

Steve **Bond:** Shlomo Goldberg (1953–), U.S. juvenile movie actor.

Beulah **Bondi:** Beulah Bondy (1892–1981), U.S. movie actress.

Manik **Bondopadhai:** Probodhkumar (1908–1956), Ind. novelist, short story writer.

Gary U.S. **Bonds:** Gary Anderson (1939–), U.S. rock composer. The musician's new name originated with his first manager, Frank Guida, who sent copies of his first single "New Orleans" to radio stations in sleeves marked "Buy U.S. Bonds."

Captain Ralph **Bonehill:** Edward Stratemeyer (1863–1930), U.S. writer of fiction for boys.

Bon Gaultier: William Edmonstone Aytoun (1813–1865), Sc. poet + [Sir] Theodore Martin (1814–1909), Sc. poet. The name was first used for the joint work, *Bon Gaultier Ballads* (1845), in which the poets parodied the verse of the day. The name comes from Rabelais, who in the Prologue to *Gargantua* used the words in a sense meaning "good fellow," "good companion," Gaultier being a generalized personal name.

Ali **Bongo:** William Wallace (? –), Eng. TV magician. The fairly traditional magician's name was first used by Wallace in a performance in a village pantomime. He was assistant to magician David Nixon (1919–1978) in TV shows.

Jacques **Bonhomme:** Guillaume Cale (or Caillet) (? –1358), Fr. peasant leader. The generic name (something like "Jack Goodfellow") was one given to the peasantry in the 14th century. Its sense was derogatory, however, not approbatory, and it implied serfdom.

[St.] **Boniface:** Wynfrith (or Winfrid) (*c.*675–754), Eng. missionary, martyr. The "Apostle of Germany" was renamed by Pope Gregory II in 719 for the 3d-century saint Boniface who had been martyred at Tarsus.

Boniface VIII: Benedetto Caetani (*c.*1235–1303), It. pope. This pope's original name was adopted as a papal name by his successor, Benedict XI (*q.v.*).

Boniface IX: Pietro Tomacelli (*c.*1350–1401), It. pope.

Jon **Bon Jovi:** John Bongiovi (1962–), U.S. rock musician.

Issy **Bonn:** Benjamin Levin (1903–1977), Eng. radio comedian, singer. A typical Jewish nickname for the comedian, who was popular on radio in the 1930s. He also occasionally appeared in the cinema as Benny Leven. "Issy" implies Israel, and "Bonn" represents Benjamin.

Richard **Bonnelli:** Richard Bunn (1894–), U.S. opera singer.

Frank **Bonner:** Frank Boers, Jr. (1942–), U.S. TV actor.

Sherwood **Bonner:** Katherine Sherwood Bonner Macdowell (1849–1883), U.S. short story writer.

Hugh **Bonneville:** Hugh Richard Bonneville Williams (1963–), Br. stage, TV actor. When the actor began his career in 1986 he felt it prudent to adopt a new name so as not to evoke an association with the actor Hugh Williams (1904–1969), who though no longer alive was still remembered by many. He thus decided to use his two middle names, Richard Bonneville. "However, my family and friends still called me Hugh, so when I worked with actors who were also friends no-one knew *what* to call me. I battled on for nine years, trying to explain to each bemused new acquaintance just who the hell I was—until last year, when I finally gave up the fight and changed my Equity [actors' union] forename to Hugh. Beats me why I didn't go with this in the first place." The form of the actor's third name on his birth certificate is actually Bonniwell [personal fax from Hugh Bonneville, March 26, 1996].

Bono: Paul Hewson (1960–), Ir. rock singer. The U2 lead singer originally used the full name Bono Vox, said to be that of a hearing-aid shop in O'Connell Street, Dublin. At first he was not keen on the name, but then realized that it was a Latin approximation of "good voice." He later used the first part of the name alone.

Jessie **Bonstelle:** Laura Justine Bonesteele (1872–1932), U.S. stage actress, theatre manager.

Roger **Bontemps:** Roger de Collerye (? 1470–1540), Fr. poet.

Betty **Boo:** Alison Moira Clarkson (1970–), Br. pop singer, of Sc.-Malayan parentage. The singer adopted her stage name from the cartoon character Betty Boop.

William **Boot:** Tom Stoppard (*q.v.*). Stoppard used the name for early pieces as a drama critic when writing for the magazine *Scene* (1962). He took it from the hero of Evelyn Waugh's *Scoop*, who was a nature columnist. As a dramatist he also used the name Boot for several characters in his plays, often complemented by another character called Moon. In 1964 he wrote a TV play called *This Way Out with Samuel Boot*, which actually featured a *pair* of Boots, representing contrary attitudes towards material possessions.

Adrian **Booth:** Virginia Mae Davis, née Pound (1918–), U.S. movie actress. The actress first adopted the name Lorna Gray. She became Adrian Booth when making a fresh start in 1946. Adrian is sometimes found as a woman's name in the U.S., as also (rarely) in the U.K.

Edwina **Booth:** Josephine Constance Woodruff (1909–1991), U.S. movie actress. The actress took her stage name from Edwin Booth, the outstanding tragedian of the 19th century, and the first American actor to make his reputation in Europe.

James **Booth:** James Geeves-Booth (1930–), Eng. stage, movie actor.

Karin **Booth:** Katharine Hoffman (1919–1992), U.S. movie actress. The actress was Katharine Booth before progressing to Karin Booth in 1947.

Shirley **Booth:** Thelma Booth Ford (1907–1992), U.S. stage, movie actress.

Matej **Bor:** Vladimir Pavšič (1913–), Slovenian writer.

Cornell **Borchers:** Cornelia Bruch (1925–), Ger. movie actress.

Olive **Borden:** Sybil Tinkle (1909–1947), U.S. movie actress.

Petrus **Borel:** Joseph-Pierre Borel d'Hauterive (1809–1859), Fr. poet, novelist.

Victor **Borge:** Börg Rosenbaum (1909–), Dan.-born U.S. pianist, comedian.

Ernest **Borgnine:** Ermes Effron Borgnino (1917–), U.S. movie actor, of It. parentage. The actor's new English first name is similar only in sound to his original Italian forename, which means "Hermes."

Inge **Borkh:** Ingeborg Simon (1917–), Ger. opera singer.

Stefan **Born:** Stefan Buttermilch (1824–1898), Ger. political reformer.

Ludwig **Börne:** Löb Baruch (1786–1837), Ger. political writer, satirist. Baruch took his new name on converting from Judaism to Christianity in 1818.

Eduard **Bornhöhe:** Eduard Brunberg (1862–1923), Estonian historical novelist. The writer adopted a name that means more or less the same (literally "well height") as his original name.

Mikhail **Borodin:** Mikhail Markovich Gruzeberg (1884–1951), Russ. Communist official, newspaper editor.

Borra: Borislav Milojkowic (1921–), Yugoslav-born Austr. magician, working in U.K.

Francesco **Borromini:** Francesco Castelli (1599–1667), It. architect.

Bos: Thomas Peckett Prest (1809–1879), Eng. author of stories for boys. Prest, and others like him, originally intended to ascribe their virtual piracies of writings by Dickens to "Boaz," after Dickens's own pen name Boz (*q.v.*). This was ruled out, however, as being rather too close, and also rather too biblical. The genre of Prest's particular fiction came to be known as the "penny dreadful."

Hieronymus **Bosch:** Jerom van Aeken (*c*.1450–1516), Du. painter. Bosch took his new name from his birthplace, the Dutch town of 's Hertogenbosch.

Abbé **Bossut:** [Sir] Richard Phillips (1767–1840), Eng. writer. Phillips was a great pseudonymist. He used "Abbé Bossut" (after the genuine French mathematician of the name, his near contemporary) for a series of French, Italian and Latin word books and phrase books; Rev. J. Goldsmith for geographical and scientific works; Rev. David Blair, Rev. C.C. Clarke, Rev. John Robinson, Rev. S. Barrow, Mrs. (or Miss) Pelham, for other writings.

Boston Bard: Robert S. Coffin (1797–1827), U.S. poet.

A **Bostonian:** Edgar Allan Poe (1809–1849), U.S. poet, short story writer. Poe was born in Boston, Massachusetts.

Sandro **Botticelli:** Alessandro di Mariano dei Filipepi (1445–1510), It. painter. The painter is said to have adopted the nickname given to his elder brother Giovanni, a rotund pawnbroker. "Botticello" means "little barrel" (Italian *botte*, "barrel"). According to Giorgio Vasari's *Lives of the Artists* (1550), however, the painter was apprenticed to a goldsmith named Botticelli and adopted his name.

Francesco **Botticini:** Francesco di Giovanni (*c*.1446–1497), It. painter. The artist took his name from his more illustrious contemporary, Sandro Botticelli (see above), on whom he based his style.

Anthony **Boucher:** William Anthony Parker White (1911–1968), U.S. editor, SF, detective story writer.

Barbara **Bouchet:** Barbara Gutscher (1943–), U.S. movie actress, of Ger. parentage.

Dion **Boucicault:** Dionysius Lardner Boursiquot (*c*.1820–1890), Ir.-born U.S. actor, dramatist. The actor, who was of Huguenot extraction, began his career under the name of Lee Moreton in 1838, subsequently adopting the new spelling of his original name in 1841, after the success (in London) of his own play *London Assurance*.

Nicolas **Boulanger:** Paul-Henri Thiry, baron d'Holbach (1723–1789), Fr. materialist, atheist writer. Holbach used this name for his antireligious work *Le Christianisme dévoilé* (1761), taking it from the French philosopher Nicolas-Antoine Boulanger, who had died two years earlier. Holbach also wrote as Abbé Bernier and Jean Mirabaud (*qq.v.*).

Houari **Boumédienne:** Mohammed Ben Brahim Boukharrouba (1927–1978), Algerian head of state. The military leader adopted his new name as a *nom de guerre* when he joined a guerrilla unit in 1955. "Boumédienne" is the French spelling of Arabic *Bum-ed-Din*, literally "owl of religion."

Benjamin **Bounce:** Henry Carey (1685–1743), Eng. poet, composer. Carey used the exuberant name for his equally lively dramatic burlesque *Chrononhotonthologos* "the Most Tragical Tragedy that ever was Tragediz'd by any Company of Tragedians" (1734). In this, Chrononhotonthologos was the king of Queerummania, and two other characters were Aldiborontiphoscophornia and Rigdum-Funnidos, names which Walter Scott later gave to his printer and publisher, the brothers James and John Ballantyne, for the pomposity of the former and the cheerfulness of the latter.

Nicolas **Bourbaki:** Henri Cartan (1904–), Fr. mathematician + Claude Chevalley (1909–1984), Fr. mathematician + Jean Dieudonné (1906–1992), Fr. mathematician + André Weil (1906–), Fr. mathematician. The named men were the nucleus of a group formed in 1933 to represent the essential "contemporary mathematician." Their group pseudonym, chosen humorously, was that of a French general, Charles Bourbaki (1816–1897), whose attempts to bridge the Prussian line during the Franco-German War (1870–71) ended in disaster. The name is chiefly associated with the group's huge reference work, *Eléments de mathématiques*, which began to appear in 1939.

Margaret **Bourke-White:** Margaret White (1906–1971), U.S. photographer. In 1926, following a brief, twelve month marriage, White added her mother's maiden name to her original surname.

George **Bourne:** George Sturt (1863–1927), Eng. writer of books on rural subjects. Sturt took his pen name from his birthplace, Lower Bourne, Farnham, Surrey.

Bourvil: André Raimbourg (1917–1970), Fr. movie comedian. The actor's screen name comes from the village of Bourville, northwest of Paris, where he was raised. At the same time it half suggests the latter half of his real surname.

B. **Bouverie:** William Ewart Gladstone (1809–1898), Br. prime minister, author.

John **Bowe:** John Wilson (1950–), Br. stage, TV actor.

Marjorie **Bowen:** Margaret Gabrielle Vere Long, née Campbell (1888–1952), Eng. novelist, biographer. The writer created her pen name from a variant of her own first name and her great-grandfather's surname. She used many other (mostly male) pseudonyms, of which the best known are Robert Paye, George R. Preedy, Joseph Shearing, and John Winch.

David **Bowie:** David Robert Hayward-Jones (1947–), Eng. rock musician. The singer changed his name to Bowie in 1966 so as not to be confused with Davy Jones of The Monkees, with his new name allegedly for the bowie knife. According to one pop music expert, "Since the bowie knife was popularised by the frontiersman Jim Bowie, … the pop star's name should most accurately be pronounced David Bo-hie, or even the down south pronunciation of Jim's name, Boo-ie" [Paul Gambaccini, *Masters of Rock*, 1982].

Debra Louise **Bowring:** Peter John Compton (1938–), Br. movie producer. The producer, a transexual, explains the choice of three new names as follows: "The name of Debra was chosen as I just liked it, Louise was an old family name, and Bowring likewise as my father's family surname was Bowring Compton" [private letter from Debra Bowring, September 14, 1995].

Edgar **Box:** Gore Vidal (1925–), U.S. novelist, playwright, writer. The writer reserved this name for three detective novels: *Death in the Fifth Position* (1952), *Death before Bedtime* (1953), and *Death Like It Hot* (1954). Vidal kept this pseudonym secret for many years, although he did confide it to one or two literary colleagues. "Edgar" contains letters in his original name.

Boxcar Willie: Lecil Travis Martin (1931–), U.S. country musician. Martin took his name after being impressed by the way in which, during the American Depression, unemployed men would climb onto the roofs of boxcars so as to travel aross the States by freight train. His own father was a railroad man, and the family house lay only a few feet from the track. On assuming the name, Boxcar Willie adopted the stage guise of an unshaven, unkempt, cigar chompin' hobo in a battered hat.

Boy: Tadeusz Żeleński (1874–1941), Pol. writer, translator, literary critic.

John **Boyd:** Boyd Bradfield Upchurch (1919–), U.S. SF writer.

Nancy **Boyd:** Edna St. Vincent Millay (1892–1950), U.S. poet.

Stephen **Boyd:** William Millar (1928–1977), Ir. movie actor, working in U.S.

Boy George: George Alan O'Dowd (1961–), Eng. pop singer. The singer adopted the name in 1982, when he first began appearing, dressed as a girl (or at least androgynously), with his group Culture Club. He had himself billed as "Boy George" on the sleeve of his first single in order to answer the inevitable initial question, "Is it a boy or a girl?" The name would ensure that the apparent "she" was correctly identified as a "he" [*Pop Focus*, 1983].

Katie **Boyle:** Caterina Irene Helen Imperiali di Francavilla (1926–), It.-born Eng. TV panelist, writer, columnist. "Katie" for Caterina; "Boyle" for her first husband, Richard Bentinck Boyle (Viscount Boyle) subsequently the Earl of Shannon. They divorced in 1955. (See also p. 18.)

René **Boylesve:** René-Marie-Auguste Tardiveau (1867–1926), Fr. novelist. The writer adopted his mother's maiden name as his pen name.

Boz: Charles Dickens (1812–1870), Eng. novelist. Dickens used this name (pronounced "Boze") in reports of debates in the House of Commons in *The Morning Chronicle* (1835) and in his collection of articles entitled *Sketches by Boz* (1836–37), as well as in other writings. The name, he explained, was "the nickname of a pet child, a younger brother [Augustus], who I had dubbed Moses (after Moses Primrose in Goldsmith's *The Vicar of Wakefield*) … which being pronounced Boses, got shortened to Boz."

Bozhidar: Bogdan Petrovich Gordeyev (1894–1914), Russ. poet. The poet's adopted name relates to his original first name: Bogdan literally means "given by God," while Bozhidar means "gift of God."

Hugh Henry **Brackenridge:** Hugh Montgomery Breckenridge (1748–1816), Sc.-born U.S. novelist, prose writer, poet.

Dame Hilda **Bracket:** Patrick Fyffe (*c.*1950–), Br. female impersonator, teaming with Dr. Evadne Hinge (*q.v.*) (as "Hinge and Bracket").

Edward P. **Bradley:** Michael Moorcock (1939–), Eng. SF writer.

Will **Bradley:** Wilbur Schwichtenberg (1912–1989), U.S. jazz trombonist. The musician changed his name because his original surname was too cumbersome for billings. "Will Bradley" presumably evolved from "Wilbur."

Scott **Brady:** Gerard Kenneth Tierney (1924–1985), U.S. movie actor.

June **Brae:** June Bear (1917–), Eng. ballet dancer.

Eric **Braeden:** Hans Gudegast (1942–), Ger. movie actor.

John **Braham:** John Abraham (1774–1856), Eng. opera singer.

Otto **Brahm:** Otto Abrahamsohn (1856–1912), Ger. stage director, literary critic.

Caryl **Brahms:** Doris Caroline Abrahams (1901–1983), Eng. writer, songwriter. The writer adopted her new name as a student in order to conceal her literary activities from her parents, "who envisaged a more domestic future for her" [*Dictionary of National Biography*].

Ernest **Bramah:** Ernest Brammah Smith (1868–1942), Br. writer. The writer used this pseudonym for all his books, and even his *Who's Who* entry is under the name. Brammah was his mother's maiden name.

Bramantino: Bartolommeo Suardi (*c.*1455–1536), It. painter. The name effectively means "little Bramante," referring to the architect and painter Donato Bramante (1444–1515), whose follower he was.

Christianna **Brand:** Mary Christianna Lewis (1907–1988), U.K. thriller writer.

Max **Brand:** Frederick Schiller Faust (1892–1944), U.S. novelist.

John **Brandane:** John MacIntyre (1869–1947), Sc. dramatist.

Georg **Brandes:** Morris Cohen (1842–1927), Dan. literary critic, historian, of Jewish parentage.

Henry **Brandon:** Henry Kleinbach (1910–1990), U.S. movie actor.

Michael **Brandon:** Michael Feldman (1945–), U.S. movie, TV actor, husband of Glynis Barber (*q.v.*).

Ivan **Brandt:** Roy Francis Cook (1903–), Eng. stage actor. Cook began his career as an architect, and took his new name when first appearing on the stage in 1927.

Marianne **Brandt:** Marie Bischoff (1842–1921), Austr. opera singer.

Willy **Brandt:** Herbert Ernst Karl Frahm (1913–1992), Ger. politician, chancellor of West Germany. The politician took his new name for articles that he wrote after joining the Socialist Workers' Party in 1931, and retained it on fleeing to Norway in 1933.

Brandy: Brandy Norwood (1979–), U.S. rhythm 'n' blues singer.

Madame Floresta A. **Brasileira:** Nísia Floresta (1810–1885), Brazilian poet, novelist, essayist. Other pseudonyms used by the writer include Une Brésilienne, Telesilla (Portuguese for "chair lift"), Floresta Augusta Brasileira, Madame Brasileira Augusta, and N.F.B.A. (initials of her original and adopted names). For ten years she owned a school called Augusto in Rio de Janeiro.

Brassaï: Gyula Halász (1899–1984), Hung.-born Fr. photographer, poet. The photographer adopted his name from that of his native city, Brassó, Hungary (now Braşov, Romania). It is tempting to think the name may also have punned on English "brass eye," referring to the lens of his camera.

Pierre **Brasseur:** Pierre-Albert Espinasse (1905–1972), Fr. stage, movie actor, playwright. The actor adopted his mother's maiden name as his stage name.

Sasthi **Brata:** Sasthibrata Chakravarti (1939–), Ind.-born Br. writer.

Ivan **Bratanov:** Ivan Marinov (1920–1968), Bulg. movie actor.

Wellman **Braud:** Wellman Breaux (1891–1966), U.S. black jazz bassist.

Nikolay **Bravin:** Nikolay Mikhaylovich Vasyatkin (1883–1956), Russ. opera singer. Possibly the baritone adopted a name intended to suggest *bravo* or *bravura*, with the same sense in Russian as in English.

Danny **Bravo:** Daniel Zaldivar (*c.*1947–), U.S. juvenile movie actor.

Brécourt: Guillaume Marcoureau (1638–1683), Fr. actor, dramatist.

Hans **Breitmann:** Charles Godfrey Leland (1824–1903), U.S. humorous writer, editor. Leland had received a university education in Germany, and he used the name for his amusing dialect poems, collected in *Hans Breitmann's Ballads* (1914).

Marie **Brema:** Minny Fehrmann (1856–1925). Eng. opera singer.

Brenda: Mrs. G. Castle Smith (*fl.*1875), Br. children's writer.

Edith **Brendall:** Eddy Charly Bertin (1944–), Ger.-born Belg. writer of horror stories.

Michel **Brenet:** Antoinette Christine Marie Bobillier (1858–1918), Fr. musical biographer.

Matthew **Brenher:** Matthew Alexander Benham (1961–), Eng. movie, TV actor.

Arvid **Brenner:** Fritz Helge Heerberger (1907–), Swe. writer, of Ger.-Swe. parentage.

Evelyn **Brent:** Mary Elizabeth Riggs (1899–1975), U.S. movie actress. The actress was initially billed as Betty Riggs before assuming her later name.

George **Brent:** George Brendan Nolan (1904–1979), Ir.-born U.S. movie actor.

Linda **Brent:** Harriet Jacobs (1818–1896), U.S. black writer. The former slave used this name for her autobiography, *Incidents in the Life of a Slave Girl* (1861).

Romney **Brent:** Romulo Larralde (1902–1976), Mexican-born U.S. stage, movie actor, dramatist.

Elinor M. **Brent-Dyer:** Gladys Elinor May Dyer (1894–1969), Eng. writer of books for girls.

Brent of Bin Bin: Stella Maria Miles Franklin (1879–1954), Austral. novelist. The novelist's pseudonym is said to represent the name of a kindly elderly gentleman writing about his experiences of Australian bush life, "Bin Bin" being a typical outback placename. The original form of the name was "Brand of Bin Bin," but the first word of this was altered as the result of a typing error.

Edmund **Breon:** Edmund MacLaverty (1882–1951), Sc. stage, movie actor, working in U.S., U.K.

Ford **Brereton:** Samuel Rutherford Crockett (1860–1914), Sc. novelist, journalist.

Jeremy **Brett:** Peter Jeremy William Huggins (1935–1995), Eng. stage, movie actor.

Lucienne **Bréval:** Berthe Agnès Lisette Schilling (1869–1935), Swiss-born Fr. opera singer.

Otokar **Březina:** Václav Ignác Jebavý (1868–1929), Cz. poet.

David **Brian:** Brian Davis (1914–1993), U.S. movie actor.

Havergal **Brian:** William Brian (1876–1972), Eng. composer. The prolific symphonic composer adopted his new first name in 1899, when he had begun to gain fame as a church organist. He probably took it from William Henry Havergal (1793–1870), English hymn composer, including the tunes familiar for "Bless'd Are the Pure in Heart," "Rejoice the Lord is King," "Ride On! Ride on in Majesty," and "Take My Life and Let It Be," the words of this last being written by his daughter.

James **Brian:** Arthur George Street (1892–1966), Eng. author of books on country life.

Mary **Brian:** Louise Byrdie Dantzler (1908–), U.S. movie actress.

Fanny **Brice:** Fannie Borach (1891–1951), U.S. singer, comedienne. Fannie Borach grew so weary of having her name mispronounced as "Bore-ache" and "Bore-act" that she changed it to something simpler. Lauren Bacall (*q.v.*) had similar problems.

Bricktop: Ada Beatrice Queen Victoria Louise Virginia Smith (1894–1984), U.S. hostess, cabaret singer, entertainer. From rolling royalty (with a common touch in "Smith") to basic brevity. Bricktop, the daughter of black parents, but with a part-Irish mother, was so nicknamed for her red hair. The name passed to the chic Chez Bricktop club in the Rue Pigalle, Paris, where she was the proprietress and where she entertained many famous expatriate U.S. writers.

Ann **Bridge:** [Lady] Mary Dolling O'Malley, née Sanders (1889–1974), Eng. novelist. Ann Bridge took her pen name from her birthplace, the hamlet of Bridge End, Surrey. (Reverse the two halves of this name, and you get something that can be turned into "Ann Bridge.")

Bonar **Bridge:** [Rev.] W.W. Tulloch (1846–1920), Sc. biographer, editor. Tulloch took his name from the Scottish village of Bonar Bridge, Sutherland (now Highland).

James **Bridie:** Osborne Henry Mavor (1888–1951), Sc. playwright. As a doctor, the writer needed a pseudonym for his distinctive dramatic writing. His first play was *The Sunlight Sonata* (1928), which he wrote under the name of Mary Henderson. He subsequently adopted his maternal grandmother's surname for later plays, with the first under the Bridie name being *The Anatomist* (1930). He continued in general medical practice until 1938.

Bright Eyes: Susette (or Susan) La Flesche (1865–1915), Native American physician, tribal leader. Susette was the daughter of Omaha chief Joseph La Flesche (Iron Eye) who was himself the son of a French trader and an Omaha woman. Bright Eyes is the English version of her Native American name, Inshta-theumba, which she came to use when involved in her people's struggle for justice. In 1894 she married Henry Picotte, half Sioux, half French, and became Susette La Flesche Picotte.

Lee **Brilleaux:** Lee Green (1953–), Eng. rock musician.

Peter **Briquette:** Patrick Lusack (1954–), Br. rock musician. The Boomtown Rats member is the cousin of Johnny Fingers (*q.v.*).

Carl **Brisson:** Carl Pedersen (1895–1958), Dan. movie actor, working in U.K. The actor's new surname evolved as a form of the original.

Elton **Britt:** James Britt Baker (1917–1972), U.S. country singer, yodeller.

May **Britt:** Maybritt Wilkens (1933–), Swe. movie actress.

Morgan **Brittany:** Suzanne Cupito (1951–), U.S. child movie, TV actress.

Barbara **Britton:** Barbara Brantingham Czukor (1919–1980), U.S. movie actress.

Colonel **Britton:** Douglas E. Ritchie (1905–), Br. radio news director.

William **Brocius:** William Graham (1851–1882), U.S. gunman, cattle rustler ("Curly Bill").

Lynn **Brock:** Alister McAllister (1877–1943), Ir. author.

Lea **Brodie:** Lea Dregham (1951–), Eng. TV actress. Lea Dregham came to adopt her husband's former pseudonym for her professional work.

Steve **Brodie:** John Stevens (1919–1992), U.S. movie actor.

Harold **Brodkey:** Aaron Roy Weintraub (1930–1996), U.S. writer. Weintraub's mother died when he was 17 months old, following which he was adopted by his father's cousins, Joseph and Doris Brodkey. They gave him his new surname, with "Harold" formed from "Aaron."

Brok: Tamara Timofeyevna Sidorkina (1910–1975), Russ. circus artist, juggler, lion tamer. An adoption of the familiar clown name "Brock," as used in England by the partner of Brick, whose own later partner was Grock (*q.v.*).

James **Brolin:** James Bruderlin (1940–), U.S. movie, TV actor.

John **Bromfield:** Farron Bromfield (1922–), U.S. movie actor.

Charles **Bronson:** Charles Buchinsky (1920–), U.S. movie actor. Bronson's grandfather was Charles Dennis Bunchinsky, the son of Russian immigrants from Lithuania. The family dropped the middle "n," and Charles Buchinsky changed to "Bronson" for his third movie, *Drum Beat* (1954). "With the hounds of McCarthyville skulking round Hollywood Slavic names didn't seem so fashionable," he reasoned [David Downing, *Charles Bronson*, 1982].

Agnolo **Bronzino:** Agnolo di Cosimo (1503–1572), It. painter. The origin of the artist's assumed nickname, meaning "bronzed," is uncertain. It probably refers to his dark complexion.

Lesley **Brook:** Lesley Learoyd (1916–), Br. movie actress. The actress adopted the middle name of her father, Reginald Brook Learoyd, as her stage name.

Hillary **Brooke:** Beatrice Sofia Mathilda Peterson (1914–), U.S. movie actress.

Harris **Brookes:** Giorgio (later George) Loraine Srampa (1875–1951), Turk.-born Br. cartoonist, illustrator, of It. descent. The artist sometimes used this name for his cartoons for the humorous weekly *Punch.*

Albert **Brooks:** Albert Einstein (1947–), U.S. movie director, screenwriter, actor, son of comedian Parkyakarkus (*q.v.*).

Beverley **Brooks:** Patricia Evelyn Beverley Brooks, née Matthews (1929–1992), Eng. aristocrat. This was the name assumed by Viscountess Rothermere.

Elkie **Brooks:** Elaine Bookbinder (1946–), Eng. popular singer. As a youngster, Bookbinder took singing lessons from the cantor of her local synagogue in Lancashire. She chose the name Elkie as a Yiddish equivalent of "Elaine," while simultaneously shortening her long surname to "Brooks" [*The Times*, March 21, 1987].

Geraldine **Brooks:** Geraldine Stroock (1925–1977), U.S. movie actress. "Brooks" is a more manageable name than "Stroock," to which it nevertheless retains a kind of resemblance.

Hadda **Brooks:** Hadda Hopgood (1916–), U.S. black boogie-woogie pianist.

Leslie **Brooks:** Leslie Gettman (1922–), U.S. movie actress. Presumably Leslie Gettman was unaware of Lesley Brook (*q.v.*).

Mel **Brooks:** Melvin Kaminsky (1926–), U.S. movie comedy writer, producer. Kaminsky changed his name so as not to be confused with trumpet player Max Kaminsky. His new name arose as a contraction of his mother's maiden name, Brookman.

Nikki **Brooks:** Nicola Ashton (1968–), Eng. popular singer, movie, TV actress.

Phyllis **Brooks:** Phyllis Weiler (or Steiller) (1914–), U.S. movie actress.

D.K. **Broster:** Dorothy Kathleen Broster (1878–1950), Eng. writer of historical novels for children. Readers of the writer's books generally assumed the author to be a man, "an impression she took no steps to correct" (Carpenter and Prichard, p. 85; see Bibliography, p. 400). Broster was thus one of several female writers using initials to mask her sex. Another was E. Nesbit (*q.v.*).

Joyce **Brothers:** Joyce Bauer (1928–), U.S. TV psychiatrist.

David **Brough:** David Bingham (1940–1997), Br. spy. The former naval officer, one of Britain's most notorious spies, was jailed for 21 years in 1971 for selling secrets to the Russians and assumed his new identity as David Brough after his release from prison in 1981.

Arthur **Brown:** Arthur Wilton (1944–), Eng. rock musician, comedian.

Carter **Brown:** Alan Geoffrey Yates (1923–1985), Br.-born Austral. thriller writer. The original form of the pen name was "Peter Carter Brown," but the writer later dropped the first part of this on the basis that "Carter Brown" alone suited his American market better. He used other names, such as Tom Conway, Caroline Farr, and Paul Valdez.

Georgia **Brown:** Lillian (or Lillie) Klot (1933–1992), Eng. stage, movie, TV actress, singer. The actress began her career as a jazz singer, and took her stage name from Maceo Pinkard's 1925 song "Sweet Georgia Brown," which featured in her act. The surname was coincidentally appropriate for her long dark hair and dark brown eyes.

Herbert **Brown:** Herbert Brovarnik (1912–), U.S. chemist, of Ukrainian parentage.

Lew **Brown:** Louis Brownstein (1893–1958), Russ.-born U.S. songwriter.

Michael **Brown:** Michael Lookofsky (1949–), U.S. rock musician.

Nappy **Brown:** Napoleon Brown Culp (1929–), U.S. black blues singer.

Roy "Chubby" **Brown:** Royston Vasey (1945–), Br. movie actor, comedian.

Teddy **Brown:** Abraham Himmebrand (1900–1946), U.S. music hall instrumentalist. "Brown" could be regarded as an assimilation of "Abraham," while also hinting at the latter half of "Himmebrand."

Vanessa **Brown:** Smylla Brind (1928–), Austr.-born U.S. movie actress. "Brown" evolved from "Brind."

Coral **Browne:** Coral Edith Brown (1913–1991), Austral. stage actress.

Henriette **Browne:** Sophie de Saux, née de Boutellier (1829–1901), Fr. painter, etcher.

Matthew **Browne:** William Brightly Rands (1823–1882), Br. writer of poems, fairy tales for children.

Henry **Brownrigg:** Douglas William Jerrold (1803–1857), Eng. author, playwright, humorist.

The writer also used the name Paul Prendergast (*q.v.*).

Thomas **Brown, the Younger:** Thomas Moore (1779–1852), Ir. poet, satirist. This is the most familiar of the poet's pseudonyms. Others include An Irish Gentleman, Thomas Little (*q.v.*), One of the Fancy, Captain Rock, and Trismegistus Rustifucius, D.D.

Arthur Loring **Bruce:** Francis Welch Crowninshield (1872–1947), U.S. editor, writer.

David **Bruce:** Andrew McBroom (1914–1976), U.S. movie actor.

Jack **Bruce:** John Symon Asher (1943–), Sc. jazz, rock musician.

Lenny **Bruce:** Leonard Alfred Schneider (1925–1966), U.S. comedian.

Leo **Bruce:** Rupert Croft-Cooke (1903–1979), Br. detective novelist.

Peter **Bruce:** Peter Robinson (1960–), Sc. TV actor. The actor took a new (typically Scottish) name to avoid confusion with another actor who bore his original name.

Virginia **Bruce:** Helen Virginia Briggs (1910–1982), U.S. movie actress.

Ferdinand **Bruckner:** Theodor Tagger (1891–1958), Austr. playwright, of Austr.-Fr. parentage.

Erik **Bruhn:** Belton Evers (1928–1986), Dan. ballet dancer, director, working in Canada.

Henri **Brûlard:** Stendhal (*q.v.*).

Gabrielle **Brune:** Gabrielle Hudson (1912–), Eng. stage actress, singer. The actress adopted the maiden name of her mother, actress and singer Adrienne (originally Phyllis Caroline) Brune, as her stage name.

Georg **Brunis:** George Clarence Brunies (1900–1974), U.S. trombonist. Brunies modified his first and last names on the advice of a numerologist.

Paul **Brunton:** Raphael Hurst (1898–1981), Eng.-born mystic, writer on mysticism, working in U.S. The writer, who introduced Indian mysticism to the West, revealed little about his personal life, and it is not clear why he adopted this particular name: "Evidently he was born with the name Raphael Hurst, and took, first Brunton Paul, then Paul Brunton as a pen name" [Jeffrey Masson, *My Father's Guru*, 1993].

Bruscambille: Jean Deslauriers (*fl.*1610–1634), Fr. comic actor. The name appears to represent French *brusque en bille*, "abrupt in the head," with *bille* a slang word for "head," something like English "nut," "noddle."

Brutus: David Owen (1795–1866), Welsh preacher, teacher, editor. This is the writer's best known pseudonym, which he used for the satirical tale *Wil Brydydd y Coed* ("Wil the rhymester of the woods") (1863–65), among other writings.

David **Bryan:** David Bryan Rashbaum (1962–), U.S. rock musician.

Dora **Bryan:** Dora May Lawton, née Broadbent (1923–), Eng. stage, movie, TV comedienne. Dora Broadbent's surname was "not a name for the stage," as Noel Coward put it. She therefore looked for an alternative, which would at the same time suggest the original. At first she selected "Bryant," from the match manufacturers, Bryant & May, but when the program arrived from the printers, the final "t" was missing and she settled for the "Bryan" instead.

Hal **Bryan:** Johnson Clark (1891–1948), Eng. stage actor.

Jane **Bryan:** Jane O'Brien (1918–), U.S. movie actress.

Rudy **Bryans:** Bernard Godet (*c.*1945–), Fr. ballet dancer.

Beulah **Bryant:** Blooma Walton (1918–1988), U.S. popular singer.

James **Bryce:** Alexander Anderson (1862–1949), Sc. novelist.

Brychan: John Davies (*c.*1784–1864), Welsh poet. The poet's name is that of the 5th-century St. Brychan.

Bryfdir: Humphrey Jones (1867–1947), Welsh poet.

Bryher: Annie Winnifred Ellerman (1894–1983), Eng. novelist. The novelist took her name from the island of Bryher, in the Isles of Scilly, where she traveled with her friend and lover, H.D. (*q.v.*).

Yul **Brynner:** Taidje Khan (1915–1985), U.S. movie actor. The actor's mother was part Russian, and his father part Swiss. At first he spelled his name Youl Bryner. Some years later, a New York theatrical agent told him that "Youl" sounded too much like "you-all," and "Bryner" as though he was soaked in brine and pickled. To clarify the pronunciation, if not the origin of the name, Youl Bryner therefore respelled his name as Yul Brynner, pronounced "Yool Brinner" [Jhan Robbins, *Yul Brynner: The Inscrutable King*, 1988].

Karl Pavlovich **Bryullov:** Charles Bruleau (1799–1852), Russ. painter. The artist was of French descent and the family name was russified only in 1821.

Bubbles: John William Sublett (1902–1986), U.S. black tapdancer. A near anagram of the dancer's real surname.

Charlie **Bubbles:** Charles Sistovaris (1971–), Br. movie actor. The actor, grandson of Charlie Chaplin, explains how he came by his name: "I don't have the Chaplin name. Although my mother [Josephine] is a Chaplin, my father was Nicolas Sistovaris, so I'm really Charlie Sistovaris. It was Annie [his actress aunt] who first called me Charlie Bubbles. When I drank from my bottle I always blew milk bubbles" [*Sunday Times Magazine*, March 28, 1993]. Presumably Aunt Annie got the nickname from the 1968 movie *Charlie Bubbles*.

Martin **Bucer:** Martin Kuhhorn (1491–1551), Ger. Protestant reformer. In the fashion of his time, the theologian translated his German name (literally "cow horn") into Greek, with "Bucer" the latinized form of Greek *boukeros* (from *bous*, "ox," and *keras*, "horn"). The name is pronounced "Bootser."

Buchan: James Boswell (1906–1971), N.Z.-born Br. painter, cartoonist, writer, of Sc. descent. The artist used this name for antifascist drawings published in the *Daily Worker* in the 1930s.

J.E. **Buckrose:** Annie Edith Jameson, née Foster (1868–1931), Eng. novelist.

Buckwheat Zydeco: Stanley Dural (1947–), U.S. accordion player. Dural first earned "Buckwheat" as a nickname, then adopted the second word of his name for his special interest in zydeco (a type of Afro-American accordion-led dance music from southern Louisiana, his own place of origin).

Buffalo Bill: William Frederick Cody (1846–1917), U.S. scout, showman. Cody was so named by Ned Buntline (*q.v.*) because he provided buffalo meat for rail construction crews.

Ken **Bugul:** Marietou Mbaye (1948–), Senegalese writer. When the writer's French-language publishers, Les Nouvelles Editions Africaines, insist she use a pseudonym for her fictionalized autobiography, *Le Baobab fou* ("The Mad Baobab") (1982), this was her answer, Wolof for "nobody wants it."

Kir **Bulychyov:** Igor Vsevolodovich Mozheyko (1934–), Russ. SF writer.

Bumble Bee Slim: Amos Easton (1905–1968), U.S. black blues singer.

Douglas **Bunn:** Douglas Henry David Honeybunn (1928–), Br. equestrian.

Bunny: Carl Emil Schultze (1866–1939), U.S. cartoonist.

Ned **Buntline:** Edward Zane Carroll Judson (1823–1886), U.S. adventurer, trapper, author. Ned Buntline, as a writer of "dime novels," simply took a random word for his pen name, with "Ned" representing his real first name, Edward. A buntline is a line fastened to the foot of a square sail when it has to be hauled up for furling. Ned Buntline named Buffalo Bill (*q.v.*), and depicted him in his writings.

Eleanor **Burford:** Eleanor Alice Hibbert, née Burford (1906–1993), Eng. novelist. The writer was here simply using her maiden name. Her best known pseudonym was Jean Plaidy (*q.v.*).

David **Burg:** Alexander Dolberg (1933–), Russ.-born Eng. writer, translator.

Annekatrin **Bürger:** Annekatrin Rammelt (1937–), Ger. movie actress.

Anthony **Burgess:** John Burgess Wilson (1917–1993), Eng. novelist, critic. Burgess explained how he came by his pen name in his autobiography: "I was christened John Burgess Wilson and was confirmed in the name of Anthony. When I published my first novel I was forced to do so in near-disguise. I was an official of the Colonial Office at the time, and it was regarded as improper to publish fiction under one's own name. So I pulled the cracker of my total name and unfolded the paper hat of Anthony Burgess. ... Burgess was the maiden name of the mother I never knew ... a dancer and singer ... named the Beautiful Belle Burgess on music hall posters. She married a Manchester Wilson but was right to insist that her slightly more distinguished surname get on to my baptismal certificate. There have always been too many plain Wilsons around" [Anthony Burgess, *Little Wilson and Big God*, 1986].

Betty **Burke:** Charles Edward Stuart (1720–1788), Sc. prince ("The Young Pretender"). One of the prince's many disguise names, in this instance when rescued by Flora Macdonald after the Battle of Culloden (1746) and taken secretly by her to the Isle of Skye disguised as her maid. The prince was 26 at the time, and Flora two years younger.

Billie **Burke:** Mary William Ethelbert Appleton Burke (1885–1970), U.S. stage, movie actress. The actress adopted the name of her father, William (Billy) Burke, a circus clown. Billie is an acceptable female name in its own right, and was popular among chorus girls at one time.

Fielding **Burke:** Olive Dargan, née Tilford (1869–1968), U.S. poet, novelist.

Marie **Burke:** Marie Holt (1894–1988), Br. stage actress.

Jonathan **Burn:** Henry Jonas Jonathan Burn-Forti (1939–), Eng. stage, TV actor.

Andreas **Burnier:** Catharina Irma Dessaur (1931–), Du. writer. The writer's new first name is created from letters in her real name.

Bobby **Burns:** Robert Müller (*c.*1920–), Ger. child movie actor.

George **Burns:** Nathan Birnbaum (1896–1996), U.S. stage, TV comedian.

Katherine **Burns:** Katharine Hepburn (1909–), U.S. stage, movie actress. Hepburn used this name for her first stage performance in New York, when she appeared in *Night Hostess* (1928). Her movie debut followed only four years later.

Tommy **Burns:** Noah Brusso (1881–1955), Can. heavyweight boxer.

Henry **Burr:** Harry H. McClaskey (1882–1941), U.S. popular singer. McClaskey used several pseudonyms. Another was Irving Gillette.

Abe **Burrows:** Abram Solman Borowitz (1910–1985), U.S. librettist.

Ellen **Burstyn:** Edna Rae Gillooly (1932–), U.S. movie actress, of Ir. parentage. The actress's stage name is that of her third husband, Neil Burstyn. She began her career as a model under the name Edna Rae. She was then a dancer in a Montreal nightclub as Keri Flynn before becoming Erica Dean for a screen test in the mid-1950s. Her first movie roles were as Ellen McRae, a name she kept until her third marriage in 1960 (aborted in 1971).

[Sir] Montague **Burton:** Meshe David Osinsky (1885–1952), Lithuanian-born Br. clothing manufacturer, retailer, of Jewish parentage. The noted British businessman, who used the full name Montague Maurice Burton, is said to have taken his English name from a public house, perhaps itself called the Montague Arms and obtaining its beer from the brewery town of Burton-on-Trent. He adopted it in 1904.

Richard **Burton:** Richard Walter Jenkins (1925–1984), Welsh stage, movie actor. When a schoolboy in Port Talbot, southern Wales, Jenkins showed signs of promise as an actor. As such, he became the protégé of the English teacher and school play producer Philip H. Burton, who made the 18-year-old his legal ward and gave him his name. The document that spelled out the change was dated December 17, 1943. Philip Burton would have adopted his pupil if it had been legally possible, but the difference between their ages was 20 days short of 21 years, the minimum required by law at that time. This ruled out official adoption.

Instead, an agreement was drawn up between Philip Burton and the real father making the "infant" a ward until he reached the age of 21. Part of the document declared that Richard Jenkins shall "absolutely renounce and abandon the use of the surname of the parent and shall bear and use the surname of the adopter and shall be held out to the world and in all respects treated as if he were in fact the child of the adopter" [Paul Ferris, *Richard Burton*, 1981].

Aleksandr Borisovich **Bushe:** Aleksandr Ksenofontovich Gnusov (1882–1970), Russ. circus artist, ringmaster.

[Sir] Alexander **Bustamante:** William Alexander Clarke (1884–1977), Jamaican prime minister. Clarke, the son of an Irish planter father and Jamaican mother, went to New York in 1932 in the guise of a Spanish gentleman named Alejandro Bustamante. He adopted the name William Alexander Bustamante by deed poll in 1943 when forming the Jamaica Labour Party in order to avoid disqualification from nomination as a candidate under a name that was not legally his. The name was that of the Cuban lawyer and politician Antonio Sánchez de Bustamante y Sirvén (1865–1951), who drew up the Bustamante Code dealing with international private law.

Prince **Buster:** Buster Campbell (1938–), Jamaican ska, rock musician.

The **Busy-Body:** Benjamin Franklin (1706–1790), U.S. statesman, scientist, philosopher. Franklin used the name for articles written in 1728.

Hilda **Butsova:** Hilda Boot (*c.*1897–1976), Eng. ballet dancer.

William **Butterworth:** Henry Schroeder (1774–1853), Eng. topographer, engraver.

Myra **Buttle:** Victor William Williams Saunders Purcell (1896–1965), Br. author of books on China.

Red **Buttons:** Aaron Schwatt (1918–), U.S. stage, movie, TV comedian. At the age of 16, Schwatt was a singing bellhop at Dinty Moore's City Island Tavern in the Bronx. For this job he had to wear a uniform with 48 prominent buttons. He had red hair, so was nicknamed after

these two distinctive features. He subsequently came to adopt the name in place of his immigrant name.

Zmitrok **Byadulya:** Samuil Yefimovich Plavnik (1886–1941), Belorussian writer. The writer came from a needy family. Hence his adopted name, meaning "poor one."

Max **Bygraves:** Walter William Bygraves (1922–), Eng. TV entertainer. On his first night in the Royal Air Force, aged 17 (and having lied about his age to enlist), Bygraves impersonated his idol, Max Miller (*q.v.*), and thereafter assumed his first name.

Robert **Byr:** Karl Robert Emmerich von Bayer (1815–1902), Austr. novelist, writer on military subjects.

James **Byrne:** Edward William Garnett (1868–1937), Br. writer, literary adviser.

Edd **Byrnes:** Edward Breitenberger (1933–), U.S. juvenile TV actor.

John **Byron:** John Heanley (1912–), Br. stage actor, dancer.

Marion **Byron:** Miriam Bilenkin (1911–1985), U.S. movie actress.

Walter **Byron:** Walter Butler (1899–1972), Br. movie actor, of Ir. descent.

E. Fairfax **Byrrne:** Emma Frances Brooke (1845–1926), Eng. novelist. An asexual pen name, with the writer's new surname punning on the original.

Byul-Byul: Martuza Rza ogly Mamedov (1897–1961), Azerbaijani opera singer, folk musician. The singer's name means "bulbul" (a songbird of the thrush family). (Compare Turkish *bülbül*, "nightingale." The word imitates the bird's warbling song.)

The same name, in its lowercase form bülbül, was adopted by the U.S. feminist cartoonist Genny Pilgrim, who points out that in Middle Eastern poetry a bülbül is a bird of protest. Of her own use of the name, she says: "I took it as a pen name when my family suffered for my outspoken opinions" [bülbül, *off our backs*, July 1984].

Roy **C:** Roy Charles Hammond (1943–), U.S. pop singer. Hammond adopted this short, distinctive name in order not to be confused with either pop musician Roy Hamilton or singer Ray Charles (*q.v.*).

James **Caan:** James Cahn (1939–), U.S. movie actor.

Fernán **Caballero:** Cecilia Böhl von Faber (1796–1877), Sp. novelist, of Ger.-Sp. parentage.

Boyd **Cable:** Ernest Andrew Ewart (1878–1943), Br. writer, journalist, screenwriter, army officer. Ewart was a tireless traveler and sea voyager, so that his assumed name may pun on "buoyed cable."

Bruce **Cabot:** Jacques Etienne de Bujac (1904–1972), U.S. movie actor, of Fr. descent.

Susan **Cabot:** Harriet Shapiro (1927–1986), U.S. movie actress.

Cadenus: Jonathan Swift (1667–1745), It. satirist, cleric. The name is an anagram of Latin *decanus* "dean." Swift had become Dean of St. Patrick's Cathedral, Dublin, in 1699, hence his common nickname of "Dean" Swift. He used the name Cadenus for his poem *Cadenus and Vanessa* (1713) addressed to Esther Vanhomrigh, thereby incidentally creating the woman's name Vanessa. (Swift formed the name from the first three letters of "Vanhomrigh" plus "Essa," a pet form of Esther.)

Cadfan: John Davies (1846–1923), Welsh poet. The poet took his bardic name from his native village of Llangadfan ("(St.) Cadfan's church"), Montgomeryshire (now Powys), where the parish church is dedicated to the 6th-century St. Cadfan.

Cadrawd: Thomas Christopher Evans (1846–1918), Welsh folklorist.

Caerfallwch: Thomas Edwards (1779–1858), Welsh lexicographer. The writer took his name from the location in Flintshire (now Clwyd) where he was born.

Caffarelli: Gaetano Maiorano (1703–1783), It. male soprano singer. The singer took his name from that of Caffaro, his teacher in Bari.

Nicolas **Cage:** Nicholas Coppola (1964–), U.S. movie actor, nephew of director Francis Ford Coppola. The actor adopted his new name to avoid any comparison with his uncle. He took it from two offbeat Cages: comic-book hero Luke Cage and composer John Cage.

Alessandro, conte di **Cagliostro:** Giuseppe Balsamo (1743–1795), It. magician, charlatan, adventurer.

Holger **Cahill:** Sveinn Kristján Bjarnarson (1887–1960), Icelandic-born U.S. folk art authority.

Sammy **Cahn:** Samuel Kahn (or Cohen) (1913–1993), U.S. movie lyricist. The songwriter describes how he and his friend, composer Saul Chaplin (*q.v.*), then still Saul Kaplan, came by their new names: "When I saw the names on that first copy of [their song] 'Rhythm Is Our Business'—Kahn, Kaplan—I said to him: 'You're going to have to change your name.' He bristled and said, 'Why? It looks good.' I said, 'It doesn't look good at all. Kahn and Kaplan, that's a dress firm.' He said, 'Why don't you change *your* name?' I: 'That's fair. From now on I'll be Cahn with a C.' He: 'Okay, I'll be Caplan with a C.' I said: 'Cahn and Caplan, that's *still* a dress firm. From now on its Cahn and Chaplin.'" [Sammy Cahn, *I Should Care*, 1975].

Claude **Cahun:** Lucy Schwob (1894–?), Fr. photographer.

Christopher **Cain:** Bruce Doggett (1943–), U.S. movie director, screenwriter.

Henry **Caine:** Henry Hawken (1888–1962), Br. stage actor. The actor probably formed his new name from the second half of his original surname.

Marti **Caine:** Lynda (or Lynne) Denise Ives, formerly Stringer, née Crapper (or Shepherd) (1945–1995), Eng. TV singer, entertainer, comedienne. The story goes that, needing a stage name, the singer opened a gardening book at random in 1968 and lighted on the entry "Tomato cane." That gave her name.

Michael **Caine:** Maurice Joseph Micklewhite (1933–), Eng. movie, TV actor, working in U.S. The actor took his first name from his nickname, Mike (no doubt itself based on his surname), and his second name from the movie *The Caine Mutiny*. He had to pick a screen name in a hurry in 1954, and happened to see a Leicester Square, London, cinema advertising the movie. The name appealed to him for its brevity and strength [*Telegraph Sunday Magazine*, May 9, 1982].

Caju: Francisca Júlia (1871–1920), Brazilian poet. A name created from the last syllable of the writer's first name and the first of her surname.

Aleksandrs **Čaks:** Aleksandrs Čadarainis (1902–1950), Latvian poet.

Calamity Jane: Martha Jane Burk (or Canary) (?1852–1903), U.S. popular heroine of the West. Calamity Jane was a colorful character who wore men's clothing, carried a gun, indulged in drinking sprees—and prophesied "doom and gloom." Hence her nickname, which became the name by which she is generally known today, having featured (in a much more attractive guise) in dime novels of the 1870s and 1880s. "Jane" has long been a nickname for a woman, especially a distinctive or disreputable one. Burk was a prostitute in various frontier towns.

Taylor **Caldwell:** Janet Miriam Taylor Reback, née Caldwell (1900–1985), Eng.-born U.S. novelist. It is not clear to what extent Taylor Caldwell wished to disguise her sex, if at all, or to what extent she wished to be associated with the contemporary novelist, Erskine Caldwell. Taylor is hardly a common woman's name.

Caledfryn: William Williams (1801–1869), Welsh poet. The poet, a Nonconformist minister, took his bardic name from the location where he lived. The placename itself literally means "hard hill." His son, a portrait painter, was known as Ab Caledfryn ("son of Caledfryn").

Louis **Calhern:** Carl Henry Vogt (1895–1956), U.S. stage, movie actor. The actor was obliged to adopt a stage name under pressure from his uncle, who regarded the profession as shameful. His new surname came from a combination of his first two names, while his first name was adopted from the city of St. Louis.

Rory **Calhoun:** Francis Timothy McCown, later Durgin (1922–), U.S. movie actor.

Randy **California:** Randy Craig Wolfe (1951–1997), U.S. rock musician. The musician was raised in Los Angeles, California, and named for that state by his first manager, Chas Chandler, bass player of the Animals.

Caligula: Gaius Julius Caesar (12–41), Roman emperor. The name means "Little Boots," and was the pet name given to Gaius Caesar by his father's soldiers when he ran around the camp as a young boy. It is strange that such an agreeable name should come to be adopted by such a cruel despot.

Calixtus II: Guido di Borgogna (c.1050–1124), It. pope. Popes of this name are also known as Callistus. The name itself derives from Greek *kallistos*, "the best," "the noblest" (literally "the most beautiful").

Calixtus III: Alfonso de Borja (Borgia) (1378–1458), Sp. pope.

Michael **Callan:** Martin Calinieff (1935–), U.S. dancer, movie actor.

Maria **Callas:** Maria Anna Cecilia Sophia Meneghini, née Kalogeropoulou (1923–1977), U.S. opera singer, of Gk. parentage. In the early 1930s, the singer's parents legally changed the family name to Callas, a name that was shorter and easier to pronounce in an English-speaking land. Although obviously based on the original lengthy surname, it is possible they saw the name as a near anagram of *La Scala*, Milan, Italy's

leading opera house. As Greeks, too, they would have made an association with Greek *kallos*, "beautiful."

Joseph **Calleia:** Joseph Alexander Herstall Vincent Spurin-Calleja (1897–1975), Maltese-born U.S. movie actor.

Emma **Calvé:** Rosa-Noémie Emma Calvet de Roquer (1858–1942), Fr. opera singer.

Phyllis **Calvert:** Phyllis Bickle (1915–), Eng. stage, movie, TV actress. Phyllis Bickle was requested to change her name by movie producer Herbert Wilcox. The actress selected Calvert as she felt it "had a sort of ring to it." She apparently felt no need to alter Phyllis.

Corinne **Calvet:** Corinne Dibos (1925–), Fr. movie actress.

Henry **Calvin:** Wimberly Calvin Goodman, Jr. (1918–1975), U.S. movie comedian.

Marie **Camargo:** Marie Anne de Cupis (1710–1770), Belg. ballet dancer, of Sp. descent. The dancer adopted her mother's Spanish maiden name as her professional name.

Camarón de la Isla: José Monge Cruz (1951–1992), Sp. flamenco singer. The singer's stage name, meaning "island shrimp," evolved from the nickname he was given as a child. Because the boy had a pale complexion, his uncle likened him to the big shrimp in the waters around the island of San Fernando, southwestern Spain, where he was born.

Elizabeth **Cambridge:** Barbara K. Hodges, née Webber (1893–1949), Br. novelist, short story writer.

John **Cameron:** Archibald Gordon Macdonell (1895–1941), Sc. crime, mystery writer. The author also used the name Neil Gordon (*q.v.*).

Rod **Cameron:** Nathan Roderick Cox (1910–1983), Can. movie actor, working in U.S.

Camillus: (1) Alexander Hamilton (1755–1804), U.S. statesman, pamphleteer, author; (2) Fisher Ames (1758–1808), U.S. statesman, orator, political writer. Both men adopted the name of Camillus, the Roman soldier and statesman who saved Rome from the Gauls and who was instrumental in securing the passage of the so-called Licinian laws, introducing measures in favor of the rights of the plebeians.

Helen Stuart **Campbell:** Helen Campbell Weeks, née Stuart (1839–1918), U.S. writer, reformer. The writer adopted her mother's maiden name (already her own middle name) as a pen name for some of her fiction in the 1860s and in 1877 assumed it legally.

Herbert Edward **Campbell:** Herbert Edward Story (1844–1904), Br. music hall artist.

Judy **Campbell:** Judy Birkin, née Gamble (1916–), Eng. stage, screen, TV actress, mother of movie actress Jane Birkin (1946–). The actress adopted the surname assumed by her father, playwright Joseph Arthur Campbell, originally Gamble.

Louise **Campbell:** Louise Weisbecker (1915–), U.S. film actress.

Maria **Campbell:** June Stifle (1940–), Can. dramatist, children's writer, of Sc., Fr., and Native American ancestry.

Mrs. Patrick **Campbell:** Beatrice Stella Campbell, née Tanner (1865–1940), Eng. stage actress. The actress was always known by her husband's name. Not really a pseudonym, of course, but a distinctive stage name of sorts. Beatrice Tanner eloped when she was 19 to marry Patrick Campbell, a London businessman.

[Sir] Henry **Campbell-Bannerman:** Henry Campbell (1836–1908), Br. politician. The British prime minister (1905–08) added his mother's maiden name of Bannerman to his own in 1872 under the will of her brother, Henry Bannerman.

Sarah **Campion:** Mary Rose Coulton (1906–), Eng.-born N.Z. novelist.

Cañadas: Henry Higgins (1944–1978), Colombian-born Eng. bullfighter, working in Spain. Henry Higgins was the only Englishman to have qualified as a matador in the Spanish bull ring. In the bullfighting tradition, he adopted a Spanish ring name. It means "glens," "narrow valleys" (related to English "canyon"). Such valleys are a feature of the countryside around Bogotá, Colombia, where Higgins was born. The Spanish themselves usually referred to him as just *El Inglés,* "the Englishman".

Canaletto: Giovanni Antonio Canal (1697–1768), It. painter. The artist's adopted name means "little Canal." It is uncertain how the painter came to acquire this version of his surname, as he was not noticeably small. Possibly it was to distinguish him from his father, Bernardo Canal, who was a theatrical scene painter. Giovanni often assisted his father in his work, so that the Italian diminutive suffix *-etto* more or less equated to "Jr."

Edward **Candy:** Barbara Alison Neville (1925–), Br. novelist.

Denis **Cannan:** Denis Pullein-Thompson (1919–), Br. playwright. The writer adopted his mother's maiden name as his pen name.

Charles **Cannell:** Evelyn Charles Vivian (1882–1947), Eng. writer of adventure, detective stories.

Effie **Canning:** Effie Carlton, née Crockett (1857–1940), U.S. stage actress.

Dyan **Cannon:** Samille Diane Friesen (1937–), U.S. movie actress. The actress was given her new name by producer Jerry Ward, who arranged her first screen test. The story goes that that one day he looked at her and exclaimed, "I see something explosive. Terrific. Bang. Cannon" [*TV Times,* June 1–7, 1985].

Freddy **Cannon:** Frederick Anthony Picariello (1940–), U.S. rock musician.

Tommy **Cannon:** Thomas Darbyshire (1938–), Eng. TV comedian, teaming with Bobby Ball (*q.v.*). The two men, formerly Lancashire welders, first performed as the Harper Brothers (after Ball's real name), working in social clubs and cabaret. They changed their joint name to "Cannon and Ball" for an appearance on the TV talent show *Opportunity Knocks* in 1973. Cannon is the bigger and older of the two, with Ball his "feed" (providing his "ammunition," as it were).

Cantinflas: Mario Moreno Reyes (1911–1993), Mexican circus clown, bullfighter, stage, movie comedian. The name looks potentially significant, but is apparently meaningless, and was given as a nickname to the performer by one of his fans. He adopted it to hide his identity from his family when he began working in variety in 1930. (The name gave colloquial Mexican Spanish *cantinflear,* "to talk much and say little.")

Eddie **Cantor:** Edward Israel (or Isidore) Itskowitz (1892–1964), U.S. singer, entertainer, movie actor. Latin *cantor* means "singer," whether understood as the Jewish leader of a synagogue service (as suitable for the actor, who was Jewish) or for the leader of some other type of worship. Cantor is anyway a Jewish surname in its own right.

Janey **Canuck:** Emily Gowan Murphy, née Ferguson (1868–1933), Can. journalist, essayist, judge. The writer used this name for a number of popular books, "Canuck" being a nickname for a Canadian. She wrote *The Black Candle* (1922), a book about narcotics, as Judge Murphy.

Robert **Capa:** Endre Ernö Friedmann (1913–1954), Hung.-born U.S. photographer. The new name was created in the mid–1930s. At that time, Friedmann was publishing his work simply as André. He felt that this made him sound like a hairdresser, however, so he and his girl friend Gerda Pohorylles, who helped him to promote this work, devised a different name. This was Robert Capa, supposedly the name of an already successful American photographer who was so rich that he refused to sell his photos at normal prices. The name itself was arbitrary in origin, although André (Endre) claimed that "Robert" came from the movies, and in particular from Robert Taylor, who in 1936 was starring as Greta Garbo's lover in *Camille*. But both words of the name were easy to pronounce, in many languages, and "Capa" looked like any nationality. Gerda could thus tell French editors that Capa was American, but also tell American editors that the photographer was French. And when the newly christened Capa went to Spain, his surname sounded conveniently Spanish. This ambiguity must have appealed to André, and the name was perfect for a stateless person. In a letter to his mother shortly after, Capa wrote: "I am working under a new name. They call me Robert Capa. One could almost say that I've been born again, but this time it didn't cause anyone any pain."

Gerda also changed her name at about this time. She became Gerda Taro, the new name borrowed from a young Japanese painter working in Paris. Not only was her new name easy to pronounce (as Capa's was), but it suggested "tarot," with its connotations of gypsies and fortune-telling. Furthermore the new name as a whole sounded rather like "Greta Garbo," who in 1936 was at the peak of her fame [Richard Whelan, *Robert Capa: A Biography*, 1985].

Judith **Cape**: Patricia K. Page (1916–), Eng.-born Can. artist, poet.

Capnio: Johannes Reuchlin (1455–1522), Ger. humanist. The scholar translated his name into the Greek equivalent (*kapnos*, "smoke"). He is now usually known by his real name, however.

Truman **Capote**: Truman Streckfus Persons (1924–1984), U.S. novelist, short story writer, playwright. The writer took his new surname in childhood from his stepfather, Joseph Garcia Capote.

Al **Capp**: Alfred Gerald Caplin (1909–1979), U.S. cartoonist.

Kate **Capshaw**: Kathy Sue Nail (1953–), U.S. movie actress.

Capucine: Germaine Lefebvre (1923 or 1933–1990), Fr. model, stage, movie actress.

Caracalla: Marcus Aurelius Severus Antoninus Augustus (188–217), Roman emperor. The infamous emperor was originally named Septimius Bassanius, for his father, Lucius Septimius Severus, and his maternal grandfather, Bassanius. He then assumed the name Marcus Aurelius Antoninus and added Caesar because his father wanted to link the family to the famous Antonine dynasty. In 198 he was given the title Augustus. The name by which he is now usually known, Caracalla, is said to refer to a new type of cloak that he designed, from a word of Gaulish origin.

Caran d'Ache: Emmanuel Poiré (1858–1909), Fr. caricaturist. The artist was born in Moscow, and took his name as a French respelling of the Russian word *karandash*, meaning "pencil." Compare the name of **Karandash.**

Caravaggio: Michelangelo Merisi (da Caravaggio) (1573–1610), It. painter. The painter's name is that of his birthplace, Caravaggio, near Bergamo in northern Italy.

Leos **Carax**: Alexandre Oscar Dupont (1961–), Fr. movie director, screenwriter, actor. The filmmaker's assumed name is an anagram of his first two names (in the form "Alex Oscar").

Francis **Carco**: François Marie Alexandre Carcopino-Tussoli (1886–1958), Fr. poet, writer.

Cardini: Richard Valentine Pitchford (1895–1973), Welsh magician, working in U.S. The illusionist was impressed as a boy by the skill of cardsharpers, and made card tricks his own special study. He began his stage career under names such as Val Raymond, Professor Thomas, and Valentine, until around 1923, when an Australian agent suggested he adopt a name like that of Houdini (*q.v.*). Hence his final name, alluding to his specialty.

The Great **Cardo**: Shree Probhat Kumar Chatterjee (1901– ?), Ind.-born Br. magician. The name alludes to the playing cards that are every illusionist's basic stock in trade.

Christine **Carère**: Christine de Borde (1930–), Fr. movie actress.

Carette: Julien Carette (1897–1966), Fr. movie actor.

Edwin **Carewe**: Jay Fox (1883–1940), U.S. movie director.

Joyce **Carey**: Joyce Lawrence (1898–1993), Eng. stage, movie actress. The actress used the name Jay Mallory for her play *Sweet Aloes*, in which she herself acted. This was filmed as *Give Me Your Heart* (1936), in which she had no part.

Jean-Pierre Cargol: Reyes Baliardo (1957–), Fr. juvenile movie actor, of Romany origin.

Karl Carl: Karl Andreas von Bernbrunn (1789–1854), Austr. actor, dramatist, impresario.

Frankie Carle: Francisco Nunzio Carlone (1903–), U.S. popular musician.

Richard Carle: Charles Carleton (1871–1941), U.S. movie actor.

Kitty Carlisle: Catherine Holtzman (1914–), U.S. opera singer, movie actress.

Carlo-Rim: Jean-Marius Richard (1905–1985), Fr. screenwriter, movie director. The name appears to be loosely based on the writer's real name, with "Carlo" representing "Richard" and the letters of "Rim" from "Marius."

Carlota: Marie-Charlotte-Amélie-Augustine-Victoire-Clémentine-Léopoldine (1840–1927), Belg.-born empress of Mexico. The wife of Emperor Maximilian adopted a Spanish version of the second word of her seven-part French name as a single name for standard use. Royal personages usually acquire strings of names like this with the aim of preserving the names of earlier family members. Léopoldine, for example, commemorated her father, Leopold I, king of the Belgians.

Richard Carlson: Albert Lea (1914–1977), U.S. movie actor, director.

Carlton: Arthur Carlton Philps (1881–1942), Eng. magician.

Felix Carmen: Frank Dempster Sherman (1860–1916), U.S. poet. The poet's adopted name translates as the Latin for "happy song."

Carmen Sylva: Elizabeth, Queen of Romania, née Pauline Elisabeth Ottilie Luise, Princess of Wied (1843–1916), Rom. verse, prose writer. The royal pen name reflected the writer's love of singing and of walks in the forest, from Latin *carmen*, "song," and *silva*,"wood." But both Carmen and Sylva are German women's names in their own right. (Elizabeth's works were mostly in German.)

T. Carmi: Charmi Charny (1925–), U.S.-born Israeli poet, editor.

Carmontelle: Louis Carrogis (1717–1806), Fr. portraitist, architect, dramatist.

Carol Carnac: Edith Caroline Rivett (1894–1958), Br. detective novelist. The writer seems to have evolved her *nom de plume* by using letters

from "Caroline," some more than once. She also wrote as E.C.R. Lorac (*q.v.*).

Judy Carne: Joyce Botterill (1939–), Eng. TV actress, working in U.S. The actress took her screen name "from a character she played years ago in a school play" [*TV Times Magazine*, June 5–11, 1982].

Dale Carnegie: Dale Carnegey (1888–1955), U.S. writer, public speaker.

Hattie Carnegie: Henrietta Kanengeiser (1886–1956), Austr.-born U.S. fashion designer. The designer adopted the surname of philanthropist Andrew Carnegie (1835–1919), as similar to her original name, on opening her first hat shop in New York in 1909. She married John Zanft in 1927 but never used his name publicly or professionally.

Mosco Carner: Mosco Cohen (1904–1985), Austr.-born Br. musicologist.

Martine Carol: Marie-Louise-Jeanne Mourer (1922–1967), Fr. movie actress.

Sue Carol: Evelyn Lederer (1907–1982), U.S. movie actress.

Francis Carpenter: Francis William Keef (1911–), U.S. child movie actor.

Catherine Carr: Rosalind Herschel Seymour, née Wade (1909–), Eng. novelist.

Glyn Carr: Frank Showell Styles (1908–), Br. detective novelist. The writer made his home in Wales, and his pseudonym is a typical Welsh placename, meaning "Carr valley."

Jane Carr: Rita Brunstrom (1909–1957). Br. movie actress, of Swe.-Eng. parentage.

Mary Carr: Mary Kennevan (1874–1973), U.S. stage, movie actress.

Michael Carr: Maurice Cohen (1904–1968), Br. songwriter.

Philippa Carr: Jean Plaidy (*q.v.*).

Vikki Carr: Florencia Bisenta de Casillas Martinez Cardona (1941–), U.S. pop singer.

Danny Carrel: Suzanne Chazelles du Chaxel (1935–), Fr. movie actress. The name evolved from the actress's first two names.

Tia Carrere: Althea Janairo (1967–), Hawaiian-born U.S. movie actress.

Arthur George Carrick: [Prince] Charles (1948–), Eng. prince. The Prince of Wales is a keen amateur painter, and this was the pseudonym he adopted for a painting of a farmhouse that he submitted to the 1988 Royal Academy Summer Show, London. His identity was revealed only after the picture was accepted. The prince's full name is Charles Philip Arthur

George. He is also Duke of Cornwall, and Carrick is an administrative district in that county.

Edward **Carrick:** Edward Anthony Craig (1905–), Br. art director, movie actor. "Carrick" means the same as "Craig," that is, "rock," the former name being a Celtic variant of the English (which itself corresponds to "crag").

John **Carrodus:** John Tiplady Carruthers (1836–1895), Br. violinist, teacher.

Norman **Carrol:** Sydney Edward Brandon (1890–), Eng. music hall comedian.

Andrea **Carroll:** Andrea Lee DeCapite (1946–), U.S. pop singer.

Diahann **Carroll:** Carol Diann Johnson (1935–), U.S. black TV singer, actress. When they were both 16, the singer and her friend Elissa Oppenheim turned up to audition for the TV show *Arthur Godfrey's Talent Scouts*, calling their act Oppenheim and Johnson. "'Before we take this any further,' the man in charge answered, 'I'd like you to go home and try to find another name. There's no way in the world we can announce, "Ladies and Gentlemen, Oppenheim and Johnson," then have you two march out there.' ... I was crestfallen, but Elissa wouldn't let herself be discouraged. Late that night ... she called with the solution to our problem. 'I've got it!' she proclaimed. 'I'm changing my name to Lisa Collins and you're going to be Diahann Carroll! D-i-a-h-a-n-n C-a-r-r-o-l-l. How does that sound to you? Is it all right?' 'It's fine, Elissa. Just fine,' I mumbled" [Diahann Carroll with Ross Firestone, *Diahann: An Autobiography*, 1986].

Elisabeth **Carroll:** Elisabeth Pfister (1937–), U.S. ballet dancer.

Joan **Carroll:** Joan Felt (1932–), U.S. child movie actress. The actress changed her name when she was only eight, choosing a name that seemed "musical."

John **Carroll:** Julian LaFaye (1905–1979), U.S. movie actor, singer.

Lewis **Carroll:** Charles Lutwidge Dodgson (1832–1898), Eng. children's writer. One of the most famous names in 19th-century English literature, that of the author of *Alice in Wonderland* (1865) and *Through the Looking-Glass* (1871), was really that of Charles Lutwidge Dodgson, a mathematical lecturer at Oxford University. His pseudonym is a transposition and translation (or rendering) of his first two names: Lutwidge to Lewis and Charles to Carroll. (Compare German Ludwig and Latin Car-

olus). He was requested to produce a pen name by Edmund Yates, editor of the humorous paper *The Train*, to which Dodgson was contributing in 1856. He first offered Yates the name Dares, after Daresbury, his Cheshire birthplace, but Yates thought this "too much like a newspaper signature." So Dodgson tried again, and on February 11, 1856, noted in his diary: "Wrote to Mr. Yates sending him a choice of names: 1. *Edgar Cuthwellis* (made by transposition out of "Charles Lutwidge"). 2. *Edgar U.S. Westhill* (ditto). 3. *Louis Carroll* (derived from Lutwidge ... Ludovic ... Louis, and Charles). 4. *Lewis Carroll* (ditto)."

Yates made his choice, saving all Alice lovers from Edgar Cuthwellis, and on March 1 Dodgson duly recorded in his diary "Lewis Carroll was chosen."

This was not actually Carroll's first pseudonym, since early contributions to *The Train* were signed as "B.B." (it was this that prompted his editor to ask for a proper *nom de plume*). The precise origin of B.B. is not clear, although Dodgson had shown a fondness for writing over mysterious initials as self-appointed editor of the Dodgson family journal, *The Rectory Magazine*. In this, as a 15-year-old schoolboy, he contributed pieces as V.X., F.L.W., J.V., F.X., Q.G.—and B.B. In her biography of Carroll, Anne Clark suggests that B.B.—which would appear to be one of the few initialized pseudonyms Dodgson retained for use in adult life—might perhaps stand for "Bobby Burns," since a number of the pieces contributed by the youthful author to *The Rectory Magazine* were mournful ballads in the style of Robert Burns. On the other hand in *Poverty Bay: A Nondescript Novel* (1905), by Harry Furniss, the illustrator chosen by Dodgson for *Sylvie and Bruno* (1889), the following is found: "He was known at Eton as "B.B.," short for Beau Brummell, the exquisite, whom he was supposed, by the boys at school, to emulate." Furniss was here perhaps consciously or unconsciously using Dodgson's own nickname, which had been confided to him some years before and which he now remembered. This seems quite a likely explanation for the strange double-letter name. Additionally, Francis King, reviewing Anne Clark's book in the *Sunday Telegraph* (September 9, 1979), points out that many of the names in Carroll's *The Hunting of the Snark* (1876) begin with B, including all the crew members (Bellman,

Barrister, Broker, Billiardmarker, Beaver, etc.) and the Snark itself, which ultimately turns out to be a Boojum!

Dodgson the don deliberately distanced himself from the persona of Lewis Carroll, and an enumeration of his factual and fictional writings in R. Farquharson Sharp's *A Dictionary of English Authors* (1897) has a footnote to the effect that "Mr. Dodgson states, with reference to this list, that he 'neither claims nor acknowledges any connection with the books not published under his name'." In other words, the man who wrote *An Elementary Treatise on Determinants* (1867) was not the creator of *Alice in Wonderland* [1. Anne Clark, *Lewis Carroll: A Biography*, 1979; 2. John Pudney, *Lewis Carroll and His World*, 1976].

Madeleine Carroll: Marie-Madeleine Bernadette O'Carroll (1906–1987), Br.-born U.S. movie actress.

Nancy Carroll: Ann Veronica La Hiff (1905–1965), U.S. movie actress. "Ann" gave "Nancy." The rest of the actress's name apparently gave the letters of "Carol," which with doubled letters produced "Carroll."

Ronnie Carroll: Ronald Cleghorn (1934–), Northern Ireland popular singer.

Sydney W. Carroll: George Frederick Carl Whiteman (1877–1958), Austral.-born Br. stage actor, critic, theatre manager. The actor's middle initial represents his surname, while his new surname is formed from his third name.

Arthur Carron: Arthur Cox (1900–1967), Eng. opera singer.

Jasper Carrott: Robert Davies (1945–), Eng. comedian. Davies explains how he came by his name: "Jasper is a nickname I picked up when I was nine, I don't know why. There is no reason for it. I added Carrott when I was 17. I was on a golf course with a friend, when he met somebody, and said: 'Oh, this is Jasper.' Carrott was the first name that came into my head. No one since school days has ever called me, or even known me, by my original name, Bob Davies" [*TV Times* February 15, 1979].

Carrott Top: Scott Thompson (1967–), U.S. stage comedian. The comedian was so nicknamed for his red hair, although the name to some extent happens to reflect his original name ("Carrot" from "Scott" and "Top" from "Thompson").

Arthur Carson: Peter Brooke (1907–), Eng.-born U.S. thriller writer.

Jeannie Carson: Jean Shufflebottom (1928–), Br. movie actress.

John Carson: John Derek Carson-Parker (1927–), Br. stage, TV actor.

Sunset Carson: Michael Harrison (1922–1990), U.S. movie actor. When the actor became a cowboy star in the 1940s, the movie company changed his name to coincide with the fictional Western hero he portrayed.

John Paddy Carstairs: John Keys (1910–1970), Eng. movie director, screenwriter.

Peter Carsten: Pieter Ransenthaler (1929–), Ger. movie actor, working in U.S.

Betty Carter: Lillie Mae Jones (1930–), U.S. black jazz singer.

Bo Carter: Armenter Chatmon (1893–1964), U.S. black blues musician.

Bruce Carter: Richard Alexander Hough (1922–), Eng. children's writer, publisher. The writer used the name Elizabeth Churchill for *Juliet in Publishing* (1956), while for *The Plane Wreckers* (1961) he was Pat Strong.

Carlene Carter: Rebecca Carlene Smith (1955–), U.S. country singer. The singer, a granddaughter of Maybelle Carter of the Carter Family, adopted her mother's maiden name as her professional name.

Helena Carter: Helen Rickerts (1923–), U.S. movie actress.

Jack Carter: John Chakrin (1922–), U.S. TV comic.

Janis Carter: Janis Dremann (1917–1994), U.S. movie actress.

Mrs. Leslie Carter: Caroline Louise Dudley (1862–1937), U.S. stage actress. An actress who, like Mrs. Patrick Campbell (*q.v.*), appeared professionally under her husband's name. She took to the stage in 1889, following the break-up of her marriage.

Nell Carter: Nell Hardy (1948–), U.S. stage, TV actress, singer.

Nick Carter: (1) John R. Coryell (1848–1924), U.S. popular fiction writer; (2) Thomas Chalmers Harbaugh (1849–1924), U.S. popular fiction writer; (3) Frederick Van Rensselaer Day (? 1861–1922), U.S. popular fiction writer. The name was adopted by the author (or authors) of a series of detective novels that appeared in the U.S. from about 1870. The character Nick Carter, who gave the name, is said to have been invented by Coryell and passed down by him to the other two.

Anna Carteret: Anna Wilkinson (1942–), Br. stage actress. The actress adopted her mother's maiden name as her stage name.

Richard Claude **Carton:** Richard Claude Critchett (1856–1928), Br. actor, dramatist.

Louise **Carver:** Louise Spilger Murray (1868–1956), U.S. movie actress.

Lynne **Carver:** Virginia Reid Sampson (1916–1955), U.S. movie actress. The actress began her screen career as Virginia Reid.

Ivan **Caryll:** Félix Tilken (1861–1921), Belg. operetta composer, working in U.K., U.S.

Maria **Casarès:** Maria Casarès Quiroga (1922–), Fr. movie actress, of Sp. parentage. The actress came to France with her family when she was 13. (This was in 1936, at the time of the civil war.)

Justin **Case:** Hugh Barnett Cave (1910–), Eng.-born U.S. horror fiction writer. A corny name, of course, but included here to show that at least one writer actually resorted to it.

Bill **Casey:** William Weldon (1909–), U.S. black blues singer, guitarist.

Alvin **Cash:** Alvin Welch (1939–), U.S. popular singer.

Jean **Casimir-Perier:** Jean Perier (1847–1907), Fr. statesman. In 1874 the future French president (from 1894 to 1895) added the first name of his grandfather, Casimir Perier (1777–1832), head of the Banque de France.

Sir Edwin **Caskoden:** Charles Major (1856–1913), U.S. novelist.

Alejandro **Casona:** Alejandro Rodríguez Álvarez (1903–1965), Sp. dramatist.

Cassandra: [Sir] William Neil Connor (1909–1967), Eng. columnist. Connor was columnist for the *Daily Mirror* from 1935, and was noted for his gloomily prophetic articles. His pen name reflects this, for in Greek mythology Cassandra was the daughter of Priam, king of Troy, who received the gift of prophecy from Apollo. However, when she refused the god's advances, he decreed that no one would believe her predictions, although they were invariably true. Her name has thus come to denote any "prophet of doom." The columnist did not choose the name himself, and it was given him by Harry Bartholomew, one of the newspaper's directors. Connor commented: "I was a bit surprised to discover that I had changed my sex; was the daughter of the King of Troy; that I could foretell in the stars when the news was going to be bad; ... that nobody believed me when I spoke the unpleasant truth" [Robert Connor, *Cassandra: Reflections in a Mirror*, 1969].

Cassandre: Adolphe-Jean-Marie Mouron (1901–1968), Fr. graphic artist, stage designer.

Jean-Pierre **Cassel:** Jean-Pierre Crochon (1932–), Fr. movie actor.

Butch **Cassidy:** Robert Le Roy Parker (1866–1909), U.S. outlaw, teaming with the Sundance Kid (*q.v.*). "Butch" was given as a nickname, since the bank and train robber worked as a butcher for a time when on the run from the law. "Cassidy" was an alias adopted from Mike Cassidy, an older outlaw from whom Parker learned cattle rustling and gunslinging.

Joanna **Cassidy:** Joanna Virginia Caskey (1944–), U.S. movie actress.

Billie **Cassin:** Joan Crawford (*q.v.*).

Andrea del **Castagno:** Andrea di Bartolo de Bargilla (*c.*1421–1457), It. painter. The artist was born near Castagno San Godenzo, Florence, and took his name from there.

Giorgione di **Castel Chiuso:** Peter Bayley (1778–1823), Eng. writer. The author used this name for *Sketches from St. George's Fields* (1820), a volume of verse with descriptions of London life. His pen name is an Italian-style rendering, literally meaning "closed castle," of his surname, since English "bailey," as a court in a castle, derives from Old French *baile*, "enclosure."

Leo **Castelli:** Leo Krauss (1907–), It.-born U.S. art dealer. The dealer adopted his mother's maiden name in 1919.

Don **Castle:** Marion Goodman, Jr. (1919–1966), U.S. movie actor.

Frances **Castle:** Evelyn Barbara Leader, née Blackburn (1898–1981), Eng. novelist, playwright.

Irene **Castle:** Irene Foote (1893–1969), U.S. cabaret dancer, teaming with Vernon Castle (see below), her husband.

Lee **Castle:** Aniello Castaldo (1915–1990), U.S. jazz trumpeter.

Vernon **Castle:** Vernon Blythe (1887–1918), Br. cabaret dancer, aviator, teaming with Irene Castle (see above), his wife.

William **Castle:** William Schloss (1914–1977), U.S. horror movie director. The English surname translates the German original.

Harry **Castlemon:** Charles Austin Fosdick (1842–1915), U.S. writer of adventure stories for boys.

Gilbert **Cates:** Gilbert Katz (1934–), U.S. movie director, uncle of Phoebe Cates (see below).

Phoebe **Cates:** Phoebe Katz (1963–), U.S. movie actress, niece of Gilbert Cates (see above).

Ambrosius **Catharinus:** Lancelot Politi (*c.*1484–1553), It. theologian. The scholar entered the Dominican order in 1517 and adopted his religious name in honor of the two Sienese saints of that order, Blessed Ambrosius Sansedone and St. Catherine (of Siena).

Willa **Cather:** Wilella Cather (1873–1947), U.S. novelist, short story writer. The writer tried out the full names Willa Love Cather and Willa Lova Cather before settling for Willa Sibert Cather, taking the middle name from an uncle on her mother's side who was killed fighting for the Confederacy. She adopted this name in 1902, three years before publishing her first book of short stories and ten years before her first novel.

Catherine I: Marta Skawronska (1684–1727), Russ. empress. The Empress of Russia was the daughter of a Lithuanian peasant named Samuil Skawronski. In 1703 she was received into the Russian Orthodox Church and rechristened Catherine (Russian Yekaterina) Alekseyevna. She married Peter the Great in 1712.

Catherine II: Sophie Friederike Auguste [Prinzessin] von Anhalt-Zerbst (1729–1796), Ger.-born Russ. empress. Catherine the Great, Empress of Russia, was born the daughter of an obscure German prince, Christian August von Anhalt-Zerbst. She assumed the title of Catherine (Russian Yekaterina) Alekseyevna on arriving in Russia in 1744 and married her cousin, the future Peter III, the following year.

[St.] **Catherine:** Alessandra Lucrezia Romola dei Ricci (1522–1590), It. mystic. The saint is known by the name she assumed on entering a Dominican convent at the age of 13. The name itself honors St. Catherine of Siena (Caterina Benincasa), who is venerated by the Dominican order.

Cat Iron: William Carradine (*c.*1896–*c.*1958), U.S. blues singer. The musician derived his name through a journalist's mishearing of his surname.

Christopher **Caudwell:** Christopher St. John Sprigg (1907–1937), Br. Marxist writer. Was Caudwell ("cold well") meant to serve as synonym for Sprigg (as if meaning "spring")?

Christopher **Caustic:** Thomas Green Fessenden (1771–1837), U.S. author, inventor, lawyer.

C.P. **Cavafy:** Konstantinos Petrou Kavafis (1863–1933), Gk. poet.

Alberto **Cavalcanti:** Alberto de Almeida-Cavalcanti (1897–1926), Brazilian movie actor.

Alain **Cavalier:** Alain Fraissé (1931–), Fr. movie director.

Francesco **Cavalli:** Pier Francesco Caletti di Bruno (1602–1676), It. opera composer. The musician assumed the name of his Venetian patron, Federico Cavalli.

Anna **Cavan:** Helen Ferguson, née Woods (1901–1968), Eng. novelist. The writer adopted the name of one of her own fictional characters. Her first novel following the creation of her new persona had the apt title *Change the Name* (1941).

Cavendish: Henry Jones (1831–1899), Br. authority on whist. The writer took his name from his club, the Cavendish, in Cavendish Square, London.

Kay **Cavendish:** Kathleen Murray (–), Br. pianist, "croonette," broadcaster.

Cawrdaf: William Ellis Jones (1795–1848), Welsh poet.

Pisistratus **Caxton:** [Lord] Edward George Earle Lytton Bulwer Lytton (1803–1873), Eng. novelist, playwright, statesman. One of several pseudonyms used at different times by the writer. This one was no doubt semi-seriously derived from Pisistratus, the 5th-century B.C. "Tyrant of Athens," and William Caxton, the first English printer.

Arthur **Cecil:** Arthur Cecil Blunt (1843–1896), Eng. actor.

Henry **Cecil:** Henry Cecil Leon (1902–1976), Br. author, playwright.

Ceiriog: John Hughes (1832–1887), Welsh poet, folk musicologist. Ceiriog was the poet's bardic name, taken from that of the village where he was born, Llanarmon Dyffryn Ceiriog, and itself named for the river on which it lies.

Paul **Celan:** Paul Leo Anschel (1920–1970), Rom.-born Ger. poet, translator, working in France. The writer appears to have created his new name from his original surname, reversing the syllables.

Madame **Céleste:** Céleste (or Céline) Elliot, née Keppler (*c.*1810–1882), Fr. dancer, actress, working in U.S., U.K. The dancer married an American, but performed mainly in England.

Celestine II: Guido di Città di Castello (? –1144), It. pope.

Celestine III: Giacinto Orsini (*c.*1106–1198), It. pope. The pontiff took his name from his former fellow-student, Celestine II (*q.v.*), who had created him cardinal in 1144.

Celestine IV: Goffredo Castiglioni (? –1241), It. pope.

[St.] **Celestine V:** Pietro da Morrone (*c.*1209–1296), It. pope.

Céline: Odette Marie Céline Hallowes (earlier Sansom, then Churchill), née Brailly (1912–1995), Fr.-born Br. wartime agent. This was the code name taken by the World War II agent better known as Odette (*q.v.*): "Every pupil, student, undergraduate, should choose a name, a Christian name, and during the period of training, she would be known only by that name. Now what name would Mrs. Sansom like? Odette thought for a moment. Her real names were Odette Marie Céline. She said cautiously: 'Would "Céline" do?' 'Certainly. We haven't got a Céline. For purposes of training, you are simply "Céline" from now on" [Jerrard Tickell, *Odette: The Story of a British Agent*, 1949]. Odette worked for Raoul (*q.v.*).

Louis-Ferdinand **Céline:** Louis-Ferdinand Destouches (1894–1961), Fr. novelist. The writer adopted his mother's first name as his new surname.

Blaise **Cendrars:** Frédéric Louis Sauser (1887–1961), Fr. novelist, poet, of Swiss parentage. The poet is said to have adopted a name that was a blend of the name of St. Blaise, French *braise*, "embers," French *cendres*, "cinders," and Latin *ars*, "skill," "art," with an overall evocation of lines from Nietzsche: "And everything of mine turns to mere cinders/What I love and what I do."

Luigia **Cerale:** Luigia Cerallo (1859–1937), It. ballet dancer.

C.W. **Ceram:** Kurt W. Marek (1915–1972), Ger.-born U.S. writer, archaeologist. The writer's pen name reversed his real name.

Ceridwen Peris: Alice Gray Jones (1852–1943), Welsh, writer, editor. The writer's new first name is that of the goddess said to have been the mother of the legendary 6th-century poet Taliesin. Her second name is that of a lake in northern Wales. Both names are forenames in their own right.

Frederick **Cerny:** Frederick Guthrie (1833–1886), Eng. physicist. The scientist used his pen name for two poems published early in his life. "Cerny" looks as if it bears some relation to "Guthrie," although it may have had some other origin.

César: César Baldaccini (1921–), Fr. sculptor.

Jacques **Chaban-Delmas:** Jacques Delmas (1915–), Fr. politician, prime minister. The politician took the first part of his surname as his cover name in World War II, when active in the Resistance. The name itself is that of the château of Chaban, at St.-Léon-sur-Vézère in the Dordogne, where he set up a network of underground agents.

Marc **Chagall:** Moyshe Segal (1887–1985), Russ.-born Fr. artist, of Jewish parentage.

Cham: [Comte] Amédée de Noé (1819–1879), Fr. caricaturist. As one might expect from an artist of this genre, the name is a quiet pun. "Cham" is the French for "Ham," second son of the biblical Noah, whose name in French is "Noé."

Champfleury: Jules-François-Félix Husson (1821–1889), Fr. novelist, journalist. Jules Husson was Jules Fleury before he became Champfleury, and the latter name seems to have developed from the former. It was no doubt suggested by *Champfleury*, a work by the 16th-century grammarian Geoffrey Tory. It encouraged the writing of learned works in French, as against the traditional Latin.

Harry **Champion:** William Henry Crump (1866–1942), Br. stage comedian, singer.

Marge **Champion:** Marjorie Celeste Belcher (1921–), U.S. movie actress, dancer. The actress was initially billed as Marjorie Bell before taking the name of her dancer, actor, and director husband, Gower Champion, with whom she featured in the 1950s.

Jackie **Chan:** Chan Kwong Sang (or Chan Gang-shen) (1954–), Hong Kong movie actor, director.

James **Chance:** James Siegfried (1953–), U.S. rock musician.

John T. **Chance:** John Carpenter (1948–), U.S. movie director, writer. Carpenter edited *Assault on Precinct 13* (1976) under this name, retaining his real name as this movie's director, screenwriter, and music composer.

Gene **Chandler:** Eugene Dixon (1937–), U.S. pop singer, record producer. The musician adopted his new name from that of his favorite actor, Jeff Chandler (see below).

Jeff **Chandler:** Ira Grossel (1918–1961), U.S. stage, movie actor.

Lane **Chandler:** Robert Lane Oakes (1899–1972), U.S. movie actor.

Fay **Chandos:** Irene Maude Swatridge, née Mossop (*c.*1905–), Eng. romantic novelist. The writer also published as Theresa Charles, Leslie Lance, and Jan Tempest.

Jung **Chang:** Er-hong Chang (1952–), Chin. writer, working in U.K. The doctor attending the writer's birth exclaimed, "Ah, another wild swan is born." Hence her original name, Erhong, "second wild swan." She acquired her new name at the age of 12, following a comment by a politics teacher that Communist China could change color "from bright red to faded red":

"It so happened that the Sichuan expression 'faded red' had exactly the same pronunciation (*er-hong*) as my name. ... I felt I must get rid of my name immediately. That evening I begged my father to give me another name. ... I told my father that I wanted 'something with a military ring to it.' ... My new name, Jung (pronounced 'Yung'), was a very old and recondite word for 'martial affairs.' ... It evoked an image of bygone battles between knights in shining armor, with tasseled spears and neighing steeds. When I turned up at school with my new name even some teachers could not recognize the [Chinese] character" [Jung Chang, *Wild Swans: Three Daughters of China*, 1991].

Stockard Channing: Susan Williams Antonia Stockard Channing Schmidt (1944–), U.S. movie, TV actress.

Mlle Chantilly: Marie-Justine-Benoiste Duronceray (1727–1772), Fr. actress.

Martin Chapender: H.M. Jones (*c*.1876-1905), Eng. conjuror.

Saul Chaplin: Saul Kaplan (1912–), U.S. movie music composer, musical director.

Jacques Chardonne: Jacques Boutelleau (1884–1968), Fr. novelist.

Yegishe Charents: Yegishe Abgarovich Sogomonyan (1897–1937), Armenian poet. The poet's adopted name means "of indomitable lineage."

Cyd Charisse: Tula Ellice Finklea (1921–), U.S. movie actress. Many filmographies give the actress's "real" name as shown here. And indeed that was how she started life. But Charisse is equally "real," as it is the name of her first husband, ballet teacher Nico Charisse. She retained the name although soon divorcing Charisse and marrying actor and singer Tony Martin. "Cyd" is the name that is not genuine. When a young child she was called "Sid" by her baby brother, in his attempt to say "sister." She adopted the name, but respelled it "Cyd." A genuine pseudonym was that of Felia Sidorova, which Tula used when she first danced (in 1939). This was derived from "Finklea" and the same "Sid" in Russian-elaborated form. For her early movie roles she took the name Lily Norwood.

Charlene: Charlene Duncan (1950–), U.S. pop singer.

Charles XIV: [Count] Jean-Baptiste Bernadotte (1763–1844), Fr.-born king of Sweden. Bernadotte rose to be a high-ranking officer in the French army and was held in favor by Napoleon when campaigning against Sweden in 1809. In 1810 he was elected Swedish crown prince, mainly through Sweden's wish to retain Napoleon's goodwill, but also as a result of financial promises from Bernadotte himself. He was adopted as son by the childless reigning king, Charles XIII, and took the name of Charles John (Karl Johan). On the death of Charles XIII in 1818 the prince became king of Sweden and Norway, taking the regnal name and number of Charles XIV.

Bobby Charles: Robert Charles Guidry (1938–), U.S. black rock songwriter.

Hugh Charles: Charles Hugh Owen Ferry (1907–1995), Br. songwriter.

Kate Charles: Carol Ann Chase, née Fosher (1950–), U.S. crime writer.

Maria Charles: Maria Zena Schneider (1929–), Br. movie, TV actress.

Pamela Charles: Pamela Foster (1932–), Eng. stage actress, singer. The actress adopted her father's first name as her stage name.

Ray Charles: Ray Charles Robinson (1930–), U.S. black popular singer. Robinson dropped his surname in order not to be confused with the champion boxer, Sugar Ray Robinson (*q.v.*).

Teddy Charles: Theodore Charles Cohen (1928–), U.S. jazz musician.

Aunt Charlotte: Charlotte Mary Yonge (1823–1901), Eng. novelist, children's writer. The author used this name for a series of historical works for children, beginning with *Aunt Charlotte's Stories of English History* (1873).

Charlotte Elizabeth: Charlotte Elizabeth Tonna, earlier Phelan, née Browne (1790–1846), Eng. writer of evangelical books for children.

John Charlton: Martin Charlton Woodhouse (1932–), Eng. novelist, mystery writer. Woodhouse selected a family name for his "rather violent detective story," *The Remington Set* (1975). This was full of cops and robbers and four-letter words, so a different name was desirable in order not to shock his regular readers.

Charo: Maria del Rosario Pilar Martinez Molina Baeza (1948–), Can. folk singer.

Mikhas Charot: Mikhail Semyonovich Kudzelka (1896–1938), Belorussian poet. The poet's adopted plant name means "reed," "rush."

Lidiya **Charskaya:** Lidiya Alekseyevna Churilova (1875–1937), Russ. writer, actress. An alteration of an awkward-sounding surname to a more euphonious one.

Leslie **Charteris:** Leslie Charles Bowyer Yin (1907–1993), Singapore-born U.S. crime novelist, of Eng.-Chin. parentage. The writer adopted his new surname from that of the colorful Scottish criminal Colonel Francis Charteris (1675–1732).

Alida **Chase:** Alida Anderson (1951–), Austral. ballet dancer.

Beatrice **Chase:** Olive Katharine Parr (1874–1911), Eng. novelist.

Borden **Chase:** Frank Fowler (1900–1971), U.S. screenwriter. The writer took his name from the familiar food company (Borden) and bank (Manhattan Chase).

Charlie **Chase:** Charles Parrott (1893–1940), U.S. movie comedian.

James Hadley **Chase:** René Brabazon Raymond (1906–1985), Eng. thriller writer. The name appears to be a fairly random one (more American than British) for a writer who also used other pseudonyms, such as James L. Docherty, Ambrose Grant, and Raymond Marshall.

Geoffrey **Chater:** Geoffrey Michael Chater Robinson (1921–), Eng. stage, movie, TV actor.

Daniel **Chaucer:** Ford Madox Ford (*q.v.*).

Mary **Chavelita:** Mary Chavelita Dunne (1860–1945), Austral. novelist.

Paddy **Chayevsky:** Sidney Stuchevsky (1923–1981), U.S. playwright, screenwriter.

Chubby **Checker:** Ernest Evans (1941–), U.S. black pop musician. The name originated as a nickname, comparing the musician to Fats Domino (*q.v.*), whom he resembled when young. ("Checker" because he checked with him, or resembled him.) The nickname is said to have been given by the wife of U.S. pop promoter Dick Clark.

Cheech: Richard Marin (1946–), U.S. movie comedian, teaming with (Thomas) Chong. Richard "Cheech" Marin is said to have earned his nickname from his fondness for the Chicano food specialty cheecharone (chicharones), a type of crackling.

Cheero: George Ernest Studdy (1878–1948), Eng. cartoonist, illustrator. The artist used this name for his drawings for comic postcards.

Cheiro: [Count] Louis Hamon (1866–1936), U.S. writer on palmistry. A name from the Greek element that gives the word "cheiro-

mancy," otherwise palmistry, Greek *kheir* meaning "hand." The title pages of some of Cheiro's books inform readers that the name is "pronounced KI-RO."

Antosha **Chekhonte:** Anton Pavlovich Chekhov (1860–1904), Russ. short story writer, dramatist. The name was humorously given to the young Anton by Father Pokrovsky, his scripture teacher at school in Taganrog, and Chekhov adopted it for several early, lighter writings in various magazines. In 1886 he explained to a journalist: "The pen name 'A. Chekhonte' may seem somewhat weird and wonderful, but it arose back in the hazy days of my youth. I have got used to it, and so no longer regard it as strange." It was not just Chekhov that Pokrovsky selected for this treatment, however, and he liked giving amusing names to his students generally.

Chekhov used the name for his first book, *Tales of Melpomene* (1884), but was advised to use his real name for his second, *Motley Stories* (1886). His response: "I don't see why the public should prefer 'An. Chekhov' to 'A. Chekhonte.' Is there really any diference? ... I have devoted my surname to medicine, which will stay with me to my dying day. Sooner or later I shall have to give up writing anyway. Secondly, medicine, which takes itself seriously, and the diversion of writing should have different names." In the event he used A. Chekhonte for *Motley Stories* but added his real name in brackets. For his third book, *In the Gloaming* (1887), he not only abandoned his pseudonym but gave his full initials, "An. P.," to avoid any confusion with his brother Alexander, also a writer [Dmitriyev, p. 95].

Chekhov used over 40 pseudonyms at one time or another, including (in translation) "A Doctor With No Patients," "A Man With No Spleen," "My Brother's Brother," and "A Prosaic Poet."

Joan **Chen:** Chen Chong (1961–), Chin.-born U.S. movie actress. Chinese "Chong" has here become English "Joan."

Pierre **Chenal:** Pierre Cohen (1903–1990), Fr. movie director.

Cher: Cherilyn Sarkisian LaPiere (1946–), U.S. pop singer, movie actress, formerly teaming with husband Sonny (*q.v.*).

Marko **Cheremshina:** Ivan Yuryevich Semanyuk (1874–1927), Ukrainian writer. The writer adopted a plant name meaning "bird-cherry tree."

Rose **Chéri:** Rose-Marie Cizos (1824–1861), Fr. actress.

Gwen **Cherrell:** Gwen Chambers (1926–), Eng. stage actress.

Neneh **Cherry:** Neneh Mariann Karlsson (1964–), Br. rock singer, of Swe.-African parentage. The singer adopted the name of her stepfather, jazz trumpeter Don Cherry.

Weatherby **Chesney:** Charles John Cutliffe Wright Hyne (1865–1944), Eng. traveler, novelist. "Chesney" presumably from letters in "Charles Hyne," and "Weatherby" perhaps from Wetherby, the Yorkshire town not far from Bradford, where the writer was born and where he lived.

Betty **Chester:** Elizabeth Grundtvig (1895– ?), Br. stage, movie actress.

Charlie **Chester:** Cecil Victor Manser (1914–1997), Br. stage actor, entertainer.

Robert **Chetwyn:** Robert Suckling (1933–), Br. stage actor.

Maria **Chevska:** Maria Elizabeth Skwarczewska (1948–), Br. painter.

Peter **Cheyney:** Reginald Evelyn Peter Southhouse-Cheyney (1896–1951), Ir. crime novelist.

Walter **Chiari:** Walter Annichiarico (1924–1991), It. movie actor.

Chic: Cyril Alfred Jacob (1926–), Eng. cartoonist, illustrator. The artist's signature arose as a contraction of his childhood nickname "Chickabiddy."

Judy **Chicago:** Judy Cohen (1939–), U.S. feminist artist. The artist took her new name from the city of her birth.

Chief Thundercloud: (1) Victor Daniels (1899–1955), Native American movie actor; (2) Scott Williams (1901–1967), U.S. radio, movie actor, of Native American descent.

Charles B. **Childs:** Charles Vernon Frost (1903–), Eng. mystery writer.

Chiquito de Cambo: Joseph Apesteguy (1881–1955), Fr. pelota player. The sportsman adopted his Spanish nickname, meaning "The Kid from Cambo." He was born in the southwest of France near the Spanish border in the small resort town of Cambo-les-Bains.

Gali **Chokry:** Mukhammetgali Gabdelsalikhovich Kiyekov (1826–1889), Russ. (Bashkir) poet. The writer adopted the name of his native village as his new surname.

Alice **Cholmondeley:** Elizabeth (*q.v.*).

Kuzma **Chorny:** Nikolay Karlovich Romanovsky (1900–1944), Belorussian writer. The writer's adoped surname means "black," presumably referring to his appearance. Compare the name of Sasha Chyorny (below).

Linda **Christian:** Blanca Rosa Welter (1923–), Mexican movie actress.

Neil **Christian:** Christopher Tidmarsh (1943–), Eng. pop musician.

Paul **Christian:** Paul Hubschmid (1917–), Ger./Sw.-born U.S. movie actor.

Christian-Jaque: Christian Albert François Maudet (1904–1994), Fr. movie director, writer.

Lou **Christie:** Lugee Alfredo Giovanni Sacco (1943–), U.S. pop singer.

Tony **Christie:** Anthony Fitzgerald (1944–), Eng. pop musician.

Christo: Christo Javacheff (1935–), Bulg.-born U.S. sculptor, designer, "package art" practitioner, teaming with Jeanne-Claude (Jeanne-Claude de Guillebon), his wife.

Dennis **Christopher:** Dennis Carelli (1955–), U.S. movie actor.

John **Christopher:** Christopher Samuel Youd (1922–), Eng. SF novelist, children's writer. Other names used by the writer include Hilary Ford, William Godfrey, Peter Graaf, Peter Nichols, and Anthony Rye.

June **Christy:** Shirley Luster (1925–1990), U.S. jazz singer. The singer first used the name Sharon Leslie before finally settling on June Christy.

Chrys: George Fraser Chrystal (1921–1972), Sc. political, sports cartoonist.

Chryssa: Varda Chryssa (1933–), Gk.-born U.S. sculptor.

Korney Ivanovich **Chukovsky:** Nikolay Vasilyevich Korneychuk (1882–1969), Russ. critic, poet. The writer used his surname to form a new first and last name, at the same time adopting a new patronymic (middle name).

Chulpan: Abdul-Khamid Suleyman ogly Yunusov (1893–1937), Uzbek writer. The writer's adopted name means "morning star."

Chung Ling Soo: William Ellsworth Campbell (1861–1918), U.S. conjuror. The artist originally used the name William E. "Billy" Robinson in the U.S. When in England in 1900, he modeled himself on a real Chinese conjuror, Ching Ling Foo, who had toured successfully in the USA. Ching accused Campbell of being an impostor, and he admitted it. However, this impersonation made him all the more popular with his audiences. The name itself was said to mean "very good luck."

Nikolay **Chuzhak:** Nikolay Fyodorovich Nasimovich (1876–1937), Russ. revolutionary, writer, literary critic. The activist's adopted name means "stranger," "alien."

Sasha **Chyorny:** Aleksandr Mikhaylovich Glikberg (Glickberg) (1880–1932), Russ. poet. The poet's adopted surname means "black," presumably referring to his appearance. Glikberg was not too pleased when in the 1910s another writer, the humorist Aleksandr Sokolov, started signing his work by exactly the same name. Compare the name of Kuzma Chorny (above).

Cicero: Elyesa Bazna (1904–1970), Ger. spy. The secret agent, one of the most famous spies of World War II, worked for Nazi Germany while employed as a valet to Sir Hughe Montgomery Knatchbull-Hugessen, British ambassador to neutral Turkey. His code name of Cicero was given him by the former German chancellor, Franz von Papen, "because his information spoke so eloquently." The Roman statesman Marcus Tullius Cicero was a noted orator. (See also next entry below.)

Marcus Tullius **Cicero:** William Melmoth the Elder (1666–1743), Eng. religious writer, lawyer. The three-part name was the full one of the famous Roman orator. (See also entry above.)

Ciceruacchio: Angelo Brunetti (1800–1849), It. revolutionary. The activist adopted his nickname, meaning "crafty Cicero."

The **Cid:** Rodrigo (or Ruy) Díaz de Vivar (*c.*1043–1099), Sp. military leader. The Castilian national hero's name, in Spanish *El Cid*, comes from Spanish Arabic *as-sī*, "the lord."

Cimabue: Bencivieni (or Cenni) di Pepo (*c.*1240–*c.*1302), It. painter, mosaicist. The name reveals something of the artist's proud and impetuous nature. It arose as a nickname, and means effectively "bullheaded," from Italian *cima*, "top," "head," and *bue*, "ox."

Cino da Pistoia: Cino dei Sighibuldi (*c.*1270–1336), It. poet, jurist. The writer is named for his native town of Pistoia, near Florence.

Paul **Cinquevalli:** Paul Kestner (1859–1918), Pol.-born U.S. juggler. The performer adopted the name of his tutor in the art, Cinquevalli.

A **Citizen of New York:** Alexander Hamilton (1737–1804), U.S. statesman + James Madison (1751–1836), U.S. president + John Jay (1745–1829), U.S. jurist, statesman. The three men adopted the unified name for their essays in the *Federalist* in favor of the new U.S. Constitution

(1787–1788). They subsequently adopted the joint name Publius (*q.v.*).

Mavis **Clair:** Mavis Tunnell (1916–), Eng. stage actress.

René **Clair:** René-Lucien Chomette (1898–1981), Fr. movie director. The director first adopted the name as an actor in 1920. He presumably aimed to avoid the associations of his surname, which to the French suggests being out of work (*chômer*, "to be unemployed").

Bernice **Claire:** Bernice Jahnigan (1911–), U.S. movie actress.

Ina **Claire:** Ina Fagan (1892–1985), U.S. stage, movie actress. The actress adopted her mother's maiden name as her stage name.

Mlle **Clairon:** Claire-Josèphe-Hippolyte Léris de la Tude (1723–1803), Fr. tragic actress. "Clairon" not only suggests the actress's first name, but is meaningful in French as the word for "bugle."

Eric **Clapton:** Eric Patrick Clapp (1945–), Eng. rock guitarist.

Ada **Clare:** Jane McElheney (1836–1874), U.S. writer of passionate poetry and fiction.

Claribel: Charlotte Alington Barnard, née Pye (1830–1869), Ir. writer of popular ballads. The name occurs occasionally for characters in classical literature. It suggests both "clear" and "beautiful" (as the voice or words of a balladeer should be), and also contains letters in the writer's real name. She also wrote as Condor.

Clarín: Leopoldo Enrique García-Alas Ureña (1852–1901), Sp. novelist, critic. The writer's pen name means "bugle," and refers to his prominent critical "voice." As a critic, Leopoldo Alas (as he was usually known) was one of the most influential of his time, and his articles were noted for their "bite" and belligerence.

Clarinda: Agnes Maclehose, née Craig (1759–1841), Sc. correspondent of Sylvander (*q.v.*). Both names are typical of classical literature. Clarinda occurs in Spenser's *Faerie Queene*, for example.

Buddy **Clark:** Samuel Goldberg (1912–1949), U.S. popular singer.

Dane **Clark:** Bernard Zanville (1913–), U.S. movie actor.

Ossie **Clark:** Raymond Clark (1942–1996), Eng. fashion designer. The artist's new first name arose as a nickname, itself from the town of Oswaldtwistle, Lancashire, where he was raised in World War II.

Susan **Clark:** Nora Golding (1940–), Can.-born U.S. movie actress.

The Rev. T. **Clark:** John Galt (1779–1839), Sc. novelist. The novelist used the name for *The Wandering Jew* (1820). For the really astute reader, he encoded his actual surname in the initial letters of the words beginning the book's last four sentences. These were "Greatness," "All," "Literally," "To."

George **Clarke:** George Broome (1886–1946), Eng. stage, movie actor.

John **Clarke:** Richard Cromwell (1626–1712), Eng. soldier, politician. The eldest son of Oliver Cromwell used this name when living in seclusion in Paris from 1659 to 1680.

Mae **Clarke:** Violet Klotz (1907–1992), U.S. movie actress.

Shirley **Clarke:** Shirley Brimberg (1925–), U.S. movie director.

Madame **Claude:** Fernande Grudet (1924–), Fr. procureuse.

Claude Lorrain: Claude Gellée (1600–1682), Fr. landscape painter. "Lorrain" is not the painter's surname, as sometimes supposed, but represents Lorraine, the region of France where he was born and where, for a short period in 1625, he worked. The name distinguished him from other artists named Claude.

Jean **Claudio:** Claude Martin (1927), Fr. juvenile movie actor. The actor was billed as simply Claudio at the start of his career, but then prefixed that with Jean as if it were a surname.

Eduard **Claudius:** Eduard Schmidt (1911–1976), Ger. writer. The writer adopted his name in honor of the 1st-century AD Roman emperor, scholar, and historian, whom he admired.

Heinrich **Clauren:** Karl G.S. Heun (1771–1854), Ger. writer. The writer used this name for his entertaining burlesque *Der Mann im Mond* ("The Man in the Moon") (1826). The name itself is loosely based on his original first name and surname, in reverse order.

Mrs. Mary **Clavers:** Caroline Matilda Kirkland, née Stansbury (1801–1864), U.S. short story writer, novelist. The author used this protective name for *A New Home—Who'll Follow?* (1839), a semifictional personal account of Michigan frontier life.

Andrew Dice **Clay:** Andrew Clay Silverstein (1958–), U.S. movie comedian.

Bertha M. **Clay:** Charlotte Monica Braeme (1836–1884), Eng. romantic noveist. It may be coincidental, but almost all of the letters in the writer's pseudonym can be found in her real full name. (And all letters if one counts "i" as "y.")

Joe **Clay:** Claiborne Joseph Cheramie (1939–), U.S. rockabilly guitarist.

Judy **Clay:** Judy Guion (–), U.S. soul singer.

Richard **Clayderman:** Philippe Pages (1954–), Fr. popular pianist. The pianist's name was altered by composers and record producers Olivier Toussaint and Paul de Senneville to one that could not be mispronounced abroad. But why cloying "Clayderman"?

Lou **Clayton:** Louis Finkelstein (1887–1950), U.S. vaudeville actor.

Lucie **Clayton:** Evelyn Florence Kark, née Gordine (1928–1997), Eng. fashion designer.

Eddy **Clearwater:** Eddy Harrington (1935–), U.S. blues musician.

Lucas **Cleeve:** Adeline Georgina Isabella Kingscote, née Wolff (? –1908), Eng. novelist.

Jedediah **Cleishbotham:** [Sir] Walter Scott (1771–1832), Sc. poet, novelist. One of the humorous pen names devised by the Scottish writer. (Others were Chrystal Croftangry and Captain Cuthbert Clutterbuck.) This particular name was used for the four series of his *Tales of My Landlord* (1816), with the author supposedly a schoolmaster and parish clerk. The name ties in well with these two occupations: "Jedediah" is a typical Puritan name, and "Cleishbotham" means "whip-bottom" (Scottish dialect *cleish*, "to whip"). A writer in the January, 1817, number of the *Quarterly Review* commented: "Why he [Scott] should industriously endeavour to elude observation by taking leave of us in one character, and then suddenly popping out upon us in another, we cannot pretend to guess without knowing more of his personal reasons for preserving so strict an incognito than has hitherto reached us."

Clement II: Suidger (? –1047), It. pope.

Clement III: Paolo Scolari (? –1191), It. pope.

Clement IV: Guy Folques (or Guido Fulconi) (*c.*1195–1268), Fr. pope.

Clement V: Bertrand de Got (*c.*1260–1314), Fr. pope.

Clement VI: Pierre Roger (1291–1352), Fr. pope.

Clement VII: Giulio de' Medici (1478–1534), It. pope.

Clement VIII: Ippolito Aldobrandini (1536–1605), It. pope.

Clement IX: Giulio Rospigliosi (1600–1669), It. pope.

Clement X: Emilio Bonaventura Altieri (1590–1676), It. pope.

Clement XI: Giovanni Francesco Albani (1649–1721), It. pope.

Clement XII: Lorenzo Corsini (1652–1740), It. pope. The pontiff adopted the name of his patron, Clement XI (above), who had created him cardinal in 1706. He himself gave the name of Clement XIII (below).

Clement XIII: Carlo della Torre Rezzonico (1693–1769), It. pope. The pontiff adopted the name of his patron, Clement XII (above), who had created him cardinal in 1737. He himself gave the name of Clement XIV (below).

Clement XIV: Giovanni Vincenzo Antonio Ganganelli (1705–1774), It. pope. The pontiff adopted the name of his patron, Clement XIII (above), who had created him cardinal in 1759.

Hal **Clement:** Harry Clement Stubbs (1922–), U.S. SF writer.

Arthur **Clements:** Andrew Clement Baker (1842–1913), Eng. journalist, writer. The writer used this name, a variant on his first two names, for articles in the *Illustrated Sporting and Dramatic News*, of which he became editor.

E. **Clerihew:** Edmund Clerihew Bentley (1875–1956), Eng. writer, inventor of the *clerihew*. The writer's unusual second name, which he used as a pen name and which has now passed into the language in its own right, was his mother's maiden name.

Jimmy **Cliff:** James Chambers (1948–), Jamaican reggae singer. The musician changed his name in the early 1960s, choosing "Cliff" because it implied the "heights" to which he aspired.

Laddie **Cliff:** Clifford Albyn Perry (1891–1937), Br. stage, movie comedian, composer.

Charles **Clifford:** William Henry Ireland (1777–1835), Eng. Shakespearean forger.

Martin **Clifford:** Frank Richards (*q.v.*).

Bill **Clifton:** William August Marburg (1931–), U.S. folk musician.

Patsy **Cline:** Virginia Patterson Hensley (1932–1963), U.S. country singer. The singer's new first name was formed from her middle name, while her new surname was that of her first husband, Gerald Cline (married 1953, marriage dissolved 1955).

Bill **Clinton:** William Jefferson Blythe IV (1946–), U.S. president. The 42nd president of the U.S. takes his surname from his stepfather, Roger Clinton. His actual father, William Jefferson Blythe, died in an automobile accident before his son was born.

Clio: (1) Joseph Addison (1672–1719), Eng. poet, dramatist, essayist; (2) Thomas Rickman (1761–1834), Eng. bookseller, reformer. These two names have different origins. For Addison, the letters represented *C*helsea, *L*ondon, *I*slington, the *O*ffice, as the places where he lived and worked. (He was a civil servant, so that "Office" means "government office.") But the letters could equally represent his initials in a signature. And of course they also stand for the name of Clio, the Muse of History, which was the sense chosen by Rickman. It arose as a nickname when he was a student, for his precocity as a poet and his taste for historical subjects.

Colin **Clive:** Colin Clive-Greig (1898–1937), Br. movie actor, working in U.S.

John **Clive:** Clive John Hambley (1938–), Br. movie, TV actor, writer.

Kitty **Clive:** Catherine Raftor (1711–1785), Eng. actress. Not exactly a pseudonym, but the actress's married name. Her brief marriage was to George Clive, a barrister, and she kept his name as an agreeably alliterative stage name.

Clodion: Claude Michel (1738–1814), Fr. sculptor. The artist fashioned his first name into a historical mold, since Clodion (or Chlodio) was a 5th-century Frankish king.

G. Butler **Clonblough:** Gustav von Seyffertitz (1863–1943), Austr.-born U.S. movie actor. The actor assumed this name, almost as esoteric as the original, in World War I with the aim of disguising his Teutonic provenance. He used it as late as 1919 as director of *The Secret Garden*.

Anacharsis **Cloots:** Jean-Baptiste du Val-de-Grâce, Baron de Cloots (1755–1794), Fr. revolutionary. The self-styled "Orator of Manking," born into a Prussian family of Dutch descent, chose a name that punningly mocked his aristocratic ancestry, since Greek *anacharsis* means "graceless."

Upton **Close:** Josef Washington Hall (1894–1960), U.S. journalist, novelist. When the journalist held a government post in Shantung in World War I, he learned of the Japanese invasion and put "up close" on his messages to indicate his position near the front. This notation later produced his pen name.

Cluff: John Longstaff (1949–), Eng. cartoonist. The artist's signature appears to be based on a shortened form of his real name.

Frank **Clune:** Francis Patrick (1909–1971), Austral. author.

June **Clyde:** June Tetrazini (1909–1987), U.S. movie actress, singer, dancer.

Lee J. **Cobb:** Leo Jacoby (1911–1976), U.S. stage, movie actor. The stage and screen name derive from the actor's real name, dropping the final "y."

William **Cobb:** Jules Hippolyte Lermina (1839–1915), Fr. novelist.

Charles **Coborn:** Colin Whitton McCallum (1852–1945), Br. music hall comedian. The performer took his name from Coborn Road, in London's East End.

Johannes **Cochlaeus:** Johannes Dobeneck (or Dobneck) (1479–1552), Ger. humanist, Roman Catholic theologian.

Eddie **Cochran:** Edward Cochrane (1938–1960), U.S. rock 'n' roll musician.

Pindar **Cockloft:** William Irving (1766–1821), U.S. poet.

Coco: Nikolai Poliakov (1900–1974), Russ.-born Eng. circus clown. The clown's ring name represents the " ko " syllable that is found in each of his real names. "Coco" has now become a popular name for any clown, both in English-speaking countries and elsewhere, as for Koko (*q.v.*), for example.

Cocoa Tea: Calvin Scott (*c.*1960), Jamaican reggae singer. The singer's name arose as a nickname, presumably based loosely on his real name.

Commander **Cody:** George Frayne (*c.*1940–), U.S. rock musician.

Lew **Cody:** Louis Joseph Côté (1884–1934), U.S. movie actor, of Fr. parentage.

Captain **Coe:** (1) Edward Card Mitchell (1853–1914), Eng. sporting writer, editor; (2) Tom Cosgrove (1902–1978), Eng. sporting writer, editor. The name, apparently inherited by Cosgrove from Mitchell, happens to suggest that of the *Echo*, the newspaper that Mitchell joined in 1883, as well as Cosgrove's own surname.

Joshua **Coffin:** Henry Wadsworth Longfellow (1807–1882), U.S. poet. The poet used this name for *A Sketch of the History of Newbury* (1845).

George M. **Cohan:** George Michael Keohane (1878–1942), U.S. stage actor, playwright, director, producer.

Emile **Cohl:** Emile Courtet (1857–1938), Fr. movie cartoonist.

Claudette **Colbert:** Lily Claudette Chauchoin (1903–1996), Fr.-born U.S. stage, movie actress.

The actress adopted her new name for her first stage appearance, at the Frazee Theatre, New York, on Christmas Eve, 1923.

Maurice **Colbourne:** Roger Middleton (1939–1989), Eng. TV actor. The actor is said to have taken his stage name from that of a Shakespearean actor whose obituary he had read.

Ann **Cole:** Cynthia Coleman (1934–), U.S. gospel singer.

Graham **Cole:** Graham Coleman Smith (1952–), Eng. TV actor.

Lester **Cole:** Lester Cohn (1904–1985), U.S. screenwriter, of Pol. parentage.

Nat "King" **Cole:** Nathaniel Adams Coles (1919–1965), U.S. singer, jazz pianist. The musician's own name, with his nickname of "King," plus the name of his group, the King Cole Trio, resulted in a performing name that was additionally associated with the "Old King Cole" of the children's nursery rhyme. Nathaniel Coles dropped the "s" of his name in 1937, when he formed his trio.

Cy **Coleman:** Seymour Kaufman (1929–), U.S. popular musician, songwriter.

Manning **Coles:** Adelaide Frances Oke Manning (1891–1959), Eng. spy, detective novelist + Cyril Henry Coles (1901–1965), Eng. spy, detective novelist, her husband. A fairly uncommon combination of two surnames to make a united first name and surname.

Colette: Sidonie-Gabrielle Claudine Colette (1873–1954), Fr. novelist. A single name that suggests a first name rather than the surname that it actually is. The writer's early books were written under the pen name of her husband, Willy (*q.v.*).

She used her own name, in combination with his (as Colette-Willy), for *Dialogues de Bêtes* (1904). She divorced Willy two years later, but continued to write as Colette-Willy until 1916, after which she wrote as Colette alone.

Bonar **Colleano:** Bonar William Sullivan II (1924–1958), U.S. movie actor. The actor joined the Colleano Circus Family as a child and adopted their name.

Constance **Collier:** Laura Constance Hardie (1878–1955), Eng. stage, movie actress. The actress adopted her mother's maiden name as her stage name.

Lois **Collier:** Madelyn Jones (1919–), U.S. movie actress.

Patience **Collier:** René Collier, née Ritcher (1910–1987), Eng. stage actress.

William **Collier:** William Senior (1866–1944), U.S. stage, movie actor.

John D. **Collins:** John Christopher Dixon (1942–), Eng. TV actor.

Michael **Collins:** Dennis Lynds (1924–), U.S. mystery writer, journalist.

Sam **Collins:** Samuel Thomas Collins Vagg (1827–1865), Eng. music hall artist, manager.

Tom **Collins:** Joseph Furphy (1843–1912), Austral. novelist. At the end of the 19th century "Tom Collins" was a slang term in Australia for a mythical rumormonger. Furphy adopted the name in 1892 and later made Collins a leading character in some of his novels.

Tommy **Collins:** Leonard Raymond Sipes (1930–), U.S. country singer.

Carlo **Collodi:** Carlo Lorenzini (1826–1890), It. writer. The author of *Le Avventure di Pinocchio* (1883) took his pen name from his mother's birthplace. He himself was born in Florence.

Bud **Collyer:** Clayton Johnson Heermanse, Jr. (1908–1969), U.S. TV personality, brother of June Collyer (see below).

June **Collyer:** Dorothy Heermanse (1907–1968), U.S. movie actress.

(la) Marquesa **Colombi:** Maria Antonietta Torriani (1846–1920), It. novelist.

Colombine: Carmen de Burgos Seguí (*c.*1870–1932), Sp. novelist.

Colon: Joseph Dennie (1768–1812), U.S. essayist, satirist, collaborating with Spondee (*q.v.*).

Jessi **Colter:** Miriam Johnson (1943–), U.S. country singer. The singer claimed to have an ancestor Jessi Colter who was a member of the Jesse James Gang. She therefore adopted his name as her stage name.

Robbie **Coltrane:** Anthony Robert McMillan (1950–), Sc. TV actor. The actor admired the U.S. jazz saxophonist John Coltrane (1926–1967) and adopted his name in the 1970s.

Coluche: Michel Gérard Josèphe Colucci (1944–1986), Fr. radio, stage, movie comedian, of It. parentage.

Christopher **Columbus:** Joseph C. Morris (1903–), U.S. black jazz drummer, bandleader.

Betty **Comden:** Elizabeth Kyle, née Cohen (1917–), U.S. movie, stage writer, actress.

Jan Ámos **Comenius:** Jan Ámos Komenský (1592–1670), Cz. educationist, Moravian bishop.

Cuthbert **Comment:** Abraham Tucker (1705–1774), Eng. moralist. For the occasion of this pleasant name, see Edward **Search.**

Perry **Como:** Pierino Roland Como (1912–), U.S. crooner, movie actor, of It. descent. The singer initially appeared under the name Nick Perido.

Fay **Compton:** Virginia Lilian Emmiline Compton (1894–1978), Br. stage actress, sister of novelist Compton Mackenzie (*q.v.*).

Frances Snow **Compton:** Henry Brooks Adams (1838–1918), U.S. historian, novelist.

Henry **Compton:** Charles Mackenzie (1805–1877), Eng. actor, grandfather of novelist Compton Mackenzie and actress Fay Compton (*qq.v.*). The actor adopted the maiden name of his Scottish paternal grandmother.

Joyce **Compton:** Eleanor Hunt (1907–), U.S. movie actress.

Comus: Robert Michael Ballantyne (1825–1894), Sc. novelist for boys. Comus was the name of the pagan god invented by Milton for his pastoral entertainment ("masque") of the name (1634).

Laure **Conan:** Marie-Louise-Félicité Angers (1845–1924), Fr.-Can. novelist.

Concolorcorvo: Alonso Carrío de la Vandera (1715–*c.*1778), Sp. colonial administrator. The official used this name for *El Lazarillo de ciegos caminantes* ("The Blind Travelers' Lazarillo") (1775), an account of his travels from Buenos Aires to Lima. The work and pseudonym were originally attributed to his Native American guide, Calixto Carlos Inca Bustamante.

Chester **Conklin:** Jules Cowles (1888–1971), U.S. movie actor.

F. Norreys **Connell:** Conal Holmes O'Connell O'Riordan (1874–1948), Ir. dramatist, novelist.

John **Connell:** John Henry Robertson (1909–1965), Br. novelist, biographer.

Marc **Connelly:** Marcus Cook (1890–1980), U.S. playwright, screenwriter, stage director.

Rearden **Conner:** Patrick Reardon Connor (1907–), Ir. novelist, short story writer. The author also wrote as Peter Malin.

J.J. **Connington:** Alfred Walter Stewart (1880–1947), Sc. crime writer.

Ralph **Connor:** Charles William Gordon (1860–1937), Can. writer of religious novels. The novelist intended to use the name "Cannor," from the letter heading "Brit. Can. Nor. West Mission," but his editor copied this as "Connor" and added "Ralph" to give a full name.

Mike **Connors:** Kreker Jay Michael Ohanian (1925–), U.S. movie, TV actor, of Armenian parentage.

George **Conquest:** George Augustus Oliver (1837–1901), Br. actor, theatrical manager. The actor adopted the same name as that used by his father, also a theatrical manager, Benjamin Oliver (1805–1872).

Owen **Conquest:** Frank Richards (*q.v.*).

Con **Conrad:** Conrad K. Dober (1891–1938), U.S. songwriter.

Jess **Conrad:** Gerald James (1936–), Br. pop singer.

Joseph **Conrad:** Józef Teodor Konrad Korzeniowski (1857–1924), Pol.-born Br. novelist, writing in English. Conrad became a British naturalized subject in 1886 and anglicized his first and third names.

Robert **Conrad:** Conrad Robert Falk (1935–), U.S. TV, movie actor.

Will **Conroy:** Harry Champion (1866–1942), Eng. music hall comedian.

Michael **Constantine:** Constantine Joanides (1927–), Gk.-born U.S. TV, movie actor.

Richard **Conte:** Nicholas Peter (1914–1975), U.S. movie actor.

Albert **Conti:** Albert de Conti Cedassamare (1887–1967), Austr. movie actor.

Gloria **Contreras:** Carmen Gloria Contreras Roeniger (1934–), Mexican ballet dancer, teacher.

Gary **Conway:** Gareth Carmody (1938–), U.S. movie, TV actor.

Hugh **Conway:** Frederick John Fargus (1847–1885), Eng. novelist. The writer took his pen name from the school frigate *Conway*, stationed on the Mersey, which he entered as a naval student at the age of 13.

Russ **Conway:** Trevor Herbert Stanford (1927–), Eng. popular pianist, composer. The musician adopted his new name in 1957 on making his first recording.

Steve **Conway:** Walter James Groom (1920–1952), Eng. popular singer.

Shirl **Conway:** Shirley Crossman (1914–), U.S. TV actress.

Tom **Conway:** Thomas Charles Sanders (1904–1967), Br.-born U.S. movie actor, brother of actor George Sanders (1906–1972).

William Augustus **Conway:** William Augustus Rugg (1789–1828), Ir. actor.

Coo-ee: William Sylvester Walker (1846–1926), Austral. novelist. "Coo-ee" was (and still is) the traditional Australian bush call.

Joe **Cook:** Joseph Lopez (1890–1959), U.S. comedian.

Susan **Coolidge:** Sarah Chauncey Woolsey (1835–1905), U.S. writer of books for girls. The author of *What Katy Did* (1872) and subsequent stories based her pen name on that of her sister, who called herself Margaret Coolidge.

Coolio: Artis Ivey (1966–), U.S. black rapper.

Alice **Cooper:** Vincent Damon Furnier (1948–), U.S. rock singer. The female name was chosen by the "shock-horror" performer in 1969 to illustrate his theory that "people are both male and female biologically." A Ouija board allegedly indicated that Alice Cooper had been a 17th-century witch, who was now reincarnated as Furnier. That is the traditional story behind the name. But when Cooper was asked in the 1984 book *Rock 'N' Roll Asylum* how he came up with it, he replied as follows: "I have no idea. I really don't. It was one day, just [snaps fingers] boom. … I could have said Mary Smith, but I said Alice Cooper. … But think about it—Alice Cooper has the same sort of ring as Lizzie Borden and Baby Jane. 'Alice Cooper.' It's sort of like a little girl with an ax. I kept picturing something in pink and black lace and blood. Meanwhile, people expected a blond folksinger" [Dolgins, p. 47].

Frank **Cooper:** William Gilmore Simms (1806–1870), U.S. novelist.

Gary **Cooper:** Frank J. Cooper (1901–1961), U.S. movie actor. The metamorphosis of the actor's first name was the work of his Hollywood agent, Nan Collins, who came from Gary, Indiana. She explained: "'My home town was named after Elbert H. Gary. I think Gary has a nice poetic sound to it. I'd like to see you take Elbert Gary's last name for your first. 'You mean,' he interrupted, 'Gary Cooper?' 'Yes—Gary Cooper. Say it again. Gary Cooper. Very nice. I like it. Don't you?' Gary Cooper. He ran the name around in his mind a few times. He spoke it again, 'Gary Cooper.' Then he smiled. 'I like it.' 'You see,' Miss Collins said. 'I knew you would. And you'll have to agree, Gary Cooper doesn't sound as tall and lanky as Frank Cooper'" [George Carpozi, Jr., *The Gary Cooper Story*, 1971].

Jackie **Cooper:** John Cooperman, Jr. (1921–), U.S. movie actor.

Jefferson **Cooper:** Gardner Francis Fox (1911–), U.S. writer of historical romances.

Natasha **Cooper:** Idonea Daphne Wright (1951–), Br. crime writer. The author also writes as Kate Hatfield.

William **Cooper:** Harry Summerfield Hoff (1910–), Eng. novelist. The writer was obliged to choose another name for his writings when employed as a civil servant. After publishing his first four novels under his real name (as H.S. Hoff), he emerged with his new literary identity for *Scenes from Provincial Life* (1950).

Joan **Copeland:** Joan Maxine Miller (1922–), U.S. stage actress, singer.

David **Copperfield:** David Kotkin (1957–), U.S. magician. The name is familiar as that of the hero of Charles Dickens's novel (1849).

Giovanni **Coprario:** John Cooper (*c.*1570–1626), Eng. composer. According to the 17th-century biographer Anthony Wood, the musician was "an Englishman borne, who having spent much of his time in Italy, was there called *Coprario*, which name he kept when he returned into England" [*Dictionary of National Biography*].

Joe **Coral:** Joseph Kagarlitski (1904–1996), Br. bookmaker, of Pol. Jewish origin. The founder of one of Britain's largest chain of betting shops smoothed his name to a word that evokes both decorativeness and durability.

Cora **Coralina:** Ana Lins dos Guimarães Peixoto Bretas (1890–1985), Brazilian writer.

Coram: Thomas Whitaker (1883–1937), Eng. ventriloquist. Latin *coram* means "openly," "in public." A ventriloquist is a paradoxical performer; he conceals his voice, but does so for public entertainment.

Glen **Corbett:** Glenn Rothenburg (1929–1993), U.S. movie actor.

Le **Corbusier:** Charles-Edouard Jeanneret (1887–1965), Swiss architect, working in France. The precise reason for the architect's adoption of this particular name is not clear. His obituary in *The Times* (August 28, 1965) claims it was his maternal grandfather's name. But another account derives it from a nickname, Le Corbeau ("the raven"), given him because of his facial resemblance to this bird.

Ellen **Corby:** Ellen Hansen (1913–), U.S. movie actress.

Alex **Cord:** Alexander Viespi (1931–), It.-born U.S. movie actor.

Mara **Corday:** Marilyn Watts (1932–), U.S. movie actress. The actress may have been influenced in her choice of name by that of the Swiss actress Paula Corday, who also used the names Rita Corday and Paule Croset. "Mara" represents "Marilyn."

Louise **Cordet:** Louise Boisot (1946–), Eng. popular singer. The singer took her mother's stage name on first signing with Decca Records in 1962.

El **Cordobés:** Manuel Benítez Pérez (*c.*1936–), Sp. bullfighter. The matador's ring name means "the Córdoba man," although he was not actually born in that city, but in Palma del Río, some 30 miles away. However, the latter town is in Córdoba province, and the name itself is said to come from a monument in the city to the great matador Manolete (*q.v.*), who inspired Benítez to excel in the bullring.

Raymond **Cordy:** Raymond Cordiaux (1898–1956), Fr. movie comedian.

Marie **Corelli:** Mary Mackay (1855–1924), Br. novelist. The writer was illegitimate, and knowing this created the myth that her father, Charles Mackay, a songwriter, was Italian. In a letter to *Blackwood's Magazine* she thus claimed to be "a Venetian, and a direct descendant (through a long line of ancestry) of the great Michael Angelo Corelli, the famous composer." She originally chose the name for a possible musical career, with a second choice of name being Rose Trevor. Earlier she had written as Vivian Earle Clifford. Arcangelo (not Michael Angelo) Corelli (1653–1713) was a noted Italian violinist and composer [Brian Masters, *Now Barabbas Was a Rotter: The Extraordinary Life of Marie Corelli*, 1978].

Jill **Corey:** Norman Jean Speranza (1935–), U.S. pop singer.

Lewis **Corey:** Luigi Carlo Fraina (1892–1953), It.-born U.S. Marxist theorist.

Corinna: Elizabeth Thomas (1675–1731), Eng. poet, letter writer. The poet was given her name by Dryden, who admired two poems she sent him in 1699 and compared her to the 6th-century BC Greek lyric poet of this name. "I would have called you Sapho," he said, "but that I hear you are handsomer." (Contemporary portraits of Sappho depict her as somewhat plain-featured.)

Fernand **Cormon:** Fernand-Anne Piestre (1845–1924), Fr. painter.

Corneille: Cornelis van Beverloo (1922–), Belg. painter, working in France. The artist's name is a French form of his original Flemish name.

Don **Cornell:** Dominico Francisco Connello (1921–), U.S. popular singer.

Corno di Bassetto: George Bernard Shaw (1856–1950), Ir. dramatist, critic, novelist. Shaw used the waggish name when writing as a music critic for *The Star* (1888–90). The corno di bassetto is (in its Italian notation, familiar in music scores) the basset horn, which two words suggest "Bernard Shaw."

Barry Cornwall: Bryan Waller Procter (1787–1874), Eng. poet, songwriter. The name chosen by the poet for his work is a near anagram of his real name.

Bernard Cornwell: Bernard Wiggins (1944–), Br. historical novelist.

Correggio: Antonio Allegri (da Correggio) (1494–1534), It. painter. As was the custom of his day, the painter adopted the name of his birthtown, Correggio, near Reggio in northern Italy.

Adrienne Corri: Adrienne Riccoboni (1930–), Sc. movie actress, of It. descent. The actress was renamed by Gordon Harbord, who also renamed Laurence Harvey (*q.v.*) and who nearly renamed Diana Dors (*q.v.*). The letters of "Corri" come from the actress's surname. Presumably Harbord selected a name like this, rather than the more obvious "Ricci," for ease of pronunciation.

Emmett Corrigan: Antoine Zilles (1868–1932), Du.-born U.S. stage, movie actor.

Ray "Crash" Corrigan: Ray Bernard (1902–1976), U.S. movie actor.

Bud Cort: Walter Edward Cox (1950–), U.S. movie actor. The actor was obliged to choose a new name because his real name already existed for the U.S. comic actor Wally Cox (1924–1973).

Dave "Baby" Cortez: David Cortez Clowney (1938–), U.S. pop musician.

Ricardo Cortez: Jacob Krantz (1899–1977), U.S. movie actor, brother of Stanley Cortez (see below).

Stanley Cortez: Stanley Krantz (1908–), U.S. cinematographer.

Baron Corvo: Frederick William Serafino Austin Lewis Mary Rolfe (1860–1913), Br. writer. The idiosyncratic author claimed to have received the title of Baron Corvo from the Duchess Sforza-Cesarini when living in Italy in the 1880s, a claim that has been neither confirmed nor disproved. The writer himself gave three versions of the origin of his pseudonym: that it was a style offered and accepted for use as a *tekhnikym* or trade name when he denied sacred orders and sought a secular livelihood, that it came from a village near Rome and was assumed when he was made a baron by the Bishop of Emmaus, who was on a visit to Rome, and that it was bestowed by the aforementioned duchess. Rolfe had other pseudonyms, as Frederick Austin, King Clement, and Fr. Rolfe. He wrote autobiographically as Nicholas Crabbe in *Nicholas Crabbe* (1958) and *The Desire and Pursuit of the Whole* (1934) and as George Arthur Rose in (and as) *Hadrian the Seventh* (1904). *Corvo* is Italian for "raven," moreover, and he had already adopted the raven as a heraldic device. (Possibly Crabbe has a similar symbolic significance.) George Arthur Rose is said to derive from St. George "of the Roses" and Duke Arthur (of Brittany) murdered by King John in 1203. C.S. Lewis's SF novel *That Hideous Strength* (1945) has a jackdaw called Baron Corvo [1. A.J.A. Symons, *The Quest for Corvo*, 1940; 2. Donald Weeks, *Corvo*, 1971].

Desmond Cory: Desmond McCarthy (1928–), Br. writer. The writer presumably adopted a name that distinguished him from the literary critic Sir Desmond MacCarthy (1877–1952).

Howard Cosell: Howard William Cohen (1918–1995), U.S. TV sports commentator.

Michael Costa: Michele Andrea Agniello (1808–1884), It. opera composer, of Sp. descent, working in U.K.

Costa-Gavras: Konstantinos Costa-Gavras (1933–), Gk.-born Fr. movie director.

Elvis Costello: Declan MacManus (1954–), Br. rock singer, songwriter. When his parents divorced and separated, MacManus took his mother's maiden name, Costello, and moved with her from London to Liverpool. He then returned to London and sang as a solo singer in folk clubs as D.P. Costello. In 1976 Jake Riviera signed him for Stiff Records and gave him the name Elvis, for Elvis Presley, if only so that he could promote him with the Presley slogan, "Elvis is King." Costello's father, band singer Ross MacManus, commented: "I didn't like it, then I realised it was probably quite good because he didn't sound anything like Elvis: I could see that Declan MacManus wasn't a very good name for a rock star" [*Sunday Times Magazine*, July 17, 1994].

Lou Costello: Louis Francis Cristillo (1906–1959), U.S. movie comedian, teaming with Bud Abbott (*q.v.*).

Tom Costello: Thomas Costellow (1863–1943), Br. music hall comedian, singer.

Al Coster: René Cardona III (1960–), Mexican juvenile movie actor.

Peter **Cotes**: Sydney Boulting (1912–), Br. stage actor, theatrical producer.

A.V. **Coton**: Edward Haddakin (1906–1969), Eng. ballet, critic, writer.

François **Coty**: Francesco Giuseppe Spoturno (1874–1934), Corsican-born Fr. perfume manufacturer.

Johnny **Cougar**: John Cougar Mellencamp (1951–), U.S. rock singer.

Nicole **Courcel**: Nicole Marie-Anne Andrieux (1930–), Fr. movie actress.

Georges **Courteline**: Georges-Victor-Marcel Moinaux (1858–1929), Fr. humorist, dramatist.

Peregrine **Courtenay**: Winthrop Mackworth Praed (1802–1839), Eng. poet. The names have an aristocratic ring for a Cambridge man, as Praed was.

Jerome **Courtland**: Jerome Jourolmon (1926–), U.S. movie actor.

John **Coventry**: John Williamson Palmer (1825–1906), U.S. journalist.

Joe **Cowell**: Joseph Leathley Hawkins-Witchett (1792–1863), Eng. stage comic, working in U.S.

Jane **Cowl**: Grace Bailey (1883–1950), U.S. playwright, stage, movie actress.

Richard **Cowper**: Colin Middleton Murry (1926–), Eng. SF writer.

Ida **Cox**: Ida Prather (1896–1967), U.S. blues singer.

Peter **Coyote**: Peter Cohon (1942–), U.S. movie actor. The actor changed his name in 1967, allegedly as the result of a vision induced by taking the drug peyote.

Buster **Crabbe**: Clarence Linden (1908–1983), U.S. movie actor, swimmer.

Charles Egbert **Craddock**: Mary Noailles Murfree (1850–1922), U.S. novelist, short story writer. Mary Murfree, who wrote novels and short stories in dialect, took her (male) name from that of the hero of an early story in *Appleton's Journal*. It was not until 1885, the year after the publication of her first collection of stories, *In the Tennessee Mountains*, that the editor of the *Atlantic Monthly*, to which she contributed, discovered the author of the tales of mountaineers and their hard life to be in reality a frail, crippled spinster.

Fanny **Cradock**: Phyllis Primrose-Pechey (1909–1994), Br. TV cook. The popular broadcaster's surname was that of her husband, John Cradock. Her new first name was that of a grandmother with whom she spent her earliest years. She used the name Frances Dale when fashion editor of the *Sunday Graphic*, and together with her husband adopted the joint *nom de plume* "Bon Viveur" for articles on travel and food in the *Daily Telegraph*.

A.A. **Craig**: Poul William Anderson (1926–), U.S. SF writer.

Alisa **Craig**: Charlotte Matilda Macleod (1922–), Can. thriller writer. The name must surely be based on the Scottish isle of Ailsa Craig, written about by Keats and Wordsworth (see Gordon Craig, below.)

David **Craig**: Allan James Tucker (1929–), Welsh crime writer. The writer adopted his wife's maiden name as his pen name. He also writes under his real name (as James Tucker).

Edith **Craig**: Edith Terry (1869–1947), Eng. stage actress, sister of Gordon Craig (see below).

Gordon **Craig**: Henry Edward Godwin Terry (1872–1966), Eng. stage actor, designer, producer. The actor was the illegitimate son of the actress Ellen Terry and Edwin Godwin, an architect. He was known as Edward Godwin until his mother married (1877) the actor Charles Wardell, when he became Edward Wardell. In 1887 his mother renamed him Henry, for the Scottish actor Henry Irving, and Gordon for her friend, Lady Gordon. Craig came from the rocky Scottish isle of Ailsa Craig, a name which appealed to her. "What a magnificent name for an actress!" she said. (Compare Alisa Craig, above.)

James **Craig**: James Henry Meador (1912–1985), U.S. movie actor. The actor took his screen name following his appearance in *Craig's Wife* (1936).

Michael **Craig**: Michael Gregson (1928–), Eng. movie actor.

Craigfryn: Isaac Hughes (1852–1928), Welsh novelist. The writer assumed a placename meaning literally "hill rock."

Tom **Crampton**: Barbara Pym (1913–1980), Eng. novelist. The writer assumed this male name for novels written in the 1960s and 1970s. They were consistently rejected by publishers. She took the name from her mother's maiden name, Thomas, and her father's middle name, Crampton, this also being one of her own names.

Lucas **Cranach** (the Elder): Lucas Müller (1472–1553), Ger. painter. The painter adopted the name of his birthtown, Cranach (now Kronach, Germany). He first indicated his adoption of the name by signing his painting *Rest on the Flight into Egypt* (1504) as "LC." His son, Lucas Cranach the Younger (1515–1586), kept the name.

Phyllis **Crane:** Phyllis Francis (1912–), U.S. movie actress.

Vincent **Crane:** Vincent Rodney Cheesman (1943–), Eng. rock musician.

Cranogwen: Sarah Jane Rees (1839–1916), Welsh poet, musician, editor. The poet took her bardic name from her native village of Llangrannog ("Carannog's church"), Cardiganshire (now Dyfed), where the parish church is dedicated to St. Carannog.

Arthur **Cravan** Fabian Lloyd (1887– ? 1920), Fr. poet, prose writer.

Hawes **Craven:** Henry Hawes Craven Green (1837–1910), Eng. theatre scene painter.

Henry Thornton **Craven:** Henry Thornton (1818–1905), Eng. actor, playwright.

José **Craveirinha:** José G. Vetrinha (1922–), Mozambiquan poet.

Joan **Crawford:** Lucille Fay LeSueur (1904–1977), U.S. movie actress. The actress first played (1925) under her real name (on which a Hollywood producer is said to have commented, "Well, honey, you certainly picked a fancy one"). She would soon become Billie Cassin, however, the latter being her stepfather's name. Later that same year she acquired her lasting stage name: "Obviously Lucille LeSueur was a comer. But Pete Smith was convinced she couldn't make it with that name. The [MGM] publicity chief laid his case before Louis Mayer. "'Lucille LeSueur' sounds too stagy, even if it is the girl's name,' argued Smith. 'And it sounds too much like "LeSewer." I think we ought to change it.' Mayer granted permission, and Smith went to work. Why not conduct a nationwide publicity contest to find a name for the promising new actress? A McFadden fan publication, *Movie Weekly*, agreed to sponsor the contest. ... The winner was 'Joan Arden,' and Lucille LeSueur became Joan Arden for a few days until a bit player protested that the name belonged to her. The second choice was submitted by Mrs. Marie M. Tisdale. ... 'Joan *Crawford!*' the former Lucille complained to her new friend William Haines. 'It sounds like "Crawfish."' "'Crawford's' not so bad,' the actor replied. 'They might have called you "Cranberry" and served you every Thanksgiving with the turkey" [Bob Thomas, *Joan Crawford*, 1979].

Kathryn **Crawford:** Kathryn Crawford Moran (1908–1980), U.S. movie actress.

Michael **Crawford:** Michael Patrick Dumble-Smith (1942–), Eng. stage, movie, TV actor. The actor initially adopted his stepfather's name, calling himself Michael Ingram. He then opted for a more distinctive stage name, and selected "Crawford" from a passing cookie truck in 1965. He subsequently adopted this name legally.

Captain **Crawley:** George Frederick Pardon (1824–1884), Eng. writer on sports, pastimes. The writer adopted the literary name of Sir Pitt Crawley, the coarse, brutal, wife-bullying old man in Thackeray's *Vanity Fair* (1847–48). It is not clear to what extent he actually wished to identify himself with the character's disagreeable nature.

Geoffrey **Crayon:** Washington Irving (1783–1859), U.S. humorous writer. Irving used the name for *The Sketch Book* (1819–20), a collection of familiar essays and tales. The pen name is appropriate for the title of the work.

Pee Wee **Crayton:** Connie Curtis (1914–1985), U.S. blues musician.

Crazy Horse: Ta-sunko-witko (c.1842–1877), U.S. Native American chief. The military leader came to be known by the English equivalent of his Sioux name, which he is said to have assumed either after dreaming of horses [Mari Sandoz, *Crazy Horse: The Strange Man of the Oglalas*, 1955] or because a wild horse ran through his camp when he was born [Stoutenburgh, p. 81].

Joseph **Crehan:** Charles Wilson (1884–1966), U.S. movie actor.

Adolphe **Crémieux:** Isaac Moïse (1796–1880), Fr. politician, Jewish leader.

Hélisenne de **Crenne:** Marguerite de Briet (c.1510–c.1550), Fr. novelist, translator. The writer took her assumed name from her husband, a *petit seigneur de Cresnes* ("little lord of Cresnes"). She apparently devised her unusual first name herself, and used it for the semiautobiographical heroine of her novel *Les Angoisses douloureuses qui procèdent d'amours* ("The grievous anxieties that proceed from love") (1538).

Kid **Creole:** August Darnell (*q.v.*).

Dormer **Creston:** Dorothy Julia Colston-Baynes (c.1900–1973), Br. biographer, writer. The author seems to have deliberately selected a sexually ambiguous pen name. "Dormer" occurs as a surname in a number of fictional works, such as the schoolmaster in Hugh Walpole's *Mr. Perrin and Mr. Traill* (1911). But "Dormer Creston" also suggests "Dorothy Colston," the author's real name. (She was originally Dorothy Baynes but legally added Colston in 1946.)

Paul **Creston:** Giuseppe Guttoveggio (1906–1985), U.S. composer, organist, of It. origin.

Creuddynfab: William Williams (1814–1869), Welsh literary critic. The writer took his name from his birthplace, Creuddyn, near Llandudno. The name thus literally means "Creuddyn man."

Paul **Creyton:** John Townsend Trowbridge (1827–1916), U.S. novelist, poet, author of books for boys.

Otis **Criblecolis:** W.C. Fields (*q.v.*).

Jimmy **Cricket:** James Mulgrew (1945–), Ir.-born Br. TV entertainer. The comedian undoubtedly based his name on the interjection of surprise, "jiminy cricket!"

Quentin **Crisp:** Dennis Pratt (1909–), Eng. eccentric, writer.

Edmund **Crispin:** Robert Bruce Montgomery (1921–1978), Eng. crime, SF writer, composer. The writer composed music under his own name, leaving this pseudonym for his crime and SF fiction. He derived his pen name from a character in the detective novel *Hamlet, Revenge!* (1937) by Hammond Innes (*q.v.*).

Peter **Criss:** Peter Crisscoula (1945–), U.S. rock musician.

Linda **Cristal:** Victoria Maya (1936–), Mexican movie actress, working in U.S.

Estil **Critchie:** Arthur J. Burks (1898–1974), U.S. fantasy fiction writer.

Monsieur **Croche:** Achille-Claude Debussy (1862–1918), Fr. composer. The composer used this name for some of his musical criticisms. He made a selection of these in 1917 and they were published posthumously as by *Monsieur Croche anti-dilettante* (1921). The name itself translates as "Mr. Quaver" (in the sense "eighth note").

David **Croft:** David Sharland (1922–), Br. TV scriptwriter. The writer adopted his mother's maiden name as his professional name.

Douglas **Croft:** Douglas Malcolm Wheatcroft (1929–), U.S. juvenile movie actor. The actor's name was originally shortened to Douglas Wheat, but when this proved unsuitable for publicity purposes he replaced it with the more marketable Croft.

Jaq **Croft:** Jacqueline Mycroft (1968–), Br. movie, TV actress.

Nita **Croft:** Nita Pycroft (1902–), Eng. stage actress.

Deas **Cromarty:** Elizabeth Sophia Watson, née Fletcher (? –1918), Eng. novelist. The writer used this name for five novels and collections of regional tales set in northern England and Scotland (where Cromarty is a region).

Richmal **Crompton:** Richmal Crompton Lamburn (1890–1969), Eng. (female) author of books for boys.

Richard **Cromwell:** (1) Richard Williams (? – ?), Welsh great-grandfather of Oliver Cromwell; (2) Roy M. Radebaugh (1910–1960), U.S. movie actor. Robert Cromwell, father of Oliver Cromwell (1599–1658), was the "grandson of a certain Richard Williams, who rose to fortune by the protection of Thomas Cromwell, earl of Essex [? 1485–1540], and adopted the name of his patron" [*Dictionary of National Biography*]. Richard Williams's own father was a Welshman, Morgan Williams, who married Katherine Cromwell, Thomas's elder sister. (See also p. 10.)

Arthur **Cronquist:** Franklin Arthur Beers (1919–1992), U.S. botanist.

Hume **Cronyn:** Hume Blake (1911–), Can. movie actor.

Alfred **Croquis:** Daniel Maclise (1806–1870), Ir. painter, caricaturist. The artist used this name for "A Gallery of Illustrious Literary Characters" published in *Fraser's Magazine* in the 1830s. French *croquis* means "sketch."

Bing **Crosby:** Harry Lillis Crosby (1904–1977), U.S. crooner, movie actor. Harry Crosby enjoyed the comic strip "Bingville Bugle" when at grade school, with its hero a character named Bing. Either because of his fondness for this character, or (some say) his resemblance to it, he was nicknamed "Bing" and later adopted the name.

David **Crosby:** David Van Cortland (1941–), U.S. rock singer.

Amanda **Cross:** Carolyn Gold Heilbrun (1926–), U.S. novelist, essayist. The writer adopted this name for mystery novels featuring the English detective Kate Fansler.

Christopher **Cross:** Christopher Geppert (1951–), U.S. pop singer. A clear play on "criss-cross" here.

Henri Edmond **Cross:** Henri Delacroix (1856–1910), Fr. neoimpressionist painter. Presumably the painter translated his name to promote his national name internationally.

Victoria **Crosse:** Vivian Cory (? –1930s), Eng. novelist, sister of Laurence Hope (*q.v.*) The writer's pen name puns on the high-ranking British gallantry award. (Cory's father was a colonel in the Indian army.) After the death of Queen Victoria (1901), she dropped the final "e" of the name.

Christopher **Crowfield:** Harriet Elizabeth Beecher Stowe (1811–1896), U.S. novelist. The author of *Uncle Tom's Cabin* (1851) used the male name for some of her lesser writings.

Aleister **Crowley:** Edward Alexander Crowley (1875–1947), Eng. occult writer, practitioner, poet ("The Great Beast"). The writer adopted his new first name in 1898, on joining the Hermetic Order of the Golden Dawn. He used a range of pseudonyms for his writings, some of the more exotic being Khaled Khan, Frater Perdurabo, Count Vladimir Svareff, Master Therion (the Greek word for "beast"), and Soror Vikaram.

Henry **Crown:** Henry Krinsky (1896–1990), U.S. industrialist, of Lithuanian parentage.

Alfred **Crowquill:** Alfred Henry Forrester (1804–1872), Eng. illustrator, comic artist + Charles Robert Forrester (1803–1850), Eng. writer, his brother. A crow quill is a special type of artist's pen, capable of drawing very fine lines. It was originally made from crows' quills.

Tom **Cruise:** Thomas Cruise Mapother IV (1962–), U.S. movie actor.

Paul **Crum:** Roger Pettiward (1906–1942), Eng. cartoonist, painter.

James **Cruze:** Jens Cruz Bosen (1884–1942), U.S. movie director, of Dan. parentage.

C3.3: Oscar Fingal O'Flahertie Wills Wilde (1854–1900), Ir. dramatist, poet. The writer used this name for his poem *The Ballad of Reading Gaol* (1898), about his experiences in the jail of the title. The name itself was his prison number (block C, 3d floor, cell 3).

Guy **Cullingford:** Constance Lindsay Taylor (1907–), Br. crime writer.

Silas Tomken **Cumberbatch:** Samuel Taylor Coleridge (1772–1834), Eng. poet, critic. The poet adopted the name, retaining his initials, on enlisting in the army (15th Dragoons) in 1793: "No objection having been taken to his height, or age, and being thus accepted, he was asked his name. He had previously determined to give one that was thoroughly Kamschatkian, but having noticed that morning over a door in Lincoln's Inn Fields (or the Temple) the name 'Cumberbatch' (not 'Comberback'), he thought this word sufficiently outlandish, and replied, 'Silas Tomken Cumberbatch', and such was the entry in the regimental book" [Joseph Cottle, *Early Recollections, chiefly relating to Samuel Taylor Coleridge*, 1837].

Constance **Cummings:** Constance Cummings Levy, née Halverstadt (1910–), U.S. stage, movie actress. The actress's middle name, which she took as her stage surname, was the maiden name of her mother, concert artist Kate Cummings.

Robert **Cummings:** Charles Clarence Robert Orville Cummings (1908–1990), U.S. movie actor. The actor's regular screen name is not as original as the one under which he passed himself off when he went to England to acquire the accent. For this purpose he was Blade Stanhope Conway, and under this name succeeded in obtaining a part in Galsworthy's last play, *The Roof* (1929).

Grace **Cunard:** Harriet Mildred Jeffries (1894–1967), U.S. movie actress.

E.V. **Cunningham:** Howard Fast (1914–), U.S. historical writer.

Robert **Cunninghame-Graham:** Robert Graham (? –c.1797), Sc. songwriter. The writer assumed the additional name of Cunninghame in 1796 on succeeding to the estates of John Cunninghame, 15th (and last) earl of Glencairn. The songwriter's great-grandson and namesake was the noted Scottish writer, politician, and adventurer, Robert Bontine Cunninghame-Graham (1852–1936).

Le **Curé d'Ars:** Jean-Baptiste-Marie Vianney (1786–1859), Fr. Roman Catholic saint. The priest and saint gains his most familiar name from the village of Ars-en-Dombes, where he was in charge of the parish from 1817 to the end of his life.

Curnonsky: Maurice Edmond Sailland (1872–1956), Fr. gastronome, cookery writer.

Finlay **Currie:** Finlay Jefferson (1878–1968), Sc. stage, movie actor.

Avon **Curry:** Jean Bowden (1920–), Sc. mystery writer, romantic novelist. Other names used by the writer are Jocelyn Barry, Jennifer Bland, and Belinda Dell.

Kid **Curry:** Harvey Logan (1865–1903), U.S. outlaw.

Alan **Curtis:** Harold Neberroth (1909–1953), U.S. movie actor.

Jean-Louis **Curtis:** Louis Laffitte (1917–1995), Fr. novelist, essayist.

Ken **Curtis:** Curtis Gates (1916–1991), U.S. TV actor.

Peter **Curtis:** Norah Lofts, née Robinson (1904–1983), Br. novelist. The novelist also wrote as Juliet Astley (*q.v.*).

Tony **Curtis:** Bernard Schwartz (1925–), U.S. movie actor, of Hung. descent. The actor explains: "When I started in movies, I knew I'd have to change my name, and I went through a whole basketful of them—every conceivable kind of name. Steven John, John Stevens. ... One of my Hungarian ancestors' names was Kertész, so I thought I'd anglicize it to Curtis. First Jimmy Curtis. Then Johnny Curtis. Finally I hit on Anthony Curtis, and it eventually got shortened to Tony" [Tony Curtis and Barry Paris, *Tony Curtis: The Autobiography*, 1994].

Michael **Curtiz:** Mihály Kertész (1888–1962), Hung.-born U.S. movie director. The director's obituary in *The Times* (April 12, 1962) records that his name "went through a number of transformations and transliterations before reaching its final American form." (Though he could have taken it even further to Curtis.)

Cusanino: Giovanni Carestini (*c*.1705–*c*.1758), It. male soprano singer. The singer took his name from the Cusani, the noble Milanese family who were his patrons.

Mieczyslawa **Ćwiklińska:** Mieczyslawa Trapszo (1880–1972), Pol. comic actress.

Cybi o Eifion: Ebenezer Thomas (1802–1863), Welsh poet and critic. The writer better known as Eben Fardd (*q.v.*) used this name as a young man. It means "Cybi of Eifionydd," the latter being his native district. Cybi was a 6th-century saint.

Cymro Gwyllt: Richard Jones (1772–1833), Welsh hymnwriter. The writer's assumed name means "wild Welshman."

Cynan: [Rev. Sir] Albert Evans-Jones (1895–1970), Welsh poet. The poet, twice Archdruid of Wales, took his bardic name from that of a Welsh saint or historical figure, such as the 6th-century traditional founder of Brittany who it is said will one day return to restore to the Welsh the right to govern the whole of Britain. The name itself means "chief," "high."

Cynddelw: Robert Ellis (1810–1875), Welsh poet, antiquary. The Baptist minister adopted a traditional bardic name for his poetry. Cynddelw was the name of a famous 12th-century Welsh court poet. The name itself means "chief image."

Cynicus: Martin Anderson (1854–1932), Sc. cartoonist, postcard publisher. The artist's name alludes to the satirical nature of his work.

Savinien de **Cyrano de Bergerac:** Savinien de Cyrano (1619–1655), Fr. writer. In 1638 the colorful and controversial writer began adding "de Bergerac" to his original name, taking it from land owned by his family in the Chevreuse valley southeast of Paris. (It is thus not the better known Bergerac in the Dordogne.) His name became widely known through Edmond Rostand's verse play *Cyrano de Bergerac* (1897), which presents him as a fictional character.

[St.] **Cyril:** Constantine (*c*.827–869), Byzantine missionary. The theologian and scholar for whom the Cyrillic alphabet is named took his religious name on becoming a monk in early 869, shortly before his death. He and his brother Methodius were jointly known as "Apostles of the Slavs."

Caran **d'Ache** *see* **Caran d'Ache.**

Morton **Da Costa:** Morton Tecosky (1914–1989), U.S. stage, musical, movie director.

Harry **Dacre:** Henry Decker (1860–1922), Br. popular composer.

Daddy Stovepipe: Johnny Watson (1867–1963), U.S. popular musician. The street musician derived his nickname from his tall top hat.

Dafydd Morganwg: David Watkin Jones (1832–1905), Welsh historian, poet. The writer's name means "David of Glamorgan," the latter being his native county.

Dafydd y Garreg Wen: David Owen (*c*.1711–1741), Welsh harpist. The musician came to be known by the name of his farm. Its own name means "white stone."

Stig **Dagerman:** Stig Halvard Jansson (1923–1954), Swe. writer.

Dagmar: Virginia Ruth Egnor (1926–), U.S. TV comedienne. Dagmar is a royal Danish name.

Dagonet: George Robert Sims (1847–1922), Br. writer. Dagonet was the name of King Arthur's fool in Malory's *Le Morte d'Arthur*.

Lil **Dagover:** Marie Antonia Sieglinde Marta Daghofer, née Liletts (1897–1980), Ger. movie actress, of Du. parentage.

Dalai Lama: Bstan-'dzin-rgya-mtsho (1935–), Tibetan religious leader, working in India. The present Dalai Lama, enthroned in 1940, is believed by Tibetans to be the 14th incarnation of the Buddhist deity Avalokiteśvara, the first of the line being Dge-'dun-grub- pa (1391–1475). It was the third of the line, Bsod-nams-rgya-mtsho (1543–1588), who was given the honorific title Dalai Lama by the Mongol chief Altan

Khan, and it has passed to each of his successors. "Dalai" is an anglicized form of Mongolian *tale*, the equivalent of Tibetan *rgya-mtsho*, "ocean," implying breadth and depth of wisdom. "Lama" represents Tibetan *blama* (with a silent *b*), "superior one," the term for a Buddhist priest.

Julian **D'Albie**: D'Albiac Luard (1892–1978), Ir.-born Eng. stage, radio, TV actor.

Alan **Dale**: (1) Alfred J. Cohen (1861–1928), Eng.-born U.S. theatre critic, playwright; (2) Aldo Sigismondi (1926–), U.S. popular singer, TV host. Both names evoke the Allan-a-Dale who was a companion of the legendary English outlaw Robin Hood.

Charles **Dale**: Charles Marks (1881–1971), U.S. vaudeville, movie actor, teaming with Joe Smith (*q.v.*).

Dick **Dale**: Richard Anthony Monsour (1937–), U.S. rock musician, "surf guitarist."

Jim **Dale**: James Smith (1935–), Br. movie actor, comedian.

Margaret **Dale**: Margaret Bolam (1922–), Br. ballet dancer, choreographer, TV director.

Cass **Daley**: Catherine Dailey (1915–1975), U.S. movie comedienne.

Vernon **Dalhart**: Marion Try Slaughter (1883–1948), U.S. country singer. The singer devised his stage name by combining the names of two Texas towns.

Dalida: Yolande Christina Gigliotti (1933–1987), Egyptian-born movie actress, singer, of It. parentage, working in France. The singer's stage name presumably derives from that of the biblical Delilah, Samson's mistress, who appears as Dalida in Wyclif's Bible (1380s) and in the works of Chaucer, including *The Court of Love*, attributed to him.

Marcel **Dalio**: Israel Moshe Blauschild (1900–1983), Fr. movie comedian, working in U.S. The actor took his screen name from the character Count Danilo, in Lehár's opera *The Merry Widow* (1905).

John **Dall**: John Jenner Thompson (1918–1971), U.S. movie actor.

Ruth **Dallas**: Ruth Mumford (1919–), N.Z. poet, children's writer. The writer adopted the name of her maternal grandmother.

Toti **dal Monte**: Antonietta Meneghelli (1893–1975), It. opera singer. "Toti" is undoubtedly a pet form of the singer's first name. She married the tenor Enzo de Muro Lomanto and "dal Monte" appears to derive from his name.

Charles **Dalmorès**: Henry Alphonse Brin (1871–1939), Fr. opera singer, working in U.S.

Ksaver Sandor **Dalski**: Ljubo Babic (1854–1935), Croatian writer.

Mamont **Dalsky**: Mamont Viktorovich Neyelov (1865–1918), Russ. actor.

Vladimir **Dalsky**: Vladimir Mikhaylovich Nesterenko (1912–), Russ. artist.

Lacy J. **Dalton**: Jill Byrem (1948–), U.S. country, rock singer. She originally used the singing name Jill Croston.

Hamlin **Daly**: Edgar Hoffman Price (1898–), U.S. adventure fiction writer.

Mark **Daly**: Mark Hobson (1887–1957), Sc. stage. movie actor.

Rann **Daly**: Edward Vance Palmer (1885–1959), Austral. writer.

Joe **D'Amato**: Aristide Massaccesi (1936–), It. movie director. Other pseudonyms used by the director, whose output centers on horror movies and porno movies, are Steve Benson, Michael Wotruba, David Hills, and Kevin Mancuso, none of them bearing any relationship to his real name.

Jacques **d'Amboise**: Jacques Joseph Ahearn (1934–), U.S. ballet dancer, choreographer.

Dame Shirley: Louise Amelia Knapp Smith Clappe (1819–1906), U.S. writer, humorist. The author assumed this persona for the writer of letters home to New England by a woman who had gone west to California for the gold rush. They were published in collected form as *The Shirley Letters* (1922).

Damian: Damian Davey (1964–), Eng. singer, entertainer.

Father **Damien**: Joseph Damien de Veuster (1840–1889), Belg. missionary, working in Hawaii.

Lili **Damita**: Liliane Marie Madeleine Carré (1901–1994), Fr. movie actress. The actress claims she changed her name after the King of Spain saw her on the beach at Biarritz and enquired after the *damita* (young lady) in the red bathing dress [*The Times*, April 4, 1993]. Hence her original stage name of Damita del Rojo, "young lady in red." She also appeared as Lily Seslys before settling for Lili Damita in 1923.

Jerry **Dammers**: Gerald Dankin (1954–), Eng. rock musician.

Mark **Damon**: Alan Mark Harris (1933–), U.S. movie actor, producer.

Stuart **Damon**: Stuart Michael Zonis (1937–), U.S. stage, TV actor, director.

Vic **Damone:** Vito Rocco Farinola (1928–), U.S. movie actor, singer.

Claude **Dampier:** Claude Cowan (1885–1955), Br. stage, movie comedian.

Fyodor **Dan:** Fyodor Ilyich Gurvich (1871–1947), Russ. Menshevik leader.

Dana: Rosemary Scallon, née Brown (1951–), Northern Ireland pop singer. The singer took her name from her nickname at school: Irish *dana* means "naughty," "mischievous." It also happens to be a first name (and even a surname) in its own right. The name rhymes with "Ghana," not "gainer."

Viola **Dana:** Violet Flugrath (1897–1987), U.S. movie actress.

Frank **Danby:** Julia Frankau, née Davis (1861–1916), Ir.-born Br. popular novelist, of Jewish parentage, sister of Owen Hall (*q.v.*).

Dancourt: Florent Carton, sieur d'Ancourt (1661–1725), Fr. actor, playwright.

Clemence **Dane:** Winifred Ashton (1888–1965), Eng. novelist, playwright. The writer took her name from the London church of St. Clement Danes, itself probably so named as it was built on an ancient Danish burial site. It stood (and stands) in a part of London that she knew well, and was where she lived for most of her life. In reply to a private enquiry she explained her choice of name as follows: "Just chance! I was talking over with a friend the type of name that I thought effective for a pseudonym—and instanced 'Bow Bells,' 'St. Mary Axe,' 'St. Clement Dane' (city churches and names that I knew) and so, in a flash, arrived my own 'umbrella'" [Marble, p. 6]. Ashton went on stage in 1913 as Diana Coris.

Hal **Dane:** Haldane M'Fall (1860–1928), Eng. soldier, author, art critic.

Karl **Dane:** Karl Daen (1886–1934), Dan. movie actor.

Pascal **Danel:** Jean-Jacques Pascal (1944–), Fr. actor, singer, entertainer. The singer originally adopted his name as a circus performer, taking it from his birthplace, Danel.

William **Danforth:** William Daniels (1869–1941), U.S. movie actor.

John **Dangerfield:** Oswald Crawfurd (1834–1909), Eng. writer. Crawfurd had several pseudonyms for his different types of writing, others being Archibald Banks, Alex Freke Turner, Joseph Strange, Humphrey St. Kayne, George Windle Sandys, and John Latouche. Using this last in *Country House Essays* (1885) he apologized for the "impertinence of an author in using a feigned name," whether from modesty or from "fear of the possible fierceness of critics" [Marble p. 7].

Rodney **Dangerfield:** Jacob Cohen (1921–), U.S. comedian, comedy writer. The actor's original stage name as a standup comic was Jack Roy.

Mlle **Dangeville:** Marie-Anne Botot (1714–1796), Fr. actress.

Dangle: Alexander Mattock Thompson (1861–1948), Ger.-born Eng. journalist, playwright. Dangle is a character in Sheridan's play *The Critic*.

Suzanne **Danielle:** Suzanne Morris (1957–), Eng. TV actress.

Henri **Daniel-Rops:** Henri Petiot (1901–1965), Fr. writer, church historian.

Bebe **Daniels:** Phyllis (or Virginia) Daniels (1901–1971), U.S. movie actress, radio entertainer, of Sc.-Sp. ancestry, teaming with Ben Lyon, her husband. The actress, originally surnamed Dougherty, made her first screen appearance as a ten-week-old baby. Ben Lyon changed her first name to "Bebe" (from "baby") and her surname to the smoother and more attractive "Daniels."

Lisa **Daniely:** Elizabeth Bodington (1930–), Anglo-Fr. movie, TV actress. The actress used this stage name for what she defined as "sexy, undistinguished movies." She reverted to her real name in the 1970s with "a new middleaged persona," as she put it.

Danilo: Danilo Dixon (1956–), U.S. hairdresser, perruquier.

Gabriele **D'Annunzio:** Gabriele Rapagnetta (1863–1938), It. poet, novelist, dramatist. The writer was almost certainly capitalizing on his first name to refer to the Archangel Gabriel, who in the Bible story told Mary of the forthcoming birth of Jesus, this happening known as the Annunciation. Italian *annunzio* means "announcement."

Dante: August Harry Jansen (1883–1955), Dan.-born U.S. conjuror. A name that alludes to the performer's nationality (and also surname) while evoking the famous Italian poet. Jansen assumed the name in 1923 on the suggestion of the U.S. conjuror Howard Thurston.

Michael **Dante:** Ralph Vitti (1935–), U.S. movie director.

Ron **Dante:** Carmine Granito (1945–), U.S. popular singer, songwriter.

Helmut **Dantine:** Helmut Guttman (1917–1982), Austr. movie actor, working in U.S.

The actor adopted the stage name, Niki Dantine, of his actress wife, whose original name was Nicola Schenck.

Caleb **D'Anvers**: Nicholas Amhurst (1697–1742), Eng. poet, political writer. The writer used the name for the influential political journal, the *Craftsman*, which he edited from 1726.

Tony **Danza**: Anthony Iandanza (1951–), U.S. heavyweight boxer, TV actor.

Lorenzo **da Ponte**: Emmanuele Conegliano (1749–1838), It. opera librettist. The librettist of three of Mozart's most famous operas was born a Jew. On being converted as a boy in 1763 to the Christian religion he took the name of the bishop who baptized him, Monsignor Lorenzo da Ponte, as was then the custom.

Kim **Darby**: Deborah Zerby (1947–), U.S. movie actress. The actress was originally a dancer and singer under the name Derby Zerby.

Terence Trent **D'Arby**: Terence Trent Darby (1962–), U.S. black soul singer. The singer retained his full name, "Trent" being his middle name, but added an apostrophe to his surname as an affectation.

Mireille **Darc**: Mireille Aigroz (1938–), Fr. movie actress.

Denise **Darcel**: Denise Billecard (1925–), Fr. movie actress, working in U.S. The actress extracted her new surname from her original one.

Hariclea **Darclée**: Hariclea Haricly Hartulari (1860–1939), Rom. opera singer. The soprano's new surname is a French-style derivative of her original name.

Alex **D'Arcy**: Alexander Sarruf (1908–1996), Egyptian movie actor.

Roy **D'Arcy**: Roy Francis de Giusti (1894–1969), U.S. movie actor.

Dardanelle: Dardanelle Breckenridge (1917–), U.S. jazz musician.

Dardmend: Zakir Ramiyev (1859–1921), Russ. (Tatar) poet. The poet's adopted name means "woeful one," alluding to the repression experienced by Tatars under czarism.

Phyllis **Dare**: Phyllis Dones (1890–1975), Eng. musical comedy actress, sister of Zena Dare (see below).

Simon **Dare**: Marjorie Huxtable (1897–), Br. author of romantic novels.

Zena **Dare**: Florence Hariette Zena Dones (1887–1975), Br. movie actress, sister of Phyllis Dare (see above). The sisters first performed together under their new name in 1899.

Georges **Darien**: Georges Adrien (1862–1921), Fr. novelist, polemicist. A simple anagram.

Bobby **Darin**: Robert Walden Cassotto (1936–1973), U.S. pop singer, movie actor. The singer is said to have found his new surname in a phone book.

Rubén **Darío**: Félix Rubén García y Sarmiento (1867–1916), Nicaraguan poet, essayist. The poet's adopted second name is the Spanish for "Darius." Possibly he chose the name for the famous king of Persia, Darius the Great.

Alexandre **Darlaine**: Alexander D'Arbeloff (1898–1996), Russ.-born (Georgian) U.S. entrepreneur, writer. The writer used this name for two novels, publishing another book, *The Word Accomplished* (1951), under the pseudonym A.B. Christopher.

Candy **Darling**: James Hope Slattery (1949–1974), U.S. transvestite movie actor. A "sweet and sugary" name to match the performer's tacky persona.

William **Darling**: Wilhelm Sandorhazi (1882–1963), Hung.-born U.S. movie art director.

August **Darnell**: Thomas August Darnell Browder (1951–), U.S. rock singer, of Dominican/Fr.-Can. parentage. The singer is also familiar as King Creole, a name referring to his mixed parentage.

Larry **Darnell**: Leo Edward Donald (1929–1983), U.S. popular singer ("Mr. Heart & Soul").

Linda **Darnell**: Monetta Eloyse Darnell (1921–1965), U.S. movie actress.

George **Darrell**: George Frederick Price (1841–1921), Eng.-born Austral. actor, playwright. The actor changed his name in 1868 on returning to Melbourne from New Zealand, where he had tried his luck as a gold digger.

Maisie **Darrell**: Maisie Hardie (1901–), Br. stage actress, dancer.

Peter **Darrell**: Peter Skinner (1929–1987), Br. dancer, choreographer.

James **Darren**: James William Ercolani (1936–), U.S. movie actor, pop singer.

Frankie **Darro**: Frank Johnson (1917–1976), U.S. movie actor.

John **Darrow**: Harry Simpson (1907–1980), U.S. movie actor.

Bella **Darvi**: Bayla Wegier (1927–1971), Pol.-Fr. movie actress, working in U.S. The actress's new surname was devised from the first names of movie mogul Darryl Zanuck and his wife

Virginia, who noticed her in Paris in 1951 and made her their protégée. Her new first name is simply a modification of the original.

Jane **Darwell**: Patti Woodward (1879–1967), U.S. movie actress. Woodward claimed to have taken her acting name from "a character in fiction." But who was Jane Darwell?

Comtesse **Dash**: Gabrielle-Anne Saint-Mars, née Cisterne (1804–1872), Fr. novelist. The countess was self-styled.

Howard **Da Silva**: Harold Silverblatt (1909–1986), U.S. movie actor, director. A neat conversion of a German (Jewish) name into a Portuguese-style one, in the process turning a silver leaf (*Silberblatt*) into a bramble bush (*silva*).

Marcel **Dassault**: Marcel Bloch (1892–1986), Fr. industrialist. The noted aircraft designer officially change his name to Bloch-Dassault in 1946 and to just Dassault in 1949. Dassault was the Resistance cover name of his brother, General Paul Bloch (1882–1969), who adopted it similarly. The name itself can be understood to mean "of the attack." (The French for "tank" is *char d'assaut*.)

Jean **Dauberval** (or d'Auberval): Jean Bercher (1742–1806), Fr. ballet dancer, choreographer.

Claude **Dauphin**: Claude Legrand (1903–1978), Fr. stage, movie actor.

Victor **d'Auverney**: Victor-Marie Hugo (1802–1885), Fr. novelist.

Dauvilliers: Nicolas Dorné (*c*.1646–1690), Fr. actor.

Lewis **Davenport**: George Ryan (1883–1916), Eng. conjuror.

Davertige: Denis Vilar (1940–), Haitian writer.

Jocelyn **Davey**: Chaim Raphael (1908–), Eng. crime novelist.

Nuna **Davey**: Margaret Symonds (1902–1977), Eng. stage actress.

David V: Khariton Dzhiboyevich Devdariani (1903–1977), Georgian catholicos. The head of the Georgian Orthodox Church bears a name, used by four predecessors, that has long been associated with Georgia and Armenia. It is traditionally understood to mean "beloved."

Hugh **David**: David Williams Hughes (1925–1987), Welsh TV director.

Joanna **David**: Joanne Elizabeth Hacking (1947–), Br. stage, movie, TV actress. The actress adopted her stage name from her mother's first name (Davida).

Thayer **David**: David Thayer Hersey (1926–1978), U.S. movie actor.

Lawrence H. **Davidson**: David Herbert Lawrence (1885–1930), Eng. novelist, short story writer. Although resembling his real name, this early pen name used by D.H. Lawrence derived from Davidson Road School, Croydon, where the future novelist taught for a brief period. Appropriately, he assumed the name for a school textbook, *Movements in European History* (1921).

Marion **Davies**: Marion Cecilia Douras (1897–1961), U.S. movie actress.

Siobhan **Davies**: Sue Davies (1950–), Eng. ballet dancer, teacher, choreographer.

Gordon **Daviot**: Elizabeth Mackintosh (1896–1952), Sc. novelist, playwright. The writer preferred to be known by this (male) name, both privately and publicly. She also wrote as Josephine Tey (*q.v.*).

Billie **Davis**: Carol Hedges (1945–), Eng. (white) soul singer.

Danny **Davis**: George Nowlan (1925–), U.S. trumpeter, popular singer.

David **Davis**: William Eric Davis (1908–1996), Eng. broadcaster, children's radio storyteller.

Gail **Davis**: Betty Jeanne Grayson (1925–), U.S. movie actress.

Nancy **Davis**: Anne Frances Robbins (1921–), U.S movie actress. "Nancy" was the actress's nickname from infancy (from "Anne Frances"). "Davis" was the name of her stepfather, a Chicago surgeon. The lady herself took on a new international role as Nancy Reagan, the former U.S. President's wife. The two married in 1952 when they were both Hollywood actors.

Skeeter **Davis**: Mary Frances Penick (1931–), U.S. country singer. Mary Penick took her singing name from that of her schoolfriend, Betty Jack Davis (1932–1953), with whom she formed the Davis Sisters group in 1953, just before Davis's death in a car crash, in which she was herself critically injured. The nickname "Skeeter" (a local term for a mosquito) was given her by her grandfather, for being as busy and active as that insect.

William **Davis**: Adolf Günther Kies (1933–), Ger.-born Eng. writer, editor. Possibly "Davis" was formed from "Adolf Kies," with the "f" serving for the "v."

Bobby **Davro**: Robert Christopher Nankeville (1958–), Eng. stage, TV comedian, impressionist. The performer explains his name: "My father needed a name for his [auto dealing] business so he took DAV from my brother David's name and RO from Robert, my first name. I liked the name so much I took it as a stage name" [John Sachs and Piers Morgan, *Secret Lives*, 1991].

Peter **Dawlish:** James Lennox Kerr (1899–1963), Br. writer of boating stories for boys. Dawlish is a Devonshire coastal resort near the mouth of the Exe River. The name also evokes that of the *Dauntless*, the 45-foot schooner which features in many of the stories.

Dolly **Dawn:** Theresa Maria Stable (1919–), U.S. popular singer.

Elizabeth **Dawn:** Sylvia Butterfield (1939–), Br. TV actress.

Geoffrey **Dawson:** George Geoffrey Robinson (1874–1944), Eng. journalist, newspaper editor. The journalist, twice editor of *The Times*, changed his name by royal licence in 1917 following an inheritance from his mother's eldest sister, Margaret Jane Dawson.

Bobby **Day:** Robert Byrd (1930–1990), U.S. rock singer.

Dennis **Day:** Eugene Denis McNulty (1917–1988), U.S. movie actor, singer, radio, TV entertainer.

Doris **Day:** Doris von Kappelhoff (1924–), U.S. movie actress, singer. The new name was suggested for the actress by Cincinnati bandleader Barney Rapp. At first he wanted to rename her Doris Kapps, based on her real name. (He himself had similarly shortened his name, from Rappaport to Rapp.) She in turn proposed Doris La Ponselle. But the final name to emerge was Doris Day: "One of Doris's numbers on her opening night was one she had been making her own on the air, 'Day after Day,' ... so when the time came for Barney Rapp to put her name on the marquee outside the club ... he suggested Day as a surname. ... Doris herself was not too excited over the proposed new name, but Barney stuck to his guns. He asked her to think about it and said, 'I think it's just right—has a nice fresh sound to it, like the dawn of a new day.' ... Her relatives liked it, but she never has—thinks it sounds phony, and several of her friends were in accord" [Eric Braun, *Doris Day*, 1991].

Frances **Day:** Frances Victoria Schenk (1908–1984), U.S. movie actress.

Jill **Day:** Yvonne Page (1930–1990), Eng. popular singer.

Josette **Day:** Josette Dagory (1914–1978), Fr. movie actress.

Laraine **Day:** Laraine Johnson (1917–), U.S. movie actress. The actress adopted the name of her drama teacher, Elias Day.

Dayananda Sarasvati: Mula Sankara (1824–1883), Ind. Hindu ascetic, social reformer.

Taylor **Dayne:** Lesley Wunderman (1963–), U.S. rock singer.

De...: Most names beginning *De* (or *de*) appear below, but a few, because of their composition, are alphabetized under the first letter of the main word. Thus Comte de Lautréamont appears under **Lautréamont**.

Henri **de Alleber:** Henri de Lapomeraye (1839–1891), Fr. critic, lecturer.

Eddie **Dean:** Edgar Dean Glossup (1907–), U.S. movie actor.

Isabel **Dean:** Isabel Hodgkinson (1918–), Eng. stage, movie actress.

Jimmy **Dean:** Seth Ward (1928–), U.S. country singer.

Charles **Deane:** Edward Saunders (1866–1910), Eng. music hall singer, songwriter.

Edna **Deane:** Edna Morton Sewell (1905–1995), Br. ballroom dancer, choreographer.

Basil **Dearden:** Basil Dear (1911–1971), Br. movie director, producer, screenwriter. The filmmaker changed his name to avoid confusion with director and producer Basil Dean (1888–1978), whose assistant he was.

Max **Dearly:** Lucien-Max Rolland (1874–1943), Fr. actor, variet artist.

Abram **Deborin:** Abram Moiseyevich Ioffe (1881–1963), Lithuanian-born Russ. philosopher.

Brian **de Breffny:** Brian Michael Leese (1931–1989), Eng. genealogist. The writer, the son of a Jewish father and an Irish mother, adopted his new name from the maiden name, Breffni, of his great-great-grandmother. He added the aristocratic prefix "de" and also styled himself "Baron," a title that he sometimes varied, so that he could be "Baron O'Rorke de Breffny" one day and simply "Count O'Rourke" the next.

Jean-Gaspard **Deburau:** Jan Kaspar Dvorák (1796–1846), Fr. pantomime actor, of Cz. parentage. A French rendering (but not translation) of the actor's original Czech name.

Chris **De Burgh:** Christopher John Davidson (1948–), Ir.-born Br. pop singer, songwriter. The singer adopted his mother's maiden name as his stage name.

Peter **Debye:** Petrus Josephus Wilhelmus Debje (1884–1966), Du.-born U.S. scientist.

Yvonne **de Carlo:** Peggy Yvonne Middleton (1922–), Can. movie actress.

Eleanora **de Cisneros:** Eleanor Broadfoot (1878–1934), U.S. opera singer.

Arturo **de Cordova:** Arturo Garcia (1908–1973), Mexican movie actor.

Jacques **Decour:** Daniel Decourdemanche (1910–1942), Fr. writer, editor.

Dave **Dee:** David Harman (1943–), Eng. pop singer, TV actor. "Dee" represents "David," the singer's first name, and originally arose as a school nickname. He first used the name on stage for his group Dave Dee and the Bostons. Later, this same group was reorganized under the cumbersome name of Dave Dee, Dozy, Beaky, Mick and Tich, those being the individual school nicknames of the classmates who formed it. (Dozy was Trevor Davies; Beaky was John Dymond; Mick was Michael Wilson; Tich was Ian Amey.) Dee left the group in 1969.

David **Dee:** David Eckford (c.1942–), U.S. blues singer.

Joey **Dee:** Joseph DeNicola (1940–), U.S. rock musician.

Kiki **Dee:** Pauline Matthews (1947–), Eng. pop singer, stage actress. The name suggests "chickadee," but may have evolved from a family pet name. The singer rejected the suggestion of Kinky Dee as her original stage name.

Nicholas **Dee:** Joan Aiken (1924–), Eng. thriller, children's book writer.

Ruby **Dee:** Ruby Ann Davis, née Wallace (1923–), U.S. black movie actress.

Sandra **Dee:** Alexandra Zuck (1942–), U.S. movie actress. The actress married Bobby Darin (*q.v.*), which presumably explains the "Dee."

André **Deed:** André Chapuis (1884–1938), Fr. movie comedian. The actor gained a remarkable collection of nicknames in different European languages, once his particular brand of destructive lunacy became popular. In France itself he was known as Boireau (from *boire*, "to drink"), in Italy Beoncelli ("little drunkard," from *beone*, "tippler"), in Spain Sanchez, and so on. When he worked for the Itala Company of Turin, Italy, he gained further names, such as Cretinetti (Italy), Gribouille (France), Toribio (Spain), Glupyshkin (Russia), Foolshead (England), all names suggesting stupidity or dumbness.

Eduardo **De Filippo:** Eduardo Passarelli (1900–1984), It. movie actor, director, playwright.

Daniel **Defoe:** Daniel Foe (? 1660–1731), Eng. journalist, novelist. It is just possible that the author of *Robinson Crusoe* (1719) was originally Daniel Defoe. But records show that he was probably Daniel Foe, and that he came to be known as "Mr. D. Foe" to distinguish himself from his father, James Foe. The initial then became the aristocratic particle "de."

Louis **de Funès:** Carlos Louis de Funès de Galarza (1908–1982), Fr. movie actor, comedian, of Port. parentage.

Cherubina **de Gabriak:** Yelizaveta Ivanovna Vasilyeva, née Dmitriyeva (1887–1928), Russ. poet. When in 1909 the poet submitted a selection of her work to the avant-garde journal *Apollo*, the poet Maksimilian Voloshin proposed this Italian-style pseudonym instead of the writer's unremarkable Russian name. It moreover disguised her modest, unprepossessing appearance. The journal's editor, S.K. Makovsky, was so entranced by her verse and seemingly exotic personality that he quite fell for her. When Voloshin disclosed the writer's true identity, however, he flew into a rage and challenged him to a duel. Some of the poems were in all probability written by Voloshin himself [Dmitriyev, p. 189].

Richard **Dehan:** Clotilde Inez Mary Graves (1863–1932), Ir. novelist, playwright. The writer used her new name for her historical works, beginning with *The Dop Doctor* (1911).

John **Dehner:** John Forkum (1915–1992), U.S. movie actor.

Elmyr **de Hory:** Palmer Hoffer (1906–1976), Hung. copier of master painters. The painter's assumed name is more or less a reworking of his original name, allowing for artistic license.

Desmond **Dekker:** Desmond Dacres (1941–), Jamaican reggae musician.

Maurice **Dekobra:** Ernest Maurice Tessier (1885–1973), Fr. novelist. The writer claimed his pen name punned on French *deux cobras*, "two cobras."

Buatier **de Kolta:** Joseph Buatier (1847–1903), Fr. magician, working in U.S., U.K.

E.M. **Delafield:** Edmée Elizabeth Monica Dashwood, née de la Pasture (1890–1943), Eng. novelist. The writer's assumed surname is essentially an English equivalent of her French original.

Theodore **de la Guard:** Nathaniel Ward (c.1578–1652), Eng. poet, novelist. The writer chose this pseudonym for *The Simple Cobler of*

Aggawam (1647), in the process translating his first name from its Hebrew original into Greek (they both mean "gift of God") and his surname from French to English. The same name, therefore, only different.

Isidore **de Lara:** Isidore Cohen (1858–1935), Eng. opera composer.

Mazo **de la Roche:** Mazo Roche (1879–1961), Can. novelist. The writer's father, William Richmond Roche, was an Irishman, and the added particle *de la* falsely implied that she was of aristocratic French descent. Her first name Mazo is a form of "Maisie."

Abbé **de la Tour:** Isabelle de Charrière, née Isabella van Tuyll van Servoskerken (1840–1905), Du.-born Fr. novelist, autobiographer. The novelist seems to have devised a pen name that worked on more levels than one. As it stands, it translates as "abbot of the tower." But "Abbé" could equally well represent "Isabelle" (or "Isabella"), and "Tour" may have evolved from "Tuyll." In other words, "Abbé de la Tour" is a sort of meaningful "Isabella van Tuyll." Servoskerken is a Dutch placename, "Servos' church," also suggesting a holy man and a tower. The writer also used the pen name Zélide (*q.v.*).

Le Vicomte Charles **de Launey:** Delphine de Girardin, née Gay (1804–1855), Fr. writer. The writer used the male name for a weekly gossip column in the 1830s, published in book form in 1842 as *Lettres parisiennes*. The name Launay (de Launay) has associations of the Bastille for French people: Bernard de Launay was the governor of the Bastille, and the diarist Rose de Launay (as Mme de Staal called herself) was long imprisoned in the Bastille.

Barbu **Delavrancea:** Barbu Stefanescu (1858–1918), Rom. writer, playwright.

Hugo **Del Carril:** Piero Bruno Ugo Fontana (1912–1989), Argentine movie actor, director.

Liviu **Deleanu:** Lipa Samuilovich Kligman (1911–1967), Moldavian poet, children's writer.

Bernard **Delfont:** Boris (later Barnet) Winogradsky (1909–1994), Russ.-born Eng. theatrical impresario, TV manager, presenter. Winogradsky began his career as a dancer, changing his name to avoid being confused with his brother, Lew Grade (*q.v.*).

Junior **Delgado:** Junior Hibbert (*c.*1958–), Jamaican reggae musician, working in England.

Délia: Maria Benedita Câmara de Bormann (1853–1895), Brazilian novelist.

Jean **de L'Isle:** Alphonse Daudet (1840–1897), Fr. novelist, short story writer.

Alan **Dell:** Alan Creighton Mandell (1924–1995), S.A.-born Br. broadcaster, dance band authority.

Belinda **Dell:** Jean Bowden (1920–), Sc. writer of romantic novels, thrillers.

Claudia **Dell:** Claudia Del Smith (1910–), U.S. movie actress.

Denis **D'Ell:** Denis Dalziel (1943–), Eng. pop musician. The singer and harmonica player respelled his surname to show its pronunciation, that is, as "Dee-ell."

Dorothy **Dell:** Dorothy Goff (1915–1934), U.S. movie actress.

Gabriel **Dell:** Gabriel Del Vecchio (1919–1988), U.S. movie actor, one of the "Dead End Kids."

Della Crusca: Robert Merry (1755–1798), Eng. poet. Merry was the leader of the so-called Della Cruscans, a band of poets who produced affected, sentimental verse in the latter half of the 18th century. They took their name (and so therefore did he) from the Della Crusca, the literary academy established in Florence in 1582 with the aim of purifying the Italian language. The name literally means "of the chaff," referring to the "sifting" process to which the academy submitted the language.

Florian **Deller:** Florian Drosendorf (1729–1773), Austr. violinist, composer.

Delly: Marie Petitjean de la Rosière (1875–1947), Fr. romantic novelist + Frédéric Petitjean de la Rosière (1876–1949), Fr. romantic novelist, her brother. The name appears to suggest a joint form of their identical aristocratic *de la* particle.

Florentina **del Mar:** Carmen Conde (1907–), Sp. poet, novelist, short story writer. The pseudonym literally means "Florentine woman of the sea," although some other allusion may actually be intended.

Nathalie **Delon:** Francine Canovas (1938–), Fr. movie actress.

Danielle **Delorme:** Gabrielle Girard (1926–), Fr. movie actress.

Joseph **Delorme:** Charles-Augustin Sainte-Beuve (1804–1869), Fr. literary critic. The writer used this name for his *Vie, Poésie et Pensées de Joseph Delorme* (1829), a collection of romantic autobiographical poems. The name is said to be that of a friend of Sainte-Beuve who had died young as a medical student.

Dolores **Del Rio:** Lolita Dolores Martinez Asunsolo Lopez Negrette (1905–1983), Mexican movie actress. The actress's real name appears in many versions, of which the one here is that given by Lloyd and Fuller (see Bibliography, p. 402). But Del Rio was actually the name of her first husband, Jaime Del Rio, and Lolita is simply a pet form of Dolores.

Michael **Delving:** Jay Williams (1914–1978), U.S. mystery writer.

Alice **Delysia:** Alice Kolb-Bernard, née Lapize (1889–1979), Fr. stage, movie actress, singer, working in U.K.

Maria **de Madeiros:** Maria de Almeida (1965–), Port. movie actress.

Angela **Demello:** Angela Joy Cox (1959–), Eng. ballet dancer. The dancer adopted her stage name in 1983 from her first husband, a Brazilian. She found it more suitable than her maiden name, which she frequently had to spell out (Cox or Cocks)? It was also more "international," and so appropriate for a dancer. Her subsequent partner was the dancer Kevin Richmond [personal telephone call from Angela Demello, March 22, 1996].

Helen **Demidenko:** Helen Darville (1971–), Austral. writer. The writer won Australia's leading literary prize in 1995 for her novel, *The Hand That Signed the Papers*, dealing with the Ukrainian massacre of Jews during World War II. She claimed to be the daughter of an illiterate Ukrainian taxi driver and a poor Irish mother, but in reality her parents were middle-class English immigrants. The imposture naturally involved a new name. She explained: "I changed my name to protect my family and friends as well as my sources." The hoax set the Australian literary establishment in considerable disarray [*The Times*, August 23, 1995].

Nikita **Demidov:** Nikita Demidovich Antufyev (1656–1725), Russ. ironmaster. The first of the wealthy Russian Demidov family, a Tula blacksmith, adapted his patronymic (middle name) as his surname, presumably on the grounds that its initial *De-* gave it an aristocratic air. It seemed to work, for in 1720 Peter the Great made him a nobleman.

Katherine **De Mille:** Katherine Lester (1911–1995), U.S. movie actress. The actress was an orphan and took her name from director Cecil B. De Mille, who adopted her when she was nine.

Louis **de Montalte:** Blaise Pascal (1623–1662), Fr. philosopher, physicist. Pascal's pen name contains a latinized reference to the "high mountain" of Puy-de-Dôme, near Clermont-Ferrand, where he conducted several of his scientific experiments into atmospheric pressure.

Peter **de Morny:** Dorothy Estelle Esmé Wynne-Tyson, née Ripper (1898–1972), Eng. novelist, dramatist, critic. From 1909 to 1920 the writer was an actress under the name Esmé Wynne. She then left the stage to concentrate on a literary career.

[Colonel] Robert **Denard:** Gilbert Bourgeaud (1929–), Fr. mercenary.

Terry **Dene:** Terence Williams (1938–), Eng. rock singer.

Catherine **Deneuve:** Catherine Dorléac (1943–), Fr. movie actress, sister of actress Françoise Dorléac (1942–1967). The actress adopted her mother's maiden name as her professional name.

[Sir] James Steuart **Denham:** James Steuart (1712–1780), Sc. economist. The noted lawyer obtained his new name in 1733, when his father inherited the estates of his uncle, Sir Archibald Denham, on condition that he and his father adopt Denham as a surname.

Denim: Frederick Joss (*c.*1909–after 1947), Eng. political cartoonist, writer.

Richard **Denning:** Ludwig (later Louis) Albert Denninger (1914–), U.S. movie actor.

Denny **Dennis:** Ronald Dennis Pountain (1913–1993), Br. dance band vocalist.

Eugene **Dennis:** Francis Xavier Waldron, Jr. (1905–1961), U.S. Communist leader.

Les **Dennis:** Leslie Heseltine (1953–), Eng. TV comedian, teaming with Dustin Gee (*q.v.*).

Will **Dennis:** Stephen Townesend (? –1914), Eng. surgeon, writer. The writer used this name for a limited but successful stage career.

Reginald **Denny:** Reginald Leigh Daymore (1891–1967), Br. stage, movie actor.

John **Denver:** Henry John Deutschendorf, Jr. (1943–1997), U.S. country singer, songwriter. The musician is said to have adopted his surname from his favorite city, though it also suggests his original name.

Karl **Denver:** Angus Mackenzie (1934–), Sc. pop musician.

Lynsey **De Paul:** Lynsey Rubin (1951–), Br. popular singer.

Madame Marguerite **de Ponti:** Stéphane Mallarmé (1842–1898), Fr. poet. The symbolist poet used this name when acting as editor of the fashion magazine *La Dernière Mode* (1897).

Dan **De Quille**: William Wright (1829–1898), U.S. humorist, historian of the Far West. There is a pun here on "quill" and "write."

Thomas **de Quincey**: Thomas Quincey (1785–1859), Eng. essayist. There is some uncertainty whether the writer added the aristocratic "de" himself, to claim Norman descent, or whether his father was already named De Quincey. According to the *Dictionary of National Biography*, the author liked to alphabetize his name under "Q," which seems to suggest otherwise.

Bo **Derek**: Mary Cathleen Collins (1957–), U.S. movie actress. "Bo" was a childhood nickname. The actress married John Derek (see below).

John **Derek**: Derek Harris (1926–), U.S. movie actor, husband of Bo Derek (see above).

Tristan **Derème**: Philippe Huc (1889–1942), Fr. poet.

José **de Rivera**: José A. Ruiz (1904–1985), U.S. sculptor. The artist adopted his maternal grandmother's name.

Francis **Derrick**: Frances Eliza Millett Notley, née Thomas (1820–1912), Eng. novelist.

Rick **Derringer**: Rick Zehringer (1947–), U.S. rock musician.

Rózsa **Déryné**: Rózsa Schenbach (1793–1872), Hung. actress, opera singer. Schenbach was the German form of the singer's original surname. The Hungarian form was Széppataki.

Sugar Pie **DeSanto**: Umpeylia Marsema Balinton (1935–), U.S. black pop singer. The singer was nicknamed "Little Miss Sugar Pie" by Johnny Otis (*q.v.*) and adopted this as her performing name.

Marceline **Desbordes-Valmore**: Marceline Félicité Joséphine Desbordes (1786–1859), Fr. poet. The poet married an actor, Prosper Lanchantin, and added his stage name, Valmore, to her maiden name.

Father **Desiderius**: Peter Lenz (1832–1928), Ger. artist, architect. Desiderio da Settignano was a famous 15th-century Florentine sculptor. Lenz, however, probably based his name on that of "Monsu" Desiderio, the pseudonym of a painter active in Naples in the 17th century. Works grouped under this name are now known to belong to at least three separate artists, including François Nomé, a painter noted for his ghostly architectural fantasies, and Didier Barra, who painted topographical views.

Gaby **Deslys**: Gabrielle Caïre (1881–1920), Fr. stage actress, revue artist.

Astra **Desmond**: Gwendolyn Mary Thomson (1893–1973), Br. opera singer. The letters of "Astra Desmond" (if one counts some twice) appear in the singer's original name. But this is no guarantee of its origin.

Eric **Desmond**: Matthew Reginald Sheffield Cassan (1901–1957), Br.-born U.S. stage, movie actor. As a child performer, the actor was billed as Reggie Sheffield, but changed his name to Eric Desmond, possibly for the Earls of Desmond, in 1913. In some of his later films, however, he is billed as Reginald Sheffield.

Florence **Desmond**: Florence Dawson (1905–1993), Eng. revue artiste, impersonator. The actress was renamed as a child dancer by a matron overseeing the group she was in at the time.

Johnny **Desmond**: Giovanni Alfredo di Simone (1920–1985), U.S. actor, singer.

Paul **Desmond**: Paul Emil Breitenfeld (1924–1977), U.S. saxophonist.

William **Desmond**: William Mannion (1878–1949), Ir. movie actor, working in U.S.

Jerry **Desmonde**: James Robert Sadler (1908–1967), Eng. music hall comedian.

Ivan **Desny**: Ivan Desnitzky (1922–), Russ. movie actor, working in France, Germany.

Oleksa **Desnyak**: Aleksey Ignatovich Rudenko (1909–1942), Ukrainian novelist, short story writer.

Des'ree: Des'ree Weeks (1968–), Br. black rock singer, of West Indian parentage.

Emmy **Destinn**: Emilie Pavlína Kittlová (1878–1930), Cz. opera singer. The singer adopted the name of her teacher, Maria Loewe-Destinn. After 1918, when Czechoslovakia was declared a republic, she patriotically adjusted her name to Ema Destinnová.

Destouches: Philippe Nicolas Néricault (1680–1754), Fr. comic playwright. The writer adopted his aunt's name.

Andre **de Toth**: Endre Antai Mihály Sásvrái Farkasfawi Tóthfalusi Toth (1913–), Hung. movie actor. If this is indeed the actor's real name (it is so quoted, albeit in garbled form, by Katz and by Lloyd and Fuller), one can hardly begrudge him his aristocratic "de."

Cristina **Deutekom**: Stientje Engel (1932–), Du. opera singer.

Jacques **Deval**: Jacques Boularan (1890–1972), Fr. playwright, working in U.S.

[Dame] Ninette **de Valois**: Edris Connell, née Stannus (1898–), Ir.-born Br. ballet dancer, director, teacher. Interviewed on her 90th birth-day, the dancer was asked, "And where did the name de Valois come from?" "My mother thought of it, because our family had French connections" [*Sunday Times Magazine*, May 29, 1988.] Valois is a historic region and duchy in northern France. The ballerina first used her new name on making her stage debut at age 13.

David Devant: David Wighton (1868–1941), Eng. magician. The illusionist was the son of a Scottish landscape painter, and the artistic con-nection may have had some bearing on his new name. As a boy, the story goes, he visited an art gallery and admired there a biblical painting by a French artist entitled *David Devant Goliath* ("David Before Goliath"). Young Wighton mis-took the second word for the subject's name and "filed it away mentally for professional purposes in later life" [John Fisher, *Paul Daniels and the Story of Magic*, 1987].

Willy DeVille: William Boray (1953–), U.S. rock singer.

Mlle de Villedieu: Marie Catherine H. Des-jardins (1631–1683), Fr. author.

Justin de Villeneuve: Nigel Davies (1939–), former Br. manager of Twiggy (*q.v.*).

Andy Devine: Jeremiah Schwartz (1905–1977), U.S. movie comedian.

Dominic Devine: David McDonald Devine (1920–1980), Eng. thriller writer.

Magenta Devine: Kim Taylor (1960–), Br. TV presenter.

Devlo: Cyril Shaw (1910–), Eng. magician. The name appears to echo that of the famous magician David Devant (*q.v.*).

Howard Devoto: Howard Trafford (*c.*1955–), Eng. punk rock musician.

Patrick Dewaere: Jean-Marie Bourdeau (1947–1982), Fr. movie actor. The actor adopted his grandmother's surname at the start of his career in 1968. He also appeared under the name Patrick Maurin.

Dewi Emlyn: David Davies (1817–1888), Welsh-born U.S. poet. The writer's name means "David of Emlyn," the latter being the historic region in which he was born.

Dewi Havhesp: David Roberts (1831–1884), Welsh poet. The writer took his bardic name, meaning "David of Havhesp," from a stream by his home near Bala.

Dewi Hefin: David Thomas (1828–1909), Welsh poet. The writer's name means "David of Hefin," this presumably being a local placename.

Dewi Wyn o Eifion: David Owen (1784–1841), Welsh poet. The writer's name means "Fair David of Eifionydd," the latter being the historic region in northwestern Wales where he was born and where many poets lived.

Billy de Wolfe: William Andrew Jones (1907–1974), U.S. stage, movie comedian, of Welsh parentage. Bill Jones (as he was usually known) was told by a theatre manager that his real name would not do for a star. He therefore simply adopted the manager's own name.

Al Dexter: Albert Poindexter (1902–1984), U.S. country singer, songwriter.

Anthony Dexter: Walter Reinhold Alfred Fleischmann (1919–), U.S. movie actor.

Aubrey Dexter: Douglas Peter Jonas (1898–1958), Br. stage, movie, TV actor.

William Dexter: William T. Pritchard (1909–), Eng. writer on magic. The writer's pen name may well have been based on "dexterous," given his specialty.

Lodewijk van Deyssel: Karel Joan Lodewijk Alberdingk Thijm (1864–1952), Du. writer, critic.

Augusto D'Halmar: Augusto Thomson (1882–1950), Chilean writer.

[Anagarika] Dharmapala: David Hewavi-tarne (1864–1933), Ceylonese Buddhist leader. The Buddhist pioneer and preacher adopted his new name in his late teens. Dharmapala means "guardian of the dharma," this being the Sanskrit word for "law," that is, the ideal truth as set forth in the teachings of the Buddha. Anagarika is a title used for a celibate, fulltime worker for Bud-dhism. Dharmapala was the first anagarika in modern times, and took his vow of celibacy (brahmacharya) at the age of eight.

Robert Dhéry: Robert Foullcy, (1921–), Fr. movie comedian. The actor took his name from that of his birthplace, Héry, France.

I.A.L. Diamond: Itek Dommnici (1920–1988), Rom.-born U.S. screenwriter. Diamond chose his new name when working on the cam-pus newspaper at Columbia University. Tongue firmly in cheek, he claimed that the initials stood for Interscholastic Algebra League, of which he had been champion in 1936 and 1937.

Neil Diamond: Noah Kaminsky (1941–), U.S. popular singer.

Fra Diavolo: Michele Pezza (1771–1806), It. brigand chief. The legendary guerrilla leader adopted his nickname, meaning "Brother Devil." This was given him by victimized peasants on account of his ferocity. It was rumored, moreover, that Pezza had originally been a monk named Fra Angelo ("Brother Angel").

Thomas John **Dibdin**: Thomas John Pitt (1771–1833), Eng. actor, playwright. The actor was illegitimate, so adopted his mother's maiden name.

Ivan Osipovich **Dic**: Jon Dicescu (1893–1938), Rom. socialist activist.

Dic Aberdaron: Richard Robert Jones (1780–1843), Welsh scholar. The eccentric linguist adopted a name meaning "Dick of Aberdaron," the latter being his birthplace.

Angie **Dickinson**: Angeline Brown (1931–), U.S movie actress. The name is that of the actress's first husband, Gene Dickinson.

Carr **Dickson**: John Dickson Carr (1905–1977), U.S. journalist, crime writer. The writer also used the name Roger Fairbairn. See also the next entry below.

Carter **Dickson**: John Dickson Carr (1905–1977), U.S. journalist, crime writer. See also the entry above.

Gloria **Dickson**: Thais Dickerson (1916–1945), U.S. movie actress.

Dic Tryfan: Richard Hughes Williams (c.1878–1919), Welsh journalist, short story writer. The writer's name means "Dick of Tryfan," the latter being a mountain near his birthplace in northwestern Wales.

Bo **Diddley**: Otha Ellas Bates (later McDaniel) (1928–), U.S. black jazz musician. McDaniel acquired his name when he was training to be a boxer at the local gym. A "bo diddley" is a one-stringed African guitar. The musician's original surname was Bates. His mother, however, was too poor to raise him and he was adopted by his mother's first cousin, Gussie McDaniel, a Sunday school teacher in Chicago, and he adopted her name.

Didi: Waldir Pereira (1928–), Brazilian footballer. A pet form of the player's first name.

Marlene **Dietrich**: Maria Magdalene Dietrich von Losch (1901–1992), Ger.-born U.S. movie actress, singer. The actress's first name is a telescoping of "Maria Magdalene." Dietrich was the name of her father, an officer in the Royal Prussian Police. A year or two after her birth, Marie's family moved from Berlin to Weimar, where her mother remarried, her new husband being Edouard von Losch. In the popular mind, the name of Marlene Dietrich is associated with that of Lilli Marlene, the girl in the German song (borrowed by the British) that was popular in World War II, as Dietrich herself was. Doubtless the German/English link helped. But the song originated in a poem written in World War I, even though it was actually composed in 1938. So the two ladies are quite distinct. ("Lilli Marlene" was sung by the Swedish singer, Lale Andersson.)

Laura **Di Falco**: Laura Carpinteri (1910–), It. novelist, painter.

Phyllis **Diller**: Phyllis Driver (1917–), U.S. movie actress, comedienne.

Isak **Dinesen**: Karen Christentze Blixen, née Dinesen (1885–1962), Dan. writer, broadcaster, working in Kenya. The author adopted her new first name, from an African word meaning "laughter," for *Seven Gothic Tales* (1934), written in English. She also wrote as Pierre Andrezel (*q.v.*), Tania B., and Osceola, the last for various Danish periodicals.

Ding: Jay Norwood Darling (1876–1962), U.S. cartoonist. From his surname.

Ding Ling: Jiang Weizhi (Chiang Wei-chih) (1904–1986), Chin. (female) novelist, Communist.

Júlio **Dinis**: Joaquim Guilherme Gomes Coelho (1839–1871), Port. poet, playwright, novelist. The writer was of English descent on his mother's side.

Ronnie James **Dio**: Ronald Padavona (c.1940–), U.S. rock singer.

Diocletian: Diocles (245–316), Roman emperor. The emperor's eventual full name, as found in official inscriptions, was Gaius Aurelius Valerius Diocletianus. Gaius was his *praenomen*, or forename, Aurelius his *nomen*, or *gens* (clan) name, Valerius his *cognomen*, or additional name (from his daughter, Valeria), and Diocletianus his second *cognomen*, created as an adjectival form of his own original name, Diocles (itself meaning "fame of Zeus").

Dion: Dion DiMucci (1939–), U.S. rock musician.

Discobolus: Donald Williams Aldous (1914–), Eng. writer on sound recording, engineering. The writer's name is Latin (from Greek) for "discus thrower," or in modern terms "disc thrower" (that is, one who "throws" discs on to a record player, or who records on such discs in the first place).

Dick **Distich**: Alexander Pope (1688–1744), Eng. poet. Pope used this pseudonym for writing in the *Guardian*, a distich being a verse couplet.

Dora **D'Istria:** Helena Gjika (1828–1882), Rom. writer, of Albanian origin.

Dito und Idem: Elizabeth, Queen of Romania (1843–1916), Romanian verse, prose writer + Mite (or Marie) Kremnitz (1852–1916), Ger. writer. This was the joint pseudonym used by the already pseudonymous Carmen Sylva (*q.v.*) and George Allan (*q.v.*) when the two ladies wrote as coauthors. The words (respectively in Italian, German, and Latin) translate as "the same and the same." An academic pun.

Carl **Ditters von Dittersdorf:** Carl Ditters (1739–1799), Ger. violinist, composer. The Vienna-born musician was ennobled in 1773 and adopted his aristocratic augmentation then.

Divine: Harris Glen Milstead (1945–1988), U.S. movie actor, drag artist. Nicknamed, with some justification, "The Filthiest Man Alive," the gross, 300-pound actor was offered a screen name that was exactly the reverse of his unpleasant persona.

Father **Divine:** George Baker (*c.*1877–1965), U.S. black evangelist. The founder of the Peace Mission movement adopted the name Major J. Devine soon after moving to New York from Georgia in 1915. This name was soon popularly modified to Divine, with "Father" indicating his leadership status.

Dorothy **Dix:** Elizabeth Meriwether Gilmer (1861–1951), U.S. journalist, women's rights pioneer. The same name was used by the English journalist Jean Nicol (died 1986) when employed by the *Daily Mirror* at the start of her career in the 1930s. The name itself was presumably borrowed from that of the social reformer and humanitarian Dorothea Dix (1802–1887).

Richard **Dix:** Ernest Carlton Brimmer (1894–1949), U.S. movie actor.

Marmaduke **Dixey:** Geoffrey Howard (1889–1973), Eng. novelist, poet.

Jean **Dixon:** Marie Jacques (1894–1981), U.S. stage, movie comedienne.

Diz: Edward Jeffrey Irving Ardizzone (1900–1979), Br. cartoonist, illustrator.

Lefty **Dizz:** Walter Williams (1937–1993), U.S. blues guitarist. Williams played a right-handed Stratocaster guitar with the strings reversed. This gave his new first name. His second name came following a spell as a trumpeter.

Assia **Djebar:** Fatima-Zohra Imalayene (1936–), Algerian novelist, movie director.

[St.] **Dmitry Donskoy:** Dmitry Ivanovich (1350–1389), Russ. prince. The grand prince of Vladimir and Moscow was given his name, meaning "of the Don," for his victory over the Golden Horde near the Don River at the Battle of Kulikovo in 1380. He was canonized in 1988.

[St.] **Dmitry Rostovsky:** Daniil Savvich Tuptalo (1651–1709), Russ. ecclesiastic, poet, playwright, of Ukrainian origin. The writer took monastic vows in 1668 and was appointed metropolitan of Rostov (hence his title) in 1702.

Anatoly **Dneprov:** Anatoly Petrovich Mitskevich (1919–), Russ. SF writer.

I. **Dniprovsky:** Ivan Danilovich Shevchenko (1895–1934), Ukrainian writer. The writer took his pen name from the Dnieper River, near which he was born.

Don Leucadio **Doblado:** Joseph Blanco White (*q.v.*).

Issay **Dobrowen:** Ishok Israelevich Barabeychik (1891–1953), Russ. conductor, pianist, working in Germany, Sweden. The musician took the name that his mother had adopted from a relative.

Lew **Dockstader:** George Alfred Clapp (1856–1924), U.S. vaudeville artist, blackface minstrel. The singer acquired his stage name through his partnership in a minstrel troupe with Charles Dockstader, billed as the Dockstader Brothers. When Charles died in 1883, Clapp kept the name, even after the troupe had disbanded.

Dr.: For names beginning thus, see the next word, e.g. Dr. **Dre**, Dr. **Feelgood**, Dr. **John**.

Charles **Dodd:** Hugh Tootel (1672–1743), Eng. Roman Catholic theologian. The cleric used this name for all his writings, notably *The Church History of England* (1737–43). Oddly, Charles Dodd (1884–1973) was the real name of a noted later English theologian, although Protestant, not Catholic.

Theo van **Doesburg:** Christian Emil Marie Küpper (1883–1931), Du. painter, architect, writer. The artist, a leader of the de Stijl movement, exhibited as a Dadaist in 1923 under the name J.K. Bonset.

Q.K. Philander **Doesticks**, P.B.: Mortimer Neal Thomson (1831–1875), U.S. humorist. The name is simply a frivolous one, although Thomson claimed that "P.B." stood for "Perfect Brick." He was the son-in-law of Fanny Fern (*q.v.*).

Sir Iliad **Doggrel:** [Sir] Thomas Burnet (1694–1753), Eng. writer + George Ducket (? –1732), Eng. writer, politician. The two used this name for their *Homerides*, a criticism of Pope's neoclassical translation of the *Iliad* (1715).

Ştefan Augustin **Doinaş:** Ştefan Popa (1922–), Rom. poet.

Dolbokov: Hannes Vayn Bok (1914–1964), U.S. SF writer, artist + Boris Dolgov (–), U.S. artist.

Thomas **Dolby:** Thomas Morgan Robertson (1958–), Br. rock musician, producer.

R. **Doleman:** Robert Parsons (1546–1610), Eng. Jesuit missionary, plotter. Parsons, who founded the English province of the Society of Jesus, used this name for *A Conference about the Next Succession to the Crown of England* (1594). He had several other pseudonyms, many of them simply initials.

Anton **Dolin:** Sydney Francis Patrick Chippendall Healey-Kay (1904–1983), Eng. ballet dancer, choreographer. Patrick Healey-Kay assumed his stage name in 1921, on joining Diaghilev's Ballets Russes: "As the programmes were being printed Pat suddenly conceived the idea of disguising himself under a Russian name. 'It will be an excellent joke. It is sure to mystify all my friends and annoy some of them intensely. What shall I be?' He reached for a volume of Tchekov. 'Anton, at any rate, is a good beginning.' The rest was not so easy. Most of the names were difficult to pronounce, and still more difficult to remember. Someone ... hit upon Dolin. 'It is simple and will look well in print. I can already hear the public calling out: "Dolin! Bravo, Dolin!"' They did the very next night" [Arnold Haskell, *Balletomania*, 1934].

Dolin is not only a genuine Russian name, appropriate for a ballet dancer, but equally suggests the common Irish surname Dolan. Healey-Kay's mother, née Healey, was Irish. An earlier name used by the dancer was Russian-style Patrikéeff, from his third name.

Jim **Dollar:** Marietta Sergeyevna Shaginyan (1888–1982), Russ. writer, playwright, literary critic. The writer used this name for her popular adventure story *Mess Mend: Yankees in Petrograd* (1923), a parody of Western detective fiction set in Russia and an imaginary New York.

Jennie **Dolly:** Janszieka Deutsch (1902–1941), Hung.-born U.S. movie actress, singer, teaming with Rosie Dolly (see below), her sister.

Rosie **Dolly:** Roszika Deutsch (1893–1970), Hung.-born U.S. movie actress, singer, teaming with Jennie Dolly (see above), her sister. Although the duo were billed as "The Dolly Sisters" from the first, they continued to use the European forms of their forenames for several years.

Evsey David **Domar:** Evsey David Domashevitsky (1914–), Pol.-born U.S. economist.

Domenichino: Domenico Zampieri (1581–1641), It. painter. The artist's name is a diminutive of his first name, so means "little Domenico."

Dominguín: Luis Miguel González Lucas (1926–1966), Sp. bullfighter. The matador inherited the name of his bullfighter father, professionally known as Domingo Dominguín.

Rey **Domini:** Audre Lorde (1934–), U.S. black poet, writer. "Rey" presumably as a pet form of "Audre," and "Domini" as a Latin-style translation of the writer's surname.

Léon **Dominique:** Léon Aronson (1893–1984), Russ.-born Fr. restaurateur, drama critic. Aronson adopted the name of the Russian restaurant he founded (in 1927) in Paris, the Dominique, as a pseudonym for his second profession as drama critic.

Fats **Domino:** Antoine Domino (1928–), U.S. black jazz musician. The musician's surname is his real one. "Fats" was the (descriptive) nickname given him by band leader Bill Diamond when he first started playing, as a ten-year-old, at the Hideaway Club, New Orleans. In 1949 his first record was called "The Fat Man." He was the inspiration for the name of Chubby Checker (*q.v.*).

Sam **Donahue:** Samuel Koontz (1918–1974), U.S. saxophonist, bandleader.

Troy **Donahue:** Merle Johnson, Jr. (1936–), U.S. movie actor.

Pauline **Donalda:** Pauline Lightstone (1882–1970), Can. opera singer.

Donatello: Donato di Niccolo di Betto Bardi (? 1386–1466), It. sculptor. The artist's adopted name arose as a straightforward nickname, "little Donato."

Lonnie **Donegan:** Anthony James Donegan (1931–), Sc. pop musician. The "King of Skiffle" took his new first name from the U.S. blues musician Lonnie Johnson (1889–1970), with whom an MC confused him when the two men were on the same London bill.

Donovan: Donovan Philip Leitch (1946–), Sc. rock musician, father of Ione Skye (*q.v.*).

Dick **Donovan:** Joyce Emmerson Preston Muddock (1843–1934), Eng. journalist, detective fiction writer.

Mr. **Dooley:** Finley Peter Dunne (1867–1936), U.S. humorist. Mr. Dooley, in a series of the writer's works, was a typical Irish saloon keeper with a typical Irish name.

Milo **Dor:** Milutin Doroslovac (1923–), Serbian writer.

Mary **Doran:** Florence Arnot (1907–), U.S. movie actress.

Jean **Dorat:** Jean Dinemandi (1508–1588), Fr. humanist, poet, translator. The scholar's change of name is explained as follows by Isaac D'Israeli (see Bibliography, p. 400): "Dorat, a French poet, had for his real name *Disnemandi*, which, in the dialect of the Limousins, signifies one who dines in the morning: that is, one who has no other dinner than his breakfast. This degrading name he changed to *Dorat*, or gilded, a nickname which one of his ancestors had for his fair tresses." The poet actually adopted the name of his birthplace, Le Dorat, near Limoges.

Roland **Dorgelès:** Roland Lecavelé (1886–1973), Fr. novelist, short story writer.

Dolores **Dorn:** Dolores Dorn-Heft (1935–), U.S. stage, movie actress.

Philip **Dorn:** Hein van der Niet (1901–1975), Du. movie actor, working in U.S. He appeared in early movies as Fritz van Dongen.

Sandra **Dorne:** Joanna Smith (1925–), Br. movie actress.

Marie **Doro:** Marie Stewart (1882–1956), U.S. movie actress.

Diana **Dors:** Diana Mary Fluck (1931–1984), Eng. stage, movie, TV actress. The actress was nearly called Diana Scarlett, a name proposed by her agent, Gordon Harbord, who also named Laurence Harvey and Adrienne Corri (*qq.v.*). But Diana was not keen on this, and her final stage name came about as described in her autobiography: "To be born with the name of Fluck, particularly if one is a girl, can be nothing less than disastrous. Originally my reason for changing it was no more than a young girl's ambition to become a movie star ... but when I was cast in my first movie the director tried gently to explain that the second part of my name would have to be altered. ... I was only fourteen and did not quite understand his well meant reasoning then, but as I wished to call myself something much more exotic anyway, I agreed willingly, and the search for a new surname was on!

My agent had suggested Scarlett ... and I toyed with that for a while. My own fantasy of Diana Carroll also seemed a possibility but my father was incensed that the family name was not to be used. ... Finally my mother in a moment of brilliance decided that I *would* stick to a family name after all, and because my grandmother's maiden name had been Dors, she felt it sounded good to have two names with the same initial. So Dors it was and we were all happy!" [Diana Dors, *Behind Closed Dors*, 1979].

Fifi **D'Orsay:** Angelina Yvonne Cecil Lussier D'Sablon (1904–1983), Can.-born U.S. stage, movie actress. The actress claimed that her new surname was adopted from a bottle of French perfume, and that "Fifi" was what other girls called her when she was in the Greenwich Village Follies chorus in the 1920s. It is certainly a typical chorus girl's name, like Gigi and Mimi. "D'Orsay" would be a "prestige" name for a commercial product, suggesting the Quai d'Orsay, the French foreign office (named after its location in Paris).

Marie **Dorval:** Marie Thomase Amélie Delaunay (1798–1849), Fr. actress. The actress's stage name is that of her husband, balletmaster Allan Dorval, whom she married at 15.

Gabrielle **Dorziat:** Gabrielle Sigrist Moppert (1886–1979), Fr. movie actress.

Stanislav **Dospevski:** Zafir Zograf (1823–1878), Bulg. painter.

Dosso Dossi: Giovanni Lutero (*c.*1490–1542), It. painter. The artist's name, which is not recorded before the 18th century, probably comes from Dosso, a place near Mantua, where he is known to have been in 1512.

Dottsy: Dorothy Brodt (1954–), U.S. country singer.

Catherine **Doucet:** Catherine Green (1875–1958), U.S. stage, movie actress.

Douglas: Thomas Douglas England (1891–1971), Eng. cartoonist.

Craig **Douglas:** Terence Perkins (1941–), Eng. popular singer.

Donald **Douglas:** Douglas Kinleyside (1905–1945), U.S. movie actor.

Donna **Douglas:** Doris Smith (1939–), U.S. TV actress.

Ellen **Douglas:** Josephine Haxton, née Ayres (1921–), U.S. novelist, short story writer.

Felicity **Douglas:** Felicity Dowson, née Tonlin (1910–), Eng. stage, movie, TV, radio author.

Part II: The Dictionary

George **Douglas:** George Douglas Brown (1869–1902), Sc. novelist.

Kirk **Douglas:** Issur Danielovitch (later Isidore Demsky) (1916–), U.S. movie actor, of Russ. Jewish parentage. The actor chose his new first name because he felt it was "snazzy," and his surname out of his admiration for Douglas Fairbanks, Jr. (*q.v.*). His adoption of "Kirk" (in 1941) gave the name a popular boost, especially with its "rugged" and respectable associations ("church").

Melvyn **Douglas:** Melvyn Edouard Hesselberg (1901–1981), U.S. stage, movie actor, producer, director, of Russ. parentage. The actor adopted his new name in 1919.

Mike **Douglas:** Michael Delaney Dowd, Jr. (1925–), U.S. TV personality, singer.

O. **Douglas:** Anna Buchan (1877–1948), Sc. novelist, sister of novelist John Buchan (1875–1940). The writer took her new name for her first book, *Olivia in India* (1913), based on her experiences while visiting her younger brother William in Calcutta: "I did not want to use my name as (in my opinion) John had given lustre to the name of Buchan which any literary efforts of mine would not be likely to add to, so I called myself 'O. Douglas'" [Anna Buchan, *Unforgettable, Unforgotten*, 1945]. The initial thus stood for "Olivia."

Robert **Douglas:** Robert Douglas Finlayson (1909–), Br. stage, movie actor, working in U.S.

Scott **Douglas:** James Hicks (1927–1996), U.S. ballet dancer.

Wallace **Douglas:** Wallace Finlayson (1911–), Can. stage director.

Frederick **Douglass:** Frederick Augustus Washington Bailey (1817–1895), U.S. black abolitionist, writer. The human rights leader escaped from slavery in Baltimore, Maryland, in 1838 and settled in New Bedford, Massachusetts, where he changed his name to avoid slave hunters.

Kent **Douglass:** Robert Douglas Montgomery (1908–1966), U.S. movie actor. The actor also used the name Robert Douglass (see below). He adopted both names as there was already a Robert Montgomery (*q.v.*), as well as a Robert Douglas (see above). Note the additional "s" to aid the distinction, essential in the second case.

Robert **Douglass:** Robert Douglas Montgomery (1908–1966), U.S. movie actor. The actor also used the name Kent Douglass (see above).

Stephen **Douglass:** Stephen Fitch (1921–), U.S. stage actor, singer. The actor adopted his mother's maiden name.

Billie **Dove:** Lillian Bohney (1900–), U.S. movie actress.

Dovima: Dorothy Virginia Margaret Juba (1927–), U.S. model, of Pol.-Ir. parentage. When the future model was confined to bed with rheumatic fever for seven years as a child she occupied herself by drawing, signing her pictures with a name formed from the first syllables of her three forenames. She kept the name in her professional career.

Peggy **Dow:** Margaret Josephine Varnadow (1928–), U.S. movie actress.

Eddie **Dowling:** Joseph Nelson Goucher (1889–1976), U.S. stage actor, producer, playwright. The actor adopted his mother's maiden name.

Major Jack **Downing:** Seba Smith (1792–1868), U.S. humorist. Major Jack Downing was the supposed name of a Down East Yankee who began to publish letters in the *Portland Courier* (founded by Smith in 1829) in 1830. He had a comic turn of speech and an essentially homespun sagacity that soon won him popularity among his readers. Note the echo of "Down East" in his name.

Dox: Jean Verdi Solomon Razkandrainy (1913–1978), Malagasy lyric poet. The poet adopted his pen name from the last syllable of *paradox*, reflecting both the indigenous and (French) colonial background against which his writing is set as well as his leading theme of love, with its duality of joy and sadness, beauty and melancholy.

Lynn **Doyle:** Leslie Alexander Montgomery (1873–1961), Ir. humorous novelist, playwright.

Rade **Drajnac:** Radojko Jovanović (1899–1943), Serbian writer, journalist.

Alfred **Drake:** Alfredo Capurro (1914–1992), It.-born U.S. stage singer, dancer.

Charles **Drake:** Charles Ruppert (1914–), U.S. movie actor.

Charlie **Drake:** Charles Springall (1925–), Eng. TV, movie, stage comedian.

Dona **Drake:** Rita Novella (1920–1989), Mexican singer, dancer, movie actress. Why did she forsake her original memorable name? An early name used by the singer was Rita Rio.

Fabia **Drake:** Ethel McGlinchy (1904–1990), Br. movie actress. The actress based her name on that of her Irish father, Alfred Drake. Her mother, Annie McGlinchy, née Dalton, was Scottish.

Frances **Drake:** Frances Dean (1908–), U.S. movie actress.

Samuel **Drake:** Samuel Drake Bryant (1768–1854), Br.-born U.S. actor-manager.

Tom **Drake:** Alfred Alderdice (1918–1982), U.S. movie actor. The "maleness" of the actor's new names may have been intended for his "boy next door" roles of the 1940s. He began his career with the screen name Richard Alden.

M.B. **Drapier:** Jonathan Swift (1667–1745), Ir. satirist, cleric. A "nonce" pseudonym adopted by the author of *Gulliver's Travels.* He used the name for *The Drapier's Letters* (1724), written in the guise of a Dublin draper. A patent had been granted to the Duchess of Kendal for supplying copper coins for use in Ireland, and this she sold to one William Wood for £10,000. The profit on the patent would have been, it is said, around £25,000, and Swift published four letters prophesying ruin to the Irish if "Wood's halfpence" were admitted into circulation. The letters were effective, and the government was forced to abandon the plan and to compensate Wood.

Sir Alexander **Drawcansir:** Henry Fielding (1707–1754), Eng. novelist, playwright. Fielding used the pseudonym as editor of *The Covent-Garden Journal* (1752). The original Drawcansir was the burlesque tyrant in Buckingham's farcical comedy *The Rehearsal* (1672), caricaturing the knight errant Almanzor in Dryden's *The Conquest of Granada* (1670). The name itself obviously puns on "Almanzor," while perhaps also intentionally implying someone who likes to *draw* a *can* of liquor. Buckingham's Drawcansir has only three lines in the play, of which two are: "He that dares drink, and for that drink dares die, And, knowing this, dares yet drink on, am I." This parodied Almanzor's: "He who dares love, and for that love must die, And, knowing this, dares yet love on, am I."

Alfred **Drayton:** Alfred Varick (1881–1949), Br. movie actor.

Dr. **Dre:** Andre Young (1965–), U.S. black rapper, DJ.

Mikey **Dread:** Michael Campbell (*c.*1958–), Jamaican reggae DJ, "toaster."

Carl **Dreadstone:** John Ramsey Campbell (1940–), Eng. writer of horror fiction.

Sonia **Dresdel:** Lois Obee (1908–1976), Eng. stage, movie actress.

Louise **Dresser:** Louise Kerlin (1878–1965), U.S. movie actress.

Marie **Dressler:** Leila Marie Koerber (1869–1934), Can.-born U.S. stage, movie comedienne. The actress adopted her new name in 1886, when making her debut as Cigarette in a stage version of *Under Two Flags* by Ouida (*q.v.*).

Ellen **Drew:** Terry Ray (1915–), U.S. movie actress. There seem to be theatrical overtones in the actress's stage name. Her substitution of "Ellen" for "Terry" suggests the name of Ellen Terry (1847–1928), the famous English stage actress, while "Drew" is also a well-known acting name, as for Mrs. John Drew (1820–1897), the U.S. actress and theatre manager.

Nancy **Drexel:** Dorothy Kitchen (1910–, U.S. movie actress.

Slim **Drifting:** Elmon Mickle (1919–1977), U.S. pop musician.

Jimmy **Driftwood:** James Morris (1907–), U.S. country singer.

Adam **Drinan:** Joseph Todd Gordon Macleod (1903–1984), Br. author, play producer, radio newsreader. The writer chose the name for three books of verse about the Hebrides, selecting the pseudonym because some of his ancestors had come from Drinan in the Isle of Skye.

Droch: Robert Seymour Bridges (1844–1930), Eng. poet. The poet's early pen name is a Celtic rendering of his surname. Scottish Gaelic *drochaid* is "bridge." He also wrote as Broch, from the Scottish word (related to English "borough") for a round stone castle.

Dromio: William John Townsend Collins (1868–1952), Br. journalist, local historian. The writer used this name for his publications on rugby football. Dromio is a messenger in Shakespeare's *Comedy of Errors*, his own name coming from Greek *dromos*, "running." Rugby is a game in which speed is of the essence.

Joanne **Dru:** Joanne Letitia LaCock (1923–1996), U.S. movie actress. When a stage actress (briefly), Joanne LaCock performed as Joanne Marshall. She later selected the name of Dru after a Welsh ancestor. It was director Howard Hawkes who encouraged her to change her name.

The **Druid:** Henry Hall Dixon (1822–1870), Eng. sporting writer.

Bill **Drummond:** William Butterworth (1953–), S.A.-born Br. rock musician.

Ivor **Drummond:** Roger Erskine Longrigg (1929–), Sc. crime, mystery writer. The name suggests that of Bulldog Drummond, the chief character in the thrillers by Sapper (*q.v.*).

Dryasdust: M.Y. Halidom (*q.v.*).

The Rev. Dr. **Dryasdust:** [Sir] Walter Scott (1771–1832), Sc. novelist. The author used the mock self-deprecatory name in the introduction to several of his novels.

Leo **Dryden:** George Dryden Wheeler (1862–1939), Eng. music hall singer.

Doggrel **Drydog:** Charles Clark (1806–1880), Br. farmer, publisher, satirist, sporting writer. Clark used other names, such as Chilly Charley, Charles William Duckett, Thomas Hood the Younger, Pe-Gas-Us, and Quintin Queerfellow, this last for *A Doctor's "Do"-ings, or the entrapped Heiress of Witham* (1848) a self-published satirical poem of racy content intended for private circulation.

Edward **Dryhurst:** Edward Roberts (1904–1989), Br. movie producer, actor.

César **Duayen:** Ema de la Barra de Llanos (1861–1947), Argentinian novelist, painter, singer. The artist used this (male) name for her writing.

Sieur **du Baudrier:** Jonathan Swift (1667–1745), Ir. satirist, cleric. Swift used the name for his *New Journey to Paris* (1711).

Alice **Dubois:** Louise de Bettignies (1880–1918), Fr. spy. The former governess adopted this cover name when working as an Allied agent in German-occupied Lille during World War I.

Jacques (or Jack) **Duchesne:** Michel Jacques Saint-Denis (1897–1971), Fr.-born Eng. stage actor, director. This was the *nom de guerre* under which the director headed a team that broadcast from London to their compatriots over the BBC French Service during World War II.

Thomas **du Clévier:** Bonaventure Des Périers (*c.*1500–1543), Fr. storyteller, humanist writer. The writer used the name for his *Cymbalum Mundi* (1537), four satirical dialogues in the style of Lucian. Du Clévier is an anagram of French *incrédule* ("unbeliever"), with Thomas alluding to the biblical Doubting Thomas. The work was supposedly translated by du Clévier, and sent by him to his friend Tryocan. But the latter was also a pseudonym used by Des Périers, and is an anagram of *croyant* ("believer"). The work is an attack on the Christian faith and its liturgy and discipline. It was officially suppressed, and only one copy survived.

Mlle **Duclos:** Marie-Anne de Châteauneuf (1668–1748), Fr. actress.

Dave **Dudley:** David Pedruska (1928–), U.S. country musician.

Pete **Duel:** Peter Deuel (1940–1972), U.S. movie actor.

Dufresne: Abraham-Alexis Quinault (1693–1767), Fr. actor.

Dugazon: Jean-Baptiste-Henri Gourgaud (1746–1809), Fr. actor.

Doris **Duke:** Doris Curry (1945–), U.S. black soul singer.

Vernon **Duke:** Vladimir Aleksandrovich Dukelsky (1903–1969), Russ.-born U.S. popular music composer. The americanized version of the composer's name was sugested by fellow musician George Gershwin. Dukelsky retained his original Russian name for his serious music.

Germaine **Dulac:** Charlotte Elisabeth Germaine Saisset-Schneider (1882–1942), Fr. movie director, actress. The actress adopted the name of her husband, engineer and novelist Marie-Louis Albert-Dulac, whom she married in 1905.

Alexandre **Dumas:** Alexandre Davy de la Pailleterie (1802–1870), Fr. novelist, playwright. The parents of the author of *The Count of Monte Cristo*, also known as "Dumas *père*", were Creoles, and Dumas was the name of his West Indian grandmother. It was actually the writer's father who adopted the name, however, rather than he himself.

Mlle **Dumesnil:** Marie-Françoise Marchand (1712–1803), Fr. tragic actress.

Carlotta **Dumont:** Clorinda Matto de Turner (1909–), Peruvian writer. A name created using letters from the writer's original name.

Margaret **Dumont:** Margaret Baker (1889–1965), U.S. movie comedienne.

Steffi **Duna:** Stephanie Berindey (1913–1992), Hung. dancer, movie actress.

Irma **Duncan:** Irma Dorette Henriette Ehrich-Grimme (1897–1977), Ger.-U.S. ballet dancer, teacher.

Jane **Duncan:** Elizabeth Jane Cameron (1910–1976), Sc. novelist. The writer took her new first name from her own middle name and her surname from the first name of her father, Duncan Cameron. She also wrote as Janet Sandison, her mother's maiden name.

Trevor **Duncan:** Leonard Trebilco (1924–), Br. popular composer.

John **Dundee:** Joseph Carrora (1893–1965), U.S. featherweight boxer ("the Scotch Wop").

Michael **Dunn:** Gary Neil Miller (1934–1973), U.S. dwarf movie actor.

Augustus **Dun-shunner:** [Professor] William Edmonstone Aytoun (1813–1865), Sc. poet. The writer used this name for his contributions to *Blackwood's Magazine.* A "dun" is a debt collector, so that a "dun-shunner" is someone who avoids debt collectors or creditors.

Amy **Dunsmuir:** Margaret Oliphant Oliphant, née Wilson (1828–1897), Sc. novelist. (Margaret Wilson married her cousin, Francis Oliphant.)

T. E. **Dunville:** Thomas Edward Wallen (1868–1924), Eng. music hall comedian, singer.

Carolus **Duran:** Charles-Auguste-Emile Durand (1837–1917), Fr. genre portrait painter.

David **Durand:** David Durrant (1921–), U.S. juvenile movie actor.

Marguerite **Duras:** Marguerite Donnadieu (1914–1996), French novelist, playwright. The writer adopted her pseudonym in the 1940s from a wine-growing village near Bordeaux where her father had once owned a house.

Deanna **Durbin:** Edna Mae Durbin (1921–), Can. movie actress, singer. The actress juggled the letters of her fairly common first two names and came up with the more esoteric "Deanna," counting "m" as "n" and losing the "y" in the process.

Henry Fowle **Durrant:** Henry Welles Smith (1822–1881), U.S. lawyer, lay preacher. The lawyer changed his name so as not to be confused with the many other Henry Smiths.

Luc **Durtain:** André Nepveu (1881–1959), Fr. writer.

Slim **Dusty:** David Gordon Kirkpatrick (1927–), Austral. singer.

Olav **Duun:** Ole Julius Raabye (1876–1939), Norw. novelist.

Frank **Duveneck:** Frank Decker (1848–1919), U.S. painter, etcher, sculptor. The artist adopted his stepfather's name, which happened to bear some resemblance to his own.

Henri **Duvernois:** Henry Schwabacher (1875–1937), Fr. novelist, playwright.

Duy Tan: Vinh San (1899–1945), Vietnamese emperor. The emperor assumed his new name on his succession in 1907. It means "reform," and as written in Chinese characters was the same as the name of the Duy Tan Hoi ("Reformation Society"), a radical nationalist organization founded around the same time.

Ann **Dvorak:** Anna McKim (1911–1979), U.S. movie actress. The actress adopted her mother's maiden name.

Dyfed: Evan Rees (1850–1923), Welsh poet. The poet and archdruid took his bardic name from the ancient province (and modern county) of Dyfed, southwestern Wales, where he was born.

Dyfnallt: [Rev.] John Owen (1873–1956), Welsh poet. The poet and archdruid took his bardic name from a favorite locality. The name itself means "deep wood."

Bob **Dylan:** Robert Allen Zimmerman (1941–), U.S. rock musician, poet, composer. The commonly held theory is that Bob Dylan adopted the name of the Welsh poet, Dylan Thomas, because he admired him. But the musician himself has specifically denied this: "No, God, no. I took the name Dylan because I have an uncle named Dillion. I changed the spelling, but only because it looked better. I've read some of Dylan Thomas's stuff, and it's not the same as mine." The popular theory persisted however, prompting Dylan to ask Robert Shelton, author of *No Direction Home: The Life and Music of Bob Dylan* (1986), to "straighten out in your book that I did not take my name from Dylan Thomas" [Dolgins, p. 74].

Osip **Dymov:** Osip Isidorovich Perelmann (1878–1959), Russ. Jewish writer, working in U.S.

Adolf **Dymsza:** Adolf Baginński (1900–1975), Pol. movie actor.

Dzerents: Ovsep Shishmanyan (1822–1888), Armenian historical novelist. The writer's name is the Armenian equivalent of Terence (as for the Roman poet).

Dzhivani: Serob Levonyan (1846–1909), Armenian poet. The poet's assumed name, meaning "handsome," was originally his father's nickname for him as a child.

Sheila **E.:** Sheila Escovedo (1959–), U.S. rock singer, percussionist, songwriter.

Vince **Eager:** Roy Taylor (c.1940–), Eng. pop singer. The singer was renamed in 1958 by manager and impresario Larry Parnes, who was impressed by Taylor's enthusiasm and energy.

Solomon **Eagle:** [Sir] John Collings Squire (1884–1958), Br. poet, essayist, short story writer.

Jean **Earle:** Doris Burge, née Stanley (1909–), Eng. poet, writer.

Sheena **Easton:** Sheena Shirley Orr (1959–), Sc. rock singer.

Eazy-E: Eric Wright (1963–1995), U.S. black "gangsta" rapper. "E" stood for "Eric," though Wright, who set up his record company with money made from drug dealing, liked to claim it stood for "entrepreneur."

Abba **Eban:** Aubrey Solomon (1915–), S.A.-born Israeli politician.

Eccles: Frank Hilton Brown (1926–1986), Eng. cartoonist. The artist used this name for his contributions to the *Daily Worker* (later renamed *Morning Star*) from 1952.

Johann **Eck:** Johann Maier (1486–1543), Ger. theologian. Martin Luther's leading Roman Catholic opponent adopted his name early in his theological career from his native village of Eck (or Egg).

Billy **Eckstine:** William Clarence Eckstein (1914–), U.S. popular singer, jazz musician.

Barbara **Eden:** Barbara Jean Huffman (1934–), U.S. movie actress.

Sir John **Edgar:** [Sir] Richard Steele (1672–1729), Eng. essayist, dramatist.

The **Edge:** David Evans (1961–), Welsh rock guitarist. The U2 musician is said to have been named by the group's lead singer, Bono (*q.v.*), after a hardware store that the latter passed on his way into Dublin city center. "The name was apparently chosen because it matched the shape of his head, although it was a very appropriate description of the original, angular way in which he approached the guitar" [Dave Bowler and Bryan Dray, *U2: A Conspiracy of Hope*, 1993]. "Evans the Edge" also sounds like a typical Welsh nickname, with "Edge" even suggesting "Evans" itself.

Paul **Edmonds:** Henry Kittner (1915–1958), U.S. fantasy fiction writer.

G.C. **Edmondson:** José Mario Garry Ordonez Edmondson y Cotton (1922–), Guatemalan-born U.S. SF writer.

Willie **Edouin:** William Frederick Bryer (1846–1908), Eng. comic actor. "Willie" from his own first name, and "Edouin" from the middle name of his father, John Edwin Bryer.

Kasimir **Edschmid:** Eduard Schmid (1890–1966), Ger. writer.

George Alden **Edson:** Paul Frederick Ernst (1902–), U.S. writer of horror stories.

Albert **Edwards:** Arthur Bullard (1879–1929), U.S. journalist, writer.

Blake **Edwards:** William Blake McEdwards (1922–), U.S. movie producer, director.

Gus **Edwards:** Gustave Edward Simon (1881–1945), U.S. songwriter, entertainer.

Vince **Edwards:** Vincenzo Edoardo Zoino (1928–1996), U.S. movie actor, of It. parentage.

Jean **Effel:** François Lejeune (1918–1982), Fr. cartoonist. The artist's new surname represented his initials, "F.L.," pronounced in French as in English. He preceded this with the most common French forename, Jean. The name as a whole was shorter than the original, too, and so more suitable for signatures on his cartoons.

Aunt **Effie:** Jane Euphemia Browne (1811–1898), Br. children's writer.

Philippe **Egalité:** Louis Philippe Joseph, duc d'Orléans (1747–1793), Fr. statesman. The duke assumed his (literally) egalitarian name in order to court the favor of the people when he became Deputy for Paris (1792) in the *Convention Nationale*. In the *Convention* he voted for the death of Louis XVI, his cousin, but was himself executed the following year. So much for egalitarianism.

Lesley **Egan:** Elizabeth Linington (1921–1988), U.S. mystery writer. The writer's pen name is a sort of part-anagram of her real name. Maybe this was intentional, for a mystery writer?

H.M. **Egbert:** Victor Rousseau Emanuel (1879–1960), Eng.-born U.S. pulp magazine writer.

George **Egerton:** Mary Chavelita Dunne (1859–1945), Austral.-born Ir. novelist, of Ir.-Welsh parentage. Dunne was married twice, and her pen name derives from that of her first husband, George Egerton Clairmonte.

Werner **Egk:** Werner Mayer (1901–1983), Ger. opera, ballet music composer. The musician apparently adopted his name as a tribute to Johann Eck (*q.v.*), who originally had the same surname.

John **Eglinton:** William Kirkpatrick Magee (1868–1961), Ir. essayist, poet, biographer.

Eglwysbach: John Evans (1840–1897), Welsh preacher, writer. The name is that of the village in Denbighshire (now Powys) where the Wesleyan minister was born. Appropriately, it means "little church."

Eifion Wyn: Eliseus Williams (1867–1926), Welsh poet. The poet took his bardic name from the historic region of Eifionydd where he was born, as were many other poets. "Wyn" means "white," "fair," "pure." Compare the next entry below.

Eifionydd: John Thomas (1848–1922), Welsh journalist, editor. The writer took his name from the historic region of Eifionydd, northwestern Wales, famous for its literary and cultural associations. It was itself named for the 5th-century ruler Eifion, son of Cunedda.

Eilir: William Eilir Owen (1852–1910), Welsh poet. The poet's bardic name means "butterfly."

Nikolay Ekk: Nikolay Vladimirovich Ivakin (1902–1976), Russ. movie director.

Britt Ekland: Britt-Marie Eklund (1942–), Swe. movie actress.

Florence Eldridge: Florence McKechnie (1901–1988), U.S. stage actress.

Gus Elen: Ernest Augustus Elen (1862–1940), Eng. music hall artist, singer of Cockney songs.

Elerydd: William John Gruffydd (1916–), Welsh poet, novelist, short story writer. The writer's name is presumably a local placename.

Elfed: Howell Elvet Lewis (1860–1953), Welsh poet, hymnwriter. The poet and arch-druid took his bardic name from his native village of Cynwyl Elfet, Carmarthenshire (now Dyfed).

Avril Elgar: Avril Williams (1932–), Eng. stage actress. The actress assumed her father's third name as her stage name.

El Hakim: Barry Walls (1937–), Eng. circus fakir. The name is a stock one for fake fakirs, and is Arabic for "the wise one."

Elia: Charles Lamb (1775–1834), Eng. writer, poet. The writer first used his pen name in his *Essays of Elia*, which appeared in *The London Magazine* in 1820–23. The subject of the first essay was an Italian clerk named Elia at South Sea House, headquarters of the East India Company, where Lamb had worked and where his brother was still employed at the time of the appearance of the *Essays*. The name is said to have been originally pronounced "Ellia."

Elidir Sais: William Hughes Jones (1885–1951), Welsh literary critic. The writer adopted the name of a 13th-century Welsh court poet. His own name meant "Elidir the Englishman," from his exile in that country. Jones was originally so called by way of a nickname, since he habitually spoke English to his Welsh-speaking friends.

Elin-Pelin: Dimitar Ivanov Stojanov (1877–1949), Bulg. short story writer. The writer's stories express the bitterness of his time. (He has been called a "singer of rural misery.") Hence his pen name, meaning "wormwood" (Bulgarian *pelin*), with Elin an alliterative prefix. (An English equivalent might be "William Wormwood" or "George Gall.") Compare the name of Maxim Gorky.

George Eliot: Mary Ann (later Marian) Evans (1819–1880), Eng. novelist. The author took her male name from that of her lover, the philosopher and writer George Henry Lewes, who himself wrote as Slingsby Lawrence (*q.v.*). Her surname she chose because it was a "full-mouthed, easily-pronounceable name." She first used the pen name for her novel *Scenes of Clerical Life* (1858). Two years after the death of Lewes in 1878 Marian Evans married John Walter Cross, an American banker. She died that same year, but Cross lived on until 1924. Such is the generally accepted story behind her name.

In his *Pribbles and Prabbles* (1906), Major-General Patrick Maxwell points out an unusual coincidence: that some time in the 1840s a young officer of the Bengal cavalry called George Donnithorne Eliot was accidentally drowned in a lake in the Himalayas. Not only does this officer's name contain the pen name assumed by Marian Evans, but in her *Adam Bede* (1859) there is a character named Arthur Donnithorne. That the Bengal officer was, however, an early flame of Marian Evans seems highly unlikely, although the novelist could have read about him.

Elisa: Lisa Barbuscia (1970–), U.S. pop singer, of Puerto Rican/It.-Ir. parentage. The singer began her career as a model, using the name Lisa B. Her comment on her singing name: "It's like a plague of Lisas out there. ... Lisa Stansfield, Lisa M, Lisa Lisa, Wendy and Lisa, Lisa Marie...." Hence the choice of something slightly different [*Sunday Times Magazine*, October 4, 1992].

Elisheva: Yelizaveta Ivanovna Zirkova (1888–1949), Russ. Jewish poet, working in Palestine. The writer's pen name is the Hebrew form of her first name (English Elizabeth).

Filinto Elísio: Francisco Manuel do Nascimento (1734–1819), Port. poet.

Elis o'r Nant: Ellis Pierce (1841–1912), Welsh novelist. The writer's pen name means "Ellis of the brook."

Elitis: Odisseas Alepudelis (1911–), Gk. poet.

Elizabeth: (1) Mary Annette, Countess von Arnim (later Russell), née Beauchamp (1866–1941), Austral. author; (2) Mary Elizabeth Jenkin (1892–1979), Eng. children's radio producer. The countess assumed her mother's first name for her novels, and it occurs in the title of her best known work, *Elizabeth and Her German Garden*, published anonymously in 1898.

Duke Ellington: Edward Kennedy Ellington (1899–1974), U.S. black jazz musician. "Duke" has long been used in the U.S. as a nickname for a smart or accomplished person, especially one who dresses and behaves stylishly. This certainly suited the greatest and most prolific jazz musician of the 20th century.

[Sir] John **Elliot:** John Elliot Blumenfeld (1898–1988), Br. railroad manager. The future head of British Railways assumed his middle name as his surname by deed poll in 1922.

Cass **Elliott:** Ellen Naomi Cohen (1942–1974), U.S. pop singer.

Gertrude **Elliott:** May Gertrude Dermot (1874–1950), U.S. stage actress, sister of Maxine Elliott (see below).

Maxine **Elliott:** Jessie Dermot (1868–1940), U.S. stage actress. Jessie Dermot adopted her stage name at the suggestion of Dion Boucicault (*q.v.*). Her sister was the actress Gertrude Elliott (see above) who married the English actor Johnston Forbes-Robertson (see under Bryan **Forbes**).

Ramblin' Jack **Elliott:** Elliott Charles Adnopoz (1931–), U.S. folksinger. The singer was embarrassed by his family name and at first called himself Buck Elliott before adopting the more homely "Jack."

William "Wild Bill" **Elliott:** Gordon Nance (1903–1965), U.S. movie actor.

Alice Thomas **Ellis:** Anna Margaret Haycraft, née Lindholm (1932), Br. writer. The writer appears to have based her pseudonymous surname on her mother's middle name, Alexandra. Thomas is the name of one of her five sons.

E. **Ellis:** Elizabeth Wolstenholme-Elmy (1834–1913), Eng. essayist, poet. A name concocted from the first half of the writer's original first name and second part of her surname. She also wrote as Ellis Ethelmer.

Mary **Ellis:** Mary Elsas (1900–), U.S. movie actress, singer.

Patricia **Ellis:** Patricia Gene O'Brien (1916–1970), U.S. movie actress.

James **Ellison:** James Ellison Smith (1910–1994), U.S. movie actor.

Ellyay: Serafim Romanovich Kulachikov (1904–1976), Russ. (Yakut) poet.

Ziggy **Elman:** Harry Finkelman (1914–1968), U.S. jazz trumpeter, bandleader.

Elphin: Robert Arthur Griffith (1860–1936), Welsh poet.

Lily **Elsie:** Lily Elsie Cotton (1886–1962), Br. musical comedy actress, singer.

Isobel **Elsom:** Isobel Reed (1893–1981), Br. stage, movie actress, working in U.S.

Willem **Elsschot:** Alfons de Ridder (1882–1960), Belg. (Flemish) writer.

Julian **Eltinge:** William Julian Dalton (1882–1941), U.S. vaudeville artist, female impersonator. The performer's stage name happens to be an anagram of "gentile." (If it did originate thus, was Julian intended to suggest "Jew," so that the name as a whole was "Jew and Gentile"?)

Geoffrey Rudolph **Elton:** Gottfried Rudolph Ehrenberg (1921–1994), Ger.-born Eng. historian. The historian changed his name to Elton in 1944 under an Army Council Instruction. This was of course in World War II. Comedian and writer Ben Elton (1959–) is his nephew.

Paul **Eluard:** Eugène Grindel (1895–1952), Fr. poet. The poet adopted his maternal grandmother's name as his pen name. In one of his tales there is a young girl called Grain d'aile, "wing seed," from his original name.

Maurice **Elvey:** William Seward Folkard (1887–1967), Br. movie director.

Violetta **Elvin:** Violetta Prokhorova (1925–), Russ. ballet dancer.

Ron **Ely:** Ronald Pierce (1938–), U.S. athlete, TV actor.

Odysseus **Elytis:** Odysseus Alepoudelis (1911–1996), Gk. poet. The poet changed his name as a young man to dissociate himself from the family soap business. The surname is said to have a range of modern Greek allusions: *Hellas*, "Greece," *elpida*, "hope," *eleftheria*, "freedom," *Heleni*, "Helen," and *alytis*, "wanderer." This last, in its classical Greek form *aletes*, is the word used by Homer to describe Odysseus (for whom the poet was already named). The sea is a common motif in the works of Elytis.

Jacob Israel **Emden:** Jacob ben Zebi (1697–1776), Ger. rabbi, Talmudic scholar. The rabbi took his name from the city in which he served four years.

Louis **Emerick:** Louis Emerick Grant (1953–), Eng. movie, TV actor.

Gilbert **Emery:** Gilbert Emery Bensley Pottle (1875–1945), U.S. stage, movie actor, playwright, of Br. parentage.

Gevork **Emin:** Karlen Grigoryevich Muradyan (1919–), Armenian poet.

Emin Pascha: Eduard Schnitzer (1840–1892), Ger. explorer, colonial official. While serving the Ottoman governor of Albania in 1870-74, Schnitzer adopted a Turkish mode of living and took the Islamic name Mehmed. He later served General Charles Gordon in Khartoum as medical officer, and became known as Emin Effendi, the latter word being a title of respect (literally "master") for an educated person. In 1878 Gordon appointed him governor of Equatoria with the title of bey, and he was subsequently promoted to the rank of pasha. Hence his final name and title, in full Mehmed Emin Pascha. Emin itself means "honorable," "trustworthy."

Emma: Emilia Ferretti Viola (1844–1929), It. novelist, essayist.

Pierre **Emmanuel:** Noël Jean Mathieu (1916–1984), Fr. religious poet. The writer's pen name epitomized the role he envisaged for the poet, as priest (St. Peter, founder of the Christian church) and prophet (Emmanuel, Christ as the coming Messiah).

Emmwood: John Musgrave-Wood (1915–), Eng. political cartoonist, painter.

El **Empecinado:** Juan Martin Diaz (1775–1825), Sp. revolutionary. The activist adopted his nickname, meaning "the stubborn one."

Caveat **Emptor:** [Sir] George Stephen (1794–1879), Eng. writer, lawyer. The writer used this name for *The Adventures of a Gentleman in Search of a Horse* (1835). The pen name is a whimsical adoption of the Latin tag, *Caveat emptor*, "Let the buyer beware."

Emrys: William Ambrose (1813–1873), Welsh poet. The poet adopted the Welsh equivalent of his surname as his bardic name. Compare the next entry below.

Emrys ap Iwan: Ambrose Jones (1851–1906), Welsh poet, writer, nationalist. The poet's bardic name is the Welsh equivalent of his English name (literally "Ambrose son of John").

Emu: William Henry Dyson (1880–1938), Austral. cartoonist, working in U.K.

Frederick **Engelheart:** Lafayette Ronald Hubbard (1911–1986), U.S. SF writer. As founder of the Church of Scientology (1954), the writer's real name is more familar in the form L. Ron Hubbard.

Isobel **English:** June Guesdon Braybrooke, earlier Orr-Ewing, née Joliffe (1920–1994), Br. novelist, short story writer.

Enya: Eithne Ni Bhraonain (1961–), Ir. popular singer. The singer's name represents a phonetic spelling of her Irish first name.

Eos Ceiriog: Huw Morys (1622–1709), Welsh poet. The poet's name means "nightingale of Ceiriog," the latter being the name of the district where he lived. Compare the next two entries below.

Eos Eyas: James Rhys Parry (*c*.1570–*c*.1625), Welsh poet. The poet's name means "nightingale of Eyas," from the parish where he lived.

Eos Gwynfa: Thomas Williams (*c*.1769–1848), Welsh poet, songwriter. The writer's name means "nightingale of Gwynfa," the latter from the name of the village, Llanfihangel-yng-Ngwynfa ("St. Michael's church in paradise") where he lived. He was also known as Eos y Mynydd, "nightingale of the mountain."

Ephemera: Edward Fitzgibbon (1803–1857), Eng. journalist, writer of books on angling. There is a pleasant pun here: "ephemera" on the one hand denotes something short-lived, such as a journalist writes about; on the other hand it is a term for the mayfly, an artificial form of which is used as bait by anglers.

Desiderius **Erasmus:** Gerhard Gerhards (or Geert Geerts) (? 1466–1536), Du. humanist, theologian. The general explanation of the scholar's name is as follows. He was born as the second child of Margaret, a physician's daughter, and Roger Gerhard (or Geert), a priest. He was thus illegitimate, or a "love child," and the name that he adopted reflects this, as both Desiderius and Erasmus means "desired one," that is, "loved one," from Latin *desiderare*, "to want," "to desire" and Greek *erasmios*, "beloved." (Compare the next name below.)

However, an interpretation of the original name may have played its part, as recounted by Isaac D'Israeli (see Bibliography, p. 400): "*Desiderius Erasmus* was a name formed out of his family name *Gerard*, which in Dutch signifies amiable; or GAR all, AERD nature. He first changed it to a Latin word of much the same signification, *desiderius*, which afterwards he refined into the Greek *Erasmus*, by which names he is now known." (But Gerard actually means "brave spear.")

Thomas **Erastus:** Thomas Lieber (or Liebler) (1524–1583), Ger.-Swiss theologian, physician. "Erastus" translates the theologian's real name, which itself means "lover." Compare the name of Desiderius Erasmus (above).

Erckmann-Chatrian: Emile Erckmann (1822–1899), Fr. writer + Charles-Louis-Alexandre Chatrian (1826–1890), Fr. writer. The two men used this joint pen name for popular historical novels set in Alsace.

Werner **Erhard:** John Paul Rosenberg (1935–), U.S. "New Age" cultist.

Leif **Erickson:** William Wycliff Anderson (1911–1986), U.S. movie actor.

John **Ericson:** Joseph Meibes (1926–), Ger.-born U.S. movie actor.

Erinni: Maria Borgese Freschi (1881–1947), It. poet, novelist. The writer's occasional pen name is the Italian for "Erinyes," the Furies of Greek mythology.

George **Ernest:** George Hjorth (1921–), U.S. juvenile movie actor, of Dan. parentage.

Erratic Enrique: Henry Clay Lukens (1838–1900), U.S. humorous writer, poet, journalist. The humorist also wrote as Heinrich Yale Snekul, each of these names being a variant of some kind on his real full name.

Erté: Romain de Tirtoff (1892–1990), Russ.-born Fr. costume designer. The designer's brief pseudonym, suitable for signing, derives from his initials "R.T." pronounced (approximately) in Russian and French as "air-tay". He first used it in contributions to the Russian magazine *Damsky Mir* ("Ladies' World"), and in France first in 1913 in the magazine *La Gazette du Bon Ton.*

Patrick **Ervin:** Robert E. Howard (1906–1936), U.S. SF writer.

Christoph **Eschenbach:** Christoph Ringmann (1940–), Ger. pianist, orchestral conductor.

Uncle **Esek:** Henry Wheeler Shaw (1818–1885), U.S. humorist. The humorist's best known pen name was Josh Billings (*q.v.*).

Carl **Esmond:** Wilhelm Eichberger (1905–), Austr. movie actor, working in U.K., U.S.

Henry Vernon **Esmond:** Henry Vernon Jack (1869–1922), Eng. stage actor, manager, dramatist. The actor appears to have been influenced in his choice of professional name by that of the central character in Thackeray's *Henry Esmond.*

Dr. **Esperanto:** [Dr.] Lazar Ludwik Zamenhof (1859–1917), Pol. doctor, inventor of Esperanto. The linguist's name translates (in Esperanto) as "Dr. Hoping One." He used it for his book introducing the language, *Langue Internationale: Préface et Manuel Complet* (1887). He also sometimes used the anagrammatic pseudonyms Gamzefon and Gofzamen. (Was he aware that *Esperanto* anagrammatizes as *personate*, as he himself did?)

David **Essex:** David Albert Cook (1947–), Eng. pop singer. The singer was born in Plaistow, now in Greater London, but at the time of his birth in Essex.

Martin **Esslin:** Martin Julius Pereszlenyi (1918–), Eng. radio producer, drama critic, of Austr.-Hung. parentage.

Luc **Estang:** Lucien Bastard (1911–1992), Fr. Catholic novelist, poet, critic. One can appreciate the need for a new name here.

Jean **Estoril:** Mabel Esther Allan (1915–), Eng. children's writer. Other names used by the writer are Priscilla Hagon and Anne Pilgrim. All three names have a slight flavor of the original, with Jean Estoril reserved for the author's series of stories about Drina, a teenage ballerina who dances her way round the world. (Perhaps significantly, Estoril is a town in Portugal.)

Partenio **Etiro:** Pietro Aretino (*q.v.*). An obvious anagram of the Italian satirist's pseudonym.

Robert **Eton:** Lawrence Walter Meynell (1899–1989), Eng. author.

Etteila: Jean-François Aliette (1738–1791), Fr. fortuneteller. The tarot practitioner's name is an obvious anagram of his original name.

Eugen: Eugen Pillatt (1879–1943), Ger. circus artist, clown, working in Russia.

Eugenius III: Bernardo Paganelli (or Pignatelli) (? –1153), It. pope.

Eugenius IV: Gabriele Condulmaro (*c.*1383–1447), It. pope.

Arthur Fritz **Eugens:** Arthur Fritz Schumacher (1930–), Ger. juvenile movie actor.

Sandro **Euli:** Aleksandr Kishvardovich Kuridze (1890–1965), Georgian poet. The poet took a name meaning "Sandro the lonely," alluding to his sense of isolation.

Eusébio: Eusébio Ferreira da Silva (1942–), Mozambiquan-born Port. footballer (the "Black Panther").

Eva: Mary Anne O'Doherty, née Kelly (1826–1910), Ir. poet.

Dale **Evans:** Frances Octavia Smith (1912–), U.S. movie actress. The actress changed her name in 1933.

Gil **Evans:** Ian Ernest Gilmore Green (1912–1988), Can.-born U.S. jazz pianist, composer, of Austral. parentage.

Joan **Evans:** Joan Eunson (1934–), U.S. movie actress.

Linda **Evans:** Linda Evenstad (1943–), U.S. TV actress, of Norw. descent.

Margiad **Evans:** Peggy Eileen Arabella Williams, née Whistler (1909–1958), Eng. novelist, poet. The writer was raised and educated near the Welsh border, and took a name to reflect her links with Wales. Her new first name is a Welsh diminutive of "Margaret," and so the equivalent of Peggy. Her surname she adopted from her paternal grandmother.

Judith **Evelyn:** Judith Evelyn Allen (1913–1967), U.S. stage, movie actress.

Chad **Everett:** Raymond Lee Cramton (1937–), U.S. TV, movie actor.

Kenny **Everett:** Maurice James Christopher Cole (1944–1995), Eng. radio, TV DJ, entertainer, presenter. Maurice Cole was working for a pirate radio station when the program controller, Ben Tony, told all on board the ship that they must change their names for legal purposes. The DJ explains how he made his own choice: "I think I'd just seen a movie with an actor called Edward Everett Horton. ... I quite liked the name Everett so that came first, followed straightaway by Kenny" [Kenny Everett, *The Custard Stops at Hatfield*, 1982]. Edward Everett Horton (1887–1970) was a U.S. comic movie actor, constantly popular from the 1920s through 1940s.

Leon **Everette:** Leon Everette Baughman (1948–), U.S. country musician.

Evoe: Edmund George Valpy Knox (1881–1971), Eng. essayist, humorist. The writer's pseudonym is a blend of the initials of two of his names and the Latin cry *evoe* (from Greek *euoi*), used as an exclamation of joy in Bacchic rites. The name had the practical purpose of distinguishing Knox from the writer E.V. Lucas, a fellow contributor to the humorous magazine *Punch*, of which Knox subsequently became editor (from 1932 through 1949).

Tom **Ewell:** Samuel Yewell Tompkins (1909–1994), U.S. movie comedian, stage actor. The actor adopted a form of his mother's maiden name, which he already had as his middle name.

Ex-Private X: Alfred McLelland Burrage (1889–1956), Eng. novelist, fantasy story writer.

Clive **Exton:** Clive Jack Montague Brooks (1930–), Eng. actor, playwright. The dramatist changed his name by deed poll in the 1950s to avoid confusion with the actor Clive Brook (1887–1974). "I chose Exton by the dodgy expedient of sticking a pin in a Shakespeare concordance and happening on Sir Piers of Exton in *Richard II*" [personal fax from Clive Exton, March 23, 1996].

An **Eye-Witness:** Charles Lamb (1775–1834), Eng. essayist, critic, poet. The writer, whose best-known pseudonym was Elia (*q.v.*), used this particular pen name for his verses entitled *Satan in Search of a Wife* (1831).

Fabian: Fabiano Forte Bonaparte (1940–), U.S. pop singer, movie actor. The actor has been billed as Fabian Forte since 1970.

Françoise **Fabian:** Michèle Cortès de Leone y Fabianera (1932–), Sp. movie actress. A French name that is more of an international draw than the Spanish original.

Colonel **Fabien:** Pierre Georges (1919–1944), Fr. Resistance agent. The name may have intentionally alluded to the 3d-century BC Roman general Fabius ("Cunctator"), who advocated delaying tactics in battle.

Nanette **Fabray:** Ruby Bernadette Nanette Fabares (1920–), U.S. movie comedienne, singer.

Philippe **Fabre d'Eglantine:** Philippe-François-Nazaire Fabre (1750–1794), Fr. playwright, revolutionary politician. The French writer assumed this name after winning the *Prix de l'églantine* ("Wild Rose Prize") at the *Jeux Floraux* of Toulouse in his youth, although some say he won by a false claim.

Napoleon **Fabri:** Avgust Fransuazovich Pyubaset (Puybasset)(1869–1932), Fr.-born Russ. circus artist, horseman, clown. The performer took his name from the Italian Fabri troupe with whom he trained as an acrobat.

Georg **Fabricius:** Georg Goldschmied (1516–1571), Ger. scholar. The scholar's assumed name is a latinization of his real name, which means "goldsmith." Compare the next two names below.

Barent **Fabritius:** Barent Pieterz (1624–1673), Du. painter, brother of Carel Fabritius (below).

Carel **Fabritius:** Carel Pieterz (1622–1654), Du. painter, brother of Barent Fabritius (above). Both brothers adopted the name Fabritius as a reference to their previous trade as carpenters (Latin *faber*, "carpenter"). Compare the name of Georg Fabricius (above).

Fabulous Moolah: Lillian Ellison (*c.*1930–), U.S. wrestler. The champion woman wrestler began her career in the ring at a tender age as "Slave Girl Moolah," the "prop" of a wrestler named Elephant Boy. Her ring name was effectively a nickname, from her announcement that she intended to wrestle for "all the moolah [money] I can get my hands on." She seems to have succeeded, and in the 1970s she claimed to be earning more than $100,000 a year.

Aleksandr **Fadeyev:** Aleksandr Aleksandrovich Bulyga (1901–1956), Russ. novelist. The writer would have readily shed a surname that is a Russian dialect word for a lout or boor.

Sammy **Fain:** Samuel Feinberg (1902–1989), U.S. composer of musicals, movie music.

A.A. **Fair:** Erle Stanley Gardner (1889–1970), U.S. crime novelist. This is the writer's best known pseudonym. Others are Charles M. Green, Carleton Kendrake, and Charles J. Kenny.

Douglas **Fairbanks, Sr.:** Douglas Elton Thomson Ulman (1883–1939), U.S. movie actor. The actor was the son of Hezekiah Charles Ulman and Ella Adelaide Marsh. When his parents divorced soon after he was born, his mother took the surname of her first husband, John Fairbanks. Ulman adopted this name himself in 1900 and in due course passed it on to his actor son, Douglas Fairbanks, Jr. (1909–).

Sydney **Fairbrother:** Sydney Tapping, later Parselle, (1873–1941), Eng. movie actress. The actress adopted her great-grandmother's name as her screen name.

Mindy **Fairchild:** Mahinder Singh Rupal (1964–), Ind.-born Br. fraudster. The bank robber and credit card heister changed his name, not necessarily with criminal intent, in order to "sound more English."

Morgan **Fairchild:** Patsy Ann McClenny (1950–), U.S. TV actress. The actress's name, perhaps intentionally, evokes that of Morgan le Fay, the beautiful young woman ("fair child") who is King Arthur's sister in the Arthurian romances.

Frank **Fairleigh:** Francis Edward Smedley (1818–1864), Eng. novelist. The writer adopted the name of the fictional hero of his own novel, *Frank Fairleigh* (1850).

Benjamin F. **Fairless:** Benjamin Franklin Williams (1890–1962), U.S. industrialist. The future president of U.S. Steel changed his name as a young boy to that of his adopted parents.

Michael **Fairless:** Margaret Fairless Barber (1869–1901), Eng. "inspirational" writer. The writer partly preserved her own name in her pseudonym, with the initial "M" of "Michael" representing that of "Margaret," and "Fairless" being her middle name, which was the first name of her father, Fairless Barber. But "Michael" was specific, in that it was the name of a young boy friend who often spent his summer holidays with her family. He was Michael McDonnell (1882–1956), who would become Sir Michael and Chief Justice of Palestine in the 1930s.

Adam **Faith:** Terence Nelhams (1940–), Eng. pop singer, actor. The singer chose the name for the radio series *Six Five Special*, taking "Adam" from the boys' section of a book of names for children, and "Faith" from the girls' section. He commented: "I liked the sound of Adam. Adam, the first man. Short. Sweet. Easily memorized." On the name as a whole: "I liked the note of courage in it. Adam Faith. Yes, they seemed to match up" [Adam Faith, *Poor Me*, 1961].

Falco: Johann Hoelzl (1957–), Austr. rock singer.

Lanoe **Falconer:** Mary Elizabeth Hawker (1848–1908), Sc.-born Eng. novelist. The writer took her new first name from the third name of her father, Peter William Lanoe Hawker, with her surname a punning allusion to her original family name. After many rejections from publishers, she finally broke into print with the appropriately titled *Mademoiselle Ixe* (1890), the first novel in Fisher Unwin's "Pseudonym Library" series.

Johan **Falkberget:** Johan Petter Lillebakken (1879–1967), Norw. writer. The writer took his name from the farm where he was born in the central eastern mountains of Norway.

Hans **Fallada:** Wilhelm Friedrich Rudolf Ditzen (1893–1947), Ger. novelist. The novelist adopted his new surname from the talking horse in the fairy tale "The Ugly Duckling," as recounted in *Grimms' Fairy Tales* (1812–22).

Mary **Fallon:** Kathleen Mary Berriman, née Denman (1951–), Austral. writer. The writer adopted her grandmother's name as her pen name.

Georgie **Fame:** Clive Powell (1943–), Eng. pop musician. The name was given to the singer by the impresario Larry Parnes, who allegedly said, "The next kid to walk through my door, I'm gonna call Georgie Fame." The next kid to do so was Clive Powell, and Parnes hired him as a member of the Blue Flames, the backing group assigned to Billy Fury (*q.v.*) on a 1960 tour. There is evidence that the name first proposed by Parnes for Powell was actually Lance Fortune (*q.v.*).

Violet **Fane:** [Baroness] Mary Montgomerie Currie, previously Singleton, née Lamb (1843–1905), Eng. novel, verse writer. The author selected the name, that of a character in Disraeli's novel *Vivian Grey* (1827), for her first publication, a volume of verse entitled *From Dawn to Noon* (1872). She first used the pseudonym to conceal her writing from her parents.

Eben **Fardd:** Ebenezer Thomas (1802–1863), Welsh poet. "Eben" represents "Ebenezer," and "Fardd" simply means "poet" (Welsh *bardd*, "poet," "bard," here in its mutated form).

Don **Fardon**: Don Maughn (*c*.1943–), Eng. pop singer.

Donna **Fargo**: Yvonne Vaughn (1949–), U.S. country singer. Presumably "Fargo" for the famous pioneer expressman, Wells Fargo, with "Donna" meaning "lady." However, it may be no coincidence that Doone Fargo was one of the many names used by the English western writer, Victor Norwood. (See Appendix 3, p. 388.) Whatever the case, the new name is somewhat similar to the original name.

Princess **Farida**: Safina Zulfikar (1920–1988), Egyptian queen. Safina Zulfikar changed her first name (Iranian for "pure rose") to Farida ("precious") in 1938, when she married King Farouk. The change complied with a tradition that all members of the Egyptian royal family must have names beginning with the same initial. King Farouk divorced his wife in 1948, however, when she failed to produce an heir to the throne, and Farida went to live in France with her three daughters.

Farinelli: Carlo Broschi (1705–1782), It. castrato singer. The singer adopted the surname of his benefactors, the brothers Farina. According to some accounts, he may have been their nephew. The brothers were of French origin, and appear to have been originally named Farinel.

Giuseppe **Farinelli**: Giuseppe Francesco Finco (1769–1836), It. opera composer.

Mukhiddin **Farkhat**: Mukhiddin Khasanov (1924–) Tajik poet. The poet's adopted name means "joy."

Ralph Milne **Farley**: Robert Sherman Hoar (1887–1963), U.S. SF writer.

Chris **Farlowe**: John Henry Deighton (1940–), Eng. pop singer. The singer took his name from the U.S. jazz guitarist Tal Farlowe.

Marianne **Farningham**: Mary Anne Hearn (1834–1909), Eng. religious writer, hymnwriter. The writer blended her first two names to form a single Christian name, then changed her surname to that of the Kent village where she was born.

Martha **Farquharson**: Martha Farquharson Finley (1828–1909), U.S children's writer.

Jamie **Farr**: Jameel Joseph Farah (1934–), U.S. TV actor.

Walli **Farrad**: Wallace D. Fard (*c*.1877– ? 1934), U.S. Black Muslim leader. This is one of the many names assumed by the founder of the Nation of Islam in the U.S. He is now revered by Black Muslims as Master Wallace Fard Muhammad, and all the attributes of God (Allah) are assigned to him, so that he is referred to as "Creator of Heaven and Earth, Most Wise, All Knowing, Most Merciful, All Powerful, Finder and Life-Giver, Master of the Day of Judgment." Understandably one of the criticisms leveled at the Black Muslims by orthodox Muslims is that they worship Wallace Fard rather than Allah of the "true" Islam. Among other names used by Fard were Professor Ford, Farrad Mohammed, F. Mohammed Ali, Wallace Fard Muhammad, and God (Allah). More importantly for the purposes of the present book, he gave his followers Arabic names to replace those that had originated in slavery and that were of Christian origin. His divinity was reinforced by his mysterious disappearance in 1934.

Louis **Farrakhan**: Louis Eugene Walcott (1933–), U.S. Black Muslim leader. The advocate of black separatism was originally a calypso performer under the name of Prince Charmer before being converted to the Nation of Islam in the mid–1950s by Malcolm X (*q.v.*).

Joe **Farrell**: Joseph Carl Firrantello (1937–1986), U.S. jazz musician.

M.J. **Farrell**: Mary ("Molly") Nesta Keane, née Skrine (1904–1996), Ir. author. Mary Skrine began to write during a long spell in bed with suspected tuberculosis. The result was a romantic tale entitled *The Knight of Cheerful Countenance* which was accepted by Mills & Boon. For this she selected the pen name M.J. Farrell, taking it from a bar she passed one day, returning home from the hunting field. She said, "I had to keep it a secret as long as I possibly could. Young men in that circle would have been afraid of you if they thought you read, let alone wrote" [*Sunday Times Magazine*, August 24, 1986].

Perry **Farrell**: Perry Bernstein (1960–), U.S. rock musician. The controversial singer took his brother's first name as his new surname.

Suzanne **Farrell**: Roberta Sue Fricker (1945–), U.S. ballet dancer.

Claude **Farrère**: Frédéric Bargone (1876–1957), Fr. novelist.

Minnesota **Fats**: Rudolf Walter Wanderone, Jr. (1913–1996), U.S. American pool player. The player's name alludes directly to his impressive dimensions: at only 5 feet 10 inches tall, he weighed 300 lb. He originally called himself New York Fats, but altered the first word following his depiction in the 1961 movie *The Hustler*, in which he is played by Jackie Gleason.

William **Faulkner:** William Cuthbert Falkner (1897–1962), U.S. writer. The writer added the "u" to his name when *The Marble Faun*, his first book of poems, was published in 1924.

Catherine **Fawcett:** Catherine Ann Cookson, née McMullan (1906–), Eng. novelist.

Eric **Fawcett:** Eric Burbidge (1904–), Br. stage actor, singer.

Marion **Fawcett:** Katherine Roger Campbell (1886–1957), Sc. stage actress.

Alice **Faye:** Alice Jeanne Leppert (1912–), U.S. movie actress, singer.

Joey **Faye:** Joseph Anthony Palladino (1910–), U.S. stage comedian.

Frank **Faylen:** Frank Ruf (1905–1985), U.S. movie actor.

Eleanor **Fayre:** Eleanor Mary Tydfil Smith-Thomas (1910–), Welsh stage actress, singer.

Irving **Fazola:** Irving Henry Prestopnik (1910–1949), U.S. jazz clarinetist. The musician's new name was created from the three musical notes *fa* (F), *so* (G), and *la* (A). No doubt one motive for a name change was that his Slavic surname Prestopnik means "criminal."

Justinus **Febronius:** Johann Nikolaus von Hontheim (1701–1790), Ger. Roman Catholic bishop. The ecclesiastic used this name for his principal work, *De statu ecclesiae et legitima potestate Romani Pontificis* ("On the state of the church and the legitimate authority of the Roman pontiff") (1763), attacking the temporal power gained by medieval popes. The pseudonym gave the name of Febronianism, a movement against the claims of the papacy. The name seems to imply a "just cleansing," in allusion to Februus, the Roman god of purification.

Dr. **Feelgood:** William Lee Perryman (1911–1985), U.S. blues singer. As a player the singer used the name Piano Red (*q.v.*).

Hans **Fehér:** Johann Anton Weiss (1922–1958), Austr. juvenile movie actor, working in U.S. The actor's new surname is the Hungarian equivalent of his German original, meaning "white." He emigrated with his family to Britain in 1933 and to the United States three years later.

Charles K. **Feldman:** Charles Gould (1904–1968), U.S. movie producer.

Félix: Félix Fernandez García (*c.*1896–1941), Sp. ballet dancer.

María **Félix:** María de los Angeles Félix Güereña (1915–), Mexican movie actress.

N. **Felix:** Nicholas Wanostrocht (1807–1876), Eng. schoolmaster, writer on cricket. The teacher and cricketer used his pen name for his writings on the "great game," including the primer *Felix on the Bat* (1845), a book at one time sometimes found in the natural history section of public libraries. He was equally "N. Felix" when playing cricket, and is believed to have adopted this name "in deference … to the feelings of parents" (*Dictionary of National Biography*).

Elisaveta **Fen:** Lydia Jackson, née Jiburtovich (1900–1983), Russ.-born Eng. writer, translator.

Freddy **Fender:** Baldemar G. Huerta (1937–), U.S.-Mexican country musician. The player took his performing name from the Fender guitar and amplifier that he used. The guitar was itself named for its developer and manufacturer, Leo Fender (1909–1991).

Shane **Fenton:** Alvin Stardust (*q.v.*).

Ferdausi (or Firdausi): Abu ul-Qasem Mansur (*c.*935–*c.*1020), Persian poet. The poet took his name from the garden of Ferdaus, owned by the governor of Khorasan, the region (now in northeastern Iran) in which he lived. He was thus "of Ferdaus." The garden name itself means "paradise" (the English word is related), and in turn represents Middle Persian *pardez*, related to Avestan *pairidaeza*, "enclosure," "park," in other words "garden," a compound of *pairi-*, "around" (Greek *peri-*), and *daeza*, "wall." (English *garden* has the same basic sense of "enclosure," from a Germanic word that also gave "yard." A "paradise garden," however poetic-sounding, is thus really an etymological tautology.) Greek *paradeisos*, from the same source, is used in the Bible for the Garden of Eden.

Lawrence **Ferlinghetti:** Lawrence Ferling (1919–), U.S. poet, writer.

Fanny **Fern:** Sara Payson Parton, earlier Eldredge, then Farmington, née Willis (1811–1872), U.S. essayist, novelist, columnist. The writer made her name with the bestselling *Fern Leaves from Fanny's Portfolio* (1853), a collection of her pieces in various magazines.

Fernandel: Fernand-Joseph-Désiré Contandin (1903–1971), Fr. movie comedian. The mother-in-law of the future comedian used to refer to him as "Fernand d'elle," that is, *her* Fernand, meaning her daughter's son, not her own. This is said to be the origin of the name.

Wilhelmenia **Fernandez:** Wilhelmenia Wiggins (1949–), U.S. opera singer.

Elizabeth X. **Ferrars:** Morna Doris Brown, née MacTaggart (1907–1995), Br. novelist, mystery writer. The writer adopted her Anglo-German mother's maiden name. (Her father was Scottish.)

José **Ferrer:** José Vincente Ferrer de Otero y Cintrón (1912–1992), Puerto Rican–born U.S. stage, movie actor.

Anna Maria **Ferrero:** Anna Maria Guerra (1931–), It. movie actress.

Afanasy **Fet:** Afanasy Afanasyevich Shenshin (1820–1892), Russ. poet. The poet was the illegitimate son of a German mother, Charlotte Fet (or Foeth), and a Russian landowner named Shenshin. He adopted his mother's name for his writing and legally assumed it in 1876.

Stepin **Fetchit:** Lincoln Theodore Monroe Andrew Perry (1902–1985), U.S. black movie actor. The actor, who made his name as a slow-moving, slow-witted black servant, originally adopted the stage name of "Skeeter" (which he wasn't). This became "Stepin Fetchit," however, when he was near destitute on one occasion, and bet his clothes against $30 on a horse of this name at an Oklahoma race. He won, saved his clothes, and would soon write a comical song about his equine savior, whose own name obviously implies "Step and fetch it," or "Run fast and win the prize."

Edwige **Feuillère:** Caroline Vivette Edwige Cunati-Koenig (1907–), Fr. stage, movie actress. The actress's stage name is that of her former husband, Pierre Feuillère (married 1929, divorced 1933). She began her stage career as Cora Lynn (from her first name, Caroline).

Jacques **Feyder:** Jacques Frédérix (1885–1948), Belg.-born Fr. movie director. A simplification of the bearer's original rather awkward surname.

Michael **ffolkes:** Brian Davis (1925–1988), Eng. cartoonist. The artist explained how his name came about: "I've always had a kind of attraction for multiple identity. I got ffolkes from *Burke's Peerage*. As an unusual name it has been very valuable. It was about the time of Sprods and Trogs [*q.v.*] and Smilbys [*q.v.*]. I wanted a distinctive name. I don't think *Punch* knows, actually. ... Originally I wanted to write and called myself Brian Chorister, horrible name. Then I tried using the name Dedalus, based on the James Joyce character. ... I had just

read Joyce. It shows a tendency to want to get away from the ordinariness of being Davis. Davis, plain Davis, is one of the commonest names in the country" [Michael Bateman, *Funny Way to Earn a Living*, 1966].

I.D. **Ffraid:** John Evans (1814–1876), Welsh translator, lexicographer. The writer and scholar took his name from the village where he was born, Llansanffraid Glan Conwy. The significance of the initials is uncertain. He also published a number of letters as Adda Jones. The first name here is the Welsh equivalent of Adam.

John **Field:** John Greenfield (1921–1991), Eng. ballet dancer, director.

Martyn **Field:** Frederick William Horner (1854– ?), Eng. politician, administrator, author. The writer took his name from the London church of St. Martin-in-the-Fields, where he was Chairman of the Works Committee.

Michael **Field:** Katharine Harris Bradley (1846–1914), Eng. poet + Edith Emma Cooper (1862–1913), Eng. poet, her niece. The poets chose a male name for their joint writings because "we have many things to say that the world will not tolerate from a woman's lips." Once their identities were revealed, their output received little attention. When writing individually they used the respective pseudonyms Arran Leigh and Isla Leigh, both forenames being adopted from Scottish islands.

Sally **Field:** Sally Field Mahoney (1946–), U.S. movie actress.

Shirley Ann **Field:** Shirley Bloomfield (1938–), Br. movie actress.

Sylvia **Field:** Harriet Johnson (1902–), U.S. stage actress. The actress was given her stage name by her first manager, Winthrop Ames, for her maiden appearance at the age of 16 at the Shubert Theatre, New York.

Virginia **Field:** Margaret St. John Field (1917–1992), Eng. movie actress.

Ann Mary **Fielding:** Anita Mostyn, née Fielding (1907–1993), Eng. novelist. Although Fielding was the writer's genuine family name, she consciously adopted a pen name that honored her ancestor, the novelist Henry Fielding (1707–1754), especially as she was born in the bicentennial year of his birth. Compare the next entry below.

Gabriel **Fielding:** Alan Gabriel Barnsley (1916–1986), Br. novelist. The writer assumed his mother's maiden name, not as a compliment to her, since she dominated his childhood, but to honor the novelist Henry Fielding (1707–1754), of whom she was a descendant. Compare the entry above.

Benny Fields: Benjamin Geisenfeld (1894–1959), U.S. movie actor, singer.

Gracie Fields: Grace Stansfield (1898–1979), Eng. popular singer, comedienne. The singer began her career in her native Rochdale, Lancashire, when only 13. After a performance one day, she raised the matter of her name. "'Mumma,' said Grace, as they walked home together after the second house, 't' manager says Grace Stansfield's a bit long as names go.' Mumma who was glowing inside with secret pride, tried it out for sound. Yes, it might be a bit costly to put a name like that up in lights. She wondered whether they should cut the name in half. 'How about, Fields?' she suggested. 'But let's get sommat posh to put in front, like Stana, or Anna!' 'What's wrong with Grace, Mumma?' Mumma rolled it over her tongue. 'Grace Fields! Bit too stiff-like. Now what about … Gracie. That's it, Gracie Fields!' The thirteen-year-old, newly-christened Gracie Fields gave a whoop of joy" [Muriel Burgess with Tommy Keene, *Gracie Fields*, 1980].

Jackie Fields: Jacob Finkelstein (1908–1987), U.S. boxer. As a youth, the boxer was trained by a former fighter, Marty Fields. He adopted his name, thus finding a simpler alternative to his original Jewish surname.

Lew Fields: Lewis Maurice Shanfield (1867–1941), U.S. stage comedian, teaming with Joseph Weber.

Stanley Fields: Walter L. Agnew (1884–1941), U.S. movie actor, former prizefighter.

Tommy Fields: Thomas Stansfield (1908–), Eng. music hall comedian.

Totie Fields: Sophie Feldman (1930–1978), U.S. nightclub, TV comedienne. "Totie" was no doubt a childish pronunciation of "Sophie."

W.C. Fields: William Claude Dukinfield (1879–1946), U.S. movie comedian. This was the comedian's standard stage name. All the many others ranged from the bizarre to the grotesque, and were in the best tradition of American humorous pseudonyms. (see p. 54.) As an appetizer, note the (admittedly rather tame) first name that he assumed when he started his career as a young juggler (1891). This was simply Whitey, the Wonder Boy. He first used W.C. Fields in 1893. Claude was a name that he had always hated; the villains in his movies were often called Claude. Many of the names that he subsequently adopted were based on the names used by Charles Dickens, whose books he admired [Carlotta Monti with Cy Rice, *W.C. Fields and Me*, 1974].

Figaro: Henry Clapp (1814–1875), U.S. journalist, editor. The name has been popular with many journalists and columnists. Another was Mariano Jose de Larra (1809–1837), the Spanish satirist and dramatist, who used the pseudonym for the contribution of humorous articles to various periodicals. *Le Figaro* is itself a leading French daily newspaper, founded in 1825. The name comes from the hero of Beaumarchais's *Le Barbier de Séville* (1775) and *Le Mariage de Figaro* (1784), where Figaro is a barber-turned-doorkeeper. Barbers (and doorkeepers), of course, hear all the gossip. The ultimate source of the name may be in Spanish *hígado*, "liver," in the sense of someone who has "pluck" and spirit.

Filandre: Jean-Baptiste Monchaingre (or Jean Mathée) (1616–1691), Fr. actor-manager. The Greek name literally means "lover of men."

Filaret: (1) Fyodor Nikitich Romanov (*c.*1554–1633), Russ. churchman, patriarch of Moscow and All Russia; (2) Vasily Mikhaylovich Drozdov (1782–1867), Russ. churchman, metropolitan of Moscow. The name is of Greek origin (properly Philarethes) and means "lover of virtue." It was assumed by each man on taking monastic vows (Romanov in 1601, Drozdov in 1808). There are several other Orthodox churchmen who assumed the name.

Filarete: Antonio Averlino (*c.*1400–*c.*1469), It. sculptor, architect, writer. The name means "lover of virtue." (Compare the entry above.)

Fin-Bec: William Blanchard Jerrold (1826–1884), Eng. playwright, novelist. French *fin-bec* (literally "fine beak") means "gourmet." Jerrold lives as much in Paris as in London, and was himself a gourmet, publishing the *Epicure's Year-Book* in 1867 and (as Fin-Bec) gastronomic works such as *Knife and Fork* (1871), *The Dinner Bell* (1878), and the like.

Peter Finch: Peter George Ingle Finch (1916–1977), Eng. stage, movie actor. The actor's name is actually as above, and *not* William Mitchell, as stated in many otherwise reliable sources, such as Halliwell, Katz, and Thomson (see Bibliography, pp. 401, 402, 403). The misnomer seems to have been initiated in Finch's obituary in *The Times* of January 15, 1977, which had: "Peter Finch, whose real name was William Mitchell..." The mixup arose from an incident when Finch was visiting Rome with the real William Mitchell, a Canadian movie actor. Mitchell became involved in a barroom brawl and the two men were taken to the police station, where they were charged. Finch had his passport but Mitchell did not. Mitchell was thus taken to be Finch, while Finch was named as Mitchell. The incident was picked up by the British press, and later led to the obituary error [Elaine Dundy, *Finch, Bloody Finch*, 1980].

Larry **Fine**: Laurence Feinberg (or Fineburg) (1911–1975), U.S. movie comedian.

Johnny **Fingers**: John Moylett (1956–), Ir. rock musician. The Boomtown Rats member, a nimble-fingered keyboardist, is the cousin of Peter Briquette (*q.v.*).

[Sir] Moses I. **Finley**: Moses Finkelstein (1912–1986), U.S.-born Br. historian. The historian adopted his new name around 1936. He had no actual middle name, but simply used the initial "I." He emigrated to England in 1954 and became a British subject in 1962.

Fiore della Neve: Martinus Gesinus Lambert van Loghem (1849–1934), Du. poet, fiction writer. The writer's Italian-style name means "flower of the snow."

Firdausi: Ferdausi (*q.v.*).

David **Firth**: David Firth Coleman (1945–), Br. stage, TV actor. The actor adopted his father's (and his own) middle name as his stage name.

Fish: Derek William Dick (1958–), Sc. rock musician. The musician adopted the nickname given him by a landlord who objected to the long time he spent in the bath.

Fred **Fisher**: Frederic Fischer (1875–1942), Ger.-born U.S. popular composer.

Nicholas **Fisk**: David Higginbottom (1923–), Eng. children's writer.

John **Fiske**: Edmund Fisk Green (1842–1901), U.S. philosopher, historian. The future historian changed his name to John Fisk when he was 13, altering the spelling to Fiske at 18.

Minnie Maddern **Fiske**: Marie Augusta Davey (1865–1932), U.S. stage actress. The actress made her stage debut with her parents when she was only three, appearing under her mother's maiden name, with "Minnie" referring to her smallness. The name of Fiske was that of her husband, playwright Harrison Grey Fiske, whom she married in 1890.

Mary **Fitt**: Kathleen Freeman (1897–1959), Br. Greek scholar, crime novelist. The writer used this name for her detective novels. She also wrote as Caroline Cory and Stuart Mary Wick.

Edward **Fitzball**: Edward Ball (1792–1873), Eng. dramatist.

George Savage **Fitz-Boodle**: William Makepeace Thackeray (1811–1863), Eng. novelist. One of the many eccentric *noms de plume* adopted by the writer. He used this one for his contributions to *Fraser's Magazine* (1842). The pseudonym itself appears to be based on the names of London clubs: the Savage Club and Boodle's still flourish. Thackeray himself was a member of the Garrick.

Barry **Fitzgerald**: William Joseph Shields (1888–1961), Ir. movie actor. When Shields began his acting career, he was working full time as a civil servant. Another name for this activity was therefore needed, and he chose a typical Irish name. By day he was thus William Shields, and by night, when he acted, Barry Fitzgerald.

Walter **Fitzgerald**: Walter Fitzgerald Bond (1896–1977), Eng. stage, movie actor.

Paul **Fix**: Paul Fix Morrison (1901–1983), U.S. movie actor.

Francis **Flagg**: Henry George Weiss (1898–1946), U.S. SF writer.

Bud **Flanagan**: Chaim Reuben (or Reeven) Weintrop (1896–1968), Eng. stage, movie comedian, of Pol. Jewish parentage, teaming with Chesney Allen (*q.v.*). The actor first trod the boards of the London music hall as Fargo the Boy Conjuror. At the age of 13 he emigrated with his family to the U.S. and, after a brief interlude as a boxer with the ring name of Luke McGluke, tried his fortune on the vaudeville stage as Bobby Wayne. Back in Britain again at the start of World War I he joined the army as Driver Robert Winthrop.

The name Flanagan was inherited from his army years. Apparently a mean sergeant-major seemed to have it in for the future singer, and when Driver Winthrop was wounded in 1918 and left the service, his last words to his sergeant-major were, "I'll remember your name as long as I live." He took the name on resuming his career on the stage. (Later the sergeant-major became a barman in London, and Bud and he were reconciled.) After Flanagan and Allen's popular song *Underneath the Arches* was published in 1932 the profits began to roll in. With his share, Bud bought a house in the village of Angmering,

Sussex, and named it *Arches*. His first break in show business was given him by Florrie Forde (*q.v.*) [Bill McGowran, "You See Him Everywhere," in *Late Extra: A Miscellany by "Evening News" Writers, Artists, and Photographers*, c. 1952].

Flavius Josephus: Joseph ben Matthias (57–100), Jewish historian, general. The historian originally had the Hebrew name *Yosef ben Mattityahu*, "Joseph son of Matthew." He added Flavius to this when the Roman emperor Titus Flavius Vespasianus (better known as Vespasian) granted him the rights of a Roman citizen and appointed him historiographer of the Flavius *gens* (clan).

Fléchelles: Hugues Guéru (*c.*1573–1633), Fr. actor. The actor usually played in farces, when he appeared as Gaultier-Garguille (*q.v.*).

George **Fleming:** Julia Constance Fletcher (1858–1938), U.S. novelist, playwright.

Ian **Fleming:** Ian Macfarlane (1888–1969), Austral.-born Br. stage, movie actor.

Oliver **Fleming:** Philip MacDonald (1900–1981), Eng. mystery writer. The writer used this name for novels written jointly with his father, Ronald MacDonald (1860–1933). He wrote independently under the names Anthony Lawless and Martin Porlock.

Rhonda **Fleming:** Marilyn Lewis (or Louis) (1922–), U.S. movie actress.

Herbert **Flemming:** Arif Nicolaiih El-Michelle (1905–), Tunisian jazz trombonist.

George U. **Fletcher:** Fletcher Pratt (1897–1956), U.S. naval, American history, fantasy writer.

Robert **Fletcher:** Robert Fletcher Wycoff (1923–), U.S. theatre designer.

Fleury: Abraham-Joseph Bénard (1750–1822), Fr. comic actor.

Evangeline **Florence:** Evangeline Crerar, née Houghton (1873–1929), U.S. opera singer.

William Jermyn (or James) **Florence:** Bernard Conlin (1831–1891), U.S. comic actor.

Lola **Flores:** Dolores Flores Ruiz (1923–1995), Sp. flamenco dancer, movie actress.

Floridor: Josias de Soulas, Sieur de Primefosse (? 1608–1671), Fr. actor.

Florizel: George IV (1762–1830), king of Great Britain. George IV adopted this name when still Prince of Wales for his correspondence with the actress Mrs. Mary Robinson. Florizel is the character in Shakespeare's *The Winter's Tale* who falls in love with Perdita.

When Mrs. Robinson first attracted the royal attention, she was playing the part of Perdita, and indeed became generally known by this name after her fine enactment of the role in 1779. She left the stage the following year to become the Prince's mistress, thus in a curious sense living up to her stage name (which means "lost one") See more at Perdita.

Flotsam: Bentley Collingwood Hilliam (1890–1968), Eng. composer, pianist, entertainer, teaming with Jetsam (*q.v.*). The comic singers always signed off their act with the phrase, "Yours very sincerely, Flotsam and Jetsam." Flotsam was a countertenor, as fitting for his name (flotsam *floats* on the surface of the water), while Jetsam was a bass (jetsam often *sinks* when thrown overboard).

Barbara **Flynn:** Barbara Joy McMurray (1948–), Eng. stage, TV actress.

Josiah **Flynt:** Josiah Flint Willard (1869–1907), U.S. writer on experiences as a tramp.

Nina **Foch:** Nina Consuelo Maud Fock (1924–), Du. stage, movie actress, working in U.S.

Jonathan Lituleson **Fogarty:** James T. Farrell (1904–1979), U.S. novelist, critic.

Helen **Foley:** Helen Rose Fowler, née Huxley (1917–), Eng. novelist. The writer attended Newnham College, Cambridge, and adopted the name of an earlier Newnham student, Helen Foley (1896–1937).

Signor **Foli:** Allan James Foley (1835–1899), Ir. opera singer. The singer adopted an italianized form of his name.

Joan **Fontaine:** Joan de Beauvoir de Havilland (1917–), Eng.-born U.S. stage, movie actress. The actress adopted the name Joan Fontaine in 1937, following her mother's divorce and subsequent remarriage to George M. Fontaine. The aim of the name change was to avoid being confused with her sister, the actress Olivia de Havilland, her senior by one year.

Wayne **Fontana:** Glyn Geoffrey Ellis (1940–), Eng. rock musician. There are two accounts to explain the musician's name. One derives it from the Philips' *Fontana* label which carried his first recording in 1963, a version of "Road Runner," by Bo Diddley (*q.v.*). The other claims he adopted the name in honor of Elvis Presley's drummer, D.J. Fontana.

Moderata **Fonte:** Modesta Pozzo (1555–1592), It. poet, religious writer.

[Dame] Margot **Fonteyn:** Margot Fonteyn de Arias, née Margaret Hookham (1919–1991), Eng. ballet dancer. The ballerina originally changed her name from Margaret Hookham to Margot Fontes, based on her Brazilian mother's maiden name. Later, on the advice of Ninette de Valois (*q.v.*), she modified this to Margot Fonteyn.

Brenda **Forbes:** Brenda Taylor (1909–), Eng. stage actress. The actress adopted her mother's maiden name as her stage name.

Bryan **Forbes:** John Theobald Clarke (1926–), Eng. movie actor, screenwriter. The actor's name was chosen for him at the start of his stage career: "[BBC radio producer] Lionel Gamlin … announced that it would be necessary for me to change my name. Another young actor, ahead of me in the game, was also named John Clarke. … He elaborated on the surname first. 'Forbes has a good theatrical ring to it,' he said. 'Forbes-Robertson, you know.' I nodded. I hadn't the vaguest idea what he was talking about. [He was talking about Johnston Forbes-Robertson (1853–1937), leading London actor and theatre manager, whose second wife was the U.S. actress Gertrude Elliott, sister of Maxine Elliott (*q.v.*). The actress Meriel Forbes (see below) is his grandniece.] Had he suggested I call myself Joseph Stalin I would have agreed without a murmur. …

Forbes it was, and then Lionel began to juggle with Christian names to go with it. 'You want a good sounding name,' he said, 'and one that *looks* right on the bills. These things are important.' … I dimly comprehended that Lionel was asking if I would accept Brian. 'Bryan with a Y, I think.' He wrote it down. … 'How does that strike you?' … I managed to blurt out my grateful acceptance of the miracle. 'Fine, that's it, then,' Lionel went on. 'From now onwards you're Bryan Forbes'" [Bryan Forbes, *Notes for a Life*, 1974].

Meriel **Forbes:** Meriel Forbes-Robertson (1913–), Eng. stage, movie actress, grandniece of Johnston Forbes-Robertson (see under Bryan **Forbes**, above).

Miranda **Forbes:** Maddalena Stephanie Weet (1946–), Br. movie, TV actress.

Ralph **Forbes:** Ralph Taylor (1902–1951), Br. movie actor, working in U.S.

Stanton **Forbes:** Deloris Stanton Forbes (1923–), U.S. mystery writer.

Clinton **Ford:** Ian George Stopford-Harrison (1931–), Eng. popular singer.

Elbur **Ford:** Jean Plaidy (*q.v.*).

Emile **Ford:** Emile Sweetman (1937–), Bahamanian rock singer.

Ford Madox **Ford:** Ford Hermann Hueffer (1873–1939), Br. novelist, editor. The writer, a grandson of the Victorian painter Ford Madox Brown, initially adopted the first names Joseph Leopold Madox. Embarrassed in World War I by his German surname, he then changed his name by deed poll (1919) to Ford Madox Ford. On the title pages of his books his name alternated between Ford Madox Ford and Ford Madox Hueffer: he used the former for his sequence of war novels with the central character Christopher Tietgens as well as for travel books and reminiscences. For *The Questions at the Well; With Sundry Other Verses for Notes of Music* (1893) he had earlier used the name Fenil Haig. A literary biographer's verdict: "Although Ford's change of name may register the wish to escape, it also recognises the impossibility of escaping, revisiting as it does its origin, and recreating the self in the process" [Max Saunders, *Ford Madox Ford: A Dual Life*, Vol. I, 1996].

Francis **Ford:** Francis O'Feeney (or O'Fearna) (1883–1953), U.S. movie actor, brother of John Ford (*q.v.*).

Frankie **Ford:** Frank Guzzo (1940–), U.S. rock singer.

Gerald Rudolph **Ford**, Jr.: Leslie Lynch King, Jr. (1913–), U.S. president. When the future 38th President of the United States was still an infant, his parents divorced and his mother moved to Grand Rapids where she married Gerald R. Ford, Sr., who adopted the child and gave him his name.

Glenn **Ford:** Gwyllyn Samuel Newton Ford (1916–), Can. movie actor, working in U.S.

John **Ford:** Sean Aloysius O'Feeney (or O'Fearna) (1895–1973), U.S. movie director, of Ir. parentage. When the director graduated from high school in 1913 his elder brother Francis Ford (*q.v.*) was working as a director and actor in Hollywood and had already adopted the name Ford. Sean (whose name is the Irish equivalent of John) therefore took the same name when he joined him, calling himself Jack Ford.

Keeley **Ford:** Mair Davies (1948–), Br. popular radio singer.

Leslie **Ford:** Zenith Brown, née Jones (1898–1983), U.S. detective novelist. The writer also used the names Brenda Conrad and David Frome.

Paul **Ford:** Paul Ford Weaver (1901–1976), U.S. stage actor. The actor adopted his mother's maiden name, which was already his middle name.

Wallace **Ford:** Samuel Jones Grundy (1897–1966), Eng.-born U.S. movie actor.

Florrie **Forde:** Florence Flanagan (1876–1940), Austral.-born Eng. music hall singer.

Walter **Forde:** Thomas Seymour (1896–1984), Br. movie director.

Keith **Fordyce:** Keith Marriott (1928–), Eng. radio, TV interviewer, DJ.

Mark **Forest:** Lou Degni (1933–), U.S. movie actor.

Cecil Scott **Forester:** Cecil Lewis Troughton Smith (1899–1966), Br. novelist. The writer, who signed himself simply C.S. Forester, took his new name for professional purposes in 1923. It was an elaboration of the middle name of his father, George Foster Smith.

Fanny **Forester:** Emily Chubbuck Judson (1817–1854), U.S. novelist.

Frank **Forester:** Henry William Herbert (1807–1858), Eng. author, editor, working in U.S.

Forez: François Mauriac (1885–1970), Fr. novelist, playwright, poet. When working for the French Resistance, Mauriac wrote *Cahier Noir* (1943), choosing for this the name of the mountainous region in the Massif Central that Resistance workers found so suitable for cover.

George **Formby:** George Hoy Booth (1904–1961), Eng. movie comedian, singer, ukelele player. The comedian, whose middle name, Hoy, was his mother's maiden name, took the same stage name as his father, James Lawler Booth. How did Booth Senior come to acquire his name? As a young millworker, James would supplement his small wages by singing in the street, where he was "discovered" by a Mr. Brown, together with another boy who had teamed up with him, and sent to different towns in the north of England to earn a shilling or two for his "manager." Mr. Brown would pay James threepence a week and the other boy sixpence. To cut his expenses, Mr. Brown transported the boys in the traveling props basket, with the lid down, to avoid paying their train fares.

"On one occasion, when they were travelling from Manchester to Bury, Jimmy happened not to be in the basket and sat watching coal wagons go by. A sign on one of the wagons showed that it came from Formby, Lancashire. The name appealed to him. He preferred it, in a theatrical sense, to his own name of Booth and decided there and then to make it his own. But Jimmy or James did not go with it. Beginning with the first letter of the alphabet he went through in his mind all the names he could think of and stopped when he got to 'G' and George. That was it—George Formby. It sounded right. It suited him. His change of name coincided with his desire to end the singing partnership" [Alan Randall and Ray Seaton, *George Formby*, 1974].

Alan **Forrest:** Allan Forrest Fisher (1889–1941), U.S. stage, movie actor.

David **Forrest:** David Denholm (1924–), Austral. novelist, short story writer.

George **Forrest**, Esq., M.A.: [Rev.] John George Wood (1827–1889), Eng. naturalist, writer. The writer used this pen name, of obvious but appropriate derivation, for the highly popular *Every Boy's Book* (1855).

George "Chet" **Forrest:** George Forrest Chichester (1915–), U.S. lyricist, composer.

Sally **Forrest:** Katharine Sally Feeney (1928–), U.S. movie actress.

Steve **Forrest:** William Forrest Andrews (1924–), U.S. movie actor.

Helen **Forrester:** June (or Jamunadevi) Bhatia (1919–), Eng. born Can. novelist.

John **Forsell:** Carl Johan Jacob (1868–1941), Swe. opera singer.

Willi **Forst:** Wilhelm Anton Frohs (1903–1980), Austr. movie actor.

Robert **Forster:** Robert Foster (1941–), U.S. movie actor.

Bruce **Forsyth:** Bruce Joseph Forsyth-Johnson (1928–), Br. entertainer, TV host.

Jean **Forsyth:** Jean Newton McIlwraith (1859–1938), Can. novelist, biographer, of Sc. parentage.

John **Forsythe:** John Lincoln Freund (1918–), U.S. stage, movie actor.

Fortis: Leslie Forse (1907–1978), Eng. journalist, editor.

Dion **Fortune:** Violet Mary Firth (1890–1946), U.S. writer of occult novels.

Lance **Fortune:** Chris Morris (1940–), Br. pop. singer. The singer's name was given him by impresario Larry Parnes, who had originally intended it for the future Georgie Fame (*q.v.*).

Lukas **Foss:** Lukas Fuchs (1922–), Ger.-born U.S. composer, conductor.

Dianne **Foster:** Dianne Laruska (1928–), Can. movie actress.

Norman **Foster:** Norman Hoeffer (1900–1976), U.S. movie actor.

Phil **Foster:** Fivel Feldman (1914–1985), U.S. TV comedian

Phoebe **Foster:** Phoebe Eager (1896– ?), U.S. stage actress.

Richard **Foster:** Kendall Foster Crossen (1910–), U.S. author, journalist.

Susanna **Foster:** Suzanne DeLee Flanders Larson (1924–), U.S. movie actress. The actress began her career as an opera singer and took her professional name from that of Stephen Foster and his song "Oh, Susanna." Compare the name of Nelly Bly.

Fougasse: Cyril Kenneth Bird (1887–1965), Eng. artist, cartoonist, editor. The former editor of *Punch* (succeeding Evoe, *q.v.*) adopted his unusual name in order to avoid confusion with another *Punch* artist calling himself W. Bird (*q.v.*). He later explained that "fougasse" was an old technical term used for a small antipersonnel landmine that might or might not go off. A cartoonist always hopes that his drawings and captions *will* "go off," or make an impact. Bird had himself been injured by a shell in World War I.

This is likely to be the true account of the artist's name, especially as the word itself became internationally known. However, French *fougasse*, a word of different origin, is also the name of a type of pie or pastry, and this has suggested an alternate source, alluded to in *The Times Magazine* of October 12, 1996, by its restaurant critic, Jonathan Meades: "Fougasse was the nom de plume of a Thirties cartoonist who drew with a thick sinuous line. He took his name from an all-purpose provençal pie." But the word is highly specialized, even to the French, and one wonders if Bird himself would even have heard of it.

Adam **Fouleweather:** Thomas Nashe (1567–1601), Eng. satirical pamphleteer, dramatist. The satirist used this name for his *Astrologicall Prognostication* (1591), in which he replied to the savage attack on him by Richard Hervey, the astrologer. His best-known pseudonym was Pasquil (*q.v.*).

Oliver **Foulis:** David Lloyd (1635–1692), Eng. miscellaneous writer.

Imro **Fox:** Isador Fuchs (1862–1910), Ger.-born U.S. magician.

Sidney **Fox:** Sidney Liefer (1910–1942), U.S. movie actress.

William **Fox:** Wilhelm Fried (1879–1952), Hung.-born U.S. movie executive (the Fox of "20th-Century Fox").

John **Foxx:** Dennis Leigh (*c.*1950–), Eng. rock musician.

Redd **Foxx:** John Elroy Sanford (1922–1991), U.S. movie, TV comedian. The comedian, a fan of the Chicago Red Sox baseball team, was already known by his nickname of Chicago Red. He added an extra "d" to the second word of this and took his new surname from the legendary baseball player Jimmie Foxx (1907–1967), who at one time played for that team. The name as a whole was further suggested by the red fox featuring in children's books.

Eddie **Foy,** Sr.: Edwin Fitzgerald (1856–1928), U.S. vaudeville artist.

Eddie **Foy,** Jr.: Edward Fitzgerald (1905–1983), U.S. stage actor, dancer, son of Eddie Foy, Sr. (see above). A good example of a necessary shortening of a lengthy name so that it fits easily on billboards.

F.P.A.: Franklin Pierce Adams (1881–1960), U.S. journalist, humorist. The writer usually signed his columns with his initials.

Harry **Fragson:** Léon Vince Philippe Pott (originally Fragmann) (1869–1913), Eng.-Belg. music hall comedian, singer.

Janet **Frame:** Janet Paterson Frame Clutha (1924–), N.Z. novelist. The writer legally adopted the additional surname of Clutha, taking it from a river that was important in her childhood. (It enters the sea south of Dunedin, where she was born.)

Celia **Franca:** Celia Franks (1921–), Eng. ballet dancer, director, choreographer.

Alexis **France:** Alexis McFarlane (1906–), Rhodesian-born Br. stage actress.

Anatole **France:** Jacques-Anatole-François Thibault (1844–1924), Fr. novelist, poet, dramatist. The writer assumed his pseudonym not so much to emphasize his nationality as to commemorate the fact that his father, who owned a bookshop, was called "Monsieur France" by his customers, this being a local form of François. (When he opened the shop in 1839 he called it the "Librairie politique de France Thibault," a name which in 1844 became "Librairie politique ancienne et moderne de France," as if referring to the country.)

Paula **Frances:** Paula Frances Muldoon (1969–), Br. TV actress.

Mother **Frances Mary Theresa:** Frances Ball (1794–1861), Eng. religious founder of Loretto nuns, Ireland.

Anthony **Franciosa:** Anthony George Papaleo (1928–), U.S. movie actor.

Arlene **Francis:** Arlene Kazanjian (1908–), U.S. TV personality.

Arthur **Francis:** Ira Gershwin (1896–1983), U.S. songwriter. Gershwin used this name when, after an abortive literary start, he began writing the lyrics for his brother George's songs in the 1920s.

Connie **Francis:** Concetta Rosa Maria Franconero (1938–), U.S. pop singer, movie actress, of It. descent. The singer appeared as a child on Arthur Godfrey's TV talent show, and he suggested her new name.

Doris **Francis:** Doris Akast (1903–), Br. stage actress, singer.

Joan **Francis:** Joan Francis Willi (1920–1995), Eng. actress.

Kay **Francis:** Katherine Edwina Gibbs (1899 or 1903–1968), U.S. stage, movie actress. The actress's stage name came from that of her first husband, James Dwight Francis (married 1922).

M.E. **Francis:** Mary Blundell, née Sweetman (1855–1930), Ir. novelist. The writer adopted the first name of her husband, Francis Blundell.

Jan **Francisci:** Janko Rimavský (1822–1905), Slovakian writer, journalist, patriot.

[St.] **Francis of Assisi:** Giovanni di Pietro di Bernadone (1182–1226), It. monk, preacher. The saint's father was away on business in France at the time of his son's birth and on his return changed the baby's name to Francesco (Francis), partly as a memorial to his visit, but also because the child's mother was a Frenchwoman, from Provence.

Franco: Franco l'Okanga La Ndju Pene Luambo Makiadi (1938–1989), Zaïrian guitarist, bandleader. The musician's original name was Okanga Luambo Makiadi. He then expanded this as above in the 1970s following President Mobutu's *authenticité* (indigenization) campaign, which involved the renaming of the country (from Congo) together with its main provinces and cities. In 1981 he converted to Islam and adopted the name Aboubakar Sidiki.

Harry **Franco:** Charles Frederick Briggs (1804–1877), U.S. journalist, author.

Jacob **Frank:** Jacob Leibowicz (1726–1791), Pol. Jewish false messiah.

Pat **Frank:** Harry Hart (1907–1964), U.S. SF writer.

Melvin **Franklin:** David English (1942–), U.S. black Motown singer.

Sydney **Franklin:** Sydney Frumkin (1905–), U.S. bullfighter, movie actor. The actor is not to be confused with the U.S. film producer and director Sidney Franklin (1893–1972).

Mary **Frann:** Mary Luecke (1943–), U.S. TV actress.

Liz **Fraser:** Elizabeth Winch (1935–), Eng. movie, TV actress. The actress originally played under her real name. She then took the name Elizabeth Fraser, but finally adopted the shorter form of her first name.

Jane **Frazee:** Mary Jane Frahse (1918–1985), U.S. singer, movie actress. An original modification of a European name for an English-speaking audience.

Liz **Frazer:** Elizabeth Winch (1933–), Eng. movie actress.

Frédérick: Antoine-Louis Prosper Lemaître (1800–1876), Fr. actor. The actor adopted his grandfather's name as his stage name.

Pauline **Frederick:** Beatrice Pauline Libbey (1883–1938), U.S. stage, movie actress.

Vera **Fredowa:** Winifred Edwards (1896–1989), Eng. ballet dancer, teacher.

Arthur **Freed:** Arthur Grossman (1894–1973), U.S. lyricist, movie producer.

Mrs. **Freeman:** Sarah Churchill, Duchess of Marlborough (1660–1744), Eng. aristocrat. This was the symbolic name adopted by the Duchess for her correspondence with Queen Anne, otherwise Mrs. Morley (*q.v.*).

Cynthia **Freeman:** Bea Feinberg (1915–1988), U.S. romantic novelist.

Bruno **Frei:** Benedikt Freistadt (1897–), Austr. journalist, writer.

Charles K. **French:** Charles E. Krauss (1860–1952), U.S. movie actor.

Peter **French:** John Nicholas ffrench (1935–), Welsh stage, TV actor.

Pierre **Fresnay:** Pierre-Jules-Louis Laudenbach (1897–1975), Fr. stage, movie actor.

Janie **Frickie:** Jane Fricke (1947–), U.S. country singer. The singer adjusted the spelling of her name to avoid any mispronunciation.

Jan **Fridegard:** Johan Fridolf Johansson (1897–1968), Swe. writer.

Egon **Friedell:** Egon Friedmann (1878–1938), Austr. stage actor, writer.

Aunt **Friendly:** Sarah S.T. Baker (1824–1906), Br. children's writer.

Trixie **Friganza:** Delia O'Callahan (1870–1955), U.S. actress, singer.

Freddie **Frinton:** Frederick Hargate (1911–1968), Eng. comedian.

Joe **Frisco:** Louis Wilson Joseph (c.1890–1958), U.S. vaudeville, movie actor.

Joachim **Frizius:** Robert Flud (1574–1637), Eng. physician, Rosicrucian.

David **Frome:** Zenith Brown, née Jones (1898–1983), U.S. detective novelist. The writer also used the names Brenda Conrad and Leslie Ford.

Fru-Fru: Teresa de la Parra (1889–1936), Fr.-born Venezuelan novelist, short story writer. The writer's full original name was Ana Teresa Parr Sanojo, but she adopted the pseudonym Fru-Fru, from a Spanish equivalent of French (now also English) *froufrou*, a word used to imitate the rustling of a dress. Presumably this came from a (possibly childhood) nickname.

Christopher **Fry:** Christopher Harris (1907–), Eng. playwright. The writer adopted his maternal grandmother's maiden name as his pen name.

Elmer **Fudpucker:** Hollis Champion (1935–), Can. country & western singer, comedian.

Fulcanelli: Jean-Julien Champagne (1877–1932), Fr. alchemist.

Blind Boy **Fuller:** Fulton Allen (1908–1941), U.S. blues singer. The blind singer based his name on his physical condition and his original name.

Fu Manchu: David Bamberg (1904–1974), U.S. magician, son of Okito (q.v.). Fu Manchu is the Chinese master villain in the stories by Sax Rohmer (q.v.), beginning in 1912.

Sofia **Fuoco:** Maria Brambilla (1830–1916), It. ballet dancer.

Furkat: Zakirdzhan Khalmukhamedov (1858–1909), Uzbek poet, polemicist. The writer was obliged to resettle in Kashgaria (Chinese Turkistan) in order to escape reprisals following his mockery of the authorities. Hence his adopted name, meaning "separation," "alienation."

Robin **Furneaux:** Frederick William Robin Smith, 3d Earl of Birkenhead (1936–1985), Br. author, historian.

Yvonne **Furneaux:** Yvonne Scatcherd (1928–), Fr. movie actress, working in U.K.

Füruzan: Füruzan Yerdelen, née Selçuk (1935–), Turk. novelist. The writer adopted her first name as her pen name following the failure of her marriage.

Billy **Fury:** Ronald Wycherley (1941–1983), Eng. pop singer. The singer was so named by impresario Larry Parnes, who also named Vince Eager, Georgie Fame, Lance Fortune, Johnny Gentle, Dickie Pride, and Marty Wilde (qq.v.). The name was an "image" one, as were the others. (It is said that the pop guitarist Joe Brown refused, however, to accept Parnes's proposed name of Almer Twitch.)

Fusbos: Henry Edward Doyle (1827–1892), Ir.-born Br. painter, cartoonist. This looks like an arbitrary name, perhaps based on Dickens's Sergeant Buzfus.

Rose **Fyleman:** Rose Amy Feilmann (1877–1957), Br. children's writer, of Ger. Jewish and Russ. parentage.

Bobby **G:** Robert Gubby (1953–), Eng. pop singer.

Johnny **G:** John Gotting (1949–), Eng. folk, pub rock singer.

Kenny **G:** Kenneth Gorelick (1959–), U.S. jazz saxophonist.

Warren **G:** Warren Griffin III (1971–), U.S. black "gangsta" rapper.

Jean **Gabin:** Jean Alexis Moncorgé (1904–1976), Fr. movie actor. The actor adopted the same professional name as that of his father, a café entertainer.

Naum **Gabo:** Naum Neemia Pevsner (1890–1977), Russ. Constructivist sculptor, working in U.S. The artist changed his name in 1915 to be distinguished from his brother, Antoine Pevsner, a painter.

Dennis **Gabor:** Dénes Gábor (1900–1979), Br. electrical engineer, physicist, of Hung. origin. The inventor of holography was the son of Bertalan Günsberg, a Hungarian of Russian and Spanish Jewish origin, who changed his name to Gábor in 1899, the year he married an actress, Adrienne Kálmán.

Zsa Zsa **Gabor:** Sari Gabor (1923–), Hung. movie actress, working in U.S.

Gabriel: James Friell (1912–), Sc. cartoonist, journalist. A name presumably based on the artist's real name.

Gabrielle: Louise Bobb (1967–), Br. pop singer.

Mazhit **Gafuri:** Gabdulmazhit Nurganiyevich Gafurov (1880–1934), Russ. (Bashkir) writer.

Zoë **Gail:** Zoë Margaret Stapleton (1920–), S.A. stage actress, dancer, working in U.K.

Sarah **Gainham:** Sarah Rachel Ames (1922–), Br. novelist.

Serge **Gainsbourg:** Lucien Ginzburg (1928–1991), Fr. popular singer, songwriter, of Russ. Jewish parentage. The singer changed his first name, as he regarded it as that of a typical hairdresser ("Lucien coiffeur pour hommes"). In any case, he had never liked it. His surname (representing the common Jewish name Ginsburg, ultimately from the Bavarian town of Gunzburg) he converted to a French-style equivalent [Lucien Roux, *Serge Gainsbourg*, 1986].

Gais: R.G. Gaisford (*fl.*1930s–1940s), Eng. cartoonist.

Nick **Gaitano:** Eugene Izzi (1953–1996), U.S. crime writer

Radola **Gajda:** Rudolf Gejdl (1892–1948), Cz. counterrevolutionary.

Gala **Galaction:** Grigore Pişculescu (1879–1961), Rom. writer.

Vincenzo **Galeotti:** Vincenzo Tomaselli (1733–1816), It. ballet dancer, teacher.

Galimafré: Auguste Guérin (1790–1870), Fr. comic actor, teaming with Bobèche (*q.v.*). The actor's stage name means "hotchpotch" (modern French *galimafrée*).

Boris **Galin:** Boris Abramovich Rogalin (1904–), Russ. writer.

Anna **Galina:** Evelyne Cournand (1936–), U.S. ballet dancer. It is tempting to think that the ballerina formed her name from those of two noted Russian artists, the dancer Anna Pavlova and the singer Galina Vishnevskaya.

G.A. **Galina:** Glafira Adolfovna Guseva-Orenburgskaya, previously Einerling, née Mamoshina (*c.*1870–1942), Russ. poet, children's writer. A name created from the writer's initials and first name.

Shaukat **Galiyev:** Shaukat Galiyevich Idiatullin (1928–), Russ. (Tatar) poet.

Junius **Gallio:** Lucius Annaeus Novatus (*c.*5 BC–AD 65), Roman consul. Famous for dismissing the charges brought by the Jews against the apostle Paul (Acts 18:12-17), Novatus assumed his new name following his adoption by the senator Junius Gallio.

Galyorka: Mikhail Stepanovich Aleksandrov (1863–1933), Russ. revolutionary, writer, historian. This was a prerevolutionary name adopted by the activist better known as Mikhail Olminsky (*q.v.*). It means "the gallery," as the writer explained at the end of his first published article: "I finished the article and thought: what pseudonym shall I use? ... I like the theatre, and for some reason always end up in the gallery. I like being with the gallery audience, and feel at home among such people. And it is to you, my gallery-going colleagues, ... that I shall address my final words: I ask you to excuse me for daring to sign my personal article with our general collective name: Galyorka" [Dmitriyev, p. 117].

Geoffrey **Gambado:** Henry William Bembury (1750–1811), Eng. artist, caricaturist.

Abram **Games:** Abram Gamse (1914–1996), Br. graphics designer, poster artist, of Latvian-Pol. parentage. The artist's father, a Latvian photographer, emigrated to London in 1904 and in 1926 changed the family name by simply transposing the last two letters.

Gamgyusar: Aliguli Alikper Nadzhafov (1880–1919), Azerbaijani satirical poet, journalist. The writer's name means "woe," "sorrow," referring to the state of the capitalist and colonialist world as he saw it.

Peter **Gan:** Richard Moering (1894–), Ger. lyric poet, writer.

Zan **Ganassa:** Alberto Naselli (*c.*1540–*c.*1584), It. actor, theatrical company manager. The actor assumed the name of a character that he had invented.

Abel **Gance:** Eugène Alexandre Péréthon (1889–1981), Fr. movie director. The filmmaker was the illegitimate son of a physician, Abel Flamant, and took his legal name from his mother, Françoise Péréthon, and his professional name from her boyfriend (later husband), Adolphe Gance.

Sir Gregory **Gander:** George Ellis (1753–1815), Eng. author. The writer used the name for his *Poetical Tales by Sir Gregory Gander* (1778), which were immediately identified as coming from his pen.

Joe **Gans:** Joseph Gaines (1874–1910), U.S. black lightweight boxer.

Pedro de **Gante:** Peeter van der Moere (*c.*1486–1572), Belg. monk, missionary, working in Mexico. The Franciscan monk came to be known by a Spanish name meaning "Peter of Ghent," the latter being his birth town in what was then Flanders.

Ilija **Garasanin:** Ilija Savić (1812–1874), Serbian prime minister.

Greta **Garbo:** Greta Lovisa Gustafsson (1905–1990), Swe.-born U.S. movie actress. The movie star's original name is in no doubt. Exactly how she acquired her well-known screen surname is more than a little uncertain. The name is generally thought to have been given to her by the Swedish movie director Mauritz Stiller. But how did he devise it? One version says that he "toyed with Gabor after Gabor Bethlen, an ancient Hungarian king, then settled on the variation, Garbo" [Norman Zierold, *Garbo*, 1970].

A detailed account of the name origin is given by one of Garbo's many biographers: "The name, which became so memorable, was the invention of Mauritz Stiller, who had long cherished it and was determined to bestow it on an actress worthy of it. In his imagination the name suggested fairyland, romance, beauty, everything he had associated in his childhood with the utmost happiness and the wildest dreams. Many explanations were later offered to explain the name. Someone wrote that he derived it from the first letters of a sentence he wrote describing Greta Gustafsson: *Gör alla roller berömvärt opersonligt* ("Plays all roles in a commendably impersonal fashion"). Others remembered that *garbo* in Spanish and Italian is a rarely used word describing a peculiar kind of grace and charm. Still others imagined it was derived from the name of Erica Darbo, a famous Norwegian singer of the time. A more plausible explanation can be found in the *garbon*, a mysterious sprite that sometimes comes out at night to dance to the moonbeams. This elfin creature was a descendant of the dreaded *gabilun* of Swedish and German folklore, who was killed by Kudrun. The *gabilun* breathed fire from its nostrils and could assume any shape at will, and some memory of his ancient power remained in the *garbon*, just as Robin Goodfellow retains some features of the Great God Pan. No one knows the true origin of the word. When asked about it, Stiller simply looked up in the air, smiled, and said, 'I really don't know. But it's right, isn't it?'" [Robert Payne, *The Great Garbo*, 1976].

This far from exhausts the theories. Another is that Greta had visited some relatives who lived on a farm called "Garboda," so that may be the source [Frederick Sands and Sven Broman, *The Divine Garbo*, 1979]. A more recent biographer claims Stiller took it from Polish *wygarbować*, "to tan" (as in making leather): "'When I saw you for the first time, you were beautiful, but your beauty was not refined. ... I said to myself, I must *wygarbovać* this girl'" [Antoni Gronowicz, *Garbo*, 1990]. This origin is dismissed as

"absurd" by a later writer, who offers his own theory. Stiller wanted a name that was "modern and elegant and international [and] says just as clearly who she is in London and Paris as in Budapest and New York." His assistant, Arthur Nordén, suggested "Mona Gabor," deriving it from Gábor Bethlen, a 17th-century Hungarian king. "Stiller rather liked it but kept trying out different variations: Gábor, GabOR, Gabro ... Garbo!" [Barry Paris, *Garbo: A Biography*, 1995]. But this takes us back to square one...

Garbo also used other pseudonyms, among them Harriet Brown (her favorite), Gussie Berger, Mary Holmquist, Jean Clark, Karin Lund, Miss Swanson, Emily Clark, Jane Emerson, Alice Smith, and the unexpected male name Karl Lund.

Jules Auguste **Garcin:** Jules Auguste Salomon (1830–1896), Fr. orchestral conductor. The musician adopted the name of his maternal grandmother.

Joyce **Gard:** Joyce Reeves (1911–), Br. children's writer, sister of poet James (originally John Morris) Reeves (1909–1978).

Helen Hamilton **Gardener:** Alice Chenoweth (1853–1925), U.S. novelist, short story writer.

Vincent **Gardenia:** Vincent Scognamiglio (1922–1992), U.S. movie actor.

Ava **Gardner:** Lucy Johnson (1922–1990), U.S. movie actress. Lucy Johnson is stated to be the actress's "real" name by many sources. But it appears that she was indeed born Ava Lavinia Gardner, the daughter of Jonas and Mary Elizabeth Gardner, of Grabtown, North Carolina [John Daniell, *Ava Gardner*, 1982].

Ed **Gardner:** Edward Poggenberg (1901–1963), U.S. TV actor.

Allen **Garfield:** Allen Goorwitz (1939–), U.S. movie actor. From 1978 through 1983 the actor was billed under his real name.

John **Garfield:** Jacob Julius Garfinkle (1912–1952), U.S. movie actor. The actor first used the stage name Jules Garfield before changing the forename to John.

N. **Garin:** Nikolay Georgiyevich Mikhaylovsky (1852–1906), Russ. novelist. The writer was obliged to take a new name to be distinguished from his near namesake, Nikolay Konstantinovich Mikhaylovsky, editor of *Russkoye bogatstvo* ("Russian riches"), the magazine in which he was first published. For his first article, "A few words about the Siberian railway," he thus took the name *Inzhener-praktik*, "Practising

Engineer." But this would obviously not be suitable for a fictional work, for which he adopted a name based on Garya, the diminutive form of Georgy, his son's name. He later joined his new name to the original, giving the surname Garin-Mikhaylovsky [Dmitriyev, p. 73].

Robert **Garioch:** Robert Garioch Sutherland (1909–1981), Sc. poet, translator.

Beverly **Garland:** Beverly Lucy Fessenden (1926–), U.S. movie, TV actress. The actress was billed as Beverly Campbell in her film debut in 1949.

Judy **Garland:** Frances Ethel Gumm (1922–1969), U.S. movie actress, singer. The actress made her stage debut at the age of three, appearing with her two elder sisters as the Gumm Sisters (on one occasion wrongly billed as the Glum Sisters). When she was nine, the sisters changed their surname to Garland, a name proposed by their agent, George Jessel, who adopted it from that of *New York Post* theatre critic Robert Garland. The following year Judy adopted her new first name. This came from Hoagy Carmichael's song so named which was popular then and her favorite, especially the line that went, "If she seems a saint, and you find she ain't, that's Judy!"

Elizabeth **Garner:** Elma Napier, earlier Gibbs, née Gordon-Cumming (1892–c.1975), Sc.-born novelist, short story writer, working in Dominica. The writer adopted her mother's maiden name for her novels, set in Dominica.

James **Garner:** James Scott Baumgarner (1928–), U.S. movie actor.

Andrew **Garran:** Andrew Gamman (1825–1901), Eng.-born Austral. journalist, politician.

Edward **Garrett:** Isabella Fyvie Mayo (1843–1914), Br. novelist, of Sc. parentage. The writer took her pen name from the elderly main characters, brother and sister Edward and Ruth Garrett, in her first novel, *Occupations of a Retired Life* (1867).

John **Garrick:** Reginald Doudy (1902–1966), Br. stage, movie actor, singer. The actor's name presumably commemorates the famous English actor David Garrick (1717–1779).

Garrincha: Manoel Francisco dos Santos (1933–1983), Brazilian footballer. The sportsman adopted his nickname, the word for a small Brazilian bird.

[Sir] Richard **Garth:** Richard Lowndes (1820–1903), Eng. colonial lawyer. The chief justice of Bengal changed his name at the same time as his father, who did so on succeeding to the property of his mother, née Elizabeth Garth, in 1837.

Tishka **Gartny:** Dmitry Fyodorovich Zhilunovich (1887–1937), Belorussian revolutionary writer. The writer based his new name on *gart*, "tempering" (as of steel).

Andrew **Garve:** Paul Winterton (1911–), Eng. journalist, mystery writer.

Gary: Gary James Smith (1963–), Eng. cartoonist.

Romain **Gary:** Roman Kacewgary (1914–1980), Fr. novelist, of Russ. (Georgian) Jewish origin.

Pierre **Gascar:** Pierre Fournier (1916–), Fr. novelist, short story writer.

Jonathan **Gash:** John Grant (1935–), Br. mystery writer.

Gassendi: [Abbé] Pierre Gassend (1592–1655), Fr. philosopher, mathematician.

Pearly **Gates:** Viola Billups (1946–), U.S. black popular singer. The singer was so named by her manager, Bruce Welch, who told her she had "better learn how to spell it." But how else could you spell such a heavenly name?

Gath: George Alfred Townsend (1841–1914), U.S. journalist, war correspondent, fiction writer. The name represents the writer's initials with also, one suspects, an oblique pun on the biblical exhortation, "Tell it not in Gath."

Henri **Gaudier-Brzeska:** Henri Gaudier (1891–1915), Fr. sculptor. The artist added the name of his companion, Sophie Brzeska, to his own.

Gaultier-Garguille: Hugues Guéru (c.1573–1633), Fr. actor. The actor mostly played in farces. For his serious plays he took the name Fléchelles (*q.v.*).

Paul **Gavarni:** Sulpice-Guillaume Chevalier (1804–1866), Fr. lithographer, painter. The artist acquired his "canvas name" by an unusual error. He once sent his drawings to a Paris exhibition from the Pyrenean village of Gavarnie. When displayed, the pictures were labeled as being by "Gavarnie," this name having appeared on the container. The exhibition was a success, and with a minor adjustment of spelling, the artist assumed the name attributed to him.

Yury Petrovich **Gaven:** Jan Ernestovich Dauman (1884–1936), Latvian Communist official.

John **Gavin:** Jack Golenor (1928–), U.S. movie actor.

Jack **Gawsworth**: Terence Ian Fytton Armstrong (1912–1970), Eng. poet, critic, editor, horror story writer.

William **Gaxton**: Arturo Antonio Gaxiola (1893–1963), U.S. stage actor, singer. The name may allude to William Caxton, the famous English printer, with the first half of the actor's surname retained for distinction.

Francis **Gay**: Herbert Leslie Gee (1901–1977), Eng. "inspirational," children's writer. The northcountry writer, famous for *The Friendship Book* and his regular feature in newspapers such as the Scottish *Sunday Post*, selected a name that matched his "couthy [friendly], heart-warming" style. His new surname also reflects his original name (another book was titled *Gay Adventure*), while "Francis" was perhaps meant to suggest "Friendship." *The Friendship Book* still appears annually, and his feature weekly, although obviously both are now written or compiled by others. A companion publication to *The Friendship Book* is *The Fireside Book* of David Hope (*q.v.*).

Maisie **Gay**: Maisie Munro-Noble (1883–1945), Eng. movie actress.

Noel **Gay**: Reginald Moxon Armitage (1898–1954), Eng. popular songwriter, music publisher. The musician adopted the name when he was director of music and organist at St. Anne's Church, London. The aim was not to embarrass the church authorities, who might not have been too pleased to discover their director writing musicals. The name itself is a sort of reversal of "Merry Christmas," though this may not have been the composer's intention.

Peter **Gay**: Peter Froelich (1923–), Ger.-born U.S. historian. The future historian emigrated to the U.S. as a teenager and translated his name to the English equivalent.

Julián **Gayarré**: Gayarré Sebastián (1844–1890), Sp. opera singer.

Arkady **Gaydar**: Arkady Petrovich Golikov (1904–1941), Russ. writer. There is some doubt concerning the origin of the novelist's name. Shortly before his untimely death in World War II, he is said to have told his colleagues in arms how he came by it in the final stages of the Civil War when serving on the Mongolian border: "A Mongolian would often run up to me, waving his cap and shouting 'gay-dar! gay-dar!' This was translated for me from the Mongolian to mean an outrider. So that was what my mates began calling me. It meant a lot to me, that word, it really did. … So you see, lads, I didn't take that pseudonym just because it sounded good!"

According to another theory, however, the name is a cryptonym, as follows: *G* is the initial of his original surname, *ay* represents the first and last letters of Arkady, and *dar* is a shortened form of *d'Arzamas*, "of Arzamas," in the French manner (like d'Artagnan), meaning the town where Golikov was raised [Dmitriyev, pp. 250–51].

Marvin **Gaye**: Marvin Pentz Gay, Jr. (1939–1984), U.S. black Motown singer. The altered form of the musician's surname first appeared in 1961 in the credits of his first single, "Let Your Conscience Be Your Guide."

Catherine **Gayer**: Catherine Ashkenasi (1937–), U.S. opera singer.

Crystal **Gayle**: Brenda Gail Webb (1951–), U.S. country singer, sister of Loretta Lynn (*q.v.*). After graduating in the late 1960s, Brenda Webb signed with her sister's record label, USA Decca. As the label already had Brenda Lee (*q.v.*), a new name was needed. The story goes that as the sisters drove past a sign for Krystal hamburgers, Lynn said, "That's your name. Crystals are bright and sunny, like you" [Larkin, p. 952]. Her new surname is a respelling of her existing middle name.

Janet **Gaynor**: Laura Gainor (1906–1984), U.S. movie actress.

Mitzi **Gaynor**: Francesca Mitzi Marlene de Charney von Gerber (1930–), U.S. movie actress. The actress is said to be a descendant of the Hungarian aristocracy. Hence the wealth of original names. Some sources give her real name as simply Francesca Mitzi Gerber.

Gayrati: Abdurakhim Abdullayev (1905–), Uzbek poet. The writer's adopted name means "energetic," "lively."

Eunice **Gayson**: Eunice Sargaison (1931–), Br. movie, stage actress.

Ibragim **Gazi**: Ibragim Zarifovich Mingazeyev (1907–1971), Russ. (Tatar) wrier.

Clara **Gazul**: Prosper Mérimée (1803–1870), Fr. novelist, historian. For the web of intrigue woven here, see the account on page 25.

Myles na **gCopaleen**: Brian O'Nolan (1912–1966), Ir. novelist. The name was used by the writer for many years for his contributions to the *Irish Times*. He took it from a character of this name, a comic vagabond, in Gerald Griffin's novel *The Collegians* (1829). Its literal meaning is "Myles of the ponies." He also wrote as Flann O'Brien (*q.v.*) and George Knowall.

George **Gé:** George Grönfeldt (1893–1962), Finnish ballet dancer, choreographer.

Ged: Gerard Melling (1934–), Sc. cartoonist.

Nicolai **Gedda:** Nicolai Ustinov (1925–), Swe. opera singer, of Russ.-Swe. parentage. The singer adopted his mother's maiden name.

Dustin **Gee:** Gerald Harrison (1942–1986), Eng. TV comedian, teaming with Les Dennis (*q.v.*).

Robbie **Gee:** Robert Grant (1970–), Br. black stage, TV actor.

Gee Bee: George Goodwin Butterworth (1905–1988), Eng. cartoonist, illustrator. The artist first used this name, representing his inititials, for sports cartoons published in the *Daily Dispatch* in the 1920s.

Will **Geer:** William Ghere (1902–1978), U.S. stage actor.

Otto **Gelsted:** Ejnar Jeppesen (1888–1968), Dan. poet.

Firmin **Gémier:** Firmin Tonnerre (1869–1933), Fr. stage actor, manager, director.

[Dame] Adeline **Genée:** Anina Margarete Kirstina Petra Jensen (1878–1970), Dan.-born Br. ballet dancer. The dancer adopted the stage name of her uncle, Alexander Genée, a ballet master and choreographer, while he chose her new first name for her, in honor of the singer Adelina Patti (1843–1919) (whose original first name was actually Adela).

Genêt: Janet Flanner (1892–1978), U.S. foreign correspondent, novelist, art critic. The name represents her first name, and was possibly influenced by that of the French dramatist and novelist Jean Genet (1910–1986).

Genghis Khan: Temujin (or Temuchin) (1162–1227), Mongol conqueror. The great fighter adopted the title Genghis (or Chingis), meaning "perfect warrior," in 1206, adding "Khan" to mean "lord," "prince."

Marcelle **Geniat:** Eugenie Martin (*c.*1879–1959), Russ.-born Fr. stage actress. A stage name loosely based on a reversal of the actress's original names.

Johnny **Gentle:** John Askew (1941–), Eng. pop singer. The singer was given his new name by the impresario Larry Parnes, who also named Billy Fury (*q.v.*), among others.

A **Gentleman of the University of Oxford:** Percy Bysshe Shelley (1792–1822), Eng. poet. Shelley used this name or title for his early "Gothic horror" verses, *St. Irvyne, or the Rosicrucian* (1811), published privately when he was a student at Oxford University.

A **Gentleman who has left his Lodgings:** [Lord] John Russell (1792–1878), Eng. poet. The earl adopted this *nom de plume* for his *Essays and Sketches of Life and Character* (1820). The preface of this work is signed "Joseph Skillet," this being the supposed lodging house keeper, who published the letters to pay the rent the "gentleman" had forgotten.

A **Gentleman with a Duster:** Harold Begbie (1871–1929), Eng. novelist, biographer, religious writer. The writer used this name for his analyses of political leaders, whom he aimed to "show up."

Bobbie **Gentry:** Roberta Lee Streeter (1944–), U.S. pop musician, of Port. descent. The singer took her stage name from the movie *Ruby Gentry* (1952), with Bobbie a pet form of her first name.

Mlle **George:** Marguerite-Joséphine Weymer (1787–1867), Fr. actress.

Ann **George:** Ann Snape (1903–1989), Eng. singer, TV actress. The actress adopted the first name of her first husband, George Snape, as her stage surname.

Chief Dan **George:** Geswanouth Slaholt (1899–1981), Can. Native American chief, movie actor.

Daniel **George:** Daniel George Bunting (1890–1967), Br. essayist, critic, anthologist.

Gladys **George:** Gladys Anna Clare (*c.*1900–1954), U.S. stage, movie actress.

Heinrich **George:** Heinrich Georg Schulz (1893–1946), Ger. stage, movie actor.

Jim **Gerald:** Jacques Guenod (1889–1958), Fr. stage, movie actor.

Geraldo: Gerald Walcan-Bright (1904–1974), Br. dance band leader. The musician added the "o" to his first name in 1930 on his return to London after a visit to Argentina and Brazil to study Latin-American music.

Steven **Geray:** Stefan Gyergyay (1899–1974), Hung. movie actor, working in U.K., U.S.

William **Gerhardie:** William Alexander Gerhardi (1895–1977), Russ.-born Eng. writer. The writer added an "e" to his name in the 1960s, saying that Dante, Shakespeare, Racine, Goethe, and Blake had "e's" so why not he? [*The Times*, July 16, 1977].

Karl **Germain:** Charles Mattmueller (1878–1959), U.S. magician, of Ger. parentage. The illusionist took his name from mysterious Comte de Saint-Germain (*c.*1707–1784), a French adventurer of unknown origin who was employed by

Louis XV as a diplomat on confidential missions and who made a special study of the occult.

[Sir] Edward **German**: Edward German Jones (1862–1936), Br. light opera composer. The composer dropped his surname, presumably for distinctiveness, some time in the 1880s, when a student at the Royal Academy of Music.

Geronimo: Goyathlay (1829–1909), Native American war leader. The chief of the Chiricahua Apache was given his familiar name by the Spanish, presumably as a phonetic approximation to his original name, which means "one who yawns." (Geronimo is actually an Italian equivalent of English Jerome.)

Gene **Gerrard**: Eugene Maurice O'Sullivan (1892–1971), Br. music hall comedian, movie actor.

Karen **Gershon**: Karen Tripp, née Loewenthal (1923–1993), Ger.-born Eng. poet, novelist. The poet was Jewish, and in 1938 was sent to England for her own safety by her parents, who subsequently perished in the Holocaust. Her new name expressed her feeling of alienation, and was the name given by Moses to a son born in Midian as a "stranger in a strange land" (Exodus 2:22).

George **Gershwin**: Jacob Gershvin (1898–1937), U.S. composer, of Russ. Jewish parentage.

Gérson: Gérson de Oliveira Nunes (1941–), Brazilian footballer.

John **Gerstad**: John Gjerstad (1924–), U.S. stage actor, producer, director, playwright.

Gertrude: Jane Cross Simpson, née Bell (1811–1886), Sc. poet, hymnwriter.

Estelle **Getty**: Estelle Scher (1923–), U.S. movie actress.

Stan **Getz**: Stanley Gayetzby (1927–1991), U.S. jazz saxophonist.

Tamara **Geva**: Tamara Gevergeyeva (1908–), Russ. ballet dancer, working in U.S. The ballerina was billed under the name Sheversheieva for her first London performance in 1924. In modern English terms her original Russian surname would be rendered Zheverzheyeva.

Michel de **Ghelderode**: Adémar Adolphe Louis Martens (1898–1962), Belg. dramatist, prose writer.

Henri **Ghéon**: Henri Léon Vangeon (1875–1944), Fr. playwright.

René **Ghil**: René-François Ghilbert (1862–1925), Fr. poet.

Domenico **Ghirlandaio**: Domenico di Tommaso Bigordi (1449–1494), It. painter. The painter's professional name pays tribute to his father's skill in making garlands (Italian *ghirlanda*).

Giacomino: Giacomo Cireni (1884–1956), It. circus artist, clown.

Lewis Grassic **Gibbon**: James Leslie Mitchell (1901–1935), Sc. novelist, short story writer. The writer adopted his pen name in the 1930s for his specifically Scottish tales, keeping his real name for scientific and historical works.

Georgia **Gibbs**: Freda Gibbons (1920–), U.S. pop singer.

Henry Gibbs: Henry St. John Clair Rumbold-Gibbs (1910–1975), Br. spy novelist.

Joe **Gibbs**: Joel Gibson (1945–), Jamaican reggae musician.

Mike **Gibbs**: Michael Clement Irving (1937–), S.A.-born composer, bandleader, working in U.S.

Terry **Gibbs**: Julius Gubenko (1924–), U.S. drummer, vibraphone player.

Chloë **Gibson**: Chloë Cawdle (1899–), Eng. stage director.

Harry **Gibson**: Harry Raab (1914–1991), U.S. jazz musician ("The Hipster").

Madeline **Gibson**: Madeline Stride (1909–), Br. stage actress.

Tim **Gidal**: Nahum Ignaz Gidalewitsch (1909–1996), Israeli photographer, of Russ. Jewish parentage.

Charles Lewis **Giesecke**: Johann Georg Metzler (1761–1833), Ger. mineralogist, working in Ireland. The mineralogist began his career as a composer and librettist, changing his name to Karl Ludwig Giesecke in 1781. He later settled in Ireland and anglicized his first two names.

John **Gifford**: (1) John Richards Green (1758–1818), Eng. writer; (2) Edward Foss (1787–1870), Eng. jurist, biographer. Green took his new name in 1781 on fleeing to France to escape his creditors. He retained it for all his writings, including an abridgment of William Blackstone's *Commentaries on the Laws of England* (1765–70), which he did not live to complete. Foss took over the work and published his own abridgement under the same name in 1820. Green also wrote as Humphrey Hedgehog.

Theo **Gift**: Theodora Boulger, née Havers (1847–1923), Eng. writer of children's stories, fantasy fiction. The writer's pen name is a half-translation of her first name Theodora, as this means "God's gift."

Marnix **Gijsen:** Johannes Alphonsius Goris (1899–), Belg. (Flemish) writer.

Gilberto **Gil:** Gilberto Passos Gil Moreira (1942–), Brazilian popular musician.

Anthony **Gilbert:** Lucy Beatrice Malleson (1899–1973), Eng. writer of detective novels, short stories.

Jean **Gilbert:** Max Winterfield (1879–1942), Ger. operetta composer.

John **Gilbert:** (1) John Gibbs (1810–1889), U.S. actor; (2) John Pringle (1895–1936), U.S. movie actor. Pringle adopted his stepfather's name, Gilbert, as his screen name.

Lou **Gilbert:** Lou Gitlitz (1909–), U.S. stage actor.

Paul **Gilbert:** Paul MacMahon (1917–1976), U.S. movie comedian, dancer.

Gilbert and George: Gilbert Proesch (1943–), It.-born Br. painter, performance artist + George Passmore (1942–), Br. painter, performance artist.

Gilderoy: Patrick Macgregor (? –1638), Sc. robber, cattlestealer. The criminal's assumed name was perhaps ironically taken by him on the understanding that it meant "servant of the king," as if from Gaelic *gille*, "lad," "servant," and French *du roy*, "of the king." It actually represents Gaelic *gille ruadh*, "ruddy-faced (or red-haired) fellow." He was hanged in the year stated, thus giving the expression "to be hung higher than Gilderoy's kite," meaning "to be punished more severely than the worst criminal." The gallows outside Edinburgh where Gilderoy met his fate were 30 feet high.

Giles: Carl Ronald Giles (1916–1995), Br. cartoonist.

Jack **Gilford:** Jacob Gellman (1907–1990), U.S. movie comedian.

André **Gill:** Louis-André Gosset (1840–1885), Fr. caricaturist.

Mildred **Gillars:** Mildred Elizabeth Sisk (1900–1988), U.S. Nazi radio propagandist ("Axis Sally").

Daniel **Gillès:** Daniel Gillès de Pelichy (1917–1981), Belg. writer.

Geneviève **Gilles:** Geneviève Gillaizeau (1946–), Fr. movie actress.

Ann **Gillis:** Alma O'Connor (1927–), U.S. child movie actress.

Werner **Gillon:** Werner Goldman (1905–1996), Ger.-born Br. art historian, of Jewish parentage.

John **Gilmore:** Willi Hirsch (1908–*c.*1961), Ger.-born Russ. spy, working in U.S. The future Soviet agent adopted this name in 1932 on marrying an American, Dorothy Baker, in Philadelphia. When sent to Moscow as art editor of the magazine *Soviet Russia Today* in 1936 he traveled with a false passport in the name of Sidney Joseph Chamberlain.

Virginia **Gilmore:** Sherman Virginia Poole (1919–1986), U.S. movie actress, of Br. parentage.

Barbara **Gilson:** Charles Gibson (1878–1943), Eng. soldier, writer of children's stories.

Maria **Ginanni:** Maria Crisi (1892–1953), It. poet, novelist, playwright. The writer took her pen name from that of her husband, the futurist painter Arnaldo Ginna (originally Arnaldo Ginanni-Corradini).

Giorgione: Giorgio Barbarelli (da Castelfranco) (1477–1510), It. painter. The painter's name, with its Italian "augmentative" suffix, means "big Giorgio." As Giorgio Vasari's *Lives of the Artists* (1550) notes: "Because of his physical appearance and his moral and intellectual stature he later came to be known as Giorgione."

Albert **Giraud:** Marie Emile Albert Kayenbergh (1860–1929), Belg. poet, playwright, critic.

Girodet-Trioson: Anne-Louis Girodet de Roucy (1767–1824), Fr. painter, illustrator. The artist adopted a name that was a combination of his own surname and that of a benefactor, one Dr. Trioson.

Dorothy **Gish:** Dorothy de Guiche (1898–1968), U.S. movie actress, sister of Lillian Gish (see below).

Lillian **Gish:** Lillian de Guiche (1899–1993), U.S. movie, stage actress, sister of Dorothy Gish (see above).

Gertie **Gitana:** Gertrude Mary Ross, née Astbury (1889–1957), Br. music hall singer. The singer derived her second name from the Spanish for "gypsy," referring both to her appearance (small, dark-haired, with ringlets) and to the pierrot costume she wore in her act. She was already performing as Little Gitana at the age of five. At about the age of 15 she substituted "Gertie" for "Little," and became established under this name.

Gizziello: Gioacchino Conti (1714–1761), It. male soprano singer. The singer took his name from that of his teacher, Domenico Gizzi.

Ksaver Sandor **Gjalski:** Ljubomir Babić (1854–1935), Croatian writer.

Glanffrwd: William Thomas (1843–1890), Welsh local historian. The scholar adopted a placename meaning literally "bank of the stream."

Henricus **Glareanus:** Heinrich Loris (1488–1563), Swiss Humanist, poet, musician. The scholar took his Latin name from his native canton of Glarus.

John **Glashan:** John McGlashan (1931–), Sc.-born Br. cartoonist, writer, painter. The artist began his career as a portrait painter, but finding work hard to come by dropped the "Mc" from his name and became a more financially rewarding cartoonist and illustrator.

Glasynys: Owen Wynne Jones (1828–1870), Welsh historian, writer. The writer adopted a placename meaning "green island" as his pen name.

Joanna **Gleason:** Joanna Hall (1950–), Can. movie actress.

Gleb **Glebov:** Gleb Pavlovich Sorokin (1899–1967), Belorussian stage actor.

Igor **Glebov:** Boris Vladimirovich Asafyev (1884–1949), Russ. composer, musicologist. The composer used his pseudonym for musical criticism.

Gary **Glitter:** Paul Francis Gadd (1944–), Eng. pop singer. According to some accounts, the singer's performing name originated as a nickname (no doubt with "Gary" deriving from his surname). Paul Gadd began his recording career as Paul Raven, probably referring to his thick, black hair. In the late 1960s, he toured clubs in Frankfurt and Hamburg, Germany, under the name of Paul Monday. After considering other alliterative names such as Turk Thrust, Terry Tinsel, Stanley Sparkle, Horace Hydrogen, and Vicky Vomit, he and his writer/producer Mike Leander (*q.v.*) settled on "Gary Glitter" in 1971.

Gluck: Hannah Gluckstein (1895–1978), U.S.-born Br. artist.

Alma **Gluck:** Reba Fiersohn (1884–1938), Rom.-born U.S. opera singer. The soprano adopted her first husband's surname.

Angela **Glynne:** Angela West (1933–), Br. stage actress. The actress took her mother's maiden name as her stage name.

Mary **Glynne:** Mary Aitken (1898–1954), Welsh-born Br. stage actress.

Tito **Gobbi:** Tito Weiss (1913–1984), It. opera singer.

Paulette **Goddard:** Pauline Marion Levy (or Levee) (1905–1990), U.S. movie actress. The actress adopted her divorced mother's maiden name as her screen name.

John **Godey:** Morton Freedgood (1912–), U.S. crime, mystery writer.

Charles **Godfrey:** Paul Lacey (1851–1900), Eng. music hall artist.

Hal **Godfrey:** Charlotte O'Conor Eccles (? –1911), Ir. journalist, novelist. The writer used this male name for her amusing novel *The Rejuvenation of Miss Semaphore* (1897).

Gog: Gordon Hogg (1912–1973), Eng. cartoonist. The artist was also racing and sports cartoonist on the *Sun*, for which he used the name Gay Gordon.

Y **Gohebydd:** John Griffith (1821–1877), Welsh journalist. The writer became the London correspondent of the Welsh newspaper *Baner Cymru* ("Banner of Wales"). Hence his byline, meaning "the correspondent."

Ziya **Gökalp:** Mehmed Ziya (1876–1924), Turk. sociologist, writer.

Michael **Gold:** Itzok Isaac Granich (1894–1967), U.S. socialist writer, critic, of Rom.-Hung. Jewish parentage.

Whoopi **Goldberg:** Caryn E. Johnson (1949–), U.S. black movie actress, comedienne. A possibly apocryphal story tells how movie colleagues nicknamed the actress Whoopi Cushion because of her problems with flatulence. She herself claims that she took her new name when "a burning bush with a Yiddish accent" suggested that her real name was boring and that she should change it [Blackwell, p. 217]. Her new surname is actually that of her first husband.

Horace **Goldin:** Hyman Goldstein (1873–1939), Pol.-born U.S. magician.

Peter **Goldsmith:** John Boynton Priestley (1894–1984), Eng. novelist, essayist, dramatist + George Billam (–), Eng. writer. Priestley used this name used for his jointly authored play *Spring Tide* (1936).

Horace **Goldwin:** Hyman Goldstein (1873–1939), Polish-born U.S. illusionist.

Samuel **Goldwyn:** Shmuel Gelbfisz (1882–1974), U.S. movie producer, of Pol. Jewish parentage. When the future producer came to England in the 1890s, he anglicized his name as Samuel Goldfish. In 1916, he and his two brothers Edgar and Arch Selwyn formed the Goldwyn Pictures Corporation, its name formed from the two elements of *Gold*fish and Sel*wyn*. He himself then adopted this name. (The other way round he would have been "Samuel Selfish.") In 1918 he officially adopted the name Samuel Goldwyn [A. Scott Berg, *Goldwyn: A Biography*, 1989]. (See also the relevant "Question of Assumed Names Passed On In Goldwyn Suit" in *Variety*, October 25, 1923, p. 19.)

Mikhail **Golodny:** Mikhail Semyonovich Epshteyn (Epstein) (1903–1949), Russ. poet. The writer's new name means "hungry," relating to the period in which he lived.

Gomer: Joseph Harris (1773–1825), Welsh writer. The Baptist minister's bardic name came from the chapel where he preached, Capel Gomer, Swansea. The name is biblical, as that of one of the grandsons of Noah (Genesis 10:2).

Agapy **Goncharenko:** Andrey Onufriyevich Gumnitsky (1832–1916), Ukrainian writer, working in U.S.

Babs **Gonzales:** Lee Brown (1919–1980), U.S. popular singer.

Lemmie B. **Good:** Limmie Snell (*c.*1945–), U.S. pop singer. This plainly punning name should be compared to the next name below.

Will B. **Good:** Rosco ("Fatty") Arbuckle (1887–1933), U.S. comic movie actor, comedy director. This is the pseudonym that Arbuckle adopted when he attempted to become a film director on resuming work in the cinema after a ban of 11 years resulting from a scandal in 1921 (in which a model, Virginia Rappe, was raped and died at a party). Arbuckle was eventually cleared by the jury, but his reputation was ruined, and his subsequent career never recovered its former success.

Louis **Goodrich:** Louis Abbot-Anderson (*c.*1873–1945), Eng. stage, movie actor, brother of Allan Aynesworth (*q.v.*).

Goodwin: Robert Frederick Goodwin Churchill (1910–), Eng. cartoonist, illustrator.

Julie **Goodyear:** Julie Kemp (1942–), Eng. TV actress.

Ivan **Gorbunov-Posadov:** Ivan Ivanovich Gorbunov (1864–1940), Russ. writer, publisher. The writer was born in the *posad* (suburb) of Kolpino, near St. Petersburg, and added a name based on this word to his surname.

C. Henry **Gordon:** Henry Racke (1883–1940), U.S. movie actor.

Gale **Gordon:** Gaylord Aldrich (1906–1995), U.S. TV actor.

Janet **Gordon:** Cecil Blanche Woodham-Smith, née Fitzgerald (1896–1977), Welsh novelist, historian.

Leon **Gordon:** Leon Lilly (1884–1960), Eng. stage actor, playwright.

Mack **Gordon:** Morris Gittler (1904–1959), Polish-born U.S. songwriter.

Marjorie **Gordon:** Marjorie Kettlewell (1893–?), Br. stage actress, singer. The actress adopted her mother's maiden name as her stage name.

Mary **Gordon:** Mary Gilmour (1882–1963), Sc. movie actress, working in U.S.

Max **Gordon:** (1) Mechel Salpeter (1892–1978), U.S. theatre manager, producer; (2) Morris Gittler (1904–1959), U.S. lyricist.

Neil **Gordon:** Archibald Gordon Macdonell (1895–1941), Sc. writer.

Rex **Gordon:** Stanley Bennett Hough (1917–), Br. SF writer.

Richard **Gordon:** Gordon Ostlere (1921–), Br. novelist.

Robert **Gordon:** Robert Gordon Duncan (1895–1971), U.S. movie actor.

Ruth **Gordon:** Ruth Gordon Jones (1896–1985), U.S. stage, movie actress, screenwriter.

Gorgeous George: George Raymond Wagner (1915–1963), U.S. wrestler.

Arshile **Gorky:** Vasdanig Manoog Adoian (1904–1948), Armenian-born U.S. Surrealist painter. The artist's adopted first name represents that of the Greek mythological hero Achilles. His second name pays tribute to the Russian writer Maxim Gorky (see below), to whom he sometimes claimed to be related.

Maxim **Gorky:** Aleksey Maksimovich Peshkov (1868–1936), Russ. writer. Early in his career, the writer identified with ordinary Russians, and for some time lived "among the people," sharing their poverty and hardship. He first used the name for his story *Makar Chudra* (1892), which he submitted to a local newspaper in Tiflis (Tbilisi), Georgia: "A journalist asked him what name he wanted to use for his first published piece of writing. Alexey hesitated; his real name, Peshkov, suggested the idea of abasement and humility to him, since the Russian word *peshka* means 'pawn.' ... He remembered that because of his 'sharp tongue' his father had been nicknamed Bitter, *gorky* in Russian. That would be a wonderful pseudonym for a young writer rebelling against society. So he chose Gorky, 'Bitter,' as his last name, and Maxim as his first" [Henri Troyat, translated by

Lowell Blair, *Gorky: A Biography*, 1986]. The name had in fact been used by writers before him, such as the poet I.A. Belousov (1863–1930).

Eydie **Gorme:** Edith Gormenzano (1932–), U.S. popular singer.

Jay **Gorney:** Daniel Jason Gornetzky (1896–1990), Russ.-born U.S. popular composer.

Goronva Camlann: Rowland Williams (1817–1870), Welsh-born Br. theologian, poet. The writer's adopted first name is now more familiar as Goronwy. (Compare the next name below.) His surname is a local placename.

Goronwy Ddu o Fôn: Goronwy Owen (1723–1769), Welsh poet. The poet's bardic name means "Black Goronwy of Anglesey," the latter being the island where he was born. The name itself was probably adopted from that of the 14th-century poet Gronw Ddu o Fôn, especially as Owen's father was Owen Gronw.

Rita **Gorr:** Marguerite Geirnaert (1926–), Belg. opera singer.

Tobio **Gorria:** Arrigo Boito (1842–1918), It. composer, librettist. A name that is both an anagram and a reversal of the two original names. "Tobio" suggests Italian *Tobia* "Toby," and the composer could have devised a name to incorporate this genuine first name. Why not "Tobia Gorrio," for example?

Sirak **Goryan:** William Saroyan (1908–1981), U.S. novelist, short story writer, of Armenian parentage.

Jeremias **Gotthelf:** Albert Bitzius (1797–1854), Swiss novelist, short story writer. The writer was a pastor professionally, with strong Christian principles. He thus changed his name in order to express his convictions, with "Jeremias" for the Old Testament prophet (whose own name means "God raise up") and "Gotthelf" as the German for "God's help."

Bernard **Gould:** [Sir] Bernard Partridge (1861–1945), Br. actor, cartoonist.

Elliott **Gould:** Elliott Goldstein (1938–), U.S. stage, movie actor. The actor was given this simpler version of his name by his mother.

Robert **Goulet:** Stanley Applebaum (1933–), Can. singer, movie, TV actor.

La **Goulue:** Louise Weber (or Wébert) (1860–1919), Fr. cancan dancer. The name means "the greedy one." The dancer was the subject of Toulouse-Lautrec's first poster, *Moulin-Rouge: La Goulue* (1891), which brought him much acclaim.

[Lama Anagarika] **Govinda:** Ernst Lother Hoffman (1898–1985), Ger.-born Buddhist leader, working in India. Precise details of the Buddhist proselytizer's life are uncertain, but he adopted his new name around 1928, when he moved from Capri, where he had gone to live after World War I, to Ceylon (modern Sri Lanka). Govinda, a Sanskrit name meaning literally "(one good at) finding cows," is an epithet of the Hindu god Krishna. Govinda was strongly influenced by Tibetan Buddhism. Hence his title of lama (monk, priest). Anagarika is the title of a celibate, fulltime worker for Buddhism.

Julien **Gracq:** Louis Poirier (1910–), Fr. novelist, essayist.

[Baron] Lew **Grade:** Louis Winogradsky (1906–), Russ.-born Br. TV executive, brother of Bernard Delfont (*q.v.*). The show business personality changed his name in the 1920s, when he entered dancing competitions in London at the height of the Charleston craze. He won several prizes, and became an increasingly popular attraction. Soon realizing that his original name was "too much of a mouthful," he shortened it to "Louis Grad." Subsequently, he became a professional dancer, and went on to perform at the Moulin Rouge, Paris. "A few days before my opening night, a big article appeared about me in the *Paris Midi* newspaper. It was great publicity, but the writer had spelt my name incorrectly. Instead of Louis Grad it came out as Lew Grade. I liked the look and sound of it—and Lew Grade it has been ever since" [Lew Grade, *Still Dancing*, 1987].

Bruce **Graeme:** Graham Montague Jeffries (1900–1982), Eng. crime, mystery writer.

Joyce **Graeme:** Joyce Platt (1918–1991), Br. ballet dancer.

Roderic **Graeme:** Roderic Graeme Jeffries (1926–), Eng. crime, mystery writer.

Bill **Graham:** Wolfgang Woldia Grajonca (1931–1991), Ger.-born U.S. rock music promoter, of Russ. Jewish parentage.

Ennis **Graham:** Mary Louise Molesworth, née Stewart (1839–1921), Br. novelist, children's writer, of Sc. parentage. The writer took her pen name from a (female) friend for her seventh book, *The Cuckoo Clock* (1877). During her lifetime her books were published as simply by "Mrs. Molesworth."

Sheilah **Graham:** Lily Sheil (1904–1988), Eng. writer, biographer. The English writer and companion (1937–40) to Scott Fitzgerald married

Major John Graham Gillam in the 1930s and went to Hollywood, where she became a gossip columnist. She once said, "The name Lily Sheil, to this day, horrifies me to a degree impossible to explain." Her new name was presumably based on her original surname and her husband's middle name.

Virginia **Graham:** Virginia Komiss (1912–), U.S. TV personality, actress.

Gloria **Grahame:** Gloria Grahame Hallward (1924–1981), U.S. stage, movie actress.

Corney **Grain:** Richard Corney (1844–1895), Br. entertainer, writer, composer. A name that probably originated as a (corny) nickname.

Otis **Grand:** Fred Bishti (1950–), Lebanese blues guitarist, working in U.S.

Sarah **Grand:** Frances Elizabeth McFall, née Clarke (1854–1943), Ir. novelist. Having initially published anonymously, the writer first used her pseudonym for her second novel, *The Heavenly Twins* (1893), claiming the name was "simple, short and emphatic—not easily forgotten."

Grandmaster Flash: Joseph Saddler (1957–), U.S. rock singer, rapper.

D.St. **Grandmixer:** Derek Howells (1960), U.S. black hip hop musician, scratch DJ. His first name represents the abbreviation of Delancey Street, New York, where he added to his collection of fashion wear. His last name alludes to his talent as a DJ.

Grandville: Jean-Ignace-Isidore Gérard (1803–1847), Fr. illustrator, caricaturist.

Stewart **Granger:** James Lablache Stewart (1913–1993), Eng.-born U.S. movie actor. The actor changed his name in the late 1930s to avoid confusion with the U.S. movie actor James Stewart (1908–1997). As a British actor, he was anyway governed by the rules of Equity, the actors' union, which states that no two actors can have the same name. Granger became a U.S. citizen in 1956.

Daniil **Granin:** Daniil Aleksandrovich German (1919–), Russ. novelist, short story writer.

Albert **Grant:** Abraham Gottheimer (1831–1899), Br. company promoter, of Ger. Jewish parentage.

Cary **Grant:** Alexander Archibald Leach (1904–1986), Eng. movie actor, working in U.S. The actor has explained how he came by his name: "I changed my name at the behest of the studio. They said Archie Leach had to go. John Monk Saunders, a friend and the author of *Nikki*, a play I'd done in New York, suggested I

take the name of the character I played in the show: Cary Lockwood. Well, Cary was all right, but Lockwood wasn't; there was already an actor named Harold Lockwood under contract to the studio. What went with 'Cary'? It was an age of short names—Gable, Brent, Cooper ... A secretary came with a list and put it in front of me. 'Grant' jumped out at me, and that was that" [Nancy Nelson, *Cary Grant*, 1991].

Gogi **Grant:** Myrtle Audrey Arinsberg (1924–), U.S. pop singer. The singer's name is said to come from a New York restaurant called Gogi La Rue. She first used the names Audrey Brown and Audrey Grant.

Jan **Grant:** Jan Jēkabson (1909–1970), Latvian novelist, short story writer.

Joan **Grant:** Joan Kelsey, née Marshall (1907–), Eng. novelist. The writer adopted the name of her first husband, Arthur Leslie Grant.

Kathryn (or Kathy) **Grant:** Olive Kathryn Grandstaff (1933–), U.S. movie actress.

Kirby **Grant:** Kirby Grant Horn (1911–1985), U.S. movie actor, of Du.-Sc. parentage.

Lee **Grant:** Lyova Haskell Rosenthal (1927–), U.S. stage, movie actress.

Peter **Graves:** Peter Aurness (1925–), U.S. movie actor, brother of James Arness (*q.v.*).

Fernand **Gravet:** (or Gravey): Fernand Martens (1904–1970), Belg.-born Fr. movie actor, working in U.S.

Gray: Gray Jolliffe (1937–), Eng. cartoonist, illustrator.

Arvella **Gray:** Walter Dixon (1906–1980), U.S. blues guitarist.

Barry **Gray:** Robert Barry Coffin (1826–1886), U.S. journalist, poet, writer.

Colleen **Gray:** Doris Jensen (1922–), U.S. movie actress, of Dan. descent.

Dobie **Gray:** Leonard Victor Ainsworth (1942–), U.S. soul singer.

Donald **Gray:** Eldred Tidbury (1914–1979), Eng. movie, TV actor.

Dulcie **Gray:** Dulcie Winifred Catherine Denison, née Bailey (1919–), Eng. stage, movie actress, novelist. The actress has described how she came by her stage name: "I ... had to change my name from Bailey as there was another Dulcie Bailey on the stage. ... I found it hard to think of a good name. At one time I decided to call myself Angela Botibol—every tube [subway] station in London had an Angel Botibol tobacconist's kiosk and I thought at least the critics wouldn't for better or worse be able to overlook me. But I eventually took my mother's maiden name of Gray" [Dulcie Gray, *Looking Forward—Looking Back*, 1991].

E. Conder **Gray**: Alexander Hay Japp (1837–1905), Sc. author, publisher. The writer used several pseudonyms, of which the best known was probably H.A. Page (*q.v.*). E. Conder Gray appears to be a fanciful reworking of "Alexander Hay."

Eileen **Gray**: Kathleen Eileen Moray Smith (1879–1976), Ir. designer, architect. The designer's mother inherited the title of Baroness Gray in 1895, and in 1897 her father changed his name by royal licence to Smith-Gray. From that time on, when Eileen was 18, all the children took the surname Gray.

Elizabeth Janet **Gray**: Elizabeth Gray Vining (1902–), U.S. children's writer.

Ellington **Gray**: Naomi Ellington Jacob (1884–1964), Eng. actress, popular novelist. The writer's mother, Nina Ellington, née Collinson, wrote novels as Nina Abbott.

George Kruger **Gray**: George Edward Kruger (1880–1943), Br. designer. The artist added Gray to his surname on his marriage in 1918 to Audrey Gordon Gray.

Gilda **Gray**: Marianna Michalska (1901–1959), Pol. dancer, movie actress, working in U.S.

Glen **Gray**: Glen Gray Knoblaugh (1906–1963), U.S. swing musician.

Jennifer **Gray**: Jennifer Skinner (1916–1962), Br. stage actress.

Jerry **Gray**: Jerry Graziano (1915–1976), U.S. popular musician, bandleader.

Linda **Gray**: Linda Baxter (1910–), Eng. stage actress, singer. The actress took her mother's maiden name as her stage name.

Mary **Gray**: Elizabeth Stuart Ward, née Phelps (1844–1911), U.S. novelist, daughter of novelist Elizabeth Wooster Phelps (1815–1852).

Maxwell **Gray**: Mary Gleed Tuttiet (1847–1923), Eng. novelist. The letters of "Gray" occur in the writer's first and middle names.

Michael **Gray**: Michael Grealis (1947–), Eng. TV reporter.

Nadia **Gray**: Nadia Kujnir-Herescu (1923–1994), Russ.-Rom. movie actress.

Sally **Gray**: Constance Vera Stevens (1916–), Br. movie actress.

Simon **Gray**: [Sir] Alexander Boswell (1775–1822), Eng. antiquary, poet.

David **Grayson**: Ray Stannard Baker (1870–1940), U.S. essayist. The writer is said to have chosen this name when he remembered having heard it "once when I was in the South" [Marble, p. 94].

Diane **Grayson**: Diane Guinibert (1948–), Flemish-born Eng. stage, movie, TV dancer, actress.

Kathryn **Grayson**: Zelma Kathryn Elizabeth Hedrick (1922–), U.S. movie actress, singer.

Larry **Grayson**: William White (1923–1995), Eng. TV entertainer, compère. The entertainer, an illegitimate child, first started acting in the music hall at the age of 14 under the name of Billy Breen. In 1956 he was spotted by agent Evelyn Taylor at London's Nuffield Centre. She signed him up, and began looking for a new name for him. "We sat there for ages going through different names. First we settled on Larry. And at the time there was a very popular Hollywood singing star Kathryn Grayson. 'That's it,' said Eve, 'Larry Grayson—write it down.' He did, liked it and has written it many thousands of times on autograph books since" [*TV Times*, August 20–26, 1983]. "Grayson" in itself suggests a kinship with "White." For the actress mentioned, see the entry above.

Rocky **Graziano**: Thomas Rocco Barbella (1919 or 1922–1990), U.S. middleweight boxer, TV actor. The boxer adopted the name of an earlier fighter in order to avoid detection when an army deserter in 1942. He quipped: "But I later found that that the original Rocky Graziano had a bigger police record than me." It was Graziano who popularized the name Rocky for boxers, and who was the model for the Rocky movies starring Sylvester Stallone.

The **Great Carmo**: Harry Cameron (1881–1944), Austral.-born Br. magician. "Carmo" is obviously extracted from "Cameron."

The **Great Lafayette**: Sigmund Neuberger (1871–1911), Ger.-born U.S. magician, working in U.K. The illusionist's early stage acts were rehearsed and produced along military lines. Hence his name, from the Marquis de Lafayette (1757–1834), the French statesman and soldier who fought against Britain in the American Revolution. He adopted the name legally by deed poll and always signed his initials "T.G.L."

The **Great Lester**: Marian Czajkowski (*c.*1880–1956), Pol.-born U.S. ventriloquist. The performer also used the fuller name Harry Lester.

The **Great Macdermott:** Gilbert Hastings Farrell (1845–1901), Br. music hall artist.

The **Great Nicola:** William Mozart Nicol (1880–1946), U.S. illusionist.

The **Great Soprendo:** Geoffrey Durham (c.1950–), Br. magician. The magician produced surprises, as his name indicates (Spanish *sorprendo*, "I surprise"). Durham studied Spanish at university and his act was as a Spaniard. He retired in 1989.

Harry **Greb:** Edward Henry Berg (1894–1926), U.S. boxer ("The Human Windmill"). A simple surname reversal here.

El **Greco:** Domenikos Theotokopoulos (1541–1614), Gr.-born Sp. painter, sculptor, architect. The name is Spanish for "the Greek." The artist usually signed his paintings with his full Greek name, however. He seems to have gained his nickname when originally working in Venice, with "El" either adopted directly from the Spanish or as a Venetian dialect form of Italian *Il*. He was first in Spain in 1577.

Harry **Green:** Henry Blitzer (1892–1958), U.S. stage, movie comedian.

Henry **Green:** Henry Vincent Yorke (1905–1973), Br. novelist.

Joseph **Green:** Joseph Greenberg (1900–1996), Pol.-born Yiddish movie director, working in U.S.

Martyn **Green:** William Martyn-Green (1899–1975), Eng. light opera singer, stage actor, working in U.S.

Mitzi **Green:** Elizabeth Keno (1920–1969), U.S. child movie actress. The actress adopted her mother's maiden name as her stage name.

Peter **Green:** Peter Greenbaum (1946–), Br. pop musician.

Max **Greene:** Mutz Greenbaum (1896–1968), Ger. cinematographer, working in U.K.

Shecky **Greene:** Fred Sheldon Greenfield (1925–), U.S. TV comedian.

Grace **Greenwood:** Sara Jane Lippincott, née Clarke (1823–1904), U.S. poet, journalist.

Richard **Greenwood:** Richard Peirse-Duncomb (c.1955–), Welsh-born Br. TV actor.

[Sir] Ben **Greet:** Philip Barling Greet (1857–1936), Br. stage actor, theatre manager. The actor first appeared on the stage in 1879 as Philip Ben, the nickname "Benjamin" having been given to him as the youngest of eight children. He later adopted the name Ben in place of his original first names.

Gregory V: Bruno (di Carinzia) (972–999), Ger.-born It. pope. The first German pope adopted the name of St. Gregory the Great (c.540–604), whom he regarded as his exemplar.

Gregory VI: Giovanni Graziano (Johannes Gratianus) (? – ? 1048), It. pope. This Gregory is said to have been given his name by popular acclaim, presumably in honor of St. Gregory the Great (c.540–604).

[St.] **Gregory VII:** Hildebrand (c.1020–1085), It. pope. The pontiff took his name in honor of St. Gregory the Great (c.540–604).

Gregory VIII: Alberto de Morra (? 1110–1187), It. pope.

Gregory IX: Ugo (or Ugolino) (dei Conti di Segni) (c.1155–1241), It. pope.

Gregory X: Tedaldo (or Tebaldo) Visconti (c.1210–1276), It. pope.

Gregory XI: Pierre Roger de Beaufort (1329–1378), Fr. pope.

Gregory XII: Angelo Correr (c.1325–1417), It. pope.

Gregory XIII: Ugo Buoncompagni (1502–1585), It. pope. It was this Gregory that gave the name of the Gregorian calendar, instituted by him.

Gregory XIV: Niccolò Sfondrati (1535–1591), It. pope. The pontiff took the name of his patron, Gregory XIII (above), who had created him cardinal in 1583.

Gregory XV: Alessandro Ludovisi (1554–1623), It. pope.

Gregory XVI: Bartolomeo Alberto Cappellari (1765–1846), It. pope. The future pontiff took the name Mauro, for one of the early saints so called, on becoming a Benedictine monk at the age of 18. In 1805 he became abbot of San Gregorio al Celio, and may have taken his papal name from this.

Frederick **Gregory:** Fritz Gugenheim (1893–1961), Br. plant physiologist, of Ger. Jewish origin. The scientist was exempted from military service in World War I on medical grounds, and began his plant studies then at an experimental station. He was subjected to abuse because of his German name—"Fritz" was a common derogatory nickname for Germans at this time—and his experimental records were sabotaged. The experience led him to change his name by deed poll in 1916.

Paul **Gregory:** Jason Lenhart (? 1905–), U.S. impresario, movie producer.

Simon **Gregson:** Simon Alan Gregory (1974–), Br. TV actor. The actor originally played under his real name, but changed his surname to Gregson in 1991 to avoid confusion with another actor named Simon Gregory.

Martin **Greif:** Friedrich Hermann Frey (1839–1911), Ger. lyric poet.

Maysie **Greig:** Maysie Sopoushek, née Greig-Smith (1901–1971), Austral. novelist.

Anna **Greki:** Colette Anna Melki, née Grégoire (1931–1966), Algerian poet.

I. **Grekova:** Yelena Sergeyevna Ventsel (Wenzel) (1907–), Russ. mathematician, writer. The mathematician used this name as a fiction writer, basing it on Russian *igrek* (itself from French), mathematical *y*, as she was an "unknown quantity" in this capacity.

Gren: Grenfell Jones (1934–), Welsh cartoonist, illustrator.

Stephen **Grendon:** August William Derleth (1909–1971), U.S. writer of horror fiction.

Madame **Grès:** Germaine Émilie Krebs (1903–1993), Fr. fashion designer. Grès was originally a signature name used by the designer's husband, the Russian artist Serge Czerefkov, who formed it from his first name.

Henry **Gréville:** Alice Durand, née Fleury (1842–1902), Fr. novelist.

Leo **Grex:** Leonard Reginald Gribble (1908–1985), Eng. crime, western novelist. Other names used by the writer were Sterry Browning, Lee Denver, Landon Grant, Louis Grey, and Dexter Muir. Some of these vaguely relate to his original name.

Anne **Grey:** Aileen Ewing (1907–), Br. movie actress.

Beryl **Grey:** Beryl Svenson, née Groom (1927–), Br. ballet dancer, artistic director. When Beryl Groom was beginning her dancing career at the age of 14, Ninette de Valois (*q.v.*) suggested this new name for her. "I called her Beryl Grey because there was an easy flow to it. If she had remained Groom people would have called her Broom or something. It's not a ballet name." Dame Ninette also suggested "Iris Grey," but Beryl resisted this. It took her about twenty years to get used to her new name [David Gillard, *Beryl Grey: a Biography*, 1977].

Denise **Grey:** Edouardine Verthiey (1896–1996), Fr. stage, movie actress.

Joel **Grey:** Joel Katz (1932–), U.S. stage actor. The actor's father formed a group called Mickey Katz and His Kittens. When the father changed this name to Mickey Kats and His Kosher Jammers, Joel Katz went on the stage alone as Joel Kaye, later changing this to Joel Grey [*The Times*, May 15, 1976]. The actress Jennifer Grey (1960–) is Joel's daughter.

Katherine **Grey:** Katherine Best (1873–1950), U.S. stage actress.

Lita **Grey:** Lillita MacMurray (1908–), U.S. juvenile movie actress.

Mary **Grey:** Ada Bevan ap Rees Bryant (1878–1974), Welsh stage actress.

Nan **Grey:** Eschal Loleet Grey Miller (1918–1993), U.S. movie actress, wife of Frankie Laine (*q.v.*).

Zane **Grey:** Pearl Zane Gray (1875–1939), U.S. novelist, writer of Westerns. The writer grew up in Zanesville, Ohio, founded in 1797 by his great-grandfather, Colonel Ebenezer Zane, and this gave his first name (originally middle name). He was usually known as "Pearl," a name then found for men as well as women, but dropped this when he overheard two young women on a train discussing his work and referring to him as "she." At the same time he modified the spelling of his last name from Gray to Grey [Jane Tompkins, Introduction to Penguin edition of *Riders of the Purple Sage*, 1990].

Grey Owl: Archibald Stansfeld Belaney (1888–1938), Eng.-born Can. writer. The writer is best known for his autobiography, *Pilgrims of the Wild* (1935). He himself was the son of an English father who had married, in the U.S., a woman said by him to be of Native American descent. His pen name, which he took in 1920 when he was adopted as a blood brother by the Ojibwa, was that of a Native American chief, and was an English equivalent of the original, Wa-sha-quon-asin.

R.E.H. **Greyson:** Henry Rogers (1806–1877), Eng. reviewer, Christian apologist. The writer's pen name is an anagram of his real name. He used it for two volumes of imaginary letters, *Selections from the Correspondence of R.E.H. Greyson, Esq.* (1857).

Gabbler **Gridiron:** Joseph Haselwood (1793–1833), Eng. antiquary.

Sydney C. **Grier:** Hilda Caroline Gregg (1868–1933), Eng. novelist. It is possible the writer based her name on those of the village and county of her birth, North Cerney, Gloucestershire.

Francis **Grierson**: Benjamin Henry Jesse Francis Shepard (1848–1927), Eng.-born U.S. writer, singer, pianist.

Ethel **Griffies**: Ethel Woods (1878–1975), Eng. stage, movie actress, working in U.S.

Arthur **Griffinhoofe**: George Colman [the Younger] (1762–1836), Eng. dramatist.

Corinne **Griffith**: Corinne Scott (1898–1979), U.S. movie actress.

Fred **Griffiths**: Frederick George Delaney (1856–1940), Eng. music hall artist.

Gritsko **Grigorenko**: Aleksandra Yevgenyevna Sudovshchikova-Kosach (1867 1924), Ukrainian short story, children's writer. Tne writer adopted a typical (male) Ukrainian name. It was used before her by another writer, Grigory Aleksandrovich Kushelev-Bezborodko (1832–1870).

Romayne **Grigorova**: Romayne Austin (1926–), Eng. ballet dancer, teacher. The dancer's name is not a contrived Slavic-style one, but her own married name, that of Grigor Grigorov, a Bulgarian journalist whom she married in 1960. "At our wedding reception several colleagues suggested I use Grigorova all the time, as it would look good on the programmes: Romayne Grigorova, Ballet Mistress to the Covent Garden Opera" [personal letter from Romayne Grigorova, November 15, 1982].

Roman **Grigoryev**: Roman Grigoryevich Katsman (Katzman) (1911–1972), Russ. movie director.

Sergey **Grigoryev**: Sergey Timofeyevich Grigoryev-Patrashkin (1875–1953), Russ. children's writer.

Dod **Grile**: Ambrose Gwinett Bierce (1842–? 1914), U.S. short story writer. The writer used this name for three collections of vitriolic sketches and witticisms published in the 1870s. The name looks anagrammatic. "Idler Dog?" "Dried Log?" "Riled God?"

Aleksandr **Grin**: Aleksandr Stepanovich Grinevsky (1880–1932), Russ. novelist, short story writer. The writer adopted a name that was originally his school nickname. For some early stories he used the name A. Stepanov, and for one or two adopted female names, among them Elsa Moravskaya and Victoria Klemm. See also entry next below.

Elmar **Grin**: Aleksandr Vasilyevich Yakimov (1909–), Russ. writer. When his father died, the writer adopted the surname of his Estonian mother, and his first stories were published as by "Al. Grin." Later editors advised him to adopt a new first name to avoid confusion with Aleksandr Grin (see entry above). "I had no time to think," he explained. "I suggested the first thing that came to mind. That was how I was landed with an Estonian name" [Dmitriyev, p. 73].

Carleton **Grindle**: Gerald W. Page (1939–), U.S. SF, horror fiction writer, editor.

Miron **Grindon**: Mondia Miron Grunberg (1909–1995), Rom.-born editor.

Harry **Gringo**: Henry Augustus Wise (1819–1869), U.S. author of melodramatic novels.

David **Grinnell**: Donald A. Wollheim (1914–), U.S. SF, fantasy writer, publisher.

Juan **Gris**: José Victoriano González (1887–1927), Sp.-born Fr. Cubist painter.

Iosif **Grishashvili**: Iosif Grigoryevich Mamulaishvili (1889 1965), Georgian poet. The poet adopted a Georgian form of his patronymic, itself deriving from his father's first name Grigory (per form Grisha). (The Georgian suffix *-shvili* corresponds to Russian-*ovich* or -*evich*, meaning "son of.")

Zanis **Griva**: Zanis Karlovich Folmanis (1910–1982), Latvian novelist. The writer's adopted name means "river mouth," denoting his birthplace near Tukums, west of Riga.

Grock: Charles Adrien Wettach (1880–1959), Swiss circus clown. Wettach had originally been a partner of another clown named Brick, whose own partner was Brock. Wettach took Brock's place when the latter left to carry out military service. "Grock" went well with "Brick" but was distinctive from "Brock." For a similar twinning of clown names see **Bim**.

Gros-Guillaume: Robert Guérin (*fl.* 1598–1634), Fr. actor. The name, meaning "Fat William," certainly described the actor's appearance. He accentuated his rotundity by strapping two belts round his middle so that he resembled a walking barrel. He used this name for farces. In serious plays he was La Fleur (*q.v.*).

George **Grosz**: Georg Groß (1893–1959), Ger.-born U.S. painter. Together with John Heartfield (*q.v.*), the artist anglicized his name in 1917 as a protest against the hatred being aroused for the enemy.

Anton **Grot**: Antocz Franziszek Groszewski (1884–1974), Pol. movie art director, working in U.S.

Frederick Philip **Grove**: Felix Paul Greve (1879–1948), Ger.-born Can. novelist. The writer adopted his new name in 1913 when he faked suicide in Germany and reappeared in Canada as a teacher named Fred Grove.

Anastasius **Grün**: Anton Alexander (Graf) von Auersperg (1806–1876), Austr. poet, statesman.

Matthias **Grünewald**: Matthias Gothardt (or Mathis Gothart Nithart) (*c.*1480–1528), Ger. painter. The painter's name arose from a 17th-century misprinting of "Gothardt" as "Grüne-wald," and this is now the standard form of his name.

Sergey **Grustny**: Sergey Mikhaylovich Arkhangelsky (1859–1921), Russ. poet. The poet's new name means "sad," "melancholy." It summarized his writing, as is evident from the following verse from one poem, "On Sleepless Nights" (1908):

The constant voice of woe unending,
The constant moan of heart that's numb.
The constant chains of iron unbending
Band hands about with shackles dumb.

Nathaniel **Gubbins**: Edward Spencer Mott (1844–1910), Eng. sporting writer. Presumably the writer based his pen name on "gubbins" as a slang word for miscellanea or oddments, although Gubbins is a surname in its own right. He also used the friendly "Gub-Gub."

Il **Guercino**: Giovanni Francesco Barbieri (1591–1666), It. painter, illustrator. The painter's name is Italian for "the squinting one," referring to an eye defect. His strabismus does not seem to have affected the quality of his paintings, however.

Jules **Guesde**: Mathieu Jules Basile (1845–1922), Fr. socialist leader, popularizer of Marxism. The politician adopted his mother's maiden name.

George **Guess**: Sequoyah (? 1770–1843), Native American language teacher, writer. The half-breed Cherokee, who devised a system of writing for his tribe, was probably the son of a British trader named Nathaniel Gist (or Guess). His native name (in the spelling Sequoia) was given to the giant redwoods of California and to Sequoia National Park in that state.

Che **Guevara**: Ernesto Guevara de la Serna (1928–1967), Argentine socialist revolutionary. Many Argentines have a verbal mannerism in that they punctuate their speech with the interjection *iche!* Guevara did this, and the word became his nickname, which he subsequently adopted as a first name. He regarded his new name as "the most important and cherished part of my life," and commented: "Everything that came before it, my surname and my Christian name, are minor, personal, and insignificant details" [Kaplan, p. 37].

Yvette **Guilbert**: Emma Laure Esther Guilbert (1865–1944), Fr. singer, diseuse. The singer was advised at the start of her career to take a new first name: "A name, it was explained to her, was important: it should have a 'ring' to it, and a 'ring' the prosaic combination of 'Emma Guilbert' clearly lacked. ... A young man who happened to know Guy de Maupassant offered to ask that celebrity's opinion. Within a few days came a laconic reply: 'Tell her to call herself Yvette,' the great man counselled. Yvette Guilbert. Completely satisfying, everyone agreed. Here was a name with a ring to it" [Bettina Knapp and Myra Chipman, *That Was Yvette*, 1966].

Robert **Guillaume**: Robert Peter Williams (1937–), U.S. TV actor.

Bonnie **Guitar**: Bonnie Buckingham (1923–), U.S. country musician. Buckingham adopted her new name in the mid-1950s, when she worked as a session guitarist in Los Angeles.

Guitar Gable: Gabriel Perrodin (1937–), U.S. guitarist.

Guitar Nubbit: Alvin Hankerson (1923–), U.S. guitarist. "Nubbit" was a nickname given the player following the loss of the tip of his right thumb at the age of three.

Guitar Shorty: John Henry Fortescue (1923–1976), U.S. guitarist, street singer.

Guitar Slim: Eddie Jones (1926–1959), U.S. blues guitarist, singer.

Friedrich **Gundolf**: Friedrich Gundelfinger (1880–1931), Ger. literary historian, poet.

Judy **Gunn**: Judy Winfindale (1914–), Br. stage actress. The actress adopted her mother's maiden name as her stage name, no doubt for reasons of brevity as much as anything.

Kristjana **Gunnars**: Kristjana Gunnarsdóttir (1948–), Icelandic-born Can. writer. The writer emigrated to the U.S. in 1964, then settled in Canada. She dropped the -*dóttir*, "daughter," that all Icelandic women have in their surname, whether married or not. (The first part of the surname is the forename of the bearer's father, in this case Gunnar.)

Norman **Gunston**: Garry McDonald (1948–), Austral. TV comedian.

Sigrid **Gurie**: Sigrid Gurie Haukelid (1911–1969), Norw.-born U.S. movie actress.

Yelena **Guro**: Yelena Genrikhovna Notenberg (1877–1913), Russ. writer.

Gus: George William Smith (1915–), Eng. cartoonist. The artist's signature represents his initials, the "W" becoming "U."

Sergey Ivanovich **Gusev:** Yakov Davidovich Drabkin (1874–1933), Russ. Communist official.

Angelina **Gushington:** Charles Wallwyn Radcliffe-Cooke (1841–1911), Br. writer.

Hon. Impulsia **Gushington:** Helena Selina Sheridan (1806–1867), Eng. song, ballad writer. Helena Sheridan, who was successively Mrs. Blackwood, Lady Dufferin, and the Countess of Blackwood, used this name (which vies with the one above) for *Lispings from Low Latitudes; or Extracts from the Journal of the Hon. Impulsia Gushington* (1863), written as a widow when she accompanied her son on his travels up the Nile.

Johannes **Gutenberg:** Johann Gensfleisch (*c.*1398–1468), Ger. printing pioneer. The inventor exchanged his original name, meaning "gooseflesh," for that of a property owned by his second wife, Else Wilse, in full *Zum Gutenberg*, literally "by the good mountain."

Albert Paris von **Gütersloh:** Albert Konrad Kichtreiber (1887–1973), Austr. writer.

Guto Nyth Bran: Griffith Morgan (1700–1737), Welsh athlete. The champion runner's first name is a form of his original name, Griffith, while the rest of the name is that of the farm, Nyth Bran, where he lived.

Gutyn Peris: Griffith Williams (1769–1838), Welsh poet. The writer's new first name is a form of his original name, Griffith, while his second name, a forename in its own right, derives from the lake of Llyn Peris, near Llanberis, where he spent his boyhood.

Gwallter Mechain: Walter Davies (1761–1849), Welsh poet. The poet took his bardic name from his native village of Llanfechain (probably originally meaning "little church," but popularly understood as "Mechain's church"), Montgomeryshire (now Powys).

Gweirydd ap Rhys: Robert John Pryse (1807–1889), Welsh writer, historian. The writer's new surname is a Welsh form of his original name, meaning literally "son of Rhys." His son, John Robert Pryse (1840–1862), known as Golyddan, and daughter, Catherine Prichard (1842–1909), known as Buddug, were both poets. The latter name means "victorious," and is related to that of Queen Boudicca (Boadicea).

Gwenallt: David James Jones (1899–1968), Welsh poet, critic, scholar. The writer was born in the village of Alltwen, near Swansea, and took

a bardic name that reversed the two elements of this. The name itself means "white hill" or "white wood."

Edmund **Gwenn:** Edmund Kellaway (1877–1959), Eng. movie actor.

Gwili: John Jenkins (1872–1936), Welsh poet. The poet and archdruid took his bardic name from the Gwili River, Carmarthenshire (now Dyfed), where he was born.

Gwylfa: [Rev.] Richard Gwylfa Roberts (1871–1935), Welsh poet. The Congregational minister took a bardic name said to mean "watching place."

Gwilym Deudraeth: William Thomas Edwards (1863–1940), Welsh poet. The writer was raised in the town of Penrhyndeudraeth. Hence his bardic name, meaning "William of Deudraeth." (This part of the placename means "two beaches.") Compare the names below.

Gwilym Gellideg: William Morgan (1808–1878), Welsh poet, musician. The writer spent most of his life in Gellideg, near Merthyr Tydfil. Hence his name, meaning "William of Gellideg."

Gwilym Hiraethog: William Rees (1802–1883), Welsh poet, preacher. The poet was born near Llansannan, Denbighshire (now Gwynedd), in a village below a mountain named Hiraethog. Hence his bardic name, "William of Hiraethog."

Gwilym Lleyn: William Rowlands (1802–1865), Welsh bibliographer, editor. The writer's name means "William of Lleyn," this being the region of Caernarvonshire (now Gwynedd) where he was born.

Gwilym Marles: William Thomas (1834–1879), Welsh poet. The writer adopted the name of his paternal uncle. (The poet Dylan Thomas was given his middle name, Marlais, in honor of the same man.)

Gwilym Morgannwg: Thomas Williams (1778–1835), Welsh poet. The writer's name means "William of Glamorgan," referring to the historic region (and county) in which he spent his childhood.

Gwilym Pant Taf: William Parry (1836–1903), Welsh poet. The writer's name means "William of the Taff valley," referring to the river that flows through the historic region of Glamorgan where he was born.

Gwilym Teilo: William Davies (1831–1892), Welsh poet, historian. The writer was born near the town of Llandeilo, and thus has a name deriving from this, meaning "William of Teilo."

The town's own name means "(St.) Teilo's church."

Gwydderig: Richard Williams (1842–1917), Welsh poet. The writer took his bardic name from that of a river in his native Carmarthenshire (now Dyfed).

Gwyndaf: Evan Gwyndaf Evans (1913–1986), Welsh poet. The poet adopted the name of a Celtic saint as his bardic name.

Anne **Gwynne:** Marguerite Gwynne Trice (1918–), U.S. movie actress.

Arthur **Gwynne:** Gwynfil Evans (1898–1938), Welsh-born Br. writer of stories for boys. The writer also used the name Barry Western.

Gwynoro: John Davies (1855–1935), Welsh poet, patriot. The poet adopted the name of a Celtic saint as his bardic name.

Gwyrosydd: Daniel James (1847–1920), Welsh poet. The writer adopted a local place-name as his bardic name.

Greta **Gynt:** Margrethe Woxholt (1916–), Norw.-born Br. movie actress.

Gyp: Sibylle-Gabrielle Marie-Antoinette de Riquetti de Mirabeau, comtesse de Martel de Janville (1849–1932), Fr. novelist. The novelist is said to have taken her name from Jip, the little dog in Charles Dickens's *David Copperfield.* She pronounced the name "Zheep." When making her writing debut in 1879 she originally called herself "Scamp." For her own illustrations to her novels she signed herself "Bob." Her mother had earlier written stories in the journal *La Vie Parisienne* under the name "Chut!"

Haakon VII: Christian Frederik Carl Georg Valdemar Axel (1872–1957), Norw. king. The king was originally called Prince Carl (Charles) of Denmark. When elected to the throne in 1905, as the first king of Norway following the restoration of the country's independence, he took the Old Norse name of Haakon, not used as a royal name since the 14th century. His son, Olaf V (*q.v.*), was similarly renamed at the time of his father's coronation.

Hans Habe: Hans Bekessy (1911–), Ger. writer, journalist.

Buddy Hackett: Leonard Hacker (1924–), U.S. movie comedian.

Albert Haddock: Alan Patrick Herbert (1890–1971), Eng. journalist, writer.

Christopher Haddon: John Leslie Palmer (1885–1944), Eng. novelist, theatre critic.

Peter Haddon: Peter Tildsley (1898–1962), Br. stage, movie actor.

Reed **Hadley:** Reed Herring (1911–1974), U.S. movie actor.

Hafetz Hayyim: Israel Meir Kagan (originally Poupko) (1838–1933), Lithuanian biblical scholar. The Talmudic and Rabbinic scholar came to be known by the title of his first book, which he published anonymously. It means "delighteth in life," a phrase from the Bible: "What man is he that delighteth in life, and loveth many days, that he may see good?" (Psalm 34:12).

Hafiz: Shams ud-Din Muhammad (*c.*1325–1389), Persian poet. The poet's adopted Arabic name means "one who remembers," that is, a Muslim who can recite the Koran by heart.

Jean **Hagen:** Jean Shirley Verhagen (1923–1977), U.S. movie actress.

William **Haggard:** Richard Henry Michael Clayton (1907–), Eng. author of spy, mystery novels. The writer assumed his mother's maiden name as his pen name.

Bob **Haggart:** Robert Sherwood (1914–), U.S. jazz musician.

Larry **Hagman:** Larry Hageman (1931–), U.S. movie, TV actor.

Jack **Haig:** Jack Coppin (1913–1989), Eng. stage comedian, TV actor.

Kevin **Haigen:** Kevin Higgenbotham (1954–), U.S. ballet dancer.

Haile Selassie: Tafari Makonnen (1892–1975), emperor of Ethiopia. The name adopted by the former Ras ("Prince") Tafari, on being crowned emperor in 1930, is effectively a title, meaning "Might of the Trinity." It was the emperor's princely name that gave the title of the Rastafarians, the Jamaican sect who believe that Blacks are the chosen people, and that Ras Tafari was God Incarnate, and that he would secure their repatriation to their African homeland. Haile Selassie's son was Amha Selassie (*q.v.*).

Olivér **Halassy:** Olivér Haltmayer (1909–1946), Hung. water polo player.

Alan **Hale:** Rufus Alan McKahan (1892–1950), U.S. movie actor.

Binnie **Hale:** Bernice Mary Hale-Monro (1899–1984), Eng. stage comedienne, sister of Sonnie Hale (see below).

Creighton **Hale:** Patrick Fitzgerald (1882–1965), U.S. movie actor.

Jonathan **Hale:** Jonathan Hatley (1891–1966), Can.-born U.S. movie actor.

Katherine **Hale:** Amelia Beers Warnock (1878–1956), Can. poet, music critic, writer. The writer adopted the first two names of her mother, Katherine Hale Warnock, née Bayard.

Keron **Hale:** Edith Joan Lyttleton (1874–1945), N.Z. novelist, poet. This was an early pseudonym used by the writer better known as G.B. Lancaster (*q.v.*).

Sonnie **Hale:** John Robert Hale-Monro (1902–1959), Eng. stage, movie comedian, brother of Binnie Hale (see above).

Fromental **Halévy:** Jacques-François-Fromental Elie Lévy (1799–1862), Fr. composer, of Jewish parentage. The first two added letters of the composer's surname are the initials of his original first names *H*enry *A*ron. In Hebrew, *ha-lewi* means "the Levite," *ha* being the definite article.

Hugh **Haliburton:** James Logie Robertson (1846–1922), Sc. poet, prose writer.

M.Y. **Halidom:** ? (? – ?), Br. (?) horror story writer(s). The identity of the writer(s) is still uncertain, although the assumed name clearly derives from the oath "by my halidom," "halidom" being an old word for "holiness." See also p. 60.

Halikarnas Balikçisi: Gevat çakir Kabaagaçli (1886–1973), Turk. writer. The writer's name means "Halicarnassus fisherman," from the ancient city that is now the Turkish port of Bodrum.

Adam **Hall:** Elleston Trevor *q.v.*

Anmer **Hall:** Alderson Burrell Horne (1863–1953), Br. stage actor, theatrical director.

Aylmer **Hall:** Norah Eleanor Lyle Hall, née Cummins (1914–), Br. children's writer. For her new first name the writer adopted the middle name of her husband, Robert Aylmer Hall, and the complete name was originally used for stories written jointly with him.

Daryl **Hall:** Daryl Hohl (1949–), U.S. rock musician, teaming with John Oates (1949–).

Gus **Hall:** Arvo Kusta Halberg (1910–), U.S. Communist leader, of Finn. parentage.

Holworthy **Hall:** Harold Everett Porter (1887–1936), U.S. novelist, short story writer.

Huntz **Hall:** Henry Hall (1920–), U.S. movie actor.

James **Hall:** James Brown (1900–1940), U.S. movie actor.

Jon **Hall:** Charles Hall Loeher (1913–1979), U.S. movie actor. The actor began his film career as Charles Locher, then changed his name to Lloyd Crane in 1936 before finally becoming Jon Hall in 1937.

Monty **Hall:** Monty Halparin (1924–), Can. TV personality.

Owen **Hall:** James Davis (1848–1907), Ir. playwright, songwriter. The singer and actress Ada Reeve (*q.v.*) recounts an amusing story about the writer's pseudonym: "Originally he intended to call himself Owen May. This caused his witty novelist sister, Frank Danby [*q.v.*] ... to remark: 'Jimmie, ... you must be doing well if you are only owing May.' After that he adopted the name of Hall, and it is on record that he and a friend collaborated under the pen-names of Owen Hall and Payne Nunn" [Ada Reeve, *Take It For A Fact*, 1954].

Radclyffe **Hall:** Marguerite Antonia Radclyffe-Hall (1880–1943), Eng. novelist, poet. The writer herself preferred to be known as "John."

Ruth **Hall:** Ruth Hale Ibanez (1912–), U.S. movie actress.

[Sir] Charles **Hallé:** Karl Halle (1819–1895), Ger.-born Br. pianist, orchestral conductor.

Joseph **Haller:** Henry Nelson Coleridge (1798–1843), Eng. lawyer, writer.

Brett **Halliday:** Davis Dresser (1904–1977), U.S. author of "private eye" stories. The writer's new surname came from the name of the detective in his first novel. His publisher, however, had not liked the name Halliday and had changed it to Burke. The publisher's own name was Brett, and this was the one adopted by Dresser as his new forename. Among other names used by Dresser for pulp magazine short stories were Matthew Blood, Peter Shelley, Anthony Scott, Don Davis, Anderson Wayne, Hal Debrett (jointly with Kathleen Rollins), Asa Baker (for his first mystery), Sylvia Carson, and Kathryn Culver.

James **Halliday:** David Symington (1904–1984), Eng. writer on India, Africa.

Michael **Halliday:** John Creasey (1908–1973), Eng. crime novelist.

Johnny **Hallyday:** Jean-Philippe Smet (1943–), Fr. pop singer. The singer was virtually abandoned by his parents, and was raised by an aunt, whose daughter and American son-in-law, Lee Halliday, were both dancers. Young Jean-Philippe accompanied his cousins on all their tours around Europe, and in due course adopted the name Halliday, but with a small distinctive change in spelling [*Sunday Times Magazine*, August 11, 1985].

Friedrich **Halm**: Eligius Franz Joseph Reichsfreiherr von Münch-Bellinghausen (1806–1871), Ger. playwright.

Margaret **Halstan**: Margaret Hertz (1879– ?), Br. stage actress.

Halston: Roy Halston Frowick (1932–1990), U.S. fashion designer.

Asger **Hamerik**: Asger Hammerich (1843–1923), Dan. composer, of Ger. parentage.

Robert **Hamerling**: Rupert Johann Hammerling (1830–1889), Austr. poet.

Cicely **Hamilton**: Cicely Mary Hammill (1872–1952), Eng. novelist, playwright, stage actress, of Eng. and Sc.-Ir. parentage. The writer first adopted the name for the stage. She also acted as Elfreda Salisbury.

Clive **Hamilton**: Clive Staples Lewis (1898–1963), Br. writer on literary, religious subjects, novelist, children's writer. C.S. Lewis adopted his mother's maiden name for his long narrative poem *Dymer* (1926).

Cosmo **Hamilton**: Cosmo Gibbs (1879–1942), Eng. playwright, novelist. The writer adopted his mother's maiden name as his pen name.

David **Hamilton**: David Pilditch (1939–), Eng. radio, TV announcer, compère. The broadcaster adopted his mother's maiden name (which is also his own middle name) when he began his career in radio. At the time he was carrying out his statutory National Service in the Royal Air Force at the base at Compton Bassett, Wiltshire, where John Dightam, the corporal who ran the services broadcasting station, Compton Forces Network, suggested he change his name. "Pilditch is too unusual. You'll need something people will remember easily if you ever make it to BFN [British Forces Network]" [David Hamilton, *The Music Game: An Autobiography*, 1986].

Dorothy **Hamilton**: Dorothy Jones (1897– ?), Br. stage actress. The actress seems to have adopted a variant of Hampton, her mother's maiden name.

[Lady] Emma **Hamilton**: Amy Lyon (1765–1815), Eng. society leader, mistress of naval hero Horatio Nelson. In 1781, when she was 16, Amy Lyon was calling herself Emily Hart (punning on Lionheart?) when she began to live with Charles Francis Greville, nephew of the man who would become her husband, Sir William Hamilton. (They married in 1791, when she was 26 and he 61.)

Gail **Hamilton**: Mary Abigail Dodge (1833–1896), U.S. popular writer, essayist. The writer, associated with women's issues, adapted her second name to provide her first name, taking her new surname from Hamilton, her Massachusetts hometown.

Russ **Hamilton**: Ronald Hulme (1933–), Eng. popular singer, songwriter.

Paul **Hamlyn**: Paul Bertrand Hamburger (1926–), Br. publisher. The publisher came to Britain as a German-Jewish refugee from Berlin in 1933, when he was only seven. He changed his name because as a child he did not like being nicknamed "Sausage" and "Wimpy." His brother is the poet Michael Hamburger (1924–) [*The Times*, July 30, 1985].

MC **Hammer**: Stanley Kirk Burrell (1962–), U.S. black rapper. The rap artist came to be so called in his teens when he took a part-time job at the Oakland A's ground in his home town, from his resemblance to that team's big hitter, Hank Aaron, known as "Hammerin' Hank." "MC" is the standard abbreviation for "master of ceremonies." (A DJ could make himself MC by means of his rapping. Hence the many rappers and rap groups using the initials.) The name happens to suggest that of Mike Hammer, the tough tec of Mickey Spillane's thrillers. From 1991 Burrell called himself simply Hammer.

Will **Hammer**: William Hinds (1897– ?), Br. movie producer, a founder (1947) of Hammer Movies, noted for their horror content.

Hans **Hammergafferstein**: Henry Wadsworth Longfellow (1807–1882), U.S. poet. The poet used this name for a minor work, *Nights Revealings from the Ancient Sclavonian, etc.*, following it up, as "H.W.L.," with *Nights Revealings from the Ancient Sclavonian of Hans Hammergafferstein*.

Alexander **Hammid**: Alexander Hackenschmied (*c.*1910–), Cz. maker of movie documentaries, working in U.S.

Kay **Hammond**: Dorothy Katherine Leon, later Clements, née Standing (1909–1980), Eng. stage, movie actress. The actress adopted the pseudonym of her mother, née Dorothy Plaskitt, as her stage name.

Pierre **Hamp**: Henri Louis Bourillon (1876–1962), Fr. novelist.

Walter **Hampden**: Walter Hampden Dougherty (1879–1955), U.S. stage, movie actor.

John **Hampson**: John Simpson (1901–1955), Br. novelist.

Robert **Hampton:** Robert Paul Toop (1962–), Sc. ballet dancer.

Olphar **Hamst:** Ralph Thomas (*fl.*1850–1880), Eng. bibliographer. The anagrammatic pseudonym masks the name of one of the leading pseudonymists of the 19th century, professionally a barrister, but for our purposes more importantly the author of the *Handbook of Fictitious Names* (1868) (see Bibliography, p. 401).

Knut **Hamsun:** Knut Pedersen (1859–1952), Norw. novelist. The writer had intended to adopt Hamsund as his pen name, this being the name of the estate on the island of Hamaroy, near Narvik, where his family moved when he was four years old. When a printer omitted the final *d*, however, he assumed the reduced name instead.

Johnny **Handle:** John Alan Pandrich (1935–), Br. folk musician. No doubt the musician evolved his new name by way of a nickname "Panhandle," punning on his surname.

Gladys **Hanson:** Gladys Cook, née Snook (1887–1973), Eng. stage actress. The actress seems to have adapted her father's middle name, Harrison, as her stage name.

John **Hanson:** John Stanley Watts (1922–), Can.-born Br. stage actor, singer.

Han Suyin: Rosalie Comber, née Chou (1917–), Br. novelist, of Chin.-Belg. parentage. The writer assumed a pseudonym meaning roughly "little voice of China." She used it for her first book, *Destination Chungking* (1943), paying tribute to the stoicism of Chinese peasants in the face of poverty and the Japanese invasion. Many sources wrongly give her real first name as Elizabeth.

Otto **Harbach:** Otto Abels Hauerbach (1873–1963), U.S. librettist, lyricist.

Robert **Harbin:** Edward Richard Charles Williams (1909–1978), S.A.-born Br. conjuror. The illusionist was obliged to take another name for distinction from the British conjuror Oswald Williams (1881–1937).

Robert **Harbinson:** Robert Harbinson Bryans (1928–), Ir. short story writer.

E.Y. "Yip" **Harburg:** Isidore Hochberg (1896–1981), U.S. lyricist, librettist. The initials E.Y. stood for Edgar Yipsel, the latter being a Yiddish nickname meaning "squirrel."

James **Harcourt:** James Hudson (1873–1951), Eng. stage actor.

Ephraim **Hardcastle:** William Henry Pyne (1769–1843), Eng. painter, author. The artist used his pseudonym for his literary activities, which he began by way of a series of anecdotes on art and artists in the 1820s.

Theo **Hardeen:** Theodore Weiss (1876–1944), U.S. illusionist, brother of Houdini (*q.v.*). The illusionist's stage name somewhat resembles Houdini's own.

Guy d'**Hardelot:** Helen Guy (1858–1936), Fr. songwriter, working in U.K.

Maximilian **Harden:** Maximilian Felix Ernst Witkowski (1861–1927), Ger. political journalist.

Kate **Hardie:** Kate Oddie (1968–), Br. movie, TV actress. The actress is the daughter of the former TV comedian (now conservationist) Bill Oddie. She changed her name to be dissociated from her father when making her first movie in 1983: "'I wasn't going to be known as Bill Oddie's bloody daughter, you could forget that!'" [*Sunday Times Magazine*, December 12, 1993]. Her new surname is a blend of those of her (separated) parents, her mother being Jean Hart, a former jazz singer.

Ty **Hardin:** Orson Whipple Hungerford II (1930–), U.S. TV, movie actor. The actor legally adopted his screen name. "Ty" was a boyhood nickname.

Wes **Hardin:** Henry John Keevill (1914–1978), Eng. writer of westerns. Other names used by Keevill are Clay Allison, Burt Alvord, Bill Bonney, Virgil Earp, Frank McLowery, Burt Mossman, Johnny Ringo, and Will Travis.

Ann **Harding:** Dorothy Walton Gatley (1901–1981), U.S. stage, movie actress.

Ernst **Hardt:** Ernst Stöckhardt (1876–1947), Ger. writer, translator.

Cyril **Hare:** Alfred Alexander Gordon Clark (1900–1958), Eng. crime novelist. The writer, professionally a lawyer and judge, took his pen name from *Cyril* Mansions, Battersea, London, where he settled after his marriage (1933), and *Hare* Court, Temple, where he worked.

David **Hare:** David Rippon (1947–), Br. playwright. The dramatist adopted his mother's maiden name as his professsional name.

[Sir] John **Hare:** John Fairs (1844–1921), Br. stage actor, theatre manager.

Martin **Hare:** Zoë Zajdler, née Girling (*c.*1907–), Ir. journalist, writer.

Marion **Harland:** Mary Virginia Terhune, née Hawes (1830–1922), U.S. popular writer.

Steve **Harley:** Steven Nice (1951–), Eng. pop musician.

Renny **Harlin**: Lauri Harjula (1959–), Finnish movie director, working in U.S.

Jean **Harlow**: Harlean Carpentier (1911–1937), U.S. movie actress. The actress adopted her mother's first name and maiden surname as her screen name. Her original first name was pronounced "Harley-Ann."

Fats **Harmonica**: Harvey Blackston (1927–), U.S. harmonica player. A straightforward descriptive nickname.

Haro: Haro Reginald Victor Hodson (1923–), Sc.-born Br. cartoonist.

Rolf **Harolde**: Rolf Harolde Wigger (1899–1974), U.S. movie actor.

Charlie **Harper**: David Charles Perez (1944–), Eng. pop musician.

Tess **Harper**: Tessie Jean Washam (1950–), U.S. movie actress.

Slim **Harpo**: James Moore (1924–1970), U.S. harmonica player, singer. The musician made his initial public appearances as Harmonica Slim before settling to a slicker version of this.

George G. **Harrington**: William Mumford Baker (1825–1883), U.S. cleric, novelist.

Barbara **Harris**: Sandra Markowitz (1935–), U.S. movie actress.

Jed **Harris**: Jacob Horowitz (1900–1979), U.S. theatrical impresario.

Johana **Harris**: Beula Aleta Duffey (1912–1995), Can.-born U.S. pianist. The pianist's surname was that of her husband, the composer Roy Harris. She assumed her new first name in honor of Johann Sebastian Bach. The single "n," instead of the expected two, was selected for numerological reasons.

Macdonald **Harris**: Donald W. Heiney (1921–1993), U.S. writer.

Mark **Harris**: Mark Finkelstein (1922–), U.S. novelist, short story writer.

Peppermint **Harris**: Harrison D. Nelson, Jr. (1925–), U.S. blues singer. The singer is said to have got his name when Bob Shand, his record manager, could not remember his real name. Harris kept the name so that his religious family would not know that he sang that kind of music.

Rex **Harrison**: Reginald Carey Harrison (1908–1990), Eng. stage, movie actor. The future actor adopted his new first name as young boy: "At the early age of six or seven [I] decided that I was not a Reggie or a Reginald, and asked my mother if she would be so kind as to address me as Rex in future. … It would be nice to think

that this regal choice was influenced by the heroic deeds of some ancient king or other. … It might even be amusing to think that perhaps I'd passed some early picture palace or place of entertainment called The Rex. Alas, I believe it was but a childish, arbitrary choice, which may, at best, have occurred because I heard someone calling his dog to heel" [Rex Harrison, *A Damned Serious Business*, 1990].

Uncle **Harry**: John Habberton (1842–1921), U.S. journalist, writer.

Dolores **Hart**: Dolores Hicks (1938–), U.S. movie actress.

Freddie **Hart**: Fred Segrest (1926–), U.S. country musician.

Gary **Hart**: Gary Warren Hartpence (1936–), U.S. political leader. The Democrat senator shortened his name when he was 25 and already married. He had tired of his real name at Yale Law School, where he was known by the nickname "Gary Hotpants."

Moss **Hart**: Robert Arnold Conrad (1904–1961), U.S. movie director, writer.

Simon **Harvester**: Henry St. John Clair Rumbold-Gibbs (1910–1975), Br. crime writer.

Laurence **Harvey**: Larushka Mischa Skikne (1928–1973), Lithuanian-born movie actor, working in U.K., U.S. The actor's name was changed by his agent, Gordon Harbord, who also created the name of Adrienne Corri (*q.v.*) and proposed Diana Scarlet for Diana Dors (*q.v.*). His first name should be changed to "Laurence," he decided, while "Skikne" was "much too continental." "He always asked actors their mothers' names or the names of their relatives. Larry Skikne's mother's name had been Zotnik. That would never do. The most English name he could think of was Harvey, as in the solid Knightsbridge store, Harvey Nichols. Not so English as Harrods perhaps, but they could hardly call him Laurence Harrods. Harbord was quite pleased with the name Laurence Harvey. 'But we have to be careful,' he told Skikne. Together they searched the pages of the theatrical directory, but they found no other actor named Harvey" [Des Hickey and Gus Smith, *The Prince, Being the Public and Private Life of Larushka Mischa Skikne, a Jewish Lithuanian Vagabond Player, otherwise known as Laurence Harvey*, 1975].

Lilian **Harvey**: Helene Lilian Muriel Pape (1906–1968), Br. movie actress, of Ger. parentage.

Paul **Harvey:** Paul Harvey Aurandt (1918–), U.S. radio journalist.

Ronald **Harwood:** Ronald Horwitz (1934–), Br. stage, TV actor, writer.

Signe **Hasso:** Signe Larsson (1910–), Swe. movie actress.

Hugh **Hastings:** Hugh Williamson (1917–), Austral. stage actor, dramatist.

Henry **Hathaway:** Marcus Henry Leopold de Fiennes (1898–1985), U.S. movie director.

Minnie **Hauk:** Amalia Mignon Hauck (1851–1929), U.S. opera singer.

June **Haver:** June McMurray, née Stovenour (1925–), U.S. movie actress.

Phyllis **Haver:** Phyllis O'Haver (1899–1960), U.S. movie actress.

June **Havoc:** Ellen Evangeline Hovick (1916–), U.S. stage, movie actress, writer, sister of Gypsy Rose Lee (*q.v.*).

Dale **Hawkins:** Delmar Allen Hawkins (1938–), U.S. rock musician.

Allan **Hawkwood:** Henry James O'Brien Bedford-Jones (1887–1949), Can.-born U.S. historical fiction, fantasy writer.

Goldie **Hawn:** Goldie Jean Studlendgehawn (1945–), U.S. movie actress.

Alice **Hawthorne:** Septimus Winner (1827–1902), U.S. popular songwriter. The writer adopted the name of a famous ancestor on his mother's side, Nathaniel Hawthorne (see next entry below).

Nathaniel **Hawthorne:** Nathaniel Hathorne (1804–1864), U.S. novelist. The writer adjusted the spelling of the family name as a young man to reflect its pronunciation. His grandfather was the Revolutionary hero Daniel Hathorne (1731–1796).

Rainey **Hawthorne:** Charlotte Eliza Lawson Riddell, née Cowan (1832–1906), Ir.-born Eng. writer. The pen name seems to be arbitrary, as probably was the writer's better-known pseudonym of F.G. Trafford (*q.v.*).

Charles **Hawtrey:** George Frederick Joffre Hartree (1914–1988), Br. radio, movie actor.

Ian **Hay:** John Hay Beith (1876–1952), Sc. novelist.

Timothy **Hay:** Margaret Wise Brown (1910–1952), U.S. children's writer. The writer also used the more original names Golden Mac-Donald and Juniper Sage. All the names have a rural ring (though Golden MacDonald can hardly relate to the McDonald's golden-arch logo!). Timothy Hay was the name for *Horses*

(1944), perhaps intentionally suggesting hay and timothy grass.

Linda **Hayden:** Linda Mary Higginson (1951–), Br. movie, TV actress.

Melissa **Hayden:** Mildred Herman (1923–), Can.-born U.S. ballet dancer, teacher.

Robert **Hayden:** Asa Bundy Sheffey (1913–1980), U.S. black poet. The poet was left as a baby with neighbors, who raised him and gave him his new name.

Russell **Hayden:** Pate Lucid (1912–1981), U.S. movie actor.

Sterling **Hayden:** Sterling Relyea Walter (1916–1986), U.S. movie actor, of Du. parentage.

Julie **Haydon:** Donella Lightfoot Donaldson (1910–), U.S. stage, movie actress.

Helen **Haye:** Helen Hay (1874–1957), Br. stage, movie actress.

Allison **Hayes:** Mary Jane Haynes (1930–1977), U.S. movie actress.

Evelyn **Hayes:** Mary Ursula Bethell (1874–1945), Br.-born N.Z. poet. The writer used this name for her early work.

Helen **Hayes:** Helen Hayes MacArthur, née Brown (1900–1993), U.S. stage, movie actress. The actress adopted her mother's maiden name, her own middle name, as her stage name.

Henry **Hayes:** Ellen Warner Kirk, née Olney (1842–1928), U.S. popular fiction writer.

Peter Lind **Hayes:** Joseph Conrad Lind (1915–), U.S. radio, TV comedian, actor. The actor adopted his mother's maiden name as his stage name.

Giant **Haystacks:** Martin Austin Ruane (1947–), Br. wrestler, actor. The wrestler's name is descriptive of his vastness, but at the same time suggests an inner softness. Compare the name of Big Daddy.

Joan **Haythorne:** Joan Mary Shankland, née Haythornthwaite (1915–1987), Eng. stage, movie actress.

Louis **Hayward:** Seafield Grant (1909–1985), S.A.-born Br. movie actor, working in U.S. The actor became a U.S. citizen in 1941.

Susan **Hayward:** Edythe Marrener (1918–1975), U.S. movie actress. How come this particular metamorphosis? Here's how Warner Brothers talent executive, Max Arnow, and talent agent Benny Medford, brought it about, after the actress's screen test in the role of Scarlett O'Hara: "The first item on the agenda was to change her name. Edythe was far too sedate for the screen image they had in mind. Edythe herself suggested the name of her grandmother, Katie Harrington, but Arnow felt it smacked of burlesque; so the brainstorming began. Another up-and-coming actress from Brooklyn, Margarita Cansino, had been doing rather well under the name Rita Hayworth. Hayworth, Haywood…. Arnow tossed it about in his mind. He had been working a lot lately with superagent Leland Hayward, and liked the sound of the name. Medford agreed. From his private garden of favorite names, Medford plucked Susan, and Susan Hayward was born. … Edythe viewed her name change with equanimity. It was, after all, a necessary step toward stardom" [Christopher P. Anderson, *A Star, Is a Star, Is a Star! The Lives and Loves of Susan Hayward*, 1981].

Richard **Haywarde:** Frederick Swartwout Cozzens (1818–1869), U.S. humorist.

Rita **Hayworth:** Margarita Carmen Cansino (1918–1987), U.S. stage, movie actress. The actress's agent, Ed Judson, created her new name when introducing her to Harry Cohn of Columbia Pictures: "The signing of Rita Cansino couldn't have been a less significant event. Cohn took no interest at all in the unknown who had already flopped at Fox—except for her name. 'Latin types are out. She sounds too Mexican,' Cohn argued, even though she had been cast as a Spanish dancer in her first Columbia programmer. 'How about her mother's maiden name?' Judson asked. 'Her uncle Vinton has done okay at RKO.' Vinton Haworth … was by this time a successful character actor and radio star. … 'Haworth. If it's pronounced Hayworth,' said Cohn, 'why the hell isn't it spelled that way?' They added the 'y' and Rita Hayworth was born" [Edward Z. Epstein and Joseph Morella, *Rita: The Life of Rita Hayworth*, 1983].

Désiré **Hazard:** Octave Feuillet (1821–1890), Fr. novelist, dramatist.

Hy **Hazell:** Hyacinth Hazel O'Higgins (1920–1970), Br. revue, musical comedy actress.

H.B.: John Doyle (1797–1868), Ir. caricaturist, painter. The initials are actually the artist's own, represented by two J's one above the other, and two D's similarly. The J's form the lefthand upright of the H. The downstroke of the D's form both its righthand upright and the downstroke of the B. The H and the B thus graphically blend to form a single figure.

H.D.: Hilda Doolittle (1886–1961), U.S. poet, novelist, filmmaker. The writer was a pupil (and briefly the fiancée) of Ezra Pound, and it was he who named and promoted her as "H.D., Imagiste."

Matthew **Head:** John Edwin Canaday (1907–1985), U.S. art critic, mystery novel writer. "Head" presumably from "Edwin."

John **Heartfield:** Helmut Herzfelde (1891–1968), Ger. painter, working in U.K. Like his compatriot, George Grosz (*q.v.*), the artist anglicized his name in World War I as a protest against German nationalistic fervor.

Nita **Heath:** Gwen Kelly, née Smith (1922–), Austral. novelist, poet. The writer adopted her mother's maiden name as her pen name.

William Least **Heat Moon:** William Trogdon (1939–), U.S. memoirist. The writer adopted his Native American name, which translates as "Least Heat Moon."

Eileen **Heckart:** Anna Eckart Herbert (1919–), U.S. stage, movie actress.

Hedd Wyn: Ellis Humphrey Evans (1887–1917), Welsh poet. The bardic name means "blessed peace." It was ironic in the event, as the poet was killed in World War I within days of winning the chair at the 1917 National Eisteddfod.

David **Hedison:** Ara Heditsian (1926–), U.S. movie, TV actor.

Jack **Hedley:** Jack Hawkins (1930–), Br. movie, TV actor.

Van **Heflin:** Emmett Evan Heflin, Jr. (1910–1971), U.S. stage, movie actor.

Heintje: Hein Nicolaas Theodoor Simons (1955–), Du. child pop singer, juvenile movie actor. The name is a diminutive of the artist's first name, to which he added his surname for his (German) film roles.

Gerard **Heinz:** Gerard Hinze (1903–1972), Ger. stage actor, working in U.K.

Ernest **Helfenstein:** Elizabeth Oakes Smith (1806–1893), U.S. popular novelist, magazine writer.

Heliogabalus (or Elagabalus): Varius Avitus Bassianus (204–222), Roman emperor. The crazed emperor was given a name which was that of the Syro-Phoenician sungod whose priest he became while still a child, with the first part of the name representing Greek *helios*, "sun," and the rest of the name said to relate to that of the Gabellus, a tributary of the Po River, Italy.

Richard **Hell:** Richard Myers (1949–), U.S. punk rock musician.

Franz **Hellens:** Frédéric van Ermenghem (1881–1972), Belg. writer.

Frank **Heller:** Gunnar Martin Serner (1886–1947), Swe. writer.

Robert **Heller:** William Henry Palmer (*c.*1830–1878), Eng. magician, working in U.S. The illusionist may have adopted a name that was a variant on that of Robert-Houdin, whom he greatly admired when young. See also **Houdini.**

Brigitte **Helm:** Gisele Eva Schittenhelm (1906–1996), Ger. movie actress.

Yr **Hen Broffwyd:** Edmund Jones (1702–1793), Welsh writer, preacher. The name by which the pious writer and zealous preacher was known means "the old prophet." He accepted and approved the nickname. Compare the name of Yr. Hen Ficer below.

Mary **Henderson:** James Bridie (*q.v.*).

Paul **Henderson:** Ruth France (1913–1968), N.Z. novelist, poet.

Ray **Henderson:** Raymond Brost (1896–1970), U.S. songwriter.

Rosa **Henderson:** Rosa Deschamps (1896–1968), U.S. vaudeville artist, blues singer. The performer had many aliases. The best known was taken from her husband and stage partner, Douglas "Slim" Henderson. Others includedFlora Dale, Rosa Green, Mae (or Mamie) Harris, Sara Johnsson, Sally Ritz, Josephine Thomas, Gladys White, and Bessie Williams, all fairly conventional.

Jimi **Hendrix:** James Marshall (originally Johnny Allen) Hendrix (1942–1970), U.S. black rock musician. On being discharged from the U.S. paratroopers in 1963 for medical reasons, Hendrix first played under the name Jimmy James. He then adopted his better known name, with this becoming prominent in 1966 on the formation of his group, the Jimi Hendrix Experience.

Yr **Hen Ficer:** Rhys Prichard (1579–1644), Welsh clergyman, poet. The popular preacher accepted his nickname, meaning "the old vicar."

Paul **Henreid:** Paul George Julius von Hernreid (1908–1992), Austr.-born U.S. stage, movie actor.

Robert **Henri:** Robert Henry Cozad (1865–1929), U.S. painter. The artist adopted his French-style name as a student at the école des Beaux-Arts in Paris.

Emile **Henriot:** Emile Maigrot (1889–1961), Fr. writer. The writer have may wished to avoid the suggestion of *maigriot,* "skinny."

Buck **Henry:** Buck Henry Zuckerman (1930–), U.S. movie actor, screenwriter, director.

John **Henry,** Jr.: Don Marion Davies (1917–), U.S. child movie actor. The actor was billed under this name for a series of Mack Sennett (*q.v.*) comedies from 1919 to 1922. He later acted as Don Marion.

O. **Henry:** William Sydney Porter (1862–1910), U.S. short story writer. It should be noted that the writer's pen name is just so, and not, as sometimes seen, "O'Henry." Porter first used the name for his story *Whistling Dick's Christmas Stocking* (1899) written in prison at Columbus, Ohio, where he was serving a sentence for embezzlement (as a result of obtaining money for his sick wife). The pseudonym is sometimes said to have been taken from one of the prison guards, Orrin Henry, but the commonly accepted version of the origin says that it is presumed to be an abbreviation of the name of a French pharmacist, Etienne-Ossian Henry, found in the *U.S. Dispensatory.* This was a reference work used by Porter when employed as a prison pharmacist.

Paul **Henry:** Paul Henry Smith (1947–), Br. TV actor.

Gladys **Henson:** Gladys Gunn (1897–1983), Ir. stage, movie actress.

Audrey **Hepburn:** Edda van Heemstra Hepburn-Ruston (1929–1993), Belg.-born U.S. movie actress, of Eng.-Du. parentage. Hepburn's father was Joseph Anthony Hepburn Ruston, an English banker. Her mother was a Dutch baroness, Ella van Heemstra. "Audrey" evolved from "Edda."

Charles **Herbert:** Charles Herbert Saperstein (1948–), U.S. child movie actor.

Evelyn **Herbert:** Evelyn Houstellier (1898 – ?), U.S. stage actress, singer.

Holmes **Herbert:** Edward Sanger (1882–1956), Br. stage, movie actor.

Herblock: Herbert Lawrence Block (1909–), U.S. cartoonist.

Hergé: George Rémi (1907–1983), Belg. cartoonist. The creator of Tintin, the boy detective, used a name that was simply the reversal of his initials in their French pronunciation ("R.G."="Hergé").

Philippe **Hériat:** Raymond Gérard Payelle (1898–1971), Fr. writer. The writer was originally an actor, and adopted his stage name as his pen name.

Eileen **Herlie**: Eileen Herlihy (1919–), Sc. stage, movie actress.

Herman: Peter Blair Denis Bernard Noone (1947–), Eng. pop singer. The lead singer of the group Herman's Hermits, formed 1963, owed his name to a nickname. Members of the local Manchester group, the Heartbeats, with whom he sang previously, claimed that Noone resembled Sherman of the *Rocky and Bullwinkle* TV cartoon series. This name was then slightly shortened to "Herman" and used to blend in nicely with that of his own band. Noone performed under his own name from 1970.

Pee-Wee **Herman**: Paul Rubenfeld (or Rubens) (1952–), U.S. movie, TV comedian. According to the actor himself: "'I had a little one inch harmonica that said "Pee-wee" on it. I just loved the way it sounded. … Growing up I knew a kid who was extremely obnoxious … and his last name was Herman'" [Blackwell, p. 258].

Stefan **Hermlin**: Rudolf Leder (1915–1997), Ger. writer, translator.

James A. **Herne**: James Ahearn (1839–1901), U.S. actor, playwright.

Herod Agrippa I: Marcus Julius Agrippa (*c.* 10 BC–AD 44), king of Judaea. The ruler is known by the same name as his grandfather, Herod the Great, through a New Testament error: "Now about that time Herod the king stretched forth his hands to vex certain of the church" (Acts 12:1).

Robert **Heron**: John Pinkerton (1758–1826), Sc. writer.

James **Herriot**: James Alfred Wight (1916–1995), Eng. writer. The Yorkshire veterinarian, who first began to publish his popular books only in 1970, when he was over 50, took his pen name quite ingenuously: "I had to have one because I didn't want to be accused of advertising by the Royal College of Veterinary Surgeons. And I was watching the telly one night when this footballer came on. He was the goalkeeper for Bristol City, I think. He was called James Herriot and I thought: 'That's a nice name.' So I used it" [*Telegraph Sunday Magazine*, June 7, 1981]. By a happy coincidence, the medieval word "heriot" was used for a death duty paid to a lord by his tenant in the form of the dead man's best beast.

Herrmann the Great: Alexandre Herman (1843–1896), Fr. magician, working in U.S.

Barbara **Hershey**: Barbara Herztine (or Herzstein) (1947–), U.S. movie actress. Barbara Hershey gained fame (or notoriety) as the Hollywood actress who in 1973 changed her name to Barbara Seagull, after accidentally killing a seagull and claiming that its spirit had entered her. She subsequently threw off her image as a typecast flower child actress, and reverted to her name of Hershey in 1975.

Carl **Hertz**: Leib (or Louis) Morgenstern (1859–1924), U.S. magician, working in U.K.

Hervé: Florimond Ronger (1825–1892), Fr. composer, organist, conductor. The musician used this name for his many operettas.

Mlle **Hervé**: Geneviève Béjart (*c.*1622–1675), Fr. actress. The actress adopted her mother's maiden name as her stage name.

Grant **Hervey**: George Henry Cochrane (1880–1933), Austral. novelist, forger.

Irene **Hervey**: Irene Herwick (1910–), U.S. movie actress.

Aleksandr Ivanovich **Herzen** (or Gertsen): Aleksandr Ivanovich Yakovlev (1812–1870), Russ. revolutionary, writer, philosopher. The writer was an illegitimate child, the son of a rich Russian merchant (Ivan Alekseyevich Yakovlev) and a poor German mother (Luise Haag). He was thus a "love child," and his new name, devised by his father, reflected this, from German *vom Herzen*, "from the heart."

Werner **Herzog**: Werner Herzog Stipetic (1942–), Ger. movie director.

Catherine **Hessling**: Andrée Madeleine Heuschling (1899–1979), Fr. movie actress.

Charlton **Heston**: John Charles Carter (1923–), U.S. stage, movie actor. The actor's stage name was adopted from that of his stepfather.

Martin **Hewitt**: Arthur Merrison (1863–1945), Eng. novelist, journalist. The writer adopted the name of the hero of his own detective stories.

Harrington **Hext**: Eden Phillpotts (1862–1960), Eng. novelist, poet, essayist, playwright. The novelist used the pen name for his mystery stories: "Hext" suggests "hexed," or "bewitched" (having a spell put on by a *hex* or witch or wizard).

Stefan **Heym**: Helmut Flieg (1913–), Ger. Communist writer, working in U.S. The writer changed his name to protect his family from reprisals following his emigration to Czechoslovakia in 1933. He is said to have chosen the name Heym on the spur of the moment, basing it on German *Heim*, "home," reflecting his homesickness.

Anne **Heywood:** Violet Pretty (1932–), Eng. movie actress.

H.H.: Helen Maria Hunt Jackson, née Fiske (1830–1885), U.S. poet, novelist, children's writer. The initials are those of the writer's first and third names. She also wrote as Saxe Holm (*q.v.*).

Ruth **Hiatt:** Ruth Redfern (1908–), U.S. movie actress.

Harry **Hieover:** Charles Bindley (1795–1859), Eng. sporting writer. Both names suggest English field sports, involving harrying and hunting. "Hieover" suggests both "hie over" (hurry over) or "high over" (of a jumping horse). "Hie" is also a command to a horse to turn.

Nehemiah **Higginbottom:** Samuel Taylor Coleridge (1772–1834), Eng. poet, critic. The poet used this name for his contributions to the *Monthly Review*, in which he parodied his own style.

Jack **Higgins:** Henry Patterson (1929–), Eng. fiction writer. The writer is said to have adopted his best known pen name from a deceased relative. Other names used by him include Martin Fallon, James Graham, Hugh Marlowe, and the barely pseudonymous Harry Paterson.

Patricia **Highsmith:** Patricia Plangman (1921–1995), U.S. crime novelist. The writer was raised by her grandparents until the age of six, then lived with her mother and stepfather, Stanley Highsmith, whose name she adopted. She published an early novel under the name Claire Morgan (*q.v.*).

Hildegarde: Hildegarde Loretta Sell (1906–), U.S. popular singer, pianist.

Benny **Hill:** Alfred Hawthorne Hill (1925–1992), Br. TV comedian. The comic took his new first name from the U.S. comedian Jack Benny (*q.v.*), an idol of his. It was Alfred's brother Leonard who suggested he adopt Benny's name, although he himself had originally favored a name such as Leslie or Vernon.

Harry **Hill:** Matthew Hall (1964–), Br. stage, TV comedian.

Headon **Hill:** Francis Edward Grainger (1857–1924), Eng. romantic novelist, detective fiction writer. The author appears to have taken his name from Headon Hill, a hill on the Isle of Wight.

Jenny **Hill:** Elizabeth Jane Woodley, née Pasta (1851–1896), Br. music hall artist ("the Vital Spark").

Joe **Hill:** Joel Emanuel Hagglund (1879–1915), Swe.-born U.S. socialist poet, songwriter. The labor activist was also known as Joe Hillstrom.

Robin **Hill:** Robert Young (1811–1908), Eng. poet.

Steven **Hill:** Solomon Berg (1924–), U.S. stage, movie actor. The actor translated his German surname into English.

Terence **Hill:** Mario Girotti (1941–), It. movie actor, of Ger. descent.

Wendy **Hiller:** Wendy Gow, née Watkin (1912–), Eng. stage, movie actress. The actress adopted her mother's maiden name as her stage name.

Harriet **Hilliard:** Peggy Lou Snyder (1914–), U.S. movie, TV actress.

Kate **Hillier:** Kate Hill (1970–), Eng. TV actress.

Morris **Hillquit:** Morris Hillkowitz (1869–1933), Latvian-born U.S. lawyer, reformer.

Roger **Hilton:** Roger Hildesheim (1911–1975), Eng. painter. The artist's family changed their name from Hildesheim to Hilton in 1916 as a result of anti-German sentiment in World War I.

Ronnie **Hilton:** Adrian Hill (1926–), Br. romantic singer, broadcaster. No doubt the singer's new first name evolved from his original name, just as his surname evolved similarly. He may well also have wished to be differentiated from his namesake, the artist Adrian Hill (1895–1977).

Thomas **Hinde:** [Sir] Thomas Willes Chitty (1926–), Br. novelist. The novelist adopted his mother's maiden name as his pseudonym.

Jerome **Hines:** Jerome Albert Link Heinz (1921–), U.S. opera singer.

Dr. Evadne **Hinge:** George Logan (*c.*1950–), Sc. female impersonator, teaming with Dame Hilda Bracket (*q.v.*). (as "Hinge and Bracket").

Mary **Hinton:** Emily Rachel Forster (1896 – ?), Eng. stage actress.

Hi-Regan: [Captain] John Joseph Dunne (1837–1910), Ir. traveler, journalist, writer on sporting subjects, father of George Egerton (*q.v.*). The author used this name for *How and Where to Fish In Ireland* (1886).

Hugo **Hirst:** Hugo Hirsch (1863–1943), Ger.-born Br. electrical engineering entrepreneur. The family of the founder of the General Electric Company (in 1889) emigrated from Munich to London in 1880 and anglicized their name soon after.

Shere **Hite:** Shirley Diana Gregory (1942–), U.S. sexologist. The writer's professional name, the subject of some punning by journalists, is her married name, with Shere, pronounced "Sherry," derived as a pet form of her first name.

H.L.L.: Jane Laurie Borthwick (1813–1897), Sc. hymnwriter. Together with her sister, Sarah Borthwick Findlater, Jane Borthwick made a series of translations (1854–62) from the German, entitled the work *Hymns from the Land of Luther*, and used the initials of this to give her own pen name.

Rose **Hobart:** Rose Kéfer (1906–), U.S. movie actress.

Meidert **Hobbema:** Meyndert Lubbertsz (or Lubbertszoon) (1638–1709), Du. painter. The artist adopted his new surname as a young man.

John Oliver **Hobbes:** Pearl Mary Teresa Craigie, née Richards (1867–1906), U.S.-born Eng. novelist. The novelist, usually referred to as simply Mrs. Craigie, chose the name Hobbes because it was "homely," suggesting "hob by the hearth" and the like. John was her father's name, while Oliver was a reference to "warring Cromwell," as she put it. Her publishers made her take a male name before publication of *Cavalry Life* (1881).

McDonald **Hobley:** Dennys Jack Valentine McDonald-Hobley (1917–1987), Br. TV presenter. In an earlier stage career, McDonald-Hobley used the name Robert Blanchard.

Ho Chi Minh: Nguyen Tat Thanh (1890–1969), North Vietnamese president. The politician first became an active socialist in France in 1917 under the name of Nguyen Ai Quoc, "Nguyen the patriot." In 1942, however, he assumed the name by which he came to be best known, Ho Chi Minh, "Ho who enlightens." He also had several party aliases in the course of his life.

Stephen **Hockaby:** Gladys Maude Winifred Mitchell (1901–1983), Eng. crime novelist.

Jakob van **Hoddis:** Hans Davidsohn (1887–1942), Ger. lyric poet. "Van Hoddis" is an exact anagram of the writer's original surname.

Johnny **Hodges:** Cornelius Hodge (1905–1970), U.S. saxophonist.

John **Hodgkinson:** John Meadowcroft (1767–1805), Br. actor, working in U.S. A pleasantly distinctive original name for some reason abandoned in favor of an unremarkable stage name.

Dennis **Hoey:** Samuel David Hyams (1893–1960), Eng. stage, movie actor, working in U.S.

Professor **Hoffmann:** Angelo Lewis (1839–1919), Eng. magician. By profession, under his real name, the magician was a lawyer and journalist. He wrote several books on magic, using both his real and his assumed name.

Fay **Holden:** Dorothy Fay Hammerton (1894–1973), Br. stage, movie actress, working in U.S. The actress played her first stage part at the age of ten under the name Gaby Fay.

Jan **Holden:** Jan Wilkinson (1931–), Eng. stage actress.

Joyce **Holden:** Jo Ann Heckert (1930–), U.S. movie actress.

Stanley **Holden:** Stanley Waller (1928–), Eng. ballet dancer.

William **Holden:** William Franklin Beedle, Jr. (1918–1981), U.S. movie actor. A Paramount executive said that the actor's real name "sounds like an insect," so renamed him in 1938 after a newspaper friend.

Billie **Holiday:** Eleanora Gough McKay, née Fagan (1915–1959), U.S. black jazz singer. The singer took her new first name from the actress Billie Dove (*q.v.*). Her surname was from her father, the guitarist Clarence Holiday (1900–1937).

Vyvyan **Holland:** Vyvyan Oscar Beresford Wilde (1886–1967), Eng. writer. The writer was the son of Oscar Wilde, and his name was changed when he was still at school to avoid association with his father following the latter's conviction for homosexual offenses in 1895. Holland was an old family name on the side of the boy's mother, Constance Mary Wilde, née Lloyd. Vyvyan's elder brother Cyril, killed in World War I, underwent the same name change.

Judy **Holliday:** Judith Tuvim (1922–1965), U.S. stage, movie actress. The actress translated her Jewish name from Hebrew to English.

Michael **Holliday:** Michael Milne (1928–1963), Eng. popular singer.

Earl **Holliman:** Anthony Numenka (1928–), U.S. movie actor.

Buddy **Holly:** Charles Hardin Holley (1936–1959), U.S. rock musician. There is a small difference between the rock pioneer's professional name and his original name. This arose when his surname was misspelled on his first recording contract in 1956, and he did not bother to have the error corrected [John J. Goldrosen, *Buddy Holly: His Life and Music*, 1979].

Hanya **Holm:** Johanna Kuntze, née Eckert (1893–1992), Ger.-born U.S. choreographer, dancer.

Ian **Holm:** Ian Holm Cuthbert (1931–), Eng. stage, movie, TV actor.

Saxe **Holm:** Helen Maria Hunt Jackson, née Fiske (1830–1885), U.S. poet, novelist, children's writer. The author used this name for her earliest writings, after the death of her first husband, Captain Edward Hunt, in 1863. She married William S. Jackson in 1875.

Libby **Holman:** Elsbeth Holzman (1904–1971), U.S. popular singer.

Gordon **Holmes:** Louis Tracy (1863–1928), Eng. journalist, fiction writer.

H.H. **Holmes:** Herman Webster Mudgett (1860–1895), U.S. mass murderer; (2) William Anthony Parker White (1911–1968), U.S. thriller writer. White adopted the serial killer's alias for his pen name.

Leon **Holmes:** Leon Sederholm (1913–), U.S. child movie actor.

Michelle **Holmes:** Corinne Michelle Cunliffe (1967–), Eng. movie, TV actress.

Stuart **Holmes:** Joseph von Liebenben (1887–1971), Ger.-born U.S. movie actor.

Patrick **Holt:** Patrick Parsons (1912–1993), Br. movie actor.

Victoria **Holt:** Jean Plaidy (*q.v.*).

Holte: Trevor Holder (1941–), Eng. cartoonist, illustrator.

Cecil **Home:** Julia Augusta Webster, née Davies (1837–1894), Br. poet, dramatist.

Evelyn **Home:** Peggy Makins, née Carn (1916–), Br. agony columnist. Evelyn Home was the long-serving agony columnist in *Woman* magazine from 1937 through 1974. The name was one that Peggy Carn inherited on the magazine, deriving from Eve, symbolizing womanhood, and (obviously) Home, suggesting domestic happiness. The name itself was first chosen by a German Jewish woman psychologist who was writing for *Woman* when Peggy Carn took over. The columnist later wrote: "The 'Evelyn' contained Eve, the archetypal mother, the temptress, the sexy side of woman; the 'home' was what every woman is supposed to want. At the time I thought the name too phony to be taken seriously ever; I was totally mistaken" [Peggy Makins, *The Evelyn Home Story*, 1975]. The name was abandoned in 1974, when Peggy Makins was succeeded in turn by Anna Raeburn (*q.v.*).

Homer: Henry D. Haynes (1917–1971), U.S. humorous country singer, teaming with Jethro (*q.v.*).

Geoffrey **Homes:** Daniel Mainwaring (1902–1978), U.S. mystery novelist, screenwriter.

Harry **Honeycomb:** James Henry Leigh Hunt (1784–1859), Eng. essayist, poet. The poet used this semiserious name, based on his second name and surname, for contributions to various journals, such as the *New Monthly Magazine*.

Honorius II: Lamberto Scannabecchi (? –1130), It. pope.

Honorius III: Cencio Savelli (? –1227), It. pope. Honorius IV (see below) was his grand-nephew.

Honorius IV: Giacomo (or Jacomus) Savelli (1210–1287), It. pope. The pontiff adopted the name of his granduncle, Honorius III (see above).

Percy **Honri:** Percy Henri Thompson (1874–1953), Eng. music hall artist. The performer adopted the misprinted version of his name "Henri" that appeared in a billing.

bell **hooks:** Gloria Jean Watkins (1952–), U.S. black feminist poet, critic. The writer adopted (and lower-cased) the name of her great-grandmother, Bell Hooks, early in her career.

Anthony **Hope:** [Sir] Anthony Hope Hawkins (1863–1933), Eng. historical novelist, playwright. The author of *The Prisoner of Zenda* (1894) wrote the popular romantic adventure novel while practicing as a barrister in London. He therefore adopted a pseudonym, using his first two names only. The book was such a success that it enabled him to give up the law as a career and become a fulltime novelist.

Ascott R. **Hope:** Ascott Robert Hope-Moncrieff (1846–1927), Br. editor, author of books for boys.

Bob **Hope:** Leslie Townes Hope (1903–), Eng.-born U.S. movie comedian. The actor originally adopted the name Lester T. Hope, reasoning: "I thought that was a little more manish... I found a lot of girls would call me Leslie and I'd call them Leslie, and there was a sort of conflict of interests there so I changed it to 'Lester.'" He then thought that this name "still looked a little ginger around the edges," so changed "Lester" to "Bob." "I thought that was more chummy and audiences would get to like me" [Charles Thompson, *Bob Hope: The Road from Eltham*, 1981].

David **Hope:** Douglas Jamieson Fraser (1910–1989), Sc. "inspirational" poet. The poet became associated with *The Fireside Book*, a selection of poems still published annually as a companion to *The Friendship Book* of Francis Gay (*q.v.*), although now obviously compiled by others.

Laura Lee **Hope:** Edward L. Stratemeyer (1863–1930), U.S. author of stories for girls. The author used various pseudonyms for his fiction for boys and girls, choosing this female one for his stories about the Bobbsey Twins for girls. The name itself was presumably random, but any name in "Hope" suggests wholesome good value, even adventure.

Laurence **Hope:** Adela Florence Nicolson, née Cory (1865–1904), Br. romantic poet. Possibly "Laurence" was adopted from the writer's second name. She first used it for *The Garden of Kama and other Love Lyrics from India* (1901), which readers took to be written by a man.

Richard **Hope:** Richard John Hope Walker (1953–), Eng. stage, movie, TV actor.

Antony **Hopkins:** Antony Reynolds (1921–), Eng. composer, conductor, broadcaster on music. Antony Hopkins (not to be confused with Anthony Hopkins, the movie actor) was adopted by Major and Mrs. Hopkins at the age of four, and thereafter assumed their name.

Hedda **Hopper:** Elda Furry (1890–1966), U.S. movie actress, gossip columnist. The actress's second name is that of her husband, De Wolf Hopper, whom she married in 1913. He had been married four times already, and his wives had been named Ella, Ida, Edna, and Nella. In view of the similarity of Elda's own name to these, a numerologist was consulted. He recommended the name Hedda, which may be different numerologically but hardly otherwise.

Trader **Horn:** Alfred Aloysius Smith (1861–1931), Eng. traveler. When living in a Johannesburg doss house in 1926, Smith made the acquaintance of a local novelist, Ethelreda Lewis, who discovered that the old man had a traveler's tale to tell. She transcribed his illiterate account of his adventures in Equatorial Africa and found a publisher for them the following year. First, however, she changed his name to protect his respectable Catholic family in England: "His first names were retained and seemed symbolic. There was 'Alfred,' a name steeped in pre-Norman days. ... And there was 'Aloysius,' a saint's name. ... His surname had to go, however, and

Mrs. Lewis cast about for a substitute. She chose 'Horn,' a name evocative of the wildness of animals, of the southern point of America and the north-eastern tip of Africa" [Tim Couzens, *Tramp Royal: The True Story of Trader Horn*, 1992]. "Trader" was thus a nickname, for when in West Africa Smith had traded in ivory.

Adam **Hornbrook:** Thomas Cooper (1805–1892), Eng. politician, author.

Horace **Hornem:** George Gordon Byron (1788–1824), Eng. poet. Byron used this name for *The Waltz; an Apostrophic Hymn* (1813). The poet was reluctant to admit authorship of this work and wrote to a friend at the time: "I fear that a certain malicious publication on waltzing is attributed to me. This report, I suppose you will take care to contradict; as the author I am sure would not like that I should wear his cap and bells" [Hamst, p. 60]. Byron also wrote as Quevedo Redivivus (*q.v.*).

Horst P. **Horst:** Horst Paul Albert Bohrmann (1906–), Ger.-born U.S. fashion photographer.

Hortencia: Hortencia Maria de Fatima Marcari Oliva (1959–), Brazilian basketball player.

Isaac **Hortibonus:** Isaac Casaubon (1559–1614), Swiss theologian, classical scholar. The scholarly pseudonym seems to have been devised to complement the theologian's real surname, with "Casaubon" (which actually means "in good state") interpreted as "good house." "Hortibonus" or "Hortusbonus," as he sometimes spelled it, thus meant "good garden."

Harry **Houdini:** Ehrich Weiss (or Weisz) (1874–1926), Hung.-born U.S. escapologist. The escapologist was keen to escape from the ties of his real name. He adopted Houdini through his admiration of the French illusionist Robert-Houdin (*q.v.*), while his new first name of Harry evolved from "Ehrie," a pet form of his original name.

John **Houseman:** Jacques Haussmann (1902–1988), Rom.-born stage, movie director, of Fr.-Eng. parentage, working in U.S.

Cissy **Houston:** Emily Drinkard (1933–), U.S. black popular singer, mother of soul singer Whitney Houston (1963–).

Renée **Houston:** Katherina Houston Gribbin (1902–1980), Sc. vaudeville artist, movie actress.

The **Howadji:** George William Curtis (1824–1892), U.S. travel writer, newspaper correspondent. The author used this name for his travel writings, such as *Nile Notes of a Howadji* (1851) and *The Howadji in Syria* (1852). The name itself was probably a corruption of Arabic *khawaja*, a form of respectful address approximating to "Sir," especially used for Christians and Westerners.

Ann **Howard:** Ann Pauline Swadling (1936–), Br. opera singer.

David **Howard:** David Paget Davis III (1896–1941), U.S. movie director.

Don **Howard:** Donald Howard Koplow (1935–), U.S. popular singer.

Elizabeth Jane **Howard:** Elizabeth Jane Liddon (1923–), Eng. writer, editor, reviewer. The writer adopted her mother's maiden name as her pen name.

H.L. **Howard:** Charles Jeremiah Wells (? 1799–1879), Eng. poet.

John **Howard:** John R. Cox, Jr. (1913–1995), U.S. movie actor.

Keble **Howard:** John Keble Bell (1875–1928), Eng. playwright, journalist.

Leslie **Howard:** Leslie Howard Steiner (1893–1943), Eng. stage, movie actor, of Hung. parentage. The actor appears to have anglicized his original Hungarian name of László Horvath.

Shemp **Howard:** Samuel Horowitz (1891–1955), U.S. movie comedian.

Susan **Howard:** Jeri Lynn Mooney (1943–), U.S. movie, TV actress.

Thomas **Howard:** Jesse Woodson James (1847–1892), U.S. desperado. This pseudonym was used by the (in)famous Jesse James in his final days while living at St. Joseph, Missouri. It seems to have been simply an "innocuous" name.

James Wong **Howe:** Wong Tung Jim (1899–1976), Chin.-born U.S. cinematographer.

Frankie **Howerd:** Francis Alick Howard (1917–1992), Eng. stage, movie, TV comedian. The actor chose the smallest of changes when adopting his stage name: "It seems [sic] to me that there were too many Howards: among them Trevor, Sidney and Arthur. So how to stay Howard, yet alter it? I hit on the idea of a change of spelling: Howerd—which, I argued, would have the added advantage of making people look twice because they assumed it to be a misprint" [Frankie Howerd, *On the Way I Lost It*, 1976]. As an aspiring comedian he had earlier tried out the totally different name Ronnie Ordex.

Howlin' Wolf: Chester Arthur Burnett (1910–1976), U.S. black blues singer, songwriter. The singer's name refers to his early singing style, with his hoarse voice and eerie "howling." According to some accounts, he was already nicknamed "The Wolf" as a child for his bad behavior, for the wicked wolf in the story of Little Red Riding Hood.

Margaret **Howth:** Rebecca Blaine Harding Davis (1831–1910), U.S. novelist. The writer adopted the name of the heroine of her own novel, *Margaret Howth* (1862).

John **Hoyt:** John Hoysradt (1905–1991), U.S. movie actor.

Rock **Hudson:** Roy Harold Fitzgerald, originally Roy Scherer (1925–1985), U.S. movie actor. Rock Hudson had a more or less standard story to account for his screen name, which he said had been given him by his first agent, Henry Willson. The following is one version: "Henry thought he knew what was best for me. I remember he said, 'we have to change your name.' 'Why?' I asked. 'I don't want one of those silly names.' 'You have to,' he said, 'so it looks good on the marquee. Roy Fitzgerald is too long.' 'What about Geraldine Fitzgerald? Is that too long?' But Henry insisted. He hit me with Hudson. Then he had some really macho, cockamamie first names. Like Dirk. Lance. Finally he said, 'What about Rock?' That clicked. 'Yeah, that sounds pretty good,' I said. It was not too far from Roy, and no one else had it. So that was it." But it is now known that it was actually Ken Hodge, Rock Hudson's friend and lover, who gave him his name, with "Rock" for strength, and "Hudson" taken from the Long Beach phone book. Even so, Willson *did* rename several famous actors, many of whom he gave names similar to "Rock Hudson." Among them were Tab Hunter, Troy Donahue, Rory Calhoun, and Rip Torn (*qq.v.*) [Rock Hudson and Sara Davidson, *Rock Hudson: His Story*, 1986]. Although born Roy Scherer, the actor subsequently adopted the name of his stepfather, Wallace Fitzgerald.

Jean **Hugard:** John G. Boyce (1872–1959), Austral. magician.

Adrian **Hughes:** Stanley Hockey (1964–), Br. TV actor, SF scriptwriter, working in U.S.

Cyril **Hughes:** Cyril Hodges (1915–1974), Welsh poet. The writer clearly preferred a recognizably Welsh name.

Hazel **Hughes:** Hazel Heppenstall (1913–1974), S.A. stage actress. The actress adopted her mother's maiden name as her stage name.

Kathleen **Hughes:** Betty von Gerlean (1928–), U.S. movie actress. Possibly the actress's surname suggested her new stage first name.

Sean **Hughes**: John Patrick (*c.*1965–), Br. stage, movie, TV, comedian, scriptwriter.

Hulda: Unnur Benedikstdóttir Bjarkling (1881–1946), Icelandic lyric poet. The Scandinavian name means "sweet," "lovable."

Josephine **Hull**: Josephine Sherwood (1884–1957), U.S. stage, movie actress. The actress's stage name was that of her actor husband, Shelley Hull.

Richard **Hull**: Richard Henry Sampson (1896–1973), Eng. crime novelist.

Engelbert **Humperdinck**: Arnold George Dorsey (1936–), Eng. pop singer. The singer borrowed the name of the German classical composer (best known for his opera *Hansel and Gretel*) for his professional name. It was suggested to Dorsey by his manager, Gordon Mills, in 1965, who was looking through some old records of works by the composer at the time. Dorsey officially assumed the name the following year.

Humph: Humphrey Richard Adeane Lyttelton (1921–), Eng. jazz musician, cartoonist. The musician used this name for cartoons published in the *Daily Mail* from 1949 to 1953.

Fritz **Hundertwasser**: Friedrich Stowasser (1928–), Austr. painter. The artist adopted his new name in 1949, taking the initial "Sto-" as the Czech word for "hundred" and translating it into German. From about 1969 he signed his work Friedensreich Hundertwasser, the first name (ostensibly based on his real name) meaning "kingdom of peace," and representing his claim to lead the observer into a new realm of peace and happiness. He often added "Regenstag" ("rainy day") to this, making the full name Friedensreich Hundertwasser Regenstag, on the basis that he felt happy on rainy days because colors glowed and sparkled then. "This exaggerated concern with the name is a symptom of the braggadocio, conceit, and talent for self-advertisement that are apparent in his work as well as his life" [Chilvers, p. 253].

Alan **Hunter**: Alan John Moore (1952–), Eng. TV actor.

Evan **Hunter**: Salvatore A. Lombino (1926–), U.S. novelist. The writer used several pseudonyms, with Ed McBain (*q.v.*) probably the best known. Others include Curt Cannon, Hunt Collins, and Richard Marsten.

Jeffrey **Hunter**: Henry Herman McKinnies, Jr. (1925–1969), U.S. movie actor.

Kim **Hunter**: Janet Cole (1922–), U.S. stage, movie actress. The actress's name was changed by David O. Selznick, who told her that Janet Cole could be anyone, but that Kim Hunter had individuality, and with a name like that she would go far.

Ross **Hunter**: Martin Fuss (1916–1996), U.S. movie actor, producer. Presumably "Fuss" became "Ross," while "Martin" was converted to "Hunter."

Tab **Hunter**: Arthur Andrew Kelm (1931–), U.S. movie actor. The actor's name was given him by his agent, Henry Willson (see Rock Hudson, above). Until he was spotted by a talent scout in 1968, the actor used his mother's maiden name, Gelien, instead of his own surname.

Peter **Hurkos**: Pieter van der Hurk (1911–1988), Du.-born U.S. clairvoyant.

Veronica **Hurst**: Patricia Wilmshurst (1931–), Br. movie actress.

Mary Beth **Hurt**: Mary Beth Supinger (1948–), U.S. movie actress. The actress's professional name is that of her former husband, actor William Hurt (1950–).

Ruth **Hussey**: Ruth Carol O'Rourke (1914–), U.S. movie actress.

Wayne **Hussey**: Jerry Lovelock (1958–), U.S. rock musician.

Hustlebuck: Clarence Lawson Wood (1878–1957), Eng. painter, cartoonist. The artist used this name for cartoons published jointly with his son-in-law Keith Sholto Douglas. The name itself is presumably a blend of "hustle" (or "hustle-bustle") and "buck up." Cartoonists often have to work hurriedly or hastily.

Walter **Huston**: Walter Houghston (1884–1950), Can.-born U.S. stage, movie actor.

Betty **Hutton**: Elizabeth June Thornburg (1921–), U.S. movie actress, singer. The actress's name was changed in 1937 by Detroit bandleader Vincent Lopez after a numerologist had been consulted. At first the singer used the name Betty Darling when touring. Betty's sister Marion also changed her surname to Hutton (see below).

Ina Ray **Hutton**: Odessa Cowan (1913–1984), U.S. jazz band leader ("The Blonde Bombshell of Rhythm").

Marion **Hutton**: Marion Thornburg (1920–1987), U.S. singer, movie actress, sister of Betty Hutton (see above).

Robert **Hutton**: Robert Bruce Winne (1920–1994), U.S. movie actor.

Joris Karl **Huysmans**: Charles-Marie-Georges Huysmans (1848–1907), Fr. novelist, of Fr.-Du.

parentage. The writer adopted the Dutch equivalents of his first and last forenames, reversing their order.

Hviezdoslav: Pál Orzságh (1849–1921), Slovakian poet. The poet's assumed name literally means "glory of the stars."

Hwfa Môn: Rowland Williams (1823–1905), Welsh poet. The writer took his bardic name from Rhos-tre-Hwfa on the island of Anglesey, where his parents moved in 1828. *Môn* is the Welsh name of Anglesey.

Père Hyacinthe: Charles-Jean-Marie Loyson (1827–1912), Fr. priest, writer.

Robin Hyde: Iris Guiver Wilkinson (1906–1939), S.A.-born N.Z. novelist, poet, of Eng./Austral. parentage. The writer adopted the name she had given a stillborn child in 1926 following an affair.

Diana Hyland: Diana Gentner (1936–1977), U.S. stage, TV actress.

Jack Hylton: Jack Hilton (1892–1965), Br. danceband leader, composer.

Jane Hylton: Gwendoline Clark (1927–1979), Br. movie actress.

Ronald Hynd: Ronald Hens (1931–), Eng. ballet dancer, choreographer, director. Hynd married the dancer Annette Page (*q.v.*).

Dorothy Hyson: Dorothy Wardell Heisen (1914–1996), U.S. stage, movie actress.

Iaco ap Dewi: James Davies (1648–1722), Welsh copyist. The scholar adopted a name that is the Welsh equivalent of the original. His surname literally means "son of David."

Iago ap Ieuan: James James (1833–1902), Welsh musician. The composer of the Welsh national anthem (known in English as "Land of My Fathers") adopted a name that means "James son of Evan." It alludes to his father, Ieuan ap Iago (*q.v.*), who wrote the words.

Janis Ian: Janis Eddy Fink (1951–), U.S. pop singer, song writer. The singer adopted her brother's first name for her new surname.

Scott Ian: Scott Rosenfeld (1963–), U.S. rock guitarist.

Ianthe: Emma Catherine Embury (1806–1863), U.S. novelist. The writer used this name for her contributions to various periodicals, perhaps borrowing it from one of the many literary Ianthes, such as the maiden in Shelley's *Queen Mab* or the young girl to whom Byron dedicated *Childe Harold's Pilgrimage*. The letters of the name also occur in her middle name, Catherine, so this may be the prime source of the pseudonym.

Juana de Ibarbourou: Juanita Fernández Morales (1895–1979), Uruguayan poet.

Abdullah Ibrahim: Adolph Johannes Brand (1934–1990), S.A. black popular pianist, composer. The musician adopted his name on converting to Islam in the 1960s.

Ice Cube: O'Shea Jackson (1968–), U.S. black rapper, movie actor.

Ice-T: Tracey Marrow (1959–), U.S. black rapper, movie actor. The rap artist, a former gang member in Los Angeles, based his name on that of a black exploitation writer, Iceberg Slim, with "T" for "Tracey."

Billy Idol: William Michael Albert Broad (1955–), Eng. punk rock singer. A music reviewer comments: "Punk pseudonyms do not mature well, as a rule, but William Broad made an inspired choice when he reinvented himself as Billy Idol. The implications of the name are simultaneously cynical, ironic and starstruck, and that sums up the contradictions of his music and career" [David Toop, *The Times*, May 4, 1990]. Idol's own comment: "It's a joke, right, but it's smart, and it's better than [Sid] Vicious [*q.v.*], or [Dee] Generate" [Jon Savage, *Time Travel*, 1996].

Idris: Arthur Mee (1860–1926), Welsh journalist, writer. The compiler of *Who's Who in Wales* (1920) took his name from the Celtic giant said to have given the name of Cader Idris ("Seat of Idris"), a mountain ridge in southern Wales.

Thomas Idris: Thomas Howell Williams (1842–1925), Welsh chemist. The pharmacist lived much of his life in southern Wales near Cader Idris, and took his name from that mountain ridge. (See Idris above.) He adopted the name on marrying in 1873 and that year set up as a mineral water manufacturer, so that the name became associated with his product. He legally assumed Idris as an additional surname in 1893. "Idris" soft drinks are still produced as a legacy of his adopted name.

Idrisyn: John Jones (1804–1887), Welsh biblical scholar. The writer based his name on that of Cader Idris, a mountain in southern Wales named for a legendary giant. (See Idris, above.) The suffix *-yn* is a diminutive, so that the name is effectively "Little Idris."

Ieuan ap Iago: Evan James (1809–1878), Welsh poet. The writer of the words of the Welsh national anthem (known in English as "Land of My Fathers") adopted the Welsh equivalent of his name. He was the father of Iago ap Ieuan (*q.v.*), who wrote the music.

Ieuan Brydydd Hir: Evan Evans (1731–1788), Welsh poet, scholar. The writer earned his name as a nickname, "Evan the tall poet." He was also known as Euean Fardd, "Evan the bard."

Ieuan Glan Alarch: John Mills (1812–1873), Welsh musician, writer. The writer took his name from a local placename, with his new first name the Welsh equivalent of the original. Compare the next name below.

Ieuan Glan Geirionydd: Evan Evans (1795–1855), Welsh poet. The writer took his name from a local placename, with his new first name the Welsh equivalent of the original. (Evan and John are related names.)

Ieuan Gwyllt: John Roberts (1822–1877), Welsh musician, writer. The hymnwriter's adopted name means literally "wild John," denoting religious fervor.

Ieuan Gwynedd: Evan Jones (1820–1852), Welsh poet, journalist. The poet was born near Dolgellau, Merionethshire, in the historic kingdom of Gwynedd (a name adopted in 1974 for the modern county in this part of Wales). Hence his bardic name, meaning "Evan of Gwynedd."

Ieuan Lleyn: Evan Prichard (1769–1832), Welsh poet. The writer took his name from his native district of Lleyn, Caernarvonshire (now Gwynedd).

Ifor Ceri: John Jenkins (1770–1829), Welsh musicologist. The musician adopted a name meaning "Ifor of Ceri," the latter (also known as Kerry) being the village where he was vicar from 1807.

Father Ignatius: Joseph Leycester Lyne (1837–1908), Eng. mission preacher. The cleric, a self-appointed Benedictine monk, took his "monastic" name and title in 1862 in the course of his campaign to revive the Benedictine order in the Anglican Church. He presumably named himself after St. Ignatius of Loyola (1491–1556), founder of the Jesuits.

Ivan Ignatyev: Ivan Vasilyevich Kazansky (1892–1914), Russ. poet.

Nina Ignatyeva: Nina Aleksandrovna Sergeyeva (1923–), Russ. movie critic.

Francis Iles: Anthony Berkeley Cox (1893–1971), Br. crime writer. Other names used by the writer were Francis Iles and A. Monmouth Platts.

I. Ilf: Ilya Arnoldovich Faynzilberberg (Feinsilberberg) (1897–1937), Russ. satirical writer,

teaming with Ye. Petrov (*q.v.*). The two writers became so closely associated in the public mind that they ceased to sign their names separately. They were simply "Ilf and Petrov." At an early stage they wrote jointly as Tolstoyevsky, a humorous blend of the names of Tolstoy and Dostoyevsky.

Iliya II: Irakly Georgiyevich Gudushauri-Shioloshvili (1933–), Georgian catholicos. The head of the Georgian Orthodox Church received his name in 1957 on taking monastic vows. The name itself corresponds to English Elijah, traditionally interpreted as "Jehovah is God."

Margaret **Illington:** Maude Ellen Light (1879–1934), U.S. stage actress. The actress's stage name was coined for her by the theatre manager, Daniel Frohman, who engaged her. He seems to have "upped" Maude to Margaret, and based "Illington" on her second name, or formed it as a sort of anagram of her two last names.

M. **Ilyin:** Ilya Yakovlevich Marshak (1895–1953), Russ. writer. The writer was the brother of Yelena Ilyina (see next entry below).

Yelena **Ilyina:** Liya Yakovlevna Preys (Preis) (1901–1964), Russ. children's writer. The writer was the sister of M. Ilyin (see previous entry).

Immerito: Edmund Spenser (? 1552–1599), Eng. poet. This was the name under which Spenser published his first major work, *The Shepheardes Calender* (1579), with the name meaning "undeservedly" in Latin.

John **Ince:** John Edwards (1887–1947), U.S. movie actor.

Fay **Inchfawn:** Elizabeth Rebecca Ward (1881– ?), Br. popular verse writer. An unusual pen name which may be based on the name of the writer Elizabeth Inchbald (1753–1821).

Robert **Indiana:** Robert Clark (1928–), U.S. pop art painter. The artist took the name of his native state as his professional name.

Ilse **Indrane:** Undina Jatniece (1927–), Latvian writer.

Frieda **Inescort:** Frieda Wightman (1900–1976), Sc.-born movie actress, working in U.S. The actress adopted her mother's maiden name as her screen name.

Colonel Frederic **Ingham:** Edward Everett Hale (1822–1909), U.S. author, editor, Unitarian clergyman. The prolific author used the name for *The Ingham Papers* (1870) and other writings.

Mona **Inglesby:** Mona Vredenburg (1918–), Br. ballet dancer.

Kathleen **Inglewood:** Kate Isitt (1876– ?), N.Z. novelist, working in England.

Ingoldsby: [Rev.] James Hildyard (1809–1897), Eng. classical scholar. The writer adopted the name of the Lincolnshire village where he had his living as a clergyman (from 1846). Compare the next name below.

Thomas **Ingoldsby:** [Rev.] Richard Harris Barham (1788–1845), Br. writer, antiquary. The author of *The Ingoldsby Legends* (1837) (full title *The Ingoldsby Legends: or Mirth and Marvels, by Thomas Ingoldsby Esquire*), took his name from the Lincolnshire village of Ingoldsby, although he never held a living there, as did James Hildyard (see entry above).

Rex **Ingram:** Reginald Ingram Montgomery Hitchcock (1893–1950), Ir.-born U.S. movie director. The director should not be confused with his U.S. namesake and near coeval, movie actor Rex Ingram (1895–1969).

Michael **Innes:** John Innes Mackintosh Stewart (1906–1994), Sc. crime writer. Stewart, professionally a university lecturer in English literature, and a distinguished literary critic, used this name for his detective fiction. The name itself consists of the first names of two of his three sons, one of whom is the economist Michael Stewart (1933–), author of *Keynes and After* (1967) and other works.

Innocent II: Gregorio Papareschi dei Guidoni (? –1143), It. pope.

Innocent III: Giovanni Lotario dei Conti di Segni (1161–1216), It. pope.

Innocent IV: Sinibaldo Fieschi (? –1254), It. pope.

Innocent V: Pierre de Tarentaise (*c.*1224–1276), Fr. pope.

Innocent VI: étienne Aubert (1282–1362), Fr. pope.

Innocent VII: Cosimo Gentile de' Migliorati (*c.*1336–1406), It. pope.

Innocent VIII: Giovanni Battista Cibò (1432–1492), It. pope.

Innocent IX: Giovanni Antonio Facchinetti (1519–1591), It. pope.

Innocent X: Giovanni Battista Pamfili (1574–1655), It. pope.

Innocent XI: Benedetto Odescalchi (1611–1689), It. pope. The pontiff took the name of his patron, Innocent X (above), who had created

him cardinal in 1645. He in turn gave the name of Innocent XII (below).

Innocent XII: Antonio Pignatelli (1615–1700), It. pope. The pontiff took the name of his patron, Innocent XI (above), who had created him cardinal in 1681 and whom he regarded as his exemplar. Both men led notably simple ("innocent") lives.

Innocent XIII: Michelangelo dei Conti (1655–1721), It. pope. The pontiff adopted the name of Innocent III (above), from whose family he was descended.

Ismet **Inönü:** Mustafa Ismet (1884–1973), Turk. statesman, army officer. The statesman adopted his surname in 1934 from his victories in the two battles of Inönü, near Ankara, in 1921.

Ioan Pedr: John Peter (1833–1877), Welsh scholar. The Nonconformist minister took a name that was the Welsh equivalent of the original. Compare the names below.

Ioan Siengcin: John Jenkin (1716–1796), Welsh poet. The writer's name is the Welsh equivalent of the original.

Ioan Tegid: Tegid (*q.v.*).

Iolo Carnarvon: John John Roberts (1840–1914), Welsh poet. The writer's name means "Iolo of Caernarvon," from his native county of Caernarvonshire (now Gwynedd).

Iolo Morganwg: Edward Williams (1746–1826), Welsh poet, antiquary. The poet was born (and died) in the historic county of Glamorganshire. Hence his bardic name, "Iolo of Glamorgan."

Ionicus: Joshua Charles Armitage (1913–), Eng. painter, illustrator. The artist's work has been described as "meticulously executed" with a "pellucid linearity." Presumably his classical name is relevant here. Latin *Ionicus* means "Ionic," itself the term for an order of architecture: fluted columns topped by volutes.

Ionoron Glan Dwyryd: Rowland Walter (1819–1884), Welsh poet. The writer's new first name derives from Welsh *Ionawr*, "January," presumably because he was born in that month. The rest of the name is a local placename.

Mikhail **Ippolitov-Ivanov:** Mikhail Mikhaylovich Ivanov (1859–1935), Russ. composer.

Bodil **Ipsen:** Bodil Louise Jensen (1889–1964), Dan. stage, movie actress. The actress's name pays tribute to Henrik Ibsen, whose heroines she played.

Miroslav **Irchan:** Andrey Dmitriyevich Babyuk (1897–1937), Ukrainian writer.

Michael **Ireland:** Darrell Figgis (1882–1925), Ir. poet, writer.

Irenaeus: Samuel Irenaeus Prime (1812–1885), U.S. clergyman, author.

Irene: Irene Lenz-Gibbons (1901–1962), U.S. movie costume designer.

William **Irish:** Cornell George Hopley-Woolrich (1903–1968), U.S. mystery writer.

Ralph **Iron:** Olive Emilie Albertina Schreiner (1855–1920), S.A. novelist, of Ger.-Eng. parentage. The writer adopted the male name for *The Story of an African Farm* (1883) (see p. 27). She is said to have taken "Ralph" as a homage to the U.S. philosopher and poet Ralph Waldo Emerson (1803–1882), whose writings she admired. "Iron" may have had a symbolic sense, but also comprises letters in her original first name and surname.

I Roy: Roy Reid (*c.*1949–), Jamaican DJ, reggae musician.

George **Irving:** George Irving Shelasky (1922–), U.S. stage actor, singer.

[Sir] Henry **Irving:** John Henry Brodribb (1838–1905), Br. stage actor, theatre manager. The actor changed his name in order to avoid embarrassing his parents, who were ashamed of his profession. The name itself was a tribute to two real Irvings: the Scottish religious writer Edward Irving (1792–1834) and the popular American writer Washington Irving (1783–1859), his favorite boyhood author.

Jules **Irving:** Jules Israel (1925–), U.S. stage director.

May **Irwin:** Ada Campbell (1862–1938), Can.-born U.S. stage actress, music hall artist, of Sc. descent. The comedienne made her professional debut at the age of 13 with her sister Georgia, who took the name Flo Irwin. The two appeared together as The Irwin Sisters until 1883.

Isfoel: Dafydd Jones (1881–1968), Welsh poet. The writer took his name from a local placename, itself meaning "under the hill."

Iskander: Aleksandr Ivanovich Herzen (*q.v.*). The Russian revolutionary writer used the Turkish form of his first name as a pseudonym for *Notes of a Young Man* (1940) and other writings. For a similar name, compare Skanderbeg.

Islwyn: William Thomas (1832–1878), Welsh poet. The poet took his bardic name from Mynydd Islwyn ("Underbush Mountain"), southern Wales, near which he was born.

Bogdan **Istru:** Ivan Spiridonovich Bodaryov (1914–), Moldavian poet. The writer appears to have extracted his name from that of his native village, Pistrueni.

Miki **Iveria:** [Princess] Gayane Mikeladze (1910–1994), Russ.-born Br. movie actress.

Burl **Ives:** Burl Icle Ivanhoe Ives (1909–1995), U.S. stage, movie actor, folk singer. The singer's name is actually his real name, which is sometimes wrongly given as Burl Icle Ivanhoe.

Maria **Ivogün:** Ilse Kempner (1891–1987), Hung.-born Ger. opera singer. The singer created her new name by taking letters from the full maiden name of her mother, Ida von Günther.

Ryurik **Ivnev:** Mikhail Aleksandrovich Kovalyov (1891–1981), Russ. poet.

Ub **Iwerks:** Ubbe Ert Iwwerks (1901–1971), U.S. movie animator.

Daniel **Jablonski:** Daniel Ernst Figulus (1660–1741), Ger. Protestant theologian.

Jac Glan-y-gors: John Jones (1766–1821), Welsh satirical poet, working in England. The writer took his name from the farm where he was born, Glan-y-gors ("bank by the marsh"), near Ruthin, Denbighshire (now Clwyd).

Wanda **Jackson:** Wanda Goodman (1937–), U.S. pop singer.

Frank **Jacson:** Ramon Mercader (1914–1978), Sp. assassinator of Leon Trotsky (*q.v.*).

Dean **Jagger:** Dean Jeffries (1903–1991), U.S. movie actor.

Jahangir: [Prince] Salim (1569–1627), Ind. emperor. The Mogul emperor's adopted name means "holder of the world."

Jairzinho: Jaïr Ventura Filho (1944–), Brazilian footballer. A diminutive form of the sportsman's first name.

Jak: Raymond Allen Jackson (1927–1997), Eng. cartoonist.

Ahmad **Jamal:** Fritz Jones (1930–), U.S. jazz pianist. The musician changed his name in the early 1950s.

Brian **James:** (1) John Tierney (1892–1972), Austral. novelist, short story writer; (2) Brian Robertson (1955–), Eng. punk rock guitarist.

Dick **James:** Isaac Vapnick (1919–1986), Eng. popular singer, music promoter. The musician began his career as a dance band singer under the name Lee Sheridan.

Elmore **James:** Elmore Brooks (1918–1963), U.S. blues guitarist.

Etta **James:** Jamesetta Hawkins (1938–), U.S. soul singer.

Francis **James:** Francis Jacobs (1907–), Austral.-born Br. stage actor.

Geraldine **James:** Geraldine Blatchley, née Thomas (1950–), Br. stage, TV actress.

James **James:** Arthur Henry Adams (1872–1936), N.Z. novelist, poet, playwright.

Jimmy **James:** James Casey (1892–1965), Eng. music hall comedian. The comedian changed his name when working in Wales, on being told that his name Casey would not be popular there.

Joni **James:** Joan Carmello Babbo (1930–), U.S. popular singer.

Polly **James:** Pauline Devaney (1941–), Eng. stage, TV actress.

Rick **James:** James Johnson (1948–), U.S. "punk funk" musician.

Sonny **James:** James Loden (1929–), U.S. country singer.

Tommy **James:** Thomas Gregory Jackson (1947–), U.S. rock singer.

Will **James:** Joseph Ernest Nephtali Dufault (1892–1942), Can. children's writer. A much more appropriate name for the writer's cowboy stories.

Jamiroquai: James Robert Kay (1970–), Br. (white) soul singer. The musician's name, which is also that of his band, is an embellished version of his full name. He also performs as Jason Kay (as if "J. son of Kay"), as Jay Kay, and as simply J.K.

Laurence M. **Janifer:** Larry Mark Harris (1933–), U.S. SF writer.

Byron **Janis:** Byron Yankelevitch (1928–), U.S. concert pianist. The musician originally shortened his surname to Yanks, then reformed this as Janis.

Dorothy **Janis:** Dorothy Jones (1912–), U.S. movie actress.

Elsie **Janis:** Elsie Bierbauer (or Bierbower) (1889–1956), U.S. stage actress.

Emil **Jannings:** Theodor Friedrich Emil Janenz (1884–1950), Swiss-born Austr. movie actor, of U.S.-Ger. parentage.

Janosch: Horst Eckert (1931–), Ger. illustrator of children's books.

Steve **Jansen:** Stephen Batt (1959–), Eng. rock drummer. The Japan member is the brother of that group's lead singer, David Sylvian (*q.v.*).

David **Janssen:** David Harold Meyer (1931–1980), U.S. movie, TV actor. The actor's stage surname is that of his stepfather, Eugene Janssen.

Sebastian **Japrisot:** Jean-Baptiste Rossi (1931–), Fr. novelist. The novelist's new surname consists of letters extracted from his original name. Presumably his new first name must have some special significance.

Jacques **Jasmin:** Jacques Boé (1798–1864), Fr. dialect (Languedoc) poet, "troubadour."

David **Jason:** David John White (1940–), Br. TV actor. The actor was obliged to choose another name as there was an existing actor David White. He therefore changed his surname to Jason, the first name of his twin brother, who died at birth.

Leigh **Jason:** Leigh Jacobson (1904–1979), U.S. movie director.

W.M.L. **Jay:** Julia Louisa Matilda Woodruff, née Curtiss (1833–1909), Eng. writer. The author's pen name consists of a reversal of her initials, with the "J" of "Julia" forming a surname.

Jennifer **Jayne:** Jennifer Jayne Jones (1932–), Br. movie, TV actress.

Michael **Jayston:** Michael James (1935–), Eng. stage, movie, TV actor.

Jazzie B: Beresford Romeo (1963–), Br. black rapper, of Antiguan parentage.

Gloria **Jean:** Gloria Jean Schoonover (1926–), U.S. movie actress.

Jean Paul: Johann Paul Friedrich Richter (1763–1825), Ger. novelist, didactic writer. The writer's adoption of the French form of his first two names is said to have expressed his admiration for the French writer Jean-Jacques Rousseau.

Ursula **Jeans:** Ursula Livesey, née McMinn (1906–1973), Eng. stage actress.

Mahatma Cane **Jeeves:** W.C. Fields (*q.v.*).

Anne **Jeffreys:** Anne Carmichael (1923–), U.S. stage actress, singer.

Fran **Jeffries:** Frances Makris (1939–), U.S. movie producer, singer.

Ladislav **Jégé:** Ladislav Nádasi (1866–1940), Slovakian novelist, short story writer.

Allen **Jenkins:** Alfred McGonegal (1900–1974), U.S. movie actor.

Caryl **Jenner:** Pamela Penelope Ripman (1917–), Eng. stage director, theatre manager.

Jenneval: Hippolyte Louis Alexandre Dechet (1801–1830), Fr. comedian, poet.

Claudia **Jennings:** Mimi Chesterton (*c.*1950–1979), U.S. movie actress. The future actress adopted her new name for her appearance as a centerfold model ("Miss November 1969") in *Playboy*.

Kid **Jensen:** David Allen Jensen (1950–), Can.-born Eng. radio, TV DJ, compère. The radio and TV personality began working as a DJ when he was only 16. In 1968 he started working for Radio Luxembourg, where he was nicknamed "Kid" for his youth and youthful appearance. He adopted the name instead of his first name until about 1980, when he felt sufficiently mature to revert to "David." Even so, he still features as David "Kid" Jensen in later reference and publicity sources.

Suzie Jerome: Suzanne Willis (1960–1986), Br. movie, TV actress.

Mary Jerrold: Mary Allen (1877–1955), Br. movie actress.

Jesulín de Ubrique: Jesús Janeiro Bazán (1974–), Sp. bullfighter. The matador's first name is a diminutive of his original name. The rest of his name means "of Ubrique," referring to his native town.

Jethro: Kenneth C. Burns (1923–), U.S. humorous country singer, teaming with Homer (*q.v.*).

Jetsam: Malcolm McEachern (1884–1945), Austral. singer, stage, radio entertainer, teaming with Flotsam (*q.v.*).

Joan Jett: Joan Larkin (1960–), U.S. rock singer.

Jimmy Jewel: James Arthur Thomas Jewel Marsh (1912–1995), Eng. music hall, radio, TV comedian, teaming with Ben Warriss, his cousin. Jimmy Jewel explains the genesis of his name: "We were really a family called Marsh, but father always worked as Jimmy Jewel. He wouldn't let me call myself Jimmy Jewel, Jr., so for years I worked as Maurice Marsh because I was always doing Chevalier impressions; then we kept changing our names on the bills so the audience wouldn't know it was all one family" [*The Times*, August 3, 1983].

Jillana: Jillana Zimmermann (1936–), U.S. ballet dancer.

Ann Jillian: Ann Jura Nauseda (1951–), U.S. TV actress.

Jodelet: Julien Bedeau (*c.*1595–1660), Fr. comic actor, brother of L'Espy (*q.v.*).

Robert Joffrey: Abdullah Jaffa Anver Bey Khan (1930–1988), U.S. ballet dancer, choreographer, of Afghan parentage.

Johannes Secundus: Jan Nikolai Everaerts (1511–1536), Du. poet. The poet wrote in Latin. Hence his name, meaning "John (or Jan) the Second."

John II: Mercurius (? –535), It. pope. Because he bore the name of a pagan god (Mercury), the pope adopted the name of John I (martyred 526). He was the first pope to assume a different name (in 533).

John III: Catelinus (? –574), It. pope.

John XII: Ottaviano (Octavian) (*c.*937–964), It. pope.

John XIV: Pietro Canepanova (? –984), It. pope. This pope took a new name to avoid repeating the name of St. Peter (*q.v.*), leader of the apostles and first bishop of Rome.

John XXI: Pedro Julião (Peter of Spain) (*c.*1210 or 1220–1277), Port. pope. Like John XIV (*q.v.*), this pope took a new name to avoid that of St. Peter (*q.v.*), first bishop of Rome.

John XXII: Jacques d'Euse (or Duèse) (*c.*1244–1334), Fr. pope.

John XXIII: Angelo Giuseppe Roncalli (1881–1963). See pp. 48–49 for a consideration of this pope's name, and those of other popes called John or John Paul.

Dr. John: Malcolm John ("Mac") Rebennack (1941–), U.S. rock musician.

Mr. John: John Pico Harberger (? 1902–1993), U.S. milliner. The designer's origins are obscure. He appears to have been born in Germany, and is said to have changed his name because Americans kept referring to him as "Hamburger."

Alix John: Alice Jones (1853–1933), Can. writer, working in France.

Elton John: Reginald Kenneth Dwight (1947–), Eng. pop musician. Reg Dwight changed his name by deed poll, adopting his new first name from Elton Dean, saxophonist for the soul group Bluesology, and his surname from Long John Baldry, the rock singer. The pop singer's *full* stage name is in Elton Hercules John, the middle name added later since, as he explained, "It gave me something to look up to and to remind me always to be strong." The singer felt that his original name "sounded like a cement mixer" [Gerald Newman with Joe Bivona, *Elton John*, 1976].

Evan John: Evan John Simpson (1901–1953), Br. playwright, novelist.

Graham John: Graham John Colmer (1887– ?), Eng. playwright, lyricist.

Jasper John: Rosalie Muspratt Jones (1913–), Br. movie, stage actress.

Katherine John: Karen Watkins, née Jones (1948–), Welsh crime writer. A version of the writer's maiden name for her new surname. She also writes as Catrin Collier.

Robert John: Robert John Pedrick, Jr. (1946–), U.S. pop singer.

Rosamund John: Nora Rosamund Jones (1913–), Br. movie actress.

John Eilian: John Tudor Jones (1904–1985), Welsh poet, editor. The writer took his name from his birthplace, the village of Llaneilian, Anglesey.

[St.] **John of the Cross:** Juan de Yepes y Alvarez (1542–1591), Sp. mystic, poet. The saint's title refers directly to his poetry, and in particular to his poem *Noche oscura del alma* ("Dark night of the soul"), in which he describes how the human soul sheds its attachment to everything and finally passes through a personal experience of the Crucifixion to attain the glory of Christ.

John Paul I: Albino Luciani (1912–1978), It. pope. The pope's name is said to have expressed his wish to combine the progressive and traditional qualities of John XXIII and Paul VI (*qq.v.*).

John Paul II: Karol Wojtyła (1920–), Pol. pope. For an account of the relationship between the various popes named John and John Paul, see pp. 48–49.

Foster Johns: Gilbert Vivian Seldes (1893–1970), U.S. journalist, drama critic, writer.

Milton Johns: John Robert Milton (1938–), Br. stage, TV actor.

Stratford Johns: Alan Edgar Stratford Johns (1925–), Br. stage, TV. movie actor.

Crockett Johnson: David Johnson Leisk (1906–1975), U.S. cartoonist, children's writer. In view of the artist's original first name, this pseudonym may have been based on a nickname ("Davy Crockett").

Don Johnson: Donald Wayne (1950–), U.S. TV actor.

Jimmy Johnson: James Thompson (1928–), U.S. blues musician, brother of Syl Johnson (*q.v.*).

John Johnson: Guy (or Guido) Fawkes (1570–1606), Eng. conspirator. The name was assumed by Guy Fawkes when he hired a house next to the Houses of Parliament with the aim of constructing a gunpowder mine in its cellars (the "Gunpowder Plot") so as to blow up the House of Lords while King James was present there for the official opening of parliament. "John Johnson" was to be the servant of one of the conspirators, Thomas Percy. The name seems arbitrary.

Kay Johnson: Catherine Townsend (1904–1975), U.S. movie actress.

Lady Bird Johnson: Claudia Alta Johnson, née Taylor (1912–), U.S. First Lady. The wife of President Lyndon B. Johnson was so nicknamed by her nurse, Alice Tittle, who said of her two-year-old charge, "Why, she's as pretty as a ladybird!" She thus grew up to be known as Lady Bird Taylor, and happened to marry a man whose first names had the same initials as her own. After the President's death in 1973, his widow maintained her bank account in the name of Mrs. L.B. Johnson and continued to sign her correspondence Lady Bird Johnson. The initials were further preserved in the names of the couple's two daughters, Linda Baines Johnson and Lucy Baines Johnson.

Rita Johnson: Rita McSean (1912–1965), U.S. movie actress. The actress "translated" her Gaelic surname into English to provide her stage name; "McSean" means "son of John."

Syl Johnson: Sylvester Thompson (1936–), U.S. blues musician, brother of Jimmy Johnson (*q.v.*).

Wilko Johnson: John Wilkinson (1947–), Eng. rock guitarist.

Benjamin F. Johnson of Boone: James Whitcomb Riley (1854–1916), U.S. poet, journalist.

Al Jolson: Asa Yoelson (1885–1950), U.S. singer, stage, movie actor, of Lithuanian Jewish descent. The singer first changed his forename Asa to Al when his elder brother changed his own name, Hirsh, to Harry. Later, in 1899, Fred E. Moore, an electrician in New York's Dewey Theatre, suggested he join him in a singing act as Harry Joelson. Eventually, four years later, the printer shortened "Joelson" to "Jolson" as the actor's original name seemed "long, foreign sounding" [Michael Freedland, *Al Jolson*, 1971].

Jon: William John Philpin Jones (1913–1992), Welsh political cartoonist.

Annie Jones: Annika Jasko (*c.*1967–), Austral. TV actress, of Hung. parentage.

Buck Jones: Charles Frederick Gebhardt (1889–1942), U.S. movie actor.

Candy Jones: Jessica Wilcox (1925–1990), U.S. model, writer on fashion. The story goes that Wilcox was renamed Candy Johnson by her agency but misremembered her name and gave it as Jones.

Casey Jones: John Luther Jones (1864–1900), U.S. railroader. The folk hero was nicknamed Casey from the town of Cayce, Kentucky, where he and his family moved when he was in his teens.

Clay Jones: David Clay-Jones (1923–1996), Welsh broadcaster on gardening. The horticulturist adopted the name by which he was known at school in order to be distinguished from the other 13 Joneses in his class of 33, many of them also David. Clay, his mother's maiden name, was a coincidentally apt name for a gardener.

Jennifer **Jones**: Phyllis Selznick, née Isley (1919–), U.S. movie actress. The actress was given her new name by producer David O. Selznick, whom she married as her second husband in 1949.

John **Jones**: Henry Cecil, 10th Earl of Exeter, Lord Burghley (1754–1804), Eng. aristocrat. The nephew and heir of the 9th Earl of Exeter adopted this name when living apart from his first wife, born Emma Vernon, who had eloped with a clergyman. He married Sarah Hoggins, a farmer's daughter, under this name when she was 17 and he 36, and subsequently obtained a divorce to legitimize the children she bore him. He abandoned his alias on succeeding to the peerage as 10th Earl (from 1801 1st Marquess) of Exeter, when his wife became a countess. The tale is touchingly told in Tennyson's poem "The Lord of Burleigh" (1842).

Johnny **Jones**: Charles Edward Peil (1907–1962), U.S. juvenile movie actor. The actor appeared under this name in a series of two-reelers in 1920–21 entitled *The Adventures and Emotions of Edgar Pomeroy*. As the son of movie actor Edward J. Peil (1888–1958), he subsequently appeared as Edward Peil, Jr.

John Paul **Jones**: (1) John Paul (1747–1792), Sc.-born U.S. naval hero. This is the man who is said to have given his name to the dance known as the Paul Jones; (2) John Baldwin (1946–), Br. rock bassist.

John Aelod **Jones**: John Roberts Williams (1914–), Welsh journalist, broadcaster, writer. A substitution of one common Welsh name for another.

L.Q. **Jones**: Justus Ellis McQueen (1927–), U.S. movie actor. The initials represents the actor's original middle name and surname.

Paul **Jones**: Paul Pond (1942–), Eng. actor, former pop musician.

Richard **Jones**: Theodore Edward Hook (1788–1841), Eng. humorist, novelist.

Sheridan **Jones**: Ada Elizabeth Chesterton, née Jones (1870–1962), Br. journalist, philanthropist. Sheridan was a family name on the paternal side, used by the writer for many of her journalistic contributions. Among her family and close friends she was known as "Keith," for the writer Gilbert Keith Chesterton (1874–

1936), her brother-in-law. She also wrote under the male name John Keith Prothero.

Sissieretta **Jones**: Matilda Sissieretta Joyner (1868–1933), U.S. black opera singer.

Spike **Jones**: Lindley Murray (1911–1965), U.S. novelty musician.

T. Percy **Jones**: William Edmonstoune Aytoun (1813–1865), Sc. humorous writer.

Tom **Jones**: Thomas Jones Woodward (1940–), Welsh popular singer. The singer was originally renamed Tommy Scott when he joined a group called the Senators. Their bass guitarist Vernon Hopkins gave the name: "We were thinking of a name when he joined the Senators and I thought I'd nip out to a telephone box and pick up the directory. I thought something with S maybe and saw the name Scott. I went back in and said 'Tommy Scott and the Senators' and they said 'Great.'" It turned out there was another singer Tommy Scott, however, so in 1964 Woodward's manager, Gordon Mills, gave him the name by which he became popularly known, taking it from the eponymous hero of Henry Fielding's novel (1749), or, more precisely, from its movie version (1963), in which Tom Jones, who undergoes many sexual escapades, is played by Albert Finney [Stafford Hildred and David Gritten, *Tom Jones: A Biography*, 1990].

Spike **Jonze**: Adam Spiegel (1969–), U.S. video director. The former photographer presumably borrowed the name of City Slickers bandleader Spike Jones (see above).

Mrs. Dorothy **Jordan**: Dorothea Bland (1762–1816), Ir. comedy actress. The actress was the illegitimate daughter of another actress by a gentleman named Francis Bland, and she first went on the stage as "Miss Francis." In 1780 she was engaged by Richard Daly, the Irish theatre manager, for the Smock Alley Theatre, Dublin, but after an affair with him fled two years later to England with her mother and sister. There, although clearly pregnant (but not married), she successfully auditioned for theatre manager Tate Williamson, who renamed her for a biblical allusion: "You have crossed the water [the Irish Sea] so I'll call you Jordan."

Sheila **Jordan**: Sheila Jeanette Dawson (1928–), U.S. (white) jazz singer.

Joselito: José Gómez (1895–1920), Sp. bullfighter.

Père **Joseph**: François Joseph Leclerc du Tremblay (1577–1638), Fr. friar, diplomat. The friar is equally well known by his nickname of *L'Eminence Grise* (as advisor to Cardinal Richelieu, *L'Eminence Rouge*), referring to his gray habit.

Joshua II: Franz Edmund Creffield (1875–1906), U.S. cult leader, "messiah," of Ger. descent.

Josiah Allen's Wife: Marietta Holley (1836–1926), U.S. humorist. In the humorist's writings, much of the homely philosophizing by Samantha, the wife of a fictional character named Josiah Allen, served as propaganda for temperance and female suffrage.

Maria **Jotuni:** Maria Kustaava Tarkiainen (1880–1943), Finn. novelist, playwright.

Louis **Jourdan:** Louis Gendre (1919–), Fr. movie actor. The actor's screen name seems to be based on his original surname.

Leatrice **Joy:** Leatrice Joy Zeidler (1894–1985), U.S. movie actress.

Brenda **Joyce:** Betty Graffina Leabo (1915–), U.S. movie actress.

Thomas **Joyce:** Arthur Joyce Lunel Carey (1888–1957), Ir. novelist.

Col **Joye:** Colin Jacobsen (1937–), Austral. popular musician.

J.R. Tryfanwy: John Richard Williams (1867–1924), Welsh poet. The poet took his name from his initials and the name of his birth place, Rhostryfan, Caernarvonshire (now Gwynedd).

J.S. of Dale: Frederic Jesup Stimson (1855–1943), U.S. lawyer, writer. The initials presumably represent the author's middle name (or middle name and surname).

Juanita: Joy Ganjou (1912–1992), Br. variety artist, dancer.

Judic: Anne-Marie-Louise Damiens (1850–1911), Fr. comic actress, singer.

Aunt **Judy:** Margaret Scott Gatty (1809–1873), Eng. children's writer. The writer (Margaret Gatty, who married a Mr. Scott) took her name from that of the popular Victorian children's periodical, *Aunt Judy's Magazine*, of which she was editor. She was the mother of the children's writer Juliana Horatia Ewing, and the magazine was itself named with the family pet name, Judy, for Juliana.

Julevno: Jules Eveno (1845–1915), Fr. occultist.

Raul **Julia:** Raúl Rafael Carlos Julia y Arcelay (1940–1994), Puerto Rican-born U.S. movie actor. Not a pseudonym in the strict sense of the word but a simplified form of a typical lengthy Hispanic name.

Julius II: Giuliano della Rovere (1443–1513), It. pope. The pontiff's new name (in Italian, Giulio) is close to his original name.

Julius III: Giovanni Maria Ciocchi del Monte (1487–1555), It. pope. The pontiff took the name of Julius II (*q.v.*), to whom he had been chamberlain as a young man.

Louis **Jullien:** Louis Georges Maurice Adolphe Roch Albert Abel Antonio Alexandre Noé Jean Lucien Daniel Eugène Joseph-le-Brun Joseph-Barême Thomas Thomas Thomas-Thomas Pierre Cerbon Pierre-Maurel Barthélemi Artus Alphonse Bertrand Emanuel Dieudonné Josué Vincent Luc Michel Jules-de-la-Plane Jules-Bazin Julio-César Jullien (1812–1860), Fr. orchestral conductor, composer. Not exactly a pseudonym, of course, but at least a masking of the musician's alleged 34 additional baptismal names.

June: June Howard Tripp (1901–1985), Eng. revue actress, singer, working in U.S.

Jennie **June:** Jane Cunningham Croly (1829–1901), Eng.-born U.S. writer. The writer's pen name was doubtless a double variation on her original first name.

Juninho: Oswaldo Giroldo Júnior (1973–), Brazilian born Br. footballer. The sportsman's surname-based professional name means "little one."

Junius: Sir Philip Francis (1740–1818), Ir. politician and writer. The named writer is generally believed to be the author of the "Letters of Junius" that appeared in the *Public Advertiser.*. If the pseudonym is not a reference to a particular Roman of note, such as one of the conspirators Lucius Junius Brutus or Marcus Junius Brutus, who plotted to kill Caesar, the aim may have been to indicate a young or *junior* person. Compare the next two entries below. (For further comments, see also p. 58.)

E. **Junius:** Adrien Emmanuel Rouquette (1813–1887), U.S. poet, novelist. The writer used the name for his *Critical Dialogue Between Aboo and Caboo* (1880), denouncing the depiction of Creoles in George Washington Cable's novel, *The Grandissimes* (1880). Rouquette, who was the son of a Creole mother, based his pen name on that of Junius (*q.v.*), with "E." presumably for "Emmanuel."

Junius Americanus: Arthur Lee (1740–1792), U.S. diplomat. The diplomat, who used the name for some letters he published, adopted the pseudonym made famous by Junius (*q.v.*).

Katy **Jurado:** María Cristina Estella Marcella Jurado García (1927–), Mexican movie actress, working in U.S.

John **Justin:** John Ledsma (1917–), Br. movie actor.

Justinian I: Petrus Sabbatius (483–565), Roman emperor. The emperor, whose full Latin name was Flavius Justinianus, took his new name from his uncle, Justin I (*c.*450–527), who preceded him and promoted him.

Tonio **K.:** Steve Krikorian (1950–), U.S. rock singer, songwriter.

Vasily **Kachalov:** Vasily Ivanovich Shverubovich (1875–1948), Russ. stage actor.

János **Kádár:** János Czermanik (or Csermanek) (1912–1989), Hung. Communist leader, premier.

Kadyr-Gulyam: Vladislav Konstantinovich Yanushevsky (1886–1970), Russ. circus artist, acrobat, athlete, husband of Nedin (*q.v.*). The performer adopted an Arabic-style name that could be loosely interpreted as "powerful young man" (although in Arabic the adjective, here *kadir*, properly follows the noun).

Kako: Francisco Angel Bastar (*c.*1937–), Puerto Rican popular musician, band leader.

Kal: Kevin Kallaugher (1955–), U.S. political cartoonist, working in U.K.

Kalanag: Helmut Schreiber (1893–1963), Ger. illusionist. The magician adopted the name from Rudyard Kipling's *Jungle Book*, where it is that of an elephant, meaning "Black Snake."

Ossip **Kalenter:** Johannes Burckhardt (1900–), Ger. writer.

Kalki: Ramasami Kirushnamurti (1899–1954), Ind. writer. The writer adopted the name of the Hindu horse god Kalki, the final avatar of Vishnu.

Valdis **Kalnroze:** Valdis Karlovich Rosenberg (1894–), Latvian painter. The artist adopted a Latvian equivalent of his original name (meaning "rose hill").

Galiaskar **Kamal:** Galiaskar Kamaletdinov (1878–1933), Russ. (Tatar) writer.

Sharif **Kamal:** Sharif Baygildiyev (1884–1942), Russ. (Tatar) writer, playwright. The writer adopted his father's name as his pen name.

Kamehameha I: Paiea (*c.*1758–1819), Hawaiian king. The king and conqueror's original name, Paiea, meant "hard-shelled crab." His new name, Kamehameha, which passed to his

sucessors in the dynasty he founded, means "very lonely one," "one set apart." The dynasty ended in 1872 with the death of Kamehameha V.

Lev Borisovich **Kamenev:** Lev Borisovich Rozenfeld (1883–1936), Russ. revolutionary, opponent of Stalin (*q.v.*). The revolutionary's name is based on Russian *kamen'*, "stone," so that he was a "man of stone," while Stalin was a "man of steel." Stalin eventually crushed him, proving that steel is stronger than stone.

Boris **Kamkov:** Boris Davidovich Kats (Katz) (1885–1938), Russ. Socialist Revolutionary leader.

Kamo: Simon Arshakovich Ter-Petrosyan (1882–1922), Georgian revolutionary.

Eden **Kane:** Richard Graham Sarstedt (1942–), Eng. pop singer. The singer is said to have derived his name from the Orson Welles movie *Citizen Kane* (1941). He used it from the early 1960s, although he also featured briefly in 1973 with his brothers Robin and Peter Sarstedt under his own name, as the Sarstedt Brothers.

Helen **Kane:** Helen Schroeder (1903–1966), U.S. singer, movie actress.

John **Kane:** John Cain (1860–1934), Sc.-born U.S. artist.

Richard **Kane:** Richard George Wright (1938–), Br. stage, TV, radio actor. The actor appears to have derived his stage name from his mother's middle name of Kathleen.

Donna **Karan:** Donna Faske (1949–), U.S. fashion designer.

Karandash: Mikhail Nikolayevich Rumyantsev (1901–1983), Russ. circus clown. The clown's name is the Russian word for "pencil." He adopted it in 1934 when appearing in Leningrad, taking it from the French cartoonist Caran d'Ache (*q.v.*). Rumyantsev had earlier worked as a commercial artist. Hence the attraction of this particular name.

Allan **Kardec:** Léon Hippolyte Rivail (1804–1869), Fr. occultist. The Breton name was given the spiritualist by a medium, who told him that in a previous existence he had been a Druid so called. His new first name appears to be based on his original name. His surname probably derives from Breton *kard*, "quarter," denoting a fourth child.

Anna **Karina:** Hanne Karin Blarke Bayer (1940–), Dan. movie actress, working in France, U.S. One can see the direct origin of the actress's name in her two first names. At the same time the screen name strongly suggests that of

Tolstoy's heroine, Anna Karenina, whether in the original novel or (more likely) in one of its filmed versions.

Barbara **Karinska:** Varvara Zhmoudsky (1886–1983), Russ.-U.S. ballet costume designer, maker.

Miriam **Karlin:** Miriam Samuels (1925–), Br. movie revue comedienne.

Boris **Karloff:** William Henry (or Charles Edward) Pratt (1887–1969), Eng. movie actor, working in Canada, U.S. The actor, noted for his portrayal of the monster in the horror movie *Frankenstein* (1931), derived his Russian-sounding name from an early family member. "I dredged up 'Karloff' from Russian ancestors on my mother's side, and I picked 'Boris' out of the chilly, Canadian air," he explained.

Phil **Karlson:** Philip N. Karlstein (1908–1985), U.S. movie director.

Dun **Karm:** Carmelo Psaila (1871–1961), Maltese poet.

Mick **Karn:** Anthony Michaelides (1958–), Br. rock saxophonist.

Maria **Karnilova:** Maria Dovgolenko (1920–), U.S. ballet dancer, of Russ. parentage. The dancer adopted (and adapted) her stage name from her mother's maiden name, which was Karnilovich.

Fred **Karno:** Frederick John Westcott (1866–1941), Eng. music hall comedian. The artist adopted his name in 1887 when he and two gymnast colleagues filled in at a London music hall for a troupe called The Three Carnos. His agent, Richard Warner, suggested they change the "C" to a more distinctive "K" [J.P. Gallagher, *Fred Karno, Master of Mirth and Tears*, 1971].

S. **Karonin:** Nikolay Yelpidiforovich Petropavlovsky (1853–1892), Russ. writer.

Ivan **Karpenko-Kary:** Ivan Karpovich Tobilevich (1845–1907), Ukrainian dramatist, actor, brother of Nikolay Sadovsky and Panas Saksagansky (*qq.v.*). The writer took the first part of his name from his father's first name, Karp (itself giving his own patronymic of Karpovich). The second part came from Gnat Kary, a character in Taras Shevchenko's poetic drama *Nazar Stodolya*.

Karro: Aleksandr Georgiyevich Karashkevich (1893–1945), Russ. circus artist, dog trainer.

Arnold **Kashtanov:** Arnold Lvovich Epshteyn (Epstein) (1938–), Russ. writer.

Garry **Kasparov:** Garri (or Harry) Kimovich Weinstein (1963–), Azerbaijan-born Russ. chess player. The world chess champion was born to a Jewish father and Armenian mother. He gained his new name at the age of seven following the death of his father in a road accident: "Many people wonder why I changed my name from Weinstein to Kasparov. After my father died I went to live with my mother's parents. It seemed natural to use the name Kasparov, particularly as they had three daughters and no son" [Garry Kasparov with Donald Trelford, *Unlimited Challenge*, 1990].

Kurt S. **Kasznar:** Kurt Serwischer (1913–1979), Austr. stage, movie actor.

Kurt **Katch:** Isser Kać (1896–1958), Pol. movie actor, working in U.S.

Cousin **Kate:** Catharine Douglass Bell (? –1861), Sc. novelist. The writer used this homely name, in the manner of her day, for *Set About It At Once, or Cousin Kate's Story* (1847) and later tales.

Anna **Kavan:** Helen Edmonds, previously Ferguson, née Woods (1901–1968), Fr.-born novelist, short story writer, working in U.S., U.K. The writer adopted her pen name in 1940 from one of her own fictional characters, the heroine of *Let Me Alone* (1930), written under her real name. The first novel she wrote as Anna Kavan was, appropriately, *Change the Name* (1941).

Dan **Kavanagh:** Julian Patrick Barnes (1946–), Eng. novelist. The writer, whose novels usually appear under his real name (Julian Barnes), adopted this name for his detective fiction, taking it from his wife, literary agent Pat Kavanagh. He has also written for the *New Review* as Edward Pygge and for *The Tatler* as Basil Seal, the latter name being that of the central character in novels by Evelyn Waugh.

Charles **Kay:** Charles Piff (1930–), Eng. stage actor.

Connie **Kay:** Conrad Henry Kirnon (1927–1994), West Indies-born U.S. jazz drummer.

John **Kay:** Joachim F. Krauledat (1944–), Ger.-born U.S. rock musician.

Karen **Kay:** Adrienne Judith Pringle (1947–), Eng. TV entertainer, singer.

Danny **Kaye:** David Daniel Kominski (1913–1987), U.S. stage, movie, TV actor, of Ukrainian parentage.

Nora **Kaye:** Nora Koreff (1920–1987), U.S. ballet dancer.

Howard **Kaylan:** Howard Kaplan (1947–), U.S. rock musician.

Elia **Kazan:** Elia Kazanjoglous (1909–), Turk.-born U.S. movie director, of Gk. parentage. The future director was taken by his family to the U.S. when he was only four, and they then shortened their name to Kazan. Later, when he was established in Hollywood, an unsuccessful attempt was made to change his name yet again to "Cezanne."

Aleksandr **Kazbegi:** Aleksandr Chopikashvili (1848–1893), Georgian writer. The writer renamed his family for nearby Mt. Kazbek.

Ernie **K-Doe:** Ernest Kador, Jr. (1936–), U.S. black rhythm 'n' blues singer.

Buster **Keaton:** Joseph Francis Keaton (1895–1966), U.S. movie comedian. It remains uncertain how the actor came by his nickname. The popular account is that it was given him by Harry Houdini (*q.v.*) after seeing the boy Keaton tumble down a flight of stairs. On the other hand, there may be a link with the comic strip character Buster Brown. Either way he was quite unrelated to the actress Diane Keaton (see below).

Diane **Keaton:** Diane Hall (1946–), U.S. stage, movie actress. The actress adopted her mother's maiden name of Keaton since there was already a Diane Hall as a member of the actors' union, Equity, which has a ruling that no two members should have the same name.

Michael **Keaton:** Michael Douglas (1951–), U.S. movie, TV actor, comedian. The actor changed his name to avoid confusion with Michael Douglas (1944–), actor son of Kirk Douglas (*q.v.*). He took his new name from Diane Keaton (see above) on seeing her picture in the *Los Angeles Times*.

Viola **Keats:** Viola Smart (1911–), Sc. stage actress. The actress adopted her mother's maiden name as her stage name.

Howard **Keel:** Harold Clifford Leek (1917–), U.S. stage, movie actor, singer.

Malcolm **Keen:** Malcolm Knee (1887–1970), Br. movie, stage actor, theatre manager.

Carolyn **Keene:** (1) Edward L. Stratemeyer (1863–1930), U.S. children's writer; (2) Harriet Stratemeyer Adams (1894–1982), U.S. children's writer, his daughter. Mrs. Adams continued, and expanded on, the many series started by her father, especially that centering on Nancy Drew, the girl detective. She was also the major author of the Hardy Boys series, begun by the Stratemeyer Syndicate, set up in 1914 to produce books that Stratemeyer himself outlined and edited.

He also wrote as Laura Lee Hope and Arthur M. Winfield (*qq.v.*). But why did he not use "Carolyn Keene" for the girl detective, and keep "Nancy Drew" for himself? They would have been much more appropriate that way round.

Laura **Keene:** Mary Frances Moss (*c.*1826–1873), Br.-born U.S. actress, theatre manager. There is some dispute about the actress's original name and date of birth, but the particulars are possibly as stated here.

Tom **Keene:** George Duryea (1896–1963), U.S. movie actor.

Oline **Keese:** Caroline Leakey (1827–1881), Eng. novelist, poet. The writer lived for a time in Tasmania, Australia, and used this name, loosely based on her real name, for *The Broad Arrow* (1859), a novel based on her experiences there.

Keith: James Barry Keefer (1949–), U.S. pop singer. The name must have originated as a nickname based on the singer's surname.

David **Keith:** Francis Steegmuller (1906–), U.S. novelist, literary critic. The author of serious literary and biographical studies used this name for his crime fiction. He also wrote as Byron Steel (*q.v.*).

Ian **Keith:** Keith Ross (1899–1960), U.S. movie actor. The actor took his mother's maiden name as his stage name.

Penelope **Keith:** Penelope Timson, née Hatfield (1940–), Eng. TV actress. The actress adopted her mother's maiden name.

Harry **Kellar:** Heinrich Keller (1849–1922), U.S. magician.

Will P. **Kellino:** William P. Gislingham (1873–1958), Br. circus clown, movie actor, director. The performer's new surname was loosely based on his original name.

Kem: Kimon Evan Marengo (1906–1988), Egyptian-born Br. political cartoonist, of Gk. parentage. A neat combination of the artist's initials and a shortened form of his first name.

Kemine: Mamedveli (*c.*1770–1840), Turkmen satirical poet. The poet's assumed name means "submissive one."

[Sir] James **Kemnal:** James Hermann Rosenthal (1864–1927), Br. engineering equipment manufacturer. The head of Babcock & Wilcox (established in 1891 as a independent British firm from the U.S. original) adopted his new name in 1915.

Jeremy **Kemp:** Edmund Jeremy James Walker (1935–), Eng. movie, TV actor. The actor adopted his mother's maiden name as his stage name.

Mirdza **Kempe:** Mirdza Yanovna Naykovskaya (1907–1974), Latvian poet.

Kempferhausen: Robert Pearse Gillies (1788–1858), Eng. litterateur and autobiographer. The writer adopted the name under which he featured in the series of dialogues known as the *Noctes Ambrosianae* published in *Blackwood's Edinburgh Magazine* between 1822 and 1835. Compare the name of Christopher North.

Joan **Kemp-Welch:** Joan Green (1906–), Eng. stage actress, theatre director. The actress took her mother's maiden name for her stage name, rather unusually preserving its lengthy (for theatrical purposes) "double-barrelling."

Geoffrey **Kendal:** Geoffrey Bragg (*c.*1910–), Br. stage actor, theatre manager, father of TV actress Felicity Kendal (1947–) and movie actress Jennifer Kendal (1934–1984). As a young man, Geoffrey Bragg was dismissed from his job as an engineering apprentice, and decided instead to try his luck on the stage with his surname changed to that of his home town in the English Lake District, Kendal. Bragg, at that time, was a name of little charisma, although today it is associated with the English novelist and broadcaster Melvyn Bragg (1939–), to whom Geoffrey Kendal may be distantly related.

The Kendal family spent some time in India in the 1940s and 1950s (interrupted by Felicity's birth) touring the country and staging Shakespeare's plays. The 1965 movie *Shakespeare Wallah* presented a version of the Kendal family's Indian adventures, and itself featured father and both daughters [1. *Sunday Times*, August 22, 1982; 2. Geoffrey Kendal with Clare Colvin, *The Shakespeare Wallah: The Autobiography of Geoffrey Kendal*, 1986].

William Hunter **Kendal:** William Hunter Grimston (1843–1917), Br. stage actor, theatre manager. The actor assumed the name Kendal for his theatrical debut as Louis XIV in *A Life's Revenge* (1861), possibly basing it on the name Kemble, that of a noted acting family. The intermingling of the names Kemble, Kendal and Kendall in the acting world generally is remarkable. See the next entries below as well as Geoffrey Kendal (above).

Kay **Kendall:** Justine Kay Kendall McCarthy (1926–1959), Eng. movie actress.

Suzy **Kendall:** Frieda Harrison (1944–), Eng. movie actress.

Merna **Kennedy:** Maude Kahler (1908–1944), U.S. movie actress.

Milward **Kennedy:** Milward Rodon X. Burge (1894–1968), Eng. journalist, mystery writer.

Dee Dee **Kennibrew:** Delores Henry (1945–), U.S. pop singer. "Dee Dee" represents "Delores," while "Kennibrew" looks like an embellished variant of "Henry."

Charles J. **Kenny:** Erle Stanley Gardner (1889–1970), U.S. crime novelist.

Barbara **Kent:** Barbara Klowtman (1906–), Can.-born U.S. movie actress.

Barry **Kent:** Barry Sautereau (1932–), Eng. stage actor.

Bruce **Kent:** William Butters (1912–1995), Eng. stage singer.

Jean **Kent:** Joan Mildred Summerfield (1921–), Eng. movie actress.

Richard **Kent:** Frank Owen (1893–1968), Eng. writer of "oriental" mystery fiction.

Jomo **Kenyatta:** Kamau wa Ngengi (? 1894–1978), Kenyan statesman, nationalist leader. Kenya's first president was orphaned early and was raised first by his uncle, Ngengi, then by his grandfather, Kongo wa Magana. He was baptized in 1914 as Johnstone Kamau, with "Jomo" a pet form of his Christian name. His second name derived from a Kikuyu word for a fancy belt which he affected.

Kenzo: Kenzo Takada (1940–), Jap. fashion designer.

Alfred **Kerr:** Alfred Kempner (1867–1948), Ger. writer, theatre critic.

Anita **Kerr:** Anita Kerr Grob (1927–), U.S. popular singer.

Deborah **Kerr:** Deborah Jane Viertel, née Kerr-Trimmer (1921–), Sc. movie actress.

Frederick **Kerr:** Frederick Grinham Keen (1858–1901), Br. stage, movie actor.

Jean **Kerr:** Bridget Jean Collins (1923–), U.S. humorist, playwright. The writer takes her name from that of her husband, drama critic Walter Francis Kerr (1913–).

M.E. **Kerr:** Marijane Meaker (1932–), U.S. novelist, writer of teenage fiction. The initials may represent the first two letters of the writer's surname or the first and last letters of her forename (or both, of course). Either way, they disguise her sex, which was presumably the intention, given her readership. She has also written as Mary James and Vin Packer.

Orpheus C. **Kerr:** Robert Henry Newell (1836–1901), U.S. humorous journalist. The humorist's pen name is an obvious pun on "office seeker," and was suggested by the many political aspirants at the time of Lincoln's inauguration. It came to be used as the name of a stock character for political lampooning subsequently.

Norman **Kerry:** Arnold Kaiser (1889–1956), U.S. movie actor.

Willette **Kershaw:** Willette Mansfield (1890–1960), U.S. stage actress, theatrical producer.

Platon **Kerzhentsev:** Platon Mikhaylovich Lebedev (1881–1940), Russ. Communist, historian. The publicist took his name from the Kerzhenets River, a tributary of the Volga.

Stanley **Ketchel:** Stanislaus Kiecal (1886–1910), U.S. middleweight boxer (the "Michigan Assassin").

Khaled: Khaled Hadj Brahim (1960–), Algerian singer ("king of rai").

Chaka **Khan:** Yvette Marie Stevens (1953–), U.S. black rock singer. The singer adopted her name in the late 1960s, when she was working on the Black Panthers' breakfast program, with "Chaka" an African name meaning "fire." It was that of the famous chief Shaka, or Chaka (c.1787–1828), founder of the Zulu nation.

Daniil **Kharms:** Daniil Ivanovich Yuvachyov (1905–1942), Russ. children's writer. The writer's assumed name was presumably intended to suggest English *charms* rather than *harms*. He also wrote as Shusterling (presumably German *Schusterling*, "little cobbler") and Shardam (apparently French *chardon*, "thistle"). Another name was Dandan (doubtless French *dindon*, "turkey"). He obviously enjoyed playing games with his young readers.

Sergey Aleksandrovich **Khudyakov:** Armenak Artyomovich Khanferyants (1901–1950), Azerbaijani-born Russ. army commander. The conscript joined the Red Army in February 1918 and adopted the full name of his commanding officer, killed defending Baku in the Civil War later that same year.

Tagir **Khuryugsky:** Tagir Alimov (1893–1958), Russ. (Lezgin) poet. The poet's adopted name is that of his birthplace, the village of Khuryug, Dagestan.

Mikola **Khvylevoy:** Mikola (or Nikolay) Grigoryevich Fitilyov (1893–1933), Ukrainian poet. The poet adopted the adjectival form of Ukrainian *khvilya*, "wave" (of the sea), as his pen name.

Leo **Kiacheli:** Leon Mikhaylovich Shengelaya (1884–1963), Georgian novelist.

Kid Creole: August Darnell (*q.v.*).

Johnny **Kidd:** Frederick Heath (1939–1966), Eng. rock singer.

Michael **Kidd:** Milton Greenwald (1919–), U.S. dancer, choreographer, theatre director. The dancer adopted the name of the hero of Aaron Copland's ballet *Billy the Kid* (1938), which was the first work in which he publicly performed.

Terry **Kilburn:** Terence Kilbourne (1926–), Br. child movie actor.

Volter **Kilpi:** Volter Adalbert Erikson (1874–1939), Finn. novelist, social critic. Finnish *kilpi* means "shield," "coat of arms," perhaps significantly here.

Kim: Kim Casali (1941–), N.Z. cartoonist, working in U.K. The artist, famous for her "Love is…" cartoons, was born Marilyn Judith Grove. In 1971 she married an Italian computer engineer, Roberto Casali, and adopted the new first name Kim.

Bobby **Kimball:** Robert Toteaux (1947–), U.S. rock singer.

Bobbie **Kimber:** Robert Kimberley (1918–), Eng. ventriloquist, female impersonator.

Jamaica **Kincaid:** Elaine Potter Richardson (1949–), Antiguan-born U.S. writer.

Viktor **Kin:** Viktor Pavlovich Surovikin (1903–1937), Russ. writer. A truncation of the writer's original surname.

Marien **Kind:** Enrica von Handel-Mazzetti (1871–1955), Austr. writer of Catholic historical novels. Given the theme of the author's writing, it seems reasonable to interpret her German pen name as "Mary's child," referring to the mother of Jesus.

Alan **King:** Irwin Alan Kinberg (1927–), U.S. cabaret performer, movie actor.

Albert **King:** Albert Nelson (1923–1992), U.S. black blues singer, guitarist.

Andrea **King:** Georgette Barry (1919–), Fr.-born U.S. movie actress.

B.B. **King:** Riley B. King (1925–), U.S. black blues guitarist. King acquired his new first name (initials) on becoming a DJ in Memphis in 1948: "He needed a catchy name that would give him an image and stick in the minds of his listeners. … Variations based on Beale Street, the main symbol of blues, were bandied about; "Beale Street Blues Boy" won out. … It was a little clumsy, and it excluded his own proper name; later he was called "Blues Boy King"; finally that was shortened to "B.B. King" [Charles Sawyer, *The Arrival of B.B. King*, 1980].

Ben E. **King:** Benjamin Earl Nelson (1938–), U.S. pop singer.

Carole **King:** Carole Klein (1942–), U.S. pop singer.

Dennis **King:** Dennis Pratt (1897–1971), Eng. opera singer, movie actor. The actor adopted his mother's maiden name as his stage name.

Earl **King:** Earl Silas (or Solomon) Johnson (1934–), U.S. black rhythm and blues singer. Somehow the two aristocratic names do not seem excessive, doubtless because they are standard first names and surnames in their own right.

Edith **King:** Edith Keck (1896–), U.S. stage actress. A name change possibly even more necessary than that made by Dennis King (above).

Freddie **King:** Billy Myles (1934–1976), U.S. black rock musician.

John "Dusty" **King:** Miller McLeod Everson (1909–), U.S. movie actor.

Kennedy **King:** George Douglas Brown (1869–1902), Sc. novelist, of Ir. parentage. The novelist, best known under his pseudonym George Douglas (*q.v.*), used this particular pen name for a book for boys, *Love and a Sword* (1899).

Larry **King:** Larry Zeiger (1933–), U.S. radio performer, TV host.

Martin Luther **King:** Michael Luther King, Jr. (1929–1968), U.S. black civil rights leader, Baptist minister. In 1935 the campaigner's father, also a Baptist minister, changed his son's and his own first name to honor the German Protestant Martin Luther (1483–1586).

Nosmo **King:** Vernon Watson (? 1887–1949), Eng. stage comedian. The comedian entered the stage through double doors on which the warning NO SMOKING appeared in large letters. Five letters were on the left-hand door and four on the right, and this made the actor's agreeable stage name.

Pee Wee **King:** Julius Frank Anthony Kuczynski (1914–), U.S. country, pop musician, of Polish parentage. He was given the nickname "Pee Wee" for his small stature (5 ft. 6 in.) and adopted it as a first name.

Robert A. **King:** Robert Keiser (1862–1932), U.S. popular composer.

Sid **King:** Sidney Erwin (1936–), U.S. rockabilly musician.

Zalman **King:** Zalman King Lefkowitz (1941–), U.S. erotic movie director.

King Curtis: Curtis Ousley (1934–1971), U.S. saxophonist.

King Pleasure: Clarence Beeks (1922–1981), U.S. popular singer.

Alice **Kingsley:** [Lady] Alice Mary Rothenstein, née Knewstub (1867–1957), Eng. stage actress. The actress adopted this name for a short stage career before her marriage in 1899 to the artist Sir William Rothenstein.

Ben **Kingsley:** Krishna Bhanji (1943–), Br. movie actor, of Br.-Ind. parentage. The actor, famous for his role in (and as) *Ghandi* (1982), reversed his Hindu names and then anglicized them. In a sense "Kingsley," suggesting "king," is a good match for "Krishna," as this is the name of the most famous of the Hindu deities.

Sidney **Kingsley:** Sidney Kirschner (1906–1995), U.S. stage, movie actor, playwright.

Hugh **Kingsmill:** Hugh Kingsmill Lunn (1889–1949), Br. novelist, short story writer, biographer. The writer's first novel, published in 1919, appeared under his original name. He then adopted his first two names as a pen name, partly to be distinguished from his elder brother, skiing pioneer Sir Arnold Lunn (1888–1974), partly to distance himself from his father, with whom he was on strained terms following the failure of his marriage in 1927.

Gertrude **Kingston:** Gertrude Silver, née Konstam (1866–1937), Eng. stage actress, theatre manager. The actress's stage name was formed from her maiden name.

King Tubby: Osbourne Ruddock (1941–1989), Jamaican musician, recording engineer.

Mme **Kinkel:** Elizabeth Sara Sheppard (1830–1862), Eng. novelist, of Jewish descent. The writer also used the name Beatrice Reynolds.

Klaus **Kinski:** Nikolaus Günther Nakszynski (1926–1991), Pol.-born Ger. stage, movie actor, father of Nastassja Kinski (see below).

Nastassja (or Nastassia) **Kinski:** Nastassja Nakszynski (1959–), Ger. movie actress, working in U.S., daughter of Klaus Kinski (see above).

Emil **Kio:** Emil Teodorovich Girshfeld-Renard (Hirschfeld-Renard) (1894–1965), Russ. circus artist, magician. The performer is said to have adopted his name from an illuminated sign "KINO" (Russian for "cinema"), in which the letter "N" was unlit. His name and profession passed down to his sons, Emil Emilyevich Kio (1938–) and Igor Emilyevich Kio (1944–).

Bruno **Kirby:** Bruno Quidaciolu, Jr. (1949–), U.S. movie actor.

Jack **Kirby:** Jacob Kurtzberg (1917–1994), U.S. cartoonist, comic book artist.

Phyllis **Kirk:** Phyllis Kirkegaard (1926–), U.S. movie actress.

Edmund **Kirke:** James Roberts Gilmore (1822–1903), U.S. businessman, author.

Sergey **Kirov:** Sergey Mironovich Kostrikov (1886–1934), Russ. statesman, Communist leader. The politician had a party name chosen for him in 1912 in the office of the Vladikavkaz newspaper *Terek* by the selection of the rare first name Kir from a calendar. He had previously signed himself S. Mironov, from his patronymic (middle name), but this was regarded as not being sufficiently "secret."

Louise **Kirtland:** Louise Isabel Jelly (1905–), U.S. stage actress.

Lord **Kitchener:** Aldwyn Roberts (*c*.1921–), Trinidad calypso singer.

Aunt **Kitty:** Maria Jane McIntosh (1803–1878), U.S. novelist, children's writer. The writer used this name for her children's stories, keeping her real name for her adult fiction.

Aleksis **Kivi:** Aleksis Stenvall (1834–1872), Finn. novelist, playwright. The writer's new name means "rock," not only as an allusion to the barrenness of his native region but as an approximate translation of his original Swedish name, which literally means "stone bank."

Kjarval: Jóhannes Sveinsson (1885–1972), Icelandic painter.

Alf **Kjellin:** Christian Keleen (1920–1988), Swe. movie actor, working in U.S.

Klabund: Alfred Henschke (1890–1928), Ger. Expressionist poet, playwright, novelist. The writer's pseudonym represents a blend of German *Klabautermann*, "hobgoblin," and *Vagabund*, "vagabond." Henschke felt such a name would be apt for the eternally seeking, wandering poet that he envisaged himself to be.

Henkie **Klein:** Heinrich Kleinmann (1921–), Du. child movie actor, working in Germany. The actor had the same name as his father, who moved to Germany in the early 1920s and directed films under the name Henk Kleinman.

Kleo Dorotti: Klavdiya Georgiyevna Karasik (1900–1974), Russ. illusionist.

Tristan **Klingsor:** Léon Leclère (1874–1966), Fr. poet, art critic. The poet loved legends and adopted the names of two legendary medieval characters. Tristan (Tristram) fell in love with Iseult (Ysolde) after they both mistakenly drank a love potion; Klingsor was an evil magician in German legend.

Sergey **Klychkov:** Sergey Antonovich Leshenkov (1889–1940), Russ. writer.

Hildegarde **Kneff:** Hildegard Knef (1925–), Ger. movie actress, working in U.S. The actress used this slightly moderated version of her name for her U.S. films. She was originally brought to Hollywood in 1947 by producer David O. Selznick, who suggested she change her name to Gilda Christian and present herself as Austrian-born. She refused.

[Sir] Godfrey **Kneller:** Gottfried Kniller (1646–1723), Ger.-born Eng. portraitist.

Diedrich **Knickerbocker:** Washington Irving (1783–1859), U.S. humorist. The great humorist used this name for the supposed Dutch author of his *History of New York* (1809). But where did he get the name itself? Very likely from a Dutch family of the name who came to live in Albany County around 1674. The family name, which may originally have been Knickerbacker, probably meant "baker of knickers," the latter being clay marbles. Irving's pseudonym became popular from the illustrations to his burlesque history drawn by George Cruickshank, showing Dutchmen in wide, loose knee breeches. Hence the adoption of "knickerbockers" (and later "knickers") as a word for breeches, or trousers, whether outerwear or (as in British use) underwear.

David **Knight:** David Mintz (1927–), U.S. stage, movie actor. The actor's stage name is his mother's maiden name.

June **Knight:** Margaret Rose Valliquietto (1911–), U.S. stage actress, dancer.

Sonny **Knight:** Joseph C. Smith (1934–), U.S. rhythm 'n' blues musician.

Ted **Knight:** Tadeusz Wladyslaw Konopka (1923–1986), U.S. TV actor. The actor's name seems to be a fairly casual anglicization of his Slavic name.

Terry **Knight:** Terry Knapp (1943–), U.S. DJ, pop musician.

Edward **Knoblock:** Edward Knoblauch (1874–1945), U.S. dramatist, working in U.K.

Edward **Knott:** Matthew Wilson (1582–1656), Eng. cleric. The disputatious Jesuit priest took his new name when entering the English College at Rome. He subsequently kept it for the rest of his life.

Gilbert **Knox:** Madge Hamilton MacBeth (*c*.1881–1965), U.S.-born Can. novelist, historian. The writer also used the name W.S. Dill.

Teddy **Knox:** Albert Edward Cromwell-Knox (1896–1974), Eng. stage comedian, teaming with Jimmy Nervo (*q.v.*).

Ruth **Kobart:** Ruth Maxine Kohn (1924–), U.S. stage actress, singer.

Rachiya **Kochar:** Rachiya Kocharovich Gabrielyan (1910–1965), Armenian writer. The writer took the father's first name (already present in his patronymic) as his new surname.

Lydia **Koidula:** Lydia Emilie Florentine Jannsen (1843–1886), Estonian poet, playwright. The writer was given her name, meaning "singer of the dawn," by the Estonian scholar and patriot Carl R. Jakobson.

Alexandre **Kojève:** Aleksandr Kozhevnikov (1902–1968), Russ.-born Fr. philosopher.

N. **Kokhanovskaya:** Nadezhda Stepanovna Sokhanskaya (1825–1884), Russ. writer. The writer appears to have based her pen name on her original name.

Koko: Alfons Frantsevich Luts (1885–1945), Russ. circus artist, clown. The name is the same as that of Coco (*q.v.*), though not for the same reason.

Kokomo: Jimmy Wisner (1931–), U.S. jazz musician. The musician presumably took his name from Kokomo, Indiana, although he himself was born in Philadelphia.

Yakub **Kolas:** Konstantin Mikhaylovich Mitskevich (1882–1956), Belorussian revolutionary writer. The writer adopted a new name in order to avoid association with the Polish revolutionary poet Adam Mickiewicz (1798–1855).

Gertrud **Kolmar:** Gertrud Chodziesner (1894–1943), Ger. lyric poet.

Kolpetti: Pyotr Andreyevich Grudzinsky (1884–1960), Russ. circus artist, clown. The performer originally used the name for a joint musical comedy act with a clown named Nikolay Morozov. Hence the name, formed from the pet names of both men, Kolya (Nikolay) and Petya (Pyotr). From 1923 he teamed with his brother, Dmitry Andreyevich Gruzinsky (1889–1944), under the same name. The name itself also happens to suggest Italian *colpetti,* "taps," "raps," "pats."

Mikhail **Koltsov:** Mikhail Yefimovich Fridlyand (Friedland) (1898–1942), Russ. writer, journalist, magazine editor.

Nikolay Pavlovich **Komarov:** Fyodor Yevgenyevich Sobinov (1886–1937), Russ. Communist official.

Komitas: Sogomon Gevorkovich Sogomonyan (1869–1935), Armenian composer, choral conductor, musicologist, working in France. The musician adopted the name of a 7th-century Armenian hymn writer.

Konimo: Daniel Amponsah (1934–), U.S. popular musician.

Wellington **Koo:** Ku Wei-chun (1888–1985), Chin. diplomat. The diplomat was the son of a wealthy merchant whose hero was said to be the first Duke of Wellington. Hence his name. ("Koo" obviously represents "Ku," while "Wellington" bears a curious similarity to "Wei-chun.")

Raymond **Kopa:** Raymond Kopaczewski (1931–), Fr. footballer, of Pol. parentage.

Erland **Kops:** Erland Olsen (1937–), Dan. badminton player.

Al **Koran:** Edward Doe (1916–1972), Br. conjuror, "mentalist." The illusionist seems to have chosen a name that simply means "The Koran," otherwise the holy book of Islam, taking the Arabic definite article as the English name "Al" (short for "Alfred"). Presumably he intended no disrespectful reference.

Janusz **Korczak:** Henryk Goldszmidt (1878–1942), Pol. writer, teacher, doctor.

[Sir] Alexander **Korda:** Sándor László Kellner (1893–1956), Hung.-born Br. movie producer. At the age of 15, Kellner moved from the Hungarian countryside to Budapest, the capital, where he was befriended by a Catholic priest who got him a job on a local paper. As the boy was legally too young to have a job, he had to find a pseudonym for himself. He chose Sándor Korda, basing this, as a compliment to his patron, on the Latin phrase *Sursum Corda,* "Lift up your hearts," from the Roman mass. This had the further advantage of being close to his original name (Sándor is the Hungarian equivalent of English Alexander), [Michael Korda, *Charmed Lives,* 1980]. Alexander Korda was the brother of Vincent Korda and Zoltán Korda (see both below).

Vincent **Korda:** Vincent Kellner (1897–1979), Hung.-born movie art director.

Zoltán **Korda:** Zoltán Kellner (1895–1961), Hung.-born movie director.

Korelli: Aleksandr Vasilyevich Peshkov (*c.*1880–1930), Russ. circus performer, trapeze artist.

David **Koresh:** Vernon Wayne Howell (1959–1993), U.S. cult leader. Koresh is the Hebrew equivalent of Cyrus, as notably for Cyrus the Great, 6th-century BC founder of the

Persian empire. The 20th-century Koresh claimed that the name was the "surname of God," and that it meant "death." He changed his name in 1990, at a time when he was already leader of the Branch Davidian cult, an offshoot of the Seventh Day Adventists. The change reflected his belief that he would father a House of David in Texas [*The Times*, March 3, 1993].

The name had already been used before him by another U.S. cult leader, Dr. Cyrus Teed (died 1908), who founded the Koreshan Unity in Chicago in 1888 and who was known to his followers as Koresh. In his case the name matched his original first name.

Alexis Korner: Alexis Koerner (1928–1984), Fr.-born jazz and pop musician, working in U.S., U.K.

Fritz Kortner: Fritz Nathan Kohn (1892–1970), Austr. stage, movie actor.

Sonia Korty: Sophia Ippar (1892–1955), Russ. ballet dancer, choreographer, teacher.

Charles Korvin: Geza Korvin Karpathi (1907–), Cz.-born U.S. movie actor.

Martin Kosleck: Nicolai Yoshkin (1907–1994), Russ.-born U.S. movie actor.

Kostandi: Yury Konstantinovich Tolchi-oglu (1876–1933), Russ. circus artist + Vladimir Konstantinovich Tolchi-oglu (1878–1915), Russ. circus artist, his brother. The brothers, who teamed as clowns and comic acrobats, adopted their ring name from their patronymic (middle name).

Henry Koster: Hermann Kosterlitz (1905–1988), Ger. movie director, working in U.S.

Marian Koval: Marian Viktorovich Kovalyov (1907–1971), Russ. composer.

Vasily Koval: Vasily Petrovich Kovalyov (1907–1937), Belorussian writer.

Kenneth Kove: John William Stevenson Bridgewater (1893–1965), Eng. stage, movie actor.

Jan Kowski: Harold Lionel Kellaway (1902–1990), Eng.-born Austral. ballet dancer.

Barbara Krafftówna: Barbara Kraft-Gazda (1928–), Pol. movie actress.

Billy J. Kramer: William Howard Ashton (1943–), Eng. pop singer. The singer's adopted name looks like a cross between those of tennis champions Billie-Jean King (actually born the same year as Ashton) and Jack Kramer. But the true origin may in reality be quite different.

Kondrat Krapiva: Kondrat Kondratyevich Atrakhovich (1896–), Belorussian satirical writer, linguist. The writer's aptly chosen plant name means "nettle."

Ivan Krasko: Ján Botto (1876–1958), Slovakian poet.

Kreskin: George Joseph Kresge, Jr. (1935–), U.S. entertainer, "mentalist."

V. Krestovsky: Nadezhda Dmitriyevna Zayonchovskaya, née Khvoshchinskaya (1824–1889), Russ. writer. The writer had already published a number of stories under her (male) pen name, when an real author Vsevolod Krestovsky became increasingly known. From then on, she signed her work as "V. Krestovsky (pseudonym)."

Vincas Kreve: Vincas Mickevičius (1884–1954), Lithuanian writer, folklorist, working in U.S. (from 1947).

Krishna Venta: Francis Pencovic (1911–), U.S. cult leader. The founder of the Fountain of the World cult changed his name on leaving the army after World War II. "Krishna" (Sanskrit, "dark one") is the name of a famous Hindu deity. "Venta" apparently relates to Ventura County, California, where the cult settled. Krishna Venta himself claimed to have been born in a valley in Nepal.

Helen Kroger: Leoninta ("Lona") Cohen, née Petka (1913–1992), U.S.-born Soviet spy, working with Peter Kroger (see below), her husband.

Peter Kroger: Morris Cohen (1910–1995), U.S.-born Soviet spy, of East European Jewish parentage, working with Helen Kroger (see above), his wife.

A. Kron: Aleksandr Aleksandrovich Kreyn (Krein) (1909–1983), Russ. writer, playwright.

Emil Krotky: Emmanuil Yakovlevich German (Herman) (1892–1963), Russ. satirical poet. The writer's adopted name means "mild," "meek," a sense that he intended ironically. Maxim Gorky (*q.v.*) said: "How could he be called mild? He's brusque and brazen!" [Dmitriyev, p. 161].

Gustav Krupp: Gustav von Bohlen und Halbach (1870–1950), Ger. industrialist. In 1906 the former diplomat married Bertha Krupp (1886–1957), heiress of the Krupp family of industrialists, and by special imperial edict was allowed to adopt her name, inserting it before the "von." It was Bertha Krupp who gave the nickname of "Big Bertha," the howitzer that shelled France in World War I.

Yury Krymov: Yury Solomonovich Beklemishev (1908–1941), Russ. writer. The writer was very attached to the Crimea (Russian *Krym*). Hence his name.

Rachid **Ksentini:** Rachid Billakadar (1887–1944), Algerian stage actor, director, playwright.

Kuba: Kurt Bartel (1914–1967), Ger. poet, writer. A name formed from the first syllables of the writer's original name.

Georgy **Kuchishvili:** Georgy Andukaparovich Chkheidze (1886–1947), Georgian poet.

Kukryniksy: Mikhail Vasilyevich Kupriyanov (1903–), Russ. satirical cartoonist + Porfiry Nikitich Krylov (1902–), Russ. satirical cartoonist + Nikolay Aleksandrovich Sokolov (1903–), Russ. satirical cartoonist. The three artists adopted a joint name comprising elements from each of their respective names, adding the Russian plural ending (*-y*).

Martin **Kukučín:** Matej Bencúr (1860–1928), Slovakian novelist.

Yanka **Kupala:** Ivan Dominikovich Lutsevich (1882–1942), Belorussian poet. The writer's new first name is a Belorussian form of Ivan, his original name. The name as a whole refers to the annual summer holiday, of religious origin, known in Russian as *Ivan Kupala*, literally "John the Bather," i.e. John the Baptist. This was held on St. John the Baptist's Day (Midsummer Day, June 24), and was marked with country customs such as leaping over a bonfire (whoever leaped highest would have the richest harvest), bathing, etc. (According to popular belief, it was on this day that John the Baptist drove evil spirits out of the water.) The rites were accompanied by singing and dancing. Hence the poetic association.

Oskar **Kurganov:** Oskar Iyeremeyevich Esterkin (1907–), Russ. writer, screenwriter.

Mitrush **Kuteli:** Dhimitër Pasko (1907–1967), Albanian writer, critic.

Grigory **Kvitka-Osnovyanenko:** Grigory Fyodorovich Kvitka (1778–1843), Ukrainian writer. The writer first used the pen name Gritzko Osnovyanenko, from a colloquial form of his own first name and the name of the village of his birth, Osnova. He later added the latter to his original surname.

Thomas **Kyd:** Alfred Bennett Harbage (1901–1976), U.S. educator, Shakespeare scholar, detective story writer. Thomas Kyd was a 16th-century English dramatist.

Elisabeth **Kyle:** Agnes Mary Robertson Dunlop (1910–1982), Sc. novelist, children's writer. The writer also used the name Jan Ralston.

Barbara **Laage:** Claire Colombat (1925–), Fr. movie actress.

Louise **Labé:** Louise Charly (or Charlien) (1526–1566), Fr. poet. The poet was known as *la belle cordière*, "the beautiful ropemaker," because of her stunning looks and the occupation of both her father and her husband (French *cordier*). Her pseudonym arose as an abbreviation of this.

Sleepy **La Beef:** Thomas Paulsley La Beff (1935–), U.S. black guitarist, singer. The musician adopted the nickname "Sleepy," given him for his drooping eyelids.

Patti **LaBelle:** Patricia Louise Holt (1944–), U.S. black rock singer. The singer's professional name arose simultaneously with that of her group, now known (since 1970) as LaBelle but formed in 1961 as Patti LaBelle and the Blue Belles.

Simon **Lack:** Simon Macalpine (1917–1980), Sc. stage actor. The actor's stage surname was extracted from the middle of his real surname (reversed).

Paul **Lacôme:** Paul-Jean-Jacques Lacôme-d'Estalenx (1838–1920), Fr. operetta composer.

Lactilla: Ann Yearsley, née Cromartie (1752–1806), Eng. poet. The writer was originally an illiterate milkwoman, and adopted a latinized equivalent of the term for her trade as a pen name.

Ed **Lacy:** Len Zinberg (1911–1968), U.S. mystery story writer.

John **Lacy:** George Darley (1795–1846), It. poet, novelist, critic.

Steve **Lacy:** Steven Lackritz (1934–), U.S. jazz saxophonist.

Cheryl **Ladd:** Cheryl Stoppelmoor (1951–), U.S. TV actress.

Diane **Ladd:** Rose Diane Ladnier (1939–), U.S. movie actress.

Léon **Ladulfi:** Noël du Fail (1520–1591), Fr. writer. Crossword buffs will readily spot the anagram here.

A **Lady of Quality:** Enid Algerine Bagnold (1889–1981), Eng. novelist, playwright. An earlyish pseudonym used by the writer who became a genuine "lady of quality" in 1920 when she married Sir Roderick Jones.

Lafayette: Sigmund Neuberger (1872–1911), Ger.-born U.S. magician.

La Fleur: Robert Guérin (*fl.*1598–1634), Fr. actor. The actor used this name for his tragic roles, keeping his other name of Gros-Guillaume (*q.v.*) for farce. His son-in-law, François Juvenon (*c.*1623–1674), adopted the same name when he played the parts of kings in succession to Montfleury (*q.v.*). Juvenon's son, also an actor, was La Tuillerie (*q.v.*).

Paul Anton de **Lagarde:** Paul Bötticher (1827–1891), Ger. Protestant theologian. The biblical scholar adopted the surname of his mother's family in 1845.

La Grange: Charles Varlet (1639–1692), Fr. actor.

Bert **Lahr:** Irving Lahrheim (1895–1967), U.S. stage, movie comedian.

Cleo **Laine:** Clementine Dinah Dankworth, née Campbell (1927–), Eng. jazz singer, actress. The singer presumably adopted her professional name from that of her first husband, George Langridge.

Denny **Laine:** Brian Arthur Haynes (or Hines) (1944–), Eng. rhythm 'n' blues musician.

Frankie **Laine:** Francis Paul LoVecchio (1913–), U.S. popular singer, actor, of Sicilian parentage, husband of Nan Grey (*q.v.*).

Hugh **Laing:** Hugh Skinner (1911–1988), Barbados-born U.S. ballet dancer.

Clara **Lair:** Mercedes Negron Muñoz (1895–), Puerto Rican poet.

Arthur **Lake:** Arthur Silverlake (1905–1987), U.S. movie actor.

Claude **Lake:** Mathilde Blind (1841–1896), Ger.-born Eng. poet, translator, literary critic. The writer used this name for her earliest poems, published in 1867.

Veronica **Lake:** Constance Frances Marie Ockleman (1919–1973), U.S. movie actress. The actress made her debut as Constance Keane in *Sorority House* (1939), taking this name from that of her stepfather. She was given her regular professional name by Paramount producer Arthur Hornblow, Jr., in 1940 for the movie *I Wanted Wings* (1941). She tells how the name came about: "'Believe me' [said Hornblow], 'the right name, a name that the public can latch on to and remember can make all the difference. It isn't just a matter, though, of creating a name that can be remembered. If that were all it took, we'd just name you Maude Mudpie or Tilly Tits or something and they'd remember the name. ... Picking a name involves coming up with something that associates in the fan's mind the person attached to that name. The name has to... well, it has to be the person, or at least what the fan thinks that person is. ... Connie, here's how I came to choose your new name. I believe that when people look into those navy blue eyes of yours, they'll see a calm coolness—the calm coolness of a lake.' The first thing that crossed my mind was that I was going to be named Lake something or other. That doesn't sound very outlandish these days with Tab and Rock, but in those days names stuck closer to the norm. ... 'And your features, Connie, are classic features. And when I think of classic features, I think of Veronica.' Lake Veronica! Oh! Veronica Lake. Of course. And then it hit me. My mother was sometimes called Veronica. Of all the goddamn names in the world to choose. ... I broke down and bawled like a baby into the couch cushions" [Veronica Lake with Donald Bain, *Veronica*, 1969].

Lamar: Lale Marinov Ponchev (1898–1974), Bulg. poet. The writer created his name from the initial syllables of his first two names.

Barbara **La Marr:** Rheatha Watson (1896–1926), U.S. movie actress. The actress was at first billed as Barbara Deely or Barbara LaMarr Deely.

Hedy **Lamarr:** Hedwig Eva Maria Kiesler (1913–), Austr. movie actress, working in U.S. The actress was given her screen name by MGM's Louis B. Mayer, after "the most beautiful star he had ever seen," which was Barbara La Marr (see above). It is not all that often that one stage name engenders another like this.

Peter **Lambda:** Peter Levy (1911–1994), Hung.-born Br. sculptor. The artist's name is the word for the Greek letter L, the initial of his surname. His father had used the same name as a writer.

Louis **Lambert:** Patrick Sarsfield Gilmore (1829–1892), Ir.-born U.S. bandmaster.

La Meri: Russell Meriwether Hughes (1898–), U.S. ballet dancer, ethnologist, writer. The dancer's name derives from the first part of her middle name.

La Messine: Juliette Adam, née Lamber (1836–1936), Fr. novelist, editor. The writer's pen name means "the woman of Metz." She also wrote as Comte Paul Vasili (*q.v.*).

Lamia: Alfred Austin (1835–1913), Eng. poet. The poet used this name for some of his autobiographical writing, as when he edited *The Poet's Diary* (1904). He presumably took it with reference to the witch of the name, who was said to suck the blood of children, and who is the subject of Keats's poem *Lamia* (1820).

Dorothy **Lamour:** Dorothy Mary Leta Lambour (earlier Slaton) (1914–1996), U.S. movie actress. Different sources give different original names for the actress. Among them are Mary Leta Dorothy Kaumeyer (Katz, Lloyd and Fuller, Thomson), Mary Leta Dorothy Slaton (Vinson), Mary Dorothy Slaton (Quinlan), Mary Dorothy Stanton (Wlaschin), and simply Dorothy Kaumeyer (Halliwell, among others). Evidence seems to suggest, however, that she was actually Dorothy Mary Leta Slaton, but that she then gained the surname of her mother's second husband, Clarence Lambour, and altered this to "Lamour" [Dorothy Lamour and Dick McInnes, *My Side of the Road*, 1980]. The name itself, of course, happens to suggest "love," blending well with Dorothy ("gift of God").

Louis **L'Amour:** Louis Dearborn LaMoore (1908–1988), U.S. novelist. The writer of Western novels also used the pen names Tex Burns and Jim Mayo.

Lana: Alan Kemp (1938–), Eng. female impersonator. By adjusting his (male) first name, the performer achieved a (female) stage name.

G.B. **Lancaster:** Edith Joan Balfour Lyttleton (1864–1945), Austral.-born N.Z. writer. The writer's initials may represent her two middle names, while Lancaster may relate in some way to Lyttleton. She also wrote as Keron Hale. Most of Lyttleton's novels were about the activities and company of men, as implied by her male-sounding name.

Elsa **Lanchester:** Elizabeth Sullivan (1902–1986), Br. stage, movie actress, working in U.S. The actress adopted her mother's maiden name as her stage name.

Jon **Land:** Nicholas Febland (1960–), Eng. popular musician.

Harald **Lander:** Alfred Bernhardt Stevnsborg (1905–1971), Dan.-Fr. ballet dancer, teacher.

Ann **Landers:** Esther Pauline Friedman (1918–), U.S. journalist. The advice columnist inherited her journalistic byname from a previous Ann Landers, competing with her twin sister, Abigail Van Buren (*q.v.*).

Lew **Landers:** Louis Friedlander (1901–1962), U.S. movie director.

Elissa **Landi:** Elisabeth-Marie-Christine Kühnelt (1904–1948), It. movie actress, novelist, of Austr. parentage. The actress's new surname derives from that of her Italian stepfather, Count Carlo Zanardi-Landi.

Carole **Landis:** Frances Lillian Mary Ridste (1919–1948), U.S. movie actress. The actress's new surname was apparently formed from letters in her original second name and surname.

Jessie Royce **Landis:** Jessie Royce Medbury (1904–1972), U.S. stage, movie actress.

Jane **Landon:** Frances Jane Leach (1947–), Austral. ballet dancer.

Michael **Landon:** Eugene Maurice Orowitz (1936–1991), U.S. movie, TV actor, producer. The actor is said to have taken his name from a Los Angeles phone book.

Avice **Landone:** Avice Spitta (1910–1976), Eng. stage actress.

Allan "Rocky" **Lane:** Harold Albershart (1904–1973), U.S. movie actor.

[Sir] Allen **Lane:** Allen Lane Williams (1902–1970), Eng. publisher. In 1919, still only 16, Williams was sent to the London publishers Bodley Head, where he was apprenticed to a distant cousin, John Lane. Lane was childless but anxious that the family name should be associated with the firm. He therefore stipulated that Williams change his surname to Lane on joining him. From then on he was known as Allen Lane, and at the same time his parents, two brothers, and sister also adopted this surname.

Burton **Lane:** Burton Levy (1912–1997), U.S. composers of musicals.

Christy **Lane:** Eleanor Johnston (1940–), U.S. country singer.

Jane **Lane:** Elaine Dakers, née Kidner (?–1978), Eng. writer of historical novels, children's books, biographies. The writer adopted her grandmother's maiden name as her pen name.

Lois **Lane:** Lois Wilkinson (1944–), Eng. popular singer.

Lola **Lane:** Dorothy Mullican (1909–1981), U.S. movie actress, elder sister of Priscilla Lane and Rosemary Lane (see below). The actress is said to have taken her new name from a Los Angeles phone book.

Lupino **Lane:** Henry Lane George Lupino (1892–1959), Br. stage, movie comedian. The actor added the surname of his actress great-aunt Sara Lane (1823–1899) to his own surname, using the latter as a first name for his new stage name.

Priscilla **Lane:** Priscilla Mullican (1917–1995), U.S. movie actress, sister of Lola Lane and Rosemary Lane (see above and below).

Rosemary **Lane:** Rosemary Mullican (1914–

1974), U.S. movie actress, sister of Lola Lane and Priscilla Lane (see above).

Eddie Lang: Salvatore Massaro (1902–1933), U.S. jazz guitarist.

June Lang: Winifred June Vlasek (1915–), U.S. movie actress.

k.d. lang: Kathryn Dawn Lang (1961–), Can. singer. The androgynous singer prefers the lower case version of her name. She explains: "I decided to change my name because Kathy is really mundane. k.d.'s genderless—it's a name, not a sexuality" [*Sunday Times Magazine*, May 3, 1992].

Ilse Langner: Ilse Siebert (1899–1988), Ger. playwright, poet, novelist.

Launcelot Langstaff: Washington Irving (1783–1859), U.S. story writer, essayist, historian + William Irving (1766–1821), U.S. politician, satirist, his brother + James Kirk Paulding (1778–1860), U.S. writer. The joint pseudonym was used by the three men for the satirical essays and poems published as *Salmagundi; or the Whim-Whams and Opinions of Launcelot Langstaff, Esq. and Others* (1808). The pen name doubtless had an implied punning reference to the satirist who uses his pen as a "lance" or a "staff" to point his barbs.

Lillie Langtry: Emilie Charlotte Le Breton (1853–1929), Eng. stage actress (the "Jersey Lily"). The actress's new first name is a pet form of her original name. Her surname is that of her first husband, Edward Langtry (married 1874, died 1897). In 1899 she married Sir Hugo de Bathe. (Her nickname, which puns on her stage name, refers to Jersey, her her birthplace in the Channel Islands, famous for its flowers. It also alludes to her beauty, and was popularized by a portrait of her by Millais, which shows her holding a lily.)

E.B. Lanin: Dr. Emile Joseph Dillon (1854–1933), Ir.-born Br. newspaper correspondent. The writer's name is a reference to his native Dublin, which is known as "Eblana" in literary imprints.

Jörg Lanner: Jörg Langenstrass (1939–), Ger. ballet dancer.

Joi Lansing: Joyce Wassmansdorf (1928–1972), U.S. movie actress.

Robert Lansing: Robert H. Brown (1929–1994), U.S. TV actor.

Meyer Lansky: Meyer Suchowljansky (*c.*1902–1983), U.S. gangster, of Pol. Jewish parentage ("the Godfather of Godfathers"). The gangster did not adopt the shorter version of his Polish name himself at the start of his law-breaking career, as popularly supposed, since he was already known as Lansky on his school record card. The new form of the name was adopted by his father, Max Suchowljansky, on bringing his family to the U.S. from Europe in 1911 [Robert Lacey, *Little Man: Meyer Lansky and the Gangster Life*, 1991].

Mario Lanza: Alfredo Arnold Cocozza (1921–1959), It.-born U.S. opera singer, movie actor. The singer took his first name from the hero of his favorite opera, Puccini's *Tosca*, in which Floria Tosca falls in love with Mario Cavaradossi, and his second name from his mother's maiden name, Maria Lanza. Her first name also accords with his.

Lanza del Vasto: Giuseppe Giovanni di Trabia Branciforte (1901–1981), It. mystic, working in France.

Eddie Large: Edward Hugh McGinnis (1942–), Sc.-born Br. TV comedian, teaming with Syd Little (*q.v.*) (as "Little and Large").

Yu. Larin: Mikhail Zalmanovich (or Aleksandrovich) Lurye (1882–1932), Russ. revolutionary.

Pierre de Larivey: Pierre de Giunti (*c.*1540–1619), Fr. comic playwright, of It. descent. The writer's name puns on his original Italian family name. Giunti means "arrived ones," so that Larivey is a version of what in modern French would be *l'arrivé*, "the arrived one."

Pete La Roca: Peter Sims (1938–), U.S. jazz musician. The musician took his new name when his professional work was with Latin bands.

Rod La Rocque: Roderick la Rocque de la Rour (1896–1969), U.S. movie actor.

Laroque: Pierre Régnault Petit-Jean (*c.*1595–1676), Fr. actor.

Rose La Rose: Rosina Dapelle (1913–1972), U.S. entertainer.

Rita La Roy: Ina Stuart (1907–), Fr. movie actress, of Eng. descent.

Larry: Terence Parkes (1927–), Eng. cartoonist, illustrator. The artist's name arose as a nickname given him by pupils when he taught art at Lincoln Road Secondary Modern School, Peterborough, in the 1950s. The nickname in turn came from the movie then showing locally, *The Jolson Story* (1946), in which Larry Parks plays Al Jolson (*q.v.*).

Danny La Rue: Daniel Patrick Carroll

(1927–), Ir.-born Br. revue artist, female impersonator. The actor was given his name by the comedian and producer Ted Gatty for his revue *Men Only* (1954). He describes the procedure in his autobiography: "When I arrived at the Irving Theatre for rehearsals that night there was a large poster on display and the name DANNY LA RUE caught my eye. 'Who's that?' I asked Ted Gatty. … 'You,' came the reply. 'Danny La Rue?' 'Yes. You *had* to have a name and a billing … so I made it up.' 'But why *Danny La Rue*?' I was intrigued, but I rather liked it. 'Well,' he said, you are very glamorous and very tall. … You look wonderful in costume and you remind me of Paris, like the Follies. You are also long and lean like a lovely French street, so I thought I would call you Danny the Street—*Danny La Rue*.' … It was a glamorous made-up name for a glamorous made-up person" [Danny La Rue, *From Drags to Riches*, 1987].

Jack La Rue: Gaspare Biondolillo (1903–1984), U.S. movie actor.

Denise **Lasalle:** Denise Craig (*c*.1947–), U.S. pop singer, songwriter.

Lady Caroline **Lascelles:** Mary Elizabeth Maxwell, née Braddon (1837–1915), Eng. novelist.

Marghanita **Laski:** Esther Pearl Laski (1915–1988), Br. writer, broadcaster. The writer's adopted first name was originally given her by her father when she was a child as an exotic variation on her middle name of Pearl.

Maiju **Lassila:** Algot Untola Tietäväinen (1868–1918), Finn. writer.

Orlando di **Lasso** (or Orlande Lassus): Roland Delattre (? 1532–1594), Belg. musical composer. Many reference sources give the composer's real name as above, although some dispute this particular origin. (The *Oxford Companion to Music*, in his entry, says specifically "not Roland de Lattre as often stated.") Perhaps it arose in the belief that his more familiar name was a latinized version of a French original, with the "true" name reconstructed from this.

Yusef **Lateef:** William Evans (1920–), U.S. popular musician. The musician changed his name on adopting the Muslim faith in the 1950s. Lateef represents Arabic *al-latif*, "the subtle," an attribute of Allah.

Emma **Lathen:** Mary J. Latsis (*c*.1917–), U.S. mystery writer + Martha Henissart (*c*.1929–), U.S. mystery writer. The writers' joint name was created by taking the first two letters of their first names to give "Emma" and combining the first two syllables of their surnames to make "Lathen." Their pseudonym long disguised their true identities, and famously led the novelist C.P. Snow to comment that Emma Lathen was "the best living writer of American detective stories."

Frank **Latimore:** Frank Kline (1925–), U.S. movie actor.

Henri de **Latouche:** Hyacinthe Thabaud de Latouche (1785–1851), Fr. poet.

La Tuillerie: Jean-François Juvenon (1650–1688), Fr. actor, dramatist, grandson of Gros-Guillaume (*q.v.*).

Horst **Laubenthal:** Horst Rüdiger Neumann (1938–), Ger. opera singer. The singer took his name from his adoptive father, tenor Rudolf Laubenthal (1886–1971), whose sole pupil he was.

Afferbeck **Lauder:** Alistair Ardoch Morrison (1911–), Austral. writer. The writer devised "Strine" as a term for the characteristic Australian pronunciation of English. "Strine" is "Australian" in Strine, and "Afferbeck Lauder" is "alphabetical order." He originally used the name as part of a mock academic title for the author of "papers" in the *Sidney Morning Herald* (1965). In full he was thus Professor Afferbeck Lauder, Professor of Strine Studies at the University of Sinny [Sydney].

Roger **Laugier:** Roger Krebs (*c*.1931–), Fr. juvenile movie actor. The actor dropped his Germanic-sounding surname to replace it with the name of the character he portrayed in his first movie, *La Cage aux rossignols* ("The Cage of Nightingales") (1943), for which he was himself billed as "Le Petit Krebs."

Laura: Mary Robinson, née Darby (1758–1810), Eng. actress, novelist, poet. The writer adopted the name used to refer to her in William Gifford's satire, *The Maeviad* (1795), directed against current poets and their schools.

Stan **Laurel:** Arthur Stanley Jefferson (1890–1965), Eng. movie comedian, working in U.S., teaming with U.S. actor Oliver Hardy (1892–1957). The "thin one" of the comic pair originally appeared on the stage as Stan Jefferson. The story goes that one day in 1912, when touring the U.S. with Fred Karno (*q.v.*), he realized that his name had 13 letters, so decided to change it. The shorter and more obviously propitious name "Laurel" is said to have been suggested by his common-law wife Mae

Dahlberg, who joined him to form a duo in vaudeville. She recalled: "I was in the dressing-room ... looking at an old history book that someone in the previous week's show must have left. ... I opened it up casual like, and I came to an etching or a drawing of a famous old Roman general, Scipio Africanus Major. ... Around his head he wore a laurel, a wreath of laurel. ... That word stayed with me. I said it aloud, Laurel. Laurel. Stan Laurel. Stan looked up from what he was doing and he said, 'What?' ... 'How about that for a name?' He repeated it aloud, too. 'Stan Laurel. Sounds very good'" [Fred Lawrence Guiles, *Stan*, 1980].

Ralph **Lauren**: Ralph Lipshitz (1939–), U.S. fashion designer.

Paula **Laurence**: Paula de Lugo (1916–), U.S. stage actress.

Piper **Laurie**: Rosetta Jacobs (1932–), U.S. movie actress, of Russ.-Pol. parentage.

Jay **Laurier**: Jay Chapman (1879–1969), Eng. music hall artist.

Comte de **Lautréamont**: Isidore-Lucien Ducasse (1846–1870), Fr. poet. The poet adopted the name and title of the eponymous hero of a novel by Eugène Sue (*q.v.*). The reason for the adoption is unknown, and many details of the poet's life remain uncertain.

Betty **Lavette**: Betty Haskin (1946–), U.S. soul singer. The singer adopted her stage name for the 1962 rhythm 'n' blues hit "My Man-He's a Loving Man."

Daliah (or Dahlia) **Lavi**: Daliah Levenbuch (1940–), Israeli movie actress.

Héctor **Lavoe**: Héctor Pérez (1946–), Puerto Rican popular singer, bandleader.

Lavrenty **Lavrov**: Lavrenty Nikitich Selyakhin (1868–1958), Russ. circus artist. The performer's ring name, based on his first name, was passed down to his children, who like him were clowns and acrobats.

Pyotr **Lavrov**: Pyotr Lavrovich Mirtov (1823–1900), Russ. revolutionary philosopher. There is an apparent pun here, since Lavrov suggests Russian *lavr*, "laurel," "bay," while Mirtov evokes *mirt*, "myrtle." Both laurel (or bay) and myrtle are evergreen shrubs specially honored by the Romans.

Peter **Lawford**: Peter Sydney Vaughn Aylen (1923–1984), Br. movie actor, working in U.S.

Anthony **Lawless**: Philip MacDonald (1900–1981), Br. writer of detective novels.

Jody **Lawrance**: Josephine Lawrence Goddard (1930–), U.S. movie actress.

Elliot **Lawrence**: Elliot Lawrence Broza (1925–), U.S. jazz pianist.

Gertrude **Lawrence**: Gertrud Alexandra Dagmar Lawrence-Klasen (1898–1952), Br. revue artist, movie actress.

Jerome **Lawrence**: Jerome Lawrence Schwartz (1915–), U.S. dramatist, screenwriter.

Lars **Lawrence**: Philip Stevenson (1896–1965), U.S. writer.

Louise **Lawrence**: Elizabeth Rhoda Holden (1943–), Br. children's writer.

Marc **Lawrence**: Max Goldsmith (1910–), U.S. movie actor.

Slingsby **Lawrence**: George Henry Lewes (1817–1878), U.S. philosopher, literary critic. This was the name used by Lewes, lover of George Eliot (*q.v.*), for adaptations of French plays. Slingsby seems to have been a vogue pseudonym with 19th-century writers. Others who used it (but as a surname) include Jonathan Freak Slingsby and Philip Slingsby (*qq.v.*). Its origin appears to be in the village schoolmaster Slingsby in Washington Irving's *Bracebridge Hall* (1823).

Steve **Lawrence**: Sidney Leibowitz (1935–), U.S. pop singer. The singer borrowed the first names of his two nephews for his professional name, with "Lawrence" at the same time not all that far removed from his original surname.

Charles **Lawson**: Quintin Charles Devenish (1959–), Ir.-born Br. stage, movie, TV actor.

[Sir] Edward Levy **Lawson**: Edward Levy (1833–1916), Br. newspaper proprietor, of Jewish parentage. The owner of the *Daily Telegraph* took his new name in 1875 by royal licence "in respect of a deed of gift from his uncle Lionel, who had also added Lawson to his surname" [Lord Burnham, *Peterborough Court: The Story of the Daily Telegraph*, 1955]. In a Jewish context, Lawson can be regarded as an equivalent of Levison, i.e. "son of Levy."

Henry Hertzberg **Lawson**: Henry Hertzberg Larsen (1867–1922), Austral. poet, short story writer.

W.B. **Lawson**: George Charles Jenks (1850–1929), Br. printer, journalist, fiction writer, working in U.S.

Wilfrid **Lawson**: Wilfrid Worsnop (1900–1966), Br. stage, movie actor.

Yank **Lawson**: John Rhea Lauson (1911–1995), U.S. jazz trumpeter.

Frank **Lawton**: Frank Lawton Mokeley, Jr. (1904–1969), Br. movie, stage actor.

Halldór **Laxness:** Halldór Kiljan Gudjónsson (1902–), Icelandic poet, novelist, playwright. The writer adopted the name of the farm near Reykjavik on which he was born.

Dilys **Lay:** Dilys Laye (1934–), Eng. stage actress.

Evelyn **Laye:** Elsie Evelyn Lay (1900–1996), Br. stage singer, movie actress.

Nikolay **Layne:** Nikolay Grigoryevich Gippiyev (1920–), Russ. (Karelian) poet. The writer's adopted name means "wave" (of the sea).

Irving **Layton:** Israel Lazarovitch (1912–), Rom.-born Can. poet, of Jewish parentage.

Joe **Layton:** Joseph Lichtman (1931–1994), U.S. choreographer, stage director.

Lazdinu Peleda: Sofia Ivanáuskaite-Psibiláuskene (1867–1926), Lithuanian writer + Maria Ivanáuskaite-Lastáuskene (1872–1957), Lithuanian writer, her sister. The sisters' joint pen name means "owl in the hazel grove," alluding to the rural themes and settings of their stories.

Ivan **Le:** Ivan Leontyevich Moysya (1895–1978), Ukrainian writer. The writer gained his pen name by chance. On submitting his first piece to a local newspaper in 1913 he signed it with his name. His signature proved difficult to read, however, and the contribution appeared as by "Ivan Le...," which was all the editor could make out. The piece itself aroused the wrath of a local dignitary, who said, "If I knew who wrote it, I'd tan the hide off him!" The young author, learning of this fearful threat, instantly appreciated the benefit of a pseudonym, and used this particular one from then on [Dmitriyev, pp. 93–94].

Leadbelly: Hudson ("Huddie") William Ledbetter (1889–1949), U.S. black folk singer. An obvious pun on the musician's surname, but also an allusion to his strength and to the buckshot wound he had in his stomach.

Leander: John Jones (1575–1635), Welsh monk. The scholar's full religious name was Leander a Sancto Martino, the latter referring to the Benedictine monastery of San Martín Pinario in Santiago, Spain, which he entered in 1599.

Mike **Leander:** Michael Farr (1941–1944), Eng. pop music composer, producer. The composer is chiefly known for his promotion of the rock star Gary Glitter (*q.v.*), whose name he helped select.

Zarah **Leander:** Zarah Hedberg (1900–1981), Swe. stage, movie actress, singer.

Amanda **Lear:** Amanda Tapp (1941–), Br. rock singer, of Russ. descent.

Evelyn **Lear:** Evelyn Schulman (1928–), U.S. opera singer.

Vasily **Lebedev-Kumach:** Vasily Ivanovich Lebedev (1898–1949), Russ. satirical poet. The poet added to his name his early pseudonym of Kumach, from Russian *kumach*, a word of Turkish origin used for a kind of red calico cloth. As he himself explained, writing about his work in the immediate postrevolutionary period: "The heroic spirit of those days, the *kumach* armbands worn by the Red Army, the *kumach* ribbons and flags, suggested my literary pseudonym of Kumach, which became permanently part of my name" [Dmitriyev, p. 119].

Pavel **Lebedev-Polyansky:** Pavel Ivanovich Lebedev (1881–1948), Russ. literary specialist. The revolutionary writer adopted the name Valerian Polyansky as both a political and literary name. On returning to Russia in 1917 from emigration in Geneva, he added Polyansky to his original surname.

Fred **Lebow:** Fischl Lebowitz (1932–1994), Rom.-born U.S. sports personality.

Major **Le Caron:** Thomas Miller Beach (1841–1894), Br. secret agent, working in U.S.

John **Le Carré:** David John Moore Cornwell (1931–), Eng. spy story writer. When starting his career as a writer, Cornwell was employed as a civil servant by the Foreign Office, and was advised to adopt another name, as it would have been frowned on for a serving diplomat to publish novels under his own name. The story goes that Cornwell saw the name on a London shoe shop one day, when riding on a bus, and decided to adopt it, although he is subsequently recorded as saying: "I have grown sick of saying I don't know where it comes from, so I usually say I saw it on a shoe shop." He first used it for *A Perfect Spy* (1962).

Jean-Paul **Le Chanois:** Jean-Paul Dreyfus (1909–1985), Fr. movie director. During World War II the actor was with the French Resistance, and adopted the undercover name Le Chanois. After 1945, he retained this as his professional name.

Jan **Lechoń:** Leszek Serafinowicz (1899–1956), Pol. poet, working from World War II in U.S.

Ginette **Leclerc:** Geneviève Manut (1912–1992), Fr. movie actress.

Philippe **Leclerc:** Jacques-Philippe-Marie de

Hauteclocque (1902–1947), Fr. army officer. The officer, a major in World War II, adopted his name when escaping to England to join the "Fighting French" in order not to jeopardize the lives of his family in German-occupied France. The name bears a resemblance to his original aristocratic surname.

Le Corbusier *see* Le **Corbusier**.

Jacques **Ledoux:** Jacques Silberberg (1921–1988), Pol.-born Belg. film archivist.

Amber **Lee:** Faith Baldwin, later Cuthrell (1893–1978), U.S. novelist. An occasional pseudonym used by the popular writer.

Andrew **Lee:** Louis (Stanton) Auchinloss (1917–), U.S. novelist.

Anna **Lee:** Joanna Boniface Winnifrith (1913–), Br. movie actress, working in U.S.

Billy **Lee:** William Lee Schlenaker (1929–1989), U.S. juvenile movie actor.

Brenda **Lee:** Brenda Mae Tarpley (1944–), U.S. country singer. Spot the "Lee": it's in the second half of the singer's original surname. She was given her new name at the age of 12, when she was promoted as "Little Miss Brenda Lee."

Bruce **Lee:** Lee Jun Fan (1940–1973), U.S. movie actor, kung fu exponent, of Chin. parentage. The actor's original name was the one given him by his mother, when he was born in San Francisco to a touring Hong Kong vaudeville family. Lee was the family name (his father was Lee Hoi Chuen), while Jun Fan means "return again." A hospital nurse, however, gave him the more American name of Bruce Lee.

Canada **Lee:** Leonard Lionel Cornelius Canegata (1907–1952), U.S. black stage, movie actor. The actor is said to have adopted his name when an announcer had difficulty pronouncing "Lee Canegata." "Lee" comes from "Leonard."

Dickie **Lee:** Richard Lipscombe (1941–), U.S. pop singer. "Lee" comes from the singer's original surname.

Dixie **Lee:** Wilma Wyatt (1911–1952), U.S. movie actress.

Dorothy **Lee:** Marjorie Millsap (1911–), U.S. movie actress.

Gwen **Lee:** Gwendolyn Le Pinski (1904–), U.S. movie actress.

Gypsy Rose **Lee:** Rose Louise Hovick (1913–1970), U.S. stage, movie actress, writer, sister of June Havoc (*q.v.*). The actress took the name "Gypsy" for her burlesque striptease acts, with "Rose Lee" based on her two first names. In her act, too, her stage mother was Madame Rose.

Rose was also her real mother's name.

Holme (or Holm) **Lee:** Harriet Parr (1828–1900), Eng. novelist. The author, who wrote around 30 "refined" but sentimental novels, adopted a *nom de plume* that was intended to be understood as "homely."

Johnny **Lee:** John Lee Ham (1946–), U.S. country singer.

Laura **Lee:** Laura Lee Rundless (1945–), U.S. black gospel singer.

Leapy **Lee:** Lee Graham (1942–), Eng. pop singer.

Lila **Lee:** Augusta Appel (1902–1973), U.S. movie actress.

Margaret **Lee:** Margaret Lightfoot (1909–), U.S. movie actress.

Michele **Lee:** Michele Lee Dusick (1942–), U.S. movie actress, singer.

Patty **Lee:** Alice Cary (1920–1971), U.S. poet, novelist.

Peggy **Lee:** Norma Deloris (or Dolores) Egstrom (1920–), U.S. nightclub singer, movie actress, of Scandinavian descent. When the singer was working on the radio station WDAY, manager Ken Kennedy nicknamed her "Peggy Lee," presumably for the contemporary singer of this name.

Steve **Lee:** Michael Patrick Parry (1947–), Eng. writer, anthologist.

Vanessa **Lee:** Winifred Ruby Moule (1920–1992), Eng. stage actress, singer. When the actress first met Ivor Novello (*q.v.*), he suggested she change her name. The story goes that when she arrived one day at the Hippodrome Theatre, London, he told he had written three names on his dressing room mirror and asked her what names she had herself chosen. She opened her handbag and showed him the three she had written: Vanessa, Virginia, and Sharon. These were identical to the ones he had written on his mirror, and she adopted the first choice [*The Times*, March 16, 1992]. Novello had earlier named Vivien Leigh (see below), "and it was Lee again, although spelt differently, that he bestowed on this new find" [W. Macqueen-Pope, *Ivor: The Story of an Achievement*, 1951].

Vernon **Lee:** Violet Paget (1856–1935), Fr.-born Eng. essayist, art critic, novelist, working in Italy. The writer adopted her pseudonym in her teens, taking "Lee" from the surname of her stepmother, Matilda Lee-Hamilton, whom her father married in 1855, when he was tutor to the widow's son Eugene Lee-Hamilton, poet and professional invalid. "Vernon" came from her first name, Violet. It is uncertain what the original name was of Lee's father, a Polish émigré who at some stage took the name Henry Ferguson Paget.

William Lee: William S. Burroughs (1914–1997), U.S. novelist. The author used this pen name for *Junkie* (1953), his frank account of his life as a drug addict. He continued the account under his real name in *The Naked Lunch* (1959).

Richard Leech: Richard Leeper McClelland (1922–), Ir. stage, movie, TV actor.

Andrea Leeds: Antoinette M. Lees (1914–1974), U.S. movie actress.

Herbert I. Leeds: Herbert I. Levy (? 1900–1954), U.S. movie director.

Thomas Leer: Thomas Wishart (*c*.1955–), Sc. new wave singer.

Lees: Peter Lees Walmesley (*c*.1908–1942), Eng. cartoonist.

Johnny Leeze: John Glen (1941–), Eng. movie, TV actor.

Ethel Leginska: Ethel Liggins (1886–1970), Eng. pianist, conductor, composer, working in U.S.

Dorian Leigh: Elizabeth Dorian Leigh Parker (1917 or 1920–), U.S. fashion model. The model shortened her name because of her parents. "My mother and father thought modeling was so low-class that I shouldn't use the last name Parker" [Michael Gross, *Model*, 1995].

Gracie Leigh: Gracie Ellis (*c*.1875–1950), U.S. vaudeville artist.

Janet Leigh: Jeanette Helen Morrison (1927–), U.S. movie, TV actress.

Jennifer Jason Leigh: Jennifer Jason Lee Morrow (1958–), U.S. movie actress.

Mitch Leigh: Irwin Mitchnick (1928–), U.S. popular composer, arranger.

Vivien Leigh: Vivian Mary Hartley (1913–1967), Eng. stage, movie actress. The actress took her new surname from her husband, Leigh Holman, whom she married in 1932. The change was not immediate, however. Her first agent, John Gliddon, to whom she signed in 1934, told her she would need a new name: "She said immediately that she'd prefer a stage name like 'Suzanne Stanley.' 'Too cold… too hard. What's your maiden name?' 'Hartley… How about Mary Hartley?' Gliddon turned it down." Later, theatre manager Gordon Courtney suggested "April Moon," which Gliddon said he would

bear in mind. He subsequently consulted with manager Ivor Novello, who finally said, "Why not call her Vivian Leigh—half her own name and half her husband's."

Impresario Sydney Carroll modified Leigh's first name in 1935 on casting her for a role in Ashley Dukes's play *The Mask of Virtue*: "'Vivian'—it's neither one thing nor the other. It'll confuse people. They won't known if you're a man or a woman. Will you agree to spelling it 'Vivien'?" [Alexander Walker, *Vivien: The Life of Vivien Leigh*, 1987]. Ivor Novello (*q.v.*) also named Vanessa Lee (see above).

Eino Leino: Armas Eino Leopold Lönnbohm (1878–1926), Finn. poet, brother of Kasimir Leino (see below).

Kasimir Leino: Kasimir Araton Lönnbohm (1866–1918), Finn. poet, brother of Eino Leino (see above).

Erich Leinsdorf: Erich Landauer (1912–), U.S. conductor, of Austr. parentage.

Murray Leinster: William Fitzgerald Jenkins (1896–1975), U.S. SF writer.

Lillian Leitzel: Leopoldina Alitza Pelikan (1892–1931), Ger.-born U.S. circus performer, gymnast. Almost every letter in the performer's professional name is to be found in her original name.

Lekain: Henri-Louis Caïn (1729–1778), Fr. tragic actor.

Leksa Manush: Aleksandr Dmitriyevich Belugin (1942–), Russ. Romany (Gypsy) poet. The poet's new first name is a Romany form of his first name. His second name means "man," so that he is "the (Gypsy) man Alex."

L.E.L.: Letitia Elizabeth Landon (1802–1838), Eng. poet, novelist.

Sara Leland: Sally Harrington (1941–), U.S. ballet dancer.

[Sir] Peter Lely: Pieter van der Faes (1618–1680), Du. portrait painter, working in England. Although some doubt remains regarding the origin of the painter's name, one account tells how his father, a military captain, was known by the nickname of "Lely" for the prominent lily on the house where he was born. The son is then said to have adopted the name as his new surname.

Francis Lemarque: Nathan Korb (1917–), Fr. popular singer, poet, of Pol. (or Latvian) Jewish parentage. The singer's new name evolved from that of "Les Frères Marc," a duo formed with his elder brother Maurice ("Marc") in 1936.

John Le Mesurier: John Elton Halliley (1912–1983), Eng. movie, TV actor. The actor adopted his mother's maiden name as his professional name.

Lemmy: Ian Kilminster (1945–), Eng. punk rock musician.

Aïcha **Lemsine:** Aïcha Laïdi (1942–), Algerian novelist, working in Mexico. The writer's surname represents the Arabic letters *lem* (L) and *sin* (S), presumably the initials of her married name and maiden name.

Le Myosotis: Charles Ratsarauelina (1910–), Madagascar poet. Although writing in Malagasy, the poet has a French name meaning "the forget-me-not."

Lenare: Leonard Green (1883– ?), Eng. society photographer. Lenare opened his studio in 1923. Since in those days a French-sounding name was the fashion for dressmakers and photographers, he took the first syllable of "Leonard" and added what he believed to be a French-style ending. When asked about the origin of the name, he would point to his bald head and say, "Look, Len no 'air" [*Sunday Times Magazine*, November 13, 1977]. It is really a variant of "Leonard."

Nikolaus **Lenau:** Nikolaus Franz Niembsch, Edler von Strehlenau (1802–1850), Austr. poet. *Edler* in the poet's original name is a title corresponding to "Lord."

Leonid **Lench:** Leonid Sergeyevich Popov (1905–), Russ. writer, dramatist. The writer regarded his surname as too ordinary, so a member of the editorial staff of the magazine where he worked, the Krasnodar *Krasnoye Znamya* ("Red Banner"), devised the name "Lench" from "Lenchik," one of the diminutive forms of his first name.

Vladimir Ilyich **Lenin:** Vladimir Ilyich Ulyanov (1870–1924), Russ. Communist party founder, head of state. The origin of the Communist leader's name, famous though it is, is still uncertain. Lenin first used it in 1901, some time before the Revolution, for an article in the revolutionary journal *Iskra* ("Spark"), then published in Munich. The traditional explanation is that the name derives from the river Lena, Siberia, where there had been disturbances. Ulyanov had been exiled to Siberia, although not to the Lena but to the village of Shushenskoye, on the Yenisey. So why this particular river? According to one authority, the choice was a more or less random one: he would have chosen a name based on the Volga, but this was already "booked" (as Volgin) by the Marxist

Plekhanov. He therefore took the next big river to the east [Louis Fisher, *The Life of Lenin*, 1966].

The uncertainty of the pseudonym's origin is emphasized by the one person who should have known its derivation—Lenin's wife. In 1924, the year of his death, she wrote a reply to the magazine *Komyacheyka*: "Dear Comrades, I don't know why Vladimir Ilyich took the name 'Lenin'; I never asked him about it. His mother was named Mariya Aleksandrovna, his late sister Olga. The events on the Lena happened after he took his pseudonym. He was never in exile on the Lena. Probably the name was chosen by chance" [Dmitriyev, p. 44]. Another tentative explanation is that the name came from a girl classmate, Lena, though this seems unlikely, given the meaningful party pseudonyms adopted by most leading activists and revolutionaries of the day.

Dan **Leno:** George Wilde Galvin (1860–1904), Eng. music hall artist. The performer was trained for the stage at an early age by his parents, who were professionally known as Mr. and Mrs. Johnny Wilde. He made his debut when he was only four, appearing as "Little George, the Infant Wonder, Contortionist and Posturer." His father died soon after, and his mother remarried another artist, whose stage name was Leno and real name Grant. Together with his mother and stepfather, George and his brother toured the country as acrobats under the billing "The Great Little Lenos." George's first name subsequently became Dan "owing to a misapprehension on the part of either the printer or deviser of a playbill. The boy's stepfather appreciated the accidental change and saw the value of it, and as Dan Leno the stage name was crystallised" [*Dictionary of National Biography*].

Jean **Lenoir:** Jean Neuberger (1891–1976), Fr. popular composer.

Rula **Lenska:** [Countess] Rozamaria Laura Leopoldyna Lubienska (1947–), Pol.-born Br. TV actress.

Julian **Leński:** Julian Leszczyński (1889–1937), Pol. revolutionary.

Aleksandr **Lensky:** Aleksandr Pavlovich Vervitsiotti (1847–1908), Russ. actor, theatrical director. The actor probably adopted the name of Pushkin's Lensky (see next entry below).

Dmitry **Lensky:** Dmitry Timofeyevich Vorobyov (1805–1860), Russ. writer, actor. The writer adopted the name of Lensky, the young romantic poet in Pushkin's *Eugene Onegin*.

Lotte **Lenya:** Karoline Wilhelmina Blamauer (1898–1981), Austr. stage actress, opera singer. "Lotte" is normally a pet form of Charlotte. "Lenya" presumably came from Karoline.

[St.] **Leo IX:** Bruno von Egisheim und Dagsburg (1002–1054), Alsatian pope. The pontiff adopted a name that recalled the ancient, pure church, as it was under St. Leo the Great (died 461).

Leo X: Giovanni de' Medici (1475–1521), It. pope, uncle of Leo XI (below).

Leo XI: Alessandro Ottaviano de' Medici (1535–1605), It. pope. The pontiff adopted the name of his uncle, Leo X (above).

Leo XII: Annibale Sermattei della Genga (1760–1829), It. pope.

Leo XIII: Vincenzo Gioacchino Pecci (1810–1903), It. pope. The pontiff adopted his name in honor of Leo XII (above), whom he had always admired and whose aims and interests he hoped to emulate.

André **Léo:** Léodile Champseix, née Béra (1824–1900), Fr. novelist, journalist. The writer adopted the first names of her two sons as her pseudonym.

Arakel **Leo:** Arakel Grigoryevich Babakhanyan (1860–1932), Armenian historian, writer.

Leon: William Downing Evans (1811–1897), Welsh poet. The writer took his name from his native town of Caerleon, Monmouthshire (now Gwent).

Benny **Leonard:** Benjamin Leiner (1896–1947), U.S. lightweight boxer.

Eddie **Leonard:** Lemuel Gordon Tooney (1875–1941), U.S. vaudeville actor, songwriter.

Hugh **Leonard:** John Keyes Byrne (1926–), Ir. playwright. The writer was illegitimate and took the name of his adoptive father as his own middle name. He is still commonly known in Ireland as Jack Byrne.

Jack E. **Leonard:** Leonard Lebitsky (1911–1973), U.S. nightclub comedian.

Sheldon **Leonard:** Sheldon Leonard Bershad (1907–), U.S. movie actor, TV producer.

Leónidas: Leónidas da Silva (1913–), Brazilian footballer.

Leonid **Leonidov:** Leonid Mironovich Volfenzon (Wolfensohn) (1873–1941), Russ. stage actor, director.

Anna **Leonowens:** Ann Harriet Edwards (1831–1914), Ind.-born U.S. travel writer. The writer took her name from that of husband, Thomas Leon Owens, whom she married in 1849.

Baby **LeRoy** *see* **Baby LeRoy.**

Phil **Lesh:** Philip Chapman (1940–), U.S. rock musician.

Carole **Lesley:** Maureen Carole Lesley Rippingdale (1935–1974), Br. movie actress. The actress worked under the name of Lesley Carol before settling to the name by which she is best known.

Frank **Leslie:** Henry Carter (1821–1880), Eng. engraver, publisher, working in U.S. The artist used the name early in his career when he was being brought up by his father and uncle to learn the glove-making business, and he did not wish to incur their wrath by his taste for drawing, sketching, and engraving. He emigrated to New York in 1848 and changed his name legally from Henry Carter to Frank Leslie.

Fred **Leslie:** Frederick Hobson (1855–1892), Eng. musical comedy actor. As an amateur actor early in his stage career Hobson used the name Owen Hobbs. He starred in some later comedies under the transparently fictitious name of A.C. Torr.

Joan **Leslie:** Joan Agnes Theresa Sadie Brodel (1925–), U.S. movie actress. The actress changed her name to escape the suggestion of "broad" in her surname, as did Amanda Barrie and Dora Bryan (*qq.v.*).

Lew **Leslie:** Lewis Lessinsky (1886–1963), U.S. vaudeville artist, theatrical producer.

Natasha **Leslie:** Nathalie Krassovska (strictly Krasovskaya) (1919–), Russ.-U.S. ballet dancer. The dancer reverted to her Russian name in 1952.

Sylvia **Leslie:** Sylvia Ward (1900– ?), Eng. stage, movie actress. For her stage name, the actress adopted the first name of her father, the illustrator Spy (*q.v.*).

L'Espy: François Bedeau (? –1663), Fr. actor, brother of Jodelet (*q.v.*).

Bruce **Lester:** Bruce Lister (1912–), S.A. movie actor, working in U.S., U.K.

Ketty **Lester:** Revoyda Frierson (1934–), U.S. popular singer, actress.

Mark **Lester:** Mark Letzer (1958–), Br. movie actor.

Daniel **Lesueur:** Jeanne Lapauze, née Loiseau (1860–1920), Fr. writer.

Letine: George Gorin (1853–1880), Eng. music hall artist, trick cyclist.

Aleksandr **Levada:** Aleksandr Stepanovich Kosyak (1909–), Ukrainian writer.

Daniel **Levans:** Daniel Levins (1953–), U.S. ballet dancer.

Levante: Leslie George Vante Cole (1892–1978), Austral. magician ("The Great Levante"). Although clearly based on his first and third names, the magician's adopted name evokes the mystery of the east (the Levant), as well as (coincidentally) levitation.

Eliphas Lévi: Alphonse Louis Constant (1810–1875), Fr. magician, mystic. The occultist's assumed name represents a Hebrew equivalent of his original first two names.

Michael Le Vell: Michael Turner (1964–), Br. TV actor. To avoid confusion with another actor of the same name, Michael Turner took his mother's maiden name, Levell, and split it into two.

John Levene: John Woods (1941–), Br. TV actor.

Phoebus Levene: Fishel Aaronovich Levin (1869–1940), Russ.-born U.S. chemist.

Sam Levene: Samuel Levine (1905–1980), U.S. stage actor.

Ethel Levey: Ethelia Fowler (1881–1955), U.S. stage actress, singer, dancer.

Eliphas Lévi: Alphonse Louis Constant (1810–1875), Fr. occultist. The practitioner adapted his original first two names to give his new name.

Vasil Levski: Vasil Ivanov Kunchev (1837–1873), Bulg. revolutionary. The patriot was nicknamed Levski ("Lionlike") for his leading role in the struggle to free Bulgaria from Ottoman rule.

Alun Lewis: Alun Bennett (c.1947–), Welsh-born Br. TV actor. The actor took his mother's maiden name as his professional name.

David Lewis: (1) David Levy (1823–1885), Br. department store owner, of Jewish parentage; (2) David Levy (1903–1987), U.S. stage actor, movie producer, of Jewish parentage. Lewis has long been a stock English substitute for Levy and similar Jewish names.

Gary Lewis: Gary Levitch (1946–), U.S. pop musician, son of Jerry Lewis (see below).

George Lewis: George Louis Francis Zeno (1900–1968), U.S. jazz clarinetist.

Huey Lewis: Hugh Cregg III (1950–), U.S. rock musician.

Jerry Lewis: Joseph Levitch (1926–), U.S. movie comedian, teaming with Dean Martin (q.v.). Jerry Lewis used the same surname as the one adopted by his parents, who were also in show business. "How could anyone called Levitch get laughs?" quipped Lewis.

Joe E. Lewis: Joseph Kleevan (1910–1971), U.S. nightclub comedian.

Mel Lewis: Melvin Sokoloff (1929–), U.S. jazz drummer.

Richard Lewis: Thomas Thomas (1914–1990), Br. opera singer, of Welsh parentage.

Shari Lewis: Shari Hurwitz (1934–), U.S. TV ventriloquist (with puppet "Lamb Chop").

Smiley Lewis: Overton Amos Lemons (1913–1966), U.S. pop musician.

Ted Lewis: Theodore Leopold Friedman (1889–1971), U.S. bandleader, entertainer, movie actor.

Ted "Kid" Lewis: Gershon Mendeloff (1894–1970), Br. boxer.

Val Lewton: Vladimir Ivan Leventon (1904–1951), Russ.-born U.S. horror movie director, novelist.

Ben Lexcen: Robert Miller (1936–1988), Austral. yachtsman, marine architect.

Edward Lexy: Edward Gerald Little (1897– ?), Eng. stage, movie actor.

George Leybourne: Joseph Saunders (1842–1884), Eng. music hall artist ("Champagne Charlie").

Lezz: Leslie Alfred Barton (1923–), Eng. cartoonist. An occasional name used by the artist as a phonetic representation of the short form of his first name.

Liberace: Wladziu Valentino Liberace (1919–1987), U.S. popular pianist, movie actor, entertainer, of It. parentage. "Call me Lee," the "Casanova of the Keyboard" would say. And somehow his real surname, which he used as his professional name, perfectly suited him, with its suggestion of "liberal," "liberty," and "libertine." He originally used the name of Walter Busterkeys when playing (as a minor attraction) in Las Vegas in the 1930s. But he soon reverted to his real name, which became well known with his TV appearances.

David Lichine: David Lichtenstein (1910–1972), Russ.-born U.S. ballet dancer, choreographer. The dancer was also a composer under the name Michael Olshansky.

Lidiya Lidina: Lidiya Stepanovna Koshkina (1900–1976), Russ. circus performer, trapeze artist.

Serge Lido: Serge Lidoff (1906–1984), Russ.-Fr. ballet photographer.

Winnie Lightner: Winifred Josephine Reeves (1899–1971), U.S. movie comedienne.

Lightnin' Slim: Otis Hicks (1915–1974), U.S. blues singer.

Leonid **Likhodeyev:** Leonid Izraylovich Lides (1921–), Russ. writer. The writer, presumably intentionally, adopted a name suggesting both Russian *likhodey,* "evildoer," and his original name.

Rosa **Liksom:** ? (1958–), Finn. writer. The writer's real name is uncertain, but her pseudonym represents Swedish *rosa,* "rose," and *liksom,* "like." She is thus "roselike," perhaps in a way relating to her original name.

Nikolai **Liliev:** Nikolai Popivanov (1885–1961), Bulg. lyric poet. The poet based his new surname on Bulgarian *liliya,* "lily."

Mariya **Lilina:** Mariya Petrovna Perevoshchikova (1866–1943), Russ. actress. The actress was the wife of the actor and theatrical director Konstantin Stanislavsky (*q.v.*).

Beatrice **Lillie:** [Lady] Constance Sylvia Peel, née Munston (1894–1989), Can.-born Eng. stage actress.

Limahl: Christopher Hamill (1958–), Eng. pop singer. An anagrammatic adaptation for the lead singer of the group Kajagoogoo, which split up in 1986.

Luke **Limner:** John Leighton (1822–1912), Sc. satirist, artist, writer on art. The writer used this name for *London Cries and Public Edifices* (1847), *Suggestions in Design* (1852), and other works. A "limner" is a portrait painter.

Frank **Lin:** Gertrude Franklin Atherton, née Horn (1857–1948), U.S. novelist.

Nora **Lin:** Dora Alonso (1910–), Cuban writer.

Abbey **Lincoln:** Anna Marie Wooldridge (1930–), U.S. black movie actress, singer. The singer originally performed in nightclubs under her real name, Anna Marie. She then sang as Gaby Lee before changing her name in 1956 to Abbey Lincoln, in tribute to Abraham Lincoln. In the 1970s she traveled and performed in Africa, and adopted a further new name, Aminata Moseka, in allusion to her African roots, but then apparently faded from the professional scene.

Charley **Lincoln:** Charles Hicks (1900–1963), U.S. blues guitarist.

Elmo **Lincoln:** Otto Elmo Linkenhelter (1889–1952), U.S. movie actor.

Kelvin **Lindemann:** Alexis Hareng (1911–), Dan. writer.

Anya **Linden:** Anya Sainsbury, née Eltenton (1933–), Eng. ballet dancer.

Hal **Linden:** Harold Lipshitz (1931–), U.S. stage actor, singer.

Max **Linder:** Gabriel-Maximilien Leuvielle (1883–1925), Fr. movie comedian, working in U.S.

Viveca **Lindfors:** Elsa Viveca Torstendotter (1920–1995), Swe. movie actress.

Margaret **Lindsay:** Margaret Kies (1910–1981), U.S. movie actress.

Robert **Lindsay:** Robert Lindsay Stevenson (1949–), Br. stage, movie actor.

Vera **Lindsay:** Vera Poliakoff (1911–), Russ.-born Br. stage actress.

David **Line:** Lionel Davidson (1922–), Br. mystery novelist, children's writer. The author reserved his pseudonym, formed by a rough reversal of his original names, for his children's writing.

Bambi **Linn:** Bambi Linnemeier (1926–), U.S. stage actress, dancer.

Carolus **Linnaeus:** Carl Nilsson Ingemarsson (1707–1778), Swe. botanist. The name Linnaeus was adopted by the botanist's father, taking it from Swedish *lind,* "lime tree." The allusion was to an ancient tree on the family estate, which was said to have magic properties. The name became official, for in 1761 the botanist was granted a patent of nobility, antedated to 1757, from which time he was known as Carl von Linné.

Johannes **Linnankoski:** Johannes Vihtori Peltonen (1869–1913), Finn. novelist, journalist. The writer adopted a local placename, itself meaning "castle falls."

Iakinte **Lisashvili:** Iakinte Barnabovich Khomeriki (1897–1972), Georgian writer.

Virna **Lisi:** Virna Lisa Pieralisi (1936–), It. movie actress.

El **Lissitzky:** Lazar Markovich Lisitsky (1890–1941), Russ. painter, designer, architect. "El" represents the first syllable of Eliezar, the Hebrew equivalent of the artist's first name by which he was known.

Emanuel **List:** Emanuel Fleissig (1890–1967), Austr.-born U.S. opera singer.

Lance **Lister:** Solomon Lancelot Inglis Watson (1901–), Br. stage actor.

Frances **Little:** Fannie Macaulay, née Caldwell (1863–1941), U.S. novelist.

Syd **Little:** Cyril John Mead (1942–), Eng. TV comedian, teaming with Eddie Large (*q.v.*) (as "Little and Large"). The comedians have descriptive names: Eddie Large is plump and taller than Syd Little, who is thin and bespectacled.

Thomas **Little:** Thomas Moore (1779–1852), Ir. poet, satirist. The author used this name on occasions to denote his small stature, and was referred to under the name by Byron in the latter's *English Bards and Scotch Reviewers* (1809). Moore's best known pseudonym was Thomas Brown, the Younger (*q.v.*).

Little Anthony: Anthony Gourdine (1941–), U.S. pop singer.

Little Egypt: Fareeda Mahzar (1873–1916), U.S. dancer, of Syrian (or Armenian) parentage. The dancer, famous for the hootchy-cootchy, adopted a stage name that suggested a generally eastern origin. Rees and Noble (see Bibliography, p. 403) give her real name as Catherine Devine, while Sharp (see also) has her as Mrs. Frieda Spyropoulos.

Little Emmie: Emma Coates (formerly Rivers) (1896–1994), Br. singer, dancer. The dancer's original name was that of the children's ballet producer Madame Pauline Rivers, who gave her her stage name and eventually adopted her. Coates was her married name.

Little Eva: Eva Narcissus Boyd (1943–), U.S. pop singer.

Little Milton: Milton James Campbell, Jr. (1934–), U.S. blues musician.

Little Richard: Richard Wayne Penniman (1935–), U.S. black rock musician.

Little Roy: Earl Lowe (*c.*1950–), Jamaican reggae musician.

Little Tich: Harry Relph (1868–1928), Br. music hall comedian. The personality is one of the few "Littles" not to take his real first name. The dwarfish comedian was nicknamed Little Tich as a child because he resembled the portly so called "Tichborne claimant." The reference is to a Victorian legal case, in which one Arthur Orton claimed in 1866 to be Roger Charles Tichborne, the heir to an English baronetcy, who had been lost at sea. Orton was eventually discredited and imprisoned in 1874. In assuming the name Little Tich, Relph bequeathed the words "titch" and "titchy" to the English language, as applied to a small thing or person.

Mark **Littleton:** John Pendleton Kennedy (1795–1870), U.S. politician, educationist, author. The writer used this pseudonym for *Swallow Barn* (1832), a series of Virginia sketches.

Little Walter: Marion Walter Jacobs (1930–1968), U.S. blues harmonica player.

Little Willie John: William John Woods (1937–1968), U.S. soul singer.

Marie **Litton:** Marie Lowe (1847–1884), Eng. actress.

Maksim Maksimovich **Litvinov:** Meir (or Max) Walach (1876–1951), Russ. revolutionary, diplomat. The Soviet politician used the name Litvinov as one of several party cover names. Others were Papasha ("Daddy"), Maximovich, and Felix, all fairly arbitrary.

Livs **Liv:** Egon Gutmanis (1924–), Latvian writer. The writer's adopted name means "Livonian," referring to the historic Finno-Ugric people who settled where Latvia is today.

Jay **Livingston:** Jacob Harold Levison (1915–), U.S. composer.

Jerry **Livingston:** Jerome Levinson (1909–1987), U.S. composer, songwriter.

Robert **Livingston:** Robert E. Randall (1906–1988), U.S. movie actor.

Mary **Livingstone:** Sadye Marks (1908–1983), U.S. radio, TV comedienne, teaming with husband, Jack Benny (*q.v.*).

Emma **Livry:** Emma-Marie Emarot (1842–1863), Fr. ballet dancer.

Michael **Lland:** Holland Stoudenmire (1924–1989), U.S. dancer, ballet master.

L.L. Cool J.: James Todd Smith (1968–), U.S. black rapper. The singer explains that his name should be understood to mean "Ladies Love Cool James."

Richard **Llewellyn:** Richard Dafydd Vivian Llewellyn Lloyd (1906–1983), Welsh novelist, dramatist.

Llewelyn Ddu o Fôn: Lewis Morris (1701–1765), Welsh scholar, poet. The writer's name means "Black Llewelyn of Anglesey," referring to the island where he was born.

Llew Llwyfo: Lewis William Lewis (1831–1901), Welsh poet, novelist, journalist. The writer took his name from the Welsh equivalent of his first name and the name of his birthplace, Llanwenllwyfo, Anglesey.

Llew Tegid: Lewis Davies Jones (1851–1928), Welsh conductor. The musician was born near Bala, a town on Lake Bala, which is known in Welsh as Llyn Tegid. This gave his name, with his new first name a Welsh equivalent of the original.

Charles **Lloyd:** [Sir] Charles Lloyd Birkin (1907–), Eng. horror story writer.

Emily **Lloyd:** Emily Lloyd Pack (1971–), Eng. movie actress.

Lucy Vaughan **Lloyd:** John Keats (1795–1821), Eng. poet. An unexpected name used by the poet for an unfinished poem, *The Cap and Bells* (1820). The adoption of a pseudonym by Keats when he was already well established suggests that he intended the poem to be somehow directed against the Lake Poets. It has been pointed out that Lucy suggests Wordsworth (real person or not, Lucy was the subject of a number of Wordsworth's poems), while Charles Lloyd was a poet and neighbor of Wordsworth. Keats's poem written under the pseudonym was first published only in 1848, 26 years after his death [Robert Gittings, *John Keats*, 1968].

Marie Lloyd: Matilda Alice Victoria Wood (1870–1922), Eng. music hall artist. The performer first used the name Bella Delmere when she began her career on the stage at the age of 14. The name probably evolved from that of the Fairy Bell Minstrels, a troup of little girl singers and actresses that she formed when herself only a young child. Six weeks later, she adopted the name Marie Lloyd, taking this from the financial journal *Lloyds Weekly News*.

Llucen: [Rev.] John Cullen (1836–1912), Eng. cleric, writer, traveler. An obvious anagram.

Llwyd o'r Bryn: Robert Lloyd (1888–1961), Welsh bardic adjudicator. The writer and speaker's name means "Lloyd of the hill."

Llyfrbryf: Isaac Foulkes (1836–1904), Welsh publisher, writer. The writer's adopted name means "bookworm."

Kenneth Lo: Hsiao Chien Lo (1913–1995), Chin.-born Eng. chef, restaurateur. Lo acquired his new first name on his first visit to England in 1919. The doctor treating him and his two brothers for flu was unable to spell or pronounce their names and for simplicity's sake decided to label their medicines Charles, Kenneth, and Walter. "Kenneth" was thus created from "Chien" [*The Times*, August 14, 1995].

Lobo: Kent Lavoie (1943–), U.S. pop guitar player, singer, of Fr.-Native American descent. The singer took the name, Spanish for "wolf," when he first recorded "Me and You and a Dog Named Boo," reasoning that he could hide behind his anonymity if he failed to make the charts. The record was in fact a smash hit on both sides of the Atlantic in 1971. Thereafter he kept the name.

Josef Locke: Joseph McLaughlin (1917–), Ir. popular singer, movie actor. The singer's new surname evolved from his original name, which was presumably popularly pronounced "McLocklin."

Malcolm Lockheed: Malcolm Loughead (*c.*1887–1958), U.S. aircraft executive. Brothers Malcolm and Allan Haines Loughead (1889–1969) jointly founded the Loughead Aircraft Manufacturing Company in 1916. Malcolm then vanished from public life. Allan cofounded the Lockheed Aircraft Company in 1926, the new spelling of his name reflecting its pronunciation. He legally adopted it in 1934.

Gary Lockwood: John Gary Yusolfsky (1937–), U.S. movie, TV actor.

Margaret Lockwood: Margaret Mary Lockwood (1916–1990), Eng. movie, TV actress. The actress's original name is given in many sources as Margaret Mary Day. However, this relates to her temporary stage name, Margie Day, that she based on a family name on leaving school at 14 in 1929.

John Loder: John Muir Lowe (1898–1988), Br. movie actor.

Cecilia (or Cissie) Loftus: Marie Cecilia M'Carthy (1876–1943), Sc. stage, movie actress, working in U.S.

Ella Logan: Ella Allan (1913–1969), Sc.-born U.S. singer, actress.

Jimmy Logan: James Short (1922–), Sc. stage, TV actor, comedian.

Herbert Lom: Herbert Charles Angelo Kuchačevič ze Schluderpacheru (1917–), Cz. stage, movie actor, working in U.K.

Carole Lombard: Jane Alice (or Janice) Peters (1908–1942), U.S. movie comedienne. The actress is said to have taken her name from the Carroll, Lombardi Pharmacy on Lexington Avenue and East 65th Street, New York.

George London: George Burnstein (1919–1985), Can. opera singer, producer, of Russ.-U.S. parentage.

Jack London: John Griffith Chaney (1876–1916), U.S. novelist, short story writer. The writer was the illegitimate son of William Henry Chaney, an itinerant astrologer, and Flora Wellman. Nine months after his birth his mother married John London, a ruined farmer. Jack London's surname is thus that of his stepfather.

Julie London: Julie Peck (1926–1992), U.S. movie actress, singer.

Pietro Longhi: Pietro Falca (1702–1785), It. painter. The artist apparently adopted the name of the well-known family of Italian architects, Longhi (or Lunghi).

Christian Longomontanus: Christian Severin (1562–1647), Dan. astronomer, astrologer. The astronomer adopted a Latin form of the name of his birthplace, Longberg, as his surname.

Frederick **Lonsdale**: Lionel Frederick Leonard (1881–1954), Eng. dramatist. The playwright adopted the name Lonsdale by deed poll in 1908, apparently basing it on his original surname.

Gordon **Lonsdale**: Konon Trofimovich Molody (1924–c.1970), Can.-born Russ. spy, working in U.K. The master spy posed as a Canadian businessman named Gordon Arnold Lonsdale. The Russians knew him as "Colonel K."

E.C.R. **Lorac**: Edith Caroline Rivett (1894–1958), Eng. writer of detective novels. One does not have to be much of a detective to deduce that the writer's pen name is a combination of her initials and a reversal of the first part of her middle name.

Violet **Loraine**: Violet Mary Tipton (1886–1956), Eng. variety actress, singer. The actress seems to have devised her new surname from letters in her original name.

Jack **Lord**: John Joseph Ryan (1928–), U.S. movie, TV actor.

Jeremy **Lord**: Ben Ray Redman (1896–1961), U.S. journalist, writer.

Lord Creator: Kentrick Patrick (c.1940–), Trinidadian reggae musician.

Traci **Lords**: Nora Louise Kuzma (1968–), U.S. porno movie actress.

Sophia **Loren**: Sofia Scicolone (1934–), It. movie actress, working in U.S. The actress was the illegitimate daughter of Riccardo Scicolone and Romilda Villani. Her original name was thus Sofia Villani Scicolone. It would not be long, however, before people would tell her that her real surname "sounded like a chunk of Italian sausage," and she soon changed it to her famous present name. The choice of name is popularly supposed to have been made by Carlo Ponti, whom she married in 1957. A biography of Loren suggests otherwise, however. Originally, it seems, a magazine editor had suggested the name Sofia Lazzaro, from the Bible story of Lazarus (with presumably a symbolic reference to a "rebirth"). Then the Italian producer, Goffredo Lombardo, who had been working with the Swedish actress Martha Toren, said that "Lazzaro" sounded more like a corpse than its resurrection and proposed a further change. Taking "Toren" as a basis, he worked through the alphabet, stopping at "Loren." "Yes," was his verdict, "Loren—it suits you...." Subsequently

Sofia became Sophia, with the changed letters "adding a touch of class" [Donald Zec, *Sophia: An Intimate Biography*, 1975].

Pilar **Lorengar**: Pilar Lorenza García (1928–1996), Sp. opera singer. The singer formed her new surname from elements of her original names.

Eugene **Loring**: LeRoy Kerpestein (1914–1982), U.S. ballet dancer, choreographer.

Constance **Lorne**: Constance MacLaurin (1914–), Sc. stage actress.

Marion **Lorne**: Marion Lorne MacDougal (1886–1968), U.S. stage, movie comedienne.

Tommy **Lorne**: Hugh Gallagher Corcoran (1890–1935), Sc. music hall comedian.

Claude **Lorrain** *see* **Claude Lorrain**

Jean **Lorrain**: Paul Duval (1855–1906), Fr. novelist.

Lillian **Lorraine**: Eulallean De Jacques (1892–1955), U.S. singer, stage actress.

Louise **Lorraine**: Louise Escovar (1901–), U.S. movie actress.

Peter **Lorre**: László Löwenstein (1904–1964), Hung.-born U.S. movie actor.

Joan **Lorring**: Magdalen Ellis (1926–), Eng.-Russ. movie actress, working in U.S.

Amy **Lothrop**: Anna Bartlett Warner (1827–1915), U.S. novelist, sister of Elizabeth Wetherell (*q.v.*).

Pierre **Loti**: Louis-Marie-Julien Viaud (1850–1923), Fr. traveler, writer. The writer's tours of duty as a naval officer took him to Tahiti, where women in the court of Queen Pomare IV (*q.v.*) nicknamed him "Loti," from the name of a local flower, a type of rose. He adopted the name professionally.

Joe **Louis**: Joseph Louis Barrow (1914–1981), U.S. black heavyweight boxer ("The Brown Bomber").

Joe Hill **Louis**: Lester Hill (1921–1957), U.S. blues musician. The musician was given his name after a boxing match, for Joe Louis (see above).

Morris **Louis**: Morris Louis Bernstein (1912–1962), U.S. painter.

Aunt **Louisa**: Laura B.J. Valentine (1814–1899), Br. children's writer.

Anita **Louise**: Anita Louise Fremault (1915–1970), U.S. stage, movie actress.

Tina **Louise**: Tina Louise Blacker (1934–), U.S. movie actress.

Pierre **Louÿs**: Pierre Félix Louis (1870–1925), Belg.-born Fr. novelist, poet. The modified spelling and added dieresis was an appropriately poetic touch. Compare the writer's pseudonym **Bilitis**, and see its story on p. 25.

Bessie **Love**: Juanita Horton (1898–1986), U.S. movie actress, working in U.K. The actress was renamed by Frank Woods, head of scenario for D.W. Griffith, right before the cast of her first movie, *The Flying Torpedo* (1916): "Bessie, because any child can pronounce it; and Love, because we want everyone to love her!" [*Sunday Times Magazine*, September 18, 1977].

Courtney **Love**: Love Michelle Harrison (1965–), U.S. rock singer, guitarist. The musician was renamed Courtney Michelle Harrison when a baby by her mother. She subsequently combined her two first names.

Darlene **Love**: Darlene Wright (1938–), U. S. pop singer, movie actress. The singer also records under her real name, but her adopted name presumably means what it looks and sounds as if it means.

Mabel **Love**: Mabel Watson (1874–1953), U.S. stage actress. The actress adopted her mother's maiden name as her stage name. It was also the name of her grandfather, William Edward Love, a popular entertainer in his time.

(Mrs.) Solomon **Lovechild**: [Lady] Eleanor (or Ellenor) Fenn, née Frere (1743–1813), Eng. writer of educational books for children. The writer, who had no children of her own, found some solace in her pen name. She also wrote as Mrs. Teachwell.

Linda **Lovelace**: Linda Boreman Marciano (1952–), U.S. porno movie actress, writer. The actress's screen name was given her by Gerry Damiano, director of her best known movie, *Deep Throat* (1972). He "came up with the name Linda Lovelace for the character in his movie. There had been a BB [Brigitte Bardot] and an MM [Marilyn Monroe] and now he wanted an LL." The actress commented: "In time I came to dislike the name, Linda Lovelace, because of what it stood for" [Linda Lovelace with Mike McGrady, *Ordeal*, 1981]. Lovelace was the name of the handsome rake who loves Clarissa Harlowe in Samuel Richardson's novel *Clarissa* (1748). It is genuine surname suggesting someone who "loves lace."

Jay **Lovestone**: Jacob Liebstein (1898–1990), Lithuanian-born U.S. political activist.

Lene **Lovich**: Marlene Premilovich (c.1955–), U.S. rock singer, of Eng.-Yugoslav parentage. It is a fortunate coincidence that the singer's stage name, extracted from her real name, happens to alliterate and to suggest "love it."

Low: [Sir] David Alexander Cecil Low (1891–1963), N.Z.-born Br. cartoonist, caricaturist, of Sc.-Ir. parentage. The artist was fortunate to have a brief surname to serve as his signature.

Robert **Lowery**: Robert Lowery Hanke (1916–1971), U.S. movie actor.

Woytec **Lowski**: Wojciech Wiesidlowski (1939–), Pol. ballet dancer.

Violet **Loxley**: Violet Humphreys (1914–), Br. stage actress.

Mina **Loy**: Mina Gertrude Lowy (1882–1966), Br.-born U.S. poet. The writer, originally an artist, changed the spelling of her name in 1903.

Myrna **Loy**: Myrna Adele Williams (1905–1993), U.S. movie actress. The actress took her new name in 1932 when she felt that "the plain old Welsh name of Williams just didn't seem flossy enough." She made the change at the suggestion of Rudolf Valentino (*q.v.*), who thought it exotic. She commented: "I didn't intend to keep it very long. But then I signed a contract and I was stuck with it."

A. **Lozovsky**: Solomon Abramovich Dridzo (1878–1952), Russ. revolutionary, historian. The Communist activist seems to have based his new surname on syllables in his original first and last names, with "A." the initial of his patronymic (middle name).

Antonella **Lualdi**: Antonietta de Pascale (1931–), It.-Gk. movie actress.

Arthur **Lucan**: Arthur Towle (1887–1954), Eng. music hall female impersonator, movie actor. The comedian was on tour in 1913 at the Lucan Dairy, Dublin, and this provided a handy stage name for the creator of his famous character "Old Mother Riley."

Victoria **Lucas**: Sylvia Plath (1932–1963), U.S. poet. The poet adopted this name for her semiautobiographical novel *The Bell Jar* (1963), reissued later (1966) under her own name. Plath was devastated when her pseudonym was revealed in the original year of publication.

William **Lucas**: William Thomas Clucas (1925–), Br. stage, movie, TV actor.

Lucas van Leyden: Lucas Hugenz (or Lucas Jacobsz) (1494–1533), Du. painter, engraver. The artist adopted the name of his birthplace (and also the place of his death), the Dutch town of Leiden.

Lucebert: Lucebert J. Swaanswijk (1924–), Du. lyric poet.

Yanka **Luchina:** Ivan Lyutsianovich Neslukhovsky (1851–1897), Belorussian poet. The writer based his pen name on a colloquial form of his first name and patronymic (middle name), the latter itself corresponding to English Lucian.

Lucius II: Gherardo Caccianemici (? –1145), It. pope.

Lucius III: Ubaldo Allucingoli (*c.*1110–1185), It. pope.

Luck & Flaw: Peter Fluck (1941–), Eng. caricaturist, animator + Roger Law (1941–), Eng. caricaturist, writer. The two men gained fame for the grotesque animated puppets they created for the weekly satirical TV program *Spitting Image* (1984–95). Their joint name not only puns on their real names but hints at the mercurial nature of the satirist's art.

Aunt **Lucy:** Lucy Bather (1836–1864), Eng. children's writer.

Johnny **Ludlow:** Ellen Wood, née Price (1814–1887), Eng. novelist. Mrs. Henry Wood (as she is still commonly known) used this name for her series of tales which appeared in the *Argosy* magazine from 1868. She did not admit to their authorship until 1879.

Aurélien **Lugné-Poe:** Aurélien Marie Lugné (1869–1940), Fr. stage actor, theatrical director, writer.

Bela **Lugosi:** Béla Ferenc Denzso Blaskó (1882–1956), Hung. movie actor, working in U.S. The actor took his name from his birthplace, Lugos, Hungary (now Lugoj, Romania). An early screen name was Arisztid Olt.

Aleksey **Lugovoy:** Aleksey Alekseyevich Tikhonov (1853–1915), Russ. writer. The writer adopted a pseudonym for distinction from his brother, V.A. Tikhonov, also a writer.

Luigi: Eugene Louis Facciuto (1925–), U.S. ballet dancer, teacher. An italianization of the dancer's second name.

Marcel **Luipart:** Marcel Fenchel (1912–), Ger.-Austr. ballet dancer, choreographer, teacher.

Luisillo: Luis Perez Davilla (1928–), Mexican ballet dancer, choreographer.

Paul **Lukas:** Pál Lukács (1894 or 1887–1971), Hung.-born U.S. movie actor.

Jean-Baptiste **Lully:** Giovanni Battista Lulli (1632–1687), It.-born Fr. composer. The composer gallicized his name after being brought to France as a teenager.

Lulu: Marie McDonald McLaughlin Lawrie (1948–), Sc. popular singer, stage, TV actress. When the singer was 14 she was appearing at various clubs in Glasgow. At one such club, the Lindella, she was recommended by her manager, Marian Massey, as being a "lulu of a kid," meaning that she was outstanding for her age. She adopted the name, and in 1964, with her group Lulu and the Luvvers, came to prominence with her version of the Isley Brothers' "Shout."

Lulu Belle: Myrtle Eleanor Cooper (1913–), U.S. country singer, teaming with Scotty (*q.v.*).

Sidney **Luska:** Henry Harland (1861–1905), U.S. novelist, working (from 1890) in U.K. Henry Harland liked to pose as a writer of Russian origin, and as having a European education. He used this Slavic-style name for his novels about immigrant Jews, including *As It Was Written: A Jewish Musician's Story* (1885).

Maksim **Luzhanin:** Aleksandr Amvrosyevich Karatay (1909–), Belorussian poet, translator. The writer has explained the origin of his name, meaning "meadowland dweller": "I feel that a poet's name should bear the scent and charm of his birthplace. I was born by the Sluch River. There are fine water meadows and dry meadows there with such hay that I can smell it every time I write the word. As for my first name, that was a tribute to Maksim Bogdanovich. When I was young I felt specially drawn to him, our native poet, who died when he was 25. And that was how Maksim Luzhanin first appeared in 1925 in the newspaper *Savetskaya Belarus* ['Soviet Belorussia']" [Dmitriyev, p. 105].

Vasily **Luzhsky:** Vasily Vasilyevich Kaluzhsky (1869–1931), Russ. stage actor, theatrical director.

Annabella **Lwin:** Myant Myant Aye (1966–), Burmese-born Br. rock singer.

Martyn **Lyadov:** Martyn Nikolayevich Mandelshtam (Mandelstam) (1872–1947), Russ. revolutionary, historian.

David **Lyall:** (1) Annie Shepherd Swann, later Burnett Smith (1860–1943), Sc. novelist; (2) Ellen Buckingham Reeves, née Mathews (1853–1920), Eng. novelist.

Edna **Lyall:** Ada Ellen Bayly (1857–1903), Eng. novelist. It is not difficult to extract the letters of the writer's pseudonym from her original name.

Nikolay **Lyashko:** Nikolay Nikolayevich Lyashchenko (1884–1953), Russ. writer.

Le **Lycanthrope:** Petrus Borel (1809–1859), Fr. poet, novelist. The writer apparently adopted this name, from the Greek word for "wolf-man," with reference to the classic saying, "Man is a wolf to man." His name is associated with melodramatic horror novels, such as *Madame Putiphar* (1839).

Viola Lyel: Violet Watson (1900–1972), Eng. stage, movie actress.

Abe **Lyman:** Abraham Simon (1897–1957), U.S. bandleader, drummer.

John **Lymington:** John Newton Chance (1911–1983), Br. SF writer.

Moura **Lympany:** Mary Defries, née Johnstone (1916–), Eng. concert pianist. The pianist's change of name was made at the suggestion of conductor Basil Cameron. She altered her Cornish mother's maiden name, Limpenny, to Lympany, at the same time modifying her own Mary to the softer Moura [*Telegraph Sunday Magazine*, June 10, 1979].

Barré **Lyndon:** Alfred Edgar (1896–1972), Br. playwright, screenwriter, working in U.S. The writer's pen name looks very much like that of the hero of Thackeray's novel *The Luck of Barry Lyndon* (1844).

Carol **Lynley:** Carolyn Lee (1942–), U.S. juvenile movie actress.

Barbara **Lynn:** Barbara Lynn Ozen (1942–), U.S. blues singer.

Cheryl **Lynn:** Cheryl Lynn Smith (1957–), U.S. black pop singer.

Diana **Lynn:** Dolores Loehr (1926–1971), U.S. movie, stage, TV comedienne.

Ethel **Lynn:** Ethelinda Beers, née Eliot (1827–1879), U.S. poet.

Dr. H.S. **Lynn:** Hugh Simmons (1836–1899), Eng. conjuror, working in U.S.

Jeffrey **Lynn:** Ragnar Godfrey Lind (1909–1995), U.S. movie actor.

Judy **Lynn:** Judy Voiten (1936–), U.S. country singer.

Loretta **Lynn:** Loretta Webb (1935–), U.S. country singer, sister of Crystal Gayle (*q.v.*).

Vera **Lynn:** Vera Margaret Welch (1917–), Eng. popular singer ("The Forces' Sweetheart"). The singer explains how she arrived at her new name: "I ought to adopt a more comfortable name than Vera Welch. My main concern was to find something that was short, easily remembered, and that would stand out on a bill — something that would allow for plenty of space round each letter. We held a kind of family conference about it, and we found the answer within the family too. My grandmother's maiden name

had been Lynn; it seemed to be everything a stage name ought to be, but at the same time it was a real one. From then on, I was to be Vera Lynn" [Vera Lynn, *Vocal Refrain: An Autobiography*, 1975].

Carole **Lynne:** Helen Violet Carolyn Haymen (1918–), Br. stage actress. The actress's third name nicely served as a full new stage name.

Gillian **Lynne:** Gillian Land, née Pyrke (1926–), Eng. ballet dancer, director, choreographer.

Lynx: Rebecca West (*q.v.*).

Leonard **Lyons:** Leonard Sucher (1906–1976), U.S. columnist.

Carmen **Lyra:** María Isabel Carvajal (1888–1951), Costa Rican writer. The writer formed her pen name from two Latin words both meaning "song."

Vera **Lysenko:** Vera Lesik (1910–1975), Can. writer, of Ukrainian parentage. The writer sought to emphasize her national ancestry by taking the typical and distinctive Ukrainian name Lysenko. She was the first Ukrainian-Canadian to write in English.

Doris **Lytton:** Doris Partington (1893–1953), Br. stage actress. The actress took her mother's maiden name as her stage name.

Henry **Lytton:** Henry Alfred Jones (1865–1936), Eng. stage actor, light opera singer. The actor first performed in 1882 in a review in which he met his future wife, Louie Webber, who was appearing under the stage name Louie Henri. They married in 1884, when she helped him gain a small part with the D'Oyly Carte Company in a Gilbert and Sullivan opera, in which he sang as H.A. Henri. In 1887 he was understudy to the great George Grossmith and took over his part when the actor fell ill. As a result of his success in the role, Gilbert himself suggested he adopt the name Lytton, a distinguished name familiar to the public from the diplomat and poet Edward Robert Bulwer-Lytton, 1st Earl of Lytton (1831–1891).

Yevsey **Lyubimov-Lanskoy:** Yevsey Osipovich Gelibter (Geliebter) (1883–1943), Russ. stage actor, theatrical director.

Maarten **Maartens:** Jozua Marius Willem van der Poorten-Schwartz (1858–1915), Du.-born Eng. novelist.

Mab Cernyw: John Hobson Mathews (1858–1914), Welsh historian. The scholar was the son of a Cornishman. Hence his name, meaning "son of Cornwall."

Mabon: William Abraham (1842–1922), Welsh politician, miners' leader. The former miner took his bardic name from Mabon, the Celtic (Welsh) god of youth, identified with Apollo. It also so happens that St. Mabon is the patron saint of Llanafan, Glamorganshire, the historic mining county in which Abraham was born.

Jan Mabuse: Jan Gossaert (or Gossart) (*c*.1478–*c*.1532), Du. painter. The artist adopted his name from Maubeuge, the town in northern France where his family made their home.

Mac: Stanley McMurtrey (1936–), Sc. cartoonist, illustrator, writer. A near generic nickname for a Scotsman, as well as a short form of this particular Scotsman's name.

Uncle Mac: Derek McCulloch (1897–1967), Eng. children's author, broadcaster.

Macarius: (1) Mikhail (*c*.1482–1564), Russ. churchman, metropolitan of Moscow and All Russia; (2) Mikhail Petrovich Bulgakov (1816–1882), Russ. churchman, ecclesiastical historian; (3) Mikhail Yakovlevich Glukharyov (1792–1847), Russ. churchman, missionary, translator. All three men adopted their new name, similar to their identical original name Mikhail (Michael), on taking their monastic vows. The name means "blessed," and specifically honors the 4th-century St. Macarius (Macarius of Egypt). Macarius (1) was himself canonized in 1988. Compare [Archbishop] Makarios III.

McArone: George Arnold (1834–1865), U.S. poet, humorist. In enjoying the (macaronic?) pun, do not overlook the echo of the humorist's real surname.

Tony Macauley: Anthony Instone (1944–), Br. pop composer.

Jock McAvoy: Joseph Bamford (1908–1971), Eng. boxer.

Ed McBain: Salvatore A. Lombino (1926–), U.S. writer, novelist. The writer assumed the "real" name of Evan Hunter before adopting this pseudonym.

Cash McCall: Maurice Dollison (1941–), U.S. rhythm 'n' blues singer.

C.W. McCall: William Fries (1928–), U.S. country singer. The singer adopted the name that he created "out of thin air" for a truck driver he played in a 1973 advertising campaign for the Metz bread company.

Greg McClure: Dale Easton (1918–), U.S. movie actor. An instance where the actor's real name looks more like a screen name.

Ewan MacColl: James Henry Miller (1915–1989), Sc.-born Br. folksinger, songwriter, playwright. In 1945 the singer adopted the name of an admired predecessor, the Scottish-born Canadian poet Evan McColl (1808–1898). Oddly, MacColl's autobiography makes no mention of his change of name, although Peggy Seeger, in her introduction to the book, comments: "He was one of a select group of Scots writers and poets who initiated the Lallans Movement in the late 1940s. Most of these men and women took the names of poets and writers from the past and Ewan did the same" [Ewan MacColl, *Journeyman: An Autobiography*, 1990].

Kent McCord: Kent McWhirter (1942–), U.S. TV actor.

F.J. McCormick: Peter Judge (1891–1947), Ir. stage, movie actor.

Kid McCoy: Norman Selby (1873–1940), U.S. boxer. According to some, the boxer was the original "real McCoy," although the term has been recorded as early as 1883, which makes Selby a tad too youthful.

Sylvester McCoy: Percy James Patrick Kent-Smith (1943–), Sc. TV actor. The actor took his name from a stage show he was once in, *Sylvester McCoy, The Human Bomb*.

Jimmy McCracklin: James David Walker (1921–), U.S. blues, soul musician.

Mickey McCune: Mickey Kuhn (*c*.1931–), U.S. child movie actor. The actor adopted this name in place of his undesirable German-sounding one in 1941 but by 1944 had reverted to Kuhn.

G.H. Macdermott: Gilbert Hastings Farrell (1845–1901), Eng. music hall singer, comedian.

Ruth McDevitt: Ruth Shoecraft (1895–1976), U.S. movie actress.

Hugh MacDiarmid: Christopher Murray Grieve (1892–1978), Sc. poet, critic, translator. The origin of the writer's pen name remains something of a mystery. He first used it in 1922, when supporting the revival of the Scots dialect as a literary medium. He commented: "It was an immediate realization of this ultimate reach of the implications of my experiment in writing in Scots which made me adopt, when I began writing Scots poetry, the Gaelic pseudonym of Hugh MacDiarmid (Hugh has a traditional association and essential rightness in conjunction with MacDiarmid)" [*The Times*, September 11, 1978].

Jock Macdonald: James Williamson Galloway (1897–1960), Sc.-born Can. painter. The artist assumed an archetypal Scottish name.

Marie **McDonald:** Cora Marie Frye (1923–1965), U.S. movie actress ("The Body").

Murray **Macdonald:** Walter MacDonald Honeyman (1899– ?), Sc. stage director, manager.

Ross **Macdonald:** Kenneth Millar (1915–1983), U.S. novelist, mystery writer.

Andie **MacDowell:** Rose Anderson Mac-Dowell (1958–), U.S. movie actress.

Geraldine **McEwan:** Geraldine Crutwell, née McKeown (1932–), Eng. stage, TV actress.

Stephen **Macfarlane:** John Keir Cross (1911–1967), Sc. fantasy fiction, children's writer.

Mike **McGear:** Peter Michael McCartney (1944–), Eng. pop musician. The singer adopted his name to avoid unwarranted associations with his stepbrother, Paul McCartney of the Beatles. At the same time, it matched those of John Gorman and Roger McGough, whom he joined in 1962 to form The Scaffold. It probably also hinted at "gear" in the slang sense of "hip." McCartney subsequently reverted to his original name.

Fibber **McGee:** James Jordan (1896–1988), U.S. movie actor, radio comedian, teaming with Molly McGee (see below), his wife.

Molly **McGee:** Marion Jordan (1898–1967), U.S. movie actress, radio comedienne.

William **McGinnis:** William Ellsworth ("Elzy") Lay (1868–1934), U.S. outlaw. The train robber, a member of the Wild Bunch, was the favorite friend and ally of Butch Cassidy (*q.v.*).

MacGregor: Leslie Gilbert Illingworth (1902–1979), Welsh-born Br. political cartoonist. The artist adopted his mother's maiden name for his cartoons appearing in the *Daily Mail* for 30 years from 1939.

Jimmy **McGriff:** James Herrell (1936–), U.S. jazz organist.

Jack **McGurn:** Jack Vincenzo de Mora (1904–1936), U.S. gangster. The Chicago gangster's assumed name was associated with "machine gun."

Arthur **Machen:** Arthur Llewellyn Jones (1863–1947), Welsh horror fiction, ghost story writer. The writer's family adopted his mother's maiden name as their surname "in order to please her Scottish relations" [*Dictionary of National Biography*].

Niccolò **Machiavelli:** Niccolò Machiavegli (1469–1527), It. politician, writer. The writer signed himself in various ways but generally favored the Tuscan original, Machiavegli. An early letter, of April 29, 1499, bears the Medieval Latin signature "Nicholaus Maclavellus." The name derives from Latin *malus*, "bad," and a diminutive form of *clavus*, "nail." A "bad nail" is generally said to be one that nailed Christ to the cross, although some authorities see an allusion to a poor sexual performance. Whatever the case, the family adopted a cross and nails symbol.

Machito: Frank Raul Grillo (1912–1984), U.S.-born Afro-Cuban jazz musician. The name suggests a diminutive of Spanish *macho* "manly," although no actual word *machito* exists as such.

Bunny **Mack:** Cecil Bunting MacCormack (*c.*1940–), African singer.

Connie **Mack:** Cornelius Alexander McGillicuddy (1862–1956), U.S. baseball manager.

Helen **Mack:** Helen McDougall (1913–1986), U.S. movie actress.

Marion **Mack:** Joey Mario McCreery (1902–1989), U.S. movie actress.

Ted **Mack:** William E. Maguiness (1904–1976), U.S. radio, TV host.

Warner **Mack:** Warner McPherson (1938–), U.S. country singer. The singer is said to have gained his name through a mistake on a record label.

Kenneth **McKenna:** Leo Mielziner (1899–1962), U.S. movie actor, director. The actor adopted his mother's middle name as his stage name.

[Sir] Compton **Mackenzie:** Edward Montague Compton (1883–1972), Eng.-born Sc. novelist. The writer assumed (or reverted to) the original family name Mackenzie to emphasize his Scottish ancestry. His maternal grandfather was the actor Henry Compton and his sister the actress Fay Compton (*qq.v.*).

Scott **McKenzie:** Philip Blondheim (1944–), U.S. rock musician.

Charles **Macklin:** Charles M'Laughlin (or McLaughlin) (*c.*1700–1797), Ir. actor, playwright. It was uncharacteristic of the quarrelsome actor to soften his original name in this way.

Bridget **MacLagan:** Mary Borden (1886–1968), U.S.-born Eng. novelist.

Shirley **MacLaine:** Shirley MacLean Beaty (1934–), U.S. movie actress, sister of Warren Beatty (*q.v.*). The actress dropped her surname and adopted the spelling of her mother's maiden name for her screen name.

Ian **Maclaren:** John Watson (1850–1907), Sc. presbyterian minister, writer. The minister first used the pseudonym, a typical Scottish name, for his highly popular collection of sketches on Scottish rural life, *Beside the Bonnie Brier Bush* (1894). Watson was actually born in England, but came from pure Highland stock.

Fiona Macleod: William Sharp (1855–1905), Sc. author. The writer used the female name for his mystic Celtic tales and romances of peasant life in the manner of the so-called "Celtic twilight" movement. The name Fiona, now a familiar (and rather "classy") girls' name, was first popularized by Sharp, and is based on Gaelic *fionn*, "white," "fair." Sharp maintained the fiction of "Fiona Macleod" until his death, and even had a bogus entry for the lady in *Who's Who*, the prestigious British record of important persons, in which he described her recreations as "boating, hill-climbing, and listening." He received many letters addressed to her, including a proposal of marriage from an ardent admirer of "her" poetry. The proposal was rejected "with a gravity befitting the occasion."

Sharp described the creation of the name in a letter to his friend Mrs. Janvier: "You have asked me once or twice about F.M., why I took her name. ... The name was born naturally: (of course I had associations with the name Macleod) it, Fiona, is very rare now. Most Highlanders would tell you it was extinct—even as the diminutive of Fionaghal (Flora). But it is not. It is an old Celtic name (meaning "a fair maid") still occasionally to be found. I know a little girl, the daughter of a Highland clergyman, who is called Fiona. ... I can write out of my heart in a way I could not do as William Sharp, and indeed I could not do so if I were the woman Fiona Macleod is supposed to be, unless veiled in scrupulous anonymity" [Elizabeth A. Sharp, *William Sharp (Fiona Macleod): A Memoir*, 1910].

Mícheál Mac Liammóir: Alfred Willmore (1899–1978), Ir. stage, movie actor. As a juvenile the actor performed under his real name. In the 1920s, however, he adopted a more romantic-sounding Gaelic name. The surname, pronounced approximately "Macleemer," corresponds to the English original, but his first name is the Irish form of Michael.

Frank McLowery: Clay Allison (1914–), Eng. writer of westerns.

Edward McLysaght: Edward Lysaght (1888–1986), Eng.-born Ir. historian, genealogist. The distinguished First Herald of Ireland was born

in England, a fact that he was never too keen to reveal. On completing his education at Oxford, he moved to Ireland and became gradually involved with the "Irish Ireland" political movement, eventually adding "Mc" to his name in 1920 so as to indicate its Gaelic origin more obviously.

Brinsley McNamara: John Weldon (1890–1963), Ir. stage actor, novelist, dramatist.

Gerald MacNamara: Harry C. Morrow (1866–1938), Ir. playwright, stage actor.

Gus McNaughton: Augustus Howard (1884–1969), Br. movie actor.

Pierre Mac Orlan: Pierre Dumarchey (1882–1970), Fr. novelist.

Butterfly McQueen: Thelma McQueen (1911–1995), U.S. black stage, movie actress. The actress's first name originated as a nickname following a production of *A Midsummer Night's Dream* in which she danced in the Butterfly Ballet. She then adopted it permanently.

Arthur Macrae: Arthur Schroepfer (1908–1962), Br. stage actor, playwright. It is possible the actor's stage name was suggested by his mother's first name, Margaret.

Georgius Macropedius: Joris van Lankveldt (1476–1558), Du. humanist. The scholar rendered his name into a classical equivalent, in the manner of his day. Latin *Georgius*, Greek *Georgios*, is English George, Dutch Joris, while *Macropedius* is "long field" (Greek *makros*, Dutch *lang*, English *long*; Greek *pedion*, Dutch *veld*, English *field*).

Seán MacStiofáin: John Edward Drayton Stephenson (1928–), Br.-born leading IRA member. The Irish name answers to the English "John Stephenson."

Ralph McTell: Ralph May (1944–), Br. folk songwriter.

Bill Macy: William Macy Garber (1922–), U.S. TV actor.

Juhan Madarik: Johannes Lauristin (1899–1941), Estonian writer. The writer's adopted plant name means "lady's bedstraw" (*Galium verum*), the Estonian word for which is *madar*.

Minnie Maddern: Minnie Maddern Fiske (*q.v.*).

Jean Madeira: Jean Browning (1918–1972), U.S. opera singer.

Madeleine: Noor Imayat Khan (1914–1944), Br. agent, working in France.

[Sister] Mary Madeleva: Mary Evaline Wolff (1887–1964), U.S. nun, poet, educator. The writer took a religious name that appears to be a blend of her original first two names and "Mary Madeleine."

Guy **Madison:** Robert Ozel Moseley (1922–1996), U.S. movie actor.

Noël **Madison:** Nathaniel Moscovitch (1898–1975), U.S. movie actor, of Russ. parentage.

Madonna: Madonna Louise Veronica Ciccone (1958–), U.S. pop singer. The singer's real first name accords with her chart-topping album of 1985, *Like a Virgin*, and at that time sharply contrasted with her hedonistic image.

Johnny **Maestro:** John Mastrangelo (1939–), U.S. rock singer.

Magic Dick: Richard Salwitz (1945–), U.S. rock harmonica player.

Magic Sam: Samuel Maghett (1937–1969), U.S. black blues musician.

Magic Slim: Morris Holt (1937–), U.S. black blues musician. He was given his name by Magic Sam (see above).

Hyacinthe **Maglanowich:** Prosper Mérimée (1803–1870), Fr. novelist, historian. Just one of the pseudonyms adopted by the writer who also deluded his readers as Clara Gazul (*q.v.*) and Joseph Létrange (see p. 25). He used it for *La Guzla* (1827), a book of ballads about murder, revenge, and vampires supposedly translated from the Illyrian.

Vasily **Magnitsky:** Vasily Konstantinovich Velelepov (1839–1901), Russ. historian, ethnographer, folklorist.

Philip **Magnus:** [Sir] Philip Magnus-Allcroft (1906–), Eng. biographer.

Magnus **Magnusson:** Magnus Sigursteinsson (1929–), Icelandic-born Br. broadcaster, writer. The well-known quizmaster was born in Scotland to Icelandic parents. His father, the Icelandic Consul-General for Scotland, was Sigursteinn Magnusson, and according to the traditional Icelandic practice, Magnus automatically acquired a surname directly based on his father's first name, as Sigursteinsson ("son of Sigursteinn"). However, he instead adopted his father's own surname, for ease of memorability and pronunciation (as well as alliteration). Just as sons add *-son* to their father's first name, so daughters add *-dóttir* (Magnus's mother was Ingibjorg Sigurdardóttir), and Icelandic women do not change their name on marriage, as conventionally elsewhere in Europe.

Lyudvig Ignatyevich **Magyar:** Lajos Milhover (or Milgorf) (1891–1940), Hung.-born Russ. rev-olutionary, historian. The activist fought for the establishment of Soviet rule in Hungary. Hence his adopted name, the Hungarian word for "Hungarian."

Taj **Mahal:** Henry Saint Clair Fredericks (1942–), U.S. black blues-rock musician. A name of obvious derivation.

Guru **Maharaj Ji:** Pratap Singh Rawat (1957–), Ind. religious leader. The leader of the Divine Light Mission assumed a Sanskrit title meaning "perfect master." He became leader in 1966 at the age of eight on the death of his father, Sri Hans Ji Maharaj, who had founded the Mission in 1960.

Gurgen **Mahari:** Gurgen Grigoryevich Adzhemyan (1903–1969), Armenian writer. The writer began his career by writing pessimistic poems, and adopted a name to match, meaning "deathward" (Armenian *mah*, "death"). His verse brought him fame, and he kept the name even when writing much more positively.

Jock **Mahoney:** Jacques O'Mahoney (1919–1989), U.S. movie actor.

Solomon **Maimon:** Solomon Heiman (1753–1800), Lithuanian-born German Jewish philosopher. The philosopher was attracted to the teachings of Maimonides (see Rambam), and adopted his name accordingly.

Maimonides *see* **Rambam**.

Marjorie **Main:** Mary Tomlinson Krebs (1890–1975), U.S. movie actress. The actress, famous in her role as "Ma Kettle," took her screen name from the title of Sinclair Lewis's novel *Main Street* (1920). She was a minister's daughter, and changed her name to avoid embarrassing her family when she joined a local stock company.

Mainbocher: Main Rousseau Bocher (1891–1976), U.S.-born Fr. fashion designer.

Charles Eric **Maine:** David McIlwaine (1921–), Br. SF writer.

Maironis: Jonas Maciulis (1862–1932), Lithuanian poet. The writer adopted a poetic plant name meaning "marjoram."

John Wilson **Maitland:** [Sir] William Watson (1858–1935), Eng. poet.

Ruth **Maitland:** Ruth Erskine (1880–1961), Br. stage actress.

Thomas **Maitland:** Robert Williams Buchanan (1841–1901), Eng. poet, novelist. The poet used the name for his article "The Fleshly School of Poetry," attacking Pre-Raphaelites, and especially Rossetti, in the October 1871 edition of the *Contemporary Review*.

Maître Adam: Adam Billaut (1602–1662), Fr. carpenter, poet.

Marie **Majerová:** Marie Stívinová, née Bartosová (1882–1967), Cz. novelist.

Tom **Major:** Abraham Thomas Ball (1879–1963), Eng. circus performer, vaudeville manager. The actor adopted his stage name in 1901 on taking up a career in variety. He was the father of British prime minister John Major (1943–), who kept the name.

Earl **Majors:** Alan Garreth (1953–1978), Eng. motorcycle stunt rider.

Lee **Majors:** Harvey Lee Yeary II (1942–), U.S. movie actor.

[Archbishop] **Makarios III:** Mikhail Khristodolou Mouskos (1913–1977), Cypriot head of state. The religious name (English Macarius) adopted by the archbishop is the Greek word for "blessed" and honors the 4th-century St. Macarius (see Macarius).

Makriyannis: Yannis Triandafillos (1797–1864), Gk. memoirist.

Vladimir Yemelyanovich **Maksimov:** Lev Alekseyevich Samsonov (1930–1995), Russ. writer, editor.

Mala: Ray Wise (1906–1952), U.S.- Eskimo movie actor.

Malachi **Malagrowther:** [Sir] Walter Scott (1771–1832), Sc. poet, novelist. Scott adopted his pen name from the character of Sir Mungo Malagrowther in his own novel *The Fortunes of Nigel* (1822).

Curzio **Malaparte:** Kurt Erich Suckert (1898–1957), It. writer, journalist. The writer adopted a surname that was intended to suggest the converse of that of (Napoleon) Bonaparte (or Buonaparte). The emperor's own name derives from a Corsican "auspicious" first name, meaning "goodly portion."

Malbim: Meir Laib ben Yehiel Michal (1809–1879), Russ. rabbi, biblical scholar. The Rabbinic scholar adopted an acronymic name formed from the initial letters of his Hebrew name: *M*eir *L*aib *b*en *Y*ehiel *M*ichal.

Karl **Malden:** Karl Mladen Sekulovich (1913–), U.S. movie, TV actor, of Yugoslav parentage.

Lucas **Malet:** Mary St. Leger Harrison, née Kingsley (1852–1931), Eng. novelist, daughter of novelist Charles Kingsley. The writer took her pseudonym from the surnames of two families related to the Kingsleys, adopting it because she did not want her work to be judged on the Kingsley name but on its own merit. She first used it for *Colonel Enderby's Wife* (1885), although this was not her first novel.

Max **Malini:** Max K. Breit (1873–1942), Pol.-born U.S. magician. The illusionist's name, suggesting "bad," "evil," matched his ugly appearance and crude approach to his acts.

David **Mallet:** David Malloch (? 1705–1765), Sc. poet, miscellaneous writer. The poet adopted an anglicized version of his Scottish name in 1724, writing in a letter to a friend at the time that "there is not one Englishman that can pronounce [Malloch]." Dr. Johnson strongly disapproved of this change, and referred to it in his definition of the word "alias" in his *Dictionary* (1755): "*alias* means otherwise, as Mallet *alias* Malloch, that is, otherwise Malloch."

Françoise **Mallet-Joris:** Françoise Lilar (1930–), Belg.-born Fr. writer. The writer adopted the maiden name of her mother, the Belgian novelist Suzanne Lilar (1901–1988).

Gina **Malo:** Janet Flynn (1909–1963), Ir.-Ger.-U.S. stage, movie actress, working in U.K.

Dorothy **Malone:** Dorothy Eloise Maloney (1925–), U.S. movie, TV actress. The actress modified her name when she joined Warner Bros. in 1945.

Louis **Malone:** Louis MacNeice (1907–1963), Ir. dramatist, poet. The writer took his early pen name from his birthplace, Malone Road, Belfast. He used it for the novel *Roundabout Way* (1932).

Conrad **Malte-Brun:** Malte Conrad Brun (1775–1826), Dan.-born Fr. geographer.

Yelizar **Maltsev:** Yelizar Yuryevich Pupko (1917–), Russ. writer. The writer adopted a more euphonious name than his original surname (suggesting Russian *pup*, "navel").

Dmitry **Mamin-Sibiryak:** Dmitry Narkisovich Mamin (1852–1912), Russ. writer. The addition to the writer's name means "Siberian." He was born near Yekaterinburg, just east of the Urals, and initially trained to be a priest. He explains how friends gave his name: "I first tried out the names Rasskazov [Russian *rasskaz*, "story"] and Tomsky [*tom*, "volume"], but they weren't right! My name was an object of fun to my fellow ordinands: why were we mummy's boys [*mamin*, "mother's"], not Tyatin ["daddy's"]? They decided that the best pseudonym was Sibiryak. After all, Yekaterinburg is the other side of the Urals, and Russians regard everywhere beyond the Urals, including Siberia, as all one!" [Dmitriyev, p. 92].

Felix **Man:** Hans Felix Sigismund Baumann (1893–1985), Ger. pioneer photojournalist, working in U.K.

Manchecourt: Henri Léon Emile Lavedan (1859–1940), Fr. playwright, novelist. The writer presumably took his name from the village of Manchecourt, south of Paris.

Georges **Mandel:** Jeroboam Rothschild (1885–1943), Fr. political leader.

Frederick **Manfred:** Frederick Feikema (1912–), U.S. novelist, of Frisian descent. The writer called himself Feike Feikema from 1944 through 1951.

Nino **Manfredi:** Nino Saturnino (1921–), It. movie actor.

Barry **Manilow:** Barry Alan Pinkus (1946–), U.S. popular singer. The singer assumed the name of his paternal grandmother. Manilow's father, Harold Kelliher, was of Irish descent, and changed his name to Pinkus to avoid conflict with the singer's grandmother, who would not have been pleased to learn that her daughter, Edna Manilow, was marrying out of the Jewish religion. Barry's father left the family when the boy was only two years old, and Edna changed his last name to Manilow when he was 13 [Stambler, p. 438].

Handsome Dick **Manitoba:** Richard Blum (1954–), U.S. rock singer.

Abby **Mann:** Abraham Goodman (1927–), U.S. screenwriter.

Anthony **Mann:** Emil Anton Bundsmann (1906–1967), U.S. movie director.

Daniel **Mann:** Daniel Chugermann (1912–1991), U.S. movie director.

Hank **Mann:** David W. Liebermann (1887–1971), U.S. movie actor.

Herbie **Mann:** Herbert Jay Solomon (1930–), U.S. popular musician.

Manfred **Mann:** Michael Lubowitz (1940–), S.A.-born Eng. pop musician.

Theodore **Mann:** Theodore Goldman (1924–), U.S. stage producer, director.

Mary **Mannering:** Florence Friend (1876–1953), Eng. stage actress, working in U.S.

Miss **Manners:** Judith Sylvia Martin, née Perlman (1938–), U.S. writer on etiquette.

Charles **Manners:** Southcote Mansergh (1857–1935), Ir. opera singer, working in U.K.

David **Manners:** Rauff de Ryther Duan Acklom (1901–), Can. stage, movie actor, novelist.

Mrs. Horace **Manners:** Algernon Charles Swinburne (1837–1909), Eng. poet. The poet used this name for his novel, *A Year's Letters*, originally serialized in 1877 but republished in 1905 as *Love's Cross Currents*.

Dick **Manning:** Samuel Medoff (1912–1991), Russ.-born U.S. songwriter.

Irene **Manning:** Inez Harvuot (1917–), U.S. movie actress, singer.

Manolete: Manuel Laureano Rodríguez Sánchez (1917–1947), Sp. bullfighter. The fighter's name is based on his first name, as that of his predecessor Joselito (*q.v.*) was based on his.

Manolo: Manuel Martínez Hugué (1872–1945), Sp. sculptor.

Jayne **Mansfield:** Vera Jayne Palmer (1932–1967), U.S. movie actress. The actress's screen name is that of her first husband, Paul Mansfield, whom she married in 1950 at the age of 16.

Katherine **Mansfield:** Kathleen Mansfield Murry, née Beauchamp (1888–1923), N.Z.-born Br. novelist, short story writer.

Eric von **Manstein:** Erich von Lewinski (1887–1973), Ger. military commander. The field marshal's surname is that of General Georg von Manstein, who adopted the boy following the untimely death of his parents.

Tsetsiliya **Mansurova:** Tsetsiliya Lvovna Vollershteyn (Wollerstein) (1897–), Russ. stage actress.

Paul **Mantee:** Paul Marianetti (1936), U.S. movie actor.

Hilary **Mantel:** Hilary Mary McEwen, née Thompson (1952–), Br. novelist. The writer adopted the name of her stepfather, Jack Mantel.

E. **Manuel:** Ernest L'Epine (1826–1893), Fr. writer. A confusing pen name, since it suggests the French poet and dramatist Eugène Manuel (1823–1901), who wrote under his real name.

[Sir] Edward **Manville:** Edward Mosley (1862–1933), Eng. electrical engineer, automobile manufacturer, of Jewish parentage. The industrialist's father changed the family's surname of Mosley to Manville in the 1870s.

Phil **Manzanera:** Philip Targett-Adams (1951–), Br. rock musician. The musician's new surname is the Spanish word for a type of apple tree. But this may not be its origin, unless there is some sort of pun on Adam and the apple.

Manzhelli: Pavel Afanasyevich Shevchenko (1872–1948), Russ. circus artist, horseman. The performer's Italian-style name (Mangelli) may be loosely based on Italian *maneggio*, "horsemanship," "manège." His sons inherited the name as jockeys.

Giacomo **Manzù:** Giacomo Manzoni (1908–1991), It. sculptor.

Mao Dun: Shen Yen-Ping (1896–1981), Chin. novelist. The writer's pseudonym means "contradiction," alluding to his stance in 1930 following the break between the Kuomintang, his previous employers, and the Chinese Communist Party.

Maori: James Inglis (1845–1908), N.Z. author, journalist, politician.

Le **Mapah:** Ganneau (1805–1851), Fr. sculptor, religious leader. The Frenchman was the originator of *Évadisme*, a quasireligion founded in about 1835 that exalted the standing of woman and preached equality of the sexes. Its name is based on the first two letters of "Eve" and "Adam," while "Le Mapah" derives from the first two letters of Latin *mater*, "mother," and *pater*, "father."

Anna **Mar:** Anna Yakovlevna Lenshina, née Brovar (1887–1917), Russ. writer, screenwriter. Mar wrote a column for the *Zhurnal dlya Zhenshchin* ("Women's Journal") as *Printsessa Grëza* ("Princess Daydream"), answering readers' inquiries.

Adele **Mara:** Adelaida Delgado (1923–), Sp.-U.S. dancer, movie actress.

Sally **Mara:** Raymond Queneau (1903–1976), Fr. writer.

Jean **Marais:** Jean Alfred Villain-Marais (1913–), Fr. movie actor.

Marc: Charles Mark Edward Boxer (1931–1988), Eng. cartoonist.

Theophilus **Marcliffe:** William Godwin (1756–1836), Eng. philosopher, novelist, dramatist. The writer used this name for *The Looking Glass; A True History of the Early History of an Artist* (1805). His new first name is a Greek equivalent of his original surname, meaning "friend of God." His main pen name was Edward Baldwin (*q.v.*).

Félicien **Marceau:** Louis Carette (1913–), Belg. novelist, dramatist.

Marcel **Marceau:** Marcel Mangel (1923–), Fr. mime artist.

Fredric **March:** Ernest Frederick McIntyre Bickel (1897–1975), U.S. stage, movie actor. The actor changed his name at the suggestion of movie director John Cromwell, who felt that "Bickel" sounded too much like "pickle." So the star of *A Star Is Born* (1937) adapted his mother's maiden name of Marcher as his screen name. Some years later he commented, "I wish I'd left it as it was—after all, [movie actor] Theodore Bickel did all right."

Jane **March:** Jane March Horwood (1973–), Br. movie actress.

Little Peggy **March:** Margaret Battavio (1948–), U.S. pop singer, songwriter. The singer's stage name evolved from her first appearance at the age of five.

Maxwell **March:** Margery Allingham (1904–1966), Br. crime novelist.

Georges **Marchal:** Georges Louis Lucot (1920–), Fr. movie actor.

Catherine **Marchant:** Catherine Cookson (1906–), Eng. novelist.

Martin **Marches:** Martin Aleksandrovich Myuller (Müller) (1894–1961), Hung.-born Russ. illusionist.

Rocky **Marciano:** Rocco Francis Marchegiano (1923–1969), U.S. heavyweight boxer.

Subcommandante **Marcos:** Rafael Sebastián Guillén (1958–), Mexican guerrilla.

Louis **Marcoussis:** Louis Markus (1878–1941), Pol.-born Fr. painter. The artist's pseudonym, although close to his original name, was suggested to him by the poet Apollinaire (*q.v.*), and came from the village of Marcoussis near Paris.

Marcus Aurelius: Marcus Annius Verus (121–180), Roman emperor, philosopher. When Marcus was adopted at the age of 17 by his uncle, the emperor Antoninus Pius, earlier named Titus Aurelius Antoninus, his name was changed to Marcus Aelius Aurelius Verus. He succeeded Antoninus as emperor in 161, when he adopted the full name and imperial title of Imperator Caesar Marcus Aurelius Antoninus Augustus.

Marevna: Maria Vorobieva (1892–1984), Russ. painter, working in France, U.K. The artist was given her professional name, based on her real name, by Maxim Gorky (*q.v.*).

Margo: María Marguerita Guadelupe Teresa Estela Bolado Castilla y O'Donnell (1918–1985), Mexican-born stage, movie actress, dancer, working in U.S.

Maria del Occidente: Maria Gowen Brooks (*c.*1794–1845), U.S. poet. The poet was dubbed "Maria of the West" by the English poet Robert Southey, who held her writing in high esteem. She herself adopted this name in a Spanish form when living in Cuba later in her life.

Edna **Marian:** Edna Mannan (1908–), U.S. movie actress.

Kelly **Marie:** Jacqueline McKinnon (1957–), Sc. pop singer. "Kelly" clearly comes from her original first name.

Marie-Jeanne: Marie-Jeanne Pelus (1920–), U.S. ballet dancer.

Mariemma: Emma Martinez (1920–), Sp. ballet dancer. A name extracted from the dancer's original name.

Marilyn: Peter Robinson (1963–), Eng. pop singer. The singer affected a blond, androgynous look, vaguely reminiscent of Marilyn Monroe (*q.v.*).

Jean **Marin:** Yves-André-Marie Morvan (1909–1995), Fr. journalist, radio commentator.

J.-J. **Marine:** René Oppitz (1904–1976), Belg. poet, critic, detective story writer.

Mario: Mario Hubert Armengol (1909–), Sp.-born Br. painter, cartoonist.

Giovanni Matteo **Mario:** Mario Cavaliere di Candia (1810–1883), It. opera singer. The romantic tenor signed his first contract in 1838 with his forename alone, and thereafter adopted it as his surname, adding new first names.

Frances **Marion:** Frances Marion Owens (1887–1973), U.S. screenwriter.

Joan **Marion:** Joan Nicholls (1908–1945), Br. stage actress. The actress took her mother's first name as her stage name.

Mona **Maris:** Maria Capdevielle (1903–1991), Fr.-Argentine movie actress, working in U.S.

Roger **Maris:** Roger Eugene Maras (1934–1985), U.S. baseball player.

Marisol: Marisol Escobar (1930–), Fr.-born U.S. sculptor, of Venezuelan parentage.

Sari **Maritza:** Patricia Detering-Nathan (1911–1987), Eng.-Austr. movie actress.

J. **Marjoram:** Ralph Hales Mottram (1883–1971), Eng. novelist, poet.

Jane **Marken:** Jane Krab (1895–1976), Fr. movie actress.

Chris **Marker:** Christian François Bouche-Villeneuve (1921–), Fr. movie director.

Mrs. **Markham:** Elizabeth Penrose, née Cartwright (1780–1837), Eng. novelist, children's writer. The writer took her pen name from the village of Markham, Nottinghamshire, where she spent much of her childhood.

David **Markham:** Peter Basil Harrison (1913–1983), Eng. stage actor.

Robert **Markham:** Kingsley Amis (1922–1995), Eng. novelist, poet, playwright, short story writer. The writer used this name for *Colonel Sun: A James Bond Adventure* (1968). "It's easy to spell and easy to remember," he said.

[Dame] Alicia **Markova:** Lillian Alice Marks (1910–), Eng. ballet dancer. The dancer was given her Russian-style name when she was only 12 and still at ballet school: "After a heated discussion and references to Tolstoi and Dostoievski, we settled on the obvious *Markova*" [Arnold Haskell, *Balletomania*, 1934].

Alfred **Marks:** Alfred Edward Touchinsky (1921–1996), Br. stage, movie comedian, singer, of Pol. Jewish parentage. The actor adopted his stage name by deed poll after World War II.

Marksman: J.C. Walker (*fl.*1920s–1940s), Welsh-born Br. cartoonist. The name is apt for an artist who aims to "hit home" in his cartoons. It was also factually fitting for Walker, who was a rifle-shooting champion.

Marky Mark: Mark Wahlberg (1971–), U.S. pop singer, movie actor.

Louis **Marlow:** Louis Umfreville Wilkinson (1881–1966), Br. novelist, biographer.

Anthony **Marlowe:** Anthony Perredita (1913–), Eng. stage actor. The actor adopted his mother's maiden name as his stage name.

Charles **Marlowe:** Harriett Jay (1857–1932), Eng. novelist, playwright, stage actress. The writer used the male name for her plays, many coauthored with her adoptive father, the poet Robert Buchanan.

Hugh **Marlowe:** Hugh Herbert Hipple (1914–1982), U.S. movie actor.

Julia **Marlowe:** Sarah Frances Frost (1866–1950), Eng.-born U.S. stage, movie actress. The actress first appeared on stage at the age of 12 under the name of Fanny Brough.

June **Marlowe:** Gisela Valaria Goetten (1903–1984), U.S. movie actress.

Vic **Marlowe:** Victor Hugh Etheridge (?–1987), Br. variety actor, dancer. All these Marlowe names, even where a genuine family name, share something of the charisma of the 16th-century English dramatist Christopher Marlowe.

Florence **Marly:** Hana Smekalova (1918–1978), Fr.-Cz. movie actress.

Jeanne **Marni:** Jeanne Marnière (1854–1910), Fr. writer.

Maroc: Robert S.E. Coram (*fl.*1930s–1940s), Eng. cartoonist. A straightforward name reversal.

Martin **Marprelate:** John Penry (1559–1593), Welsh Puritan writer + John Udall (?1560–1592), Eng. Puritan preacher + Henry Barrow (?–1593), Eng. church reformer + Job Throckmorton (1545–1601), Eng. Puritan. The name, with its pun on "mar prelate" (i.e. "attack the episcopacy"), was used for a number of anonymous (or pseudonymous) tracts directed against the bishops and defending the Presbyterian system of discipline. The tracts were issued from a secret press in the two years from 1588, and the suspected authors were the Puritan pamphleteers mentioned. Penry and Barrow were executed, Udall died in prison, but Throckmorton, denying his complicity, escaped punishment.

J.J. Marric: John Creasey (1908–1973), Eng. crime novelist. Creasey used around two dozen pen names. This one, less orthodox than most, may have been intended to suggest his own first name and a version of "crime."

Moore Marriott: George Thomas Moore-Marriott (1885–1949), Br. movie comedian.

Mlle Mars: Anne-Françoise-Hippolyte Boutet (1779–1847), Fr. actress.

Marjorie Mars: Marjorie Brown (1903–), Br. stage actress.

Beryl Marsden: Beryl Hogg (1947–), Eng. popular singer.

Carol Marsh: Norma Simpson (1926–), Br. movie actress.

Garry Marsh: Leslie Marsh Geraghty (1902–1981), Eng. stage, movie actor. The actor seems to have used his surname as the basis of his new first name, retaining his middle name for his new surname.

Joan Marsh: Nancy Ann Rosher (1913–), U.S. movie actress.

Marion Marsh: Violet Krauth (1913–), U.S. movie actress.

Brenda Marshall: Ardis Anderson Gaines (1915–1992), U.S. movie actress.

Frank Marshall: Frank Marzalkiewicz (c.1895–1969), U.S. stage puppet maker.

Garry Marshall: Garry Marscharelli (1934–), U.S. movie director, brother of Penny Marshall (see below).

James Marshall: James Greenblatt (1969–), U.S. movie, TV actor. The actor originally changed his name to James Green. He then decided to adopt the middle name of Jimi Hendrix (q.v.) as his surname.

Owen Marshall: Owen Marshall Jones (1941–), N.Z. short story writer.

Penny Marshall: Carole Penny Marscharelli (1942–), U.S. movie director, actress, sister of Garry Marshall (see above).

Peter Marshall: Pierre La Cock (1930–), U.S. TV host.

Tully Marshall: William Phillips (1864–1943), U.S. movie actor.

Charles Martel: Thomas Delf (1812–1866), Eng. writer. The writer, who also made translations from the French, appears to have adopted the name of the Frankish king Charles Martel ("Charles the Hammer") (c.688–741).

Paul Martens: Stephen H. Critten (1887–1964), Eng. novelist, short story writer.

Fred Marteny: Feodor Neumann (1931–), Cz.-Austr. ballet dancer, choreographer.

Martin IV: Simon de Brie (c.1210–1285), Fr. pope. The pontiff took the name of France's patron saint, St. Martin, especially as he had been treasurer of St. Martin's, Tours, where the saint had been bishop and where his shrine now is.

Martin V: Oddo Colonna (1368–1431), It. pope. The pontiff took the name of St. Martin, on whose feastday (November 11, 1417) he was elected pope.

Billy Martin: Alfred Manuel Pesano (1928–1989), U.S. baseball player, manager, of It. descent. "Billy" evolved from "Belli" ("beautiful"), a nickname given Martin as a young child by his Italian grandmother.

Claire Martin: Claire Montreuil (1914–), Can. writer. The writer adopted her mother's maiden name as her pen name.

David Martin: Ludwig Detsinyi (1915–), Hung.-born Austral. journalist, writer. The writer used the name Spinifex for his book of verse, *Rob the Robber, His Life and Vindication* (1954), from the Australian grass so called.

Dean Martin: Dino Paul Crocetti (1917–1995), U.S. movie actor, of It. parentage, teaming with Jerry Lewis (q.v.). The actor put himself over as a "cousin" of the Metropolitan Opera star Nino Martini, although quite unrelated to him. The adoption of this particular name and ruse was suggested by band leader Ernie McKay, at Walkers Café, Columbus, Ohio [Michael Freedland, *Dino: The Dean Martin Story*, 1984].

Derek Martin: Derek William Rapp (1933–), Br. TV actor.

Ernest H. Martin: Ernest H. Markowitz (1919–), U.S. stage manager, producer.

George Madden Martin: Georgia May Madden (1866–1946), U.S. short story writer, novelist.

Quinn Martin: Martin Cohn, Jr. (1922–1987), U.S. TV producer, scriptwriter. "Quinn" presumably represents "Cohn."

Ross Martin: Martin Rosenblatt (1920–1981), Pol.-U.S. movie actor.

Stella **Martin:** Georgette Heyer (1902–1974), Br. author of historical romances, detective novels.

Tony **Martin:** Alvin Maris (or Morris) (1913–), U.S. cabaret singer, movie actor. The singer changed his name to Anthony Martin in 1934. His new first name then settled to its standard diminutive.

Jean Paul Egide **Martini:** Johann Paul Ägidius Schwarzendorf (1741–1816), Ger.-born Fr. composer.

Al **Martino:** Alfred Cini (1927–), U.S. pop singer, of It. parentage.

Mary **Martlew:** Mary Greenhalgh (1919–), Eng. stage actress.

L. **Martov:** Yuly Osipovich Tsederbaum (1873–1923), Russ. Menshevik leader. The politician's name appears to represent Russian *mart*, "March," possibly referring to a key date in his activities.

Ik **Marvel:** Donald Grant Mitchell (1822–1908), U.S. essayist. The writer adopted the name J.K. Marvel in 1846 for his contributions to the *Morning Courier and New York Enquirer*. This was misprinted as "Ik Marvel," and he stuck with it. "Ik" would have been a short form of "Isaac." The origin of the initials is uncertain, but "Marvel" presumably derived from his surname.

Hank **Marvin:** Brian Rankin (1941–), Br. rock guitarist.

Chico **Marx:** Leonard Marx (1886–1961), U.S. movie comedian (see below).

Groucho **Marx:** Julius Henry Marx (1890–1977), U.S. movie comedian (see below).

Gummo **Marx:** Milton Marx (1893–1977), U.S. vaudeville artist (see below).

Harpo **Marx:** Adolph (known as Arthur) Marx (1888–1964), U.S. movie comedian (see below).

Zeppo **Marx:** Herbert Marx (1901–1979), U.S. movie comedian. The Marx Brothers began their career as a vaudeville team in which Gummo was replaced by Zeppo. Their names grew out of their characters. Chico, it seemed, had a reputation for always being "after the chicks"; Harpo, of course, played the harp; Groucho "had a naturally caustic view of life" (and according to another theory was characterized by the grouch bag or briefcase in which he carried his stage equipment); Gummo always had holes in his shoes and wore rubbers, or gumshoes, over them; Zeppo—although nobody is quite sure—was born around the time the first

Zeppelin was built. Asked about his own name in a TV interview, Groucho explained: "I always had a grim visage, because I handled the money, and the others didn't have too much confidence in me, and it became Groucho, and it was a nice name" [*The Listener*, August 16, 1979].

According to another theory, however, Groucho took his first name from a comic strip character called Groucho Monk. Chico, Harpo, and Gummo were other characters in the strip, itself called *Mager's Monks*.

Aunt **Mary:** Mary Hughes, née Robson (*fl.*1820), Br. children's writer.

Maryan: Maria Descard (1847–1927), Fr. novelist. The writer used this pseudonym for her first novel, *Mlle de Kervallez*, published when she was 30, taking it from the first names, Mary Ann, of her English maternal grandmother.

Mary of the Incarnation: Mme Acarie (*q.v.*).

Masaccio: Tommaso di ser Giovanni di Simone Cassai (Guidi) (1401–1428), It. painter. The artist's name, formed from the second syllable of his first name with the Italian pejorative ("bad") suffix *-accio*, can be understood as "slovenly Tom." Giorgio Vasari's *Lives of the Artists* (1550) writes of him thus: "He was very absent-minded and erratic, and he devoted all his mind and thoughts to art and paid little attention to himself and still less to others. He refused to give any time to worldly cares and possessions, even to the way he dressed, let alone anything else. ... So instead of calling him by his proper name, which was Tommaso, everyone called him Masaccio." Compare the name of Masolino (below).

Masaniello: Tommaso Aniello d'Amalfi (1620–1647), It. political agitator. A single name formed from the bearer's first two names.

Masolino: Tommaso di Cristoforo Fini (*c.*1383–*c.*1447), It. painter. The painter's name, formed from the accented syllable of his first name with the Italian dimunutive suffix *-olino*, can be understood to mean "little Tom." The reference is presumably to his size or stature, possibly by comparison with Masaccio (see above), with whom he was closely linked, and by whom he was influenced.

Edith **Mason:** Edith Barnes (1898–1973), U.S. opera singer.

Jackie **Mason:** Yacov Moshe Maza (1934–), U.S. rabbi, comedian. The performer's name represents a loose anglicization of his first name and a blend of his other two names.

Shirley **Mason:** Leonie Flugrath (1901–1979), U.S. movie actress.

Stuart **Mason:** Christopher Sclater Millard (1872–1927), Br. biographer. The writer used this name for his three books on Oscar Wilde (1914, 1915, 1920), but kept his real name for *The Printed Work of Claud Lovat Fraser* (1923).

Massachusettensis: Daniel Leonard (1740–1829), U.S. Loyalist writer. The writer used this pseudoclassical pen name for a series of contributions to *The Massachusetts Gazette and Post Boy* (1774–75). These were replied to by Novanglus (*q.v.*).

Lea **Massari:** Anna Maria Massatani (1933–), Fr.-It. movie actress.

Fritzi **Massary:** Friederike Massaryk (1882–1969), Austr. operetta singer, working in U.S. The Jewish singer fled Hitler in 1933 and went to London. She later settled in California.

Ilona **Massey:** Ilona Hajmassy (1910–1974), Hung.-born U.S. movie actress. Although the actress's screen name clearly resembles her real name, it may well have been additionally suggested by the existing name of movie actor Raymond Massey (1896–1983).

Léonide **Massine:** Leonid Fyodorovich Miassin (1896–1979), Russ. ballet dancer, choreographer. A gallicized form of the dancer's original name.

Charles **Masson:** James Lewis (1800–1853), Br. traveler, archaeologist. The traveler adopted his new name in the late 1820s when embarking for a ten-year period of archaeological exploration and investigation in Afghanistan.

Kitty **Masters:** Katherine Masterson (1902–1994), Br. popular singer.

Masuccio Salernitano: Tommaso Guardati (*c.*1475–*c.*1475), It. writer. The writer's first name is a diminutive of his original name, so means something like "Tommy." His second name means "of Salerno," his birthtown.

Mata Hari: Margarethe Geertruida MacLeod, née Zelle (1876–1917), Du.-born Fr. dancer, spy. The dancer's name for her exotic Eastern temple performance on the French stage derives from Malay *matahari*, "sun," literally "eye of the day" (from *mata*, "eye," and *hari*, "day"). She took the name in 1898. Before her arrival in Paris in 1904, Zelle had been married briefly to a Dutch colonial officer, Rudolph MacLeod, and with him had stayed, equally briefly, in the Dutch East Indies. She had retained enough of the language to adopt the name for her new life in the theatre.

The dancer's stage name may have been simply evocative. However, it happens to relate to her given name "Margarethe" (Margaret). This name, meaning "pearl," derives from French *marguerite*, "daisy," and English *daisy* literally means "day's eye," otherwise "eye of the day" or "sun."

Carmen **Mathé:** Margaretha Matheson (1938–), Sc. ballet dancer. The dancer adopted a Spanish-style name rather cleverly from her existing two names, adding "Carmen" as a clincher, the name of the alluring Spanish gypsy girl made famous by Bizet's opera.

Berkley **Mather:** John (later Jasper) Evan Weston-Davies (1909–1996), Eng. TV scriptwriter. The author spent many years in India as an army officer, and after World War II sold his first radio play to the BBC. To disguise his professional military status he devised a pseudonym from the (misspelled) Berkeley Grill and Mathers' drugstore, Poona, India.

Helen **Mathers:** Ellen Buckingham Reeves, née Mathews (1853–1921), Eng. novelist. The writer also used the name David Lyall (*q.v.*).

Mathetes: John Jones (1821–1878), Welsh Baptist minister, writer.

Anna **Matilda:** (1) Hannay Cowley (1743–1809), Eng. dramatist, poet; (2) Hester Lynch Piozzi, née Salusbury (1741–1821), Eng. writer. The same name was used by both women in their correspondence with the Della Cruscans (see Della Crusca). Hester Piozzi, better known as Mrs. Thrale, after her first husband, had been called "Matilda" by William Gifford in his two satires, *The Baviad* (1794) and *The Maeviad* (1795), both directed against the Dellacruscan school of English poetry.

Julia **Matilda:** Julia Clara Byrne, née Busk (1819–1894), Eng. author.

Matt: Matthew Pritchett (1965–), Eng. cartoonist.

Matta: Roberto Sebastian Antonio Matta-Echaurren (1911–), Chilean painter, sculptor.

Matteo: Matteo Marcellus Vittucci (1919–), U.S. dancer.

Walter **Matthau:** Walter Matuschanskayasky (1920–), U.S. stage, movie actor, of Russ. Jewish parentage. Sources vary on the actor's original impressive Slavic surname, but it seems to have been as stated here.

Thomas **Matthew:** John Rogers (1505–1555), Eng. Protestant divine, martyr. The Protestant convert used this name for his English translation of the Bible (1537), assuming a pseudonym for fear of meeting the same fate as his friend William Tyndale, who had earlier translated the New Testament (1525), the Pentateuch (1530) and the Book of Jonah (1531), and who had been burnt at the stake in 1536 as a heretic. But Rogers was accorded exactly the same judgment. His translation is now usually referred to as "Matthew's Bible."

Iain Matthews: Ian Matthew MacDonald (1946–), Eng. folk rock musician. The musician change his surname to avoid confusion with Ian McDonald, a saxophonist.

Camille Mauclair: Camille Faust (1872–1945), Fr. poet, novelist, art critic, of Dan. descent.

[Sir] Edward Maufe: Edward Brantwood Muff (1883–1974), Eng. architect. The architect changed his name by deed poll in 1908 from the common or garden Muff to the more distinctive Maufe.

Thierry Maulnier: Jacques Louis Talagrand (1909–1988), Fr. writer, journalist. The writer used this name for his articles in the political daily *Action Française*. The name itself evokes that of the central character of Alain-Fournier's novel *Le Grand Meaulnes*, although this may not have been the origin.

Maupin: Julie (or Emilie) d'Aubigny (*c.*1670–1707), Fr. opera singer. The singer's (sole) stage name was her married surname.

Molly Maureen: Elizabeth Mary Campfield (1904–1987), Br. stage, movie actress.

Furnley Maurice: Frank Leslie Thompson Wilmot (1881–1942), Austral. poet. The writer based his pseudonym on the names of two of his favorite Melbourne haunts: Ferntree Gully and Beaumaris.

Walter Maurice: [Sir] Walter Besant (1836–1901), Eng. novelist.

André Maurois: Emile Salomon Wilhelm Herzog (1885–1967), Fr. writer. The writer was a liaison officer in the British army in World War I and first used the name for *Les Silences du Colonel Bramble* (1918), humorously depicting British officers in their mess. In his autobiography he tells how his publisher advises him to adopt a pseudonym in order to avoid being recognized by the officers concerned:

"I resigned myself and selected the first name André, in memory of my cousin who had been killed in action, and Maurois, the name of a village near Cambrai, because I liked its sad sonor-ity... André Maurois... How strange and new those syllables sounded to me then!" [André Maurois, *Memoirs*, translated by Denver Lindley, 1970].

Yanka Mavr: Ivan Mikhaylovich Fyodorov (1883–1971), Belorussian children's writer. The writer adopted a colloquial form of his first two names.

[St.] Maxim the Greek: Mikhail Trivolis (*c.*1475–1556), Gr. churchman, translator, working in Russia. The scholar was nicknamed for his nationality, but it seems strange that his first name was altered in this way, as both Greek and Russian share a common version of "Michael." He was canonized in 1988.

Lois Maxwell: Lois Hooker (1927–), Can. movie actress, working in U.S., U.K. A name change was clearly desirable here.

Robert Maxwell: Jan Ludvik Hoch (1923–1991), Cz.-born Eng. publisher, politician, press baron. The newspaper owner had a fairly complex naming history. He was born near the Czech-Romanian border as the son of a Jewish peasant, Mechel Hoch, who called him Abraham Lyabi. But when the father went to register the boy at the local town hall, the Czech government official insisted on a Czech name for the record. He was thus renamed Jan Ludvik Hoch. Later, in World War II, he joined the Czech Pioneer Corps and was posted to Britain, where in 1943 he joined the North Staffordshire Regiment, taking the name of Private L.I. du Maurier, a name he had chosen from a cigarette packet in order to disguise his true identity if captured by the Germans. A year later, after the D-Day landings, he was working in the intelligence field in Paris, France, using the cover name Private Jones (although his actual rank was now higher than this).

In due course, his work so impressed the military authorities that he was promoted to second lieutenant and recommended to choose yet another name, as du Maurier and Jones were not regarded as fitting. The Scottish name of Robert Maxwell was suggested, and he adopted it, adding the English form of Jan (Ian) as a first name. He was long undecided whether to use Ian or Robert as his first name [Tom Bower, *Maxwell, the Outsider*, 1988].

Roger Maxwell: Roger D. Latham (1900–), Eng. stage, movie, TV actor.

Vera Maxwell: Vera Huppé (1901–1995), U.S. fashion designer.

Ada **May:** Ada Mae Weeks (earlier Potter) (1900–), U.S. stage actress. dancer.

Edna **May:** Edna May Pettie (1878–1948), U.S. stage actress, singer, working in U.K.

Elaine **May:** Elaine Berlin (1932–), U.S. movie actress, director.

Joe **May:** Joseph Otto Mandel (1880–1954), Austr. director of movie adventure serials.

Sophie **May:** Rebecca Sophia Clarke (1833–1906), U.S. children's writer.

Thomas **Maybank:** Hector Thomas Maybank Webb (*fl.*1900–1937), Br. painter, illustrator, cartoonist.

Louis B. **Mayer:** Lazar Meir (1885–1957), Russ.-born U.S. movie producer.

Bill **Maynard:** Walter Williams (1928–), Eng. movie, TV actor.

Walter **Maynard:** Thomas Willert Beale (1828–1894), Eng. lawyer, musician, impresario. The writer used this name for *The Enterprising Impresario* (1867), a personal account of the world of theatre managers and opera singers.

Ferdy **Mayne:** Ferdinand Mayer-Boerckel (1916–), Ger.-born Br. movie actor.

Rutherford **Mayne:** Samuel J. Waddell (1879–1967), Ir. actor, playwright.

James **Mayo:** Stephen Coulter (1914–), Br. writer of thrillers and spy novels.

Virginia **Mayo:** Virginia May Jones (1920–), U.S. movie actress. The actress's screen name almost certainly comes from her real name, although one theory claims she took it from a pantomime horse that she appeared with as a showgirl. The front and back legs of the horse were two Mayo brothers. An old Hollywood joke says that the name arose from a café counterman's call "Virginia, mayo" when the actress ordered a (Virginia) ham sandwich with mayonnaise while waiting at a bus station.

Augusta **Maywood:** Augusta Williams (1825–1876), U.S. ballet dancer. The dancer took the name of her stepfather, theatrical manager Robert Campbell Maywood, who adopted her when she was three.

Joseph **Mazilier:** Giulio Mazarini (1901–1968), Fr. ballet dancer, choreographer, teacher.

Mike **Mazurki:** Mikhail Mazurwsky (or Mazurkiewicz) (1909–1990), U.S. movie, TV actor, of Ukrainian descent.

Lillie Thomas (or L.T.) **Meade:** Elizabeth Thomasina Meade Smith (1854–1914), Eng. author of books for girls, mystery, detective fiction writer.

Audrey **Meadows:** Audrey Cotter (1929–), U.S. movie, TV comedienne, sister of Jayne Meadows (see below).

Jayne **Meadows:** Jayne Cotter (1925–), U.S. movie actress.

Meat Loaf: Marvin Lee Aday (1947–), U.S. rock singer. The singer was so nicknamed by his Dallas school friends on account of his gross size, with the name itself allegedly originating from a football coach. Aday landed on the coach's foot in the course of a training session, prompting a response on the lines of, "Get off me, you great hunk of meat loaf!" [Baker, p. 7]. Whatever the case, the singer adopted the name, calling his first band alternately Meat Loaf Soul and Popcorn Blizzard. The name's initials happen to repeat those of his first two names.

Kay **Medford:** Kay Regan (1918–1980), U.S. stage actress.

Grigory **Medynsky:** Grigory Aleksandrovich Pokrovsky (1899–1984), Russ. writer.

Ralph **Meeker:** Ralph Rathgeber (1920–1988), U.S. stage, movie actor.

Mehboob: Ramjankhan Mehboobkhan (1907–1964), Ind. movie director.

Meher Baba: Merwan Sheriar Irani (1894–1969), Ind. spiritual leader, of Persian parentage. The leader was given his name, meaning "compassionate father," by his first disciples in the early 1920s.

Hannes **Meinkema:** Hannemieke Stamperius (1943–), Du. writer. The writer's new first name comes from her original forename and surname initial, while her new surname is formed from letters in this same forename. She uses her real name for her academic writing.

Golda **Meir:** Goldie Myerson, née Mabovitch (1898–1978), Russ.-born Israeli prime minister. After emigrating to the U.S. at the age of eight, Goldie Mabovitch met (in 1917) Morris Myerson, a Russian Jewish immigrant, whom she later married. Back later with her husband in Palestine, Golda changed her name to Meir at the insistence of David Ben Gurion (*q.v.*) when she was appointed (1956) Israeli foreign minister. She chose a name that still suggested "Myerson" (although her marriage had by now broken up), knowing that Meir means "enlightener" in Hebrew. (The familiar European form of the Jewish name is Mayer.)

George **Melachrino:** George Militiades (1909–1965), Br. danceband leader, composer, arranger, of Gk. parentage. The musician may have meant his name to suggest "black-haired," from Greek *melas*, "black," and Latin *crinis*, "hair."

Philipp Melanchthon: Philipp Schwartzerd (1497–1560), Ger. humanist, Protestant theologian. In the manner of his day, the theologian translated his German name (literally "black earth") into Greek.

Melanie: Melanie Safka (1947–), U.S. pop singer, songwriter, of Ukrainian-It. parentage.

[Dame] Nellie Melba: Helen Porter Armstrong, née Mitchell (1861–1931), Austral. opera singer. The singer took her name from Melbourne, the city near which she was born. She first used the name in Brussels in 1887, for her debut as Gilda in *Rigoletto*. She in turn gave her name to those dietetic opposites, Melba toast and peach Melba, the former because she fancied it, the latter because it was as bright and colorful as she was.

Lauritz Melchior: Lebrecht Hommel (1890–1973), U.S. opera singer, of Dan. parentage.

Melchizedek III: Mikhail Pkhaladze (1876–1960), Georgian catholicos. The head of the Georgian Orthodox Church took the name of two of his predecessors, traditionally interpreted as "king of righteousness."

Jill Melford: Jill Melford-Melford (1934–), U.S. stage actress.

Melissa: Jane Brereton, née Hughes (1685–1740), Welsh poet. The poet adopted her Greek name because of its literal sense of "bee," "honey."

Melissanthi: Ivi Skandalaki, née Kouyia (1910–1990), Gk. poet. The poet's pen name means "honeyflower."

Marisa Mell: Marlies Moitzi (1929–1992), Fr. movie actress.

Courtney Melmoth: Samuel Jackson Pratt (1749–1814), Br. poet, prose writer. The writer used the rather flamboyant name for his unsuccessful acting debut in 1773, but later adopted it more generally for his literary pennings. His American wife was more fortunate in her stage career, appearing always as Mrs. Charlotte Melmoth after their brief marriage. Her maiden name is unknown.

Sebastian Melmoth: Oscar Wilde (1854–1900), Ir. playwright, author, poet. The writer adopted this name after his release from Reading Gaol in 1897. He took it from the hero of *Melmoth the Wanderer*, a novel by Charles Maturin, who was a remote ancestor on Wilde's maternal side. The first name Sebastian was suggested by the arrows on his prison uniform, as an allusion to paintings showing St. Sebastian being shot to death by arrows.

Alan Melville: Alan Caverhill (1910–), Eng. lyric writer, dramatist.

Jean-Pierre Melville: Jean-Pierre Grumbach (1917–1973), Fr. movie director. The actor admired American culture and took his new name in honor of his favorite writer, Herman Melville (1819–1891).

Jennie Melville: Gwendoline Butler (1922–), Br. mystery novelist.

Lewis Melville: Lewis Samuel Benjamin (1874–1932), Br. author.

Mary Melwood: Eileen Mary Lewis, née Hall (*c.*1920–), Br. children's writer.

Memphis Minnie: Lizzie Douglas (1897–1973), U.S. guitarist, singer. The guitarist, born in Louisiana and raised in Mississippi, ran away from home at the age of 13 to play music in Memphis, Tennessee.

Memphis Slim: Peter Chatman (1915–1988), U.S. black blues singer, musician. The singer, who lived in France from the 1960s, was born in Memphis, Tennessee.

Menander: Charles Langbridge Morgan (1894–1958), Br. novelist, essayist. The writer used the name for a series of articles entitled "Menander's Mirror" in the *Times Literary Supplement* during World War II. Menander was an Athenian poet of the 3d century B.C.

Mendele Moykher-Sforim: Sholom Yakov Abramovich (1835–1917), (Russ.) Jewish writer. The creator of modern literary Yiddish adopted his name, meaning "Mendele the itinerant bookseller," in 1879. The name implies his life's aim to enlighten and educate.

Menelik II: Sahle Miriam (1844–1913), Ethiopian emperor. The ruler took his crown name from that of Menelik I, the legendary son of King Solomon and the Queen of Sheba.

Adah Isaacs Menken: Dolores Adios Fuertes (1835–1868), U.S. actress, poet. The actress married Alexander Isaacs Menken in 1856 and kept his name through all subsequent alliances and marriages. Menken was a Jew, and this may have prompted her to change her first two names to something more specifically Jewish, although she herself was the daughter of a Spanish Jew. Facts regarding her family name and early life remain uncertain, and some sources give her original name as Adelaide McCord.

Gerhardus **Mercator:** Gerhard Kremer (1512–1594), Flemish cartographer, mathematician. In the style of his time, the scholar translated his surname, which literally means "tradesman," to its Latin equivalent.

T. **Merchant:** Thomas John Dibdin (1771–1841), Eng. playwright, operatic composer, songwriter. The writer used this punning name for some of his work, but mostly used the name Thomas Pitt, from his mother's maiden name. He was illegitimate, and only adopted his father's name of Dibdin to annoy him, as he accused him of having neglected himself and his two brothers when they were children. His elder brother, playwright Charles Pitt (1768–1833), kept his mother's name.

Vivien **Merchant:** Ada Thomson (1929–1982), Eng. stage, movie actress.

Melina **Mercouri:** Maria Amalia Mercouris (1923–1994), Gk. movie actress, politician.

Freddie **Mercury:** Farok Bulsara (1946–1991), Zanzibar-born Br. rock singer, of Ind. parentage. Queen's flamboyant lead singer's original forename gave English "Frederick" (and so "Freddie"). He early used the "glam rock" name Larry Lurex. His surname has been the subject of some speculation: "I had assumed Farok Bulsara had chosen the name Mercury because he imagined himself to be as uncatchable as quicksilver. ... The official Queen biography says he named himself in 1970 after the messenger of the gods. [Mercury's brother-in-law] Roger, however, insists that he chose the name because Mercury was his rising planet" [*Sunday Times Magazine*, November 17, 1996].

Anne **Meredith:** Lucy Beatrice Malleson (1899–1973), Eng. crime novelist.

Burgess **Meredith:** George Burgess (1908–), U.S. movie actor.

Isabel **Meredith:** Olivia Frances Maddox Agresti, née Rossetti (1875–1960), Eng. writer + Helen Maria Maddox Angeli, née Rossetti (1879–1969), Eng. writer, her sister.

Owen **Meredith:** Edward Robert Bulwer Lytton (1831–1891), Br. statesman, poet. The politician adopted the name for his first book, *Clytemnestra, the Earl's Return and Other Poems* (1855), written when employed in the diplomatic service. There was a family tradition that Anne Meredith, who had married a Lytton ancestor, was a sister or niece of Owen Tudor (*c.*1400–1461), Welsh founder of the English Tudor dynasty, and this is said to be the origin of the name.

Bess **Meredyth:** Helen McGlashan (1890–1969), U.S. movie scriptwriter.

Merlinus Anglicus: William Lilly (1602–1681), Eng. astrologer. Lilly used the name, meaning "English Merlin," for the many astrological almanacs he published.

Ethel **Merman:** Ethel Agnes Zimmerman (1908–1984), U.S. stage, movie actress.

Mary **Merrall:** Mary Lloyd (1890–1976), Eng. stage, movie actress. The actress almost certainly changed her name in order to avoid being confused with Marie Lloyd (*q.v.*). She first appeared on the stage in 1907 as Queenie Merrall.

David **Merrick:** David Margulois (1912–), U.S. theatrical producer.

Judith **Merril:** Josephine Juliet Zissman, later Pohl, née Grossman (1923–), U.S. SF writer, working in Canada (from 1968).

Bob **Merrill:** Henry Robert Merrill Levan (1921–), U.S. popular composer, lyricist.

Dina **Merrill:** Nedenia Hutton (1925–), U.S. movie, TV actress, socialite.

Helen **Merrill:** Helen Milcetic (1930–), U.S. jazz singer.

Robert **Merrill:** Henry Lavan (1921–), U.S. movie music composer, lyricist.

Henry Seton **Merriman:** Hugh Stowell Scott (1862–1903), Eng. writer of historical fiction. The writer was obliged by his father to become an underwriter at Lloyds of London, a commercial position that was not to his liking. He chose the name, loosely based on his real name, in order not to incur his family's displeasure, first using it for his novel *The Phantom Future* (1889).

LeRoy Charles **Merritt:** LeRoy Charles Schimmelpfennig (1912–1970), U.S. librarian, educator.

Felix **Merry:** Evert Augustus Duychinck (1816–1878), U.S. editor.

Tom **Merry:** William Mecham (1853–1902), Eng. caricaturist.

Billy **Merson:** William Henry Thompson (1881–1947), Eng. music hall artist, movie actor. The actor toured early in his career as a clown named Ping-Pong.

Ambrose **Merton:** William John Thomas (1803–1885), Eng. antiquary. The founder of the academic journal *Notes and Queries* used this name for a collection of tales and ballads that he published in 1846.

Paul **Merton:** Paul Martin (1957–), Br. TV humorist. The comic panelist adopted the name of the London borough where he was raised. He made the change on discovering that there was another Paul Martin, a comedy magician in Leeds.

William **Mervyn:** William Mervyn Pickwoad (1912–1976), Eng. stage, movie, TV actor.

Pietro **Metastasio:** Pietro Antonio Domenico Bonaventura Trapassi (1698–1782), It. dramatist, librettist. At the age of ten, Pietro was made the heir adoptive of Gian Vincenzo Gravina, a man of letters who rendered his Italian surname, meaning literally "passing," "transition," into its Greek equivalent. There is a sort of learned pun here, since a name change is itself a metastasis or transformation.

[Sir] Algernon **Methuen:** Algernon Methuen Marshall Stedman (1856–1924), Eng. publisher. A former schoolmaster, Stedman founded the publishing house of Methuen (using his second name) in 1889, and in 1899 changed his own name from Stedman to Methuen to celebrate its first decade.

Mait **Metsanurk:** Eduard Hubel (1879–1957), Estonian novelist. The writer's adopted name means "forest corner."

Metsarents: Misak Metsaturyan (1886–1908), Armenian poet.

Meudwy Môn: Owen Jones (1806–1889), Welsh writer, preacher. The writer was born on the island of Anglesey. Hence his adopted Welsh name, meaning "hermit of Anglesey."

Meuryn: Robert John Rowlands (1880–1967), Welsh poet, journalist.

[Sir] Hedworth **Meux:** Hedworth Lambton (1856–1929), Eng. naval officer. In 1899 the future admiral of the fleet supplied guns as reinforcements for the defence of Ladysmith in the Boer War. His timely action met with the approval of Lady Valerie Meux, wife of brewer Sir Henry Meux, who herself sent similar guns. Lambton subsequently called on Lady Meux to return the compliment. Touched by his tribute, and after many changes of will, Lady Meux bequeathed her large fortune to Lambton on the sole condition he change his name to Meux. He did so by royal license in 1911 at the relatively late age of 55.

Giacomo **Meyerbeer:** Jakob Liebmann Meyer Beer (1791–1864), Ger. opera composer, working in Italy, France.

Gustav **Meyrink:** Gustav Meyer (1868–1932), Austr. writer.

Mezz **Mezzrow:** Milton Mesirow (1899–1972), U.S. jazz musician.

George **Michael:** Yorgos Kyriakou Panayiotou (1963–), Br. pop singer, of Gk.-Cypriot/Eng. parentage. "George" is recognizably Yorgos, and "Michael" presumably evolved loosely from "Kyriakou," perhaps as a result of a mishearing or "mangling" of this name. The lead singer of the now defunct group Wham! changed his name when he changed his image at the age of 18, in 1982.

Kathleen **Michael:** Kathleen Smith (1917–), Eng. stage actress.

Ralph **Michael:** Ralph Michael Champion Shotter (1907–1994), Eng. movie actor.

Michelangelo: Michelagniolo di Lodovico Buonarroti Simoni (1475–1564), It. sculptor, painter, architect, poet. It is uncertain whether the artist's first name was originally Michelangelo or Michelagniolo. The former is more likely, suggesting "Michael the Archangel." The latter name means the same (Italian *angelo* and *agnolo* both mean "angel"), but also suggests "lamb" (*agnello*).

Miching Mallecho, Esq.: Percy Bysshe Shelley (1792–1822), Eng. poet. Shelley used this name for his satirical poem *Peter Bell the Third* (1839), a parody of Wordsworth's poem *Peter Bell* (1819). He took the name from Shakespeare's *Hamlet* (III.ii.148):

Ophelia. What means this, my lord?

Hamlet. Marry, this is miching mallecho; it means mischief.

(The words themselves mean "lurking mischief," as Shelley of course intended.)

Josephine **Middleton:** Josephine Alcock (1886–1971), U.S. stage actress.

Robert **Middleton:** Samuel G. Messer (1911–1977), U.S. movie actor.

Mary **Midnight:** John Newbery (1713–1767), Eng. children's writer, publisher + Christopher Smart (1722–1771), Eng. poet. The joint pseudonym was used by publisher and poet for a threepenny journal, *The Midwife, or the Old Woman's Magazine*, issued between 1751 and 1753. The name itself is said to have been borrowed from a booth at London's annual Bartholomew Fair. Smart, who himself used the pseudonym Pentweazle, was one of Newbery's literary clients and married his stepdaughter.

Ludwig **Mies van der Rohe:** Maria Ludwig Michael Mies (1886–1969), Ger.-born U.S. architect. The artist added his mother's maiden name to his surname once he had established himself as an architect.

Pavel Aleksandrovich **Mif**: Mikhail Aleksandrovich Fortus (1901–1939), Russ. Communist official, historian. The official formed his new name from the first two letters of his original first name and initial of his surname.

Mighty Sam: Sam McClain (1943–), U.S. blues singer.

Mighty Sparrow: Slinger Francisco (1935–), Grenada calypso singer. The singer was so called because he hopped about the stage like a sparrow.

Migjeni: Millosh Gjergj Nikolla (1911–1938), Albanian poet, short story writer. The writer's pen name is formed from letters in his full name.

Lev **Mikhaylov**: Lev Mikhaylovich Yelinson (1872–1928), Russ. revolutionary.

Sergeant Pyotr **Mikhaylov**: Peter I (the Great) (1672–1725), Russ. czar. This was the name and rank assumed by the Russian ruler when traveling incognito in western Europe in the 1690s. His full name was Pyotr Alekseyevich, the latter being a patronymic, "son of Aleksey," referring to his father, Aleksey Mikhaylovich, commonly known in English as Czar Alexis. Peter based his adopted name on his father's second name, itself a patronymic derived from his father, Peter's grandfather, Mikhail Fyodorovich, the first Romanov czar of Russia.

Solomon **Mikhoels**: Solomon Mikhaylovich Vovsi (1890–1948), Russ. Jewish stage actor.

Hans **Mikkelsen**: Ludvig von Holberg (1684–1754), Norw.-born Dan. dramatist ("Father of Danish Drama").

Zinka **Milanov**: Zinka Kunc (1906–1989), Yugoslav opera singer.

Annie **Miles**: Anne Miller (1958–), Eng. stage, TV actress.

Butch **Miles**: Charles Thornton (1944–), U.S. jazz drummer.

Garry **Miles**: James E. Cason (1939–), U.S. popular singer.

Lizzie **Miles**: Elizabeth Mary Pajaud (1895–1963), U.S. black blues singer.

Miska **Miles**: Patricia Miles Martin (1899–1986), U.S. children's writer. The writer also used the name Jerry Lane.

Peter **Miles**: Gerald Richard Perreau-Saussine (1938–), U.S. movie actor, of Fr.-U.S. parentage, brother of Gigi Perreau (*q.v.*). As a child artist, the actor was billed as Gerald Perreau until 1948, when he adopted the friendlier screen name of Peter Miles.

Susan **Miles**: Ursula Roberts, née Wyllie (1887–1970), Eng. poet, novelist, memoirist.

Vera **Miles**: Vera Ralston (1929–), U.S. movie actress. The actress might have been content to retain her original name had it not been for the Czech ice skater Vera Ralston (*q.v.*).

Lewis **Milestone**: Lev Milshtein (1895–1980), Russ.-born U.S. movie director.

Geo **Milev**: Georgi Milev Kasabov (1895–1925), Bulg. poet. The writer adopted his father's name, which was his own patronymic (middle name).

Ray **Milland**: Reginald Truscott-Jones (1905–1986), Welsh-born Br. movie actor, working in U.S. The actor's first change of name was to Mullane, the surname of his stepfather after his mother's second marriage. Later, a studio publicity man suggested a further change, and recommended the name Percival Lacy. Ray (or Reg), however, was nostalgically thinking back to the rural beauty of his Welsh childhood, and proposed "Mill-land." The publicity man, more reasonable this time, advised that a name with three "l"'s might present difficulties, whereupon the actor modified it to the form in which it became popularly known [Ray Milland, *Wide-eyed in Babylon*, 1975].

Mary **Millar**: Mary Wetton (1936–), Eng. stage actress, singer. The actress adopted (and adapted) her stage name from her mother's maiden name, which was Mellow.

Ann **Miller**: Lucille Ann Collier (1919–), U.S. tap dancer, movie actress. The actress's screen name is that of her first husband, Reese Miller.

Eddie **Miller**: Edward Raymond Müller (1911–1991), U.S. jazz musician.

Gary **Miller**: Neville Williams (1924–1968), Br. popular singer, dancer.

Joaquin **Miller**: Cincinnatus Hiner Miller (1841–1913), U.S. poet. The poet had the ambition of being "the American Byron." The first name he adopted was originally a nickname, as his earliest writing defended the Mexican bandit Joaquin Murietta. He later preferred to spell his middle name as "Heine," perhaps in allusion to the German poet.

Kristine **Miller**: Jacqueline Olivia Eskeson (1925–), Dan. movie actress, working in U.S.

Marilyn **Miller**: Mary Ellen Reynolds (1898–1936), U.S. movie actress. The actress's new first name, which gave that of Marilyn Monroe (*q.v.*), is a blend of her two original first names.

Martin **Miller:** Rudolf Muller (1899–1969), Cz. movie actor, working in U.K.

Marvin **Miller:** Marvin Mueller (1913–1985), U.S. movie actor.

Max **Miller:** Thomas Henry Sargent (1895–1963), Eng. music hall comedian (the "Cheeky Chappie").

Punch **Miller:** Ernest Burden (1894–1971), U.S. jazz trumpeter.

Wade **Miller:** Robert Wade (1920–), U.S. mystery writer + Bill Miller (1920–1961), U.S. mystery writer.

Carl **Milles:** Wilhelm Carl Emil Andersson (1875–1955), Swe. sculptor.

Millie: Millicent Small (1942–), Jamaican pop singer.

Spike **Milligan:** Terence Alan Milligan (1918–), Br. humorist, comedian, of Ir. parentage. How did the oddball writer and performer come by his new name? "The story goes that he had been talking to [his friend] Harry Edgington about his musical ambitions. 'I'd like to play the trumpet as well as Spike Hughes does,' said the young, enthusiastic Terence. 'Oh, I see. We're going to have Spike Milligan next, are we?' So Terence became Spike" [Pauline Scudamore, *Spike Milligan*, 1985]. Jazz musician Spike Hughes (1908–1987) was born Patrick Cairns Hughes.

Powell **Millington:** [Major] Mark Synge (1871–1921), Br. soldier, military writer. The army officer used this name for his unofficial publications, his official writings being for the Indian government. He seems to have adopted his pen name from his coeval, the Irish dramatist John Millington Synge (1871–1909). They were born only nine days apart. Synge's father's surname was actually Sing.

Alan **Mills:** Albert Miller (1914–1977), Can. folk singer.

Donna **Mills:** Donna Jean Miller (1943–), U.S. TV actress.

[Sir] John **Mills:** Lewis Ernest Watts (1908–), Br. movie actor. The distinguished actor changed his name when still at school because he considered it "too sissy" [*Sunday Times Magazine*, August 31, 1986]. It may be no coincidence that "Mills" is graphically somewhat similar to "Watts." (Compare the name of Lireve Monett, below.)

George **Milner:** George Edward Charles Hardinge, Baron Hardinge of Penshurst (1921–), Eng. crime novelist.

Sandra **Milo:** Alessandra Marini (1935–), It. movie actress.

Robert **Milton:** Robert Davidor (*c.*1886–1956), Russ.-born theatrical producer, movie director, working in U.S.

Mina: Anna Maria Mazzini (1940–), It. popular singer.

[Cardinal] József **Mindszenty:** József Pehm (1892–1975), Hung. church leader. The archbishop adopted the Magyar name in 1940 from his native village of Mindszent as a protest against Hungary's pro-Hitler stand in the 1930s. The placename means "all saints" (Hungarian *mind*, "all," and *szent*, "saint"), with the final -*y* equal to "of."

Nikolay **Minsky:** Nikolay Maksimovich Vilenkin (1855–1937), Russ. writer, translator. The writer adopted his name from his native city of Minsk.

Mary Miles **Minter:** Juliet Reilly (1902–1984), U.S. movie actress. The actress began her screen career as a child star, billed as "Little Juliet Shelby." When she was 13, she changed her name to Mary Miles Minter (presumably a random alliteration) and continued under the name as an adult actress until 1923, when she quit the cinema for good after a scandal involving the murder of former director (and her reputed lover) William Desmond Taylor.

DJ **Minute Mix:** Jarrett Cordes (1968–),U.S. black "hip-hop" musician, turntable artist (mixer). The musician, nicknamed J.C. the Eternal, is the brother of Prince Be (*q.v.*).

Miölnir Nanteos: George Powell (1842–1882), Welsh poet. The writer became interested in Scandinavian mythology and in particular in Iceland and its struggle for independence. Hence his adopted name. Mjöllnir is the hammer thrown by Thor, the Nordic god of war and thunder, as his "bolt." (Its name is related to Welsh *mellt*, "lightning.") Nanteos is the name of the village where Powell was born.

Miou-Miou: Sylvette Arri (or Herry) (1950–), Fr. movie actress. The actress's name probably arose from a nursery nickname.

Jean **Mirabaud:** Paul Thiry, Baron d'Holbach (1723–1789), Fr. materialist, atheist philosopher. Holbach frequently used the names of important deceased persons as pseudonyms for his books. This one, which he used for his most important book, *Système de la nature* (1770), he took from the writer and member of the French Academy, Jean Baptiste de Mirabaud, who had died ten years previously. (He should not be confused with the much more eminent French revolutionary, the Comte de Mirabeau, who was his contemporary.)

Carmen Miranda: Maria do Carmo Miranda da Cunha (1909–1955), Port.-born U.S. popular singer, movie actress. Objectively, the actress's name comes from her middle names; subjectively it evokes the musical gypsy singer heroine of Bizet's *Carmen* and the romantic heroine of Shakespeare's *The Tempest*.

Isa Miranda: Ines Isabella Sampietro (1909–1982), It. stage, movie actress. No doubt the actress took "Miranda" from the same source as Carmen Miranda (see above).

Mireille: Mireille Hartuch (1906–1996), Fr. stage actress, singer, composer, of Pol.-Eng. parentage. The actress was advised to drop her surname by the theatrical director Firmin Gémier.

Stratis Mirivilis: Efstratios Stamatopulos (1890–1969), Gk. novelist.

Panas Mirny: Afanasy Yakovlevich Rudchenko (1849–1920), Ukrainian writer. The writer made it his business to expose the social injustices that existed in Ukrainian rural life. He was therefore obliged to mask his real name behind the cloak of another, disarmingly meaning "peaceful." His new first name is simply a colloquial form of the original.

Miroslava: Miroslava Stern (1926–1955), Cz. movie actress, working in Mexico.

Yevstigney Mirovich: Yevstigney Afinogenovich Dunayev (1878–1952), Belorussian stage actor, director, playwright.

Helen Mirren: Ilyena Lydia Mironoff (1945–), Br. movie actress, of Russ. descent. The actress, daughter of a Russian-born father and Scottish mother, adopted her present surname at the age of ten.

Mishima Yukio: Hiraoka Kimitake (1925–1970), Jap. novelist.

Mistinguett: Jeanne-Marie Florentine Bourgeois (1873–1956), Fr. music hall singer, actress. The singer, popularly known simply as "Miss," was originally named "Miss Hélyett" by a revue writer of the day, Saint-Marcel, who used to travel with her regularly on the same train to Enghien, outside Paris, where she lived. Edmond Audran's light opera *Miss Hélyett* (1890) was in vogue at the time. He then suggested the variation "Miss Tinguette," rhyming this with a character in a popular song called Vertinguette. The

singer adopted the name in the form "Mistinguette," later dropping the final "e" [France Vernillat and Jacques Charpentreau, *Dictionnaire de la chanson française*, 1968]. The English-style name is said to have alluded to her prominent front teeth, a characteristic of the English aristocracy.

Gabriela Mistral: Lucila Godoy de Alcayaga (1889–1957), Chilean poet. The poet derived her *nom de plume* from two fellow poets, the Italian Gabriele d'Annunzio (1863–1938) and the Provençal Frédérick Mistral (1830–1914). She began to use the name soon after Mistral's death. Thirty years later she was awarded the Nobel prize for literature, as he had been.

Cameron Mitchell: Cameron Mizell (1918–1994), U.S. movie actor, of Sc.-Ger. parentage.

Eddy Mitchell: Claude Moine (1942–), Fr. rock singer. The singer adopted the American-style name in 1960 in order to give his persona a more "international" image.

Guy Mitchell: Albert Cernick (1927–), U.S. pop singer, movie actor. The singer's real name can be seen reflected, somewhat distortedly, in his professional name.

Joni Mitchell: Roberta Joan Anderson (1943–), Can. pop musician. Many sources give the singer's real name thus. But "Joni Mitchell" is just as real, since the first name is a pet form of "Joan" and she married fellow folksinger Chuck Mitchell in 1965 (although soon separating from him).

Warren Mitchell: Warren Misell (1926–), Eng. movie, TV actor.

Yvonne Mitchell: Yvonne Joseph (1925–1979), Eng. stage, movie actress, writer. The actress adopted her mother's maiden name as her stage name.

Jean Mitry: Jean-René-Pierre Goetgheluck Le Rouge Tillard des Acres de Presfontaines (1907–1988), Fr. movie director, film theoretician.

Mit (or **Mot**) **Yenda:** Timothy (or Thomas) Adney (*fl.*1785), Eng. poet of the Dellacruscan school. The poet simply reversed his name(s). See also **Della Crusca.**

Mobutu Sese Seko: Joseph-Désiré Mobutu (1930–1997), African statesman, president of Zaire (from 1965). In 1972 the president dropped his baptismal name and expanded his surname, which thus officially became Mobutu Sese Seko Kuku Ngbendu wa za Banga. According to the *Sunday Times Magazine* (March 7, 1972), this means "invincible warrior cockerel who leaves no chick intact."

Moby: Richard Melville Hall (1965–), U.S. rock musician, dancer. The former punk musician and DJ is a distant relative of novelist Herman Melville, famous for *Moby-Dick* (1851).

Jean-Pierre **Mocky:** Jean Mokiejewski (1929–), Fr. movie director, actor, of Pol. descent.

Helen **Modjeska:** Helena Modrzejewska, née Opid (1840–1909), Pol. actress, working in U.S.

Moebius: Jean Giraud (1938–), Fr. cartoonist. The comic-book artist also works under the name Gir, from his real surname. His regular name evokes the one-sided continuous Möbius strip. Giraud began his career as an illustrator of strip westerns.

Moelona: Elizabeth Mary Jones (1878–1953), Welsh novelist. The writer's name may have been based on a placename or else created from letters in her original name.

Léonide **Moguy:** Leonid Moguilevsky (1899–1976), Russ. newsreel producer, movie director, working in France, U.S.

Johnny **Moke:** John Rowley (1945–), Br. shoe designer. The designer explains how he came by his name: "I owned a white Mini Moke car. The car became the symbol of Swinging London. In London's Chelsea district I became known as Johnny Moke. The actress Katy Manning ... was the first to actually call me Johnny Moke" [private fax from Johnny Moke, August 25, 1995].

Stevan **Mokranjas:** Stevan Stojanovic (1856–1914), Serbian composer, folklorist.

Nicholas **Moldwarp:** Anne Manning (1807–1879), Eng. novelist, historian. The writer used this name for *The Lincolnshire Tragedy: Passages in the Life of the Faire Gospeller, Mistress Anne Askew* (1866), a historical novel based on the life of the Protestant martyr Anne Askew (1520–1546). Manning also wrote as Margarita More (*q.v.*).

Molière: Jean-Baptiste Poquelin (1622–1673), Fr. dramatist. This classic pseudonym is also a classic mystery. How did the author of *Tartuffe* and *Le Malade imaginaire* acquire his new name? We know that he must have first used it in 1643 or 1644, for it is found in a document dated June 28, 1644. It at least has a much more theatrical ring than Poquelin. The name Molière was in fact also that of a second-rank writer who died in the same year that Jean-Baptiste was born (1622). But the commonly held theory is that he derived it not from his lesser fellow dramatist, but from a place of this name, or something like this name, that was visited by the touring company to which young Poquelin belonged. (There are several villages named Molières, for example, and at least one Molères.)

Ferenc **Molnár:** Ferenc Neumann (1878–1952), Hung. dramatist, working in U.S.

Vyacheslav **Molotov:** Vyacheslav Mikhaylovich Skryabin (1890–1986), Russ. diplomat. The politician assumed his party name in 1906, when he became a Bolshevik. It means "hammer," in the significant, symbolic manner of the Bolsheviks. Compare the name of **Stalin**. Molotov's father, a storekeeper, was related to the composer and pianist Aleksandr Skryabin (1871–1915).

Momus: Nicholas Currie (1960–), Sc. singer, songwriter. The earthy singer presumably adopted the name of the Greek god of ridicule.

Franz **Mon:** Franz Löffelholz (1926–), Ger. writer.

Monarque: Jean Arnolis (1905–), Belg. magician. The magician's name is French for "monarch," suggesting he is "king" in his art.

Patrick **Monckton:** Patrick Arnold (1945–), Br. movie, TV actor.

Pierre **Mondy:** Pierre Cuq (1925–), Fr. movie actor.

Lireve **Monett:** Everil Worrell (1893–1969), U.S. (female) writer of horror stories. The writer's first name is a reversal of her original name, while "Monett" is graphically somewhat similar to "Worrell." Compare the name of John Mills (above).

Eddie **Money:** Edward Mahoney (1949–), U.S. rock singer.

Phyllis **Monkman:** Phyllis Harrison (1892– ?), Eng. stage actress, dancer.

Matt **Monro:** Terence Edward Parsons (1930–1985), Eng. popular singer. The singer took his new first name from Matt White, the first journalist to write about him, and his second name from the first name of the father of Winifred Atwell, the popular pianist who encouraged him. An earlier name that he used was Al Jordan, while a name for a comedy recording was Fred Flange.

Marilyn **Monroe:** Norma Jeane Dougherty, née Mortensen, later Baker (1926–1962), U.S. movie actress. Dougherty was the name of Monroe's first husband, whom she married at the age of 16; Baker was a name (not that of a husband) that she used later as her "real" name. When Darryl F. Zanuck signed up the actress in 1946, Ben Lyon wanted to change her name to Carole Lind, but this was "a rather obvious composite of an opera singer and a dead actress," and didn't sound right. Lyon and his actress wife, Bebe Daniels (*q.v.*), decided they could do better. They invited Norma Jeane to tea. Lyon recalled: "I finally said to her, 'I know who you are. You're Marilyn!' I told her that once there was a lovely actress named Marilyn Miller [*q.v.*] and that she reminded me of her. 'But what about the last name?' Marilyn said, 'My grandmother's name was Monroe and I'd like to keep that.' I said 'Great! That's got a nice flow, and two Ms should be lucky.' That's how she got her name" [Anthony Summers, *Goddess: The Secret Lives of Marilyn Monroe*, 1985].

Nicholas **Monsarrat**: Nicholas John Turney Montserrat (1910–1979), Eng. novelist. The novelist's name had been incorrectly registered at his birth, with a spelling that was preferred by his mother, who claimed that the family went back to a French nobleman, the Marquis de Montserrat. In his autobiography, Monsarrat recalls that the discrepancy between spellings was to embarrass him both at school and later on joining the Royal Navy [Nicholas Monsarrat, *Life Is a Four-Letter Word*, 1966].

Ashley **Montagu**: Israel Ehrenberg (1905–), Br.-born U.S. anthropologist. The scholar's adopted name appears to have been loosely based on the original, with the first half of his new surname, meaning "hill," translating the latter half of his old name.

Samuel **Montagu**: Montagu Samuel (1832–1911), Br. merchant banker, of Ger. Jewish descent. The parents of the future Baron Swaythling reversed his original names on the completion of his education. The rest of the family kept the surname of Samuel.

Henry James **Montague**: Henry James Mann (1844–1878), U.S. actor.

Bull **Montana**: Luigi Montagna (1887–1950), It.-U.S. movie actor.

Patsy **Montana**: Rubye Blevins (1912–1996), U.S. country singer, yodeller. Blevins was born in Arkansas, not Montana. But in 1931 she joined singing cowboy Stuart Hamblen's show, and appeared on radio and at rodeos as part of the Montana Showgirls. This gave her new surname. Hamblen renamed her Patsy as it was "a good Irish name."

Montana Slim: Wilfred Arthur Charles Carter (1904–1996), Can. country singer. ("Slim" in names of this type means "smart.")

Yves **Montand**: Ivo Livi (1921–1991), It.-born Fr. movie actor, singer. When the singer began his career in Marseille, appearing at the Alcazar, his manager told him that "Ivo Livi" was not right for a professional name: "It's too foreign and it doesn't have a proper ring to it." Montand tells how he arrived at his new name: "When I was a kid, my mother didn't like me to hang around in the street in front of our house. She spoke bad French and would shout, 'Yvo monta, Yvo monta.' [Yvo, come upstairs.] That came back to me, so I frenchified my christian name, Yves, and monta became Montand" [Simone Berteaut, *Piaf*, translated by Ghislaine Boulanger, 1970]. But maybe his name was actually suggested by that of his birthplace, Monsumano, near Montecatini?

Mlle **Montansier**: Marguerite Brunet (1730–1820), Fr. actress, theatre manager. The actress adopted the name of the aunt who raised her as her stage name.

G. **Montbard**: Charles Auguste Loye (1841–1901), Fr. painter, cartoonist, working in U.K. The artist took his name from Montbard, his birthtown in east central France. The initial presumably comes from his middle name.

Montdory: Guillaume des Gilberts (1594–1651), Fr. tragic actor.

Felipa **Monterro**: Philippa Schuyler (1931–1967), U.S. colored concert pianist. The musician temporarily adopted this name when performing in Europe, hoping that audiences there would take her to be Spanish or Greek. If someone recognized her, she wrote home to her mother, "I could always say that Miss Monterro developed laryngitis, or leprosy or bubonic plague or something and couldn't come at the last minute and asked me to fill in for her" [Kathryn Talalay, *Composition in Black and White: The Life of Philippa Schuyler*, 1996].

Lola **Montez**: Marie Dolores Eliza Rosanna Gilbert (1818–1861), Ir. actress, dancer, courtesan, working in France and U.S. Soon after marrying Ensign Thomas James, of the Indian army, Marie Gilbert called herself Rose Anne Gilbert, and indeed signed the marriage register thus when the two eloped to Ireland. Later, as a "Spanish" dancer, she adopted the typical Spanish name of Lola Montez, "Lola" being a pet form of her second name.

Maria **Montez:** María Africa Vidal de Santo Silas (1918–1951), U.S. movie actress, born in Dominican Republic ("The Caribbean Cyclone").

Montfleury: (1) Zacharie Jacob (*c.*1600–1667), Fr. actor; (2) Antoine Jacob (1639–1685), Fr. actor, his son. The stage name presumably originated from a French placename.

George **Montgomery:** George Montgomery Letz (1916–), U.S. movie actor.

K.L. **Montgomery:** Kathleen Montgomery (*c.*1863–1960), Ir.-born Eng. novelist, translator + Letitia Montgomery (? –1930), Ir.-born Eng. novelist, translator, her sister. The writers used this joint name for eight novels and various historical translations.

L.M. **Montgomery:** Lucy Maud Montgomery (1874–1942), Can. writer of novels for girls.

Robert **Montgomery:** Henry Montgomery, Jr. (1904–1981), U.S. movie actor, politician.

Sarita **Montiel:** Maria Antonia Abad (1927–), Sp. movie actress.

Muriel **Montrose:** Muriel Andrews (*c.*1900–), Eng. stage actress, dancer.

Gloria **Monty:** Gloria Montemuro (1921–), U.S. TV producer.

Ron **Moody:** Ronald Moodnick (1924–), Eng. stage, TV comedian.

Moondog: Louis Thomas Hardin (1916–), U.S. blind "popular classical" street musician. The composer explains: "I began using Moondog as a pen name in 1947, in honor of a dog I had in Hurley, who used to howl at the moon more than any dog I knew of" [liner notes of album *Moondog*, 1969].

Harry **Mooney:** Harry Goodchild (1889–1972), Eng. music hall comedian.

Dmitry **Moor:** Dmitry Stakhiyevich Orlov (1883–1946), Russ. illustrator, poster artist.

Archie **Moore:** Archibald Lee Wright (1916–), U.S. light heavyweight boxer, movie actor. The actor took his name from an uncle who had helped to raise him, Cleveland Moore.

Colleen **Moore:** Kathleen Morrison (1900–1988), U.S. movie actress.

Demi **Moore:** Demi Guynes (1962–), U.S. movie actress. The actress's name is that of rock musician Freddy Moore, whom she married as a teenager.

Garry **Moore:** Thomas Garrison Morfit (1915–1993), U.S. TV comedian, linkman. The TV comic tired of people mispronouncing his surname. In 1940 a contest was therefore held to select a new name for him. A Pittsburgh woman

suggested "Garry Moore" and won the prize of $50 and a trip to Chicago.

Kieron **Moore:** Kieron O'Hanrahan (1925–), Ir. movie actor.

Maggie **Moore:** Margaret Sullivan (1851–1926), U.S.-born stage actress, working in Australia.

Terry **Moore:** Helen Koford (1929–), U.S. movie actress. The actress used the names of Judy Ford and Jan Ford before settling for Terry Moore in 1948.

Wentworth **Moore:** William Hurrell Mallock (1849–1923), Eng. author, poet.

Lois **Moran:** Lois Darlington Dowling (1908–1990), U.S. movie actress.

Alberto **Moravia:** Alberto Pincherle (1907–1990), It. novelist, short story writer.

Elinor **Mordaunt:** Evelyn May Clowes (1877–1942), Eng. popular novelist. The writer is said to have adopted the name of her husband, a planter named Mordaunt, but there is evidence that his name was actually Wiehe.

Margarita **More:** Anne Manning (1807–1879), Eng. novelist, historian. The prolific writer used this name for *The Household of Sir Thomas More* (1851), a fictional account of the life of More told from the point of view of his daughter, Margaret Roper. The pen name is thus essentially that of the narrator, although also echoing the writer's mother's maiden name, Whatmore. She also wrote as Nicholas Moldwarp (*q.v.*).

Jean **Moréas:** Iannis Papadiamantopoulos (1856–1910), Gk.-born Fr. Symbolist poet.

Hégésippe **Moreau:** Pierre Jacques Rouillot (1810–1838), Fr. poet.

Eric **Morecambe:** John Eric Bartholomew (1926–1984), Eng. TV comedian, teaming with Ernie Wise (*q.v.*). The popular comedian described how he came by his name in his and Ernie Wise's joint autobiography: "An early problem was my stage name. Nobody liked Bartholomew and Wise. [Manager] Bryan Michie wanted to call us Bartlett and Wise or Barlow and Wise. The matter was finally settled in Nottingham. My mother was talking to Adelaide Hall, the colored American singer on the bill, when her husband, Bert Hicks, came up. My mother said, 'We're trying to think of a name for Eric.' Bert ... said, 'There's this friend of mine, a colored boy who calls himself Rochester because he comes from Rochester, Minnesota. Where do you come from?' 'Morecambe.' 'That's a good name. Call him Morecambe.' My mother liked it and I liked it, and from there on I was Morecambe on the bill" [Dennis Holman, *Eric & Ernie: The Autobiography of Morecambe and Wise*, 1973].

André **Morell:** André Mesritz (1909–1978), Eng. stage, movie actor.

Sir Charles **Morell:** James Ridley (1736–1765), Eng. writer. Ridley used this name, purportedly that of a "one time ambassador from the British settlements in India to the Great Mogul," for his best known work, *The Tales of the Genii* ("faithfully translated from the Persian Manuscript") (1764).

Antonio **Moreno:** Antonio Garride Monteagudo (1886–1967), Sp.-born U.S. movie actor.

Rita **Moreno:** Rosita Dolores Alverio (1931–), Puerto Rican stage, movie actress, dancer. Spanish *moreno* means "brown," "dark-haired," as many West Indian people are. Rita Moreno has black hair and brown eyes.

Louis **Moresby:** Eliza Louisa Moresby Beck (? –1931), Eng. novelist. The writer obviously took the male name from her middle name and maiden name, Beck being her married name. She also wrote as E. Barrington and Lily Adams Beck (*qq.v.*).

Claire **Morgan:** Patricia Highsmith (1921–1995), U.S. novelist. Patricia Highsmith (*q.v.*) used this name for an early novel, *The Price of Salt* (1952).

Claudia **Morgan:** Claudeigh Louise Wupperman (1912–), U.S. stage actress, daughter of Ralph Morgan (see below).

Dennis **Morgan:** Stanley Morner (1910–1994), U.S. movie actor. The actor used the name Richard Stanley before settling for Dennis Morgan in 1939.

Fidelis **Morgan:** Fidelis Horswill (1952–), Br. stage, TV actress, writer. The actress adopted the name of her mother, also Fidelis Morgan.

Frank **Morgan:** Francis Philip Wupperman (1890–1949), U.S. movie actor, brother of Ralph Morgan (see below).

Harry **Morgan:** Henry Bratsburg (1915–), U.S. movie actor. The actor originally appeared as Henry Morgan but later became Harry Morgan to avoid confusion with his coeval namesake, comedian Henry Morgan (see below).

Helen **Morgan:** Helen Riggins (1900–1941), Can. movie actress, singer.

Henry **Morgan:** Henry Lerner von Ost (1915–1994), U.S. radio, TV comedian.

Jane **Morgan:** Jane Currier (1920–), U.S. popular singer

Michèle **Morgan:** Simone Roussel (1920–), Fr. movie actress. The actress is said to have called herself Michèle to please a young man of her acquaintance who liked the name. The story goes that she then took the name Morgan, for reasons of euphony, from the main branch of Morgan & Co.'s bank in the Place Vendôme, Paris.

Ralph **Morgan:** Ralph Kuhner Wupperman (1882–1956), U.S. movie actor, brother of Frank Morgan, father of Claudia Morgan (see above).

Ted **Morgan:** Sanche de Gramont (1932–), Swiss-born U.S. writer, journalist.

Mori Ogai: Mori Rintaro (1862–1922), Jap. novelist, playwright, translator. The writer used ten different pseudonyms over the course of his career.

Gaby **Morlay:** Blanche Fumoleau (1897–1964), Fr. movie actress.

Mrs. **Morley:** Anne (1665–1714), queen of England. This is the name that Queen Anne used for her correspondence with the Duchess of Marlborough, who called herself Mrs. Freeman (*q.v.*).

Karen **Morley:** Mildred (or Mabel) Linton (1905–), U.S. movie actress.

Susan **Morley:** Sarah Frances Spedding (1836–1921), Eng. novelist.

Clara **Morris:** Clara Morrison (1848–1925), U.S. stage actress.

Jan **Morris:** James Humphrey Morris (1926–), Br. journalist, travel writer. The writer underwent a sex-change operation in 1972, having long felt the "victim of a genetic mix-up," and thus needed a name change. She comments: "My new name, though just right for me, I thought, was sometimes itself confusing. 'I thought Jan Morris was a man,' said a jolly Australian at a *Spectator* lunch one day. 'What happened, d'you change your sex or something?' Just that, I replied" (Jan Morris, *Conundrum*, 1974].

[Sir] John **Morris-Jones:** John Jones (1864–1929), Welsh poet, teacher. The scholar was the son of Morris Jones, a shopkeeper, and adopted his father's name as his new surname when he was knighted in 1918.

Morrissey: Steven Patrick Morrissey (1959–), Eng. pop musician.

Boris **Morros:** Boris Mikhailovitch (1891–1963), Russ.-born U.S. movie producer.

Buddy **Morrow:** Muni "Moe" Zudekoff (1919–), U.S. trombonist.

Jelly Roll **Morton:** Ferdinand Joseph La Menthe (or Lamothe, or Lemott) (1885–1941), U.S. black jazz composer, pianist. To his original surname, whatever it was, the musician added Morton, the name of the porter who married his mother after her husband left her. "Jelly Roll" is a black slang term (not exclusive to Morton) implying sexual prowess. (In the comestible sense, a jelly roll is a cylindrical cake containing jelly or jam, the equivalent of the British Swiss roll.)

Tex **Morton:** Robert William Lane (1916–1983), N.Z. popular musician, entertainer, working in Australia. The story goes that one day, when busking on the streets, the teenager was asked by a policeman if his name was Bobby Lane. He noticed a nearby garage sign that gave the name "Morton" and quickly informed the officer that he was Bob Morton and a street singer and entertainer. "Tex" came later when he adopted a country style of music.

Cenydd **Morus:** Kenneth Vennor Morris (1879–1937), Welsh fantasy writer. The writer's name is a Welsh equivalent of the original.

Morus Cyfannedd: Morus Jones (1895–1982), Welsh poet. The writer's adopted name means "Morus of the habitation."

Maurice **Moscovitch:** Morris Maascoff (1871–1940), Russ.-born U.S. movie actor, father of Noël Madison (*q.v.*).

Mihály **Mosonyi:** Michael Brand (1815–1870), Hung. composer, music critic. The musician magyarized his German name in 1859.

Mickie **Most:** Michael Peter Hayes (1938–), Eng. record company director, promoter. The record producer first used the name in 1958 for a double act, the Most Brothers, with his friend Alex Murray. The name suggests "Mickey Mouse," and possibly the singer was so called by way of a nickname.

Zero **Mostel:** Samuel Joel Mostel (1915–1977), U.S. stage, movie actor. The actor adopted his school nickname, given him for his repeated zero marks.

Mounet-Sully: Jean Sully Mounet (1841–1916), Fr. actor.

[Lord] Louis **Mountbatten:** [Prince] Louis Francis Albert Victor Nicholas of Battenberg (1900–1979), Eng. soldier, statesman. Queen Victoria's grandson adopted the English part-translation of "Battenberg" in 1917, when his father, Louis Alexander Mountbatten, relinquished the title at the request of George V. Other members of his branch of German counts living in England did likewise.

Movita: Movita Castenada (1915–), Mexican movie actress.

Natalie **Moya:** Natalie Mullaly (1900–), Ir.-born Br. stage actress.

George **Mozart:** David Gillins (1864–1947), Eng. music hall comedian, musician.

Sergey **Mstislavsky:** Sergey Dmitriyevich Maslovsky (1876–1943), Russ. novelist.

Leonard **Mudie:** Leonard Mudie Cheetham (1884–1965), Br. stage, movie actor, working in U.S.

Mudrooroo: Colin Johnson (1938–), Austral. novelist, of part Aborigine origin. The writer has also used the fuller names Mudrooroo Narogin and Mudrooroo Nyoongah.

Elijah **Muhammad:** Elijah (or Robert) Poole (1897–1975), U.S. Black Muslim leader. The meeting of Elijah (or Robert) Poole with Walli Farrad (*q.v.*) started him on a career which took him to the top of the Black Muslim movement. It was he who converted, and named, both Malcolm X and Muhammad Ali (*qq.v.*). His own change of name to that of the founder of Islam is self-evident.

Jean **Muir:** Jean Muir Fullarton (1911–1996), U.S. stage, movie actress. The actress originally performed in the theatre under her real name, Jean Fullarton, but became Jean Muir when turning to the cinema in the mid-1930s.

Maria **Muldaur:** Maria Grazia Rosa Domenica d'Amato (1943–), U.S. pop singer. The singer's professional name is actually her married name, after Geoff Muldaur, whom she married in the mid–1960s and divorced in 1972.

Arthur **Mullard:** Arthur Mullord (1910–1995), Br. comedian.

Multatuli: Eduard Douwes Dekker (1820–1887), Du. writer. The writer's pen name represents Latin *multa tuli*, "I have borne many things," alluding to his personal experiences. In 1838 he went to the Dutch East Indies where he held various government posts. In 1856 he was obliged to resign when he was not supported by the colonial government in his endeavors to protect the Javanese from their own bosses. He returned to Europe and spent many years in a nomadic and impoverished existence, braving cold and hunger and losing his family in the process. His main work was the 7-volume *Ideeën*

("Ideas") (1862–77), expressing his radical views on a wide range of topics.

Claude **Muncaster:** Grahame Hall (1903–1974), Eng. landscape, marine painter. The painter changed his name to avoid being confused with his father, Oliver Hall, who was also an artist.

Baron **Münchhausen:** Rudolfe Erich Raspe (1737–1794), Ger. scientist, antiquary, writer. The author of the well-known *Marvellous Travels and Campaigns in Russia* (1785), based his fantastic stories on the tales of a real Baron Münchhausen, who had written highly colored accounts of his adventures in the Russian war against the Turks and whose given name was Karl Friedrich Hieronymus von Münchhausen (1720–1797).

Talbot **Mundy:** William Lancaster Gribbon (1879–1940), Eng.-born U.S. writer of adventure novels, historical fantasies.

Paul **Muni:** Muni Weisenfreund (1895–1967), U.S. stage, movie actor, of Austr.-Hung. Jewish parentage.

Kai **Munk:** Harald Leininger (1898–1944), Dan. writer.

Mihály **Munkácsy:** Leo Lieb (1844–1900), Hung. painter. The artist adopted the name of his birth town, Munkács (now Mukachevo, Ukraine), presumably adding Mihály (Michael) for euphony.

C.K. **Munro:** Charles Walden Kirkpatrick MacMullan (1889–1973), Ir. playwright.

Ona **Munson:** Ona Wolcott (1906–1955), U.S. movie actress.

Murad Efendi: Franz von Werner (1836–1881), Austr. poet. The poet was long in the Turkish diplomatic service, and adopted a pen name that reflected this: "Murad" was the name of several Turkish sultans, and "Efendi" (or "Effendi") was a title of respect. He may have based the name specifically on that of Murad Bey, the Egyptian Mameluke chief who fought with the French against the Turks and who died in 1801.

Grigor **Muratsan:** Grigor Ter-Ovanisyan (1854–1908), Armenian writer. Many of the writer's stories center on the injustice and poverty borne by the Armenian peasantry. Others relate to corruption in the local press. Hencehis adopted name, which literally means "blackening."

Friedrich Wilhelm (or F.W.) **Murnau:** Friedrich Wilhelm Plumpe (1888–1931), Ger. movie director, working in U.S. The director took his name from the German town of Murnau, where he lived for some time (but not where he was born, which was Bielefeld).

Dennis Jasper **Murphy:** [Rev.] Charles Robert Maturin (1782–1824), Ir. playwright, novelist. The writer adopted the pseudonym when working as an impoverished curate in Dublin, first using it for three romances published between 1807 and 1812.

Isaac **Murphy:** Isaac Burns (1861–1896), U.S. black jockey. The horseman adopted the name of his maternal grandfather, who raised him following the death of his father in the Civil War.

Murray: Leo Norman Maurien Murray Stuart Carrington Walters (1901–), Austral. magician, escapologist.

Arthur **Murray:** Moses Teichman (1895–1991), U.S. dancing instructor.

Braham **Murray:** Braham Goldstein (1943–), Eng. stage director.

Brian **Murray:** Brian Bell (1937–), S.A. stage actor, working in U.K. The actor adopted his mother's maiden name as his stage name.

Hon. Mrs. **Murray:** Sarah Aust (1741–1811), Eng. topographical writer. The writer's pen name was effectively her real name, for her first husband was the Hon. William Murray. But after his death, in 1786, she married George Aust, and most of her writing was done subsequently. The full title under which she wrote was "The Hon. Mrs. Murray, of Kensington," a name almost as lengthy as that of her best known work, *A Companion and Useful Guide to the Beauties of Scotland, to the Lakes of Westmoreland, Cumberland, and Lancashire, and to the Curiosities in the District of Craven, in the West Riding of Yorkshire; to which is added a more particular description of Scotland, especially that part of it called the Highlands* (1799).

Ken **Murray:** Kenneth Doncourt (1903–1988), U.S. movie comedian, radio, TV entertainer.

Mae **Murray:** Marie Adrienne Koenig (1885–1965), U.S. movie actress, of Austr.-Belg. parentage. Both the actress's screen names appear to come from her original first name.

Sinclair **Murray:** Edward Alan Sullivan (1868–1947), Can. novelist.

Fakir **Musafar:** Roland Loomis (1930–), U.S. Modern Primitive ("body modification") leader.

Gavriil **Musicescu:** Gavriil Vakulovich Musychenko (1847–1903), Russ. composer, choirmaster. The musician was fortunate to have a name that so readily adapted to indicate his profession.

Musidora: Jeanne Roques (1889–1957), Fr. music hall singer, dancer, movie actress. The actress took her professional name at the start of her stage career (in 1910) from the heroine of Théophile Gautier's novel *Fortunio* (1836), an "Arabian Nights"-like tale set in Paris. The name is found in earlier literature, such as the Musidora who loves Damon in James Thomson's poem *The Seasons* ("Summer," 1727). It means "gift of the Muses," suitably enough for the actress, who later wrote novels, a play, and poetry.

P. **Mustapää:** Martti Haavio (1899–?), Finn. poet. Haavio was professor of poetry at Helsinki university, and used his real name for his academic writing.

Ornella **Muti:** Francesca Romana Rivelli (1955–), It. movie actress. The actress won her first movie role when she was 14. The schedule required her absence from school for two months: "While I was shooting in Sicily I told my teachers I was sick. To stop them finding me I changed my name from Francesca Rivelli" [*Telegraph Magazine*, July 6, 1991]. "Ornella," a regular Italian forename, appears to have been extracted from her original name. "Muti" is presumably a family name.

R. **Mutt:** Marcel Duchamp (1887–1968), Fr. artist. The unconventional artist used this name for *Fountain* (1917), a so called "readymade" that was simply a urinal. The name may mean something or nothing. If pronounced in the French fashion it suggests *ermite*, "hermit," perhaps with some private reference.

Eadweard **Muybridge:** Edward James Muggeridge (1830–1904), Eng.-born U.S. photographer, motion picture pioneer. The inventor, who photographed people and animals in motion, was born in Kingston-on-Thames, Surrey, and grew up with a keen interest in local history, as many Saxon kings were said to have been crowned in his birthtown (as its name implies). His interest came to a head in 1850, when a special commemorative "coronation" stone was set up in the Market Place. On the plinth were carved the names of the kings who, it was believed, had been crowned in Kingston, among them Eadweard the Elder (crowned 900) and Eadweard the Martyr (975), their names spelled the Saxon way. "This spelling seemed a lot more romantic than plain Edward so the young man

decided to adopt the Saxon version and for good measure changed his East-Anglian surname of Muggeridge ... to Muybridge. The only reason for this change of name seems to have been sheer romanticism" [Kevin MacDonnell, *Eadweard Muybridge: The Man Who Invented the Moving Picture*, 1972].

Myfyr Morganwg: Evan Davies (1801–1888), Welsh poet. The poet and archdruid took a bardic name meaning "muse of Glamorgan," referring to the historic region in which he was born. Welsh *myfyr*, "muse," "thought," is related to English *memory*. Compare the next name below.

Myfyr Wyn: William Williams (1849–1900), Welsh poet, blacksmith, historian. The poet's bardic name means "fair muse." Compare the name above.

Mynyddog: Richard Davies (1833–1877), Welsh poet, singer. The poet and conductor took a bardic name meaning "mountain one."

Myrander: James Alexander Stevenson (1881–1937), Br. sculptor. The classical-style name appears to be based on the name of the artist's wife, née Ethel Myra Scott, whom he married in 1913. If so, and with a Greek sense, the meaning would be "Myra's husband."

Odette **Myrtil:** Odette Quignard (1898–?), Fr. stage actress, violinist, working in UK, U.S.

Harriet **Myrtle:** Lydia Falconer Miller, née Fraser (1811–1876), Sc. children's writer. The writer seems to have based her pen name on that of her husband, Hugh Miller. It was also used by another writer, Mary Gillies, for *More Fun for our Little Friends* (1864). Gillies appears to have borrowed the name from Miller, who first used it in 1846. Hamst (see Bibliography, p. 401) comments: "One person employing a pseudonym already used by another, is much to be deprecated," but adds of Gillies, "We do not believe this lady had any intention to deceive." Compare the Myrtle names below.

Marmaduke **Myrtle:** [Sir] Richard Steele (1672–1729), Br. essayist, dramatist. The writer used this name for his editorship of *The Lover* (1714), a periodical similar to the better known *Spectator*.

Minnie **Myrtle:** Anna Cummings Johnson (1818–1892), U.S. writer. The writer used this name for *The Myrtle Wreath, or Stray Leaves recalled* (1854), as well as subsequent works.

Mystic Meg: Margaret Lake (1942–), Eng. astrologer. The astrologer, familiar as a TV fortune-teller for the weekly National Lottery, is usually known by this name but also predicts as Meg Markova.

Myushfik: Mikail Kadyr ogly Ismailadze (1908–1939), Azerbaijani lyrical poet. The writer's adopted name means "soft-hearted."

Ilya **Nabatov:** Ilya Semyonovich Turovsky (1896–), Russ. music hall artist, popular versifier.

Nadar: Félix Tournachon (1820–1910), Fr. photographer, illustrator, writer. The following account has appeared of the writer's pen name: "He had also found his name: from Tournachon to Tournadard, an obscure epistemological gallic joke, referring either to his satirical *sting*, or else to the tongue of *flame* (also *dard*) above his brow; and thence to the more economical, and generally more marketable, Nadar. This signature now began to appear below little matchstick drawings, and at the age of 27, Nadar published a first caricature on the inside page of *Charivari*" [*The Times*, October 12, 1974].

Nadira: Makhlar-oyim (1791–1842), Uzbek poet. The poet's adopted name means "rare one." She also wrote as Kamila.

Anne **Nagel:** Ann Dolan (1912–1966), U.S. movie actress.

Nahmanides *see* **Ramban.**

Jimmy **Nail:** James Michael Aloysius Bradford (1954–), Br. TV actor, singer. The actor's stage name arose as a nickname given him when he stepped on a six-inch nail at a time when he was working in a glassworks.

Laurence **Naismith:** Lawrence Johnson (1908–1992), Eng. stage, movie actor.

Nita **Naldi:** Anita Donna Dooley (1899–1961), U.S. movie actress. "Nita" from "Anita," and "Naldi" presumably from letters in her full name.

Lewis Bernstein **Namier:** Ludwik Bernsztajn (1888–1960), Pol.-born Eng. historian. Namier's father's surname was originally Niemirowski, both his parents being Polish Jews who no longer adhered to the Jewish religion. He came to Britain as a young man, entering Oxford University in 1908. On taking British nationality in 1913, he changed his name by deed poll to Lewis Namier, a version of his father's name.

Alan **Napier:** Alan Napier-Clavering (1903–1988), Br. movie actor, working in U.S.

Diana **Napier:** Molly Ellis (1908–1982), Br. movie actress.

Mark **Napier:** John Laffin (1922–), Austral. novelist, journalist.

Nar-Dos: Mikael Zakharyevich Ovanisyan (1867–1933), Armenian writer. When in the late 1880s the writer delivered his first novel (*Nune*) to the magazine *Nor-dar* ("New Century"), the editor told him he would have to choose a pen name, as was then customary. The writer recalled: "I had no objection. The secretary took a dictionary and started to pick out names. He finally came to the word 'nardos,' lavender. 'If we hyphenate it, it'll look even better!' he said. I agreed, and since then Nar-Dos has been my pseudonym" [Dmitriyev, pp. 92–93].

Owen **Nares:** Owen Nares Ramsay (1888–1943), Br. movie actor.

Datt **Nargis:** Fatima Rashid (1929–1981), Ind. movie actress. The actress first appeared as "Baby Rani" at the age of six.

Petroleum Vesuvius **Nasby:** David Ross Locke (1833–1888), U.S. humorous journalist. The writer adopted the droll pseudonym in 1861 when he became editor of the Findlay, Ohio, *Jeffersonian*. The origin of the surname is uncertain. See also p. 25.

Daniel **Nash:** William Reginald Loader (1916–), Br. novelist.

Mary **Nash:** Mary Ryan (1885–1976), U.S. movie actress.

N. Richard **Nash:** Nathaniel Richard Nusbaum (1913–), U.S. playwright.

Alcofribas **Nasier:** François Rabelais (1495–1553), Fr. satirist. The writer used this anagrammatic version of his real name for *Pantagruel* (1532), one of his most famous works. He also used it for its successor, *Gargantua*, the story of Pantagruel's father, now usually read first. After that he used his real name for the third (1546) and fourth (1548) books in the series, as well as for the posthumous fifth book (1562), which may not actually be by him, however.

Marie-José **Nat:** Marie-José Benhalassa (1940–), Fr. movie actress.

Anna **Natarova:** Anna Petrovna Chistyakova (1835–1917), Russ. circus artist, bareback rider.

John-Antoine **Nau:** Antoine Torquet (1860–1918), U.S.-born Fr. poet, novelist. The writer spent some years "before the mast," and took a surname that means "boat." (It is a form of French *nef*, related to the Greek root that gave English *nautical*). Compare the next entry below.

Nauticus: (1) [Sir] William Laird Clowes (1856–1905), Eng. naval writer, historian; (2) [Sir] Owen Seaman (1861–1936), Eng. editor, humorist. The name is appropriate for both men: academically for the first, and punningly for the second.

André Navarre: Alexander Wright (?–1940), Austral. music hall performer.

Martina Navratilova: Martina Subert (1956–), Cz.-born U.S. tennis player. The sportswoman changed her surname to that of her grandfather (properly Navrátilová) when she was 10. She became a U.S. citizen in 1981.

Sergey Naydyonov: Sergey Aleksandrovich Alekseyev (1868–1922), Russ. writer.

Eliot Naylor: Pamela Frankau (1908–1967), Br. novelist, short story writer, working in U.S.

Jerry Naylor: Jerry Naylor Jackson (1939–), U.S. country singer.

Alla Nazimova: Alla Aleksandrovna Leventon (1879–1945), Russ.-born U.S. stage, movie actress.

Amedeo Nazzari: Salvatore Amedeo Buffa (1907–1979), It. movie actor.

[Dame] Anna Neagle: Marjorie Wilcox, née Robertson (1904–1986), Eng. stage, movie actress. When the actress was beginning to become established in the theatre, after appearing as a chorus girl in Charles Cochran's shows, her manager commented one day: "'I think your name "Marjorie Robertson" has been too much publicized as a "Cochran Young Lady." Now you are turning to serious acting, you must change it.' I stared at him. In my childhood when I had daydreamed of a stage career, I'd invented the most incredible professional names; but now I'd spent five years putting my real name on to playbills and programs and didn't much like the idea of wasting all that publicity. … 'It's rather a long name, too,' Mr. Williams went on tentatively. … I began to see his point. … If I'd remained 'Marjorie Robertson, Chorus Girl' much longer I would have been type-cast for life. … 'My mother's name was Neagle...?' 'Nagle?' 'No—Neagle,' I protested. 'Don't worry—they'll call it Nagle,' he said. 'What about Anna Neagle?' I suggested. 'Oh, fine. That's just fine. Anna Neagle? That's it.' And so Marjorie Robertson, successful chorus girl, was quietly, and a little sadly, disposed of in a teashop on the corner of Wardour and Old Compton Streets, on August 21st, 1930. And Anna Neagle, embryo actress and star, was born" [Anna Neagle, *There's Always Tomorrow*, 1974].

Hilary Neal: Olive Marion Norton (1913–), Br. children's writer.

Johann August Wilhelm Neander: David Mendel (1789–1850), Ger. Protestant church historian. The scholar was born a Jew, and adopted his new name (from the Greek meaning "new man") on being baptized a Christian in 1806.

Ivan Nechuy-Levitsky: Ivan Semyonovich Levitsky (1838–1918), Ukrainian writer.

Nedin: Nadezhda Aleksandrovna Yanushevskaya (1896–1959), Russ. circus artist, animal trainer, wife of Kadyr-Gulyam (*q.v.*).

Neera: Anna Radius Zuccari (1846–1919), It. novelist, poet. The writer seems to have based her name on her original first name and middle name initial.

Hildegard Neff: Hildegard Knef (1925–), Ger. movie actress.

Pola Negri: Barbara Apollonia Chalupiec (1897–1987), Pol.-born U.S. movie actress. "Pola" comes from the actress's middle name, while also suggesting her nationality. "Negri" comes from the Italian poet Ada Negri (1870–1965). "The very name summons up the exoticism that was her stock-in-trade" (Joseph Arkins, in Vinson, p. 466).

Roy William Neill: Roland de Gostrie (1886–1946), Ir.-born U.S. movie director.

Thomas Neill: Thomas Neill Cream (1850–1892), Sc. physician, murderer. The murderer poisoned his (female) victims with strychnine, and used his cover name when obtaining the necessary drugs from the pharmacy.

Donald Neilson: Donald Nappey (1936–), Eng. murderer ("The Black Panther"). The killer took his name from an icecream van, mainly as he had never liked his original name, but also to avoid any future embarrassment for his daughter. (The British baby's nappy is the American diaper.) He should not be confused with Dennis Nilsen (1945–), another British murderer.

Lilian Adelaide Neilson: Elizabeth Ann Brown (1846–1880), Br. actress. The actress's mother had originally had the name Brown but was later known as Mrs. Bland. Her father's name is unknown. On working as a nurse as a young woman, she learned of the somewhat dubious circumstances of her birth, and decided to make her way to London. For the purposes of this she assumed the name Lizzie Ann Bland. She began her stage career in 1865, and soon after felt confident enough to bloom forth from Lizzie Ann Bland to "Lilian Adelaide Lessont," subsequently changing this last name to "Neilson."

Perlita **Neilson:** Margaret Sowden (1933–), Eng. stage actress.

Barry **Nelson:** Robert Haakon Neilsen (1920–), U.S. stage, movie actor, of Scandinavian descent.

Gene **Nelson:** Leander Berg (1920–1996), U.S. stage, movie actor, dancer.

Harriet **Nelson:** Peggy Lou Snyder (1909–1994), U.S. singer, actress.

Oscar **Nelson:** Oscar Nielsen (1882–1954), Dan.-born U.S. lightweight boxer ("The Durable Dane").

Nemo: Phiz (*q.v.*).

Nadia **Nerina:** Nadine Judd (1927–), S.A. ballet dancer, of Russ. parentage. The dancer took her new surname from the South African scarlet flower called the Nerine (pronounced "ne-rye-nee"), which grew around Cape Town, where she was born. Her first name, Nadia, is a pet form of her real name, with this in turn a form of her mother's first name, Nadezhda.

Salomeja **Neris:** Salomeja Bacinskáite- Buciene (1904–1945), Lithuanian poet. The poet took her name from the river where she lived.

Nero: Lucius Domitius Ahenobarbus (37–68), Roman emperor. When the future emperor was 13, his mother married her uncle, Tiberius Claudius Drusus Nero Germanicus, otherwise the Emperor Claudius, who adopted the boy and renamed him as Nero Claudius Caesar Drusus Germanicus. Nero was thus a Roman cognomen (surname), not meaning "black," as might be supposed, but "strong," "warlike" (English *nerve*).

Franco **Nero:** Francesco Spartanero (1941–), It. movie actor.

Peter **Nero:** Peter Bernard Nierow (1934–), U.S. popular pianist.

Pablo **Neruda:** Neftalí Ricardo Reyes Basoalto (1904–1973), Chilean poet. The poet adopted a pen name in 1920 so as not to embarrass his father, a railroad worker. He took the name from the Czech writer Jan Neruda (1834–1891), whose story *By the Three Lilies* he had greatly admired. He adopted the name legally in 1946.

Gérard de **Nerval:** Gérard Labrunie (1808–1855), Fr. poet, traveler, story writer. Nerval was the name of a property near Paris owned by the writer's parents. Moreover, his mother's maiden name was Laurent, and if this name is read backwards (minus its final "t" and counting "u" as "v"), one ends up with Nerval. Finally, Nerval is a near anagram of the writer's original surname, Labrunie. The writer himself was deeply interested in the "hidden meaning" of language.

Jimmy **Nervo:** James Henry Holloway (1897–1975), Eng. stage comedian, teaming with Teddy Knox (*q.v.*). The actor began his career in the circus, as an artist whose specialty was balancing and buffoonery, and thus in consequence falling and fractures. For such a way of life he needed "nerve." Hence his professional name.

E. **Nesbit:** Edith Bland, née Nesbit (1858–1924), Eng. children's writer. "The use of the bare initial 'E.' led ... at least one library to assume that she was a man, which delighted her; she liked the masculine role, and assumed it happily in her writing" (Carpenter & Prichard, p. 372; see Bibliography, p. 400). The author thus deliberately used this strategy to conceal her sex, although retained her real maiden name as her true identity. Nesbit used the name Fabian Bland (*q.v.*) for work written jointly with her husband.

Nesimi: Seid Imadeddin (*c.*1369–1417), Azerbaijani poet, scholar. The writer's adopted Arabic name means "waft," "breath of wind."

Emma **Nevada:** Emma Wixom (1859–1940), U.S. opera singer. The singer was born in Alpha, near Nevada City, California, and took her name from that city. (Sources claiming she was born in Austin, Nevada, and that she is named for that state, are incorrect.) Her daughter, soprano Mignon Nevada (1886–1971), kept the name.

Aleksandr **Neverov:** Aleksandr Sergeyevich Skobelev (1886–1923), Russ. writer.

Vladimir Ivanovich **Nevsky:** Feodosy Ivanovich Krivobokov (1876–1937), Russ. Communist official historian. The Marxist historian spent his prerevolutionary career in Petrograd (St. Petersburg). Hence his name, for the Neva River, on which that city stands.

Igor **Newerly:** Igor Abramow (1903–), Pol. writer.

Ne Win: Maung Shu Maung (1911–), Myanmar (Burmese) statesman. The former leader of Burma (now Myanmar) adopted a name meaning "brilliant sun."

Aristarchus **Newlight:** Richard Whately (1786–1863), Eng. logician, theologian. The theologian, who became Archbishop of Dublin, used this meaningful name to attack German neologism, that is, the German tendency to rationalistic views in religious matters. The name was thus ironic. Aristarchus was a Greek critic of the 2d century B.C.

Ernest **Newman:** William Roberts (1868–1959), Eng. music critic. The critic first used the pseudonym for his book *Gluck and the Opera* (1895). It was intended to be punningly meaningful, and indicate his innovative approach, but it also seems to have been representative of his attitude to life generally, because he used the name both in his private life and in his writings. He never legally adopted it, however.

Tom Newman: Thomas Pratt (1894–1943), Eng. billiards player. One can appreciate the need for a new name (and new image) here.

Julie Newmar: Julia Charlene Newmeyer (1930–), U.S. movie actress, dancer.

Juice Newton: Judy Kaye Cohen (1952–), U.S. country singer. The progression of the first name was presumably "Judy" to "Juicy" to "Juice."

Marie Ney: Marie Fix (1895–1981), Eng. stage, movie actress.

Fred Niblo: Federico Nobile (1874–1948), U.S. movie director, of It. parentage.

Nicander: Morris Williams (1809–1874), Welsh hymnwriter. The writer adopted this name at the 1849 National Eisteddfod, when he won the chair. It is (unusually) Greek in origin, meaning "man of victory."

Nicholas II: Gérard de Bourgogne (*c.*1010–1061), Fr. pope. The pontiff named himself for Nicholas I (*c.*820–867).

Nicholas III: Giovanni Gaetano Orsini (*c.*1220–1280), It. pope. The pope took this name because he had been cardinal deacon of the church of S. Niccolò in Carcere (St. Nicholas in Prison), Rome.

Nicholas IV: Girolamo Masci (1227–1292), It. pope. The pontiff named himself for his patron, Nicholas III (see above).

Nicholas V: Tommaso Parentucelli (1397–1455), It. pope. The pontiff named himself Nicholas as a mark of respect for his patron, Bishop Niccolò (Nicholas) Albergati of Bologna, whom he had served for 20 years.

Horatio Nicholls: Lawrence Wright (1888–1964), Br. popular composer, music publisher. The musician used this and many other pseudonyms for his prodigious output of popular songs. Other names included Victor Ambroise, Haydon Augarde, Everett Lynton, Paul Paree, Gene Williams (for his million-selling "Wyoming"), Betsy O'Hogan (for "Old Father Thames"), and W. Kerrigan.

Barbara Nichols: Barbara Nickerauer (1929–1976), U.S. movie actress.

Mike Nichols: Michael Igor Peschkowsky (1931–), Ger.-born U.S. cabaret entertainer,

movie director. The entertainer's Russian father anglicized his patronymic, Nikolayevich, when he left Germany on the rise of Hitler to become a physician (as Nichols) in the U.S.

Niclas y Glais: Thomas Evan Nicholas (1878–1971), Welsh poet. The writer was a Nonconformist minister and served for ten years at Glais near Swansea. Hence his name, meaning "Nicholas of Glais."

Nico: Christa Päffgen (1938–1988), Ger. model, pop singer, movie actress. The model's new name was given her by her "mentor," the German photographer Herbert Tobias: "'You cannot carry on calling yourself Christa Päffgen. Even Christa is wrong. It's not international. Krista is better, but it doesn't suit your character. ... Models have one name, just like photographers and designers have one name. I am Tobias. I have a name for you, and you must use it from now on.'" He explained: "'The most wonderful man I have ever seen lives in Paris. I am in love with him. ... His name is Nico Papatakis.' From that day, in the Berlin of 1956, Christa was Nico, taking the name of a man loved by another. ... She recognised even then that Nico as a name was a brilliant, indefinite, ambiguous choice" [Richard Witts, *Nico: The Life and Lies of an Icon*, 1993].

Nico would later offer the media four different versions of how she came by her name, the first being the real one: (1) she took the name from the best friend of a photographer; (2) her real name was Nico Pavlovsky, but she shortened this difficult name to Nico; (3) she was so named by Salvador Dali as an anagram of "icon"; (4) she was given the name by the fashion designer Coco Chanel, who based it on her own name.

Abioseh Nicol: Davidson Sylvester Hector Willoughby Nicol (1924–1994), Sierra Leonean diplomat, writer, working in England. The scholar adopted a native name in place of his English one.

Nicolini (or Nicolino): Nicolò Grimaldi (1673–1732), It. male alto singer.

Ernest Nicolini: Ernest Nicolas (1834–1898), Fr. opera singer.

Flora Nielsen: Sybil Crawley (1900–1976), Can. opera singer, teacher.

Niger: Ivan Vasiliyevich Dzhanayev (1896–1947), Russ. (Ossetian) poet, literary critic. The writer's adopted name means "black," referring to his dark complexion.

Shmuel **Niger**: Shmuel Charmi (1884– ?), Russ.-born Jewish literary critic, essayist, working in U.S.

Robert **Nighthawk**: Robert McCollum (1909–1967), U.S. blues guitarist. The musician took his professional name from his own release of "Prowlin' Nighthawk."

Nikodim: Boris Georgievich Rotov (1929–1978), Russ. Orthodox churchman. The metropolitan of Leningrad may have deliberately chosen a religious name meaning "victory of the people." Compare the name of Nikon (below).

Galina **Nikolayeva**: Galina Yevgenyevna Volyanskaya (1911–1963), Russ. writer.

Nikon: Nikita Minov (1605–1681), Russ. Orthodox churchman. The patriarch of Moscow and All Russia seems to have based his religious name on his original name. It would have been regarded as meaningful, from the Greek word for "victory." Compare the name of Nikodim (above).

Nilsson: Harry Edward Nelson III (1941–1994), U.S. pop singer.

Nimrod: Charles James Apperley (1777–1843), Eng. sporting writer. The writer punningly adopted the name of the biblical Nimrod, the "mighty hunter" (Genesis 19:9). He may additionally have seen a meaning "taking the rod," from the old English word *nim* meaning "take." The three traditional English field sports are hunting, shooting, and fishing.

Nina: Ethel Florence Nelson (1923–), Can. travel writer.

Egnate **Ninoshvili**: Egnate Fomich Ingorokva (1859–1894), Georgian writer. The writer was orphaned as a child and took his pen name from the aunt who raised him, Nina, with *-shvili* the Georgian suffix meaning "son of."

Sir Nicholas **Nipclose**, Bart: David Garrick (1717–1779), Eng. actor, dramatist. The actor used this frivolous name for some of his farces and stage adaptations.

Red **Nirt**: Tommy Trinder (1909–1989), Eng. stage, radio comedian. The comedian used this whimsical reversal of his surname early in his career.

Shota **Nishnianidze**: Shota Georgiyevich Mamageyshvili (1929–), Georgian poet.

Greta **Nissen**: Grethe Rutz-Nissen (1906–1988), Norw. movie actress, working in U.S.

Der **Nister**: Pinkhos Mendeleyevich Kaganovich (1884–1950), Ukrainian Jewish writer. The writer was born in Berdichev and in 1905 moved to Zhitomir, where he became a teacher of Hebrew under an assumed name. Hence his pseudonym, Yiddish for "the hidden one."

David **Niven**: James David Nevins (1909–1983), Sc.-born Br. movie actor.

Marni **Nixon**: Marni McEathron (1929–), U.S. movie actress, singer.

Kwame **Nkrumah**: Francis Nwia Kofi (1909–1972), Ghanaian political leader.

Nobody: William Stevens (1732–1807), Eng. biographer. This, the ultimate in anonymous names, was originally used by the writer in its Hebrew equivalent form of "Ain," as the author of one of his many religious publications, *Review of the Review of a New Preface to the Second Edition of Mr. Jones's Life of Bishop Horne* (1800). The name in turn suggested his pseudonym for a collection of his pamphlets, published with the Greek and English title *Oudenos erga, Nobody's Works* (1805). At about the same time, a club was founded in Stevens' honor entitled the "Society of Nobody's Friends." Anyone who calls himself Nobody is, of course, somebody. Compare the next name below.

A. **Nobody**: Gordon Frederick Browne (1858–1932), Eng. illustrator, painter. The artist, who was the son of Phiz (*q.v.*), used this mock selfdeprecatory name for three books of nonsense rhymes that he wrote and illustrated for children.

Magali **Noël**: Magali Guiffrai (1932–), Turk.-born movie actress, working in France, Italy.

Marie **Noël**: Marie Rouget (1883–1967), Fr. writer of religious verse.

Philip **Noel-Baker**: Philip John Baker (1889–1982), Br. politician. The Labor politician married Irene Noel in 1915 and added her name to his then.

Noël-Noël: Lucien Noël (1897–1989), Fr. movie comedian.

Victor **Noir**: Yvan Salmon (1848–1870), Fr. journalist.

Mary **Nolan**: Mary Imogen Robertson (1905–1948), U.S. movie actress.

Emile **Nolde**: Emil Hansen (1867–1956), Ger. Expressionist painter. The artist adopted the name of his birthplace, the village of Nolde, in what is now southern Denmark.

Nomad: Norman Ellison (1893–1976), Eng. naturalist, writer, broadcaster. The name not only indicates the naturalist's "roaming" activity but also reflects his real first name.

Non Con Quill: John Cynddylan Jones (1840–1930), Welsh theologian, biblical scholar. Jones was a Nonconformist ("Noncon") minister. Hence his name, which he used for articles published in the *Western Mail*.

Ed **Noon:** Michael Angelo Avallone, Jr. (1924–), U.S. thriller, horror story writer. Other names used by the novelist include Troy Conway, Priscilla Dalton, Mark Dane, J.A. DePre, Dorothea Nile, Vance Stanton, and Sidney Stuart.

Jeremiah **Noon:** John Calvin (1828–1871), Br. boxer. The boxer based his name on that of Anthony Noon, who had been killed in a fight against Owen Swift in 1834.

T.R. **Noon:** Olive Marion Norton (1913–), Br. children's writer. An anagram of the writer's surname gave the genderless pen name that some children's writers formerly favored.

Tommy **Noonan:** Thomas Patrick Noon (1922–1958), U.S. movie comedian.

Oodgeroo **Noonuccal:** Kathleen Mary Jean Walker (Kath Walker), née Ruska (1920–1993), Austral. Aboriginal poet. The writer adopted her Aboriginal name in 1988 when Australia celebrated its bicentennial. Her new first name derives from a word for the paper bark tree. Her surname was that of the Noonuccal tribe to which her parents belonged.

Max Simon **Nordau:** Max Simon Südfeld (1849–1923), Hung.-Ger. physician, writer. The name shows a swing of polarity, since the writer's original surname means "southern field," while his pen name means "northern meadow." The "volte face" may have been designed to represent the physician's switch from medicine to literature.

Charles **Norden:** Lawrence George Durrell (1912–1990), Br. novelist, poet. The writer adopted this name for his early novel *Panic Spring* (1937). This was actually his second novel, but as his first, *Pied Piper of Lovers* (1935), had been a failure, his publishers suggested he adopt a pseudonym as a precautionary measure. Later, the huge success of *The Alexandria Quartet* (1957–60) ensured that false names were a thing of the past.

Christine **Norden:** Mary (or Molly) Lydia Thornton (1924–1988), Br. movie actress.

Lillian **Nordica:** Lillian Norton (1859–1914), U.S. opera singer.

Norman **Norell:** Norman Levinson (1900–1972), U.S. fashion designer. The designer seems to have formed his new surname from the first syllables of his real two names.

Eidé **Norena:** Kaja Hanson Eidé (1884–1968), Norw. opera singer.

Géo **Norge:** Georges Mogin (1898–1990), Belg. poet. A pseudonym extracted from the poet's original name.

Assia **Noris:** Anastasia von Gerzfeld (1912–), Russ.-born movie actress, of Ger.-Ukrainian parentage.

Norma Jean: Norma Jean Beasler (1938–), U.S. country singer.

Karyl **Norman:** George Podezzi (1897–1947), U.S. male impersonator ("The Creole Fashion Plate").

Mabel **Norman:** Mabel Fortescue (1894–1930), U.S. movie comedienne.

Normski: Normon Anthony Anderson (1967–), Br. TV presenter, of Jamaican parentage. Rapper brother Kevin explains: "I just called him Normon as a kid, then he went off to America and came back with a belt saying Normski on it and started using the name all the time. It's just an aka, a street name, everyone has one. Mine is Kzee, Killer Zone" [*Sunday Times Magazine*, December 6, 1992].

Normyx: George Norman Douglas (1868–1952), Sc. novelist + Elizabeth (or Elsa) Theobaldina Douglas, née FitzGibbon, his wife (also cousin). The pair used this joint name for *Unprofessional Tales* (1901). Until about 1908, Douglas used the name G. Norman Douglass (preserving the spelling of his father's name) for all his writings, changing this to Norman Douglas thereafter.

Nedra **Norris:** Nedra Gullette (1914–), U.S. movie actress.

Harold **Norse:** Harold George Rosen (1916–), U.S. poet, of Lithuanian-Ger. parentage. An obvious anagram here, from a name that lent itself readily to this.

Captain George **North:** Robert Louis Stevenson (1850–1894), Sc. essayist, novelist, poet. This was the name assumed by Stevenson for *Treasure Island* when the novel first appeared serially in the magazine *Young Folks* (1881–82). He used his real name a year later when the story was published in book form. The name may have been intended to indicate a Scot, who came from "north of the border" (with England). Or possibly he based it on the name of Christopher North (see next entry below).

Christopher **North:** John Wilson (1785–1854), Sc. literary critic. The writer used this name for his contributions to many of the dialogues that appeared in the *Noctes Ambrosianae*, published in *Blackwood's Magazine* (1822–35). "North" relates to Scotland, to the north of England.

Danby **North:** Daniel Owen Madden (1815–1852), Ir. writer. The author used this name for *The Mildmayes, or the Clergymen's Secret* (1856).

Sheree **North:** Dawn Bethel (1933–), U.S. movie actress.

André **Norton:** Alice Mary Norton (1912–), U.S. SF, children's writer. The author also used the similar male name Andrew North.

Barry **Norton:** Alfredo de Biraben (or de Biartsen) (1905–1956), Argentine-born U.S. movie actor.

Fleming **Norton:** Frederic Mills (1836–1895), Br. actor, entertainer.

Jack **Norton:** Mortimer J. Naughton (1889–1958), U.S. movie actor.

Red **Norvo:** Kenneth Norville (1908–), U.S. jazz musician.

Eille **Norwood:** Anthony Brett (1861–1948), Br. stage actor.

Jack **Norworth:** John Knauff (1879–1959), U.S. stage actor, singer, dancer.

Max **Nosseck:** Alexander Norris (1902–1972), Pol. movie director, actor, working in U.S.

Nostradamus: Michel de Nostre-Dame (1503–1566), Fr. astrologer, doctor. The name appears to be a simple latinization of Nostre-Dame (or Notre- Dame, "Our Lady"). But the astrologer could have intended something more significant. One possible interpretation is "we give what is ours," from Latin *nostra*, "our things," and *damus*, "we give (them)."

Kim **Novak:** Marilyn Pauline Novak (1933–), U.S. movie actress. The actress adopted a first name that she felt went well with her surname. Among other names she considered, but rejected, were Kavon Novak (one name reversing the other), Iris Green (the color shade), and Windy City (the nickname of Chicago, where she was born).

Novalis: Friedrich Leopold von Hardenberg (1772–1801), Ger. romantic poet, novelist. The writer's pseudonym derives from the name of the family estate of Grossenrode, itself meaning "great clearing." His ancestors devised a Latin form of this name, from *novalis*, "fallow land," ultimately from *novus*, "new." The Hardenberg family were known as "de Novalis" as far back as the 13th century.

Novanglus: John Adams (1735–1828), U.S. statesman, president. The name, obviously meaning "New Englander," was used by Adams for letters of his published in 1775 in the *Boston Gazette* rebutting letters by the Loyalist writer Daniel Leonard, otherwise Massachusettensis (*q.v.*).

Ramon **Novarro:** Jose Ramon Gil Samaniegos (1899–1968), Mexican movie actor, working in U.S. The actor's name was given him by director Rex Ingram, who needed a replacement for Rudolph Valentino (*q.v.*) when the latter left the company. Ingram cast Samaniegos as Rupert of Henzau in his version of *The Prisoner of Zenda* (1922). The name suggests a new persona and new role in life, while possibly also hinting at Spanish *varón*, "man" (in the "macho" sense).

Alec **Nove:** Alexander Novakovsky (1915–1994), Russ.-born Br. economist.

Ivor **Novello:** David Ivor Davies (1893–1951), Welsh stage actor-manager, playwright, composer. The actor inherited the Italian name from his mother, Clara Novello Davies, née Davies, whose own second name had been given her by her father in admiration of the singer Clara Anastasia Novello (to whom she was not actually related, as sometimes stated). Clara Novello was the daughter of the English organist and music publisher Vincent Novello (1781–1861), who in turn was the son of an Italian father and English mother. David Ivor Davies's professional name thus reached him by a rather roundabout route.

Davies was known as Ivor from childhood, and in 1909 was signing himself Ivor Novello Davies as a piano teacher. He adopted the name officially by deed poll in 1927. "There were two men in that one person. There was David Ivor Davies, the dark-eyed handsome youth from Wales, and there was Ivor Novello, whom the public knew and adored and whom David Ivor Davies created. That creation was one of his major successes. So complete did it become that it was almost impossible to say where one finished and the other began" [W. Macqueen-Pope, *Ivor: The Story of an Achievement*, 1951].

Novello's play *The Rat* (1924) was coauthored with Constance Collier (*q.v.*) under the joint pseudonym David L'Estrange, from a combination of his original first name and her married name.

Aleksey **Novikov-Priboy:** Aleksey Silych Novikov (1877–1944), Russ. novelist, short story writer. The writer's fiction regularly had a naval or maritime setting. Hence his addition to his original name of Russian *priboy,* "surf."

Karel **Nový**: Karel Novák (1890–1980), Cz. novelist.

Owen **Nox**: Charles Barney Cory (1857–1921), U.S. ornithologist.

Nuitter: Charles-Louis-Etienne Truinet (1828–1899), Fr. playwright, librettist. An anagrammatic name.

Gary **Numan**: Gary Anthony James Webb (1958–), Eng. pop singer. A symbolic name, with a new-style (or nu-style) spelling. There happens also to be a British actor Gary Oldman, Numan's exact coeval.

Bill **Nye**: Edgar Wilson Nye (1850–1896), U.S. humorist, editor. The writer used his part-pseudonymous name for a successful series of books beginning with *Bill Nye and Boomerang* (1881). (The latter was the *Laramie Boomerang,* the Wyoming newspaper that he edited.)

Alfonsas **Nyka-Niliunas**: Alfonsas Cipkus (1919–), Lithuanian writer, critic.

Jack **Oakie**: Lewis Delaney Offield (1903–1978), U.S. movie comedian. The actor was born in Sedalia, Missouri, but later his family moved to Muskogee, Oklahoma, where his schoolfriends nicknamed him "Oakie." He added "Jack" to this to fix himself up with a suitable screen name.

Vivian **Oakland**: Vivian Anderson (1895–1958), U.S. movie actress.

Annie **Oakley**: Phoebe Anne Oakley Moses (1860–1926), U.S. sharpshooter. The famous markswoman tried out the name Annie Mozee when still a girl, but later settled on a more conventional form of her two names.

Wheeler **Oakman**: Vivian Eichelberger (1890–1949), U.S. movie actor. The actor indirectly translated part of his original name, German *Eichel* meaning "acorn."

Merle **Oberon**: Estelle Merle O'Brien Thompson (1911–1979), Eng. movie actress. The popular account of the actress's origins states that she was born in Tasmania, Australia, of Irish, French, and Dutch descent. However, it emerged in a 1983 biography that she had invented this genesis, and that she was actually born in Bombay, India, to a part Irish, part Singhalese mother, Charlotte Constance Selby, and a British army officer, Arthur Terrence O'Brien Thompson. She moved to England in 1928 and played bit parts on stage and in films under the name Queenie O'Brien. She was then discovered by Alexander Korda (*q.v.*), whom she subsequently married, and adopted her permanent screen name: "She began with Merle O'Brien, then O'Bryan, then Auberon (but that was the name of a firm in Bond Street), then Overell, then Avril Oberon, then Merle Oberon" [Charles Higham and Roy Moseley, *Merle: A Biography of Merle Oberon*, 1983].

Hugh **O'Brian**: Hugh J. Krampke (1925–), U.S. movie actor.

Dave **O'Brien**: David Barclay (1912–1969), U.S. movie actor.

David **O'Brien**: David Herd (1930–), Eng. stage actor.

Flann **O'Brien**: Brian O'Nolan (1912–1966), Ir. novelist. This is the name the writer, also familiar as Myles na gCopaleen (*q.v.*), used for his first novel, *At Swim-Two-Birds* (1939), and for subsequent fiction. Flann is an established Irish first name.

John **O'Brien**: Patrick Joseph Hartigan (1878–1952), Austral. poet, balladist.

Margaret **O'Brien**: Angela Maxine O'Brien (1937–), U.S. child movie actress.

Richard **O'Brien**: Richard Morley-Smith (1942–), N.Z.-born Br. stage actor, writer, TV presenter. The actor adopted his mother's maiden name as his professional name.

Robert C. **O'Brien**: Robert Leslie Conly (1918–1973), U.S. writer.

W.J. **O'Bryen**: Wilfrid James Wheeler-O'Bryen (1898– ?), Br. theatre manager.

Dermot **O'Byrne**: [Sir] Arnold Bax (1883–1953), Br. composer, writer. The composer visited Ireland at the age of 19 and, falling under its Celtic spell, adopted the Irish name "Diarmid" for some early love letters. He then expanded and anglicized this name to "Dermot McDermott," and finally became Dermot O'Byrne. He was first "Diarmid" in print for a poem, "The Glen of Starry Peace," in the October 1908 issue of the art magazine *Orpheus,* of which he was editor (under his real name), while "Dermot O'Byrne" made his bow for the poem "To my little friend Donall Gillespie" in the April 1910 issue.

Richard **O'Callaghan**: Richard Hayes (1945–), Br. TV actor. The actor is the son of the actress Patricia Hayes (1910–), and chose a name to express his individuality and to distinguish his own career and approach from his mother's. He commented: "I've always had to do things my way, which is why I wanted a different name from hers. I didn't want people giving me jobs because I was her son" [*Sunday Times Magazine*, June 28, 1987].

Sean **O'Casey**: John Casey (1880–1964), Ir. dramatist. When he began writing, in 1918, the playwright used an Irish version of his name, Sean O'Cathasaigh. Later, in the early 1920s, when his plays were first produced at the Abbey Theatre, Dublin, he part-reverted to an anglicized form of this.

Jehu **O'Cataract**: John Neal (1793–1876), U.S. romantic novelist, poet. This name, a typical 19th-century American literary whimsy, originally arose as a nickname, given the writer for his impetuosity. He first adopted it for two narrative poems published in 1918, *Battle of Niagara* and *Goldau, or the Maniac Harper*. His feverish, flamboyant writing and editing continued unabated until he was in his 80s.

Billy **Ocean**: Leslie Sebastian Charles (1950–), Trinidad rhythm 'n' blues singer, working in U.K., U.S. Other early pseudonyms used by the singer include Joshua and Sam Spade.

Humphrey **Ocean**: Humphrey Butler-Bowdon (1951–), Br. portrait artist.

Marie **Ochs**: Gloria Steinem (1934–), U.S. feminist writer. This was the name the writer adopted when infiltrating the Playboy Club as a bunny girl in 1963: "I've decided to call myself Marie Catherine Ochs. It is, may my ancestors forgive me, a family name. I have some claim to it, and I'm well versed in its European origins. Besides, it sounds much too square to be phony" [Gloria Steinem, *Outrageous Acts and Everyday Rebellions*, 1983].

Frank **O'Connor**: Michael O'Donovan (1903–1966), Ir. short story writer. The writer adopted his mother's maiden name as his pen name.

Patrick **O'Connor**: Leonard Patrick O'Connor Wibberley (1915–1983), Ir.-born U.S. journalist, novelist, children's writer.

Una **O'Connor**: Agnes Teresa McGlade (1880–1959), Ir. movie actress, working in U.S.

Anita **O'Day**: Anita Colton (1919–), U.S. popular singer. The singer changed her name as a teenager, when she was a professional marathon dancer.

Dawn **O'Day**: Anne Shirley (*q.v.*).

Molly **O'Day**: Suzanne Dobson Noonan (1911–), U.S. movie actess.

Kenny **O'Dell**: Kenneth Gist, Jr. (*c.*1940–), U.S. country singer, songwriter.

Odetta: Odetta Holmes Felious Gorden (1930–), U.S. folk singer.

Odette: Odette Marie Céline Churchill (later Hallowes, earlier Sansom), née Brailly (1912–1995), Fr.-born Br. wartime agent. When training for her work in the field, Odette took the code name Céline (*q.v.*). She also operated as Lise, while in prison in Paris she was Madame Odette Chambrun and in Ravensbrück women's camp, Germany, she was Frau Schurer. "Chambrun" was an alias of Raoul (*q.v.*), her group leader, who later became her second husband.

Mary **Odette**: Odette Goimbault (1901–), Fr.-born Br. movie actress.

Cathy **O'Donnell**: Ann Steely (1923–1970), U.S. movie actress.

Cornelius **O'Dowd**: Charles James Lever (1806–1872), Eng.-born Ir. novelist. This pseudonym was one of several used by the writer for his series of essays entitled *Cornelius O'Dowd upon Men, Women and Other Things in General*, published in *Blackwood's Magazine* in 1864.

Irina Vladimirovna **Odoyevtseva**: Iraida Gustavovna Geynike (Heinicke) (1901–), Russ. writer.

Odysseus: [Sir] Charles Norton Edgcumbe Eliot (1862–1931), Br. diplomat. The diplomat, whose duties took him on travels to many parts of the world, used this significant pseudonym for *Turkey in Europe* (1901), an account of Macedonia and its different races under the old regime.

John **Oecolampadius**: Johannes Huszgen (or Husschyn) (1482–1531), Ger. Humanist, preacher. In the manner of his day the scholar translated his German name into Greek. The equivalent of modern German *Haus* thus gave Greek *oikos*, "house," and the equivalent of *Schein* gave *lampas*, *lampados*, "light." The theologian would further have seen his preaching as bringing light (truth) into the house of God (church).

Sean **O'Faolain**: John Francis Whelan (1900–1991), Ir. writer. The writer changed his name to its Irish equivalent in order to express his political convictions.

Ofelia: Mercedes Matamoros (1851–1906), Cuban poet.

[Cardinal] Tomás **O'Fiaich**: Thomas Seamus Fee (1923–1990), Ir. Roman Catholic church leader. The future cardinal adopted the Irish (Gaelic) form of his name in 1977, when appointed Archbishop of Armagh and Primate of All Ireland.

Talbot **O'Farrell:** William Parrot (1878–1952), Eng. music hall comedian. The performer's adopted name resembles a sort of anagrammatized reversal of his two original names.

Jacques **Offenbach:** Jakob Eberst (1819–1880), Ger.-born Fr. composer. The composer's father, Isaac Juda Eberst, a cantor at the Cologne Synagogue, was born in Offenbach, and was thus known as "Der Offenbacher." When Jakob was 14, his family moved to France, and he himself adopted his father's nickname, modifying his own first name to its French equivalent.

Gavin **Ogilvy:** [Sir] James Matthew Barrie (1860–1937), Sc. novelist, dramatist. The author of *Peter Pan* adopted this name, from his mother's maiden name, for *When a Man's Single, A Tale of Literary Life*, published serially in the *British Weekly* over the two years 1887–88.

N. **Ognev:** Mikhail Grigoryevich Rozanov (1888–1938), Russ. writer. The writer adopted a pseudonym (apparently based on letters from his original name) in order to be distinguished from his brother, Sergey Grigoryevich Rozanov (1894–1957), also a writer.

George **O'Hanlon:** George Rice (1917–1989), U.S. movie actor.

Kevin **O'Hara:** Marten Cumberland (1892–1971), Br. thriller writer.

Mary **O'Hara:** Mary O'Hara Alsop (1885–1980), U.S. novelist.

Maureen **O'Hara:** Maureen FitzSimons (1920–), Ir.-born U.S. movie actress.

Pixie **O'Harris:** Rona Olive Pratt (1903–), Welsh-born Austral. children's writer, illustrator. Harris is a family name. The Australian entertainer and TV artist Rolf Harris (1930–) is the writer's nephew.

Dennis **O'Keefe:** Edward Vanes Flanagan (1908–1968), U.S. movie, TV actor, of Ir. parentage. The actor appeared in several films as Bud Flanagan before changing his name to Dennis O'Keefe in 1937 after joining MGM as a contract player. This earlier name was identical to that of the British actor Bud Flanagan (*q.v.*).

Lorenz **Oken:** Lorenz Ockenfuss (1779–1851), Ger. natural scientist, philosopher.

Okito: Theodore Bamberg (1875–1963), U.S. magician, of Du. descent. The illusionist originally wore a Japanese costume. Hence his name, as an anagram of "Tokio" (as Tokyo was sometimes spelled). His son was Fu Manchu (*q.v.*).

Olaf V: Alexander Edward Christian Frederik (1903–1991), Norw. king. The king was the son of Haakon VII (*q.v.*) and Princess Maud, daughter of Edward VII of England, and was actually born in England. He was christened Alexander but in 1905 was renamed Prince Olaf when his father became king of Norway and took his own new Norse name.

Pierre **Olaf:** Pierre-Olaf Trivier (1928–), Fr. stage actor.

Warner **Oland:** Johan Werner Öhlund (1880–1938), Swe. movie actor, working in U.S.

Ivan **Olbracht:** Kamil Zeman (1882–1952), Cz. writer, son of Antal Stašek (*q.v.*).

Chauncey **Olcott:** John Chancellor (1858–1932), U.S. popular singer, composer.

Sidney **Olcott:** John Sidney Alcott (1873–1949), Ir.-Can. movie director, working in U.S. The slight spelling change was probably made to ensure the surname's correct pronunciation.

Old Block: Alonzo Delano (? 1801–1874), U.S. playwright, humorist. The writer used this name, somewhat predictably, for *Penknife Sketches, or Chips of the Old Block* (1853).

An **Old Boy:** Thomas Hughes (1822–1896), Eng. author. This was the name under which the writer first published his famous novel of school life, *Tom Brown's Schooldays* (1857). It was semiautobiographical, evoking Rugby School, which Hughes had himself attended as a boy.

Humphrey **Oldcastle:** (1) Henry St. John (1672–1751), Eng. magazine contributor; (2) Nicholas Amhurst (1697–1742), Eng. poet, politician. Henry St. John, Viscount Bolingbroke, contributed to *The Craftsman* under this pen name, as did the magazine's originator, Nicholas Amhurst, who actually founded it as Caleb D'Anvers (*q.v.*). There is still some doubt about the precise authorship of the articles attributed to Amhurst.

John **Oldcastle:** Wilfrid Meynell (1852–1948), Br. writer, poet. The writer used this name for *Journals and Journalism* (1880). The name punningly refers to his birth city, Newcastle upon Tyne.

Old Humphrey: George Mogridge (1787–1854), Eng. writer of moral and religious works for children and adults. Mogridge used more than one pseudonym. His best known was Peter Parley (*q.v.*). As "Old Humphrey" he wrote over 40 tracts or tales. He probably took the name from some literary character, although it is uncertain who this was. Or possibly he adopted the name from an existing pseudonym, such as the next below.

Jonathan **Oldstyle:** Washington Irving (1783-1859), U.S. essayist, short story writer, historian. This was an early pseudonym used by the writer, who later wrote as (alone) Geoffrey Crayon and (jointly) Launcelot Langstaff (*qq.v.*). He used it for the *Letters of Jonathan Oldstyle, Gent.*, a series of satires on New York society which appeared in the New York *Morning Chronicle* over the period 1802–03.

Patrick Albert **O'Leary:** [Dr.] Albert-Marie Edmond Guérisse (1911–1989), Belg. army officer, serving with Br. navy. Guérisse adopted this name from a peacetime Canadian friend in 1940, when he became first officer of the "Q" ship HMS *Fidelity*, with the naval rank of lieutenant commander.

Ole Luk-Oie: [Sir] Ernest Dunlop Swinton (1868–1951), Br. soldier, writer. The unusual pseudonym is a Danish phrase meaning roughly "Olaf Shut-Eye." It was adopted by the army officer for his book of short stories *The Green Curve* (1909) and other writings. He also wrote as Backsight-Forethought (*q.v.*).

Olenka: Olga Augusta Maria Savary (1933–), Brazilian poet, writer, of Russ. parentage. The writer's adopted name is a diminutive of her original Russian first name.

Konstantin **Olimpov:** Konstantin Konstantinovich Fofanov (1889–1940), Russ. Decadent poet. The poet adopted a somewhat outlandish name (implying Olympic prowess) to be distinguished from his father, Konstantin Mikhaylovich Fofanov (1862–1911), also a poet.

Oliver: William Oliver Swofford (1945–), U.S. folk-rock singer.

Edith **Oliver:** Edith Goldsmith (1913–), U.S. drama critic. The critic took her new surname from the first name of the dramatist whose surname she shared, Oliver Goldsmith (1728–1784).

Edna May **Oliver:** Edna May Cox-Oliver, née Nutter (1883–1942), U.S. movie actress.

George **Oliver:** George Oliver Onions (1873–1961), Eng. novelist. This was not the adoption of a pseudonym but a legal name change, made in 1918.

Jane **Oliver:** Helen Rees (1903–1970), Sc. novelist.

Stephen **Oliver:** Stephen John Walzig (*c.*1950–), U.S. juvenile TV actor.

Susan **Oliver:** Charlotte Gercke (1937–1990), U.S. movie, TV actress, director, aviator.

Vic **Oliver:** Viktor Oliver van Samek (1898–1964), Austr.-born Br. comedian, musician.

Olivia: Dorothy Bussy, née Strachey (1866–1960), Br. writer, translator, working in France. The writer used this name for her sole novel *Olivia* ("by Olivia") (1949), a fictional autobiography of a French schoolgirl, preceded by an outline of her earlier years. The account covers a year, involves a passionate affair, and ends in the narrator's suicide. The name Olivia has long been regarded as a romantic one, and even suggests "I love you" if spoken rapidly.

Ollie: Clive Hugh Austin Collins (1942–), Eng. cartoonist, illustrator. A name based on the artist's surname.

Mikhail **Olminsky:** Mikhail Stepanovich Aleksandrov (1863–1933), Russ. revolutionary, writer, historian. In 1898 the activist was exiled to the Siberian town of Olyokminsk, and this gave the name by which he became regularly known. A prerevolutionary name used by the writer was Galyorka (*q.v.*).

Olnem: Varvara Nikolayevna Tsekhovskaya, née Menshchikova (1872– ?), Russ. writer. The writer created her pen name from a syllable in her patronymic (middle name) and the first (reversed) syllable of her maiden name.

John **O'London:** Wilfred Whitten (? –1942), Br. editor, author, founder of *John O'London's Weekly*. Whitten founded the popular literary weekly in 1919, but it ceased publication in 1936.

April **Olrich:** Edith April Oelrichs (1941–), Br. stage, movie, TV actess.

Ipay **Olyk:** Ipaty Stepanovich Stepanov (1912–1943), Russ. (Mari) poet. The poet adopted a surname meaning "meadow."

Omar Khayyám: Ghiyāthuddīn Abulfath 'Omar bin Ibrāhīmal-Khayyāmi (? 1048–1122), Persian poet, astronomer. The famous author of the *Rubáiyát* (which name means "Quatrains" in Arabic) has a name that literally means "Omar Tentmaker," the latter indicating his father's occupation. (The second half of his name, as given here, spells him out more fully as "Omar son of Ibrahim the Tentmaker." Omar was the name of an early caliph of the 7th century.)

Innokenty **Omulevsky:** Innokenty Vasilyevich Fyodorov (1836–1883), Russ. writer. The writer lived in Irkutsk, not far from Lake Baykal.

His adopted name derives from Russian *omul'*, "omul," a fish of the salmon family found in that lake.

Anny Ondra: Anna Sofia Ondráková (1903–1987), Pol. movie actress, working in U.K., Germany. The actress adopted the simplified version of her original name in the late 1920s.

Siri O'Neal: Siri Willow Ceridwen Neal (1972–), Welsh stage, movie, TV actress. The actress adopted her family's original name of O'Neal in 1996. This was her grandmother's name, which her mother had altered to Neal.

Philothée O'Neddy: Théophile Dondey (1811–1875), Fr. poet, short story writer, dramatic critic. To the author's literary accomplishments we might have added "anagrammatist." He was fortunate in having a classical-style first name that could be inverted like this, from "loved of God" (in the original Greek) to "loving God."

Sigrid Onegin: Sigrid Elisabeth Elfriede Emilie Hoffmann (1889–1943), Swe.-born Russ. opera singer, of Ger.-Fr. parentage. The singer took her first husband's adopted name of Onegin as her professional name.

Sally O'Neil: Virginia Louise Concepta Noonan (1908–1968), U.S. movie actress.

Egan O'Neill: Elizabeth Linington (1921–1988), U.S. mystery writer. The writer's pen name, evoking that of the better known Eugene O'Neill, was possibly formed from letters of her real name.

Maire O'Neill: Molly Allgood (1885–1952), Ir. movie actress.

L. Onerva: Hilja Onerva Lehtinen (1882–1971), Finn. writer. The initial "L." could derive either from the writer's first name or from the initial of her maiden name.

Colette O'Niel: [Lady] Constance Malleson, née Annesley (1886–1975), Ir. stage actress, writer. The actress's stage name appears to reflect either her married name or her maiden name. Her husband was the English actor Miles Malleson (1888–1969).

Marcel Ophüls: Marcel Oppenheimer (1927–), Ger. movie director, son of Max Ophüls (see below).

Max Ophüls: Max Oppenheimer (1902–1957), Ger.-born Fr. movie director, father of Marcel Ophüls (see above). The filmmaker began his career as a stage actor at the age of 17 and changed his name then to avoid embarrassing his parents.

Oliver Optic: William Taylor Adams (1822–1897), U.S. novelist, children's writer. The author, who wrote around 1000 short stories and over 100 novels, adopted a name that seems to have been randomly enjoyable. He used it notably for *Oliver Optic's Magazine for Boys and Girls* (1867–75). Adams reserved this name for his children's writing. His other main pseudonyms were Irving Brown for romantic novels and Clinham Hunter, M.D., for travel writing.

William Orbit: William Wainwright (1959–), Br. music composer, arranger, record company owner.

Andrea Orcagna: Andrea di Cione (*c*.1308–*c*.1368), It. artist. The artist is known by his nickname, said to derive from a local form of Italian *arcangelo*, "archangel." The reference is presumably to his religious paintings, or even to his appearance.

Robin Ordell: Robert Dowe (1918–1942), Austral. juvenile movie actor. The actor was the son of the popular writer and comedian Athol Dowe, who worked under the name Tal Ordell. Later in life he took the full name Robert Athol Buntine.

Ordovex: John Humphreys (or Humffreys) Parry (1786–1825), Welsh editor. The writer used this name for his journalism. It means "Ordovician," that is, a member of the pre-Roman Ordovices tribe who inhabited northern Wales. Parry was born in Mold, Flintshire, in this part of Wales.

Ordubady: Mamed Hadzha-aga ogly (1872–1950), Azerbaijani writer. The writer adopted the name of his birthtown, Ordubad.

Katherine O'Regan: Kathleen Melville (1903–), Ir. stage actress.

Miles O'Reilly: Charles Graham Halpine (1829–1868), Ir. humorist, soldier, working in U.S. The writer used the name specifically for his humorous description of Civil War events, *The Life and Adventures ... of Private Miles O'Reilly* (1864).

Max O'Rell: Léon Paul Blouet (1848–1903), Fr.-born Eng. humorous writer.

Zaharije Orfelin: Zaharije Stefanovic (1726–1785), Serbian scholar, writer, historian.

Orhan Kemal: Mehmet Raşit Ogutçü (1914–1970), Turk. writer.

Orinda: Katherine Philips, née Fowler (1631–1664), Eng. poet, letter-writer. The poet adopted the name Orinda as her pseudonym, and this in turn gave her literary sobriquet, the

"Matchless Orinda." She moved in a society where it was the fashion to adopt a colorful and preferably classical-style name: her husband, James Philips, was "Antenor," and among other friends were "Silvander" (Sir Edward Dering) and "Palaemon" (Jeremy Taylor, the Irish bishop and theological writer). The name Orinda occurs in the writings of Philips' contemporary, the poet Abraham Cowley, and he may have invented it on classical lines.

Orion: Jimmy Ellis (1945–), U.S. rock singer. The famous Elvis Presley lookalike and sounda-like is said to have adopted his name after received a phone call from a woman who had written a book titled *Orion*, a fictionalized account of the Presley story. The original Orion was a great hunter of Greek mythology.

Władysław **Orkan:** Franciszek Smreczyński (1875–1930), Pol. writer. The writer adopted a name meaning "hurricane," "whirlwind."

Tony **Orlando:** Michael Anthony Orlando Cassivitis (1944–), U.S. rock singer, of Gk.-Puerto Rican descent.

Pavel **Orlenev:** Pavel Nikolayevich Orlov (1869–1932), Russ. actor.

Boris **Orlovsky:** Boris Ivanovich Smirnov (1796–1837), Russ. sculptor.

Eugene **Ormandy:** Jenö Ormandy Blau (1899–1985), Hung.-born U.S. orchestral con-ductor.

Mary **Orme:** Mary Sargent Nichols, earlier Gove, née Neal (1810–1884), U.S. writer, health reformer.

Orris: Jean Ingelow (1820–1897), Eng. poet, novelist. The writer's pseudonym is a plant name, that of a type of iris.

Orry-Kelly: John Orry Kelly (1897–1964), Austral.-born U.S. movie costume designer.

Jiří **Orten:** Jiří Ohrenstein (1918–1941), Cz. poet.

Orwell: Walter Chalmers Smith (1824–1908), Sc. poet, preacher. The poet, who was a minis-ter of the Free Church of Scotland, took his name from the parish of Orwell, Kinross-shire, to which he was appointed in 1853.

George **Orwell:** Eric Arthur Blair (1903–1950), Eng. novelist, satirist. The writer first used his pen name for *Down and Out in Paris and London* (1933). He felt that Eric was too "Norse" and Blair too Scottish, and that a more suitable English name was one composed of the name of the patron saint of England and that of the river in Suffolk on whose banks he had lived. He also said that he wished to avoid embarrassing his parents, although friends felt that he was really trying to escape from his genteel middle-class background. Mixed motives, therefore, seem to have prompted him to take a new name.

The reviewer of a book on Rebecca West (*q.v.*) summarized the choice of name thus: "George Orwell—a commonplace Christian name and an English river—together name the plain-speaking Englishman that Eric Blair chose to be in his work" [Samuel Hynes, "In communion with reality," *Times Literary Supplement*, December 21, 1973]. Blair had initially considered other names, among them P.S. Burton, Kenneth Miles, and H. Lewis All-ways, and some sources, such as Peter Stansky and William Abrahams, in *Orwell: The Trans-formation* (1979), claim that Blair's publisher, Victor Gollancz, made the final choice of name. Richard Mayne, reviewing a later book on Orwell, and noting that he had a sense of humor, commented, "I've sometimes wondered whether he concealed a pun in his pen name: jaw-jaw well" [*Times Literary Supplement*, November 26, 1982].

Early in his writing career, Orwell was asked by a friend, novelist Anthony Powell, whether he had considered legally adopting his pseudonym. "Well, I have," he replied, "but then, of course, I'd have to *write* under another name if I did" [Goodman, p. 41].

Ozzy **Osbourne:** John Michael Osbourne (1948–), Br. rock musician. The name almost certainly arose as a nickname.

Henry **Oscar:** Henry Wale (1891–1969), Br. stage actor, director.

N. **Osinsky:** Valerian Valerianovich Obolen-sky (1887–1938), Russ. Communist official, economist.

Ossian Gwent: John Davies (1839–1892), Welsh poet. The poet's name means "Ossian of Gwent," from Ossian, the legendary Gaelic bard, and Gwent, the historic region (now county) in which he was born.

Juliusz **Osterwa:** Juliusz Maluszek (1885–1947), Pol. stage actor, director.

Aleksandr **Ostuzhev:** Aleksandr Alekseyevich Pozharov (1874–1953), Russ. stage actor. The actor appears to have chosen a name suggesting an opposite sense to the original: Russian *pozharit'* means "to burn," while *ostuzhat'* means "to cool."

Gilbert **O'Sullivan:** Raymond Edward O'Sullivan (1946–), Ir. pop musician. The musician originally intended to call himself simply "Gilbert," but his manager, Gordon Mills, who also produced the name of Engelbert Humperdinck (*q.v.*), suggested he keep his surname, no doubt seeking to retain the association with Gilbert and Sullivan, the comic operetta writers.

Seumas **O'Sullivan:** James Sullivan Starkey (1879–1958), Ir. poet, literary editor. "Seumas" is an Irish form of "James."

Richard **Oswald:** Richard Ornstein (1880–1963), Ger. movie director, producer.

Ossi **Oswalda:** Oswalda Sräglich (1897–1948), Ger. film actress. The actress adopted a pet form of her first name as her new first name and her original first name as her new surname.

La Belle **Otero:** Caroline Puentovalga (1868–1965), Sp. courtesan, dancer. The dancer's stage name ("The Beautiful Otero") apparently derives from her husband, an Italian tenor whom she married when she was 14.

James **Otis:** James Otis Kaler (1848–1912), U.S. writer of stories for boys.

Johnny **Otis:** John Veliotes (1921–), U.S. rhythm 'n' blues musician, of Gk. parentage.

Nikolay **Otrada:** Nikolay Karpovich Turochkin (1918–1940), Russ. poet. The poet's adopted surname means "joy," "delight." One of his first works was a collection of verse entitled *Happiness* (1939). Ironically, he was killed in World War II on the Finnish frontier.

Rudolf **Otreb:** Robert Fludd (1574–1634), Eng. Rosicrucian, philosopher, physician. A straightforward anagrammatic name, with a convincing first name but contrived surname.

Ouida: Marie Louise de la Ramée (1839–1908), Eng. novelist, of Eng.-Fr. parentage. The writer adopted her own childhood pronunciation of her name "Louise." The pseudonym happens to combine the words for "yes" in French and Russian.

Gérard **Oury:** Max-Gérard Houry Tannenbaum (1919–), Fr. movie actor, director.

Mosheh **Oved:** Edward Goodack (1885–1958), Pol.-born Br. antiquary, writer. The jeweller's name was the one by which he was known in London's Polish Jewish community. His original name was shortened by a London signwriter to Edward Good.

Owain **Alaw:** John Owen (1821–1883), Welsh singer, composer. The musician's adopted name

means "Owen of melody." Alaw is a forename in its own right.

Owain **Myvyr:** Owen Jones (1741–1814), Welsh antiquary. The writer took his name from his birthplace, the village of Llanfihangel Glyn Myfyr, Denbighshire (now Gwynedd). (The name is that of a small river.)

Ashford **Owen:** Anne Charlotte Ogle (1832–1918), Eng. novelist. The writer's pen name preserves her initials, if not her gender.

Bill **Owen:** William John Owen Rowbotham (1914–), Eng. stage, movie, TV comedian. Unusually, the actor adopted a new professional name only late in his career.

Seena **Owen:** Signe Auen (1894–1966), U.S. movie actress, of Dan. descent. A simplification of a Scandinavian name that many would wonder how to pronounce.

Sid **Owen:** David John Sutton (1972–), Eng. movie, TV actor.

Owen Rhoscomyl: Robert Scourfield Mills (1863–1919), Eng.-born Welsh adventurer, writer. The writer devised his pen name from the (genuine) Welsh first name Owen and the initial letters of his three original names. Later in life he adopted the name Arthur Owen Vaughan.

Jesse **Owens:** John (or James) Cleveland Owens (1913–1980), U.S. black athlete. The athlete's first name was created from his first two initials.

Rochelle **Owens:** Rochelle Bass (1936–), U.S. dramatist.

Elsie J. **Oxenham:** Elsie Jeanette Dunkerley (? –1960), Br. writer of stories for girls, daughter of John Oxenham (see below).

John **Oxenham:** William Arthur Dunkerley (1852–1941), Eng. poet, novelist.

Platon **Oyunsky:** Platon Alekseyevich Sleptsov (1893–1939), Russ. (Yakut) writer, politician. The writer based his name on a local word *oyun*, "wizard," "shaman," with direct reference to his own verse play *The Red Shaman* (1918). This concerned the "reforging" of one such cult leader. Shamans played a key role in Yakut society.

Amos **Oz:** Amos Klausner (1939–), Israeli writer, of Russ. parentage.

Frank **Oz:** Frank Richard Oznowicz (1944–), U.S. puppeteer, movie director.

Augustus **Pablo:** Horace Swaby (*c.*1954–), Jamaican reggae musician.

Pach-Pach: Pavel Maksimovich Yesikovsky (originally Yesikov) (1900–1961), Russ. circus artist, horseman, movie actor. The name is a reduplicated shortening of the performer's first two names. He would have been known as Pavel Maksimovich (pronounced "Pavel Maksimich") as a standard form of address and in rapid speech this would have been shortened even further.

Pacificus: Alexander Hamilton (1757–1804), U.S. statesman, lawyer ("King of the Feds").

Philo **Pacificus:** Noah Worcester (1758–1837), U.S. clergyman, editor, pacifist. The mock-classical name means "peacelover," and was used by Worcester for *A Solemn Review of the Custom of War* (1814) and other pacifist works.

Suzanne **Packer:** Suzanne Jackson (1962–), Br. black TV actress. The actress took her grandmother's maiden name as her professional name.

Anita **Page:** Anita Pomares (1910–), U.S. movie actress.

Annette **Page:** Annette Hynd, née Lees (1932–), Eng. ballet dancer. The dancer adopted her mother's maiden name as her stage name. Her husband is Ronald Hynd (*q.v.*).

Ashley **Page:** Ashley Laverty (1956–), Br. ballet dancer.

Emma **Page:** Honoria Tirbutt (*c.*1930–), Br. detective writer.

Gale **Page:** Sally Perkins Rutter (1911–1983), U.S. movie actress.

Geneviève **Page:** Geneviève Bonjean (1931–), Fr. stage, movie actress.

H. A. **Page:** Alexander Hay Japp (1837–1905), Sc. writer, publisher. This is one of several pseudonyms used by the writer, as an approximate reversal of his initials and surname. He also wrote as E. Conder Gray (*q.v.*), Benjamin Orme, A.F. Scot, and A.N. Mount Rose.

Larry **Page:** Leonard Davies (*c.*1938–), Eng. pop musician. The musician changed his name as a teenager in honor of the U.S. movie actor Larry Parks (1914–1975), star of *The Jolson Story*.

Marco **Page:** Harry Kurnitz (1909–1968), U.S. playwright, novelist, moviewriter.

Patti **Page:** Clara Ann Fowler (1927–), U.S. pop singer. It is possible the singer took her first name from the surname of Adelina Patti, the (Spanish-born) Italian operatic soprano who died in 1919. She was given her new surname by the Page Milk Company, a dairy in Tulsa, Oklahoma, when she appeared in a show that they sponsored, KTUL's *The Patti Page Show*.

Debra **Paget:** Debralee Griffin (1933–), U.S. movie actress.

Nicola **Pagett:** Nicola Mary Scott (1945–), Eng. TV actress. The actress was obliged to change her name on discovering that Nicola Scott, daughter of the conservationist Sir Peter Scott, was a stage manager at the Chichester Festival Theatre. She chose a family name instead.

Pagu: Patricia Galvão (1910–1962), Brazilian poet, novelist. The writer's pen name is based on the first syllables of her original names.

Elaine **Paige:** Elaine Bickerstaff (1951–), Eng. singer, actress.

Janis **Paige:** Donna Mae Tjaden (1922–), U.S. movie actress, singer. The actress took her new first name from the musical comedy star Elsie Janis (*q.v.*) and her surname from a grandparent.

Robert **Paige:** John Arthur Page (1910–1987), U.S. movie actor.

Teuvo **Pakkala:** Teodor Oskar Frosterus (1862–1925), Finn. writer. The writer adopted an equivalent of his original Swedish name, Finnish *pakkanen* meaning "frost." He also wrote as Taustan Kalle (Swedish *kall*, "cold").

Lucila **Palacios:** Mercedes Carvajal de Arocha (1902–), Venezuelan writer. The writer adopted her pen name in 1932.

Jack **Palance:** Walter (earlier Vladimir) Jack Palahnuik (1920–), U.S. movie actor, of Russ. parentage. The actor's original name is variously given, depending which source one consults. This seems as likely as any.

Madame **Palatine:** Elisabeth-Charlotte von der Pfalz (1652–1722), Fr. writer, of Ger. origin. French *Palatine* translates German *Pfalz*.

Aldo **Palazzeschi:** Aldo Giurlani (1885–1974), It. writer.

Peter **Palette:** Thomas Onwhyn (*fl.*1837–1886), Br. illustrator, cartoonist. The artist used this name, of obvious origin, for his etchings in an unauthorized edition of Dickens's *Nicholas Nickleby* published in 1838. He had earlier used the name Sam Weller for a similar edition of *Pickwick Papers*, the name being that of a leading character in this work.

Palinurus: Cyril Vernon Connolly (1903–1974), Br. literary critic, novelist. The writer used the name for *The Unquiet Grave* (1944), which he described as "a word-cycle in three or four rhythms: art, love, nature and religion." In classical mythology, Palinurus was the pilot of Aeneas's ship, famous for his fall from the ship into the sea. Connolly thought that Palinurus fell through the typically modern will to failure.

Andrea **Palladio:** Andrea di Pietro della Gondola (1508–1580), It. architect. The artist was named by his patron and tutor, the humanist poet and scholar Count Gian Giorgio Trissino. It was an allusion to the Greek goddess Pallas Athene and to a character in Trissino's own poem, "Italia liberata dai goti" ("Italy liberated from the Goths"). The name also aimed to indicate the hopes that Trissino had for his protégé.

Betsy **Palmer:** Patricia Brumek (1929–), U.S. movie actress, TV panelist.

Gregg **Palmer:** Palmer Lee (1927–), U.S. movie actor.

Lillie **Palmer:** Lillie Marie Peiser (1911–1986), Ger. movie actress.

Luciana **Paluzzi:** Luciana Paoluzzi (1937–), It. movie actress.

Hermes **Pan:** Hermes Panagiotopoulos (1910–1990), U.S. ballet dancer, choreographer, of U.S.-Gk. parentage. A name that is not only a necessary shortening of a lengthy surname, but that immediately evokes two Greek gods. In Greek mythology, Pan, the god of pastures, was actually the son of Hermes, herald and messenger of the gods.

Petro **Panch:** Pyotr Iosifovich Panchenko (1891–1978), Ukrainian writer.

Vijaya Lakshmi **Pandit:** Swarup Kumari Nehru (1900–1990), Ind. politician, diplomat. The political leader's new last name is that of her husband, Ranjit Sitaram Pandit, whom she married in 1921. At the same time, in accordance with Hindu custom, she changed the rest of her name to reflect her husband's clan.

Anton **Pann:** Antonie Pantoleon Petroveanu (1796–1854), Rom. poet, folklorist, composer.

Pansy: Isabella MacDonald Alden (1841–1930), U.S. children's magazine editor. The writer, noted for her sentimental religious fiction, used the name that had been given her as a pet name in childhood.

L. **Panteleyev:** Aleksey Ivanovich Yeremeyev (1908–), Russ. writer.

Pantycelyn: William Williams (1717–1791), Welsh hymnwriter. The writer adopted his name from that of a neighboring farm where his mother had lived before her marriage. The name itself means "holly valley."

Paul **Panzer:** Paul Wolfgang Panzerbeiter (1872–1958), Ger.-born U.S. movie actor.

Irene **Papas:** Irene Lelekou (1926–), Gk. movie actress. The actress's screen name is that of her first husband, Alkis Papas (married 1947, marriage dissolved 1951).

Papillon: Henri Charrière (1906–1973), Fr. criminal. The alleged murderer, author of the 1969 bestseller titled with his name, adopted the nickname given him for the design of a butterfly (French *papillon*) tattooed on his chest.

Joseph **Papp:** Yosl Papirofsky (1921–1991), U.S. theatrical producer, director.

Papus: Gérard Encausse (1865–1916), Fr. occultist writer. The practitioner took his name from the genius of medicine in Apollonius of Tyana's *Nuktemeron* ("Night and Day")(1st century AD).

Paracelsus: Philippus Aureolus Theophrastus Bombastus von Hohenheim (1493–1541), Swiss-Ger. physician, alchemist. The medical genius and philosopher regarded himself as superior to the famous 1st-century physician Celsus. He was therefore "beyond Celsus," or "para-Celsus." But at the same time his name may allude to his original surname (a placename), as both Latin *celsus* and German *hohen* mean "high," "lofty." Paracelsus appears to have fancied the *para-* prefix, and used it in the titles of his *Paramirum* and *Paragranum*.

Judith **Paris:** Judith Franklin (1944–), Br. stage, TV actress. The actress appears to have adopted the name of the fictional Judith Paris, a central character in the series of popular historical novels by Hugh Walpole, including *Judith Paris* (1931) itself.

Mica **Paris:** Michelle Warren (1969–), Br. black soul singer, of Caribbean parentage.

Harry **Parke:** Parkyakarkus (*q.v.*).

Cecil **Parker:** Cecil Schwabe (1897–1971), Br. movie actor.

Jean **Parker:** Lois Mae Greene, originally Luise-Stephanie Zelinska (1912–), U.S. movie actress. (The English surname Greene roughly equates to the Slavic surname Zelinska.)

John **Parker:** Jacob Solomons (1875–1952), U.S.-born Br. theatre historian, of Pol.-Welsh parentage. The founder and editor of *Who's Who in the Theatre* (1912), originally a shipping agent, changed his Jewish name on the advice of his mother. He legalized it in 1917.

Lew **Parker:** Austin Lewis Jacobs (1906–), U.S. stage actor.

Suzy **Parker:** Cecilia Parker (1933–), U.S. fashion model, movie actress.

"Colonel" Tom **Parker:** Andreas Cornelius van Kuijk (1909–1997), Du.-born U.S. music promoter. The promoter, famously Elvis Presley's manager, stowed away at the age of 16 and sailed for America, where he reinvented himself under his new name. His honorary title of "Colonel" was bestowed on him in 1948 by the governor of Louisiana.

Willard **Parker:** Worster van Eps (1912–), U.S. movie actor.

Norman **Parkinson:** Ronald William Parkinson Smith (1913–1990), Eng. society photographer ("Parks"). The photographer derived his name from the Norman Parkinson Portrait Studio that he set up with a colleague in 1934. The first name was that of the colleague, Norman Kibblewhite; the surname was his own third name. The business was short lived, but when it ended Parkinson continued to use the name himself.

Parkyakarkus: Harry Einstein (1904–1958), U.S. radio, movie comedian. Einstein originally worked as Harry Parke. Later, he expanded and embellished this surname to "Parkyakarkus." He reckoned this would be a name easily remembered by Americans, who would recognize it as an invitation to take a seat: "Park your carcass!" The comic's son was Albert Brooks (*q.v.*).

Peter **Parley:** (1) Samuel Griswold Goodrich (1793–1860), U.S. bookseller, writer of moral tales for children; (2) Thomas Tegg (1776–1845), Eng. bookseller, publisher; (3) George Mogridge (see **Old Humphrey**); (4) John Bennett (1865–1956), U.S. writer of books for boys; (5) William Martin (1801–1867), Eng. children's writer. A popular name for tellers of children's tales, as the name itself suggests. Goodrich was the first to use it, however, beginning with *The Tales of Peter Parley About America* (1827), which opens with the words, "Here I am! My name is Peter Parley! I am an old man. I am very gray and lame." It was then adopted by other writers on both sides of the Atlantic (first by Tegg in 1832 in England), which did not please its originator. Goodrich may have based the name itself on *Parley the Porter*, a moral tract by the English writer Hannah More, although according to his daughter he took it from French *parler*, "to talk."

Dita **Parlo:** Grethe Gerda Kornstadt (or Kornwald) (1906–1971), Ger. movie actress. If taken to be Italian, the romantic actress's name translates as "Fingers, I speak." Possibly this was the intended interpretation, referring to the eloquence of gestures made with the fingers?

Martine **Parmain:** Martine Hemmerdinger (1942–), Fr. ballet dancer. Although French *par main* happens to mean "by hand," appropriately enough for a ballerina, whose hands are as important as her feet, Hemmerdinger was born in the village of Parmain, north of Paris, and took her name from there.

Parmigianino: Girolamo Francesco Mazzola (1503–1540), It. painter, etcher. The artist takes his name from Parma, the city of his birth. (The word is strictly speaking the adjectival diminutive of the name, so equates to "little Parmesan.")

Kostas **Paroritis:** Leonidas Sureas (1878–1931), Gk. writer.

Gram **Parsons:** Cecil Ingram Connor (1946–1973), U.S. country rock musician. Connor's father died when he was only 13. His mother then married Robert Ellis Parsons, who shortened his stepson's middle name to "Gram" and provided him with a new surname at the same time.

Louella **Parsons:** Louella Rose Oettinger (1884–1972), U.S. movie columnist, actress.

Fidalma **Partenide:** Petronilla Paolini Massimi (1663–1726), It. poet. The poet assumed this classical-style name, suggesting Latin *fidelis*, "faithful," and Greek *partheneion*, "maiden song," for her pastoral verse.

Mrs. **Partington:** Benjamin Penhallow Shillaber (1814–1890), U.S. humorist. The humorist created this lady as a kind of Mrs. Malaprop for his *Life and Sayings of Mrs. Partington* (1854) and other books in which Mrs. Partington chats pleasantly yet ignorantly on a whole range of topics. There had been a real Mrs. Partington, it seems, who during a storm at Sidmouth, England (in 1824), had tried to brush back the sea with her mop. References to her abortive effort became legendary and metaphorical, so that the House of Lords had been compared to her in a speech (1831) attacking the body's opposition to the progress of reform. Shillaber admitted that he borrowed his own character from the English archetype. He first used her in 1847 for a newspaper on which he was employed.

Paschal II: Rainerius (? –1118), It. pope.

Jules **Pascin:** Julius Pincas (1885–1930), Bulg.-born Fr. painter. The painter adopted a more obviously French first name, then anagrammatized his surname likewise.

Teixeira de **Pascoaes:** Joaquim Pereira Teixeira de Vasconcelos (1877–1952), Port. writer.

La **Pasionaria:** Dolores Ibárruri (1895–1989), Sp. Communist leader, writer. The politician first used the name, literally "Passion Flower," when writing an anticlerical diatribe in the local Communist paper that was to appear in Passion Week. The name also implied her "impassioned" stance generally regarding social conditions and injustices. She herself was a miner's daughter.

Anthony **Pasquin:** John Williams (1761–1818), Eng. critic, satirist, working in U.S. The writer took the name from the statue called Pasquin in Rome. This was unearthed in 1501 as an incomplete Roman bust, and a habit became established of attaching satirical Latin verses to it on St. Mark's Day. From this practice came the term "pasquinade" to apply to any brief but anonymous satirical comment. It is not certain how the statue itself acquired its name. One theory is that it was named after a local shopkeeper whose premises were near the site where it was discovered.

Joe **Pass:** Joseph Anthony Jacobi Passalaqua (1929–1994), U.S. guitarist.

Passo: Pavel Alekseyevich Sokolov (1876–1947), Russ. conjurer. The illusionist also performed as Sokolov-Passo. His name represents syllables from his first and last names, but also suggests French *passe*, "pass," a word associated with card games and tricks, Sokolov's specialty.

George **Paston:** Emily Morse Symonds (*c.*1860–1936), Br. novelist, dramatist, cousin of the critic John Addington Symonds.

Tony **Pastor:** Antonio Pestritto (1907–1969), U.S. popular musician.

Wally **Patch:** Walter Vinnicombe (1888–1971), Eng. stage, movie comedian.

Jason **Patric:** Jason Patric Miller, Jr. (1966–), U.S. movie actor.

Gail **Patrick:** Margaret LaVelle Fitzpatrick (1911–1980), U.S. movie actress, TV producer.

John **Patrick:** John Patrick Goggan (1905–1995), U.S. playwright, screenwriter.

Nigel **Patrick:** Nigel Dennis Wemyss (1913–1981), Eng. stage actor, director.

Ted **Pauker:** George Robert Acworth Conquest (1917–), Eng. poet, editor, writer on Russia. This is the standard pen name of the British editor and writer Robert Conquest. Its exact origin is not clear, although *Pauker* is German for "kettle-drummer" and also has a slang sense "schoolteacher," "crammer." Conquest had some of his poems included under this name in *The New Oxford Book of Light Verse* (1978).

Shortly before his contribution, there appears in the book a selection of limericks by one Victor Gray. Gray is given the same birth year as Pauker (1917). A *Sunday Times* columnist, in an informal review of the book (June 4, 1978), pointed out that if you take the initials of Conquest's first three names and precede the name of the unknown rhymster by them you get G.R.A. Victory, otherwise an anagram of Victor Gray, with a victory of course being a conquest. This sleuthwork may not have pleased the venerable Oxford University Press.

Juozas **Paukštelis:** Juozas Ptasìnskas (1899–1981), Lithuanian writer.

Paul: Ray Hildebrand (1940–), U.S. pop singer, teaming with Paula (*q.v.*).

[St.] **Paul:** Saul (? –*c.*69), Christian theologian, missionary. When the disciple and missionary was still a Jew he was known by the name of Saul. After his dramatic conversion he took the Roman name Paul, which he used for preference as a proud Roman citizen. (His binominal state is alluded to in Acts 13:9: "Saul, also called Paul.") Why did Saul choose this particular name? In Hebrew "Saul" means "asked for"; in Latin "Paul" (Paulus) means "little," and as such was a standard Roman name. The meaning of the new name may perhaps have been significant in some way, possibly as a sign of humility, but Paul could have chosen it simply because it was close in sound to his previous name. It certainly marked a transition: both from Jew to Christian, and to Paul's new role as leader when Barnabas, formerly the leader, delegated it to him.

Paul II: Pietro Barbo (1417–1471), It. pope. A name adopted to avoid repeating that of St. Peter, leader of the apostles and first bishop of Rome. (Barbo was vain about his appearance, and toyed with the idea of calling himself Formosus II, this name meaning "handsome".)

Paul III: Alessandro Farnese (1468–1549), It. pope.

Paul IV: Gian Pietro Carafa (1476–1559), It. pope.

Paul V: Camillo Borghese (1552–1621), It. pope.

Paul VI: Giovanni Battista Montini (1897–1978), It. pope. The pontiff chose a name intended to suggest an "outgoing" approach, that of the great missionary St. Paul.

Andrew **Paul:** Paul Andrew Herman (1961–), Eng. movie, TV actor.

John **Paul:** Charles Henry Webb (1834–1905), U.S. journalist, editor.

Les **Paul:** Lester Polfuss (1915–), U.S. guitarist.

Paula: Jill Jackson (1942–), U.S. pop singer, teaming with Paul (*q.v.*). Paul and Paula originally teamed up to sing for a radio station's charity drive in Texas in the early 1960s, becoming a popular attraction with their matching sweaters embroidered with the letter "P."

Madame **Paulette:** Pauline de la Bruyère (1900–1984), Fr. hat designer.

Pav: Francis Minet (1913–), Eng. cartoonist, stained glass artist. The name may have arisen as a sort of esoteric pun or nickname on "pavan" and "minuet," both types of stately dance.

Marisa **Pavan:** Marisa Pierangeli (1932–), It. movie actress, working in U.S., sister of Pier Angeli (*q.v.*).

Pax: Mary Cholmondeley (1859–1925), Br. novelist.

Katina **Paxinou:** Katina Konstantinopolou (1900–1973), Gk. stage, movie actress, working in U.S.

Philip **Paxton:** Samuel Adams Hammett (1816–1865), U.S. humorist, writer of adventure stories.

Johnny **Paycheck:** Donald Eugene Lytle (1941–), U.S. country singer. The singer's name is popularly believed to pun on the name of his fellow country singer Johnny Cash (1932–). It is actually that of a heavyweight boxer knocked out by Joe Louis in 1940, and is moreover close to Paycheck's original Polish name.

Payrav: Atadzhan Sulaymoni (1899–1933), Tajik poet. The poet adopted a name meaning "faithful follower."

Olyona **Pchilka:** Olga Petrovna Kosach, née Dragomanova (1849–1930), Ukrainian writer. The writer's adopted name means "little bee," with Olyona a pet form of her first name Olga. She was the mother of Lesya Ukrainka (*q.v.*).

Minnie **Pearl:** Sarah Ophelia Colley Cannon (1912–1996), U.S. country singer, entertainer.

Drew **Pearson:** Andrew Russell (1897–1969), U.S. political columnist.

Pedrog: John Owen Williams (1853–1932), Welsh poet. The writer took his name from the village of Llanpedrog ("St. Petroc's church") where he was raised.

John **Peel:** John Robert Parker Ravenscroft (1939–), Eng. radio DJ. There may be an implicit pun here. One thinks of the well-known literary John Peel, the huntsman in the Victorian song by John Woodcock Graves ("D'ye ken John Peel with his coat so gray? D'ye ken John Peel at the break of the day?"), and one has it in mind that a DJ is a disc *jockey* (often "at the break of the day," too). As the song continues: "D'ye ken John Peel when he's far far away with his hounds and his horn in the morning?"

Jan **Peerce:** Jacob Pincus Perlemuth (1904–1984), U.S. opera singer.

Baby **Peggy** *see* **Baby Peggy**.

Pelé: Edson Arantes do Nascimento (1940–), Brazilian footballer. The player claimed that he never knew the origin of his "game name," and that it has no meaning in any language known to him. He was apparently nicknamed thus from the age of seven. He points out that it is easy to say in many languages [Pelé and Robert L. Fish, *My Life and the Beautiful Game*, 1977].

A. **Pen,** Esq.: John Leech (1817–1864), Eng. caricaturist.

Pencerdd Gwalia: John Thomas (1826–1913), Welsh harpist. The musician's name means "chief musician of Wales." Pencerdd has long been the title of an officer of the Bardic Order who is in the employ of the king. Thomas was himself appointed harpist to Queen Victoria in 1871 and played for many of the royal courts of Europe. Gwalia is a half-Latin, half-Welsh name for Wales.

Mike **Pender:** Michael Prendergast (1942–), Eng. pop musician.

Pendragon: Henry Sampson (1841–1891), Eng. newspaper proprietor, editor, sporting writer. Pendragon was the title given to an ancient British or Welsh chief, and meant literally "head dragon," the "dragon" being the war standard. Possibly Sampson used the name with an implied pun on "dragon with a pen."

Amabel **Penfeather:** Susan Fenimore Cooper (1813–1894), U.S. novelist, writer, daughter of novelist James Fenimore Cooper (1789–1851). The author used this name for her first novel, *Elinor Wyllys; or the Young Folk of Longbridge* (1845). The name itself suggests one writing a romantic tale, which was essentially true.

Dan **Penn:** Wallace Daniel Pennington (1941–), U.S. popular songwriter.

Joe **Penner:** Joe Pinter (1904–1941), Hung.-U.S. radio comedian, movie actor.

Dennis **Pennis:** Paul Kaye (1965–), Br. spoof celebrity TV interviewer. The name matches the supposedly American interviewer's nerdish persona, and evokes a blend of the cartoon character Dennis the Menace and something rather ruder.

Pennsylvania Farmer: John Dickinson (1732–1800), U.S. lawyer, political writer. The Philadelphia lawyer led the conservative group in the Pennsylvania legislature during the debates on proprietary government, and used the name for his *Letters from a Farmer in Pennsylvania* (1768), published in the *Pennsylvania Chronicle*. The letters criticized England's continuing assertion of its rights of taxation, saying that this was contrary to that country's own constitutional principles.

Richard **Penrose:** Richard James Jackson Pace (1941–), Br. psychiatrist. The specialist adopted his mother's maiden name by deed poll in 1968.

Hugh **Pentecost:** Judson Pentecost Philips (1903–1989), U.S. crime, mystery writer. Philips also wrote as Philip Owen.

Willie **Pep:** Gugliermo Papeleo (1922–), U.S. featherweight boxer. Better "Pep" (for vigor) than "Pap" (for softness), of course.

K.N. **Pepper:** James W. Morris (*fl.* 1858), U.S. journalist, humorist. The writer used this name for *The K.N. Pepper Papers* (1858), the name itself a fairly obvious pun on "cayenne pepper," implying pungency and wit.

Pip **Pepperpod:** Charles Warren Stoddard (1843–1909), U.S. traveler, poet.

Philemon **Perch:** Richard Malcolm Johnson (1822–1909), U.S. humorous writer, educator.

Percival: Julian Ralph (1853–1903), U.S. journalist.

Edward **Percy:** Edward Percy Smith (1891–1968), Br. playwright, novelist.

Florence **Percy:** Elizabeth Chase Allan, formerly Taylor, then Akers (1832–1911), U.S. poet, literary editor. The author used the name for the one poem for which she is now remembered, "Rock me to sleep, Mother" first printed in the *Saturday Evening Post* in 1860. Because of the pseudonym, the authorship was disputed, but Mrs. Akers (as she then was) successfully defended her claim.

Reuben **Percy:** Thomas Byerley (? –1826), Eng. writer, journalist. Together with Joseph Clinton Robertson (1788–1852), who adopted the name Sholto Percy, Byerley published the popular *Percy Anecdotes*, which appeared in 20 volumes from 1821 to 1823. The cover announced that the collection was by "Sholto and Reuben Percy, brothers of the Benedictine monastery of Mount Benger." The name actually came from the Percy coffee house in Rathbone Place, London, where the two men regularly met. Byerley also used the name Stephen Collet for another collection of miscellanies, *Relics of Literature* (1823).

Thomas **Percy:** Thomas Piercy (1729–1811), Eng. churchman, poet. The literary scholar, famous for his collection of ballads, sonnets, historical songs, and metrical romances entitled *Reliques of Ancient English Poetry* (popularly, "Percy's *Reliques*") (1765), was a selfmade man (with a selfmade name) who rose to be a bishop. The slight but subtle name change enabled him to claim descent from the aristocratic Percy family.

Essayist Alpha of the Plough (*q.v.*) wryly commented: "I have never thought so well of Bishop Percy ... since I discovered that his real name was Piercy, and that, being the son of a grocer, he knocked his 'i' out and went into the Church, in order to set up a claim to belong to the house of the Duke of Northumberland. He even put the Percy arms on his monument in Dromore Cathedral, and, not content with changing his own name, altered the maiden name of his wife from Gutteridge to Godriche. I am afaid Bishop Percy was a snob" ["On Being Called Thompson," *Leaves in the Wind*, 1920].

La **Peregrina:** Gertrudis Gómez de Avellaneda (1814–1873), Cuban-born Sp. playwright, poet. The writer adopted this name, meaning "The Pilgrim," for her early poems, collected in 1841.

Shimon **Peres:** Shimon Perski (1923–), Pol.-born Israeli politician.

Giovanni Battista **Pergolesi:** Giovanni Battista Draghi (1710–1736), It. composer. The composer was born in the family home at Jesi. When the family moved from Jesi to Pergola, however, they became known as the *Pergolesi*, the "Pergola people."

François **Périer:** François-Gabriel-Marie Pilu (1919–), Fr. stage, movie actor.

Carl **Perkins:** Carl Lee Perkings (1932–), U.S. country, rockabilly singer.

Eli **Perkins:** Melville de Lancey Landon (1839–1910), U.S. journalist, humorous lecturer.

Perley: Benjamin Perley Poore (1820–1897), U.S. journalist, author, biographer.

Barry **Perowne:** Philip Atkey (1908–1985), Eng. crime, adventure, mystery story writer. The author adopted his uncle's name as his pen name.

Gigi **Perreau:** Ghislaine Elizabeth Marie Thérèse Perreau-Saussine (1941–), U.S. movie actress, of Fr.-U.S. parentage, sister of Peter Miles (*q.v.*).

Lynne **Perrie:** Jean Dudley (1931–), Br. TV actress.

Jacques **Perrin:** Jacques Simonet (1941–), Fr. movie director, producer.

Edgar A. **Perry:** Edgar Allan Poe (1809–1849), U.S. poet, storywriter. This was the name under which the writer enlisted in the U.S. Army in 1827.

Lynne **Perry:** Jean Dudley (1931–), Eng. TV actress.

Margaret **Perry:** Margaret Hall Frueauff (1913–), U.S. stage actress, theatrical director. The actress took her mother's maiden name as her stage name.

Peregrine **Persic:** James Justinian Morier (1780–1849), Turk.-born Eng. traveler, writer. The writer used this name for his oriental tale *The Adventures of Hajji Baba of Ispahan* (1824). The name itself means "Persian pilgrim."

Camille **Pert:** Louise Hortense Grillet (1865–1952), Fr. romantic novelist.

Pietro **Perugino:** Pietro di Cristoforo Vannucci (1446–1523), It. painter. The artist was mainly active in the city of Perugia, near which he was born. Hence his name.

Leonid Solomonovich **Pervomaysky:** Ilya Shlyomovich Gurevich (1908–1973), Ukrainian writer. The writer's assumed name means "First of May." He was born on May 4.

Pesellino: Francesco di Stefano (*c*.1422–1457), It. painter. The painter was raised by his grandfather, Giuliano il Pesello, who was also a painter, and worked as his assistant until the old man's death in 1446. His name comes from him, with the diminutive *-ino* suffix implying "little."

Rose **Pesotta:** Rachelle Peisoty (1896–1965), Ukrainian-born U.S. labor organizer, autobiographer.

[St.] **Peter:** Simon (or Simeon) (? –*c*.65), Christian leader, pope. Peter was the first of the disciples to be called by Jesus, and his "primacy" was affirmed at Caesarea Philippi when, as Simon, son of Jonah, he acknowledged Jesus as "The Christ, the Son of the living God." It was then that he was given his new name, with Jesus saying to him, "Thou art Peter, and upon this rock I will build my church" (Matthew 16:18). The name is a play on words, for Greek *petros*, Latin *petrus*, and Aramaic (Christ's vernacular tongue) *képha* all mean "rock." The Aramaic word gave Peter's alternate name: "And when Jesus beheld him, he said, Thou art Simon, the son of Jona: thou shalt be called Cephas, which is by interpretation, A stone" (John 1:42). The popularity of the name Peter stems entirely from this origin.

Peter III: Karl Peter Ulrich [Herzog] von Holstein-Gottorp (1728–1762), Ger.-born Russ. emperor. The heir to the Russian throne was renamed in 1742 on being received into the Russian Orthodox Church. He was the grandson of Peter the Great, and already bore his name.

Peter Martyr: (1) Pietro Martire d'Anghiera (1457–1526), It. historian; (2) Pietro Martire Vermigli (1500–1562), It. ecclesiastic. Both men have come to be known by the English equivalent of their two first names. Vermigli's father had lost many children and had vowed to dedicate to the 13th-century St. Peter Martyr any that lived.

Bernadette **Peters:** Bernadette Lazzara (1948–), U.S. stage actress, singer, of It.-U.S. parentage. The actress changed her name at the age of ten.

Brock **Peters:** Brock Fisher (1927–), U.S. movie actor.

Elizabeth **Peters:** Barbara Mertz (1927–), U.S. mystery writer.

Ellis **Peters:** Edith Pargeter (1913–1995), Br. mystery writer. Pargeter published her first mystery novel in 1951 under her own name. For greater distinction, she subsequently devised her pen name: Ellis was the name of her brother, while Peters was an adaptation of Petra, the daughter of a close friend in Czechoslovakia [*The Times*, October 16, 1995].

Susan **Peters:** Suzanne Carnahan (1921–1952), U.S. movie actress.

Miska **Petersham:** Mihaly Petrezselyen (1888–1960), Hung.-born U.S. writer, illustrator of children's books. The artist collaborated with his U.S. wife, Maud Petersham, née Fuller (1889–1971).

Ivailo **Petrov:** Prodan Kyuchukov (1923–), Bulg. writer.

Ivan **Petrov:** Ivan Ivanovich Krause (1920–), Russ. opera singer.

Valeri **Petrov:** Valeri Nisim Mevorakh (1920–), Bulg. screenwriter, poet.

Ye. **Petrov:** Yevgeny Petrovich Katayev (1903–1942), Russ. satirical writer, teaming with I. Ilf (*q.v.*).

Olga **Petrova:** Muriel Harding (1886–1977), Eng. movie actress, working in U.S.

Ludmila **Petrowa:** Ludmila Petrovna Nacheyeva (1942–), Russ. ballet dancer, teacher, working in Austria. The dancer dropped her surname for professional purposes, then modified her patronymic (Petrovna) to resemble a surname, with a westernized spelling ("w" for "v").

Gypsy **Petulengro:** ? (? –1957), Br. herbalist, broadcaster. The identity of the "gypsy king," as he came to be called, is still uncertain. His childhood was spent in Hungary and Romania, and it is possible he was born there. He himself claimed to be the grandson of the English gypsy Ambrose Smith (1804–1878), fictionalized as Jasper Petulengro in George Borrow's novels *Lavengro* (1851) and its sequel *The Romany Rye* (1857). He spent some time in America, where he sold herbal remedies under the name Professor Thompson-Thompson. The name Petulengro itself means "shoesmith," "farrier."

K.M. **Peyton:** Kathleen Wendy Peyton (1929–), Eng. children's writer. There is more to this name than meets the eye. When the writer was only 15, she completed her first novel, *Sabre, the Horse from the Sea*, which was published four years later under her true maiden name of Kathleen Herald. By then she was studying at Manchester Art School, where she eloped with a fellow student, Michael Peyton. They began producing "potboiler" adventure stories together for a Boy Scout magazine, and these were published under the name of K. and M. Peyton. Three of the stories were subsequently published in book form, and their publisher, Collins, did not want two authors' names on the title page, so they were stated to be by K.M. Peyton.

Carlos **Pezoa Véliz:** Carlos Moyano Yaña (1879–1908), Chilean poet.

Phelix: Hugh Burnett (1924–), Eng. TV producer, cartoonist, writer. The artist adopted this name for his work as a freelance cartoonist.

Phiber Optik: Marke Abene (1972–), U.S. computer hacker. The telephone and computer technician took a (respelled) self-descriptive name. Fiber optics play a key role in telecommunications.

Jacob **Philadelphia:** Jacob Meyer (1721–*c.*1800), U.S. conjuror, of Pol. Jewish parentage.

Alazonomastix **Philalethes:** [Dr.] Henry More (1614–1687), Eng. philosopher. More used this mock-Greek name, meaning "impostor Philalethes," for an attack on the alchemical work

Anthroposophia Theomagica by Eugenius Philalethes (see next entry below).

Eugenius **Philalethes:** Thomas Vaughan (1622–1666), Eng. alchemist. The mock-Greek name literally means "noble-born truth-lover," and was used by Vaughan for the majority of his works. The name should not be confused with that of Eireneaus Philalethes, another 17th-century alchemist of uncertain identity. His own name means "peaceful truth-lover." Carty (see Bibliography, p. 400) lists no less than 33 different writers calling themselves Philalethes, as well as four Philalethes Cantabrigiensis (from Cambridge) and various writers Phileleutharus followed by an identifying Latin placename (Dubliniensis, Londoniensis, Norfolciensis and the like). See Phileleutharus Norfolcienses (below).

Kim **Philby:** Harold Adrian Russell Philby (1912–1988), Br. intelligence officer, Soviet spy. Philby was born in India as the son of an English officer of the Indian Civil Service. "Kim" was a childhood nickname, alluding to the boy hero of Rudyard Kipling's *Kim* (1901).

Phileleutharus Norfolciensis: [Dr.] Samuel Parr (1747–1825), Eng. pedagogue, classical scholar. Most of Parr's works were virtually unreadable even in his own time, let alone today. But this is just one of the typical, pompous, classical pseudonyms that he used, in this instance for a *Discourse on the Late Fast* (1781), in which the theme (or one of them) is the American Revolution. The name itself is part-Greek, part-Latin, and means "Norfolk freedom-lover." At the time of writing, Parr was a curate in Norwich. For a later work, published in 1809, he was Philopatris Varvicensis, otherwise "Warwick country-lover."

Philenia: Sarah Wentworth Morton, née Apthorp (1759–1846), U.S. novelist, poet. Mrs. Morton used the full pen name "Philenia, a Lady of Boston" for *Ouâbi; or, The Virtues of Nature* (1790), a tale in four cantos celebrating the Native American as "noble savage," as well as other, similar works. The name Philenia is clearly based on the Greek root element *phil-*, meaning "fond of," "loving," with apparently an arbitrary ending.

François-André **Philidor:** François-André Danican (1726–1795), Fr. composer, chessplayer. Both François-André and his father André took their name from the sobriquet, Philidor, originally given to an ancestor, Michel Danican (died *c.*1659), by Louis XIII as a compliment to his

musical skill. The name itself was that of Fili-
dori, a famous Italian oboist. As a name in its
own right, Philidor can be apropriately understood to mean "fond of giving," "bountiful."

King Philip: Metacom (*c.*1638–1676), Native
American chief. The leader of the worst Indian
war in New England history was so named by
English colonists. The conflict itself thus came
to be known as King Philip's War (1675–76).

Philippe: Jacques Talon (1802–1878), Fr.
magician.

Conrad **Phillips:** Conrad Philip Havord
(1925–), Eng. movie, TV actor.

Esther **Phillips:** Esther May Jones (1935–
1984), U.S. black rhythm 'n' blues singer. The
singer's career began in 1949, at age 13, when
she won a talent contest in Los Angeles, singing
under the name Little Esther. She was then out
of show business for much of the 1950s, and on
resuming her career in the early 1960s was too
old to continue as Little Esther. She thus needed
a new name, and is said to have picked it after
noticing a Phillips 66 gasoline billboard at a gas
station.

John **Phillips:** William John Vassall (1920–
1996), Eng. Soviet spy. The former British
Embassy official was convicted of espionage in
1962 and adopted this unremarkable name on
his release from jail ten years later.

Lou Diamond **Phillips:** Lou Upchurch
(1962–), U.S. movie actor.

Rog **Phillips:** Roger Phillips Graham (1909–
1965), U.S. SF writer.

René **Philombe:** Philippe-Louis Ombede
(1930–), Cameroonian writer.

Philomela: Elizabeth Rowe, née Singer
(1674–1737), Eng. writer, poet. Mrs. Rowe used
this name for a collection of verse published in
1696, *Poems on Several Occasions, by Philomela*.
The name is not exactly original, and derives
from the Philomela of classical mythology, who
was the daughter of Pandion, king of Athens.
But at least it is appropriate enough for a poet,
both because (in the story) Philomela was
changed into a nightingale, which sings sweetly,
and because it literally means "sweet song." In
this case it also nicely accords with the writer's
maiden name.

Phiz: Hablot Knight Browne (1815–1882),
Eng. painter, illustrator, cartoonist. The artist
originally used the name Nemo (Latin for
"nobody") to illustrate some plates for Dickens's
Pickwick Papers (1836). Later, he chose a name

designed to match Dickens's own pseudonym,
Boz (*q.v.*). At the same time, "phiz" is (or was)
a colloquial word meaning "face" ("physiog-
nomy"), so is suitable in its own right for one
who draws portraits and concentrates on facial
expressions. Phiz's son was A. Nobody (*q.v.*).

John **Phoenix:** George Horatio Derby (1823–
1861), U.S. humorous writer, satirist.

Pat **Phoenix:** Patricia Pilkington (1923–
1986), Ir.-born Br. TV actress. The actress who
became familiar to millions as the blowzy Elsie
Tanner in British TV's longest running soap
opera, *Coronation Street*, originally acted under
her own name, Pat Pilkington. (She was actually
the illegitimate daughter of a man named
Mansfield, who claimed to have been married to
her mother for 16 years while remaining the husband of his first wife, whom he had never
divorced. Later, Pat's mother married Richard
Pilkington.)

In 1955, the actress temporarily changed her
name from Pilkington to Dean so as not to
embarrass family and friends when she appeared
in the lead role in the sex crime play *A Girl
Called Sadie* that year, at the same time dyeing
her hair blonde to complete the physical disguise. She later fell on hard times, and even
attempted suicide. But she felt that a change of
name might change her fortune, and as she later
recounted, "Pat Pilkington did, after all,
officially die in London. I changed my name to
Phoenix. I took the new name from the book I
was reading, Marguerite Steen's *Phoenix Rising*"
[*TV Times*, November 1–7, 1986]. And this did
seem to help, for she began to get small parts in
movies and stage shows from then on, rising
slowly but surely phoenix-like from her days of
depression and hunger in her basement apart-
ment in London.

River **Phoenix:** River Jude Dunetz (1970–
1993), U.S. movie actor. The actor's hippie parents, Arlyn and John, changed their surname in
1977 to mark a new beginning on settling in
Florida. River was their firstborn. Subsequent
children had similar names: Rain Joan of Arc
(later Rainbow), Leaf Joaquin Raphael (later
Leaf), Libertad Mariposa (later Liberty Butterfly,
or Liberty), Summer Joy (or Summer).

Phranc: Susan Gottlieb (*c.*1958–), U.S. folk
singer. The singer changed her name symbolically (in sense and spelling) when she came out
as a lesbian at the age of 17, at the same time
leaving home, dropping out of high school and

cutting off her waist-length hair. For a time she was involved in punk rock, but later progressed to a gentler and more meaningful role as a folksinger, although retaining the name Phranc.

Duncan Phyfe: Duncan Fife (1768–1854), Sc.-born U.S. furniture designer. The cabinetmaker changed the spelling of his name in about 1793, a year after moving to New York.

Edith Piaf: Edith Giovanna Gassion (1915–1963), Fr. singer, entertainer. The singer was given her stage name in 1935 by the Paris nightclub owner Louis Leplée. After an audition one day, he asked her her name. When she told him (all three real names) he protested that a name like that was not a show business name: "'The name is very important. What's your real name again?' 'Edith Gassion, but when I sing I call myself Huguette Elias.' He swept these names aside with a wave of his hand. ... 'Well, *mon petit*, I've got a name for you—*la môme Piaf* [The Little Sparrow].' We weren't wild about *la môme Piaf*, it didn't sound very artistic. That evening, Edith asked [her half-sister], 'Do you like *la môme Piaf*?' 'Not much.' Then she started to think. 'You know, Momone, *la môme Piaf* doesn't sound all that bad. I think Piaf has style. It's cute, it's musical, it's gay, it's like spring, it's like us. That Leplée isn't so dumb after all.'" [Simone Berteaut, translated by Ghislaine Boulanger, *Piaf*, 1970].

Thus the small, birdlike singer, with her peaked face and half-starved look, became the "little sparrow of Paris." (The author of the biography quoted above is the half-sister mentioned in the passage itself.) The singer adopted the name Edith in memory of Edith Cavell (1865–1915), the British nurse shot by the Germans for harboring allied soldiers and helping them escape. Piaf was born in the year of her death.

Piano Red: William Lee Perryman (1911–1985), U.S. popular pianist. The pianist apparently took his name from his elder brother, blues musician Rufus "Speckled Red" Perryman (1892–1973), with "Piano" differentiating and distinguishing him.

Alfred Piccaver: Alfred Peckover (1884–1958), Br. opera singer.

Slim Pickens: Louis Bert Lindley, Jr. (1919–1983), U.S. movie actor. The name suggests "slim pickings."

Jack Pickford: Jack Smith (1896–1933), Can. movie actor, brother of Mary Pickford (*q.v.*).

Mary Pickford: Gladys Mary Smith (1893–1979), Can.-born U.S. movie actress ("America's Sweetheart"). Gladys Smith's name was changed by Broadway producer David Belasco, with the actress adopting a family name that was more distinctive than plain "Smith." The Canadian-born U.S. movie actress also born Gladys Smith (1921–1993) changed her first name to Alexis.

Pickle: Alastair Ruadh Macdonell (*c*.1725–1761), Sc. spy. The secret agent used this name for his communications with the government on the activities of Prince Charles Edward Stuart ("The Young Pretender") and the Jacobites. He is usually known as "Pickle the Spy," as in the title of Andrew Lang's book (1897) about him.

Peregrine Pickle: George Putnam Upton (1834–1919), U.S. journalist, music critic. The writer adopted the name of the eponymous hero of Tobias Smollett's *Adventures of Peregrine Pickle* (1751).

Pictor Ignotus: William Blake (1757–1827), Eng. artist, poet, mystic. The name is Latin for "Painter Unknown," used on paintings that cannot be confidently attributed to a particular artist. Blake used it occasionally, just as the Anglo-American etcher Joseph Pennell (1857–1926) later used the initials "A.U." ("Artist Unknown").

De De Pierce: Joseph De Lacrois (1904–1973), U.S. jazz musician.

Piero di Cosimo: Piero di Lorenzo (1462–1521), It. painter. The artist took his name from his master, Cosimo Rosselli, whom he assisted in work on certain frescoes in the Sistine Chapel (1481).

Abbé Pierre: Henri Antoine Grouès (1912–), Fr. priest, Resistance fighter.

Pietro da Cortona: Pietro Berrettini (1596–1669), It. painter, architect. The artist adopted the name of his birthtown, Cortona, northwest of Perugia, central Italy.

Pigault-Lebrun: Charles-Antoine-Guillaume Pigault de l'épinoy (1753–1835), Fr. playwright, novelist.

Alexandra Pigg: Sandra McKibbin (1963–), Eng. TV actress. The actress's screen name presumably originated as a nickname (punning on her surname).

Pigpen: Ronald McKernan (1946–1973), U.S. rock musician. The name arose as a nickname, alluding to the singer's gross and untidy habits. (Britons usually call a pigpen a "pigsty.")

Morton **Pike:** David Harold Parry (1868–1950), Eng. writer of boys' stories, military articles.

Robert L. **Pike:** Robert Lloyd Fish (1912–1981), U.S. crime writer.

Nova **Pilbeam:** Margery Pilbeam (1919–), Br. movie actress. The actress had the same first name as her mother, so changed it to Nova, for her mother's family associations with Nova Scotia. It is also, of course, a "new" name in the literal sense.

David **Pilgrim:** John Leslie Palmer (1895–1944), Br. thriller writer + Hilary Aidan St. George Saunders (1895–1951), Br. thriller writer. A particular sort of pilgrim is a "palmer," who has been to the Holy Land and returns bearing a palm branch. Hence the punning name. The two men also wrote jointly as Francis Beeding (*q.v.*).

Boris **Pilnyak:** Boris Andreyevich Vogau (1894–1937), Russ. writer, of Volga Ger.-Russ. parentage. The name appears to be based on Russian dialect *pil'nyy*, "diligent."

Pimen: Sergey Mikhaylovich Izvekov (1910–1990), Russ. churchman, patriarch of Moscow and All Russia. The head of the Russian Orthodox Church adopted his religious name on taking monastic vows in 1927. The name itself comes from Greek *poimen*, "shepherd," "pastor."

Paul **Pindar:** John Yonge Akerman (1806–1873), Eng. antiquary, numismatist. The scholar presumably adopted a pen name based on that of Peter Pindar (*q.v.*). There were others of the same name.

Peter **Pindar:** (1) John Wolcot (1738–1819), Eng. satirical verse writer; (2) C.F. Lawler (1728–1819), Eng. writer. The name was adopted by more than one writer, but notably by Wolcot. Pindar was a Greek lyric poet of the 4th century B.C., and in his first book, *Lyric Odes to the Royal Academicians for 1782*, Wolcot described himself as "a distant relation to the poet of Thebes." Most of the other Peter Pindars were imitators of Wolcot, some very palely so. Lawler clearly hoped to be taken as the original: "A poetaster of little or no art unwarrantably assumed this name, merely to deceive the public and to bring profit to the writer and his bookseller" [*Biographical Dictionary*, 1816].

Theodore **Pine:** Emil Pataja (1915–), U.S. SF writer.

[Sir] Arthur Wing **Pinero:** Arthur Wing Pinheiro (1855–1934), Br. dramatist, stage actor, of Port. Jewish descent.

Harold **Pinter:** Harold da Pinta (1930–), Br. dramatist, stage actor.

Pinturicchio: Bernardino di Bette di Biago (1454–1513), It. painter. The painter's name arose as a nickname, meaning "little painter," referring to his small stature. It is also spelled Pintoricchio.

Padre **Pio:** Francesco Forgione (1887–1968), It. stigmatic friar, spiritual healer. The future priest entered a Franciscan friary at the age of 16 and took the religious name of the father provincial, Pio da Benevento.

Jacki **Piper:** Jacki Crump (1948–), Eng. movie, TV actress.

Jeems **Pipes of Pipesville:** Stephen G. Massett (1820–1898), U.S. author.

Pisanello: Antonio Pisano (*c*.1395–*c*.1455), It. painter. The artist's name is a diminutive of his original name, itself indicating that his family came from Pisa. He himself spent his early years in Verona and was associated with that city for most of the rest of his life.

Nikolaas **Piscator:** Nikolaas Johannes Visscher (*c*.1586–1652), Du. publisher, engraver. The publisher translated his name, meaning "fisherman," into Latin, as was the custom in his day.

Marie-France **Pisier:** Claudia Chauchat (1944–), Fr. movie actress.

Pistocchio: Francesco Antonio Mamiliano Pistocchi (1659–1726), It. male soprano singer. The singer's name arose as an emotive nickname formed from his surname.

Pitcher: Arthur Morris Binstead (1861–1914), Eng. humorist, sporting writer. The name presumably alludes to someone who sets out his pitch, or who "pitches" (throws out) his offerings. Or possibly it relates to a pitcher (jug) and its mixed contents. The writer was founder and editor of the gossip magazine *Town Topics*.

Molly **Pitcher:** Mary McCauly (*c*.1753–1832), U.S. battle heroine. The intrepid woman was so nicknamed because she carried a pitcher of water back and forth to the weary and wounded American soldiers at the Battle of Monmouth (June 28, 1778), having accompanied her first husband, William Hays, a gunner in a Pennsylvania artillery regiment. Her real original name is uncertain. That given above is of her second husband, John McCauly, whom she married in 1793.

Ingrid **Pitt:** Ingoushka Petrova (1944–), Pol. movie actress, of Russ. parentage, working in U.K.

Augustus Henry **Pitt-Rivers:** Augustus Henry Lane Fox (1827–1900), Eng. soldier, archaeologist. The soldier and scholar was known by his father's name of Fox until 1880, when he eventually inherited the estates of his greatuncle, George Pitt, 2d Baron Rivers, and assumed his name (and title).

ZaSu **Pitts:** Eliza Susan Pitts (1898–1963), U.S. movie, stage actress. The actress's original name is frequently given thus, but biographical sources suggest she had her unusual name from the first. It was formed from syllables of the first names of her father's sisters (not her own sisters, as also found), Eliza and Susan.

Pius II: Enea Silvio Piccolomini (or Aeneas Silvius) (1405–1464), It. pope. The pontiff chose the name Pius in memory of Virgil's *pius Aeneas*, "dutiful Aeneas."

Pius III: Francesco Todeschini Piccolomini (*c.*1440–1503), It. pope. The pontiff was the nephew of Pius II (above), and took his name.

Pius IV: Giovanni Angelo de' Medici (1499–1565), It. pope.

[St.] **Pius V:** Antonio Michele Ghislieri (1504–1572), It. pope.

Pius VI: Giovanni Angelo Braschi (1717–1799), It. pope.

Pius VII: Gregorio Luigi Barnaba Chiaramonte (1742–1823), It. pope.

Pius VIII: Francesco Saverio Castiglione (1761–1830), It. pope. The pontiff took the name of Pius VII (above), whom he regarded as his exemplar.

Pius IX: Giovanni Maria Mastai-Ferretti (1792–1878), It. pope. *Pio Nono*, as he is mellifluously known in Italy, took his name in memory of Pius VII (above), who had been his friend and who, like him, had been bishop of Imola.

[St.] **Pius X:** Giuseppe Melchiorre Sarto (1835–1914), It. pope.

Pius XI: Ambrogio Damiano Achille Ratti (1857–1939), It. pope.

Pius XII: Eugenio Maria Giuseppe Giovanni Pacelli (1876–1958), It. pope.

Benjamin **Place:** Edward Thring (1821–1887), Eng. schoolmaster, educationist. The school teacher, famous as the headmaster of Uppingham School, used this pen name for one of his early works, *Thoughts on Life Science* (1869). He took it from the name of the house, Ben Place, Grasmere, in the Lake District, where he went for his summer vacations and where he wrote much of the book.

Plácido: Gabriel de la Concepción Valdés (1809–1844), Cuban poet. The poet adopted a name meaning "mild," "placid."

Jean **Plaidy:** Eleanor Alice Hibbert, née Burford (1906–1993), Br. novelist, mystery writer. The prolific writer used a range of pseudonyms for her different genres of historical, romantic, and "Gothic" novels. Her best known is the one given here. Plaidy is the name of a beach in Cornwall, where she lived, while she liked Jean for its brevity. Other names were Victoria Holt, Philippa Carr, Ellalice Tate, Elbur Ford, and Kathleen Kellow. (The third and fourth of these have their genesis in her original name.)

Andrey **Platonov:** Andrey Platonovich Klimentov (1899–1951), Russ. writer.

Yuliya **Platonova:** Yuliya Fyodorovna Tvaneva, née Garder (1841–1892), Russ. opera singer.

Martha **Plimpton:** Martha Carradine (1971–), U.S. movie actress.

Jacquest **Plowert:** Paul Adam (1862–1920), Fr. novelist. The pen name was only an occasional one, and was used by the writer in particular for his *Petit Glossaire pour servir à l'intelligence des auteurs décadents et symbolistes* (1888).

Vilis **Plūdonis:** Vilis Janovic Lejnieks (1874–1940), Latvian poet.

James **Plunkett:** James Plunkett Kelly (1920–), Ir. novelist, short story writer.

Pocahontas: Matoaka (? 1595–1617), Native American princess. Matoaka, famous for allegedly saving the life of the English colonist John Smith, was nicknamed Pocahontas, "sportive," and assumed this name on her marriage (in 1614) to the Englishman John Rolfe. Little might have been heard of her had she not gone with him to England in 1616, where she died the following year of smallpox. She had been converted to Christianity in 1612 and renamed Lady Rebecca. Hence the entry in the parish register of St. George's Church, Gravesend, the town where she died, which reads: "1616, May 2j, Rebecca Wrothe, wyff of Thomas Wroth, gent., a Virginia lady borne, here was buried in ye chauncell" [*Dictionary of National Biography*].

William **Poel:** William Pole (1852–1934), Br. stage actor, director. The actor respelled his surname when his father, an engineer and musician, disapproved of his chosen profession.

Nikolay **Pogodin:** Nikolay Fyodorovich Stukalov (1900–1962), Russ. playwright, screenwriter.

Antony **Pogorelsky:** Aleksey Alekseyevich Perovsky (1787–1836), Russ. writer. The writer, the illegitimate son of Count Razumovsky, based his name on that of his estate, Pogoreltsy.

Robert **Pointon:** Daphne Rooke (1914–), S.A. novelist. The writer used this male name for her first novel, *The Sea Hath Bounds*, published in 1946. Four years later it was reissued under her real name with the title *A Grove of Fever Trees*.

Polaire: Emilie-Marie Bouchard, née Zouzé (1877–1939), Algerian-born Fr. actress, singer.

Lou **Polan:** Lou Polansky (1904–), U.S. stage director.

Yan **Poldi:** Ivan Konstantinovich Podrezov (1889–1913), Russ. circus artist, trick cyclist. The name Poldi was originally used for a group of acrobatic cyclists formed by Podrezov in 1909. He was killed performing one of his acts.

Boris **Polevoy:** Boris Nikolayevich Kampov (1908–1981), Russ. novelist, journalist. The writer's original name, Kampov, was changed by the editor of the newspaper *Tverskaya Pravda*, in which he had had an article published (using the name B. Ovod) as a 14-year-old schoolboy. The editor regarded Kampov as too "Latin," so he russianized it as Polevoy, i.e. translated Latin *campus* "field," by the adjectival form of Russian *pole* with the same meaning.

Poliarchus: [Sir] Charles Cotterell (1615– ? 1687), Eng. politician, courtier. The courtier used this name, meaning "ruler of many," for his correspondence with Orinda (*q.v.*).

Polidor: Ferdinando Guillaume (1887–1977), Fr. movie comedian, stage clown. The performer's stage and screen name means "many-gifted," "multitalented."

Polin: Pierre-Paul Marsalès (1863–1927), Fr. music hall artist, stage actor.

Politian: Angelo Poliziano (*q.v.*).

Kosmas **Politis:** Paris Taveloudis (1888–1974), Gk. novelist. The writer's name seems to suggest "cosmopolitan," literally "citizen of the world."

Angelo **Poliziano:** Angelo Ambrogini (1454–1494), It. poet, scholar. The poet is often known in English as Politian.

Antonio **Pollaiuolo:** Antonio di Jacopo d'Antonio Benci (1433–1498), It. painter, sculptor, engraver. The name was borne by both Antonio and his elder brother Piero (1443–1496), who worked together as artists, and is said to derive from Italian *pollaio*, "hen coop," since their father is supposed to have been a poulterer.

Records indicate, however, that he was probably a goldsmith.

Harry "Snub" **Pollard:** Harold Fraser (1886–1962), Austral. movie comedian, working in U.S.

Michael J. **Pollard:** Michael J. Pollack (1939–), U.S. movie actor.

Vyacheslav **Polonsky:** Vyacheslav Pavlovich Gusin (1886–1932), Russ. critic, journalist, historian. The writer adopted the name of the poet Yakov Petrovich Polonsky (1819–1898), with whom he felt he had an affinity.

Dimitr **Polyanov:** Dimitr Ivanov Popov (1876–1953), Bulg. poet.

Pomare IV: Aimata (1813–1877), Tahitian queen. The original bearer of the dynastic name was King Pomare I (reigned 1797–1803), originally Vairaatoa. The name itself means "night of the cough," from Tahitian *po*, "night," and *mare*, "cough." The king was seized by a coughing fit one night when waging war. It was ladies in the court of Queen Pomare IV who gave the name of the French writer Pierre Loti (*q.v.*).

Jay **Pomeroy:** Joseph Pomeranz (1895–1955), Russ.-born Br. theatrical director. Pomeranz went to England in 1915 and became a naturalized British subject in 1929. The name change is more subtle than it appears, since Pomeranz comes from a word meaning "orange," while Pomeroy derives from a source meaning "apple."

Aleksandr **Pomorsky:** Aleksandr Nikolayevich Linovsky (1891–1977), Russ. poet. At the start of his career the writer lived on the coast near St. Petersburg. Hence his name, meaning "coast dweller" (Russian *pomor*). (English *Pomeranian* is related.)

Doc **Pomus:** Jerome Solon Felder (1925–1991), U.S. lyricist.

Rosa **Ponselle:** Rosa Ponzillo (1897–1981), U.S. opera singer.

Pont: Graham Graham Laidler (1908–1940), Br. cartoonist. The artist originally intended to take up a career as an architect, and to this end adopted the name Pontifex Maximus, literally "great bridge-builder," the title of the Roman pontiff or president, which was already a family nickname for him after he had paid an early visit to Italy. This later became shortened to "Pont," a name familiar to readers of *Punch*, where his cartoons appeared. He did not thus adopt his name from London's Pont Street, as has been sometimes suggested [R.G.G. Price, *A History of Punch*, 1957].

Pontormo: Jacopo Carucci (1494–1557), It. painter. The artist took his name from his birthplace, the village of Pontormo, near Empoli, west of Florence.

Poor Richard: Benjamin Franklin (1709–1790), U.S. statesman, philosopher. Franklin was the author and publisher of *Poor Richard's Almanack* (1733–58), the most famous of the American almanacs, although he signed the prefaces as "Richard Saunders." The name was almost certainly based on that of the English *Poor Robin's Almanack* (see next entry below), especially as Richard Saunders was the name of the English editor of *Apollo Anglicanus*.

Poor Robin: (?) William Winstanley (? 1628–1698), Eng. compiler. The precise identity of the author of the various works by "Poor Robin," especially the almanacs published in England from about 1663, is uncertain. William Winstanley seems the most likely candidate, although others support his brother, Robert Winstanley, possibly simply through the similarity between the names Robert and Robin. Othes again suggest that the actual author was the poet Robert Herrick. Either way, the title almost certainly inspired the name of its American equivalent, *Poor Richard's Almanack* (see entry above).

Iggy Pop: James Newell Osterberg, Jr. (1947–), U.S. rock musician. Osterberg adopted the name "Iggy" from an early group, The Iguanas. In 1965 he left the group and joined the Prime Movers. That same year he adopted the name Iggy Pop, taking the second word from a local junkie, Jim Popp.

Faith Popcorn: Faith Plotkin (1948–), U.S. businesswoman. The cultural trend watcher explains how she came by her name: "I was born Faith Plotkin but in my first job my boss called me Popcorn and it stuck. I made up a story that when my great-grandfather came from Italy with the name Corne, he was so old that everyone called him Papa and that's where Poppacorne came from. The truth is that my nickname felt so much more me. I changed my name legally to Popcorn" [*Sunday Times Magazine*, February 13, 1994].

Popski: Vladimir Peniakoff (1897–1951), Belg. military commander, of Russ. parentage. The name was a cover name used for military intelligence work in World War II. Peniakoff published an account of this work in *Popski's Private Army* (1950), and this publicized the name. It was in fact in use before the war for a cartoon character, a little Russian with a beard holding a bomb, created by Low (*q.v.*) in the London *Evening Standard*.

Lasgush **Poradeci:** Lazar Gusho (1899–1985), Albanian poet.

Peter **Porcupine:** William Cobbett (1763–1835), Eng. journalist, politician. The writer used this name for *The Life and Adventures of Peter Porcupine* (1796), published in Philadelphia, a provocatively pro-English work. A porcupine, after all, has prickly spines that "sting."

Pordenone: Giovanni Antonio de' Sacchis (*c.*1483–1539), It. painter. The artist is named for the city of his birth, Pordenone, in northern Italy.

Porphyry: Malchas (*c.*234–*c.*305), Gk. scholar. The scholar's original Syrian name of Malchas meant "king." This was hellenized at Athens by Cassius Longinus, his teacher of logic, to Porphyry, meaning "purple," alluding to the imperial color (royal purple) associated with kings.

Porporino: Antonio Uberti (1697–1783), It. male soprano singer. The singer took his name from Nicola Porpora (1686–1768), the composer and chapelmaster in whose class he had studied in Naples.

Porte-Crayon: David Hunter Strother (1816–1888), U.S. artist, illustrator. The artist's pen name (literally) is French for "pencil-holder."

Sandy **Posey:** Martha Sharp (1945–), U.S. country-pop singer, songwriter.

George **Posford:** Benjamin George Ashwell (1906–1976), Br. popular composer, conductor.

Adrienne **Posta:** Adrienne Poster (1948–), Eng. juvenile movie actress.

Posy: Rosemary Elizabeth Simmonds (1945–), Eng. strip cartoonist, illustrator. An adoption of the artist's pet name, as a form of her first name.

Gillie **Potter:** Hugh William Peel (1888–1975), Eng. humorist, stage, radio comedian. "Gillie" presumably from Hugh William, and "Potter" perhaps as a family name.

Arthur **Pougin:** François Auguste Arthur Paroisse-Pougin (1834–1921), Fr. musical biographer, critic. As well as simplifying his original name, the writer also used the pseudonym Pol Dax.

Liane de **Pougy:** Marie Chassaigne, later Princess Ghika (*c.*1870–1950), Fr. novelist, courtesan.

Jane **Powell:** Suzanne Burce (1929–), U.S. movie actress, singer, dancer.

Richard Stillman **Powell:** Ralph Henry Barbour (1870–1944), U.S. novelist, writer of boys' stories. The writer explains the origin of his name: "As I recall it, I simply picked three names from the contents table of a *Century Magazine* which happened to be in my hands at the moment of inspiration … and arranged them in a sequence that satisfied my ear. Richard Powell Stillman *looked* just as good but it didn't *sound* so well!" [Marble, p. 177].

James T. **Powers:** James McGovern (1862–1943), U.S. stage comedian, singer.

Stefanie **Powers:** Stefania Zofia Federkiewicz (1942–), U.S. movie, TV actress.

Stephen **Powys:** Virginia Bolton, née de Lanty (1907–), U.S. playwright, short story writer.

Poy: Percy Hutton Fearon (1874–1945), Eng. political cartoonist, editor. The artist's name is said to have originated from the American pronunciation of his first name (as "Poycee") when he was a student at the Chase School of Art in New York.

Launce **Poyntz:** Frederick Whittaker (1838–1889), U.S. writer of adventure stories. The name suggests a pun on "lance" and "points."

P.P.C.R.: Thomas Watts (1811–1869), Eng. bibliographer, librarian. The writer, keeper of printed books in the British Museum, London, used these initials for letters published in the *Mechanics' Magazine* (1836) regarding improvements to the British Museum Library. Hamst (see Bibliography, p. 401) comments: "What the initials mean we do not know, though we do know that they mean something." They in fact stood for "Peerless Pool, City Road," referring to an open-air swimming pool owned by the Watts family in Islington, north London [Edward J. Miller, *That Noble Cabinet: A History of the British Museum*, 1973].

Swami **Prabhupada:** Abhay Charanaravinda Bhaktivedanta (1896–1977), Ind. religious leader, working in U.S. The founder of the Hare Krishna movement is commonly known by his religious title, which is of Sanskrit origin and means literally "Lord Master Footstep." This never entirely replaced his original name, however, which is usually cited with the first two names as initials (A.C. Bhaktivedanta).

Michael **Praetorius:** Michael Schultheiss (or Schulz) (1571–1621), Ger. musician, composer. The musician latinized his German name as nearly as possible. German *Schultheiss*, the former title of a village mayor, literally meant "debt orderer," "one who tells others to pay dues,"

from *Schuld*, "debt," and *heissen*, "to tell." Latin *praetorius* was the adjectival form of *praetor*, the term for a Roman magistrate.

Prem Chand: Dhanpat Rai Srivastava (1880–1936), Ind. novelist, short story writer. The writer adopted a symbolic name meaning "moon of love."

Paul **Prendergast:** Douglas William Jerrold (1803–1857), Eng. novelist, journalist, playwright. The writer used the name for his series of sketches titled *Heads of the People* (1840–41). The name itself appears to be randomly alliterative.

Paula **Prentiss:** Paula Ragusa (1939–), U.S. movie actress.

E. Livingston **Prescott:** Edith Katharine Spicer Jay (? –1901), Br. military novelist.

John **Presland:** Gladys Skelton, née Bendit (1889–1975), Austral. novelist. The writer commented on her choice of male name: "Presland was my mother's name. … When I began to publish I was anxious to enter the lists as anonymously as possible. I disliked all kinds of publicity … and I thought that if sex, as well as personality, were hidden behind a pseudonym, the author stood a better chance of being judged solely on merit" [Marble, p. 217].

Micheline **Presle:** Micheline Chassagne (1922–), Fr. movie actress. The actress made her screen debut at the age of 16 under the name Micheline Michel. In American films she is usually billed as Micheline Prelle.

George F. **Preston:** [Baron] John Byrd Leicester Warren (1835–1895), Eng. poet. The writer used this name for some volumes of verse published between 1859 and 1862. The first part of the name is almost certainly a tribute to his close friend and fellow student at Oxford, George Fortescue, who was killed in an accident in 1859. Warren also used the name William Lancaster, and the surnames of both pseudonyms appear to derive from the Lancashire cities of Preston and Lancaster, not far from his native Cheshire.

Johnny **Preston:** John Preston Courville (1939–), U.S. pop, rock singer.

Kelly **Preston:** Kelly Smith (1962–), U.S. movie actress.

Mike **Preston:** Jack Davis (1934–), Eng. pop singer. The singer was given his stage name in a competition by readers of a regular pop music column in the *Daily Mirror*. Presumably readers were told he had been discovered by London agent Dennis Preston.

Robert **Preston:** Robert Preston Meservey (1917–1987), U.S. stage, movie actor.

Préville: Pierre-Louis Dibus (1721–1799), Fr. comic actor.

André **Previn:** Andreas Ludwig Priwin (1929–), Ger.-born U.S. pianist, conductor, of Russ. Jewish descent.

Marie **Prévost:** Marie Bickford Dunn (1893–1937), Can.-born U.S. movie actress.

Voranc **Prežihov:** Lovro Kuhar (1893–1950), Slovenian poet.

Dennis **Price:** Dennistoun John Franklyn Rose-Price (1915–1973), Eng. stage, movie actor.

Evadne **Price:** Helen Zenna Smith (1896–1985), Eng. journalist, children's writer. The writer used this name for a series of books for children about a mischievous little girl called Jane, beginning with *Just Jane* (1928).

Dickie **Pride:** Richard Knellar (*c.*1940–*c.*1970), Eng. pop singer ("The Sheik of Shake"). Knellar was "discovered" by Russ Conway (*q.v.*) singing rock 'n' roll in a pub in 1958 and passed on by him to impresario Larry Parnes, who renamed him.

Suzy **Prim:** Suzanne Arduini (1895–1991), Fr. movie, stage, actress.

Dorothy **Primrose:** Dorothy Buckley (1916–), Sc. stage actress.

Prince: Prince Roger Nelson (1958–), U.S. black rock musician. The artist was originally named for the Prince Roger Trio, of which his father, John L. Nelson, was a member. On June 7, 1993, his 35th birthday, he changed his name to an unpronounceable but supposedly significant symbol. The Artist Formerly Known As Prince, as the media thereafter referred to him, commented: "Changing my name's made perfect sense to me. I'm not Nel's son, Nelson, that's a slave name. I was ridiculed for that, but they did the same to Muhammad Ali and Malcolm X [*qq.v.*]. ...What should you call me? My wife just says, 'Hey.' If she said, 'Prince, get me a cup of tea,' I'd probably drop the cup'" [*Sunday Times Magazine,* December 22, 1996].

Richard **Prince:** Richard Miller Archer (1858–?), Eng. actor. The performer's growing grudge against William Terriss (*q.v.*) eventually unhinged his mind and drove him to murder the popular actor.

Prince Be: Attrell Cordes (1970–), U.S. black "hip-hop" musician, "daisy-age" rapper, brother of DJ Minute Mix (*q.v.*).

Prince Buster: Cecil Bustamente Campbell (1938–), Jamaican popular singer.

Prince Far I: Michael Williams (*c.*1944–1983), Jamaican DJ, reggae rapper. He was originally given the name "King Cry-Cry" but soon renamed himself as "Prince Far I."

Prince Jazzbo: Linval Carter (*c.*1950–), Jamaican reggae musician.

Aileen **Pringle:** Aileen Bisbee (1895–1989), U.S. movie actress. The actress adopted the name of her first husband, Sir Charles MacKenzie Pringle. She made her screen debut in 1919 as Aileen Savage.

Yvonne **Printemps:** Yvonne Wigniolle (1894–1977), Fr. singer, movie, stage comedienne.

James **Prior:** James Prior Kirk (1851–1922), Eng. novelist.

Pro: Peter Clive Probyn (1915–1991), Eng. cartoonist, animator. The artist's name not only represents his surname but also implies one who is a "pro," or a professional.

P.J. Proby: James Marcus Smith (1938–), U.S. rock singer. The singer began his performing career as Jett Powers, an arbitrary "dynamic" name, and the reversed initials of this gave "P.J." "Proby" appears to have originated as some kind of nickname, although it could have tied in with the name of his friend Elvis Presley, who dated his sister. He first used it in 1963.

Professor Longhair: Henry Roeland Byrd (1918–1980), U.S. black jazz pianist. The musician took his name from a nickname given him by a club owner.

Sofya **Prokofyeva:** Sofya Leonidovna Korovina (1928–), Russ. children's writer. No doubt the writer wished to avoid a name that suggested "cow" (Russian *korova*), so altered it to one with apter associations.

Lozania **Prole:** Ursula Bloom (1893–1984), Eng. novelist. The pen name was one of the more unusual adopted by the writer, who mainly used conventional names such as Sheila Burnes, Mary Essex, and Rachel Harvey. Possibly it arose from a mishearing or miswriting of her original name?

Marjorie **Proops:** Rebecca Marjorie Israel (*c.*1911–1996), Br. journalist. The popular "agony aunt" changed her surname to Rayle and dropped her first name at a time of anti-Semitic abuse. Proops was her married name. She began her career with the *Daily Mirror* as a fashion artist under the byline Silvaine: "I was horrified. It made me sound like a flower shop," said "Marje."

Perch **Proshyan:** Ovanes Stepanovich Ter-Arakelyan (1837–1907), Armenian writer, teacher.

Robert **Prosky:** Robert Porzuczek (1931–), U.S. movie actor.

Father **Prout:** Francis Sylvester Mahoney (1804–1866), Ir. humorist. The writer adopted the name for his *Prout Papers* (1834–36), which purported to be the autobiography of a rural Irish priest. Mahoney had abandoned the priesthood for literary pursuits after being expelled from the Jesuit order in 1830. He is said to have taken the name from a real Father Prout, a parish priest in Co. Cork, whom he had known as a boy, and who had died in 1830, the year of his expulsion.

Marcel **Provence:** Marcel Jouhandeau (1888–1979), Fr. novelist, short story writer, playwright. The writer took his name from Provence, where he was born, disguising his native town of Guéret in his works as "Chaminadour."

Joseph **Prunier:** Guy de Maupassant (1850–1893), Fr. short story writer. Maupassant used this name for his first story, *La Main d'écorché* (1875).

Bolesław **Prus:** Aleksander Głowacki (1847–1912), Pol. novelist.

Kozma **Prutkov:** Aleksey Konstantinovich Tolstoy (1817–1875), Russ. writer + Aleksey Mikhaylovich Zhemchuzhnikov (1821–1908), Russ. poet + Vladimir Mikhaylovich Zhemchuzhnikov (1830–1884), Russ. poet, his brother. The three writers first combined under this name in 1854 when contributing verse and literary parodies to the journal *Sovremennik* ("Contemporary"). Kozma Prutkov was presented as a civil servant turned comic poet, well-intentioned and benign, but smug and unimaginative, judging everything from an official point of view. His character was popularly enhanced by an "autobiography" and he even had his portrait painted. His name was adopted from that of the Zhemchuzhnikov brothers' valet.

Paul **Pry:** William Heath (1795–1840), Eng. caricaturist, illustrator. The artist's name implies one who "pries" into society. It was originally that of a popular stage character, the hero of John Poole's comedy of the same name (1825). Heath adopted the name in 1827 but abandoned it two years later when it became plagiarized.

Anthony **Pryde:** Agnes Russell Weekes (1880– ?), Eng. novelist. The writer gained her pseudonym by chance. In 1919 her publisher published both her own first American novel and

James Branch Cabell's *Jurgen*, with particularly high hopes for the latter. However, Cabell's novel was suppressed by the reformer Anthony Comstock. So, "Pride goes before a fall," and Anthony caused that fall, just as in history Mark Antony caused his own downfall. Hence the pseudonym.

Maureen **Pryor:** Maureen Pook (1924–1977), Ir. stage, movie, TV actress.

Nicholas **Pryor:** Nicholas David Probst (1935–), U.S. movie actor.

George **Psalmanazar:** ? (*c.*1679–1763), Fr. (or Swiss) literary impostor. The impostor apparently took his name from the Assyrian king (mentioned in the Bible) Shalmaneser, adding an initial "P." For a fuller consideration, see p. 59.

Pseudoplutarch: John Milton (1608–1674), Eng. poet. Milton used this name for addressing Charles II in his *Pro Populo Anglicano Defensio* (1651), written in Latin, in which he replied to the *Defensio Regia* (1649) by the French scholar Salmasius (Claude de Saumaise). The overall work was written under his real name, however.

Publius: Alexander Hamilton (1757–1804), U.S. statesman + James Madison (1751–1804), U.S. statesman, president + John Jay (1745–1829), U.S. lawyer, statesman. The joint name was adopted by the three influential men for their essays in *The Federalist* in support of the Constitution. These were published in collected form in 1788. The name "Publius" referred to the intention of the writers to address New York voters publicly, and to persuade them to accept the Constitution. The three had earlier used the name A Citizen of New York (*q.v.*).

Puck: John Proctor (1836–after 1898), Sc.-born Br. cartoonist, illustrator. The artist first used the well known Shakespearean name in the late 1850s for some children's book illustrations.

Punjabee: William Delafield Arnold (1828–1859), Eng. novelist. The Anglo-Indian official was in India as an army officer from 1848, and subsequently became a commissioner in the Punjab. His pseudonym relates to this, and was adopted for his best known work, *Oakfield, or Fellowship in the East* (1853). He was the brother of the poet Matthew Arnold (1822–1888).

Giovanni **Punto:** Jan Václav Stich (1746–1803), Bohemian horn player. The musician italianized his name, with Giovanni the equivalent of Jan ("John"), and Punto translating German Stich ("stitch").

Reginald **Purdell**: Reginald Grasdorf (1896–1953), Br. stage, music hall, movie actor. The actor adopted his mother's maiden name as his stage name.

Bobby **Purify**: Robert Lee Dickey (1939–), U.S. black soul singer, teaming with cousin James Purify. The two teamed up as a duo in 1965, with Bobby assuming his cousin's (real) name.

Yazep **Pushcha**: Iosif Pavlovich Plashchinsky (1902–1964), Belorussian poet.

Eleanor **Putnam**: Harriet Leonora Bates, née Vose (1856–1886), U.S. writer.

Isra **Putnam**: Greye La Spina, née Fanny Greye Bragg (1880–1969), U.S. horror story writer. The writer apparently based her name on that of the U.S. Revolutionary commander, Israel Putnam (1718–1790).

Iosif **Pyatnitsky**: Iosif (or Osip) Aronovich Tarshis (1882–1938), Russ. revolutionary.

Q: (1) Arthur Thomas Quiller-Couch (1863–1944), Br. novelist, short story writer; (2) Douglas William Jerrold (1803–1857), Br. playwright, humorist. "Q" as a pseudonym often means "query," otherwise "guess who wrote this." (Compare the next entry below.) In the case of Quiller-Couch it was his genuine initial.

Jerrold also used the name Paul Prendergast (*q.v.*), keeping "Q" for sociopolitical contributions to the humorous journal *Punch*, with which he was associated from its launch in 1841.

Q.Q.: Jane Taylor (1783–1824), Eng. children's writer. Taylor used this name, probably meaning "query (first name), query (surname)," for her contributions to *The Youth's Magazine*, an evangelical periodical published monthly from 1805 through 1865.

M. **Quad**: Charles Bertrand Lewis (1842–1924), U.S. printer, journalist, humorist. The pseudonym reveals the writer's original profession, since an "M quad" is a block of type metal the width of a capital "M", used in printing for spacing.

John **Qualen**: John Mandt Kvalen (1899–1987), Can. movie actor, of Norw. parentage, working in U.S.

Suzi **Quatro**: Suzi Quatrocchio (1950–), U.S. rock singer, guitarist, of It. descent. An early name used by the musician was Suzi Soul (*q.v.*).

Ellery **Queen**: Frederic Dannay (1905–1982), U.S. crime novelist + Manfred Bennington Lee (1905–1971), U.S. crime novelist. The two novelists, whose original names were respectively Daniel Nathan and Manford Lepofsky, were Brooklyn cousins. (Dannay's name thus derived from the first syllables of "Daniel" and "Nathan," while Manfred evolved from "Manford" and Lee from the first syllable of "Lepofsky.") The duo based the name Ellery Queen on a mutual boyhood friend named Ellery. To this they added "Queen" as they reasoned this would make the name memorable, especially as it occurs throughout their books as the name of the main detective anyway. They had considered other names, such as James Griffen and Wilbur See, but eventually rejected these.

Rita de **Queluz**: Raquel de Queirós (1910–), Brazilian novelist.

Peter **Query**, Esq.: Martin Farquhar Tupper (1810–1899), Eng. versifier. The author of the once popular *Proverbial Philosophy* (1838–76, 4 series), a bestseller on both sides of the Atlantic for more than a generation, used this name for *Rides and Reveries of Mr. Aesop Smith* (1858), now long forgotten, like all his other works. The name is a transparent attempt to disguise a real name.

Quevedo Redivivus: George Gordon Byron (1788–1824), Eng. poet. Byron used this name for *The Vision of Judgment* (1822), a parody of Southey's identically named poem published the previous year. The pseudonym means "Quevedo renewed," referring to the Spanish poet and satirist Francisco Gómez de Quevedo y Villegas (1580–1645), imprisoned for his political attacks. Byron also wrote as Horace Hornem (*q.v.*).

La **Quica**: Francisca González (1907–1967), Sp. ballet dancer, teacher. The flamenco dancer adopted a name that probably arose as a nickname, from a form of Portuguese *cuica*, the four-eyed opossum, with its distinctive big head and small body. The dancer made her debut as a child in a café chantant and was presumably fancifully compared to this animal.

Dan **Quin**: Alfred Henry Lewis (*c*.1858–1914), U.S. journalist, novelist. The writer used this name for his volumes of "Wolfville" stories, presenting a series of whimsical reminiscences of cowboy and mining life in the Southwest by an "Old Cattleman." The first to appear was *Wolfville* itself (1897).

Peter **Quince**: (1) Isaac Story (1774–1803), U.S. satirist, poet; (2) John William McWean Thompson (1920–), Eng. newspaper editor, writer. Story adopted his name from the character in Shakespeare's *A Midsummer Night's*

Dream, in which Peter Quince, the carpenter, is stage manager of the "Pyramus and Thisbe" interlude. It seems likely that Thomson used the same source, rather than taking the pseudonym from his American namesake. He used the name for his book *Country Life* (1975).

Freddy Quinn: Manfred Petz (1932–), Austr. popular guitarist.

Simon Quinn: Martin Cruz Smith (1942–), U.S. mystery writer.

Quiz: (1) Charles Dickens (1812–1870), Eng. novelist, short story writer; (2)[Sir] Max Beerbohm (1872–1956), Eng. essayist, caricaturist; (3) Powys Arthur Lenthall Evans (1899–1981), Eng. caricaturist, painter, of Welsh parentage. The name is a patent disguise or simply a token anonymity. Dickens used the name for *Sketches of Young Couples* (1840). The name happens to blend in well with his better known pseudonym, Boz (*q.v.*), as well as with that of his illustrator, Phiz (*q.v.*).

John Quod: John Treat Irving (1812–1906), U.S. writer on frontier life, nephew of Washington Irving. The writer used this name for *The Quod Correspondence* (1842), also titled *The Attorney*, a novel about legal affairs. For the name itself he may have had the generic name "John Q. Public" or "John Q. Citizen" in mind. These themselves are said to be based on the name of John Quincy Adams (1767–1848), sixth U.S. president.

Richard Quongti: Thomas Babington Macaulay (1800–1859), Eng. writer, statesman. "Quongti" is presumably an anagram of "quoting."

Paco Rabanne: Francisco Rabaneda-Cuervo (1934–), Sp.-born Fr. fashion designer, esotericist. Paco is a regular Spanish pet form of Francisco.

William Rabbit: Katay Don Sasorith (1904–1959), Laotian nationalist, writer of resistance pamphlets. Sasorith adopted the English name from his own name, as "Katay" is Laotian for "rabbit." He used the pseudonym for *Contribution à l'histoire du mouvement d'indépendance national Lao* (1948).

Istvan Rabovsky: Istvan Rab (1930–), Hung.-U.S. ballet dancer, teacher.

Rachel: Rachel Bluwstein (1890–1931), Russ.-born Israeli poet.

Mlle Rachel: Élisabeth (or Élisa) Félix (1820–1858), Fr. tragedienne. The actress's sisters also took new stage names: Sophie (1819–1877) was Sarah, Adelaide (1828–1872) was Lia, Rachel (the real one) (1829–1854) was Rebecca, and Mélanie Emilie (1836–1909) was Dinah. Her brother Raphaël (1825–1872) acted under his real name.

Rachilde: Marguerite Vallette, née Eymery (1860–1953), Fr. novelist, literary critic. The writer claimed that her androgynous pseudonym came to her from a 16th-century Swedish medium in a seance.

John Rackham: John Thomas Phillifent (1916–1976), Br. SF writer.

Radbaz: David ben Zimra (1479–1573), Egyptian Jewish scholar. The Halakhic authority came to be known by an acronymic name formed from the initial letters of his Hebrew name and title: *R*abbi *D*avid *b*en *Z*imra.

Karl Radek: Karl Bernardovich Sobelsohn (1885– ? 1939), Russ. Communist propagandist.

Sheila Radley: Sheila Mary Robinson (1928–), Eng. crime writer.

Charlotte Rae: Charlotte Rae Lubotsky (1926–), U.S. stage, TV actress, singer.

Anna Raeburn: Sally Taylor (1944–), Eng. "agony aunt." The name is not quite such a disguise as it seems. The journalist began life as Sally Taylor, but later changed Sally to "Anna" in order to avoid confusion with a flatmate. She then married Michael Raeburn, so that she had a new surname. She subsequently remarried, but by then was well established as Anna Raeburn, so kept this name.

Raff: William John Hooper (1916–), Eng. cartoonist, writer, broadcaster. The artist adopted the name of his dog, which he had when serving in the RAF (Royal Air Force) in World War II.

Chips Rafferty: John William Goffage (1909–1971), Austral. movie actor. The actor originally considered the name Slab O'Flaherty, but later rejected this in favor of the name by which he became popularly established as a "rugged" character actor.

Raffi: Akop Melik-Akopyan (Hakob Meliq-Hakobian) (1835–1888), Armenian novelist. The writer adopted a name meaning "teacher" (related to English *rabbi*, itself from Hebrew), as which he began his career.

George Raft: George Ranft (1895–1980), U.S. movie actor, of Ger.-It. parentage.

James Raglan: Thomas James Raglan Cornewall-Walker (1901–1961), Eng. stage actor.

C.E. Raimond: Elizabeth Robins (1865–1952), Eng. stage actress, novelist. The actress used her real name on the stage, keeping the pseudonym for her novels. She took the name from her brother, Raymond, her search for whom inspired her bestseller, *The Magnetic North* (1904). C.E. were her father's initials.

Raimu: Jules-Auguste-César Muraire (1883–1946), Fr. stage, movie actor. The actor formed his professional name from his surname, reversing the first two syllables.

Ferdinand **Raimund:** Ferdinand Jakob Raimann (1790–1836), Austr. playwright, actor.

Allen **Raine:** Anne Adaliza Beynon Puddicombe, née Evans (1836–1908), Welsh novelist. The writer's pseudonym is said to have been suggested to her in a dream. She did not begin writing until she was in her 50s, and used it for her first and best known novel *A Welsh Singer* (1897).

Ella **Raines:** Ella Wallace Raubes (1921–1988), U.S. movie actress.

Gertrude "Ma" **Rainey:** Gertrude Malissa Pridgett (1886–1939), U.S. black blues singer. Rainey was actually the singer's married name, that of William "Pa" Rainey, who married her when she was 18 and he was already an established dancer, singer, and comedian. The couple toured as Rainey & Rainey. "Ma" was a compliment to her authority as "Mother of the Blues," while also hinting at her mature style. She did not make her first recording until she was 37.

W.B. Rainey: Wyatt Rainey Blassingame (1909–), U.S. writer of children's books, reference works. A switching of initials enabled the writer to use his middle name as a new surname.

Ralph **Rainger:** Ralph Reichenthal (1901–1942), U.S songwriter.

Jānis **Rainis:** Jānis Pliekšāns (1865–1929), Latvian poet, playwright. The poet adopted the name of the hamlet of Raini that he noticed one day on a roadside signpost. His wife was Aspazija (*q.v.*).

Marvin **Rainwater:** Marvin Karlton Percy (1925–), U.S. country singer, of Cherokee descent. The singer adopted his mother's maiden name as his professional name.

Rosa **Raisa:** Rose Burchstein (1893–1963), Pol.-born U.S. opera singer.

Bhagwan Shree **Rajneesh:** Mohan Chandra Jain (1931–1990), Ind. cult leader, "sex guru." Sources differ regarding the cultist's original name, but it is usually given as above. It may equally have been Acharya Rajneesh. Bhagwan represents the Hindi word for "god," while Shree is a Sanskrit title of respect meaning literally "majesty." Rajneesh took his new name in 1970 on settling in Poona with seven disciples. He came to the U.S. in 1981 but was expelled in 1985 and returned to Poona, where he dropped the honorific Bhagwan and instead adopted the name Osho, "teacher" (otherwise "he on whom the heavens shower flowers").

Sabit **Rakhman:** Sabit Kerim ogly Makhmudov (1910–1970), Azerbaijani writer.

David **Raksin:** John Sartain (1912–), U.S. movie music composer, conductor.

Jessie **Ralph:** Jessie Ralph Chambers (1864–1944), U.S. movie actress.

Vera **Ralston:** Vera Helena Hruba (1919–), Cz. ice skater, movie actress, working in U.S. The actress originally appeared as Vera Hruba. She then starred as Vera Hruba Ralston and finally as Vera Ralston. Her screen name is identical to the original name of Vera Miles (*q.v.*).

Ramakrishna: Gadadhar Chatterji (1836–1886), Ind. (Bengali) Hindu religious leader. The leader's name combines those of Rama and Krishna, respectively the seventh and eight avatars (incarnations), each meaning "dark one," of the god Vishnu. Rama and Krishna were formerly two of the most widely worshipped Hindu deities. The Ramakrishna Missionary Society that bears the mystic's name was founded in Calcutta in 1897 by Vivekananda (*q.v.*), his most important disciple.

Walter **Ramal:** Walter de la Mare (1873–1956), Eng. poet, short story writer. The writer used the name, a part inversion of his surname, for an early volume of poems for children, *Songs of Childhood* (1902).

Ramana Maharishi: Venkataraman Aiyer (1879–1950), Ind. Hindu philosopher, yogi. The guru's name is properly a title meaning "Raman the great sage," from Hindi *maha*, "great," and *rishi*, "sage."

Rambam: Moshe ben Maimon (1135–1204), Sp. Jewish thinker. The Talmudic authority came to be known by an acronymic name formed from the initial letters of his Hebrew name and title: *Rabbi Moshe ben Maimon*. He is also known as Maimonides, a Medieval Latin form of his original name, in which the Greek suffix *-ides*, meaning "son of," translates Hebrew *ben*. Compare the name below.

Ramban: Moshe ben Nahman (1194–1270), Sp. Jewish scholar. The Talmudist and Kabbalist adopted an acronymic name formed from the initial letters of his Hebrew name and title: *R*abbi *M*oshe *b*en *N*ahman. He is also known as Nahmanides, a Medieval Latin form of his original name, with the Greek suffix *-ides*, meaning "son of," translating Hebrew *ben*. Compare the name above.

Eddie **Rambeau:** Edward Cletus Fluri (1943–), U.S. pop singer.

Marie **Rambert:** Myriam Ramberg (1888–1982), Pol.-born Br. ballet dancer, teacher. The dancer's birth certificate showed her first name to be Cyvia. Myriam was thus originally a nickname, given her by her French poet friend, Edmée Delbecque. Myriam's father's family name was Rambam (see this name above), and her father and his brothers had this name changed to make them seem only children, and thus escape military service. One son thus retained the name Rambam, one (her father) took the name Ramberg, one took Rambert, as Myriam herself did, and the fourth, to represent their Polish nationality, assumed the name Warszawski ("of Warsaw") [Marie Rambert, *Quicksilver: An Autobiography*, 1972].

Dack **Rambo:** Norman Rambeau (1941–1994), U.S. TV actor. Rambeau was raised on a cotton farm with his twin brother Orman. The two decided to change their names to Dack and Dirk and launched themselves on a singing career in the mold of the Everley Brothers as the Rambo Twins. Dirk was killed in an auto accident in 1967.

"Ram" **Ramirez:** Roeger Ameres (*c.*1915–), West Indian jazz pianist. The musician hispanicized his name, with his nickname of "Ram" in turn derived from this.

Laon **Ramon:** Leon Janney (1917–1980), U.S. juvenile movie actor. The actor was given his screen name by his mother, using her own maiden name. In 1928, however, a numerologist advised her that this was not an auspicious name, and he reverted to the original.

Dee Dee **Ramone:** Douglas Colvin (1952–), Can.-born U.S. punk rock musician, teaming with Joey, Johnny, and Tommy Ramone (see below) to form the Ramones. The group took their collective name from Paul McCartney of the Beatles, who had briefly performed as Phil Ramone when the Beatles were still the Silver Beatles. Possibly McCartney's own name was meant to suggest "philharmonic."

Joey **Ramone:** Jeffrey Hyman (1952–), U.S. punk rock musician (see above).

Johnny **Ramone:** John Cummings (1951–), U.S. punk rock musician (see above).

Tommy **Ramone:** Tom Erdelyi (1952–), Hung.-born U.S. punk rock musician (see above).

Grace **Ramsay:** Kathleen O'Meara (1839–1888), Ir. biographer, novelist, working in France. The writer reserved this name for her novels.

Ayn **Rand:** Alice Rosenbaum (1905–1982), Russ.-born U.S. novelist.

Sally **Rand:** Helen (or Hazel) Gould Beck (1904–1979), U.S. fan dancer, movie actress.

Tony **Randall:** Leonard Rosenberg (1920–), U.S. movie actor. The actor's new surname is an approximate anagram of his original first name.

James **Randi:** Randall James Hamilton Zwinge (1928–), Can.-born U.S. magician, lecturer.

Frank **Randle:** Arthur McEvoy (1901–1957), Eng. music hall, movie comedian.

Otto **Rank:** Otto Rosenfeld (1884–1939), Austr. psychologist. The psychologist assumed his pen name while studying at Vienna University, and subsequently adopted it legally.

Shabba **Ranks:** Rexton Fernando Gordon (1966–), Jamaican reggae musician. The singer adopted the name Shabba as a youth: "I was 15 when I got this name. It comes from King Shabba of Africa. It is a revolutionary name and a powerful name" [*Sunday Times Magazine*, December 13, 1992]. "Ranks" is from "Rexton." Ranks named his first child, born 1992, Shabboo.

Abram **Ranovich:** Abram Borisovich Rabinovich (1885–1948), Russ. ancient historian.

Raoul: (1) Peter Morland Churchill (1909–1972), Br. wartime agent, working in France; (2) Hugh Duff McLauchlan (1920–), Sc. music hall dancer, teaming with Babette (*q.v.*). Churchill led the group joined by Odette (*q.v.*), and both were captured by the Gestapo. She saved him by claiming to be his wife, and was herself spared because the Germans believed she was the niece of Winston Churchill. The two in fact married in 1947, but both later remarried. "On the 28th of August, 1942, Captain Peter Morland Churchill, *alias* Monsieur Pierre Chauvet, *alias* Monsieur Pierre Chambrun, known in the field as 'Raoul', had arrived in France for the third time since the outbreak of hostilities" [Jerrard Tickell, *Odette: The Story of a British Agent*, 1949].

Renato **Rascel:** Renato Ranucci (1912–), It. movie actor.

Rashba: Solomon ben Abraham Adret (1235–1310), Sp. rabbi, theologian. The name by which the Jewish authority came to be known is an acronym of the initial letters of his Hebrew name and title: *Rabbi Shlomo ben Abraham Adret*. Compare the two names below.

Rashbam: Shemuel ben Meir (? –*c*.1174), Fr. rabbi, biblical commentator. The scholar's name is an acronym of his Hebrew name and title: *Rabbi Shemuel ben Meir*. Compare the name above and that below.

Rashi: Shlomo Yitzhaki (1040–1105), Fr. rabbi, biblical commentator. The scholar's acronymic name represents the initial letters of his Hebrew name and title: *Rabbi Shlomo Yitzhaki*. Compare the two names above.

Atilla **Rasikh:** Atilla Kadyrovich Rasulev (1916–), Russ. (Tatar) writer.

Rasputin: Grigoriy Yefimovich Novykh (? 1864–1916), Russ. monk, court favorite, religious fanatic. Rasputin was born in Siberia as the son of a peasant named Yefim Novykh. He came to lead a dissolute life, and was given the name by which he became known and which he adopted as a surname. It derives from Russian *rasputnyy*, "dissolute." An earlier uncomplimentary nickname had been "Varnak," a Siberian word meaning "vagabond." Rasputin was the son of a horse thief and became one himself [Prince Yousoupoff, *Rasputin*, 1974].

Alexis **Rassine:** Alexis Rays (1919–), Lithuanian-Br. ballet dancer. The dancer may have based his name on that of Leonid Massine (*q.v.*).

Thalmus **Rasulala:** Jack Crowder (1939–1991), U.S. black movie actor.

Rasul Rza: Rasul Ibragim ogly Rzayev (1910–1981), Azerbaijani poet. The poet adopted a conventional curtailment of his original name.

Master **Ratan:** Syed Nazir Ali (1942–), Ind. child movie actor.

Jonatan **Ratosch:** Uriel Halpern (1909–), Pol. Jewish poet, working in Israel. The writer also used the name Uriel Schelach.

Rattlesnake Annie: Rosanne McGowan, née Gallimore (1941–), U.S. country singer, of Cherokee descent. The singer acquired her name as a nickname, for the rattlesnake's tail that she took to wearing on her right ear.

Mlle **Raucourt:** Françoise-Marie-Antoinette-Josèphe Saucerotte (1756–1815), Fr. actress. The actress appears to have based her stage name on her surname.

Rausch: Francis Peter Whitford (1941–), Eng. cartoonist, illustrator. The artist's name may have arisen from some incident or personal characteristic. German *Rausch* means "intoxication," "ecstasy."

Genya **Ravan:** Goldie Zelkowitz (1942–), Pol.-born U.S. rock musician.

Mike **Ravan:** Churton Fairman (1927–), Eng. radio DJ, movie actor.

Eddie **Raven:** Edward Garvin Futch (1944–), U.S. country musician.

Ray: Raymond Wilson Chesterton (1912–), Eng. cartoonist, illustrator, writer.

Aldo **Ray:** Aldo da Re (1926–1991), U.S. movie actor.

Cyril **Ray:** Cyril Rotenberg (1908–1991), Eng. writer on wine. The oenophile was given his simpler name by his father.

Jean **Ray:** Jean-Raymond De Kremer (1887–1964), Belg. novelist, short story writer.

Man **Ray:** Emmanuel Rabinovich Rudnitsky (1890–1976), U.S. surrealist painter, photographer, of Russ. Jewish descent. The painter changed his name when at art school in Manhattan so as to avoid the taunts of his fellow students. His real name long remained unknown, and was publicly revealed only after his death.

Michel **Ray:** Michel Ray Popper (1944–), Br. juvenile movie actor, working in U.S.

Nicholas **Ray:** Raymond Nicholas Kienzle (1911–1979), U.S. movie director, of Norw. descent.

René **Ray:** Irene Creese (1911–1993), Eng. stage, movie actress.

Ted **Ray:** Charles Olden (1905–1977), Eng. comedian, violinist. The comedian's original name remains rather uncertain. His surname at birth seems to have been Alden, changed by his parents when he was still a boy to Olden. It is at least known that Olden appeared early in his career as Nedlo (his surname reversed) and as a comic violinist cornily named Hugh Neek ("unique"). Not long after, he selected his permanent stage name, adopting it from a noted golfer of the day, Ted Ray, British winner of the 1920 U.S. Open Golf Championship.

Carol **Raye:** Kathleen Mary Corkrey (1923–), Br. stage, movie actress.

Don **Raye:** Donald McRae Wilhoite, Jr. (1909–1985), U.S. popular singer, songwriter.

Martha **Raye:** Margaret Teresa Yvonne O'Reed (1916–1994), U.S. radio, TV comedienne, singer.

Raymond: Peter Raymond (originally Raymondo Pietro Carlo Bessone) (1911–1992), Eng. hair stylist, of It. parentage ("Mr. Teazy-Weazy"). The coiffeur later gallicized his first two original names and added a second "Raymond" as a surname, so that his full name was Raymond Pierre Carlo Bessone Raymond.

Derek **Raymond:** Robin (originally Robert) Cook (1931–1994), Br. crime writer. The writer adopted the name of a drinking companion in order to avoid being confused with another Robin Cook, author of the medical thriller *Coma* (1978).

Fred **Raymond:** Friedrich Vesely (1900–1954), Austr. popular composer, lyricist.

Gene **Raymond:** Raymond Guion (1908–), U.S. stage, movie, TV actor. The actor adopted his new name in 1931, although he was on the stage as a small child in 1913 and subsequently played juvenile roles.

Jack **Raymond:** John Caines (1892–1953), Br. movie producer.

John T. **Raymond:** John O'Brien (1836–1887), U.S. comedian.

Paul **Raymond:** Geoffrey Anthony Quinn (1925–), Eng. musician, impresario, nightclub owner.

Paula **Raymond:** Paula Ramona Wright (1923–), U.S. movie actress.

Andy **Razaf:** Andreamenentania Razafinkeriefo (1895–1973), U.S. lyricist, of Madagascan descent. Madagascan personal names and placenames are notoriously lengthy, and in this case a radical curtailment was clearly required.

Miss **Read:** Dora Jessie Saint, née Shafe (1913–), Eng. writer. The author, a former school teacher, became popular for her gentle accounts of life centering on a village school, beginning with *Village School* itself (1955). She has described how she chose her pen name: "That book, *Village School*, was being written in the first person and I remember trying to think of an ordinary kind of name by which this central character would be known. My mother's maiden name was Read. There seemed no reason to seek further. When the time came for it to be published, ... one of the directors of the firm ... which was to publish the book ...

suggested that it would be a good idea to let it appear under the pseudonym of 'Miss Read,' thus creating a modest secret" [Dora Saint, "The Birth of Miss Read," *The Countryman*, Winter 1978].

Janet **Reade:** Helen Rulon (1910–), U.S. movie actress.

Pauline **Réage:** Dominique Aury (? – ?) Fr. writer. Aury was the mistress of the critic and essayist Jean Paulhan (1884–1968) and adopted this name for her pornographic classic *L'Histoire d'O* (1954), written in an attempt to retain the favors of her unfaithful lover. Paulhan promoted the book and wrote its introduction but claimed not to know who the actual author was.

Martin **Redfield:** Alice Brown (1857–1948), U.S. novelist, short story writer, playwright.

Red River Dave: Dave McEnery (1914–), U.S. cowboy singer.

Alan **Reed:** Edward Bergman (1908–1977), U.S. movie actor.

Donna **Reed:** Donna Belle Mullenger (1921–1986), U.S. movie, TV actress, hostess. The actress used the name Donna Adams when she began her screen career, later changing the second name to Reed.

Jerry **Reed:** Jerry Hubbard (1937–), U.S. country singer, guitarist.

Jimmy **Reed:** Mathis James Reed Leland (1925–1976), U.S. rhythm 'n' blues musician.

Lou **Reed:** Louis Firbank (1943–), U.S. rock musician.

Robert **Reed:** John Robert Rietz (1932–1992), U.S. TV actor.

Harry **Reems:** Herbert Streicher (1947–), U.S. porno movie actor.

Dilwyn **Rees:** Glyn Edmund Daniel (1914–1986), Welsh archaeologist, writer. The archaeologist, a popularizer of his specialty on radio and TV, used this pseudonym for two detective novels: *The Cambridge Murders* (1945) and *Welcome Death* (1954).

Robert **Rees:** Alfred Neobard Palmer (1847–1915), Welsh historian. The scholar used this pseudonym for his novel *Owen Tanat* (1897).

Della **Reese:** Dellareese Taliaferro, née Early (1931–), U.S. black gospel, pop singer.

Ada **Reeve:** Adelaide Mary Isaacs (1874–1966), Eng. music hall artist, of Fr.-Du. Jewish parentage. The singer was registered at birth as above, although her father had already changed his name: "Father was born in Norwich as Samuel Isaacs, but he changed his name to

Charles Reeves when he left home at the age of sixteen to go on the stage. … He once told me that he chose the name of Reeves because of his mother's friendship with [John] Sim[s] Reeves, the great tenor of those days. Looking at some old programmes I find myself billed as 'Little Ada Reeve*s*,' with the final '*s*' to my name, and it was not until some years later that it disappeared and I finally became Ada R*eeve*. I do not recollect how or why this came about—it just happened" [Ada Reeve, *Take It For A Fact*, 1954].

George Reeves: George Besselo (1914–1959), U.S. movie actor.

Vic Reeves: James Roderick Moir (1959–), Br. entertainer, teaming with Bob Mortimer. The comedian comments: "Jim Moir is not a showbiz name. In the first place, it's hard to say and it's also difficult to spell. Anyway, the head of BBC Light Entertainment is called Jim Moir. I think Vic Reeves is a good name. It was the first that came into my head" [*Telegraph Magazine*, July 6, 1991].

Seeley Regester: Metta Victoria Victor, née Fuller (1831–1886), U.S. romantic, humorous writer.

Régine: Rachel Zylberbeg (1929–), Fr. nightclub owner.

José Réglo: José María dos Reis Pereira (1901–1969), Port. poet.

Regiomontanus: Johann Müller (1436–1476), Ger. astronomer, mathematician. The name is the latinized equivalent, meaning "king's mountain," of the astronomer's birthplace, Königsberg, now Kaliningrad, Russia.

Frédéric Regnal: [Baron] Frédéric d'Erlanger: (1868–1943), Br. composer, of Ger.-U.S. parentage. The composer, a banker by profession, used this royal-looking reversal of most of his surname for some early works.

Ada Rehan: Ada Crehan (1860–1916), U.S. stage actress.

Sidney Reilly: Sigmund Rosenblum (1874–1925), Russ.-born Br. intelligence officer. The spy changed his original name to Sidney George Reilly in 1899.

Max Reinhardt: Max Goldmann (1873–1943), Austr. stage actor, manager, director, working in U.S. The actor changed his Orthodox Jewish name for a name that would not be regarded as specifically Jewish.

Hans Reinmar: Hans Wochinz (1895–1961), Austr. opera singer, working in Germany.

Réjane: Gabrielle-Charlotte Réju (1857–1920), Fr. stage actress, theatre manager.

Erich Maria Remarque: Erich Paul Remark (1898–1970), Ger. novelist.

Ede Reményi: Eduard Hoffman (1828–1898), Hung. violinist. The player adopted a Hungarian equivalent of his German name: Hungarian *remény* means "hope," and so corresponds to German *hoffen*, "to hope."

Uncle Remus: Joel Chandler Harris (1848–1908), U.S. writer. The white writer created the character of Uncle Remus, a wise and friendly old Negro, who told stories about Brer Rabbit, Brer Fox and other animals to the small son of a plantation owner. The formula was new, and was immensely popular. Harris's first Uncle Remus story appeared in the *Atlanta Constitution* in 1879. In 1907 he founded his own *Uncle Remus's Magazine.*

Colonel Rémy: Gilbert Renault (1904–1984), Fr. Resistance hero, writer, politician.

M.C. Ren: Lorenzo Patterson (*c.*1965–), U.S. black "gangsta" rapper.

Duncan Renaldo: Renault Renaldo Duncan (1904–1980), U.S. movie actor, painter.

Renaud: Renaud Séchan (1952–), Fr. singer, songwriter.

Mary Renault: Eileen Mary Challans (1905–1983), Br. novelist, working in South Africa. Mary Challans began writing when a nurse before World War II, and was obliged to keep her activity secret from Matron, her "presiding deity" in the hospital, who might not have approved. She is generally said to have taken the name from a character in the *Chroniques* of Froissart, the 14th-century French historian and poet. However, according to another account, she adopted it from a character in Thomas Otway's play *Venice Preserv'd* (1682). "I never thought of the car!" she said. She herself pronounced the name "Renolt."

Liz Renay: Pearl Elizabeth Dobbins (1934–), U.S. movie actress.

W.S. Rendra: Willibrodus Surenda Broto (1935–), Indonesian poet, playwright.

Renée: Renée Taylor, née Jones (1929–), N.Z. playwright, novelist. The writer rejected her married name in 1981, and instead adopted just her (significant) first name.

Ludwig Renn: Arnold Friedrich Vieth von Golssenau (1889–1979), Ger. writer.

Nicolas Restif de la Bretonne: Nicolas-Edmé Rétif (1734–1806), Fr. writer. The writer's new surname is a historical form of his original name, suffixed by the name of the farm where he was born, La Bretonne, southeast of Paris.

Jean de **Reszke**: Jan Mieczyslaw (1850–1925), Pol. opera singer. The famous tenor began his singing career in Italy as a baritone under the name Giovanni di Reschi. This was later modified to a French form.

Elisabeth **Rethberg**: Elisabeth Sättler (1894–1976), Ger. opera singer, working in U.S.

Werdna **Retnyw**: Andrew Wynter (1819–1876), Eng. doctor, writer on medicine. The writer used this name, a reversal of the original, for books such as *Odds and Ends from an Old Drawer* (1855) and *Pictures of Town from my Mental Camera* (1855).

[Freiherr von] Paul Julius **Reuter**: Israel Beer Josaphat (1816–1899), Ger. founder of Reuters news agency. Originally a Jew, Josaphat became a Christian in 1844 and adopted the name of Reuter, substituting Christian names for Jewish. It is not known why he chose this particular surname.

Reginald **Reverie**: Grenville Mellen (1799–1841), U.S. author, poet.

Imre **Révész**: Imre Csebray (1859–1945), Hung. painter.

Dorothy **Revier**: Doris Velegra (1904–1994), U.S. movie actress. The actress's new surname is that of her first husband, Harry J. Revier, who directed her first film, *The Broadway Madonna* (1922).

Alvino **Rey**: Alvin McBurney (1911–), U.S. guitarist, bandleader.

Fernando **Rey**: Fernando Casado Arambillet Veiga (1917–1994), Sp. movie actor. If taken literally, the actor's screen name means "King Ferdinand." Rey actually played kings in several films, including Philip I and Philip II.

H.A. **Rey**: Hans August Reyersbach (1898–1977), Ger.-born U.S. children's writer, illustrator. The writer also used the name Uncle Gus.

Monte **Rey**: James Montgomery Fife (1900–1982), Sc. radio singer. The singer's name reflects his second name, while punning on Monterrey, the Mexican city.

Judith **Reyn**: Judith Fisher (1944–), Rhodesian-born Eng. ballet dancer.

Debbie **Reynolds**: Mary Frances Reynolds (1932–), U.S. movie actress. The actress's new first name was given her by Jack Warner, of Warner Brothers, when she was starting her stage career in 1948. (Perhaps he thought it suggested "debutante"?) She is said to dislike it to this day.

Gene **Reynolds**: Eugene Reynolds Blumenthal (1923–), U.S. juvenile movie actor.

Marjorie **Reynolds**: Marjorie Goodspeed (1921–), U.S. movie actress. The actress, a child star of silent films, performed as Marjorie Moore in the early 1930s. She changed her name to Reynolds in 1937.

Peter **Reynolds**: Peter Horrocks (1926–1975), Br. movie actor.

Václav **Řezáč**: Václav Voňavka (1901–1956), Cz. novelist.

Rhäticus: Georg Joachim von Lauchen (or de Porris) (1514–1576), Austr. astronomer, mathematician. The astronomer adopted a name derived from his native district of Rhaetia.

Robert Barnwell **Rhett**: Robert Barnwell Smith (1800–1876), U.S. senator. The political campaigner adopted the surname of an ancestor in 1837.

John **Rhode**: (1) Honoré de Balzac (*q.v.*); (2) [Major] Cecil John Charles Street (1884–1965), Br. crime writer. For Balzac, the pseudonym was one of many, with this one possibly inspired by another, Lord R'Hoone, itself an anagram of his first name. For Street, the pun of the name is fairly transparent. He also wrote as Miles Burton.

Erik **Rhodes**: Ernest Sharpe (1906–1990), U.S. movie comedian.

Sonny **Rhodes**: Clarence Edward Smith (1940–), U.S. pop guitarist.

Madlyn **Rhue**: Madeleine Roche (1934–), U.S. movie actress. A rather esoteric refashioning of the actress's real name.

Siôn **Rhydderch**: John Roderick (1673–1735), Welsh grammarian, publisher. The name is the Welsh equivalent of the English original.

Jean **Rhys**: Ella Gwendolen Rees Williams (1890–1979), Br. novelist, of white Dominican-Welsh parentage. The writer was given her pen name by Ford Madox Ford (*q.v.*), who admired her (unpublished) fictionalized diary of the years 1910–19.

Paul **Ricca**: Felice Delucia (1897–1972), It.-born U.S. gangster.

Ruggiero **Ricci**: Woodrow Wilson (later, Roger) Rich (1918–), U.S. concert violinist, of It. descent. The musician's father italianized Roger Rich to Ruggiero Ricci, hoping that such a professional-looking name would bring "riches."

Il **Riccio:** Andrea Briosco (*c.*1470–1532), It. sculptor, goldsmith. The name means "the curlyhead." The artist was also known as Andrea Crispus, from the Latin equivalent.

Anne **Rice:** Howard Allen Frances O'Brien (1941–), U.S. novelist. The writer of novels on vampires was originally named after her father, Howard O'Brien. She legally changed this to Anne at around the age of seven. Her new surname is that of her husband, Stanley Rice, whom she married in 1961. She has also written mildly titillating novels as Anne Rampling, and an erotic trilogy, *The Claiming of Sleeping Beauty* (1983), *Beauty's Punishment* (1984), and *Beauty's Release* (1985), as A.N. Roquelaure. This name derives from *roquelaure*, a type of masquerade cloak.

Craig **Rice:** Georgiana Ann Randolph Craig (1908–1957), U.S. thriller, short story writer. The writer took her surname from that of the aunt who raised her, Mrs. Elton Rice, with her original surname serving as her new forename. She also wrote as Daphne Saunders and Michael Venning.

Dan **Rice:** Daniel McLaren (1823–1900), U.S. circus clown.

Elmer **Rice:** Elmer Leopold Reizenstein (1892–1967), U.S. playwright, novelist. The writer simplified his name like this in 1914, after becoming tired of constantly having to spell out his real name over the telephone. There is scope for confusion between several similar Jewish names, such as Einstein, Eisenstein, Reichstein, Rosenstein and this one.

Irene **Rich:** Irene Luther (1891–1988), U.S. movie actress.

Tony **Rich:** Anthony Jeffries (1971–), U.S. rhythm 'n' blues musician.

Cliff **Richard:** Harold Rodger Webb (1940–), Eng. pop musician, movie actor.

How did the pop star come to choose his name? In his own words: "Harry Webb! Fine for a plumber. Ideal for a policeman. But for a pop singer, the kiss of death. So we sat round a table in a pub and threw out ideas. After an hour we got near it. Russ Clifford... Cliff Russord. Ten minutes later, Cliff Richards. Then the brainwave. 'If you leave off the "s",' someone said, 'you'll be paying tribute to Little Richard, and be out of the ordinary with two christian names at the same time. When you're interviewed on air ... the interviewer's bound to get it wrong and call you "Richards." You can correct him and that gets the name mentioned twice!' That clinched it. Back home I announced the big news to my parents and sisters. From now on I was Cliff Richard. No-one must call me Harry again. 'OK, Cliff,' they said—and they never did!" [Baker, p. 4]. He first used the name in 1958 when appearing with The Drifters in Derby.

Francis **Richard:** Frank R. Stockton (1834–1902), U.S. novelist, short story writer.

Pierre **Richard:** Maurice Charles Léopold Defays (1934–), Fr. movie actor, director.

Frank **Richards:** Charles Harold St. John Hamilton (1875–1961), Eng. author of school stories. This was the best known pseudonym of the creator of Billy Bunter and a host of other immortal characters who peopled the writer's fictional Greyfriars School. The choice of the name may appear arbitrary, but in fact the author took much trouble over its selection, as he has recorded: "The chief thing was to select a name totally different from those under which he had hitherto written: so that when he used the name, he would feel like a different person, and in consequence write from a somewhat different angle. I have been told—by men who do not write—that this is all fanciful. ... This only means that they don't understand" [*The Autobiography of Frank Richards*, 1952]. He introduced the name for the first Greyfriars story, published in the school story magazine *The Magnet* in 1908.

Hamilton derived the name itself from Frank Osbaldistone, a character in Scott's *Rob Roy*, and his own brother Richard. He identified so closely with it that his entry in *Who's Who* appeared under the name, and he even used it for his autobiography, as already seen. Among other pseudonyms used by Hamilton were Owen Conquest, Martin Clifford, Ralph Redway, and Hilda Richards, this last for some stories featuring Bessie Bunter, the sister of Billy Bunter. However, Hamilton's characterization of Bessie was too crude for his girl readers, and he was replaced by other writers, who continued the stories about the schoolgirl under Hamilton's original name of Hilda Richards.

Jeff **Richards:** Richard Mansfield Taylor (1922–1989), U.S. movie actor.

Johnny **Richards:** John Cascales (1911–1968), U.S. jazz musician.

Renee **Richards:** Richard Raskind (1935–), U.S. transexual. The tennis-playing ophthalmologist made his much publicized sex change in 1975. The new first name is significant, as Renee (or Renée) means "reborn." "*The New York Times* … cheerfully changed not only the name of Renee Richards (and other transsexuals) but also the gender of every single pronoun in news stories" [Gloria Steinem, *Outrageous Acts and Everyday Rebellions,* 1984]. An earlier transsexual, George Jorgensen (1926–1989), the first to make her sex change public (in 1952), merely changed his first name to Christine.

Stan **Richards:** Stanley Richardson (1930–), Eng. stage, movie, TV actor.

Henry Handel **Richardson:** Ethel Florence Lindesay Robertson, née Richardson (1870–1946), Austral. novelist, short stort writer. The writer adopted a male name (that of an uncle) on the basis that "there had been much talk in the press about the ease with which a woman's work could be distinguished from a man's; and I wanted to try out the truth of the assertion."

Lee **Richardson:** Lee David Richard (1926–), U.S. TV actor.

Richelieu: William Erigena Robinson (1814–1892), U.S. journalist, politician.

Shane **Richie:** Shane Patrick Roache (1964–), Eng. TV comedian, singer, presenter.

Harry **Richman:** Harold Reichman (1895–1972), U.S. entertainer, movie actor.

Fiona **Richmond:** Julia Harrison (1947–), Eng. stage, movie actress.

Kane **Richmond:** Frederick W. Bowditch (1906–1973), U.S. movie actor.

Harry **Rickards:** Benjamin Leete (1843–1911), Br. music hall artist.

Jehan **Rictus:** Gabriel Randon de Saint-Amand (1867–1933), Fr. poet, novelist, dramatist.

John **Riddell:** Corey Ford (1902–1969), U.S. humorist, playwright. The writer described the genesis of his name in typical whimsical style: "Unfortunately, its origin is not the least mysterious nor significant. To be perfectly frank, I neither dreamt it in a dream, chose it after my dead great-grandmother, nor formed it by spelling backward the letters of my name. It happened that when I decided to do critical parodies for *Vanity Fair,* I thought it might be more successful if their author were anonymous. I wanted some name that sounded as if it might be a real person, and so I turned to that magnificent compendium of real names, the New York Telephone Directory. I lit a small jar

of incense, closed all the windows and summoned three Dyak witch doctors to beat on drums. I then blindfolded myself, took three paces, flung open the telephone book, and placed my forefinger on a name (any name) then removed the blindfold, turned on the light and saw the name was none other than Runkleschmelz. In as much as Runkleschmelz was not a very good name for a reviewer, I dismissed the witch doctors and went backward through the telephone book until I found Riddell. The name John I thought of myself" [Marble, pp. 82–83].

John **Ridgely:** John Huntington Rea (1909–1968), U.S. movie actor.

Laura **Riding:** Laura Jackson, née Reichenthal (1901–1991), U.S. writer, poet. The author adopted her new surname in 1926. She was married to Schuyler B. Jackson (her second husband) from 1941 to his death in 1970, and also wrote as Laura (Riding) Jackson. A pen name was Madeleine Vara.

Robert **Rietty:** Robert Rietti (1923–), Eng. stage actor, playwright, director.

Edward **Rigby:** Edward Coke (1879–1951), Eng. stage, movie actor. The actor took his mother's maiden name as his stage name.

Joachim **Ringelnatz:** Hans Bötticher (1883–1934), Ger. poet, novelist.

Jeremiah **Ringletub:** John Styles (1770–1860), Eng. preacher. The writer used this name for *The Legend of the Velvet Cushion* (1815), a reply to the Rev. J.W. Cunningham's *The Velvet Cushion,* published the previous year.

John **Ringling:** John Rüngeling (1866–1936), U.S. circus impresario, of Ger. parentage. "Ringling" is a somehow appropriate name for the circus.

Johnny **Ringo:** Henry John Keevill (1914–1978), Eng. writer of westerns. The name has the right associations for the world of westerns, with the various senses of "ring" involving animals, especially horses and cattle. For some other pen names used by Keevill, see Wes **Hardin.**

Ringuet: [Dr.] Philippe Panneton (1895–1960), Fr.-Can. novelist.

A. **Riposte:** Elinor Mordaunt, née Evelyn May Clowes (1877–1942), Eng. novelist, travel writer. The author used this name for the U.S. edition, entitled *Gin and Bitters,* of her novel *Full Circle* (1931). The book was intended as a counterblast ("riposte") to Somerset Maugham's *Cakes and Ale* (1930). She hardly carried the guns, however, for this daunting assault.

Arthur **Riscoe:** Arthur Boorman (1896–1954), Br. stage, movie comedian.

Elizabeth **Risdon:** Elizabeth Evans (1887–1958), Br. stage, movie actress.

Rita: Eliza Margaret Humphreys, née Gollan (1860–1938), Sc. novelist. The writer's pen name reflects her second name of Margaret, and may well have been her pet name among her family and friends. She also wrote as E. Jayne Gilbert.

Ritba: Yom Tov ben Avraham Ishbili (? –1330), Sp. Jewish scholar. The Talmudic and Halakhic authority came to be known by an acronymic name formed from the initial letters of his Hebrew name and title: *R*abbi *Yom Tov* ben *A*vraham. (Ishbili is a locational suffix meaning "of Seville.")

Al **Ritz:** Al Joachim (1901–1965), U.S. movie comedian, of Austr. parentage, teaming with Harry and Jimmy Ritz (see below) as The Ritz Brothers.

Harry **Ritz:** Herschel Joachim (1906–1986), U.S. movie comedian (see above).

Jimmy **Ritz:** James Joachim (1904–1985), U.S. movie comedian (see above). The brothers used the glitzy name of Ritz, the famous hotelkeeper, for their original vaudeville act, first as precision dancers, then as zany comedians.

Chita **Rivera:** Dolores Conchita Figueroa del Rivero (1933–), U.S. stage, movie actress, dancer.

Joan **Rivers:** Joan Alexandra Rosenberg, née Molinsky (1933–), U.S. TV comedienne, chat show host.

Johnny **Rivers:** John Ramistella (1942–), U.S. pop musician, record company executive. The musician's new name was suggested by DJ Alan Freed, who felt it would suggest the river bayou country where he was raised (Baton Rouge, Louisiana).

Larry **Rivers:** Yitzroch Loiza Grossberg (1923–), U.S. painter, sculptor.

Yakov **Rives:** Jakov Yudovich Baskin (1886–1975), Russ. Jewish writer.

Sue **Robbie:** Susan Jennifer Robinson (1949–), Eng. TV presenter.

Harold **Robbins:** Francis Kane (1916–1997), U.S. novelist. The writer took the name Harold Rubin when he was adopted in 1927 and later legally modified the surname to Robbins.

Jerome **Robbins:** Jerome Rabinowitz (1918–), U.S. stage director, choreographer.

Marty **Robbins:** Martin David Robertson (1925–1982), U.S. country singer.

Rob Donn: Robert Mackay (1714–)1778), Sc. Gaelic poet. The poet's name means "Rob the Brown," referring to his brown hair and brown eyes, which distinguished him from the redheaded highlanders. Compare **Rob Roy.**

Robert ap Gwilym Ddu: Robert Williams (1766–1850), Welsh poet, hymnwriter. The writer's bardic name means "Robert son of Black William."

Robert-Houdin: Jean-Eugène Robert (1805–1871), Fr. conjuror. The illusionist married Josèphe Cécile Houdin in 1830, and added his wife's maiden name to his own to give his stage name. He in turn gave the name of Houdini (*q.v.*).

Ben **Roberts:** Benjamin Eisenberg (1916–1984), U.S. screenwriter.

Ewan **Roberts:** Thomas McEwan Hutchison (1914–1983), Sc. stage actor.

James Hall **Roberts:** Robert Lipscomb Duncan (1927–), U.S. thriller writer.

Joan **Roberts:** Josephine Seagrist (1920–), U.S. stage actress, singer. The actress adopted her mother's maiden name as her stage name.

Lionel **Roberts:** Robert Lionel Fanthorpe (1935–), Eng. SF writer.

Luckey **Roberts:** Charles Luckyeth (1887–1968), U.S. black jazz pianist.

Lynne **Roberts:** Mary Hart (1919–), U.S. movie actress.

Robertson: Etienne-Gaspard Robert (1763–1837), Fr. illusionist.

E. Arnot **Robertson:** [Lady] Eileen Arbuthnot Turner, née Robertson (1903–1961), Eng. novelist.

Gilles **Roberval:** Gilles Peronnier (or Personne) (1602–1675), Fr. mathematician. The mathematician took his name from his birthplace, Roberval, near Beauvais, northern France.

[Sir] George **Robey:** George Edward Wade (1869–1954), Eng. stage, movie comedian ("The Prime Minister of Mirth"). Wade's family disapproved when he began appearing in amateur theatrical performances at an early age. He therefore decided to adopt another name, and took "Robey" (originally "Roby") from a builder's business in Birmingham, where he was employed as a clerk in a tram (streetcar) company. He liked the name for its simple, robust appearance and its ease of pronunciation, and later adopted it by deed poll [*Dictionary of National Biography*].

Henri **Robin:** Henrik Joseph Donckel (1811–1874), Du. illusionist, working in France ("The

French Wizard"). The magician's name half suggests that of his French rival, Robert-Houdin (*q.v.*).

Denise **Robins:** Naomi Klein (*c.*1897–1985), Br. romantic novelist. The writer adopted her main pen name from her mother's first name and the surname of her first husband, Arthur Robins. She also wrote as Denise Chesterton, Ashley French, Harrie Gray, Hervey Hamilton, Julia Kane, and Francesca Wright.

Edward H. **Robins:** Edward Haas (1880–1951), U.S. stage actor. The actor took his mother's maiden name for his stage surname. His middle initial represents his original surname.

Mr. and Master **Robinson:** Henry Hawley Crippen (1868–1910), Br. murderer + Ethel Le Neve (1893–1967), his mistress. Following the murder of his wife in London in 1910, Dr. Crippen and his mistress fled to the U.S., of which he was a citizen. They boarded a boat to Quebec with Ethel Le Neve posing as "Master Robinson" and Crippen as "his" father. The master of the ship, however, saw through her disguise and sent a message to the ship's owners in Liverpool. On the ship's arrival in Quebec, the couple were arrested by the police. Crippen was subsequently executed.

Various other aliases were used throughout the affair. Crippen's wife, the daughter of a German mother and a Polish father, was christened Kunigunde Mackamotzki. When she was in her late teens in Brooklyn, she began calling herself Cora Turner. Soon after marrying Crippen, she used the name Cora Motzki, hoping this would help with a proposed operatic career. For a time she also appeared on the stage as Belle Elmore. Ethel Le Neve, meanwhile, called herself "Miss Allen" when she again sailed for North America after the trial, and "Miss Nelson" when she returned to England in World War I. Under this latter name she married one Stanley Smith.

Edward G. **Robinson:** Emanuel Goldenberg (1893–1973), U.S. movie actor. The name change is described in interesting detail in the actor's autobiography. Given the need for a change, since Emanuel Goldenberg was "not a name for an actor, ... too long, too foreign and ... too Jewish, ... the obvious ploy was translation, but Emanuel Goldenhill didn't work and Goldenmount was too pretentious. ... I continued to debate lists of names in the phone book, catalogs, and encyclopedias I picked up in the

Astor Place Library ... and none would satisfy me. Then one night I went to see a play, a highly urbane English drawing room comedy, and from my perch in the rear of the second balcony I heard a butler on stage announce to a lady ..., 'Madam, a gentleman to see you—a Mr. Robinson.'"

"Mr. Robinson. I liked the ring and strength of it. And, furthermore, it was a common change. I knew many Rosenbergs, Rabinowitzes, and Roths who'd switched to Robinson. Yes, that was it. From this time forward I would be Robinson—Emanuel Robinson. That decision was greeted at the Academy with something less than enthusiasm. Emanuel and Robinson were an odd coupling. What other names began with *E*? Edgar? Egbert? Ellery? Ethan? Edward? Why not Edward, then King of England? ... Edward Robinson. But I could not desert the Goldenberg entirely. That became the *G*, my private treaty with my past. But that wasn't enough. Some managers didn't like the *G*, and quite arbitrarily one of them translated it to Gould. And so, if you ever look at the early programs, you will see me billed as Edward Gould Robinson..." [Edward G. Robinson with Leonard Spigelglass, *All My Yesterdays: An Autobiography*, 1973].

Madeleine **Robinson:** Madeleine Svoboda (1916–), Fr. stage, movie actress, of Cz. origin.

Ralph **Robinson:** George III (1738–1820), king of England ("Farmer George"). George III used this name, that of his shepherd at Windsor, for his contributions to the *Annals of Agriculture*, the monthly journal published from 1784 to 1809 by the agriculturist Arthur Young. The king was a keen, progressive farmer. Hence his nickname.

Sugar Ray **Robinson:** Walker Smith, Jr. (1921–1989), U.S. black middleweight boxer. The boxer turned professional in 1940 and acquired his new name that year. Watching a small promotion from ringside one day, he was suddenly asked to substitute for a fighter named Ray Robinson, who had failed to turn up for one of the bouts. Smith won in style, and assumed that boxer's name himself. Later, an observer remarked to Robinson's trainer that he seemed to have a "sweet" fighter. The trainer, George Gainsford, replied, "Yes, he's as sweet as sugar." Hence his first name.

Rob Roy: (1) Robert MacGregor (1671–1734), Sc. Highland outlaw; (2) John MacGregor (1825–1892), Eng. traveler, writer, canoe designer.

The usual explanation behind the name is that the outlaw signed himself as "Rob Roy," meaning "red Rob" and referring to his thick, dark red hair. (Compare Rob Donn, above.) However, the motto of the MacGregors is "My race is royal," and "Roy" could have derived from this. This origin seems to be supported by the use of the same name by the second MacGregor above, although he originally applied the name "Rob Roy" to the canoe he designed and built in 1865. This was built of oak but covered fore and aft in cedar, which is a red wood.

Frederick **Robson:** Thomas Robson Brownhill (1821–1864), Eng. music hall actor.

May **Robson:** Mary Jeanette Robison (1858–1942), Austral.-born U.S. stage, movie actress.

Stuart **Robson:** Henry Robson Stuart (1836–1903), U.S. comedian.

Patricia **Roc:** Felicia Riese (1918–), Eng. movie actress. The actress's adopted name is probably an adaptation of her real name. But it may be no coincidence that German *Riese* means "giant," and the roc is a legendary gigantic bird.

Blas **Roca:** Francesco Calederío (1908–1987), Cuban government official. When the political activist joined the Communist Party in 1929, he took the name "Roca," Spanish for "rock." This evokes the names of other Communist leaders, such as Kamenev (stone) and Stalin (steel) (*qq.v*).

J.W. **Rochester:** Vera Ivanovna Kryzhanovskaya (1861–1924), Russ. novelist, short story writer.

Mark **Rochester:** William Charles Mark Kent (1823–1902), Eng. author, journalist. Charles Kent (as he was usually known) became editor of the evening newspaper *The Sun* in 1845, and used his pen name for political sketches that he published separately, such as *The Derby Ministry* (1858), later reissued as *Conservative Statesmen*. No doubt the name was inspired by the town of Rochester, Kent. He himself was born in London.

Rockin' Dopsie: Alton Jay Rubin (1932–1993), U.S. black zydeco accordionist. Rubin was known as "Dopsie" or "Dupsee" from an early age, and is said to have taken the name from "Doopsie," a Chicagoan dancer.

Rockin' Sidney: Sidney Semien (1938–), U.S. black zydeco musician.

Rockwell: Kenneth Gordy (1964–), U.S. rock musician, son of Motown Records head Berry Gordy. The singer adopted the name of his school band, itself no doubt implying players who "rock well."

Alexander **Roda Roda:** Sandór Friedrich Rosenfeld (1872–1945), Austr. humorist, working in U.S.

Julius **Rodenberg:** Julius Levy (1831–1914), Ger. journalist, novelist. The writer assumed the name of his birthplace, Rodenberg, western Germany.

Jimmy **Rodgers:** James Snow (1933–), U.S. folksinger. The singer took his name in memory of the country singer Jimmie Rodgers (1897–1933), the "Singing Brakeman," who died in the year that Snow was born.

Red **Rodney:** Robert Roland Chudnick (1927–1994), U.S. jazz trumpeter.

William **Roerick:** William Roehrich (1912–), U.S. playwright, stage actor.

Ginger **Rogers:** Virginia Katherine McMath (1911–1995), U.S. stage, movie actress, dancer. The actress's first name evolved from "Virginia," the creation being the work of a young cousin who could not pronounce her "v"s. She was thus first "Dinda," then "Ginger." Her surname came from her mother's second marriage to John Rogers in 1920.

Jean **Rogers:** Eleanor Lovegren (1916–1991), U.S. movie actress.

Julie **Rogers:** Julie Rolls (1943–), Br. popular singer.

Roy **Rogers:** Leonard Franklin Slye (1912–), U.S. movie actor. As a singer early in his career, the future cowboy star called himself Dick Weston. He later adopted the name Roy Rogers, which may have been prompted by either Ginger Rogers (*q.v.*) or, more likely, Will Rogers (1879–1935), the movie actor who had formerly been a cowboy.

Shorty **Rogers:** Milton Michael Rajonsky (1924–1994), U.S. jazz musician.

Mikhail **Rogov:** Mikhail Ivanovich Ivanov (1880–1942), Russ. revolutionary, Communist official.

Criena **Rohan:** Deidre Cash (1925–1963), Austral. novelist, of Ir. parentage.

Eric **Rohmer:** Jean-Marie-Maurice Scherer (1920–), Fr. movie director.

Sax **Rohmer:** Arthur Sarsfield Ward (1886–1959), Eng. writer of "oriental" mystery stories. The writer was originally Arthur Henry Ward, but substituted Sarsfield for Henry when he was 15. His pen name has a somewhat convoluted origin. "Sax" came from what he believed was the Anglo-Saxon word for "blade" (which may have given the name of the Saxons themselves, as the word for their weapon, although made of stone, not steel). "Rohmer" he interpreted as meaning "roamer," "wanderer." In other words, he was a "roaming blade," otherwise a freelance.

Pablo de Rokha: Carlos Díaz Loyola (1894–1968), Chilean poet.

Betty Roland: Elizabeth Maclean (1903–), Austral. writer. The writer adopted her father's first name as her new surname.

Gilbert Roland: Luis Antonio Dámaso de Alonso (1905–1994), Mexican-born U.S. movie, TV actor. The actor devised his screen name from the names of two of his favorite movie stars, John Gilbert (*q.v.*) and Ruth Roland (1892–1937).

Rolant o Fôn: Rowland Jones (1909–1962), Welsh poet. The writer's name means "Roland of Anglesey," alluding to the island where he was born and where he spent his professional life as a solicitor (lawyer).

Henry Rollins: Henry Garfield (1961–), U.S. punk musician, poet.

Anthony Rolls: Colwyn Edward Vulliamy (1886–1971), Welsh writer. He also used the Welsh name Twm Teg ("Handsome Tom") for a comic novel of Welsh village life: *Jones, A Gentleman of Wales* (1954).

C.H. Rolph: Cecil Rolph Hewitt (1901–1994), Eng. writer, editor.

Yvonne Romain: Yvonne Warren (1938–), Br.-born (Fr.-raised) movie actress. "Romain" may have evolved from a Gallic attempt to pronounce the alien English "Warren."

Jules Romains: Louis-Henri-Jean Farigoule (1885–1972), Fr. playwright, novelist, poet.

Stella Roman: Stella Blasiu (1904–1992), Rom.-born U.S. opera singer. The singer's performing name denotes her nationality.

Viviane Romance: Pauline Ronacher Ortmans (1912–1991), Austr.-born Fr. movie actress. The actress's new surname neatly combines her real second name and surname. As her name implies, she starred in romantic roles, such as the alluring but faithless wife in *La Belle Equipe*, screened in the U.S. as *They Were Five* (1936).

Michael (or Mike) Romanoff: Harry F. Gerguson (*c.*1892–1971), Lithuanian-born U.S. restaurateur, impostor. Harry Gerguson posed (to 1958) as His Imperial Highness Prince Michael Alexandrovitch Dmitry Obolensky Romanoff. Any émigré Russian will tell you what weight such names carried in the ancien régime. (Earlier, he had used the try-out noble names of William Wellington, Arthur Wellesley, and Count Gladstone.) When once at a party in his role of royal Russian, someone spoke Russian to him. He turned away and said to a friend, "How vulgar, we only spoke French at court."

Romany: George Bramwell Evens (1884–1943), Eng. writer, broadcaster on the countryside. "Romany" suggests gypsies, of course, as well as someone who roams romantically over the country. In her biography of her late husband, who was actually of Gypsy descent, Evens's widow describes how he came to take his name: "When the day of my husband's first [BBC radio] engagement arrived, he was received by the organizer and asked, 'How do you wish to be announced?' for, at that time, all those who took part were either Uncles or Aunties. ... Certainly not "Uncle Bramwell" nor "The Rev. Bramwell Evens." On the spur of the moment he replied, "Romany," and Romany he became. What a fortunate choice it was! ... The only person who disapproved of it was our small nine-year-old daughter, who had been christened Romany June, for she felt that she had a prior claim to it" [Eunice Evens, *Through the Years with Romany*, 1946].

Romário: Romário de Souza Farias (1966–), Brazilian footballer.

Romark: Ronald Markham (1927–1982), Eng. TV hypnotist. The entertainer formed his professional name rather unusually from the respective first syllables of his first name and surname, in the manner of a commercial name. The name hardly hints at his specialty, which another performer might have chosen to indicate.

Stewart Rome: Septimus Wernham Ryott (1887–1965), Br. movie actor. The actor appears to have devised his screen name from letters in his original name.

Max Romeo: Max Smith (*c.*1947–), Jamaican reggae musician.

Edana Romney: Edana Rubenstein (1919–), S.A. movie actress.

Landon Ronald: Landon Ronald Russell (1873–1938), Eng. conductor, composer.

William Ronald: William Ronald Smith (1926–), Can. painter, radio, TV presenter.

Edward Ronns: Edward Sidney Aarons (1916–1975), U.S. writer of detective fiction.

Valentine Rooke: Valentine Brooke (1912–), Eng. stage actor.

Mickey Rooney: Joe Yule, Jr. (1920–), U.S. movie actor. The actor's original screen name was Mickey McGuire, which he legally adopted from the comic-strip character he played as a child in two-reel comedies. In 1932 he took the name by which he became famous. According to Rooney himself, it was suggested by Kenneth Wilson, a publicity man at Universal Studios, when they needed him for a part in a new movie but wanted to distinguish him from Mickey McGuire: "'How about "Mickey Yule"?' He savored it for a moment. 'Nah. It doesn't sound right. The rhythm is wrong. I like Mickey. But Yule? No. We need another last name. Something with a "y" in it. That would sound better. Mickey Maloney? Mickey Downey? Mickey Looney?' ... 'How about Rooney?' asked my mother. 'I knew a guy in vaudeville, Pat Rooney.' 'Not bad,' said Wilson. 'Mickey Rooney. I'll run it by my boss and see what he says.' He never bothered to ask me whether *I* liked it. ... Wilson returned a few minutes later with a smile on his face. 'Well, kid, that's your new name—Mickey Rooney'" [Mickey Rooney, *Life Is Too Short*, 1991].

Henry **Root**: William Donaldson (1935–), Eng. writer. The writer adopted this name for his epistolary spoof, *The Henry Root Letters* (1980), which, together with its sequel, *The Further Letters of Henry Root* (1980), reproduced correspondence between the author and various celebrities and government officials. Root himself was created in the guise of a jingoistic retired wet-fish merchant, with wife, Doris, 19-year-old daughter, Doreen, and 15-year-old son, Henry Jr. Only a very few recipients of the letters suspected the actual legpull.

Amanda **Ros**: Anna Margaret Ross, née McKittrick (1860–1939), Ir. novelist, poet. The writer claimed to have been originally named Amanda Malvina Fitzalan Anna Margaret McLelland McKittrick, but some of these names are in fact from Regina Maria Roche's novel, *Children of the Abbey* (1796), a favorite book from Ross's childhood.

Carl **Rosa**: Karl Rose (1842–1889), Ger. conductor, impresario, founder of Carl Rosa Opera Company.

Rosa **Rosà**: Edyth von Haynau (1894–1978), Austr.-born It. writer, illustrator.

Rosario: Florencia Pérez Podilla (1918–), Sp. ballet dancer, teaming with cousin Antonio (*q.v.*).

Françoise **Rosay**: Françoise Bandy de Nalèche (1891–1974), Fr. stage, movie actress.

Axl **Rose**: William Bailey (1962–), U.S. rock singer. Rose is the Guns n' Roses member's real name, which he discovered when he was 17, having been raised under the name of his stepfather, L. Stephen Bailey. He allegedly called himself Axl after a band for which he played in his home state of Indiana. However, it can hardly be a coincidence that the name as a whole is an anagram of "oral sex."

Billy **Rose**: William Samuel Rosenberg (1899–1966), U.S. theatre manager, composer.

Calypso **Rose**: McCartha Lewis (1940–), Tobago calypso singer.

Philip **Rose**: Philip Rosenberg (1921–), U.S. stage producer.

Peter **Rosegger**: Peter Kettenfeier (1843–1918), Austr. writer.

Fedora **Roselli**: Edith Dora Bernard, née Hodges (1896–1950), Eng. opera singer. The singer was the mother of the writer Jeffrey Bernard (*q.v.*).

[St.] **Rose of Lima**: Isabel de Flores y del Oliva (1586–1617), Peruvian virgin recluse, of Sp. parentage.

Nikolay **Roshchin-Insarov**: Nikolay Petrovich Pashenny (1861–1899), Russ. actor.

Rosimond: Claude La Roze (*c.*1640–1686), Fr. actor.

Carl **Rosini**: John Rosen (1882–?), Pol.-born magician, working in Germany, U.S.

Emperor **Rosko**: Michael Pasternak (1942–), Eng. radio DJ.

Natalia **Roslavleva**: Natalia Petrovna René (1907–1977), Russ. born Br. writer on ballet. The writer used the name for her contributions to the journal *Ballet Today* in the 1940s, so commemorating the Russian dancer Lyubov Roslavleva (1874–1904).

Ernst **Rosmer**: Elsa Bernstein (1866–1925), Ger. playwright. The dramatist was influenced by Ibsen, and adopted her name from his *Rosmersholm* (1886). The British writer Rebecca West (*q.v.*) took her name from a character in the same play.

Milton **Rosmer**: Arthur Milton Lunt (1881–1971), Br. stage, movie actor, director. The actor took his stage name from that of Johannes Rosmer, the central character in Ibsen's play *Rosmersholm*. For a similar borrowing, compare the name of Rebecca West.

J.-H. **Rosny**: Joseph-Henri Boex (1856–1940), Fr. novelist + Séraphin-Justin François Boex (1859–1948), Fr. novelist, his brother. The initials are those of the elder brother ("Rosny aîné"), while the surname appears to have been taken from that of "Baron de Rosny," the name by which the Duc de Sully (1559–1641), the famous minister of Henri IV, was known during the early part of his career.

Ross: Harry Ross Thomson (1938–), Sc. cartoonist, illustrator. The artist adopted the shortest of his names for his work, signing it distinctively as "roSS."

Adrian **Ross:** Arthur Reed Ropes (1859–1933), Eng. lyricist, librettist. Ropes used the name Arthur Reed for the libretto of a vaudeville entertainment, *A Double Event* (1884), written jointly (a "double event") with Arthur Law. He later adopted the name Adrian Ross, first using it for the libretto of *Joan of Arc* (1891).

Annie **Ross:** Annabelle Macauley Lynch, née Short (1930–), Eng. jazz singer. Possibly "Ross" evolved out of the singer's maiden name, of which it is a sort of reversal.

Barnaby **Ross:** Ellery Queen (*q.v.*). The Ellery Queen partnership used this name for various crime novels featuring a detective named Drury Lane. Rather surprisingly, the two men did not use this name as their own pseudonym. But no doubt it would have looked too obvious.

Barney **Ross:** Barnet David Rosofsky (1909–1967), U.S. welterweight boxer.

Jerry **Ross:** Jerold Rosenberg (1926–1955), U.S. popular composer, lyricist.

John Hume **Ross:** Thomas Edward Lawrence (1888–1935), Eng. soldier, archaeologist, writer ("Lawrence of Arabia"). This was the name chosen by Lawrence to escape publicity when he enlisted in the Royal Air Force in 1922. A year later he joined the Tank Corps as T.E. Shaw, adopting the name by deed poll in 1927. The latter name was intended as a mark of respect to Bernard Shaw.

Leonard Q. **Ross:** Leo Calvin Rosten (1908–1997), Pol.-born U.S. writer. Rosten used this name for his best known book, *The Education of Hyman Kaplan* (1937), a humorous account of the torments unwittingly inflicted on the English language and his long-suffering English teacher by the immigrant student of the title.

Martin **Ross:** Violet Florence Martin (1861–1915), Ir. author. The writer used her surname as her first name, taking "Ross" from her birthplace, Ross House, County Galway. In collaboration with her cousin, Edith Somerville (1858–1949), she wrote many books and stories

about Irish life under the joint name of Somerville and Ross.

Mike **Ross:** Colin John Novelle (1948–), Br. radio DJ.

Oriel **Ross:** Muriel Swinstead (1907–), Br. stage actress.

Peggy **Ross:** Margaret Campbell (1912–), Can. movie actress.

Shirley **Ross:** Bernice Gaunt (1909–1975), U.S. pianist, singer, movie actress.

Robert **Rossen:** Robert Rosen (1908–1966), U.S. movie director, screenwriter.

Eleanora **Rossi-Drago:** Palmira Omiccioli (1925–), It. movie actress.

Rossini: Pyotr Akimovich Ogluzdin (1887–1939), Russ. circus artist, acrobat. Members of the performer's family followed in his footsteps under the same name, itself first used in 1902 for the three Rossini Brothers.

Gene **Roth:** Gene Stuttenroth (1903–1976), U.S. movie actor.

Lillian **Roth:** Lillian Rutstein (1910–1980), U.S. movie actress, singer.

Paul **Rotha:** Roscoe Treeve Fawcett Thompson (1907–1984), Br. documentary movie producer, director, film critic. The filmmaker's parents altered his first name to Paul at any early age. He then changed his name by deed pool to Paul Rotha when starting a career as an artist, the new surname apparently based on the first syllables of his original first name and surname.

Mark **Rothko:** Marcus Rothkovich (1903–1970), Latvian-born U.S. painter.

Contessa Anna **Roti:** Regina di Luanto (*c.*1862–1914), It. novelist. The writer's assumed name (but not title) is a part-anagram of her real name.

Ola **Rotimi:** Emmanuel Gladstone Olawole (1938–), Nigerian playwright.

Johnny **Rotten:** John Joseph Lydon (1956–), Br. punk rock musician, of Ir. parentage. The former Sex Pistols member explains in his autobiography: "I got the name Rotten because I had green teeth. It was Steve [Jones]'s nickname for me: "You're fucking Rotten!" That's what he used to say. It was, and it wasn't an affectionate nickname" [John Lydon with Keith and Kent Zimmerman, *Rotten: No Irish, No Blacks, No Dogs*, 1993].

The antiestablishment name chimed with those of his fellow punk rockers, as illustrated in a contemporary news item: "They call themselves names designed to alienate society: Rat

Scabies, Dee Generate, Johnny Rotten, Sid Vicious" [*Sunday Mirror*, June 12, 1977]. (See the first and last of these names individually.) After the group's breakup in 1978, followed soon after by the death of Vicious, Lydon reverted to his real name and formed his own group, Public Image Limited (PiL).

Roland W. ("Tiny") **Rowland:** Roland Fuhrhop (1917–), Br. businessman, newspaper owner. The entrepreneur adopted (and slightly adapted) his own first name as his new surname.

Effie Adelaide **Rowlands:** Effie Marie Albanesi, née Henderson (1859–1936), Br. romantic novelist ("Madame Albanesi").

Jimmy **Rowles:** James George Hunter (1918–1996), U.S. jazz pianist, composer. The musician adopted his stepfather's name as his professional name.

Thomas **Rowley:** Thomas Chatterton (1752–1770), Eng. poet, writer. The precocious poet, a suicide at age 18, adopted the name and persona of Thomas Rowley, an imaginary 15th-century monk, "prieste of St. Johan's, Bristowe," for a number of his poems. It is possible he selected the surname after reading about Charles II, who was nicknamed "Old Rowley" (after a prize racehorse), but it is more likely he took the complete name from a memorial in the church mentioned (St. John's, Bristol) to Thomas Rowley, a merchant who died in 1478.

Samuel **Roxy:** Samuel Lionel Rothafel (1882–1936), U.S. movie distributor. The name became famous to the public at large through the Roxy cinema chain, typified by New York's Roxy Theatre, which opened in 1927.

Claude **Roy:** Claude Orland (1915–), Fr. poet, essayist.

Harry **Roy:** Harry Lipman (1900–1971), Br. dance band leader.

Manabendra Nath **Roy:** Narendranath Bhattacharya (1887–1954), Ind. Communist leader. The politician changed his name on seeking support in San Francisco in 1916.

Frank **Royde:** Frank Howroyd (1882– ?), Eng. stage actor.

Roy **Royston:** Roy Charles Crowden (or Chown) (1899–1976), Br. juvenile stage, movie actor.

Marie **Roze:** Hippolyte Ponsin (1846–1926), Fr. opera singer.

Gennadi **Rozhdestvensky:** Gennadi Nikolayevich Anosov (1931–), Russ. orchestral conductor. The musician adopted his mother's maiden name to avoid trading on the reputation of his father, the noted conductor Nikolay Anosov (1900–1962).

Alma **Rubens:** Alma Smith (1897–1931), U.S. movie actress. The actress was also billed early in her career as Alma Reuben or Alma Reubens.

Harry **Ruby:** Harry Rubenstein (1895–1974), U.S. stage, movie songwriter.

Jack L. **Ruby:** Jacob Rubenstein (1911–1967), U.S. assassin.

Steele **Rudd:** Arthur Hoey Davis (1868–1935), Austral. novelist, playwright. The writer began contributing magazine articles in about 1890 under the name Steele Rudder, the first word expressing his admiration for the essayist Sir Richard Steele, the second alluding to his love of boating. The second word was soon shortened to "Rudd."

Patrick **Ruell:** Reginald Charles Hill (1936–), Br. crime novelist. Other names used by the writer include Dick Morland and Charles Underhill.

Titta **Ruffo:** Ruffo Titta (1878–1953), It. opera singer. Unusually, the opera singer's name was taken from a family pet dog. Oresta Titta frequently took his dog, Ruffo, out hunting. One day, on such an expedition, the dog was accidentally shot and killed. Grief-stricken, his master vowed to preserve the dog's name, and later, when his son was born, named him Ruffo commemoratively. In due course the boy grew up and started an operatic career. He had come to dislike his dog-derived name, but not wishing to offend his father, chose a new professional name by simply turning his original name around. Thus Ruffo Titta became Titta Ruffo, family honor was satisfied, and the canine commemoration was preserved.

Sig **Ruman:** Siegfried Alban Rumann (1884–1967), Ger. movie actor, working in U.S.

RuPaul: RuPaul Andre Charles (1960–), U.S. drag entertainer. The performer's first name, if original, is presumably a blend of names such as Rupert and Paul.

Jia **Ruskaya:** Eugenia Borisenko (1902–1970), Russ.-It. ballet dancer. The dancer adopted a name that indicated her Russian parentage, with "Jia" an Italian pet form of her first name.

Anna **Russell:** Anna Claudia Russell-Brown (1911–), Br. stage entertainer.

Billy **Russell:** Adam George Brown (1893–1971), Eng. music hall comedian.

Fred **Russell:** Thomas Frederic Parnell (1862–1957), Eng. ventriloquist, variety artist. The performer changed his name to avoid any undesirable associations with the Irish politician Charles Parnell (1846–1891), who had been involved in a scandal with Kitty O'Shea, the wife of a prominent party member. He took the name Russell from his local Member of Parliament, Charles Russell (1832–1900), later Lord Russell of Killowen and Lord Chief Justice of England.

Hal **Russell:** Harold Russell Luttenbacher (1926–), U.S. jazz saxophonist.

Johnny **Russell:** John Russell Countryman (1933–), U.S. child movie actor.

Leon **Russell:** Hank Wilson (1941–), U.S. rock musician.

Lillian **Russell:** Helen Louise Leonard (1861–1922), U.S. stage actress, singer.

Mark **Russell:** Mark Ruslander (1932–), U.S. comedian.

Sarah **Russell:** Marghanita Laski (1915–1988), Br. novelist. The writer used the name for her second novel, *To Bed with Grand Music* (1946).

Theresa **Russell:** Theresa Paup (1957–), U.S. movie actress.

William **Russell:** William Lerche (1884–1929), U.S. movie actor.

Russo: Pyotr Dmitriyevich Poluparnev (1894–1972), Russ. circus artist, clown.

An **Rutgers:** An Rutgers van der Loeff-Basenau (1910–), Du. children's writer.

Mark **Rutherford:** William Hale White (1831–1913), Eng. novelist.

Salomon van **Ruysdael:** Salomon de Goyer (*c*.1600–1670), Du. painter.

Ward **Ruyslinck:** Raimond de Belser (1929–), Belg. writer.

Ruzante (or **Ruzzante**): Angelo Beolco (*c*.1496–1542), It. comic actor, playwright. The actor's stage name means "playful one."

Irene **Ryan:** Irene Riordan (1903–1973), U.S. movie comedienne.

Meg **Ryan:** Margaret Mary Emily Hyra (1961–), U.S. movie actress.

Sheila **Ryan:** Katherine Elizabeth McLaughlin (1921–1975), U.S. movie actress.

David **Ryazanov:** David Borisovich Goldendakh (Goldendach) (1870–1938), Russ. revolutionary.

Bobby **Rydell:** Robert Ridarelli (1942–), U.S. pop musician.

Alfred **Ryder:** Alfred Jacob Corn (1919–), U.S. stage actor, director.

Mitch **Ryder:** William Levise, Jr. (1945–), U.S. (white) soul singer.

Winona **Ryder:** Winona Laura Horowitz (1971–), U.S. movie actress.

Poul **Rytter:** Parmo Carl Ploug (1813–1894), Dan. poet, politician.

Saadi (or **Sa'di**): Musharrif od-Din Muslih od-Din (*c*.1213–1292), Persian poet. The poet took his name in honor of the ruler of Shiraz, his contemporary, Abu Bakr ibn-Sa'd ibn-Zangi (ruled 1231–1260), and alludes to him by name in his book of ethics in verse *Bustan* ("The Orchard"). The name itself means "happy," "lucky."

Martha **Saalfeld:** Martha vom Scheidt (1898–), Ger. writer.

Umberto **Saba:** Umberto Poli (1883–1957), It. poet.

Sabicas: Agustín Castellón (1917–1990), Sp. flamenco guitarist. The musician's name evolved from a nickname. As a child he was known as *el niño de las habicas*, "little broad bean boy," for his liking for this vegetable. The last two words of this were subequently smoothed to the single word "Sabicas."

Sabir: Mirza Alekper Tairzade (1862–1911), Azerbaijani satirical writer, poet. The writer's adopted name means "patient," alluding indirectly to the potential censorship that he risked for his criticism of the repressive society of his day.

Sabrina: Norma Sykes (1928–), Eng. movie, TV actress. The actress may have taken her name arbitrarily, rather than from the Samuel A. Taylor play (or subsequent movie) *Sabrina Fair* (1954).

Sabu: Sabu Dastagir (1924–1963), Ind. juvenile movie actor, working in U.K., U.S.

Maurice **Sachs:** Jean-Maurice Etting Lausen (1906– ? 1944), Fr. essayist, novelist.

Sade: Helen Folasade Adu (1959–), Br. pop singer, of Nigerian-Eng. parentage.

Michael **Sadleir:** Michael Thomas Harvey Sadler (1888–1957), Br. writer, publisher. The writer adopted an earlier spelling of the family name to be distinguished from his father, Sir Michael Sadler (1861–1943), educationist and art patron, and "my best and wisest friend," as his son called him in his biography.

Nikolay **Sadovsky:** Nikolay Karpovich Tobilevich (1856–1933), Ukrainian stage actor, director, brother of Ivan Karpenko-Kary and Panas Saksagansky (*qq.v.*).

Prov **Sadovsky:** Prov Mikhaylovich Yermilov (1818–1872), Russ. actor. Following the death of his father, the actor was reared and trained by his mother's brothers, provincial actors G.V. and D.V. Sadovsky, and adopted their name as his stage name.

Françoise **Sagan:** Françoise Quoirez (1935–), Fr. novelist. The author of *Bonjour Tristesse*, published when she was 19, was urged by her editor to assume a pen name. She took it, somewhat at random, from the Princesse de Sagan, a character in Proust's *A la Recherche du Temps Perdu*.

Leontine **Sagan:** Leontine Schlesinger (1889–1974), Austr. stage actress, theatre, movie director, working in South Africa.

Sagittarius: (1) Olga Miller, née Katzin (1896–1987), Br. author, satirist, of Russ. Jewish parentage; (2) Heinrich Schütz (1585–1672), Ger. church music composer. The pseudonym was chosen for quite different reasons by the two different people. Miller used the name for satirical verses in the weekly *New Statesman* (from 1934). These were "barbed," like the arrows shot by the mythological Sagittarius, the Archer. Schütz, on the other hand, was simply translating his German name into Latin, in the manner of his time. Miller (known to her friends as "Saj") used other names for her satirical sociopolitical contributions to other publications. For *Time and Tide* she wrote as Fiddlestick, for the *Manchester Guardian* she was Mercutio, and in the *Daily Herald* she appeared as Scorpio.

Amo **Sagiyan:** Amayak Saakovich Grigoryan (1915–), Armenian poet.

Alexandru **Sahia:** Alexandru Stanescu (1908–1937), Rom. writer.

Sathya **Sai Baba:** Sathyanarayana (1926–), Ind. spiritual leader. The leader claimed to be the reincarnation of the Hindu saint Sai Baba of Shirdi (died 1918), and assumed his new name, meaning roughly "saintly father," at the age of 14 on recovering from an illness.

Saib Tebrizi: Mirza Mukhammed Ali (1601–1677), Azerbaijani poet. The poet's adopted name is that of his birthplace, the city of Tabriz, northwestern Iran.

Michael **St. Clair:** Michael Sinclair MacAuslan Shea (1938–), Sc. spy fiction writer. The writer used this name to distinguish his literary activities from his official duties. He was press secretary to Queen Elizabeth from 1978 through 1987.

Marian **St. Claire:** Marian Beare, née Allsopp (1946–), Br. ballet dancer.

Lillian **Saint Cyr:** Marie Van Shaak (1917–), U.S. entertainer.

Renée **St. Cyr:** Marie-Louise Vittore (1907–), Fr. movie actress.

Michel **Saint-Denis:** Jacques Duchesne (1897–1971), Fr. theatre director, playwright, actor.

Ruth **St. Denis:** Ruth Dennis (1879–1968), U.S. ballet dancer, choreographer. The joint founder, with her husband, Ted Shawn, of the Denishawn School of Dancing changed her name in about 1906.

Teddie **St. Denis:** June Catherine Church Denham (1909–), Sc. variety artist, singer.

Ivy **St. Helier:** Ivy Aitchison (1890–1971), Br. popular composer, singer, actress. The actress was born in the Channel Islands and took her stage name from her birthtown, St. Helier, Jersey.

Raymond **St. Jacques:** James Arthur Johnson (1930–1990), U.S. black movie actor. The actor explained that he took his name from a white French boy who later became a "milkman in New Haven."

Susan **Saint James:** Susan Jane Miller (1946–), U.S. movie, TV actress. The actress has said that her name was "French-Inspired." It evolved following a high-school year on a French exchange-student program.

Betta **St. John:** Betty Streidler (1930–), U.S. movie actress.

Christopher Marie **St. John:** Christabel Marshall (*c.*1875–1960), Br. novelist, playwright, biographer.

Jeff **St. John:** Jeff Newton (1946–), Austral. soul singer.

Jill **St. John:** Jill Oppenheim (1940–), U.S. movie actress.

Saint-John Perse: Marie-René-Auguste-Alexis Saint-Léger Léger (1887–1975), Fr. poet, diplomat.

Crispian **St. Peters:** Robin Peter Smith (1943–), Eng. pop musician.

Saint-Pol-Roux: Paul Roux (1861–1940), Fr. Symbolist poet.

S.Z. **Sakall:** Eugene Geró Szakall (1884–1955), Hung. movie actor, working in U.S. ("Cuddles"). The actor's screen initials are the first two letters of his real surname.

Alexander **Sakharoff:** Alexander Zuckermann (1886–1963), Russ. ballet dancer, teacher, working in Italy. The dancer translated his name from German to Russian, basically *Zucker* ("sugar") to *sakhar*. People named Sugarman will often be found, in the English-speaking world, to have had a similar Jewish name origin, such as the Welsh-born TV actress Sara Sugarman (1962–).

Saki: Hector Hugh Munro (1870–1916), Eng. short story writer. The writer first used the name for his short story collection entitled *Reginald* (1904). According to his sister, the pseudonym comes from a line in Fitzgerald's version of *The Rubáiyát* of Omar Khayyám: "And when like her, O Saki, you shall pass." But another theory claims that the name is a contraction of "Sakya Muni," one of the names of the Buddha [J.W. Lambert, Introduction to *The Bodley Head Saki*, 1963].

Panas **Saksagansky:** Afanasy Karpovich Tobilevich (1859–1940), Ukrainian stage actor, director, brother of Ivan Karpenko-Kary and Nikolay Sadovsky (*qq.v.*).

Saladin: William Stewart Ross (1844–1906), Sc. author of poems, works on agnosticism. Ross used this name for his contributions to the *Agnostic Journal and Secular Review*, of which he was the editor. The name is a symbolic one, that of the 12th-century sultan of Egypt who invaded Palestine and defeated the Christians.

Soupy **Sales:** Milton Hines (1926–), U.S. TV entertainer, movie actor. "Soupy" arose as a childhood nickname, as his surname, Hines, sounded like "Heinz." He changed his surname to "Sales" to match this, and adopted his new name as his screen name in 1952.

Felix **Salten:** Siegmund Salzmann (1869–1945), Hung. novelist, journalist, critic, working in Switzerland.

Mikhail **Saltykov-Shchedrin:** N. Shchedrin (*q.v.*).

Francesco **Salviati:** Francesco de' Rossi (1510–1563), It. painter. The artist entered the service of Cardinal Giovanni Salviati in about 1531 and adopted his name. It was for his patron that he painted the work that made his reputation, the fresco of the *Visitation* (1538).

Antonina **Samarina:** Antonina Nikolayevna Sobolshchikova-Samarina (1896–1971), Russ. stage actress. The actress was the daughter of the actor and theatrical director Nikolay Sobolshchikov-Samarin (*q.v.*), and adopted the name that he added to his original surname (and that had thus passed to her).

Olga **Samaroff:** Lucie Hickenlooper (1882–1969), U.S. concert pianist. The pianist was the first wife of the orchestral conductor Leopold Stokowski (*q.v.*) (married 1911, divorced 1923).

Emma **Samms:** Emma Samuelson (1960–), Eng.-born U.S. TV actress.

David **Samoylov:** David Samuilovich Kaufman (1920–), Russ. poet. The writer adopted a russianized form of his Jewish patronymic (middle name) as his new surname.

Samson **Samsonov:** Samson Iosifovich Edelshteyn (Edelstein) (1921–), Russ. movie director.

Galina **Samsova:** Galina Ursuliak (later, Prokovsky), née Samtsova (1937–), Russ.-born ballet dancer, working in Canada.

Sonia **Sanchez:** Wilsonia Driver (1934–), U.S. black poet, playwright, activist.

George **Sand:** Amandine-Aurore-Lucile Dudevant, née Dupin (1804–1876), Fr. writer. One of the most famous of literary pseudonyms. The novelist derived it from her liaison with the writer Jules Sandeau. "George," she would write later, she chose spontaneously "because George seemed to me to be synonymous with Berrichon [a native of Berry, the region of central France where she was born]." (Possibly she subconsciously associated the name with its original Greek sense of "tiller of the earth.") The spelling of French *Georges* without the final "s," in the English manner, may have been an intended compliment to England, or at least to the English nuns of the Augustinian convent in Paris that she attended.

Mme Dudevant first used the name in 1831 for writing done jointly with Sandeau: some articles for *Le Figaro* and their first joint novel *Rose et Blanche*. She herself first used the name independently the following year, for her novel *Indiana*. Earlier she had used the name Blaise Bonnain, taken from a carpenter she had known as a girl. The abbreviated form "Sand" was devised by Jules, and used both by him (as Jules Sand) and by Maurice Sand, George Sand's son.

Paul **Sand:** Paul Sanchez (1944–), U.S. movie actor.

Dominique **Sanda:** Dominique Varaigne (1951–), Fr.-born U.S. movie actress. It may not be a coincidence that the actress's screen surname suggests English "Sunday," as does her first name (Latin *dominica dies*, "the Lord's day"). She was actually born on a Sunday (March 11, 1951).

Cora Sandel: Sara Fabricius (1880–1974), Norw. novelist, short story writer.

Eugen Sandow: Friedrich Müller (1867–1925), Ger. strong man, working in U.K., U.S.

Baby **Sandy** *see* **Baby Sandy.**

Frederick Sandys: Anthony Frederick Augustus Sands (1829–1904), Eng. painter. The Pre-Raphaelite artist is said to have modified his name in order to imply a blood relationship with the aristocratic Sandys family.

Sangharakshita: Dennis Philip Edward Lingwood (1925–), Eng. Buddhist monk. The founder of the Friends of the Western Buddhist Order (1967) first went east in 1943 when serving in the army. He was already attracted to Buddhism, and on leaving the army in 1946 met with Buddhist gurus in India and abandoned his English name to call himself by the Sanskrit name Dharmapriya, "lover of the law," i.e., of the ideal truth as set forth in the teachings of the Buddha. His constant companion was Satyapriya, "lover of truth," an Indian convert to Buddhism originally named Rabindra Kumar Banerjee. In 1949 both men were ordained into the Buddhist religion, Dharmapriya receiving the name Sangharakshita, "protected by the community," and Satyapriya becoming Buddharakshita, "protected by the Buddha."

In 1962 Sangharakshita had been given the new name Urgyen by the Indian guru Khachu Rimpoche. This is the Tibetan form of *Udyana*, the Sanskrit name of a land (now Swat, Pakistan) in northwestern India where the legendary Buddhist mystic Padmasambhava is said to have reigned. Sangharakshita did not adopt it then, but began using it in 1985, on the occasion of his 60th birthday. A life of Sangharakshita, *Bringing Buddhism to the West* (1995), has been written by his former personal secretary, Subhuti ("good fortune"), an English Buddhist born Alex Kennedy in 1947.

Aleksandr Sanin: Aleksandr Akimovich Shenberg (Schönberg) (1869–1956), Russ. stage, movie actor, director.

Andrea Sansovino: Andrea Contucci (*c.*1467–1529), It. sculptor, architect. The artist took his name from his birthplace, near Monte San Savino, Florence. He gave his adopted name in turn to his pupil, Jacopo Sansovino (see below).

Jacopo Sansovino: Jacopo Tatti (1486–1570), It. sculptor, architect. The artist studied in the Florence workshop of Andrea Sansovino (see above) from the age of 16 and adopted the name of his master out of admiration for him and his work.

Santana: Carlos Santana (1947–), U.S. rock musician.

Bernardo Santareno: António Martinho do Rosário (1924–1980), Port. poet, playwright. The writer's adopted name comes from his birthplace, the city of Santarém, central Portugal.

George Santayana: Jorge Ruiz de Santayana y Borrais (1863–1952), Sp.-born U.S. writer, philosopher.

Fernando Santiván: Fernández Santibáñez Puga (1898– ?), Chilean writer.

Joseph Santley: Joseph Mansfield (1889–1971), U.S. movie director. The filmmaker adopted the name of his stepfather, veteran stage actor Eugene Santley.

Rahel Sanzara: Johanna Bleschke (1894–1936), Ger. novelist.

Sapper: Herman Cyril McNeile (1888–1937), Eng. novelist. The creator of Bulldog Drummond, the ex-army officer who foils the activities of the international crook, Carl Peterson, adopted his pseudonym when an officer in the Royal Engineers, a sapper being a soldier who digs saps (tunnels or trenches to conceal an approach to a fortified place). (In the Royal Engineers, "sapper" is still the official term for a private.) The name was devised for him by Lord Northcliffe, as no regular serving officer was allowed to publish under his real name. McNeile attempted to use his real name after World War I, but the public would have none of it, and demanded their familiar "Sapper."

Susan Sarandon: Susan Abigail Tomaling (1946–), U.S. movie actress. The actress's professional name is that of her first husband, actor Chris Sarandon (married 1967, divorced 1979).

Vasily Saratovets: Vasily Frolovich Yefimov (1885–1912), Russ. revolutionary. The Bolshevik worker's name means "(native) of Saratov." He was born near that city and was politically active there.

Gene Sarazen: Eugenio Saraceni (1902–), U.S. golfer, of It. parentage.

Joseph Sargent: Giuseppe Danielle Sorgente (1925–), U.S. movie director.

Frank Sargeson: Norris Frank Davey (1903–1982), N.Z. novelist, short storywriter.

Michael Sarne: Michael Schener (1940–), Br. TV, movie actor, singer.

Sarnicol: Thomas Jacob Thomas (1873–1945), Welsh poet. The writer's bardic name is derived from a local placename.

Leslie **Sarony:** Leslie Legge Sarony Frye (1897–1985), Eng. songwriter, entertainer. The music hall artist adopted his mother's maiden name (his own third name) at the age of 14, when he became a professional entertainer in juvenile variety acts.

Andrea del **Sarto** *see* **Andrea del Sarto**

Sassoferrato: Giovanni Battista Salvi (1609–1685), It. painter. The artist took his name from the town of his birth, Sassoferrato, in central Italy.

Lu **Säuberlich:** Liselotte Säuberlich-Lauke (1911–1976), Ger. stage, movie actress.

Ernest **Saunders:** Ernest Walter Schleyer (1935–), Austr.-born Br. businessman. The former Guinness chairman, jailed in 1990 for fraud, fled with his Jewish family from Vienna to England in 1938 to escape Hitler. When he was bullied at school in World War II because of his German name, his family adopted the English name of Saunders. They chose this name because they all liked it and because it "seemed to go with Schleyer" [*Sunday Times*, February 11, 1990].

Marshall **Saunders:** Margaret Marshall Saunders (1861–1947), Can. writer of animal stories for children.

Richard **Saunders:** Poor Richard (*q.v.*).

George **Sava:** Georgi Alexei Bankoff (1901–1996), Bulg.-born Br. author, consulting surgeon. The prolific writer of medical mystery novels claimed to have been born George Alexis Milkomanovich Milkomane, a name allegedly acquired from his uncle, Prince Alexander Milkomanovich Milkomane. In fact he was fostered when five years old by his mother's brother, General Alexis Ignatiev, who took him to Russia. His two best known pseudonyms were George Sava and George Borodin, but he also wrote as George Braddin, Peter Conway, and Alex Redwood, as well as under his real name of George Bankoff. The name Sava appears to have been created from letters in his uncle's name.

Ann **Savage:** Bernie Lyon (1921–), U.S. movie actress.

John **Savage:** John Youngs (1950–), U.S. movie actor.

Laura **Savage:** Frederic George Stephens (1828–1907), Eng. art critic. The writer used this name early for some contributions on Italian painting to the Pre-Raphaelite journal *The Germ* (1850). He also used the name John Seward for his papers that this organ published.

Lily **Savage:** Paul O'Grady (1955–), Br. drag artist, comedian.

Dany **Saval:** Danielle Nadine Suzanne Salle (1940–), Fr. movie actress.

Lee **Savold:** Lee Hulver (? 1914–1972), U.S. heavyweight boxer.

Bert **Savoy:** Everett Mackenzie (1888–1923), U.S. female impersonator.

Hanna **Sawicka:** Anna Krystyna Szapiro (1917–1943), Pol. World War II resistance worker.

Joseph **Sawyer:** Joseph Sauer (1901–1982), U.S. movie comedian.

John **Saxon:** Carmen Orrico (1935–), U.S. movie actor.

Peter **Saxon:** Wilfred McNeilly (1921–), Sc. SF, occult fiction writer. A blatantly Sassenach name for a Scot!

Sayat-Nova: Arutyun Sayadyan (1712–1795), Armenian troubadour. The poet, famous for his love songs, adopted his melodious nickname, meaning "king of song" or "master of music."

Leo **Sayer:** Gerard Hugh Sayer (1948–), Eng. rock singer. The singer was given his nickname by the wife of Adam Faith (*q.v.*), who when she first met him commented on his "mane" of hair, "Hey, he's like a little lion." Sayer liked the name, and adopted it [*Reveille*, January 12, 1979].

Rat **Scabies:** Chris Miller (1957–), Eng. punk rock drummer.

Scaeva: John Stubbes (1541–1600), Eng. Puritan zealot. The writer published a pamphlet entitled *The Discovery of a Gaping Gulf* (1579) condemning Queen Elizabeth's proposed marriage with Henry, Duke of Anjou. For this traitorous act, his right hand was ordered to be cut off. *Scaeva* is Latin for "lefthanded."

Boz **Scaggs:** William Royce Scaggs (1944–), U.S. rock musician. The musician spent his boyhood in Dallas, Texas, where he was nicknamed Boxley. This evolved into Boz, which replaced his original first names.

Gia **Scala:** Giovanna Sgoglio (1934–1972), Br. movie actress, of Ir.-It. parentage, working in U.S. The actress's screen name suggests both her own surname and the name of La Scala, Italy's chief opera house, in Milan.

Prunella **Scales:** Prunella Margaret Rumney West, née Illingworth (1932–), Eng. stage, TV actress. The actress adopted her mother's maiden name when she became a professional. Her mother had been on the stage before her marriage, and "I felt my father's name of Illingworth was rather long with Prunella" (personal letter from Prunella Scales, October 6, 1988).

Julius Caesar Scaliger: Julius Caesar Bordone (1484–1558), It. doctor, scholar. The physician claimed descent from the Veronese della Scala family, whose latinized name was Scaligerus, and changed his name accordingly.

Oda Schaefer: Oda Lange, née Kraus (1900–), Ger. poet, writer.

Fritzi Scheff: Friederike Yager (1879–1954), Austr.-born U.S. operetta singer, actress.

Andrea Schiavone: Andrea Meldolla (c.1510–1563), It. painter. The artist's adopted name means "Slav," referring to the fact that he came from Zara, Dalmatia (now Zadar, Croatia), then under Venetian jurisdiction.

Tito Schipa: Raffaele Attilio Amadeo (1888–1965), It. opera singer.

Leon Schiller: Leon de Schildenfeld (1887–1954), Pol. theatrical director, designer.

Dr. Schmidt: Johann Christoph Friedrich von Schiller (1759–1805), Ger. poet, playwright. The dramatist was originally a military surgeon in a Württemberg regiment. In 1781 he went absent without leave to attend a performance of his first play, *Die Räuber*. He was arrested by order of the regimental commander-in-chief, the Duke of Württemberg, and condemned to publish nothing but medical treatises. However, the following year he escaped from the Duke under the assumed name of Dr. Schmidt and spent several years, his so-called *Wanderjahre*, outside the country. Presumably the choice of name was an arbitrary one.

Karl Schmidt-Rottluff: Karl Schmidt (1884–1976), Ger. Expressionist painter. In 1906 the artist added the name of the town of his birth, Rottluff, near Chemnitz, to his surname, presumably for purposes of distinction.

Romy Schneider: Rosemarie Magdalena Albach-Retty (1938–1982), Austr. movie actress. Although the actress's father was actor Wolf Albach-Retty, her mother was film star Magda Schneider. Rosemarie (pet name Romy) adopted her mother's name as her screen name when she made her film debut in 1953. Her career took off immediately, and by 1955 Magda Schneider was playing supporting roles to those of her daughter.

Matitjahu Schoham: Matithau Poliakewitsch (1893–1937), Pol. Jewish playwright.

A Scholar: Samuel Wesley (1662–1735), Eng. clergyman, poet. The father of John Wesley, the founder of Methodism, used this name for a collection of poems published in 1685, when he was a student at Exeter College, Oxford. The exact title of the work was *Maggots: or, Poems on Several Subjects, never before handled. By a Schollar.*

Lotte Schöne: Charlotte Bodenstein (1891–1977), Austr.-born Fr. opera singer.

Paul Schott: Erich Wolfgang Korngold (1897–1957), Cz.-born U.S. composer + Julius Korngold (1860–1945), Cz. music critic, his father. The composer used this name for the libretto that he and his father jointly wrote for his opera *Die Tote Stadt* ("The Dead City") (1920).

Ossip Schubin: Aloiysia Kirschner (1854–1934), Ger. writer.

Scipione: Gino Bonichi (1904–1933), It. painter. The artist was the son of a soldier and adopted his name in honor of Scipio Africanus, the great Roman general who defeated Hannibal.

Agnes Neill Scott: Wilhelmina ("Willa") Johnstone Muir, née Anderson (1890–1970), Sc. poet, novelist, translator.

Gabriel Scott: Holst Jensen (1874–1958), Norw. writer.

Gordon Scott: Gordon M. Werschkul (1927–), U.S. movie actor.

Hennie Scott: Hendrik Momberg (1948–), Br. juvenile movie actor, of S.A. parentage.

Jack Scott: Jack Scafone, Jr. (1936–), Can. rock singer.

Jack S. Scott: Jonathan Escott (1922–), Br. crime novelist. The writer's assumed middle initial and surname phonetically reproduce his original surname.

Jay Scott: Jeffrey Scott Beaven (1949–1993), Can.-born U.S. movie critic.

Leader Scott: Lucy Baxter, née Barnes (1837–1902), Eng. writer on art. The writer derived her pen name from the maiden surnames of her two grandmothers: Isabel Leader was her mother's mother and Grace Scott her father's.

Linda Scott: Linda Joy Sampson (1945–), U.S. pop singer.

Lizabeth Scott: Emma Matzo (1922–), U.S. movie actress.

Randolph Scott: George Randolph Crane (1903–1987), U.S. movie actor.

Raymond **Scott:** Harry Warnow (1910–), U.S. popular music composer, arranger.

Ronnie **Scott:** Ronald Schatt (1927–1996), Eng. jazz club owner.

Sheila **Scott:** Sheila Christine Hopkins (1927–1988), Eng. aviator, lecturer, actress, writer.

Tony **Scott:** Anthony Sciacca (1921–), U.S. clarinetist.

Sir Walter **Scott:** James Kirke Paulding (1779–1860), U.S. author. Several writers and plagiarists adopted the name of the great Scottish author for their own works. Paulding, a close friend of Washington Irving, used the name for *The Lay of the Scotch Fiddle, a Tale of Havre de Grace* (1813), which was thus itself a "Scotch fiddle." A joint pseudonym shared by Paulding was Launcelot Langstaff (*q.v.*).

Scotty: Scott Wiseman (1909–1981), U.S. country singer, teaming with Lulu Belle (*q.v.*).

The **Scout:** Clive Graham (1913–1974), Eng. racing correspondent. The correspondent assumed the byname used by Cyril Luckham, his predecessor on the *Daily Express*. Graham began his journalistic career as Bendex in 1931, this name presumably referring to the curve in a racecourse (where one can spot the leaders as they enter the straight).

Annibal **Scratch:** Samuel Collings (*fl.*1780–1793), Eng. painter, caricaturist. The name is appropriate for an engraver of humorous plates, as Collings was.

H. **Scriblerus Secundus:** Henry Fielding (1707–1754), Eng. novelist, playwright. Fielding adopted this name for *The Tragedy of Tragedies, or Tom Thumb the Great* (1731), taking it from the name Martinus Scriblerus used by members of the so-called Scriblerus Club. This was a group of writers, including Pope, Swift, and Arbuthnot, formed in about 1713 with the aim of discussing topics of the day, enjoying witty conversation, and ridiculing "all false tastes in learning." They invented a character called Martinus Scriblerus, a pedantic hack, whose intellectual limitations and literary lapses were the central theme of their joint *Memoirs of Martinus Scriblerus* (1741). The character's name was apparently based on a punning nickname given Swift when at Oxford University. (The martin is a bird resembling the swift.)

While Fielding was Scriblerus Secundus, as the second of the name, Scriblerus Tertius and Scriblerus Quartus were both names used by the poet and pamphleteer Thomas Cooke (1703–1756). Martin Scriblerus was itself used by the satirist Thomas James Mathias (1754–1835).

George Julius Poulett **Scrope:** George Julius Poulett Thomson (1797–1876), Eng. geologist, politician. The scientist and political economist married Emma Phipps Scrope, heiress of William Scrope, in 1821, and thereupon assumed her name and the Scrope family's arms. William Scrope was the last of the old earls of Wiltshire, and had inherited not only his own father's family estates but those of another branch of the family in Lincolnshire. These all now passed to Emma, and so to the former George Thomson.

Thomas **Scrutiny:** Samuel De Wilde (1748–1832), Du.-born Br. painter, caricaturist. The artist used this name for his political caricatures in the *Satirist* in the early years of the 19th century.

Barbara **Seagull:** Barbara Hershey (*q.v.*).

Seal: Henry Samuels (1963–), Br.-born black rock musician, of Nigerian, Brazilian, and West Indian ancestry. The artist is said to have taken his name from his collection of porcelain seals. But it may have arisen as a nickname variant of his original surname, perhaps with reference to Sammy the Seal, the main character in a children's reading book of this name (1960) by the American writer Syd Hoff.

Charles **Sealsfield:** Karl Anton Postl (1793–1864), Swiss-born U.S. novelist. The writer was originally a monk, but in 1823 fled the monastery and went to the U.S. His adopted name was revealed to be a pseudonym only after his death.

Edward **Search:** Abraham Tucker (1705–1774), Eng. philosopher. The writer first used this intentionally meaningful name for his short philosophical work, *Freewill, Foreknowledge, and Fate* (1763). But he also used it for the work by which he is best known, *The Light of Nature Pursued* (1768–1778). Similar names were used by other thinkers and writers, such as Archbishop Whately, who published *Religion and her Name* (1847) as John Search. Tucker used the name Cuthbert Comment for a good-humored little pamphlet, *Man in Quest of Himself* (1763), written in reply to some critics.

January **Searle:** George Searle Phillips (1815–1889), Eng. miscellaneous writer, working in U.S. If "January" does not derive from "George" it presumably alludes to a significant month in the writer's life. It so happened that he died in January.

George **Seaton:** George Stenius (1911–1979), U.S. movie writer, director.

John **Sedges:** Pearl S. Buck (1892–1973), U.S. novelist, biographer. The writer used this male name for five books.

Paul **Sédir:** Yvon Le Loup (1871–1926), Fr. occultist. The practitioner's new surname is an anagram of French *désir*, "desire."

George **Seferis:** Giorgios Stylianou Seferiadis (1900–1971), Gk. poet, essayist, diplomat.

Anna **Seghers:** Netti Radványi, née Reiling (1900–1983), Ger. novelist, working in U.S. The writer took her name from the Flemish painter Hercules Seghers (1589–*c*.1638), a pupil of Rembrandt, whom she had always admired. She also used the name in an early story.

Lea **Seidl:** Caroline Mayrseidl (1895–1987), Austr. stage, movie actress, singer, working in U.K.

Steve **Sekely:** Istvan Szekely (1899–1979), Hung. movie director, working in U.S.

P.T. **Selbit:** Percy Thomas Tibbles (1881–1938), Eng. magician. A little hocus pocus with the illusionist's surname, and hey presto: a new name emerges (but with his original initials). Before World War I, the magician presented an act with an Egyptian theme under the name Joad Hereb, "The Wizard of the Sphinx."

Percival M. **Selby:** Percival M. Short (1886–1955), Br. stage actor, theatrical manager.

George **Selden:** George Selden Thomspon (1929–), U.S. biographer, children's writer.

Selena: Selena Quintanilla Perez (1971–1995), U.S. "Tex-Mex" singer.

Connie **Sellecca:** Concetta Sellecchia (1955–), U.S. TV actress.

Arthur **Sellings:** Robert Arthur Ley (1921–1968), Br. SF writer.

Selmar: [Baron] Karl Gustav von Brinckman (1764–1847), Swe. diplomat, poet.

Morton **Selten:** Morton Richard Stubbs (1860–1940), Eng. stage, movie actor.

Lewis J. **Selznick:** Lewis Zeleznik (1870–1933), Russ.-born U.S. movie distributor, impresario, father of movie producers David O. Selznick (1902–1965) and Myron Selznick (1898–1944).

Marcella **Sembrich:** Prakseda Marcelina Kochańska (1858–1935), Pol. opera singer, working in U.S.

Semprini: Fernando Riccardo Alberto Semprini (1908–1990), Br. popular pianist, entertainer, of It. parentage.

Senesino: Francesco Bernardi (*c*.1680–*c*.1750), It. male alto singer. The singer took his professional name from Siena, his birthplace.

Mack **Sennett:** Michael (or Mikail) Sinnott (1880–1960), Can.-born U.S. comedy movie director, producer, actor ("King of Comedy").

Captain **Sensible:** Raymond Burns (1957–), Eng. pop singer. The singer adopted his name in about 1977. Its origins are somewhat vague, but it appears to have had something to do with his habit of wearing a peaked cap, playing the fool on an airplane trip to France with his punk group, The Damned, and announcing himself as "your captain speaking." He later admitted that he would have preferred a more macho name, "something like Duane Zenith or Bert Powerhouse, but I'm lumbered with Captain Sensible" [*Observer Magazine*, February 3, 1985].

[St.] **Serafim Sarovsky:** Prokhor Isidorovich Moshnin (1759–1833), Russ. monk. The holy hermit, one of Russia's most popular saints, made his monastic vows at an early age, adopting the name Serafim (Seraphim, from the same word as the biblical seraphim, or order of angels). The second word of his name is the adjectival form of Sarov, the location of the monastery southeast of Moscow where he lived until 1825 and where he died. He was canonized in 1903 by order of Czar Nicholas II.

Aleksandr **Serafimovich:** Aleksandr Serafimovich Popov (1863–1949), Russ. writer. The writer adopted his own patronymic (middle name) as his pen name, but changed the stress (accent) from the third syllable to the fourth.

Seranus: Susie Frances Harrison, née Riley (1859–1935), Can. writer. The writer's Latin-looking name appears to have been based on her first two names, which contain all its letters.

Séraphine: Séraphine Louis (1864–1934), Fr. painter. The artist is also known as Séraphine de Senlis, from the name of the town where she was in domestic service before being "discovered."

Massimo **Serato:** Giuseppe Segato (1917–1989), It. movie actor.

Victor **Serge:** Viktor Kibalchich (1890–1947) Belg.-born Fr. revolutionary politician, of Russ. origin.

Mark **Sergeyev:** Mark Davidovich Gantvarger (Handwarger) (1926–), Russ. writer. The writer replaced his Jewish surname by a somewhat similar Russian one.

Sergey **Sergeyev-Tsensky:** Sergey Nikolayevich Sergeyev (1875–1958), Russ. writer. The writer was born and raised in Tambov, on the Tsna River. Hence the addition to his original surname, as the adjectival form of the river name.

Sergius: (1) Barfolomey Kirillovich (1314–1392), Russ. saint, monk ("Sergius of Radonezh"); (2) Ivan Nikolayevich Stragorodsky (1867–1944), Russ. churchman, patriarch of Moscow and All Russia. St. Sergius of Radonezh was one of Russia's most important spiritual leaders, and was subsequently regarded as the saint protector of Russia. Stragorodsky almost certainly took his religious name in his honor. This means that the monk must have taken his own name from an earlier Sergius. He was possibly the 3d-century Christian martyr St. Sergius, who with St. Bacchus was put to death by the Romans in about 303. Sergius of Radonezh adopted his religious name in 1337, on taking monastic vows. Stragorodsky similarly took his name in 1890. See also the next name below.

Sergius IV: Pietro Buccaporci (? –1012), It. pope. The pope's original surname was actually a nickname, meaning "pig's snout," and referring to his appearance. He was no doubt ready enough to take a name that had been used by three popes before him. (He would not have kept his original name in any case, out of respect for St. Peter, leader of the apostles and first bishop of Rome.)

Sergo: Aleksey Ivanovich Sergeyev (1915–1976), Russ. circus artist, clown.

Mikhail Sergeyevich **Sergushev:** Markel Prokopyevich Aksyonov (1886–1930), Russ. revolutionary.

German **Serrano:** José Ricardo Ruíz (1960–1992), Salvadorean guerrilla commander.

Jean Nicolas **Servan:** Giovanni Niccolò Servandoni (1695–1766), It. architect, working in France. The artist gallicized his name on settling in France.

Mishshi **Sespel:** Mikhail Kuzmich Kuzmin (1899–1922), Russ. (Chuvash) poet. The founder of Chuvash poetry took a plant name meaning "snowdrop," with Mishshi a Chuvash form of his original Russian name Mikhail (Michael).

Sesshu: Oda (1420–1506), Jap. artist. The artist's original personal name is unknown, but his family name was Oda. In 1431, when he was ten, he was enrolled at a local Zen temple and given the name Toyo, "willowlike," perhaps because he was graceful and slender. In about

1466 he became chief priest of a temple in Yamaguchi, and it was then that he began calling himself Sesshu, literally "snow boat."

John **Sessions:** John Gibb Marshall (1953–), Sc.-born Br. stage, TV comedian.

Ernest Thompson **Seton:** Ernest Evan Seton-Thompson (1860–1946), Eng. author, artist, naturalist, working in Canada. The writer inverted the two parts of his last name when he began his Canadian career as naturalist to the Government of Manitoba.

Dr. **Seuss:** Theodor Seuss Geisel (1904–1991), U.S. children's writer, illustrator. The popular author called himself "Dr." by way of a self-conferred title. In 1955, however, his old college, Dartmouth, awarded him a genuine doctorate. His name as a whole to some young readers would suggest "Dr. Sweet" as an added allure. Seuss wrote verse as Theo le Sieg (reversing his surname).

Paruyr **Sevak:** Paruyr Rafaelovich Kazaryan (1924–1971), Armenian poet, literary critic. The poet's name means "black-eyed," describing his appearance. Compare the next entry below.

Ruben **Sevak:** Ruben Chilinkaryan (1885–1915), Armenian writer. The writer's name means "black-eyed," as this is what he was. Compare the entry above.

Steve **Severin:** Steven Bailey (1955–), Br. punk rock musician. The bassist member of Siouxsie and the Banshees, lead singer Siouxsie Sioux (*q.v.*), took his new name from Séverin, the narrator of Leopold von Sacher-Masoch's perverse novel *Venus in Furs* (1870).

Séverine: Caroline Guebhard, née Rémy (1855–1929), Fr. journalist, novelist.

David **Severn:** David Storr Unwin (1918–), Eng. novelist, children's writer.

Igor **Severyanin:** Igor Vasilyevich Lotarev (1887–1941), Russ. poet. The poet was born in St. Petersburg. Hence his new surname, meaning "Northerner." He is the best known of this name, which was adopted by other writers similarly.

Carmen **Sevilla:** Carmen Galisteo (1930–), Sp. movie actress, dancer, singer. The actress took her stage name from her birthplace, Seville.

David **Seville:** Ross Bagdassarian (1919–1972), U.S. music, record company executive.

Gagerin **Sevunts:** Gagerin Seviyevich Grigoryan (1911–1969), Armenian writer.

Anne **Seymour:** (1) Anne Ekert (1909–1988), U.S. movie actress; (2) Phyllis Digby Morton, née Panting (? –1984), Eng. journalist, broadcaster.

Carolyn **Seymour**: Carolyn von Benckendorff (*c.*1955–), Br. movie, TV actress.

Gordon **Seymour**: [Sir] Charles Waldstein (later, Watson) (1856–1927), U.S.-born Br. archaeologist.

Jane **Seymour**: Joyce Penelope Wilhelmina Frankenberg (1951–), Eng. movie actress, working in U.S. If the actress's screen name is not derived from the name of Henry VIII's third wife, possibly it is a compliment to Jane Seymour Fonda, her fellow actress?

Lynn **Seymour**: Lynn Berta Springbett (1939–), Can. ballet dancer. Despite the possible aptness of her real surname (although it does suggest "bedsprings"), the dancer was advised to find a new name by choreographer Kenneth Macmillan. It was he who proposed "Seymour." The name seems to appeal as a pseudonym (see the entries above and the one below). If its attraction does not stem from Jane Seymour, Henry VIII's third wife, possibly the lure lies in its suggestion of "see more," which could be regarded as promising or propitious. It is also an English aristocratic name in its own right (that of the dukes of Somerset and marquises of Hertford).

William **Seymour**: William Gorman Cunningham (1855–1933), U.S. stage actor.

Shabba-Doo: Adolfo Quinones (1955–), U.S. black movie actor, dancer. The performer is presumably named Shabba from the same source as Shabba Ranks (*q.v.*).

John **Shadow**: John Byrom (1692–1763), Eng. poet. The poet used this appropriate name for two papers on dreams that he contributed to the *Spectator* (Nos. 586, 593) in 1714.

Mighty **Shadow**: Winston Bailey (*c.*1939–), U.S. black calypso singer. The singer is usually known simply as Shadow.

Ivan **Shadr**: Ivan Dmitriyevich Ivanov (1887–1941), Russ. sculptor. The artist took his name from his birthplace, the town of Shadrinsk, southern Russia.

Shag: Anatoly Sergeyevich Novozhilov (1910–), Russ. conjuror, circus artist. The performer originally teamed up with a colleague named Shvetsov as a pair of acrobats, calling their act "Dva Moreno" ("The Two Morenos"). This then became "Dva Shaga" ("The Two Steps"), and Novozhilov kept the name in the singular for his solo acts.

Abdulla **Shaik**: Abdulla Mustafa ogly Talybzade (1881–1959), Azerbaijani novelist, poet, critic.

Shakey Jake: James D. Harris (1921–1990), U.S. blues musician. When not playing harmonica Harris was a professional gambler. Hence his name, from the crapshooters' call "Shake 'em, Jake."

Yitzhak **Shamir**: Yitzhak Jazernicki (or Yezernitzky) (1915–), Pol.-born Israeli prime minister.

Bud **Shank**: Clifford Everett, Jr. (1926–), U.S. jazz musician.

Shannon: Shannon Greene (1958–), U.S. pop singer.

Dell **Shannon**: Elizabeth Linington (1921–1988), U.S. mystery writer. Other names used by the writer include Anne Blaisdell, Lesley Egan, and Egan O'Neill.

Del **Shannon**: Charles Weedon Westover (1934–1990), U.S. popular musician, songwriter. The musician is said to have derived his first name from his boss's car, a Cadillac Coupe de Ville, and his surname from a wrestler that he met in a night club, Mark Shannon. The name is virtually identical to that of Dell Shannon (above), and it is hard to believe this is simply a coincidence.

Peggy **Shannon**: Winona Sammon (1909–1941), U.S. stage, movie actress.

Levon **Shant**: Levon Segbosyan (1869–1951), Armenian writer.

Roxanne **Shante**: Lolita Gooden (1969–), U.S. black rapper. Is the singer's name meant to suggest "rocks an' shanty"?

Omar **Sharif**: Michael Shalhoub (1932–), Egyptian movie actor, of Syrian-Lebanese descent. The actor explains in his autobiography how he arrived at his screen name: "I'd changed my name to do 'The Blazing Sun.' At birth, I was Michael Shalhoub. My first name, Michael, annoyed me. Anybody could be a Michael. I'd tried to come up with something that sounded Middle Eastern and that could still be spelled in every language. Omar! Two syllables that had a good ring to them and reminded Americans of General Omar Bradley. Next I thought of combining Omar with the Arabic Sherif, but I realized that this would evoke the word 'sheriff,' which was bit too cowboyish. So I opted for a variant—I became Omar Sharif" [Omar Sharif with Marie-Thérèse Guinchard, *The Eternal Male*, 1977]. (Arabic *sherif* is a form of title applied to one of noble ancestry in a Middle Eastern country.)

Jack **Sharkey:** Joseph Paul Zukauskas (1902–1994), U.S. heavyweight boxer, of Lithuanian parentage. The boxer took his name from a former leading heavyweight, Sailor Tom Sharkey. Like him, Zukauskas was a sailor before entering the ring.

Dee Dee **Sharp:** Diana (or Dione) LaRue (1945–), U.S. soul singer. The singer's name may pun on the musical note (D sharp).

Luke **Sharp:** Robert Barr (1850–1912), Sc. novelist, working in Canada, U.K. A name in the same punning category as Justin Case (*q.v.*).

Sharpshooter: John Phillips (*fl.*1825–1842), Eng. caricaturist, illustrator. The name is apt for a caricaturist, who aims to "score a hit" on his subject.

Mikhail **Shatrov:** Mikhail Filippovich Marshak (1932–), Russ. playwright.

Samuel **Shattock:** Samuel George Betty (1852–1924), Eng. pathologist. The medical specialist changed his name in about 1882, presumably in order to claim a kinship with a bearer of the new name.

Artie **Shaw:** Arthur Jacob Arshawsky (1910–), U.S. jazz musician.

Brian **Shaw:** Brian Earnshaw (1928–1992), Eng. ballet dancer.

Fiona **Shaw:** Fiona Mary Wilson (1958–), Ir.-born Br. stage actress. As she was about to leave the Royal Academy of Dramatic Art, the actress discovered that there was another Fiona Wilson: "I wanted a name that connected my Irish family with me and passing the statue of George Bernard Shaw on the lower staircase and knowing there were many Shaws in my family, I opted for its short succinctness. ... I have never regretted it. It is easy to spell, to pronounce and identifies my family and nation the way Wilson never would" [private undated letter from Fiona Shaw, received October 5, 1995].

Jane **Shaw:** Jean Bell Shaw Patrick (1910–), Sc. writer of books for girls. Shaw was the writer's mother's maiden name, as well as her own third name.

Roger **Shaw:** Roger Ollerearnshaw (1931–), Eng. TV announcer.

Run Run **Shaw:** Shao Yi-fu (1906–), Chin. movie producer, working in Hong Kong.

Sandie **Shaw:** Sandra Goodrich (1947–), Eng. pop singer. A pleasantly punning seaside name, with "Sandie," of course, from her first name. The name was given by her first manager, Eve Taylor.

Susan **Shaw:** Patsy Sloots (1929–1978), Eng. movie actress. The future actress was spotted at a London Camera Club demonstration by a film agent, who changed her name to Pat Fanshawe and secured her a test. After a year's "grooming," she was given a small part in *The Upturned Glass* (1947), for which she was further renamed Susan Shaw.

T.E. **Shaw:** John Hume Ross (*q.v.*).

Victoria **Shaw:** Jeanette Elphick (1935–1988), Austral. movie actress, working in U.S. In view of the actress's nationality, this sounds like a state-inspired name.

Wini **Shaw:** Winfred Lei Momi (1899–1982), U.S. movie actress, singer, of Hawaiian descent.

Dick **Shawn:** Richard Schulefand (1928–1987), U.S. movie comedian. The actor made his debut in 1948 as Richy Shawn.

William **Shawn:** William Chon (1907–1992), U.S. journalist, editor.

Robert **Shayne:** Robert Shaen Dawe (*c.*1910–1992), U.S. movie actor.

Tamara **Shayne:** Tamara Nikoulin (1897–1983), Russ.-U.S. movie actress.

N. **Shchedrin:** Mikhail Yevgrafovich Saltykov (-Shchedrin) (1826–1889), Russ. writer. Saltykov's son has explained how his father came by his pseudonym, which is based on the Russian word *shchedryy*, "generous": "It was like this. When he was in government service, he was advised that it was not done to sign one's work with one's real name. So he had to find a pen name, but could not hit on anything suitable. My mother suggested that he should choose a pseudonym based on the word 'shchedryy,' as in his writings he was extraordinarily generous with any kind of sarcasm. My father liked his wife's idea, and from then on he called himself Shchedrin." It is possible, however, that the name could have come from a servant in the employ of Saltykov's family, or from a local merchant T. Shchedrin, or some acquaintance of Saltykov, or it could even derive from the word *shchedrina* "pockmarks," with reference to the "pockmarks" on the face of Russia at the time (1870s) [Dmitriyev, pp. 58–59].

Al **Shean:** Alfred Schoenberg (1868–1949), Ger.-born U.S. stage, movie comedian.

Moira **Shearer:** Moira Shearer King (1926–), Sc. ballet dancer, stage, movie actress.

Norma **Shearer:** Edith Norma Fisher (1900–1983), Can. movie actress.

Charlie **Sheen:** Carlos Irwin Estevez (1965–), U.S. movie actor, son of Martin Sheen (see below). His elder brother, actor Emilio Estevez (1960–), has retained the family name.

Martin **Sheen:** Ramon Estevez (1940–), U.S. stage actor. The actor adopted the maiden name of his wife, née Janet Sheen.

Sheila: Anna Chancel (1946–), Fr. pop singer. The singer took her name in 1962 when she sang a version of Tommy Roe's hit "Sheila."

Barbara **Shelley:** Barbara Kowin (1933–), Br. movie actress.

Paul **Shelley:** Paul Matthews (1942–), Eng. stage, TV actor.

Pete **Shelley:** Peter McNeish (1955–), Eng. "electro-pop" musician.

Anne **Shelton:** Patricia Sibley (1924–), Eng. popular singer.

John **Shelton:** John Price (1917–1972), U.S. movie actor.

Paul **Shelving:** Paul North (c.1889–1968), Br. theatrical designer.

Sam **Shepard:** Samuel Shepard Rogers VII (1943–), U.S. playwright, movie actor.

Michael **Shepley:** Michael Shepley-Smith (1907–1961), Br. stage, movie actor.

T.G. **Sheppard:** William Browder (1944–), U.S. country singer. The origin of the singer's name is told as follows. "T.G. was loathe [sic] to use his real name, Bill Browder, feeling that it might conflict with his promotion work. Inspiration struck when looking out of his office window across the street, he saw some dogs of the German Shepherd breed. An office colleague jokingly suggested he call himself 'The German Shepherd.' T.G. was amused at the thought, but on later reflection, decided he liked the idea" [Kash, p. 408]. (Another account claims he saw the name as "The Good Shepherd.")

John **Shepperd:** Shepperd Strudwick (1907–1983), U.S. movie actor.

Ann **Sheridan:** Clara Lou Sheridan (1915–1967), U.S. movie actress (the "Oomph Girl"). The actress's new first name is nicely echoed in her surname.

Dinah **Sheridan:** Dinah Mec (1920–), Br. movie actress, of Ger.-Russ. parentage.

Mary **Sheridan:** Daphne Graham (1903–), Eng. stage, movie actress.

Paul **Sheriff:** Paul Schouvalov (or Schouvaloff) (1903–1962), Russ.-born movie art director, working in U.K.

Allan **Sherman:** Allan Copelon (1924–1973), U.S. comedian, folk humorist.

Bim **Sherman:** Jarret Tomlinson (1952–), Jamaican pop musician.

Vincent **Sherman:** Abram Orovitz (1906–), U.S. movie director.

Billy **Sherrill:** Philip Campbell (1936–), U.S. pop, country musician.

Lydia **Sherwood:** Lily Shavelson (1906–1989), Br. stage, movie actress.

Madeleine **Sherwood:** Madeleine Thornton (1926–), Can. movie actress.

Lev **Shestov:** Lev Isaakovich Shvartsman (Schwarzman) (1866–1938), Russ. existentialist philosopher, man of letters.

Ella **Shields:** Ella Buscher (1879–1952), U.S.-born Br. music hall singer, male impersonator.

George **Shiels:** George Morsheil (1881–1949), Ir. playwright.

Sahib **Shihab:** Edmund Gregory (1925–1989), U.S. jazz musician. The musician changed his name in 1947 on adopting the Muslim faith.

Mother **Shipton:** Ursula Shipton, née Southill (or Southiel) (*fl.*1486), Eng. prophetess. The lady is probably quite fictional, but her popular biographical data are as here.

Ovanes **Shiraz:** Ovanes Tatevosovich Karapetyan (1914–1984), Armenian poet. The poet adopted as his new name that of the Iranian city of Shiraz, birthplace of two famous Persian poets, Saadi (Sa'di) (*q.v.*) and Hafez.

Talia **Shire:** Talia Rosa Coppola (1946–), U.S. movie actress, sister of director Francis Ford Coppola (1939–). The actress's name is that of her former husband, composer David Shire.

Shirley: [Sir] John Skelton (1831–1897), Sc. lawyer, author, literary critic. The writer adopted his pen name from the main character of *Shirley* (1849), the novel by Charlotte Brontë, whose earlier *Jane Eyre* (1847) he had favorably reviewed. (Miss Brontë had written to thank him.) He used the name for his essays and reviews in *The Guardian*, a short lived Edinburgh periodical, as well as for contributions to the longer lived *Fraser's Magazine*. A pseudonym was necessary in order not to jeopardize his professional prospects as an up-and-coming lawyer.

Anne **Shirley:** Dawn Evelyeen Paris (1918–1993), U.S. movie actress. The actress began her career in silent movies, in which she was billed under such names as Dawn O'Day, Lenn Fondre, and Lindley Dawn. In 1934, at the age of 16, she was given the title role in *Anne of Green Gables*, a screen version of the novel by L.M. Montgomery, and legally adopted the name of the young girl who is its heroine.

Steve **Shirley**: Vera Stephanie Shirley (1933–), Ger.-born Br. businesswoman. The former computer company executive now has the name of the Englishman she married in 1959. She was born Vera Stephanie Buchthal, but went to England as a child refugee in 1939. She subsequently changed her name on naturalization to Brook in honor of the English poet Rupert Brooke.

Aleksandr **Shirvanzade**: Aleksandr Minasovich Movsisyan (1858–1935), Armenian writer. The writer was born in Shemakha, historic capital of the khanate of Shirvan. Hence his adopted name, with the Azerbaijani patronymic suffix -*zade*, so that he was "son of Shirvan."

M. **Shketan**: Yakov Pavlovich Mayorov (1898–1937), Russ. (Mari) writer. Mayorov was the first Mari prose writer. Hence his adopted name, meaning "lonely."

Michelle **Shocked**: Michelle Schacht (1962–), U.S. folk singer. The singer adopted her new name when she ran away from her Mormon parents at the age of 15. In 1996, on settling a legal dispute with her record company, Mercury Records, she adopted a softer, more "spiritual" persona, prompting one commentator to quip: "At this rate she might even have to change her name again—although Michelle Mellowed doesn't have quite the same ring" [*The Times*, November 22, 1996].

Sholem Aleichem: Sholem (or Shalom) Yakov Rabinowitz (1859–1916), Russ.-born Yiddish novelist, working in U.S. The name is a familiar Yiddish greeting derived from Hebrew, meaning "peace be with you." (Hebrew *shalom* is pronounced "sholem" by the Ashkenazim.) The writer adopted the name in 1883, the year he decided to abandon Hebrew as a literary medium and instead write stories and sketches in Yiddish (then regarded as bad form).

Georgy **Sholokhov-Sinyavsky**: Georgy Filippovich Sholokhov (1901–1967), Russ. writer. The writer was born in the hamlet of Sinyavsky, and added its name to his original surname.

Troy **Shondell**: Gary Shelton (1940–), U.S. pop singer, producer.

Dinah **Shore**: Frances Rose Shore (1917–1994), U.S. singer, radio, TV actress. The singer's change of name was initially prompted

when "everybody down in Nashville" suggested she should use the pet form of her first name, Fanny, quipping and quoting: "Fanny sat on a tack. Fanny Rose. Fanny Rose sat on a tack. Did Fanny rise?" "I had to do something," sighed Frances Rose Shore, so changed her first two names to "Dinah," from the song of that name. Even so, as a child star, she *had* performed as "Fanny Rose" for some time.

Bob **Short**: (1) Augustus Baldwin Longstreet (1790–1870), U.S. lawyer, educationist, author; (2) Alexander Pope (1688–1744), Eng. poet. Pope used the name for some contributions to the short-lived periodical *The Guardian* (1713), and it is possible that Longstreet borrowed the pseudonym from him, enjoying the pun on his own surname.

Bobby **Short**: Robert Waltrip (1926–), U.S. popular singer, pianist.

Abel **Shufflebottom**: Robert Southey (1774–1843), Eng. poet. A frivolous name used by the poet for some minor love poems.

Shukhrat: Gulyam Alimov (1918–), Uzbek writer. The writer's pen name means "glory," "fame."

Sergey **Shumsky**: Sergey Vasilyevich Chesnokov (1820–1878), Russ. actor.

Yury **Shumsky**: Yury Vasilyevich Shomin (1887–1954), Ukrainian actor.

Shusha: Shusha Guppy (1940–), Iranian-born singer, songwriter, author. The singer emigrated to France as a teenager, then married an English writer and relocated to London. She writes under her full name.

Nevil **Shute**: Nevil Shute Norway (1899–1960), Br. novelist, working in Australia. "My full name is Nevil Shute Norway," runs an "Author's Note" prefacing the writer's autobiography. "Readers will find on page 71 an explanation of the reasons that made me use my Christian names alone when writing my books." Here is that explanation: "During the daytime I was working in a fairly important position on a very important engineering job. ... It seemed to me that Vickers would probably take a poor view of an employee who wrote novels on the side. ... For these reasons I made up my mind to do what many other authors in a similar case have done in the past, and to write under my Christian names. ... Nevil Shute was quite a good, euphonious name for a novelist, and Mr. Norway could go on untroubled by his other interest and build up a sound reputation as an engineer. So it started, and so it has gone on to this day" [Nevil Shute, *Slide Rule: The Autobiography of an Engineer*, 1954].

Timothy **Shy:** Dominic Bevan Wyndham Lewis (1891–1969), Br. journalist, novelist, biographer. The writer used this pseudonym for his contributions to the *News Chronicle* from 1936. His better known pen name was Beachcomber (*q.v.*).

Siamanto: Atom Yardzhanyan (1878–1915), Armenian poet.

Sice: Simon Rowbottom (1969–), Eng. rock musician.

Edward William **Sidney:** Nathaniel Beverley Tucker (1784–1851), U.S. novelist.

George **Sidney:** Samuel Greenfield (1878–1945), U.S. movie comedian.

Margaret **Sidney:** Harriet Mulford Lothrop, née Stone (1844–1924), U.S. children's writer. The writer adopted her daughter's name as her first name, with Sidney simply a name that she liked.

Sylvia **Sidney:** Sophia Kosow (1910–), U.S. stage, movie actress, of Russ. Jewish parentage. The actress adopted her stepfather's name, Sidney, as her professional surname, moderating her first name at the same time to harmonize with it.

Siface: Giovanni Francesco Grossi (1653–1697), It. male alto singer. The castrato sang so superbly in a 1678 performance of Cavalli's opera *Scipione Africano* in Venice that he came to be known by the part he took, that of Siface (Syphax).

Siful Sifadda: Henrik Arnold Wergeland (1808–1845), Norw. poet. Norway's national poet used this name for some early satirical farces.

Sigma: [Sir] Douglas Straight (1844–1914). Eng. author. The writer's pen name represents the Greek letter corresponding to his initial "S."

Simone **Signoret:** Simone-Henriette-Charlotte Kaminker (1921–1985), Ger.-born Fr. movie actress. The actress adopted her mother's maiden name during the German occupation of France in World War II in place of her original Jewish name.

Sikhkhat: Abbasguli Ali-abbas ogly Mekhtizade (1874–1918), Azerbaijani poet, translator. The writer's adopted name means "truthful," "upright."

Albert **Siklós:** Albert Schönwald (1878–1942), Hung. cellist, composer.

The **Silent Traveller:** Chiang Yee (1903–), Chin.-born Eng. writer of popular travel books. The writer, famous for his travel books in the series *The Silent Traveler in...* (London, Oxford, New York, Edinburgh, etc.) derived his English pen name from his Chinese pseudonym, Yahsin-che, which meant "dumb walking man."

Beverly **Sills:** Belle Miriam Greenough, née Silverman (1929–), U.S. opera singer. The singer's professional name is clearly based on her original first name and surname. She was a child radio performer under the name Bubbles, a pet form of her first name.

Ignazio **Silone:** Secondo Tranquilli (1900–1978), It. anti-fascist writer, novelist. The writer adopted a pseudonym to protect his family from Fascist persecution.

Silurist: Henry Vaughan (1622–1695), Welsh poet. The poet was born in Breconshire (now Powys), in a historic region of southern Wales named for the people known as the Silures. Hence his pseudonym.

James **Silvain:** James Sullivan (? –1856), Eng. ballet dancer, working in France, U.S.

Ron **Silver:** Ron Zimelman (1946–), U.S. movie, TV actor.

Jay **Silverheels:** Harold J. Smith (1919–1980), Can. Native American movie actor. The actor's name alludes to his roles in westerns.

Silverpen: Eliza Meteyard (1816–1879), Eng. novelist, writer. The writer was given the name by editor Douglas Jerrold when she contributed an article to the first number of *Douglas Jerrold's Weekly Newspaper* (1846).

Phil **Silvers:** Philip Silversmith (1912–1985), U.S. movie, TV comedian, of Russ. parentage.

Silvia: Zanetta-Rosa-Giovanni Benozzi (*c.*1701–1758), It. actress.

Silyn: Robert Roberts (1871–1930), Welsh poet. The writer took his name from Cwm Silyn, the name of a valley in his native Caernarvonshire (now in Gwynedd). The name is now a forename in its own right.

Georges **Sim:** Georges-Joseph-Christian Simenon (1903–1989), Belg. writer of detective fiction.

Simeon Polotsky: Samuil Yemelyanovich (or Gabrilovich) Petrovsky-Sitnianovich (1629–1680), Belorussian-born Russ. ecclesiastic, poet, playwright. The writer, also known as Simeon of Polotsk, adopted his name in 1656 on taking his monastic vows in his birthtown of Polotsk.

John **Simm:** John Simmon (1920–), U.S. theatre critic.

Al **Simmons:** Aloys Szymanski (1902–1956), U.S. baseball player.

Gene **Simmons:** Chaim Witz (1949–), Israeli-born Br. rock musician. The musician adopted a name that paid tribute to his favorite film star, English actress Jean Simmons (1929–).

Ginny **Simms:** Virginia Sims (1916–1994), U.S. singer, movie actress.

Hilda **Simms:** Hilda Moses (1920–), U.S. stage actress.

Madame **Simone:** Pauline Benda Porché (1877–1985), Fr. stage actress, author. The actress, whose stage and writing career lasted almost a century, married the actor Charles le Bargy in 1897, and it was he who persuaded her to adopt a stage name derived from that of the Musset heroine.

Nina **Simone:** Eunice Kathleen Waymon (1933–), U.S. black jazz singer, pianist, composer. The musician's stage name appears to be loosely based on her original first name and surname.

Simplicissimus: Georgy Valentinovich Plekhanov (1857–1918), Russ. socialist. A name adopted for a while by the Russian socialist Plekhanov, who also wrote as Volgin (see Lenin). It derives from the title of the best known book by the 17th-century German novelist Hans Jakob Christoffel von Grimmelshausen, in full: *Der Abenteuerliche Simplicissimus Teutsch, das ist: Beschreibung des Lebens eines Seltzamen Vagantens Genannt Melchior Sternfels von Fuchshaim* ("The Adventurous German Simpleton, that is: Description of the life of a Strange Wanderer Named Melchior Sternfels von Fuchshaim") (1669). Canny readers will have noticed that the name of the hero is an anagram of that of the author; moreover, the book was supposedly published by one Hermann Scheifhaim von Sulsfort, a similarly anagrammatic name. And as if this wasn't enough, the author purported to be a certain Samuel Greifensohn von Hirschfeld (*q.v.*). The book itself is a picaresque novel about the adventures of a simple youth in various guises (soldier, robber, slave) and gives a vivid picture of the havoc wrought in Germany by the Thirty Years' War (1618–48).

Rogelio **Sinán:** Bernardo Domínguez Alba (1904–), Panamanian writer.

Alexander (or Terry) **Sinclair:** Terence Clark (1945–1983), N.Z. criminal. The drug trafficker was a partner in crime of Robert Trimbole (*q.v.*).

Arthur **Sinclair:** Francis Quinto McDonnell (1883–1951), Ir. stage actor.

Clive **Sinclair:** Joshua Smolinsky (1950–), Br. writer, of Pol. Jewish parentage. The writer tells how he came by his English name: "My mother's father came from Stashev in South-West Poland. How the family got there no one knows. His name in Hebrew was Joshua, though he was known as Shia, its Yiddish diminutive. When he settled in England it was Anglicized and he became Charles. I am named after him, the initial letter sufficing. ... My father's mother was named Shaindel. In England Shane became plain Jane. My middle name, John, comes from her. Smolinsky was her married name, which my father changed to Sinclair when he joined the army in 1939. Thus my disguise, my *nom de vivre*, Clive Sinclair. Joshua Smolinsky (whom I might have been) lives, but only in my stories, as a down-at-heel private eye on the seamy side of Los Angeles. Joshua Ben David, by which I am known to God, has not been heard since ... my bar mitzvah. ... The last named ought to be the essential me, but isn't. I am stuck as Clive Sinclair, because my mother tongue is English" [*Times Literary Supplement*, May 3, 1985].

Jo **Sinclair:** Ruth Seid (1913–), U.S. writer, of Russ. Jewish parentage.

Ronald **Sinclair:** (1) Reginald Teague-Jones (1889–1988), Eng. intelligence officer, working in India, Russia; (2) Richard Arthur Hould (1924–1992), N.Z.-born juvenile movie actor, of N.Z.-Eng. parentage, working in U.S. Teague-Jones became so closely associated with his pseudonym that his obituary was published under his adopted name in *The Times* of November 22, 1988. A revised obituary, giving his true identity and the reasons for his change of name, appeared three days later: "Born Reginald Teague-Jones, he changed his name to Ronald Sinclair. ... The reason was his fear ... of being liquidated by Bolshevik agents, or even of being kidnapped and brought back to the Soviet Union for trial" [Peter Hopkirk, "Ronald Sinclair: Carrying his true identity to the grave," *The Times*, November 25, 1988].

Isaac Bashevis **Singer:** Icek-Hersz Zynger (1904–1991), Pol.-born U.S. writer, working in Yiddish.

Anne **Singleton:** Ruth Benedict, née Fulton (1887–1948), U.S. anthropologist, poet.

Penny **Singleton:** Mariana Dorothy McNulty (1908–), U.S. movie actress. The actress used her married name as her screen name.

Sinitta: Sinitta Renay Malone (1966–), U.S. black pop singer.

John **Sinjohn:** John Galsworthy (1867–1933), Eng. novelist, playwright. The name was an early one used by Galsworthy for his collection of stories, *From the Four Winds* (1897). The name itself refers to his identically named father, John Galsworthy, with "Sin-" apparently intended to mean "son."

Siôn Wyn o Eifion: John Thomas (1786–1859), Welsh poet. The writer's name means "Fair John of Eifionydd," the latter being the historic region in northwestern Wales where he was born and where many poets lived.

Siouxsie **Sioux:** Susan Dallion (1957–), Eng. rock singer.

Siranuysh: Merobe Kantardzhyan (1857–1932), Armenian actress.

Siras: Amayak Saakovich Voskanyan (1902–), Armenian writer.

Sirin: Vladimir Vladimirovich Nabokov (1899–1977), Russ.-born U.S. novelist. This was an early pseudonym used by the author when he was still writing in Russian, although already an immigrant resident in the U.S. (from 1919). In Old Russian literature, "Sirin" was the name of a mythical bird with a woman's head and torso, similar to a harpy (but not malignant in the same way). Nabokov used the name to avoid being confused with his father, Vladimir Dmitriyevich Nabokov (1869–1922), a criminologist and political figure who was one of the founders of the "Kadets," the Constitutional Democratic Party led by Milyukov.

Douglas **Sirk:** Claus (later Hans) Detlef Sierck (1900–1987), Ger. movie director, of Dan. parentage, working in U.S. "Claus" gave "Douglas."

Sirone: Norris Jones (1940–), U.S. jazz musician. A virtual reversal of the musician's original first name, with a suggestion of his surname thrown in.

Sitting Bull: Tatanka Iyotake (*c.*1831–1890), U.S. Native American chief. The Teton Dakota chief was originally known by a name translating as Jumping Badger. He took his present name (the English translating the Dakota) in 1857 following a battle.

Sixtus IV: Francesco della Rovere (1414–1484), It. pope. This is the pope who built the Sistine Chapel, the papal chapel in the Vatican, named for him.

Sixtus V: Felice Peretti (1520–1590), It. pope. The pontiff took the name out of regard for Sixtus IV (see above), who had been a Franciscan, like himself.

Skanderbeg: Gjergj (or George) Kastrioti (1405–1468), Albanian national hero. The national leader acquired this name when, as Iskander (for Alexander the Great), he was converted to Islam with the rank of bey. Hence "Skander*beg*." He subsequently rejected his Islam faith and embraced Christianity. Compare Iskander.

Arthur **Sketchley:** George Rose (1817–1882), Eng. cleric, playwright, humorist. The writer used this name for his stage comedies and witty sketches (hence perhaps the name) published in such periodicals as *Fun* and *Cassell's Magazine.* Many of them involved the doings of an eccentric old woman called Mrs. Brown.

Alison **Skipworth:** Alison Groom (1863–1952), Eng. movie actress, working in U.S. The actress adopted her husband's name as her screen name.

Stepan **Skitalets:** Stepan Gavrilovich Petrov (1869–1941), Russ. writer. The writer's name means "wanderer," "rover." He relates: "In 1897 I submitted my first, unsigned article to a newspaper and asked if I should sign with my real name or devise a pseudonym. The editor replied that for topical articles a pseudonym was necessary. But that day I was in a real hurry somewhere and didn't have a moment to think of a name. 'You think one up, I can't stop!' I said, and left. The next day I saw my first piece printed in the paper over the name Rover. 'Is that the name you gave me?' I asked the editor. 'Yes,' he replied. 'We all of us here in the office discussed the matter and in view of your article decided to call you Rover. From now on you'll be a Rover in literature just as I expect you've been a rover in real life... Do you like the name?' 'Not bad!' I replied. 'It's a good name!' 'So, you can carry on now under that pen name.' And I set to in earnest..." [Dmitriyev, p. 93].

Skitt: Harden E. Taliaferro (1818–1875), U.S. editor, sketch writer. The link is that between "skit" and "sketch," of course. (The two words are actually quite unrelated in origin.)

Ione **Skye:** Ione Skye Leitch (1971–), Br. movie actress, working in U.S. The actress is the out-of-wedlock daughter of rock singer

Donovan (*q.v.*), whom she never met, and an American mother. Her second name refers to the Scottish island that was the place of her conception. (Her first name presumably relates similarly to the Scottish island of Iona.)

Andrej **Sládkovič**: Ondrej Braxatoris (1820–1872), Slovakian poet.

Slash: Saul Hudson (1965–), Br.-born U.S. rock guitarist. The letters of the name happen to occur in the player's original name, but this was probably not the origin of his nickname.

Christian **Slater**: Christian Hawkins (1969–), U.S. movie actor. The actor adopted his mother's maiden name as his screen name.

Mia **Slavenska**: Mia Corak (1914–), Yugoslav-born ballet dancer, working in U.S. The dancer took her stage name from her birthplace, Slavonski-Brod, west of Belgrade. The name happens to indicate her Slavic origins, which is a bonus.

Patsy **Sledd**: Patsy Randolph (1944–), U.S. country musician.

Grace **Slick**: Grace Wing (1939–), U.S. rock singer.

Jonathan **Slick**: Ann Sophia Stephens (1810–1886), U.S. historical novelist. The writer used this name for her quite different *High Life in New York* (1842), based on typical Down East humor.

Sam **Slick**: Thomas Chandler Haliburton (1796–1865), Can. jurist, humorist.

Jonathan Freke **Slingsby**: John Francis Waller (1810–1894), Ir. journalist, poet. The writer used this name, based partly on his real name, for his contributions to the *Dublin University Magazine*, of which he was a staff member. He called his articles the *Slingsby Papers*. They were pieces somewhat in the style of the *Noctes Ambrosianae* (see Christopher North), or at any rate an Irish equivalent.

Philip **Slingsby**: Nathaniel Parker Willis (1806–1867), U.S. journalist, poet.

Xero **Slingsby**: Matthew Coe (1957–1988), Br. jazz musician. The musician's name is a typical creation of the punk rock era.

Eric **Sloane**: Everard Jean Hinrichs (1905–1985), U.S. artist, writer, meteorologist. The artist took his name from the U.S. Ashcan School painter John Sloan, who had influenced him as a student, substituting "Eric" for "Everard" and adding an "e" to the other artist's surname.

Olive **Sloane**: Olive Atkins (1896–1963), Eng. music hall artist, movie actress. The actress

began her career as a child performer called Baby Pearl. She later appeared with a partner as the Sisters Love.

Ally **Sloper**: Charles H. Ross (? 1842–1897), Eng. humorist. The writer was the original creator of this name, which soon became well known as that of a popular comic cartoon character who was "noted for his dishonest or bungling practices" (*Oxford English Dictionary*). The character's full name was Alexander Sloper F.O.M., the letters standing for "Friend of Man." He and his partner in various adventures Isaac Moses (otherwise known as "Ikey Mo") were seedy conmen who planned to become rich but who never did. The character of the name seems to have appeared in a fullpage strip entitled "Some of the Mysteries of Loan and Discount," published in the comic paper *Judy* in 1867. It was not long before Ross's name and that of Ally Sloper became synonymous, especially through the titles of such comics as (the best-known) *Ally Sloper's Half Holiday*, published from 1844 to 1914. Ross's son, Charles Ross, Jr., wrote for this particular comic under the name of Tootsie Sloper. "Sloper" itself implies someone who "slopes," that is, sneaks off or departs furtively (presumably following or prior to some misdeed).

Tony **Slydini**: Quintino Marucci (*c.*1900–?), It.-born U.S. magician. The illusionist first performed as Tony Foolem before adopting his permanent stage name.

Jurkšas **Smalaūsys**: Antanas Baranauskas (1835–1902), Lithuanian poet, linguist.

Chas **Smash**: Cathal Smyth (1959–), Br. rock musician.

Smectymnuus: Stephen Marshall (*c.*1594–1655), Eng. Presbyterian leader, preacher + Edmund Calamy (1600–1666), Eng. Puritan clergyman + Thomas Young (1587–1655), Sc. clergyman + William Spurstowe (*c.*1605–1666), Eng. clergyman. A somewhat unattractive joint pseudonym for the five Presbyterian ministers who in a pamphlet of 1641 attacked Bishop Joseph Hall's claim of divine right for the episcopacy. The name is formed from the men's initials, with Spurstowe's "W" provided the double "u" of the name.

Wentworth **Smee**: George Brown Burgin (1856–1944), Eng. novelist, journalist, critic. The journalist used the name for his contributions to the *Sunday Sun*.

Smilby: Francis Wilford-Smith (1927–), Eng. cartoonist. The artist's name seems to represent elements from his surname and from his birthplace, Rugby.

Smiley Culture: David Emmanuel (*c.*1960–), Br. reggae musician, of Jamaican-S.A. parentage. The singer was given his nickname at school for his method of chatting up girls: he simply asked for a smile.

Khristo **Smirnenski:** Khristo Dimitrov Izmirliyev (1898–1923), Bulg. poet.

Yakov **Smirnoff:** Yakov Pokhis (1951–), U.S. TV comedian.

Nikolay **Smirnov-Sokolsky:** Nikolay Pavlovich Smirnov (1898–1962), Russ. music hall artist, writer. The writer added his stage name (Sokolsky) to his original surname, if only to be distinguished from the many other Smirnovs.

Betty **Smith:** Elizabeth Keogh (1896–1972), U.S. novelist.

Cal **Smith:** Calvin Grant Shofner (1932–), U.S. country singer.

Cordwainer **Smith:** Paul Myron Anthony Linebarger (1913–1966), U.S. SF writer.

Gamaliel **Smith:** Jeremy Bentham (1748–1832), Eng. jurist, philosopher. The writer used this name for *Not Paul but Jesus* (1823), a didactic work setting out to prove that St. Paul had distorted true Christianity as taught and practiced by Christ. Gamaliel, in the Bible, is the man who had taught Paul (Acts 22:3).

Jimmy **Smith:** James Mellilo (1882–1946), U.S. bowler.

Joe **Smith:** Joseph Sultzer (1884–1981), U.S. vaudeville comedian, teaming with Charles Dale (*q.v.*).

John **Smith:** Robert Earl Van Orden (1931–1995), U.S. movie, TV actor. The actor adopted this particular name in order to be "the only John Smith in the business."

Johnston **Smith:** Stephen Crane (1871–1900), U.S. fiction writer. Crane used this name for his first novel, *Maggie: A Girl of the Streets*, published privately in 1893.

Martin Cruz **Smith:** Martin William Smith (1942–), U.S. crime, mystery writer. The novelist used his original name for *The Indians Won* (1970), about an imaginary American Indian nation. An editor suggested he capitalize on his Native American ancestry by substituting his Pueblo Indian maternal grandmother's name, Cruz, for his middle name. He thus appeared as Martin Cruz Smith on the title page of his first

bestseller, *Nightwing* (1977), about vampire bats in a Hopi reservation. He had earlier used the pseudonym Jake Logan for all-action westerns.

Pete **Smith:** Peter Schmidt (1892–1979), U.S. movie producer.

Rosamond **Smith:** Joyce Carol Oates (1938–), U.S. novelist, poet, playwright. The prolific novelist used this name for her distinctive thriller *Kindred Passions* (1987), basing it on the name of her husband, Raymond Smith (married 1961).

S.S. **Smith:** Thames Ross Williamson 1894– ?), U.S. writer. The author used this name for mystery stories, basing it on the name of Simmons and Smith College, where he had taught for a time after graduating from the University of Iowa (1917) and studying at Harvard. Other names used by Williamson, mainly for children's stories, include Edward Dagonet, Waldo Fleming, De Wolfe Morgan, and Gregory Trent.

Stevie **Smith:** Florence Margaret Smith (1902–1971), Eng. poet. The poet's new first name arose from an incident one day in the 1920s when she was riding over a London common. "Some boys called out 'Come on, Steve,' alluding to the well-known jockey, Steve Donaghue, whose fringe stood on end when he rode, and the friend with her thought the name apt. Steve became Stevie, a sobriquet that took over from 'Peggy,' the name by which up till then she had been known to family and friends" [Frances Spalding, *Stevie Smith: A Critical Biography*, 1988].

James **Smithson:** James Lewes Macie (1765–1829), Eng. scientist. The provider of funds for the founding of the Smithsonian Institution, Washington, D.C. (1846), was the illegitimate son of Hugh Smithson Percy, 1st Duke of Northumberland, and Elizabeth Keate Macie. It was through his mother's family that Macie inherited his substantial fortune. It is uncertain when he received royal permission to change his name, but it first occurs publicly in a scientific publication of 1802. It is believed his bequest to the United States was prompted by his illegitimacy, which he resented, and he is on record as stating: "My name shall live in the memory of man when the titles of the Northumberlands and Percys are extinct and forgotten."

Harry **Smolka:** Harry Peter Smollett (1912–), Austr.-born Eng. author, journalist.

Ján **Smrek:** Ján Čietek (1898–1982), Slovakian poet.

Conn **Smythe:** Constantine Falkland Cary (1895–1980), Can. ice hockey player. The sportsman was also known as Karry Smythe.

Snaffles: Charlie Johnson Payne (1884–1967), Eng. sporting artist, caricaturist. The artist probably took his name from a character in the sporting novels of R.S. Surtees. A "snaffle" in any case is a type of horse's bit.

The **Snark:** Starr Wood (1870–1944), Eng. cartoonist. The artist adopted the name of the fictional creature in Lewis Carroll's nonsense poem *The Hunting of the Snark* (1876). The name may have originated as a nickname based on his own first name.

Snookums: Lawrence McKeen (1924–1933), U.S. child movie actor, of Ir. origin. The sadly shortlived actor began his screen career at the age of eighteen months under this name.

Snoop Doggy Dogg: Calvin Broadus (1971–), U.S. black "gangsta" rapper. The rap artist was given the idea for his unusual name by his mother, who said his long face reminded her of the cartoon dog Snoopy. The second part of his name was borrowed from his cousin's nickname, Tate Doggy Dogg.

Phoebe **Snow:** Phoebe Laub (1952–), U.S. pop musician. The singer was given her new name in 1972, when she signed up to Shelter Records.

[Sir] Henry F.R. **Soame:** [Sir] Henry Edward Bunbury (1778–1860), Eng. historical writer. There is an apparent case of mistaken identity here. This name is usually given as the pseudonym of the soldier, historian, and Member of Parliament Sir Henry Edward Bunbury. The *Dictionary of National Biography* points out, however, that it is the *real* name of Sir Henry Bunbury's cousin, Henry Francis Robert Soame, born ten years earlier (1768). In the 1990s neither man may seem significant, but the instance is an example of the shaky historical attribution some pseudonyms can attract.

Nikolay **Sobolshchikov-Samarin:** Nikolay Ivanovich Sobolshchikov (1868–1945), Russ. theatrical director, actor. The director's actress daughter, Antonina Samarina (*q.v.*), dropped the original family surname and adopted the addition.

Sócrates: Sócrates Brasileiro Sampaio de Sousa Vieira de Oliveira (1954–), Brazilian footballer.

Sodoma: Giovanni Antonio Bazzi (1477–1549), It. painter. The artist's name, meaning "sodomite," has been explained in a possibly embellished account by Giorgio Vasari in his *Lives of the Artists* (1530) as follows: "His manner of life was licentious and dishonorable, and as he always had boys and beardless youths about him of whom he was inordinately fond, this earned him the nickname of Sodoma; but instead of feeling shame, he gloried in it, writing stanzas and verses on it, and singing them to the accompaniment of the lute." The painter (who was married and had children) indeed adopted the name and signed his pictures with it.

Grigory **Sokolnikov:** Grigory Yakovlevich Brilliant (1888–c.1939), Russ. revolutionary, politician, of Jewish origin.

Lydia **Sokolova:** Hilda Munnings (1896–1974), Eng. ballet dancer. The dancer was given her name by Diaghilev himself. He told her, "I have signed your photograph ... with the name Lydia Sokolova, and I hope you will live up to the name of Sokolova, as it is that of a great dancer in Russia" [Richard Buckle, *Dancing for Diaghilev: The Memoirs of Lydia Sokolova*, 1960]. The tribute was to Yevgenia Pavlovna Sokolova (1850–1925), one of the most famous Russian ballerinas of the 1870s and 1880s, and subsequently a noted teacher. (Munnings studied under Pavlova, who had herself been one of Sokolova's pupils.)

Philippe **Sollers:** Philippe Joyaux (1936–), Fr. writer.

Madeleine **Sologne:** Madeleine Vouillon (1912–1995), Fr. movie actress.

Fyodor **Sologub:** Fyodor Kuzmich Teternikov (1863–1927), Russ. novelist, poet. The writer based his name on that of an admired literary namesake, Count Vladimir Aleksandrovich Sollogub (1813–1882), but dropped one "l."

Solomon: Solomon Cutner (1902–1988), Br. concert pianist, of Pol. Jewish origin. The pianist was the son of Harris Cutner, a master tailor, whose original name was appropriately Schneiderman (German *Schneider*, "tailor"). The surname Cutner suggests a blend of English "cutter," as an alternate word for a tailor, and Cutnow, the Polish town where the family originated.

Ikey **Solomons,** Jun.: William Makepeace Thackeray (1811–1863), Eng. novelist. Thackeray used this name for his story "Catherine" in *Fraser's Magazine* (1839–40).

Nikolay **Solovtsov:** Nikolay Nikolayevich Fyodorov (1857–1902), Russ. actor, theatrical director.

Vasily **Solovyov-Sedoy:** Vasily Pavlovich Solovyov (1907–1979), Russ. composer.

Ludwik **Solski:** Ludwik Napoleon Sosnowski (1855–1954), Pol. stage actor, producer.

Suzanne **Somers:** Suzanne Mahoney (1946–), U.S. TV actress. The name is that of the actress's first husband, Bruce Somers.

Franca **Somigli:** Marin Bruce Clark (1901–1974), U.S.-It. opera singer.

Elke **Sommer:** Elke Schletz (1940–), Ger. movie actress, working in U.S.

Sonderborg: Kurt R. Hoffmann (1923–), Dan.-Ger. painter. The artist adopted the name of his home town, the Danish port of Sonderborg, as his professional name.

Sonny: Salvatore Bono (1935–), U.S. pop singer, formerly teaming with wife Cher (*q.v.*).

Henriette **Sontag:** Gertrud Walpurgis Sonntag, Countess Rossi (1806–1854), Ger. opera singer

Jack **Soo:** Goro Suzuki (1916–1979), Jap. movie actor, working in U.S.

Kaikhosru Shapurji **Sorabji:** Leon Dudley Sorabji (1892–1988), Eng. pianist, keyboard composer, of Parsee and Sp.-Sicilian parentage. Many reference works give the musician's original name as simply Leon Dudley, as which he at first signed himself. But his surname was always Sorabji, that of his Parsee father, Shapurji Sorabji, whose first name he adopted as a middle name, adding Kaikhosru as his own first name.

Jean **Sorel:** Jean de Rochbrune (1934–), Fr. movie actor. The actor may have adopted his screen name from that of Julien Sorel, hero of the novel *Le Rouge et le Noir* (1830) by Stendhal (*q.v.*).

Tabitha **Soren:** Tabitha Sornberger (1967–), U.S. TV journalist.

Agnes **Sorma:** Martha Karoline Zaremba (1865–1927), Ger. stage actress.

Ann **Sothern:** Harriette Lake (1909–), U.S. stage, movie actress. The actress adopted her new name in 1933 at the start of her screen career.

Alain **Souchon:** Alain Kienast (*c.*1950–), Fr. pop singer.

David **Soul:** David Solberg (1943–), U.S. pop singer, TV actor.

Jimmy **Soul:** James McCleese (1942–1988), U.S. black pop singer. The singer was nicknamed "Soul" by his congregations when a boy preacher.

Suzi **Soul:** Suzi Quatro (1950–), U.S. pop singer, of It. descent, working in U.K. Suzi Quatro (*q.v.*) used this early name when she was a TV go-go dancer at the age of 14, and retained it for a while with her group Suzi Soul and the Pleasure Seekers.

Sister **Souljah:** Lisa Williamson (1964–), U.S. black rapper, "raptivist." The name of the rapper and community activist is probably a blend of "soul" and "soldier."

Joe **South:** Joe Souter (1940–), U.S. popular musician.

Theophilus **South:** Edward Chitty (1804–1863), Eng. legal reporter. The barrister and legal writer used this name for a publication quite distinct from his professional work, the *Fly Fisher's Text Book* (1841).

Jeri **Southern:** Genevieve Hering (1926–1991), U.S. popular singer.

Southside Johnny: John Lyon (1948–), U.S. rock musician. The musician doubtless took his name from jazz jargon, where "Southside" implies playing in small bands in unpromising or unattractive locations (like Chicago's South Side, with its swarming immigrant population). Lyon himself came from New Jersey.

Stephen **Southwold:** Stephen H. Critten (1887–1964), Eng. novelist, short story writer. The writer, who also used the name Neil Bell (*q.v.*), kept this name for his children's fiction. It alludes to his birthplace, the town of Southwold, Suffolk.

E.D.E.N. **Southworth:** Emma Dorothy Eliza Southworth, née Nevitte (1819–1899), U.S. novelist. The writer used her (maiden name) initials, suggesting a male name, to disguise her sex. She first used the name in 1846 two years after separating from her husband (married 1840).

Boris **Souvarine:** Boris Lifschitz (1895–1984), Russ.-born Fr. Communist. The political activist, who was prominent in the foundation of the French Communist party, adopted the name, Souvarine, of the intellectual revolutionary depicted in Emile Zola's novel *Germinal* (1885). He also used the name in the form Boris Souvart. Zola himself may have based his character's name on those of two real Russian revolutionaries, Bakunin and Kropotkin.

E. **Souza:** Evelyn Scott (1893–1963), U.S. novelist, poet, short story writer. The writer used this name for her adventure story *Blue Rum* (1930). This was set in Portugal, so merited a Portuguese-style pen name.

Gérard **Souzay:** Gérard Marcel Tisserand (1918–), Fr. lieder, opera singer.

Bob B. **Soxx:** Robert Sheen (1943–), U.S. rock musician. A punning name with a patent origin.

Raphael **Soyer:** Raphael Schoar (1899–1987), U.S. artist.

Sissy **Spacek:** Mary Elizabeth Spacek (1949–), U.S. movie actress. The actress retained her kid sister's pet name "Sissy," given her by her elder brothers, for her screen name.

Mark **Spade:** Nigel Marlin Balchin (1908–1970), Br. novelist. The novelist used this name for his humorous contributions to *Punch* collected in *How to Run a Bassoon Factory, or Business Explained* (1934) and *Pleasures of Business* (1935). The name itself suggests a reference to card-playing.

Georg **Spalatin:** Georg Burkhardt (1484–1545), Ger. humanist, writer. The writer took his name from his birthplace, Spalt, Bavaria (now Germany).

Tony **Spargo:** Anthony Sbarbaro (1897–1969), U.S. jazz musician.

Ned **Sparks:** Edward A. Sparkman (1883–1957), Can. movie comedian, working in U.S.

Spartakus: Karl Liebknecht (1871–1919), Ger. lawyer, Communist leader. The activist took his name from the Spartacus League, founded by him as the nucleus of the German Communist Party, and itself named for the Roman slave leader, Spartacus.

[Sir] Edward **Spears:** Edward Louis Spiers (1886–1974), Eng. army officer. The future major general altered the spelling of his name on marrying in 1918. The aim was to ensure its correct pronunciation, since his original name was frequently mispronounced as "Spires."

Speckled Red: Rufus G. Perryman (1892–1973), U.S. black jazz pianist. A pleasant pun on the musician's first name, while borrowing the name of the breed of hens.

Bud **Spencer:** Carlo Pedersoli (1929–), It. movie actor. Possibly "Bud" evolved from the first syllable of the actor's surname. He would have needed an English-sounding name for the "spaghetti westerns" he played in.

Bruno **Sperani:** Beatrice Speraz (1843–?), It. novelist.

Speranza: [Lady] Jane Francisca Speranza Wilde, née Elgee (1826–1896), Ir. writer, literary hostess, mother of Oscar Wilde.

Olga **Spessiva:** Olga Aleksandrovna Spessivtseva (1895–1991), Russ.-born U.S. ballet dancer. The ballerina mostly danced under her original name.

Spike: Leslie David Gibbard (1945–), N.Z.-born Br. political cartoonist, motion picture animator. The artist used this name for his occasional work as a freelance cartoonist after his arrival in London in 1967.

Spinifex: David Martin (*q.v.*).

Spondee: Royall Tyler (1757–1826), U.S. playwright, essayist, satirist, teaming with Colon (*q.v.*). A spondee is a metrical foot of two long syllables, and as such is an apt name for a (satirical) verse writer.

Jack **Spot:** Jack Comer (1912–), Br. criminal, of Pol. Jewish parentage. The London gangster always gave his real name thus, but the actual original may well have been entirely different.

Dusty **Springfield:** Mary O'Brien (1939–), Eng. pop singer, musician, working in U.S. The singer's new surname comes from the name of an early folk group, the Springfields, consisting of "Dusty" herself (so nicknamed because as a girl she was a tomboy, playing football with the boys), her brother Dion, who became Tom Springfield, and her friend Tim Feild.

Rick **Springfield:** Richard Springthorpe (1949–), Austral. rock musician, movie actor.

Mercurius **Spur:** Cuthbert Shaw (1739–1771), Eng. poet. The poet used this name, which is possibly loosely based on his real name, for *The Race* (1766), in which the poets of the day were made to compete for pride of place by running a race. "Mercurius" of course also suggests Mercury, the fleet-footed messenger of the gods in classical mythology, and "Spur" is a sporting term associated with racing.

Spy: [Sir] Leslie Matthew Ward (1851–1922), Eng. caricaturist, portrait painter. The artist made many contributions to the topical illustrated magazine *Vanity Fair*, founded in 1868 as a periodical designed to "display the vanities of the week." Ward was asked to choose a pen name by the magazine's editor, Thomas Gibson Bowles, and is said to have done so by opening a copy of Dr. Johnson's *Dictionary* at random and selecting the first word his eye fell on. This was "spy," a highly apt name for a man whose professional job was to "spy" on society and produce his observations in pictorial form. Other artists contributing to *Vanity Fair* were Ape (*q.v.*), Sir Max Beerbohm (as Ruth, Sulto, and

Max), and Walter Sickert (as Sic). (Editor Bowles wrote as Jehu Junior, a name retained by his successors until the magazine closed in 1929.) [1. Leslie Ward, *Forty Years of "Spy"*, 1915; 2. John Arlott, "Ape, Spy, and Jehu Junior," in *Late Extra: A Miscellany by "Evening News" Writers, Artists, and Photographers, c.* 1952].

Squibob: George Horatio Derby (1823–1861), U.S. humorist, satirist. The writer, professionally an army officer, was a noted perpetrator of practical jokes as well as a penner of satirical verse. He thus enjoyed "squibs," or verbal attacks. He also wrote as John Phoenix (*q.v.*).

Ronald **Squire:** Ronald Lancelot Squirl (1886–1958), Eng. stage, movie actor.

Lilian **Stacey:** Lili Szecsi (1892–1996), Hung. refugee. The name of the longlived diplomatic negotiator is an anglicized form of that of her husband, businessman Marius Szecsi, whom she married in 1912, subsequently saving his company from expropriation and securing his freedom. (He died in 1945.) She adopted it on escaping to England in 1956 at the time of the Hungarian Revolution. The new name is merely a conventional equivalent of the original, which would have been pronounced more like "Saichy."

Robert **Stack:** Robert Langford Modini (1919–), U.S. movie, TV actor.

Hanley **Stafford:** Alfred John Austin (1899–1968), U.S. radio actor.

Mary **Stafford:** Flora M. Mayor (1872–1931), Eng. novelist, short story writer.

Stainless Stephen: Arthur Clifford Baynes (1892–1971), Eng. music hall comedian. The performer was born in Sheffield, a city long famous for its manufacture of stainless steel.

Black **Stalin:** Leroy Calliste (1941–), Trinidad calypso singer.

Joseph **Stalin:** Iosif Vissarionovich Dzhugashvili (1879–1953). Russ. Communist leader. The famous name took some time to evolve. Dzhugashvili was contributing to Bolshevik magazines such as *Zvezda* ("Star") under the names K.S. and K. Salin, for example, two or three years before Stalin itself first appeared (in 1913). Opinions are divided regarding the symbolic intention of the name. Russian *stal'* means "steel," and certainly, after repeated arrest, banishment, and imprisonment in czarist days, Dzhugashvili's spirit was unbroken, but it is unlikely that the name was given him by Lenin (*q.v.*), as legend has it, because of his "steel-like" nature.

Another early favorite pseudonym of the Bolshevik activist was Koba, said to mean "fearless," and at one time he also used the name Kato, possibly alluding to the forthrightness of Cato the Elder. Other names used by the revolutionary were David Bars, Gayoz Nizheradze, I. Besoshvili, Zakhar Gregoryan Melikyants, Ogoness Vartanovich Totomyants, K. Solin (possibly from Russian *sol'*, "salt"), and K. Stefin. Some of these names suggest his own original Georgian name [Robert Payne, *Stalin*, 1966].

William **Stallybrass:** William Teulon Swan Sonnenschein (1883–1948), Eng. academic, college principal, of Austr. descent. The vice chancellor of Oxford University adopted his grandmother's maiden name in 1917, at a time when German names were out of favor. Friends and colleagues nevertheless continued to nickname him "Sonners."

John **Standing:** [Sir] John Ronald Leon (1934–), Eng. stage, movie actor, son of Kay Hammond (*q.v.*). The actor adopted his mother's maiden name as his stage name.

Burt L. **Standish:** William Gilbert Patten (1866–1945), U.S. writer of dime novels.

Yemilian **Stanev:** Nikola Stoyanov (1907–1979), Bulg. writer.

Konstantin **Stanislavsky:** Konstantin Sergeyevich Alekseyev (1865–1938), Russ. stage actor, director, teacher. The actor adopted his new name in 1885: "It was because of the unsavory atmosphere at some of the vaudeville performances with which he became associated that Constantin Sergeyevich Alexeiev ... decided it would be wiser to conceal his identity from the public. He therefore assumed the name of Stanislavsky, which had belonged to a young amateur whom he had once known and who had stopped playing. He thought that such a Polish-sounding name would be a complete disguise" [Christine Edwards, *The Stanislavsky Heritage*, 1965].

M. **Stanitsky:** Avdotya Yakovlevna Panayeva (1819–1893), Russ. writer. The author used this male name for two novels written jointly with the poet Nikolay Nekrasov, as well as alone.

Viktor **Stanitsyn:** Viktor Yakovlevich Gёze (1897–), Russ. actor, theatrical director.

[Sir] Albert **Stanley:** Albert Henry Knattriess (1874–1948), Br. transport chief. The future head of the London Passenger Transport Board emigrated as a small child with his family to the

U.S., where his father changed their surname to Stanley, presumably basing this on the original name.

[Sir] Henry Morton **Stanley:** John Rowlands (1841–1904), Welsh-born U.S. explorer of Africa. The explorer was the illegitimate son of John Rowlands and Elizabeth Parry. When in the U.S.A. at the age of 18 he was adopted by a New Orleans merchant, Henry Morton Stanley, who gave him his own name.

Kim **Stanley:** Patricia Kimberly Reid (1921–), U.S. stage, movie actress.

Paul **Stanley:** Paul Stanley Eisen (1950–), U.S. rock musician.

Phyllis **Stanley:** Phyllis Knapman (1914–), Eng. stage actress, singer, dancer. The actress took her new surname from the first name of her father, Stanley Evans Knapman.

Frank **Stanmore:** Francis Henry Pink (1887– ?), Br. movie actor.

Barbara **Stanwyck:** Ruby Stevens (1907–1990), U.S. movie, TV actress. The actress was given her new name by producer, director, and playwright Willard Mack, when he cast her for the stage play *The Noose* (1926). "Ruby Stevens is no name for an actress," he told her. He got the name from an old theatre program, which listed Jane Stanwyck in Clyde Fitch's play *Barbara Frietchie* (1899) [Jane Ellen Wayne, *Stanwyck*, 1986].

Jean **Stapleton:** Jeanne Murray (1923–), U.S. movie, TV actress.

Alvin **Stardust:** Bernard William Jewry (1942–), Eng. rock singer. The singer began his career under the name Shane Fenton. Later, he took the present name from his favorite performers, *Elv*is Presley and Gene *Vin*cent (*q.v.*), adding "Stardust" as he thought it more "1974."

Richard **Stark:** Donald E. Westlake (1933–), U.S. suspense writer.

Edwin **Starr:** Charles Hatcher (1942–), U.S. pop singer.

Freddie **Starr:** Frederick Leslie Fowell (1953–), Eng. TV, movie entertainer. The comedian is said to have changed his name because his friends kept calling him "Foul Freddie."

Kay **Starr:** Katherine LaVerne Starks (1922–), U.S. popular radio singer.

Kenny **Starr:** Kenneth Trebbe (1953–), U.S. pop singer.

Ringo **Starr:** Richard Starkey (1940–), Eng. pop musician. The former Beatles drummer, who later took up a solo career, changed his name in 1961, when appearing with Rory Storm

(*q.v.*). His new second name derives from his original surname, with its implicit "star" quality, while "Ringo" was a nickname referring to his fondness for wearing rings. It also resembles his original first name.

Lovebug **Starski:** Keven Smith (1961–), U.S. DJ, rapper. The rap artist took his name from the popular television series *Starsky and Hutch*.

Grigory **Stary:** Grigory Ivanovich Borisov (1880–1937), Russ. Communist official. The revolutionary's adopted name means "old," presumably in some symbolic sense.

Antal **Stašek:** Antonin Zeman (1843–1931), Cz. writer.

Vargo **Statten:** John Russell Fearn (1908–1960), Eng. SF writer.

Vladimir **Stavsky:** Vladimir Petrovich Kirpichnikov (1900–1943), Russ. writer.

Maggie **Steed:** Margaret Baker (1946–), Eng. movie, TV actress.

Byron **Steel:** Francis Steegmuller (1906–), U.S. crime novelist, literary critic. The writer used the name for his lesser critical studies.

Dawn **Steel:** Dawn Spielberg (1947–), U.S. motion picture executive.

Bob **Steele:** Robert North Bradbury, Jr. (1907–1988), U.S. movie actor. The actor took his screen name from the cowboy character he played in *The Mojave Kid* (1927).

Tommy **Steele:** Thomas Hicks (1936–), Eng. pop singer, stage, movie actor. Hicks was signed up in the mid-1950s by two young promoters, Larry Parnes and John Kennedy, who gave him a more charismatic name in the process. The name is typical of Parnes, who often combined a "soft" forename with a "hard" surname, as he did for Marty Wilde (*q.v.*) and others.

Stefán frá Hvítadal: Stefán Sigurdsson (1887–1933), Icelandic poet. The poet's adopted name means "Stefán of Hvítadal," denoting his birthplace.

Steinn **Steinarr:** Adalsteinn Kristmundsson (1908–1958), Icelandic poet.

Saul **Steinberg:** Saul Jacobson (1914–), Rom.-born U.S. cartoonist, illustrator. An unusual substitution of one Jewish name for another.

Charles Proteus **Steinmetz:** Karl August Rudolf Steinmetz (1865–1923), Ger.-born U.S. electrical engineer. The electrical pioneer immigrated to the U.S. in 1889 and anglicized his first name at this time, simultaneously substituting Proteus, a university nickname, for his original two middle names.

Henry **Steinway:** Heinrich Engelhardt Steinweg (1797–1871), Ger. pianomaker, working in U.S. A general anglicization, although the "Stein" did not produce a "Stone," as it might otherwise have done. The craftsman modified his name on moving to New York with his three sons in 1849.

Yury **Steklov:** Yury Mikhaylovich Nakhamkis (1873–1941), Russ. revolutionary, historian.

Stella: (1) Esther Johnson (1681–1738), Eng. letter writer, correspondent of Jonathan Swift; (2) Estella Anna Lewes (1824–1880), U.S. author. Swift used this name to address Esther Johnson through his *Journal to Stella* (1710–13). The name hints at "Esther," while also meaning "star." For Lewes the name was even closer to her first name. Because of its propitious meaning, the name has been used by other writers. In the poetry of Sir Philip Sidney, for example, "Stella," in the sonnet sequence *Astrophel and Stella* (1591), was Penelope Rich, sister of the Earl of Essex. "Astrophel" was Sidney himself. The latter name, significantly, means "star-loving."

Anna **Sten:** Annel (or Anjuschka) Stenskaya Sujakevich (1908–1993), Ukrainian-born U.S. movie actress, of Swe.-Ukrainian parentage.

Stendhal: Marie-Henri Beyle (1783–1842), Fr. novelist. This is the best known pseudonym of the many used by the writer. He adopted it in 1817 from the small Prussian town of Stendal (sic), the birthplace of Jean-Joachim Winckelmann (1717–1768), a German archaeologist and historian admired by Beyle, and first used it for his travel account *Rome, Naples et Florence* (1817–26). (He added an "h" to make it look more German.) Altogether Stendhal had around 200 pseudonyms, many of them Italian. They include: Dominique, Salviati, Cotonnet, Chamier, Baron de Cutendre, William Crocodile, Lizio, and Viscontini. For his first book, *Vies de Haydn, de Mozart et de Métastase* (1814), Beyle wrote as L.-A.-C. Bombet. For his autobiography, published posthumously (1890), he was Henri Brûlard, alluding to his passion (French *brûler*, "to burn").

Steno: Stefano Vanzina (1915–1988), It. screenwriter. Although obviously deriving from his first name, the writer's pseudonym also suggests "writing" itself, from the Greek element found in such words as "stenographer."

Stephen IX: Frederick of Lorraine (*c.*1000–1058), Fr. pope. The pope took the name of St. Stephen, on whose feastday (August 2, 1057) he was elected.

Martin **Stephens:** Martin Angel Keller (1948–), Br. juvenile movie actor.

Henry **Stephenson:** Henry Stephenson Garroway (1871–1956), Br. stage, movie actor, working in U.S. The actor's stage name, his own middle name, originated as his mother's maiden name.

Yakov **Stepovoy:** Yakov Stepanovich Yakimenko (1883–1921), Ukrainian composer.

Ford **Sterling:** George Ford Stitch (1883–1939), U.S. movie comedian.

Jan **Sterling:** Jane Sterling Adriance (1923–), U.S. movie actress.

Richard **Sterling:** Albert G. Leggatt (1880–1959), U.S. stage actor.

Robert **Sterling:** William Sterling Hart (1917–), U.S. movie actor.

Daniel **Stern:** Marie Catherine Sophie de Flavigny, Comtesse d'Agoult (1805–1876), Fr. writer. The writer was the mistress of Liszt and in 1854 published her novel *Nélida*, based on her relations with him. The pseudonym she adopted for it was based on an anagram of its title.

Karl **Stern:** Julia Daudet (1844–1940), Fr. poet, essayist. The writer used this male name for critical articles.

Paul Frederick **Stern:** Paul Frederick Ernst (1902–), U.S. SF writer. The writer had a surname that readily lent itself to apt anagrammatization.

Stesichorus: Teisias (*c.*632–*c.*556 BC), Gk. lyric poet. The poet came to be known by his nickname, meaning "choir setter."

Stet: Thomas Earle Welby (1881–1933), Br. journalist, essayist, literary critic. The writer adopted the proofreader's instruction meaning "let it stand" as used for a deleted word or passage that should remain undeleted after all.

Cat **Stevens:** Steven Giorgiou (1947–), Eng. pop musician, of Gk.-Swe. parentage. In 1977 the musician converted to Islam, ceased recording, and changed his name yet again to Yusef Islam.

Connie **Stevens:** Concetta Rosalie Ann Ingolia (1938–), U.S. movie actress.

Craig **Stevens:** Gail Shikles, Jr. (1918–), U.S. movie actor.

Dodie **Stevens:** Geraldine Ann Pasquale (1947–), U.S. popular singer, movie actress.

Inger **Stevens:** Inger Stensland (1934–1970), Swe.-born U.S. movie, TV actress.

K.T. **Stevens:** Gloria Wood (1919–), U.S. movie actress.

Margaret Dean Stevens: Bess Streeter Aldrich (1881–1954), U.S. novelist, short story writer. The writer used her name for stories published in the *American Magazine* and other periodicals. She explained: "In a sort of foolish fashion (ostrich-like) I hid behind the pen name of Margaret Dean Stevens for several years. It was a combination of my grandmother's names. I felt a timidity in having my stuff read—the typical amateur's print-fright, which is the writer's stage-fright" [Marble, p. 208].

Onslow Stevens: Onslow Ford Stevenson (1902–1977), U.S. stage, movie actor.

Ray Stevens: Ray Ragsdale (1941–), U.S. country pop writer, performer.

Risë Stevens: Risë Steenberg (1913–), U.S. opera singer.

Shakin' Stevens: Michael Barratt (1948–), Welsh-born Br. pop singer ("Shaky").

Stella Stevens: Estelle Eggleston (1936–), U.S. movie actress.

Stu Stevens: Wilfred Pierce (*c.*1937–), Eng. country musician.

Juliet Stevenson: Juliet Anne Virginia Stevens (1956–), Br. stage, movie actress.

Stevo: Steven Pearse (1962–), Eng. DJ, pop music entrepreneur.

Douglas Stewart: Edward Askew Sothern (1926–1981), Eng. actor. The actor used this stage name when first appearing in the provinces.

Ed Stewart: Edward Stewart Mainwaring (1941–), Eng. radio DJ, TV performer ("Stewpot").

Elaine Stewart: Elsa Steinberg (1929–), U.S. movie actress.

Michael Stewart: Michael Rubin (1924–1987), U.S. popular composer, lyricist.

Paul Stewart: Paul Sternberg (1908–1986), U.S. movie actor.

Jan Stewer: Albert John Coles (1876– ?), Eng. dialect writer. The writer was born and bred in Devon, southwestern England, and adopted a name from the local ballad "Widdicombe Fair," where it is that of one of the villagers who borrowed Tom Pearse's gray mare to ride to the fair: "For I want for to go to Widdicombe Fair,/ Wi' Bill Brewer, Jan Stewer, Peter Gurney, Peter Davey, Dan'l Whiddon, Harry Hawk,/ Old Uncle Tom Cobbleigh and all." (The names are those of real people, and there is still an annual fair at Widecombe in the Moor, as the village is now usually known.)

Georg Stiernhielm: Jöran Oloffson (1598–1672), Swe. poet, scholar.

Sting: Gordon Mathew Sumner (1951–), Eng. rock singer. The singer acquired his name by way of a school nickname referring not only to his "buzzing" energy but to a black and yellow hooped T-shirt that he habitually wore.

Max Stirner: Johann Kaspar Schmidt (1806–1856), Ger. philosopher, translator.

Wilhelmina Stitch: Ruth Collie (1889–1936), Br. writer of sentimental verse.

Alan Stivell: Alan Cochevelou (1943–), Fr. folk musician. The musician's name is based on a Breton word meaning "spring," "fountain."

Leopold Stokes: Leopold Antoni Stanislaw Boleslawowicz Stokowski (1882–1977), Br. orchestral conductor, of Pol.-Ir. parentage, working in U.S. Was the conductor at one time known by this English version of his name? His father was Polish, and his mother Irish, and in his obituary notice in *The Times* (1977) it was mentioned that his father had so anglicized his name to 1905, from which year the conductor worked mainly in the U.S. under his more familiar Polish name. However, a few days later (September 24, 1977), *The Times* printed the following correction: "We have been asked to point out that Leopold Stokowski was registered at birth under that name and not under that of Stokes: and that, similarly, he studied at the Royal College of Music under the name of Stokowski." Leopold Stokes would thus seem to have been short-lived, if indeed he lived at all. Stokowski's first wife was Olga Samaroff (*q.v.*).

[Sir] Oswald Stoll: Oswald Gray (1866–1942), Eng. theatre manager. The impresario's mother was widowed when the boy was only three years old, but remarried when he was 13 and gave her son the name of her new Danish husband, John George Stoll.

Rosine Stoltz: Victoire Noël (1815–1903), Fr. opera singer. The singer adopted a form of her mother's maiden name of Stoll.

Cliffie Stone: Clifford Gilpin Snyder (1917–), U.S. country musician.

George E. Stone: George Stein (1903–1967), Pol. movie actor, working in U.S.

Hampton Stone: Aaron Marc Stein (1906–), U.S. mystery writer. The author also wrote as George Bagby.

I.F. Stone: Isidor Feinstein (1907–1989), U.S. journalist, newspaper owner, of Russ. Jewish parentage. The journalist adopted his new name at the age of 30, forming it from the initials of his original name with a translation of "Stein" as "Stone."

Irving Stone: Irving Tennenbaum (1903–1989), U.S. fictional biographer. The writer legally adopted the surname of his stepfather.

Jesse Stone: Charles Calhoun (*c*.1930–), U.S. pop music arranger.

Lew Stone: Louis Steinberg (1898–1969), Br. bandleader, composer, arranger, of Jewish parentage.

Sly Stone: Sylvester Stewart (1944–), U.S. black rock musician.

Stonehenge: John Henry Walsh (1810–1888), Eng. sporting writer, editor. The ancient monument of Stonehenge, on Salisbury Plain, Wiltshire, was a popular venue for hunting and riding in Victorian times. The surrounding area is now largely owned by the army, although local hunts still have the right to hold their meets there on specified occasions.

Tom Stoppard: Tomas Straussler (1937–), Cz.-born Br. dramatist, theatre critic. When the future playwright was still only nine years old, his mother remarried, and he took his new name from his stepfather, Major Kenneth Stoppard. See also William Boot.

Gale Storm: Josephine Cottle (1922–), U.S. movie, TV actress, singer.

Lesley Storm: Mabel Margaret Clark, née Cowie (1904–1975), Sc. novelist, playwright.

Rory Storm: Alan Caldwell (1941–), Br. pop singer. The singer tried out the name Jet Storme early on in his career, then settled for for a more plausible Rory Storm.

Lyudmil Stoyanov: Georgi Stoyanov Zlatarov (1886–1973), Bulg. writer. The writer based his pen name on that of his father, Stoyan Zlatarov, whose first name already formed his patronymic (middle name).

Izzy Stradlin: Jeffrey Isbell (1962–), U.S. rock guitarist. Presumably a punning nickname gave this name.

Mary Strafford: Flora Macdonald Mayor (1872–1932), Eng. novelist. The writer used this name not only for her writing but for a short-lived career in her early thirties as an actress.

Mark Straker: Mark Williams (1956–), Eng. movie, TV actor.

Herbert Strang: George Herbert Ely (1866–1958), Eng. children's writer + Charles James L'Estrange (1867–1944), Eng. children's writer. The two men were staff members of the Oxford University Press, writing adventure stories and historical novels for children in the first three decades of the 20th century. Their joint name is extracted from their real names, as can be seen. They also wrote for girls under the not very original name of Mrs. Herbert Strang.

Steve Strange: Stephen John Harrington (1959–), Welsh rock singer. The singer acquired his name thanks to a postman (mailman): "I was living in West Hampstead [London] and my hair was white and cut spiky on top. The other girl [sic] I was living with, Suzy, also had white hair and so the postman used to call us Mr. and Mrs. Strange. The name just stuck" [*Observer Colour Supplement*, August 22, 1982].

Joyce Stranger: Joyce Muriel Wilson, née Judson (1924–), Eng. writer of animal stories for children.

Lee Strasberg: Israel Strassberg (1901–1982), Austr.-born U.S. theatrical director.

Teresa Stratas: Anastasia Stratakis (1938–), Can. opera singer, of Gk. descent.

Dorothy Stratten: Dorothy Ruth Hoogstratten (1960–1980), U.S. movie actress, model.

L.B. Stratten: Louise B. Hoogstratten (1969–), U.S. movie actress.

Eugene Stratton: Eugene Augustus Rühlmann (1861–1918), U.S.-born music hall dancer, singer, of Alsatian parentage, working in U.K. The dancer began his career under the name Master Jean. He then joined a blackface group called the Four Arnolds, but decided that he was not an Arnold and instead took the name of Stratton, suggested by a fellow dancer.

Gene Stratton-Porter: Geneva Grace Porter, née Stratton (1863–1924), U.S. writer of books for girls.

Oscar Straus: Oskar Strauss (1870–1954), Austr. composer. The operetta composer dropped one "s" from his name so as not to be confused with the famous Strauss family of musicians.

Paul Patrick Streeten: Paul Patrick Hornig (1917–), Austr.-born Br. economist. The writer changed his Germanic name to an English one in 1943, under the Army Council Instruction that year which regulated some name changes. At the time he was serving in the Commandos, but returned to England on being wounded in Sicily.

Hesba Stretton: Sarah Smith (1832–1911), Eng. children's writer. The writer took her first name from the initials (HESBA) of the names of her brothers and sisters, in order of age (the "E" was Elizabeth, her lifelong companion; the "A" was her younger sister Ann), while her new surname came from the Shropshire village of All Stretton, near Church Stretton, where Ann Smith had been left property by her uncle. Sarah Smith adopted the name in 1858, before her writing career began, choosing the new name because she felt that her real name lacked distinction.

Stijn Streuvels: Frank Lateur (1871–1969), Belg. (Flemish) writer.

Stringbean: David Akeman (1914–1973), U.S. country singer. The singer's name arose as a nickname, referring to his gangling appearance. According to one story, this originated from a radio announcer, who came to introduce him but forgot his real name.

Pauline Strogova: Prudence Hyman (1914–1995), Br. ballet dancer.

Patience Strong: Winifred Emma May (1907–1990), Eng. "inspirational" poet. The writer took her name from *Patience Strong* (1870), a homely moral (fictional) autobiography by the U.S. author Adeline D. T. Whitney. Winifred May was very impressed by the book and its spiritual content. "No words can describe what it did for me. ... The main character, the fictitious Patience Strong, moves through the book with a simplicity that only partially hides a philosophy that is as practical as it is profound. I had found more than a pseudonym. I had turned a corner and found, by chance, my true vocation. ... The charm and the power of that book, *Patience Strong*, is something I cannot define. ... I place it reverently on a pedestal alongside Mrs. Gaskell's *Cranford*, Jane Austen's *Emma* and *Our Village* by Nancy Russell Mitford" [Patience Strong, *With a Poem in My Pocket*, 1981]. The import of the fictional name itself is, of course, transparent enough, and is meaningful for the book's central character, the 38-year-old spinster who shares the old New England home with her mother, and who is thus at a significant stage in her spiritual and personal life.

Sheppard Strudwick: John Shepperd (1907–1983), U.S. movie actor.

Strube: Sidney Strube (1891–1956), Br. cartoonist. The artist addressed everyone, both male and female, as "George," so it was generally assumed this was his own name. His surname rhymes with "ruby," not "tube."

Andrzej Strug: Tadeusz Gałecki (1871–1937), Pol. writer.

Joe Strummer: John Mellor (1953–), Eng. punk rock musician.

Jan Struther: Joyce Maxtone Graham, née Anstruther (1901–1953), Eng. poet, short story writer, novelist.

Esmé Stuart: Amélie Claire LeRoy (1851–1934), Fr.-born Br. novelist, children's writer.

Gloria Stuart: Gloria Stuart Finch (1909–1983), U.S. movie actress.

Ian Stuart: Alistair Maclean (1922–1987), Sc. novelist. The writer used this name for his SF writing, such as *The Dark Crusader* (1961) and *The Satan Bug* (1962).

Jeanne Stuart: Jeanne Sweet (1908–), Br. stage actress.

John Stuart: John Croall (1898–1979), Sc. movie, stage actor.

Leslie Stuart: Thomas Augustine Barrett (1864–1928), Eng. songwriter, popular composer. The musician at first wrote songs as Lester Barrett before becoming Leslie Stuart.

Nick Stuart: Nicholas Pratza (1904–1973), Rom.-born U.S. movie actor.

Theodore Sturgeon: Edward Hamilton Waldo (1918–1985), U.S. SF writer. The writer legally adopted his stepfather's name. U.S. novelist Kurt Vonnegut is said to have based his SF writer character Kilgore Trout on Sturgeon.

Preston Sturges: Edmond Preston Biden (1898–1959), U.S. movie director, screenwriter. The writer took his new name from his mother's second husband (his stepfather), Solomon Sturges, at the same time dropping his first name.

Jule Styne: Jules (or Julius) Kerwin Stein (1905–1994), Br.-born U.S. stage producer, songwriter. A fairly original variation on the familiar "Stein-to-Stone" transition.

Poly Styrene: Marion Elliott (1956–), Eng. punk rock musician. The singer, who formed the band X-Ray Spex in 1977, adopted the name because she felt it was suitable for the "plastic" culture and values of the 1970s. She abandoned punk soon after, however, and went on to become Maharani Devi, as a member of the International Society of Krishna Consciousness. The band subsequently reformed.

Styx: Leslie Clifford Harding (1914–1991), Eng. cartoonist. The artist began his career drawing sporting strips. Hence presumably his name, alluding both to the river crossed by the souls of the dead in classical mythology and the "sticks" or fences that horses jump in a steeplechase.

André **Suarès:** Félix-André-Yves Scantrel (1868–1948), Fr. critic, poet.

Jānis **Sudrabkalns:** Arvīds Peine (1894–1975), Latvian poet, journalist.

Edzus **Sudrabu:** Eduard Zilber (1860–1941), Latvian writer. The writer translated his Germanic surname, meaning "silver," to the Latvian equivalent.

Eugène **Sue:** Marie-Joseph Sue (1804–1857), Fr. novelist. The writer took his new first name in honor of one of his patrons, Prince Eugène de Beauharnais (1781–1824).

Suggs: Graham McPherson (1961–), Br. rock singer.

Sukarno: Kusnasosro (1901–1970), Indonesian politician. Indonesia's first president was the son of a Javanese teacher, Raden Sukemi Sosrodihardjo, and his Balinese wife, Ida Njoman Rai. He was originally named Kusnasosro, after his father, but following a series of illnesses was renamed with the more auspicious name Sukarno, "son of Karna," for a hero of the epic poem *Mahabharata,* in which he is the son of the Hindu sun god Surya. Sukarno's childhood nickname was Djago ("cock," "champion"), and as an adult revolutionary hero he was known as Bung Karno (Brother Karno, Comrade Karno).

N. **Sukhanov:** Nikolay Nikolayevich Gimmer (1882–1940), Russ. revolutionary, economist.

Frants **Sukhoverkhov:** Mikhail Ivanovich Sychyov (1883–1918), Russ. revolutionary.

Naim **Suleymanoglü:** Naim Suleimanov (1967–), Bulg.-Turk. weightlifter. The athlete was born a member of the Turkish minority in Bulgaria, and at an early age was forced to take a Bulgarian form of his name, Naum Shalamanov. He sought political asylum in Turkey after the 1986 World Cup, competing first for Bulgaria as Shalamanov, then for Turkey as Suleymanoglü. The *-oglü* suffix in the latter name is a form of Turkish *ogul*, meaning "son," and corresponding to the Slavic *-ov* suffix of Suleimanov (and Shalamanov). The Jewish surname itself corresponds to Salomonson.

Margaret **Sullavan:** Margaret Brooke (1911–1960), U.S. movie actress.

Barry **Sullivan:** Patrick Barry (1912–1994), U.S. movie actor.

Maxine **Sullivan:** Marietta Williams (1911–1987), U.S. jazz singer. The singer's assumed name is graphically related to her original name.

Yma **Sumac:** Zoila Imperatriz Charrari Sumac del Castillo (1928–), Peruvian-born U.S. singer. Despite reports to the contrary, the singer is *not* a housewife originally named Amy Camus.

Donna **Summer:** LaDonna Andrea Sommer, née Gaines (1948–), U.S. pop singer. The singer married a German, Helmut Sommer, when she was 19, and (regularly) took his surname, while (irregularly) altering its spelling to make it look more English. She divorced him in 1976, but kept the anglicized name.

Charles **Summerfield:** Alfred W. Arrington (1810–1967), U.S. lawyer, writer.

Felix **Summerly:** [Sir] Henry Cole (1808–1882), Eng. art patron, educator. The artist first used the name for *Felix Summerly's Home Treasury* (1841), a series of children's stories illustrated with woodcuts based on well known paintings. The name seems to be to be simply propitious and agreeable: Latin *felix* means "fruitful," "lucky," and "Summerly" obviously evokes summer. As Hamst comments (see Bibliography, p. 399): "This gentleman's pseudonym, though longer, is much pleasanter than his own name."

Slim **Summerville:** George J. Sommerville (1892–1946), U.S. comedy movie actor.

Barney **Sumner:** Bernard Dicken (1956–), Br. rock musician. This was the name used by Dicken when a member of the group New Order. Earlier, in Joy Division, he called himself Bernard Albrecht.

Joe **Sun:** James J. Paulson (1943–), U.S. country singer. The singer's new surname is an imaginative development of the latter half of his original surname.

Sun Bear: Vince Laduke (1929–1992), U.S. "New Age" Native American Chieftain.

Sundance Kid: Harry Longabaugh (or Longbaugh) (1870–1909), U.S. outlaw, teaming with Butch Cassidy (*q.v.*). The bank robber and gunslinger took his nickname from the town of Sundance, Wyoming, where he was imprisoned from 1887 to 1889 for stealing a horse.

Sunnyland Slim: Albert Luandrew (1907–1995), U.S. black blues musician. The pianist is said to have taken his name from one of his own songs, "Sunnyland Train." He was also known as Sunny Land Slim, Delta Joe (for the Mississippi Delta style of blues), and Dr. Clayton's Buddy (for the singer Peter J. "Doctor" Clayton).

Sun Ra: Herman Blount (1914–1993), U.S. black jazz musician. The musician's name may have actually evolved from the nickname "Sonny," and he was certainly known at one time as Sonny Lee, as well as Herman Lee, Sonny Bourke, and Le Sony'r Ra. However, the man himself would doubtless point to higher things, especially as he claimed to be an angel from outer space. Ra (or Re) was the Egyptian sun god. Sun Ra would frequently announce to concert audiences: "Some call me Mr. Ra, some call me Mr. Re, but you can call me Mr. Mystery" [*The Times*, June 2, 1993].

Marion Sunshine: Mary Tunstall Ijames (1894–1963), U.S. vaudeville, movie actress, singer, songwriter.

Franz von Suppé: Francesco Ezechiele Ermenegildo Cavaliere Suppé-Demelli (1819–1895), Dalmatian-born Austr. composer, conductor, of Belg. parentage.

Master Suresh: Nasir Ahmed Khan (1929–), Ind. juvenile movie actor.

Surfaceman: Alexander Anderson (1845–1909), Sc. poet, librarian. The writer was a surfaceman (railbed laborer) on the Glasgow and South-Western Railway for 17 years.

John Surrebutter: John Anstey (? –1819), Eng. poet. The poet used this name for "a didactic poem" entitled *The Pleader's Guide* (1796), described in the subtitle as "containing the conduct of a Suit of Law, with the Arguments of Counsellor Bother'um and Counsellor Bore'um in an action between John-a-Gull and John-a-Gudgeon for assault and battery at a late contested election." The poem is witty, but the humor mainly legal. A "surrebutter" is a little-used legal term for a plaintiff's reply to a defendant's rebutter.

Colonel Surry: John Esten Cooke (1830–1886), U.S. novelist, essayist. The writer used the name for a series of romances, in which the Civil War was seen through the eyes of "Colonel Surry," a fictitious aide of Stonewall Jackson.

Joan Sutherland: Joan Maisie Kelly, née Collings (1890–1947), Eng. popular novelist. The writer began her career as a singer. By coincidence she chose a name identical to that of the Australian soprano Joan Sutherland (1926–).

Suzy: Aileen Mehle (1952–), U.S. "queen of aristocratic tittle-tattle."

Svatopluk T.: Svatopluk Turek (1900–1972), Cz. writer.

Karolína Světlá: Johanna Rottová, née Mužáková (1830–1899), Cz. writer. The writer took her pseudonym from her husband's birthplace.

Nikolay Svetlovidov: Nikolay Afanasyevich Sedykh (1889–1970), Russ. stage actor. The actor seems to have adopted a name related in sense to his original surname: Sedykh means literally "gray-haired," while Svetlovidov, more agreeably, is "of fair countenance."

Italo Svevo: Ettore Schmitz (1861–1928), It. novelist, short story writer. The writer's pseudonym means "Italian Swabian," and was chosen by him to express his feeling of being a hybrid: he was Italian-speaking, Austrian in citizenship, and German in ancestry and education. The name does to an extent reflect or resemble his real name.

Swamp Dogg: Jerry Williams, Jr. (1942–), U.S. pop musician.

Bettye Swann: Betty Jean Champion (1944–), U.S. country, soul singer.

Gloria Swanson: Gloria Josephine Mae Swenson (or Svensson) (1899–1983), U.S. movie actress, of Swe.-It. descent.

Emanuel Swedenborg: Emanuel Swedberg (1688–1772), Swe. scientist, philosopher, religious writer. The scientist enhanced his name in 1719 when the family was ennobled.

Tom Swift: Thomas Kneafcy (1928–), Br. opera singer.

Nora Swinburne: Nora (or Elinore) Swinburne Johnson (1902–), Eng. stage actress.

Basil Sydney: Basil Sydney Nugent (1894–1968), Br. movie actor.

Ilena Sylva: Ilena Thimblethorpe (1916–), Br. stage actress. The actress based her stage name on the maiden name of her mother, Karenhappuch Silvester.

Vernon Sylvaine: Vernon Scotchburn (1897–1957), Eng. stage actor, playwright.

Urbanus Sylvan: Henry Charles Beeching (1859–1919), Eng. poet, essayist. The name was almost certainly adopted from that of Sylvanus Urban (*q.v.*), and similarly evokes the town and the country (or forest).

Sylvander: Robert Burns (1756–1796), Sc. poet. This was the name used by Burns when corresponding with Clarinda (*q.v.*). It was probably intended to mean "forest man," and resembles the Sylvanus of classical mythology as the name of different sylvan beings or deities.

Sylvester: Sylvester James (1946–1988), U.S. rock singer. An earlier name used by the musician was Ruby Blue.

Sylvester II: Gerbert of Aurillac (*c.*945–1003), Fr. pope. The pontiff took the name of

St. Silvester I (died 335), whose papal partnership with the Roman emperor Constantine the Great is regarded as exemplary (as Sylvester's also was with Otto III).

Sylvester III: John of Sabina (? –1063), It. pope (or antipope).

Sylvia: (1) Sylvia Kirby Allen (1956–), U.S. country singer; (2) Sylvia Vanderpool (1936–), U.S. pop singer.

David **Sylvian:** David Batt (1958–), Eng. rock musician. The lead singer of Japan is the brother of that group's drummer, Steve Jansen (*q.v.*).

Sylvie: Louise Sylvain (1883–1970), Fr. movie actress.

Sylvia **Syms:** Sylvia Blagman (1917–1992), U.S. cabaret, jazz singer, of half-Russ. parentage.

Dr. **Syntax:** William Combe (1741–1823), Eng. pamphleteer, satirist, writer. This is probably the best known of the many names used by the writer, famous for his verse satire *The Tour of Dr. Syntax in Search of the Picturesque* (1809), relating the comic adventures of a village schoolmaster. Other names used by Combe include Belphegor, Isaac Brandon, Johannes Scriblerus, and descriptives such as A Country Gentleman, An Italian Nun, and A Retired Officer.

Syreeta: Rita Wright (? –), U.S. black rock singer, former wife (1970–72) of Stevie Wonder (*q.v.*).

Władysław **Syrokomla:** Ludwik Kondratowicz (1823–1862), Pol. poet.

T: Joseph Peter Thorp (1873–1962), Br. writer, biographer.

Mr. **T:** Lawrence Tureaud (or Tero) (1952–), U.S. black TV actor.

Kamil Amin **Taabes:** Elie Cohen (? –1965), Israeli spy. Cohen, a Jew, was given a Muslim name for his operations in the Zionist cause in Syria.

Tabarin: Antoine Girard (? –1626), Fr. actor. Sources differ concerning the true identity of the actor. Some say that Tabarin was his real name, and that his full name and dates were thus Jean Salomon Tabarin (1584–1633). Either way, his name gave the standard French expression *faire le tabarin*, "play the fool."

Jamaaladeen **Tacuma:** Rudy McDaniel (1956–), U.S. rock musician. The musician adopted his new name on coverting to Islam.

Tad: Thomas Aloysius Dorgan (1877–1929), U.S. cartoonist, sports commentator. The cartoonist's initials conveniently gave his acronymic pseudonym. The name has the added advantage of being a short personal name (for "Thaddeus") in its own right.

Taffrail: [Captain] Henry Taprell Dorling (1883–1968), Br. naval writer, broadcaster. The captain's name is obviously based on his middle name, but at the same time is a nautical term for the upper part of a ship's stern timbers.

Koki **Taiho** Koki Naya (1940–), Jap. sumo wrestler. The athlete adopted his Japanese nickname, meaning "great bird."

John **Taine:** Eric Temple Bell (1883–1960), Sc.-born U.S. SF writer.

Aleksandr **Tairov:** Aleksandr Yakovlevich Kornblit (1885–1950), Russ. theatrical director.

Takamura Koun: Nakajima Kozo (1852–1934), Jap. sculptor. The artist studied Buddhist sculpture under Takamura Koun and subsequently adopted his master's name.

Takis: Panayotis Vassilakis (1925–), Gk. experimental artist.

Talbert: Talbert McLean (1906–1992), Sc. painter, cartoonist.

Howard **Talbot:** Richard Lansdale Munkittrick (1865–1928), U.S.-born Br. popular composer, of Ir. parentage. The musician's father wanted him to be a doctor and for a time he trained for this profession. He decided it was not for him, however, and instead studied music. His father disowned him, and it was at this point that he adopted his new name, taking his mother's maiden name.

Lyle **Talbot:** Lysle Hollywood Henderson (1904–1987), U.S. movie actor.

Nita **Talbot:** Anita Sokol (1930–), U.S. TV comedienne.

Dimitr **Talev:** Dimitr Talev Petrov (1898–1966), Bulg. writer.

Talfryn: Iorwerth Hefin Lloyd (1920–1986), Welsh poet. The writer's bardic name is that of his birthplace near Denbigh, northern Wales.

Talhaiarn: John Jones (1810–1869), Welsh poet. The writer's bardic name comes from his birthplace, the village of Llanfair Talhaiarn, near Abergele, Denbighshire (now Clwyd).

Hal **Taliaferro:** Floyd Taliaferro Alderson (1895–1980), U.S. movie actor.

Taliesin ab Iolo: Taliesin Williams (1787–1847), Welsh poet. The writer's name means "Taliesin son of Iolo," the latter being Iolo Morganwg (*q.v.*). His first name is that of the legendary 6th-century poet Taliesin.

Talis Qualis: Carl Vilhelm August Strandberg (1818–1877), Swe. poet, journalist. The pseudonym represents the Latin phrase meaning "of such a kind as."

Talma: Mary Ann Ford (*c.*1870–1944), Eng. magician, "Queen of Coins." The illusionist married the Belgian-British magician Jean Henri Servais Le Roy (1865–1953) in 1890 and performed jointly with him and Leon Bosco as "Leroy-Talma-Bosco."

Richard **Talmadge:** Ricardo Metzetti (1896–1981), U.S. movie actor, stunt man.

Aino **Talvi:** Aino Augustovna Pindam (1905–), Estonian stage actress.

Talvj: Therese Albertine Louise Robinson, née von Jakob (1797–1870), Ger. author, writing in English. The writer's pseudonym represents the initials of her full maiden name, and was pronounced by her as "Talvey." Her husband was Professor Edward Robinson, the U.S. biblical scholar.

Rabbenu **Tam:** Jacob ben Meir (1100–1171), Fr. Talmudic scholar. The Jewish authority came to be known by a name alluding to the biblical line: "Jacob was a mild man [*ish tam*], dwelling in tents" (Genesis 25:27). This is interpreted in the Rabbinic tradition to mean that Jacob was a "perfect" man, dwelling in the tents of the Torah. Hence the scholar's full name, interpreted as "Our Teacher the Perfect One." Rabbenu Tam was the grandson of Rashi and younger brother of Rashbam (*qq.v.*).

Tamara: Tamara Swann Drasin (1907–1943), Russ.-born U.S. stage, movie actress, singer.

Tamara Khanum: Tamara Artyomovna Petrosyan (1906–), Uzbek dancer, singer, of Armenian parentage.

Helen **Tamiris:** Helen Becker (1905–1966), U.S. ballet dancer, choreographer, teacher.

A.H. **Tammsaare:** Anton Hansen (1878–1940), Estonian writer. The writer took the name of the farmhouse where he was born as his new surname, then added the initials of his original name.

Tampa Red: Hudson Woodbridge (or Whittaker) (*c.*1904–1981), U.S. black blues singer. The singer was raised in Tampa, Florida, by his grandmother. Hence his name.

V.G. **Tan:** Vladimir Germanovich Bogoraz (1865–1936), Russ. writer, anthropologist. The writer adopted his pseudonym from his original first name, Natan (Nathan). He spelled this out with an alternate form, N.A. Tan.

Tania (or Tanya): (1) Zoya Anatolyevna Kosmodemyanskaya (1923–1941), Russ. partisan; (2) Haydee Tamara Bunke (1937–1967), Argentine-born Soviet agent, of Ger. parentage; (3) Patricia Campbell Shaw, née Hearst (1954–), U.S. liberationist. Tania (Tanya), a name of Russian origin (the pet form of Tatiana), was at first one of many Soviet cover names in revolutionary circles. It became more widely known from its association with Russian partisan Kosmodemyanskaya, executed by the Germans in World War II, who herself adopted it in memory of Tanya Solomakha, a Civil War agent. It was in turn taken up by non-Russian activists such as Bunke, who worked in South America with Che Guevara (*q.v.*). In 1964, on leaving Cuba for Europe, she assumed the identity of either Vittoria Pancini, the daughter of German parents living on the Italian-German border, or of Marta Iriarte, an Argentine. When in Havana she operated as Laura Gutierrez Bauer. Her Cuban cover name was the outcome: an Italian-Argentine-German compromise. Like Kosmodemyanskaya, she also lost her life in the field. The name was subsequently adopted in her honor by Symbionese Liberation Army agent Patty Hearst [1. *Sunday Telegraph*, July 21, 1968; 2. Marta Royas and Mirta Rodriguez Calderon, *Tania*, 1973; 3. David Boulton, *The Making of Tania: The Patty Hearst Story*, 1975; 4. V.D. Uspensky, *Zoya Kosmodemyanskaya*, 1989].

Maksim **Tank:** Evgeny Ivanovich Skurko (1912–), Belorussian revolutionary poet. The poet has given his own account of his name: "I first had my work printed in 1932 in the irregular newspaper *Na perelome* ["Turning Point"] published in Lvov. The poem was called "Factory Chimneys." I was young and green then. Almost all the established poets that I admired had pen names. I followed their example, of course. Moreover, writing at that time under your real name was not without risk. By then I had already been using a number of undercover names: Zhenka, Viktor, Maksim... This last was in honor of Gorky [*q.v.*]. I kept this name for my published writing. But what for a surname? I was raised in the country and at first thought of adopting a plant name. However, it turned out that many of the plant names were already bespoken by poets: Kolas, Krapiva, Charot, Vasilyok... Moreover, if you follow someone's example, aren't you doing just the same? So I took something that was the opposite—

powerful, steel, dynamic, something that matched, I felt, the measure and restless mood of the time. And ever since then I have been Tank. There is something rather juvenile about the pseudonym, of course. But that was how it was. Later, too, at the front, the name was really quite appropriate" [Dmitriyev, p. 217].

Tanti: Konstantin Konstantinovich Ferroni (1888–1974), Russ. circus artist + Leon Konstantinovich Ferroni (1892–1973), Russ. circus artist, his brother. The two brothers, who performed as musical clowns, originated from an Italian circus family. Hence their Italian surname. Their ring name comes from their patronymic (middle name), but also happens to mean "so much."

Tantia Topi: Ramchandra Panduranga (c.1819–1859), Ind. guerrilla leader.

Tanya *see* Tania.

Tanymarian: [Rev.] Edward Stephen (1882–1885), Welsh hymnwriter. The musician took his name from the house in northwestern Wales where he lived. The name itself means "below the strand" (Welsh *tan*, "below," *y*, "the," and *marian*, "strand").

Marguerite **Taos:** Marie-Louise Taos Amrouche (1913–1976), Algerian writer, working in France.

[Princess] Elizaveta **Tarakanova:** ? (c.1745–1775), Russ. adventuress, royal pretender. For the story of the mystery, see p. 59.

Tarheel Slim: Alden Bunn (1924–1977), U.S. blues, gospel singer, guitarist. The singer came from North Carolina, the "Tarheel State."

Yury **Tarich:** Yury Viktorovich Alekseyev (1885–1967), Russ. movie director, screenwriter. The filmmaker's adopted name represents a casual pronunciation of his first name and patronymic (Yury Viktorovich), which would be a standard way of addressing him. (The patronymic is conventionally shortened in speech, so that "Viktorovich" would sound as "Viktarich" or even as just "Tarich.")

Mikhail **Tarkhanov:** Mikhail Mikhaylovich Moskvin (1877–1948), Russ. stage, movie actor.

William **Tarmey:** William Cleworth Piddington (1941–), Br. TV actor, singer. Advised that his original name was too long for billing purposes, the actor adopted a shorter name based on that of the U.S. singer Mel Tormé (1925–).

Niccolò **Tartaglia:** Niccolò Fontana (1499–1557), It. mathematician. During the French sacking of Brescia, his birthtown, 12-year-old Niccolò was slashed in the jaws and palate by a

saber. As a result, his speech was impaired, and he was nicknamed *Tartaglia*, "stammerer." He later adopted the name.

Tasma: Jessie Couvreur, née Huybers (1848–1897), Br. novelist, journalist. The writer took her name from Tasmania, Australia, where she was raised.

Agostino **Tassi:** Agostino Buonamici (c.1580–1644), It. painter.

Harry **Tate:** Ronald MacDonald Hutchison (1873–1940), Sc. music hall comedian. The actor took his name from his former employers, the sugar refiners Henry Tate & Sons (now Tate & Lyle).

Simon **Tate:** Simon Neil Tattersall (1956–), Br. radio presenter.

Jacques **Tati:** Jacques Tatischeff (1908–1982), Fr. comic movie actor. The actor was the grandson of Count Dmitri Tatischeff, an attaché at the Russian embassy in Paris who had married a Frenchwoman. His screen name was a shortening of his real name (in its original Russian form, Tatishchev), but at the same time sounds engagingly affectionate to the French ear.

Richard **Tauber:** Ernst Seiffert (1891–1948), Austr.-born Br. operetta singer, conductor. The musician was illegitimate, and initially bore his mother's maiden name. He was later adopted by his father, Anton Richard Tauber, and took his name.

Léo **Taxil:** Gabriel Antoine Jogand-Pagès (1854–1907), Fr. journalist, anticlerical writer. The writer appears to have based his name on that of the Greek general Taxiles.

Vic **Tayback:** Victor Tabback (1929–1990), U.S. movie actor.

Chip **Taylor:** James Wesley Voight (1940–), U.S. pop singer, composer.

Estelle **Taylor:** Estelle Boylan (1899–1958), U.S. stage, movie actress.

Eva **Taylor:** Irene Gibbons (1895–1977), U.S. theatre, radio singer.

Gwen **Taylor:** Gwendoline Allsop (1939–), Eng. stage, movie, TV actress.

Kent **Taylor:** Louis Weiss (1907–1987), U.S. movie actor.

Koko **Taylor:** Cora Walton (1935–), U.S. black blues singer. Presumably "Koko" from Cora and "Taylor" loosely from Walton.

Laurette **Taylor:** Helen Laurette Magdalene Cooney (1884–1946), U.S. stage, movie actress.

Little Johnny **Taylor:** Johnny Young (1943–), U.S. soul, blues singer. The singer took his name from the established soul singer, Ted Taylor (1934–1987).

Pat **Taylor**: Pat Pope (1918–), Eng. stage actress, singer.

Robert **Taylor**: Spangler Arlington Brugh (1911–1969), U.S. movie actor. The actor was given his screen name in 1934 by MGM head Louis B. Mayer. Later, the Australian movie actor Robert Taylor (1929–) shortened his first name to Rod and moved to England.

Theodore **Taylor**: John Camden Hotten (1832–1873), Eng. writer, publisher. The writer, whose original name was John William Hotten, and who introduced many American authors to the British public, assumed this name for a rather slight biography of Thackeray, published in 1864.

Taylor: Vince/Maurice Brian Holden (1939–1991), Br. rock musician, working in France.

Bram **Tchaikovsky**: Peter Bramall (1950–), Eng. rock guitarist.

Ludmilla **Tcherina**: Monique Avenirovna Tchemerzine (1924–), Fr. ballet dancer, movie actress.

Conway **Tearle**: Frederick Levy (1878–1938), U.S. movie actor.

Teena Marie: Mary Christine Brockert (1957–), U.S. soul, jazz musician. The singer reversed her first two names before adapting forms of them as her stage name.

Teffi: Nadezhda Aleksandrovna Buchinskaya, née Lokhvitskaya (1872–1952), Russ. short story writer, poet, working in France. The writer took her pen name from Taffy, the little prehistoric girl in Rudyard Kipling's story "How the Alphabet Was Made" in the *Just So Stories* (1902).

Tegid: John Jones (1792–1852), Welsh poet, antiquary. The poet was born near Lake Bala, Merionethshire (now Gwynedd), and took his bardic name from the Welsh name of the lake, Llyn Tegid. He was also known as Ioan Tegid, with the Welsh equivalent of his first name.

Tegla: Edward Davies (1880–1967), Welsh writer. The writer took his name from his birthplace, the village of Llandegla-yn-Iâl ("St. Tegla's church in Yale"), near Denbigh. (The latter district gave the name of Elihu Yale, benefactor of Yale University, New Haven, Connecticut.)

Telynog: Thomas Evans (1840–1865), Welsh poet. The poet's bardic name means "harper."

[Dame] Marie **Tempest**: Mary Susan Etherington (1864–1942), Eng. stage actress, singer. The actress adopted her name from Lady Susan Vane-Tempest, whom she claimed to be her godmother.

Ann **Temple**: Penelope Ruth Mortimer, earlier Dimont, née Fletcher (1918–), Welsh novelist. The writer used this name for her "lonely hearts" column in the London *Daily Mail*. For her first novel, *Johanna* (1947), she wrote as Penelope Dimont, from her first husband (married 1937), Charles Dimont.

Hope **Temple**: Dotie Davies (1859–1938), Ir. songwriter, of Eng. parentage. The name suggests a "temple of hope." The writer married the French composer André Messager (1853–1929).

Neville **Temple**: [Hon.] Julian Charles Henry Fane (1827–1870), Eng. diplomat, poet. The writer used this name (a temple being poetically a "fane") for the joint authorship, with "Edward Trevor" (Hon. Edward Robert Bulwer Lytton), of the poem *Tannhäuser; or the Battle of the Bards* (1861).

Paul **Temple**: Francis Durbridge (1912–), Eng. crime writer + James Douglas Rutherford McConnell (1915–), Ir. crime, mystery writer. The two writers used this name for mystery novels which did *not* feature Paul Temple, the famous detective created by Durbridge.

William **Tenn**: Philip Klass (1920–), U.S. SF writer. This looks like a pun on "William Penn," but verification is needed.

Kylie **Tennant**: Kylie Tennant Rodd (1912–1988), Austral. novelist, playwright.

Madison **Tensas**, M.D.: [Dr.] Henry Clay Lewis (1825–1850), U.S. humorist.

Tenzing Norgay: Namgyal Wangdi (1914–1986), Nepalese Sherpa mountaineer. The mountaineer's adopted Nepalese name means literally "wealthy-fortunate religion-follower."

Teresa: Teresa Viera-Romero (1929–), U.S.-Sp. ballet dancer.

Mother **Teresa**: Agnes Gonxha Bojaxhiu (1910–1997), Albanian-born Ind. missionary. The founder of the Missionaries of Charity went to Ireland in 1928 to join the Loreto Sisters, an order noted for its missionary work. She was transferred as a teacher to St. Mary's Loreto Convent High School in Calcutta, and when taking her vows as a Sister of Loreto in 1931 chose the name Teresa for St. Theresa of Lisieux (*q.v.*). "Mother Teresa gives us a first sign of the contemplative side of her mission by picking St.

Theresa of Lisieux as a saintly guide" [Lucinda Varley, Introduction to Mother Teresa, *A Simple Path*, 1995].

Teresah: Teresa Corinna Ubertis Gray (1877–1964), It. novelist, poet.

Max **Terpis:** Max Pfister (1889–1958), Swiss ballet dancer, choreographer, teacher. The dancer's professional surname is a near anagram of his real name.

Tammi **Terrell:** Thomasina Montgomery (1945–1970), U.S. pop singer. The singer's alliterative name was derived from her first husband, heavyweight boxer Ernie Terrell (married 1965). It is therefore a real name, on the same lines as that of Cyd Charisse (*q.v.*).

Norma **Terris:** Norma Allison (1904–1989), U.S. stage actress, singer.

Ellaline **Terriss:** Ellen Hicks, née Lewin (1871–1971), Eng. stage, movie actress, daughter of William Terriss (see next entry below).

William **Terriss:** William Charles James Lewin (1847–1897), Eng. actor. The actor's best work was done at the Adelphi Theatre, London, and consequently he was nicknamed "No. 1, Adelphi Terrace," after a street in this region. He subsequently altered "Terrace" to a spelling that more closely resembled that of a surname. The name also happens to suggest "Terry," a noted theatrical surname. (Terriss actually acted opposite Ellen Terry, his exact contemporary.) He was murdered by a deranged actor, Richard Prince (*q.v.*).

Alice **Terry:** Alice Frances Taafe (1899–1987), U.S. movie actress.

C.V. **Terry:** Frank Gill Slaughter (1908–), U.S. novelist.

Don **Terry:** Donald Locher (1902–1988), U.S. movie actor.

Megan **Terry:** Marguerite Duffy (1932–), U.S. playwright. The writer's first name is the Welsh equivalent of her own (and her mother's) first name, Marguerite. Her surname both honors the actress Ellen Terry and suggests the earth (things terrestrial).

Sonny **Terry:** Saunders Terrell (1911–1986), U.S. black jazz, blues musician.

Terry-Thomas: Thomas Terry Hoar-Stevens (1911–1990), Eng. comic stage, movie actor. The actor began his career as Mot Snevets (reverse it), then he tried Thomas Terry. He explained: "I quite liked the sound of Thomas Terry but I decided I had to kill that one fast. I didn't want people to think I was trying to cash in on Ellen Terry's name and fame. So I turned my christian names round and added a hyphen for an individual touch" [Terry-Thomas with Terry Daum, *Terry-Thomas Tells Tales*, 1990]. The gap-toothed actor also quipped: "The hyphen's the gap between my teeth." Ellen Terry (1848–1928) came from a famous acting family (see William Terris, above).

Peter **Terson:** Peter Patterson (1932–), Br. playwright. The writer adopted the clipped form of his name in the 1960s when he was resident dramatist at the Victoria Theatre, Stoke-on-Trent, Britain's first theatre-in-the-round.

Phillida **Terson:** Phyllis Neilson-Terry (1892–1977), Eng. stage actress. The actress's new surname combines syllables from her original surname.

Abram **Tertz:** Andrey Donatovich Sinyavsky (1925–1997), Russ. dissident novelist, short story writer, critic. The writer adopted this pseudo-Jewish name, from a character in a song about the criminal underworld, for fiction published in the West. The choice of such a name was probably intended to suggest that he was an "outsider," as a criminal is.

Vaan **Teryan:** Vaan Sukiasovich Ter-Grigoryan (1885–1920), Armenian poet. The poet abbreviated his surname, combining the prefixed particle *Ter-*, frequently found in Armenian names to denote a clerical origin, with the second half of the surname proper (itself representing the first name Grigor, "Gregory").

Laurent **Terzieff:** Laurent Tchemerzine (1935–), Fr. movie actor.

Teutha: William Jerdan (1782–1869), Sc. journalist, editor, writer. The writer used this name for a number of contributions to journals, taking it from the historic name of the Tweed. He was born in Kelso, which stands on this river.

Joe **Tex:** Joseph Arrington, Jr. (1933–1982), U.S. soul singer, composer. The musician was born in Texas, as his name readily implies. In 1966 he converted to the Muslim faith and took the name Yusuf Hazziez.

Josephine **Tey:** Elizabeth Mackintosh (1897–1952), Sc. playwright, novelist, short story writer. The writer adopted her great-great-grandmother's name for her pen name. She also wrote as Gordon Daviot (*q.v.*).

[Dame] Maggie **Teyte:** [Dame] Margaret Cottingham, née Tate (1888–1976), Eng. singer. When the soprano went to Paris at the age of 20 she changed the spelling of her surname to ensure the correct pronunciation of "Tate" by the French. This led to doubts about her name's pronunciation in English-speaking countries, a situation that was commented on in the following piece of doggerel (of American origin):

Tell us ere it be too late,
Art thou known as Maggie Teyte?
Or, per contra, art thou hight
As we figure, Maggie Teyte?

Zare **Thalberg:** Ethel Western (1858–1915), Eng. opera singer, stage actress.

Elswyth **Thane:** Elswyth Thane Ricker Beebe (1900–), U.S. playwright, novelist. The writer married William Beebe.

Octave **Thanet:** Alice French (1850–1934), U.S. novelist. The writer has explained her name: "Octave was the name of a school-friend of mine. It is both French and Scotch. I thought if I could find another name to go with it, that was both French and Scotch, I would adopt that. I was riding on a train one time when we stopped at a way station, and on a siding near where I sat was a freight car painted red. On the side was chalked the word, 'Thanet.' What it meant or how it got there, I have not the slightest idea, but I decided then and there to adopt it. Lots of people still think that Octave Thanet is a man and I frequently get letters like this: 'My dear Mr. Thanet: I have read your works and I am sure you are a manly man.' They usually contain a request for a small loan, to be repaid in the near future" [Marble, p. 207].

Mlle **Théodore:** Marie-Madeleine Crépé (1760–1796), Fr. ballet dancer.

Theodosia: Anne Steel (1716–1778), Eng. writer of religious verse, hymns. The name, which means "gift of God," was doubtless significant for the writer, who adopted it for *Poems on Subjects Chiefly Devotional* (1760).

Sylvanus **Theophrastus:** John Thelwall (1764–1834), Eng. reformer, politician, lecturer on elocution. The writer's pseudonym is a classical concoction, but may have had specific reference to Johannes Sylvanus, the 16th-century German reformer and theologian, and the 3d-century BC Greek philosopher Theophrastus. The latter gained vogue from the 16th century thanks to translations of his works, and his name was employed by other writers, e.g. as a pen name of the Scottish publisher William Creech (1745–1815) and in the title of a volume of essays by George Eliot (*q.v.*), *The Impressions of Theophrastus Such* (1879).

Thérésa: Eugénie Emma Valdon (1837–1913), Fr. music hall artist.

[St.] **Theresa of Lisieux:** Marie-Françoise-Thérèse Martin (1873–1897), Fr. virgin, Carmelite nun (the "Little Flower of Jesus").

David **Thewlis:** David Wheeler (1963–), Br. stage, TV actor. The actor's stage name is his mother's maiden name.

Alan **Thicke:** Alan Jeffery (1948–), U.S. TV actor, writer. The actor adopted his stepfather's surname.

Thinks-I-to-Myself, Who?: [Rev.] Edward Nares (1762–1841), Eng. cleric, novelist, historian. The writer used this name for *Thinks-I-to-Myself* (1811), a "serio-ludicro-tragico-comico tale," and *I Says, Says I* (1812), a novel. Nares had himself complained when others used this pseudo-pseudonym.

Bel **Thistlethwaite:** Agnes Ethelwyn Wetherald (1857–1940), Can. poet, journalist. The writer adopted her maternal grandmother's maiden name as her pen name.

Caroline **Thomas:** Julia Caroline Dorr, née Ripley (1825–1913), U.S. poet, novelist. The writer adopted her mother's maiden name for her first novel, *Farmingdale* (1854). Later novels were published under her married name.

Danny **Thomas:** Muzyad Yakhoob (later Amos Jacobs) (1912–1991) U.S. nightclub comedian, TV actor, of Lebanese parentage. For his stage name, the actor adopted the first names of his two brothers. The actress Marlo Thomas (Margaret Julia Thomas) (1938–) is his daughter.

E.H. Francis **Thomas:** David Tecwyn Lloyd (1914–), Welsh editor, writer. The writer used this pseudonym for two collections of short stories.

Idris **Thomas:** Robert Thomas Jenkins (1881–1969), Eng.-born Welsh historian, writer. The writer used this name for short stories and a novel.

Kid **Thomas:** Thomas Valentine (1896–1987), U.S. jazz musician.

Olive **Thomas:** Oliveretta Elaine Duffy (1884–1920), U.S. movie actress.

Thomas à Kempis: Thomas Hemerken (*c.*1380–1471), Du. theologian. The reputed author of *De Imitatione Christi* takes his name from his birthtown of Kempen, now in Germany northwest of Cologne.

Carlos **Thompson:** Juan Carlos Mundin Schafter (or Mundanschaffter) (1916–1990), Argentine stage, movie actor, of Ger. descent.

Daley **Thompson:** Francis Morgan Thompson (1958–), Br. black athlete. The decathlete's adopted first name is a colloquial form of Ayodele, a Nigerian name given him by his father, meaning "joy comes home."

Jack **Thompson:** John Payne (1940–), Austral. movie actor.

Sue **Thompson:** Eva Sue McKee (1926–), U.S. pop singer.

James **Thomson, B.V.:** James Thomson (1834–1882), Sc. poet. The poet added the initials to his name in order to be distinguished from the Scottish poet who was his namesake, James Thomson (1700–1748). The letters stand for "Bysshe Vanolis," with the first of these names the middle name of Percy Bysshe Shelley, and the second an anagram of the name of Novalis (*q.v.*). Thomson greatly admired both writers.

Ismay **Thorn:** Edith Caroline Pollock (*fl.*1890), Br. children's writer.

Ronald Scott **Thorn:** Ronald Scotthorn Wilkinson (1920–1996), Br. playwright, novelist. The writer used this (fairly transparent) name early in his career for distinction from his professional work as a doctor.

Frank **Thornton:** Francis Thornton Ball (1921–), Eng. stage, TV actor. The actor adopted his mother's maiden name (his own middle name) as his stage name.

Henry **Thornton:** Henry Ford (1750–1818), Eng. theatre manager.

Jim **Thorpe:** Wa-tho-huck (1888–1943), U.S. athlete, American footballer. The sportsman's father was part Irish and part Native American, while his mother was part Native American and part French. His original Native American name meant "bright path." His full English name was James Frances Thorpe.

Linda **Thorson:** Linda Robinson (1947–), Can. stage, TV actress. The actress extracted her stage name from the surname of her first husband, Barry Bergthorson, whom she married at the age of 16.

General Tom **Thumb:** Charles Sherwood Stratton (1838–1883), U.S. midget showman. For his professional name, Charles Stratton adopted the name of the traditional folktale character, who dates back at least to the 16th century. His assumed title of "General" was designed to add to his stature, so to speak.

Johnny **Thunder:** Gil Hamilton (1941–), U.S. pop singer.

Captain **Thunderbolt:** Frederick Ward (1835–1870), Austral. bushranger.

Chief **Thundercloud:** Victor Daniels (1899–1955), Native American movie actor.

Johnny **Thunders:** John Anthony Genzale, Jr. (1952–1991), U.S. rock musician.

Henry T. **Thurston:** Francis Turner Palgrave (1824–1897), Eng. poet, anthologist, critic. The compiler of *Palgrave's Golden Treasury* (1861) adopted this name for *The Passionate Pilgrim; or, Eros and Anteros* (1858). Palgrave was the son of the historian Sir Francis Palgrave (1788–1861), who was himself of Jewish origin, with the original surname Cohen. In 1823 he adopted the Christian faith, and in that same year married, changing his name to Palgrave, the maiden name of his mother-in-law.

Lawrence **Tibbett:** Lawrence Tibbet (1896–1960), U.S. classical singer. The singer adopted a misspelling of his original name as his stage name.

Tiberius: Tiberius Claudius Nero (42 BC–AD 37), Roman emperor. The emperor's original full name was as above, and was the same as that of his father. His later full name was Tiberius Caesar Augustus (or Tiberius Julius Caesar Augustus), for Augustus (*q.v.*), whose stepson, adopted son, and successor he was. His own successor was Caligula (*q.v.*).

Tiffany: Tiffany Renee Darwish (1971–), U.S. pop singer.

Pamela **Tiffin:** Pamela Wonso (1942–), U.S. movie actress, former child model.

Tiger: Norman Jackson (*c.*1965–), Jamaican reggae rapper.

Dick **Tiger:** Dick Ihetu (1929–1971), Nigerian middleweight boxer.

[St.] **Tikhon:** Vasily Ivanovich Belavin (1865–1925), Russ. churchman, patriarch of Moscow and All Russia. The head of the Russian Orthodox Church, who was canonized in 1989, adopted his religious name on taking monastic vows in 1891. The name itself means "successful," from the Greek.

Vesta **Tilley:** Matilda Alice Powles (1864–1952), Br. singing comedienne, male impersonator. The actress began her performing career at the age of three, when she was billed as Little Tilley (as a pet form of her first name, which she shared with her mother). This was a provincial debut, made at the Star Music Hall, Gloucester, where her father, William Henry Powles (known as Harry Ball), was the manager. When she was

14, she made her first London appearance, now being billed as The Great Little Tilley. It was soon after this that she adopted the name Vesta, using Tilley as a surname. That way she intrigued even more those members of her audiences who were puzzled as to whether she was male or female. The selection of this name may have been arbitrary, although it has been related to the type of wax match known as a "Vesta" (after the Greek goddess of the hearth). Appropriately, it happens to suggest "transvestite," although this word was not current when Tilley first took the name. (However, the now rare verb "to transvest," meaning to dress in the clothes of the opposite sex, is recorded by the *Oxford English Dictionary* in 1652.)

Alice Tilton: Phoebe Atwood Taylor (1909–1976), U.S. detective story writer.

Tim: William Timyn (1902–1990), Austr.-born Br. cartoonist.

Timothy: Timothy Birdsall (1936–1963), Eng. cartoonist, illustrator.

Timrava: Božena Slánčiková (1867–1951), Slovakian writer.

Tina: Philomena Josephine Veronica Quinn (1948–), Ir. pop singer.

Dick Tinto: Frank Booth Goodrich (1826–1894), U.S. writer, son of Peter Parley (1) (*q.v.*). The writer adopted the name of the artist who is the supposed narrator of the story told in Scott's *The Bride of Lammermoor* (1819).

Tintoretto: Jacopo Robusti (1518–1594), It. painter. The painter's name arose as nickname meaning "little dyer," referring to his father, who by profession was a silk dyer (Italian *tintore*).

Tiny Tim: Herbert Kauhry (1922–1996), U.S. popular singer, of Lebanese Jewish parentage. The oddball entertainer is said to have adopted his name from an incident in 1965: "As he was shambling out of a New York night spot whose management had decided that his lanky 6 ft figure and bizarre clothes did not 'fit,' a voice from the audience called out, 'Hey, Tiny, do us a set.' Kauhry returned, performed, and from that moment grew swiftly to fame as Tiny Tim" [*The Times*, December 2, 1996]. Kauhry had also played Greenwich Village clubs as Darry Dover and Larry Love.

Tippa Irie: Anthony Henry (1965–), Br. reggae rapper.

James Tiptree, Jr.: Alice Sheldon, née Bradley (1915–1987), U.S. SF writer. The writer took her (male) name from Wilkin's "Tiptree" jam. She also wrote as Raccoona Sheldon.

Tiradentes: Joaquin José da Silva Xavier (1748–1792), Brazilian revolutionary. The activist had many jobs as a young man, one of them being a dentist. Hence his nickname which he adopted as his pseudonym, meaning literally "tooth-puller" (Portuguese *tirar*, "to pull," and *dente*, "tooth").

Hans Tisdall: Hans John Knox Aufseeser (1910–1997), Ger.-born artist, designer, working in U.K.

Timothy Titcomb: Josiah Gilbert Holland (1819–1881), U.S. doctor, novelist, poet, editor. The writer used this name for *Titcomb's Letters to Young People, Single and Married* (1858).

Tirso de Molina: [Frey] Gabriel Téllez (*c.*1571–1648), Sp. dramatist. When censorship threatened his writing early in his career, the playwright named himself Tirso de Molina, "Tirso of Molina."

Titian: Tiziano Vecellio (1488–1576), It. painter. Unlike some of his contemporaries, Titian did not assume (and was apparently not given) a name or nickname that differed from his basic first name.

Michael Angelo Titmarsh: William Makepeace Thackeray (1811–1863), Eng. novelist. The writer used this name for various tales published from the 1840s. He is said to have been humorously nicknamed "Michael Angelo" for his broken nose and his aspirations to be an artist. To this famous name, Thackeray then added "Titmarsh" as an absurd contrast.

[Marshal] Tito: Josip Broz (1892–1980), Yugoslav soldier, statesman. There are various accounts claiming to explain the famous leader's name. One maintains that it derives from Serbo-Croat *ti to*, literally "you this," meaning "you do this." Tito was apparently always saying "You do this," "You do that." But Tito himself is said to have adopted the name after reading a book by two Serbo-Croatian writers who had "Tito" as their first name. (As such, it was, and is, a standard Serbo-Croat forename, simply meaning "Titus.") Josip Broz is said to have wished to adopt the name "Rudi," but someone else had already claimed it. The second of these two rival explanations for the name seems the more likely. In the world of partisan warfare in which Tito was involved, he had several underground names, although in Comintern communications he was always "Comrade Walter." The hazardous conditions of guerrilla combat sometimes necessitated a change of cover name as often as three times a *day* [Jules Archer, *Red Rebel: Tito of Yugoslavia*, 1968].

Harriet **Toby:** Harriet Katzman (1929–1952), U.S. ballet dancer.

(Uncle) Simeon **Toby:** George Trask (1798–1875), U.S. cleric, reformer. The writer used this name for *Thoughts and Stories on Tobacco, for American Lads* (1852), subtitled Uncle Toby's Anti- Tobacco Advice to his Nephew, Billy Bruce.

Toby, M.P.: [Sir] Henry William Lucy (1845–1924), Eng. journalist, humorist, satirist. The writer used this name for his contributions to *Punch*. Toby, of course, is the name of Punch's dog in the traditional "Punch and Judy" puppet show. The initials were intended to stand for "Member of Parliament," although Lucy was not an M.P. but a J.P. (Justice of the Peace).

Ann (E.) **Todd:** Anne Todd Mayfield (1932–), U.S. child movie actress. The actress added the "E." to her name in the 1940s to avoid confusion with the British actress Ann Todd (1909–1993).

Mike **Todd:** Avram Hirsch Goldbogen (or Goldenbogen) (1907–1958), U.S. movie producer, of Pol. Jewish parentage. When Goldbogen's father died, in 1931, he assumed the first name of his own son, Michael, at the same time changing his surname to "Todd." This represented his own nickname, "Toat."

Nick **Todd:** Nicholas Boone (1935–), U.S. pop singer. The singer was signed to Dot Records, and took his stage name by reversing the company name.

Togare: Georg Kulovits (1900–1988), Hung.-born/Austr. animal tamer, circus artist. The performer adopted the character name of his act, an exotic and fearless oriental lion tamer.

Togolok Moldo: Bayymbet Abdyrakhmanov (1860–1942), Kirgiz folk poet. The poet's adopted name was self-descriptive and means "round-faced scholar."

Samuel **Tolansky:** Samuel Turlausky (1907–1973), Br. physicist, of Lithuanian Jewish origin. The family name was changed for ease of pronunciation some time before 1912.

Svetlana **Toma:** Svetlana Andreyevna Fomicheva (1947–), Russ. movie actress.

Tom and Jerry: Art Garfunkel (1937–), U.S. pop singer + Paul Simon (1940–), U.S. pop singer. The singers and composers called themselves thus for the four years 1956–59, having started in show business as, respectively, Tom Graph and Jerry Landis. In 1959 they vanished from the music scene until 1964, when they re-emerged under their own names (Simon and Garfunkel), subsequently splitting in 1970. The popular pair name Tom and Jerry goes back a good deal further than the well-known cartoon cat and mouse. In 1821 Pierce Egan, an English sports writer, published *Life in London; or, The Day and Night Scenes of Jerry Hawthorn, Esq., and his Elegant Friend Corinthian Tom*, and the names came to typify a couple of roistering young men-about-town.

Isaac **Tomkins,** Gent.: [Sir] Henry Peter Brougham, Baron Brougham and Vaux (1778–1868), Sc.-born Br. statesman, writer. The politician, Lord Chancellor of England, used this name for *We Can't Afford It!, being Thoughts on the Aristocracy of England* (1834).

Tommaseo: Niccolò Tomasiç (1802–1874), It. (Dalmatian) writer, philologist, patriot.

István **Tömörkény:** István Steingasner (1866–1917), Hung. writer, folklorist, ethnographer.

Tomos Glyn Cothi: Thomas Evans (1764–1833), Welsh poet, writer. The writer's name derives from a local placename in his native Carmarthenshire, so means "Thomas of Glyncothi."

Jacob **Tonson:** Enoch Arnold Bennett (1867–1931), Br. novelist. The writer's early pseudonym was borrowed from that of an 18th-century bookseller.

Horne **Tooke:** John Horne (1736–1812), Eng. politician, philologist. Horne added the name of William Tooke, a friend and political supporter, to his own in 1782, so that from then on he was John Horne Tooke (familiarly, Horne Tooke). Tooke had a sizeable estate in Surrey, and Horne had added his name with the intention of indicating that he would be his friend's heir. When Tooke died in 1802, however, Horne Tooke discovered that instead of making him his heir, William Tooke had merely left him £500, apart from canceling certain outstanding debts.

Topol: Chaim (or Haym) Topol (1935–), Israeli stage, movie actor. The actor made his name on the London stage playing Tevye in the U.S. musical *The Fiddler on the Roof* (1967). He dropped his first name on discovering that it confused the English.

Friedrich **Torberg:** Friedrich Kantor-Berg (1908–), Austr. novelist, essayist.

Peter **Tordenskjold:** Peter Wessel (1691–1720), Dan.-born Norw. naval commander, of

Du. parentage. The commander was raised to the aristocracy following a battle victory in 1716 in the Great Northern War against the Swedes, and took his new name then.

Miguel Torga: Adolfo Correia da Rocha (1907–1995), Port. poet, diarist.

Peter Tork: Peter Torkelson (1942–), U.S. pop musician.

Rip Torn: Elmore Rual Torn, Jr. (1931–), U.S. stage, movie, TV actor. The actor retained his high school nickname (of obvious origin) for his professional name.

Torquemada: Edward Powys Mathers (1892–1939), Br. crossword compiler. The compiler adopted the name of the infamous Spanish Grand Inquisitor, since he aimed to torture his victims, as his historic namesake had done in the 15th century. (The Inquisitor's name itself happens to suggest torturing, from Latin *torquere*, "to twist," "to torture." It actually derives from his place of origin, itself from Spanish *torre*, "tower," and *quemada*, "burnt.")

David Torrence: David Torrence Tayson (1880–1942), Sc. movie actor.

Johannes Torrentius: Jan van der Beeck (1589–1644), Du. painter. The artist translated his Dutch name (in English amounting to "John of the Brook") into a Latin equivalent.

Raquel Torres: Paula Marie Osterman (1908–1987), Mexican-born U.S. movie actress. "Torres" presumably as an anagrammatic evolution from "Osterman."

Malcolm Torrie: Gladys Maude Winifred Mitchell (1901–1983), Eng. writer of detective novels, children's fiction. Another male name used by the writer was Stephen Hockaby.

Peter Tosh: Winston Hubert McIntosh (1944–1987), Jamaican reggae musician.

Tostão: Eduardo Gonçalves de Andrade (1947–), Brazilian footballer. The player's Portuguese name means "tanned," "sunburned" (literally "toasted").

Toto: (1) Antonio de Curtis-Gagliardi Ducas Comneno di Bizanzio (1898–1967), It. stage, movie comedian, circus clown; (2) Armando Novello (? –1938), Swiss circus clown. The first Toto here, more correctly Totò, added the names of two leading Byzantine families, Ducas and Comneno ("of Byzantium"), to his real name, before abandoning this long-winded nomenclature for the short name that was a pet form of his first name. Novello borrowed his own name from him.

Dave Tough: David Jarvis (1907–1948), U.S. jazz drummer.

Kwame Touré: Stokely Carmichael (1941–), Trinidad-born U.S. activist. The former Black Panthers leader changed his Western name for an African one on leaving the United States for Guinea in 1969.

Jennie Tourel: Jennie Davidson (or Davidovich) (1899–1973), Russ.-born U.S. opera singer. The singer is said to have taken her professional name from that of a teacher, Anna El-Tour.

Maurice Tourneur: Maurice Thomas (1876–1961), Fr. movie director.

Toussaint-Louverture: François Dominique Toussaint (1743–1803), Haitian black political leader. The liberator and independence fighter took his additional name in 1793 at the time of the French Revolution. It represents French *l'ouverture*, "the opening," and alludes to the breaches that he bravely made in the ranks of his enemies.

Jean Tousseul: Olivier Degée (1890–1944), Belg. writer.

Peter Towry: David Towry Piper (1918–1990), Eng. writer on art, novelist.

Toyah: Toyah Ann Willcox (1958–), Br. rock singer, stage, movie actress. The singer reverted to her full name when concentrating on an acting career from the early 1990s.

Arthur Tracy: Abraham Tratsefofski (1900-1997), Ukrainian-born U.S. popular singer.

F.G. Trafford: Charlotte Eliza Lawson Riddell, née Cowan (1832–1906), Ir. novelist. The writer used this name for her first novel, *The Moors and the Fens* (1858), and retained it until 1864, after which she used her real (married) name, Mrs. J.H. Riddell, as well as other pseudonyms. One was Rainey Hawthorne.

Peter Traill: Guy Mainwaring Morton (1896–1968), Eng. novelist, playwright.

Chris Tranchell: Christopher Peter John Small (1941–), Br. stage actor.

B. (or Ben) Traven: Albert Otto Max Feige (*c*.1882–1969), U.S. novelist, of Ger. parentage. The writer was a recluse, and he rarely revealed any personal details. His true identity was revealed only in 1979. From 1917 through 1920 he edited the revolutionary German magazine *Der Ziegelbrenner* ("The Tile Burner") under the name of Ret Marut. The origin of this is uncertain. He also wrote as Traven Torsvan and, as a Hollywood scriptwriter, Hal Croves.

Bill **Travers**: William Lindon-Travers (1922–1994), Br. movie actor, brother of Linden Travers (see below).

Graham **Travers**: Margaret Georgina Todd (1859–1918), Sc. doctor, novelist. Possibly "Graham" was suggested by letters in the writer's real first name.

Henry **Travers**: Travers John Heagerty (1874–1965), Br. stage, movie actor, working in U.S.

John **Travers**: Eva Mary Bell, née Hamilton (1878–1959), Eng. novelist.

Linden **Travers**: Florence Lindon-Travers (1913–), Br. stage, movie actress, sister of Bill Travers (see above).

P.L. **Travers**: Helen Lyndon Goff (1899–1996), Austral.-born writer, of Ir. parentage, working in U.K. The creator of the fictional children's nanny Mary Poppins adopted a family name for her pen name (her father was Travers Robert Goff). She invariably used initials for her writing, with P.L. actually representing Pamela Lyndon.

Randy **Travis**: Randy Bruce Traywick (1959–), U.S. country singer. The singer originally performed as Randy Traywick. He then appeared as Randy Ray before adopting his eventual stage name.

Richard **Travis**: William Justice (1913–1989), U.S. movie actor.

Arthur **Treacher**: Arthur Treacher Veary (1894–1975), Br. movie actor, working in U.S.

Lawrence **Treat**: Lawrence Arthur Goldstone (1903–), U.S. crime writer.

Zélia **Trebelli**: Gloria Caroline Gillebert (or Lebert) (1834–1892), Fr. opera singer. The singer apparently formed her stage surname by reversing her original name.

Trebor Mai: Robert Williams (1830–1877), Welsh poet. The writer's bardic name, more playful than most, reads "I am Robert" in reverse.

Pirmin **Trecu**: Pirmon Aldabaldetrecu (1930–), Sp. ballet dancer, teacher.

[Sir] Herbert **Tree**: Herbert Draper Beerbohm (1853–1917), Br. theatre actor, manager. The actor was the son of Julius Beerbohm, a naturalized English grain merchant of Lithuanian parentage. His stage name of "Tree" represented the English equivalent of the second half of his original surname, itself a form of German *Birnbaum*, "pear tree." He retained the original surname in his full name, which was thus Herbert Draper Beerbohm Tree, and first used the stage name Beerbohm Tree in 1876. Tree was the half-brother of the dramatist and critic Max Beerbohm (1872–1956).

Trefin: Edgar Phillips (1889–1962), Welsh poet. The writer took his bardic name from his native village of Tre-fin (Trevine), Pembrokeshire (now Dyfed).

Robert **Tressell**: Robert P. Noonan (1868–1911), Ir. writer, working in U.K. The writer is famous for a single novel, *The Ragged-Trousered Philanthropists*, an attack on life and conditions in the building trade, published posthumously in abbreviated form in 1914 (with the pen name misspelled "Tressall") and in a full version in 1955. The author was a housepainter by trade. The origin of his pseudonym is uncertain (possibly it was meant to suggest "trestle"), as is much about his own background. His original middle name may have been Philippe.

Trevanian: Rodney William Whitaker (1931–), U.S. novelist, writer.

Hilda **Trevelyan**: Hilda Marie Antoinette Anna Blow, née Tucker (1880–1959), Br. stage actress.

John **Trevena**: Ernest George Henham (1870–1946), Eng. poet, novelist, working in Canada.

Ann **Trevor**: Ann Trilnick (1899–1970), Br. movie actress.

Austin **Trevor**: Austin Schilsky (1897–1978), Ir.-born Br. movie, stage, radio actor.

Claire **Trevor**: Claire Wemlinger (1909–), U.S. movie actress.

Elleston **Trevor**: Trevor Dudley Smith (1920–1995), Br. spy thriller writer, working in U.S. Like many thriller writers, Smith had several pseudonyms. He used Adam Hall (said to have been taken from a telephone directory) for his novels featuring the British Secret Service agent Quiller. Other names included Roger Fitzalan, Trevor Burgess, Caesar Smith, Warwick Scott, Mansell Black, and Simon Rattray.

William **Trevor**: William Trevor Cox (1928–), Ir. novelist, short story writer.

Tricky: Adrian Thaws (*c*.1970– ?), Br. black rapper. The musician's name was his street name as a nimble-minded, agile-bodied teenager. In 1996 he released an album under a new pseudonym: Nearly God. This resulted from a German interviewer who asked him: "So, how does it feel to be God—well, nearly God?"

Trilussa: Carlo Alberto Salustri (1873–1950), It. poet. A straight anagram of the poet's surname.

Robert **Trimbole:** Bruno Trimboli (1931–1987), It.-born Austral. criminal. Australia's most wanted man was a partner in crime of Alexander Sinclair (*q.v.*).

A. Stephen **Tring:** Laurence Walter Meynell (1899–1989), Eng. novelist, children's writer. The writer reserved this name for boys' books, while for girls he wrote as Valerie Baxter. For adults he wrote either as Robert Eton or Geoffrey Ludlow, or under his real name. Tring, Eton, and Ludlow are all names of English towns.

Tristan l'Hermite: François l'Hermite (*c.*1601–1655), Fr. dramatist, poet. The classical dramatist is said to have taken his new name through a family connection with Louis XI's counsellor Tristan l'Hermite (died after 1475).

Johannes **Trithemius:** Johannes von Heidenberg (1462–1516), Ger. monk, magician. The occultist took his name from a Latin form of the name of his birthplace, Trittenheim, on the Mosel River.

Trog: Walter ("Wally") Ernest Fawkes (1924–), Can.-born Br. cartoonist. The artist, famous for his magical creature Flook, took his name from the Troglodytes, the jazz band of which he had formerly been a member. As their name implies, the band played in a cellar.

Frances **Trollope:** Paul Feval (1817–1887), Fr. writer of sentimental novels. The writer adopted the name of the mother of the English novelist Anthony Trollope (1815–1882).

Sven **Trost:** [Count] Carl Johan Gustav Snoilsky (1841–1903), Swe. lyric poet.

Leon **Trotsky:** Lev Davidovich Bronstein (1879–1940), Russ. revolutionary leader, of Jewish parentage. There has been considerable controversy as to the precise origin of this famous (infamous) name. A popular theory is that the revolutionary picked it at random, writing it in a blank passport handed him by friends, when emerging from exile in Siberia in 1902. It is known, however, that Trotsky was the name of a jailer in the prison at Odessa, where the young Bronstein had been before this. Trotsky is certainly not an invented Russian name, but one existing in its own right. Even so, with his knowledge of German, Bronstein may have been consciously or subconsciously thinking of the German word *Trotz*, with its symbolic meaning

of "defiance," "insolence," "intrepidity." Some of his other pseudonyms seem to be more obviously meaningful. At one stage he was Antid-Oto, a word found (*antidoto*) in an Italian dictionary when he started to weigh up different pen names, and seen by him as suitable since he "wanted to inject a Marxist antidote into the legal press." For a time in 1936 he was Crux, a name he used for articles in the *Bulletin of the Opposition*. He had also been Ensign, Arbuzov, Mr. Sedov (when leaving incognito for Europe in 1932), Pyotr Petrovich (to local Petersburg revolutionaries), Vikentyev (his "official" name in Petersburg in 1905), and Yanovsky (from Yanovka Farm, itself named for the colonel who had sold it to his father) [1. Joel Carmichael, *Trotsky: An Appreciation of His Life*, 1975; 2. *Observer Colour Magazine*, October 21, 1979].

Kilgore **Trout:** Philip Jose Farmer (1918–), U.S. SF writer. The writer took his pen name from the fictitious SF writer appearing in stories by Kurt Vonnegut, Jr. See Theodore Sturgeon.

Ben **Trovato:** Samuel Lover (1797–1868), Ir. songwriter, novelist, printer. The writer adopted his pseudonym from the Italian phrase *ben trovato*, literally "well found," in other words, "happy invention," like the pen name itself.

Doris **Troy:** Doris Payne (1937–), U.S. pop singer, songwriter.

Henri **Troyat:** Levon Aslanovich Tarasov (1911–), Russ.-born Fr. novelist. The writer selected a new name at the request of his first editor. He came up with Troyat (allegedly from a telephone directory), a name that had the same initial as his surname. For reasons of euphony and clarity, the editor then asked him to choose a new first name. The novelist proposed Henri.

Nikolay **Trublaini:** Nikolay Petrovich Trublayevsky (1907–), Ukrainian children's writer. The writer adapted his surname so that he would appear to be Italian.

Truong Chinh: Dang Xuan Khu (1907–1988), Vietnamese scholar, statesman. The leading Communist intellectual adopted a name meaning "long march," alluding to the famous Long March led by Mao Tse-tung in 1934–35 from Kiangsi to Shensi.

Basil **Truro:** Vassilie Trunoff (1929–1985), Austral.-born Russ. ballet dancer. During the Australian tour of the Ballet Rambert in 1948, Trunoff was invited to fill a vacancy caused when another dancer returned to England. Marie Rambert (*q.v.*) asked him to appear with an

English stage name instead of his Russian one, thus rather unusually reversing the usual ballet practice of the day.

Bruce **Truscot**: Edgar Allison Peers (1891–1952), Eng. authority on Spanish religious history, educationist. The academic used this pen name for two books: *Redbrick University* (1943) and *Redbrick and These Vital Days* (1945).

H. **Trusta**: Elizabeth Stuart Phelps (1815–1852), U.S. novelist. The writer used this name, formed anagrammatically from her middle name and the "h" of her surname, for two semiautobiographical novels, *A Peep at Number Five* (1851) and *The Angel Over the Right Shoulder* (1851).

Sojourner **Truth**: Isabella Baumfree (later Van Wagener) (1797–1883), U.S. black evangelist, reformer. In 1843 the evangelist announced that "voices" had commanded her to adopt her new name and to "travel up and down the land" singing and preaching. She was born a slave, and her legal name was that of the family who bought her. They freed her just before the abolition of slavery in New York state in 1827.

Tsuruya Namboku IV: Ebiya Genzo (1755–1829), Jap. playwright. In about 1780 the writer married the daughter of Tsuruya Namboku III, a noted actor of the day, and adopted his name in 1811.

Jerry **Tucker**: Jerry Schatz (1926–), U.S. juvenile movie actor.

Richard **Tucker**: Reuben Ticker (1913–1975), U.S. opera singer.

Sophie **Tucker**: Sophia Abuza (originally Kalish) (1884–1966), U.S. vaudeville, movie actress, of Russ. Jewish parentage. The actress's father was originally named Kalish, but when he absconded from Russian military service to go to America, he fell in with an Italian named Charles Abuza, also absent without leave. Abuza fell ill and died, whereupon Sophie's father, fearing detection by the Russian authorities, took the Italian's identity papers and also adopted his name. He thus arrived in the U.S. as Charles Abuza.

When she was still a teenager, Sophie Abuza married Louis Tuck, a dancer in Hartford, Connecticut, where her family then lived. Meanwhile, she had gained local success as a singer, and in 1906 went to New York to be auditioned by songwriter Harry Von Tilzer (*q.v.*). While waiting for his verdict, she called in at the Café Monopol, on Eighth Street, and asked the proprietor if she could "sing for her supper," as she was hungry and low on funds. He agreed, and asked her name. Tucker tells what happened next: "I had my mail sent to Mrs. Louis Tuck, care of General Delivery, as of course that was my name. But 'Mrs. Tuck' didn't sound right for a singer. 'Sophie Tucker,' I told him. Right like that a career was born" [Sophie Tucker, *Some of These Days: An Autobiography*, 1948].

Tommy **Tucker**: Robert Higginbotham (1933–1982), U.S. blues singer, pianist. In the nursery rhyme, "Little Tommy Tucker / Sings for his supper," just as any singer has to do if he is to eat. Presumably the blues singer borrowed the name from this well known source.

Antony **Tudor**: William Cook (1908–1987), Eng. ballet dancer, choreographer, teacher.

Stepan **Tudor**: Stepan Iosifovich Oleksyuk (1892–1941), Ukrainian writer.

Tasha **Tudor**: Starling Burgess (1915–), U.S. children's writer, illustrator. The writer adopted a pet version of her first name and added the maiden name of her mother, portrait painter Rosamond Tudor.

Tenpole **Tudor**: Edward Felix Tudor-Pole (1956–), Br. actor, TV presenter, former pop singer. "Tenpole" looks like a nickname. Perhaps it evolved via "Ted Tudor-Pole," from the singer's real name.

Sonny **Tufts**: Bowen Charleston Tufts (1911–1970), U.S. movie actor.

Friedebert **Tuglas**: Friedebert Mihkelson (1886–1971), Estonian writer. The writer adopted his new name in 1923, when he became editor of the journal *Looming* ("Creation").

Iosif **Tumanov**: Iosif Mikhaylovich Tumanishvili (1909–), Georgian-born Russ. theatrical director. The artist russified his Georgian name.

Semyon **Tumanov**: Semyon Isayevich Tseytlin (Zeitlin) (1921–1973), Russ. movie director.

Boris **Tumarin**: Boris Tumarinson (1910–), Latvian stage actor, director, working in U.S.

Sven **Tumba**: Sven Johansson (1931–), Swe. ice hockey player. The player adopted his nickname, that of the Stockholm suburb where he was raised.

Tupac Amaru II: José Gabriel Condorcanqui (*c.*1740–1781), Peruvian Native American revolutionary. The activist was a descendant of the last Inca ruler, Tupac Amaru, and adopted his name when leading a peasant rebellion against Spanish rule.

Yevgeniya **Tur:** Yelizaveta Vasilyevna Salhias-de-Tournemire (1815–1892), Russ. writer, editor, critic. The writer's son tells how his mother came by her name: "It has been said that 'Yevgeniya Tur' is 'Turgenev' turned round. By sheer coincidence this is so, and you get an almost complete anagram. But there is no secret in this: the stories about my mother's affair with Turgenev are complete nonsense. My mother was called Yelizaveta, but she was extremely fond of the names 'Yevgeny' and 'Yevgeniya.' She was a passionate admirer of Pushkin and of *Eugene Onegin* in particular. That's where I get my own name of Yevgeny from… The way her pen name came about is as follows: 'Yevgeniya' was chosen with little hesitation. Then the search was on for a surname. 'Yevgeniya Sal' was an abbreviation of 'Salhias,' but *sale* in French is 'dirty.' 'Yevgeniya Lhias' doesn't sound well, 'Yevgeniya Nemir' is too long. … Everyone liked 'Yevgeniya Tur'" [Dmitriyev, p. 53].

Tur Brothers: Leonid Davidovich Tubelsky (1905–1961), Russ. playwright, screenwriter + Pyotr Lvovich Ryzhey (1908–1978), Russ. playwright, screenwriter. The writers' joint name comprises the first letters of their surnames.

Turlupin: Henri Legrand (c.1587–1637), Fr. actor. The actor used the name Belleville (*q.v.*) for serious tragic roles, keeping Turlupin for farces. The name itself is of obscure origin.

Gil **Turner:** Gilbert Strunk (1933–1974), U.S. folk singer, guitarist.

Lana **Turner:** Julia Jean Mildred Frances Turner (1920–1995), U.S. movie actress (the "Sweater Girl"). It is uncertain whether Judy Turner (as she usually called herself) chose her new first name, or whether it was given by her Warner Brothers agent, Mervyn LeRoy. If the latter, LeRoy is said to have taken the unusual name from a girl he knew when he was at school. Either way, she adopted the name, and was anxious that it should be "pronounced Lana as in lah-de-da, not lady" [Joe Morella and Edward Z. Epstein, *Lana: The Public and Private Lives of Miss Turner*, 1983]. She was said to be wearing a figure-clinging sweater at the time of her discovery, and this led to her nickname, which was used to promote her. By a coincidence Italian (also Spanish) *lana* happens to mean "wool."

Sammy **Turner:** Samuel Black (1932–), U.S. pop singer.

Tina **Turner:** Anna Mae (or Mabel) Bullock (1938–), U.S. black rock singer. It is really only the first name of the singer that is different, for her surname is that of her husband, Ike Turner (married 1958, divorced 1976), with whom she initially made her name, recording and touring as the Ike and Tina Turner Revue. It was Ike that named her Tina. He was keen on movies with "jungle girl" heroines such as Sheena, and gave his wife a name to match, seeing her as a "wild woman."

Tutankhamun: Tutankhaten (*fl.*14th century BC), Egyptian pharaoh. The young king was originally known as Tutankhaten, "living image of the [sun disk] Aten," but later changed his name, apparently in order to distance himself from the Atenist heresies of the reigns of his father-in-law Akhenaten (*q.v.*) and of Akhenaten's successor, Smenkhkara. His new name thus meant "living image of [the god] Amun." Tutankhamun's wife, Ankhesenpa'aten, Akhenaten's third daughter, similarly changed her name to Ankhesenamun.

Mark **Twain:** Samuel Langhorne Clemens (1835–1910), U.S. novelist, short story writer. Most people know that the real name behind this famous pseudonym was Samuel Langhorne Clemens. It is generally believed, too, that the writer derived his pen name from the call, "Mark twain!" of pilots on the Mississippi River when they wanted a depth sounding (i.e., "mark two fathoms"). But perhaps it is less well known that there was a Mississippi pilot, one Captain Isaiah Sellers (c.1802–1863), who used the name earlier for contributions to the *New Orleans Picayune*. Twain himself claimed that he was the source of the pseudonym: "He died in 1863, and as he could no longer need that signature, I laid violent hands upon it without asking the permission of the proprietor's remains" [Kaplan, p. 39]. Whatever the case, Clemens first used the name for a humorous travel letter to the Virginia City *Territorial Enterprise* that same year, signing it, "Yours, dreamily, Mark Twain."

Brother **Twelve:** Edward Arthur Wilson (1878–1934), Br. cult leader, working in Canada. The significance of the name is obscure. Wilson assumed it in the 1920s, claiming it was given him by the mysterious author of a book called *The Three Truths*.

Twiggy: Lesley Lawson, née Hornby (1950–), Eng. fashion model, movie actress, singer. When the former fashion model was still at school, she was nicknamed "Sticks," for her thin and skinny appearance. This name was later revamped as

"Twiggy," and she adopted this professionally in 1964 for her fashion career. Her near-anorexic look was regarded as appropriate for the miniskirt modes of the day. In 1988 she married Leigh Lawson and took his name. She says: "Twiggy is a stupid name for a woman in her 40s, but it would be hard to drop. At least a full name makes me sound like a person, instead of a strange animal" [*Telegraph Magazine*, July 6, 1991].

Twinkle: Lynne Annette Ripley (1947–), Br. pop singer. Possibly the name arose as a nickname for a "little star."

Conway Twitty: Harold Lloyd Jenkins (1933–1993), U.S. folk singer. The singer has explained how he got his name: "So we started thinking about all kinds of names, and to make a long story short, what I finally wound up doing was, I got the map out and there's a place called Twitty, Texas. Then I thought if I could get something different to go with this, it might be something. I finally got the map of Arkansas and started looking through that, and there're towns in Arkansas like Baldknob, Walnut Creek, Smackover, and all kinds of crazy names like that. But right outside of Little Rock there's a town called Conway, and that's how it came about—Conway, Arkansas, and Twitty, Texas. So we all agreed that that was an unusual name, and my first record was ... under the name of Conway Twitty. I didn't agree with the idea first because my main interest was I was worried about the people in my hometown that wouldn't know who Conway Twitty is, and I wanted them all to know I had a new record out. ... But I finally realized what the fellow was talking about and I decided he was right, so we went with Conway Twitty" [Shestack, p. 285].

Twm Carnabwth: Thomas Rees (*c.*1806–1876), Welsh pugilist. The fighter's name, "Tom of Carnabwth," comes from that of his farm.

Twm Chwarae Teg: Thomas Williams (1737–1802), Welsh industrialist. The copper-mine owner derived his name by way of a nickname. It means "Tom Fair Play," alluding to his honest dealings with workers and rivals.

Twm o'r Nant: Thomas Edwards (1739–1810), Welsh poet, playwright. The writer's name, meaning "Tom of the brook," derives from the village of Nant Ganol, where he was raised. Its own name means "middle stream."

Twm Siôn Cati: Thomas Jones (*c.*1530–1609), Welsh poet, antiquary. The so called

"Welsh Robin Hood" was popularly known by this name, which means "Tom (son of) John (and) Catherine."

Twym: Alexander Stuart Boyd (1854–1930), Sc. illustrator, cartoonist. The artist used this name at the start of his career in the 1880s. Perhaps it arose as some sort of nickname or private pun.

Bonnie **Tyler:** Gaynor Sullivan (or Hopkins) (1951–), Welsh pop singer.

Steven **Tyler:** Steven Tallarico (1948–), U.S. rock musician.

Tom **Tyler:** Vincent Markowski (1903–1954), U.S. movie actor.

T. Texas **Tyler:** David Luke Myrick (1916–1972), U.S. country singer. As his name implies, the singer came from Texas.

Rob **Tyner:** Robert Derminer (1944–), U.S. rock singer.

Tyotka: Eloiza (or Aloiza) Stepanovna Pashkevich (1876–1916), Belorussian poet. The poet was of peasant stock and adopted a name meaning "Auntie," identifying her with ordinary people and especially country folk. In World War I, during the German occupation, she journeyed widely helping combat a typhus epidemic, but died of the disease herself.

Jan **Tyszka:** Leo Jogiches (1867–1919), Lithuanian-born Pol. revolutionary, working in Germany.

Sarah **Tytler:** Henrietta Keddie (1827–1914), Sc. novelist.

Sbrui **Tyusab:** Sbrui Vaganyan (1841–1901), Armenian (female) writer.

Tristan **Tzara:** Samuel Rosenstock (1896–1963), Rom.-born Fr. poet.

Paolo **Uccello:** Paolo di Dono (1397–1475), It. painter. The artist's adopted surname is the Italian word for "bird," from the nickname given him for his love of animals, and birds in particular.

Gustav **Ucicky:** Gustav Klimt (1899–1961), Austr. movie director, working in Germany. The director presumably changed his name to avoid being associated with his namesake, the Austrian painter Gustav Klimt (1862–1918).

Lynn **Udall:** John Henry Keating (1870–1963), U.S. songwriter.

Uesugi Kenshin: Nagao Torachiyo (1530–1578), Jap. military leader. The leader adopted the name of a local governor general, Uesugi Norimasa, who adopted him as his son in 1552.

Vorea **Ujko:** Domenico Belizzi (1918–), It.-Albanian poet.

Lesya **Ukrainka:** Larisa Petrovna Kvitko, née Kosach (1871–1913), Ukrainian poet, playwright, daughter of Olyona Pchilka (*q.v.*). The writer adopted a surname meaning "Ukrainian woman" to emphasize her nationality.

Ulanhu: Yun-Tse (1906–1988), Mongolian political leader. The former vice president of the Chinese People's Republic changed his aristocratic name Yun-Tse to Ulanfu in the 1920s, this being the Wade-Giles spelling (the Pinyin spelling is Ulanhu). The change was intended as a tribute both to Lenin (*q.v.*), whose family name was Ulyanov (*fu* being the Chinese character which transliterates the Russian suffix *-ov*), and to his Communist beliefs, as *ulan* is the Mongolian word for "red."

Lenore **Ulric:** Lenore Ulrich (1892–1970), U.S. stage, movie actress.

Ultra Violet: Isabelle Collin-Dufresne (1934–), Fr. movie actress.

Michael **Underwood:** John Michael Evelyn (1916–1992), Eng. crime novelist. The writer adopted his mother's maiden name as his pen name.

Urban II: Odo (or Eudes) (*c.*1035–1099), Fr. pope.

Urban III: Uberto Crivelli (? –1187), It. pope.

Urban IV: Jacques Pantaléon (*c.*1200–1264), Fr. pope.

Urban V: Guillaume de Grimoard (1310–1370), Fr. pope.

Urban VI: Bartolomeo Prignano (*c.*1318–1389), It. pope.

Urban VII: Giambattista Castagna (1521–1590), It. pope.

Urban VIII: Maffeo Vincenzo Barberini (1568–1644), It. pope.

Sylvanus **Urban:** Edward Cave (1691–1754), Eng. printer, founder (1731) of *The Gentleman's Magazine*. The writer and editor's pseudoclassical name was designed to reflect his dual interest in both town and country affairs, in other words, things "sylvan" (relating to woodland) and "urban" (relating to cities). The name was passed down to subsequent editors of the magazine until it closed in 1914. Compare the name of Urbanus Sylvan.

Urmuz: Demetru Demetrescu-Buzau (1883–1923), Rom. writer. A name created from the writer's full original name.

Maurice **Utrillo:** Maurice Valadon (1883–1955), Fr. painter. The artist was born as the illegitimate son of the model Suzanne Valadon. When he was eight years old, Maurice was formally adopted by the Spanish art critic Miguel Utrillo (1863–1934), who recognized him as his son in order to help him and who gave him his own name. The young artist was devoted to his mother and initially disowned his new name, signing his pictures "Maurice Valadon." Even when finally persuaded to adopt the name, he still retained his mother's initial, so that his signature was "Maurice Utrillo V."

Khveder **Uyar:** Fyodor Yermilovich Afanasyev (1914–), Russ. (Chuvash) poet. The poet's adopted surname means "bright," "shining." His new first name is a Chuvash form of his original name Fyodor (Theodore).

Uygun: Rakhmatulla Atakuziyev (1905–), Uzbek poet, playwright.

Mishshi **Uyp:** Mikhail Danilovich Shumilov (1911–1970), Russ. (Chuvash) poet. The poet's adopted surname means "bullfinch," while his new first name is a Chuvash form of his original name Mikhail (Michael).

Roger **Vadim:** Roger Vadim Plemiannikow (1928–), Fr. movie director, of Ukrainian-Fr. descent.

Vera **Vague:** Barbara Jo Allen (? 1904–1974), U.S. movie, radio comedienne.

Svetozar **Vajanský:** Svetozar Hurban (1847–1916), Slovakian writer.

Vakeli: Iona Lukich Megrelidze (1900–), Georgian poet, playwright. The writer's name derives from the village of his birth, Vake.

Katri **Vala:** Karin Alice Wadenström-Heikel (1901–1944), Finn. lyric poet.

Ricky **Valance:** David Spencer (*c.*1939–), Welsh pop singer.

Freddie **Vale:** Frederick Veale (1925–1989), Br. stage, TV actor, theatrical agent.

Ritchie **Valens:** Richard Stephen Valenzuela (1941–1959), U.S. pop guitarist.

Karl **Valentin:** Valentin Ludwig Fey (1882–1948), Ger. stage, movie comedian, writer.

Valentina: Valentina Nikolayevna Sanina (1899–1989), Russ.-born U.S. fashion designer.

Basil **Valentine:** (? 1394– ?), Ger. alchemist. The identity of the supposed monk and alchemist whose works bear his name (all edited long after his death) is unknown. The name may mask more than one person. It can anyway be seen to be a pun, since it represents Greek *basileus*, "king," and Latin *valens*, "healthy." The so called "royal art" of alchemy centered on the philosopher's stone, which was said to reveal the "elixir of life."

Dickie **Valentine**: Richard Brice (1929–1971), Br. pop singer.

Joseph **Valentine**: Giuseppe Valentino (1900–1949), It.-U.S. cinematographer.

Valentino: Valentino Garavani (1932–), It. fashion designer.

Rudolph **Valentino**: Rodolfo Alfonzo Raffaelo Pierre Filibert Guglielmi di Valentina d'Antonguolla (1895–1926), It.-born U.S. movie actor. Of this impressive string of names, the first three (Rodolfo Alfonzo Raffaelo) came from ancestors of Giovanni Gugliemi, the actor's father, while the next two (Pierre Filibert) derived from his mother's family. His cognomen (di Valentina d'Antonguolla) combined an old papal title with a claim asserted by the Guglielmis to certain estates. Thus, of all these names, the actor's basic original surname was Guglielmi. He originally called himself Rodolfo di Valentina. This then settled to the less specifically Italian Rudolph Valentino. The association with "Valentine" (in the "sweetheart" sense) is thus fortuitous, but could have been suggested to some by the actor's dark, Latin looks.

Sal **Valentino**: Sal Spampinato (1942–), U.S. pop singer.

N. **Valentinov**: Nikolay Vladislavovich Volsky (1879– ?), Russ. revolutionary journalist.

Simone **Valere**: Simone Gondoff (1923–), Fr. movie actress.

Valezi: Valentina Yakovlevna Shchetinina, née Borisovna (1916–), Russ. circus artist + Yelena Pavlovna Lebedinskaya (1910–), Russ. circus artist + Zinaida Stepanovna Lesnevskaya (1911–1974), Russ. circus artist. The three bareback riders formed their joint name from the first syllables of the pet forms of their names: Valya, Lëlya, and Zina.

Peet **Vallak**: Peeter Pedajas (1893–1959), Estonian writer.

Juvenco **Valle**: Gilberto Concha Riffo (1900–), Chilean poet.

Rudy **Vallee**: Hubert Prior Vallee (1901–1986), U.S. movie actor, singer. The singer took his new first name to express his admiration for saxophonist Rudy Weidoft.

Alwina **Valleria**: Alwina Schoening (1848–1925), U.S. opera singer.

Alida **Valli**: Alida Maria Altenburger (1921–), It. movie actress, of Austr.-It. parentage. The actress's screen surname suggests "valley" (Italian *valle*), as if a counterpart to her original German surname, popularly understood as "high mountain" (though actually meaning "old town").

Frankie **Valli**: Frank Castelluccio (1937–), U.S. rock musician. As a youngster, Castelluccio was taken under the wing of the Texas country singer Jean Valley, who passed him off as his kid brother, Frankie Valley. Hence his name.

Virginia **Valli**: Virginia McSweeney (1898–1968), U.S. movie actress.

Arvo **Valton**: Arvo Vallikivi (1935–), Estonian writer.

Bobby **Van**: Robert King (1930–1980), U.S. dancer, singer, stage actor.

Richard **Van Allan**: Alan Philip Jones (1935–), Br. opera singer

Jan **Van Avond**: Francis Carey Salter (1876–1958), S.A. poet, novelist.

[Dame] Irene **Vanbrugh**: Irene Barnes (1872–1949), Br. stage actress, sister of Violet Vanbrugh (see below).

Violet **Vanbrugh**: Violet Augusta Mary Barnes (1867–1942), Br. stage actress. The actress adopted her stage name at the suggestion of Ellen Terry, the compliment being to the architect and dramatist Sir John Vanbrugh (1664–1726). Violet's sister Irene, also an actress (see above), followed suit.

Abigail **Van Buren**: Pauline Esther Philips, née Friedman (1918–), U.S. journalist. The advice specialist, famous for her "Dear Abby" column, was the twin of her rival "sob sister" Ann Landers (*q.v.*).

Alfred Glenville **Vance**: Alfred Peck Stevens (1839–1888), Eng. music hall actor, singer. Presumably "Vance" evolved from "Stevens."

Charles **Vance**: Charles Ivan Goldblatt (1929–), Br. stage actor, theatrical director. "Vance" appears to have evolved from letters in the actor's first two names.

Ethel **Vance**: Grace Stone, née Zaring (1891–1991), U.S. novelist.

Vivian **Vance**: Vivian Jones (1913–1979), U.S. TV actress.

Jean-Claude **Van Damme**: Jean-Claude Van Varenberg (1961–), Belg. movie actor, working in U.S.

Margaret **Vandegrift**: Margaret Thomson Janvier (1844–1913), U.S. children's writer, sister of

Ivory Black (*q.v.*). There is a hint of "Vandegrift" in the writer's original surname, although the actual origin may lie elsewhere.

Trish Van Devere: Patricia Dressel (1943–), U.S. movie actress.

S.S. Van Dine: Willard Huntington Wright (1888–1939), U.S. literary critic, detective story writer. The writer adopted an old family name, Van Dyne, adding the initials whimsically to mean "steamship," as they commonly do before a ship name.

Mamie Van Doren: Joan Lucille Olander (1933–), U.S. movie actress. Presumably the actress's new surname evolved out of her original name.

Peter Van Eyck: Götz von Eick (1913–1969), Ger. movie actor.

Vangelis: Evangelos D. Papathanassiou (1943–), Gk. pop musician, working in U.K.

James Van Heusen: Edward Chester Babcock (1913–1990), U.S. composer of musicals, movie music. The musician took his surname from the shirt manufacturers and chose James as a new first name simply because he liked it.

Dave Vanian: David Letts (1956–), Eng. punk rock singer.

Vanilla Ice: Robert Van Winckle (1968–), U.S. rapper, of Du. descent. The singer was nicknamed "Vanilla" by his black rapping friends, from "Van" and the fact that he was white. He himself added "Ice" because it sounded better as a name. It also happens to comprise letters from his last name.

Vanity: Denise Matthews (1958–), U.S. movie actress. The actress has also used the name D.D. Winters.

Eric Van Lhin: Lester del Rey (or Rámon Álvarez del Rey) (1915–), U.S. SF writer. More conventional names used by the writer include Edson McCann, Philip St. John, and Kenneth Wright.

Marda Vanne: Marda van Hulsteyn (? – 1970), S.A. stage actress, working in U.K.

Vano Romano: Ivan Mikhaylovich Panchenko (1941–), Russ. Gypsy poet. The poet's adopted Romany name means "Ivan the Gypsy."

Nikola Vapcarov: Nikola Yonkov (1909–1942), Bulg. revolutionary poet.

Victor Varconi: Mihaly Várkonyi (1896–1976), Hung. movie actor, working in U.S.

Inna Varlamova: Klavdiya Gustavovna Landau (1922–), Russ. writer.

John Philip Varley: Langdon Elwyn Mitchell (1862–1935), U.S. playwright.

Marcel Varnel: Marcel le Bozec (1894–1947), Fr.-born Br. theatrical producer.

Daniel Varudzhan: Daniel Chebukaryan (1884–1915), Armenian poet. The poet's adopted name means "canary." Many of his writings had the word "song" in the title.

M. Vasalis: Margaretha Droogleever Fortuyn-Leenmans (1909–), Du. poet.

Gillan Vase: Elizabeth Palmer, later Palmer Pacht Newton (1841–1921), Eng. novelist. The writer was born in the seaside town of Falmouth, Cornwall, and took her pseudonym from a local variant of the name of a Falmouth beach (properly Gyllyngvase).

Vasilchenko: Stepan Vasilyevich Panasenko (1879–1932), Ukrainian writer.

Comte Paul Vasili: Juliette Adam, née Lamber (1836–1936), Fr. novelist, editor. The founder of *La Nouvelle Revue* assumed a name that ran counter to reality: she was not a count, but a commoner; not Russian, but French; not male, but female.

Pal Vasvári: Pal Fejér (1827–1849), Hung. socialist, historian.

Vatvat (or Vatvot): Rashididaddin Mohammed bin Abd al-Jalal al-Umari (1087–1182 or 1177), Persian poet. The poet's assumed name means "eagle owl."

Jeanne Vaubernier: Marie-Jeanne Bécu [comtesse] du Barry (1743–1793), Fr. mistress of Louis XV. This was the name adopted by the future Madame du Barry when a shop assistant in a Paris fashion house. While there, she became the mistress of the Gascon nobleman Jean du Barry, and took his name.

Frankie Vaughan: Francis Abelsohn (1928–), Eng. popular singer, dancer, movie actor.

Kate Vaughan: Catherine Candelin (*c.*1852–1903), Br. stage actress, dancer, sister of Susie Vaughan (see below). The sisters made their debut as the Sisters Vaughan dancers in 1870.

Peter Vaughan: Peter Ewart Ohm (1923–), Eng. movie, TV actor.

Richard Vaughan: Ernest Lewis Thomas (1904–1983), Welsh novelist.

Susie Vaughan: Susan Mary Charlotte Candelin (1853–1950), Br. stage actress, sister of Kate Vaughan (see above).

Jean Vautran: Jean Herman (1933–), Fr. movie director, writer.

Vava: Edvaldo Izidio Neto (1934–), Brazilian football player. The name is a pet form of the player's first name.

Vazekh: Mirza Shafi Sadykh-ogly (1796–1852), Azerbaijani poet, teacher. The poet's name means "clear," "expressive," denoting the ideal attribute of a teacher, if not necessarily of a poet.

Vazgen: Levon Karapet Baljian (1908–1994), Armenian churchman. The head of the Armenian Orthodox Church took his religious name at his ordination in 1943.

Vazha Pshavela: Luka Pavlovich Razikashvili (1861–1915), Georgian balladist. The greatest of Georgia's poets took a name meaning "brave young Pshav" (this being the ethnic name of a Georgian mountain people).

Bobby **Vee:** Robert Thomas Velline (1943–), U.S. pop singer.

Irina **Velembovskaya:** Irina Aleksandrovna Shukhgalter (Schuhhalter) (1922–), Russ. writer.

Lupe **Velez:** Maria Guadalupe Velez de Villalobos (1908–1944), Mexican movie actress ("the Mexican Spitfire").

Lino **Ventura:** Angelino Borrini (1919–1987), It.-born Fr. movie actor. The actor adopted his name as a professional wrestler, who needs fortune (Italian *ventura*) in the ring.

Benay **Venuta:** Venuta Rose Crooke (1911–), U.S. stage actress, singer.

Vera: (1) [Lady] Gertrude Elizabeth Campbell, née Blood (? –1911), Br. art critic, author; (2) Charlotte Louisa Hawkins Dempster (1835–1913), Br. author; (3) Vera Neumann (1910–1993), U.S. artist, designer. The name may have a symbolic attraction, since Latin *vera* means "true," while Russian *vera* means "faith."

Vera-Ellen: Vera-Ellen Westmeyr Rohe (1920–1981), U.S. popular singer, dancer, movie actress.

Vercors: Jean-Marcel Bruller (1902–1991), Fr. writer, illustrator. The writer used this name for his secretly distributed *Le Silence de la Mer* (1942) when running an underground press in Paris. Vercors is the name of an Alpine plateau which was a Resistance center in World War II. (For a similar name, compare Forez.)

Violette **Verdy:** Nelly Guillerm (1933–), Fr.-born U.S. ballet dancer.

Diana **Vere:** Diana Fox (1942–), Trinidad-born Br. ballet dancer.

V. **Veresaeff:** Vikenty Vikentievich Smidovich (1867–1945), Russ. writer. The writer originally used the pen name Vikentyev, formed from his patronymic (middle name). In 1892 he adopted the name by which he was subsequently known, taking it from the name of a character in a story by the Russian writer P.P. Gnedich. He felt the name was "attractive and not pretentious" [Dmitriyev, p. 61].

Tom **Verlaine:** Thomas Miller (1949–), U.S. rock musician. The musician adopted the name of the French poet, Paul Verlaine.

Adela **Verne:** Adela Wurm (1877–1952), Br. concert pianist, of German parentage, sister of Alice Verne and Mathilde Verne (see below). Adela was taught piano by Mathilde, and to negate the family relationship called herself "Clara Jenkins" during lessons, at the same time insisting on being treated as a stranger.

Alice **Verne:** Alice Wurm (1868–1938), Br. concert pianist, sister of Adela Verne (see above) and Mathilde Verne (see below).

Karen **Verne:** Ingabor Katrine Klinckerfuss (1915–1967), Ger. movie actress, working in U.S.

Mathilde **Verne:** Mathilde Wurm (1865–1936), Br. concert pianist, sister of Adela Verne and Alice Verne (see above). Their elder sister, pianist and conductor Marie Wurm (1860–1938), retained her original German surname.

Gerald **Verner:** Donald Stuart (1896–1980), Br. thriller writer.

Henri **Verneuil:** Achod Malakian (1920–), Turk. movie director, of Armenian parentage, working in France.

Anne **Vernon:** Edith Antoinette Alexandrine Vignaud (1925–), Fr. movie actress, working in U.K., U.S.

Bobby **Vernon:** Silvion de Jardins (1897–1939), U.S. movie comedian. "Vernon" perhaps from letters in the performer's original name.

Dai **Vernon:** David Frederick Wingfield Werner (1894–1992), Can.-born U.S. magician.

John **Vernon:** Adolphus Vernon Agopsowicz (1932–), Can. movie actor.

Konstanze **Vernon:** Konstanze Herzfeld (1939–), Ger. ballet dancer.

Paolo **Veronese:** Paolo Cogliari (or Caliari) (1528–1588), It. painter. The artist is named for Verona, the city of his birth. He was mainly active in Venice, however, and is considered to belong to the Venetian school.

Andrea del **Verrocchio:** Andrea di Michele Cioni (*c.*1435–1488), It. sculptor, painter, metalworker. The artist is said to have taken his name either from the ecclesiastic whose protégé he was or from his teacher, a goldsmith named Giuliano Verrocchi. It was in the goldsmith's trade that he was initially trained. Appropriately for an artist or craftsman, the name itself means "true eye."

Odile Versois: Katiana de Poliakoff-Baidarov (1930–1980), Fr. movie actress, of Russ. parentage, sister of actresses Marina Vlady (*q.v.*) and Hélène Vallier (originally Militza de Poliakoff-Baidaroff) (1932–).

Dziga Vertov: Denis Arkadyevich Kaufman (1896–1954), Russ. documentary movie director.

Veruschka: [Countess] Vera von Lehndorff (1939–), Ger. fashion model, movie actress. The actress adopted her professional name when beginning her career as a model. She explains: "Veruschka was a nickname I had when I was a child. It means 'little Vera.' And as I was always too tall, I thought it would be nice to say that I'm little Vera. And it was also nice to have a Russian name because I came from the East" [Michael Gross, *Model*, 1995].

Stanley Vestal: Walter Stanley Campbell (1887–1957), U.S. author, educator. The author used this name mostly for his writings about the Southwestern frontier, and possibly "Vestal" is meant to suggest "West."

Madame Vestris: Lucy Elizabeth Vestris, née Bartolozzi (1787–1856), Eng. actress, singer. As was the tradition of her day, the actress used her married name for her stage name. Her husband was the French ballet dancer, Armand Vestris (1787–1825). (He deserted her when she was only 23.)

Artyom Vesyoly: Nikolay Ivanovich Kochkurov (1899–1939), Russ. writer. The writer's adopted surname means "merry," although his stories of Russia rent asunder by revolution and civil war show this to be ironic.

Victoria Vetri: Angela Dorian (1944–), Austral. movie actress, model. The actress's assumed and original name are given thus in Walker (see Bibliography, p. 403). However, it seems the names are really the other way around: "Being named for a shipwreck doesn't sound appealing, but a young actress named Victoria Vetri went for the idea, which was hatched by an agent who must have been haunted by the sinking of the Italian liner *Andrea Doria* [in 1956]" [Gretchen Edgren, *The Playmate Book*, 1996].

Andris Vejan: Donat Kalnač (1927–), Latvian poet. The poet's adopted name is based on Russian *veter*, "wind."

Pavel Vezhinov: Nikola Delchev Gugov (1914–1983), Bulg. novelist, short stort writer.

Lodovico Viadana: Lodovico Grossi (*c.*1560–1627), It. composer. The musician and friar came to be known by the name of his birthplace, Viadana, near Mantua, northern Italy.

Sid Vicious: John Simon Ritchie (later, Beverly) (1957–1979), Eng. punk rock musician. The Sex Pistols member is said to have received his antiestablishment name following an attack on a journalist. However, a fellow Pistols member, Johnny Rotten (*q.v.*), recounts the following in his autobiography: "I called him Sid, after my pet, ... this soppy white hamster that used to live in a cage on the corner table in my parents' living room. One day ... the hamster took a bite out of my father's hand. ...We dubbed Sid the hamster 'Vicious' after that. Sid's real name was Simon Ritchie or John Beverly; even he wasn't sure which. It all depended on his mother's whim at the time" [John Lydon with Keith and Kent Zimmerman, *Rotten: No Irish, No Blacks, No Dogs*, 1993].

Martha Vickers: Martha MacVicar (1925–1971), U.S. movie actress.

Vicky: Victor Weisz (1913–1966), Ger.-born Br. political cartoonist. The artist used other signatures during his career, among them Pierrot and Smith.

Victor II: Gebhard of Dollnstein-Hirschberg (*c.*1018–1057), Ger. pope.

Victor III: Dauferi (later, Desiderius) (1027–1087), It. pope. The pontiff named himself for Victor II (see above), guardian of the emperor Henry IV, as a token of conciliation with that monarch.

Josephine Victor: Josephine Guenczler (1885– ?), Hung.-born U.S. stage actress.

Victoria: Lilli Ursula Barbara Victoria Davidson, née Commichau (1915–), Ger.-born Br. humorous illustrator.

Vesta Victoria: Victoria Lawrence (1873–1951), Br. music hall singer. The singer based her name, and its formation, on that of Vesta Tilley (*q.v.*).

Florence Vidor: Florence Cobb (1895–1977), U.S. movie actress. The actress's surname changed to Arto when her mother remarried and became Vidor when she married director King Vidor in 1915.

Luandinu Vieira: José Vieira Mateus da Graça (1935–), Port.-born (white) Angolan writer. The writer's new first name relates to Luanda, where his family came to settle in 1938.

Antanas **Vienuolis:** Antanas Žukauskas (1882–1957), Lithuanian writer. The writer explained in his autobiography: "My road through life has mostly been a lonely one, and I have had few friends. Hence my choice of the literary name Vienuolis, i.e., all on my own" [Dmitriyev, p. 121].

Jacomo da **Vignola:** Jacomo Barozzi (1507–1573), It. architect. The architect came to be known by the name of his birthtown of Vignola, northern Italy.

Jean **Vigo:** Jean Almereyda (1905–1934), Fr. movie director.

Irina **Vilde:** Darya Dmitriyevna Polotnyuk (1907–1982), Ukrainian writer.

Charles **Vildrac:** Charles Messager (1882–1971), Fr. poet, novelist, dramatist. The writer adopted a literary name for his pen name, that of Roger Wildrake, the reckless cavalier ("wild rake") in Walter Scott's novel *Woodstock*, with the English name rendered in a French manner.

Lettie **Viljoen:** Ingrid Gouws, née Winterbach (1948–), S.A. writer.

Evald **Vilks:** Evald Latsis (1923–1976), Latvian writer. The writer was obliged to take a new name so as not to be confused with the better known Latvian novelist Vilis Latsis (1904–1966). His new surname means "wolf."

Francisco "Pancho" **Villa:** Doroteo Arango (1877–1923), Mexican revolutionary, guerrilla leader.

Frank **Villard:** François Drouineau (1917–1980), Fr. movie actor.

Henry **Villard:** Ferdinand Heinrich Gustav Hilgard (1835–1900), Ger.-born U.S. financier, publisher. The journalist came to New York in 1853, changing his name to avoid being forced back to Germany. His new surname is loosely based on his original third name and surname.

Caroline **Villiers:** Carol Friday (1949–), Eng. stage, TV actress.

François **Villon:** François de Montcorbier (1431–after 1463), Fr. poet. Some uncertainty remains about the real name of the French poet, and his date of death is also not accurately recorded. He seems to have been born as either François de Montcorbier or François des Loges, these two "surnames" being respectively the name of a village on the borders of Burgundy where his father was born and, probably, the name of his father's farm. The name by which he is now generally known is that of the man who adopted him, Guillaume de Villon, a Paris chaplain. Villon used other pseudonyms, among them Michel Mouton.

Jacques **Villon:** Gaston Emile Duchamp (1875–1963), Fr. painter. The artist adopted the latter half of the name of his half-brother, Raymond Duchamp-Villon, a sculptor. The name also expressed his admiration for the poet François Villon (see above).

Gene **Vincent:** Vincent Eugene Craddock (1935–1970), U.S. rock musician.

Harl **Vincent:** Harl Vincent Schoelphfin (1893–1968), U.S. SF writer.

William **Vincent:** Thomas Holcroft (1745–1809), Eng. dramatist, writer. The writer used the name (in the form "William Vincent of Gray's Inn," suggesting the author was a barrister) for a work published in 1780 which included a "Narrative of the Late Riots in London" and an "Account of the commitment of Lord G. Gordon to the Tower."

Barbara **Vine:** Ruth Rendell (1930–), Eng. crime novelist. The writer mostly uses her real name, but began to use her pen name in the 1980s, first for *A Dark-Adapted Eye* (1986), when she was "looking for a new voice." It derives from an alternate first name by which she was known as a child and the maiden name of her great-grandmother. "I know it sounds odd," says Rendell, "but I feel different when I use it. It is more feminine."

Vinkbooms: Thomas Griffiths Wainewright (1794–1852), Eng. art critic, writer, forger. This was one of the pseudonyms used by Wainewright for his contributions to the *London Magazine*, others being Egomet Bonmot and Janus Weathercock. The name itself was presumably based on that of the Flemish painter David Vinckboons (1576–c.1630).

Helen **Vinson:** Helen Rulfs (1907–), U.S. movie actress.

Georges **Virrès:** Henri Briers (1869–1946), Belg. writer.

Edvards **Virza:** Edvards Lieknis (1883–1940), Latvian poet.

Visal: Mohammed Shafi (1779–1846), Iranian poet.

Ostap **Vishnya:** Pavel Mikhaylovich Gubenko (1889–1956), Ukrainian satirical writer, humorist. The writer's assumed surname means "cherry." When he first appeared in print in a local newspaper at the age of 22, his editor, a woman named Oksana (Oxana), asked him how he wished to sign himself. He hesitated, since choosing a pseudonym on the spur of the moment was not so easy, then took a pen and wrote "Oksana." This female name was subsequently ousted by his male one.

Vitalis: Erk Sjöberg (1794–1825), Swe. poet. The poet adopted a Latin name meaning "likely to live," implying a life struggle. He died when only 31, the struggle having been too much.

Yuozas **Vitas:** Jonas Valunas (1899–1943), Lithuanian Communist official.

Vasil **Vitka:** Timofey Vasilyevich Krysko (1911–), Belorussian poet, playwright. The writer's adopted name means "branch," "twig."

Monica **Vitti:** Maria Luisa Ceciarelli (1931–), It. stage, movie actress.

Viva: Janet Sue Hoffman (1941–), U.S. movie actress, associated with Andy Warhol (*q.v.*).

[Swami] **Vivekananda:** Narendranath Datta (or Dutt) (1863–1902), Ind. religious leader. The Hindu sage, who propagated the teaching of his master Ramakrishna (*q.v.*), took his religious name from a blend of Sanskrit *viveka*, "reason," "discernment," and *nanda*, "joy," "pleasure." Swami is a title meaning "master," "prince."

Renée **Vivien:** Pauline Mary Tarn (1877–1909), Eng.-born Fr. poet, prose writer, of U.S.-Eng. parentage. The poet first wrote as (genderless) "R. Vivien," then as (male) "René Vivien," and finally as (female) "Renée Vivien." The revelation of her sex caused something of a scandal, since her writing was highly sensual.

Vivienne: Florence Vivienne Entwistle (1887–1982), Br. portrait photographer.

Miron **Vladimirov:** Miron Konstantinovich Sheynfinkel (Scheinfinkel) (1879–1925), Russ. revolutionary, Communist official.

Ignaty **Vladislavlev:** Ignaty Vladislavovich Gulbinsky (1880–1962), Russ. bibliographer.

Vladimir **Vladomirsky:** Vladimir Iosifovich Maleyko (1893–1971), Belorussian stage actor.

Marina **Vlady:** Marina de Poliakoff-Baidarov (1938–), Fr. movie actress, of Russ. parentage, sister of Odile Versois (*q.v.*). The actress began her career as a ballet dancer under the name Marina Versois. Her screen surname suggests a Russian family name such as Vladimirova.

Boris **Volin:** Boris Mikhaylovich Fradkin (1886–1957), Russ. Communist official.

Ivan **Volnov:** Ivan Yegorovich Vladimirov (1885–1931), Russ. writer. The writer derived his pen name from Russian *vol'nyy*, "free," alluding to the desired freeing of peasant folk from poverty under czarist rule.

V. **Volodarsky:** Moisey Markovich Goldshteyn (Goldstein) (1891–1918), Russ. revolutionary.

Aleksandr **Volodin:** Aleksandr Moiseyevich Lifshits (1919–), Russ. playwright.

Vladimir **Volodin:** Vladimir Sergeyevich Ivanov (1891–1968), Russ. movie actor. The actor's new surname is based on the colloquial form, Volodya, of his own first name. He presumably adopted it for distinction from the many other Ivanovs, this being the commonest Russian surname.

Maksimilian **Voloshin:** Maksimilian Aleksandrovich Kiriyenko-Voloshin (1877–1932), Russ. poet.

Vitaly **Volsky:** Vitaly Fridrikhovich Zeydel (Seidel) (1901–), Belorussian writer.

Voltaire: François Marie Arouet (1694–1778), Fr. philosopher, poet, dramatist. Possibly the best known of all pseudonyms. The commonly held theory is that the name is an anagram of the writer's surname, with "l.j." standing for *le jeune* (i.e. "The Young") added. (One must allow that the 'u' of Arouet becomes 'v,' and the initial 'j' shifts to 'i.') An alternate theory is that the writer adopted (and adapted) the name of Veauterre, a property he had acquired near Asnières-sur-Seine. Voltaire first used the name on his release from the Bastille in 1718. Appendix 1, p. 384, gives a complete list of his 173 pseudonyms.

Daniele da **Volterra:** Daniele Ricciarelli (1509–1566), It. painter, sculptor. The artist's name is that of his birthplace, Volterra, Florence.

Claus **von Bülow:** Cecil Borberg (1926–), Dan.-born U.S. socialite. The wealthy Dane was in the news in 1983, when he was found guilty of attempting to murder his wife. He was acquitted two years later. His adopted aristocratic name matched his jet-set lifestyle.

Samuel Greifensohn **von Hirschfeld:** Hans Jakob Christoffel von Grimmelshausen (? 1620–1676), Ger. writer. The writer revelled in anagrammatic pseudonyms, of which this is one example. Others were Erich Stainfels von Grufensholm, Israel Fromschmit von Hugenfels, Filarhus Grossus von Trommenhaim, and even A.c.eee.ff.g.hh.ii.ll.mm.nn.oo.rr.sss.t.uu, which appeared on the title page of *Das wunderbarliche Vogelsnest* (1672). His best known pen name, however, was Simplicissimus (*q.v.*).

W.O. **von Horn:** Philip Friedrich Wilhelm Örtel (1798–1867), Ger. writer of popular stories. The writer's pseudonym stands for

"Wilhelm Örtel of Horn," the latter being his native town in Germany.

Baron von Schlicht: [Count] Wolf Heinrich von Baudissin (1789–1878), Ger. literary critic, translator. No doubt significantly, German *schlicht* means "homely," "unpretentious."

Sasha von Scherler: Alexandra-Xenia Elizabeth Anne Marie Fiesola von Schoeler (1939–), U.S. stage actress. The actress adopted the pet form of her first name and a simplified form of her surname.

Josef von Sternberg: Josef Sternberg (1894–1969), Austr. Jewish movie director, working in U.S. The aristocratic "von" was added to the director's name by a Hollywood producer who thought it would look better on a cinema marquee.

Erich von Stroheim: Erich Oswald Stroheim (1885–1957), Austr. movie actor, director, working in U.S. The actor's original name is given in many sources as Erich Hans Carl Maria Stroheim von Nordenwall, supposedly the descendant of a noble Prussian military family. However, his name was actually as stated above, and he was the son of a Jewish hatter from Prussia who had settled in Vienna.

Baron Arminius von Thunder-ten-Tronckh: Matthew Arnold (1822–1888), Eng. poet, critic. Arnold used this early pen name for some satirical contributions to the *Pall Mall Gazette*, subsequently published collectively as *Friendship's Garland* (1871). The name is that of the principal imaginary correspondent, the descendant of a fictional baron in Voltaire's *Candide* (1759), himself named for his estate, Thunder-ten-Tronckh, an "earthly paradise."

Albert Von Tilzer: Albert Gumm (1878–1956), U.S. popular music publisher, songwriter. The musician changed his name following the success of his brother, Harry Von Tilzer (see below), as a composer and song publisher.

Harry Von Tilzer: Harry Gumm (1872–1946), U.S. popular music publisher, songwriter, brother of Albert Von Tilzer (see above). The composer took his mother's maiden name of Tilzer for his professional name.

Aleksandr Vostokov: Aleksandr Khristoforovich Ostenek (1781–1864), Russ. philologist, poet. The writer was the illegitimate son of Count Osten-Sacken, a name that he subsequently modified to Ostenek. His new surname is a part translation of this, since German *Ost* and Russian *vostok* both mean "east."

Marko Vovchok: Mariya Aleksandrovna Vilinskaya-Markovich (1833–1907), Ukrainian writer, of Russ.-Pol. descent. The writer took her new surname from the village where she lived. Her new first name is a shortened form of the surname of her husband, ethnographer and political activist A.V. Markovich.

Bono Vox *see* Bono.

Grigory Voytinsky: Grigory Naumovich Zarkhin (1893–1953), Russ. Communist, sinologist.

Stanko Vraz: Jakob Frass (1810–1851), Croatian poet, critic.

Jaroslav Vrchlický: Emil Bohus Frída (1853–1912), Cz. poet, playwright.

Theun de Vries: Theunis Milke (1907–), Du. poet, novelist.

Vakhtang Vronsky: Vakhtang Ivanovich Nadiradze (1905–), Georgian-born Russ. ballet master.

Azat Vshtuni: Azat Setovich Mamikonyan (1894–1958), Armenian poet.

Samed Vurgun: Samed Yusif ogly Vekilov (1906–1956), Azerbaijani folk poet. The poet's adopted name means "enamored."

Vydunas: Vilius Storasta (1868–1953), Lithuanian playwright, philosopher. The writer's adopted name means "noble one."

Henry Wade: [Major Sir] Henry Lancelot Aubrey Fletcher (1887–1969), Eng. crime novelist. The writer adopted his mother's maiden name as his pen name.

Michael Wager: Emanuel Weisgal (1925–), U.S. stage actor, director.

Bunny Wailer: Neville O'Reilly Livingston (1947–), Jamaican pop singer, songwriter.

Anton Walbrook: Adolf Anton Wilhelm Wohlbrück (1900–1967), Austr. movie actor, working in U.S., U.K. The actor dropped the then unpopular first name of Adolf when in Hollywood in the 1930s.

Jersey Joe Walcott: Arnold Raymond Cream (1914–1994), U.S. black heavyweight boxer. Cream took his ring name from his boyhood hero, welterweight champion Joe Walcott, adding "Jersey" because he was born in New Jersey.

Herwarth Walden: Georg Levin (1878–1941), Ger. writer, art critic, working in Russia.

Robert Walden: Robert Wolkowitz (1943–), U.S. TV actor.

Claire Waldoff: Clara Wortmann (1884–1957), Ger. music hall artist.

Emile **Waldteufel:** Charles Emile Lévy (1837–1915), Fr. composer, conductor. The musician's assumed surname had earlier been used by his grandfather, father, and two uncles, who were all dance musicians. Its origin is uncertain. As an Alsatian surname it literally means "forest devil."

Hubert **Wales:** William Pigott (1870–1943), Br. novelist, writer on psychical research.

Arthur **Waley:** Arthur David Schloss (1889–1966), Eng. oriental scholar, translator. The writer's family adopted his mother's maiden name as their legal name in 1914, at the outbreak of World War I.

Gary **Walker:** Gary Leeds (1944–), U.S. pop singer.

Jerry Jeff **Walker:** Paul Crosby (1942–), U.S. country singer, songwriter.

John **Walker:** John Joseph Mans (1943–), U.S. pop singer.

Junior **Walker:** Autry DeWalt II (1931–1995), U.S. rhythm 'n' blues musician. The saxophonist adopted the nickname given him by his stepfather for his performing name.

Kath **Walker:** Oodgeroo Noonuccal (*q.v.*).

Nancy **Walker:** Anna Myrtle Swoyer (1922–1992), U.S. TV actress. The actress got her stage name by accident. Richard Rodgers and his producer George Abbott were holding auditions in 1942 and Swoyer was one of those seeking a break on Broadway. Among the applicants was a singer named Helen Walker, hoping to land a minor five-line role. When Swoyer came on, she was announced in her place as "Miss Walker." The song she belted out, "Bounce Me Brother With a Solid Four," was not the one they had been expecting, but they changed their minds and offered her a leading part. She kept the other singer's surname, with "Nancy" a form of her real name Anna.

Scott **Walker:** Noel Scott Engel (1944–), U.S. pop musician.

Syd **Walker:** Sidney Kirman (1887–1945), Eng. radio comedian.

Max **Wall:** Maxwell George Lorimer (1908–1990), Sc.-born Br. stage, TV actor, comedian. The actor derived his stage name not simply from his first name, split into two, but as a compound of the first half of this name and the first half of his stepfather's name, Wallace.

Edgar **Wallace:** Richard Horatio Edgar Wallace (1875–1932), Eng. novelist, playwright. The writer was born as the son of Polly Richards, née Mary Jane Blair, and Richard Horatio Edgar, both of whom were in the acting business. (His mother had married a Mr. Richards, and was known as "Polly" instead of her actual first name, Marie, which she had "upgraded" from Mary.) The question is: who gave the novelist the "Wallace" of his name? When Polly Richards registered her son's birth, she could not resist giving him the full name of his father, but in the paternity column of the register wrote "Walter Wallace, comedian," in order to disguise the actual identity of the father. It seems likely that "William Wallace, comedian" never existed, and no actor of this name has been traced in theatrical records. Even if he had lived, it seems unlikely that he would have agreed to give his name to a child that was certainly not his. No doubt Polly Richards was giving the boy the name of "a convenient father who could never be traced, and who had his beginning and his end solely in her own imagination" [Margaret Lane, *Edgar Wallace: The Biography of a Phenomenon*, 1939]. One of Wallace's detective plays was in fact titled *The Man Who Changed His Name*. It was not a great success, and was full of improbable coincidences.

Irving **Wallace:** Irving Wallechinsky (1916–1990), U.S. novelist, encyclopedist. The writer was well known for the various editions of *The Book of Lists* (1977), among other works, with this particular publication compiled by a family foursome: Irving Wallace, David Wallechinsky (Irving's son), Amy Wallace (his daughter), and Sylvia Wallace (his wife).

Jean **Wallace:** Jean Wallasek (1923–1990), U.S. movie actress.

Julie T. **Wallace:** Julie Therese Keir (1961–), Br. stage, TV actress. The actress adopted her mother's maiden name.

Nellie **Wallace:** Eleanor Jane Liddy (1870–1948), Br. music hall artist.

Lester **Wallack:** John Johnstone Wallack (1820–1888), U.S. actor, playwright, theatre manager.

Fats **Waller:** Thomas Wright Waller (1904–1943), U.S. jazz pianist, composer. The musician's nickname is a descriptive one, and was given him for his plump appearance. He adopted it as his professional name.

Lewis **Waller:** William Waller Lewis (1860–1915), Br. actor, theatre manager. The actor was fortunate enough to have a surname that could readily be adopted as a first name for stage name use.

Max **Waller:** Léopold-Nicolas-Maurice-Edouard Warlomont (1860–1889), Belg. poet.

Walneerg: Thomas Knox (1835–1896), U.S. journalist, traveler. The writer used this name for *Rhymed Convictions in Song* (1852). It is a reversal of his birthplace, Greenlaw, New Hampshire.

Stella **Walsh:** Stanislawa Walasiewicz (1911–1980), Pol.-born U.S. athlete. The athlete's original first name was actually Stefania. Her parents emigrated to the U.S. when she was only two. As she was unable to obtain American citizenship then, she competed for Poland until 1947, when she became a naturalized American. (She eventually became a U.S. citizen on marrying an American in 1956, by which time, at age 45, she was unable to make the U.S. team.)

Walter: Walter Goetz (1911–), Ger.-born Br. cartoonist, painter.

Bruno **Walter:** Bruno Walter Schlesinger (1876–1962), Ger.-born orchestral conductor, working in U.S.

Joseph **Walton:** Joseph Losey (1909–1984), U.S.-born Br. movie director. This was one of the pseudonyms under which Losey worked in London in the 1950s when hoping to attract the attention of the critics. He used it for *The Intimate Stranger* (1956), having earlier directed *The Sleeping Tiger* (1954) as Victor Hanbury.

Waif **Wander:** Mary Helena Fortune, née Wilson (*c*.1833–*c*.1909), Ir.-born crime writer, novelist, poet, working in Australia. The name, suggesting a "wandering waif," was used by the writer for her romantic novels and poetry. For her crime fiction she was simply "W.W."

Walter **Wanger:** Walter Feuchtwanger (1894–1968), U.S. movie producer.

Hank **Wangford:** Samuel Hutt (1940–), Br. country singer. The singer took his name from the village of Wangford, Suffolk, where he was born. He commented: "Hank Wangford was a good name for the classic country star. He sings about pain, he sings about heartache, and that was good because Sam could go on living and being normal" [Larkin, p. 2622].

Artemus **Ward:** Charles Farrar Browne (1834–1867), U.S. humorist. The writer is said to have adopted his pen name from that of an eccentric showman known by him. The name was first used for a character who gave illiterate "commentaries" on various subjects in his letters. In 1861 Browne took to lecturing as Artemus Ward. By a coincidence, there had earlier been

an American Revolutionary commander named Artem*as* Ward (1727–1800) and this same name was also that of the advertising manager who gave King C. Gillette valuable advice about advertising when the inventor of the disposable razor blade visited London in the 1880s.

Burt **Ward:** Herbert John Gervais, Jr. (1945–), U.S. juvenile movie actor.

Fannie **Ward:** Frances Buchanan (1872–1952), U.S. stage actress.

Polly **Ward:** Byno Poluski (1908–), Br. movie actress.

Margaret **Warde:** Edith Kellogg Dunton (1875–1944), U.S. novelist. The writer used the name for her series of books about the college girl Betty Wales. She explained: "I chose a pen name because I had a sister at Smith College who, I thought, might be annoyed by a connection with anyone writing stories about college life. Also, I didn't want Smith to be embarrassed by a graduate's impressions, wholly fictional but never so regarded by one's friends. I chose Margaret because I always felt as if my name ought to have been Margaret, and Warde, with an *e*, because it wasn't in the Smith Alumnae of names. I didn't know it was so rare; a Margaret Warde in California wrote me that she had never seen it except in her own family and in one other case, Frederick Warde, and wished to trace a relationship" [Marble, p. 180].

Florence **Warden:** Florence Alice James, née Price (1857–1929), Eng. novelist.

David **Warfield:** David Wollfeld (or Wohlfelt) (1866–1951), U.S. stage actor.

Andy **Warhol:** Andrew Warhola (1927–1987), U.S. pop artist, filmmaker, of Cz. parentage.

Barbara **Waring:** Barbara Gibb (1912–), Br. stage actress. The actress took her stage name from the maiden name of her mother, Louise Waring Colley.

Richard **Waring:** Richard Stephens (1912–), Eng. stage actor. The actor adopted his mother's maiden name as his stage name.

Peter **Warlock:** Philip Arnold Heseltine (1894–1930), Eng. composer, writer. The writer's name, adopted around 1921, was intended to signify a change to a new, aggressive personality, one of "wine, women and song." A warlock, after all, is a wizard, a practicer of black magic. Heseltine had first used the name in 1919, after the failure of his early work and a number of rejects. Reviewing a new book on Warlock in the *Times Literary Supplement* (July 11, 1980),

Eric Sams points out that the assumed name may be even more meaningful, since Heseltine is said to derive from "hazel," and thus, by means of an associative switch, via "witch hazel," and a sex change ("witch" to "warlock"), the composer arrived at his new name. A literary pseudonym Warlock used was Rab Noolas for *Merry-Go-Down: A Gallery of Gorgeous Drunkards Through the Ages* (1929). Reversed, it reveals the sober truth.

Charles **Warner**: Charles John Lickfold (1846–1909), Br. stage actor.

Harry **Warner**: Harry Morris Eichelbaum (1881–1958), Pol.-born U.S. movie exhibitor, producer, brother of Jack L. Warner (see below).

Jack **Warner**: Horace John Waters (1894–1981), Eng. stage, movie, TV actor. The actor changed his name to avoid trading on the name of his sisters, Elsie Waters (1895–1990) and Doris Waters (? –1978), teaming together as radio comediennes (in the characters of Cockney gossips, Gert and Daisy).

Jack L. **Warner**: Jack Leonard Eichelbaum (1892–1978), U.S. movie producer, brother of Harry Warner (see above). Jack Warner was the youngest and best known of the four Warner brothers, who in 1923 founded one of the world's leading motion picture companies, Warner Brothers Pictures. His son was the movie and TV producer Jack Warner, Jr. (1916–1995).

Betty **Warren**: Babette Hilda Hogan (1905–1990), Br. stage, movie actress.

Harry **Warren**: Salvatore Guaragna (1893–1981), U.S. movie songwriter, of It. parentage. The English surname evolved from the Italian original.

Leonard **Warren**: Leonard Warenoff (1911–1960), U.S. opera singer, of Russ. Jewish parentage.

Lavinia **Warren**: Mercy Lavinia Warren Bumpus (1841–1919), U.S. midget, wife of General Tom Thumb (*q.v.*).

Dionne **Warwick**: Marie Dionne Warrick (1940–), U.S. black soul singer.

John **Warwick**: John McIntosh Beattie (1905–1972), Austral. movie actor, working in U.K.

Robert **Warwick**: Robert Taylor Bien (1878–1964), U.S. stage, movie actor.

Washboard Doc: Joseph Doctor (1911–1988), U.S. black street musician.

Washboard Sam: Robert Brown (1910–), U.S. black washboard player, blues singer.

Washboard Slim: Robert Young (1900–1990), U.S. black street musician.

Washboard Willie: William Paden Hensley (1909–), U.S. black blues musician. All these names of course imply an involvement with the washboard and its associated kitchen implements as a rhythm instrument. Washboard Slim embellished his with frying pans and cowbells.

Booker T. **Washington:** Booker Taliaferro (1856–1915), U.S. black educator. The teacher and lecturer was born into slavery and took the name Booker Washington as a schoolboy.

Dinah **Washington:** Ruth Lee Jones (1924–1963), U.S. black blues singer. The singer adopted her new name around 1942.

Donna Day **Washington:** Donna Day Washington-Smith (1942–), Can. ballet dancer.

Hugo **Wast:** Gustavo Martínez Zuviría (1883–1962), Argentine novelist. The writer created his pen name from his original first name, with an added "h" and with "v" giving the "w."

William **Wastle:** John Gibson Lockhart (1794–1854), Sc. biographer, magazine contributor. The writer used this name for his contributions to *Blackwood's Magazine*, adopting it from that of Willie Wastle, a character in Robert Burns's poem *Willie's Wife* (1792). This was the name under which Lockhart featured in the *Noctes Ambrosianae* (see Christopher North).

Watcyn Wyn: Watkin Hezekiah Williams (1844–1905), Welsh poet, preacher, teacher. The poet's popular name means "Watkin the fair." It also reflects the name of the school for budding Nonconformist ministers that he set up in 1888. He called it "Gwynfryn" ("white hill").

Muddy **Waters:** McKinley Morganfield (1915–1983), U.S. blues singer, musician. The musician was given this name as a nickname by his grandmother, who raised him on Stovell plantation, near Clarksdale, Mississippi. The name referred to the boy's habit of fishing and playing in a nearby muddy creek.

Arena **Wati:** Dahlan bin Buyung (1925–), Malaysian writer.

Arthur **Watkyn:** Arthur Thomas Levi Watkins (1907–1965), Welsh-born Br. playwright.

Dilys **Watling:** Dilys Rhys-Jones (1946–), Eng. stage actress.

Claire **Watson:** Claire McLamore (1927–), U.S. opera singer.

Robert (or Bobby) **Watson:** Robert Watson Knucher (1888–1965), U.S. movie actor.

Wylie **Watson:** John Wylie Robertson (1889–1966), Sc.-born Br. movie actor.

Jonathan **Watts:** John B. Leech (1933–), U.S. ballet dancer, teacher.

Theodore **Watts-Dunton:** Walter Theodore Watts (1832–1914), Eng. novelist. The writer added his mother's maiden name of Dunton to his original surname in 1897.

Mansie **Wauch:** David MacBeth Moir (1798–1851), Sc. doctor, essayist. The writer used this name for the purported autobiography of a Dalkeith tailor, *The Life of Mansie Wauch* (1828). He also wrote as Gabriel Cowitch and Joseph Thomson, and was a contributor to *Blackwood's Magazine* as Δ (a capital Greek letter delta, the initial of his first name).

Edward Bradwardine **Waverley:** John Wilson Croker (1780–1857), Ir.-born Br. politician, essayist. The writer adopted this name in two letters (published 1826) replying to Malachi Mala growther (*q.v.*), concocting the name itself from those of two characters in Scott's *Waverley:* Edward Waverley and the Baron of Bradwardine.

Franz **Waxman:** Franz Wachsmann (1906–1967), Ger. movie music composer, working in U.S.

David **Wayne:** Wayne David McKeekan (1914–1995), U.S. stage, movie actor.

Dennis **Wayne:** Dennis Wayne Wendelken (1945–), U.S. ballet dancer.

John **Wayne:** Marion Michael Morrison (1907–1979), U.S. movie actor. The movie star's name change was prompted by head of production Sheehan for the movie *The Big Trail* (1930), Sheehan commenting, "I don't like this name, Duke Morrison, it's no name for a leading man." (Earlier Morrison had adopted the first name Duke. This was the name of his Airedale, and the nickname used by firemen in a nearby fire station when young Morrison and dog went past.) Director Raoul Walsh, who admired "Mad Anthony" Wayne, the American Revolutionary War general, suggested Anthony Wayne. Sheehan said that this "sounded too Italian." "Then Tony Wayne," countered Walsh. Here Sol Wurtzel, head of production at Fox, protested that this "sounds like a girl." So Sheehan decreed, "What's the matter with just plain John? John Wayne." Wurtzel approved, "It's American" [Maurice Zolotow, *John Wayne: Shooting Star*, 1974].

Johnny **Wayne:** John Louis Weingarten (1918–1990), Can. radio, TV comedian, teaming with Frank Shuster (1916–).

Naunton **Wayne:** Henry Wayne Davies (1901–1970), Welsh stage, movie, radio, TV actor. The actor changed his name by deed poll in 1933.

Thomas **Wayne:** Thomas Wayne Perkins (1940–1971), U.S. pop musician.

Putnam **Weale:** Bertram Lenox Simpson (1877–1930), Eng. writer. Simpson's maternal grandfather, John Weale, married Sarah Hollis Putnam, granddaughter of the U.S. Revolutionary commander Israel Putnam (1718–1790). Hence Simpson's pen name, which he used when writing about political conditions in the Far East, e.g. in *Indiscreet Letters from Peking* (1905) and *Why China Sees Red* (1925).

Charley **Weaver:** Clifford Arquette (1905–1974), U.S. entertainer.

Sigourney **Weaver:** Susan Alexandra Weaver (1949–), U.S. movie actress. The actress adopted a new first name for distinctiveness when she was 14, renaming herself for Sigourney Howard, Jordan Baker's aunt in Scott Fitzgerald's novel *The Great Gatsby* (1925).

Clifton **Webb:** Webb Parmallee Hollenbeck (1893–1966), U.S. movie actor.

Jane **Webb:** Mary Young (? –1740), Eng. pickpocket ("Jenny Diver").

Lizbeth **Webb:** [Lady] Elizabeth Campbell, née Wills-Webber (1926–), Br. stage actress, singer.

Katie **Webster:** Kathryn Thorne (1939–), U.S. blues pianist.

Weegee: Arthur H. Felling (1899–1968), Pol.-born U.S. photographer. The story goes that Felling was nicknamed "Ouija" for his apparent psychic ability to sniff out a good story. He altered this to "Weegee."

Ted **Weems:** Wilfred Theodore Weymes (1901–1963), U.S. bandleader.

Awfly **Weirdly:** Charles Robinson (1870–1937), Eng. illustrator, cartoonist. The artist used this name for *Christmas Dreams* (1896), a book of Chrismas cards, menus, and the like, in which he parodied the mannered style of Aubrey Beardsley. The name itself is thus a punning parody of that artist's style and name.

Barbara **Weisberger:** Barbara Linshen (*c.*1926–), U.S. ballet dancer.

Raquel **Welch:** Raquel Tejada (1940–), U.S. movie actress, of Bolivian parentage. The actress's new surname is that of her first husband, James Welch, her high school sweetheart. The couple separated in 1961, but she retained the name.

Ronald **Welch:** Ronald Oliver Felton (1909–1982), Welsh-born Br. children's writer. The writer took his pen name from the Welch Regiment, with whom he served in World War II.

Tuesday **Weld:** Susan Ker Weld (1943–), U.S. movie actress. The actress has explained her first name in different ways at different times, but it seems likely that "Tuesday" is a corruption of "Susan," presumably originating as a childish pronunciation of this name.

Ljuba **Welitsch:** Ljuba Velichkova (1913–1996), Bulg. opera singer. The soprano's adopted name is a germanicized form of the original. Her name as a whole coincidentally suggests the Bulgarian for "great love," appropriately enough for a singer who took the part of passionate heroines, notably Strauss's Salome.

Ehm **Welk:** Thomas Trimm (1884–1966), Ger. novelist, playwright.

Colin **Welland:** Colin Williams (1934–), Eng. actor, playwright.

Sylvia **Welling:** Sylvia Galloway (1901–), Br. stage actress, singer. The actress adopted her mother's maiden name as her stage name.

Junior **Wells:** Amos Blackmore (1934–), U.S. black blues singer.

Kitty **Wells:** Muriel Ellen Deason (1919–), U.S. country singer. The singer's name was chosen for her by her husband, Johnny Wright, who when courting her recalled the song popularized by the Carter Family, "I'm A-Goin' to Marry Kitty Wells."

Sandra **Wells:** Ruth Lilian Clarke (1906–1992), Br. variety artist. As a flamenco dancer the performer took the name Janita, while as a ventriloquist and subsequently pantomime cat she was Joy Wilby.

Freddie **Welsh:** Frederick Hall Thomas (1886–1927), Welsh lightweight boxer ("The Welsh Wizard"). The champion was clearly keen to stress his nationality.

John **Wengraf:** Johann Wenngraft (1897–1974), Austr. movie actor, working in U.S.

Bessie **Wentworth:** Elizabeth Andrews (1874–1901), Eng. music hall singer.

Patricia **Wentworth:** Dora Amy Elles (1878–1961), Indian-born Eng. crime novelist.

Oskar **Werner:** Oskar Josef Bschliessmayer (1922–1984), Austr. stage, movie actor.

Lina **Wertmüller:** Arcangela Felice Assunta Wertmüller von Elgg (1928–), It. movie writer, director, of Swiss descent. The writer's new first

name presumably evolved as a diminutive of Arcangela.

Mary **Wesley:** Mary Aline Farmar (1912–), Eng. novelist, children's writer. The writer is descended from the eldest brother of the Duke of Wellington, whose surname was Wellesley, and her adopted name is a legitimate variant of this.

Adam **West:** William West Anderson (1928–), U.S. movie actor.

Billy **West:** Roy B. Weissberg (1893–1975), U.S. movie comedian.

Elizabeth **West:** Margaret Wilson (1882–1973), U.S. novelist, poet, missionary, working in England. The writer used this name for some early poetry. She wrote as "An Elderly Spinster" for stories published between 1917 and 1921, when she was still a spinster but hardly elderly. (She settled in England in 1923 on marrying an Englishman she had met as a missionary in India.)

Keith **West:** Keith Hopkins (1943–), Eng. pop singer.

Leslie **West:** Leslie Weinstein (1945–), U.S. rock singer, guitarist.

Nathanael **West:** Nathan Wallenstein Weinstein (1903–1940), U.S. novelist, screenwriter. "West" can be easily picked out of both "Wallenstein" *and* "Weinstein," with the last three letters of "Nathanael" also found in the former name.

Nigel **West:** Rupert Allason (1951–), Br. spy writer, politician. The writer chose the name before becoming a Member of Parliament. He comments: "I wanted an identity that was bland, neutral and classless. The only book I wrote under my own name did not sell at all."

[Dame] Rebecca **West:** Cicily Isabel Andrews, née Fairchild (1892–1983), Ir.-born Eng. novelist, critic. The writer took her pen name from her character namesake in Ibsen's play *Rosmersholm* (1886), where "*Rebecca West*" stood for "*Rights of Women*," her own cause. Fairchild had actually played this part in a London performance of the play. She first used the name in 1911.

Reviewing a new book on West, a writer commented: "The brilliant and rebellious Ibsen heroine is chosen to replace Cicily Fairfield (a name that in itself seems almost too good an example of English gentility). To choose that name was to claim the ideas and the radical posture of Ibsen, and particularly his ideas about women, as one's own public identity. The choice suggests an exceptional woman, willing her life to be an example of woman's situation" [Samuel Hynes, "In communion with reality," *Times Literary Supplement*, December 21, 1973].

Helen Westcott: Myrthas Helen Hickman (1928–), U.S. movie actress.

Netta Westcott: Netta Lupton (*c.*1893–1953), Br. stage actress.

Helen Westley: Henrietta Remsen Meserole Manney (1875–1942), U.S. stage, movie actress.

Mary Westmacott: [Dame] Agatha Christie (1890–1976), Br. detective novelist (the "Queen of Crime"). The writer used this name for six romantic novels, distinctive from her detective genre, the first published in 1930, the last in 1956.

Arthur Weston: Peggy Webling (*c.*1870–?), Eng. journalist, fiction writer. The writer used this name for her Canadian tales, written following a spell as an actress in Canada. She used her real name for her English fiction.

Jack Weston: Jack Weinstein (1925–1996), U.S. movie actor.

Paul Weston: Paul Wetstein (1912–), U.S. popular composer, pianist.

Karen Westwood: Karen Smith (1964–), Sc. movie, TV actress.

Agnes Ethelwyn Wetherald: Bel Thistlethwaite (1857–1940), Can. poet, journalist. The writer's new name appears to be loosely based on her original surname.

Elizabeth Wetherell: Susan Bogert Warner (1819–1885), U.S. sentimental novelist, sister of Amy Lothrop (*q.v.*). The writer's new name may have been intended to suggest "weather all," since her novels were mostly about young girls coping bravely (and usually prayerfully) with the rigors of a predominantly male world.

Joan Wetmore: Joan Dixon, née Deery (1911–), Austral. stage actress.

Michael Whalen: Joseph Kenneth Shovlin (1899–1974), U.S. movie actor.

Anthony Wharton: Alister McAllister (1877–1943), Ir. author.

Grace Wharton: Katharine Thomson, née Byerley (1797–1862), Br. author. The Byerley family were descended from Colonel Anthony Byerley (died 1667), the father of Robert Byerley (1660–1714) who married Mary Wharton, great-niece of Philip, 4th Lord Wharton. Hence Mrs. Thomson's pen name, also adopted by her son, Philip Wharton (see below).

Philip Wharton: John Cockburn Thomson (1834–1860), Br. author, son of Grace Wharton (see above).

William Wharton: Albert du Aime (1925–), U.S. novelist. Many of the writer's novels deal with aspects of identity and self-definition, and his pseudonym, although known to be such, long concealed his own real identity.

Peetie Wheatstraw: William Bunch (1902–1941), U.S. black blues singer, musician.

Jimmy Wheeler: Ernest Remnant (1910–1973), Eng. music hall comedian.

Albert Whelan: Albert Waxman (1875–1961), Austral. music hall entertainer.

Whigfield: Sannie Charlotte Carlson (1970–), Dan. pop singer. The singer adopted the surname of her singing teacher as her sole stage name.

William and Robert Whistlecraft: John Hookham Frere (1769–1846), Eng. diplomat, author. The writer used this double pen name for his humorous poem *The Monks and the Giants* (1817–18). This itself sprang from two cantos entitled *Prospectus and Specimen of an Intended National Work, by William and Robert Whistlecraft of Stowmarket in Suffolk, Harness and Collar Makers. Intended to comprise the most interesting particulars relating to King Arthur and his Round Table* (1817). The work inspired Byron, no less, who wrote to a friend that year: "Mr. Whistlecraft has no greater admirer than myself. I have written a story in eighty-nine stanzas in imitation of him, called 'Beppo.'" Whistlecraft is a genuine Suffolk surname.

Antonia White: Eirene Adeline Botting (1899–1980), Eng. novelist, translator, journalist. The writer adopted her mother's maiden name, as she never considered her original name "sufficiently imposing to suit her personality" (*Times Literary Supplement*, August 26–September 1, 1988).

Babington White: Mary Elizabeth Maxwell, née Braddon (1837–1915), Eng. novelist. The writer adopted her mother's maiden name as her pen name.

Chris White: Chris Costner Sizemore (1927–), U.S. "split personality." In 1978 an unusual autobiography was published. It was entitled *Eve*, and the author was Chris Costner Sizemore (with Elen Sain Pittillo). In it, the writer describes how she developed a multiple personality, telling the story of one woman who effectively became 12 different people, all existing within the body of a single human being. Naturally, the personalities assumed different names. The three main women were Chris White, a "sad, dowdy woman," Chris Costner, a "flamboyant party-goer," and Jane Doe, a "well-bred, refined Southern lady." (Of these, the first is Sizemore's dominant alter ego, the second her real self, with her maiden name, and the third, Jane Doe, the average woman, the female equivalent of John Doe.) Costner's case history had earlier been described by two psychiatrists, Corbett H. Thigpen and Hervey M. Cleckley. Their account was a bestseller, and was turned into a movie, *The Three Faces of Eve* (1957), in which all three women were played by Joanne Woodward.

George **White**: George Weitz (1890–1968), U.S. movie actor, director, producer.

Jesse **White**: Jesse Weidenfeld (1918–), U.S. comic movie actor.

Joseph Blanco **White**: José María Blanco y Crespo (1775–1841), Sp.-born Eng. poet, journalist, churchman. The writer fled to England as a Roman Catholic priest in 1810. There he took Anglican orders and anglicized his surname while retaining the Spanish original. He referred to this arrangement in another pseudonym, Don Leucadio Doblado, where "Don" indicates his Spanish origin, "Leucadio" (via Greek) means "white," and Spanish "Doblado" means "doubled."

Matthew **White**: William Prynne (1600–1669), Eng. Puritan pamphleteer.

Pearl **White**: Victoria Evans White (1889–1938), U.S. movie actress (the "Queen of the Silent Serials").

Roma **White**: Blanche Winder, née Oram (1866–1930), Eng. novelist, children's writer. The writer translated her first name to form her new surname, and rearranged her maiden surname to form her new first name.

Vanna **White**: Vanna Marie Rosich (1957–), U.S. actress. Her actress's adopted surname is that of her stepfather, Herbert Stackley White, Jr. (Her parents split up before she was a year old, and she was raised by her grandparents. Vanna was her grandmother's goddaughter, with a second "n" added to the original by her mother. Marie was her mother's middle name.)

Slim **Whitman**: Otis Dewey, Jr. (1924–), U.S. country singer, yodeller. The singer was a self-styled protégé of Montana Slim (*q.v.*).

Peter **Whitney**: Peter King Engle (1916–1972), U.S. movie actor.

Violet **Whyte**: Henrietta Eliza Vaughan Stannard, née Palmer (1856–1911), Eng. novelist. The writer's better known pen name was John Strange Winter (*q.v.*).

Mary **Wickes**: Mary Isabelle Wickenhauser (1910–1995), U.S. movie comedienne.

Anna **Wickham**: Edith Alice Mary Hepburn, née Harper (1884–1947), Eng. poet. The writer grew up in Australia, and at the age of ten made a vow to her father that she would be a poet. She later took her pen name from the Brisbane street, Wickham Terrace, where the vow was made.

Martina **Wied**: Alexandrina Martina Augusta Schnabel (1882–1957), Austr. writer.

Mary **Wigman**: Marie Wiegmann (1886–1973), Ger. ballet dancer, choreographer.

Helene **Wildbrunn**: Helene Wehrenpfennig (1882–1972), Austr. opera singer.

Kim **Wilde**: Kim Smith (1960–), Eng. pop singer, songwriter, daughter of Marty Wilde (*q.v.*). The singer originally found her father's fame a burden: "When I was at art college I changed my name [back] to Kim Smith because I wanted to escape. For a whole year no one knew who I was, and I found that sense of anonymity very exciting. But when I had my first hit [*Kids in America* (1981), coproduced by her father], I realised that I'd been fighting something I couldn't change and I chose to embrace being Marty's daughter completely" [*The Times*, December 4, 1995].

Marty **Wilde**: Reginald Leonard Smith (1936–), Eng. pop singer. The singer tells how he came to adopt his new name: "I was 17 when I became Marty Wilde and I've always said that's when I really came alive. Previously I'd been Reg Smith, but Reg Smith was never me. ... Larry Parnes, my manager at the time, did the name change. It was done on the toss of a coin. He tossed the coin and up came Wilde which I hated, and he tossed another coin and that decided Marty which I didn't mind but wasn't mad about. I think I wanted to be Marty Patterson after the World Heavyweight Champion, Floyd Patterson. ... I still say it's important to have a name that looks fantastic in print. The Boomtown Rats— star name. Siouxsie and the Banshees—star name. Cliff Richard is a star-quality name. ... Reg Smith isn't a star-quality name" [*TV Times Magazine*, November 28–December 4, 1981].

The combination of "soft" forename and "hard" surname is typical of Parnes, who also named Tommy Steele (*q.v.*).

Patricia **Wilde:** Patricia White (1930–), Can.-born U.S. ballet dancer. The dancer changed her name (slightly) so as to be distinguished from her sister, Nora White, who was also a ballerina.

Herman **Wildenvey:** Herman Theodor Portaas (1886–1959), Norw. poet.

Gene **Wilder:** Jerome (or Jerry) Silberman (1935–), U.S. movie comedian, of Russ. Jewish parentage.

John **Wilder:** Keith Magaurn (1936–), U.S. movie, TV producer.

Wilhelmina: Gertrude Wilhelmina Behmenburg Cooper (1939–1980), Du.-born U.S. fashion model, of Du.- Ger. parentage. The model began her career as Winnie Hart: "Gertrude just wouldn't do, Behmenburg was too long and awkward to remember, and her middle name, Wilhelmina, was too foreign." Subsequently, however, an agency decided that Wilhelmina was the right name after all. The model's friends knew her as Willie [Michael Gross, *Model*, 1995].

Warren **William:** Warren William Krech (1895–1948), U.S. movie actor, of Ger. parentage.

Williams Sidney William Martin (1919–1993), Austral. cartoonist, working in U.K. The artist used this name when drawing for *Sporting Life*.

Andy **Williams:** Howard Andrew (1930–), U.S. pop singer.

Barney **Williams:** Bernard O'Flaherty (1824–1876), U.S. actor, of Ir. parentage.

Bert **Williams:** Egbert Austin (*c.*1876–1922), U.S. black stage comedian, songwriter.

Bill **Williams:** Herman William Katt (1916–1992), U.S. movie actor.

Bransby **Williams:** Bransby William Pharez (1870–1961), Br. music hall actor.

Cara **Williams:** Bernice Kamiat (1925–), U.S. TV, radio, movie comedienne.

Daniel **Williams:** Daniel Grossman (1942–), U.S. ballet dancer, teacher.

Deniece **Williams:** Deniece Chandler (1951–), U.S. black gospel, soul singer.

Frances **Williams:** Frances Jellinek (1903–1959), U.S. stage actress, singer.

Guy **Williams:** Guy Catalano (1924–1989), U.S. movie, TV actor.

Joe **Williams:** Joseph Goreed (1918–), U.S. black blues singer.

John **Williams:** George Mackay (1884–1913), Br. murderer, of Sc. parentage.

Otis **Williams:** Otis Miles (1949–), U.S. black Motown singer.

Tennessee **Williams:** Thomas Lanier Williams (1911–1983), U.S. playwright. The writer was born in Mississippi, not Tennessee. His father, however, was directly descended from John Williams, first senator of Tennessee, from the brother Valentine of Tennessee's first governor John Sevier (whose own name was itself changed from Xavier by the Huguenots), and from Thomas Lanier Williams I, first chancellor of the Western Territory, as Tennessee was called before it became a state. So, explained the dramatist, "I've just indulged myself in the Southern weakness for climbing a family tree" [Tennessee Williams, *Memoirs*, 1976].

Sonny Boy **Williamson:** Aleck (or Alex) Ford (1899–1965), U.S. blues harmonica player, singer. In order to gain greater popularity, Aleck Ford, also known as Aleck Miller (nickname "Rice" Miller), after his stepfather, claimed to be "the original Sonny Boy Williamson" following the murder of masterly blues harmonica player John Lee "Sonny Boy" Williamson (1914–1948). He began by performing as Little Boy Blue, and later played as Willie Williamson, Willie Williams, and Willie Miller.

Boxcar **Willie** *see* **Boxcar Willie**.

Bruce **Willis:** Walter Willison (1955–), U.S. movie actor.

Brember **Wills:** Brember Le Couteur (*c.*1883–1948), Br. stage, movie actor.

Meredith **Willson:** Robert Meredith Reiniger (1902–1984), U.S. songwriter, lyricist, composer.

Willy: Henri Gauthier-Villars (1859–1931), Fr. novelist, music critic, husband of Colette (*q.v.*). The name derives from the latter half of the writer's surname.

Henry **Wilson:** Jeremiah Jones Colbath (1812–1875), U.S. statesman, abolitionist. The Republican senator and U.S. vice president was indentured as a farm laborer at the age of 10. When he was freed at the age of 21 he legally changed his name, and soon after determined to devote his life to the antislavery cause.

J. Arbuthnot **Wilson:** Grant Allen (1848–1899), Can.-born Eng. author. The writer began his career as a scientist, and down to 1883 all his writings were on scientific subjects. He then found that he could not earn a living on science alone, and took to fiction. It was thus as J. Arbuthnot Wilson that he first published some short stories, issued under the collective title of *Strange Stories* in 1884.

Jennifer **Wilson**: Jennifer Wenda Lohr (1935–), Eng. stage, movie, TV actress.

Marie **Wilson**: Katherine Elizabeth White (1916–1972), U.S. movie actress.

Romer **Wilson**: Florence Roma Muir O'Brien, née Wilson (1891–1930), Br. novelist.

Whip **Wilson**: Charles Meyer (1915–1964), U.S. cowboy movie actor.

Robb **Wilton**: Robert Wilton Smith (1881–1957), Eng. music hall comedian.

Barbara **Windsor**: Barbara Anne Deeks (1937–), Eng. movie, TV actress, singer. The actress has explained that she took the name Windsor from that of her Aunt Dolly. It is also, of course, the name of the royal family. "I'm very, *very* pro-Royal," Miss Windsor has said. She actually adopted the name in 1953, the year of the Coronation of Queen Elizabeth II.

Claire **Windsor**: Clara Viola Cronk (1898–1972), U.S. movie actress.

Marie **Windsor**: Emily Marie Bertelson (1922–), U.S. movie actress.

Arthur M. **Winfield**: Edward L. Stratemeyer (1863–1930), U.S. author of stories for boys. *Life* magazine carried a letter from the writer explaining how he came by his pen name: "One evening when writing, with my mother sitting near sewing, I remarked that I wanted an unusual name—that I wasn't going to use my own name on the manuscript. She thought a moment and suggested Winfield. 'For then,' she said, 'you may win in that field.' I thought that good. She then supplied the first name saying, 'You are going to be an author, so why not make it Arthur?'" Stratemeyer added the middle "M." himself, reasoning that as it stood for "thousand," it might help to sell thousands of books" [Atkinson, p. 8].

Winna **Winifred**: Amelia Nielsen (1914–), Dan.-born movie actress, working in France, U.K., U.S.

George **Winslow**: George Wentzlaff (1946–), U.S. child movie actor.

John Strange **Winter**: Henrietta Eliza Vaughan Stannard, née Palmer (1856–1911), Eng. novelist. The author began her literary career under the name Violet Whyte (*q.v.*), with her first writing appearing in the *Family Herald*

in 1874. In 1881 her *Cavalry Life* was published, as a collection of regimental sketches, and two years later her *Regimental Legends*. The publisher refused to issue these books under a female name, so she selected John Strange Winter for them, this being the name of a character in the earlier work. Her readers assumed that the books were by a cavalry officer. The writer then kept this name for the rest of her career.

Bernie **Winters**: Bernard Weinstein (1932–1991), Br. TV comedian, of Russ. Jewish parentage, teaming with Mike Winters (1930–), his brother.

Shelley **Winters**: Shirley Shrift (1922–), U.S. stage, movie actress. When the actress was about 15, she was in the office of the Group Theatre in New York to read for an understudy in a play by Irwin Shaw. "The secretary asked me my name. 'Shirley Schrift.' ... 'Shirley Schrift isn't a very good name for an actress,' she told me. 'Let's see if we can figure out another one. ... What's your mother's maiden name?' 'Winter,' I told her. She wrote it down. 'Do you like "Shirley"?' she asked. 'God, no, there's millions of Shirleys all over Brooklyn, all named after Shirley Temple.' 'Well, wouldn't you like a name that sounds like Shirley in case someone calls you?' I thought for a moment. 'Shelley is my favorite poet, but that's a last name, isn't it?' She wrote it on the card in front of 'Winter.' She looked at it. 'Not anymore it isn't. Shelley Winter. That's your name.' She handed me the card, and I looked at it. It felt like me. Half poetic and half cold with fright. 'Okay,' I told her. 'Send it in.' Years later, in their infinite wisdom, Universal Studios added an *S* to 'Winter' and made me plural" [Shelley Winters, *Shelley: Also Known as Shirley*, 1981].

Eduard von **Winterstein**: Eduard von Wangenheim (1871–1961), Ger. movie actor.

Frances **Winwar**: Francesca Vinciguerra Grebanier (1900–), Sicilian-born U.S. novelist. The writer, who came to the U.S. when she was seven, translated her Italian maiden name (Vinciguerra) to provide her pen name, using it for her romantic novels, popular biographies, and books on famous poets.

Estelle **Winwood**: Estelle Goodwin (1882–1984), Eng. stage, movie actress, working in U.S. A neat transposition of the two halves of the actress's surname, a slight adjustment, and a new stage name emerges.

Norman **Wisdom**: Norman Wisden (1920–), Eng. stage, movie, radio comedian.

Ernie **Wise:** Ernest Wiseman (1925–), Eng. TV comedian, teaming with Eric Morecambe (*q.v.*).

Herbert **Wise:** Herbert Weisz (1924–), Austr.-born stage actor, TV director, working in U.K.

Stephen Samuel **Wise:** Stephen Samuel Weiss (1874–1949), U.S. social activist, Zionist leader.

Vic **Wise:** Donald Victor Bloom (1900– ?), Eng. music hall comedian.

Witkacy: Stanisław Ignacy Witkiewicz (1885–1939), Pol. playwright. A pen name formed from the first part of the writer's surname and second part of his middle name.

Googie **Withers:** Georgette Lizette Withers (1917–), Eng. stage, movie, TV actress. Miss Withers has stuck by her story that the nickname "Googie" was given her by her Indian nurse during her childhood in Karachi, and that it derives from a Punjabi word meaning "dove," or else a Bengali word meaning "clown." But could it not have simply arisen as a pet form of her first name? (Some sources give this as Georgina, rather than Georgette.)

Jah **Wobble:** John Wardle (*c.*1958–), Br. rock musician. The name represents a casual (possibly Cockney) pronunciation of the musician's real name.

Peter **Wolf:** Peter Blankfield (1946–), U.S. rock singer.

Humbert **Wolfe:** Umberto Wolff (1886–1940), Br. poet, of Ger.-It. Jewish parentage. The writer and civil servant adopted the new version of his name in 1918.

[Sir] Donald **Wolfit:** Donald Woolfitt (1902–1968), Br. stage, movie actor, theatre manager.

Wolfman Jack: Robert Weston Smith (1938–1995), U.S. radio DJ. Smith changed his name several times before finally becoming Wolfman Jack in 1963. The name alludes to the "banshee howl" that was his trademark.

Wols: Alfred Otto Wolfgang Schulze (1913–1951), Ger. painter, working in France. The artist created his name from letters in his third name and surname and originally used it as a photographer in Paris from 1932.

Stevie **Wonder:** Steveland Judkins (or Steveland Morris Hardaway) (1950–), U.S. black Motown singer. The singer was born Steveland Judkins, later acquiring the surname Morris after his mother's remarriage. He became a singing star at the early age of 12, when he was called "Little Stevie Wonder." Two years later, he had grown to six feet tall, and although he kept the name, he dropped "Little" [Constantine Elsner, *Stevie Wonder*, 1977].

Anna May **Wong:** Wong Liu-Tsong (1907–1961), U.S. movie actress, of Chin. parentage. The actress's original Chinese name meant "Frosted Yellow Willow."

Arthur **Wontner:** Arthur Smith (1875–1960), Eng. stage actor, theatre manager. The actor adopted his mother's maiden name as his stage name.

John **Woo:** Wu Yusen (1948–), Hong Kong movie director.

Brenton **Wood:** Alfred Jesse Smith (1941–), U.S. pop singer. The singer adopted his professional name from Brenton Wood, his home district in Los Angeles.

Del **Wood:** Adelaide Hazelwood (1920–), U.S. jazz pianist, singer.

Kerry **Wood:** Edgar Allardyce Wood (1907–), U.S. born Can. journalist, children's writer.

Natalie **Wood:** Natasha Virapaeff (later, Gurdin) (1938–1981), U.S. movie actress, of Russ.-Fr. parentage. The actress's new surname came from movie director Sam Wood, a friend of her own first director, Irving Pichel.

Wee Georgie **Wood:** George Bramlett (1895–1979), Eng. music hall comedian.

Henry **Woodhouse:** Mario Terenzio Enrico Casalegno (1884– ?), It.-born U.S. aeronautics expert. The engineer was able to translate his Italian name into English just as successfully as Frances Winwar (*q.v.*) would do later.

Holly **Woodlawn:** Harold Ajzenberg (1947–), Puerto Rican-born U.S. transvestite movie actor.

Donald **Woods:** Ralph L. Zink (1904–), U.S. movie actor.

Sara **Woods:** Sara Bowen-Judd, née Hutton (1922–1985), Eng.-born Can. detective novelist. The writer adopted her mother's maiden name as her pen name.

[Sir] Peregrine **Worsthorne:** Peregrine Gerard Koch de Gooreynd (1923–), Br. newspaper editor. "He changed his name for snobbish reasons because his mother lived in a village called Worsthorne when she was married to the governor of the Bank of England" [Nigel Dempster, in *Punch*, October 26–November 1, 1996].

The genealogical background is actually as follows. Worsthorne's father, Colonel Alexander Koch de Gooreynd, assumed the name of Worsthorne by deed poll in 1921, on the birth of Peregrine's elder brother, Sir Simon Towneley, but reverted to Koch de Gooreynd in 1937. The

Worsthorne name derives from Sir Simon's estate near Burnley, Lancashire. Sir Simon himself discontinued the name by deed poll and in 1955 assumed by royal licence the arms of Towneley through his descent from the eldest daughter and coheiress of Colonel Charles Towneley of Towneley.

Harry Worth: Harold Burlon Illingsworth (1917–1989), Eng. radio, TV comedian.

Helen Worth: Cathryn Helen Wigglesworth (1951–), Eng. TV actress.

Nicholas Worth: Walter Hines Page (1855–1918), U.S. journalist, diplomat.

George Wostenholm: George Wolstenholme (1800–1876), Eng. cutlery manufacturer. The manufacturer slightly shortened the family name to facilitate its inclusion on knife blades.

John Wray: John Griffith Malloy (1888–1940), U.S. movie director, actor.

Belinda Wright: Brenda Wright (1927–), Eng. ballet dancer. A small verbal uplift can work wonders for a name in this way, and "Belinda" has the added beauty of French *belle* and the neatness of Italian *linda*, both highly desirable assets for a ballerina (which word is itself also suggested by the name).

Dale Wright: Harlan Dale Reiffe (1938–), U.S. pop singer.

Józef Wroński: Józef Hoene (1776–1853), Pol. mathematician, philosopher.

Jeffrey Wyatville: Jeffrey Wyatt (1766–1840), Eng. architect.

Margaret Wycherly: Margaret De Wolfe (1881–1956), Br. stage actress.

John Wyckham: John Suckling (1926–), Eng. theatre consultant, lighting designer.

Gretchen Wyler: Gretchen Wienecke (1932–), U.S. stage, movie actress.

Julian Wylie: Julian Samuelson (1878–1934), Br. theatre manager.

Bill Wyman: William George Perks (1936–), Eng. rock musician. The Rolling Stones bassist took his new surname from Lee Whyman, a friend made in the 1950s during National Service in the Royal Air Force. He adopted the name by deed poll in 1964.

Jane Wyman: Sarah Jane Faulks (1914–), U.S. movie actress. The actress began her show career in 1933 as a radio singer under the name Jane Durrell.

Patrick Wymark: Patrick Cheeseman (1926–1970), Eng. TV, movie actor. The actor's son, Tristram Wymark (1961–), also an actor, has preserved his father's name and explains its origin: "I'm the only one to keep Dad's original name, Cheeseman. I keep it for its nostalgia. On my passport I have a nice little a.k.a. ... The name Wymark was borrowed initially from my mum's grandfather" [*Sunday Times Magazine*, August 14, 1988].

[Sir] Charles Wyndham: Charles Culverwell (1837–1919), Eng. stage actor, theatre manager. The actor took his new surname in 1860, the year of his first marriage. He legalized the name change in 1886.

Esther Wyndham: Mary Links, née Lutyens (1908–), Eng. novelist. The writer used this name for her magazine serials.

John Wyndham: John Wyndham Parkes Lucas Beynon Harris (1903–1969), Eng. SF, short story writer. The writer used all his many names as pen names at one stage or another, the best known apart from John Wyndham being John Beynon, Lucas Parkes, and Johnson Harris, this last denoting "John, son of Harris."

Tammy Wynette: Virginia Wynette Byrd, née Pugh (1942–), U.S. country singer. The singer was asked by Billy Sherrill, her agent in Nashville, what name she wanted to use professionally. She explained: "It had never occurred to me to change my name but he said, 'I didn't think you'd want to use Byrd since you're getting a divorce, and Pugh doesn't fit you.' I said, 'Well, what does fit me?' He thought for a minute, then said, 'With that blond ponytail you look like a Tammy to me,' I said, 'Well, can I at least keep Wynette?' He said, 'Sure. How about Tammy Wynette?' I left his office saying the name over and over under my breath. It sounded strange, but it sounded right too. 'Tammy Wynette.' I said it out loud. It didn't sound like me, but it sounded like someone I wanted to be. I sensed it was more than just a new name. I felt I was also about to start a new life" [Tammy Wynette, *Stand by Your Man*, 1979].

Peter Wyngarde: Cyril Louis Goldbert (1928–), Br. stage, movie, TV actor, of Eng.-Fr. parentage.

Ed Wynn: Isaiah Edwin Leopold (1886–1966), U.S. stage, movie, radio, TV comedian.

May Wynn: Donna Lee Hickey (1931–), U.S. movie actress.

May Wynne: Mabel Winifred Knowles (1875–1949), Br. writer of popular fiction.

Dana Wynter: Dagmar Spencer-Marcus (1930–), Br.-born S.A. movie actress, working in U.S.

Mark **Wynter:** Terence Lewis (1943–), Eng. pop singer.

Diana **Wynyard:** Dorothy Isobel Cox (1906–1964), Br. stage, movie actress. The actress made her debut on the stage under her new name in 1925 and officially adopted it by deed poll in 1936.

John **Wyse:** John Wise (1904–), Eng. stage actor.

X: Eustace Budgell (1686–1737), Br. essayist. The writer can hardly have been the first to adopt this disguise, and he is unlikely to be the last. He himself used it for contributions to *The Spectator*.

Flying Officer **X:** Herbert Ernest Bates (1905–1974), Eng. novelist. The writer used this rather obvious pseudonym for short stories about the Royal Air Force (in which he was serving as an officer in World War II) collected as *The Greatest People in the World* (1942) and *How Sleep the Brave* (1943). He usually wrote under his real name (in the form H.E. Bates).

Malcolm **X:** Malcolm Little (1925–1965), U.S. black militant leader. The noted nationalist received the conventional Muslim 'X' from Elijah Muhammad (*q.v.*) in 1952. As he explained: "The Muslim's 'X' symbolized the true African family name that he could never know. For me, my 'X' replaced the white slavemaster name of 'Little' which some blue-eyed devil named Little had imposed upon my paternal forebears. ... Mr. Muhammad taught that we would keep this 'X' until God Himself returned and gave us a Holy Name from His own mouth." In 1964 Malcolm broke from the Nation of Islam, the Black Muslim group to which he belonged, and following his hajj (Muslim pilgrimage to Mecca) that year called himself El-Hajj Malik El-Shabazz.[1. Malcolm X, *The Autobiography of Malcolm X*, 1965; 2. *The Listener*, August 8, 1974; 3. *The Times*, November 13, 1992]. See also Michael X (below) and Muhammad Ali.

Michael **X:** Michael de Freitas Abdul Malik (1933–1975), Br. black power leader. The Trinidad-born activist was the son of a black mother and a Portuguese father, originally named Michael de Freitas. On his conversion to the Muslim religion, this became Michael Abdul Malik and subsequently Michael X.

Xanrof: Léon-Alfred Fourneau (1867–1953), Fr. composer, songwriter, by profession a lawyer. The name is certainly distinctive, and was arrived at by translating French *fourneau* ("furnace") into Latin *fornax* and then reversing it. The musician officially adopted the name in 1896.

Xariffa: Mary Ashley Townsend, née Van Voorhis (1832–1901), U.S. poet, essayist, novelist. This is the writer's best known pseudonym. She also wrote as Crab Crossbones, Michael O'Quillo, and Henry Rip. The name is clearly an anagram of "Fairfax," presumably with some private reference.

Xavier: Joseph Xavier Boniface Saintine (1798–1865), Fr. novelist, poet, dramatist.

Ximenes: Derrick Somerset Macnutt (1902–1971), Eng. crossword compiler. Perhaps one of the most imposing and appropriate of all pseudonyms, in view of the significant capital letter. Its bearer, professionally a classics teacher, was responsible for the "Everyman" (to 1963) and harder "Ximenes" puzzles in *The Observer* (from 1939). The name itself is that of Francisco Jiménez de Cisneros (1436–1517), better known in English as Ximenes, the Spanish prelate who became Grand Inquisitor of Castile. Macnutt assumed the name in 1943 when he succeeded to the compilership vacated by doyen cruciverbalist Torquemada (*q.v.*). In the 1930s he contributed crosswords to *The Listener* as Tesremos, his middle name reversed.

X.L.: Julian Field (1849–1925), Br. novelist, writer. An obviously meaningful duo of initials, apparently quite unrelated to the writer's real name.

Yigael **Yadin:** Yigael Sukenik (1917–1984), Israeli archaeologist, military leader.

Yakov **Yakovlev:** Yakov Arkadyevich Epshteyn (Epstein) (1896–1938), Russ. Communist official.

Mari **Yan:** María Flora Yáñez de Echeverria (1898– ?), Chilean novelist, short story writer.

Vasily **Yan:** Vasily Grigoryevich Yanchevetsky (1874–1954), Russ. writer. A rather radical pruning of an original surname.

Yana: Pamela Guard (1932–1989), Br. stage, movie actress, TV singer.

Tukhvat **Yanabi:** Tukhvatulla Kalimullovich Kalimullin (1894–1939), Russ. (Bashkir) poet. The poet adopted the name of his native village as his pen name.

Jean **Yanne:** Jean Gouyé (or Gouillé) (1933–), Fr. movie actor, director.

Yanni: Yanni Chryssomallis (1954–), Gk.-born U.S. popular musician.

Yan Tsygan: Ivan Karpovich Kuksenko (1911–1958), Russ. wrestler, circus artist. The performer's name, meaning "Jan the Gypsy," hardly reflects his strongman feats, which included bending an iron girder across his shoulders and tying a tie made of iron bars.

Yemelyan Mikhaylovich **Yaroslavsky:** Miney Izrailevich Gubelman (Hubelman) (1878–1943), Russ. historian, revolutionary, Communist. The activist abandoned his Jewish name in favor of a "Christian" one (ironically, as he was a militant atheist).

Kamil **Yashen:** Kamil Nugmanov (1909–), Uzbek writer. The writer's adopted name means "lightning."

Aleksandr **Yashin:** Aleksandr Yakovlevich Popov (1913–1968), Russ. writer. The writer's adopted name was based on Yasha, the familiar form of Yakov. This was the name of the father he had never known, for he was killed in World War I when his baby son was only a year old.

Dornford **Yates:** [Major] Cecil William Mercer (1885–1960), Eng. novelist. The author of a series of books about "Berry" Pleydell and his family, popular between the wars, adopted the maiden names of his grandmothers to form his pen name. He first used it for a piece published in *Punch* in 1910.

Peyo **Yavorov:** Peyo Kracholov (1877–1914), Bulg. poet, playwright. The writer adopted a plant name meaning "sycamore."

Yana **Yazova:** Lyuba Gancheva (1912–1974), Bulg. poet, novelist.

Yazz: Yasmin Marie Evans (1960–), Jamaican-Eng. pop singer.

Yefrem II: Grigory Shiovich Sidamonidze (1896–1972), Georgian catholicos. The head of the Georgian Orthodox Church received his name on taking monastic vows in 1922. The name itself corresponds to English Ephraim, said to mean "fruitful."

Dominik Ivanovich **Yefremov:** Mikhail Yefremovich Shteynman (Steinman) (1881–1925), Latvian-born Russ. Communist official.

D.J. **Yella:** Antoine Carraby (*c.*1967–), U.S. black "gangsta" rapper. "Yella" relates to the artist's vocal delivery.

Yellow Bird: John Rollin Ridge (1827–1867), U.S. writer, journalist. The writer was the son of a Cherokee and a white woman, and his pen name was the translation of his Cherokee name.

Sydney **Yendys:** Sydney Thompson Dobell (1824–1874), Br. poet, critic. The writer was for-tunate to have a first name that lent itself reasonably readily to reversal like this.

Yerukhan: Yervand Srmakeshkhanlyan: (1870–1915), Armenian writer. A practical shortening of a lengthy original name.

Yetim Emin: Magomed-Emin, son of Sevzikhan (1838–1884), Dagestani (Lezgian) poet. The writer replaced the first part of his personal name by a word meaning "hapless," "orphaned."

Irodion **Yevdoshvili:** Irodion Isakiyevich Khositashvili (1873–1916), Georgian poet. The poet based his new surname on his mother's first name, Yevdokiya (Eudocia). The Georgian suffix -*shvili* corresponds to English -*son*.

Mr. **Yorick:** Laurence Sterne (1713–1768), Ir. writer. The author of *Tristram Shandy* used this name for sermons and other writings, as well as in his *Sentimental Journey*, taking it from the "lively, witty, sensible, and heedless parson" in the former work. The character himself believes he was probably descended from Hamlet's gravedigger of this name.

Andrew **York:** Christopher Robin Nicole (1930–), Guyanese crime, mystery writer. The writer has used a range of male and female pseudonyms. The former include Daniel Adams, Leslie Arlen, Robin Cade, Peter Grange, Mark Logan and the above; the latter embrace Caroline Gray, Christina Nicolson, and Alison York.

Michael **York:** Michael Hugh Johnson (1942–), Eng. movie actor.

Susannah **York:** Susannah Yolande Fletcher (1941–), Eng. movie actress. There are two vying accounts behind the name. York herself claims that it arose when she was learning about the Wars of the Roses as a child and started calling herself Susannah York Fletcher, substituting "York" for her middle name. But the actress's sister is on record as saying that she got her name by simply opening a telephone directory and sticking a pin in [ITV program, *This Is Your Life* November 11, 1983]. The first version is perhaps nearer the truth.

Stephen **Yorke:** Mary Linskill (1840–1891), Eng. novelist. The writer was born in Yorkshire, and many of her novels are set in that county.

Banana **Yoshimoto:** Mahoko Yoshimoto (1964–), Jap. novelist. The popular novelist chose a new name with a view to a world market for her writing: "It is sexless, it's funny and it can be used abroad" [*The Times Magazine*, November 9, 1996].

Bernard **Youens:** Bernard Popley (1914–1984), Br. stage, TV actor.

Gig **Young:** Byron Ellsworth Barr (1913–1978), U.S. stage, movie, TV actor. The actor took his name from the character that he played in the movie *The Gay Sisters* (1942). He had earlier used the name Bryant Fleming. The change was necessary because there was another actor appearing under the name Byron Barr.

Jesse Colin **Young:** Perry Miller (1944–), U.S. rock musician.

Loretta **Young:** Gretchen Michaela Young (1913–), U.S. movie actress, sister of Sally Blane (*q.v.*). The actress's first name was changed to Loretta by Colleen Moore (*q.v.*), who discovered her as a 14-year-old extra in *Her Wild Oat* (1928). Miss Moore explained that Loretta was the name of "the most beautiful doll I ever had."

Marian **Young:** Martha Deane (1908–1973), U.S. radio host.

Stephen **Young:** Stephen Levy (1939–), Can. movie actor.

Irving **Younger:** Irving Yoskowitz (1932–1988), U.S. lawyer, writer.

Marguerite **Yourcenar:** Marguerite de Crayencour (1903–1987), Fr. historical novelist, of Belg.-Fr. parentage, working in U.S. The writer's pen name is a near anagram of her real surname (omitting one "c").

Sakari **Yrjö-Koskinen:** Georg Zacharias Forsman (1830–1903), Finn. historian, politician. The politician adopted his grandiose name when he was made a baron.

Ysgafell: Jane Williams (1806–1885), Eng.-born Welsh writer. The writer was a distant relative of the Puritan preacher, Henry Williams (1624–1684), and took her pseudonym from the name of his farm, Ysgafell, near Newtown, Montgomeryshire (now Powys).

P.B. **Yuill:** Gordon Williams (1939–), Sc. journalist, crime writer + Terry Venables (1943–), Br. footballer, crime writer. The name looks like an anagram. But of what? Perhaps "Billy" is involved.

Yuriko: Yuriko Kikuchi (1920–), U.S. ballet dancer, teacher, choreographer, of Jap. parentage.

Blanche **Yurka:** Blanche Jurka (1887–1974), U.S. stage, movie actress. Presumably the actress modified the spelling of her surname to ensure its proper pronunciation, i.e. not as "Jerker."

Aleksandr **Yuzhin:** Aleksandr Ivanovich Sumbatov (1857–1927), Russ. playwright, actor, theatrical director.

Y.Y.: Robert Lynd (1879–1949), Ir. essayist. The writer used this name for his contributions to weekly magazines, first in the *Nation*, then in the *New Statesman*. Presumably the pseudonym was an elaboration of the vowel in his surname, unless it was intended to suggest "wise."

Zadkiel: Richard James Morrison (1795–1874), Eng. naval officer, astrologer. The writer used the name for his astrological predictions, published in *Zadkiel's Almanack*. The name itself is that of the angel of the planet Jupiter in Rabbinical angelology.

Zagorka: Maria Jurić (1873–1957), Croatian novelist, playwright.

Vladimir **Zagorsky:** Vladimir Mikhaylovich Lubotsky (1883–1919), Russ. revolutionary.

[Sir] Basil **Zaharoff:** Basileios Zacharias (1849–1936), Turk.-born Fr. armament contractor, intelligence agent, of Gk. parentage.

Tony **Zale:** Anthony Florian Zaleski (1913–1997), U.S. boxer of Pol. descent.

Máté **Zalka:** Béla Frankl (1896–1937), Hung. writer, revolutionary.

Pyotr **Zamoysky:** Pyotr Ivanovich Zevalkin (1896–1958), Russ. writer. The writer adopted a name that had pleasanter connotations than his original surname (which suggests Russian *zevaka*, "idler," "gaper").

Mariya **Zankovetskaya:** Mariya Konstantinovna Adasovskaya (1860–1934), Ukrainian stage actress, theatre manager. The actress took her stage name from the village of her birth, Zanki.

Zanne: Auguste van Dekerkove (1838–1923), Fr. occultist. The practitioner assumed his new name in 1894, claiming it had been given him by "spiritual masters."

Gabriela **Zapolska:** Maria Gabriela Janowska, née Korwin-Piotrowska (1857–1921), Pol. novelist, playwright. The writer's assumed name emphasizes her nationality. An earlier name was Józef Maskoff.

Pantaley **Zarev:** Pantaley Yordanov Pantov (1911–), Bulg. literary critic.

Mikhas **Zaretsky:** Mikhail Yefimovich Kosenkov (1901–), Belorussian writer.

Yefrosiniya **Zarnitskaya:** Yefrosiniya Filippovna Azguridi (1867–1936), Ukrainian stage actress.

Nairi **Zaryan:** Ayastan Yegiazaryan (1900–1969), Armenian writer.

Yanis **Zébgos:** Yanis Talagánes (1899–1947), Gk. Communist, historian.

Franco **Zeffirelli:** Gianfranco Corsi (1923–), It. movie director, designer, operatic producer.

Zélide: Isabelle Agnès Élizabeth de Charrière, née Isabella van Tuyll van Servooskerken van Zuylen (1740–1805), Du.-born Fr. novelist, autobiographer. The writer gave herself the name in an early self-portrait, apparently basing it on her birthplace, Zuylen, near Utrecht. See also Abbé de la Tour.

Zelda: Zelda Shneurson Mishkovsky (1914–1984), Ukrainian-born Israeli poet.

Eugen **Zetternam:** Jos Josef Diricksens (1826–1855), Belg. writer.

Alexandre **Zevaès:** Gustave Alexandre Bourson (1873–1953), Fr. politician, lawyer, historian. The writer seems to have based his new surname on reversed syllables in his first two names.

Praskovya **Zhemchugova:** Praskovya Ivanovna Kovalyova (1768–1803), Russ. actress, opera singer.

Iosif **Zhinovich:** Iosif Iosifovich Zhidovich (1907–), Russ. conductor, composer. The musician altered one letter of his name to avoid the suggestion of Russian *zhid*, an offensive word for a Jew (akin to English *Yid*).

Vladimir **Zhirinovsky:** Vladimir Volfovich Eydelshteyn (Edelstein) (1946–), Russ. nationalist leader. The populist politician changed his surname in 1964 to conceal his Jewish origins.

Zico: Artur Antunes Coimbra (1953–), Brazilian footballer.

Pavle **Zidar:** Zdravko Slamnik (1932–), Slovakian writer.

Kamen **Zidarov:** Todor Sibev Manov (1902–), Bulg. writer.

Anne **Ziegler:** Irene Frances Eastwood (1910–), Eng. romantic singer, teaming with Webster Booth (1902–1984), whom she married in 1938. An unusual substitution of a foreign-sounding name for an English one.

Grigory **Zinoviev:** Ovsel Gershon Aronov Radomyslsky (1883–1936), Russ. revolutionary, of Jewish parentage.

Zito: Jose Eli de Miranda (1932–), Brazilian footballer.

Jovan **Zmaj:** Jovan Jovanović (1833–1904), Serbian poet. The poet adopted the name of the satirical journal for which he wrote. Its own name means "Snake."

Zoke: Michael Attwell (1943–), Eng. political cartoonist. The artist devised his name from those of his children, Zoe and Jake.

Miro **Zolan:** Miroslav Zlochovsky (1926–), Cz.-Br. ballet dancer, choreographer.

Zoli: Zoltán Rendessy (1941–1982), Hung.-born U.S. male model.

A. **Zorich:** Vasily Timofeyevich Lokot (1899–1937), Russ. writer.

Vera **Zorina:** Eva Brigitta Hartwig (1917–), Ger. ballet dancer, stage, movie actress, of Norw. parentage, working in U.S. The dancer adopted the Russian-sounding name in 1934 on joining the Monte Carlo Ballets Russes of Colonel de Basil (*q.v.*).

Stefan **Zoryan:** Stefan Arakelyan (1890–1967), Armenian writer.

Zouzou: Danielle Ciarlet (1944–), Fr. movie actress. The actress adopted a childhood nickname as her screen name. The name itself is a characteristic pet doublet name, and may have derived from the repeated second syllable of *oiseau*, "bird."

Zozimus: Michael Moran (*c*.1794–1846), Ir. balladist, street entertainer. The Dublin performer took his name from a character in Bishop Anthony Cole's "Life of St. Mary of Egypt," which he recited in a verse version.

Zucchero: Aldelmo Fornaciari (1956–), It. pop singer. The singer adopted his childhood nickname, meaning "sugar."

Z.Z.: Louis Zangwill (1869–1938), Eng. novelist, of Russ. Jewish parentage. The writer, brother of the better-known Israel Zangwill (1864–1926), adopted a name that capitalized (literally) on his initial, at the same time ensuring his exclusive position at the end of any alphabetical listing.

Part III
Appendices

A Prefatory Note

An investigation into the 3,000 aliases used by Mr. Sidney Phserowsky ... is to be undertaken (news item, *The Times,* June 7, 1986).

The five appendices that follow are effectively a bonus to the rest of the book. But they are an interesting bonus, and in many ways an important one.

Appendix 1 is a complete list of the 173 pseudonyms used at one time or another by Voltaire (which is itself a pseudonym, of course). They are taken from the Bibliothèque Nationale *Catalogue Général,* ccxiv (1978), i, pp. 162–166 (*Pseudonymes de Voltaire, noms sur lesquels il a écrit, formules ou qualifications sous lesquelles il s'est déguisé* [Pseudonyms of Voltaire, names under which he has written, phrases or designations under which he has disguised himself]. Many of the names were for satirical writings, hence the predominance of religious and professional names and titles for this most outspoken critic of his age. English translations are provided for some of the more obscure (and translatable) French names and titles adopted.

Appendix 2 is a similar list of 198 pseudonyms adopted by Daniel Defoe. The listing is probably not entirely complete, but it is full

enough, and in quantity overvaults Voltaire's total. Many of the names were used for Defoe's pamphlets, and reflect the passion and prolificity of his political writings, as well as his vivid imagination and attention to detail. In many ways Defoe's pseudonyms can be compared to those of Voltaire, and both men were outspoken thinkers and polemicists who were active at approximately the period, the first half of the 18th century.

Appendix 3 is a listing of recent or current writers' multiple pen names. It has its own introduction.

Appendix 4 is a select listing of French official name changes. It, too, has its own introduction.

Appendix 5 concerns *real* names, meaning those that their bearers retained but that in some cases are wrongly taken to be pseudonyms. A listing follows of sports personalities who kept their surnames but adopted their nicknames as their new first name. Such names blend the real with the pseudonymous.

1. Pseudonyms Used by Voltaire
*With translations where appropriate**

Firmin Abauzit
Abbé***
Abbé B**

Un académicien de Berlin (An Academician
    from Berlin)
Un académicien de Londres, de Boulogne, de

*Where pseudonyms resemble first-plus-last-name or contain a surname, they are entered alphabetically under that last name; otherwise arrangement is alphabetical by first main word.

Pétersbourg, de Berlin, etc. (An Academician from London, Boulogne, Petersburg, Berlin, etc.)

Un académicien de Lyon (An Academician from Lyons)

Jacques Aimon

Le Docteur Akakia, médecin du pape (Doctor Akakia, physician to the Pope)

Le Rabbin Akib (Rabbi Akib)

Irénée Aléthès, professor du droit dans le canton suisse d'Uri (Irénée Aléthès, professor of law in the Swiss canton of Uri)

Ivan Aléthof, secrétaire de l'Ambassade russe (Ivan Aléthof, secretary at the Russian embassy)

Alexis, archevêque de Novogorod (Alexis, archbishop of Novgorod)

Amabed

Un Amateur de belles-lettres (A Lover of the Humanities)

Archevêque de Cantorbéry (Archbishop of Canterbury)

Abbé d'Arty

Un auteur célèbre qui s'est retiré de France (A Famous Author Who Has Left France)

L'Auteur de "L'Homme aux quarante écus" (The Author of "The Man with Forty Crowns")

L'Auteur de la tragédie de "Sémiramis" (The Author of the Tragedy "Semiramis")

L'Auteur de la tragédie des "Guèbres" (The Author of the Tragedy "The Gabars")

L'Auteur du "Compère Marhieu" (The Author of "Comrade Mathieu") Le Sieur Aveline

George Avenger

Un avocat de Besançon (An Advocate from Besançon)

Un avocat de province (A Provincial Advocate)

Un bachelier ubiquiste (A Ubiquitous Graduate)

Feu l'abbé Bazin (The Late Father Bazin)

Beaudinet, citoyen de Neufchâtel (Beaudinet, citizen of Neufchâtel)

Une belle dame (A Beautiful Lady)

Ancien avocat Belleguier (Former Advocate Belleguier)

Un bénédictin (A Benedictine)

Un bénédictin de Franche-Comté (A Benedictine from Franche-Comté)

Abbé Bigex

Abbé Bigore

Lord Bolingbroke

Joseph Bourdillon, professeur en droit public (Joseph Bourdillon, professor of civil law)

Un bourgeois de Genève (A Townsman of Geneva)

Le Pasteur Bourn (Pastor Bourn)

Abbé Caille

Caius Memmius Gemellus

Dom Calmet

Jérôme Carré

Cass***, avocat au Conseil du Roi (Cass***, advocate to the King's Council)

Cassen, avocat au Conseil du Roi (Cassen, advocate to the King's Council)

M. de Chambon

Chapelain du Cte de Chesterfield (Chaplain to the Count of Chesterfield)

Le Papa Nicolas Charisteski

Un chrétien... (A Christian...)

Le Chrétien errant (The Wandering Christian)

Les Cinquante (The Fifty)

Un Citoyen de Genève (A Citizen of Geneva)

Claire

Clocpitre

Cte de Corbera

Lord Cornsbury

Le Corps des Pasteurs du Gévaudan (The Pastors of Gévaudan)

Robert Covelle

Cubstorf, pasteur de Helmstad (Cubstorf, pastor of Helmstad)

Le Curé de Frêne (The Vicar of Frêne)

D., chapelain de S.E. Mgr le Cte de K... (D., chaplain to His Eminence Monseigneur the Count of K...)

D*** M***

Cte Da...

Damilaville

George Aronger Dardelle

M. de la Caille

De la Lindelle

M. de La Visclède

M. de L'Ècluse

Chevr de M...re

Chevr de Molmire

Chevr de Morton

M. de Morza

Démad

Feu M. de Saint-Didier (The Late M. de Saint-Didier)

Chevr de Saint-Gile

Abbé de Saint-Pierre

Des Amateurs (Some Devotees)

Desjardins

Desmahis

Gaillard d'Ètallonde de Morival

Abbé de Tilladet
Cte de Tournay
Mis de Villette (Marquis de Villette)
Mis de Ximénez (Marquis de Ximenez)
John Dreamer
Anne Dubourg
Dumarsais [Du Marsay], philosophe
Dumoulin
M. le Chevr Durand (Knight Durand)
Un ecclésiastique (An Ecclesiastic)
R.P. Èlie, carme chaussé (The Reverend Father
    Elias, calced Carmelite)
Èratou
Èvhémère
Fatema
Formey
Le P. Fouquet (Father Fouquet)
Un Frère de la Doctrine chrétienne (A Brother
    of the Christian Doctrine)
Le Gardien des Capucins de Raguse (The
    Guardian of the Capuchins of Ragusa)
Un gentilhomme (A Gentleman)
Gérofle
Dr Good Natur'd Wellwisher
Dr Goodheart
Charles Gouju
Gabriel Grasset et associés (Gabriel Grasset
    and Partners)
Un homme de lettres (A Man of Letters)
Hude, échevin d'Amsterdam (Hude, deputy
    mayor of Amsterdam)
M. Huet [Hut]
L'Humble Èvêque d'Alétopolis (The Humble
    Bishop of Alétopolis)
Hume, prêtre écossais (Hume, a Scottish
    priest)
L'Ignorant (The Ignorant One)
Imhof
Le Jésuite des anguilles (The Jesuit of the Eels)
Un jeune abbé (A Young Priest)
Major Kaiserling
M. L***
Joseph Laffichard
Lantin, neveu de M. Lantin et de feu l'abbé
    Bazin (Lantin, Nephew of M. Lantin and of
    the Late Father Bazin)
Le Neveu de l'abbé Bazin (The Nephew of
    Father Bazin)
R.P. L'Escarbotier
Mairet
M. Mamaki
Abbé Mauduit
M. de Mauléon

Maxime de Madaure
Un membre du Conseil de Zurich (A Member
    of the Zurich Council)
Un membre des nouveaux conseils (A Member
    of the New Council)
Un membre d'un corps (A Member of a Body)
Le Curé Meslier
Prêtre Montmolin
Le Muphti
Naigeon
Needham
Docteur Obern
Cte Passeran
Le Physicien de Saint-Flour
Plusieurs Aumôniers (Several Chaplains)
Jean Plokof
R.P. Polycarpe, prieur des Bernardins de
    Chésery (The Reverend Father Polycarp,
    prior of the Bernardines of Chésery)
Un professeur de droit public (A Professor of
    Civil Law)
Un proposant (A Divinity Student)
Un quaker (A Quaker)
Le P. Quesnel
Le Dr Ralph
Genest Ramponeau
Rapterre [Parterre]
Don Apuleius Risorius
Josias Rossette
La Roupilière
Sadi
Saint-Hiacinte
Scarmentado
Le Secrétaire de M. de Voltaire (The Secretary
    to M. de Voltaire)
Le Secrétaire du prince Dolgorouki (The Sec-
    retary to Prince Dolgoruky)
Mr. Sherloc
Une société de bacheliers en théologie (A
    Group of Theology Graduates)
Soranus, médecin de Trajan (Soranus, Physi-
    cian to Trajan)
Abbé Tamponet
Sieur Tamponet, docteur en Sorbonne (Mr.
    Tamponet, doctor at the Sorbonne)
Théro
Thomson
Tompson [Thomson]
Trois avocats d'un Parlement (Three Advocates
    of One Parliament)
Un Turc (A Turk)
Antoine Vadé
Catherine Vadé

Guillaume Vadé
Verzenot
Le Vieillard du Mont-Caucase (The Old Man
    of Mt. Caucasus)

Un vieux capitaine de cavalerie (An Old Cav-
    alry Captain)
Youssouf
Dominico Zapata

2. Pseudonyms Used by Daniel Foe, Better Known as Daniel Defoe

A.A.A.
A B.
A Citizen Who Lives the
    Whole Time in London
A.G.
A.M.G.
A.Z.
Abed
Abigail
All-Hide
Aminadab
Ancient
Andronicus
Anglipolski of Lithuania
Anne
Antiaethiops
Anti-Bubble
Anti-Bubbler
Anticationist
Hen. Antifogger, Jr.
Anti-Italik
Anti-Jobber
Anti-King-Killer
Anti-Pope
Antiplot
Anthony Antiplot
Antisycoph
The Author of the "Trueborn
    Englishman"
Bankrupt
Tom Bankrupt
Barinda
Tom Beadle
Tom A. Bedlam
Obadiah Blue Hat
Betty Blueskin

Nicholas Boggle
William Bond
Anthony Broadheart
Bubble
C.M.
Callipedia
Christopher Carefull
Cataline
Caution
Henry Caution, Jr.
Sir Timothy Caution
Celibacy
Sir Malcontent Chagrin
Chesapeake
Combustion
Conscientia
A Converted Thief
The Corporal
Coventry
Credulous
D —
D.D.F.
D.F., Gent.
Daniel De Foe
Daniel DeFoe
Democritus
Diogenes
Jeremiah Dry-Boots
E.S.
Eleanor
Elevator
Mr. Eminent
An English Gentleman
An Englishman at the Court
    of Hanover
Enigma

The Enquirer
Epidemicus
T. Experience
Eye Witness
Dan D.F — e
Count Kidney Face
Frank Faithfull
A Familiar Spirit
Henry Fancy, Jr.
The Farmer
The Father of Modern Prose
    Fiction
Penelope Firebrand
Floretina
A Freeholder
Harry Freeman
Furioso
Furious
G.
G.B.
G.M.
G.T.
G.Y.
A Gentleman
Grateful
Gunpowder
Gyaris
H.
H.R.
Thomas Horncastle
Autho' Hubble Bubble
Hubble-Bubble
Humanity
Hushai
Anthony Impartiality
Jack Indifferent

The Inoculator
Insolvent
P. Ivy
John-Joan
Journal
L.L.L.
A Layman
Leicestershire
Libertas
Liberty
Leonard Love-Wit
Theophilus Lovewit
Lionel Lye-Alone
Livery Man
M.G.
Tom Manywife
Lady Marjory
Miranda Meanwell
Meeting House
A Member
A Member of the Honourable
    House of Commons
Meteor
A Ministering Friend of the
    People Called Quakers
Miser
Misericordia
Modern
Moll
Andrew Moreton, Merchant
Myra
N.B.
N — Upon Trent

Nelly
The New Convert
New Whig
Andrew Newport
Nicety
Oliver Oldway
One, Two, Three, Four
Orthodox
Patience
Abel Peaceable
Phil — Arguros
Mrs. Philo — Britannia
Philo — Royalist
Philygeia
Jonathan Problematick
Protestant Neutrality
Prudential
Quarantine
Anthony Quiet
Quietness
Quinquampoix
Arina Donna Quixota
R.R.
R.S.
Rebel
L.M. Regibus
Anthony Tom Richard
S.
S.B.
T. Sadler
Same Friend Who Wrote to
    Thomas Bradbury, etc.
Fello De Se

Sempronicus
Sincerity
Jeffrey Sing-Song
Spanish
A Sufferer
The Sunny Gentleman
T.B.
T.E.
T.L.
Talionis
T. Taylor
Tea-Table
Termagant
Theo-Philo
Thunder-Bolt
Sir Fopling Tittle-Tattle
Tranquillity
Timothy Trifle
Boatswain Trinkolo
True Love
The Trustee
Tom Turbulent
Urgentissimus
Vale
W.L.
Wallnutshire
Solomon Waryman
Weeping Winifred
White Witch
Woman Witch'd
A Young Cornish Gentleman

3. Writers with Multiple Pen Names

A very large number of writers have pen-names (J.A. Cuddon, A Dictionary of Literary Terms, 1977).

"Pen name" is an English translation of French *nom de plume*, a term that has also entered English in the same sense to denote a literary pseudonym. (It is no longer used by the French, however, who know it by the broader and less specific word *pseudonyme*).

For the reasons considered in the introductory chapters to this book, some writers assume a number of pen names, and it is interesting to see what they are. In many cases there is no obvious link with the bearer's real name, although there may well be a similarity between one pen name and another. From the practical point of view, the writer simply employs the same skill as that used to create names for a novel's fictional characters. The current state of the art may be judged by what follows, as the 20th-century equivalent of the many names and titles devised by Daniel Defoe and Voltaire (in Appendices 1 and 2 above).

The names are often unremarkable, although some clearly have associations. Thus, two of Ballard's names are Parker Bonner, evoking Bonnie Parker, of "Bonnie and Clyde" notoriety, and Sam Bowie, suggesting Jim Bowie, of Bowie knife fame. Norwood actually uses Jim Bowie as one of his names. He also has Vince Destry, from his first name and the surname of Tom Destry, the fictional lawman who is the hero of Faust's novel *Destry Rides Again* (1930), written under his own pen name of Max Brand.

Readers scanning the names may have an apparent sense of déjà vu on finding Volsted Gridban listed twice, for both Fearn and Tubb. But this is correct, since it was one of the "house names" assigned to Tubb by his publishers, Scion Press. (Gridban, incidentally, appears to be an anagram of "brigand." However, only the name's deviser can vouch for this origin.)

Note that, unlike the main entries in this book, the writer's *real* name is given first, followed by his or her nationality, birth and death years, and type of fiction. (Where there are no death years, the writers were living at the time their names were recorded.) The pen names are then given. As will be seen, their bearers are chiefly crime, fantasy, or SF writers or else the authors of westerns or romantic fiction. Some of the names feature in the main entries in the book, where their origins may be found.

Michael Angelo **Avallone**, Jr. (U.S. popular novelist, 1924): James Blaine, Nick Carter, Troy Conway, Priscilla Dalton, Mark Dane, Jean-Anne De Pre, Dora Highland, Steve Michaels, Dorothea Nile, Ed Noon, Edwina Noone, John Patrick, Vance Staton, Sidney Stuart.

Willis Todhunter **Ballard** (U.S. western writer, 1903–1980): Brian Agar, P.D. Ballard, Todhunter Ballard, Parker Bonner, Sam Bowie, Hunter D'Allard, Brian Fox, Harrison Hunt, George Hunter, John Hunter, Neil McNeil, John Shepherd, Jack Slade, Clay Turner.

David Ernest **Bingley** (Eng. crime, western novelist, 1920): Bart Adams, Adam Benson, Adam Bridger, Abe Canuck, Dave Carver, Larry Chatham, Henry Chesham, Will Coltman, Ed Coniston, Luke Dorman, George Fallon, David Horsley, Bat Jefford, Syd Kingston, Eric Lynch, James Martell, Colin North, Ben Plummer, Caleb Prescott, Mark Remington, John Roberts, Steve Romney, Frank Silvester, Henry Starr, Link Tucker, Christopher Igan, Roger Yorke.

Henry Kenneth **Bulmer** (Eng. historical novelist, SF writer, 1921): Alan Burt Akers, Ken Blake, Frank Brandon, Ernest Corley, Arthur Frazier, Kenneth Johns, Philip Kent, Bruno Krauss, Neil Langholm, Karl Maras, Charles R. Pike, Andrew Quiller, Nelson Sherwood, Richard Silver, Philip Stratford, Tully Zetford.

John **Creasey** (Eng. crime novelist, 1908–1973): Gordon Ashe, Margaret Cooke, M.E. Cooke, Henry St. John Cooper, Norman Deane, Elise Fecamps, Robert Caine Frazer, Patrick Gill, Michael Halliday, Charles Hogarth, Brian Hope, Colin Hughes, Kyle Hunt, Abel Mann, Peter Manton, J.J. Marric, James Marsden, Richard Martin, Rodney Mattheson, Anthony Morton, Ken Ranger, William K. Reilly, Tex Riley, Jeremy York.

Dorothy **Daniels** (U.S. romantic novelist, 1915): Danielle Dorsett, Angela Gray, Cynthia Kavanaugh, Helaine Ross, Suzanne Somers, Geraldine Thayer, Helen Gray Weston.

Leslie Purnell **Davies** (Eng. mystery, fantasy writer, 1914): Leo Berne, Robert Blake, Richard Bridgeman, Morgan Evans, Ian Jefferson, Lawrence Peters, Thomas Philips, G.K. Thomas, Leslie Vardre, Rowland Welch.

Robert Lionel **Fanthorpe** (Eng. SF writer, 1935): Erle Barton, Lee Barton, Thornton Bell, Leo Brett, Bron Fane, Victor La Salle, Robert Lionel, J.E. Muller, Philip Nobel, Lionel Roberts, Neil Thanet, Trebor Thorpe, Pel Torro, Olaf Trent, Karl Ziegfried.

Frederic Schiller **Faust** (U.S. mystery, western novelist, 1892–1944): Frank Austin, George Owen Baxter, Lee Bolt, Max Brand, Walter C. Butler, George Challis, Peter Dawson, Martin Dexter, Evin Evan, Evan Evans, John Frederick,

Frederick Frost, Dennis Lawton, David Manning, M.B., Peter Henry Morland, Hugh Owen, Nicholas Silver, Henry Uriel.

John Russell **Fearn** (Eng. SF writer, 1908–1960): Geoffrey Armstrong, Thornton Ayre, Hugo Blayn, Dennis Clive, John Cotton, Polton Cross, Astron del Martia, Spike Gordon, Volsted Gridban, Conrad G. Holt, Frank Jones, Paul Lorraine, Jed McNab, Dom Passante, Laurence F. Rose, John Russell, Brian Shaw, John Slate, Vargo Statten, Earl Titan, Ephraim Winiki.

Lee **Floren** (U.S. western novelist, 1910): Brett Austin, Lisa Franchon, Claudia Hall, Wade Hamilton, Matt Harding, Matthew Whitman Harding, Felix Lee Horton, Stuart Jason, Grace Lang, Marguerite Nelson, Lew Smith, Maria Sandra Sterling, Lee Thomas, Len Turner, Will Watson, Matthew Whitman, Dave Wilson.

John **Glassco** (Can. writer, poet, 1909–1981): Sylvia Beyer, Buffy, George Colman, S. Colson-Haig, Grace Davignon, W.P.R. Eady, Albert Eddy, Silas M. Gooch, George Henderson, Nordyk Nudleman, Hideki Okada, Jean de Saint-Luc, Miles Underwood.

Terence William **Harknett** (Eng. crime, western novelist, 1936): Frank Chandler, David Ford, George G. Gilman, Adam Hardy, Jane Harman, Joseph Hedges, William M. James, Charles R. Pike, William Pine, James Russell, Thomas H. Stone, William Terry.

Henry John **Keevill** (Eng. western novelist, 1914–1978): Clay Allison, Burt Alvord, Bill Bonney, Virgil Earp, Wes Harding, Frank McLowery, Burt Mossman, Mark Reno, Johnny Ringo, Will Travis.

Albert **King** (Eng. SF writer, 1934): Ken Albion, Mark Bannon, Walt Brennan, Catherine Brent, Wade Bronson, Jim Cleveland, Paul Conrad, Craig Cooper, Joel Creedi, Steve Dallas, Reece Doan, Eli Driscoll, Wallace Ford, Lee Foreman, Evan Foster, Floyd Gibson, Matt Gifford, Simon Girty, Brad Hammond, Ross Harlan, Gil Harmon, Art Hoffman, Tom Holland, Scott Howell, Nelson Hoyt, Mark Kane, Janice Kelsey, Lee Kimber, Ames King, Berta King, Christopher King, Carl Mason, Paul Muller, Clint Ogden, Ray Owen, Bart Prender, Alvin Ripley, Walt Santee, Grover Scott, Cole Shelby, Dean Taggart, Ellis Tyler, Simon Waldron, Agnes Wallace, Lewis Wetzel, Steve Yarbo.

Leonard **Levinson** (U.S. crime novelist, 1935): Nicholas Brady, Lee Chang, Glen Chase,

Richard Hale Curtis, Gordon Davis, Clay Dawson, Nelson De Mille, Josh Edwards, Richard Gallagher, March Hastings, J. Farragut Jones, Leonard Jordan, Philip Kirk, John Mackie, Robert Novak, Philip Rawls, Bruno Rossi, Jonathon Scofield, Jonathon Trask, Cynthia Wilkerson.

John **Marsh** (Eng. romantic, mystery novelist, 1907): Julia Davis, John Elton, John Harvey, Irene Lawrence, Joan Marsh, Grace Richmond, Petra Sawley, Monica Ware, Lilian Woodward.

Christopher Robin **Nicole** (Guyanese-born Br. crime, mystery writer, 1930): Daniel Adams, Leslie Arlen, Robin Cade, Peter Grange, Nicholas Grant, Caroline Gray, Mark Logan, Simon McKay, Christina Nicholson, Robin Nicolson, Alan Savage, Alison York, Andrew York.

Victor G.C. **Norwood** (Eng. western novelist, 1920): Coy Banton, Shane V. Baxter, Jim Bowie, Clay Brand, Victor Brand, Paul Clevinger, Walt Cody, Shayne Colter, Craig Corteen, Wes Corteen, Clint Dangerfield, Johnny Dark, Vince Destry, Doone Fargo, Mark Fenton, Wade Fisher, G. Gearing-Thomas, Mark Hampton, Hank Jansen, Nat Karta, Whip McCord, Brett Rand, Brad Regan, Shane Russell, Mark Shane, Rhondo Shane, Victor Shane, Jim Tressidy.

Lauran Bosworth **Paine** (U.S. western novelist, 1916): Roy Ainsworthy, Clay Allen, Rosa Almonte, A.A. Andrews, John Armour, Kathleen Bartlett, Reg Batchelor, Harry Beck, Kenneth Bedford, Will Benton, Frank Bosworth, Will Bradford, Concho Bradley, Will Brennan, Mark Carrel, Nevada Carter, Claude Cassady, Richard Clarke, Robert Clarke, Clint Custer, Amber Dana, Richard Dana, Audrey Davis, J.F. Drexler, Antoinette Duchesne, John Durham, Margot Fisher, Betty Fleck, Joni Frost, Donn Glendenning, James Glenn, Angela Gordon, Beth Gorman, Francis Hart, Jay Hayden, Helen Holt, Will Houston, Elizabeth Howard, Roy Howard, John Hunt, Jared Ingersol, Ray Kelley, Kack Ketchum, John Kilgore, Hunter Liggett, J.K. Lucas, Buck Lyon, Bruce Martin, Tom Martin, Angela Morgan, Arlene Morgan, Frank Morgan, John Morgan, Valerie Morgan, Clint O'Connor, Jon Pindell, Arthur St. George, Helen Sharp, Jim Slaughter, Buck Standish, Margaret Stuart, Russ Thompson, Barbara Thorne, P.F. Undine.

William Edward Daniel **Ross** (Can. novelist, 1912): Leslie Ames, Laura Frances Brooks, Alice Colby, Lydia Colby, Rose Dana, Jan Daniels, Jane Daniels, Ruth Dorset, Ann Gilmer, Charlotte McCormack, Ellen Randolph, Jane Randolph, Dan Roberts, Clarissa Ross, Dan Ross, Dana Ross, Marilyn Ross, W.E.D. Ross, Jane Rossiter, Tex Steele, Rose Williams.

Donald Sydney **Rowland** (Eng. western, romantic novelist, 1928): Annette Adams, Jack Bassett, Hazel Baxter, Karla Benton, Helen Berry, Lewis Brant, Alison Bray, William Brayce, Fenton Brockley, Oliver Bronson, Chuck Buchanan, Rod Caley, Roger Carlton, Janita Cleve, Sharon Court, Vera Craig, Wesley Craile, John Dryden, Freda Fenton, Charles Field, Burt Kroll, Helen Langley, Henry Lansing, Harvey Lant, Irene Lynn, Stuart McHugh, Hank Madison, Chuck Mason, Edna Murray, Lorna Page, Olive Patterson, Alvin Porter, Alex Random, W.J. Rimmer, Donna Rix, Matt Rockwell,

Charles Roscoe, Minerva Rossetti, Norford Scott, Valerie Scott, Bart Segundo, Frank Shaul, Clinton Spurr, Roland Stan, J.D. Stevens, Mark Suttling, Kay Talbot, Will Travers, Elaine Vinson, Rick Walters, Neil Webb.

Edwin Charles **Tubb** (Eng. SF, western writer, 1919): Chuck Adams, Jud Cary, J.F. Clarkson, James S. Farrow, James R. Fenner, Charles S. Graham, Charles Grey, Volsted Gridban, Alan Guthrie, George Holt, Gill Hunt, E.F. Jackson, Gregory Kern, King Lang, Mike Langtry, P. Lawrence, Chet Lawson, Arthur MacLean, Carl Maddox, M.L. Powers, Paul Schofield, Brian Shaw, Roy Sheldon, John Stevens, Edward Thomson, Douglas West, Eric Wilding.

Emily Kathleen **Walker** (Eng. journalist, 1913): Pauline Ash, Eileen Barry, Sara Devon, Anne Durham, Louise Ellis, Delia Foster, Christine Lawson, Jane Lester, Cora Mayne, Jill Murray, Quenna Tilbury, Kathleen Treves, Heather Vincent, Honor Vincent, Kay Winchester.

4. Name Changes in France

They order, said I, this matter better in France (Laurence Sterne, *A Sentimental Journey*, 1768).

It is instructive, after the consideration and exemplification of name changes that are mostly in the English-speaking world, to see how things operate in a non-English-speaking country. The following are examples of legal 19th- and 20th-century name changes recorded in the two volumes by "l'Archiviste Jérôme" (itself an obvious pseudonym) listed in the Bibliography, p. 399. These date from 1803 to 1962, and are for the most part abstracted from the *Journal Officiel*, the French government publication that records such pronouncements and decrees and that itself approximately corresponds to the British *London Gazette*.

A full typical announcement of such a name change appears in the following form (translated from an actual entry extracted by

Jérôme from the October 1, 1955, issue of the *Journal Officiel*):

ROSENSTOCK-FRANCK (Louis-Joseph-Emile), born April 28, 1906, in Jaffa (Palestine), residing in Neuilly-sur-Seine (Seine), 31, Boulevard du Commandant-Charcot, and his children: a) Guillaume, born October 8, 1937, in Neuilly-sur-Seine (Seine); b) Anne, born July 28, 1939, in Neuilly-sur-Seine (Seine); c) Doris, born November 20, 1942, in Washington (United States), are authorized to substitute for their patronymic name that of "FRANCK", in order to call themselves legally henceforth "FRANCK" instead of "ROSENSTOCK-FRANCK".

This particular name change is simply a shortening of a lengthy name. Others listed are more radical. In many cases they are a gallicized (and simplified) form of a Germanic, Polish or other non-French name, in many instances probably Jewish, such as Aubale for Hausenball, or Colot for Kolodziejski. As these examples themselves suggest, in most cases the new name is based in some way on the old. There are times, however, when the new name is quite different, such as Camus for Grodner, Grandval for Hirsch-Ollendorff, or Moura for Zlatopolsky. There are also French-for-French substitutions, such as Louit for Moncouyoux.

Arabic names beginning Ben ("son") equally undergo a gallicization. Examples are Ben Azerat to Benat, Ben Yaya to Beniard, Ben Kemoun to Benque, and Ben Saïd to Bansart.

Certain German names, especially of the "toponymic" variety, lend themselves to a French translation, such as Beauchamp ("beautiful field") for Schonfeld, Châtaigner ("chestnut tree") for Kestenbaum, Fermont ("iron mountain") for Ajzenberg, and Neuville ("new town") for Neustadt. In some cases the original denotes an occupation or other descriptive, giving for example Lebon ("good man") for Gouttman, Lejeune ("young") for Jung, Maçon ("stonemason") for Steinmetzer, or Petit ("little") for Klein.

In a number of instances it has clearly been necessary to distinguish between families of identical name, especially where the name is a common one. One method of making the distinction is to add (by hyphenation) another family name. Thus for families who were originally simply Durand, one now finds Durand-Barthez, Durand-Chaumont, Durand-Couppel, Durand-Dubief, Durand-Saint-Amand, Durand-Viel and the like. The same goes for a common name such as Martin, giving Martin-Caille, Martin-Laval, Martin-Prével, etc. A more unusual change here is from Martin to Martin le Neuf de Neufville (as if "Martin the New from Newtown"), legalized in 1877. Some already lengthy compound names become even longer, so that in 1923 a lady named Marie-Eugène-Léonce-Renaud-Martin Martin de Boulancy expanded her surname, as did the rest of her family, to Martin de Boulancy d'Escayrac-Lauture.

A particularly common Jewish name in France is Lévy (or some similar spelling), and this has necessitated hundreds of name changes. A favorite substitution is Leroy, a name that is not only similar in form but almost in meaning ("the king" for "the priest"). Other substitutes recorded for this particular name are Lamy, Lancy, Larue, Leclerc (even closer in meaning), Lefebvre, Lepage, Léry, Lhéry, and Louis. There are also many (such as Franc or Tissot) that bear no resemblance to it.

The French name Cocu (or some form of it) is also fairly common and has brought about a wide variety of replacements. It actually means "cuckoo" (modern French coucou), but has clearly become popularly associated with cocu, "cuckold." Hence one finds both similar-looking substitutions, such as Cocy, Colin, Cossu, Cotty, Cucy, and Lecoq, as well as totally dissimilar names, such as Boulat, Jollivet, and Ruette.

Running through both of Jérôme's volumes one finds names that have clearly been changed because of the undesirable meanings, or supposed meanings, of the originals. A process of amelioration has thus occurred, replacing the bad with the good, or at least the acceptable. The following are individual examples. The reader should take the colloquial or "taboo" sense of the translated original name, so that "cock" does not mean the barnyard bird, and "ball" not the sports requisite. Other "four-letter words" have their accepted (often anatomical) sense.

Batton for Bâtard ("bastard")
Baudin for Boudin ("fatso")
Bertel for Bestiale ("bestial")
Bertrand for Couille ("ball")
Bessac for Bécasse ("silly goose")
Borde for Bordel ("brothel")
Bordet for Bidet ("bidet")
Caume for Con ("cunt," "schmuck")
Calvet for Caca ("pooh")
Coullon for Couillon ("cretin")
Brémard for Pochard ("drunk")
Chevin for Schwein (German, "pig")

Cieux for Chieux (*chier*, "to shit")
Cochot for Cochon ("pig")
Cornic for Cornichon ("nitwit")
Crestant for Crétin ("cretin")
Darrier for Derrière ("rear," "behind")
Euverte for Cimetière ("cemetery")
Faure for Pet ("fart")
Fortin for Infortuné ("wretch")
Grenoville for Grenouille ("frog")
Hidène for Hideux ("hideous")
Lacotte for Lacrotte (*crotte*, "bogey")
Lafitte for Labitte (*bitte*, "cock")
Larisse for Lapisse (*pisse*, "piss")
Laurisse for Saucisse ("sausage," "ninny")
Lavalle for Lavache (*vache*, "cow," "bitch," "sod")
Lecup for Lecul (*cul*, "ass")
Lesage for Lesinge (*singe*, "monkey")
Massin for Assassin ("assassin")
Mérida for Merda (*merde*, "shit")
Mock for Moch (*moche*, "ugly," "nasty")
More for Mort ("death")
Morus for Morue ("codfish," "whore")

Nesmon for Pédal (*pédale*, "queer")
Papy for Pipi ("pee")
Patin for Putin (*putain*, "whore")
Péant for Puant ("stinking")
Pline for Pine ("cock," "prick")
Rivollet for Pissoir ("urinal")
Roche for Boche ("Boche," "Kraut")
Saland for Salaud ("bastard," "sod")
Soulappe for Saloppe (*salope*, "bitch," "tart")
Tissier for Titi ("cocky Parisian kid")
Vente for Ventre ("belly")

The reasons for these renamings is not stated, but many were doubtless for general purposes of assimilation in a francophone community, no doubt in several cases by immigrants, or descendants of immigrants. It would be interesting to learn, however, why a family called Zissu renamed themselves Willoughby in 1948. It can hardly have been for purposes of distinctiveness.

5. Real Names

I never tell people my real name. It gives me more privacy (Patrick Malahide [1945–], Eng. TV actor, in *TV Times*, June 4–10, 1988).

This book has concentrated on those people who have changed their name or adopted a pseudonym. Yet there are several well known personalities and individuals who have not done so, and who in some cases have resolutely stuck by their real name, however unwieldy, unsuitable or incongruous it may have been for their professional career.

In some instances the persons concerned have taken pains to put the facts about their real name on the record —*for* the record. Here are some examples.

• When Sydne Rome, the U.S. movie actress, once inquired at an airport whether she could stop off in Nice, the clerk, after asking her name, looked at her carefully and said, "Madam, I think you would do better to transfer to Qantas" (*Telegraph Sunday Magazine*, June 3, 1979).

• The U.S. movie actor Bradford Dillman commented, "Bradford Dillman sounded like a distinguished, phoney, theatrical name, so I kept it" (Clarke, p. 250).

• When a Hollywood executive wanted to change the name of Jack Lemmon to "Lennon," the U.S. movie comedian said, "I told him it had taken me most of my life to get used to the traumatic effects of being called Jack U. Lemmon, and that I was used to it now and I wasn't going to change it" (Clarke, p. 250).

• Louella Parsons, the U.S. movie columnist, said of the movie actress Rita Gam, "I *do* wish she would change her name" (Clarke, p. 249).

• The South African actress Janet Suzman adamantly refused to accede to suggestions that she change her surname when she first went on the stage because it was too "foreign." Instead, she sent a telegram to the theatre director: "Imperative remain Suzman" (*TV Times*, April 9, 1976).

• Together with Dustin Hoffman, actress and singer Barbra Streisand was one of the 1960s generation of Hollywood stars who refused to change their names, although Barbara Joan Streisand did drop an "a" (Charles Derry, in Vinson, p. 594).

• Bridget Fonda, the actress daughter of Peter Fonda and the granddaughter of the famous Henry Fonda, has been frequently tempted to change her name since her childhood, when her father divorced her mother (and attempted to persuade his wife to drop the Fonda name similarly). Bridget acknowledges that having this particular name has its problems: "I did consider changing my name but it does no good to run away and I am proud to be part of the Fonda family," she says (*The Times*, August 1, 1988).

• As a child, the British theatre and TV actress Frances Cuka told her ballerina aunt that she wanted to go on stage and change her name to "Gloria La Raine." "What's wrong with Cuka?" said her aunt sternly. "I was Cuka; your Aunt Eileen acted under the name Cuka. No one can spell it, no one can pronounce it properly — but no one will ever forget it." Says Frances (who actually pronounces her name "Chewka"), "I was too scared to change my name, and I am pleased now I was frightened into keeping it" (*TV Times*, February 14–20, 1987).

• "Of course it's my real name," retorts U.S. TV star Cloris Leachman, when interviewers raised doubts about it. "Would anyone in his right mind change it *to* Cloris Leachman?" (Andersen, p. 247).

• When Helena Michell, daughter of Australian TV actor Keith Michell, first followed in her father's professional footsteps, and was asked how she aimed to preserve her distinct identity, she replied: "What do people want me to do? Change my name? I think my Dad

would be upset if I did, as if I were ashamed of it" (*TV Times*, October 22–28, 1988).

• Playwright Timberlake Wertenbaker, who grew up in the French Basque country, finds that critics react with suspicion to her work, since they see her name as an anagram. Yet it is her real name, with her first name a former family surname (*Sunday Times*, April 6, 1986).

• British radio and TV presenter Gloria Hunniford says: "A lot of people think it's a stage name but it isn't. When my husband told his family he was marrying me, they said: 'No wonder — she wants to change her name!'" (John Sachs and Piers Morgan, *Secret Lives*, 1991).

• British TV comedian and presenter Bob Monkhouse comments on his name: "Americans never get it right, they always call me Mongoose. If I'd had my wits about me I would have changed it at the start. People like Ted Ray and Lulu had it right" (John Sachs and Piers Morgan, *Secret Lives*, 1991).

• Popular U.S. singer Frank Sinatra, at the age of 22, was a singing waiter in New Jersey, calling himself Frank Trent. He kept this name until it was pointed out to him that his real name was much more musical. It evokes "sonata," among other words (*Times Literary Supplement*, March 1, 1996).

• U.S. movie actress Sandra Bullock has (so far) resolutely kept her original name. "There is something about the name Sandra Bullock that just isn't Hollywood," opined a British journalist. "It sounds grimly ordinary, plain and tough. It lacks the delicate beauty of a Michelle Pfeiffer, the take-no-prisoners hit of a Jamie Lee Curtis or the languorous sexiness of a Kim Basinger. In an industry where changing your name is as routine as changing your socks these things matter. If a name says something about a person, then Sandra Bullock could be an installation artist, a sprint-hurdler or a gum-chewing bully at school. But a Hollywood starlet? Surely not" (Sasha Miller, *Sunday Times Magazine*, September 25, 1994).

For similar reasons, and simply because we expect the names of movie actors and actresses, among others, to be pseudonyms, we tend to imagine non-existent linguistic contrivances and manipulations when we see a real name. Why, Candice Bergen's name clearly contains "iceberg," and must denote her cool, calm beauty and screen presence, while Clara Bow had bow-shaped lips, as the old publicity photos show.

How fitting that Primo Carnera, the heavyweight boxer and wrestler, had such a "meaty" name, suggesting prime beef, or even carnage, while as a kind of converse, Celeste Holm has a name that conjures up a kind of "heavenly home." Thora Hird, the English TV actress, must surely have a name that is an anagram (could it be "Horrid Hat"?), and maybe Anita Loos has a name of this type, too (perhaps she was born Tina Olosa or Ilsa Anoto?). Danielle Darrieux, Mireille Mathieu, and Simone Simon have such alliteratively attractive French names that they cannot be their true names, and we all know that William Tubbs was a portly actor.

And so on. Our doubt is also prompted by the knowledge that names such as "Grey" and "Martin" are frequently assumed names. Beryl Grey was originally Beryl Groom, for example, and Joel Grey was Noel Katz. But Zane Grey always used his real name for the westerns that he wrote. Similarly Dean Martin was originally Dino Crocetti, Ross Martin was Martin Rosenblatt, and Tony Martin was Alvin Morris. Yet Mary Martin and Millicent Martin have always performed under their true names. Such duplication of names can cause confusion, so that we tend to think that Audrey Hepburn and Katherine Hepburn are related, or that there is some family relationship between Gloria Holden, Fay Holden and William Holden. But Audrey Hepburn was originally Edda van Heemstra Hepburn-Ruston, while Fay Holden began life as Fay Hammerton and William Holden was born William Beedle.

So there is the apparent artificiality of the name on the one hand or the seeming family kinship on the other, either of which can raise our suspicions.

A particular folklore has developed around one or two well known names, which are pop-ularly regarded as not being the bearer's original. It is commonly supposed, for instance, that the "real" name of Adolf Hitler (1889–1945) was actually Adolf Schicklgruber, and during World War II much satirical play was made of this fact. In fact Adolf's father, Alois Hitler (1837–1903), was the illegitimate son of Anna Maria Schicklgruber (1796–1847), and bore her name until he was 39. (Her husband, whom she married five years after she bore Alois, was actually surnamed Hiedler.) But Alois then established his claim to the name Hitler, which naturally was passed on to his son. (The dictator always used this name, and never referred to himself as Schicklgruber.)

Again, it was frequently said of the English entertainer Joyce Grenfell (1910–1979) that she was "really" Joyce Phipps. But this was simply her maiden name, and she chose to perform professionally under her married name, that of her husband, Reginald Grenfell.

Sometimes an unlikely looking but genuine name may inadvertently be adopted for a fictional character, or coincide with one. This actually happened in the case of novelist Berta Ruck, whose unusual name appeared as that of a character in Virginia Woolf's novel *Jacob's Room* (1922). This caused a dispute between the two women, although subsequently they were reconciled. The matching of real names with fictional names is essentially a topic outside the scope of the present book, however, although this one incidence of it can be mentioned here.

In general, therefore, it can be assumed that if the name of a well known person or celebrity does *not* appear in this book (allowing for authorial fallibility, of course), it is likely to be genuine.

Many personalities, while retaining their original surname, adopt a new first name that arose as a nickname. They then appear with this name in regular billings, reviews, publicity, media news items, and the like, as well as in reference publications or "who's whos." A selection of sports celebrities who came to be known by a name of this type follows below. (Their new or modified first name could in one sense qualify them for admission to the main body of the book. They are here in this "real" section, however, since they did not change their surname and remained true to the family name of their birth. They did not even actively aim to adopt a new first name, but simply passively accepted the nickname that was given them.)

The nicknames themselves are varied in origin and do not necessarily relate to the individual's sporting activity or performance. Thus Bear Bryant came to be so called because, as a boy, he wrestled a bear in Fordyce, Arkansas, for money. But many nicknames *do* arise only when the figure appears in the public eye. The names are in many cases descriptive, relating to a person's size (Tich Freeman, Pee Wee Reese, Tiny Thompson), age (Babe Ruth), resemblance to another (Rube Marquard to pitcher Rube Waddell, Dally Messenger to New South Wales premier William Dalley), color or complexion (Dixie Dean was swarthy), habits or nature (Gabby Hartnett was loquacious), physical performance (Punch Broadbent was a hard hitter, Lefty Gomez and Lefty Grove pitched left-handed, Rabbit Maranville leaped like a rabbit), general superiority (Magic Johnson). Some nicknames derives from incidents. Pitcher Cy ("Cyclone") Young was so called when one of his vicious fastballs shattered a backstop. The name may also be a tribute to another, as for Australian jockey Scobie Breasley to the Australian-born British racehorse trainer N.C. Scobie.

In most instances the nicknamed person not only readily acknowledges and uses the name but may even adopt it legally, as did Cash Asmussen.

Sometimes the "nickname" by which an individual comes to be known is a regular forename (Mickey Cochrane, Sam Huff, Sam Rice, Gene Tunney, Mickey Walker, Cy Young). (Legendary baseballer Mickey Mantle was named for Mickey Cochrane.) Some nicknames are "stock" names, and as such approach being standard forenames (Bunny Austin, King Clancy, Buster Crabbe, Red Faber, Sonny Liston, Budge Rogers). However, such names differ from the person's original first name, although sometimes suggesting it ("Red" suggests "Ed," "Bunny" resembles "Henry"). In certain cases a person's nickname simply alliterates with the original surname (Goose Goslin, Minnie Minoso, Sandy Saddler), and as such may have little real significance.

For this reason, the list below does not include names that are regular "pet" or diminutive forms of the original first name (such as Chick and Chuck from Charles, or Hank from Henry).

Phog Allen: Forrest Clare Allen (1885–1974), U.S. baseballer.

Sparky Anderson: George Lee Anderson (1934–), U.S. baseballer.

Cap Anson: Adrian Constantine Anson (1852–1922), U.S. baseballer.

Cash Asmussen: Brian Keith Asmussen (1962–), U.S. jockey.

Red Auerbach: Arnold Auerbach (1917–), U.S. basketballer.

Bunny Austin: Henry Wilfred Austin (1906–), Br. tennis player.

Kork Ballington: Hugh Neville Ballington (1951–), S.A. motorcycle racer.

Chief Bender: Charles Albert Bender (1884–1954), U.S. baseballer, of Native American descent.

Yogi Berra: Lawrence Peter Berra (1925–), U.S. baseballer.

Scobie Breasley: Arthur Edward Breasley (1914–), Austral. jockey.

Punch Broadbent: Harry Broadbent (1892–1971), Can. ice hockey player.

Bear Bryant: Paul William Bryant (1913–1983), U.S. American footballer.

Hopalong Cassady: Howard Cassady (1934–), U.S. American footballer.

King Clancy: Francis Michael Clancy (1903–), Can. ice hockey player.

Dit Clapper: Aubrey Victor Clapper (1907–1978), Can. ice hockey player.

Dutch Clark: Earl Harry Clark (1906–1978), U.S. American footballer.

Mickey Cochrane: Gordon Stanley Cochrane (1903–1962), U.S. baseballer.

Buster Crabbe: Clarence Linden Crabbe (1910–1983), U.S. swimmer.

Candy Cummings: William Arthur Cummings (1848–1924), U.S. baseballer.

Dixie Dean: William Ralph Dean (1907–1980), Br. footballer.

Dizzy Dean: Jay Hanna Dean (1911–1974), U.S. baseballer.

Red Faber: Urban Charles Faber (1888–1976), U.S. baseballer.

Whitey Ford: Edward Charles Ford (1928–), U.S. baseballer.

Tich Freeman: Alfred Percy Freeman (1888–1965), Eng. cricketer.

Rowdy Gaines: Ambrose Gaines IV (1959–), U.S. swimmer.

Lefty Gomez: Vernon Louis Gomez (1908–1989), U.S. baseballer.

Pancho Gonzales: Richard Alonzo Gonzales (1928–), U.S. tennis player.

Wentworth Gore: Arthur William Charles Gore (1868–1928), Br. tennis player.

Goose Goslin: Leon Allen Goslin (1900–1971), U.S. baseballer.

Red Grange: Harold Edward Grange (1903–1991), U.S. American footballer.

Lefty Grove: Robert Moses Grove (1900–1975), U.S. baseballer.

Chip Hanauer: Lee Edward Hanauer (1954–), U.S. powerboat racer.

Dusty Hare: William Henry Hare (1952–), Br. rugby player.

Gabby Hartnett: Charles Leo Hartnett (1900–1972), U.S. baseballer.

Patsy Hendren: Elias Henry Hendren (1889–1962), Eng. cricketer.

Babe Herman: Floyd Caves Herman (1903–1987), U.S. baseballer.

Sam Huff: Robert Lee Huff (1934–), U.S. American footballer.

Catfish Hunter: James Augustus Hunter (1946–), U.S. baseballer.

Bo Jackson: Vincent Edward Jackson (1962–), U.S. baseballer, American footballer.

Magic Johnson: Earvin Johnson, Jr. (1959–), U.S. basketballer.

Choo-Choo Justice: Charles Justice (1924–), U.S. American footballer.

Red Kelly: Leonard Patrick Kelly (1927–), Can. ice hockey player.

Curly Lambeau: Earl Louis Lambeau (1898–1965), U.S. American footballer.

Sonny Liston: Charles Liston (1932–1970), U.S. boxer.

Pop Lloyd: John Henry Lloyd (1884–1965), U.S. baseballer.

Rabbit Maranville: Walter James Vincent Maranville (1891–1954), U.S. baseballer.

Rube Marquard: Richard William Marquard (1889–1980), U.S. baseballer.

Dally Messenger: Herbert Henry Messenger (1883–1959), Austral. rugby player.

Minnie Minoso: Saturnino Orestes Armas Minoso Arrieta (1922–), Cuban-born U.S. baseballer.

Satchel Paige: Leroy Robert Paige (1906–), U.S. baseballer.

Ace Parker: Clarence McKay Parker (1913–), U.S. American footballer.

Budge Patty: John Edward Patty (1924–), U.S. tennis player.

Atty Persse: Henry Seymour Persse (1869–1960), Ir. racehorse trainer, working in U.K.

Pee Wee Reese: Harold Henry Reese (1918–), U.S. baseballer.

Butch Reynolds: Harry Lee Reynolds, Jr. (1964–), U.S. athlete.

Sam Rice: Edgar Charles Rice (1890–1974), U.S. baseballer.

Budge Rogers: Derek Prior Rogers (1939–), Eng. rugby player.

Red Ruffing: Charles Herbert Ruffing (1904–1986), U.S. baseballer.

Babe Ruth: George Herman Ruth (1895–1948), U.S. baseballer.

Bunny Ryan: Elizabeth Montague Ryan (1892–1979), U.S.-born Br. tennis player.

Sandy Saddler: Joseph Saddler (1926–), U.S. boxer.

Tod Sloan: James Forman Sloan (1873–1933), U.S. jockey.

Duke Snider: Edward Donald Snider (1926–), U.S. baseballer.

Major Taylor: Marshall Walter Taylor (1878–1932), U.S. cyclist.

Tiny Thompson: Cecil Thompson (1905–1981), Can. ice hockey player.

Gene Tunney: James Joseph Tunney (1897–1978), U.S. boxer.

Rube Waddell: George Edward Waddell (1876–1914), U.S. baseballer.

Honus Wagner: John Peter Wagner (1874–1955), U.S. baseballer.

Mickey Walker: Edward Patrick Walker (1901–1981), U.S. boxer.

Dutch Warmerdam: Cornelius Anthony Warmerdam (1915–), U.S. athlete, of Du. parentage.

Pop Warner: Glenn Scobey Warner (1871–1954), U.S. American footballer.

Whizzer White: Byron Raymond White (1917–), U.S. footballer and Supreme Court justice.

Bluey Wilkinson: Arthur George Wilkinson (1911–1940), Austral. speedway racer.

Hack Wilson: Lewis Robert Wilson (1900–1948), U.S. baseballer.

Jocky Wilson: John Thomas Wilson (1950–), Sc. darts player.

Cy Young: Denton True Young (1867–1955), U.S. baseballer.

Bibliography

Clearly, any bibliography on the vast subject of pseudonyms and name changes is bound to be selective. The bibliography that follows concentrates on those works that were found to be the most helpful in establishing a pseudonymous person's real name, or in recording permanent name changes. If anything, it is weighted towards the everyday rather than the esoteric, since such names are the most readily documented.

At the same time, the reader of this book should know that many more books than those actually listed here were consulted during its compilation. This particularly applies to books shown as published in a numbered edition ("2d ed.," "4th ed." and so on), where the earlier editions will also have been consulted and exploited.

In the main, the books are English-language publications. A few, however, are in a foreign language, and in such cases an English translation of the title is also provided for case of reference.

For enjoyable reading, Americans (and not only Americans) are urged to see Sections 1 ("Surnames") and 2 ("Given-Names") of Chapter X, "Proper Names in America," in Mencken (pp. 474–525 in the edition listed below), where there is a wealth of illustrative material, spiced with anecdotes.

Agee, Patrick. *Where Are They Now?* London, Everest, 1977.

Andersen, Christopher P. *The Book of People.* New York: Perigee, 1981.

Arnold, Denis, gen. ed. *The New Oxford Companion to Music.* Oxford: Oxford University Press, 1983. 2 vols.

Ash, Brian. *Who's Who in Science Fiction.* London: Sphere, rev. ed., 1977.

Ashley, Leonard R.N. "Flicks, Flacks, and Flux: Tides of Taste in the Onomasticon of the Moving Picture Industry," *Names (Journal of the American Name Society)* 23:4 (December 1975).

Ashley, Mike. *Who's Who in Horror and Fantasy Fiction.* London: Elm Tree, 1977.

Atkinson, Frank. *Dictionary of Literary Pseudonyms.* London: Clive Bingley, 4th enl. ed., 1987.

Attwater, Donald. *The Penguin Dictionary of Saints.* Harmondsworth: Penguin, 1965.

Baker, Glenn A. *The Name Game: Their Real Names Revealed.* London: GRR/Pavilion, 1986.

Banham, Martin, ed. *The Cambridge Guide to World Theatre.* Cambridge: Cambridge University Press, 1988.

Baring-Gould, S. *Family Names and Their Story.* London: Seeley & Co., 1910.

Bauer, Andrew, comp. *The Hawthorn Dictionary of Pseudonyms.* New York: Hawthorn, 1971.

Bego, Mark. *The Rock & Roll Almanac.* New York: Macmillan, 1996.

Benét, William Rose. *The Reader's Encyclopedia.* London: A. & C. Black, 3d ed., 1988.

Blackwell, Earl. *Earl Blackwell's Entertainment Celebrity Register.* New York: Visible Ink, 1991.

Blain, Virginia, Patricia Clements, and Isobel Grundy. *The Feminist Companion to Literature in English.* London: Batsford, 1990.

Blake, Lord, and C.S. Nicholls, eds. *The Dictionary of National Biography: 1971–1980.* Oxford: Oxford University Press, 1986.

____, eds. *The Dictionary of National Biography: 1981–1985.* Oxford: Oxford University Press, 1990.

Bottomley, Roy. *This Is Your Life.* London: Methuen, 1993.

Bowden, John. *Who's Who in Theology: From the First Century to the Present.* London: SCM Press, 1990.

Bowman, John S., ed. *The Cambridge Dictionary of American Biography.* Cambridge: Cambridge University Press, 1995.

Briggs, Asa, cons. ed. *A Dictionary of Twentieth Century World Biography.* Oxford: Oxford University Press, rev. ed., 1992.

Brosse, Jacques. *Les Maîtres spirituels [Religious Leaders].* Paris: Bordas, 1988.

Browning, D.C., comp. *Everyman's Dictionary of Literary Biography, English and American.* London: Dent, 1969.

Bryant, Mark, and Simon Heneage, comps. *Dictionary of British Cartoonists and Caricaturists 1730–1980.* Aldershot: Scolar Press, 1994.

Buck, Claire, ed. *Bloomsbury Guide to Women's Literature.* London: Bloomsbury, 1992.

Busby, Roy. *The British Music Hall: An Illustrated Who's Who from 1850 to the Present Day.* London: Paul Elek, 1976.

Callahan, J. Kenneth, comp. *A Dictionary of Sporting Pen Names.* Peterborough, N.H.: Callahan, 1995.

Camden, William. *Remains Concerning Britain: Their Languages, Names, Surnames, Allusions, Anagramms, Armories, Moneys, Impresses, Apparel, Artillerie, Wise Speeches, Proverbs, Poesies, Epitaphs.* London: Charles Harper, 1674 [1586].

Carpenter, Humphrey, and Mari Pritchard. *The Oxford Companion to Children's Literature.* Oxford: Oxford University Press, 1984.

Carty, T.J. *A Dictionary of Literary Pseudonyms in the English Language.* London: Mansell, 1995.

Case, Brian, and Stan Britt. *The Illustrated Encyclopaedia of Jazz.* London: Salamander, 1978.

Chaneles, S., and A. Wolsky. *The Movie Makers.* London: Octopus, 1974.

Cherpillod, André. *Dictionnaire étymologique des noms d'hommes et de dieux [Etymological Dictionary of the Names of Men and Gods].* Paris: Masson, 1988.

Chilton, John. *Who's Who of Jazz.* London: Macmillan, 5th ed., 1989.

Chilvers, Ian. *The Concise Oxford Dictionary of Art and Artists.* Oxford: Oxford University Press, 2d ed., 1996.

Chilvers, Ian, and Harold Osborne, eds. *The Oxford Dictionary of Art.* Oxford: Oxford University Press, 1988.

Clarke, Donald, ed. *The Penguin Encyclopedia of Popular Music.* London: Viking Penguin, 1989.

Clarke, J.F. *Pseudonyms.* London: Elm Tree, 1977.

Clifford, Mike, consult. *The Illustrated Rock Handbook.* London: Salamander, 1983.

The Compact Edition of the Dictionary of National Biography. Oxford: Oxford University Press, 1975 [complete text, reproduced micrographically, of 22 volumes of main work and of six volumes covering respective periods 1901–1911, 1912–1921, 1922–1930, 1931–1940, 1941–1950, 1951–1960].

The Complete Guide to the Stars on Video. Peterborough: The Home Entertainment Corporation, 1994.

Connors, Martin, Beth A. Fhaner, and Kelly M. Cross, eds. *The VideoHound & All-Movie Guide StarGazer.* Detroit: Visible Ink, 1996.

Coston, Henri. *Dictionnaire des pseudonymes [Dictionary of Pseudonyms].* Paris: Lectures Françaises, 1965 (vol. I), 1969 (vol. II).

Crosland, Margaret. *Ballet Carnival: A Companion to Ballet.* London: Arco, 1977.

Cross, F.L., and E.A. Livingstone, eds. *The Oxford Dictionary of the Christian Church.* Oxford: Oxford University Press, 2d ed., 1974.

Crowther, Jonathan, ed. *The AZED Book of Crosswords.* London: Pan, 1977.

Cushing, William. *Initials and Pseudonyms: A Dictionary of Literary Disguises.* New York: Crowell, 1886.

Daly, Steven, and Nathaniel Wice. *Alt. Culture: An A-Z Guide to 90s America.* London: Fourth Estate, 1995.

Dawson, Lawrence H. *Nicknames and Pseudonyms: Including Sobriquets of Persons in History, Literature, and the Arts Generally, Titles Given to Monarchs, and the Nicknames of the British Regiments and the States of North America.* London: Routledge, 1908.

De Bekker, L.J. *Black's Dictionary of Music & Musicians.* London: A. & C. Black, 1924.

D'Israeli, Isaac. "Influence of Names," *Curiosities of Literature.* London: George Routledge and Sons, 1866 [1791–1834].

Dmitriyev, V.G. *Pridumannyye imena (rasskazy o psevdonimakh) [Invented Names (Stories of Pseudonyms)].* Moscow: Sovremennik, 1986.

_____. *Skryvshiye svoë imya (iz istorii anonimov i psevdonimov) [The Name Concealers (A History of Anonyms and Pseudonyms)].* Moscow: Nauka, 2d enl. ed., 1977.

Dolgins, Adam. *Rock Names.* New York: Carol Publishing, 1993.

Drabble, Margaret, ed. *The Oxford Companion to English Literature.* Oxford: Oxford University Press, rev. ed., 1995.

Dupuy, Trevor N., Curt Johnson, and David L. Bongard. *The Harper Encyclopedia of Military Biography.* Edison, NJ: Castle Books, 1995.

Elson, Howard, and John Brunton. *Whatever Happened To...? The Great Rock and Pop Nostalgia Book.* London: Proteus, 1981.

Encyclopaedia Britannica. 15th ed., 1993.

Erlewine, Michael, Vladimir Bogdanov, and Chris Woodstra, eds. *All Music Guide to Rock.* San Francisco: Miller Freeman Books, 1995.

Ewen, C. L'Estrange. *A History of Surnames of the British Isles*. London: Kegan Paul, 1931.

____. *A Guide to the Origin of British Surnames*. London: John Gifford, 1938.

Farmer, David Hugh. *The Oxford Dictionary of Saints*. Oxford: Oxford University Press, 4th ed., 1997.

Fisher, John. *Funny Way to Be a Hero*. St. Albans: Paladin, 1976.

France, Peter, ed. *The New Oxford Companion to Literature in French*. Oxford: Clarendon, 1995.

Freestone, Basil. *Harrap's Book of Nicknames and Their Origins*. London: Harrap, 1990.

Gammond, Peter. *The Oxford Companion to Popular Music*. Oxford: Oxford University Press, 1991.

____, and Peter Clayton. *A Guide to Popular Music*. London: Phoenix, 1960.

Goldston, Will. *Will Goldston's Who's Who in Magic*. London: Will Goldston, n.d. [*c.*1935].

Goodman, Jonathan. *Who He?* London: Buchan & Enright, 1984.

Gowing, Sir Lawrence, gen. ed. *A Biographical Dictionary of Artists*. London: Grange Books, 1994.

Gregory, Hugh. *Who's Who in Country Music*. London: Weidenfeld & Nicolson, 1993.

Greif, Martin. *The Gay Book of Days*. London: W.H. Allen, 1985.

Gribben, Lenore. *Who's Whodunit: A List of 3,128 Detective Story Writers and Their 1,100 Pseudonyms*. Chapel Hill, N.C.: University of North Carolina, 1969.

Hall, Tony, ed. *They Died Too Young*. Bristol: Parragon, 1996.

Halliwell, Leslie. *Halliwell's Filmgoer's Companion*. London: Paladin, 9th ed., 1988.

____, with Philip Purser. *Halliwell's Television Companion*. London: Grafton, 3d ed., 1986.

Hamst, Olphar. *Handbook of Fictitious Names (Being a Guide to Authors, Chiefly in the Lighter Literature of the XIXth Century, Who Have Written Under Assumed Names; and to Literary Forgers, Imposters, Plagiarists, and Imitators)*. London: John Russell Smith, 1868.

Hanks, Patrick, and Flavia Hodges. *A Dictionary of Surnames*. Oxford: Oxford University Press, 1988.

Hardy, Phil, and Dave Laing, eds., with additional material by Stephen Barnard and Don Perretta. *Encyclopaedia of Rock*. London: Macdonald Orbis, 1987.

Hardy, Phil, and Dave Laing. *The Faber Companion to 20th-Century Popular Music*. London: Faber and Faber, 1990.

Hart, James D., with revisions and additions by Phillip W. Leininger. *The Oxford Companion to American Literature*. Oxford: Oxford University Press, 6th ed., 1995.

Hartnoll, Phyllis, ed. *The Oxford Companion to the Theatre*. Oxford: Oxford University Press, 4th ed., 1983.

Harvey, Sir Paul, and J.E. Heseltine, comps. and eds. *The Oxford Companion to French Literature*. Oxford: Oxford University Press, 1961.

Hayward, Anthony, ed. *Who's Who on Television*. London: Boxtree, 5th ed., 1990.

____, ed. *The Boxtree A-Z of TV Stars*. London: Boxtree, 1992.

____. *Who's Who on Television*. London: Boxtree, 1996.

____, and Deborah Hayward. *TV Unforgettables*. Enfield: Guinness Publishing, 1993.

Herbert, Ian, ed. *Who's Who in the Theatre. Vol 1: Biographies*. Detroit: Gale, 17th ed., 1981.

Hildreth, Peter. *Name Dropper*. London: McWhirter, 1970.

Hinnells, John R. (ed). *Who's Who of World Religions*. London: Macmillan, 1992.

Holmstrom, John. *The Moving Picture Boy: An International Encyclopaedia from 1895 to 1995*. Wilby: Michael Russell, 1996.

Illustrated Encyclopaedia of World Theatre. London: Thames & Hudson, 1977.

International Authors and Writers Who's Who. Cambridge: International Biographical Centre, 15th ed., 1997.

Jacobs, Arthur. *The Penguin Dictionary of Musical Performers*. London: Penguin Books, 1990.

Jacobs, Louis. *The Jewish Religion: A Companion*. Oxford: Oxford University Press, 1995.

Jares, Joe. *Whatever Happened to Gorgeous George?* New York: Grosset & Dunlap, 1974.

Jeremy, David J., ed. *Dictionary of Business Biography*. London: Butterworths, 1984–86. 5 vols.

Jerôme, l'Archiviste. *Dictionnaire des changements de noms de 1803 à 1956* [*Dictionary of Name Changes from 1803 to 1956*]. Paris: Henry Coston, 1957.

____. *Dictionnaire des changements de noms 1957–1962* [*Dictionary of Name Changes 1957–1962*]. Paris: La Librairie Française, 1979.

Jones, Maldwyn A. *Destination America*. London: Weidenfeld & Nicolson, 1976.

Josling, J.F. *Change of Name*. London: Longman, 14th ed., 1989.

Kaganoff, Benzion C. *A Dictionary of Jewish Names and Their History*. London: Routledge & Kegan Paul, 1978.

Kamm, Antony. *Collins Biographical Dictionary of English Literature*. Glasgow: HarperCollins, 1993.

Kaplan, Justin. "The Naked Self and Other Problems," in Marc Pachter, ed. *Telling Lives, The*

Biographer's Art. Philadelphia: University of Pennsylvania Press, 1981.

Karney, Robyn, ed. *Who's Who in Hollywood.* London: Parragon, 1993.

Kash, Murray. *Murray Kash's Book of Country.* London: W.H. Allen, 1981.

Katz, Ephraim. *The Macmillan International Film Encyclopedia.* London: Macmillan, new ed., 1994.

Keating, H.R.F., ed. *Whodunit? A Guide to Crime, Suspense and Spy Fiction.* London: Windward, 1982.

Kelly, J.N.D. *The Oxford Dictionary of Popes.* Oxford: Oxford University Press, 1986.

Kennedy, Michael. *The Concise Oxford Dictionary of Music.* Oxford: Oxford University Press, 4th ed., 1996.

Kidd, Charles. *Debrett Goes to Hollywood.* New York: St. Martin's Press, 1986.

Klymasz, R.B. *A Classified Dictionary of Slavic Surname Changes in Canada.* Winnipeg: Ukrainian Free Academy of Sciences, 1961. (Onomastica No. 22).

Koegler, Horst. *The Concise Oxford Dictionary of Ballet.* Oxford: Oxford University Press, 2d rev. ed., 1987.

Kupper, Susan J. *Surnames for Women: A Decision-Making Guide.* Jefferson, N.C.: McFarland, 1990.

Lamb, Geoffrey. *Magic Illustrated Dictionary.* London: Kaye & Ward, 1979.

Larkin, Colin, ed. *The Guinness Encyclopedia of Popular Music.* Enfield: Guinness Publishing, 1992. 4 vols.

____, ed. *The Guinness Who's Who of Stage Musicals.* Enfield: Guinness Publishing, 1994.

Lloyd, Ann, and Graham Fuller, eds. *The Illustrated Who's Who of the Cinema.* London: Orbis, 1983.

McCormick, Donald. *Who's Who in Spy Fiction.* London: Elm Tree, 1977.

Marble, Annie Russell. *Pen Names and Personalities.* New York: Appleton, 1930.

Masanov, I.F. *Slovar' psevdonimov russkikh pisateley, uchënykh i obshchestvennykh deyateley* [*Dictionary of Pseudonyms of Russian Writers, Scholars and Public Figures*]. Moscow: Izdatel'stvo Vsesoyuznoy Knizhnoy Palaty, 1956. 4 vols.

Massingberd, Hugh, ed. *The Daily Telegraph Book of Obituaries.* London: Macmillan, 1995.

Massingberd, Hugh (ed.) *The Daily Telegraph Third Book of Obituaries: Entertainers.* London: Macmillan, 1997.

Matthews, Peter, Ian Buchanan, and Bill Mallon. *The Guinness International Who's Who of Sport.* Enfield: Guinness, 1993.

Meades, Jonathan. *This Is Your Life: An Insight into the Unseen Lives of Your Favourite TV Personalities.* London: Salamander, 1979.

Mencken, H.L. *The American Language.* New York: Alfred A. Knopf, 4th ed., 1936.

Miller, Compton: *Who's Really Who.* London: Sphere, 3d ed., 1987.

Miller, Maud M., ed. *Winchester's Screen Encyclopedia.* London: Winchester Publications, 1948.

Moran, Caitlin. "Turning up the watts in a name." *The Times,* May 6, 1994.

Morgan, Jane, Christopher O'Neill, and Rom Harré. *Nicknames: Their Origins and Social Consequences.* London: Routledge & Kegan Paul, 1979.

Mossman, Jennifer, ed. *New Pseudonyms and Nicknames.* Detroit: Gale, supp. to 1st ed., 1981.

____, ed. *Pseudonyms and Nicknames Dictionary.* Detroit: Gale, 1st ed., 1980.

Neuburg, Victor E. *The Batsford Companion to Popular Literature.* London: Batsford Academic and Educational, 1982.

New Catholic Encyclopedia. New York: McGraw-Hill, 1967.

Nicholls, C.S., ed. *The Dictionary of National Biography: Missing Persons.* Oxford: Oxford University Press, 1993.

____, ed. *The Dictionary of National Biography: 1986–1990.* Oxford: Oxford University Press, 1996.

____, ed. *The Hutchinson Encyclopedia of Biography.* Oxford: Helicon, 1996.

Osborne, Harold, ed. *The Oxford Companion to Art.* Oxford: Oxford University Press, 1970.

Ousby, Ian, ed. *The Cambridge Guide to Literature in English.* Cambridge: Cambridge University Press, rev. ed. 1993.

Panassié, Hugues, and Madeleine Gautier. *Dictionary of Jazz.* London: Cassell, 1956.

Pareles, Jon, and Patricia Romanowski, eds. *The Rolling Stone Encyclopedia of Rock & Roll.* London: Rolling Stone/Michael Joseph, 1983.

Parish, James Robert. *Great Child Stars.* New York: Ace, 1976.

Park, James, ed. *Cultural Icons.* London: Bloomsbury, 1991.

Parker, John, comp. and ed. *Who's Who in the Theatre.* London: Sir Isaac Pitman, 10th ed., 1947.

Parker, Jonathan, ed. *People of Today.* London: Debrett's Peerage, 9th ed., 1996.

Parker, Peter, ed. *The Reader's Companion to Twentieth Century Writers.* London: Fourth Estate/Oxford: Helicon, 1995.

Parry, Melanie (ed.). *Chambers Biographical Dictionary.* Edinburgh: Chambers, 8th ed., 1997.

Pascall, Jeremy, and Rob Burt. *The Stars and Superstars of Black Music.* London: Phoebus, 1977.

Pedder, Eddie, ed. *Who's Who on Television*. London: ITV, 4th ed., 1988.

Perkins, George, Barbara Perkins, and Phillip Leininger, eds. *Benét's Reader's Encyclopedia of American Literature*. Glasgow: HarperCollins, 1992.

Phoebus Publishing Co., comps. *The Story of Pop*. London: Octopus, 1974.

The Picturegoer's Who's Who and Encyclopaedia of the Screen To-Day. London: Odhams Press, 1st ed., 1933.

Pynsent, Robert B., and S.I. Kanikova, eds. *The Everyman Companion to East European Literature*. London: J.M. Dent, 1993.

Quinlan, David. *Quinlan's Illustrated Directory of Film Stars*. London: B.T. Batsford, 3d ed., 1991.

Rees, Dafydd, and Luke Crampton. *The Guinness Book of Rock Stars*. Enfield: Guinness Publishing, 3d ed., 1994.

_____. *Q Encyclopedia of Rock Stars*. London: Dorling Kindersley, 1996.

Rees, Nigel, and Vernon Noble. *A Who's Who of Nicknames*. London: George Allen & Unwin, 1985.

Reyna, Ferdina. *Concise Encyclopedia of Ballet*. London: Collins, 1974.

Rigdon, Walter, ed. *The Biographical Encyclopedia and Who's Who of the American Theatre*. New York: J.H. Heinemann, 1966.

Roberts, Frank C., comp. *Obituaries from The Times 1961–1970*. Reading: Newspaper Archive Developments, 1975; *...1971–75*, 1978; *...1951–1960*, 1979.

Robertson, Patrick. *The Guinness Book of Almost Everything You Didn't Need to Know About the Movies*. Enfield: Guinness Superlatives, 1986.

Robinson, Roger, comp. *Who's Hugh? An SF Reader's Guide to Pseudonyms*. Harold Wood: Beccon Publications, 1987.

Rose, Simon. *One FM Essential Film Guide*. Glasgow: HarperCollins, 1993.

Romanowski, Patricia, and Holly George-Warren, eds. *The New Rolling Stone Encyclopedia of Rock & Roll*. New York: Simon and Schuster, 1995.

Roxon, Lillian. *Rock Encyclopedia*. New York: Grosset & Dunlap, 1971.

Sachs, John, and Piers Morgan. *Private Files of the Stars*. London: Angus & Robertson, 1991.

_____. *Secret Lives*. London: Blake, 1991.

Seth, Ronald. *Encyclopedia of Espionage*. London: New English Library, 1972.

Shankle, George Earie. *American Nicknames: Their Origin and Significance*. New York: Wilson, 1955.

Sharp, Harold S., comp. *Handbook of Pseudonyms and Personal Nicknames*. Metuchen, N.J.: Scarecrow, 1972. *First Supplement*, 1975.

Shestack, Melvin. *The Country Music Encyclopaedia*. London: Omnibus, 1977.

Shneyer, A. Ya., and R. Ye. Slavsky. *Tsirk. Malen'kaya entsiklopediya* [*The Circus: A Little Encyclopedia*]. Moscow: Sovetskaya Entsiklopediya, 1979.

Smith, Benjamin E., ed. *The Century Cyclopedia of Names*. London: The Times/New York: The Century Co., 1904.

Stacey, Chris, and Darcy Sullivan. *Supersoaps*. London: Independent Television Publications, 1988.

Stambler, Irwin. *Encyclopaedia of Pop, Rock and Soul*. New York: St. Martin's Press, 1989.

Stephens, Meic, comp. and ed. *The Oxford Companion to the Literature of Wales*. Oxford: Oxford University Press, 1986.

Stetler, Susan. *Actors, Artists, Authors & Attempted Assassins*. Detroit: Visible Ink, 1991.

Stevens, Andy. *World of Stars: Your 200 Favourite Personalities*. London: Fontana, 1980.

Stoutenburgh, Jr., John. *Dictionary of the American Indian*. New York: Philosophical Library, 1960.

Stringer, Jenny, ed. *The Oxford Companion to Twentieth Century Literature in English*. Oxford: Oxford University Press, 1996.

Thomson, David. *A Biographical Dictionary of the Cinema*. London: Secker & Warburg, 1975.

_____. *A Biographical Dictionary of Film*. London: André Deutsch, 1994.

Thomson, Ronald W. *Who's Who of Hymn Writers*. London: Epworth, 1967.

Tobler, John, ed. *Who's Who in Rock & Roll*. London: Hamlyn, 1991.

Todd, Janet. *A Dictionary of British and American Women Writers 1660–1800*. London: Methuen, 1987.

_____, ed. *Dictionary of British Women Writers*. London: Routledge, 1989.

Uglow, Jennifer, comp. and ed. *The Macmillan Dictionary of Women's Biography*. London and Basingstoke: Macmillan, 2d ed., 1989.

Vinson, James, ed. *The International Dictionary of Films and Filmmakers. Vol. III: Actors and Actresses*. London: St. James, 1986.

Walker, John, ed. *Halliwell's Filmgoer's Companion*. London: HarperCollins, 2nd ed., 1997.

Ward, A.C. *Longman Companion to Twentieth Century Literature*. London: Longman, 3d ed., 1981.

Warrack, John, and Ewan West. *The Oxford Dictionary of Opera*. Oxford: Oxford University Press, 1992.

Webster's Biographical Dictionary. Springfield, Mass.: Merriam, 1976.

Webster's New Biographical Dictionary. Springfield, Mass.: Merriam-Webster, 1988.

Wheeler, William A. *A Dictionary of the Noted Names of Fiction (Including Also Familiar Pseudonyms, Surnames Bestowed on Eminent Men, and Analogous Popular Appellations Often Referred to in Literature and Conversation).* London: George Bell, 1892.

Who Was Who. London: A. & C. Black, decennially (1920–1991). 8 vols.

Who Was Who in the Theatre: 1912–1976. Detroit: Gale, 1978. 4 vols.

Who's Who. London: A. & C. Black, annually (from 1897).

Wilde, William H., Joy Hooton, and Barry Andrews. *The Oxford Companion to Australian Literature.* Oxford: Oxford University Press, 1995.

Williams, E.T., and C.S. Nicholls, eds. *The Dictionary of National Biography: 1961–1970.* Oxford: Oxford University Press. 1981.

Wlaschin, Ken. *The World's Great Movie Stars and Their Films.* London: Peerage, rev. ed., 1984.

Yutkevich, S.I., chief ed. *Kino: Entsiklopedicheskiy slovar'* [*The Cinema: An Encyclopedic Dictionary*]. Moscow: Sovetskaya Entsiklopediya, 1986.

Zec, Donald. *Some Enchanted Egos.* London: Allison & Busby, 1972.

Articles and Essays

Aside from the few included above, numerous articles and essays on pseudonyms and name changes have appeared over the years, and readers who wish for a fuller listing than can be provided here are referred to the relevant sections of the two following annotated bibliographies:

Lawson, Edwin D., comp. *Personal Names and Naming.* Westport, CT: Greenwood Press, 1987.

_____. *More Names and Naming.* Westport, CT: Greenwood Press, 1995.